Essential System Administration

THIRD EDITION

Essential System Administration

Æleen Frisch

O'REILLY®

Beijing · Cambridge · Farnham · Köln · Paris · Sebastopol · Taipei · Tokyo

Essential System Administration, Third Edition
by Æleen Frisch

Published by O'Reilly Media, Inc., 1005 Gravenstein Highway North, Sebastopol, CA 95472.

O'Reilly Media, Inc. books may be purchased for educational, business, or sales promotional use. Online editions are also available for most titles (*safari.oreilly.com*). For more information contact our corporate/institutional sales department: (800) 998-9938 or *corporate@oreilly.com*.

Editor:	Michael Loukides
Production Editor:	Leanne Clarke Soylemez
Cover Designer:	Edie Freedman
Interior Designer:	David Futato

Printing History:

August 2002:	Third Edition.
September 1995:	Second Edition.
October 1991:	First Edition.

Library of Congress Cataloging-in-Publication Data

Frisch, AEleen
    Essential System Administration/by AEleen Frisch.--3rd ed.
      p. cm.
    Includes index.
    ISBN 0-596-00343-9
    1. UNIX (Computer file) 2. Operating systems (Computers) I. Title.

QA76.76.O63 F75 2002
005.4'32--dc21
                                                2002023321

For Frank Willison

"Part of the problem is passive-aggressive behavior, my pet peeve and bête noire, and I don't like it either. Everyone should get off their high horse, particularly if that horse is my bête noire. We all have pressures on us, and nobody's pressure is more important than anyone else's."

***

"Thanks also for not lending others your O'Reilly books. Let others buy them. Buyers respect their books. You seem to recognize that 'lend' and 'lose' are synonyms where books are concerned. If I had been prudent like you, I would still have Volume 3 (Cats–Dorc) of the Encyclopedia Britannica."

Table of Contents

Preface

*This book is an agglomeration of lean-tos and annexes
and there is no knowing how big the next addition will
be, or where it will be put. At any point, I can call the
book finished or unfinished.*
—Alexander Solzhenitsyn

A poem is never finished, only abandoned.
—Paul Valery

This book covers the fundamental and essential tasks of Unix system administration. Although it includes information designed for people new to system administration, its contents extend well beyond the basics. The primary goal of this book is to make system administration on Unix systems straightforward; it does so by providing you with exactly the information you need. As I see it, this means finding a middle ground between a general overview that is too simple to be of much use to anyone but a complete novice, and a slog through all the obscurities and eccentricities that only a fanatic could love (some books actually suffer from both these conditions at the same time). In other words, I won't leave you hanging when the first complication arrives, and I also won't make you wade through a lot of extraneous information to find what actually matters.

This book approaches system administration from a task-oriented perspective, so it is organized around various facets of the system administrator's job, rather than around the features of the Unix operating system, or the workings of the hardware subsystems in a typical system, or some designated group of administrative commands. These are the raw materials and tools of system administration, but an effective administrator has to know when and how to apply and deploy them. You need to have the ability, for example, to move from a user's complaint ("This job only needs 10 minutes of CPU time, but it takes it three hours to get it!") through a diagnosis of the problem ("The system is thrashing because there isn't enough swap space"), to the particular command that will solve it (swap or swapon). Accordingly, this book covers all facets of Unix system administration: the general concepts, underlying structure, and guiding assumptions that define the Unix environment, as well as the commands, procedures, strategies, and policies essential to success as a system administrator. It will talk about all the usual administrative tools that Unix provides and also how to use them more smartly and efficiently.

Naturally, some of this information will constitute advice about system administration; I won't be shy about letting you know what my opinion is. But I'm actually much more interested in giving you the information you need to make informed decisions for your own situation than in providing a single, univocal view of the "right way" to administer a Unix system. It's more important that you know what the issues are concerning, say, system backups, than that you adopt anyone's specific philosophy or scheme. When you are familiar with the problem and the potential approaches to it, you'll be in a position to decide for yourself what's right for your system.

Although this book will be useful to anyone who takes care of a Unix system, I have also included some material designed especially for system administration professionals. Another way that this book covers essential system administration is that it tries to convey the essence of what system administration is, as well as a way of approaching it when it is your job or a significant part thereof. This encompasses intangibles such as system administration as a profession, professionalism (not the same thing), human and humane factors inherent in system administration, and its relationship to the world at large. When such issues are directly relevant to the primary, technical content of the book, I mention them. In addition, I've included other information of this sort in special sidebars (the first one comes later in this Preface). They are designed to be informative and thought-provoking and are, on occasion, deliberately provocative.

The Unix Universe

More and more, people find themselves taking care of multiple computers, often from more than one manufacturer; it's quite rare to find a system administrator who is responsible for only one system (unless he has other, unrelated duties as well). While Unix is widely lauded in marketing brochures as the "standard" operating system "from microcomputers to supercomputers"—and I must confess to having written a few of those brochures myself—this is not at all the same as there being a "standard" Unix. At this point, Unix is hopelessly plural, and nowhere is this plurality more evident than in system administration. Before going on to discuss how this book addresses that fact, let's take a brief look at how things got to be the way they are now.

Figure P-1 attempts to capture the main flow of Unix development. It illustrates a simplified Unix genealogy, with an emphasis on influences and family relationships (albeit Faulknerian ones) rather than on strict chronology and historical accuracy. It traces the major lines of descent from an arbitrary point in time: Unix Version 6 in 1975 (note that the dates in the diagram refer to the earliest manifestation of each version). Over time, two distinct flavors (strains) of Unix emerged from its beginnings at AT&T Bell Laboratories—which I'll refer to as System V and BSD—but there was also considerable cross-influence between them (in fact, a more detailed diagram would indicate this even more clearly).

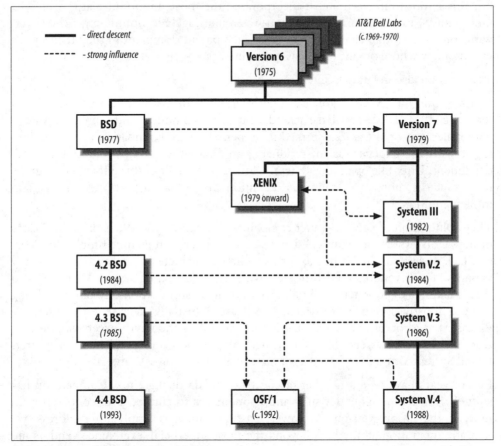

Figure P-1. Unix genealogy (simplified)

 For a Unix family tree at the other extreme of detail, see *http://perso. wanadoo.fr/levenez/unix/*. Also, the opening chapters of *Life with UNIX*, by Don Libes and Sandy Ressler (PTR Prentice Hall), give a very entertaining overview of the history of Unix. For a more detailed written history, see *A Quarter Century of UNIX* by Peter Salus (Addison-Wesley).

The split we see today between System V and BSD occurred after Version 6.* developers at the University of California, Berkeley, extended Unix in many ways, adding virtual memory support, the C shell, job control, and TCP/IP networking, to name just a few. Some of these contributions were merged into the AT&T code lines at various points.

System V Release 4 was often described as a merger of the System V and BSD lines, but this is not quite accurate. It incorporated the most important features of BSD (and SunOS) into System V. The union was a marriage and not a merger, however, with some but not all characteristics from each parent dominant in the offspring (as well as a few whose origins no one is quite sure of).

The diagram also includes OSF/1.

In 1988, Sun and AT&T agreed to jointly develop future versions of System V. In response, IBM, DEC, Hewlett-Packard, and other computer and computer-related companies and organizations formed the Open Software Foundation (OSF), designing it with the explicit goal of producing an alternative, compatible, non-AT&T-dependent, Unix-like operating system. OSF/1 is the result of this effort (although its importance is more as a standards definition than as an actual operating system implementation).

The proliferation of new computer companies throughout the 1980s brought dozens of new Unix systems to market—Unix was usually chosen as much for its low cost and lack of serious alternatives as for its technical characteristics—and also as many variants. These vendors tended to start with some version of System V or BSD and then make small to extensive modifications and customizations. Extant operating systems mostly spring from System V Release 3 (usually Release 3.2), System V Release 4, and occasionally 4.2 or 4.3 BSD (SunOS is the major exception, derived from an earlier BSD version). As a further complication, many vendors freely intermixed System V and BSD features within a single operating system.

Recent years have seen a number of efforts at standardizing Unix. Competition has shifted from acrimonious lawsuits and countersuits to surface-level cooperation in unifying the various versions. However, existing standards simply don't address system administration at anything beyond the most superficial level. Since vendors are free to do as they please in the absence of a standard, there is no guarantee that

---

* The movement from Version 7 to System III in the System V line is a simplification of strict chronology and descent. System III was derived from an intermediate release between Version 6 and Version 7 (CB Unix), and not every Version 7 feature was included in System III. A word about nomenclature: The successive releases of Unix from the research group at Bell Labs were originally known as "editions"—the Sixth Edition, for example—although these versions are now generally referred to as "Versions." After Version 6, there are two distinct sets of releases from Bell Labs: Versions 7 and following (constituting the original research line), and System III through System V (commercial implementations started from this line). Later versions of System V are called "Releases," as in System V Release 3 and System V Release 4.

system administrative commands and procedures will even be similar under different operating systems that uphold the same set of standards.

Unix Versions Discussed in This Book

How do you make sense out of the myriad of Unix variations? One approach is to use computer systems only from a single vendor. However, since that often has other disadvantages, most of us end up having to deal with more than one kind of Unix system. Fortunately, taking care of n different kinds of systems doesn't mean that you have to learn as many different administrative command sets and approaches. Ultimately, we get back to the fact that there are really just two distinct Unix varieties; it's just that the features of any specific Unix implementation can be an arbitrary mixture of System V and BSD features (regardless of its history and origins). This doesn't always ensure that there are only two different commands to perform the same administrative function—there are cases where practically every vendor uses a different one—but it does mean that there are generally just two different approaches to the area or issue. And once you understand the underlying structure, philosophy, and assumptions, learning the specific commands for any given system is simple.

When you recognize and take advantage of this fact, juggling several Unix versions becomes straightforward rather than impossibly difficult. In reality, lots of people do it every day, and this book is designed to reflect that and to support them. It will also make administering heterogeneous environments even easier by systematically providing information about different systems all in one place.

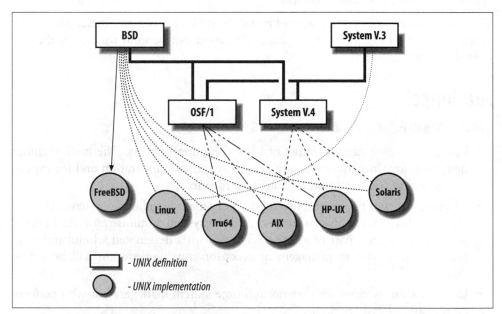

Figure P-2. Unix versions discussed in this book

The Unix versions covered by this book appear in Figure P-2, which illustrates the influences on the various operating systems, rather than their actual origins. If the version on your system isn't one of them, don't despair. Read on anyway, and you'll find that the general information given here applies to your system as well in most cases.

The specific operating system levels covered in this book are:

- AIX Version 5.1
- FreeBSD Version 4.6 (with a few glances at the upcoming Version 5)
- HP-UX Version 11 (including many Version 11i features)
- Linux: Red Hat Version 7.3 and SuSE Version 8
- Solaris Versions 8 and 9
- Tru64 Version 5.1

This list represents some changes from the second edition of this book. We've dropped SCO Unix and IRIX and added FreeBSD. I decided to retain Tru64 despite the recent merger of Compaq and Hewlett-Packard, because it's likely that some Tru64 features will eventually make their way into future HP-UX versions.

When there are significant differences between versions, I've made extensive use of headers and other devices to indicate which version is being considered. You'll find it easy to keep track of where we are at any given point and even easier to find out the specific information you need for whatever version you're interested in. In addition, the book will continue to be useful to you when you get your next, different Unix system—and sooner or later, you will.

The book also covers a fair amount of free software that is not an official part of any version of Unix. In general, the packages discussed can be built for any of the discussed operating systems.

Audience

This book will be of interest to:

- Full or part-time administrators of Unix computer systems. The book includes help both for Unix users who are new to system administration and for experienced system administrators who are new to Unix.
- Workstation and microcomputer users. For small, standalone systems, there is often no distinction between the user and the system administrator. And even if your workstation is part of a larger network with a designated administrator, in practice, many system management tasks for your workstation will be left to you.
- Users of Unix systems who are not full-time system managers but who perform administrative tasks periodically.

Why Vendors Like Standards

Standards are supposed to help computer users by minimizing the differences between products from different vendors and ensuring that such products will successfully work together. However, standards have become a weapon in the competitive arsenal of computer-related companies, and vendor product literature and presentations are often a cacophony of acronyms. Warfare imagery dominates discussions comparing standards compliance rates for different products.

For vendors of computer-related products, upholding standards is in large part motivated by the desire to create a competitive advantage. There is nothing wrong with that, but it's important not to mistake it for the altruism that it is often purported to be. "Proprietary" is a dirty word these days, and "open systems" are all the rage, but that doesn't mean that what's going on is anything other than business as usual.

Proprietary features are now called "extensions" and "enhancements," and defining new standards has become a site of competition. New standards are frequently created by starting from one of the existing alternatives, vendors are always ready to argue for the one they developed, and successful attempts are then touted as further evidence of their product's superiority (and occasionally they really are).

Given all of this, though, we have to at least suspect that it is not really in most vendors' interest for the standards definition process to ever stop.

This book assumes that you are familiar with Unix user commands: that you know how to change the current directory, get directory listings, search files for strings, edit files, use I/O redirection and pipes, set environment variables, and so on. It also assumes a very basic knowledge of shell scripts: you should know what a shell script is, how to execute one, and be able to recognize commonly used features like if statements and comment characters. If you need help at this level, consult *Learning the UNIX Operating System*, by Grace Todino-Gonguet, John Strang, and Jerry Peek, and the relevant editions of *UNIX in a Nutshell* (both published by O'Reilly & Associates).

If you have previous Unix experience but no administrative experience, several sections in Chapter 1 will show you how to make the transition from user to system manager. If you have some system administration experience but are new to Unix, Chapter 2 will explain the Unix approach to major system management tasks; it will also be helpful to current Unix users who are unfamiliar with Unix file, process, or device concepts.

This book is not designed for people who are already Unix wizards. Accordingly, it stays away from topics like writing device drivers.

Organization

This book is the foundation volume for O'Reilly & Associates' system administration series. As such, it provides you with the fundamental information needed by everyone who takes care of Unix systems. At the same time, it consciously avoids trying to be all things to all people; the other books in the series treat individual topics in complete detail. Thus, you can expect this book to provide you with the essentials for all major administrative tasks by discussing both the underlying high-level concepts and the details of the procedures needed to carry them out. It will also tell you where to get additional information as your needs become more highly specialized.

These are the major changes in content with respect to the second edition (in addition to updating all material to the most recent versions of the various operating systems):

- Greatly expanded networking coverage, especially of network server administration, including DHCP, DNS (BIND 8 and 9), NTP, network monitoring with SNMP, and network performance tuning.

- Comprehensive coverage of email administration, including discussions of sendmail, Postfix, procmail, and setting up POP3 and IMAP.

- Additional security topics and techniques, including the secure shell (ssh), one-time passwords, role-based access control (RBAC), chroot jails and sandboxing, and techniques for hardening Unix systems.

- Discussions of important new facilities that have emerged in the time since the second edition. The most important of these are LDAP, PAM, and advanced file-system features such as logical volume managers and fault tolerance features.

- Overviews and examples of some new scripting and automation tools, specifically Cfengine and Stem.

- Information about device types that have become available or common on Unix systems relatively recently, including USB devices and DVD drives.

- Important open source packages are covered, including the following additions: Samba (for file and printer sharing with Windows systems), the Amanda enterprise backup system, modern printing subsystems (LPRng and CUPS), font management, file and electronic mail encryption and digital signing (PGP and GnuPG), the HylaFAX fax service, network monitoring tools (including RRD-Tool, Cricket and NetSaint), and the GRUB boot loader.

Chapter Descriptions

The first three chapters of the book provide some essential background material required by different types of readers. The remaining chapters generally focus on a single administrative area of concern and discuss various aspects of everyday system operation and configuration issues.

Chapter 1, *Introduction to System Administration*, describes some general principles of system administration and the *root* account. By the end of this chapter, you'll be thinking like a system administrator.

Chapter 2, *The Unix Way*, considers the ways that Unix structure and philosophy affect system administration. It opens with a description of the man online help facility and then goes on to discuss how Unix approaches various operating system functions, including file ownership, privilege, and protection; process creation and control; and device handling. This chapter closes with an overview of the Unix system directory structure and important configuration files.

Chapter 3, *Essential Administrative Tools and Techniques*, discusses the administrative uses of Unix commands and capabilities. It also provides approaches to several common administrative tasks. It concludes with a discussion of the cron and syslog facilities and package management systems.

Chapter 4, *Startup and Shutdown*, describes how to boot up and shut down Unix systems. It also considers Unix boot scripts in detail, including how to modify them for the needs of your system. It closes with information about how to troubleshoot booting problems.

Chapter 5, *TCP/IP Networking*, provides an overview of TCP/IP networking on Unix systems. It focuses on fundamental concepts and configuring TCP/IP client systems, including interface configuration, name resolution, routing, and automatic IP address assignment with DHCP. The chapter concludes with a discussion of network troubleshooting.

Chapter 6, *Managing Users and Groups*, details how to add new users to a Unix system. It also discusses Unix login initialization files and groups. It covers user authentication in detail, including both traditional passwords and newer authentication facilities like PAM. The chapter also contains information about using LDAP for user account data.

Chapter 7, *Security*, provides an overview of Unix security issues and solutions to common problems, including how to use Unix groups to allow users to share files and other system resources while maintaining a secure environment. It also discusses optional security-related facilities such as dialup passwords and secondary authentication programs. The chapter also covers the more advanced security configuration available by using access control lists (ACLs) and role-based access control (RBAC). It also discusses the process of hardening Unix systems. In reality, though, security is something that is integral to every aspect of system administration, and a good administrator consciously considers the security implications of every action and decision. Thus, expecting to be able to isolate and abstract security into a separate chapter is unrealistic, and so you will find discussion of security-related issues and topics in every chapter of the book.

Chapter 8, *Managing Network Services*, returns to the topic of networking. It discusses configuring and managing various networking daemons, including those for

DNS, DHCP, routing, and NTP. It also contains a discussion of network monitoring and management tools, including the SNMP protocol and tools, Netsaint, RRDTool, and Cricket.

Chapter 9, *Electronic Mail*, covers all aspects of managing the email subsystem. It covers user mail programs, configuring the POP3 and IMAP protocols, the sendmail and Postfix mail transport agents, and the procmail and fetchmail facilities.

Chapter 10, *Filesystems and Disks*, discusses how discrete disk partitions become part of a Unix filesystem. It begins by describing the disk mounting commands and filesystem configuration files. It also considers Unix disk partitioning schemes and describes how to add a new disk to a Unix system. In addition, advanced features such as logical volume managers and software striping and RAID are covered. It also discusses sharing files with remote Unix and Windows systems using NFS and Samba.

Chapter 11, *Backup and Restore*, begins by considering several possible backup strategies before going on to discuss the various backup and restore services that Unix provides. It also covers the open source Amanda backup facility.

Chapter 12, *Serial Lines and Devices*, discusses Unix handling of serial lines, including how to add and configure new serial devices. It covers both traditional serial lines and USB devices. It also includes a discussion of the HylaFAX fax service.

Chapter 13, *Printers and the Spooling Subsystem*, covers printing on Unix systems, including both day-to-day operations and configuration issues. Remote printing via a local area network is also discussed. Printing using open source spooling systems is also covered, via Samba, LPRng, and CUPS.

Chapter 14, *Automating Administrative Tasks*, considers Unix shell scripts, scripts, and programs in other languages and environments such as Perl, C, Expect, and Stem. It provides advice about script design and discusses techniques for testing and debugging them. It also covers the Cfengine facility, which provides high level automation features to system administrators.

Chapter 15, *Managing System Resources*, provides an introduction to performance issues on Unix systems. It discusses monitoring and managing use of major system resources: CPU, memory, and disk. It covers controlling process execution, optimizing memory performance and managing system paging space, and tracking and apportioning disk usage. It concludes with a discussion of network performance monitoring and tuning.

Chapter 16, *Configuring and Building Kernels*, discusses when and how to create a customized kernel, as well as related system configuration issues. It also discusses how to view and modify tunable kernel parameters.

Chapter 17, *Accounting*, describes the various Unix accounting services, including printer accounting.

The Appendix covers the most important Bourne shell and bash features.

The Afterword contains some final thoughts on system administration and information about the System Administrator's Guild (SAGE).

Conventions Used in This Book

The following typographic and usage conventions are used in this book:

italic

> Used for filenames, directory names, hostnames, and URLs. Also used liberally for annotations in configuration file examples.

`constant width`

> Used for names of commands, utilities, daemons, and other options. Also used in code and configuration file examples.

`constant width italic`

> Used to indicate variables in code.

`constant width bold`

> Used to indicate user input on a command line.

`constant width bold italic`

> Used to indicate variables in command-line user input.

 Indicates a warning.

 Indicates a note.

 Indicates a tip.

he, she

> This book is meant to be straightforward and to the point. There are times when using a third-person pronoun is just the best way to say something: "This setting will force the user to change his password the next time he logs in." Personally, I don't like always using "he" in such situations, and I abhor "he or she" and "s/he," so I use "he" some of the time and "she" some of the time, alternating semi-randomly. However, when the text refers to one of the example users who appear from time to time throughout the book, the appropriate pronoun is always used.

Comments and Questions

Please address comments and questions concerning this book to the publisher:

O'Reilly & Associates, Inc.
1005 Gravenstein Highway North
Sebastopol, CA 95472
(800) 998-9938 (in the United States or Canada)
(707) 829-0515 (international/local)
(707) 829-0104 (fax)

There is a web page for this book, which lists errata, examples, or any additional information. You can access this page at:

http://www.oreilly.com/catalog/esa3/

To comment or ask technical questions about this book, send email to:

bookquestions@oreilly.com

For more information about books, conferences, Resource Centers, and the O'Reilly Network, see the O'Reilly web site at:

http://www.oreilly.com

Acknowledgments

Many people have helped this book at various points in its successive incarnations. In writing this third edition, I'm afraid I fell at times into the omnipresent trap of writing a different book rather than revising the one at hand; although this made the book take longer to finish, I hope that readers will benefit from my rethinking many topics and issues.

I am certain that few writers have been as fortunate as I have in the truly first-rate set of technical reviewers who read and critiqued the manuscript of the third edition. They were, without doubt, the most meticulous group I have ever encountered:

- Jon Forrest
- Peter Jeremy
- Jay Kreibich
- David Malone
- Eric Melander
- Jay Migliaccio
- Jay Nelson
- Christian Pruett
- Eric Stahl

Luke Boyett, Peter Norton and Nate Williams also commented on significant amounts of the present edition.

My thanks go also to the technical reviews of the first two editions. The second edition reviewers were Nora Chuang, Clem Cole, Walt Daniels, Drew Eckhardt, Zenon Fortuna, Russell Heise, Tanya Herlick, Karen Kerschen, Tom Madell, Hanna Nelson, Barry Saad, Pamela Sogard, Jaime Vazquez, and Dave Williams; first edition reviewers were Jim Binkley, Tan Bronson, Clem Cole, Dick Dunn, Laura Hook, Mike Loukides, and Tim O'Reilly. This book still benefits from their comments.

Many other people helped this edition along by pointing out bugs and providing important information at key points: Jeff Andersen, John Andrea, Jay Ashworth, Christoph Badura, Jiten Bardwaj, Clive Blackledge, Mark Burgess, Trevor Chandler, Douglas Clark, Joseph C. Davidson, Jim Davis, Steven Dick, Matt Eakle, Doug Edwards, Ed Flinn, Patrice Fournier, Rich Fuchs, Brian Gallagher, Michael Gerth, Adam Goodman, Charles Gordon, Uri Guttman, Enhua He, Matthias Heidbrink, Matthew A. Hennessy, Derek Hilliker, John Hobson, Lee Howard, Colin Douglas Howell, Hugh Kennedy, Jonathan C. Knowles, Ki Hwan Lee, Tom Madell, Sean Maguire, Steven Matheson, Jim McKinstry, Barnabus Misanik, John Montgomery, Robert L. Montgomery, Dervi Morgan, John Mulshine, John Mulshine, Darren Nickerson, Jeff Okimoto, Guilio Orsero, Jerry Peek, Chad Pelander, David B. Perry, Tim Rice, Mark Ritchie, Michael Saunby, Carl Schelin, Mark Summerfield, Tetsuji Tanigawa, Chuck Toporek, Gary Trucks, Sean Wang, Brian Whitehead, Bill Wisniewski, Simon Wright, and Michael Zehe.

Any errors that remain are mine alone.

I am also grateful to companies who loaned me or provided acccss to hardware and/or software:

- Gaussian, Inc. gave me access to several computer systems. Thanks to Mike Frisch, Jim Cheeseman, Jim Hess, John Montgomery, Thom Vreven and Gary Trucks.

- Christopher Mahmood and Jay Migliaccio of SuSE, Inc. gave me advance access to SuSE 8.

- Lorien Golarski of Red Hat gave me access to their beta program.

- Chris Molnar provided me with an advance copy of KDE version 3.

- Angela Loh of Compaq arranged for an equipment loan of an Alpha Linux system.

- Steve Behling, Tony Perraglia and Carlos Sosa of IBM expedited AIX releases for me and also provided useful information.

- Adam Goodman and the staff of *Linux Magazine* provided feedback on early versions of some sections of this book. Thanks also for their long suffering patience with my habitual lateness.

I'd also like to thank my stellar assistant Cat Dubail for all of her help on this third edition. Felicia Bear also provided important editorial help. Thanks also to Laura Lasala, my copy editor for the second edition.

At O'Reilly & Associates, my deepest gratitude goes to my amazing editor Mike Loukides, whose support and guidance brought this edition to completion. Bob Woodbury and Besty Waliszewski provided advice and help at key points. Darren Kelly helped with some technical issues regarding the index. Finally, my enthusiastic thanks go to the excellent production group at O'Reilly & Associates for putting the finishing touches on all three editions of this book.

Finally, no one finishes a task of this size without a lot of support and encouragement from their friends. I'd like to especially thank Mike and Mo for being there for me throughout this project. Thanks also to the furry Frischs: Daphne, Susan, Lyta, and Talia.

—ÆF; Day 200 of 2002; North Haven, CT, USA

## CHAPTER 1

Introduction to System Administration

The traditional way to begin a book like this is to provide a list of system administration tasks—I've done it several times myself at this point. Nevertheless, it's important to remember that you have to take such lists with a grain of salt. Inevitably, they leave out many intangibles, the sorts of things that require lots of time, energy, or knowledge, but never make it into job descriptions. Such lists also tend to suggest that system management has some kind of coherence across the vastly different environments in which people find themselves responsible for computers. There are similarities, of course, but what is important on one system won't necessarily be important on another system at another site or on the same system at a different time. Similarly, systems that are very different may have similar system management needs, while nearly identical systems in different environments might have very different needs.

But now to the list. In lieu of an idealized list, I offer the following table showing how I spent most of my time in my first job as full-time system administrator (I managed several central systems driving numerous CAD/CAM workstations at a Fortune 500 company) and how these activities have morphed in the intervening two decades.

Table 1-1. Typical system administration tasks

Then: early 1980s	Now: early 2000s
Adding new users.	I still do it, but it's automated, and I only have to add a user once for the entire network. Converting to LDAP did take a lot of time, though.
Adding toner to electrostatic plotters.	Printers need a lot less attention—just clearing the occasional paper jam—but I still get my hands dirty changing those inkjet tanks.
Doing backups to tape.	Backups are still high priority, but the process is more centralized, and it uses CDs and occasionally spare disks as well as tape.
Restoring files from backups that users accidentally deleted or trashed.	This will never change.
Answering user questions ("How do I send mail?"), usually not for the first or last time.	Users will always have questions. Mine also whine more: "Why can't I have an Internet connection on my desk?" or "Why won't IRC work through the firewall?"

Table 1-1. Typical system administration tasks (continued)

Then: early 1980s	Now: early 2000s
Monitoring system activity and trying to tune system parameters to give these overloaded systems the response time of an idle system.	Installing and upgrading hardware to keep up with monotonically increasing resource appetites.
Moving jobs up in the print queue, after more or less user whining, pleading, or begging, contrary to stated policy (about moving jobs, not about whining).	This is one problem that is no longer an issue for me. Printers are cheap, so they are no longer a scare resource that has to be managed.
Worrying about system security, and plugging the most noxious security holes I inherited.	Security is always a worry, and keeping up with security notices and patches takes a lot of time.
Installing programs and operating system updates.	Same.
Trying to free up disk space (and especially contiguous disk space).	The emphasis is more on high performance disk I/O (disk space is cheap): RAID and so on.
Rebooting the system after a crash (always at late and inconvenient times).	Systems crash a lot less than they used to (thankfully).
Straightening out network glitches ("Why isn't *hamlet* talking to *ophelia*?"). Occasionally, this involved physically tracing the Ethernet cable around the building, checking it at each node.	Last year, I replaced my last Thinnet network with twisted-pair cabling. I hope never to see the former again. However, I now occasionally have to replace cable segments that have malfunctioned.
Rearranging furniture to accommodate new equipment; installing said equipment.	Machines still come and go on a regular basis and have to be accommodated.
Figuring out why a program/command/account suddenly and mysteriously stopped working yesterday, even though the user swore he changed nothing.	Users will still be users.
Fixing—or rather, trying to fix—corrupted CAD/CAM binary data files.	The current analog of this is dealing with email attachments that users don't know how to access. Protecting users from potentially harmful attachments is another concern.
Going to meetings.	No meetings, but lots of casual conversations.
Adding new systems to the network.	This goes without saying: systems are virtually always added to the network.
Writing scripts to automate as many of the above activities as possible.	Automation is still the administrator's salvation.

As this list indicates, system management is truly a hodgepodge of activities and involves at least as many people skills as computer skills. While I'll offer some advice about the latter in a moment, interacting with people is best learned by watching others, emulating their successes, and avoiding their mistakes.

Currently, I look after a potpourri of workstations from many different vendors, as well as a couple of larger systems (in terms of physical size but not necessarily CPU power), with some PCs and Macs thrown in to keep things interesting. Despite these significant hardware changes, it's surprising how many of the activities from the early 1980s I still have to do. Adding toner now means changing a toner cartridge in a laser printer or the ink tanks in an inkjet printer; backups go to 4 mm tape and CDs rather than 9-track tape; user problems and questions are in different areas but are still very much on the list. And while there are (thankfully) no more meetings, there's probably even more furniture-moving and cable-pulling.

Some of these topics—moving furniture and going to or avoiding meetings, most obviously—are beyond the scope of this book. Space won't allow other topics to be treated exhaustively; in these cases, I'll point you in the direction of another book that takes up where I leave off. This book will cover most of the ordinary tasks that fall under the category of "system administration." The discussion will be relevant whether you've got a single PC (running Unix), a room full of mainframes, a building full of networked workstations, or a combination of several types of computers. Not all topics will apply to everyone, but I've learned not to rule out any of them *a priori* for a given class of user. For example, it's often thought that only big systems need process-accounting facilities, but it's now very common for small businesses to address their computing needs with a moderately-sized Unix system. Because they need to be able to bill their customers individually, they have to keep track of the CPU and other resources expended on behalf of each customer. The moral is this: take what you need and leave the rest; you're the best judge of what's relevant and what isn't.

Thinking About System Administration

I've touched briefly on some of the nontechnical aspects of system administration. These dynamics will probably not be an issue if it really is just you and your PC, but if you interact with other people at all, you'll encounter these issues. It's a cliché that system administration is a thankless job—one widely-reprinted cartoon has a user saying "I'd thank you but system administration is a thankless job"—but things are actually more complicated than that. As another cliché puts it, system administration is like keeping the trains on time; no one notices except when they're late.

System management often seems to involve a tension between authority and responsibility on the one hand and service and cooperation on the other. The extremes seem easier to maintain than any middle ground; fascistic dictators who rule "their system" with an iron hand, unhindered by the needs of users, find their opposite in the harried system managers who jump from one user request to the next, in continual interrupt mode. The trick is to find a balance between being accessible to users and their needs—and sometimes even to their mere wants—while still maintaining your authority and sticking to the policies you've put in place for the overall system welfare. For me, the goal of effective system administration is to provide an environment where users can get done what they need to, in as easy and efficient a manner as possible, given the demands of security, other users' needs, the inherent capabilities of the system, and the realities and constraints of the human community in which they all are located.

To put it more concretely, the key to successful, productive system administration is knowing when to solve a CPU-overuse problem with a command like:[*]

```
# kill -9 `ps aux | awk '$1=="chavez" {print $2}'
```

(This command blows away all of user *chavez*'s processes.) It's also knowing when to use:

```
$ write chavez
You've got a lot of identical processes running on dalton.
Any problem I can help with?
^D
```

and when to walk over to her desk and talk with her face-to-face. The first approach displays Unix finesse as well as administrative brute force, and both tactics are certainly appropriate—even vital—at times. At other times, a simpler, less aggressive approach will work better to resolve your system's performance problems in addition to the user's confusion. It's also important to remember that there are some problems no Unix command can address.

To a great extent, successful system administration is a combination of careful planning and habit, however much it may seem like crisis intervention at times. The key to handling a crisis well lies in having had the foresight and taken the time to anticipate and plan for the type of emergency that has just come up. As long as it only happens once in a great while, snatching victory from the jaws of defeat can be very satisfying and even exhilarating.

On the other hand, many crises can be prevented altogether by a determined devotion to carrying out all the careful procedures you've designed: changing the root password regularly, faithfully making backups (no matter how tedious), closely monitoring system logs, logging out and clearing the terminal screen as a ritual, testing every change several times before letting it loose, sticking to policies you've set for users' benefit—whatever you need to do for your system. (Emerson said, "A foolish consistency is the hobgoblin of little minds," but not a wise one.)

My philosophy of system administration boils down to a few basic strategies that can be applied to virtually any of its component tasks:

- Know how things work. In these days, when operating systems are marketed as requiring little or no system administration, and the omnipresent simple-to-use tools attempt to make system administration simple for an uninformed novice, someone has to understand the nuances and details of how things really work. It should be you.

- Plan it before you do it.

- Make it reversible (backups help a lot with this one).

---

[*] On HP-UX systems, the command is ps -ef. Solaris systems can run either form depending on which version of ps comes first in the search path. AIX and Linux can emulate both versions, depending on whether a hyphen is used with options (System V style) or not (BSD style).

- Make changes incrementally.
- Test, test, test, before you unleash it on the world.

I learned about the importance of reversibility from a friend who worked in a museum putting together ancient pottery fragments. The museum followed this practice so that if better reconstructive techniques were developed in the future, they could undo the current work and use the better method. As far as possible, I've tried to do the same with computers, adding changes gradually and preserving a path by which to back out of them.

A simple example of this sort of attitude in action concerns editing system configuration files. Unix systems rely on many configuration files, and every major subsystem has its own files (all of which we'll get to). Many of these will need to be modified from time to time.

I never modify the original copy of the configuration file, either as delivered with the system or as I found it when I took over the system. Rather, I always make a copy of these files the first time I change them, appending the suffix *.dist* to the filename; for example:

```
# cd /etc
# cp inittab inittab.dist
# chmod a-w inittab.dist
```

I write-protect the *.dist* file so I'll always have it to refer to. On systems that support it, use the cp command's -p option to replicate the file's current modification time in the copy.

I also make a copy of the current configuration file before changing it in any way so undesirable changes can be easily undone. I add a suffix like *.old* or *.sav* to the filename for these copies. At the same time, I formulate a plan (at least in my head) about how I would recover from the worst consequence I can envision of an unsuccessful change (e.g., I'll boot to single-user mode and copy the old version back).

Once I've made the necessary changes (or the first major change, when several are needed), I test the new version of the file, in a safe (nonproduction) environment if possible. Of course, testing doesn't always find every bug or prevent every problem, but it eliminates the most obvious ones. Making only one major change at a time also makes testing easier.

 Some administrators use the a revision control system to track the changes to important system configuration files (e.g., CVS or RCS). Such packages are designed to track and manage changes to application source code by multiple programmers, but they can also be used to record changes to configuration files. Using a revision control system allows you to record the author and reason for any particular change, as well as reconstruct any previous version of a file at any time.

The remaining sections of this chapter discuss some important administrative tools. The first describes how to become the superuser (the Unix privileged account). Because I believe a good system manager needs to have both technical expertise and an awareness of and sensitivity to the user community of which he's a part, this first chapter includes a section on Unix communication commands. The goal of these discussions—as well as of this book as a whole—is to highlight how a system manager thinks about system tasks and problems, rather than merely to provide literal, cookbook solutions for common scenarios.

Important administrative tools of other kinds are covered in later chapters of this book.

Becoming Superuser

On a Unix system, the superuser refers to a privileged account with unrestricted access to all files and commands. The username of this account is *root*. Many administrative tasks and their associated commands require superuser status.

There are two ways to become the superuser. The first is to log in as *root* directly. The second way is to execute the command su while logged in to another user account. The su command may be used to change one's current account to that of a different user after entering the proper password. It takes the username corresponding to the desired account as its argument; *root* is the default when no argument is provided.

After you enter the su command (without arguments), the system prompts you for the *root* password. If you type the password correctly, you'll get the normal root account prompt (by default, a number sign: #), indicating that you have successfully become superuser and that the rules normally restricting file access and command execution do not apply. For example:

```
$ su
Password:    Not echoed
#
```

If you type the password incorrectly, you get an error message and return to the normal command prompt.

You may exit from the superuser account with exit or Ctrl-D. You may suspend the shell and place it in the background with the suspend command; you can return to it later using fg.

When you run su, the new shell inherits the environment from your current shell environment rather than creating the environment that *root* would get after logging in. However, you can simulate an actual *root* login session with the following command form:

```
$ su -
```

Unlike some other operating systems, the Unix superuser has all privileges all the time: access to all files, commands, etc. Therefore, it is entirely too easy for a superuser to crash the system, destroy important files, and create havoc inadvertently. For this reason, people who know the superuser password (including the system administrator) should *not* do their routine work as superuser. *Only use superuser status when it is needed.*

The *root* account should always have a password, and this password should be changed periodically. Only experienced Unix users with special requirements should know the superuser password, and the number of people who know it should be kept to an absolute minimum.

To set or change the superuser password, become superuser and execute one of the following commands:

```
# passwd        Works most of the time.
# passwd root   Solaris and FreeBSD systems when su'd to root.
```

Generally, you'll be asked to type the old superuser password and then the new password twice. The *root* password should also be changed whenever someone who knows it stops using the system for any reason (e.g., transfer, new job, etc.), or if there is any suspicion that an unauthorized user has learned it. Passwords are discussed in detail in Chapter 6.

I try to avoid logging in directly as *root*. Instead, I su to *root* only as necessary, exiting from or suspending the superuser shell when possible. Alternatively, in a windowing environment, you can create a separate window in which you su to *root*, again executing commands there only as necessary.

For security reasons, it's a bad idea to leave any logged-in session unattended; naturally, that goes double for a *root* session. Whenever I leave a workstation where I am logged in as *root*, I log out or lock the screen to prevent anyone from sneaking onto the system. The xlock command will lock an X session; the password of the user who ran xlock must be entered to unlock the session (on some systems, the *root* password can also unlock sessions locked by other users).* While screen locking programs may have security pitfalls of their own, they do prevent opportunistic breaches of system security that would otherwise be caused by a momentary lapse into laziness.

 If you are logged in as *root* on a serial console, you should also use a locking utility provided by the operating system. In some cases, if you are using multiple virtual consoles, you will need to lock each one individually.

---

* For some unknown reason, FreeBSD does not provide xlock. However, the xlockmore (see *http://www.tux.org/~bagleyd/xlockmore.html*) utility provides the same functionality (it's actually a follow-on to xlock).

Controlling Access to the Superuser Account

On many systems, any user who knows the root password may become superuser at any time by running su. This is true for HP-UX, Linux, and Solaris systems in general.* Solaris allows you to configure some aspects of how the command works via settings in the */etc/default/su* configuration file.

Traditionally, BSD systems limited access to su to members of group 0 (usually named *wheel*); under FreeBSD, if the *wheel* group has a null user list in the group file (*/etc/group*), any user may su to root; otherwise, only members of the *wheel* group can use it. The default configuration is a *wheel* group consisting of just *root*.

AIX allows the system administrator to specify who can use su on an account-by-account basis (no restrictions are imposed by default). The following commands display the current groups that are allowed to su to *root* and then limit that same access to the *system* and *admins* groups:

```
# lsuser -a sugroups root
root sugroups=ALL
# chuser sugroups="system,admins" root
```

Most Unix versions also allow you to restrict direct *root* logins to certain terminals. This topic is discussed in Chapter 12.

An Armadillo?

The armadillo typifies one attribute that a successful system administrator needs: a thick skin. Armadillos thrive under difficult environmental conditions through strength and perseverance, which is also what system administrators have to do a lot of the time (see the colophon at the back of the book for more information about the armadillo). System managers will find other qualities valuable as well, including the quickness and cleverness of the mongoose (Unix is the snake), the sense of adventure and playfulness of puppies and kittens, and at times, the chameleon's ability to blend in with the surroundings, becoming invisible even though you're right in front of everyone's eyes.

Finally, however, as more than one reader has noted, the armadillo also provides a cautionary warning to system administrators not to become so single-mindedly or narrowly focused on what they are doing that they miss the big picture. Armadillos who fail to heed this advice end up as roadkill.

---

* When the PAM authentication facility is in use, it controls access to su (see "User Authentication with PAM" in Chapter 6).

Running a Single Command as root

su also has a mode whereby a single command can be run as *root*. This mode is not a very convenient way to interactively execute superuser commands, and I tend to see it as a pretty unimportant feature of su. Using su -c can be very useful in scripts, however, keeping in mind that the target user need not be *root*.

Nevertheless, I have found that it does have one important use for a system administrator: it allows you to fix something quickly when you are at a user's workstation (or otherwise not at your own system) without having to worry about remembering to exit from an su session.* There are users who will absolutely take advantage of such lapses, so I've learned to be cautious.

You can run a single command as *root* by using a command of this form:

```
$ su root -c "command"
```

where *command* is replaced by the command you want to run. The command should be enclosed in quotation marks if it contains any spaces or special shell characters. When you execute a command of this form, su prompts for the *root* password. If you enter the correct password, the specified command runs as *root*, and subsequent commands are run normally from the original shell. If the command produces an error or is terminated (e.g. with CTRL-C), control again returns to the unprivileged user shell.

The following example illustrates this use of su to unmount and eject the CD-ROM mounted in the */cdrom* directory:

```
$ su root -c "eject /cdrom"
Password:     root password entered
```

Commands and output would be slightly different on other systems.

You can start a background command as *root* by including a final ampersand within the specified command (*inside* the quotation marks), but you'll want to consider the security implications of a user bringing it to the foreground before you do this at a user's workstation.

sudo: Selective Access to Superuser Commands

Standard Unix takes an all-or-nothing approach to granting *root* access, but often what you actually want is something in between. The freely available sudo facility allows specified users to run specific commands as *root* without having to know the *root* password (available at *http://www.courtesan.com/sudo/*).†

---

* Another approach is always to open a new window when you need to do something at a user's workstation. It's easy to get into the habit of always closing it down as you leave.

† Administrative roles are another, more sophisticated way of partitioning *root* access. They are discussed in detail in "Role-Based Access Control" in Chapter 7.

For example, a non-*root* user could use this sudo command to shut down the system:

```
$ sudo  /sbin/shutdown ...
Password:
```

sudo requires only the user's own password to run the command, not the *root* password. Once a user has successfully given a password to sudo, she may use it to run additional commands for a limited period of time without having to enter a password again; this period defaults to five minutes. A user can extend the time period by an equal amount by running sudo -v before it expires. She can also terminate the grace period by running sudo -K.

sudo uses a configuration file, usually */etc/sudoers*, to determine which users may use the sudo command and the other commands available to each of them after they've started a sudo session. The configuration file must be set up by the system administrator. Here is the beginning of a sample version:

```
# Host alias specifications: names for host lists
Host_Alias    PHYSICS = hamlet, ophelia, laertes
Host_Alias    CHEM = duncan, puck, brutus

# User alias specifications: named groups of users
User_Alias    BACKUPOPS = chavez, vargas, smith

# Command alias specifications: names for command groups
Cmnd_Alias    MOUNT = /sbin/mount, /sbin/umount
Cmnd_Alias    SHUTDOWN = /sbin/shutdown
Cmnd_Alias    BACKUP = /usr/bin/tar, /usr/bin/mt
Cmnd_Alias    CDROM = /sbin/mount /cdrom, /bin/eject
```

These three configuration file sections define sudo aliases—uppercase symbolic names—for groups of computers, users and commands, respectively. This example file defines two sets of hosts (PHYSICS and CHEM), one set of users (BACKUPOPS), and four command aliases. For example, the MOUNT command alias is defined as the mount and umount commands. Following good security practice, all commands include the full pathname for the executable.

The final command alias illustrates the use of arguments within a command list. This alias consists of a command to mount a CD at */cdrom* and to eject the media from the drive. Note, however, that it does not grant general use of the mount command.

The final section of the file (see below) specifies which users may use the sudo command, as well as what commands they can run with it and which computers they may run them on. Each line in this section consists of a username or alias, followed by one or more items of the form:

```
host = command(s) [: host = command(s) ...]
```

where *host* is a hostname or a host alias, and *command(s)* are one or more commands or command aliases, with multiple commands or hosts separated by commas. Multiple access specifications may be included for a single user, separated by colons. The alias ALL stands for all hosts or commands, depending on its context.

Here is the remainder of our example configuration file:

```
# User specifications: who can do what where
root            ALL = ALL
%chem           CHEM = SHUTDOWN, MOUNT
chavez          PHYSICS = MOUNT : achilles = /sbin/swapon
harvey          ALL = NOPASSWD: SHUTDOWN
BACKUPOPS       ALL, !CHEM = BACKUP, /usr/local/bin
```

The first entry after the comment grants *root* access to all commands on all hosts. The second entry applies to members of the *chem* group (indicated by the initial percent sign), who may run system shutdown and mounting commands on any computer in the CHEM list.

The third entry specifies that user *chavez* may run the mounting commands on the hosts in the PHYSICS list and may also run the swapon command on host *achilles*. The next entry allows user *harvey* to run the shutdown command on any system, and sudo will not require him to enter his password (via the NOPASSWD: preceding the command list).

The final entry applies to the users specified for the BACKOPS alias. On any system except those in the CHEM list (the preceding exclamation point indicates exclusion), they may run the command listed in the BACKUP alias as well as any command in the */usr/local/bin directory*.

Users can use the sudo -l command form to list the commands available to them via this facility.

 Commands should be selected for use with sudo with some care. In particular, shell scripts should not be used, nor should any utility which provides *shell escapes*—the ability to execute a shell command from within a running interactive program (editors, games, and even output display utilities like more and less are common examples). Here is the reason: when a user runs a command with sudo, that command runs as *root*, so if the command lets the user execute other commands via a shell escape, any command he runs from within the utility will also be run as *root*, and the whole purpose of sudo—to grant *selective* access to superuser command—will be subverted. Following similar reasoning, because most text editors provide shell escapes, any command that allows the user to invoke an editor should also be avoided. Some administrative utilities (e.g., AIX's SMIT) also provide shell escapes.

The sudo package provides the visudo command for editing */etc/sudoers*. It locks the file, preventing two users from modifying the file simultaneously, and it performs syntax checking when editing is complete (if there are errors, the editor is restarted, but no explicit error messages are given).

There are other ways you might want to customize sudo. For example, I want to use a somewhat longer interval for password-free use. Changes of this sort must be made by rebuilding sudo from source code. This requires rerunning the configure script with options. Here is the command I used, which specifies a log file for all sudo operations, sets the password-free period to ten minutes, and tells visudo to use the text editor specified in the *EDITOR* environment variable:

```
# cd sudo-source-directory
# ./configure --with-logpath=/var/log/sudo.log \
        --with-timeout=10 --with-env-editor
```

Once the command completes, use the make command to rebuild sudo.[*]

sudo's logging facility is important and useful in that it enables you to keep track of privileged commands that are run. For this reason, using sudo can sometimes be preferable to using su even when limiting *root*-level command access is not an issue.

 The one disadvantage of sudo is that it provides no integrated remote-access password protection. Thus, when you run sudo from an insecure remote session, passwords are transmitted over the network for any eavesdropper to see. Of course, using SSH can overcome this limitation.

Communicating with Users

The commands discussed in this section are simple and familiar to most Unix users. For this reason, they're often overlooked in system administration discussions. However, I believe you'll find them to be an indispensable part of your repertoire. One other important communications mechanism is electronic mail (see Chapter 9).

Sending a Message

A system administrator frequently needs to send a message to a user's screen (or window). write is one way to do so:

```
$ write username [tty]
```

where *username* indicates the user to whom you wish to send the message. If you want to write to a user who is logged in more than once, the *tty* argument may be used to select the appropriate terminal or window. You can find out where a user is logged in using the who command.

Once the write command is executed, communication is established between your terminal and the user's terminal: lines that you type on your terminal will be transmitted to him. End your message with a CTRL-D. Thus, to send a message to user *harvey* for which no reply is needed, execute a command like this:

---

[*] A couple more configuration notes: sudo can also be integrated into the PAM authentication system (see "User Authentication with PAM" in Chapter 6). Use the --use-pam option to configure. On the other hand, if your system does not use a shadow password file, you must use the --disable-shadow option.

```
$ write harvey
The file you needed has been restored.
```
Additional lines of message text
```
^D
```

In some implementations (e.g., AIX, HP-UX and Tru64), write may also be used over a network by appending a hostname to the username. For example, the command below initiates a message to user *chavez* on the host named *hamlet*:

```
$ write chavez@hamlet
```

When available, the rwho command may be used to list all users on the local subnet (it requires a remote who daemon be running on the remote system).

The talk command is a more sophisticated version of write. It formats the messages between two users in two separate spaces on the screen. The recipient is notified that someone is calling her, and she must issue her own talk command to begin communication. Figure 1-1 illustrates the use of talk.

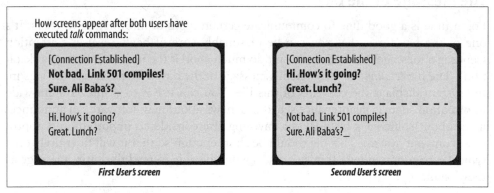

Figure 1-1. Two-way communication with talk

Users may disable messages from both write and talk by using the command mesg n (they can include it in their *.login* or *.profile* initialization file). Sending messages as the superuser overrides this command. Be aware, however, that sometimes users have good reasons for turning off messages.

> In general, the effectiveness of system messages is inversely proportional to their frequency.

Sending a Message to All Users

If you need to send a message to every user on the system, you can use the wall command. wall stands for "write all" and allows the administrator to send a message to all users simultaneously.

To send a message to all users, execute the command:

```
$ wall
```
Followed by the message you want to send, terminated with CTRL-D on a separate line
```
^D
```

Unix then displays a phrase like:

```
Broadcast Message from root on console ...
```

to every user, followed by the text of your message. Similarly, the `rwall` command sends a message to every user on the local subnet.

Anyone can use this facility; it does not require superuser status. However, as with `write` and `talk`, only messages from the superuser override users' `mesg n` commands. A good example of such a message would be to give advance warning of an imminent but unscheduled system shutdown.

The Message of the Day

Login time is a good time to communicate certain types of information to users. It's one of the few times that you can be reasonably sure of having a user's attention (sending a message to the screen won't do much good if the user isn't at the workstation). The file */etc/motd* is the system's message of the day. Whenever anyone logs in, the system displays the contents of this file. You can use it to display system-wide information such as maintenance schedules, news about new software, an announcement about someone's birthday, or anything else considered important and appropriate on your system. This file should be short enough so that it will fit entirely on a typical screen or window. If it isn't, users won't be able to read the entire message as they log in.

On many systems, a user can disable the message of the day by creating a file named *.hushlogin* in her home directory.

Specifying the Pre-Login Message

On Solaris, HP-UX, Linux and Tru64 systems, the contents of the file */etc/issue* is displayed immediately before the login prompt on unused terminals. You can customize this message by editing this file.

On other systems, login prompts are specified as part of the terminal-related configuration files; these are discussed in Chapter 12.

About Menus and GUIs

For several years now, vendors and independent programmers have been developing elaborate system administration applications. The first of these were menu-driven, containing many levels of nested menus organized by subsystem or administrative task. Now, the trend is toward independent GUI-based tools, each designed to manage some particular system area and perform the associated tasks.

Whatever their design, all of them are designed to allow even relative novices to perform routine administrative tasks. The scope and aesthetic complexity of these tools vary considerably, ranging from shell scripts employing simple selections lists and prompts to form-based utilities running under X. A few even offer a mouse-based interface with which you perform operations by dragging icons around (e.g., dropping a user icon on top of a group icon adds that user to that group, dragging a disk icon into the trash unmounts a filesystem, and the like).

In this section, we'll take a look at such tools, beginning with general concepts and then going on to a few practical notes about the tools available on the systems we are considering (usually things I wish I had known about earlier). The tools are very easy to use, so I won't be including detailed instructions for using them (consult the appropriate documentation for that).

Ups and Downs

Graphical and menu-based system administration tools have some definite good points:

- They can provide a quick start to system administration, allowing you to get things done while you learn about the operating system and how things work. The best tools include aids to help you learn the underlying standard administrative commands.

  Similarly, these tools can be helpful in figuring out how to perform some task for the first time; when you don't know how to begin, it can be hard to find a solution with just the manual pages.

- They can help you get the syntax right for complex commands with lots of options.

- They make certain kinds of operations more convenient by combining several steps into a single menu screen (e.g., adding a user or installing an operating system upgrade).

On the other hand, they have their down side as well:

- Typing the equivalent command is usually significantly faster than running it from an administrative tool.

- Not all commands are always available through the menu system, and sometimes only part of the functionality is implemented for commands that are included. Often only the most frequently used commands and/or options are available. Thus, you'll still need to execute some versions of commands by hand.

- Using an administrative tool can slow down the learning process and sometimes stop it altogether. I've met inexperienced administrators who had become convinced that certain operations just weren't possible simply because the menu system didn't happen to include them.

- The GUI provides unique functionality accessible only through its interface, so creating scripts to automate frequent tasks becomes much more difficult or impossible, especially when you want to do things in a way that the original author did not think of.

In my view, an ideal administrative tool has all of these characteristics:

- The tool must run normal operating system commands, not opaque, undocumented programs stored in some obscure, out-of-the-way directory. The tool thus makes system administration easier, leaving the thinking to the human using it.

- You should be able to display the commands being run, ideally before they are executed.

- The tool should log of all its activities (at least optionally).

- As much as possible, the tool should validate the values the user enters. In fact, novice administrators frequently assume that the tools do make sure their selections are reasonable, falsely thinking that they are protected from anything harmful.

- All of the options for commands included in the tool should be available for use, except when doing so would violate the next item.

- The tool should not include every administrative command. More specifically, it should deliberately omit commands that could cause catastrophic consequences if they are used incorrectly. Which items to omit depends on the sort of administrators the tool is designed for; the scope of the tool should be directly proportional to the amount of knowledge its user is assumed to have. In the extreme case, dragging a disk icon into a trash can icon should never do anything other than dismount it, and there should not be any way to, say, reformat an existing filesystem. Given that such a tool is consciously designed for minimally-competent administrators, including such capabilities is just asking for trouble.

In addition, these features make using an administrative tool much more efficient, but they are not absolutely essential:

- A way of specifying the desired starting location within a deep menu tree when you invoke the tool.

- A one-keystroke exit command that works at every point within menu system.

- Context-sensitive help.

- The ability to limit access to subsections of the tool by user.

- Customization features.

If one uses these criteria, AIX's SMIT comes closest to an ideal administrative tool, a finding that many have found ironic.

As usual, using menu interfaces in moderation is probably the best approach. These applications are great when they save you time and effort, but relying on them to lead you through every situation will inevitably lead to frustration and disappointment somewhere down the line.

The Unix versions we are considering offer various system administration facilities. They are summarized and compared in Table 1-2. The table columns hold the Unix version, tool command or name, tool type, whether or not the command to be run can be previewed before execution, whether or not the facility can log its actions and whether or not the tool can be used to administer remote systems.

Table 1-2. Some system administration facilities

Unix Version	Command/tool	Type	Command preview?	Creates logs?[a]	Remote admin?
AIX	smit	menu	yes	yes	no
	WSM	GUI	no	no	yes
FreeBSD	sysinstall	menu	no	no	no
HP-UX	sam	both	no	yes	yes
Linux	linuxconf	both	no	no	no
Red Hat Linux	redhat-config-*	GUI	no	no	no
SuSE Linux	yast	menu	no	no	no
	yast2	GUI	no	no	no
Solaris	admintool	menu	no	no	no
	CDE admin tools	GUI	no	no	no
	AdminSuite/SMC	menu	no	yes	yes
Tru64	sysman	menu	no	no	no
	sysman -station	menu	no	no	yes

[a] Some tools do some rather half-hearted logging to the syslog facility, but it's not very useful.

There are also some other tools on some of these systems that will be mentioned in this book when appropriate, but they are ignored here.

AIX: SMIT and WSM

AIX offers two main system administration facilities: the System Management Interface Tool (SMIT) and the Workspace System Manager (WSM) facility. Both of them run in both graphical and text mode.

SMIT consists of a many-leveled series of nested menus. Its main menu is illustrated in Figure 1-2.

One of SMIT's most helpful features is command preview: if you click on the Command button or press F6, SMIT displays the command to be executed by the current dialog. This feature is illustrated in the window on the right in Figure 1-2.

You can also go directly to any screen by including the corresponding *fast path* keyword on the smit command line. Many SMIT fast paths are the same as the command

Why Menus and Icons Aren't Enough

Every site needs at least one experienced system administrator who can perform those tasks that are beyond the abilities of the administrative tool. Not only does every current tool leave significant amounts of uncovered territory, but they also all suffer from limitations inherent in programs designed for routine operations under normal system conditions. When the system is in trouble, and these assumptions no longer hold, the tools don't work.

For example, I've been in a situation where the administrative tool couldn't configure a replacement because the old disk hadn't been unconfigured properly before being removed. One part of the tool thought the old disk was still on the system and wouldn't replace it, while another part wouldn't delete the old configuration data because it couldn't access the corresponding physical disk.

I was able to solve this problem because I understood enough about the device database on that system to fix things manually. Not only will such things happen to every system from time to time, they will happen to everyone, sooner or later. It's a lot easier to coax a system back to life from single user mode after a power failure when you understand, for example, what the Check Filesystem Integrity menu item actually does. In the end, *you* need to know how things really work.

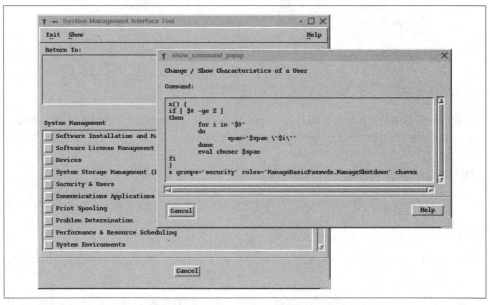

Figure 1-2. The AIX SMIT facility

executed from a particular screen. Many other fast paths fall into a predictable pattern, beginning with one of the prefixes mk (make or start), ch (change or reconfigure), ls (list), or rm (remove or stop), to which an object code is appended: mkuser, chuser, lsuser, rmuser for working with user accounts; mkprt, chprt, lsprt, rmprt for working with printers, and so on. Thus, it's often easy to guess the fast path you want.

You can display the fast path for any SMIT screen by pressing F8 in the ASCII version of the tool:

```
Current fast path:
    "mkuser"
```

If the screen doesn't have a fast path, the second line will be blank. Other useful fast paths that are harder to guess include the following:

chgsys
> View/change AIX parameters.

configtcp
> Reconfigure TCP/IP.

crfs
> Create a new filesystem.

lvm
> Main Logical Volume Manager menu.

_nfs
> Main NFS menu.

spooler
> Manipulate print jobs.

Here are a few additional SMIT notes:

- The smitty command may be used to start the ASCII version of SMIT from within an X session (where the graphical version is invoked by default).

- Although I like them, many people are annoyed by the SMIT log files. You can use a command like this one to eliminate the SMIT log files:

  ```
  $ smit -s /dev/null -l /dev/null ...
  ```

  You can define an alias in your shell initialization file to get rid of these files permanently (C shell users would omit the equals sign):

  ```
  alias smit="/usr/sbin/smitty -s /dev/null -l /dev/null"
  ```

- smit -x provides a command preview mode. The commands that would be run are written to the log file but not executed.

- Newer versions of smit have the following annoying feature: when a command has successfully completed, and you click Done to close the output window, you are taken back to the command setup window. At this point, to exit, you must click Cancel, not OK. Doing the latter will cause the command to run again, which is not what you want and is occasionally quite troublesome!

The WSM facility contains a variety of GUI-based tools for managing various aspects of the system. Its functionality is a superset of SMIT's, and it has the advantage of being able to administer remote systems (it requires that remote systems be running a web server). You can access WSM via the Common Desktop Environment's Applications area: click on the file cabinet icon (the one with the calculator peeking out of it); the system administration tools are then accessible under the System_Admin icon. You can also run a command-line version of WSM via the wsm command.

The WSM tools are run on a remote system via a Java-enabled web browser. You can connect to the tools by pointing the browser at *http://*hostname*/wsm.html*, where *hostname* corresponds to the desired remote system. Of course, you can also run the text version by entering the wsm command into a remote terminal session.

HP-UX: SAM

HP-UX provides the System Administration Manager, also known as SAM. SAM is easy to use and can perform a variety of system management tasks. SAM operates in both menu-based and GUI mode, although the latter requires support for Motif.

The items on SAM's menus invoke a combination of regular HP-UX commands and special scripts and programs, so it's not always obvious what they do. One way to find out more is to use SAM's built-in logging feature. SAM allows you to specify the level of detail in log file displays, and you can optionally keep the log open as you are working in order to monitor what is actually happening. The SAM main window and log display are illustrated in Figure 1-3.

If you really want to know what SAM is doing, you'll need to consult its configuration files, stored in the subdirectories of */usr/sam/lib*. Most subdirectories have two-character names, closely related to a top-level icon or menu item. For example, the *ug* subdirectory contains files for the Users and Groups module, and the *pm* subdirectory contains those for Process Management. If you examine the *.tm* file there, you can figure out what some of the menu items do. This example illustrates the kinds of items to look for in these files:

```
#egrep '^task [a-z]|^ *execute' pm.tm
task pm_get_ps {
   execute "/usr/sam/lbin/pm_parse_ps"
task pm_add_cron {
   execute "/usr/sam/lbin/cron_change ADD /var/sam/pm_tmpfile"
task pm_add_cron_check {
   execute "/usr/sam/lbin/cron_change CHECK /var/sam/pm_tmpfile"
task pm_mod_nice {
   execute "unset UNIX95;/usr/sbin/renice -n %$INT_ID% %$STRING_ID%"
task pm_rm_cron {
   execute "/usr/sam/lbin/cron_change REMOVE /var/sam/pm_tmpfile"
```

The items come in pairs, relating a menu item or icon and an actual HP-UX command. For example, the fourth pair in the previous output allows you to figure out what the Modify Nice Priority menu item does (runs the renice command). The second pair indicates that the item related to adding cron entries executes the listed shell script; you can examine that file directly to get further details.

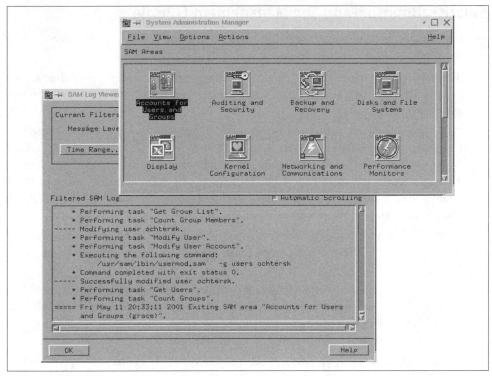

Figure 1-3. The HP-UX SAM facility

There is another configuration file for each main menu item in the */usr/sam/lib/C* subdirectory, named *pm.ui* in this case. Examining the lines containing "action" and "do" provides similar information. Note that "do" entries that end with parentheses (e.g., *do pm_forcekill_xmit()*) indicate a call to a routine in one of SAM's component shared libraries, which will mean the end of the trail for your detective work.

SAM allows you to selectively grant access to its functional areas on a per-user basis. Invoke it via sam -r to set up user privileges and restrictions. In this mode, you select the user or group for which you want to define allowed access, and then you navigate through the various icons and menus, enabling or disabling items as appropriate. When you are finished, you can save these settings and also save groups of settings as named permission templates that can subsequently be applied to other users and groups.

In this mode, the SAM display changes, and the icons are colored indicating the allowed access: red for prohibited, green for allowed, and yellow when some features are allowed and others are prohibited.

You can use SAM for remote administration by selecting the Run SAM on Remote System icon from the main window. The first time you connect to a specific remote system, SAM automatically sets up the environment.

Solaris: admintool and Sun Management Console

From a certain point of view, current versions of Solaris actually offer three distinct tool options:

- admintool, the menu-based system administration package available under Solaris for many years. You must be a member of the *sysadmin* group to run this program.

- A set of GUI-based tools found under the System_Admin icon of the Applications Manager window under the Common Desktop Environment (CDE), which is illustrated on the left in Figure 1-4. Select the Applications → Application Manager menu path from the CDE's menu to open this window. Most of these tools are very simple, one-task utilities related to media management, although there is also an icon there for admintool.

- The Solaris AdminSuite, whose components are controlled by the Sun Management Console (SMC). The facility's main window is illustrated on the right in Figure 1-4.

  In some cases, this package is included with the Solaris operating system. It is also available for (free) download (from *http://www.sun.com/bigadmin/content/ adminpack/*). In fact, it is well worth the overnight download required if you have only a slow modem (two nights if you want the documentation as well).

  This tool can be used to perform administrative tasks on remote systems. You specify the system on which you want to operate when you log in to the facility.

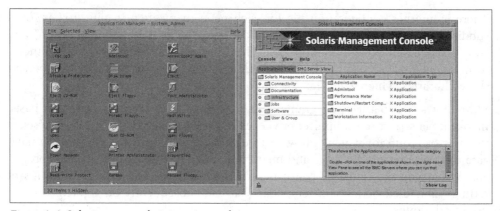

Figure 1-4. Solaris system administration tools

Linux: Linuxconf

Many Linux systems, including some Red Hat versions, offer the Linuxconf graphical administrative tool written by Jacques Gélinas. This tool can also be used with other Linux distributions (see *http://www.solucorp.qc.ca/linuxconf/*). It is illustrated in Figure 1-5.

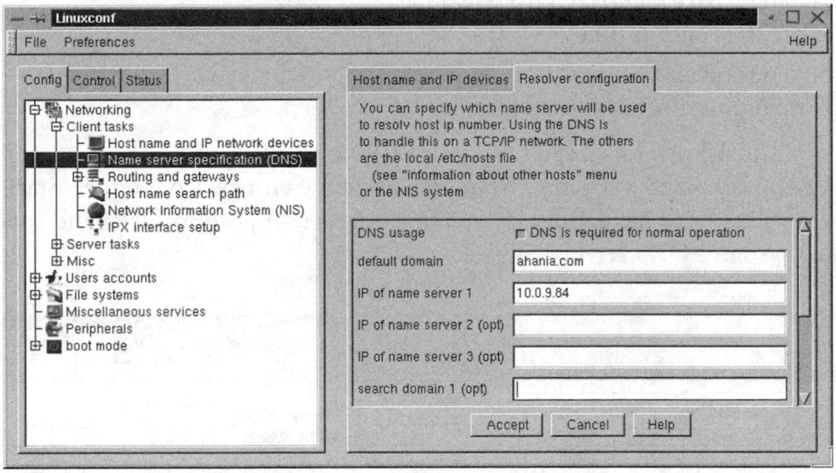

Figure 1-5. The Linuxconf facility

The tool's menu system is located in the area on the left, and forms related to the current selection are displayed on the right. Several of the program's subsections can be accessed directly via separate commands (which are in fact just links to the main `linuxconf` executable): `fsconf`, `mailconf`, `modemconf`, `netconf`, `userconf`, and `uucpconf`, which administer filesystems, electronic mail, modems, networking parameters, users and groups and UUCP, respectively.

Early versions of Linuxconf were dreadful: bug-rich and unbelievably slow. However, more recent versions have improved quite a bit, and the current version is pretty good. Linuxconf leans toward supporting all available options at the expense of novice's ease-of-use at times (a choice with which I won't quarrel). As a result, it is a tool that can make many kinds of configuration tasks easier for an experienced administrator; less expert users may find the number of settings in some dialogs to be somewhat daunting. You can also specify access to Linuxconf and its various subsections on a per-user basis (this is configured via the user account settings).

Red Hat Linux: redhat-config-*

Red Hat Linux provides several GUI-based administration tools, including these:

redhat-config-bindconf
    Configure the DNS server (redhat-config-bind under Version 7.2).

redhat-config-network
    Configure the networking on the local host (new with Red Hat Version 7.3).

redhat-config-printer-gui
    Configure and manage print queues and the print server.

redhat-config-services
    Select servers to be started at boot time.

redhat-config-date *and* redhat-config-time
    Set the date and/or time.

redhat-config-users
    Configure user accounts and groups.

There are often links to some of these utilities with different (shorter) names. They can also be accessed via icons from the System Settings icon under Start Here. Figure 1-6 illustrates the dialogs for creating a new user account (left) and specifying the local system's DNS server (right).

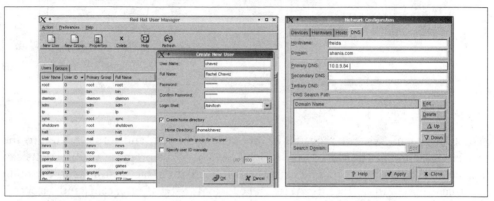

Figure 1-6. Red Hat Linux system configuration tools

SuSE Linux: YaST2

The "YaST" in YaST2 stands for "yet another setup tool." It is a follow-on to the original YaST, and like the previous program (which is also available), it is a somewhat prettied up menu-based administration facility. The program's main window is illustrated in Figure 1-7.

The yast2 command is used to start the tool. Generally, the tool is easy to use and does its job pretty well. It does have one disadvantage, however. Whenever you add a new package or make other kinds of changes to the system configuration, the *SuSEconfig* script runs (actually, a series of scripts in */sbin/conf.d*). Before SuSE Version 8, this process was fiendishly slow.

SuSEconfig's actions are controlled by the settings in the */etc/rc.config* configuration file, as well as those in */etc/rc.config.d* (SuSE Version 7) or */etc/sysconfig* (SuSE Version 8). Its slowness stems from the fact that every action is performed every time anything changes on the system; in other words, it has no intelligence whatsoever that would allow it to operate only on items and areas that were modified.

Even worse, on SuSE 7 systems, *SuSEconfig*'s actions are occasionally just plain wrong. A particularly egregious example occurs with the Postfix electronic mail package. By default, the primary Postfix configuration file, *main.cf*, is overwritten

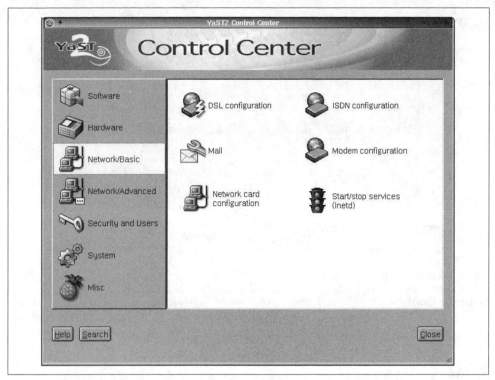

Figure 1-7. The SuSE Linux YaST2 facility

every time the Postfix *SuSEconfig* subscript is executed.* The latter happens every time *SuSEconfig* runs, which is practically every time you change anything on the system with YaST or YaST2 (regardless of its lack of relevance to Postfix). The net result is that any local customizations to *main.cf* get lost. Clearly, adding a new game package, for example, shouldn't clobber a key electronic-mail configuration file.

Fortunately, these problems have been cleared up in SuSE Version 8. I do also use YaST2 on SuSE 7 systems, but I've examined all of the component subscripts thoroughly and made changes to configuration files to disable actions I didn't want. You should do the same.

FreeBSD: sysinstall

FreeBSD offers only the sysinstall utility in terms of administrative tools, the same program that manages operating system installations and upgrades (its main menu is illustrated in Figure 1-8). Accordingly, the tasks that it can handle are limited to the ones that come up in the context of operating system installations: managing disks and partitions, basic networking configuration, and so on.

---

* You can prevent this by setting POSTFIX_CREATECF to no in */etc/rc.config.d/postfix.rc.config*.

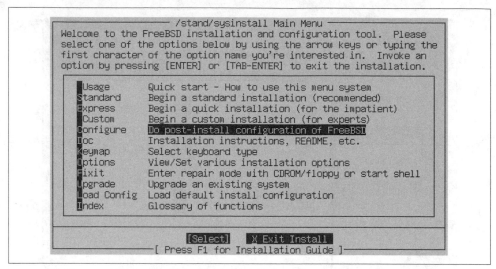

Figure 1-8. The FreeBSD sysinstall facility

Both the Configure and Index menu items are of interest for general system administration tasks. The latter is especially useful in that it lists individually all the available
operations the tool can perform.

Tru64: SysMan

The Tru64 operating system offers the SysMan facility. This tool is essentially menu
driven despite the fact that it can run in various graphical environments, including via
a Java 1.1–enabled browser. SysMan can run in two different modes, as shown in
Figure 1-9: as a system administration utility for the local system or as a monitoring
and management station for the network. These two modes of operations are selected
with the sysman command's -menu and -station options, respectively; -menu is the
default.

This utility does not have any command preview or logging features, but it does have
a variety of "accelerators": keywords that can be used to initiate a session at a particular menu point. For example, sysman shutdown takes you directly to the system shutdown dialog. Use the command sysman -list to obtain a complete list of all defined
accelerators.

One final note: the insightd daemon must be running in order to be able to access
the SysMan online help.

Other Freely Available Administration Tools

The freely available operating systems often provide some additional administrative
tools as part of the various window manager packages that they include. For example, both the Gnome and KDE desktop environments include several administrative

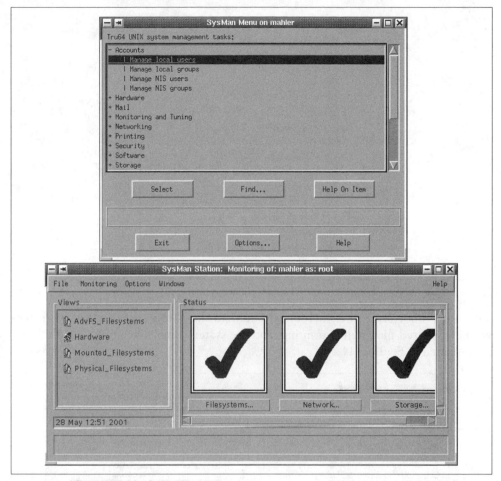

Figure 1-9. The SysMan facility

applets and utilities. Those available under KDE on a SuSE Linux system are illustrated in Figure 1-10.

We will consider some of the best of these tools from time to time in this book.

The Ximian Setup Tools

The Ximian project brings together the latest release of the Gnome desktop, the Red Carpet web-based system software update facility, and several other items into what is designed to be a commercial-quality desktop environment. As of this writing, it is available for several Linux distributions and for Solaris systems. Additional ports, including to BSD, are planned for the future.

The Ximian Setup Tools are a series of applets designed to facilitate system administration, ultimately in a multiplatform environment. Current modules allow you to

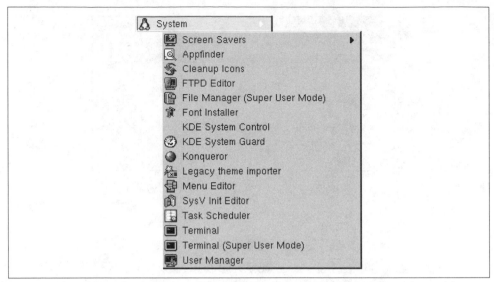

Figure 1-10. KDE administrative tools on a SuSE Linux system

administer boot setup (i.e., kernel selection), disks, swap space, users, basic networking, shared filesystems, printing, and the system time. The applet for the latter is illustrated in Figure 1-11.

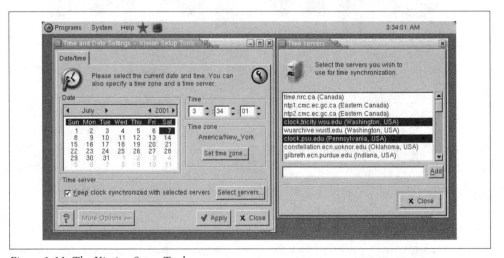

Figure 1-11. The Ximian Setup Tools

This applet, even in this early incarnation, goes well beyond a simple dialog allowing you to set the current date and time; it also allows you to specify time servers for Internet-based time synchronization. The other tools are of similar quality, and the package seems very promising for those who want GUI-based system administration tools.

VNC

I'll close this section by briefly looking at one additional administrative tool that can be of great use for remote administration, especially in a heterogeneous environment. It is called VNC, which stands for "virtual network computing." The package is available for a wide variety of Unix systems* at *http://www.uk.research.att.com/vnc/*. It is shown in Figure 1-12.

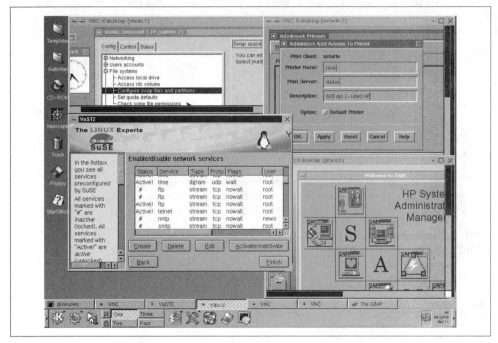

Figure 1-12. Using VNC for remote system administration

The illustration depicts the entire desktop on a SuSE Linux system. You can see several of its icons along the left edge, as well as the tool bar at the bottom of the screen (where you can determine that it is running the KDE window manager).

The four open windows are three individual VNC sessions to different remote computers, each running a different operating system and a local YaST session. Beginning at the upper left and moving clockwise, the remote sessions are a Red Hat Linux system (Linuxconf is open), a Solaris system (we can see admintool), and an HP-UX system (running SAM).

VNC has a couple of advantages over remote application sessions displayed via the X Windows system:

---

* Official binary versions of the various tools are available for a few systems on the main web page. In addition, consult the *contrib* area for ports to additional systems. It is also usually easy to build the tools from source code.

- With VNC you see the entire desktop, not just one application window. Thus, you can access applications via the remote system's own icons and menus (which may be much less convenient to initiate via commands).

- You eliminate missing font issues and many other display and resource problems, because you are using the X server on the remote system to generate the display images rather than the one on the local system.

In order to use VNC, you must download the software and build or install the five executables that comprise it (conventionally, they are placed in */usr/local/bin*). Then you must start a server process on systems that you want to administer remotely, using the vncserver command:

```
garden-$ vncserver
You will require a password to access your desktops.

Password:    Not echoed.
Verify:

New 'X' desktop is garden:1

Creating default startup script /home/chavez/.vnc/xstartup
Starting applications specified in /home/chavez/.vnc/xstartup
Log file is /home/chavez/.vnc/garden:1.log
```

This example starts a server on host *garden*. The first time you run the vncserver command, you will be asked for a password. This password, which is independent of your normal Unix password, will be required in order to connect to the server.

Once the server is running, you connect to it by running the vncviewer command. In this example, we connect to the vncserver on *garden*:

```
desert-$ vncviewer garden:1
```

The parameter given is the same as was indicated when the server was started. VNC allows multiple servers to be running simultaneously.

In order to shut down a VNC server, execute a command like this one on the remote system (i.e., the system where the server was started):

```
garden-$ vncserver -kill :1
```

 Only the VNC server password is required for connection. Usernames are not checked, so an ordinary user can connect to a server started by *root* if she knows the proper password. Therefore, it is important to select strong passwords for the server password (see "Administering User Passwords" in Chapter 6) and to use a different password from the normal one if such cross-user connections are needed.

Additionally, VNC passwords are sent in plain text over the network. Thus, using VNC is problematic on an insecure network. In such circumstances, VNC traffic can be encrypted by tunneling it through a secure protocol, such as SSH.

Where Does the Time Go?

We'll close this chapter with a brief look at a nice utility that can be useful for keeping track of how you spend your time, information that system administrators will find comes in handy all too often. It is called `plod` and was written by Hal Pomeranz (see *http://bullwinkle.deer-run.com/~hal/plod/*). While there are similar utilities with a GUI interface (e.g., `gtt` and `karm`, from the Gnome and KDE window manager packages, respectively), I prefer this simpler one that doesn't require a graphical environment.

`plod` works by maintaining a log file containing time stamped entries that you provide; the files' default location is *~/.logdir/yyyymm*, where *yyyy* and *mm* indicate the current year and month, respectively. `plod` log files can optionally be encrypted.

The command has lots of options, but its simplest form is the following:

```
$ plod [text]
```

If some text is included on the command, it is written to the log file (tagged with the current date and time). Otherwise, you enter the command's interactive mode, in which you can type in the desired text. Input ends with a line containing a lone period.

Once you've accumulated some log entries, you can use the command's -C, -P, and -E options to display them, either as continuous output, piped through a paging command like `more` (although `less` is the default), or via an editor (`vi` is the default). You can specify a different paging program or editor with the *PAGER* and *EDITOR* environment variables (respectively).

You can also use the -G option to search `plod` log files; it differs from `grep` in that matching entries are displayed in their entirety. By default, searches are not case sensitive, but you can use -g to make them so.

Here is an example command that searches the current log file:

```
$ plod -g hp-ux
-----
05/11/2001, 22:56 --
Starting to configure the new HP-UX box.
-----
05/11/2001, 23:44 --
Finished configuring the new HP-UX box.
```

Given these features, `plod` can be used to record and categorize the various tasks that you perform. We will look at a script which can read and summarize `plod` data in Chapter 14.

CHAPTER 2
The Unix Way

It's easy to identify the most important issues and concerns system managers face, regardless of the type of computers they have. Almost every system manager has to deal with user accounts, system startup and shutdown, peripheral devices, system performance, security—the list could go on and on. While the commands and procedures you use in each of these areas vary widely across different computer systems, the general approach to such issues can be remarkably similar. For example, the process of adding users to a system has the same basic shape everywhere: add the user to the user account database, allocate some disk space for him, assign a password to the account, enable him to use major system facilities and applications, and so on. Only the commands to perform these tasks are different on different systems.

In other cases, however, even the *approach* to an administrative task or issue will change from one computer system to the next. For example, "mounting disks" doesn't mean the same thing on a Unix system that it does on a VMS or MVS system (where they're not always even called disks). No matter what operating system you're using—Unix, Windows 2000, MVS—you need to know something about what's happening inside, at least more than an ordinary user does.

Like it or not, a system administrator is generally called on to be the resident guru. If you're responsible for a multiuser system, you'll need to be able to answer user questions, come up with solutions to problems that are more than just band-aids, and more. Even if you're responsible only for your own workstation, you'll find yourself dealing with aspects of the computer's operation that most ordinary users can simply ignore. In either case, you need to know a fair amount about how Unix really works, both to manage your system and to navigate the eccentric and sometimes confusing byways of the often jargon-ridden technical documentation.

This chapter will explore the Unix approach to some basic computer entities: files, processes, and devices. In each case, I will discuss how the Unix approach affects system administration procedures and objectives. The chapter concludes with an overview of the standard Unix directory structure.

If you have managed non-Unix computer systems, this chapter will serve as a bridge between the administrative concepts you know and the specifics of Unix. If you have some familiarity with user-level Unix commands, this chapter will show you their place in the underlying operating system structure, enabling you to place them in an administrative context. If you're already familiar with things like file modes, inodes, special files, and fork-and-exec, you can probably skip this chapter.

Files

Files are central to Unix in ways that are not true for some other operating systems. Commands are executable files, usually stored in standard locations in the directory tree. System privileges and permissions are controlled in large part via access to files. Device I/O and file I/O are distinguished only at the lowest level. Even most inter-process communication occurs via file-like entities. Accordingly, the Unix view of files and its standard directory structure are among the first things a new administrator needs to know about.

Like all modern operating systems, Unix has a hierarchical (tree-structured) directory organization, know collectively as the *filesystem*.* The base of this tree is a directory called the *root directory*. The root directory has the special name / (the forward slash character). On Unix systems, all user-available disk space is transparently combined into a single directory tree under /, and the physical disk a file resides on is not part of a Unix file specification. We'll discuss this topic in more detail later in this chapter.

Access to files is organized around file ownership and protection. Security on a Unix system depends to a large extent on the interplay between the ownership and protection settings on its files and the system's user account and group† structure (as well as factors like physical access to the machine). The following sections discuss the basic principles of Unix file ownership and protection.

File Ownership

Unix file ownership is a bit more complex than it is under some other operating systems. You are undoubtedly familiar with the basic concept of a file having an owner: typically, the user who created it and has control over it. On Unix systems, files have two owners: a user owner and a group owner. What is unusual about Unix file ownership is that these two owners are decoupled. A file's group ownership is independent of the user who owns it. In other words, although a file's group owner is often,

---

* Or *file system*—the two forms refer to the same thing. To make things even more ambiguous, these terms are also used to refer to the collection of files on an individual formatted disk partition.

† On Unix systems, individual user accounts are organized into *groups*. Groups are simply collections of users, defined by the entries in */etc/passwd* and */etc/group*. The mechanics of defining groups and designating users as members of them are described in Chapter 6. Using groups effectively to enhance system security is discussed in Chapter 7.

perhaps even usually, the same as the group its user owner belongs to, this is not required. In fact, the user owner of a file does need not even need to be a member of the group that owns it. There is no necessary connection between them at all. In such a case, when file access is specified for a file's group owner, it applies to members of that group and not to other members of its user owner's group, who are treated simply as part of "other": the rest of the world.

The motivation behind this group ownership of files is to allow file protections and permissions to be organized according to your needs. The key point here is flexibility. Because Unix lets users be in more than one group, you are free to create groups as you need them. Files can be made accessible to almost completely arbitrary collections of the system's users. Group file ownership means that giving someone access to an entire set of files and commands is as simple as adding her to the group that owns them; similarly, taking access away from someone else involves removing her from the relevant group.

To consider a more concrete example, suppose user *chavez*, who is in the *chem* group, needs access to some files usually used by the *physics* group. There are several ways you can give her access:

- Make copies of the files for her. If they change, however, her copies will need to be updated. And if she needs to make changes too, it will be hard to avoid ending up with two versions that need to be merged together. (Because of inconveniences like these, this choice is seldom taken.)
- Make the files world-readable. The disadvantage of this approach is that it opens up the possibility that someone you don't want to look at the files will see them.
- Make *chavez* a member of the *physics* group. This is the best alternative and also the simplest. It involves changing only the group configuration file. The file permissions don't need to be modified at all, since they already allow access for *physics* group members.

Displaying file ownership

To display a file's user and group ownership, use the long form of the ls command by including the -l option (-lg under Solaris):

```
$ ls -l
-rwxr-xr-x  1 root     system       120   Mar 12 09:32  bronze
-r--r--r--  1 chavez   chem          84   Feb 28 21:43  gold
-rw-rw-r--  1 chavez   physics    12842   Oct 24 12:04  platinum
-rw-------  1 harvey   physics      512   Jan  2 16:10  silver
```

Columns three and four display the user and group owners for the listed files. For example, we can see that the file *bronze* is owned by user *root* and group *system*. The next two files are both owned by user *chavez,* but they have different group owners; *gold* is owned by group *chem*, while *platinum* is owned by group *physics*. The last file, *silver*, is owned by user *harvey* and group *physics*.

Who owns new files?

When a new file is created, its user owner is the user who creates it. On most Unix systems, the group owner is the current* group of the user who creates the file. However, on BSD-style systems, the group owner is the same as the group owner of the directory in which the file is created. Of the versions we are considering, FreeBSD and Tru64 Unix operate in the second manner by default.

Most current Unix versions, including all of those we are considering, allow a system to selectively use BSD-style group inheritance from the directory group ownership by setting the set group ID (setgid) attribute on the directory, which we discuss in more detail later in this chapter.

Changing file ownership

If you need to change the ownership of a file, use the chown and chgrp commands. The chown command changes the user owner of one or more files:

```
# chown new-owner files
```

where *new-owner* is the username (or user ID) of the new owner for the specified files. For example, to change the owner of the file *brass* to user *harvey,* execute this chown command:

```
# chown harvey brass
```

On most systems, only the superuser can run the chown command.

If you need to change the ownership of an entire directory tree, you can use the -R option (*R* for *recursive*). For example, the following command will change the user owner to *harvey* for the directory */home/iago/new/tgh* and all files and subdirectories contained underneath it:

```
# chown -R harvey /home/iago/new/tgh
```

You can also change both the user and group owner in a single operation, using this format:

```
# chown new-owner:new-group files
```

For example, to change the user owner to *chavez* and the group owner to *chem* for *chavez*'s home directory and all the files underneath it, use this command:

```
# chown -R chavez:chem /home/chavez
```

If you just want to change a file's group ownership, use the chgrp command:

```
$ chgrp new-group files
```

where *new-group* is the group name (or group ID) of the desired group owner for the specified files. chgrp also supports the -R option. Non-*root* users of chgrp must be

---

* See "Unix Users and Groups" in Chapter 6 for information about how the user's primary group is determined.

both the owner of the file and a member of the new group to change a file's group ownership (but need not be a member of its current group).

File Protection

Once ownership is set up properly, the next natural issue to consider is how to protect files from unwanted access (or the reverse: how to allow access to those people who need it). The protection on a file is referred to as its *file mode* on Unix systems. File modes are set with the chmod command; we'll look at chmod after discussing the file protection concepts it relies on.

Types of file and directory access

Unix supports three types of file access: read, write, and execute, designated by the letters *r*, *w*, and *x*, respectively. Table 2-1 shows the meanings of those access types.

Table 2-1. File access types

Access	Meaning for a file	Meaning for a directory
r	View file contents.	Search directory contents (e.g., use ls).
w	Alter file contents.	Alter directory contents (e.g., delete or rename files).
x	Run executable file.	Make it your current directory (cd to it).

The file access types are fairly straightforward. If you have read access to a file, you can see what's in it. If you have write access, you can change what's in it. If you have execute access and the file is a binary executable program, you can run it. To run a script, you need both read and execute access, since the shell has to read the commands to interpret them. When you run a compiled program, the operating system loads it into memory for you and begins execution, so you don't need read access yourself.

The corresponding meanings for directories may seem strange at first, but they do make sense. If you have execute access to a directory, you can cd to it (or include it in a path that you want to cd to). You can also access files in the directory by name. However, to list all the files in the directory (i.e., to run the ls command without any arguments), you also need read access to the directory. This is consistent because a directory is just a file whose contents are the names of the files it contains, along with information pointing to their disk locations. Thus, to cd to a directory, you need only execute access since you don't need to be able to read the directory file itself. In contrast, if you want to run any command lists or use files in the directory via an explicit or implicit wildcard—e.g., ls without arguments or cat *.dat—you do need read access to the directory file itself to expand the wildcards.

Table 2-2 illustrates the workings of these various access types by listing some sample commands and the minimum access you would need to successfully execute them.

Table 2-2. File protection examples

	Minimum access needed	
Command	On file itself	On directory file is in
cd /home/chavez	N/A	x
ls /home/chavez/*.c	(none)	r
	r	x
ls -l /home/chavez/*.c	(none)	rx
	r	x
cat myfile	r	x
cat >>myfile	w	x
runme (executable)	x	x
cleanup.sh (script)	rx	x
rm myfile	(none)	wx

Some items in this list are worth a second look. For example, when you don't have access to any of the component files, you still need only read access to a directory in order to do a simple ls; if you include -l (or any other option that lists file sizes), you also need execute access to the directory. This is because the file sizes must be determined from the disk information, an action which implicitly changes the directory in question. In general, any operation that involves more than simply reading the list of filenames from the directory file is going to require execute access if you don't have access to the relevant files themselves.

Note especially that write access on a file *is not required* to delete it; write access to the directory where the file resides is sufficient (although in this case, you'll be asked whether to override the protection on the file):

```
$ rm copper
rm: override protection 440 for copper? y
```

If you answer yes, the file will be deleted (the default response is no). Why does this work? Because deleting a file actually means removing its entry from the directory file (among other things), which is a form of altering the directory file, for which you need only write access to the directory. The moral is that write access to directories is very powerful and should be granted with care.

Given these considerations, we can summarize the different options for protecting directories as shown in Table 2-3.

Table 2-3. Directory protection summary

Access granted	Resulting availability
--- (no access)	Does not allow any activity of any kind within the directory or any of its subdirectories.
r-- (read access only)	Allows users to list the names of the files in the directory, but does not reveal any of their attributes (i.e., size, ownership, mode, and so on).

Table 2-3. Directory protection summary (continued)

Access granted	Resulting availability
--x (execute access only)	Lets users work with programs in the directory specified by full pathname, but hides all other files.
r-x (read and execute access)	Lets users work with programs in the directory and list the contents of the directory, but does not allow them to create or delete files in the directory.
-wx (write and execute access)	Used for a drop-box directory. Users can change to the directory and leave files there, but can't discover the names of files placed there by others. The sticky bit is also usually set on such directories (see below).
rwx (full access)	Lets users work with programs in the directory, look at the contents of the directory, and create or delete files in the directory.

Access classes

Unix defines three basic classes of file access for which protection may be specified separately:

User access (u)
> Access granted to the owner of the file.

Group access (g)
> Access granted to members of the same group as the group owner of the file (but does not apply to the owner himself, even if he is a member of this group).

Other access (o)
> Access granted to all other normal users.

Unix file protection specifies the access types available to members of each of the three access classes for the file or directory.

The long version of the ls command also displays file permissions in addition to user and group ownership:

```
$ ls -l
-rwxr-xr-x  1 root     system      120 Mar 12 09:32  bronze
-r--r--r--  1 chavez   chem         84 Feb 28 21:43  gold
-rw-rw-r--  1 chavez   physics   12842 Oct 24 12:04  platinum
```

The set of letters and hyphens at the beginning of each line represents the file's mode. The 10 characters are interpreted as indicated in Table 2-4.

Table 2-4. Interpreting mode strings

File	type 1	User access			Group access			Other access		
		read 2	write 3	exec 4	read 5	write 6	exec 7	read 8	write 9	exec 10
bronze	-	r	w	x	r	-	x	r	-	x
gold	-	r	-	-	r	-	-	r	-	-
platinum	-	r	w	-	r	w	-	r	-	-
/etc/passwd	-	r	w	-	r	-	-	r	-	-

Table 2-4. *Interpreting mode strings (continued)*

File	type 1	User access read 2	write 3	exec 4	Group access read 5	write 6	exec 7	Other access read 8	write 9	exec 10
/etc/shadow	-	r	-	-	-	-	-	-	-	-
/etc/inittab	-	r	w	-	r	w	-	r	-	-
/bin/sh	-	r	-	x	r	-	x	r	-	x
/tmp	d	r	w	x	r	w	x	r	w	t

The first character indicates the file type: a hyphen indicates a plain file, and a *d* indicates a directory (other possibilities are discussed later in this chapter). The remaining nine characters are arranged in three groups of three. Moving from left to right, the groups represent user, group, and other access. Within each group, the first character denotes read access, the second character write access, and the third character execute access. If a certain type of access is allowed, its code letter appears in the proper position within the triad; if it is not granted, a hyphen appears instead.

For example, in the previous listing, read access and no other is granted for all users on the file *gold*. On the file *bronze,* the owner—in this case, *root*—is allowed read, write, and execute access, while all other users are allowed only read and execute access. Finally, for the file *platinum,* the owner (*chavez*) and all members of the group *physics* are allowed read and write access, while everyone else is granted only read access.

The remaining entries in Table 2-4 (below the line) are additional examples illustrating the usual protections for various common system files.

Setting file protection

The chmod command is used to specify the access mode for files:

```
$ chmod access-string files
```

chmod's second argument is an *access string*, which states the permissions you want to set (or remove) for the listed files. It has three parts: the code for one or more access classes, the operator, and the code for one or more access types.

Figure 2-1 illustrates the structure of an access string. To create an access string, you choose one or more codes from the access class column, one operator from the middle column, and one or more access types from the third column. Then you concatenate them into a single string (no spaces). For example, the access string *u+w* says to add write access for the user owner of the file. Thus, to add write access for yourself for a file you own (*lead,* for example), use:

```
$ chmod u+w lead
```

To add write access for everybody, use the *all* access class:

```
$ chmod a+w lead
```

To remove write access, use a minus sign instead of a plus sign:

```
$ chmod a-w lead
```

This command sets the permissions on the file *lead* to allow only read access for all users:

```
$ chmod a=r lead
```

If execute or write access had previously been set for any access class, executing this command removes it.

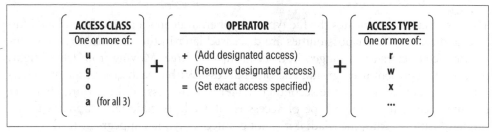

Figure 2-1. Constructing an access string for chmod

You can specify more than one access type and more than one access class. For example, the access string *g-rw* says to remove read and write access from the group access. The access string *go=r* says to set the group and other access to read-only (no execute access, no write access), changing the current setting as needed. And the access string *go+rx* says to add both read and execute access for both group and other users.

You can also include more than one set of operation–access type pairs for any given access class specification. For example, the access string *u+x-w* adds execute access and removes write access for the user owner. You can combine multiple access strings by separating them with commas (no spaces between them). Thus, the following command adds write access for the file owner and removes write access and adds read access for the group and other classes for the files *bronze* and *brass*:

```
$ chmod u+w,og+r-w bronze brass
```

The chmod command supports a *recursive* option (-R), to change the mode of a directory and all files under it. For example, if user *chavez* wants to protect all the files under her home directory from everyone else, she can use the command:

```
$ chmod -R go-rwx /home/chavez
```

Beyond the basics

So far, this discussion has undoubtedly made chmod seem more rigid than it actually is. In reality, it is a very flexible command. For example, both the access class and the access type may be omitted under some circumstances.

When the access class is omitted, it defaults to *a*. For example, the following command grants read access to all users for the current directory and every file under it:

```
$ chmod -R +r .
```

On some systems, this form operates slightly differently than a chmod a+r command. When the *a* access class is omitted, the specified permissions are compared against the default permissions currently in effect (i.e., as specified by the umask). When there is disagreement between them, the current default permissions take precedence. We'll look at this in more detail when we consider the umask a bit later.

The access string may be omitted altogether when using the = operator; this form has the effect of removing all access. For example, this command prevents any access to the file *lead* by anyone other than its owner:

```
$ chmod go= lead
```

Similarly, the form chmod = may be used to remove all access from a file (subject to constraints on some systems, to be discussed shortly).

The *X* access type grants execute access to the specified access classes only when execute access is already set for some access class. A typical use for this access type is to grant group or other read and execute access to all the directories and executable files within a subtree while granting only read access to all other types of files (the first group will all presumably have user execute access set). For example:

```
$ ls -lF
-rw-------   1 chavez chem609 Nov 29 14:31 data_file.txt
drwx------   2 chavez chem512 Nov 29 18:23 more_stuff/
-rwx------   1 chavez chem161 Nov 29 18:23 run_me*
$ chmod go+rX *
$ ls -lF
-rw-r--r--   1 chavez chem609 Nov 29 14:31 data_file.txt
drwxr-xr-x   2 chavez chem512 Nov 29 18:23 more_stuff/
-rwxr-xr-x   1 chavez chem161 Nov 29 18:23 run_me*
```

By specifying *X*, we avoid making *data_file.txt* executable, which would be a mistake.

chmod also supports the *u*, *g*, and *o* access *types*, which may be used as a shorthand form for the corresponding class's current settings (determined separately for each specified file). For example, this command makes the other access the same as the current group access for each file in the current directory:

```
$ chmod o=g *
```

If you like thinking in octal, or if you've been around Unix a long time, you may find numeric modes more convenient than incantations like *go+rX*. Numeric modes are described in the next section.

Specifying numeric file modes

The method just described for specifying file modes uses *symbolic* modes, since code letters are used to refer to each access class and type. The mode may also be set as an *absolute* mode by converting the symbolic representation used by ls to a numeric form. Each access triad (for a different user class) is converted to a single digit by setting each individual character in the triad to 1 or 0, depending on whether that type of access is permitted or not, and then taking the resulting three-digit binary number and converting it to an integer (which will be between 0 and 7). Here is a sample conversion:

	user			group			other		
Mode	r	w	x	r	-	x	r	-	-
Convert to binary	1	1	1	1	0	1	1	0	0
Convert to octal digit		7			5			4	
Corresponding absolute mode					754				

To set the protection on a file to match those above, you specify the numeric file mode 754 to chmod as the access string:

```
$ chmod 754 pewter
```

Specifying the default file mode

You can use the umask command to specify the default mode for newly created files. Its argument is a three-digit numeric mode that represents the access to be *inhibited*—masked out—when a file is created. Thus, the value is the octal complement of the desired numeric file mode.

If masks confuse, you can compute the umask value by subtracting the numeric access mode you want to assign from 777. For example, to obtain the mode 754 by default, compute 777 − 754 = 023; this is the value you give to umask:

```
$ umask 023
```

Note that leading zeros are included to make the mask three digits long.

Once this command is executed, all future files created are given this protection automatically. You usually put a umask command in the system-wide login initialization file and in the individual login initialization files you give to users when you create their accounts (see Chapter 6).

As we mentioned earlier, the chmod command's actions are affected by the default permissions when no explicit access class is specified, as in this example:

```
% chmod +rx *
```

In such cases, the current umask is taken into account before the file access mode is changed. More specifically, an individual access permission is not changed unless the umask allows it to be set.

It takes a concrete example to fully appreciate this aspect of chmod:

```
$ umask              Displays the current value.
23
$ ls -l gold silver
----------   1 chavez   chem        609 Oct 24 14:31  gold
-rwxrwxrwx   1 chavez   chem      12874 Oct 22 23:14  silver
$ chmod +rwx gold
$ chmod -rwx silver
$ ls -l gold silver
-rwxr-xr--   1 chavez   chem        609 Nov 12 09:04  gold
-----w--wx   1 chavez   chem      12874 Nov 12 09:04  silver
```

The current umask of 023 allows all access for the user, read and execute access for the group, and read-only access for other users. Thus, the first chmod command acts as one would expect, setting access in accordance with what is allowed by the umask. However, the interaction between the current umask and chmod's "–" operator may seem somewhat bizarre. The second chmod command clears only those access bits that are *permitted* by the umask; in this case, write access for group and write and execute access for other remain turned on.

Special-purpose access modes

The simple file access modes described previously do not exhaust the Unix possibilities. Table 2-5 lists the other defined file modes.

Table 2-5. Special-purpose access modes

Code	Name	Meaning
t	save text mode, sticky bit	Files: Keep executable in memory after exit. Directories: Restrict deletions to each user's own files.
s	setuid bit	*Files*: Set process user ID on execution.
s	setgid bit	Files: Set process group ID on execution. Directories: New files inherit directory group owner.
l	file locking	Files: Set mandatory file locking on reads/writes (Solaris and Tru64 and sometimes Linux). This mode is set via the group access type and requires that group execute access is off. Displayed as S in ls -l listings.

The *t* access type turns on the *sticky bit* (the formal name is *save text mode,* which is where the *t* comes from). For files, this traditionally told the Unix operating system to keep an executable image in memory even after the process that was using it had exited. This feature is seldom implemented in current Unix implementations. It was designed to minimize startup overhead for frequently used programs like vi. We'll consider the sticky bit on directories below.

When the set user ID (setuid) or set group ID (setgid) access mode is set on an executable file, processes that run it are granted access to system resources based upon the file's user or group owner, rather than based on the user who created the process. We'll consider these access modes in detail later in this chapter.

Save-text access on directories

The sticky bit has a different meaning when it is set on directories. If the sticky bit is set on a directory, a user may only delete files that she owns or for which she has explicit write permission granted, even when she has write access to the directory (thus overriding the default Unix behavior). This feature is designed to be used with directories like */tmp,* which are world-writable, but in which it may not be desirable to allow any user to delete files at will.

The sticky bit is set using the user access class. For example, to turn on the sticky bit on */tmp,* use this command:

```
# chmod u+t /tmp
```

Oddly, Unix displays the sticky bit as a "t" in the other execute access slot in long directory listings:

```
$ ls -ld /tmp
drwxrwxrwt   2 root          8704  Mar 21 00:37  /tmp
```

Setgid access on directories

Setgid access on a directory has a special meaning. When this mode is set, it means that files created in that directory will have the same group ownership as the directory itself (rather than the user owner's primary group), emulating the default behavior on BSD-based systems (FreeBSD and Tru64). This approach is useful when you have groups of users who need to share a lot of files. Having them work from a common directory with the setgid attribute means that correct group ownership will be automatically set for new files, even if the people in the group don't share the same primary group.

To place setgid access on a directory, use a command like this one:

```
# chmod g+s /pub/chem2
```

Numerical equivalents for special access modes

The special access modes can also be set numerically. They are set via an additional octal digit prepended to the mode whose bits correspond to the sticky bit (lowest bit: 1), setgid/file locking (middle bit: 2), and setuid (high bit: 4). Here are some examples:

```
# chmod 4755 uid         Setuid access
# chmod 2755 gid         Setgid access
# chmod 6755 both        Setuid and setgid access: 2 highest bits on
# chmod 1777 sticky      Sticky bit
# chmod 2745 locking     File locking (note that group execute is off)
# ls -ld
-rwsr-sr-x  1 root   chem        0 Mar 30 11:37 both
-rwxr-sr-x  1 root   chem        0 Mar 30 11:37 gid
-rwxr-Sr-x  1 root   chem        0 Mar 30 11:37 locking
drwxrwxrwt  2 root   chem     8192 Mar 30 11:39 sticky
-rwsr-xr-x  1 root   chem        0 Mar 30 11:37 uid
```

How to Recognize a File Access Problem

My first rule of thumb about any user problem that comes up is this: it's usually a file ownership or protection problem.* Seriously, though, the majority of the problems users encounter that aren't the result of hardware problems really are file access problems. One classic tip-off of a file protection problem is something that worked yesterday, or last week, or even last year, but doesn't today. Another clue is that something works differently for *root* than it does for other users.

In order to work properly, programs and commands must have access to the input and output files they use, any scratch areas they access, and any permanent files they rely on, including the special files in */dev* (which act as device interfaces).

When such a problem arises, it can come from either the file permissions being wrong or the protection being correct but the ownership (user and/or group) being wrong.

The trickiest problem of this sort I've ever seen was at a customer site where I was conducting a user training course. Suddenly, their main text editor, which happened to be a clone of the VAX/VMS editor EDT, just stopped working. It seemed to start up fine, but then it would bomb out when it got to its initialization file. But the editor worked without a hitch when *root* ran it. The system administrator admitted to "changing a few things" the previous weekend but didn't remember exactly what. I checked the protections on everything I could think of, but found nothing. I even checked the special files corresponding to the physical disks in */dev*. My company ultimately had to send out a debugging version of the editor, and the culprit turned out to be */dev/null*, which the system administrator had decided needed protecting against random users!

There are at least three morals to this story:

- For the local administrator: *always* test every change before going on to the next one—multiple, random changes almost always wreak havoc. Writing them down as you do them also makes troubleshooting easier.
- For me: if you *know* it's a protection problem, check the permissions on *everything*.
- For the programmer who wrote the editor: *always* check the return value of system calls (but that's another book).

If you suspect a file protection problem, try running the command or program as *root*. If it works fine, it's almost certainly a protection problem.

A common, inadvertent way of creating file ownership problems is by accidentally editing files as *root*. When you save the file, the file's owner is changed by some editors. The most obscure variation on this effect that I've heard of is this: someone was

---

* At least, this was the case before the Internet.

editing a file as *root* using an editor that automatically creates backup files whenever the edited file is saved. Creating a backup file meant writing a new file to the directory holding the original file. This caused the ownership on the *directory* to be set to *root*.* Since this happened in the directory used by UUCP (the Unix-to-Unix copy facility), and correct file and directory ownership are crucial for UUCP to function, what at first seemed to be an innocuous change to an inconsequential file broke an entire Unix subsystem. Running chown uucp on the directory fixed everything again.

Mapping Files to Disks

This section will change our focus from files as objects to files as collections of data on disk. Users need not be aware of the actual disk locations of files they access, but administrators need to have at least a basic conception of how Unix maps files to disk blocks in order to understand the different file types and the purpose and functioning of the various filesystem commands.

An *inode* (pronounced "eye-node") is the data structure on disk that describes and stores a file's attributes, including its physical location on disk. When a filesystem is initially created, a specific number of inodes are created. In most cases, this becomes the maximum number of files of all types, including directories, special files, and links (discussed later) that can exist in the filesystem. A typical formula is one inode for every 8 KB of actual file storage. This is more than sufficient in most situations.† Inodes are given unique numbers, and each distinct file has its own inode. When a new file is created, an unused inode is assigned to it.

Information stored in inodes includes the following:

- User owner and group owner IDs.
- File type (regular, directory, etc., or 0 if the inode is unused).
- Access modes (permissions).
- Most recent inode modification, data access, and data modification times. If the file's metadata does not change, the first item will correspond to the file creation time.

---

* Clearly, the system itself was somewhat "broken" as well, since adding a file to a directory should never change the directory's ownership. However, it is also possible to do this accidentally with text editors that allow you to edit a directory.

† There are a couple of circumstances where this may not hold. One is a filesystem containing an enormous number of very small files. The traditional example of this is the USENET news spool directory tree (although some modern news servers now use a better storage scheme). News files are typically both very small and inordinately numerous, and their numbers have been known to exceed normal inode limits. A second potential problem situation occurs with facilities that make extensive use of symbolic links for functions such as source code version control, again characterized by many, many tiny files. In such cases, you can run out of inodes before disk capacity is exhausted. You will want to take these factors into account when preparing the disk (see Chapter 10). At the other extreme, filesystems that are designed to hold only a few very large files might save a nontrivial amount of space by being configured with far fewer than the normal number of inodes.

- Number of hard links to the file (links are discussed later in this chapter). This is 0 if the inode is unused, and one for most regular files.
- Size of the file.
- Disk addresses of:
  - Disk locations for the data blocks that make up the file, and/or
  - Disk locations of disk blocks that hold the disk locations of the file's data blocks (*indirect blocks*), and/or
  - Disk locations of disk blocks that hold the disk locations of indirect blocks (*double indirect blocks*: two disk addresses removed from the actual data blocks).*

In short, inodes store all available information about the file except its name and directory location. The inodes themselves are stored elsewhere on disk.

On Unix systems, it is reasonably safe to say that "everything is a file": the operating system even represents I/O devices as files. Accordingly, there are several different kinds of files, each with a different function.

Regular files

Regular files are files containing data. They are normally called simply "files." These may be ASCII text files, binary data files, executable program binaries, program input or output, and so on.

Directories

A *directory* is a binary file consisting of a list of the other files it contains, possibly including other directories (try running od -c on one to see this). Directory entries are filename-inode number pairs. This is the mechanism by which inodes and directory locations are associated; the data on disk has no knowledge of its (purely logical) location within its filesystem.

Special files: character and block device files

Special files are the mechanism used for device I/O under Unix. They reside in the directory */dev* and its subdirectories, as well as the directory */devices* under Solaris.

Generally, there are two types of special files: *character special files*, corresponding to character-based or raw device access, and *block special files*, corresponding to block I/O device access. Character special files are used for unbuffered data transfers to and from a device (e.g., a terminal). In contrast, block special files are used when data is transferred in fixed-size chunks known as *blocks* (e.g., most file I/O). Both kinds of special files exist for some devices (including disks). Character special files

---

* In traditional System V filesystems, inode disk addresses can point to triple indirect blocks. FreeBSD also uses triple indirect blocks.

generally have names beginning with *r* (for "raw")—*/dev/rsd0a*, for example—or reside in subdirectories of */dev* whose names begin with *r*—*/dev/rdsk/c0t3d0s7*, for example. The corresponding block special files have the same name, minus the initial *r*: */dev/disk0a*, */dev/dsk/c0t3d0s7*. Special files are discussed in more detail in later in this chapter.

Links

A *link* is a mechanism that allows several filenames (actually, directory entries) to refer to a single file on disk. There are two kinds of links: hard links and symbolic or soft links. A hard link associates two (or more) filenames with the same inode. Hard links are separate directory entries that all share the same disk data blocks. For example, the command:

```
$ ln index hlink
```

creates an entry in the current directory named *hlink* with the same inode number as *index*, and the link count in the corresponding inode is increased by 1. Hard links may not span filesystems, because inode numbers are unique only within a filesystem. In addition, hard links should be used only for files and not for directories, and correctly implemented versions of ln won't let you create the latter.

Symbolic links, on the other hand, are pointer files that refer to a different file or directory elsewhere in the filesystem. Symbolic links may span filesystems, because they point to a Unix pathname, not to a specific inode.

Symbolic links are created with the -s option to ln.

The two types of links behave similarly, but they are not identical. As an example, consider a file *index* to which there is a hard link *hlink* and a symbolic link *slink*. Listing the contents using either name with a command like cat will result in the same output. For both *index* and *hlink*, the disk contents pointed to by the addresses in their common inode will be accessed and displayed. For *slink*, the disk contents referenced by the address in its inode contain the pathname for *index*; when it is followed, *index*'s inode will be accessed next, and finally its data blocks will be displayed.

In directory listings, *hlink* will be indistinguishable from *index*. Changes made to either file will affect both of them, since they share the same disk blocks. However, moving either file with the mv command will not affect the other one, since moving a file involves only altering a directory entry (keep in mind that pathnames are not stored in the inode). Similarly, deleting *index* will not affect *hlink*, which will still point to the same inode (the corresponding disk blocks are only freed when an inode's link count reaches zero).

If a new file in the current directory named *index* is subsequently created, there will be no connection between it and *hlink*, because when the new file is created, it will be assigned a free inode. Although they are initially created by referencing an existing file, hard links are linked only to an inode, not to the other file. In fact, all regular files are technically hard links (i.e., inodes with a link count ≥ 1).

In contrast, a symbolic link *slink* to *index* will behave differently. The symbolic link appears as a separate entry in directory listings, marked as a link with an "l" as the first character in the mode string:

```
% ls -l
-rw------- 2 chavez  chem  5228 Mar 12 11:36 index
-rw------- 2 chavez  chem  5228 Mar 12 11:36 hlink
lrwxrwxrwx 1 chavez  chem     5 Mar 12 11:37 slink -> index
```

Symbolic links are always very small files, while every hard link to a given file (inode) is exactly the same size (*hlink* is naturally the same length as *index*).

Changes made by referencing either the real filename or the symbolic link will affect the contents of *index*. Deleting *index* will also break the symbolic link; *slink* will point nowhere. But if another file *index* is subsequently recreated, *slink* will once again be linked to it.* Deleting *slink* will have no effect on *index*.

Figure 2-2 illustrates the differences between hard and symbolic links. In the first picture, *index* and *hlink* share the inode N1 and its associated data blocks. The symbolic link *slink* has a different inode, N2, and therefore different data blocks. The contents of inode N2's data blocks refer to the pathname to *index*.† Thus, accessing *slink* eventually reaches the data blocks for inode N1.

When *index* is deleted (in the second picture), *hlink* is associated with inode N1 by its own directory entry. Accessing *slink* will generate an error, however, since the pathname it references does not exist. When a new *index* is created (in the third picture), its gets a new inode, N3. This new file clearly has no relationship to *hlink*, but it does act as the target for *slink*.

Using the cd command can be a bit tricky when dealing with symbolic links to directories, as these examples illustrate:

```
$ pwd; cd ./htdocs
/home/chavez
$ cd ../bin
../bin: No such file or directory.
$ pwd
/public/web2/apache/htdocs
$ ls -l /home/chavez/htdocs
lrwxrwxrwx   1 chavez chem   18 Mar 30 12:06 htdocs ->
                             /public/web2/apache/htdocs
```

The subdirectory *htdocs* in the current directory is a symbolic link (its target is indicated in the final command). Accordingly, the second cd command does not work as

---

* Symbolic links are actually interpreted only when accessed, so they can't really be said to point anywhere at other times. But conceptually, this is what they do.

† Some operating systems, including FreeBSD, store the target of the symbolic link in the inode itself, provided the target is short enough.

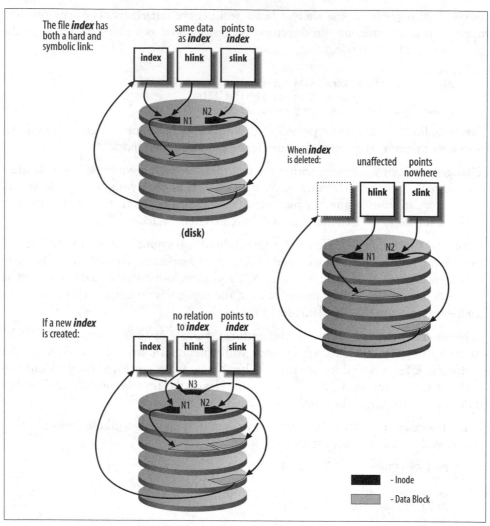

Figure 2-2. Comparing hard and symbolic links

expected, and the current directory does not change to */home/chavez/bin*. Similar effects would occur with a command like this one:

```
$ cd /home/chavez/htdocs/../cgi-bin; pwd
/public/web2/apache/cgi-bin
```

For more information about links, see the ln manual page, and experiment with creating and modifying linked files.

Tru64 Context-Dependent Symbolic Links. In a Tru64 clustered environment, many standard system files and directories are actually a type of symbolic link known as *context-dependent symbolic links* (CDSLs). They are symbolic links with a variable component that is resolved to a specific cluster host at access time. For example, consider this directory listing (the output is wrapped to fit):

```
$ ls -lF /var/adm/c*
-rw-r--r--   1 root     system  91 May 30 13:07  cdsl_admin.inv
-rw-r--r--   1 root     adm    232 May 30 13:07  cdsl_check_list
lrwxr-xr-x   1 root     adm     43 Jan  3 12:09  collect.dated@ ->
                        ../cluster/members/{memb}/adm/collect.dated
lrwxr-xr-x   1 root     adm     35 Jan  3 12:04  crash@          ->
                        ../cluster/members/{memb}/adm/crash/
lrwxr-xr-x   1 root     adm     34 Jan  3 12:04  cron@           ->
                        ../cluster/members/{memb}/adm/cron/
```

The first two files are regular files that reside in the */var/adm* directory. The remaining three files are context-dependent symbolic links, indicated by the *{memb}* component. When such a file is accessed, this component is resolved to a directory named *member*n, where *n* indicates the host's number within the cluster.

Occasionally, you may need to create such a link. The mkcdsl command serves this purpose, as in this example (output is wrapped):

```
# cd /var/adm
# mkcdsl pacct
# ls -l pacct
lrwxr-xr-x   1 root     adm     43 Jan  3 12:09  pacct ->
                ../cluster/members/{memb}/adm/pacct
```

The ln -s command may also be used to create context-dependent symbolic links:

```
# ln -s "../cluster/members/{memb}/adm/pacct" ./pacct
```

The cdslinvchk -verify command may be used to verify that all expected CDSLs are present on a system. It reports its findings to the file */var/adm/cdsl_check_list*. Here is some sample output (wrapped to fit):

```
Expected CDSL: ./usr/var/X11/Xserver.conf ->
  ../cluster/members/{memb}/X11/Xserver.conf
An administrator or application has replaced this CDSL with:
-rw-r--r-- 1 root system 4545   Jan 3 12:41
                            /usr/var/X11/Xserver.conf
```

This report indicates that there is one missing CDSL.

Sockets

A socket, whose official name is a *Unix domain socket*, is a special type of file used for communications between processes. A socket may be thought of as a communications end point, tied to a particular local system port, to which processes may attach. For example, on a BSD-style system, the socket */dev/printer* is used by processes to send messages to the program lpd (the line-printer spooling daemon), informing it that it has work to do.

Named pipes

Named pipes are pipes opened by applications for interprocess communication (they are "named" in the sense that applications refer to them by their pathname). They are a System V feature that has migrated to all versions of Unix. Named pipes often reside in the *dev* directory. They are also known as FIFOs (for "first-in, first-out").

Using ls to identify file types

The long directory listing (produced by the ls -l command) identifies the type of each file it lists via the initial character of the permissions string:

-     Plain file (hard link)
- d   Directory
- l   Symbolic link
- b   Block special file
- c   Character special file
- s   Socket
- p   Named pipe

For example, the following ls -l output includes each of the file types discussed above, in the same order:

```
-rw------- 2 chavez  chem     28 Mar 12 11:36  gold.dat
-rw------- 2 chavez  chem     28 Mar 12 11:36  hlink.dat
drwx------ 2 chavez  chem    512 Mar 12 11:36  old_data
lrwxrwxrwx 1 chavez  chem      8 Mar 12 11:37  zn.dat -> gold.dat
brw-r----- 1 root    system    0 Mar  2 15:02  /dev/sd0a
crw-r----- 1 root    system    0 Jun 12  1989  /dev/rsd0a
srw-rw-rw- 1 root    system    0 Mar 11 08:19  /dev/log
prw------- 1 root    system    0 Mar 11 08:32  /usr/lib/cron/FIFO
```

Note that the -l option also displays the target file for symbolic links (following the -> symbol).

ls has other options to make identifying file types easy. On many systems, the -F option will append a special character to each filename, indicating its type:

```
-rw------- 2 chavez  chem     28 Mar 12 11:36  gold.dat
-rw------- 2 chavez  chem     28 Mar 12 11:36  hlink.dat
drwx------ 2 chavez  chem    512 Mar 12 11:36  old_data/
-rwxr-x--- 1 chavez  chem  23478 Feb 23 09:45  test_prog*
lrwxrwxrwx 1 chavez  chem      8 Mar 12 11:37  zn.dat@ -> gold.dat
srw-rw-rw- 1 root    system    0 Mar 11 08:19  /dev/log=
prw------- 1 root    system    0 Mar 11 08:32  /usr/lib/cron/FIFO|
```

Note than an asterisk indicates an executable file (program or script). Some versions of ls also support a -o option, which color-codes filenames in the output based on their file type.

You can use the -i option to ls to determine the equivalent file in the case of hard links. Using -i tells ls to display the inode number associated with each filename. Here is an example:

```
$ ls -i /dev/rmt0 /dev/rmt/*
290 /dev/rmt0 293 /dev/rmt/c0d6l n
292 /dev/rmt/c0d6h291 /dev/rmt/c0d6m
295 /dev/rmt/c0d6hn294 /dev/rmt/c0d6mn
290 /dev/rmt/c0d6l
```

From this display, we can determine that the special files */dev/rmt0* (the default tape drive for many commands, including tar) and */dev/rmt/c0d6l* are equivalent, because they both reference inode number 290.

ls can't distinguish between text and binary files (both are "regular" files). You can use the file command to do so. Here is an example:

```
# file *
appoint: ... executable not stripped
bin: directory
clean: symbolic link to bin/clean
fort.1: empty
gold.dat: ascii text
intro.ms:   [nt]roff, tbl, or eqn input text
run_me.sh: commands text
xray.c: ascii text
```

The file *appoint* is an executable image; the additional information provided for such files differs from system to system. Note that file tries to figure out what the contents of ASCII files are, with varying success.

Processes

In simple terms, a *process* is a single executable program that is running in its own address space.* It is distinct from a job or a command, which, on Unix systems, may be composed of many processes working together to perform a specific task. Simple commands like ls are executed as a single process. A compound command containing pipes will execute one process per pipe segment. For Unix systems, managing CPU resources must be done in large part by controlling processes, because the resource allocation and batch execution facilities available with other multitasking operating systems are underdeveloped or missing.

Unix processes come in several types. We'll look at the most common here.

Interactive Processes

Interactive processes are initiated from and controlled by a terminal session. Interactive processes may run either in the *foreground* or the *background*. Foreground processes remain attached to the terminal; the foreground process is the one with which

---

* I am not distinguishing between processes and threads at this point.

the terminal communicates directly. For example, typing a Unix command and waiting for its output means running a foreground process.

While a foreground process is running, it alone can receive direct input from the terminal. For example, if you run the diff command on two very large files, you will be unable to run another command until it finishes (or you kill it with CTRL-C).

Job control allows a process to be moved between the foreground and the background at will. For example, when a process is moved from the foreground to the background, the process is temporarily stopped, and terminal control returns to its parent process (usually a shell). The background job may be resumed and continue executing unattached to the terminal session that launched it. Alternatively, it may eventually be brought to the foreground, and once again become the terminal's current process. Processes may also be started initially as background processes.

Table 2-6 reviews the ways to control foreground and background processes provided by most current shells.

Table 2-6. Controlling processes

Form	Meaning and examples
&	Run command in background.
	`$ long_cmd &`
^Z	Stop foreground process.

	`$ long_cmd`
	`^Z   Stopped`
	`$`

jobs	List background processes.

	`$ jobs`
	`[1] - Stopped emacs`
	`[2] - big_job &`
	`[3] + Stopped long_cmd`

%*n*	Refers to background job number *n*.
	`$ kill %2`
fg	Bring background process to foreground.
	`$ fg %1`
%?*str*	Refers to the background job command containing the specified characters.
	`$ fg %?em`
bg	Restart stopped background process.

	`$ long_cmd`
	`^Z Stopped`
	`$ bg`
	`[3] long_cmd &`

~^Z	Suspend rlogin session.

	`bridget-27 $ ~^Z`
	`Stopped`
	`henry-85 $`

Table 2-6. Controlling processes (continued)

Form	Meaning and examples
~~^Z	Suspend second-level `rlogin` session. Useful for nested `rlogin`s; each additional tilde says to pop back to the next highest level of `rlogin`. Thus, one tilde pops all the way back to the lowest level job (the job on the local system), two tildes pops back to the first `rlogin` session, and so on.

```
bridget-28 $ ~~^Z
Stopped
peter-46 $
```

Batch Processes

Batch processes are not associated with any terminal. Rather, they are submitted to a queue, from which jobs are executed sequentially. Unix offers a very primitive `batch` command, but vendors whose customers require queuing have generally implemented something more substantial. Some of the best known are the Network Queuing System (NQS), developed by NASA and used on many high-performance computers including Crays, as well as several network-based process-scheduling systems from various vendors. These facilities usually support heterogeneous as well as homogeneous networks, and they attempt to distribute the aggregate CPU load evenly among the workstations in the network, a process known as *load balancing* or *load leveling*.

Daemons

Daemons are server processes, often initiated at boot time, that run continuously while the system is up, waiting in the background until a process requires their service.* For example, network daemons are idle until a process requests network access.

Table 2-7 provides a brief overview of the most important Unix daemons.

Table 2-7. Important Unix daemons

Facility	Description	Daemon Names
init	First created process	init
syslog	System status/error message logging	syslogd
email	Mail message transport	sendmail
printing	Print spooler	lpd, lpsched, qdaemon, rlpdaemon

---

* Daemon is an ancient Greek word meaning "divinity" or "spirit" (but keep the character of the Greek gods in mind). The OED defines it as a "tutelary deity": the guardian of a particular person, place or thing. More recently, the poet Yeats wrote at length about daemons, defining them as that which we continually struggle against yet paradoxically need in order to survive, simultaneously the source of our pain and of our strength, even in some sense, the very essence of our being. For Yeats, the daemon is "of all things not impossible the most difficult."

Table 2-7. *Important Unix daemons (continued)*

Facility	Description	Daemon Names
cron	Periodic process execution	`crond`
tty	Terminal support.	`getty` (and similar)
sync	Disk buffer flushing	`update`, `syncd`, `syncher`, `fsflush`, `bdflush`, `kupdated`
paging and swapping	Daemons to support virtual memory management	`pagedaemon`, `vhand`, `kpiod`, `pageout`, `swapper`, `kswapd`, `kreclaimd`
inetd	Master TCP/IP daemon, responsible for starting many others on demand: `telnetd`, `ftpd`, `rshd`, `imapd`, `pop3d`, `fingerd`, `rwhod` (see */etc/inetd.conf* for a full list)	`inetd`
name resolution	DNS server process	`named`
routing	Routing daemon	`routed`, `gated`
DHCP	Dynamic network client configuration	`dhcpd`, `dhcpsd`
RPC	Remote procedure call facility network port-to-service mapper	`portmap`, `rpcbind`
NFS	Network File System: native Unix network file sharing	`nfsd`, `rpc.mountd`, `rpc.nfsd`, `rpc.statd`, `rpc.lockd`, `nfsiod`
Samba	File/print sharing with Windows systems	`smbd`, `nmbd`
WWW	HTTP server	`httpd`
network time	Network time synchronization	`timed`, `ntpd`

Process Attributes

Unix processes have many associated attributes. Some of the most important are:

Process ID (PID)
> A unique identifying number used to refer to the process.

Parent process ID (PPID)
> The PID of the process's *parent* process (the process that created it).

Nice number
> The process's scheduling priority, which is a number indicating its importance relative to other processes. This needs to be distinguished from its actual execution priority, which is dynamically changed based on both the process's nice number and its recent CPU usage. See "Managing CPU Resources" in Chapter 15 for a detailed discussion of nice numbers and their effect on execution priority.

TTY
> The terminal (or pseudo-terminal) device associated with the process.

Real and effective user ID (RUID, EUID)
> A process's real UID is the UID of the user who started it. Its effective UID is the UID that is used to determine the process's access to system resources (such as

files and devices). Usually the real and effective UIDs are the same, and the process accordingly has the same access rights as the user who launched it. However, when the setuid access mode is set on an executable image, then the EUIDs of processes executing it are set to the UID of the file's user owner, and they are accorded corresponding access rights.

Real and effective group ID (RGID, EGID)
A process's real GID is the user's primary or current group. Its effective GID, used to determine the process's access rights, is the same as the real GID except when the setgid access mode is set on an executable image. The EGIDs of processes executing such files are set to the GID of the file's group owner, and they are given corresponding access to system resources.

The life cycle of a process

A new process is created in the following manner. An existing process makes an exact copy of itself, a procedure known as *forking*. The new process, called the *child process*, has the same environment as its *parent process*, although it is assigned a different process ID. Then, this image in the child process's address space is overwritten by the one the child will run; this is done via the exec system call. Hence, the often-used phrase *fork-and-exec*. The new program (or command) completely replaces the one duplicated from the parent. However, the environment of the parent still remains, including the values of environment variables; the assignments of standard input, standard output, and standard error; and its execution priority.

Let's make this picture a bit more concrete. What happens when a user runs a command like grep? First, the user's shell process forks, creating a new shell process to run the command. Then, the new shell process execs grep, which overlays the shell's executable image in memory with grep's, which begins executing. When the grep command finishes, the process dies.

This is the way that all Unix processes are created. The ultimate ancestor for every process on a Unix system is the process with PID 1, init, created during the boot process (see Chapter 4). init creates many other processes (all by fork-and-exec). Among them are usually one or more executing the getty program. The gettys are each assigned to a different serial line; they display the login prompt and wait for someone to respond to it. When someone does, the getty process execs the login program, which validates user logins, among other activities.[*]

Once the username and password are verified,[†] login execs the user's shell. Forking is not always required to run a new program, and login does not fork in this case. After

---

[*] The process is similar for an X terminal window. In the latter case, the xterm or other process is created by the window manager in use, which was itself started by a series of other X-related processes, ultimately deriving from a command issued from the login shell (e.g., startx) or as part of the login process itself.

[†] If the login attempt fails, login exits, sending a signal to its parent process, init, indicating it should create a new getty process for the terminal.

logging in, the user's shell is the same process as the getty that was watching the unused serial line. That process changed programs twice by execing a new executable, and it will go on to create new processes to execute the commands that the user types. Figure 2-3 illustrates Unix process creation in the context of initial user login.

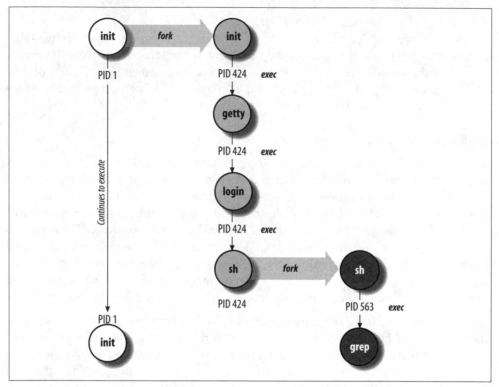

Figure 2-3. Unix process creation: fork and exec

When any process exits, it sends a signal to inform its parent process that is has completed. So, when a user logs out, her login shell sends a signal to its parent, init, as it dies, letting init know that it's time to create a new getty process for the terminal. init forks again and starts the getty, and the whole cycle repeats itself again and again as different users use that terminal.

Setuid and setgid file access and process execution

The purpose of the setuid and setgid access modes is to allow ordinary users to perform tasks requiring privileges and access rights that are ordinarily denied to them. For example, on many systems the write command is owned by the *tty* group, which also owns all of the terminal and pseudo-terminal device files. The write command has setgid access, allowing any user to use it to write a message to another user's terminal or window (to which they do not normally have any access). When users execute write, their effective GID is set to that of the group owner of the executable file (often */usr/bin/write*) for the duration of the command.

Setuid and/or setgid access are also used by the printing subsystem, by programs like mailers, and by some other system facilities. However, setuid programs are also notorious security risks. In practice, setuid almost always means setuid to *root,* and the danger is that somehow, through program stupidity or their own cleverness or both, users will figure out a way to perform additional, unauthorized functions while the setuid command is running or to retain their inherited *root* status after the command ends. In general, setuid access should be avoided since it involves greater security risks than setgid, and almost any function can be performed by using the latter in conjunction with carefully designed groups. See Chapter 7 for a more detailed discussion of the security issues involved with setuid and setgid programs. Keep in mind, though, that while setgid programs are safer than setuid ones, they are not risk-free themselves.

The relationship between commands and files

The Unix operating system does not distinguish between commands and files in the ways that some systems do. Aside from a few commands that are built into each Unix shell, Unix commands are executable files stored in one of several standard locations within the filesystem. Access to commands is exactly equivalent to access to these files. By default, there is no other privilege mechanism. Even I/O is handled via *special files,* stored in the directory */dev,* which function as interfaces to the device drivers. All I/O operations look just like ordinary file operations from the user's point of view.

Unix shells use *search paths* to locate the executable's images for commands that users enter. In its simplest form, a search path is simply an ordered list of directories in which to look for command executables, and it is typically set in an initialization file *($HOME/.profile* or *$HOME/.login*). A faulty (incomplete) search path is the most common cause for "Command not found" error messages.

Search paths are stored in the *PATH* environment variable. Here is a typical *PATH*:

```
$ echo $PATH
/bin:/usr/ucb:/usr/bin:/usr/local/bin:.:$HOME/bin
```

The various directories in the *PATH* are separated by colons. The search path is used whenever a command name is entered without an explicit directory location. As an example, consider the following command:

```
$ od data.raw
```

The od command is used to display a raw dump of a file. To locate this command, the operating system first looks for a file named od in */bin.* If such a file exists, it is executed. If there is no od file in the */bin* directory, */usr/ucb* is checked next, followed by */usr/bin* (where od is in fact usually located). If it were necessary, the search would continue in */usr/local/bin,* the current directory, and finally the *bin* subdirectory of the user's home directory.

The order of the directories in the search path is important when more than one version of a command exists. Such effects come into play most frequently when both the BSD and the System V versions of commands are available on a system. In this case, you should put the directory holding the versions you want to use first in your search path. For example, if you want to use the BSD versions of commands such as ls and ln on a System V–based system, then put */usr/ucb* ahead of */usr/bin* in your search path. Similarly, if you want to use the System V–compatible commands available on some systems, put */usr/5bin* ahead of */usr/bin* and */usr/ucb* in your search path. These same considerations will obviously apply to users' search paths that you define for them in their initialization files (see "Initialization Files and Boot Scripts" in Chapter 4).

Most of the Unix administrative utilities are located in the directories */sbin* and */usr/ sbin*. However, the locations of administrative commands can vary widely between Unix versions. These directories typically aren't in the search path unless you put them there explicitly. When executing administrative commands, you can either add these directories to your search path or provide the full pathname for the command, as in the example below:

```
# /usr/sbin/ping hamlet
```

I'm going to assume in my examples that the administrative directories have been added to the search path. Thus, I won't be including the full pathname for any of the commands I'll be discussing.

The Unix Way of System Administration

System administrators are stereotypically arrogant, single-minded, and opinionated. For Unix system administrators, the stereotype was born in the days when Unix was this bizarre operating system that ran on only a few systems, and the local Unix guru was some guy who generally kept to himself, locked away with his system—or so the story goes.

The skepticism I'm exhibiting with this view of Unix system managers does not mean that there is no truth in it at all. Like most caricatures, this one has roots in reality. For example, it is all too easy to find people who will tell you that there is one right editor to use, one right shell for writing scripts, one right way to do anything you care to name. Discussing the advantages and liabilities of alternative approaches to problems can be both useful and entertaining, but only within reason.

Since you're reading this introductory chapter, I'm assuming that you are only beginning your exploration of Unix administration. I certainly want to encourage you to consider for yourself all the tasks and issues you will face as you proceed and to provide help when I can. You'll quickly form your own opinions and define what system administration is for you. Doing so is a process, which can continue for as long and range as widely as you want it to. However, if you get to a point where fanaticism replaces thinking, you've gone too far.

Devices

One of the strengths of Unix is that users don't need to worry about the specific characteristics of devices and device I/O very often. They don't need to know, for example, what disk drive a file they want to access physically sits on. And the Unix special file mechanism allows many device I/O operations to look just like file I/O. As we've noted, the administrator doesn't have these same luxuries, at least not all the time. This section discusses Unix device handling and then surveys the special files used to access devices.

Device files are characterized by their *major* and *minor numbers*, which allow the kernel to determine which device driver to use to access the device (via the major number), as well as its specific method of access (via the minor number).

Major and minor numbers appear in place of the file size in long directory listings. For example, consider these device files related to the mouse from a Linux system:

```
$ cd /dev; ls -l *mouse
crw-rw-r--   1 root     root      10,  10 Jan 19 03:36 adbmouse
crw-rw-r--   1 root     root      10,   4 Jan 19 03:35 amigamouse
crw-rw-r--   1 root     root      10,   5 Jan 19 03:35 atarimouse
crw-rw-r--   1 root     root      10,   8 Jan 19 03:35 smouse
crw-rw-r--   1 root     root      10,   6 Jan 19 03:35 sunmouse
crw-rw-r--   1 root     root      13,  32 Jan 19 03:36 usbmouse
```

The major number for all but the last special file is 10; only the minor number differs for these devices. Thus, all of these mouse device variations are handled by the same device driver, and the minor number indicates the variation within that general family. The final item, corresponding to a USB mouse, has a different major number, indicating that a different device driver is used.

Device files are created with the mknod command, and it takes the desired device name and major and minor numbers as its arguments. Many systems provide a script named *MAKEDEV* (located in */dev*), which is an easy-to-use interface to mknod.

An In-Depth Device Example: Disks

We'll use disk drives as an example in this overview discussion of Unix devices.* As we've noted before, Unix organizes all user-accessible files into a single hierarchical directory structure. The files and directories it contains may be spread across several different disk drives.

On most Unix systems, disks are divided into one or more fixed-size *partitions*: physical subsets of the disk drive that are separately accessed by the operating system.

---

* This discussion will describe traditional ways of handling disks and filesystems. Unix versions that require or offer a logical volume manager do things quite differently at the lowest level, but this overview is still conceptually true for those systems (for "disk partition," read "logical volume"). See Chapter 10 for details.

There may be several partitions or just one on each physical disk. The disk partition containing the root filesystem is called the *root partition* and sometimes the *root disk*, although it obviously needn't comprise the entire disk drive. The disk containing the root partition is generally called the *system disk*.

The root filesystem is the first one *mounted*, early in the Unix boot process, and the remaining ones are mounted afterwards. On many operating systems, mounting a disk refers to the process of making the device's contents available. For Unix, it means something more. Like the overall Unix filesystem, the files and directories physically located on each disk partition are arranged in a tree structure.* An integral part of the process of mounting a disk partition involves grafting its local directory structure into the overall Unix directory tree. Once this is done, the files physically residing on that device may be accessed via the usual Unix pathname syntax; Unix takes care of mapping pathnames to the correct physical device and data blocks.

For administrators, however, there are a few times when the disk partition must be accessed directly. The actual mount operation is the most common. Remember that disk partitions may be accessed in two modes, block mode and raw (or character) mode, and different special files are used from each mode. Character access mode does unbuffered I/O, generally making a data transfer to or from the device with every read or write system call. Block devices do buffered I/O on a block basis, collecting data in a buffer until the operating system can transfer an entire block of data at one time.

For example, the disk partition containing the root filesystem traditionally corresponded to the special files */dev/disk0a* and */dev/rdisk0a*, specifying the first partition on the first disk (disk 0, partition a), accessed in block and raw mode respectively,† with the *r* designating raw device access.

 Most disk partition–related commands require a specific type of special file and won't accept the other kind.

---

* For this reason, each separate disk partition may also be referred to as a filesystem. Thus, "filesystem" is used to refer both to the overall system directory tree (as in "the Unix filesystem"), comprising every user-accessible disk partition on the system, and to the files and directories on individual disk partitions (as in "build a filesystem on the disk partition" or "mounting the user filesystems"). Whether the overall Unix directory tree or an individual disk partition is meant will be clear from the context. On a related note, the terms partition and filesystem are often used synonymously. Thus, while technically only filesystems can be mounted, common usage often refers to "mounting a disk" or "mounting a partition."

† The names given to the two types of special files are overdetermined. For example, the special file */dev/disk0a* is referred to as a *block special file*, and */dev/rdisk0a* is called a *character special file*. However, block special files are also sometimes called *block devices*, and character special files may be referred to as *character devices* or *raw devices*.

Note that most Linux versions and newer versions of BSD do not distinguish between the two types of special files for IDE disks and provide only one special file per disk partition.

As an example of the use of special files to access disk partitions, consider the mount commands below:

```
# mount /dev/disk0a /
# mount /dev/disk1e /home
```

Naturally, the command to mount a disk partition needs to specify the physical disk partition to be mounted (mount's first argument) and the location to place it in the filesystem, its *mount point* (the second argument).* Thus, the first command makes the files in the first partition on drive 0 available, placing them at the root of the Unix filesystem. The second command accesses a partition on drive 1, placing it at */home* in the overall directory tree. Thus, regular files in the top-level directory on this second disk partition will appear in */home*, and top-level directories on the disk partition become subdirectories of */home*. The mount command is discussed in greater detail in Chapter 10.

Fixed-disk special files

Currently used special file names for disk partitions are highly implementation-dependent. However, a common logic underlies all of the various naming schemes. Disk special files can encode the type of disk, the disk controller, the disk location on its controller, and the disk partition within the physical disk (as well as the access mode) within the special file name.

Let's take the Tru64 special files for disks as an example; these special files have names of the following form, where *n* is the disk number (beginning at 0), and *x* is a letter from a to h designating the partition on the physical disk:

*/dev/disk/dsk*nx
    Block device

*/dev/rdisk/dsk*nx
    Character (raw) device

The partitions have conventional uses, and not all partitions are used on every disk (see Chapter 10 for more details). Traditionally, the a partition on the root disk contains the root filesystem. b partitions are conventionally used as swap partitions. On the root disk, other partitions might be used for various system directories: for example, e for */usr*, h for */var*, d for other filesystems, and so on.

---

* In fact, on most Unix systems, mount is smarter than this. If you give it a single argument—either the physical disk partition or the mount point—it will look up the other argument in a table. But you can always supply both arguments, which means that you can rearrange your filesystem at will. (Why you would want to is a different question.)

The c partition often refers to the entire disk as a whole: every bit of space on the disk, including areas that should be accessed only by the kernel (such as the partition table at the beginning of the drive). For this reason, using the c partition for a filesystem was not allowed under older versions of Unix. More recent versions generally do not have this restriction.

System V-based systems use a similar naming philosophy, although the actual names differ. Special filenames for disk partitions are often of the form */dev/dsk/cktmdpsn,* where k is the controller number, m is the drive number on that controller (often the SCSI target ID), and n is the partition (section) number on that drive (all numbers start at 0). p refers to the logical unit number (LUN) for SCSI devices and is thus usually 0. HP-UX uses this form but typically omits the s component.

In this scheme, character and block special files have the same names, but they are stored in two different subdirectories of */dev*: */dev/dsk* and */dev/rdsk*, respectively. Thus, the special file */dev/dsk/c1t4d0s2* is the block special file for the third partition on the disk with SCSI ID 4 on controller 1 (the second controller). The corresponding character device is */dev/rdsk/c1t4d0s2*.

Names in this format, known as *controller-drive-section identifiers*, are specified for all disk and tape devices under the System V.4 standard. Actual System V–based implementations start with this framework and may vary it somewhat according to the devices actually supported. Sometimes, they also provide links to more mnemonically or intuitively-named special files. For example, on some (mostly older) Solaris systems, */dev/sd0a* might be linked to */dev/dsk/c0t3d0s0*, allowing the conventional SunOS name to be used for the 0 partition on the disk with SCSI ID 3 on the first controller.[*]

Table 2-8 illustrates the similarities among disk special file names. The special files in the table all refer to a partition on the second SCSI disk drive on the first controller, using SCSI ID 4.

Table 2-8. Interpreting disk special file names

	FreeBSD	HP-UX	Linux	Solaris	Tru64[a]
Special file	*/dev/rda1d*	*/dev/rdsk/c0t4d0*	*/dev/sdb1*	*/dev/rdsk/c0t4d0s3*	*/dev/rdisk/dsk1c*
Raw access	*/dev/rda1d*	*/dev/rdsk/c0t4d0*	*/dev/sdb1*	*/dev/rdsk/c0t4d0s3*	*/dev/rdisk/dsk1c*
Device = Disk	*/dev/rda1d*	*/dev/r**dsk**/c0t4d0*	*/dev/**sdb**1*	*/dev/r**dsk**/c0t4d0s3*	*/dev/r**disk**/dsk1c*
Type = SCSI	*/dev/rda1d*		*/dev/**sdb**1*		
Controller #		*/dev/rdsk/c**0**t4d0*		*/dev/rdsk/c**0**t4d0s3*	
SCSI ID		*/dev/rdsk/c0t**4**d0*		*/dev/rdsk/c0t**4**d0s3*	

Table 2-8. *Interpreting disk special file names (continued)*

	FreeBSD	HP-UX	Linux	Solaris	Tru64[a]
Device #	*/dev/rda1d*		*/dev/sdb1*		*/dev/rdisk/dsk1c*
Disk Partition	*/dev/rda1d*	assumed	*/dev/sdb1*	*/dev/rdsk/c0t4d0s3*	*/dev/rdisk/dsk1c*

[a] Older Tru64 systems use the now-obsolete device names of the form */dev/rz**, */dev/ra**, and */dev/re**.

In yet another twist, systems that use logical volume managers (including AIX by default) allow the system administrator to specify names for the special files for logical volumes—virtual disk partitions—when they are created. These special files often have names of the form */dev/*name, where *name* is chosen when the filesystem is created. On such systems, it is logical volumes rather than physical partitions that hold filesystems. We'll leave the rest of the gory details about these topics until Chapter 10.

Special Files for Other Devices

Other device types have special files named differently, but they follow the same basic conventions. Some of the most common are summarized in Table 2-9 (they will be discussed in more detail as appropriate in later chapters). In some cases, only the more commonly used form (block versus character) of the file is listed. For example, tape drives are seldom, if ever, accessed via the block device, and on many systems, the block special files do not even exist.

Table 2-9. *Common Unix special file names*

Device/use	Special file forms	Example
Floppy disk	/dev/[r]fd*n** /dev/floppy	/dev/fd0
Tape devices[a]	/dev/rmt*n*	/dev/rmt1
	/dev/rmt/*n*	/dev/rmt/0
nonrewinding	/dev/nrmt*n*	/dev/nrmt0
SCSI	/dev/rst*n*	/dev/rst0
default tape drive	/dev/tape	
CD-ROM devices	/dev/cd*n* /dev/cdrom	/dev/cd0
Serial lines	/dev/tty*n* /dev/term/*n*	/dev/tty1 /dev/tty01 /dev/term/01
Slave virtual terminal (windows, network sessions, etc.)	/dev/tty[p-s]*n* /dev/pts/*n*	/dev/ttyp1 /dev/pts/2
Master/control virtual terminal devices	/dev/pty[p-s]*n*	/dev/ptyp3
Console device	/dev/console	
some System V	/dev/syscon	
AIX	/dev/lft0	

Table 2-9. Common Unix special file names (continued)

Device/use	Special file forms	Example
Process controlling TTY (used to ensure I/O comes from/goes to terminal, regardless of any I/O redirection)	/dev/tty	

Memory maps:
    physical
    kernel virtual
	
	/dev/mem
	/dev/kmem	

Mouse interface	/dev/mouse	
Null devices: all output is discarded; reads return nothing (0 characters, 0 bytes) or a zero-filled buffer, respectively.	/dev/null /dev/zero	

[a] Tape devices often have suffixes that specify the tape density.

Commands for listing the devices on a system

Most Unix versions provide commands that make it easy to quickly determine what devices are present on the system, as well as their current status. Table 2-10 lists the commands for the systems we are considering.

Table 2-10. Device listing and information commands

Unix Version	Command(s)	Description
AIX	lscfg	List all devices.
	lscfg -v -l device	Device configuration detail.
	lsdev -C -s scsi	List all SCSI IDs.
	lsattr -E -H -l device	Display device attributes.
FreeBSD	pciconf -l -v	List PCI devices
	camcontrol devlist	List SCSI devices.
HP-UX	ioscan -f -n	Detailed device listing.
	ioscan -f -n -C disk	Limit to device class.
Linux	lsdev	List major devices.
	scsiinfo -l	List SCSI devices.
	lspci	List PCI devices.
Solaris[a]	dmesg[b]	Boot messages identify all devices.
	getdev	List devices.
	getdev type=disk	Limit to device class.
	devattr -v device	Device detail.
Tru64	dsfmgr -s	List devices.

[a] Unfortunately, the *getdev* and *devattr* commands are often of limited use.
[b] *dmesg* is also available under FreeBSD, HP-UX, and Linux.

The AIX Object Data Manager

Under AIX, information about the devices on the system and other system configuration is stored in a binary database. The management apparatus for this database is known as the Object Data Manager (ODM), although "ODM" is also used colloquially to refer to the database itself, as well. Information is stored in the ODM as *objects*: items of various predefined types, with a collection of attributes and their associated sets or ranges of legal values.

Here is a textual representation of a sample entry for a disk drive:

```
name = "hdisk0"
status = 1
chgstatus = 2
ddins = "scdisk"
location = "00-00-0S-0,0"
parent = "scsi0"
connwhere = "0,0"
PdDvLn = "disk/scsi/1000mb"
```

This entry illustrates the general form for a device; most devices use the same fields, although their meaning varies somewhat depending on the device type. This entry describes a 1 GB SCSI disk drive.

The preceding entry came from the current devices database, stored in */etc/objrepos/CuDv*. The attributes for this object (as well as those for the other objects on the system) are stored in a separate, current attributes database (found in */etc/objrepos/CuAt*). This database may have several entries for any given object, one for each defined attribute for that class of object for which a nondefault value is set. For example, here are two of the attributes for the logical volume *hd6* (one of the disk partitions on *hdisk0*):

```
name = "hd6"
attribute = "type"
value = "paging"
type = "R"
generic = "DU"
rep = "s"
nls_index = 639
name = "hd6"
attribute = "size"
value = "16"
type = "R"
generic = "DU"
rep = "r"
nls_index = 647
```

The first entry indicates that this is a paging space, and the second indicates that its size is 16 logical partitions (64 MB, assuming the default partition size).

SMIT and the AIX commands it runs retrieve information from the ODM, as well as adding and modifying entries as necessary.

The Unix Filesystem Layout

Now that we've considered the Unix approach to major system components, it's time to acquaint you with the structure of the Unix filesystem. This brief tour will begin with the root directory and its most important subdirectories.

The basic layout of traditional Unix filesystems is illustrated in Figure 2-4, which shows an idealized directory structure (actually a superset of the items found on any one system). Note that in practice, there are lots of variations with respect to this paradigm.

You'll find small deviations from this on most Unix systems you encounter, but the basic structure will be quite similar. We'll consider each of the major directories in turn.

The Root Directory

This is the base of the filesystem's tree structure; all other files and directories, regardless of their physical disk locations, are logically contained underneath the root directory (described in detail in Chapter 10).

There are a variety of important first-level directories under the / directory:

/bin

> The traditional location for executable (binary) files for the various Unix user commands and utilities. On many current systems, some files within /bin are merely symbolic links to files in /usr/bin, and /bin is sometimes a link to /usr/bin. Other directories that hold Unix commands are /usr/bin and /usr/ucb.

/dev

> The device directory, containing special files as described previously. The /dev directory is divided into subdirectories in most System V–based versions of Unix, with each subdirectory holding special files of a given type. Subdirectory names indicate the type of devices it contains: dsk and rdsk for disks accessed in block and raw mode, mt and rmt for tape drives, term for terminals (serial lines), pts and ptc for pseudo-terminals, and so on.

> Solaris introduces a new device directory tree, beginning at /devices, and many files under /dev are links to files in subdirectories of /devices.

/etc and /sbin

> System configuration files and executables. These directories contain many administrative files and configuration files. Among the most important files are the System V–style boot script subdirectories, named rcn.d and init.d, which are located under one of these two locations on systems using this style of booting.

> /etc also traditionally contained the executable binaries for most administrative commands. In recent Unix versions, these files have moved to /sbin and /usr/sbin. Conventionally, the former is used for files required to boot the system, and the latter contains all other administrative commands.

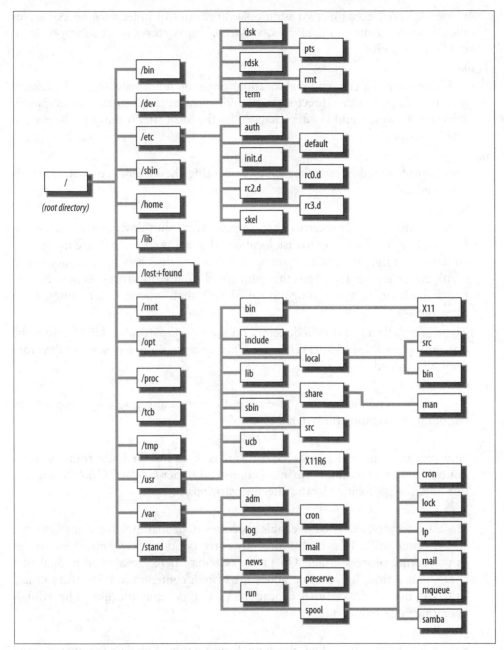

Figure 2-4. Generic Unix directory structure

On many systems, /etc also contains a subdirectory *default*, which holds files containing default parameter values for various commands.

On Linux systems, the *sysconfig* subdirectory holds network configuration and other package-specific, boot-related configuration files.

Under AIX, */etc* contains two additional directories of note: */etc/objrepos* stores the device configuration databases, and */etc/security* stores most security-related configuration files.

/home

This directory is a conventional location for users' home directories. For example, user *chavez*'s home directory is often */home/chavez*. The name is completely arbitrary, however, and is often changed by the local site. It may also be a separate filesystem.

/lib

Location of shared libraries required for booting the system (i.e., before */usr* is mounted).

/lost+found

Lost files directory. Disk errors or incorrect system shutdown may cause files to become *lost*: lost files refer to disk locations that are marked as in use in the data structures on the disk, but that are not listed in any directory (i.e., an inode with a link count greater than zero that isn't listed in any directory). When the system is booting, it runs a program called fsck that, among other things, finds these files.

There is usually a *lost+found* directory on every disk partition; */lost+found* is the one on the root disk. However, some Unix systems do not create the directory until it is needed.

/mnt

Temporary mount directory: an empty directory conventionally designed for temporarily mounting filesystems.

/opt

Directory tree into which optional software is often installed. On some systems, optional software products are installed instead under */var/opt*. On AIX systems, this function is provided by the directory */usr/lpp*.

/proc

Process directory, designed to enable processes to be manipulated using Unix file access system calls. Files in this directory correspond to active processes (entries in the kernel process table). On Linux systems, there are also additional files containing various information about the system configuration: interrupt usage, I/O port use, DMA channel allocation, CPU type, and the like. The HP-UX operating system does not use */proc*.

/stand

Boot-related files, including the kernel executable. Solaris uses */kernel*, and Linux systems use */boot* for the same purpose. FreeBSD systems use */stand* for installation and system configuration–related programs and use */boot* for kernels and related files used for booting.

/tcb

Directory tree for security-related database files on some systems offering enhanced security features, including HP-UX and Tru64 (the name stands for "trusted computing base"). Configuration files related to the TCB are also stored under */etc/auth*. */usr/tcb* may also be used for this purpose.

/tmp

Temporary directory, available to all users as a scratch directory. The system administrator should see that all the files in this directory are deleted occasionally. Normally, one of the Unix startup scripts will clear */tmp*.

/usr

This directory contains subdirectories for locally generated programs, executables for user and administrative commands, shared libraries, and other parts of the Unix operating system. The most important subdirectories of */usr* are discussed in more detail in the next section. */usr* also sometimes contains application programs.

/var

Spooling and other volatile directories (*varying* data). Important subdirectories are described below.

The /usr Directory

The directory */usr* contains a number of important subdirectories:

/usr/bin

Command binary files and shell scripts. This directory contains public executable programs that are part of the Unix system. Many executables for the X Window System are stored in */usr/bin/X11* or */usr/X11R6/bin*.

/usr/include

Include files. This directory contains C-language header files that define the C programmer's interface to standard system features and program libraries. For example, it contains the file *stdio.h*, which defines the user's interface to the C standard I/O library. The directory */usr/include/sys* contains operating system include files.

/usr/lib

Library directory, for public library files. Among other things, this directory contains the standard C libraries for mathematics and I/O. Library files generally have names of the form *libx.a* or *libx.so*, where *x* is one or more characters related to the library's contents; the extensions specify a regular (statically linked) and shared library, respectively.

/usr/local

Local files. By convention, the directory */usr/local/bin* holds executable programs that were developed locally or retrieved from the Internet and any sources other than the operating-system vendor. There may be other subdirectories here to hold related files: *man* (manual pages), *lib* (libraries), *src* (source code), *doc* (documentation), and so on.

/usr/sbin

Administrative commands (except ones required for booting, which are in */sbin*).

/usr/share

Shared data. On some recent systems, certain CPU architecture-independent static data files (such as the online manual pages, font directories, the dictionary files for spell, and the like) are stored in subdirectories under */usr/share*. The name *share* reflects the idea that such files could be shared among a group of networked systems, eliminating the need for separate copies on every system.

/usr/share/man

One location for the manual pages directory tree. This directory contains the online version of the Unix reference manuals. It is divided into subdirectories for the various sections of the manual.

Traditionally, the subdirectory structure contains several *man*n subdirectories holding the raw source for the manual pages in that section and corresponding *cat*n subdirectories storing the formatted versions. On many current systems, however, the latter are eliminated, and manual pages are formatted as needed. In many cases, the source files are stored in compressed form to save even more space.

The significance of the manual sections is described in the Table 2-11.

Table 2-11. Manual-page sections

Contents	BSD style	System V style
User commands	1	1
System calls	2	2
Functions and library routines	3	3
Special files and hardware	4	7
Configuration files and file formats	5	4
Games and demos	6	6 or 1
Miscellaneous: character sets, filesystem types, data type definitions, etc.	7	5
System administration commands	8	1m
Maintenance commands	8	8
Device drivers	4	7 or 9

Among the systems we are considering, the BSD-style organization is used by FreeBSD, Linux, and Tru64, and the System V–style organization is more or less followed by AIX, HP-UX, and Solaris.

/usr/src

Source code for locally built software packages (FreeBSD and Linux). FreeBSD also uses the */usr/ports* directory tree for retrieving and building additional software packages.

/usr/ucb

A directory that contains standard Unix commands originally developed under BSD. Recent System V–based systems also provide BSD versions of commands so that users may use the form that they prefer. Some BSD-based versions have similar directories for System V versions of commands, conventionally */usr/5bin*. */usr/opt/s5/bin* and */usr/opt/s5/sbin* perform a similar function under Tru64.

The /var Directory

As we noted, the */var* directory tree holds data that changes over time. These are its most important subdirectories:

/var/adm

Administrative directory (home directory of the special *adm* user). This directory traditionally contains the Unix accounting files although many Unix versions have moved them.

/var/cron, /var/news

/var contains subdirectories used by many system facilities. These examples are used by the cron and Usenet news facilities, respectively.

/var/log

Location for log files maintained by many system facilities.

/var/mail

User mailbox location.

/var/run

Contains files holding the current process IDs of various system daemons and other server and/or execution instance-specific data.

/var/spool

Contains subdirectories for Unix subsystems that provide different kinds of spooling services. Some of the tools using */var/spool* subdirectories are the print spooling system, the mail system, and the cron facility.

CHAPTER 3
Essential Administrative Tools and Techniques

The right tools make any job easier, and the lack of them can make some tasks almost impossible. When you need an Allen wrench, nothing but an Allen wrench will do. On the other hand, if you need a Phillips head screwdriver, you might be able to make do with a pocket knife, and occasionally it will even work better.

The first section of this chapter will consider ways the commands and utilities that Unix provides can make system administration easier. Sometimes that means applying common user commands to administrative tasks, sometimes it means putting commands together in unexpected ways, and sometimes it means making smarter and more efficient use of familiar tools. And, once in a while, what will make your life easier is creating tools for users to use, so that they can handle some things for themselves. We'll look at this last topic in Chapter 14.

The second section of this chapter will consider some essential administrative facilities and techniques, including the cron subsystem, the syslog facility, strategies for handling the many system log files, and management software packages. We'll close the chapter with a list of Internet software sources.

Getting the Most from Common Commands

In this section, we consider advanced and administrative uses of familiar Unix commands.

Getting Help

The manual page facility is the quintessentially Unix approach to online help: superficially minimalist, often obscure, but mostly complete. It's also easy to use, once you know your way around it.

Undoubtedly, the basics of the man command are familiar: getting help for a command, specifying a specific section, using -k (or apropos) to search for entries for a specific topic, and so on.

There are a couple of man features that I didn't discover until I'd been working on Unix systems for years (I'd obviously never bothered to run `man man`). The first is that you can request multiple manual pages within a single `man` command:

```
$ man umount fsck newfs
```

man presents the pages as separate files to the display program, and you can move among them using its normal method (for example, with `:n` in more).

On FreeBSD, Linux, and Solaris systems, man also has a `-a` option, which retrieves the specified manual page(s) from every section of the manual. For example, the first command below displays the introductory manual page for every section for which one is available, and the second command displays the manual pages for both the chown command and system call:

```
$ man -a intro
$ man -a chown
```

Manual pages are generally located in a predictable location within the filesystem, often */usr/share/man*. You can configure the man command to search multiple *man* directory trees by setting the MANPATH environment variable to the colon-separated list of desired directories.

Changing the search order

The man command searches the various manual page sections in a predefined order: commands first, followed by system calls and library functions, and then the other sections (i.e., 1, 6, 8, 2, 3, 4, 5, and 7 for BSD-based schemes). The first manual page matching the one specified on the command line is displayed. In some cases, a different order might make more sense. Many operating systems allow this ordering scheme to be customized via the *MANSECTS* entry within a configuration file. For example, Solaris allows the search order to be customized via the *MANSECTS* entry in the */usr/share/man/man.cf* configuration file. You specify a list of sections in the order in which you want them to be searched:

```
MANSECTS=8,1,2,3,4,5,6,7
```

This ordering brings administrative command sections to the beginning of the list.

Here are the available ordering customization locations for the versions we are considering that offer this feature:

FreeBSD
    MANSECT environment variable (colon-separated)

Linux (Red Hat)
    MANSECT in */etc/man.config* (colon-separated)

Linux (SuSE)
    SECTION in */etc/manpath.config* (space-separated)

Solaris
> MANSECTS in */usr/share/man/man.cf* and/or the top level directory of any manual page tree (comma-separated)

Setting up man −k

It's probably worth mentioning how to get man -k to work if your system claims to support it, but nothing comes back when you use it. This command (and its alias apropos) uses a data file indexing all available manual pages. The file often must be initially created by the system administrator, and it may also need to be updated from time to time.

On most systems, the command to create the index file is makewhatis, and it must be run by *root*. The command does not require any arguments except on Solaris systems, where the top-level manual page subdirectory is given:

```
# makewhatis                 Most systems
# makewhat /usr/share/man     Solaris
```

On AIX, HP-UX, and Tru64, the older catman -w command is used instead.

Piping into grep and awk

As you undoubtedly already know, the grep command searches its input for lines containing a given pattern. Users commonly use grep to search files. What might be new is some of the ways grep is useful in pipes with many administrative commands. For example, if you want to find out about all of a certain user's current processes, pipe the output of the ps command to grep and search for her username:

```
% ps aux | grep chavez
chavez   8684 89.5  9.627680 5280 ?   R N  85:26 /home/j90/1988
root    10008 10.0  0.8 1408  352 p2 S       0:00 grep chavez
chavez   8679  0.0  1.4 2048  704 ?   I N    0:00 -csh (csh)
chavez   8681  0.0  1.3 2016  672 ?   I N    0:00 /usr/nqs/sc1
chavez   8683  0.0  1.3 2016  672 ?   I N    0:00 csh -cb rj90
chavez   8682  0.0  2.6 1984 1376 ?   I N    0:00 j90
```

This example uses the BSD version of ps, using the options that list every single process on the system,[*] and then uses grep to pick out the ones belonging to user *chavez*. If you'd like the header line from ps included as well, use a command like:

```
% ps -aux | egrep 'chavez|PID'
```

Now that's a lot to type every time, but you could define an alias if your shell supports them. For example, in the C shell you could use this one:

```
% alias pu "ps -aux | egrep '\!:1|PID'"
% pu chavez
```

---

[*] Under HP-UX and for Solaris' */usr/bin/ps*, the corresponding command is ps -ef.

```
USER     PID %CPU  %MEM SZ    RSS TT  STAT TIME   COMMAND
chavez  8684 89.5  9.6 27680 5280 ?   R N   85:26 /home/j90/1988
...
```

Another useful place for grep is with man -k. For instance, I once needed to figure out where the error log file was on a new system—the machine kept displaying annoying messages from the error log indicating that disk 3 had a hardware failure. Now, I already knew that, and it had even been fixed. I tried man -k error: 64 matches; man -k log was even worse: 122 manual pages. But man -k log | grep error produced only 9 matches, including a nifty command to blast error log entries older than a given number of days.

The awk command is also a useful component in pipes. It can be used to selectively manipulate the output of other commands in a more general way than grep. A complete discussion of awk is beyond the scope of this book, but a few examples will show you some of its capabilities and enable you to investigate others on your own.

One thing awk is good for is picking out and possibly rearranging columns within command output. For example, the following command produces a list of all users running the quake game:

```
$ ps -ef | grep "[q]uake" | awk '{print $1}'
```

This awk command prints only the first field from each line of ps output passed to it by grep. The search string for grep may strike you as odd, since the brackets enclose only a single character. The command is constructed that way so that the ps line for the grep command itself will not be selected (since the string "quake" does not appear in it). It's basically a trick to avoid having to add grep -v grep to the pipe between the grep and awk commands.

Once you've generated the list of usernames, you can do what you need to with it. One possibility is simply to record the information in a file:

```
$ (date ; ps -ef | grep "[q]uake" | awk '{print $1 " [" $7 "]"}' \
      | sort | uniq) >> quaked.users
```

This command sends the list of users currently playing quake, along with the CPU time used so far enclosed in square brackets, to the file *quaked.users*, preceding the list with the current date and time. We'll see a couple of other ways to use such a list in the course of this chapter.

awk can also be used to sum up a column of numbers. For example, this command searches the entire local filesystem for files owned by user *chavez* and adds up all of their sizes:

```
# find / -user chavez -fstype 4.2 ! -name /dev/\* -ls | \
    awk '{sum+=$7}; END {print "User chavez total disk use = " sum}'
User chavez total disk use = 41987453
```

The awk component of this command accumulates a running total of the seventh column from the find command that holds the number of bytes in each file, and it prints out the final value after the last line of its input has been processed. awk can also compute averages; in this case, the average number of bytes per file would be given by the expression *sum/NR* placed into the command's *END* clause. The denominator *NR* is an awk internal variable. It holds the line number of the current input line and accordingly indicates the total number of lines read once all of them have been processed.

awk can be used in a similar way with the date command to generate a filename based upon the current date. For example, the following command places the output of the *sys_doc* script into a file named for the current date and host:

```
$ sys_doc > `date | awk '{print $3 $2 $6}'`.`hostname`.sysdoc
```

If this command were run on October 24, 2001, on host *ophelia*, the filename generated by the command would be *24Oct2001.ophelia.sysdoc*.

Recent implementations of date allow it to generate such strings on its own, eliminating the need for awk. The following command illustrates these features. It constructs a unique filename for a scratch file by telling date to display the literal string *junk_* followed by the day of the month, short form month name, 2-digit year, and hour, minutes and seconds of the current time, ending with the literal string *.junk*:

```
$ date +junk_%d%b%y%H%M%S.junk
junk_08Dec01204256.junk
```

We'll see more examples of grep and awk later in this chapter.

Is All of This Really Necessary?

If all of this fancy pipe fitting seems excessive to you, be assured that I'm not telling you about it for its own sake. The more you know the ins and outs of Unix commands—both basic and obscure—the better prepared you'll be for the inevitable unexpected events that you will face. For example, you'll be able to come up with an answer quickly when the division director (or department chair or whoever) wants to know what percentage of the aggregate disk space in a local area network is used by the *chem* group. Virtuosity and wizardry needn't be goals in themselves, but they will help you develop two of the seven cardinal virtues of system administration: *flexibility* and *ingenuity*. (I'll tell you what the others are in future chapters.)

Finding Files

Another common command of great use to a system administrator is find. find is one of those commands that you wonder how you ever lived without—once you learn it. It has one of the most obscure manual pages in the Unix canon, so I'll spend a bit of time explaining it (skip ahead if it's already familiar).

find locates files with common, specified characteristics, searching anywhere on the system you tell it to look. Conceptually, find has the following syntax:[*]

```
# find starting-dir(s) matching-criteria-and-actions
```

Starting-dir(s) is the set of directories where find should start looking for files. By default, find searches all directories underneath the listed directories. Thus, specifying / as the starting directory would search the entire filesystem.

The *matching-criteria* tell find what sorts of files you want to look for. Some of the most useful are shown in Table 3-1.

Table 3-1. find command matching criteria options

Option	Meaning
-atime *n*	File was last accessed exactly *n* days ago.
-mtime *n*	File was last modified exactly *n* days ago.
-newer *file*	File was modified more recently than *file* was.
-size *n*	File is *n* 512-byte blocks long (rounded up to next block).
-type *c*	Specifies the file type: *f*=plain file, *d*=directory, etc.
-fstype *typ*	Specifies filesystem type.
-name *nam*	The filename is *nam*.
-perm *p*	The file's access mode is *p*.
-user *usr*	The file's owner is *usr*.
-group *grp*	The file's group owner is *grp*.
-nouser	The file's owner is not listed in the password file.
-nogroup	The file's group owner is not listed in the group file.

These may not seem all that useful—why would you want a file accessed exactly three days ago, for instance? However, you may precede time periods, sizes, and other numeric quantities with a plus sign (meaning "more than") or a minus sign (meaning "less than") to get more useful criteria. Here are some examples:

```
-mtime +7      Last modified more than 7 days ago
-atime -2      Last accessed less than 2 days ago
-size +100     Larger than 50K
```

You can also include wildcards with the -name option, provided that you quote them. For example, the criteria -name '*.dat' specifies all filenames ending in *.dat*.

Multiple conditions are joined with AND by default. Thus, to look for files last accessed more than two months ago and last modified more than four months ago, you would use these options:

```
-atime +60 -mtime +120
```

---

[*] Syntactically, find does not distinguish between file-selection options and action-related options, but it is often helpful to think of them as separate types as you learn to use find.

Options may also be joined with -o for OR combination, and grouping is allowed using escaped parentheses. For example, the matching criteria below specifies files last accessed more than seven days ago or last modified more than 30 days ago:

```
\( -atime +7 -o -mtime +30 \)
```

An exclamation point may be used for NOT (be sure to quote it if you're using the C shell). For example, the matching criteria below specify all *.dat* files except *gold.dat*:

```
! -name gold.dat -name \*.dat
```

The -perm option allows you to search for files with a specific access mode (numeric form). Using an unsigned value specifies files with exactly that permission setting, and preceding the value with a minus sign searches for files with *at least* the specified access. (In other words, the specified permission mode is XORed with the file's permission setting.) Here are some examples:

-perm 755	*Permission = rwxr-xr-x*
-perm -002	*World-writeable files*
-perm -4000	*Setuid access is set*
-perm -2000	*Setgid access is set*

The *actions* options tell find what to do with each file it locates that matches all the specified criteria. Some available actions are shown in Table 3-2.

Table 3-2. find actions

Option	Meaning
-print	Display pathname of matching file.
-ls[a]	Display long directory listing for matching file.
-exec cmd	Execute command on file.
-ok cmd	Prompt before executing command on file.
-xdev	Restrict the search to the filesystem of the starting directory (typically used to bypass mounted remote filesystems).
-prune	Don't descend into directories encountered.

[a] Not available under HP-UX.

The default on many newer systems is -print, although forgetting to include it on older systems like SunOS will result in a successful command with no output. Commands for -exec and -ok must end with an escaped semicolon (\;). The form {} may be used in commands as a placeholder for the pathname of each found file. For example, to delete each matching file as it is found, specify the following option to the find command:

```
-exec rm -f {} \;
```

Note that there are no spaces between the opening and closing curly braces. The curly braces may only appear once within the command.

Now let's put the parts together. The command below lists the pathname of all C source files under the current directory:

```
$ find . -name \*.c -print
```

The starting directory is "." (the current directory), the matching criteria specify file-names ending in .c, and the action to be performed is to display the pathname of each matching file. This is a typical user use for find. Other common uses include searching for misplaced files and feeding file lists to cpio.

find has many administrative uses, including:

- Monitoring disk use
- Locating files that pose potential security problems
- Performing recursive file operations

For example, find may be used to locate large disk files. The command below displays a long directory listing for all files under /chem larger than 1 MB (2048 512-byte blocks) that haven't been modified in a month:

```
$ find /chem -size +2048 -mtime +30 -exec ls -l {} \;
```

Of course, we could also use -ls rather than the -exec clause. In fact, it is more efficient because the directory listing is handled by find internally (rather than having to spawn a subshell for every file). To search for files not modified in a month or not accessed in three months, use this command:

```
$ find /chem -size +2048 \( -mtime +30 -o -atime +120 \) -ls
```

Such old, large files might be candidates for tape backup and deletion if disk space is short.

find can also delete files automatically as it finds them. The following is a typical administrative use of find, designed to automatically delete old junk files on the system:

```
# find / \( -name a.out -o -name core -o -name '*~'\
    -o -name '.*~' -o -name '#*#' \) -type f -atime +14 \
    -exec rm -f {} \; -o -fstype nfs -prune
```

This command searches the entire filesystem and removes various editor backup files, core dump files, and random executables (a.out) that haven't been accessed in two weeks and that don't reside on a remotely mounted filesystem. The logic is messy: the final -o option ORs all the options that preceded it with those that followed it, each of which is computed separately. Thus, the final operation finds files that match either of two criteria:

- The filename matches, it's a plain file, and it hasn't been accessed for 14 days.
- The filesystem type is *nfs* (meaning a remote disk).

If the first criteria set is true, the file gets removed; if the second set is true, a "prune" action takes place, which says "don't descend any lower into the directory tree."

Thus, every time `find` comes across an NFS-mounted filesystem, it will move on, rather than searching its entire contents as well.

Matching criteria and actions may be placed in any order, and they are evaluated from left to right. For example, the following `find` command lists all regular files under the directories */home* and */aux1* that are larger than 500K and were last accessed over 30 days ago (done by the options through -print); additionally, it removes those named *core*:

```
# find /home /aux1 -type f -atime +30 -size +1000 -print \
    -name core -exec rm {} \;
```

`find` also has security uses. For example, the following `find` command lists all files that have setuid or setgid access set (see Chapter 7).

```
# find / -type f \( -perm -2000 -o -perm -4000 \) -print
```

The output from this command could be compared to a saved list of setuid and setgid files, in order to locate any newly created files requiring investigation:

```
# find / \( -perm -2000 -o -perm -4000 \) -print | \
    diff - files.secure
```

`find` may also be used to perform the same operation on a selected group of files. For example, the command below changes the ownership of all the files under user *chavez*'s home directory to user *chavez* and group *physics*:

```
# find /home/chavez -exec chown chavez {} \; \
                    -exec chgrp physics {} \;
```

The following command gathers all C source files anywhere under */chem* into the directory */chem1/src*:

```
# find /chem -name '*.c' -exec mv {} /chem1/src \;
```

Similarly, this command runs the script *prettify* on every C source file under */chem*:

```
# find /chem -name '*.c' -exec /usr/local/bin/prettify {} \;
```

Note that the full pathname for the script is included in the -exec clause.

Finally, you can use the `find` command as a simple method for tracking changes that have been made to a system in the course of a certain time period or as the result of a certain action. Consider these commands:

```
# touch /tmp/starting_time
# perform some operation
# find / -newer /tmp/starting_time
```

The output of the final `find` command displays all files modified or added as a result of whatever action was performed. It does not directly tell you about deleted files, but it lists modified directories (which can be an indirect indication).

Repeating Commands

`find` is one solution when you need to perform the same operation on a group of files. The `xargs` command is another way of automating similar commands on a group of objects; `xargs` is more flexible than `find` because it can operate on any set of objects, regardless of what kind they are, while `find` is limited to files and directories.

`xargs` is most often used as the final component of a pipe. It appends the items it reads from standard input to the Unix command given as its argument. For example, the following command increases the nice number of all quake processes by 10, thereby lowering each process's priority:

```
# ps -ef | grep "[q]uake" | awk '{print $2}' | xargs renice +10
```

The pipe preceding the `xargs` command extracts the process ID from the second column of the `ps` output for each instance of quake, and then `xargs` runs `renice` using all of them. The `renice` command takes multiple process IDs as its arguments, so there is no problem sending all the PIDs to a single `renice` command as long as there are not a truly inordinate number of quake processes.

You can also tell `xargs` to send its incoming arguments to the specified command in groups by using its -n option, which takes the number of items to use at a time as its argument. If you wanted to run a script for each user who is currently running quake, for example, you could use this command:

```
# ps -ef | grep "[q]uake" | awk '{print $1}' | xargs -n1 warn_user
```

The `xargs` command will take each username in turn and use it as the argument to `warn_user`.

So far, all of the `xargs` commands we've look at have placed the incoming items at the end of the specified command. However, `xargs` also allows you to place each incoming line of input at a specified position within the command to be executed. To do so, you include its -i option and use the form {} as placeholder for each incoming line within the command. For example, this command runs the System V `chargefee` utility for each user running quake, assessing them 10000 units:

```
# ps -ef | grep "[q]uake" | awk '{print $1}' | \
   xargs -i chargefee {} 10000
```

If curly braces are needed elsewhere within the command, you can specify a different pair of placeholder characters as the argument to -i.

Substitutions like this can get rather complicated. `xargs`'s -t option displays each constructed command before executing, and the -p option allows you to selectively execute commands by prompting you before each one. Using both options together provides the safest execution mode and also enables you to nondestructively debug a command or script by answering no for every offered command.

-i and -n don't interact the way you might think they would. Consider this command:

```
$ echo a b c d e f | xargs -n3 -i echo before {} after
before a b c d e f after
$ echo a b c d e f | xargs -i -n3 echo before {} after
before {} after a b c
before {} after d e f
```

You might expect that these two commands would be equivalent and that they would both produce two lines of output:

```
before a b c after
before d e f after
```

However, neither command produces this output, and the two commands do not operate identically. What is happening is that -i and -n conflict with one another, and the one appearing last wins. So, in the first command, -i is what is operative, and each *line* of input is inserted into the echo command. In the second command, the -n3 option is used, three arguments are placed at the end of each echo command, and the curly braces are treated as literal characters.

Our first use of -i worked properly because the usernames are coming from separate lines in the ps command output, and these lines are retained as they flow through the pipe to xargs.

If you want xargs to execute commands containing pipes, I/O redirection, compound commands joined with semicolons, and so on, there's a bit of a trick: use the -c option to a shell to execute the desired command. I occasionally want to look at the final lines of a group of files and then view all of them a screen at a time. In other words, I'd like to run a command like this and have it "work":

```
$ tail test00* | more
```

On most systems, this command displays lines only from the last file. However, I can use xargs to get what I want:

```
$ ls -1 test00* | xargs -i /usr/bin/sh -c \
  'echo "****** {}:"; tail -15 {}; echo ""' | more
```

This displays the last 15 lines of each file, preceded by a header line containing the filename and followed by a blank line for readability.

You can use a similar method for lots of other kinds of repetitive operations. For example, this command sorts and de-dups all of the *.dat* files in the current directory:

```
$ ls *.dat | xargs -i /usr/bin/sh -c "sort -u -o {} {}"
```

Creating Several Directory Levels at Once

Many people are unaware of the options offered by the mkdir command. These options allow you to set the file mode at the same time as you create a new directory and to create multiple levels of subdirectories with a single command, both of which can make your use of mkdir much more efficient.

For example, each of the following two commands sets the mode on the new directory to *rwxr-xr-x*, using mkdir's -m option:

```
$ mkdir -m 755 ./people
$ mkdir -m u=rwx,go=rx ./places
```

You can use either a numeric mode or a symbolic mode as the argument to the -m option. You can also use a relative symbolic mode, as in this example:

```
$ mkdir -m g+w ./things
```

In this case, the mode changes are applied to the default mode as set with the umask command.

mkdir's -p option tells it to create any missing parents required for the subdirectories specified as its arguments. For example, the following command will create the subdirectories *./a* and *./a/b* if they do not already exist and then create *./a/b/c*:

```
$ mkdir -p ./a/b/c
```

The same command without -p will give an error if all of the parent subdirectories are not already present.

Duplicating an Entire Directory Tree

It is fairly common to need to move or duplicate an entire directory tree, preserving not only the directory structure and file contents but also the ownership and mode settings for every file. There are several ways to accomplish this, using tar, cpio, and sometimes even cp. I'll focus on tar and then look briefly at the others at the end of this section.

Let's make this task more concrete and assume we want to copy the directory */chem/olddir* as */chem1/newdir* (in other words, we want to change the name of the *olddir* subdirectory as part of duplicating its entire contents). We can take advantage of tar's -p option, which restores ownership and access modes along with the files from an archive (it must be run as *root* to set file ownership), and use these commands to create the new directory tree:

```
# cd /chem1
# tar -cf - -C /chem olddir | tar -xvpf -
# mv olddir newdir
```

The first tar command creates an archive consisting of */chem/olddir* and all of the files and directories underneath it and writes it to standard output (indicated by the - argument to the -f option). The -C option sets the current directory for the first tar command to */chem*. The second tar command extracts files from standard input (again indicated by -f -), retaining their previous ownership and protection. The second tar command gives detailed output (requested with the -v option). The final mv command changes the name of the newly created subdirectory of */chem1* to *newdir*.

If you want only a subset of the files and directories under *olddir* to be copied to *newdir*, you would vary the previous commands slightly. For example, these commands copy the *src*, *bin*, and *data* subdirectories and the *logfile* and *.profile* files from *olddir* to *newdir*, duplicating their ownership and protection:

```
# mkdir /chem1/newdir
set ownership and protection for newdir if necessary
# cd /chem1/olddir
# tar -cvf - src bin data logfile.* .profile  |\
   tar -xvpf - -C /chem/newdir
```

The first two commands are necessary only if */chem1/newdir* does not already exist.

This command performs a similar operation, copying only a single branch of the subtree under *olddir*:

```
# mkdir /chem1/newdir
set ownership and protection for newdir if necessary
# cd /chem1/newdir
# tar -cvf - -C /chem/olddir src/viewers/rasmol | tar -xvpf -
```

These commands create */chem1/newdir/src* and its *viewers* subdirectory but place nothing in them but *rasmol*.

If you prefer cpio to tar, cpio can perform similar functions. For example, this command copies the entire *olddir* tree to */chem1* (again as *newdir*):

```
# mkdir /chem1/newdir
set ownership and protection for newdir if necessary
# cd /chem1/olddir
# find . -print | cpio -pdvm /chem1/newdir
```

On all of the systems we are considering, the cp command has a -p option as well, and these commands create *newdir*:

```
# cp -pr /chem/olddir /chem1
# mv /chem1/olddir /chem1/newdir
```

The -r option stands for recursive and causes cp to duplicate the source directory structure in the new location.

Be aware that tar works differently than cp does in the case of symbolic links. tar recreates links in the new location, while cp converts symbolic links to regular files.

Comparing Directories

Over time, the two directories we considered in the last section will undoubtedly both change. At some future point, you might need to determine the differences between them. dircmp is a special-purpose utility designed to perform this very operation.* dircmp takes the directories to be compared as its arguments:

```
$ dircmp /chem/olddir /chem1/newdir
```

* On FreeBSD and Linux systems, diff -r provides the equivalent functionality.

`dircmp` produces voluminous output even when the directories you're comparing are small. There are two main sections to the output. The first one lists files that are present in only one of the two directory trees:

```
Mon Jan 4 1995  /chem/olddir only and /chem1/newdir only  Page 1
./water.dat                   ./hf.dat
./src/viewers/rasmol/init.c  ./h2f.dat
...
```

All pathnames in the report are relative to the directory locations specified on the command line. In this case, the files in the left column are present only under */chem/olddir*, and those in the right column are present only at the new location.

The second part of the report indicates whether the files present in both directory trees are the same or different. Here are some typical lines from this section of the report:

```
same       ./h2o.dat
different   ./hcl.dat
```

The default output from `dircmp` indicates only whether the corresponding files are the same or not, and sometimes this is all you need to know. If you want to know exactly what the differences are, you can include the `-d` to `dircmp`, which tells it to run `diff` for each pair of differing files (since it uses `diff`, this works only for text files). On the other hand, if you want to decrease the amount of output by limiting the second section of the report to files that differ, include the `-s` option on the `dircmp` command.

Deleting Pesky Files

When I teach courses for new Unix users, one of the early exercises consists of figuring out how to delete the files *–delete_me* and *delete me* (with the embedded space in the second case).[*] Occasionally, however, a user winds up with a file that he just can't get rid of, no matter how creative he is in using `rm`. At that point, he will come to you. If there is a way to get `rm` to do the job, show it to him, but there are some files that `rm` just can't handle. For example, it is possible for some buggy application program to put a file into a bizarre, inconclusive state. Users can also create such files if they experiment with certain filesystem manipulation tools (which they probably shouldn't be using in the first place).

One tool that can take care of such intransigent files is the directory editor feature of the GNU `emacs` text editor. It is also useful to show this feature to users who just can't get the hang of how to quote strange filenames.

This is the procedure for deleting a file with `emacs`:

1. Invoke `emacs` on the directory in question, either by including its path on the command line or by entering its name at the prompt produced by Ctrl-X Ctrl-F.

---

[*] There are lots of solutions. One of the simplest is `rm delete\ me ./-delete_me`.

2. Opening the directory causes emacs to automatically enter its directory editing mode. Move the cursor to the file in question using the usual emacs commands.

3. Enter a d, which is the directory editing mode subcommand to mark a file for deletion. You can also use u to unmark a file, # to mark all auto-save files, and ~ to mark all backup files.

4. Enter the x subcommand, which says to delete all marked files, and answer the confirmation prompt in the affirmative.

5. At this point the file will be gone, and you can exit from emacs, continue other editing, or do whatever you need to do next.

emacs can also be useful for viewing directory contents when they include files with bizarre characters embedded within them. The most amusing example of this that I can cite is a user who complained to me that the ls command beeped at him every time he ran it. It turned out that this only happened in his home directory, and it was due to a file with a Ctrl-G in the middle of the name. The filename looked fine in ls listings because the Ctrl-G character was being interpreted, causing the beep. Control characters become visible when you look at the directory in emacs, and so the problem was easily diagnosed and remedied (using the r subcommand to emacs's directory editing mode that renames a file).

Putting a Command in a Cage

As we'll discuss in detail later, system security inevitably involves tradeoffs between convenience and risk. One way to mitigate the risks arising from certain inherently dangerous commands and subsystems is to isolate them from the rest of the system. This is accomplished with the chroot command.

The chroot command runs another command from an alternate location within the filesystem, making the command think that that the location is actually the root directory of the filesystem. chroot takes one argument, which is the alternate top-level directory. For example, the following command runs the sendmail daemon, using the directory */jail* as the new root directory:

```
# chroot /jail sendmail -bd -q10m
```

The sendmail process will treat */jail* as its root directory. For example, when sendmail looks for the mail aliases database, which it expects to be located in */etc/aliases*, it will actually access the file */jail/etc/aliases*. In order for sendmail to work properly in this mode, a minimal filesystem needs to be set up under */jail* containing all the files and directories that sendmail needs.

Running a daemon or subsystem as a user created specifically for that purpose (rather than *root*) is sometimes called *sandboxing*. This security technique is recommended wherever feasible, and it is often used in conjunction with chrooting for added security. See "Managing DNS Servers" in Chapter 8 for a detailed example of this technique.

FreeBSD also has a facility called jail, which is a stronger versions of chroot that allows you to specify access restrictions for the isolated command.

Starting at the End

Perhaps it's appropriate that we consider the tail command near the end of this section on administrative uses of common commands. tail's principal function is to display the last 10 lines of a file (or standard input). tail also has a -f option that displays new lines as they are added to the end of a file; this mode can be useful for monitoring the progress of a command that writes periodic status information to a file. For example, these commands start a background backup with tar, saving its output to a file, and monitor the operation using tail -f:

```
$ tar -cvf /dev/rmt1 /chem /chem1 > 24oct94_tar.toc &
$ tail -f 24oct94_tar.toc
```

The information that tar displays about each file as it is written to tape is eventually written to the table of contents file and displayed by tail. The advantage that this method has over the tee command is that the tail command may be killed and restarted as many times as you like without affecting the tar command.

Some versions of tail also include a -r option, which will display the lines in a file in reverse order, which is occasionally useful. HP-UX does not support this option, and Linux provides this feature in the tac command.

Be Creative

As a final example of the creative use of ordinary commands, consider the following dilemma. A user tells you his workstation won't reboot. He says he was changing his system's boot script but may have deleted some files in /etc accidentally. You go over to it, type ls, and get a message about some missing shared libraries. How do you poke around and find out what files are there?

The answer is to use the simplest Unix command there is, *echo*, along with the wildcard mechanism, both of which are built into every shell, including the statically linked one available in single user mode.

To see all the files in the current directory, just type:

```
$ echo *
```

This command tells the shell to display the value of "*", which of course expands to all files not beginning with a period in the current directory.

By using echo together with cd (also a built-in shell command), I was able to get a pretty good idea of what had happened. I'll tell you the rest of this story at the end of Chapter 4.

Essential Administrative Techniques

In this section, we consider several system facilities with which system administrators need to be intimately familiar.

Periodic Program Execution: The cron Facility

cron is a Unix facility that allows you to schedule programs for periodic execution. For example, you can use cron to call a particular remote site every hour to exchange email, to clean up editor backup files every night, to back up and then truncate system log files once a month, or to perform any number of other tasks. Using cron, administrative functions are performed without any explicit action by the system administrator (or any other user).[*]

For administrative purposes, cron is useful for running commands and scripts according to a preset schedule. cron can send the resulting output to a log file, as a mail or terminal message, or to a different host for centralized logging. The cron command starts the crond daemon, which has no options. It is normally started automatically by one of the system initialization scripts.

Table 3-3 lists the components of the cron facility on the various Unix systems we are considering. We will cover each of them in the course of this section.

Table 3-3. Variations on the cron facility

Component	Location and information
crontab files	**Usual:** */var/spool/cron/crontabs*
	FreeBSD: */var/cron/tabs, /etc/crontab*
	Linux: */var/spool/cron* (Red Hat) */var/spool/cron/tabs* (SuSE), */etc/crontab* (both)
crontab format	**Usual:** System V (no username field)
	BSD: */etc/crontab* (requires username as sixth field)
cron.allow and *cron.deny* files	**Usual:** */var/adm/cron*
	FreeBSD: */var/cron*
	Linux: */etc* (Red Hat), */var/spool/cron* (SuSE)
	Solaris: */etc/cron.d*
Related facilities	**Usual:** none
	FreeBSD: periodic utility
	Linux: */etc/cron.** (*hourly,daily,weekly,monthly*)
	Red Hat: anacron utility[a]

---

[*] Note that cron is not a general facility for scheduling program execution off-hours; for the latter, use a batch processing command (discussed in "Managing CPU Resources" in Chapter 15).

Table 3-3. Variations on the cron facility (continued)

Component	Location and information
cron log file	**Usual:** */var/adm/cron/log* **FreeBSD:** */var/log/cron* **Linux:** */var/log/cron* (Red Hat), not configured (SuSE) **Solaris:** */var/cron/log*
File containing PID of crond	**Usual:** not provided **FreeBSD:** */var/run/cron.pid* **Linux:** */var/run/crond.pid* (Red Hat), */var/run/cron.pid* (SuSE)
Boot script that starts cron	**AIX:** */etc/inittab* **FreeBSD:** */etc/rc* **HP-UX:** */sbin/init.d/cron* **Linux:** */etc/init.d/cron* **Solaris:** */etc/init.d/cron* **Tru64:** */sbin/init.d/cron*
Boot script configuration file: cron-related entries	**AIX:** none used **FreeBSD:** */etc/rc.conf*: *cron_enable="YES"* and *cron_flags="args-to-cron"* **HP-UX:** */etc/rc.config.d/cron: CRON=1* **Linux:** none used (Red Hat, SuSE 8), */etc/rc.config: CRON="YES"* (SuSE 7) **Solaris:** */etc/default/cron: CRONLOG=yes* **Tru64:** none used

a The Red Hat Linux anacron utility is very similar to cron, but it also runs jobs missed due to the system being down when it reboots.

crontab files

What to run and when to run it are specified by *crontab entries*, which comprise the system's cron schedule. The name comes from the traditional cron configuration file named *crontab*, for "cron table."

By default, any user may add entries to the cron schedule. Crontab entries are stored in separate files for each user, usually in the directory called */var/spool/cron/crontabs* (see Table 3-3 for exceptions). Users' crontab files are named after their username: for example, */var/spool/cron/crontabs/root*.

> The preceding is the System V convention for crontab files. BSD systems traditionally use a single file, */etc/crontab*. FreeBSD and Linux systems still use this file, in addition to those just mentioned.

Crontab files are not ordinarily edited directly but are created and modified with the crontab command (described later in this section).

Crontab entries direct cron to run commands at regular intervals. Each one-line entry in the crontab file has the following format:

```
minutes  hours  day-of-month  month  weekday  command
```

Whitespace separates the fields. However, the final field, *command*, can contain spaces within it (i.e., the *command* field consists of everything after the space following *weekday*); the other fields must not contain embedded spaces.

The first five fields specify the times at which cron should execute *command*. Their meanings are described in Table 3-4.

Table 3-4. Crontab file fields

Field	Meaning	Range
minutes	Minutes after the hour	0-59
hours	Hour of the day	0-23 (0=midnight)
day-of-month	Numeric day within a month	1-31
month	The month of the year	1-12
weekday	The day of the week	0-6 (0=Sunday)

Note that hours are numbered from midnight (0), and weekdays are numbered beginning with Sunday (also 0).

An entry in any of these fields can be a single number, a pair of numbers separated by a dash (indicating a range of numbers), a comma-separated list of numbers and/or ranges, or an asterisk (a wildcard that represents all valid values for that field).

If the first character in an entry is a number sign (#), cron treats the entry as a comment and ignores it. This is also an easy way to temporarily disable an entry without permanently deleting it.

Here are some example crontab entries:

```
0,15,30,45 * * * *  (echo ""; date; echo "") >/dev/console
0,10,20,30,40,50 7-18 * * * /usr/sbin/atrun
0 0 * * *  find / -name "*.bak" -type f -atime +7 -exec rm {} \;
0 4 * * *  /bin/sh /var/adm/mon_disk 2>&1 >/var/adm/disk.log
0 2 * * *  /bin/sh /usr/local/sbin/sec_check 2>&1 | mail root
30 3 1 * * /bin/csh /usr/local/etc/monthly 2>&1 >/dev/null
#30 2 * * 0,6  /usr/local/newsbin/news.weekend
```

The first entry displays the date on the console terminal every fifteen minutes (on the quarter hour); notice that the multiple commands are enclosed in parentheses in order to redirect their output as a group. (Technically, this says to run the commands together in a single subshell.) The second entry runs */usr/sbin/atrun* every 10 minutes from 7 A.M. to 6 P.M. daily. The third entry runs a find command to remove all *.bak* files not accessed in seven days.

The fourth and fifth lines run a shell script every day, at 4 A.M. and 2 A.M., respectively. The shell to execute the script is specified explicitly on the command line in both cases; the system default shell, usually the Bourne shell, is used if none is explicitly specified. Both lines' entries redirect standard output and standard error, sending both of them to a file in one case and as electronic mail to *root* in the other.

The sixth entry executes the C shell script */usr/local/etc/monthly* at 3:30 A.M. on the first day of each month. Notice that the command format—specifically the output redirection—uses Bourne shell syntax even though the script itself will be run under the C shell.

Were it not disabled, the final entry would run the command */usr/local/newsbin/ news.weekend* at 2:30 A.M. on Saturday and Sunday mornings.

The final three active entries illustrate three output-handling alternatives: redirecting it to a file, piping it through mail, and discarding it to */dev/null*. If no output redirection is performed, the output is sent via mail to the user who ran the command.

The *command* field can be any Unix command or group of commands (properly separated with semicolons). The entire crontab entry can be arbitrarily long, but it must be a single physical line in the file.

If the command contains a percent sign (%), cron will use any text following this sign as standard input for *command*. Additional percent signs can be used to subdivide this text into lines. For example, the following crontab entry:

```
30 11 31 12 * /usr/bin/wall%Happy New Year!%Let's make it great!
```

runs the wall command at 11:30 A.M. on December 31, using the text "Happy New Year! Let's make it great!" as standard input.

Note that the day of the week and day of the month fields are effectively ORed: if both are filled in, the entry is run on that day of the month *and* on matching days of the week. Thus, the following entry would run on January 1 and every Monday:

```
* * 1 1 1 /usr/local/bin/test55
```

In most implementations, the cron daemon reads the crontab files when it starts up and whenever there have been changes to any of the crontab files. In some, generally older versions, cron reads the crontab files once every minute.

 The BSD crontab file, */etc/crontab*, uses a slightly different entry format, inserting an additional field between the *weekday* and *command* fields: the user account that should be used to run the specified command. Here is a sample entry that runs a script at 3:00 A.M. on every weekend day:

```
0 3 * * 6-7 root /var/adm/weekend.sh
```

As this example illustratess, this entry format also encodes the days of the week slightly differently, running from 1=Monday through 7=Sunday.

FreeBSD and Linux crontab entry format enhancements. FreeBSD and Linux systems use the cron package written by Paul Vixie. It supports all standard cron features and includes enhancements to the standard crontab entry format, including the following:

- Months and days of the week may be specified as names, abbreviated to their first three letters: *sun*, *mon*, *jan*, *feb*, and so on.

- Sunday can be specified as either 0 or 7.

- Ranges and lists can be combined: e.g., 2,4,6–7 is a legal entry. HP-UX also supports this enhancement.

- *Step values* can be specified with a /*n* suffix. For example, the hours entry 8-18/2 means "every two hours from 8 A.M. to 6 P.M." Similarly, the minutes entry */5 means "every five minutes."

- Environment variables can be defined within the crontab file, using the usual Bourne shell syntax. The environment variable MAILTO may be used to specify a user to receive any mail messages that cron thinks are necessary. For example, the first definition below sends mail to user *chavez* (regardless of which crontab the line appears in), and the second definition suppresses all mail from cron:

  ```
  MAILTO=chavez
  MAILTO=
  ```

  Additional environment variables include *SHELL*, *PATH*, and *HOME*.

- On FreeBSD systems, special strings may be used to replace the scheduling fields entirely:

@reboot	Run at system reboots
@yearly	Midnight on January 1
@monthly	Midnight on the first of the month
@weekly	Midnight each Sunday
@daily	Midnight
@hourly	On the hour

Adding crontab entries

The normal way to create crontab entries is with the crontab command.* In its default mode, the crontab command installs the text file specified as its argument into the cron spool area, as the crontab file for the user who ran crontab. For example, if user *chavez* executes the following command, the file *mycron* will be installed as */var/spool/cron/crontabs/chavez*:

```
$ crontab mycron
```

If *chavez* had previously installed crontab entries, they will be replaced by those in *mycron*; thus, any current entries that *chavez* wishes to keep must also be present in *mycron*.

The -l option to crontab lists the current crontab entries, and redirecting the command's output to a file will allow them to be captured and edited:

```
$ crontab -l >mycron
$ vi mycron
$ crontab mycron
```

---

* Except for the BSD-style */etc/crontab* file, which must be edited manually.

The -r option removes all current crontab entries.

The most convenient way to edit the crontab file is to use the -e option, which lets you directly modify and reinstall your current crontab entries in a single step. For example, the following command creates an editor session on the current crontab file (using the text editor specified in the *EDITOR* environment variable) and automatically installs the modified file when the editor exits:

```
$ crontab -e
```

Most crontab commands also accept a username as their final argument. This allows *root* to list or install a crontab file for a different user. For example, this command edits the crontab file for user *adm*:

```
# crontab -e adm
```

The FreeBSD and Linux versions of this command provide the same functionality with the -u option:

```
# crontab -e -u adm
```

When you decide to place a new task under cron's control, you'll need to carefully consider which user should execute each command run by cron, and then add the appropriate crontab entry to the correct crontab file. The following list describes common system users and the sorts of crontab entries they conventionally control:

root
: General system functions, security monitoring, and filesystem cleanup

lp
: Cleanup and accounting activities related to print spooling

sys
: Performance monitoring

uucp
: Running tasks in the UUCP file exchange facility

cron log files

Almost all versions of cron provide some mechanism for recording its activities to a log file. On some systems, this occurs automatically, and on others, messages are routed through the syslog facility. This is usually set up at installation time, but occasionally you'll need to configure syslog yourself. For example, on SuSE Linux systems, you'll need to add an entry for cron to the syslog configuration file */etc/syslog.conf* (discussed later in this chapter).

Solaris systems use a different mechanism. cron will keep a log of its activities if the *CRONLOG* entry in */etc/default/cron* is set to *YES*.

If logging is enabled, the log file should be monitored closely and truncated periodically, as it grows extremely quickly under even moderate cron use.

Using cron to automate system administration

The sample crontab entries we looked at previously provide some simple examples of using cron to automate various system tasks. cron provides the ideal way to run scripts according to a fixed schedule.

Another common way to use cron for regular administrative tasks is through the use of a series of scripts designed to run every night, once a week, and once a month; these scripts are often named *daily*, *weekly*, and *monthly*, respectively. The commands in *daily* would need to be performed every night (more specialized scripts could be run from it), and the other two would handle tasks to be performed less frequently.

daily might include these tasks:

- Remove junk files more than three days old from */tmp* and other scratch directories. More ambitious versions could search the entire system for old unneeded files.
- Run accounting summary commands.
- Run calendar.
- Rotate log files that are cycled daily.
- Take snapshots of the system with df, ps, and other appropriate commands in order to compile baseline system performance data (what is normal for that system). See Chapter 15 for more details.
- Perform daily security monitoring.

weekly might perform tasks like these:

- Remove very old junk files from the system (somewhat more aggressively than *daily*).
- Rotate log files that are cycled weekly.
- Run fsck -n to list any disk problems.
- Monitor user account security features.

monthly might do these jobs:

- List large disk files not accessed that month.
- Produce monthly accounting reports.
- Rotate log files that are cycled monthly.
- Use makewhatis to rebuild the database for use by man -k.

Additional or different activities might make more sense on your system. Such scripts are usually run late at night:

```
0 1 * * *  /bin/sh /var/adm/daily    2>&1 | mail root
0 2 * * 1  /bin/sh /var/adm/weekly   2>&1 | mail root
0 3 1 * *  /bin/sh /var/adm/monthly 2>&1 | mail root
```

In this example, the *daily* script runs every morning at 1 A.M., *weekly* runs every Monday at 2 A.M., and *monthly* runs on the first day of every month at 3 A.M.

---

cron need not be used only for tasks to be performed periodically forever, year after year. It can also be used to run a command repeatedly over a limited period of time, after which the crontab entry would be disabled or removed. For example, if you were trying to track certain kinds of security problems, you might want to use cron to run a script repeatedly to gather data. As a concrete example, consider this short script to check for large numbers of unsuccessful login attempts under AIX (although the script applies only to AIX, the general principles are useful on all systems):

```
#!/bin/sh
# chk_badlogin - Check unsuccessful login counts

date >> /var/adm/bl
egrep '^[^*].*:$|gin_coun' /etc/security/user | \
   awk 'BEGIN {n=0}
       {if (NF>1 && $3>3) {print s,$0; n=1}}
       {s=$0}
       END {if (n==0) {print "Everything ok."}}' \
>> /var/adm/bl
```

This script writes the date and time to the file */var/adm/bl* and then checks */etc/security/user* for any user with more than three unsuccessful login attempts. If you suspected someone was trying to break in to your system, you could run this script via cron every 10 minutes, in the hopes of isolating that accounts that were being targeted:

```
0,10,20,30,40,50 * * * * /bin/sh /var/adm/chk_badlogin
```

Similarly, if you are having a performance problem, you could use cron to automatically run various system performance monitoring commands or scripts at regular intervals to track performance problems over time.

The remainder of this section will consider two built-in facilities for accomplishing the same purpose under FreeBSD and Linux.

FreeBSD: The periodic command. FreeBSD provides the periodic command for the purposes we've just considered. This command is used in conjunction with the cron facility and serves as a method of organizing recurring administrative tasks. It is used by the following three entries from */etc/crontab*:

```
1   3   *   *   *   root    periodic daily
15  4   *   *   6   root    periodic weekly
30  5   1   *   *   root    periodic monthly
```

The command is run with the argument *daily* each day at 3:01 A.M., with *weekly* on Saturdays at 4:15 A.M., and with *monthly* at 5:30 A.M. on the first of each month.

The facility is controlled by the */etc/defaults/periodic.conf* file, which specifies its default behavior. Here are the first few lines of a sample file:

```
#!/bin/sh
#
# What files override these defaults ?
periodic_conf_files="/etc/periodic.conf /etc/periodic.conf.local"
```

This entry specifies the files that can be used to customize the facility's operation. Typically, changes to the default settings are all that appear in these files. The system administrator must create a local configuration file if desired, because none is installed by default.

The command form periodic *name* causes the command to run all of the scripts that it finds in the specified directory. If the latter is an absolute pathname, there is no doubt as to which directory is intended. If simply a name—such as *daily*—is given, the directory is assumed to be a subdirectory of */etc/periodic* or of one of the alternate directories specified in the configuration file's *local_periodic* entry:

```
# periodic script dirs
local_periodic="/usr/local/etc/periodic /usr/X11R6/etc/periodic"
```

/etc/periodic is always searched first, followed by the list in this entry.

The configuration file contains several entries for valid command arguments that control the location and content of the reports that periodic generates. Here are the entries related to *daily*:

```
# daily general settings
daily_output="root"              Email report to root.
daily_show_success="YES"         Include success messages.
daily_show_info="YES"            Include informational messages.
daily_show_badconfig="NO"        Exclude configuration error messages.
```

These entries produce rather verbose output, which is sent via email to *root*. In contrast, the following entries produce a minimal report (just error messages), which is appended to the specified log file:

```
daily_output="/var/adm/day.log"   Append report to a file.
daily_show_success="NO"
daily_show_info="NO"
daily_show_badconfig="NO"
```

The bulk of the configuration file defines variables used in the scripts themselves, as in these examples:

```
# 100.clean-disks
daily_clean_disks_enable="NO"# Delete files daily
daily_clean_disks_files="[#,]* .#* a.out *.core .emacs_[0-9]*"
daily_clean_disks_days=3# If older than this
daily_clean_disks_verbose="YES"# Mention files deleted
# 340.noid
weekly_noid_enable="YES# Find unowned files
weekly_noid_dirs="/"# Start here
```

The first group of settings are used by the */etc/periodic/daily/100.clean-disks* script, which deletes junk files from the filesystem. The first one indicates whether the script should perform its actions or not (in this case, it is disabled). The next two entries specify specific characteristics of the files to be deleted, and the final entry determines whether each deletion will be logged or not.

The second section of entries apply to */etc/periodic/weekly/340.noid*, a script that searches the filesystem for files owned by an unknown user or group. This excerpt from the script itself will illustrate how the configuration file entries are actually used:

```
case "$weekly_noid_enable" in
    [Yy][Ee][Ss])        Value is yes.
        echo "Check for files with unknown user or group:"
        rc=$(find -H ${weekly_noid_dirs:-/} -fstype local \
            \( -nogroup -o -nouser \) -print | sed 's/^/ /' |
            tee /dev/stderr | wc -l)
        [ $rc -gt 1 ] && rc=1;;

    *)  rc=0;;            Any other value.
esac
exit $rc
```

If *weekly_noid_enable* is set to "yes," then a message is printed with echo, and a pipe comprised of find, sed, tee and wc runs (which lists the files and then the total number of files), producing a report like this one:

```
Check for files with unknown user or group:
 /tmp/junk
 /home/jack
        2
```

The script goes on to define the variable *rc* as the appropriate script exit value depending on the circumstances.

You should become familiar with the current periodic configuration and component scripts on your system. If you want to make additions to the facility, there are several options:

- Add a crontab entry running periodic */dir*, where periodic's argument is a full pathname. Add scripts to this directory and entries to the configuration file as appropriate.

- Add an entry of the form periodic *name* and create a subdirectory of that name under */etc/periodic* or one of the directories listed in the configuration file's *local_ periodic* entry. Add scripts to the subdirectory and entries to the configuration file as appropriate.

- Use the directory specified in the *daily_local* setting (or *weekly* or *monthly*, as desired) in */etc/defaults/periodic.conf* (by default, this is */etc/{daily,weekly,monthly}. local*). Add scripts to this directory and entries to the configuration file as appropriate.

I think the first option is the simplest and most straightforward. If you do decide to use configuration file entries to control the functioning of a script that you create, be sure to read in its contents with commands like these:

```
if [ -r /etc/defaults/periodic.conf ]
then
    . /etc/defaults/periodic.conf
```

```
        source_periodic_confs
    fi
```

You can use elements of the existing scripts as models for your own.

Linux: The /etc/cron.* directories. Linux systems provide a similar mechanism for organizing regular activities, via the */etc/cron.* subdirectories. On Red Hat systems, these scripts are run via these crontab entries:

```
01 * * * * root run-parts /etc/cron.hourly
02 4 * * * root run-parts /etc/cron.daily
22 4 * * 0 root run-parts /etc/cron.weekly
42 4 1 * * root run-parts /etc/cron.monthly
```

On SuSE systems, the script */usr/lib/cron/run-crons* runs them; the script itself is executed by cron every 15 minutes. The scripts in the corresponding subdirectories are run slightly off the hour for */etc/cron.hourly* and around midnight (SuSE) or 4 A.M. (Red Hat). Customization consists of adding scripts to any of these subdirectories.

Under SuSE 8, the */etc/sysconfig/cron* configuration file contains settings that control the actions of some of these scripts.

cron security issues

cron's security issues are of two main types: making sure the system crontab files are secure and making sure unauthorized users don't run commands using cron. The first problem may be addressed by setting (if necessary) and checking the ownership and protection on the crontab files appropriately. (In particular, the files should not be world-writeable.) Naturally, they should be included in any filesystem security monitoring that you do.

The second problem, ensuring that unauthorized users don't run commands via cron, is addressed by the files *cron.allow* and *cron.deny*. These files control access to the crontab command. Both files contain lists of usernames, one per line. Access to crontab is controlled in the following way:

- If *cron.allow* exists, a username must be listed within it in order to run crontab.
- If *cron.allow* does not exist but *cron.deny* does exist, any user not listed in *cron. deny* may use the crontab command. *cron.deny* may be empty to allow unlimited access to cron.
- If neither file exists, only *root* can use crontab, except under Linux and FreeBSD, where the default build configuration of cron allows everyone to use it.

 These files control *only* whether a user can use the crontab command or not. In particular, they do not affect whether any existing crontab entries will be executed. Existing entries will be executed until they are removed.

The locations of the cron access files on various Unix systems are listed in Table 3-3.

System Messages

The various normal system facilities all generate status messages in the course of their normal operations. In addition, error messages are generated whenever there are hardware or software problems. Monitoring such messages—and acting upon important ones—is one of the system administrator's most important ongoing activities.

In this section, we first consider the syslog subsystem, which provides a centralized system message collection facility. We go on to consider the hardware-error logging facilities provided by some Unix systems, as well as tools for managing and processing the large amount of system message data that can accumulate.

The syslog facility

The syslog message-logging facility provides a more general way to specify where and how some types of system messages are saved. Table 3-5 lists the components of the syslog facility.

Table 3-5. Variations on the syslog facility

Component	Location and information
`syslogd` option to reject nonlocal messages	**AIX:** `-r` **FreeBSD:** `-s` **HP-UX:** `-N` **Linux:** `-r` to *allow* remote messages **Solaris:** `-t` **Tru64:** List allowed hosts in */etc/syslog.auth* (if if doesn't exist, all hosts are allowed)
File containing PID of `syslogd`	**Usual:** */var/run/syslog.pid* **AIX:** */etc/syslog.pid*
Current general message log file	**Usual:** */var/log/messages* **HP-UX:** */var/adm/syslog/syslog.log* **Solaris:** */var/adm/messages* **Tru64:** */var/adm/syslog.dated/current/*.log*
Boot script that starts `syslogd`	**AIX:** */etc/rc.tcpip* **FreeBSD:** */etc/rc* **HP-UX:** */sbin/init.d/syslogd* **Linux:** */etc/init.d/syslog* **Solaris:** */etc/init.d/syslog* **Tru64:** */sbin/init.d/syslog*
Boot script configuration file: syslog-related entries	**Usual:** none used **FreeBSD:** */etc/rc.conf*: *syslogd_enable="YES"* and *syslogd_flags="opts"* **SuSE Linux:** */etc/rc.config* (SuSE 7), */etc/sysconfig/syslog* (SuSE 8); *SYSLOGD_PARAMS="opts"* and *KERNEL_LOGLEVEL*=n

Configuring syslog

Messages are written to locations you specify by syslogd, the system message logging daemon. syslogd collects messages sent by various system processes and routes them to their final destination based on instructions given in its configuration file /etc/syslog.conf. Syslog organizes system messages in two ways: by the part of the system that generated them and by their importance.

Entries in *syslog.conf* have the following format, reflecting these divisions:

```
facility.level      destination
```

where *facility* is the name of the subsystem sending the message, *level* is the severity level of the message, and *destination* is the file, device, computer or username to send the message to. On most systems, the two fields must be separated by tab characters (spaces are allowed under Linux and FreeBSD).

There are a multitude of defined facilities. The most important are:

kern
> The kernel.

user
> User processes.

mail
> The mail subsystem.

lpr
> The printing subsystem.

daemon
> System server processes.

auth
> The user authentication system (nonsensitive information).

authpriv
> The user authentication system (security sensitive information). Some systems have only one of *auth* and *authpriv*.

ftp
> The FTP facility.

cron
> The cron facility.

syslog
> Syslog facility internal messages.

mark
> Timestamps produced at regular intervals (e.g., every 15 minutes).

local*
> Eight local message facilities (0-7). Some operating systems use one or more of them.

Note that an asterisk for the facility corresponds to all facilities except *mark*.

The severity levels are, in order of decreasing seriousness:

emerg
> System panic.

alert
> Serious error requiring immediate attention.

crit
> Critical errors like hard device errors.

err
> Other errors.

warning
> Warnings.

notice
> Noncritical messages.

info
> Informative messages.

debug
> Extra information helpful for tracking down problems.

none
> Ignore messages from this facility.

mark
> Selects timestamp messages (generated every 20 minutes by default). This facility is not included by the asterisk wildcard (and you wouldn't really want it to be).

Multiple facility-level pairs may be included on one line by separating them with semi-colons; multiple facilities may be specified with the same severity level by separating them with commas. An asterisk may be used as a wildcard throughout an entry.

Here are some sample destinations:

/var/log/messages	*Send to a file (specify full pathname).*
@scribe.ahania.com	*Send to syslog facility on a different host.*
root	*Send message to a user…*
root,chavez,ng	*…or list of users.*
*	*Send message via wall to all logged-in users.*

All of this will be much clearer once we look at a sample *syslog.conf* file:

```
*.err;auth.notice                      /dev/console
*.err;daemon,auth.notice;mail.crit     /var/log/messages
lpr.debug                              /var/adm/lpd-errs
mail.debug                             /var/spool/mqueue/syslog
*.alert                                root
*.emerg                                *
auth.info;*.warning                    @hamlet
*.debug                                /dev/tty01
```

The first line prints all errors, as well as notices from the authentication system (indicating successful and unsuccessful su commands) on the console. The second line sends all errors, daemon and authentication system notices, and all critical errors from the mail system to the file */var/log/messages*.

The third and fourth lines send printer and mail system debug messages to their respective error files. The fifth line sends all alert messages to user *root*, and the sixth line sends all emergency messages to all users.

The final two lines send all authentication system nondebugging messages and the warnings and errors from all other facilities to the syslogd process on host *hamlet*, and it displays all generated messages on *tty01*.

You may modify this file to suit the needs of your system. For example, to create a separate *sulog* file, add a line like the following to *syslog.conf*:

```
auth.notice     /var/adm/sulog
```

All messages are appended to log files; thus, you'll need to keep an eye on their size and truncate them periodically when they get too big. This topic is discussed in detail in "Administering Log Files," later in this chapter.

 On some systems, a log file must already exist when the syslogd process reads the configuration file entry referring to it in order for it to be recognized. In other words, on these systems, you'll need to create an empty log file, add a new entry to *syslog.conf*, and signal (kill -HUP) or restart the daemon in order to add a new log file.

Don't make the mistake of using commas when you want semicolons. For example, the following entry sends all cron messages at the level of *warn* and above to the indicated file (as well as the same levels for the printing subsystem):

```
cron.err,lpr.warning     /var/log/warns.log
```

Why are warnings included for cron? Each successive severity applies in order, replacing previous ones, so *warning* replaces *err* for *cron*. Entries can include lists of facility-severity pairs and lists of facilities at the same severity level, but not lists including both multiple facilities and severity levels. For these reasons, the following entry will log all error level and higher messages for all facilities:

```
*.warning,cron.err     /var/log/errs.log
```

Enhancements to syslog.conf

Several operating systems offer enhanced versions of the syslog configuration file, which we will discuss by example.

AIX. On AIX systems, there are some additional optional fields beyond the destination:

```
facility-level destination rotate size s  files n time t  compress archive path
```

For example:

```
*.warn        @scribe      rotate size 2m files 4 time 7d compress
```

The additional parameters specify how to handle log files as they grow over time. When they reach a certain size and/or age, the current log file will be renamed to something like name.*0*, existing old files will have their extensions incremented and the oldest file(s) may be deleted.

The *rotate* keyword introduces these parameters, and the others have the following meanings:

size s
Size threshold: rotate the log when it is larger than this. *s* is followed by k or m for KB and MB, respectively.

time t
Time threshold: rotate the log when it is older than this. *t* is followed by h, d, w, m, or y for hours, days, weeks, months, or years, respectively.

files n
Keep at most *n* files.

compress
Compress old files.

archive path
Move older files to the specified location.

FreeBSD and Linux. Both FreeBSD and Linux systems extend the *facility.severity* syntax:

.=severity
Severity level is exactly the one specified.

.!=severity
Severity level is anything other than the one specified (Linux only).

.<=severity
Severity level is lower than or equal to the one specified (FreeBSD only). The .< and .> comparison operators are also provided (as well as .>= equivalent to the standard syntax).

Both operating systems also allow pipes to programs as message destinations, as in this example, which sends all *error*-severity messages to the specified program:

```
*.=err|/usr/local/sbin/save_errs
```

FreeBSD also adds another unusual feature to the *syslog.conf* file: sections of the file which are specific to a host or a specific program.[*] Here is an example:

---

[*] Naturally, this feature will probably not work outside of the BSD environment.

```
# handle messages from host europa
+europa
mail.>debug/var/log/mailsrv.log

# kernel messages from every host but callisto
-callisto
kern.*/var/log/kern_all.log

# messages from ppp
!ppp
*.*/var/log/ppp.log
```

These entries handle non-debug mail messages from *europa*, kernel messages from every host except *callisto*, and all messages from ppp from every host but *callisto*. As this example illustrates, host and program settings accumulate. If you wanted the ppp entry to apply only to the local system, you'd need to insert the following lines before its entries to restore the host context to the local system:

```
# reset host to local system
+@
```

A program context may be similarly cleared with !*. In general, it's a good idea to place such sections at the end of the configuration file to avoid unintended interactions with existing entries.

Solaris. Solaris systems use the m4 macro preprocessing facility to process the *syslog.conf* file before it is used (this facility is discussed in Chapter 9). Here is a sample file containing m4 macros:

```
# Send mail.debug messages to network log host if there is one.
mail.debug      ifdef(`LOGHOST', /var/log/syslog, @loghost)

# On non-loghost machines, log "user" messages locally.
ifdef(`LOGHOST', ,
user.err/var/adm/messages
user.emerg*
)
```

Both of these entries differ depending on whether macro *LOGHOST* is defined. In the first case, the destination differs, and in the second section, entries are included in or excluded from the file based on its status:

Resulting file when LOGHOST is defined (i.e., this host is the central logging host):
```
# Send mail.debug messages to network log host if there is one.
mail.debug/var/log/syslog
```

Resulting file when LOGHOST is undefined:
```
# Send mail.debug messages to network log host if there is one.
mail.debug@loghost

user.err/var/adm/messages
user.emerg*
```

On the central logging host, you would need to add a definition macro to the configuration file:

```
define(`LOGHOST',`localhost')
```

The Tru64 syslog log file hierarchy. On Tru64 systems, the syslog facility is set up to log all system messages to a series of log files named for the various syslog facilities. The *syslog.conf* configuration file specifies their location as, for example, */var/adm/syslog. dated/*/auth.log*. When the syslogd daemon encounters such a destination, it automatically inserts a final subdirectory named for the current date into the pathname. Only a week's worth of log files are kept; older ones are deleted via an entry in *root*'s crontab file (the entry is wrapped to fit):

```
40 4 * * * find /var/adm/syslog.dated/* -depth -type d
              -ctime +7 -exec rm -rf {} \;
```

The logger utility

The logger utility can be used to send messages to the syslog facility from a shell script. For example, the following command sends an alert-level message via the *auth* facility:

```
# logger -p auth.alert -t DOT_FILE_CHK \
    "$user's $file is world-writeable"
```

This command would generate a syslog message like this one:

```
Feb 17 17:05:05 DOT_FILE_CHK: chavez's .cshrc is world-writable.
```

The logger command also offers a -i option, which includes the process ID within the syslog log message.

Hardware Error Messages

Often, error messages related to hardware problems appear within system log files. However, some Unix versions also provide a separate facility for hardware-related error messages. After considering a common utility (dmesg), we will look in detail at those used under AIX, HP-UX, and Tru64.

The dmesg command is found on FreeBSD, HP-UX, Linux, and Solaris systems. It is primarily used to examine or save messages from the most recent system boot, but some hardware informational and error messages also go to this facility, and examining its data may be a quick way to view them.

Here is an example from a Solaris system (output is wrapped):

```
$ dmesg | egrep 'down|up'
Sep 30 13:48:05 astarte eri: [ID 517527 kern.info] SUNW,eri0 :
No response from Ethernet network : Link down -- cable problem?
Sep 30 13:49:17 astarte last message repeated 3 times
Sep 30 13:49:38 astarte eri: [ID 517527 kern.info] SUNW,eri0 :
```

```
No response from Ethernet network : Link down -- cable problem?
Sep 30 13:50:40 astarte last message repeated 3 times
Sep 30 13:52:02 astarte eri: [ID 517527 kern.info] SUNW,eri0 :
100 Mbps full duplex link up
```

In this case, there was a brief network problem due to a slightly loose cable.

The AIX error log

AIX maintains a separate error log, */var/adm/ras/errlog*, supported by the errdemon daemon. This file is binary, and it must be accessed using the appropriate utilities: errpt to view reports from it and errclear to remove old messages.

Here is an example of errpt's output:

```
IDENTIFIER TIMESTAMP  T C RESOURCE_NAME  DESCRIPTION
C60BB505   0807122301 P S SYSPROC        SOFTWARE PROGRAM ABNORMALLY TERMINATED
369D049B   0806104301 I O SYSPFS         UNABLE TO ALLOCATE SPACE IN FILE SYSTEM
112FBB44   0802171901 T H ent0           ETHERNET NETWORK RECOVERY MODE
```

This command produces a report containing one line per error. You can produce more detailed information using options:

```
LABEL:          JFS_FS_FRAGMENTED
IDENTIFIER:     5DFED6F1

Date/Time:      Fri Oct  5 12:46:45
Sequence Number: 430
Machine Id:     000C2CAD4C00
Node Id:        arrakis
Class:          O
Type:           INFO
Resource Name:  SYSPFS

Description
UNABLE TO ALLOCATE SPACE IN FILE SYSTEM

Probable Causes
FILE SYSTEM FREE SPACE FRAGMENTED

        Recommended Actions
        CONSOLIDATE FREE SPACE USING DEFRAGFS UTILITY

Detail Data
MAJOR/MINOR DEVICE NUMBER
000A 0006
FILE SYSTEM DEVICE AND MOUNT POINT
/dev/hd9var, /var
```

This error corresponds to an instance where the operating system was unable to satisfy an I/O request because the */var* filesystem was too fragmented. In this case, the recommended actions provide a solution to the problem.

A report containing all of the errors would be very lengthy. However, I use the following script to summarize the data:

```
#!/bin/csh

errpt | awk '{print $1}' | sort | uniq -c | \
        grep -v IDENT > /tmp/err_junk
printf "Error \t# \tDescription: Cause (Solution)\n\n"
foreach f (`cat /tmp/err_junk | awk '{print $2}'`)
  set count = `grep $f /tmp/err_junk | awk '{print $1}'`
  set desc = `grep $f /var/adm/errs.txt | awk -F: '{print $2}'`
  set cause = `grep $f /var/adm/errs.txt | awk -F: '{print $3}'`
  set solve = `grep $f /var/adm/errs.txt | awk -F: '{print $4}'`
  printf "%s\t%s\t%s: %s (%s)\n" $f $count \
                                 "$desc" "$cause" "$solve"
end
rm -f /tmp/err_junk
```

The script is a quick-and-dirty approach to the problem; a more elegant Perl version would be easy to write, but this script gets the job done. It relies on an error type summary file I've created from the detailed errpt output, */var/adm/errs.txt*. Here are a few lines from that file (shortened):

```
071F4755:ENVIRONMENTAL PROBLEM:POWER OR FAN COMPONENT:RUN DIAGS.
0D1F562A:ADAPTER ERROR:ADAPTER HARDWARE:IF PROBLEM PERSISTS, ...
112FBB44:ETHERNET NETWORK RECOVERY MODE:ADAPTER:VERIFY ADAPTER ...
```

The advantage of using a summary file is that the script can produce its reports from the simpler and faster default errpt output.

Here is an example report (wrapped):

```
Error          #        Description: Cause (Solution)

071F4755       2        ENVIRONMENTAL PROBLEM: POWER OR FAN
                        COMPONENT (RUN SYSTEM DIAGNOSTICS.)
0D1F562A       2        ADAPTER ERROR: ADAPTER HARDWARE (IF
                        PROBLEM PERSISTS, CONTACT APPROPRIATE
                        SERVICE REPRESENTATIVE)
112FBB44       2        ETHERNET NETWORK RECOVERY MODE: ADAPTER
                        HARDWARE (VERIFY ADAPTER IS INSTALLED
                        PROPERLY)
369D049B       1        UNABLE TO ALLOCATE SPACE IN FILE SYSTEM:
                        FILE SYSTEM FULL (INCREASE THE SIZE OF THE
                        ASSOCIATED FILE SYSTEM)
476B351D       2        TAPE DRIVE FAILURE: TAPE DRIVE (PERFORM
                        PROBLEM DETERMINATION PROCEDURES)
499B30CC       3        ETHERNET DOWN: CABLE (CHECK CABLE AND
                        ITS CONNECTIONS)
5DFED6F1       1        UNABLE TO ALLOCATE SPACE IN FILE SYSTEM:
                        FREE SPACE FRAGMENTED (USE DEFRAGFS UTIL)
C60BB505       268      SOFTWARE PROGRAM ABNORMALLY TERMINATED:
                        SOFTWARE PROGRAM (CORRECT THEN RETRY)
```

The errclear command may be used to remove old messages from the error log. For example, the following command removes all error messages over two weeks old:

```
# errclear 14
```

The error log is a fixed-size file, used as a circular buffer. You can determine the size of the file with the following command:

```
# /usr/lib/errdemon -l
Error Log Attributes
--------------------------------------------
Log File                   /var/adm/ras/errlog
Log Size                   1048576 bytes
Memory Buffer Size         8192 bytes
```

The daemon is started by the file */sbin/rc.boot*. You can modify its startup line to change the size of the log file by adding the -s option. For example, the following addition would set the size of the log file to 1.5 MB:

```
/usr/lib/errdemon -i /var/adm/ras/errlog -s 1572864
```

The default size of 1 MB is usually sufficient for most systems.

Viewing errors under HP-UX . The HP-UX xstm command may be used to view errors on these systems (stored in the files */var/stm/logs/os/log*.raw**). It is illustrated in Figure 3-1.

The main window appears in the upper left corner of the illustration. It shows a hierarchy of icons corresponding to the various peripheral devices present on the system. You can use various menu items to determine information about the devices and their current status.

Selecting the Tools → Utility → Run menu path and then choosing logtool from the list of tools initiates the error reporting utility (see the middle window of the left column in the illustration). Select the File → Raw menu path and then the current log file to view a summary report of system hardware status, given in the bottom window in the left column of the figure. In this example, we can see that there have been 417 errors recorded during the lifetime of the log file.

Next, we select File → Formatted Log to view the detailed entries in the log file (the process is illustrated in the right column of the figure). In the example, we are looking at an entry corresponding to a SCSI tape drive. This entry corresponds to a power-off of the device.

Command-line and menu-oriented versions of xstm can be started with cstm and mstm, respectively.

The Tru64 binary error logger. Tru64 provides the binlogd binary error logging server in addition to syslogd. It is configured via the */etc/binlog.conf* file:

```
*.*                        /usr/adm/binary.errlog
dumpfile                   /usr/adm/crash/binlogdumpfile
```

The first entry sends all error messages that binlogd generates to the indicated file. The second entry specifies the location for a crash dump.

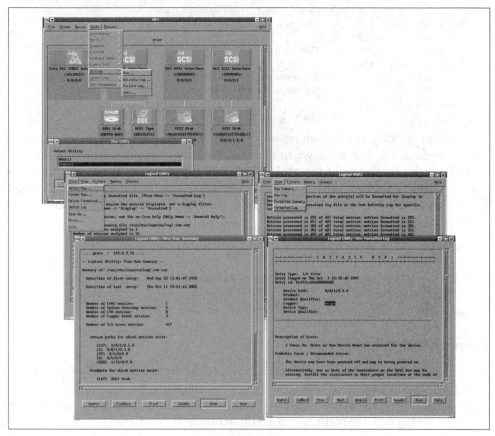

Figure 3-1. View hardware errors under HP-UX

Messages may also be sent to another host. The */etc/binlog.auth* file controls access to the local facility. If it exists, it lists the hosts that are allowed to forward messages to the local system.

You can view reports using the uerf and dia commands. I prefer the latter, although uerf is the newer command.

dia's default mode displays details about each error, and the -o brief option produces a short description of each error.

I use the following pipe to get a smaller amount of output:*

```
# dia | egrep '^(Event seq)|(Entry typ)|(ASCII Mes.*[a-z])'
Event sequence number  10.
Entry type             300. Start-Up ASCII Message Type
Event sequence number  11.
```

---

* The corresponding uerf command is uerf | egrep '^SEQU|MESS'.

```
Entry type            250. Generic ASCII Info Message Type
ASCII Message              Test for EVM connection of binlogd
Event sequence number  12.
Entry type            310. Time Stamp
Event sequence number  13.
Entry type            301. Shutdown ASCII Message Type
ASCII Message              System halted by root:
Event sequence number  14.
Entry type            300. Start-Up ASCII Message Type
```

This command displays the sequence number, type, and human-readable description (if present) for each message. In this case, we have a system startup message, an event manager status test of the binlogd daemon, a timestamp record, and finally a system shutdown followed by another system boot. Any messages of interest could be investigated by viewing their full record. For example, the following command displays event number 13:

```
# dia -e s:13 e:13
```

 You can send a message to the facility with the logger -b command.

Administering Log Files

There are two more items to consider with respect to managing the many system log files: limiting the amount of disk space they consume while simultaneously retaining sufficient data for projected future requirements, and monitoring the contents of these log files in order to identify and act upon important entries.

Managing log file disk requirements

Unchecked, log files grow without bounds and can quickly consume quite a lot of disk space. A common solution to this situation is to keep only a fraction of the historical data on disk. One approach involves periodically renaming the current log file and keeping only a few recent versions on the system. This is done by periodically deleting the oldest one, renaming the current one, and then recreating it.

For example, here is a script that keeps the last three versions of the *su.log* file in addition to the current one:

```
#!/bin/sh
cd /var/adm
if [ -r su.log.1 ]; then
    mv -f  su.log.1 su.log.2
fi
if [ -r su.log.0 ]; then
    mv -f  su.log.0 su.log.1
fi
if [ -r su.log ]; then
```

```
        cp su.log su.log.0        Copy the current log file.
    fi
    cat /dev/null > su.log        Then truncate it.
```

There are three old *su.log* files at any given time: *su.log.0* (the previous one), *su.log.1*, and *su.log.2*, in addition to the current *su.log* file. When this script is executed, the *su.log.n* files are renamed to move them back: 1 becomes 2, 0 becomes 1, and the current *su.log* file becomes *su.log.0*. Finally, a new, empty file for current su messages is created. This script could be run automatically each week via cron, and the last month's worth of *su.log* files will always be on the system (and no more).

 Make sure that all the log files get backed up on a regular basis so that older ones can be retrieved from backup media in the event that their information is needed.

Note that if you remove active log files, the disk space won't actually be released until you send a HUP signal to the associated daemon process holding the file open (usually syslogd). In addition, you'll then need to recreate the file for the facility to function properly. For these reasons, removing active log files is not recommended.

As we've seen, some systems provide automatic mechanisms for accomplishing the same thing. For example, AIX has built this feature into its version of syslog.

FreeBSD provides the newsyslog facility for performing this task (which is run hourly from cron by default). It rotates log files based on the directions in its configuration file, */etc/newsyslog.conf*:

```
# file        [own:grp]  mode  #  sz  when [ZB] [/pid_file] [sig]
/var/log/cron            600   3  100  *    Z
/var/log/amd.log         644   7  100  *    Z
/var/log/lpd-errs        644   7  100  *    Z
/var/log/maillog         644   7  *    $D0  Z
```

The fields hold the following information:

- the pathname to the log file
- the user and group ownership it should be assigned (optional)
- the file mode
- the number of old files that should be retained
- the size at which the file should be rotated
- the time when the file should be rotated
- a flag field (Z says to compress the file; B specifies that it is a binary log file and should be treated accordingly)
- the path to the file holding the process ID of the daemon that controls the file
- the numeric signal to send to that daemon to reinitialize it

The last three fields are optional.

Thus, the first entry in the previous example configuration file processes the cron log file, protecting it against all non-*root* access, rotating it when it is larger than 100 KB, and keeping three compressed old versions on the system. The next two entries rotate the corresponding log file at the same point, using a seven-old-files cycle. The final entry rotates the mail log file every day at midnight, again retaining seven old files. The "when" field is specified via a complex set of codes (see the manual page for details).

If both an explicit size and time period are specified (i.e., not an asterisk), rotation occurs when either condition is met.

Red Hat Linux systems provide a similar facility via logrotate, written by Erik Troan. It is run daily by default via a script in */etc/cron.daily*, and its operations are controlled by the configuration file, */etc/logrotate.conf*.

Here is an annotated example of the logrotate configuration file:

```
# global settings
errors root                     Mail errors to root.
compress                        Compress old files.
create                          Create new empty log files after rotation.
weekly                          Default cycle is 7 days.

include /etc/logrotate.d        Import the instructions in the files here.

/var/log/messages {             Instructions for a specific file.
  rotate 5                      Keep 5 files.
  weekly                        Rotate weekly.
  postrotate                    Run this command after rotating,
    /sbin/killall -HUP syslogd  to activate the new log file.
  endscript
  }
```

This file sets some general defaults and then defines the method for handling the */var/log/messages* file. The *include* directive also imports the contents of all files in the */etc/logrotate.d* directory. Many software packages place in this location files containing instructions for how their own log files should be handled.

 logrotate is open source and can be built on other Linux and Unix systems as well.

Monitoring log file contents

It is very easy to generate huge amounts of logging information very quickly. You'll soon find that you'll want some tool to help you sift through it all, finding the few entries of any real interest or importance. We'll look at two of them in this subsection.

The swatch facility, written by E. Todd Atkins, is designed to do just that. It runs in a variety of modes: examining new entries as they are added to a system log file, moni-

---

toring an output stream in real time, checking through a file on a one-time basis, and so on. When it recognizes a pattern you have specified in its input, it can perform a variety of actions. Its home page (at the moment) is *http://oit.ucsb.edu/~eta/swatch/*.

Swatch's configuration file specifies what information the facility should look for and what it should do when it finds that information. Here is an example:

```
# Syntax:
# event               action
#
# network events
/refused/             echo,bell,mail=root
/connect from iago/   mail=chavez
#
# other syslog events
/(uk|usa).*file system full/exec="wall /etc/fs.full"
/panic|halt/exec="/usr/sbin/bigtrouble"
```

The first two entries search for specific syslog messages related to network access control. The first one matches any message containing the string "refused". Patterns are specified between forward slashes using regular expressions, as in sed. When such an entry is found, swatch copies it to standard output (*echo*), rings the terminal bell (*bell*), and sends mail to *root* (*mail*). The second entry watches for connections from the host *iago* and sends mail to user *chavez* whenever one occurs.

The third entry matches the error messages generated when a filesystem fills up on host *usa* or host *uk*; in this case, it runs the command wall /etc/fs.full (this form of wall displays the contents of the specified file to all logged-in users). The fourth entry runs the bigtrouble command when the system is in severe distress.

This file focuses on syslog events, presumably sent to a central logging host, but swatch can be used to monitor any output. For example, it could watch the system error log for memory parity errors.

The following swatch command could be used to monitor the contents of the */var/adm/messages* file, using the configuration file specified with the -c option:

```
# swatch -c /etc/swatch.config -t /var/adm/messages
```

The -t option says to continuously examine the tail of the file (in a manner analogous to tail -f). This command might be used to start a swatch process in a window that could be periodically monitored throughout the day. Other useful swatch options are -f, which scans a file once for matching entries (useful when running *swatch* via *cron*), and -p, which monitors the output from a running program.

Another great, free tool for this purpose is logcheck from Psionic Software (*http://www.psionic.com/abacus/logcheck/*). We'll consider its use in Chapter 7.

Managing Software Packages

Most Unix versions provide utilities for managing software packages: bundled collections of programs that provide a particular feature or functionality, delivered via a single archive. Packaging software is designed to make adding and removing packages easier. Each operating system we are considering provides a different set of tools.* The various offerings are summarized in Table 3-6.

Table 3-6. Software package management commands

Function	Command[a]
List installed packages	**AIX:** lslpp -l all
	FreeBSD: pkg_info -a -I[b]
	HP-UX: swlist
	Linux: rpm -q -a
	Solaris: pkginfo
	Tru64: setld -i
Describe package	**FreeBSD:** pkg_info
	HP-UX: swlist -v
	Linux: rpm -q -i
	Solaris: pkginfo -l
List package contents	**AIX:** lslpp -f
	FreeBSD: pkg_info -L
	HP-UX: swlist -l file
	Linux: rpm -q -l
	Solaris: pkgchk -l
	Tru64: setld -i
List prerequisites	**AIX:** lslpp -p
	Linux: rpm -q ---requires
Show file's original package	**AIX:** lslpp -w
	Linux: rpm -q ---whatprovides
	Solaris: pkgchk -l -p
List available packages on media	**AIX:** installp -l -d *device*
	FreeBSD: sysinstall Configure → Packages
	HP-UX: swlist -s *path* [-l *type*]
	Linux: ls */path-to-RPMs* yast2 Install/Remove software (SuSE)
	Solaris: ls */path-to-packages*
	Tru64: setld -i -D *path*

---

* The freely available epm utility can generate native format packages for many Unix versions including AIX, BSD and Linux. It is very useful for distributing locally developed packages in a heterogeneous environment. See *http://www.easysw.com/epm/* for more information.

Table 3-6. Software package management commands (continued)

Function	Command[a]
Install package	**AIX:** `installp -acX`
	FreeBSD: `pkg_add`
	HP-UX: `swinstall`
	Linux: `rpm -i`
	Solaris: `pkgadd`
	Tru64: `setld -l`
Preview installation	**AIX:** `installp -p`
	FreeBSD: `pkg_add -n`
	HP-UX: `swinstall -p`
	Linux: `rpm -i --test`
Verify package	**AIX:** `installp -a -v`
	Linux: `rpm -V`
	Solaris: `pkgchk`
	Tru64: `fverify`
Remove package	**AIX:** `installp -u`
	FreeBSD: `pkg_delete`
	HP-UX: `swremove`
	Linux: `rpm -e`
	Solaris: `pkgrm`
	Tru64: `setld -d`
Menu/GUI interface for package management	**AIX:** `smit`
	HP-UX: `sam swlist -i swinstall`
	Linux: `xrpm, gnorpm, yast2` (SuSE)
	Solaris: `admintool`
	Tru64: `sysman`

[a] On Linux systems, add the -p pkg option to examine an uninstalled RPM package.

[b] Note that this option is an uppercase I ("eye"). All similar-looking option letters in this table are lowercase l's ("ells").

These utilities all work in a very similar manner, so we will consider only one of them in detail, focusing on the Solaris commands and a few HP-UX commands as examples.

We'll begin by considering the method to list currently installed packages. Generally, this is done by running the general listing command, possibly piping its output to grep to locate packages of interest. For example, this command searches a Solaris system for installed packages related to file compression:

```
# pkginfo | grep -i compres
system      SUNWbzip     The bzip compression utility
system      SUNWbzipx    The bzip compression library (64-bit)
system      SUNWgzip     The GNU Zip (gzip) compression utility
system      SUNWzip      The Info-Zip (zip) compression utility
system      SUNWzlib     The Zip compression library
system      SUNWzlibx    The Info-Zip compression lib (64-bit)
```

To find out more information about a package, we add an option and package name to the listing command. In this case, we display information about the bzip package:

```
# pkginfo -l SUNWbzip
PKGINST:  SUNWbzip
    NAME:  The bzip compression utility
CATEGORY:  system
    ARCH:  sparc
 VERSION:  11.8.0,REV=2000.01.08.18.12
 BASEDIR:  /
  VENDOR:  Sun Microsystems, Inc.
    DESC:  The bzip compression utility
  STATUS:  completely installed
   FILES:      21 installed pathnames
                9 shared pathnames
                2 linked files
                9 directories
                4 executables
              382 blocks used (approx)
```

Other options allow you to list the files and subdirectories in the package. On Solaris systems, this produces a lot of output, so we use grep to reduce it to a simple list (a step that is unnecessary on most systems):

```
# pkgchk -l SUNWbzip | grep ^Pathname: | awk '{print $2}'
/usr                  Subdirectories in the package are created on
/usr/bin              install if they do not already exist.
/usr/bin/bunzip2
/usr/bin/bzcat
/usr/bin/bzip2
...
```

It is also often possible to find out the name of the package to which a given file belongs, as in this example:

```
# pkgchk -l -p /etc/syslog.conf
Pathname: /etc/syslog.conf
Type: editted file
Expected mode: 0644
Expected owner: root
Expected group: sys
Referenced by the following packages:
        SUNWcsr
Current status: installed
```

This configuration file is part of the package containing the basic system utilities.

When you want to install a new package, you use a command like this one, which installs the GNU C compiler from the CD-ROM mounted under /cdrom (*s8-software-companion* is the Companion Software CD provided with Solaris 8):

```
# pkgadd -d /cdrom/s8-software-companion/components/sparc/Packages SFWgcc
```

Removing an installed package is also very simple:

```
# pkgrm SFWbzip
```

You can use the pkgchk command to verify that a software package is installed correctly and that none of its components has been modified since then.

Sometimes you want to list all of the available packages on a CD or tape. On FreeBSD, Linux, and Solaris systems, you accomplish this by changing to the appropriate directory and running the ls command. On others, an option to the normal installation or listing command performs this function. For example, the following command lists the available packages on the tape in the first drive:

```
# swlist -s /dev/rmt/0m
```

HP-UX: Bundles, products, and subproducts

HP-UX organizes software packages into various units. The smallest unit is the *fileset* which contains a set of related file that can be managed as a unit. *Subproducts* contain one or more filesets, and *products* are usually made up of one or more subproducts (although a few contain the filesets themselves). For example, the fileset MSDOS-Utils.Manuals.DOSU-ENG-A_MAN consists of the English language manual pages for the Utils subproduct of the MSDOC-Utils product. Finally, *bundles* are groups of related filesets from one or more products, gathered together for a specific purpose. They can, but do not have to, be comprised of multiple complete products.

The swlist command can be used to view installed software at these various levels by specifying the corresponding keyword to its -l option. For example, this command lists all installed products:

```
# swlist -l product
```

The following command lists the subproducts that make up the MS-DOS utilities product:

```
# swlist -l subproduct MSDOS-Utils

# MSDOS-Utils                 B.11.00        MSDOS-Utils
  MSDOS-Utils.Manuals         Manuals
  MSDOS-Utils.ManualsByLang   ManualsByLang
  MSDOS-Utils.Runtime         Runtime
```

You could further explore the contents of this product by running the swlist -l fileset command for each subproduct to list the component filesets. The results would show a single fileset per subproduct and would indicate that the MSDOS-Utils product is made up of runtime and manual page filesets.

AIX: Apply versus commit

On AIX systems, software installation is a two-step process. First, software packages are *applied*: new files are installed, but the previous system state is also saved in case you change your mind and want to roll back the package. In order to make an installation permanent, applied software must be *committed*.

You can view the installation state of software packages with the `lslpp` command. For example, this command displays information about software compilers:

```
# lslpp -l all | grep -i compil
  vacpp.cmp.C    5.0.2.0  COMMITTED  VisualAge C++ C Compiler
  xlfcmp         7.1.0.2  COMMITTED  XL Fortran Compiler
  vac.C          5.0.2.0  COMMITTED  C for AIX Compiler
  ...
```

Alternatively, you can display applied but not yet committed packages with the `installp -s all` command.

The `installp` command has a number of options controlling how and to what degree software is installed. For example, use a command like this one to apply and commit software:

```
# installp -ac -d device [items | all]
```

Other useful options to `installp` are listed in Table 3-7.

Table 3-7. Options to the AIX installp command

Option	Meaning
-a	Apply software.
-c	Commit applied software.
-r	Reject uncommitted software.
-t dir	Use alternate location for saved rollback files.
-u	Remove software
-C	Clean up after a failed installation.
-N	Don't save files necessary for recovery.
-X	Expand filesystems as necessary.
-d dev	Specify installation source location.
-p	Preview operation.
-v	Verbose output.
-l	List media contents.
-M arch	Limit listing to items for the specified architecture type.

 Using apply without commit is a good tactic for cautious administrators and delicate production systems.

FreeBSD ports

FreeBSD includes an easy-to-use method for acquiring and building additional software packages. This scheme is known as the Ports Collection. If you choose to install it, its infrastructure is located at */usr/ports*.

The Ports Collection provides all the information necessary for downloading, unpacking, and building software packages within its directory tree. Installing such pre-setup packages is then very simple. For example, the following commands are all that is needed to install the Tripwire security monitoring package:

```
# cd /usr/ports/security/tripwire
# make && make install
```

The make commands automatically take all steps necessary to install the package.

Building Software Packages from Source Code

There are a large number of useful open source software tools. Sometimes, thoughtful people will have made precompiled binaries available on the Internet, but there will be times when you will have to build them yourself. In this section, we look briefly at building three packages in order to illustrate some of the problems and challenges you might encounter. We use will HP-UX as our example system.

mtools: Using configure and accepting imperfections

We begin with mtools, a set of utilities for directly accessing DOS-format floppy disks on Unix systems. After downloading the package, the first steps are to uncompress the software archive and extract its files:

```
$ gunzip mtools-3.9.7.tar.gz
$ tar xvf mtools-3.9.7.tar
x mtools-3.9.7/INSTALL, 737 bytes, 2 tape blocks
x mtools-3.9.7/buffer.c, 8492 bytes, 17 tape blocks
x mtools-3.9.7/Release.notes, 8933 bytes, 18 tape blocks
x mtools-3.9.7/devices.c, 25161 bytes, 50 tape blocks
...
```

Note that we are not running these commands as *root*.

Next, we change to the new directory and look around:

```
$ cd mtools-3.9.7; ls
COPYING        floppyd_io.c      mmount.c
Changelog      floppyd_io.h      mmove.1
INSTALL        force_io.c        mmove.c
Makefile       fs.h              mpartition.1
Makefile.Be    fsP.h             mpartition.c
Makefile.in    getopt.h          mrd.1
Makefile.os2   hash.c            mread.1
NEWPARAMS      htable.h          mren.1
README         init.c            msdos.h
...
```

We are looking for files named *README*, *INSTALL*, or something similar, which will tell us how to proceed.

Here is the relevant section in this example:

```
Compilation
-----------
To compile mtools on Unix, first type ./configure, then make.
```

This is a typical pattern in a well-crafted software package. The configure utility checks the system for all the items needed to build the package, often selecting among various alternatives, and creates a make file based on the specific configuration.

We follow the directions and run it:

```
$ ./configure
checking for gcc... cc
checking whether the C compiler works... yes
checking whether cc accepts -g... yes
checking how to run the C preprocessor... cc -E
checking for a BSD compatible install... /opt/imake/bin/install -c
checking for sys/wait.h that is POSIX.1 compatible... yes
checking for getopt.h... no
...
creating ./config.status
creating Makefile
creating config.h
config.h is unchanged
```

At this point, we could just run make, but I always like to look at the make file first. Here is the first part of it:

```
$ more Makefile
# Generated automatically from Makefile.in by configure.
#         Makefile for Mtools

MAKEINFO = makeinfo
TEXI2DVI = texi2dvi
TEXI2HTML = texi2html

# do not edit below this line
# ============================================================
SHELL = /bin/sh

prefix      = /usr/local
exec_prefix = ${prefix}
bindir      = ${exec_prefix}/bin
mandir      = ${prefix}/man
```

The *prefix* item could be a problem if I wanted to install the software somewhere else, but I am satisfied with this location, so I run make. The process is mostly fine, but there are a few error messages:

```
cc  -Ae -DHAVE_CONFIG_H -DSYSCONFDIR=\"/usr/local/etc\" -DCPU_hppa1_0 -DVENDOR_hp -
DOS_hpux11_00 -DOS_hpux11 -DOS_hpux  -g -I.  -I.   -c floppyd.c
cc: "floppyd.c", line 464: warning 604: Pointers are not assignment-compatible.

cc -z    -o floppyd   -lSM -lICE -lXau -lX11 -lnsl
```

```
/usr/ccs/bin/ld: (Warning) At least one PA 2.0 object file (buffer.o) was detected.
The linked output may not run on a PA 1.x system.
```

It is important to try to understand what the messages mean. In this case, we get a compiler warning, which is not an uncommon occurrence. We ignore it for the moment. The second warning simply tells us that we are building architecture-dependant executables. This is not important as we don't plan to use them anywhere but the local system.

Now, we install the package, using the usual command to do so:

```
$ su
Password:
# make -n install        Preview first!
./mkinstalldirs /usr/local/bin
/opt/imake/bin/install -c mtools /usr/local/bin/mtools
     ...
# make install           Proceed if it looks ok.
./mkinstalldirs /usr/local/bin
/opt/imake/bin/install -c mtools /usr/local/bin/mtools
 ...
/opt/imake/bin/install -c floppyd /usr/local/bin/floppyd
cp: cannot access floppyd: No such file or directory
 ...
Make: Don't know how to make mtools.info.  Stop.
```

We encounter two problems here. The first is a missing executable: floppyd, a daemon to provide floppy access to remote users. The second problem is a make error that occurs when make tries to create the info file for mtools (a documentation format common on Linux systems). The latter is unimportant since the info system is not available under HP-UX. The first problem is more serious, and further efforts do not resolve what turns out to be an obscure problem. For example, modifying the source code to correct the compiler error message does not fix the problem. The failure actually occurs during the link phase, which simply fails without comment. I'm always disappointed when errors prevent a package from working, but it does happen occasionally.

Since I can live without this component, I ultimately decide to just ignore its absence. If it were an essential element, it would be necessary to resolve the problem to use the package. At that point, I would either try harder to fix the problem, check news groups and other Internet information sources, or just decide to live without the package.

 Don't let a recalcitrant package become a time sink. Give up and move on.

bzip2: Converting Linux-based make procedures

Next, we will look at the bzip2 compression utility by Julian Seward. The initial steps are the same. Here is the relevant section of the *README* file:

```
HOW TO BUILD -- UNIX

Type `make'.  This builds the library libbz2.a and then the
programs bzip2 and bzip2recover.  Six self-tests are run.
If the self-tests complete ok, carry on to installation:

To install in /usr/bin, /usr/lib, /usr/man and /usr/include, type
   make install
To install somewhere else, eg, /xxx/yyy/{bin,lib,man,include}, type
   make install PREFIX=/xxx/yyy
```

We also read the *README.COMPILATION.PROBLEMS* file, but it contains nothing relevant to our situation.

This package does not self-configure, but simply provides a make file designed to work on a variety of systems. We start the build process on faith:

```
$ make
gcc -Wall -Winline -O2 -fomit-frame-pointer -fno-strength-reduce
-D_FILE_OFFSET_BITS=64 -c blocksort.c
sh: gcc:  not found.
*** Error exit code 127
```

The problem here is that our C compiler is cc, not gcc (this make file was probably created under Linux). We can edit the make file to reflect this. As we do so, we look for other potential problems. Ultimately, the following lines:

```
SHELL=/bin/sh
CC=gcc
BIGFILES=-D_FILE_OFFSET_BITS=64
CFLAGS=-Wall -Winline -O2 -fomit-frame-pointer ... $(BIGFILES)
```

are changed to:

```
SHELL=/bin/sh
CC=cc
BIGFILES=-D_FILE_OFFSET_BITS=64
CFLAGS=-Wall +w2 -O  $(BIGFILES)
```

The *CFLAGS* entry specifies options sent to the compiler command, and the original value contains many gcc-specific ones. We replace those with their HP-UX equivalents.

The next make attempt is successful:

```
cc -Wall +w2 -O  -D_FILE_OFFSET_BITS=64 -c blocksort.c
cc -Wall +w2 -O  -D_FILE_OFFSET_BITS=64 -c huffman.c
cc -Wall +w2 -O  -D_FILE_OFFSET_BITS=64 -c crctable.c
...

Doing 6 tests (3 compress, 3 uncompress) ...
   ./bzip2 -1  < sample1.ref > sample1.rb2
   ./bzip2 -2  < sample2.ref > sample2.rb2
   ...
```

```
If you got this far, it looks like you're in business.

To install in /usr/bin, /usr/lib, /usr/man and /usr/include,
  type: make install
To install somewhere else, eg, /xxx/yyy/{bin,lib,man,include},
  type: make install PREFIX=/xxx/yyy
```

We want to install into */usr/local*, so we use this make install command (after pre-viewing the process with -n first):

```
# make install PREFIX=/usr/local
```

If the facility had not provided the capability to specify the install directory, we would have had to edit the make file to use our desired location.

jove: Configuration via make file settings

Lastly, we look at the jove editor by Jonathan Payne, my personal favorite editor. Here is the relevant section from the *INSTALL* file:

```
Installation on a UNIX System.
------------------------------

To make JOVE, edit Makefile to set the right directories for the binaries, on line
documentation, the man pages, and the TMP files, and select the appropriate load
command (see LDFLAGS in Makefile).  (IMPORTANT! read the Makefile carefully.)
"paths.h" will be created by MAKE automatically, and it will use the directories you
specified in the Makefile.  (NOTE: You should never edit paths.h directly because
your changes will be undone by the next make.)

You need to set "SYSDEFS" to the symbol that identifies your system, using the
notation for a macro-setting flag to the C compiler. If yours isn't mentioned, use
"grep System: sysdep.h" to find all currently supported system configurations.
```

This package is the least preconfigured of those we are considering. Here is the part of the make file I needed to think about and modify (from the original). Our changes are highlighted in boldface:

```
JOVEHOME = /usr/local
SHAREDIR = $(JOVEHOME)/lib/jove
BINDIR = $(JOVEHOME)/bin
...
# Select the right libraries for your system.
LIBS = -ltermcap          We uncommented the correct one.
#LIBS = -lcurses
...
# define a symbol for your OS if it hasn't got one. See sysdep.h.
SYSDEFS = -DHPUX -Ac      −Ac says to use the K&R Edition 1 version of C.
```

Once this configuration of the make file is completed, running make and make install built and installed the software successfully.

Internet software archives

I'll close this chapter with this short list of the most useful of the currently available general and operating system-specific software archives (in my opinion). Unless otherwise noted, all of them provide freely-available software.

General	*http://sourceforge.net*
	http://www.gnu.org
	http://freshmeat.net
	http://www.xfree86.org
	http://rtfm.mit.edu
AIX	*http://freeware.bull.net*
	http://aixpdslib.seas.ucla.edu/aixpdslib.html
FreeBSD	*http://www.freebsd.org/ports/*
	http://www.freshports.org
HP-UX	*http://hpux.cs.utah.edu*
	http://www.software.hp.com (drivers and commercial packages)
Linux	*http://www.redhat.com*
	http://www.suse.com
	http://www.ibiblio.org/Linux
	http://linux.davecentral.com
Solaris	*http://www.sun.com/bigadmin/downloads/*
	http://www.sun.com/download/
	ftp://ftp.sunfreeware.com/pub/freeware/
	http://www.ibiblio.org/pub/packages/solaris/
Tru64	*http://www.unix.digital.com/tools.html*
	ftp://ftp.digital.com
	http://gatekeeper.dec.com
	http://www.tru64.compaq.com (demos and commercial software)
	(Compaq also offers a low-cost freeware CD for Tru64.)

## CHAPTER 4

Startup and Shutdown

Most of the time, bringing up or shutting down a Unix system is actually very simple. Nevertheless, every system administrator needs to have at least a conceptual understanding of the startup and shutdown processes in order to, at a minimum, recognize situations where something is going awry—and potentially intervene. Providing you with this knowledge is the goal of this chapter. We will begin by examining generic boot and shutdown procedures that illustrate the concepts and features common to virtually every Unix system. This will be followed by sections devoted to the specifics of the various operating systems we are discussing, including a careful consideration of the myriad of system configuration files that perform and control these processes.

About the Unix Boot Process

Bootstrapping is the full name for the process of bringing a computer system to life and making it ready for use. The name comes from the fact that a computer needs its operating system to be able to do anything, but it must also get the operating system started all on its own, without having any of the services normally provided by the operating system to do so. Hence, it must "pull itself up by its own bootstraps." *Booting* is short for bootstrapping, and this is the term I'll use.*

The basic boot process is very similar for all Unix systems, although the mechanisms used to accomplish it vary quite a bit from system to system. These mechanisms depend on both the physical hardware and the operating system type (System V or BSD). The boot process can be initiated automatically or manually, and it can begin when the computer is powered on (a *cold boot*) or as a result of a reboot command from a running system (a *warm boot* or *restart*).

---

* IBM has traditionally referred to the bootstrapping process as the IPL (initial program load). This term still shows up occasionally in AIX documentation.

The normal Unix boot process has these main phases:

- Basic hardware detection (memory, disk, keyboard, mouse, and the like).
- Executing the firmware system initialization program (happens automatically).
- Locating and running the initial boot program (by the firmware boot program), usually from a predetermined location on disk. This program may perform additional hardware checks prior to loading the kernel.
- Locating and starting the Unix kernel (by the first-stage boot program). The kernel image file to execute may be determined automatically or via input to the boot program.
- The kernel initializes itself and then performs final, high-level hardware checks, loading device drivers and/or kernel modules as required.
- The kernel starts the init process, which in turn starts system processes (daemons) and initializes all active subsystems. When everything is ready, the system begins accepting user logins.

We will consider each of these items in subsequent sections of this chapter.

From Power On to Loading the Kernel

As we've noted, the boot process begins when the instructions stored in the computer's permanent, nonvolatile memory (referred to colloquially as the BIOS, ROM, NVRAM, and so on) are executed. This storage location for the initial boot instructions is generically referred to as *firmware* (in contrast to "software," but reflecting the fact that the instructions constitute a program*).

These instructions are executed automatically when the power is turned on or the system is reset, although the exact sequence of events may vary according to the values of stored parameters.† The firmware instructions may also begin executing in response to a command entered on the system console (as we'll see in a bit). However they are initiated, these instructions are used to locate and start up the system's *boot program*, which in turn starts the Unix operating system.

The boot program is stored in a standard location on a bootable device. For a normal boot from disk, for example, the boot program might be located in block 0 of the root disk or, less commonly, in a special partition on the root disk. In the same way, the boot program may be the second file on a bootable tape or in a designated location on a remote file server in the case of a network boot of a diskless workstation.

---

* At least that's my interpretation of the name. Other explanations abound.

† Or the current position of the computer's key switch. On systems using a physical key switch, one of its positions usually initiates an automatic boot process when power is applied (often labeled "Normal" or "On"), and another position (e.g., "Service") prevents autobooting and puts the system into a completely manual mode suitable for system maintenance and repair.

There is usually more than one bootable device on a system. The firmware program may include logic for selecting the device to boot from, often in the form of a list of potential devices to examine. In the absence of other instructions, the first bootable device that is found is usually the one that is used. Some systems allow for several variations on this theme. For example, the RS/6000 NVRAM contains separate default device search lists for normal and service boots; it also allows the system administrator to add customized search lists for either or both boot types using the `bootlist` command.

The boot program is responsible for loading the Unix kernel into memory and passing control of the system to it. Some systems have two or more levels of intermediate boot programs between the firmware instructions and the independently-executing Unix kernel. Other systems use different boot programs depending on the type of boot.

Even PC systems follow this same basic procedure. When the power comes on or the system is reset, the BIOS starts the master boot program, located in the first 512 bytes of the system disk. This program then typically loads the boot program located in the first 512 bytes of the active partition on that disk, which then loads the kernel. Sometimes, the master boot program loads the kernel itself. The boot process from other media is similar.

The firmware program is basically just smart enough to figure out if the hardware devices it needs are accessible (e.g., can it find the system disk or the network) and to load and initiate the boot program. This first-stage boot program often performs additional hardware status verification, checking for the presence of expected system memory and major peripheral devices. Some systems do much more elaborate hardware checks, verifying the status of virtually every device and detecting new ones added since the last boot.

The *kernel* is the part of the Unix operating system that remains running at all times when the system is up. The kernel executable image itself, conventionally named *unix* (System V–based systems), *vmunix* (BSD-based system), or something similar. It is traditionally stored in or linked to the root directory. Here are typical kernel names and directory locations for the various operating systems we are considering:

AIX	*/unix* (actually a link to a file in */usr/lib/boot*)
FreeBSD	*/kernel*
HP-UX	*/stand/vmunix*
Linux	*/boot/vmlinuz*
Tru64	*/vmunix*
Solaris	*/kernel/genunix*

Once control passes to the kernel, it prepares itself to run the system by initializing its internal tables, creating the in-memory data structures at sizes appropriate to current system resources and kernel parameter values. The kernel may also complete the hardware diagnostics that are part of the boot process, as well as installing loadable drivers for the various hardware devices present on the system.

When these preparatory activities have been completed, the kernel creates another process that will run the init program as the process with PID 1.*

Booting to Multiuser Mode

As we've seen, init is the ancestor of all subsequent Unix processes and the direct parent of user login shells. During the remainder of the boot process, init does the work needed to prepare the system for users.

One of init's first activities is to verify the integrity of the local filesystems, beginning with the root filesystem and other essential filesystems, such as /usr. Since the kernel and the init program itself reside in the root filesystem (or sometimes the /usr filesystem in the case of init), you might wonder how either one can be running before the corresponding filesystem has been checked. There are several ways around this chicken-and-egg problem. Sometimes, there is a copy of the kernel in the boot partition of the root disk as well as in the root filesystem. Alternatively, if the executable from the root filesystem successfully begins executing, it is probably safe to assume that the file is OK.

In the case of init, there are several possibilities. Under System V, the root filesystem is mounted read-only until after it has been checked, and init remounts it read-write. Alternatively, in the traditional BSD approach, the kernel handles checking and mounting the root filesystem itself.

Still another method, used when booting from tape or CD-ROM (for example, during an operating system installation or upgrade), and on some systems for normal boots, involves the use of an in-memory (RAM) filesystem containing just the limited set of commands needed to access the system and its disks, including a version of init. Once control passes from the RAM filesystem to the disk-based filesystem, the init process exits and restarts, this time from the "real" executable on disk, a result that somewhat resembles a magician's sleight-of-hand trick.

Other activities performed by init include the following:

- Checking the integrity of the filesystems, traditionally using the fsck utility
- Mounting local disks
- Designating and initializing paging areas
- Performing filesystem cleanup activities: checking disk quotas, preserving editor recovery files, and deleting temporary files in /tmp and elsewhere
- Starting system server processes (*daemons*) for subsystems like printing, electronic mail, accounting, error logging, and cron

---

* Process 0, if it exists, is really part of the kernel itself. Process 0 is often the scheduler (controls which processes execute at what time under BSD) or the swapper (moves process memory pages to and from swap space under System V). However, some systems assign PID 0 to a different process, and others do not have a process 0 at all.

- Starting networking daemons and mounting remote disks
- Enabling user logins, usually by starting getty processes and/or the graphical login interface on the system console (e.g., xdm), and removing the file */etc/nologin*, if present

These activities are specified and carried out by means of the system *initialization scripts*, shell programs traditionally stored in */etc* or */sbin* or their subdirectories and executed by init at boot time. These files are organized very differently under System V and BSD, but they accomplish the same purposes. They are described in detail later in this chapter.

Once these activities are complete, users may log in to the system. At this point, the boot process is complete, and the system is said to be in *multiuser mode*.

Booting to Single-User Mode

Once init takes control of the booting process, it can place the system in *single-user mode* instead of completing all the initialization tasks required for multiuser mode. Single-user mode is a system state designed for administrative and maintenance activities, which require complete and unshared control of the system. This system state is selected by a special boot command parameter or option; on some systems, the administrator may select it by pressing a designated key at a specific point in the boot process.

To initiate single-user mode, init forks to create a new process, which then executes the default shell (usually */bin/sh*) as user *root*. The prompt in single-user mode is the number sign (#), the same as for the superuser account, reflecting the *root* privileges inherent in it. Single-user mode is occasionally called *maintenance mode*.

Another situation in which the system might enter single-user mode automatically occurs if there are any problems in the boot process that the system cannot handle on its own. Examples of such circumstances include filesystem problems that fsck cannot fix in its default mode and errors in one of the system initialization files. The system administrator must then take whatever steps are necessary to resolve the problem. Once this is done, booting may continue to multiuser mode by entering CTRL-D, terminating the single-user mode shell:

```
# ^D                              Continue boot process to multiuser mode.
Tue Jul 14 14:47:14 EDT 1987      Boot messages from the initialization files.
...
```

Alternatively, rather than picking up the boot process where it left off, the system may be rebooted from the beginning by entering a command such as reboot (AIX and FreeBSD) or telinit 6. HP-UX supports both commands.

Single-user mode represents a minimal system startup. Although you have *root* access to the system, many of the normal system services are not available at all or are not set up. On a mundane level, the search path and terminal type are often not set correctly. Less trivially, no daemons are running, so many Unix facilities are shut down (e.g., printing). In general, the system is not connected to the network. The available filesystems may be mounted read-only, so modifying files is initially disabled (we'll see how to overcome this in a bit). Finally, since only some of the filesystems are mounted, only commands that physically reside on these filesystems are available initially.

This limitation is especially noticeable if */usr* was created on a separate disk partition from the root filesystem and is not mounted automatically under single-user mode. In this case, even commands stored in the root filesystem (in */bin*, for example) will not work if they use shared libraries stored under */usr*. Thus, if there is some problem with the */usr* filesystem, you will have to make do with the tools that are available. For such situations, however rare and unlikely, you should know how to use the ed editor if vi is not available in single-user mode; you should know which tools are available to you in that situation before you have to use them.

On a few systems, vendors have exacerbated this problem by making */bin* a symbolic link to */usr/bin*, thereby rendering the system virtually unusable if there is a problem with a separate */usr* filesystem.

Password protection for single-user mode

On older Unix systems, single-user mode does not require a password be entered to gain access. Obviously, this can be a significant security problem. If someone gained physical access to the system console, he could crash it (by hitting the reset button, for example) and then boot to single-user mode via the console and be automatically logged in as *root* without having to know the *root* password.

Modern systems provide various safeguards. Most systems now require that the root password be entered before granting system access in single-user mode. On some System V–based systems, this is accomplished via the sulogin program that is invoked automatically by init once the system reaches single-user mode. On these systems, if the correct *root* password is not entered within some specified time period, the system is automatically rebooted.*

Here is a summary of single-user mode password protection by operating system:

AIX	Automatic
FreeBSD	Required if the console is listed in */etc/ttys* with the *insecure* option:

```
console none unknown off insecure
```

---

* The front panel key position also influences the boot process, and the various settings provide for some types of security protection. There is usually a setting that disables booting to single-user mode; it is often labeled "Secure" (versus "Normal") or "Standard" (versus "Maintenance" or "Service"). Such security features are usually described on the init or boot manual pages and in the vendor's hardware or system operations manuals.

HP-UX	Automatic
Linux	Required if */etc/inittab* (discussed later in this chapter) contains a *sulogin* entry for single-user mode. For example: `sp:S:respawn:/sbin/sulogin`
Tru64	Required if the *SECURE_CONSOLE* entry in */etc/rc.config* is set to ON.
Solaris	Required if the *PASSREQ* setting in */etc/default/sulogin* is set to YES.

 Current Linux distributions include the `sulogin` utility but do not always activate it (this is true of Red Hat Linux as of this writing), leaving single-user mode unprotected by default.

Firmware passwords

Some systems also allow you to assign a separate password to the firmware initialization program, preventing unauthorized persons from starting a manual boot. For example, on SPARC systems, the `eeprom` command may be used to require a password and set its value (via the *security-mode* and *security-password* parameters, respectively).

On some systems (e.g., Compaq Alphas), you must use commands within the firmware program itself to perform this operation (`set password` and `set secure` in the case of the Alpha SRM). Similarly, on PC-based systems, the BIOS monitor program must generally be used to set such a password. It is accessed by pressing a designated key (often F1 or F8) shortly after the system powers on or is reset.

On Linux systems, commonly used boot-loader programs have configuration settings that accomplish the same purpose. Here are some configuration file entries for `lilo` and `grub`:

```
password = something          /etc/lilo.conf
password -md5 xxxxxxxxxxxx     /boot/grub/grub.conf
```

The grub package provides the `grub-md5-crypt` utility for generating the MD5 encoding for a password. Linux boot loaders are discussed in detail in Chapter 16.

Starting a Manual Boot

Virtually all modern computers can be configured to boot automatically when power comes on or after a crash. When autobooting is not enabled, booting is initiated by entering a simple command in response to a prompt: sometimes just a carriage return, sometimes a b, sometimes the word boot. When a command is required, you often can tell the system to boot to single-user mode by adding a `-s` or similar option to the boot command, as in these examples from a Solaris and a Linux system:

```
ok boot -s              Solaris
boot: linux single      Linux
```

In the remainder of this section, we will look briefly at the low-level boot commands for our supported operating systems. We will look at some more complex manual-boot examples in Chapter 16 and also consider boot menu configuration in detail.

AIX

AIX provides little in the way of administrator intervention options during the boot process.* However, the administrator does have the ability to preconfigure the boot process in two ways.

The first is to use the `bootlist` command to specify the list and ordering of boot devices for either normal boot mode or service mode. For example, this command makes the CD-ROM drive the first boot device for the normal boot mode:

```
# bootlist -m normal cd1 hdisk0 hdisk1 rmt0
```

If there is no bootable CD in the drive, the system next checks the first two hard disks and finally the first tape drive.

The second configuration option is to use the `diag` utility to specify various boot process options, including whether or not the system should boot automatically in various circumstances. These items are accessed via the Task Selection submenu.

FreeBSD

FreeBSD (on Intel systems) presents a minimal boot menu:

```
F1  FreeBSD
F2  FreeBSD
F5  Drive 1     Appears if there is a second disk with a bootable partition.
```

This menu is produced by the FreeBSD boot loader (installed automatically if selected during the operating system installation, or installed manually later with the `boot0cfg` command). It simply identifies the partitions on the disk and lets you select the one from which to boot. Be aware, however, that it does not check whether each partition has a valid operating system on it (see Chapter 16 for ways of customizing what is listed).

The final option in the boot menu allows you to specify a different disk (the second IDE hard drive in this example). If you choose that option, you get a second, similar menu allowing you to select a partition on that disk:

```
F1  FreeBSD
F5  Drive 0
```

In this case, the second disk has only one partition.

---

* Some AIX systems respond to a specific keystroke at a precise moment during the boot process and place you in the System Management Services facility, where the boot device list can also be specified.

Shortly after selecting a boot option, the following message appears:*

```
Hit [Enter] to boot immediately, or any other key for the command prompt
```

If you strike a key, a command prompt appears, from which you can manually boot, as in these examples:

```
disk1s1a:> boot -s            Boot to single-user mode

disk1s1a:> unload             Boot an alternate kernel
disk1s1a:> load kernel-new
disk1s1a:> boot
```

If you do not specify a full pathname, the alternate kernel must be located in the root directory on the disk partition corresponding to your boot menu selection.

FreeBSD can also be booted by the grub open source boot loader, which is discussed—along with a few other boot loaders—in the Linux section below.

HP-UX

HP-UX boot commands vary by hardware type. These examples are from an HP 9000/800 system. When power comes on initially, the greater-than-sign prompt (>)† is given when any key is pressed before the autoboot timeout period expires. You can enter a variety of commands here. For our present discussion, the most useful are search (to search for bootable devices) and co (to enter the configuration menu). The latter command takes you to a menu where you can specify the standard and alternate boot paths and options. When you have finished with configuration tasks, return to the main menu (ma) and give the reset command.

Alternatively, you can boot immediately by using the bo command, specifying one of the devices that search found by its two-character path number (given in the first column of the output). For example, the following command might be used to boot from CD-ROM:

```
> bo P1
```

The next boot phase involves loading and running the initial system loader (ISL). When it starts, it asks whether you want to enter commands with this prompt:

```
Interact with ISL? y
```

If you answer yes, you will receive the ISL> prompt, at which you can enter various commands to modify the usual boot process, as in these examples:

```
ISL> hpux -is                 Boot to single user mode
ISL> hpux /stand/vmunix-new   Boot an alternate kernel
ISL> hpux ll /stand           List available kernels
```

---

* We're ignoring the second-stage boot loader here.

† Preceded by various verbiage.

Linux

When using lilo, the traditional Linux boot loader, the kernels available for booting are predefined. When you get lilo's prompt, you can press the TAB key to list the available choices. If you want to boot one of them into single-user mode, simply add the option single (or -s) to its name. For example:

```
boot: linux single
```

You can specify kernel parameters generally by appending them to the boot selection command.

If you are using the newer grub boot loader, you can enter boot commands manually instead of selecting one of the predefined menu choices, by pressing the c key. Here is an example sequence of commands:

```
grub> root (hd0,0)                              Location of /boot
grub> kernel /vmlinuz=new ro root=/dev/hda2
grub> initrd /initrd.img
grub> boot
```

The root option on the kernel command locates the partition where the root directory is located (we are using separate / and /boot partitions here).

If you wanted to boot to single-user mode, you would add single to the end of the kernel command.

In a similar way, you can boot one of the existing grub menu selections in single-user mode by doing the following:

1. Selecting it from the menu
2. Pressing the e key to edit it
3. Selecting and editing the kernel command, placing single at the end of the line
4. Moving the cursor to the first command and then pressing b for boot

The grub facility is discussed in detail in Chapter 16.

On non-Intel hardware, the boot commands are very different. For example, some Alpha Linux systems use a boot loader named aboot.* The initial power-on prompt is a greater-than sign (>). Enter the b command to reach aboot's prompt.

Here are the commands to boot a Compaq Alpha Linux system preconfigured with appropriate boot parameters:

```
aboot> p 2      Select the second partition to boot from.
aboot> 0        Boot predefined configuration 0.
```

The following command can be used to boot Linux from the second hard disk partition:

```
aboot> 2/vmlinux.gz root=/dev/hda2
```

---

* This description will also apply to Alpha hardware running other operating systems.

You could add single to the end of this line to boot to single-user mode.

Other Alpha-based systems use quite different boot mechanisms. Consult the manufacturer's documentation for your hardware to determine the proper commands for your system.

Tru64

When power is applied, a Tru64 system generally displays a console prompt that is a triple greater-than sign (>>>). You can enter commands to control the boot process, as in these examples:

```
>>> boot -fl s            Boot to single-user mode

>>> boot dkb0.0.0.6.1     Boot an alternate device or kernel
>>> boot -file vmunix-new
```

The -fl option specifies boot flags; here, we select single-user mode. The second set of commands illustrate the method for booting from an alternate device or kernel (the two commands may be combined).

Note that there are several other ways to perform these same tasks, but these methods seem the most intuitive.

Solaris

At power-on, Solaris systems may display the ok console prompt. If not, it is because the system is set to boot automatically, but you can generate one with the Stop-a or L1-a key sequence. From there, the boot command may be used to initiate a boot, as in this example:

```
ok boot -s        Boot to single user mode
ok boot cdrom     Boot from installation media
```

The second command boots an alternate kernel by giving its full drive and directory path. You can determine the available devices and how to refer to them by running the devalias command at the ok prompt.

Booting from alternate media

Booting from alternate media, such as CD-ROM or tape, is no different from booting any other non-default kernel. On systems where this is possible, you can specify the device and directory path to the kernel to select it. Otherwise, you must change the device boot order to place the desired alternate device before the standard disk location in the list.

Boot Activities in Detail

We now turn to a detailed consideration of the boot process from the point of kernel initialization onward.

Boot messages

The following example illustrates a generic Unix startup sequence. The messages included here are a composite of those from several systems, although the output is labeled as for a mythical computer named the Urizen, a late-1990s system running a vaguely BSD-style operating system. While this message sequence does not correspond exactly to any existing system, it does illustrate the usual elements of booting on Unix systems, under both System V and BSD.

We've annotated the boot process output throughout:

```
> b                                        Initiate boot to multiuser mode.
Urizen Ur-Unix boot in progress...
testing memory                            Output from boot program.
checking devices                          Preliminary hardware tests.
loading vmunix                            Read in the kernel executable.


Urizen Ur-Unix Version 17.4.2: Fri Apr 24 23 20:32:54 GMT 1998
Copyright (c) 1998 Blakewill Computer, Ltd.   Copyright for OS.
Copyright (c) 1986 Sun Microsystems, Inc.     Subsystem copyrights.
Copyright (c) 1989-1998 Open Software Foundation, Inc.
...
Copyright (c) 1991 Massachusetts Institute of Technology
All rights reserved.                      Unix kernel is running now.

physical memory = 2.00 GB                 Amount of real memory.

Searching SCSI bus for devices:           Peripherals are checked next.
rdisk0 bus 0 target 0 lun 0
rdisk1 bus 0 target 1 lun 0
rdisk2 bus 0 target 2 lun 0
rmt0 bus 0 target 4 lun 0
cdrom0 bus0 target 6 lun 0
Ethernet address=8:0:20:7:58:jk           Ethernet address of network adapter.


Root on /dev/disk0a                       Indicates disk partitions used as /,...
Activating all paging spaces              ...as paging spaces and...
swapon: swap device /dev/disk0b activated.
Using /dev/disk0b as dump device          ...as the crash dump location.


                                          Single-user mode could be entered here,...
INIT: New run level: 3                    ...but this system is booting to run level 3.
                                          Messages produced by startup scripts follow.
The system is coming up. Please wait.     Means "Be patient."
Tue Jul 14 14:45:28 EDT 1998


Checking TCB databases                    Verify integrity of the security databases.
Checking file systems:                    Check and mount remaining local filesystems.
fsstat: /dev/rdisk1c (/home) umounted cleanly;  Skipping check.
fsstat: /dev/rdisk2c (/chem) dirty        This filesystem needs checking.
Running fsck:
/dev/rdisk2c: 1764 files, 290620 used, 110315 free
Mounting local file systems.
```

```
Checking disk quotas: done.                    Daemons for major subsystems start first,...
cron subsystem started, pid = 3387
System message logger started.
Accounting services started.
                                               ...followed by network servers,...
Network daemons started: portmap inetd routed named rhwod timed.
NFS started: biod(4) nfsd(6) rpc.mountd rpc.statd rpc.lockd.
Mounting remote file systems.
Print subsystem started.                       ...and network-dependent local daemons.
sendmail started.

Preserving editor files.                        Save interrupted editor sessions.
Clearing /tmp.                                  Remove files from /tmp.
Enabling user logins.                           Remove the /etc/nologin file.
Tue Jul 14 14:47:45 EDT 1998                    Display the date again.

Urizen Ur-Unix 9.1 on hamlet                    The hostname is hamlet.

login:                                          Unix is running in multiuser mode.
```

There are some things that are deliberately anachronistic about this example boot sequence—running fsck and clearing */tmp*, for instance—but we've retained them for nostalgia's sake. We'll consider the scripts and commands that make all of these actions happen in the course of this section.

Saved boot log files

Most Unix versions automatically save some or all of the boot messages from the kernel initialization phase to a log file. The system message facility, controlled by the syslogd daemon, and the related System V dmesg utility are often used to capture messages from the kernel during a boot (syslog is discussed in detail Chapter 3). In the latter case, you must execute the dmesg command to view the messages from the most recent boot. On FreeBSD systems, you can also view them in the */var/run/dmesg.boot* file.

It is common for syslogd to maintain only a single message log file, so boot messages may be interspersed with system messages of other sorts. The conventional message file is */var/log/messages*.

The syslog facility under HP-UX may also be configured to produce a *messages* file, but it is not always set up at installation to do so automatically. HP-UX also provides the */etc/rc.log* file, which stores boot output from the multiuser phase.

Under AIX, */var/adm/ras/bootlog* is maintained by the alog facility. Like the kernel buffers that are its source, this file is a circular log that is maintained at a predefined fixed size; new information is written at the beginning of the file once the file is full, replacing the older data. You can use a command like this one to view the contents of this file:

```
# alog -f /var/adm/ras/bootlog -o
```

General considerations

In general, init controls the multiuser mode boot process. init runs whatever initialization scripts it has been designed to run, and the structure of the init program determines the fundamental design of the set of initialization scripts for that Unix version: what the scripts are named, where they are located in the filesystem, the sequence in which they are run, the constraints placed upon the scripts' programmers, the assumptions under which they operate, and so on. Ultimately, it is the differences in the System V and BSD versions of init that determines the differences in the boot process for the two types of systems.

Although we'll consider those differences in detail later, in this section, we'll begin by looking at the activities that are part of every normal Unix boot process, regardless of the type of system. In the process, we'll examine sections of initialization scripts from a variety of different computer systems.

Preliminaries

System initialization scripts usually perform a few preliminary actions before getting down to the work of booting the system. These include defining any functions and local variables that may be used in the script and setting up the script's execution environment, often beginning by defining *HOME* and *PATH* environment variables:

```
HOME=/; export HOME
PATH=/bin:/usr/bin:/sbin:/usr/sbin; export PATH
```

The path is deliberately set to be as short as possible; generally, only system directories appear in it to ensure that only authorized, unmodified versions of commands get executed (we'll consider this issue in more detail in "Protecting Files and the Filesystem" in Chapter 7).

Alternatively, other scripts are careful always to use full pathnames for every command that they use. However, since this may make commands excessively long and scripts correspondingly harder to read, some scripts take a third approach and define a local variable for each command that will be needed at the beginning of the script:

```
mount=/sbin/mount
fsck=/sbin/fsck
rm=/usr/bin/rm
...
```

The commands would then be invoked in this way:

```
${rm} -f /tmp/*
```

This practice ensures that the proper version of the command is run while still leaving the individual command lines very readable.

Whenever full pathnames are not used, we will assume that the appropriate *PATH* has previously been set up in the script excerpts we'll consider.

Preparing filesystems

Preparing the filesystem for use is the first and most important aspect of the multiuser boot process. It naturally separates into two phases: mounting the root filesystem and other vital system filesystems (such as /usr), and handling the remainder of the local filesystems.

Filesystem checking is one of the key parts of preparing the filesystem. This task is the responsibility of the fsck* utility.

 Most of the following discussion applies only to traditional, non-journaled Unix filesystems. Modern filesystem types use journaling techniques adapted from transaction processing to record and, if necessary, replay filesystem changes. In this way, they avoid the need for a traditional *fsck* command and its agonizingly slow verification and repair procedures (although a command of this name is usually still provided).

For traditional Unix filesystem types (such as ufs under FreeBSD and ext2 under Linux), fsck's job is to ensure that the data structures in the disk partition's superblock and inode tables are consistent with the filesystem's directory entries and actual disk block consumption. It is designed to detect and correct inconsistencies between them, such as disk blocks marked as in use that are not claimed by any file, and files existing on disk that are not contained in any directory. fsck deals with filesystem structure, but not with the internal structure or contents of any particular file. In this way, it ensures filesystem-level integrity, not data-level integrity.

In most cases, the inconsistencies that arise are minor and completely benign, and fsck can repair them automatically at boot time. Occasionally, however, fsck finds more serious problems, requiring administrator intervention.

System V and BSD have very different philosophies of filesystem verification. Under traditional BSD, the normal practice is to check all filesystems on every boot. In contrast, System V–style filesystems are not checked if they were unmounted normally when the system last went down. The BSD approach is more conservative, taking into account the fact that filesystem inconsistencies do on occasion crop up at times other than system crashes. On the other hand, the System V approach results in much faster boots.†

If the system is rebooting after a crash, it is quite normal to see many messages indicating minor filesystem discrepancies that have been repaired. By default, fsck fixes problems only if the repair cannot possibly result in data loss. If fsck discovers a

---

* Variously pronounced as "fisk" (like the baseball player Carlton, rhyming with "disk"), "ef-es-see-kay," "ef-es-check," and in less genteel ways.

† FreeBSD Version 4.4 and higher also checks only dirty filesystems at boot time.

more serious problem with the filesystem, it prints a message describing the problem and leaves the system in single-user mode; you must then run fsck manually to repair the damaged filesystem. For example (from a BSD-style system):

```
/dev/disk2e: UNEXPECTED INCONSISTENCY;
RUN fsck MANUALLY                       Message from fsck.
Automatic reboot failed . . . help!     Message from /etc/rc script.
Enter root password:                    Single-user mode.
# /sbin/fsck -p /dev/disk2e             Run fsck manually with –p.
...                                     Many messages from fsck.
BAD/DUP FILE=2216 OWNER=190 M=120777    Mode=> file is a symbolic link, so deleting it is safe.
S=16 MTIME=Sep 16 14:27 1997
CLEAR? y
*** FILE SYSTEM WAS MODIFIED ***
# ^D                                    Resume booting.
Mounting local file systems.            Normal boot messages
...
```

In this example, fsck found a file whose inode address list contained duplicate entries or addresses of known bad spots on the disk. In this case, the troublesome file was a symbolic link (indicated by the mode), so it could be safely removed (although the user who owned it will need to be informed). This example is intended merely to introduce you to fsck; the mechanics of running fsck are described in detail in "Managing Filesystems" in Chapter 10.

Checking and mounting the root filesystem

The root filesystem is the first filesystem that the boot process accesses as it prepares the system for use. On a System V system, commands like these might be used to check the root filesystem, if necessary:

```
/sbin/fsstat ${rootfs} >/dev/null 2>&1
if [ $? -eq 1 ] ; then
    echo "Running fsck on the root file system."
    /sbin/fsck -p ${rootfs}
fi
```

The shell variable *rootfs* has been defined previously as the appropriate special file for the root filesystem. The fsstat command determines whether a filesystem is clean (under HP-UX, fsclean does the same job). If it returns an exit value of 1, the filesystem needs checking, and fsck is run with its -p option, which says to correct automatically all benign errors that are found.

On many systems, the root filesystem is mounted read-only until after it is known to be in a viable state as a result of running fsstat and fsck as needed. At that point, it is remounted read-write by the following command:

```
# mount -o rw,remount /
```

On FreeBSD systems, the corresponding command is:

```
# mount -u -o rw /
```

Preparing other local filesystems

The traditional BSD approach to checking the filesystems is to check all of them via a single invocation of fsck (although the separate filesystems are not all checked simultaneously), and some System V systems have adopted this method as well. The initialization scripts on such systems include a fairly lengthy case statement, which handles the various possible outcomes of the fsck command:

```
/sbin/fsck -p
retval=$?
case $retval in                                 Check fsck exit code.
0)                                              No remaining problems,
  ;;                                               so just continue the boot process
4)                                              fsck fixed problems on root disk.
  echo "Root file system was modified."
  echo "Rebooting system automatically."
  exec /sbin/reboot -n
  ;;
8)                                              fsck failed to fix filesystem.
  echo "fsck -p could not fix file system."
  echo "Run fsck manually."
  ${single}                                     Single-user mode.
  ;;
12)                                             fsck exited before finishing.
  echo "fsck interrupted ... run manually."
  ${single}
  ;;
*)                                              All other fsck errors.
  echo "Unknown error in fsck."
  ${single}
  ;;
esac
```

This script executes the command fsck -p to check the filesystem's consistency. The -p option stands for *preen* and says that any needed repairs that will cause no loss of data should be made automatically. Since virtually all repairs are of this type, this is a very efficient way to invoke fsck. However, if a more serious error is found, fsck asks whether to fix it. Note that the options given to fsck may be different on your system.

Next, the case statement checks the status code returned by fsck (stored in the local variable *retval*) and performs the appropriate action based on its value.

If fsck cannot fix a disk on its own, you need to run it manually when it dumps you into single-user mode. Fortunately, this is rare. That's not just talk, either. I've had to run fsck manually only a handful of times over the many hundreds of times I've rebooted Unix systems, and those times occurred almost exclusively after crashes due to electrical storms or other power loss problems. Generally, the most vulnerable disks are those with continuous disk activity. For such systems, a UPS device is often a good protection strategy.

Once all the local filesystems have been checked (or it has been determined that they don't need to be), they can be mounted with the mount command, as in this example from a BSD system:

```
mount -a -t ufs
```

mount's -a option says to mount all filesystems listed in the system's filesystem configuration file, and the -t option restricts the command to filesystems of the type specified as its argument. In the preceding example, all ufs filesystems will be mounted. Some versions of mount also support a nonfs type, which specifies all filesystems other than those accessed over the network with NFS.

Saving a crash dump

When a system crashes due to an operating system–level problem, most Unix versions automatically write the current contents of kernel memory—known as a *crash dump*—to a designated location, usually the primary swap partition. AIX lets you specify the dump location with the sysdumpdev command, and FreeBSD sets it via the *dumpdev* parameter in */etc/rc.conf*. Basically, a crash dump is just a core dump of the Unix kernel, and like any core dump, it can be analyzed to figure out what caused the kernel program—and therefore the system—to crash.

Since the swap partition will be overwritten when the system is booted and paging is restarted, some provision needs to be made to save its contents after a crash. The savecore command copies the contents of the crash dump location to a file within the filesystem. savecore exits without doing anything if there is no crash dump present. The HP-UX version of this command is called savecrash.

savecore is usually executed automatically as part of the boot process, prior to the point at which paging is initiated:

```
savecore /var/adm/crash
```

savecore's argument is the directory location to which the crash dump should be written; */var/adm/crash* is a traditional location. On Solaris systems, you can specify the default directory location with the dumpadm command.

The crash dumps themselves are conventionally a pair of files named something like *vmcore*.n (the memory dump) and *kernel*.n, *unix*.n, or *vmunix*.n (the running kernel), where the extension is an integer that is increased each time a crash dump is made (so that multiple files may exist in the directory simultaneously). Sometimes, additional files holding other system status information are created as well.

HP-UX creates a separate subdirectory of */var/adm/crash* for each successive crash dump, using names of the form *crash*.n. Each subdirectory holds the corresponding crash data and several related files.

The savecore command is often disabled in the delivered versions of system initialization files since crash dumps are not needed by most sites. You should check the files on your system if you decide to use savecore to save crash dumps.

Starting paging

Once the filesystem is ready and any crash dump has been saved, paging can be started. This normally happens before the major subsystems are initialized since they might need to page, but the ordering of the remaining multiuser mode boot activities varies tremendously.

Paging is started by the `swapon -a` command, which activates all the paging areas listed in the filesystem configuration file.

Security-related activities

Another important aspect of preparing the system for users is ensuring that available security measures are in place and operational. Systems offering enhanced security levels over the defaults provided by vanilla Unix generally include utilities to verify the integrity of system files and executables themselves. Like their filesystem-checking counterpart `fsck`, these utilities are run at boot time and must complete successfully before users are allowed access to the system.

In a related activity, initialization scripts on many systems often try to ensure that there is a valid password file (containing the system's user accounts). These Unix versions provide the `vipw` utility for editing the password file. `vipw` makes sure that only one person edits the password file at a time. It works by editing a copy of the password file; `vipw` installs it as the real file after editing is finished. If the system crashes while someone is running `vipw`, however, there is a slight possibility that the system will be left with an empty or nonexistent password file, which significantly compromises system security by allowing anyone access without a password.

Commands such as these are designed to detect and correct such situations:

```
if [ -s /etc/ptmp ]; then              Someone was editing /etc/passwd.
    if [ -s /etc/passwd ]; then        If passwd is non-empty, use it...
        ls -l /etc/passwd /etc/ptmp >/dev/console
        rm -f /etc/ptmp                ...and remove the temporary file.
    else                               Otherwise, install the temporary file.
        echo 'passwd file recovered from /etc/ptmp'
        mv /etc/ptmp /etc/passwd
    fi
elif [ -r /etc/ptmp ]; then            Delete any empty temporary file.
    echo 'removing passwd lock file'
    rm -f /etc/ptmp
fi
```

The password temporary editing file, */etc/ptmp* in this example, also functions as a lock file. If it exists and is not empty (`-s` checks for a file of greater than zero length), someone was editing */etc/passwd* when the system crashed or was shut down. If */etc/passwd* exists and is not empty, the script assumes that it hasn't been damaged, prints a long directory listing of both files on the system console, and removes the password lock file. If */etc/passwd* is empty or does not exist, the script restores */etc/*

ptmp as a backup version of */etc/passwd* and prints the message "passwd file recovered from /etc/ptmp" on the console.

The elif clause handles the case where */etc/ptmp* exists but is empty. The script deletes it (because its presence would otherwise prevent you from using vipw) and prints the message "removing passwd lock file" on the console. Note that if no */etc/ ptmp* exists at all, this entire block of commands is skipped.

Checking disk quotas

Most Unix systems offer an optional disk quota facility, which allows the available disk space to be apportioned among users as desired. It, too, depends on database files that need to be checked and possibly updated at boot time, via commands like these:

```
echo "Checking quotas: \c"
quotacheck -a
echo "done."
quotaon -a
```

The script uses the quotacheck utility to check the internal structure of all disk quota databases, and then it enables disk quotas with quotaon. The script displays the string "Checking quotas:" on the console when the quotacheck utility begins (suppressing the customary carriage return at the end of the displayed line) and completes the line with "done." after it has finished (although many current systems use fancier, more aesthetically pleasing status messages). Disk quotas are discussed in "Monitoring and Managing Disk Space Usage" in Chapter 15.

Starting servers and initializing local subsystems

Once all the prerequisite system devices are ready, important subsystems such as electronic mail, printing, and accounting can be started. Most of them rely on daemons (server processes). These processes are started automatically by one of the boot scripts. On most systems, purely local subsystems that do not depend on the network are usually started before networking is initialized, and subsystems that do need network facilities are started afterwards.

For example, a script like this one (from a Solaris system) could be used to initialize the cron subsystem, a facility to execute commands according to a preset schedule (cron is discussed in Chapter 3):

```
if [ -p /etc/cron.d/FIFO ]; then
  if /usr/bin/pgrep -x -u 0 -P 1 cron >/dev/null 2>&1; then
      echo "$0: cron is already running"
      exit 0
  fi
elif [ -x /usr/sbin/cron ]; then
    /usr/bin/rm -f /etc/cron.d/FIFO
    /usr/sbin/cron &
fi
```

The script first checks for the existence of the cron lock file (a named pipe called *FIFO* whose location varies). If it is present, the script next checks for a current cron process (via the pgrep command). It the latter is found, the script exits because cron is already running. Otherwise, the script checks for the existence of the cron executable file. If it finds the file, the script removes the cron lock file and then starts the cron server.

The precautionary check to see whether cron is already running isn't made on all systems. Lots of system initialization files simply (foolishly) assume that they will be run only at boot time, when cron obviously won't already be running. Others use a different, more general mechanism to determine the conditions under which they were run. We'll examine that shortly.

Other local subsystems started in a similar manner include:

update
> A process that periodically forces all filesystem buffers (accumulated changes to inodes and data blocks) to disk. It does so by running the sync command, ensuring that the disks are fairly up-to-date should the system crash. The name of this daemon varies somewhat: bdflush is a common variant, AIX calls its version syncd, the HP-UX version is syncer, and it is named fsflush on Solaris systems. Linux runs both update and bdflush. Whatever its name, don't disable this daemon or you will seriously compromise filesystem integrity.

syslogd
> The system message handling facility that routes informational and error messages to log files, specific users, electronic mail, and other destinations according to the specifications in its configuration file (see Chapter 3).

Accounting
> this subsystem is started using the accton command. If accounting is not enabled, the relevant commands may be commented out.

System status monitor daemons
> some systems provide daemons that monitor the system's physical conditions (e. g., power level, temperature, and humidity) and trigger the appropriate action when a problem occurs. For example, the HP-UX ups_mond daemon watches for a power failure, switching to an uninterruptible power supply (UPS) to allow an orderly system shutdown, if necessary.

Subsystems that are typically started after networking (discussed in the next section) include:

- Electronic mail: the most popular electronic mail server is sendmail, which can route mail locally and via the network as needed. Postfix is a common alternative (its server process is also called sendmail).
- Printing: the spooling subsystem also may be entirely local or used for printing to remote systems in addition to (or instead of) locally connected ones. BSD-type printing subsystems rely on the lpd daemon, and System V systems use lpsched. The AIX printing server is qdaemon.

There may be other subsystems on your system with their own associated daemon processes; some may be vendor enhancements to standard Unix. We'll consider some of these when we look at the specific initialization files used by the various Unix versions later in this chapter.

The AIX System Resource Controller. On AIX systems, system daemons are controlled by the System Resource Controller (SRC). This facility starts daemons associated with the various subsystems and monitors their status on an ongoing basis. If a system daemon dies, the SRC automatically restarts it.

The srcmstr command is the executable corresponding to the SRC. The lssrc and chssys commands may be used to list services controlled by the SRC and change their configuration settings, respectively. We'll see examples of these commands at various points in this book.

Connecting to the network

Network initialization begins by setting the system's network hostname, if necessary, and configuring the network interfaces (adapter devices), enabling it to communicate on the network. The script that starts networking at boot time contains commands like these:

```
ifconfig lo0 127.0.0.1
ifconfig ent0 inet 192.168.29.22 netmask 255.255.255.0
```

The specific ifconfig commands vary quite a bit. The first parameter to ifconfig, which designates the network interface, may be different on your system. In this case, *lo0* is the loopback interface, and *ent0* is the Ethernet interface. Other common names for Ethernet interfaces include *eri0*, *dnet0,* and *hme0* (Solaris); *eth0* (Linux); *tu0* (Tru64); *xl0* (FreeBSD); *lan0* (HP-UX); *en0* (AIX); and *ef0* and *et0* (some System V). Interfaces for other network media will have different names altogether. Static routes may also be defined at this point using the route command. Networking is discussed in detail in Chapter 5.

Networking services also rely on a number of daemon processes. They are usually started with commands of this general form:

```
if [ -x server-pathname ]; then
   preparatory commands
   server-start-cmd
   echo Starting server-name
fi
```

When the server program file exists and is executable, the script performs any necessary preparatory activities and then starts the server process. Note that some servers go into background execution automatically, while others must be explicitly started in the background. The most important network daemons are listed in Table 4-1.

Table 4-1. Common network daemons

Daemon(s)	Purpose
`inetd`	Networking master server responsible for responding to many types of network requests via a large number of subordinate daemons, which it controls and to which it delegates tasks.
`named, routed, gated`	The name server and routing daemons, which provide dynamic remote hostname and routing data for TCP/IP. At most, one of `routed` or `gated` is used.
`ntpd, xntpd, timed`	Time-synchronization daemons. The `timed` daemon has been mostly replaced by the newer `ntpd` and the latest `xntpd`.
`portmap, rpc.statd, rpc.lockd`	Remote Procedure Call (RPC) daemons. RPC is the primary network interprocess communication mechanism used on Unix systems. `portmap` connects RPC program numbers to TCP/IP port numbers, and many network services depend on it. `rpc.lockd` provides locking services to NFS in conjunction with `rpc.statd`, the status monitor. The names of the latter two daemons may vary.
`nfsd, biod, mountd`	NFS daemons, which service file access and filesystem mounting requests from remote systems. The first two take an integer parameter indicating how many copies of the daemon are created. The system boot scripts also typically execute the `exportfs -a` command, which makes local filesystems available to remote systems via NFS.
`automount`	NFS automounter, responsible for mounting remote filesystems on demand. This daemon has other names on some systems.
`smbd, nmbd`	SAMBA daemons that handle SMB/CIFS-based remote file access requests from Windows (and other) systems.

Once basic networking is running, other services and subsystems that depend on it can be started. In particular, remote filesystems can be mounted with a command like this one, which mounts all remote filesystems listed in the system's filesystem configuration file:

```
mount -a -t nfs      On some systems, –F replaces –t.
```

Housekeeping activities

Traditionally, multiuser-mode boots also include a number of cleanup activities such as the following:

- Preserving editor files from `vi` and other ex-based editors, which enable users to recover some unsaved edits in the event of a crash. These editors automatically place checkpoint files in */tmp* or */var/tmp* during editing sessions. The `expreserve` utility is normally run at boot time to recover such files. On Linux systems, the `elvis` vi-clone is commonly available, and `elvprsv` performs the same function as `expreserve` for its files.

- Clearing the */tmp* directory and possibly other temporary directories. The commands to accomplish this can be minimalist:

```
rm -f /tmp/*
```

utilitarian:

```
cd /tmp; find . ! -name . ! -name .. ! -name lost+found \
                    ! -name quota\* -exec rm -fr {} \;
```

or rococo:

```
# If no /tmp exists, create one (we assume /tmp is not
# a separate file system).
if [ ! -d /tmp -a ! -l /tmp ]; then
    rm -f /tmp
    mkdir /tmp
fi
for dir in /tmp /var/tmp /usr/local/tmp ; do
    if [ -d $dir ] ; then
        cd $dir
        find . \( \( -type f \( -name a.out -o          \
                -name \*.bak -o -name core -o -name \*~ -o    \
                -name .\*~ -o -name #\*# -o -name #.\*# -o    \
                -name \*.o -o \( -atime +1 -mtime +3 \) \) \) \
                -exec rm -f {} \; -o -type d -name \*       \
                -prune -exec rm -fr {} \; \)
    fi
cd /
done
```

The first form simply removes from /tmp all files other than those whose names begin with a period. The second form might be used when /tmp is located on a separate filesystem from the root filesystem to avoid removing important files and subdirectories. The third script excerpt makes sure that the /tmp directory exists and then removes a variety of junk files and any subdirectory trees (with names not beginning with a period) from a series of temporary directories.

On some systems, these activities are not part of the boot process but are handled in other ways (see Chapter 15 for details).

Allowing users onto the system

The final boot-time activities complete the process of making the system available to users. Doing so involves both preparing resources users need to log in and removing barriers that prevent them from doing so. The former consists of creating the getty processes that handle each terminal line and starting a graphical login manager like xdm—or a vendor-customized equivalent facility—for X stations and the system console, if appropriate. On Solaris systems, it also includes initializing the Service Access Facility daemons sac and ttymon. These topics are discussed in detail in Chapter 12.

On most systems, the file /etc/nologin may be created automatically when the system is shut down normally. Removing it is often one of the very last tasks of the boot scripts. FreeBSD uses /var/run/nologin.

/etc/nologin may also be created as needed by the system administrator. If this file is not empty, its contents are displayed to users when they attempt to log in. Creating the file has no effect on users who are already logged in, and the root user can always log in. HP-UX versions prior to 11i do not use this file.

Initialization Files and Boot Scripts

This section discusses the Unix initialization files: command scripts that perform most of the work associated with taking the system to multiuser mode. Although similar activities take place under System V and BSD, the mechanisms by which they are initiated are quite different. Of the systems we are considering, FreeBSD follows the traditional BSD style, AIX is a hybrid of the two, and all the other versions use the System V scheme.

Understanding the initialization scripts on your system is a vital part of system administration. You should have a pretty good sense of where they are located and what they do. That way, you'll be able to recognize any problems at boot time right away, and you'll know what corrective action to take. Also, from time to time, you'll probably need to modify them to add new services (or to disable ones you've decided you don't need). We'll discuss customizing initialization scripts later in this chapter.

Although the names, directory locations, and actual shell program code for system initialization scripts varies widely between BSD-based versions of Unix and those derived from System V, the activities accomplished by each set of scripts as a whole differs in only minor ways. In high-level terms, the BSD boot process is controlled by a relatively small number of scripts in the /etc directory, with names beginning with rc, which are executed sequentially. In contrast, System V executes a large number of scripts (as high as 50 or more), organized in a three-tiered hierarchy.

Unix initialization scripts are written using the Bourne shell (/bin/sh). As a convenience, Bourne shell programming features are summarized in Appendix A.

Aspects of the boot process are also controlled by configuration files that modify the operations of the boot scripts. Such files consist of a series of variable definitions that are read in at the beginning of a boot script and whose values determine which commands in the script are executed. These variables can specify things like whether a subsystem is started at all, the command-line options to use when starting a daemon, and the like. Generally, these files are edited manually, but some systems provide graphical tools for this purpose. The dialog on the left in Figure 4-1 shows the utility provided by SuSE Linux 7 as part of its YaST2 administration tool.

The dialog on the right shows the new run-level editor provided by YaST2 on SuSE 8 systems. In this example, we are enabling inetd in run levels 2, 3, and 5.

Initialization Files Under FreeBSD

The organization of system initialization scripts on traditional BSD systems such as FreeBSD is the essence of simplicity. In the past, boot-time activities occurred via a series of only three or four shell scripts, usually residing in /etc, with names beginning

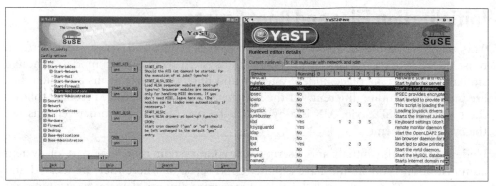

Figure 4-1. Editing the boot script configuration file on a SuSE Linux system

with *rc*. Under FreeBSD, this number has risen to about 20 (although not all of them apply to every system).

Multiuser-mode system initialization under BSD-based operating systems is controlled by the file */etc/rc*. During a boot to multiuser mode, init executes the rc script, which in turn calls other *rc.** scripts. If the system is booted to single-user mode, rc begins executing when the single-user shell is exited.

The boot script configuration files */etc/default/rc.conf*, */etc/rc.conf*, and */etc/rc.conf. local* control the functioning of the *rc* script. The first of these files is installed by the operating system and should not be modified. The other two files contain overrides to settings in the first file (although the latter is seldom used).

Here are some example entries from */etc/rc.conf*:

```
accounting_enable="YES"
check_quotas="YES"
defaultrouter="192.168.29.204"
hostname="ada.ahania.com"
ifconfig_xl0="inet 192.168.29.216 netmask 255.255.255.0"
inetd_enable="YES"
nfs_client_enable="YES"
nfs_server_enable="YES"
portmap_enable="YES"
sendmail_enable="NO"
sshd_enable="YES"
```

This file enables the accounting, inetd, NFS, portmapper, and ssh subsystems and disables sendmail. It causes disk quotas to be checked at boot time, and specifies various network settings, including the Ethernet interface.

Initialization Files on System V Systems

The system initialization scripts on a System V–style system are much more numerous and complexly interrelated than those under BSD. They all revolve around the notion of the current system run level, a concept to which we now turn.

System V run levels

At any given time, a computer system can be in one of three conditions: off (not running, whether or not it has power), single-user mode, or multiuser mode (normal operating conditions). These three conditions may be thought of as three implicitly defined system states.

System V–based systems take this idea to its logical extreme and explicitly define a series of system states, called *run levels*, each of which is designated by a one-character name that is usually a number. At any given time, the system is at one of these states, and it can be sent to another one using various administrative commands. The defined run levels are listed in Table 4-2.

Table 4-2. System V–style run levels

Run Level	Name and customary purpose
0	Halted state: conditions under which it is safe to turn off the power.
1	System administration/maintenance state.
S *and* s	Single-user mode.
2	Multiuser mode: the normal operating state for isolated, non-networked systems or networked, non-server systems, depending on the version of Unix.
3	Remote file sharing state: the normal operating state for server systems on networks that share their local resources with other systems (irrespective of whether networking and resource sharing occurs via TCP/IP and NFS or some other protocol).
4, 7, 8, 9	Administrator-definable system states: a generally unused run level, which can be set up and defined locally.
5	Same as run level 3 but running a graphical login program on the system console (e.g., xdm).
6	Shutdown and reboot state: used to reboot the system from some running state (s, 2, 3, or 4). Moving to this state causes the system to be taken down (to run level 0) and then immediately rebooted back to its normal operating state.
Q *and* q	A pseudo-state that tells init to reread its configuration file */etc/inittab*.
a, b, c	Pseudo–run levels that can be defined locally. When invoked, they cause init to run the commands in */etc/inittab* corresponding to them without changing the current (numeric) run level.

In most implementations, states 1 and s/S are not distinguished in practice, and not all states are predefined by all implementations. State 3 is the defined normal operating mode for networked systems. In practice, some systems collapse run levels 2 and 3, supporting all networking functions at run level 2 and ignoring run level 3, or making them identical so that 2 and 3 become alternate names for the same system state. We will use separate run levels 2 and 3 in our examples, making run level 3 the system default level.

Note that the pseudo–run levels (a, b, c, and q/Q) do not represent distinct system states, but rather function as ways of getting init to perform certain tasks on demand.

Table 4-3 lists the run levels defined by the various operating systems we are considering. Note that FreeBSD does not use run levels.

Table 4-3. Run levels defined by various operating systems

	AIX	HP-UX	Linux	Tru64	Solaris
Default run level	2	3	3 or 5	3	3
Q	yes	yes	yes	yes	yes
7, 8, 9	yes	no	yes	yes	no
a, b, c	yes	yes	yes	no	yes

The command who -r may be used to display the current run level and the time it was initiated:

```
$ who -r
.   run level 3   Mar 14 11:14   3   0   S      Previous run level was S.
```

The output indicates that this system was taken to run level 3 from run level S on March 14. The 0 value between the 3 and the S indicates the number of times the system had been at the current run level *immediately* prior to entering it this time. If the value is nonzero, it often indicates previous unsuccessful boots.

On Linux systems, the runlevel command lists the previous and current run levels.

Now for some concrete examples. Let's assume a system whose normal, everyday system state is state 3 (networked multiuser mode). When you boot this system after the power has been off, it moves from state 0 to state 3. If you shut the system down to single-user mode, it moves from state 3 through state 0 to state s. When you reboot the system, it moves from state 3 through state 6 and state 0, and then back to state 3.*

Using the telinit command to change run levels

The telinit utility may be used to change the current system run level. Its name comes from the fact that it *tells* the init process what to do next. It takes the new run level as its argument. The following command tells the system to reboot:

```
# telinit 6
```

Tru64 does not include the telinit command. However, because telinit is just a link to init that has been given a different name to highlight what it does, you can easily create it if desired:

```
# cd /sbin
# ln init telinit
```

You can also just use init itself: init 6.

AIX also omits the telinit command, since it does not implement run levels in the usual manner.

---

* In practice, booting to state 3 often involves implicitly moving through state 2, given the way that *inittab* configuration files employing both states are usually set up.

Initialization files overview

System V–style systems organize the initialization process in a much more complex way, using three levels of initialization files:

- */etc/inittab*, which is init's configuration file.
- A series of primary scripts named *rcn* (where *n* is the run level), typically stored in */etc* or */sbin*.
- A collection of auxiliary, subsystem-specific scripts for each run level, typically located in subdirectories named *rcn.d* under */etc* or */sbin*.
- In addition, some systems also provide configuration files that define variables specifying or modifying the functioning of some of these scripts.

On a boot, when init takes control from the kernel, it scans its configuration file, */etc/inittab*, to determine what to do next. This file defines init's actions whenever the system enters a new run level; it contains instructions to carry out when the system goes down (run level 0), when it boots to single-user mode (run level S), when booting to multiuser mode (run level 2 or 3), when rebooting (run level 6), and so on.

Each entry in the *inittab* configuration file implicitly defines a process to be run at one or more run levels. Sometimes, this process is an actual daemon that continues executing as long as the system remains in a given run level. More often, the process is a shell script that is executed when the system enters one of the run levels specified in its *inittab* entry.

When the system changes run levels, init consults the *inittab* file to determine the processes that should be running at the new run level. It then kills all currently running processes that should not be running at the new level and starts all processes specified for the new run level that are not already running.

Typically, the commands to execute at the start of each run level are contained in a script named *rcn*, where *n* is the run level number (these scripts are usually stored in the */etc* directory). For example, when the system moves to run level 2, init reads the */etc/inittab* file, which tells it to execute *rc2*. *rc2* then executes the scripts stored in the directory */etc/rc2.d*. Similarly, when a running system is rebooted, it moves first from run level 2 to run level 6, a special run level that tells the system to shut down and immediately reboot, where it usually executes *rc0* and the scripts in */etc/rc0.d*, and then changes to run level 2, again executing *rc2* and the files in */etc/rc2.d*. A few systems use a single *rc* script and pass the run level as its argument: rc 2.

A simple version of the System V rebooting process is illustrated in Figure 4-2 (assuming run level 2 as the normal operating state). We will explain all of the complexities and eccentricities in it as this section progresses.

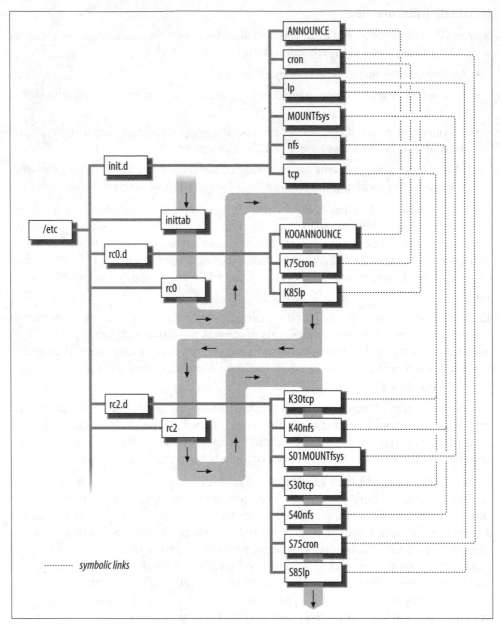

Figure 4-2. Executing System V–style boot scripts

The init configuration file

As we've seen, top-level control of changing system states is handled by the file */etc/ inittab*, read by init. This file contains entries that tell the system what to do when it enters the various defined system states.

Entries in the *inittab* have the following form:

```
cc:levels:action:process
```

where *cc* is a unique, case-sensitive label identifying each entry (subsequent entries with duplicate labels are ignored).* *levels* is a list of run levels to which the entry applies; if it is blank, the entry applies to all of them. When the system enters a new state, init processes all entries specified for that run level in the *inittab* file, in the order they are listed in the file.

process is the command to execute, and *action* indicates how init is to treat the process started by the entry. The most important *action* keywords are the following:

wait
> Start the process and wait for it to finish before going on to the next entry for this run state.

respawn
> Start the process and automatically restart it when it dies (commonly used for getty terminal line server processes).

once
> Start the process if it's not already running. Don't wait for it.

boot
> Execute entry only at boot time; start the process but don't wait for it.

bootwait
> Execute entry only at boot time and wait for it to finish.

initdefault
> Specify the default run level (the one to reboot to).

sysinit
> Used for activities that need to be performed before init tries to access the system console (for example, initializing the appropriate device).

off
> If the process associated with this entry is running, kill it. Also used to comment out unused terminal lines.

Comments may be included on separate lines or at the end of any entry by preceding the comment with a number sign (#).

Here is a sample *inittab* file:

```
# set default init level -- multiuser mode with networking
is:3:initdefault:

# initial boot scripts
```

---

* Conventionally, labels are 2 characters long, but the actual limit is usually four characters, and some systems allow labels of up to 14 characters.

```
fs::bootwait:/etc/bcheckrc </dev/console >/dev/console 2>&1
br::bootwait:/etc/brc </dev/console >/dev/console 2>&1

# shutdown script
r0:06:wait:/etc/rc0  >/dev/console 2>&1 </dev/console

# run level changes
r1:1:wait:/sbin/shutdown -y -iS -g0 >/dev/console 2>&1
r2:23:wait:/etc/rc2 >/dev/console 2>&1 </dev/console
r3:3:wait:/etc/rc3  >/dev/console 2>&1 </dev/console
pkg:23:once:/usr/sfpkg/sfpkgd    # start daemon directly

# off and reboot states
off:0:wait:/sbin/uadmin 2 0 >/dev/console 2>&1 </dev/console
rb:6:wait:/sbin/uadmin 2 1 >/dev/console 2>&1 </dev/console

# terminal initiation
co:12345:respawn:/sbin/getty console console
t0:234:respawn:/sbin/getty tty0 9600
t1:234:respawn:/sbin/getty tty1 9600
t2:234:off:/sbin/getty tty2 9600

# special run level
acct:a:once:/etc/start_acct       # start accounting
```

This file logically consists of seven major sections, which we've separated with blank lines. The first section, consisting of a single entry, sets the default run level, which in this case is networked multiuser mode (level 3).

The second section contains processes started when the system is booted. In the sample file, this consists of running the */etc/bcheckrc* and */etc/brc* preliminary boot scripts commonly used on System V systems in addition to the *rcn* structure. The bcheckrc script's main function is to prepare the root filesystem and other critical filesystems like */usr* and */var*. Both scripts are allowed to complete before init goes on to the next *inittab* entry.

The third section of the sample *inittab* file specifies the commands to execute whenever the system is brought down, either during a system shutdown and halt (to run level 0) or during a reboot (run level 6). In both cases, the script */etc/rc0* is executed, and init waits for it to finish before proceeding.

The fourth section, headed "run level changes," specifies the commands to run when system states 1, 2, and 3 begin. For state 1, the shutdown command listed in the sample file takes the system to single-user mode. Some systems execute the *rc1* initialization file when the system enters state 1 instead of a shutdown command like the one above.

For state 2, init executes the *rc2* initialization script; for state 3, init executes *rc2* followed by *rc3*. In all three states, each process is allowed to finish before init goes on to the next entry. The final entry in this section starts a process directly instead of calling a script. The sfpkgd daemon is started only once per run level, when the system first enters run level 2 or 3. Of course, if the daemon is already running, it will not be restarted.

The fifth section specifies commands to run (after *rc0*) when the system enters run levels 0 and 6. In both cases, `init` runs the `uadmin` command, which initiates system shutdown. The arguments to `uadmin` specify how the shutdown is to be handled. Many modern systems have replaced this legacy command, folding its functionality into the `shutdown` command (as we'll see shortly). Of the System V systems we are considering, only Solaris still uses `uadmin`.

The sixth section initializes the system's terminal lines via `getty` processes (which are discussed in Chapter 12).

The final section of the *inittab* file illustrates the use of special run level a. This entry is used only when a `telinit a` command is executed by the system administrator, at which point the *start_acct* script is run. The run levels a, b, and c are available to be defined as needed.

The rcn initialization scripts

As we've seen, `init` typically executes a script named *rcn* when entering run level *n* (*rc2* for state 2, for example). Although the boot (or shutdown) process to each system state is controlled by the associated *rcn* script, the actual commands to be executed are stored in a series of files in the subdirectory *rcn.d*. Thus, when the system enters state 0, `init` runs *rc0* (as directed in the *inittab* file), which in turn runs the scripts in *rc0.d*.

The contents of an atypically small *rc2.d* directory (on a system that doesn't use a separate run level 3) are listed below:

```
$ ls -C /etc/rc2.d
K30tcp          S15preserve    S30tcp    S50RMTMPFILES
K40nfs          S20sysetup     S35bsd    S75cron
S01MOUNTFSYS    S21perf        S40nfs    S85lp
```

All filenames begin with one of two initial filename characters (S and K), followed by a two-digit number, and they all end with a descriptive name. The *rcn* scripts execute the K-files (as I'll call them) in their associated directory in alphabetical order, followed by the S-files, also in alphabetical order (this scheme is easiest to understand if all numbers are the same length; hence the leading zeros on numbers under 10). Numbers do not need to be unique.

In this directory, files would be executed in the order *K30tcp*, *K40nfs*, *S01MOUNTFSYS*, *S15preserve*, and so on, ending with *S75cron* and *S85lp*. K-files are generally used to kill processes (and perform related functions) when transitioning to a different state; S-files are used to start processes and perform other initialization functions.

The files in the *rc*.d* subdirectories are usually links to those files in the subdirectory *init.d*, where the real files live. For example, the file *rc2.d/S30tcp* is actually a link to *init.d/tcp*. You see how the naming conventions work: the final portion of the name in the *rcn.d* directory is the same as the filename in the *init.d* directory.

The file *K30tcp* is also a link to *init.d/tcp*. The same file in *init.d* is used for both the kill and start scripts for each subsystem. The K and S links can be in the same *rcn.d* subdirectory, as is the case for the TCP/IP initialization file, or in different subdirectories. For example, in the case of the print spooling subsystem, the S-file might be in *rc2.d* while the K-file is in *rc0.d*.

The same file in *init.d* can be put to both uses because it is passed a parameter indicating whether it was run as a K-file or an S-file. Here is an example invocation, from an *rc2* script:

```
# If the directory /etc/rc2.d exists,
# run the K-files in it ...
if [ -d /etc/rc2.d ]; then
    for f in /etc/rc2.d/K*
    {
        if [ -s ${f} ]; then
#           pass the parameter "stop" to the file
            /bin/sh ${f} stop
        fi
    }
# and then the S-files:
    for f in /etc/rc2.d/S*
    {
        if [ -s ${f} ]; then
#           pass the parameter "start" to the file
            /bin/sh ${f} start
        fi
    }
fi
```

When a K-file is executed, it is passed the parameter *stop*; when an S-file is executed, it is passed *start*. The script file will use this parameter to figure out whether it is being run as a K-file or an S-file.

Here is a simple example of the script file, *init.d/cron*, which controls the cron facility. By examining it, you'll be able to see the basic structure of a System V initialization file:

```
#!/bin/sh
case $1 in
    # commands to execute if run as "Snncron"
    'start')
        # remove lock file from previous cron
        rm -f /usr/lib/cron/FIFO
        # start cron if executable exists
        if [ -x /sbin/cron ]; then
            /sbin/cron
```

```
        echo "starting cron."
    fi
;;

# commands to execute if run as "Knncron"
'stop')
        pid=`/bin/ps -e | grep ' cron$' | \
            sed -e 's/^ *//' -e 's/ .*//'`
        if [ "${pid}" != "" ]; then
            kill ${pid}
        fi
;;

# handle other arguments
*)
    echo "Usage: /etc/init.d/cron {start|stop}"
    exit 1
;;
esac
```

The first section in the case statement is executed when the script is passed *start* as its first argument (when it's an S-file); the second section is used when it is passed *stop*, as a K-file. The start commands remove any old lock file and then start the cron daemon if its executable is present on the system. The stop commands figure out the process ID of the cron process and kill it if it's running. Some scripts/operating systems define additional valid parameters, including *restart* (equivalent to *stop* then *start*) and *status*.

The file */etc/init.d/cron* might be linked to both */etc/rc2.d/S75cron* and */etc/rc0.d/K75cron*. The cron facility is then started by *rc2* during multiuser boots and stopped by *rc0* during system shutdowns and reboots.

Sometimes scripts are even more general, explicitly testing for the conditions under which they were invoked:

```
set `who -r`                        Determine previous run level.
if [ $8 != "0" ]                    The return code of the previous state change.
then
    exit
fi
case $arg1 in 'start')
    if [ $9 = "S" ]                 Check the previous run level.
    then
        echo "Starting process accounting"
        /usr/lib/acct/startup
    fi
;;
...
```

This file uses various parts of the output from `who -r`:

```
$ who -r
.    run level 2   Mar 14 11:14    2    0    S
```

The set command assigns successive words in the output from the who command to the shell script arguments *$1* through *$9*. The script uses them to test whether the current system state was entered without errors, exiting if it wasn't. It also checks whether the immediately previous state was single-user mode, as would be the case on this system on a boot or reboot. These tests ensure that accounting is started only during a successful boot and not when single-user mode has been entered due to boot errors or when moving from one multiuser state to another.

Boot script configuration files

On many systems, the functioning of the various boot scripts can be controlled and modified by settings in one or more related configuration files. These settings may enable or disable subsystems, specify command-line arguments for starting daemons, and the like. Generally, such settings are stored in separate files named for the corresponding subsystem, but sometimes they are all stored in a single file (as on SuSE Linux systems, in */etc/rc.config*).

Here are two configuration files from a Solaris system; the first is */etc/default/ sendmail*:

```
DAEMON=yes      Enable the daemon.
QUEUE=1h        Set the poll interval to 1 hour.
```

The next file is */etc/default/samba*:

```
# Options to smbd
SMBDOPTIONS="-D"
# Options to nmbd
NMBDOPTIONS="-D"
```

The first example specifies whether the associated daemon should be started, as well as one of its arguments, and the second file specifies the arguments to be used when starting the two Samba daemons.

File location summary

Table 4-4 summarizes the boot scripts and configuration files used by the various System V–style operating systems we are considering. A few notes about some of them will follow.

Table 4-4. Boot scripts for System V–style operating systems

Component	Location
inittab file	**Usual:** */etc*
rc* files	**Usual:** */sbin/rcn*
	AIX: */etc/rc.**
	HP-UX: */sbin/rc n[a]*
	Linux: */etc/rc.d/rc n[a]*

Table 4-4. Boot scripts for System V–style operating systems (continued)

Component	Location
rcn.d and *init.d* subdirectories	**Usual:** */sbin/rcn.d* and */sbin/init.d* **AIX:** */etc/rc.d/rcn.d* (but they are empty) **Linux:** */etc/rc.d/rcn.d* and */etc/rc.d/init.d* (Red Hat); */etc/init.d/rcn.d* and */etc/init.d* (SuSE) **Solaris:** */etc/rcn.d* and */etc/init.d*
Boot script configuration files	**AIX:** none used **FreeBSD:** */etc/rc.conf*, and/or */etc/rc.conf.local* **HP-UX:** */etc/rc.config.d/** **Linux:** */etc/sysconfig/** (Red Hat, SuSE 8); */etc/rc.config* and */etc/rc.config.d/** (SuSE 7) **Solaris:** */etc/default/** **Tru64:** */etc/rc.config*

ᵃ *n* is the parameter to *rc*.

Solaris initialization scripts

Solaris uses a standard System V boot script scheme. The script *rcS* (in */sbin*) replaces bcheckrc, but it performs the same functions. Solaris uses separate *rcn* scripts for each run level from 0 through 6 (excluding *rc4*, which a site must create on its own), but the scripts for run levels 0, 5, and 6 are just links to a single script, called with different arguments for each run level. There are separate *rcn.d* directories for run levels 0 through 3 and S.

Unlike on some other systems, run level 5 is a "firmware" (maintenance) mode, defined as follows:

```
s5:5:wait:/sbin/rc5        >/dev/msglog 2>&1 </dev/console
of:5:wait:/sbin/uadmin 2 6 >/dev/msglog 2>&1 </dev/console
```

These entries illustrate the Solaris *msglog* device, which sends output to one or more console devices via a single redirection operation.

Solaris *inittab* files also usually contain entries for the Service Access Facility daemons, such as the following:

```
sc:234:respawn:/usr/lib/saf/sac -t 300 ...
co:234:respawn:/usr/lib/saf/ttymon ...
```

Run level 3 on Solaris systems is set up as the remote file-sharing state. When TCP/IP is the networking protocol in use, this means that general networking and NFS client activities—such as mounting remote disks—occur as part of run level 2, but NFS server activities do not occur until the system enters run level 3, when local filesystems become available to other systems. The *rc2* script, and thus the scripts in *rc2.d*, are executed for both run levels by an *inittab* entry like this one:

```
s2:23:wait:/sbin/rc2 ...
```

Tru64 initialization scripts

Tru64 feels generally like a BSD-style operating system. Its initialization scripts are one of the few places where its true, System V–style origins are revealed. It uses bcheckrc to check (if necessary) and mount the local filesystems.

Tru64 defines only four run levels: 0, S, 2, and 3. The latter two differ in that run level 3 is the normal, fully networked state and is usually init's default run level. Run level 2 is a nonnetworked state. It is designed so that it can be invoked easily from a system at run level 3. The */sbin/rc2.d* directory contains a multitude of K-files designed to terminate all of the various network servers and network-dependent subsystems. Most of the K-files operate by running the ps command, searching its output for the PID of a specific server process, and then killing it if it is running. The majority of the S-files in the subdirectory exit immediately if they are run at any time other than a boot from single-user mode. Taken together, the files in *rc2.d* ensure a functional but isolated system, whether run level 2 is reached as part of a boot or reboot, or via a transition from run level 3.

Linux initialization scripts

Most Linux systems use a vanilla, System V–style boot script hierarchy. The Linux init package supports the special action keyword *ctrlaltdel* that allows you to trap CTRL-ALT-DELETE sequences (the standard method of rebooting a PC), as in this example, which calls the shutdown command and reboots the system:

```
ca::ctrlaltdel:/sbin/shutdown -r now
```

Linux distributions also provide custom initial boot scripts (run prior to *rc*). For example, Red Hat Linux uses */etc/rc.d/rc.sysinit* for this purpose, and SuSE Linux systems use */etc/init.d/boot*. These scripts focus on the earliest boot tasks such as checking and mounting filesystems, setting the time zone, and initializing and activating swap space.

AIX: Making System V work like BSD

It's possible to eliminate most of the layers of initialization scripts that are standard under System V. Consider this AIX *inittab* file:

```
init:2:initdefault:
brc::sysinit:/sbin/rc.boot 3 >/dev/console 2>&1
rc:2:wait:/etc/rc 2>&1 | alog -tboot > /dev/console srcmstr:2:respawn:/usr/sbin/srcmstr
tcpip:2:wait:/etc/rc.tcpip > /dev/console 2>&1
nfs:2:wait:/etc/rc.nfs > /dev/console 2>&1
ihshttpd:2:wait:/usr/HTTPServer/bin/httpd > /dev/console 2>&1
cron:2:respawn:/usr/sbin/cron
qdaemon:2:wait:/usr/bin/startsrc -sqdaemon
cons::respawn:/etc/getty /dev/console
tty0:2:respawn:/etc/getty /dev/tty0
```

Other than starting a server process for the system console and executing the file /etc/bcheckrc at boot time, nothing is defined for any run level other than state 2 (multiuser mode).

This is the approach taken by AIX. When the system enters state 2, a series of initialization files are run in sequence: in this case, /etc/rc, /etc/rc.tcpip, and /etc/rc.nfs (with the System Resource Controller starting up in the midst of them). Then several daemons are started via their own *inittab* entries. After the scripts complete, getty processes are started. Since /etc/rcn.d subdirectories are not used at all, this setup is a little different from that used on BSD systems.

More recent AIX operating system revisions do include hooks for other run levels, modifying the preceding *inittab* entries in this way:

```
# Note that even run level 6 is included!
tcpip:23456789:wait:/etc/rc.tcpip > /dev/console 2>&1
```

The /etc/rc.d/rcn.d subdirectories are provided, but they are all empty.

Customizing the Boot Process

Sooner or later, you will want to make additions or modifications to the standard boot process. Making additions is less risky than changing existing scripts. We'll consider the two types of modifications separately.

 Before adding to or modifying system boot scripts, you should be very familiar with their contents and understand what every line within them does. You should also save a copy of the original script so you can easily restore the previous version should problems occur.

Adding to the boot scripts

When you want to add commands to the boot process, the first thing you need to determine is whether there is already support for what you want to do. See if there is an easy way to get what you want: changing a configuration file variable, for example, or adding a link to an existing file in *init.d*.

If the operating system has made no provisions for the tasks you want to accomplish, you must next figure out where in the process the new commands should be run. It is easiest to add items at the end of the standard boot process, but occasionally this is not possible.

It is best to isolate your changes from the standard system initialization files as much as possible. Doing so makes them easier to test and debug and also makes them less vulnerable to being lost when the operating system is upgraded and the previous boot scripts are replaced by new versions. Under the BSD scheme, the best way to accomplish this is to add a line to *rc* (or any other script that you need to change) that calls a separate script that you provide:

```
. /etc/rc.site_specific >/dev/console 2>&1
```

Ideally, you would place this at the end of *rc*, and the additional commands needed on that system would be placed into the new script. Note that the script is sourced with the dot command so that it inherits the current environment from the calling script. This does constrain it to being a Bourne shell script.

 Some systems contain hooks for an *rc.local* script specifically designed for this purpose (stored in */etc* like *rc*). FreeBSD does—it is called near the end of *rc*—but you will have to create the file yourself.

On System V systems, there are more options. One approach is to add one or more additional entries to the *inittab* file (placing them as late in the file as possible):

```
site:23:wait:/etc/rc.site_specific >/dev/console 2>&1
h96:23:once:/usr/local/bin/h96d
```

The first entry runs the same shell script we added before, and the second entry starts a daemon process. Starting a daemon directly from *inittab* (rather than from some other initialization file) is useful in two circumstances: when you want the daemon started only at boot time and when you want it to be restarted automatically if it terminates. You would use the *inittab* actions *once* and *respawn*, respectively, to produce these two ways of handling the *inittab* entry.

Alternatively, if your additions need to take place at a very specific point in the boot process, you will need to add a file to the appropriate *rcn.d* subdirectories. Following the System V practice is best in this case: place the new file in the *init.d* directory, giving it a descriptive name, and then create links to other directories as needed. Choose the filenames for the links carefully, so that your new files are executed at the proper point in the sequence. If you are in doubt, executing the ls -1 command in the appropriate directory provides you with an unambiguous list of the current ordering of the scripts within it, and you will be able to determine what number to use for your new one.

Eliminating certain boot-time activities

Disabling parts of the boot process is also relatively easy. The method for doing so depends on the initialization scripts used by your operating system. The various possibilities are (in decreasing order of preference):

- Disable a subsystem by setting the corresponding control variable to no or 0 in one of the boot script configuration files. For example:

    ```
    sendmail_enable="no"
    ```

- Remove the link in the *rcn.d* directory to the *init.d* directory in the case of System V–style boot scripts. Alternatively, you can rename the link, for example, by adding another character to the beginning (I add an underscore: *_K20nfs*). That way, it is easy to reinstate the file later.

- In some cases, you will need to comment out an entry in */etc/inittab* (when a daemon that you don't want is started directly).

- Comment out the relevant lines of initialization scripts that you don't want to use. This is the only option under FreeBSD when no *rc.conf* parameter has been defined for a command or subsystem.

Linux systems often provide graphical utilities for adding and removing links to files in *init.d*. Figure 4-3 illustrates the ksysv utility running on a Red Hat Linux system.

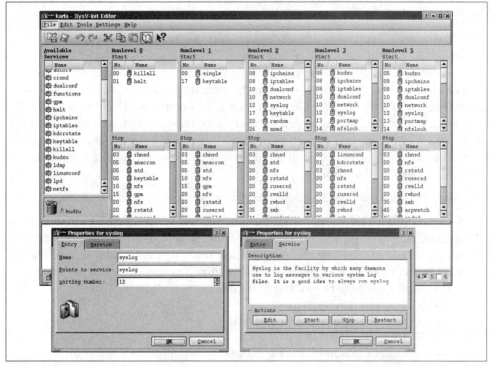

Figure 4-3. Modifying boot script links

The main window lists the scripts assigned as S-files (upper lists) and K-files for each run level. The Available Services list shows all of the files in *init.d*. You can add a script by dragging it from that list box to the appropriate run level pane, and you can remove one by dragging it to the trash can (we are in the process of deleting the annoying Kudzu hardware detection utility in the example).

Clicking on any entry brings up the smaller dialog at the bottom of the figure (both of whose panels are shown as separate windows). You can specify the location within the sequence of scripts using the Entry panel. The Service panel displays a brief description of the daemon's purpose and contains buttons with which you can start, stop, and restart it. If appropriate, you can use the Edit button to view and potentially modify the startup script for this facility.

Modifying standard scripts

While it is usually best to avoid it, sometimes you have no choice but to modify the commands in standard boot scripts. For example, certain networking functions stopped working on several systems I take care of immediately after an operating system upgrade. The reason was a bug in an initialization script, illustrated by the following:

```
# Check the mount of /. If remote, skip rest of setup.
mount | grep ' / ' | grep ' nfs ' 2>&1 > /dev/null
if [ "$?" -eq 0 ]
then
    exit
fi
```

The second line of the script is trying to figure out whether the root filesystem is local or remote—in other words, whether the system is a diskless workstation or not. It assumes that if it finds a root filesystem that is mounted via NFS, it must be a diskless system. However, on my systems, lots of root filesystems from other hosts are mounted via NFS, and this condition produced a false positive for this script, causing it to exit prematurely. The only solution in a case like this is to fix the script so that your system works properly.

Whenever you change a system script, keep these recommendations in mind:

- As a precaution, *before modifying them in any way*, copy the files you intend to change, and write-protect the copies. Use the -p option of the cp command, if it is supported, to duplicate the modification times of the original files as well as their contents; this data can be invaluable should you need to roll back to a previous, working configuration. For example:

  ```
  # cp -p /etc/rc /etc/rc.orig
  # cp -p /etc/rc.local /etc/rc.local.orig
  # chmod a-w /etc/rc*.orig
  ```

  If your version of cp doesn't have a -p option, use a process like this one:

  ```
  # cd /etc
  # mv rc rc.orig; cp rc.orig rc
  # mv rc.local rc.local.orig; cp rc.local.orig rc.local
  # chmod a-w rc.orig rc.local.orig
  ```

  Similarly, when you make further modifications to an already customized script, save a copy before doing so, giving it a different extension, such as *.save*. This makes the modification process reversible; in the worst case, when the system won't boot because of bugs in your new versions—and this happens to everyone—you can just boot to single-user mode and copy the saved, working versions over the new ones.

- Make some provision for backing up modified scripts regularly so that they can be restored easily in an emergency. This topic is discussed in detail in Chapter 11.

- For security reasons, the system initialization scripts (including any old or saved copies of them) should be owned by *root* and not be writable by anyone but the owner. In some contexts, protecting them against any non-*root* access is appropriate.

Guidelines for writing initialization scripts

System boot scripts often provide both good and bad shell programming examples. If you write boot scripts or add commands to existing ones, keep these recommended programming practices in mind:

- Use full pathnames for all commands (or use one of the other methods for ensuring that the proper command executable is run).

- Explicitly test for the conditions under which the script is run if it is relying on the system being in some known state. Don't assume, for example, that there are no users on the system or that a daemon the script will be starting isn't already running; have the script check to make sure. Initialization scripts often get run in other contexts and at times other than those for which their writers originally designed them.

- Handle all cases that might arise from any given action, not just the ones that you expect to result. This includes handling invalid arguments to the script and providing a usage message.

- Provide lots of informational and error messages for the administrators who will see the results of the script.

- Include plenty of comments within the script itself.

Shutting Down a Unix System

From time to time, you will need to shut the system down. This is necessary for scheduled maintenance, running diagnostics, hardware changes or additions, and other administrative tasks.

During a clean system shutdown, the following actions take place:

- All users are notified that the system will be going down, preferably giving them some reasonable advance warning.

- All running processes are sent a signal telling them to terminate, allowing them time to exit gracefully, provided the program has made provisions to do so.

- All subsystems are shut down gracefully, via the commands they provide for doing so.

- All remaining users are logged off, and remaining processes are killed.

- Filesystem integrity is maintained by completing all pending disk updates.

- Depending on the type of shutdown, the system moves to single-user mode, the processor is halted, or the system is rebooted.

After taking these steps, the administrator can turn the power off, execute diagnostics, or perform other maintenance activities as appropriate.

Unix provides the shutdown command to accomplish all of this. Generally, shutdown sends a series of timed messages to all users who are logged on, warning them that the system is going down; after sending the last of these messages, it logs all users off the system and places the system in single-user mode.

 All Unix systems—even those running on PC hardware—should be shut down using the commands described in this section. This is necessary to ensure filesystem integrity and the clean termination of the various system services. If you care about what's on your disks, never just turn the power off.

There are two main variations of the shutdown command. The System V version is used by Solaris and HP-UX (the latter slightly modified from the standard), and the BSD version is used under AIX, FreeBSD, Linux, Solaris (in */usr/ucb*), and Tru64.

 On systems that provide it, the telinit command also provides a fast way to shut down (telinit S), halt (telinit 0) or reboot the system (telinit 6).

The System V shutdown Command

The standard System V shutdown command has the following form:

```
# shutdown [-y] [-g grace] [-i new-level]  message
```

where -y says to answer all shutdown prompts with yes automatically, *grace* specifies the number of seconds to wait before starting the process (the default is 60), *new-level* is the new run level in which to place the system (the default is single-user mode) and *message* is a text message sent to all users. This is the form used on Solaris systems.

Under HP-UX, the shutdown command has the following modified form:

```
# shutdown [-y] grace
```

where -y again says to answer prompts automatically with yes, and *grace* is the number of seconds to wait before shutting down. The keyword now may be substituted for *grace*. The shutdown command takes the system to single-user mode.

Here are some example commands that take the system to single-user mode in 15 seconds (automatically answering all prompts):

```
# shutdown -y -g 15 -i s "system going down"    Solaris
# shutdown -y 15                                HP-UX
```

The HP-UX shutdown also accepts two other options, -r and -h, which can be used to reboot the system immediately or to halt the processor once the shutdown is complete (respectively).

For example, these commands could be used to reboot the system immediately:

```
# shutdown -y -g 0 -i 6 "system reboot"          Solaris
# shutdown -y -r now                             HP-UX
```

HP-UX shutdown security

HP-UX also provides the file */etc/shutdown.allow*. If this file exists, a user must be listed in it in order to use the shutdown command (and *root* must be included). If the file does not exist, only *root* can run shutdown. Entries in the file consist of a hostname followed by a username, as in these examples:

```
hamlet     chavez     Chavez can shut down hamlet.
+          root       Root can shut down any system.
dalton     +          Anyone can shut down dalton.
```

As these examples illustrate, the plus sign serves as a wildcard. The *shutdown.allow* file also supports the percent sign as an additional wildcard character denoting all systems within a cluster; this wildcard is not valid on systems that are not part of a cluster.

The BSD-Style shutdown Command

BSD defines the shutdown command with the following syntax:

```
# shutdown [options] time message
```

where *time* can have three forms:

```
+m      Shut down in m minutes.
h:m     Shut down at the specified time (24-hour clock).
now     Begin the shutdown at once.
```

now should be used with discretion on multiuser systems.

message is the announcement that shutdown sends to all users; it may be any text string. For example, the following command will shut the system down in one hour:

```
# shutdown +60 "System going down for regular maintenance"
```

It warns users by printing the message "System going down for regular maintenance" on their screens. shutdown sends the first message immediately; as the shutdown time approaches, it repeats the warning with increasing frequency. These messages are also sent to users on the other systems on the local network who may be using the system's files via NFS.

By default, the BSD-style shutdown command also takes the system to single-user mode, except on AIX systems, where the processor is halted by default. Under AIX, the -m option must be used to specify shutting down to single-user mode.

Other options provide additional variations to the system shutdown process:

- shutdown -r says to reboot the system immediately after it shuts down. The reboot command performs the same function.

- `shutdown -h` says to halt the processor instead of shutting down to single-user mode. Once this process completes, the power may be safely turned off. You can also use the `halt` command to explicitly halt the processor once single-user mode is reached.

- `shutdown -k` inaugurates a fake system shutdown: the shutdown messages are sent out normally, but no shutdown actually occurs. I suppose the theory is that you can scare users off the system this way, but some users can be pretty persistent, preferring to be killed by `shutdown` rather than log out.

The Linux shutdown Command

The version of `shutdown` found on most Linux systems also has a -t option which may be used to specify the delay period between when the kernel sends the TERM signal to all remaining processes on the system and when it sends the KILL signal. The default is 30 seconds. The following command shuts down the system more rapidly, allowing only 5 seconds between the two signals:

```
# shutdown -h -t 5 now
```

The command version also provides a -a option, which provides a limited security mechanism for the `shutdown` command. When it is invoked with this option, the command determines whether any of the users listed in the file */etc/shutdown.allow* are currently logged in on the console (or any virtual console attached to it). If not, the `shutdown` command fails.

The purpose of this option is to prevent casual passers-by from typing Ctrl-Alt-Delete on the console and causing an (unwanted) system reboot. Accordingly, it is most often used in the *inittab* entry corresponding to this event.

Ensuring Disk Accuracy with the sync Command

As we've noted previously, one of the important parts of the shutdown process is syncing the disks. The sync command finishes all disk transactions and writes out all data to disk, guaranteeing that the system can be turned off without corrupting the files. You can execute this command manually if necessary:

```
# sync
# sync
```

Why is sync executed two or three times (or even more*)? I think this is a bit of Unix superstition. The sync command schedules but does not necessarily immediately perform the required disk writes, even though the Unix prompt returns immediately. Multiple sync commands raise the probability that the write will take place before

---

* Solaris administrators swear that you need to do it five times to be safe; otherwise, the password file will become corrupted. I have not been able to reproduce this.

you enter another command (or turn off the power) by taking up the time needed to complete the operation. However, the same effect can be obtained by waiting a few seconds for disk activity to cease before doing anything else. Typing "sync" several times gives you something to do while you're waiting.

There is one situation in which you do not want sync to be executed, either manually or automatically: when you have run fsck manually on the root filesystem. If you sync the disks at this point, you will rewrite the bad superblocks stored in the kernel buffers and undo the fixing fsck just did. In such cases, on BSD-based systems and under HP-UX, you must use the -n option to reboot or shutdown to suppress the usual automatic sync operation.

FreeBSD and System V are smarter about this issue. The fsck command generally will automatically remount the root filesystem when it has modified the root filesystem. Thus, no special actions are required to avoid syncing the disks.

Aborting a Shutdown

On most systems, the only way to abort a pending system shutdown is to kill the shutdown process. Determine the shutdown process' process ID by using a command like the following:

```
# ps -ax | grep shutdown        BSD-style
# ps -ef | grep shutdown        System V–style
```

Then use the kill command to terminate it:

```
# ps -ef | grep shutdown
25723 co S      0:01 /etc/shutdown -g300 -i6 -y
25800 co S      0:00 grep shutdown
# kill -9 25723
```

It's only safe to kill a shutdown command during its grace period; once it has actually started closing down the system, you're better off letting it finish and then rebooting.

The Linux version of shutdown includes a -c option that cancels a pending system shutdown. Every version should be so helpful.

Troubleshooting: Handling Crashes and Boot Failures

Even the best-maintained systems crash from time to time. A *crash* occurs when the system suddenly stops functioning. The extent of system failure can vary quite a bit, from a failure affecting every subsystem to one limited to a particular device or to the kernel itself. System *hang-ups* are a related phenomenon in which the system stops responding to input from any user or device or stops producing output, but the operating system nominally remains loaded. Such a system also may be described as *frozen*.

There are many causes of system crashes and hangups. These are among the most common:

- Hardware failures: failing disk controllers, CPU boards, memory boards, power supplies, disk head crashes, and so on.
- Unrecoverable hardware errors, such as double-bit memory errors. These sorts of problems may indicate hardware that is about to fail, but they also just happen from time to time.
- Power failures or surges due to internal power supply problems, external power outages, electrical storms, and other causes.
- Other environmental problems: roof leaks, air conditioning failure, etc.
- I/O problems involving a fatal error condition rather than a device malfunction.
- Software problems, ranging from fatal kernel errors caused by operating system bugs to (much less frequently) problems caused by users or third-party programs.
- Resource overcommitment (for example, running out of swap space). These situations can interact with bugs in the operating system to cause a crash or hang-up.

Some of these causes are easier to identify than others. Rebooting the system may seem like the most pressing concern when the system crashes, but it's just as important to gather the available information about why the system crashed while the data is still accessible.

Sometimes it's obvious why the system crashed, as when the power goes out. If the cause isn't immediately clear, the first source of information is any messages appearing on the system console. They are usually still visible if you check immediately, even if the system is set to reboot automatically. After they are no longer on the screen, you may still be able to find them by checking the system error log file, usually stored in */var/log/messages* (see Chapter 3 for more details), as well as any additional, vendor-supplied error facilities.

Beyond console messages lie crash dumps. Most systems automatically write a dump of kernel memory when the system crashes (if possible). These memory images can be examined using a debugging tool to see what the kernel was doing when it crashed. Obviously, these dumps are of use only for certain types of crashes in which the system state at the time of the crash is relevant. Analyzing crash dumps is beyond the scope of this book, but you should know where crash dumps go on your system and how to access them, if only to be able to save them for your field service engineers or vendor technical support personnel.

Crash dumps are usually written to the system disk swap partition. Since this area may be overwritten when the system is booted, some provisions need to be made to save its contents. The savecore command solves this problem, as we have seen (the command is called savecrash under HP-UX).

If you want to be able to save crash dumps, you need to ensure that the primary swap partition is large enough. Unless your system has the ability to compress crash dumps as they are created (e.g., Tru64) or selectively dump only the relevant parts of memory, the swap partition needs to be at least as large as physical memory.

If your system crashes and you are *not* collecting crash dumps by default, but you want to get one, boot the system to single-user mode and execute `savecore` by hand. Don't let the system boot to multiuser mode before saving the crash dump; once the system reaches multiuser mode, it's too late.

AIX also provides the `snap` command for collecting crash dump and other system data for later analysis.

Power-Failure Scripts

There are two other action keywords available for *inittab* that we've not yet considered: *powerfail* and *powerwait*. They define entries that are invoked if a *SIGPWR* signal is sent to the `init` process, which indicates an imminent power failure. This signal is generated only for detectable power failures: those caused by faulty power supplies, fans, and the like, or via a signal from an uninterruptable power supply (UPS). *powerwait* differs from *powerfail* in that it requires `init` to wait for its process to complete before going on to the next applicable *inittab* entry.

The scripts invoked by these entries are often given the name `rc.powerfail`. Their purpose is to do whatever can be done to protect the system in the limited time available. Accordingly, they focus on syncing the disks to prevent data loss that might occur if disk operations are still pending when the power does go off.

Linux provides a third action, *powerokwait*, that is invoked when power is restored and tells `init` to wait for the corresponding process to complete before going on to any additional entries.

When the System Won't Boot

As with system crashes, there can be many reasons why a system won't boot. To solve such problems, you first must figure out what the specific problem is. You'll need to have a detailed understanding of what a normal boot process looks like so that you can pinpoint exactly where the failure is occurring. Having a hard copy of normal boot messages is often very helpful. One thing to keep in mind is that boot problems always result from some sort of change to the system; systems don't just stop working. You need to figure out *what* has changed. Of course, if you've just made modifications to the system, they will be the prime suspects.

This section lists some of the most common causes of booting problems, along with suggestions for what to do in each case.

Bad or flaky hardware

Check the obvious first. The first thing to do when there is a device failure is to see if there is a simple problem that is easily fixed. Is the device plugged in and turned on? Have any cables connecting it to the system come loose? Does it have the correct SCSI ID (if applicable)? Is the SCSI chain terminated? You get the idea.

Try humoring the device. Sometimes devices are just cranky and can be coaxed back to life. For example, if a disk won't come on line, try power-cycling it. If that doesn't work, try shutting off the power to the entire system. Then power up the devices one by one, beginning with peripherals and ending with the CPU if possible, waiting for each one to settle down before going on to the next device. Sometimes this approach works on the second or third try even after failing on the first. When you decide you've had enough, call field service. When you use this approach, once you've turned the power off, leave it off for a minute or so to allow the device's internal capacitors to discharge fully.

Device failures. If a critical hardware device fails, there is not much you can do except call field service. Failures can occur suddenly, and the first reboot after the system power has been off often stresses marginal devices to the point that they finally fail.

Unreadable filesystems on working disks

You can distinguish this case from the previous one by the kind of error you get. Bad hardware usually generates error messages about the hardware device itself, as a whole. A bad filesystem tends to generate error messages later in the boot process, when the operating system tries to access it.

Bad root filesystem. How you handle this problem depends on which filesystem is damaged. If it is the root filesystem, then you may be able to recreate it from a bootable backup/recovery tape (or image on the network) or by booting from alternate media (such as the distribution tape, CD-ROM, or diskette from which the operating system was installed), remaking the filesystem and restoring its files from backup. In the worst case, you'll have to reinstall the operating system and then restore files that you have changed from backup.

Restoring other filesystems. On the other hand, if the system can still boot to single-user mode, things are not nearly so dire. Then you will definitely be able to remake the filesystem and restore its files from backup.

Damage to non-filesystem areas of a disk

Damaged boot areas. Sometimes, it is the boot partition or even the boot blocks of the root disk that are damaged. Some Unix versions provide utilities for restoring these areas without having to reinitialize the entire disk. You'll probably have to boot from a bootable backup tape or other distribution media to use them if you discover the problem only at boot time. Again, the worst-case scenario is having to reinstall the operating system.

Corrupted partition tables. On PCs, it is possible to wipe out a disk's partition tables if a problem occurs while you are editing them with the `fdisk` disk partitioning utility. If the power goes off or `fdisk` hangs, the disk's partition information can be incorrect or wiped out entirely. This problem can also happen on larger systems as well, although its far less common to edit the partition information except at installation (and often not even then).

The most important thing to do in this case is not to panic. This happened to me on a disk where I had three operating systems installed, and I really didn't want to have to reinstall all of them. The fix is actually quite easy: simply rerun `fdisk` and recreate the partitions as they were before, and all will be well again. However, this does mean that you need to have complete, detailed, and accessible (e.g., hardcopy) records of how the partitions were set up.

Incompatible hardware

Problems with a new device. Sometimes, a system hangs when you try to reboot it after adding new hardware. This can happen when the system does not support the type of device that you've just added, either because the system needs to be reconfigured to do so or because it simply does not support the device.

In the first case, you can reconfigure the system to accept the new hardware by building a new kernel or doing whatever else is appropriate on your system. However, if you find out that the device is not supported by your operating system, you will probably have to remove it to get the system to boot, after which you can contact the relevant vendors for instructions and assistance. It usually saves time in the long run to check compatibility before purchasing or installing new hardware.

Problems after an upgrade. Hardware incompatibility problems also crop up occasionally after operating system upgrades on systems whose hardware has not changed, due to withdrawn support for previously supported hardware or because of undetected bugs in the new release. You can confirm that the new operating system is the problem if the system still boots correctly from bootable backup tapes or installation media from the previous release. If you encounter sudden device-related problems after an OS upgrade, contacting the operating system vendor is usually the best recourse.

Device conflicts. On PCs, devices communicate with the CPU using a variety of methods: interrupt signals, DMA channels, I/O addresses/ports, and memory addresses (listed in decreasing order of conflict likelihood). All devices that operate at the same time must have unique values for the items relevant to it (values are set via jumpers or other mechanisms on the device or its controller or via a software utility provided by the manufacturer for this purpose). Keeping detailed and accurate records of the settings used by all of the devices on the system will make it easy to select appropriate ones when adding a new device and to track down conflicts should they occur.

System configuration errors

Errors in configuration files. This type of problem is usually easy to recognize. More than likely, you've just recently changed something, and the boot process dies at a clearly identifiable point in the process. The solution is to boot to single-user mode and then correct the erroneous configuration file or reinstall a saved, working version of it.

Unbootable kernels. Sometimes, when you build a new kernel, it won't boot. There are at least two ways that this can occur: you may have made a mistake building or configuring the kernel, or there may be bugs in the kernel that manifest themselves on your system. The latter happens occasionally when updating the kernel to the latest release level on Linux systems and when you forget to run lilo after building a new kernel.

In either case, the first thing to do is to reboot the system using a working, saved kernel that you've kept for just this contingency. Once the system is up, you can track down the problem with the new kernel. In the case of Linux kernels, if you're convinced that you haven't made any mistakes, you can check the relevant newsgroups to see if anyone else has seen the same problem. If no information is available, the best thing to do is wait for the next patch level to become available (it doesn't take very long) and then try rebuilding the kernel again. Frequently, the problem will disappear.

Errors in initialization files are a very common cause of boot problems. Usually, once an error is encountered, the boot stops and leaves the system in single-user mode. The incident described in Chapter 3 about the workstation that wouldn't boot ended up being a problem of this type. The user had been editing the initialization files on his workstation, and he had an error in the first line of */etc/rc* (I found out later). So only the root disk got mounted. On this system, */usr* was on a separate disk partition, and the commands stored in */bin* used shared libraries stored under */usr*. There was no ls, no cat, not even ed.

As I told you before, I remembered that echo could list filenames using the shell's internal wildcard expansion mechanism (and it didn't need the shared library). I typed:

```
# echo /etc/rc*
```

and found out there was an *rc.dist* file there. Although it was probably out of date, it could get things going. I executed it manually:

```
# . /etc/rc.dist
```

The moral of this story is, of course, *test, test, test*. Note once more that obsessive prudence is your best hope every time.

CHAPTER 5

TCP/IP Networking

Since very few computers exist in isolation, managing networks is an inextricable part of system administration. In fact, in some circles, the designations "system administrator" and "network administrator" are more or less synonymous.

This chapter provides an overview of TCP/IP networking on Unix systems. It begins with a general discussion of TCP/IP concepts and procedures and then covers basic network configuration for client systems, including the variations and quirks of each of our reference operating systems. There are other discussions of network-related topics throughout the remainder of the book, including in-depth treatments of network security issues in Chapter 7 and coverage of administering and configuring network facilities and services in Chapter 8.

For a book-length discussion of TCP/IP networking, consult Craig Hunt's excellent book, *TCP/IP Network Administration* (O'Reilly & Associates).

Understanding TCP/IP Networking

The term "TCP/IP" is shorthand for a large collection of protocols and services that are used for internetworking computer systems. In any given implementation, TCP/IP encompasses operating system components, user and administrative commands and utilities, configuration files, and device drivers, as well as the kernel and library support upon which they all depend. Many of the basic TCP/IP networking concepts are not operating system–specific, so we'll begin this chapter by considering TCP/IP networking in a general way.

Figure 5-1 depicts an example TCP/IP network including several kinds of network connections. Assuming that these computers are in reasonably close physical proximity to one another, this network would be classed as a *local area network* (LAN).*

---

* You may wonder whether this is one LAN or two LANs. In fact, the term LAN is not precisely defined, and usage varies.

In contrast, a wide area network (WAN) consists of multiple LANs, often widely separated geographically (see Figure 5-5, later in this chapter). Different physical network types are also characteristic of the LAN/WAN distinction (e.g., Ethernet versus frame relay).

Each computer system on the network is known as a *host** and is identified by both a name and an IP address (more on these later). Most of the hosts in this example have a permanent name and IP address. However, two of them, *italy* and *chile*, have their IP address dynamically assigned when they first connect to the network (typically, at boot time), using the DHCP facility (indicated by the highlighted final element in the IP address).

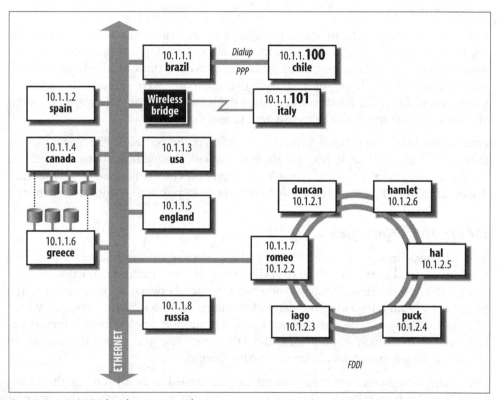

Figure 5-1. TCP/IP local area network

If I am logged in to, say, *spain* (either by direct connection or via a modem), *spain* is said to be the *local* system, and *brazil* is a *remote* system with respect to processes running on *spain*. A system that performs a task for a remote host is called a *server*; the host for whom the task is performed is called the *client*. Thus, if I request a file from *brazil*, that system is a server for the client *spain* during that transfer.

---

* The term *node* is sometimes used as a synonym for host in non-Unix networking lexicons.

In our example, the network is divided into two *subnets* that communicate via the host *romeo*. The systems named for countries are all connected to an Ethernet backbone, and those named for Shakespearean characters are connected via FDDI.

The host *romeo* serves as a *gateway* between the two subnets. It is part of both subnets and passes data from one to the other. In this case, the gateway is a computer with two network interfaces (adapters). However, it is probably more common to use a special-purpose computer known as a *router* for this purpose.

The host named *italy* connects to the network using a wireless connection. The wireless bridge (colored black in the illustration) accepts wireless connections and connects their originating computers to the hosts in the LAN by serving as the conduit to the Ethernet.

Host *chile* connects to the network by dialing up a modem connected to *brazil*, using the PPP facility. Unlike a regular dialup session, which simply starts a normal login session on the server, *dialup networking* connections like this one allow full network participation by the dialing-in host, as if that computer were directly connected to the network. Once the initial connection is made, the fact that the connection actually goes through *brazil* will be transparent to users on *chile*.

Finally, the illustration shows Unix disk sharing via the Network File System (NFS) facility. NFS allows TCP/IP hosts to share disks, with remote filesystems merged into the local directory tree. Users on *canada* and *greece* potentially have access to four disk drives, even though both systems only have three disks physically connected to them.

Media and Topologies

TCP/IP networks can run over a variety of *physical media*. Traditionally, most networks have used some sort of coaxial cable (thick or thin), twisted pair cable, or fiber optic cable. Network *adapters* provide the interface between a computer and the physical medium comprising the network connection. In hardware terms, they usually consist of a single board. Network adapters support one or more communication protocols, which specify how the computers use the physical medium to exchange data. Most protocols are not media-specific.

For example, Ethernet communications can be carried over all four of the media types mentioned previously, and FDDI networks can run over either fiber optic or twisted pair cable. Such protocols specify networking characteristics, such as the structure of the lowest level data unit, the way that data moves from host to host across the physical medium, how multiple simultaneous network accesses are handled, and the like. Currently, Ethernet accounts for more than 80% of all networks.

Figure 5-2 illustrates the various types of connectors you may see on Ethernet network cables. These days, the one at the bottom is the most prevalent: unshielded twisted pair (UTP) cable with an RJ-45 connector. The type of cable required for 100 Mb/sec communication is known as Category 5. Category 5E cable is used for 1000 Mb/sec (Gigabit) Ethernet.

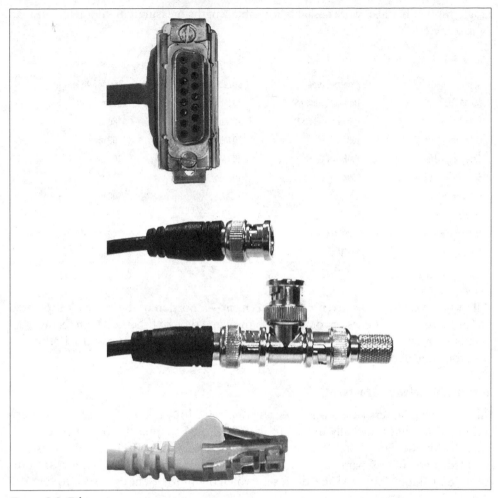

Figure 5-2. Ethernet connectors

The other items in Figure 5-2 illustrate older cable types, which you may still run into. The top item is the most common connector for RG-11 coax. The middle two items are connectors used for RG-58 coax (Thinnet). The upper item in the pair is a simple connector. The lower item illustrates the tap design used for a computer connector. The connector is part of a T junction attached to the coaxial cable. In the illustration, there is a terminator on the right side of the tap, but a continuation of the cable could also be placed there.

Table 5-1 summarizes some useful characteristics of the various Ethernet media. Note that the maximum cable length for UTP at any speed is 100 meters. Longer distances require fiber optic cable, of which there are two main varieties. Single-mode fiber equipment is technically more complex than multimode fiber because it uses a laser to force the light traveling within the cable to a single frequency ("mode"), making the optical system and the connectors much more expensive to produce. However, single-mode fiber also works reliably for cable lengths measured in kilometers instead of just meters.

Table 5-1. Popular media characteristics

Media	Ethernet type	Speed	Maximum length
RG-11 coax	Thicknet (10Base5)	10 Mb/sec	500 m
RG-58 coax	Thinnet (10Base2)	10 Mb/sec	180 m
Category 3 UTP	10BaseT	10 Mb/sec	100 m
Category 5 UTP	100BaseTX	100 Mb/sec	100 m
Single-mode fiber	100BaseFX	100 Mb/sec	20 km
Category 5E UTP	Gigabit (1000BaseT)	1 Gb/sec	100 m
Single-mode fiber	1000BaseLX	1 Gb/sec	3 km
Multimode fiber	1000BaseSX	1 Gb/sec	440 m
Wireless	802.11b[a]	11 Mb/sec	100 m

[a] Not an Ethernet medium.

All of the hosts within a given *network segment*—a portion of the network separated from the rest by switches or routers—use the same type of Ethernet. Connecting segments with different characteristics requires special hardware that can use both types and translate between them.

Identifying network adapters

All network adapters have a *Media Access Control (MAC) address*, which is a numerical identifier that is globally unique to that individual adapter. For Ethernet devices, MAC addresses are 48-bit values expressed as twelve hexadecimal digits, usually divided into colon-separated pairs: for example, 00:00:f8:23:31:a1. There are thus over 280 trillion distinct MAC addresses (which ought to be enough, even for us).

MAC addresses were formerly referred to as *Ethernet addresses* and are occasionally called *hardware addresses*. The first 24 bits of the MAC address is a hardware vendor–specific prefix called an Organizationally Unique Identifiier (OUI). Knowing the OUI can be helpful if you ever have to figure out which device corresponds to a specific MAC address. OUIs are assigned by the IEEE, which maintains the master database of OUI-to-vendor mappings.

You can find the MAC address for an adapter on a Unix system using these commands:[*]

---

[*] The term *network interface* is commonly used as a synonym for network adapter (as in NIC). In the Unix world, an interface is really a logical entity consisting of an adapter plus its operating system level configuration. On AIX systems, adapters and interfaces have different names (e.g., *ent0* and *en0*, respectively).

AIX	entstat *adapter* (for Ethernet adapters)
FreeBSD	ifconfig *interface*
HP-UX	lanscan
Linux	ifconfig *interface*
Solaris	ifconfig *interface* (must be run as *root*)
Tru64	ifconfig -v *interface*

There is also a special network interface present on every computer, known as the *loopback interface*. There is no physical network adapter corresponding to the loopback interface, but even so, it is sometimes called the *loopback device*. The loopback interface allows a computer to send network packets to itself: implemented in software, it intercepts the packets and redirects them back to the local host, as if they had arrived from an external source.

Hosts within a local area network can be connected in a variety of arrangements known as *topologies*. For example, the 10.1.1 subnet in Figure 5-1 uses a bus topology in which each host taps into a backbone, which is standard for coax Ethernet networks. Often, the backbone is not a cable at all but merely a junction point where connections from the various hosts on the network converge, commonly known as a *hub* or a *switch*, depending on its capabilities. The 10.1.2 subnet uses a ring topology.

One of the fundamental characteristics of Ethernet is also illustrated in the diagram. Each host on an Ethernet is logically connected to every other host: to communicate with any other host, a system sends a message out on the Ethernet, where it arrives at the target host directly. By contrast, for the other network, messages between *duncan* and *puck* must be handled by two other hosts first. At typical network speeds, however, this difference is not significant.

Networking protocols may include a required topology as part of their specification, as in the 10.1.2 subnet in Figure 5-1. For example, full FDDI networks are composed of two counter-rotating rings (two duplicate rings through which data flows in opposite directions), an arrangement designed to enable a network to easily bypass breaks in one ring and to scale well as network load increases.

 Although I've used FDDI quite a bit here for illustration purposes, general-purpose FDDI networks are pretty rare. FDDI is currently used in storage area networks (SANs) to interconnect the storage media (disks) and the one or two hosts to which they are attached.

The Ethernet protocol is based on a communication strategy known as Carrier Sense Multiple Access/Collision Detection (CSMA/CD). On an Ethernet, a device that wants to transmit a message is able to determine if any other device is already using the medium (*carrier sense*). In other words, a device waits until there is a lull in activity before trying to "talk." If two or more devices both start to talk at the same time, both of them stop (*collision detection*), and they each wait a semi-random amount of time before trying again in the hopes of avoiding a second collision. "Multiple access" refers to the fact that any host is able to use the communication medium.

This is a lightweight protocol that works very well for most common networking uses. Its one disadvantage is that it does not perform as well under heavy loads as do some other topologies (e.g., token rings). In fact, under heavy network loads, the overhead caused by frequent collisions and the resulting wait times can become a significant factor in actual network throughput (although this is less true of current UTP-based 100 Mb networks than it is of older, coax-based 10 Mb networks).

Protocols and Layers

Network communication is organized as a series of layers. With the exception of the layer referring to the physical transmission medium, these layers are logical or conceptual rather than literal or physical, and they are implemented in the networking software running on computers and other network devices. Every network message moves down through the layers on its originating system, travels across the physical medium, and then moves up through the same stack of layers on the destination system. In addition, as it passes through various network devices, it may travel partway up and down the stack (as we'll see).

No discussion of any network architecture is complete without at least a brief mention of the Open Systems Interconnection (OSI) Reference Model. This description of networking has seldom been the basis of actual network implementations, but it can be quite helpful in clearly identifying the distinct functions necessary for network communications to occur. Things are not really divided up according to its specification in real networks, because many of the distinct communication phases and functions that it identifies are handled equally well or more efficiently by a single network layer (with correspondingly lower overhead). The OSI Reference Model is probably best thought of as an after-the-fact, generalized, logical description of network communications.

Figure 5-3 lists the layers in the OSI Reference Model and those actually used in TCP/IP implementations, including the most important protocols defined for each layer.

When a network operation is initiated by a user command or program, it travels down the protocol stack on the local host (via software), across the physical medium to the destination host, and then back up the protocol stack on the remote host to the proper recipient process. For example, a network transmission originating from a user program like rcp moves down the stack on the local system from the Application layer to Network Access layer, travels across the wire to the destination system, and then moves up the stack from the Network Access layer to the Application layer, finally communicating with a daemon process in the latter. Replies to this message travel the same route in reverse.

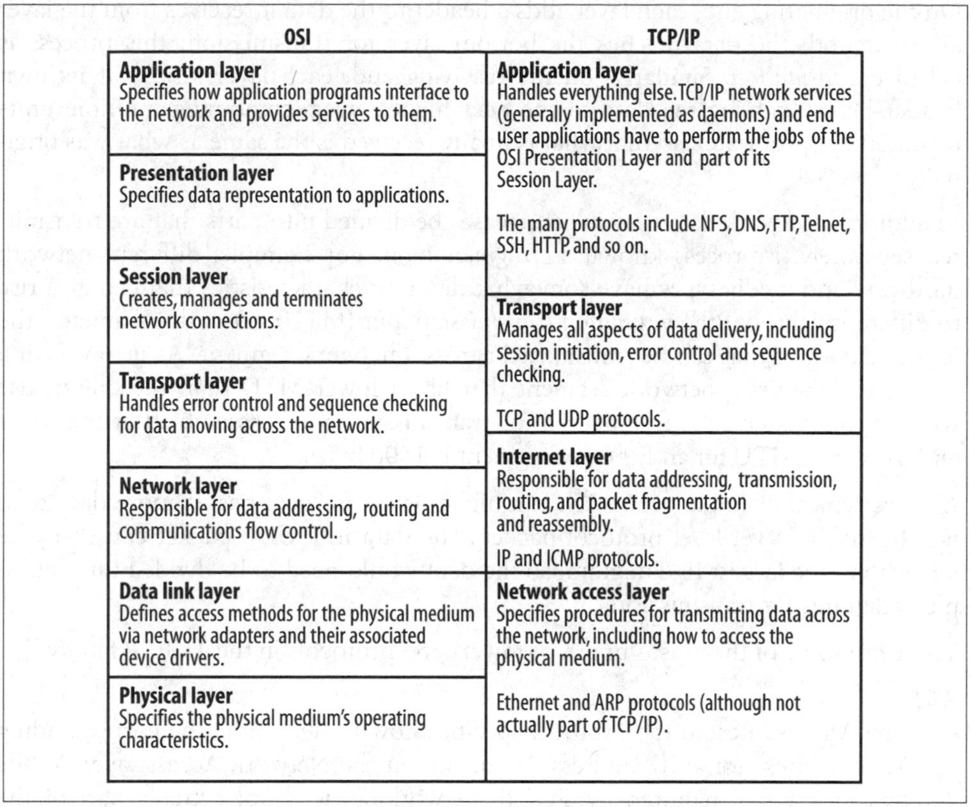

OSI	TCP/IP
Application layer Specifies how application programs interface to the network and provides services to them.	**Application layer** Handles everything else. TCP/IP network services (generally implemented as daemons) and end user applications have to perform the jobs of the OSI Presentation Layer and part of its Session Layer. The many protocols include NFS, DNS, FTP, Telnet, SSH, HTTP, and so on.
Presentation layer Specifies data representation to applications.	
Session layer Creates, manages and terminates network connections.	**Transport layer** Manages all aspects of data delivery, including session initiation, error control and sequence checking. TCP and UDP protocols.
Transport layer Handles error control and sequence checking for data moving across the network.	
Network layer Responsible for data addressing, routing and communications flow control.	**Internet layer** Responsible for data addressing, transmission, routing, and packet fragmentation and reassembly. IP and ICMP protocols.
Data link layer Defines access methods for the physical medium via network adapters and their associated device drivers.	**Network access layer** Specifies procedures for transmitting data across the network, including how to access the physical medium.
Physical layer Specifies the physical medium's operating characteristics.	Ethernet and ARP protocols (although not actually part of TCP/IP).

Figure 5-3. Idealized and real network protocol stacks

Each network layer is equipped to handle data in particular predefined units. The traditional names of these units for the two main transport protocols are listed in Table 5-2.

Table 5-2. Traditional[a] network data unit names

Layer	TCP Protocol	UDP Protocol
Application	stream	message
Transport	segment	packet
Internet	datagram	
Network Access	frame	

[a] To complicate things even further, current usage seems to be moving toward calling the UDP transport layer unit a "datagram" and the IP layer data unit a "packet."

The term *packet* is also used generically to refer to any network transmission (including in this book).

On the originating end, each layer adds a header to the data it receives from the layer above it until the data reaches the bottom layer for transmission; this process is called *encapsulation*. Similarly, on the receiving end, each layer strips off its own header before passing the data to the next higher layer (combining multiple units together if appropriate), so that what is finally received is the same as what was originally sent.

In addition, network data may in some cases be divided into parts that are transmitted separately, a process known as *fragmentation*. For example, different network hardware and media types have somewhat different characteristics that can give rise to different values of the *maximum transmission unit* (MTU) network parameter: the largest data unit that can be transmitted across a network segment. As it travels, if a packet encounters a network segment that has a lower MTU than the one in use where it originated, it is fragmented for transmission and reassembled at the other end. A typical MTU for an Ethernet segment is 1500 bytes.

A more typical example occurs when a higher-level protocol passes more data than will fit into a lower-level protocol packet. The data in a UDP packet can easily be larger than the largest IP datagram, so the data would need to be divided into multiple datagrams for transmission.

These are some of the most important lower-level protocols in the TCP/IP family:

ARP

> The Address Resolution Protocol specifies how to determine the corresponding MAC address for an IP address. It operates at the Network Access layer. While this protocol is required by TCP/IP networking, it is not actually part of the TCP/IP suite.

IP

> The Internet Protocol manages low-level data transmission, routing, and fragmentation/reassembly. It operates at the Internet layer.

TCP

> The Transmission Control Protocol provides reliable network communication sessions between applications, including flow control and error detection and correction. It operates at the Transport layer.

UDP

> The User Datagram Protocol provides "connectionless" communication between applications. In contrast to TCP, data transmitted using UDP is not delivery-verified; if expected data fails to arrive, the application simply requests it again. UDP operates at the Transport layer.

We'll consider other protocols when we look at network services in Chapter 8.

Ports, Services, and Daemons

Network operations are performed by a variety of network *services*, consisting of the software and other facilities needed to perform a specific type of network task. For example, the *ftp* service performs file transfer operations using the FTP protocol; the software program that does the actual work is the FTP daemon (whose actual name varies).

A *service* is defined by the combination of a transport protocol—TCP or UDP—and a port: a logical network connection endpoint identified by a number. The TCP and UDP port numbering schemes are part of the definition of these protocols.

 Port numbers need be unique only within a given transport protocol. TCP and UDP each define a unique set of ports, even though they use the same port numbers. However, recent practice is to assign both the UDP and TCP ports to standard services.

Various configuration files in the */etc* directory indicate the standard mappings between port numbers and TCP/IP services:

- */etc/protocols* lists the protocol numbers assigned to the various transport protocols in the TCP/IP family. Although this list is large, most systems need to use only the TCP, UDP, and ICMP protocols.
- */etc/services* lists the port numbers assigned to the various TCP and UDP services.

Individual TCP/IP connections are defined by a pair of host-port combinations, each known as a *socket*, which is unique during the connection's lifetime: source IP address, source port, destination IP address, destination port (as seen from the client's point of view). For example, when a user first connects to a remote host using ssh, it contacts that computer on the standard port 22 (such ports are commonly referred to as *well-known ports*). The process is assigned a random (*dynamically allocated* or *ephemeral*) port which is used as the *source* (outgoing) port by the client. Multiple simultaneous ssh sessions on the destination system are possible using this scheme since each one will have a different source port/source IP address combination and thus a unique socket.

For example, the first ssh connection might use port 2222 as the source port. The next ssh connection might use port 3333. In this way, the messages intended for the two sessions can be easily distinguished, even if they came from the same user on the same remote system.

Most standard services usually use ports below 1024, and such ports are restricted to *root* (at least on Unix systems). Table 5-3 lists some common services and their associated ports. In most cases, both the TCP and UDP ports are assigned to the service; for the few exceptions, the protocol follows the port number (as in */etc/services* entries). The shaded portion of the table contains port numbers for commonly used services from non-Unix operating systems.

Table 5-3. Important services and their associated ports

Service	Port(s)	Service	Port(s)
FTP	21 (also 20), 990 (secure; also 989)	NetBIOS SAMBA	137-139
SSH	22	SRC (AIX)	200/udp
TELNET	23, 992 (secure)	Remote Exec	512/tcp
SMTP	25, 465 (secure)	Remote Login	513/tcp
DNS	53	Remote Shell	514/tcp
DHCP (BOOTP)	67 (server), 68 (client)	SYSLOG	514/udp, 601 (reliable)
TFTP	69	LPD	515
FINGER	79	ROUTE	520
HTTP	80, 443 (secure)	NFS	2049, 4045/udp (Solaris)
Kerberos	88, 749-50	RSYNC	873
POP-2	109	X11	6000-19, 6063, 7100 (fonts)
POP-3	110, 995 (secure)	AppleTalk	201-208
RPC	111	IPX	213
NTP	123	SMB	445
IMAP	143 (v2), 220 (v3), 993 (v4 secure)	QuickTime	458
SNMP	161, 162 (traps)	Active Directory Global Catalog	3268, 3269 (secure)
LDAP	389, 636 (secure)	America Online	5190-5193

Administrative Commands

Unix operating systems include a number of generic TCP/IP user commands that may be used to display various network-related information, including the following:

hostname
> Display the name of the local system

ifconfig
> Display information about network interfaces (also configure them)

ping
> Perform a simple network connectivity test

arp
> Display or modify the IP-to-MAC address-translation tables

netstat
> Display various network usage statistics

route
> Display or modify the static routing tables

```
traceroute
```
Determine the route to a specified target host

```
nslookup
```
Determine IP address-to-hostname and other translations produced by the Domain Name Service

We'll see examples of many of these commands later in this chapter.

A Sample TCP/IP Conversation

All of these concepts will come together when we look at a sample TCP/IP conversation. We'll consider what must happen in order for the following command to be successfully executed:

```
hamlet> finger chavez@greece
Login name: chavez                    In real life: Rachel Chavez
Directory: /home/chem/new/chavez      Shell: /bin/csh
On since Apr 28 08:35:42 on pts/3 from puck
No Plan.
```

This finger command causes a network connection to be formed between the hosts *hamlet* and *greece*, and more specifically between the finger client process running on *hamlet* and the fingerd daemon on *greece* (which will be started by *greece*'s inetd process).

The finger service uses the TCP transport protocol (number 6) and port 79. TCP connections are always created via a three-step handshaking process. Here is a dump of the packet corresponding to Step 1, in which the most important fields have been highlighted:[*]

```
ETH: ====( 60 bytes recd on en0 )====Sun Apr 28 13:38:27 1996
ETH: [ 32:21:a6:e1:7f:c1   18:33:e4:2a:43:2d ]  type 800  (IP)
IP:  < SRC =      192.168.2.6   (hamlet)
IP:  < DST =      192.168.1.6   (greece)
IP:  ip_v=4, ip_hl=20, ip_tos=0, ip_len=44, ip_id=56107, ip_off=0
IP:  ip_ttl=60, ip_sum=f84, ip_p = 6 (TCP)
TCP: <source port=1031, destination port=79(finger)>
TCP: th_seq=d83ab201, th_ack=0
TCP: th_off=6, flags<SYN>
TCP: th_win=16384, th_sum=3577, th_urp=0        data in ASCII
data: 00000000      020405b4                    |....          |
```

Each line of this packet display is labeled with the protocol that created it: ETH lines were created at the Ethernet level (Network Access layer), IP lines by the IP protocol (Internet layer), and TCP lines by the TCP protocol (Transport layer).

Lines labeled as data are used by whatever layer is sending data in the packet. The data is dumped in hex and ASCII (the latter at the extreme right between the two

---

[*] Slightly modified from that created with AIX's iptrace and ipreport utilities.

vertical bars). In this case, the data consists of TCP options (negotiating a maximum segment length of 1460 bytes) and not finger-related data.

The initial ETH line is actually created by the packet dumping software, and it lists the date and time of the message. The actual data from the packet begins with the second ETH line, which lists the MAC addresses of the two hosts.

The IP lines indicate that the packet comes from the TCP transport protocol (*ip_p*), as well as its source and destination hosts. The TCP header indicates the destination port, allowing the network service to be identified. The *th_seq* field in this header indicates the sequence number for this packet. The TCP protocol requires that all packets be acknowledged by the receiving host (although not necessarily individually). The SYN flag (for synchronize) by itself indicates an attempt to create a new network connection, and in this case, the sequence number is an initial sequence number for the conversation. It will be incremented by one for each byte of data transmitted.

Here are the next two packets in the sequence, which complete the handshake:

```
ETH: ====( 60 bytes trans on en0 )====Sun Apr 28 13:38:27 1996
ETH: [ 18:33:e4:2a:43:2d -> 32:21:a6:e1:7f:c1 ]  type 800  (IP)
IP:  < SRC =      192.168.1.6 >  (greece)
IP:  < DST =      192.168.2.6 >  (hamlet)
IP:  ip_v=4, ip_hl=20, ip_tos=0, ip_len=44, ip_id=54298, ip_off=0
IP:  ip_ttl=60, ip_sum=1695, ip_p = 6 (TCP)
TCP: <source port=79(finger), destination port=1031 >
TCP: th_seq=d71b9601, th_ack=d83ab202
TCP: th_off=6, flags<SYN | ACK>
TCP: th_win=16060, th_sum=c98c, th_urp=0
data: 00000000      020405b4                    |....          |

ETH: ====( 60 bytes recd on en0 )====Sun Apr 28 13:38:27 1996
ETH: [ 32:21:a6:e1:7f:c1 -> 18:33:e4:2a:43:2d ]  type 800  (IP)
IP:  < SRC =      192.168.2.6 >  (hamlet)
IP:  < DST =      192.168.1.6 >  (greece)
IP:  ip_v=4, ip_hl=20, ip_tos=0, ip_len=40, ip_id=56108, ip_off=0
IP:  ip_ttl=60, ip_sum=f87, ip_p = 6 (TCP)
TCP: <source port=1031, destination port=79(finger) >
TCP: th_seq=d83ab202, th_ack=d71b9602
TCP: th_off=5, flags<ACK>
TCP: th_win=16060, th_sum=e149, th_urp=0
```

In the packet with sequence number d71b9601, sent from *greece* back to *hamlet*, both the SYN and ACK (acknowledge) flags are set. The ACK is the acknowledgement of the previous packet, and the SYN establishes communication from *greece* to *hamlet*. The contents of the *th_ack* field indicate the last byte of data that has been received (one byte so far). The *th_seq* field indicates *greece*'s starting sequence number. The next packet simply acknowledges *greece*'s SYN, and the connection is complete.

Now we are ready to get some work done (packets are abbreviated from here on):

```
IP:  < SRC =      192.168.2.6 >  (hamlet)
IP:  < DST =      192.168.1.6 >  (greece)
```

```
TCP: <source port=1031, destination port=79(finger) >
TCP: th_seq=d83ab202, th_ack=d71b9602
TCP: th_off=5, flags<PUSH | ACK>
TCP: th_win=16060, th_sum=4c86, th_urp=0
data: 00000000 61656C65 656E3A29              |chavez        |
```

This packet sends the data "chavez" to fingerd on *greece* (the final characters don't print); user data is indicated by the presence of the PUSH flag. In this case, the data is from the Application layer. The packet also acknowledges the previous packet from *greece*. This data is passed up the various network layers, to be delivered ultimately to fingerd.

greece acknowledges this packet and eventually sends fingerd's response:

```
IP:   < SRC =      192.168.1.6 >  (greece)
IP:   < DST =      192.168.2.6 >  (hamlet)
TCP: <source port=79(finger), destination port=1031 >
TCP: th_seq=d71b9602, th_ack=d83ab20c
TCP: th_off=5, flags<PUSH | ACK>
TCP: th_win=16060, th_sum=e29b, th_urp=0
data: |Login name: chavez ..In real life: Rachel Chavez..Director|
data: |y: /home/chem/new/chavez ..Shell:/bin/csh. On since Apr 28|
data: | 08:35:42 on pts/3 from puck..No Plan...                  |
```

The output from the finger command constitutes the data in this packet (the hex version is omitted). The packet also acknowledges data received from *hamlet* (10 bytes since the previous packet).

All that remains is to close down the connection:

```
IP:   < SRC =      192.168.1.6 >  (greece)
IP:   < DST =      192.168.2.6 >  (hamlet)
TCP: th_off=5, flags<FIN | ACK>

IP:   < SRC =      192.168.2.6 >  (hamlet)
IP:   < DST =      192.168.1.6 >  (greece)
TCP: th_off=5, flags<FIN | ACK>

IP:   < SRC =      192.168.1.6 >  (greece)
IP:   < DST =      192.168.2.6 >  (hamlet)
TCP: th_off=5, flags<ACK>
```

The FIN flag indicates that a connection is to be terminated. *greece* indicates that it is finished first. *hamlet* sends its own FIN (also acknowledging that packet), which *greece* acknowledges.

Names and Addresses

Every system on a network has a *hostname*. When fully qualified, this name must be unique within the relevant naming space. Hostnames let users refer to any computer on the network by using a short, easily remembered name rather than the host's network address.

Each system on a TCP/IP network also has an *IP address* that is unique for all hosts on the network. Systems with multiple network adapters usually have a separate IP address for each adapter.

When an actual network operation occurs, the hostnames of the systems involved are used to determine their numerical IP addresses, either by looking them up in a table or requesting translation from a server designated for this task.

A traditional Internet network address is a sequence of 4 bytes* (32 bits). Network addresses are usually written in the form *a.b.c.d*, where *a*, *b*, *c*, and *d* are all decimal integers: e.g. 192.168.10.23. Each component is 8 bits long and thus runs from 0 to 255. The address is split into two parts: the first part—highest-order bits—identifies the local network, specifically those hosts that may be connected directly (without the need for any routing information. The second part of the IP address (i.e., all remaining bits) identifies the host within the network.

The size of the two parts vary. The first byte of the address (*a*) determines the address type (called its *class*), and hence the number of bytes allocated to each part. Table 5-4 gives more specific details about how this scheme traditionally works.

Table 5-4. Traditional Internet address types

Initial Bits	Range of *a*	Address class	Network part	Host part	Maximum networks	Maximum hosts/net
0...	1–126	Class A	*a*	*b.c.d*	126	16,777,214
10...	128–191	Class B	*a.b*	*c.d*	16,384	65,534
110...	192–223	Class C	*a.b.c*	*d*	2,097,152	254
1110...	224-239	Class D	Multicast addresses			
1111...	240-254	Class E	Reserved for research			

Class A addresses provide millions of hosts per network, since 24 bits can be used for host addresses: 1 through $2^{24}-1$ (0 is not allowed as a host address). There are, however, only a total of 126 of them (these network numbers were typically assigned to major national networks and very large organizations). At the other extreme, Class C addresses traditionally support only 254 hosts per network (since only 8 bits are used for the host address), but there are over two million of them. Class B addresses fall in between these two types.

Multicast addresses are part of the reserved range of addresses (*a*=224–254). They are used to address a group of hosts as a single entity and are designed for applications such as video conferencing. They are assigned on a temporary basis. Normal IP addresses are sometimes referred to as *unicast* addresses in contrast to multicast addresses.

---

* More precisely, *octets* (since standardized bytes are more recent than IP addresses).

Some values of the various network address bytes have special meanings:

- The address with a host part of 0 refers to the network itself, as in 192.168.10.0. The 0.0.0.0 network is sometimes used to refer to the local network.
- The 127.0.0.1 address is always assigned to the loopback interface. The remainder of the 127.0 network is reserved.
- A host part of all ones defines the *broadcast address* for the network: the destination address used when a computer wants to send a query to every host on the local network. For example, the broadcast address for the network containing the Class C address 192.168.10.23 is 192.168.10.255, and the broadcast address for the network containing the Class A address 10.1.12.43 is 10.255.255.255.

Network addresses for networks connected to the Internet must be obtained from some official source. These days, network addresses for new sites are obtained from one of the ISPs that is authorized to assign them. Every host that will communicate directly with a host on the Internet must have an officially assigned IP address.

Networks that are not directly connected to the Internet also use network addresses that obey the Internet numbering conventions. The following IP address blocks are reserved for private networks:*

- 10.0.0.0 through 10.255.255.255
- 172.16.0.0 through 172.31.255.255
- 192.168.0.0 through 192.168.255.255

Sites that connect to the Internet via an ISP or other dedicated gateway frequently use Network Address Translation (NAT) to map internal IP addresses to their external ("real") IP address space. NAT can be performed by a computer and many routers. It is often used to map a large number of private addresses to a small number of real IP addresses, often just one.

NAT processes all Internet-bound packets, transforming their original source addresses into the address appropriate for use on the Internet. This may be done to translate private addresses to the organization's actual assigned IP address space or to conflate/hide the internal network structure from the outside world. It also keeps track of this mapping data so that it can perform the reverse translation process for incoming packets (responses).

 So far, we've assumed that IP addresses are permanently assigned to each host within a network, but this need not be true for all hosts within a network. The Dynamic Host Configuration Protocol (DHCP) is a facility that allows IP addresses to be assigned to systems dynamically when they require network access. It is discussed later in this chapter.

---

* Traditionally, many sites that were not on the Internet used IP addresses of the form 192.0.*x.y* or 193.0.*x.y*. Some probably still do.

Subnets and Supernets

A site can divide its block of addresses—also known as its *address space*—in any way that makes sense. For example, consider the block of addresses that begin with 192. 168. Traditionally, this is a Class B address and so would be interpreted as 256 networks of 254 hosts each: the networks are 192.168.0.0, 192.168.1.0, 192.168.2.0, ..., 192.168.255.0, and the hosts are numbered 1 through 254 for each network. However, this is not the only way of dividing the 16 site-specific bits. In this case, the theoretical possibilities range from one network with over two million hosts (all 16 bits are used for the host part) to 16,384 networks of 2 hosts each (only the lowest two bits are used for the host part, and the remaining 14 bits are used for the subnet).

 The number of hosts per subnet is always 2^n-2 where n is the number of bits in the host part of the IP address. Why -2? We must exclude the invalid host addresses consisting of all zeros and all ones.

A *subnet mask* specifies how the 32-bit IP address is divided between the network part (including the subnet) and the host part, and all computers participating in a TCP/IP network have one assigned to them. Computers and other devices on the same subnet always use the same subnet mask.

The subnet mask is a 32-bit value constructed by placing 1 in each bit location for the network portion of the IP address and 0 in all the bit locations for the host part of the address. This results in a string of ones followed by a string of zeros. For example, a traditional Class A IP address would use a subnet mask of 11111111000000000000000000000000, conventionally written as 4 period-separated decimal integers: 255.0.0.0. Similarly, traditional Class B and Class C addresses would use a subnet mask of 255.255.0.0 and 255.255.255.0, respectively.

The subnet mask can also be used to further subdivide one network ID among several local networks. For example, if you use a subnet mask of 255.255.255.192 for the network 192.168.10.0, you are making the highest 2 bits of the final address byte part of the network address (the final byte is 11000000), thereby subdividing the 192.168.10 network into 4 subnets, each of which can have up to 62 hosts on it (since the host ID is coded into the remaining 6 bits). Contrast this with the normal interpretation, which yields 256 networks of 254 hosts each.

 In contrast to host addresses, subnet addresses of all ones or all zeros are legal.

You can also use fewer than the standard number of bits for the network part of the address (this strategy is known as *supernetting*). For example, for the network address 192.168.0.0, you could use only 4 bits for the subnet part rather than the usual 8, yielding 16 subnets of up to 1022 hosts each.

Memorizing all the powers of 2 from 2^0 to 2^{16} makes all of this much easier.

Classless Inter-Domain Routing (CIDR, usually pronounced like apple *cider*) addressing is the more common way of expressing the subnet mask these days.* CIDR appends a suffix indicating the number of bits in the host part to the IP address. For example, 192.168.10.212/24 designates a subnet mask of 255.255.255.0, and the /27 suffix specifies a subnet mask of 255.255.255.224.

Table 5-5 shows how this works in detail. In the first example, we divide the 192.168.10 network into 8 subnets of 30 hosts each. In the second example, we organize a block of 256 traditional Class C addresses into 64 subnets of 1022 hosts each with supernetting by assigning the upper 6 bits of the third IP address byte to the network address, thereby leaving 10 bits for the host part.

Table 5-5. Subnetting and supernetting examples

Subnet Bits	Subnet Address[a]	Broadcast Address[b]	Host Addresses
Subnetting: subnets of 192.168.10.0/27 (subnet mask: 255.255.255.224)			
000	192.168.10.0	192.168.10.31	192.168.10.1-30
001	192.168.10.32	192.168.10.63	192.168.10.33-62
010	192.168.10.64	192.168.10.95	192.168.10.65-94
011	192.168.10.96	192.168.10.127	192.168.10.97-126
100	192.168.10.128	192.168.10.159	192.168.10.129-158
101	192.168.10.160	192.168.10.191	192.168.10.161-190
110	192.168.10.192	192.168.10.223	192.168.10.193-222
111	192.168.10.224	192.168.10.255	192.168.10.225-254
Supernetting: subnets of 192.168.0.0/22 (subnet mask: 255.255.248.0)			
000000	192.168.0.0	192.168.3.255	192.168.0.1-3.254
000001	192.168.4.0	192.168.7.255	192.168.4.1-7.254
000010	192.168.8.0	192.168.11.255	192.168.8.1-11.254
...			
111101	192.168.244.0	192.168.247.255	192.168.244.1-247.254

---

* CIDR's primary purpose is not to make notation more compact but to decrease the number of entries in the routing tables at major Internet hubs. CIDR minimizes the number of routing table entries required per site (often to just one) by allowing sites to be assigned a block of contiguous IP addresses that can be addresses via a single CIDR address. While CIDR was developed to address this specific problem arising from the uncontrolled growth of the Internet, it has also helped to stave off feared address shortages (for example, the entire traditional Class C address space supports only around 530 million hosts). For more information on the current status of available Internet address space consumption, consult the report at *http://www.caida. org/outreach/resources/learn/ipv4space/*.

Table 5-5. Subnetting and supernetting examples (continued)

Subnet Bits	Subnet Address[a]	Broadcast Address[b]	Host Addresses
111110	192.168.248.0	192.168.251.255	192.168.248.1-251.254
111111	192.168.252.0	192.168.255.255	192.168-252.1-255.254

[a] Host part=all 0's
[b] Host part=all 1's

Note that some of the host addresses in the second part of Table 5-5 have 255 as their last byte. These are legal host addresses with the specified subnet mask since the entire host part is not all ones (write one of these addresses, say 192.168.0.255/22, out in binary if you're not sure). With CIDR addresses, there is nothing special about the byte boundaries, and classes really are irrelevant.

Table 5-6 lists commonly used CIDR suffixes and their associated subnet masks.

Table 5-6. CIDR suffixes and subnet masks

Suffix	Subnet mask	Maximum hosts
/22	255.255.252.0	1022
/23	255.255.254.0	510
/24	255.255.255.0	254
/25	255.255.255.128	126
/26	255.255.255.192	62
/27	255.255.255.224	30
/28	255.255.255.240	14
/29	255.255.255.248	6
/30	255.255.255.252	2

If you'd rather avoid the math, there are tools that can help with these calculations. Figure 5-4 illustrates the output from a Perl script named *ipcalc.pl* (this one is from *http://jodies.de/ipcalc/*, written by *krischan@jodies.de*; there are several versions of the script by different authors[*]). It takes a CIDR address as its input and prints a variety of useful information about the local network that can be derived from it. The Wildcard field displays the inverted netmask (used by Cisco).

Introducing IPv6 host addresses

At some point in the future, Internet addresses may switch over to the next-generation design, IPv6 (the current one is IPv4). IPv6 was designed in the 1990s to address the perceived future shortage of Internet addresses (which fortunately has not yet arrived). In this brief subsection, we'll take a look at the major features of IPv6 addresses. All the vendors we are considering support IPv6 addresses.

---

[*] For a Palm Pilot version, see *http://www.ajw.com* (written by Alan Weiner).

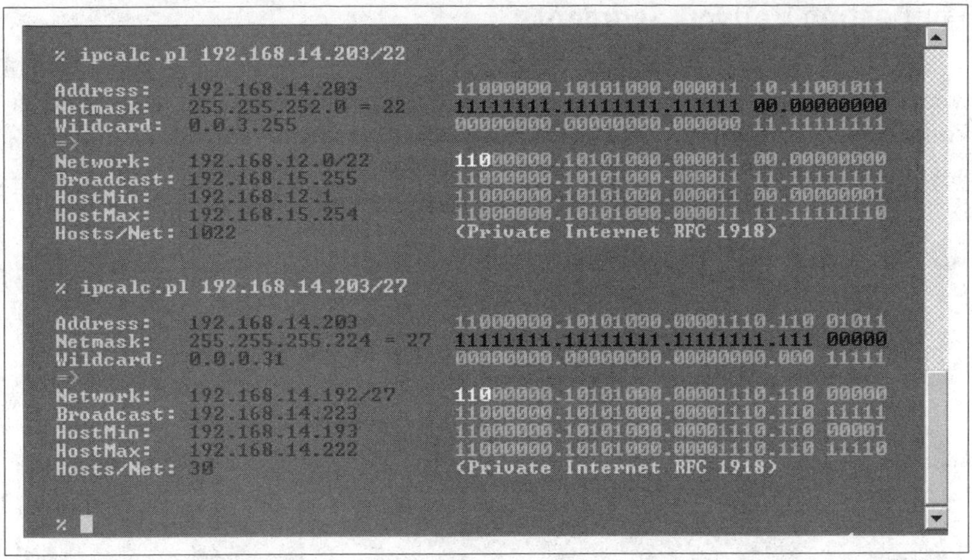

```
% ipcalc.pl 192.168.14.203/22

Address:    192.168.14.203         11000000.10101000.000011 10.11001011
Netmask:    255.255.252.0 = 22     11111111.11111111.111111 00.00000000
Wildcard:   0.0.3.255              00000000.00000000.000000 11.11111111
=>
Network:    192.168.12.0/22        11000000.10101000.000011 00.00000000
Broadcast:  192.168.15.255         11000000.10101000.000011 11.11111111
HostMin:    192.168.12.1           11000000.10101000.000011 00.00000001
HostMax:    192.168.15.254         11000000.10101000.000011 11.11111110
Hosts/Net:  1022                   (Private Internet RFC 1918)

% ipcalc.pl 192.168.14.203/27

Address:    192.168.14.203         11000000.10101000.00001110.110 01011
Netmask:    255.255.255.224 = 27   11111111.11111111.11111111.111 00000
Wildcard:   0.0.0.31               00000000.00000000.00000000.000 11111
=>
Network:    192.168.14.192/27      11000000.10101000.00001110.110 00000
Broadcast:  192.168.14.223         11000000.10101000.00001110.110 11111
HostMin:    192.168.14.193         11000000.10101000.00001110.110 00001
HostMax:    192.168.14.222         11000000.10101000.00001110.110 11110
Hosts/Net:  30                     (Private Internet RFC 1918)

% ▮
```

Figure 5-4. Output from the ipcalc.pl Script

IPv6 addresses are 128 bits long, expressed as a series of 8 colon-separated 16-bit values written in hexadecimal, e.g., 1111:2222:3333:4444:5555:6666:7777:8888. Each value runs from 0x0 to 0xFFFF (from 0 to 65535 in decimal). The network host boundary is fixed at 64 bits, and there is some additional internal structure defined, described in Table 5-7.

Table 5-7. IPv6 host address interpretation

Bits	Name	Purpose (Example use)
1-3	Format Prefix (FP)	Address type (unicast, multicast)
4-16	Top-level aggregation ID (TLA ID)	Highest-level organization (major upstream ISP)
17-24		Reserved
25-48	Next-level aggregation ID (NLA ID)	Regional organization (local ISP)
49-64	Site-level aggregation ID (SLA ID)	Site-specific subdivision (subnet)
65-128	Interface ID	Specific device address: a transformation of the MAC address

As the table indicates, sites get 16 bits for subnetting. The entire initial prefix of 48 bits is provided by the ISP. One advantage of IPv6 is that host addresses may be automatically derived from the device's MAC address, so that aspect of host configuration can be eliminated (optionally).

IPv6 allows for backward compatibility with IPv4 by assigning addresses of the form 0:0:0:FFFF:*a.b.c.d* to IPv4-only devices, where *a.b.c.d* is the IPv4 address. This is generally written as ::FFFF:*a.b.c.d*, where :: replaces a contiguous block of zeros (any length) in the IPv6 address (but the double colon may be used only once). Finally, the loopback address is always defined as ::1, and the broadcast address is FF02::1.

Connecting Network Segments

At the physical level, individual networks can be organized, subdivided and joined in a variety of ways, as illustrated in Figure 5-5 (constructed to include many different connectivity examples and not as a general model for network design).

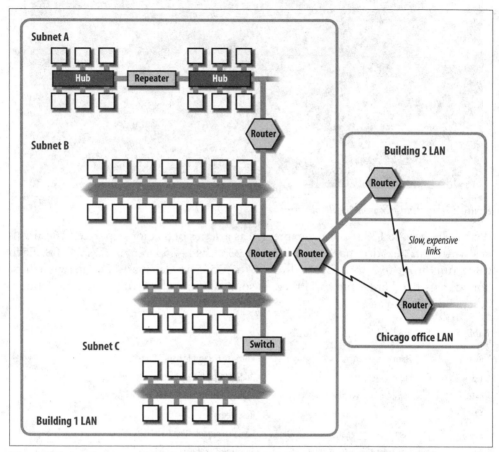

Figure 5-5. A wide area network and its component LANs

The Chicago office LAN in the figure is geographically separated from the organization's main site in San Francisco—the Building 1 and Building 2 LANs—and it is connected to it via relatively slow links. The two LANs at the main site are connected via high-speed fiber optic cable, so that site's entire network runs at the same speed, despite the separation of the two buildings. Collectively, these three LANs comprise the WAN for this organization.

The Building 1 LAN illustrates several hardware networking devices. All the hosts in Subnet A are connected to devices called *hubs*. Traditional hubs serve as an Ethernet backbone, linking all of the connected hosts together. In this case, there are two hubs in this network segment, as well as a *repeater*. The latter device connects hosts that are farther apart than the maximum cable length, passing all signals from one wire to the other. Actually, a repeater is also a hub; in this case, it has only two ports. Ethernet imposes a maximum number of four hubs between the most distant hosts. Subnet A follows this rule.

Subnet B is another network segment, connected to the other two subnets by routers. Although its internal structure is not shown, the various hosts in this subnet are all connected to hubs or switches. The same is true for the two parts of subnet C.

The two branches of subnet C are connected by a *switch*, a somewhat more intelligent device than a hub, which selectively passes only the data destined for the other segment between the two. A hub is just a point where connections come together, while a switch includes some ability to decide which "side" a given packet is destined for. Two-port switches like the one in the figure are sometimes called *bridges*.

 These days, plain hubs/repeaters are seldom used. Switches are generally used as the central connector to which individual hosts are attached. (I've used hubs in the diagram for illustrative purposes.) Occasionally, devices that are really switches are labeled as hubs, presumably for marketing purposes.

More complex switches can handle more than one media type or have the ability to filter the traffic in a variety of ways, and some are capable of connecting networks of different types—say, TCP/IP and SNA—by translating or encapsulating the data from one protocol family to/within the other as it is passed across. These tasks, performed by such devices, overlap those traditionally assigned to routers.

The various subnets and the three local LANs in Figure 5-5 are connected to one another via *routers*, a still more sophisticated network linking device that is essentially a small computer. In addition to selectively handling data based on its destination, routers also have the ability to determine the current best path to that destination; finding a path to a destination is known as *routing*.* The best routers are highly programmable and can also perform very complex filtering of the data they receive, accepting or rejecting it based upon criteria specified by the network administrator.

The routers that connect our three locations are arranged so that there are multiple paths to every destination; losing any one of them will cause no harm to communications between the two unaffected networks.

Hubs/repeaters, switches/bridges, and routers can be distinguished by where their operations fall within the TCP/IP protocol stack. Repeaters operate at the Network

---

* Both common pronunciations of this word are technically correct. However, I still believe that *rooting* is something humans do at baseball games and pigs do when looking for truffles. *Routing* is what partisans do to occupying armies, and its homonym is what enables packets to travel across a network.

Access layer, bridges use the Internet layer,[*] and routers operate within the Transport layer. A full network host, which obviously supports all four TCP/IP layers, can thus perform the functions of any of these types of devices. Note that many devices labeled with one name may actually function like lower-end versions of the next higher device (e.g., high end switches are simple routers).

 Although inexpensive dual-speed (e.g., 10BaseT and 100BaseT) switches exist, I don't recommend using them. The network will provide better performance if you segregate devices by speed and don't mix speeds on the same (low-end) switch.[†] The low-speed switch will thus be the only low-speed device on the high speed switch.

Adding a New Network Host

To add a new host to the network, you must:

- Install networking software and build a kernel capable of supporting networking and the installed networking hardware (if necessary). These days, basic networking is almost always installed by default with the operating system, but you may have to add some features manually.

- Physically connect the system to the network and enable the hardware network interface. Occasionally, on older PC systems, the latter may involve setting jumpers or switches on the network adapter board or setting low-level system parameters (usually via the pre-boot monitor program).

- Assign a hostname and network address to the system (or find out what has been assigned by the network administrator). When you add a new host to an existing network, the unique network address you assign it must fit in with whatever addressing scheme is already in use at your site. You can also decide to use DHCP to assign the IP address and other networking parameters dynamically instead of specifying a static address.

- Ensure that necessary configuration tasks occur at boot time, including starting all required networking-related daemons.

- Configure name resolution (hostname-to-IP address translation).

- Set up any static routes and configure any other routing facilities in use. This includes defining a default gateway for packets destined beyond the local subnet.

---

[*] The smartest switches intrude a tiny bit into the Transport layer.

[†] One of the book's technical reviewers notes that this problem occurs *only* with inexpensive switches and is not a problem on high quality (higher priced) ones.

- Test the network connection.
- Enable and configure any additional network services that you plan to use on that computer.

Configuring the Network Interface with ifconfig

The `ifconfig` command ("if" for interface) is used to set the basic characteristics of the network adapter, the most important of which is associating an IP address with the interface. Here are some typical commands:

```
# ifconfig lo0 localhost up
# ifconfig eth0 inet 192.168.1.9 netmask 255.255.255.0
```

The first command configures the loopback interface, designating it as up (active). In many versions of `ifconfig`, up is the default when the first IP address is assigned to an interface, and thus it is usually omitted.

The second command configures the Ethernet interface on this system, named *en0*, assigning it the specified Internet address and netmask.

The second parameter in the second `ifconfig` command designates the address family. Here, `inet` refers to IPv4; `inet6` is used to refer to IPv6. This parameter is optional and defaults to IPv4.

The first example command above also illustrates the use of a hostname to specify the IP address. If you do so, the IP address corresponding to the hostname must be available when the `ifconfig` command is run, generally because it is in */etc/hosts*.

FreeBSD, Solaris, and Tru64 systems allow you to replace the IP address and netmask parameters with a CIDR address:

```
# ifconfig tu0 192.168.9.6/24
```

Ethernet interface names

The loopback interface is almost always named *lo0* (but Linux calls it simply *lo*). Ethernet interface names vary tremendously among systems. Here are some common names for the first Ethernet interface on the various systems:*

AIX	*en0*
FreeBSD	*xl0*, *de0*, and others (depends on hardware)
HP-UX	*lan0*
Linux	*eth0*
Solaris	*hme0*, *dnet0*, *eri0*, *le0*
Tru64	*tu0*, *ln0*

---

* AIX uses different interface names for other networking types: *et0* for so-called 803.2 (a related but slightly different protocol), *tr0* for Token Ring etc.

Other uses of ifconfig

Without any other options, ifconfig displays the configuration of the specified network interface, as in this example:

```
$ ifconfig eth0
en0: flags=c63<UP,BROADCAST,NOTRAILERS,RUNNING,FILTMULTI,MULTICAST>
inet 192.168.1.9 netmask 0xffffff00 broadcast 192.168.1.255
```

You can display the status of all configured network interfaces with ifconfig -a except under HP-UX. On AIX, FreeBSD, and Tru64 systems, the -l option can be used to list all network interfaces:

```
$ ifconfig -l
en0 en1 lo0
```

This system has two Ethernet interfaces installed, as well as the loopback interface.

The HP-UX lanscan command provides similar functionality.

ifconfig on Solaris systems

Solaris systems provide two versions of ifconfig, one in */sbin* and another in */usr/sbin*. Their syntax is identical. They differ only in the way in which they attempt to resolve hostnames specified as arguments. The */sbin* version always checks */etc/hosts* before consulting DNS, while the other version uses whatever name resolution order is specified in the network switch file (discussed below). The former is used at boot time, when DNS may not be available.

Solaris also requires that an interface be "plumbed" before it is configured, via commands like the following:

```
# ifconfig hme0 plumb
# ifconfig hme0 inet 192.168.9.2 netmask + up
```

The first command sets up the kernel data structures needed for the device to be used with IP. Other operating systems also perform this setup function, but they do so automatically when the first IP address is assigned to an interface. The plus sign parameter to the netmask keyword is shorthand that tells the command to look up the default netmask for the specified subnet in the file */etc/inet/netmasks*. The file has entries like the following:

```
#subnet       netmask
192.168.9.0   255.255.255.0
```

Interface configuration at boot time

Table 5-8 lists the configuration files that store the parameters for ifconfig for each Unix version we are considering and also provides some example entries from the file, using the first interface of a common type. The third column in the table indicates which boot script actually performs the interface configuration operation and where in the boot process it occurs.

Table 5-8. *Boot-time network interface configuration*

Unix version	Configuration file	Boot script (Invoked by)
AIX	Data is stored in the ODM; use `smit mktcpip` or the `mktcpip` command to modify it (not `ifconfig` commands).	*/sbin/rc.boot* (first */etc/inittab* entry)
FreeBSD	*/etc/rc.conf*: ```hostname="clarissa"\nifconfig_xl0="192.168.9.2 netmask\n 255.255.255.0"```	*/etc/rc.network* (called from */etc/rc*)
HP-UX	*/etc/rc.config.d/netconf*: ```HOSTNAME="acrasia"\nINTERFACE_NAME[0]=lan0\nIP_ADDRESS[0]=192.168.9.55\nSUBNET_MASK[0]=255.255.255.0\nINTERFACE_STATE[0]="up"```	*/sbin/init.d/net* (link in */sbin/rc2.d*)

Linux (Red Hat)	*/etc/sysconfig/network-scripts/ifcfg_eth0*:
	
	```DEVICE=eth0\nBOOTPROTO=static\nIPADDR=192.168.9.220\nNETMASK=255.255.255.0\nONBOOT=yes```
	
	/etc/sysconfig/network:
	
	```HOSTNAME="selene"```
		/etc/init.d/network (link in */etc/rc2.d*)

Linux (SuSE 7)	*/etc/rc.config*:
	
	```NETCONFIG="_0" Number of interfaces\nIPADDR_0="192.168.9.220"\nNETDEV_0="eth0"\nIFCONFIG_0="192.168.9.220 broadcast\n 192.0.9.255 netmask 255.255.255.0"```
	
	/etc/HOSTNAME:
	
	```sabina```
		/etc/init.d/network (link in */etc/rc2.d*)

Linux (SuSE 8)	*/etc/sysconfig/network/ifcfg_eth0*
	
	```BOOTPROTO=static\nIPADDR=192.168.9.220\nNETMASK=255.255.255.0\nSTARTMODE=yes```
	
	/etc/HOSTNAME:
	
	```sabina```
		/etc/init.d/network (link in */etc/rc2.d*)

Solaris	*/etc/hostname.hme0*: ```ishtar```	*/etc/init.d/network* (link in */sbin/rcS.d*)
Tru64	*/etc/rc.config*: ```HOSTNAME="ludwig"\nNETDEV_0="tu0"\nIFCONFIG_0="192.168.9.73 netmask\n 255.255.255.0"\nNUM_NETCONFIG="1" Number of interfaces\nexport HOSTNAME NETDEV_0 ...```	*/sbin/init.d/inet* (link in */sbin/rc3.d*)

These files and their entries are quite straightforward and self-explanatory. Multiple interfaces are configured in the same manner. Parameters for additional interfaces are defined in the same way as the first one, typically using the next element in the array (e.g., IP_ADDRESS[1] (HP-UX), NETDEV_1 (Tru64), and the like), corresponding syntax (e.g., ifconfig_xl1 for FreeBSD), or an analogous filename (e.g., *hostname.hme1* for Solaris or *ifcfg_eth1* for Linux).

The Solaris */etc/hostname*.interface (where *interface* is the interface name, e.g., *hme0*) file merits additional comment. In general, this file requires only a hostname as its contents, but you can also place specific parameters to ifconfig on additional lines if desired, as in this example:

```
kali
192.168.24.37 netmask 255.255.248.192 broadcast 192.168.191.255
```

Generally, Solaris attempts to locate the system's IP address automatically by consulting all the available name services, but you can specify specific parameters in this way if you choose. The */etc/init.d/network* script will append each additional line in turn to ifconfig *interface* inet to form a complete command, which is then executed immediately. The hostname still needs to be the first line in the file or other parts of the script will break.

The file */etc/nodename* also contains the hostname of the local host; it is used when the system is in standalone mode and in other circumstances within the boot scripts. If you decide to change a system's hostname, you'll need to change it in both */etc/nodename* and the */etc/hostname.** file (as well as in */etc/hosts*, DNS and any other directory service you may be running).

Dynamic IP Address Assignment with DHCP

The Dynamic Host Configuration Protocol (DHCP) facility is used to dynamically assign IP addresses and configuration settings to network hosts.* This facility is designed to decrease the amount of individual workstation configuration necessary for a system to be successfully connected to the network. It is especially suited to computer systems that change network locations frequently (e.g., laptops).

Never use dynamic addressing for any system that shares any of its resources—filesystems (via NFS or SAMBA), printers, or other devices—or provides any network resources (DNS, DHCP, electronic mail services, and so on). It is OK to use DHCP to assign static addresses to servers (see "Configuring a DHCP Server" in Chapter 8).

---

* DHCP is a follow-on to the BOOTP remote booting facility.

The DHCP facility assigns an IP address to a requesting host for a specified period of time known as a *lease*, via a process like the following:

- The requesting (client) system broadcasts a DHCP Discover* message to UDP port 67. At this point, the system does not need to know anything about the local network, not even the subnet mask (the source address for this message is 0.0.0.0, and the destination is 255.255.255.255).

- One or more DHCP servers reply with a DHCP Offer message (to UDP port 68), containing an IP address, subnet mask, server IP address, and lease duration (and possibly other parameters). The server reserves the offered address until it is accepted or rejected by the requesting client or a timeout period expires.

- The client selects an offered IP address and broadcasts a DHCP Request message. All servers other than the successful one release the pending reservation.

- The selected server sends a DHCP Acknowledge message to the client.†

- When the lease is 50% expired, the client attempts to renew it (via another DHCP Request). If it cannot do so at that time, it will try when it reaches 87.5% of the lease period; if the second renewal attempt also fails, the client looks for a new server. During the lease period, DHCP-assigned parameters persist across boots on most systems. On some systems, the client tries to extend its lease each time it boots.

As this description indicates, the DHCP facility depends heavily on broadcast messages, but it does not generate an inordinate amount of network traffic if it is configured properly. Typical default lease periods are a few hours, but the time period can be shortened or lengthened as appropriate (see "Configuring a DHCP Server" in Chapter 8).

DHCP can also be used to assign other parameters related to networking to the client, including the default gateway (router), the hostname, and which server(s) to use for a variety of functions, including DNS, syslog message destination, X fonts, NTP, and so on. In addition, DHCP clients can request that specific parameters be supplied by the server and optionally reject offers that do not fulfill them. Some clients can also specify terms for the lease, such as the time period. DHCP additional parameters are known as *options*, and they are identified via standard identifying numbers.

In the remainder of this section, we'll look at configuring DHCP clients. We'll discuss DHCP servers in Chapter 8.

---

* More precisely, it is a DHCPDISCOVER message, but I've tried to make the text more readable by adding a space and changing letter case.

† Occasionally, things don't work out after an offer has been selected. The server also has the option of sending a Negative Acknowledgement if there is some problem with the request. Also, the client can send a Decline message to the server if its initial test of the IP address fails. In either case, the client restarts the discovery process from the beginning.

Table 5-9 summarizes the various files and settings involved in DHCP client configuration on the various systems we are considering, using the first Ethernet interface of a common type as an example in each case. The table is followed by discussions of the specifics for each Unix version.

Table 5-9. DHCP client configuration summary

Item	Location and/or configuration
Enable DHCP	**AIX:** ODM; `interface stanza` (*/etc/dhcpcd.ini*)
	FreeBSD: `ifconfig_xl0="DHCP"` (*/etc/rc.conf*)
	HP-UX: `DHCP_ENABLE=1` (*/etc/rc.config.d/netconf*)
	Linux: `IFCONFIG_0="dhcpclient"` in */etc/rc.config* (SuSE 7); `BOOTPROTO='dhcp'` (*ifcfg_eth0* in */etc/sysconfig/network-scripts* in Red Hat, */etc/sysconfig/network* in SuSE 8)
	Solaris: Create */etc/dhcp.hme0*
	Tru64: `IFCONFIG_0="DYNAMIC"` (*/etc/rc.config*)
Additional Configuration Files	**FreeBSD:** */etc/dhclient.conf*
	Solaris: */etc/default/dhcpagent*
	Tru64: */etc/join/client.pcy*
Primary Command or Daemon	**AIX:** `dhcpcd` daemon
	FreeBSD: `dhclient` command
	HP-UX: `dhcpclient` daemon
	Linux: `dhcpcd` daemon
	Solaris: `dhcpagent` daemon
	Tru64: `joinc` daemon
Boot Script where DHCP Configuration Occurs	**AIX:** */etc/rc.tcpip*
	FreeBSD: */etc/rc.network*
	HP-UX: */sbin/rc*
	Linux: */etc/init.d/network*
	Solaris: */etc/init.d/network*
	Tru64: */sbin/init.d/inet*
Automated/ Graphical Configuration Tool	**AIX:** `smit usedhcp`
	FreeBSD: `sysinstall`
	HP-UX: SAM
	Linux: Linuxconf (Red Hat), YAST2 (SuSE)
	Solaris: Solaris Management Console
	Tru64: `netconfig`
Current Lease Information	**AIX:** */usr/tmp/dhcpcd.log*
	FreeBSD: */var/db/dhclient.leases*
	HP-UX: */etc/auto_parms.log*
	Linux: */etc/dhcp/dhcpcd-eth0.info* (Red Hat); */var/lib/dhcpcd/dhcpcd-eth0.info* (SuSE)
	Solaris: */etc/dhcp/hme0.dhc*
	Tru64: */etc/join/leases*

AIX

The easiest way to enable DHCP on an AIX system is to use SMIT, specifically the
smit usedhcp command. The resulting dialog is illustrated in Figure 5-6.

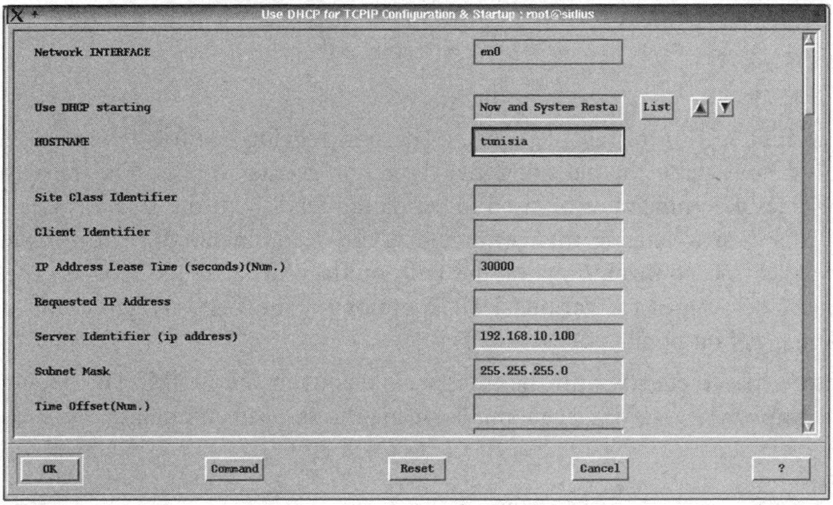

Figure 5-6. Enabling DHCP with SMIT

As the figure illustrates, SMIT allows you not only to enable DHCP but also to specify a desired lease length and other DHCP parameters. In this example, we request a
lease length of 30,000 seconds (5 hours), and we also specify a specific DHCP server
to contact (giving its IP address and subnet mask). This second item is not necessary
and in fact is usually omitted; it is included here only for illustrative purposes.

AIX DHCP client configuration consists of three parts:

- Configuring and starting the dhcpcd daemon, which requests configuration information and keeps track of the lease status. In particular, the relevant lines in */etc/
  rc.tcpip* must be activated by removing the initial comment marker:

  ```
  # Start up dhcpcd daemon
  start /usr/sbin/dhcpcd "$src_running"
  ```

- Adding a stanza for the network interface and other settings to dhcpcd's config
  file */etc/dhcpcd.ini*. Here is an example of this file:

  ```
  # Use 4 log files of 500KB each and log lots of info
  numLogFiles     4
  logFileSize     500
  logFileName     /usr/tmp/dhcpcd.log
  logItem         SYSERR
  logItem         OBJERR
  logItem         WARNING
  logItem         EVENT
  logItem         ACTION
  ```

```
updateDNS "/usr/sbin/dhcpaction '%s' '%s' '%s' '%s' A NONIM
  >> /tmp/updns.out 2> &1 "      Command is wrapped.
clientid MAC      Identify client via its MAC address.

interface en0
{
option 12 "lovelace"      Hostname.
option 51 30000      Requested lease period in seconds.
...
}
```

The first section of the file specifies desired logging options. Here we request substantial detail by selecting five types of events to log. The next section includes a command to be used for updating DNS with the IP address assigned to this host (changing this command is not recommended). The final section specifies the configuration for the *en0* interface. The items between the curly braces set values for various DHCP options. (The file */etc/options.file* defines DHCP option numbers.)

- Setting parameters within the interface's record in the ODM. This step can be accomplished via SMIT or manually, using the `mktcpip` command.

FreeBSD

FreeBSD uses the DHCP implementation created by the Internet Software Consortium (ISC). The dhclient command requests DHCP services when they are needed. At boot time, it is called from *rc.network*. It uses the configuration file, */etc/dhclient. conf*. Here is a simple example:

```
interface "xl0" {
  request subnet-mask, broadcast-address, host-name,
    time-offset, routers, domain-name, domain-name-servers;
  require subnet-mask;
  send requested-lease-time 360000;
  media "media 10baseT/UTP", "media 10base2/BNC";
  }
```

This file configures DHCP for the interface *xl0*, for which DHCP is enabled in */etc/rc. conf* (ifconfig_xl0='DHCP'). This example specifies a list of options for which to request values from the DHCP server. Leases without most of these options will still be acceptable, but the subnet mask parameter is required. The client also requests a lease time of 360,000 seconds (100 hours).

All the items within the braces apply only to this particular interface. However, these same commands can appear independently within the configuration file, in which case they apply to all specified interfaces. Many other options are provided, including the ability to specify a specific DHCP server.

 The default version of */etc/dhclient.conf* usually works fine unmodified.

HP-UX

Once DHCP has been enabled for an interface in */etc/rc.config.d/netconf*, it will be started at boot time automatically. The auto_parms script is called from */etc/rc*, and it performs the actual DHCP operations, with help from set_parms. The script also calls dhcpdb2conf, which merges the configuration data provided by DHCP into the network configuration file mentioned above, and the ifconfig process proceeds in the same way it does for hosts with static IP addresses. In addition, auto_parms starts the dhcpclient daemon, which oversees the lease and its renewal.

Other than enabling DHCP for the network interface, HP-UX provides nothing in terms of DHCP client configuration. When you enable DHCP, you will also need to set the corresponding *IP_ADDRESS* and *SUBNET_MASK* variables to an empty string.

Linux

DHCP configuration differs slightly among different Linux distributions. However, both Red Hat and SuSE use the file *ifcfg.eth0* to hold configuration information for the first Ethernet interface (see Table 5-8 for the directory locations), and DHCP is enabled in this file as well, via the BOOTPROTO parameter. The actual interface configuration happens in the */etc/init.d/network* boot script, which is called during a boot, during the transition to run level 2.

On both systems, the network script calls additional scripts and commands to help it perform its tasks. The most important of these is */sbin/ifup* which is responsible for network interface activation both for systems with static IP addresses and for DHCP clients.

On Red Hat Linux systems, ifup starts the dhcpcd daemon, which monitors and renews the DHCP lease as necessary. On SuSE Linux systems, it calls another command, ifup-dhcp (also in */sbin*) to perform the core configuration tasks, including starting the daemon.

On SuSE systems, there is also another option for DHCP clients: the dhclient command, part of the same Internet Software Consortium (ISC) DHCP implementation used by FreeBSD. It uses a similar */etc/dhclient.conf* configuration file to the one described above for FreeBSD. The default on SuSE systems is to use dhcpcd, but dhclient can be selected using the following entry in the */etc/sysconfig/network/dhcp* configuration file:

```
DHCLIENT_BIN="dhclient"
```

On older Red Hat systems, the default DHCP client is pump. This facility is still available as an option if you want to use it (currently, it is not included in an installation unless you specifically request it).

Solaris

On a Solaris system, you can specify that a network interface be configured using DHCP by issuing a command like the following:

```
# ifconfig hme0 dhcp
```

(You can change back to a static configuration by adding drop to this command.)

Initiating DHCP in this way automatically invokes the dhcpagent daemon. It will initiate and manage the DHCP lease.

For an interface to be configured with DHCP at boot time, a file of the form */etc/dhcp*.interface must exist. Such files can be empty. If one of these files contains the word "primary" as its contents, the corresponding interface will be configured first (if more than one includes the word "primary," the first one listed in the file will be used as the primary interface).

The dhcpagent daemon uses the configuration file */etc/default/dhcpagent*. The following is the most important entry within it:

```
PARAM_REQUEST_LIST=1,3,12,43
```

This entry specifies the list of parameters that the client will request from the DHCP server. The standard DHCP parameter numbers are translated to descriptive strings in the */etc/dhcp/inittab* file.

Tru64

Tru64 also uses a daemon to manage DHCP client leases. Its name is joinc, and it is started at boot time by the dhcpconf command; the latter is invoked by */sbin/init.d/inet* when moving to run level 3.

The DHCP client configuration file is */etc/join/client.pcy* Here is a simple example of this file:

```
use_saved_config          Use existing lease if still valid.
lease_desired 604800      One week lease.

# options to request from server
request   broadcast_address
request   dns_servers
request   dns_domain_name
request   routers
request   host_name
request   lease_time
```

The bulk of this file consists of a list of options to be requested from the server. The full list of supported options is given in the *client.pcy* manual page.

Name Resolution Options

The term *name resolution* refers to the process of translating a hostname to its corresponding IP address. Hostnames are much more convenient for users and administrators within commands and configuration files, but actual network operations require IP addresses.* Thus, when a user enters a command like finger chavez@hamlet, one of the first things that must happen is that the hostname *hamlet* gets translated to its IP address (say, 192.168.2.6). There are several ways that this can happen, but the two most prevalent are:

- The IP address can be looked up in a file. The list of translations is traditionally stored in */etc/hosts*. When a directory service is in use, the contents of the local hosts file may be integrated into it, and a common master file can be automatically propagated throughout a network (e.g., NIS).

- The client can contact a Domain Name System (DNS) server and ask it to perform the translation.

In the first case, the hostnames and IP addresses of all hosts with which the local host will need to communicate must be entered into */etc/hosts* (or another central location). In the second case, a host trying to translate a name will contact a local or remote named server process to determine the corresponding IP address.

For a relatively small network not on the Internet, using just */etc/hosts* may not be a problem. For even a medium-sized network, however, this strategy may result in a lot of work every time a new host is added, because the master *hosts* file must be propagated to every system in the network. For networks on the Internet, using DNS is the only practical way to translate hostnames for systems located beyond the local domain.

The /etc/hosts file

The file */etc/hosts* traditionally contains a list of the hosts in the local network (including the local host itself). If you use this file for name resolution, whenever you add a new system to the network, you will have to edit it on (or copy a master version to) every system on the Unix local network (and take whatever action is equivalent for hosts running other operating systems).

 Even systems that use DNS for name resolution typically have a small hosts file for use during booting.

Here is a sample */etc/hosts* file for a small LAN:

```
# Loopback address for localhost
127.0.0.1      localhost

# Local hostname and address
192.168.1.2    spain
```

---

* And, ultimately, MAC addresses.

```
# Other hosts
192.168.1.3    usa
192.168.1.4    canada england uk
192.168.1.6    greece olympus
10.154.231.42  paradise
```

Lines beginning with # are comments and are ignored. Aside from the comments, each line has three fields: the IP address of a host in the network, its hostname, and any *aliases* (synonyms) for the host.

Every */etc/hosts* file should contain at least two entries: the loopback address and the address by which the local system is known to the rest of the network. The remaining lines describe the other hosts in your local network. This file may also include entries for hosts that are not on your immediate local network.

On Solaris systems, the hosts file has moved to the */etc/inet* directory (as have several other standard network configuration files), but a link to the standard location is provided.

Configuring a DNS client

On the client side, DNS configuration is very simple and centers around the */etc/resolv.conf* configuration file. This file lists the local domain name and the locations of one or more name servers to be used by the local system.

Here is a simple resolver configuration file:

```
search ahania.com      DNS domains to search for names.
nameserver 192.168.9.44
nameserver 192.168.10.200
```

The first entry specifies the DNS domain(s) in which to search for name translations. Up to six domains can be specified (separated by spaces), although listing only one is quite common. In general, they should be ordered from most to least specific (e.g., subdomains before their parent domain). On some systems, *domain* will replace the *search* keyword in the installed configuration file version; this is an older resolver configuration convention, and such entries are used to specify only the name of the local domain (i.e., a list is not accepted).

Name servers are identified by IP address, and up to three may be listed. When a name server needs to be located, they are contacted in the order in which they are listed in the file. However, once a server has successfully replied to a query, it will continue to be used. Thus, the best practice is to place servers in preferential order within this file. Usually, this means from closest to most distant, but when there are multiple local name servers, clients are generally configured so that each server is preferred by the appropriate fraction of clients (e.g., half of the clients in the case of two local name servers).

There are two other configuration file entries which are useful in some special circumstances:

sortlist *network-list*

> This entry specifies how to select among multiple responses that may be returned by a DNS query when the target has multiple network interfaces.

options ndots:*n*

> This entry determines when the domain name will be automatically added to a hostname. The domain name will be added only when the target name has less than *n* periods within it. The default for *n* is 1, causing the domain name to be added only to bare hostnames.

On most systems, removing (or renaming) */etc/resolv.conf* will disable DNS lookups from the system.

The name service switch file

Some operating systems, including Linux, HP-UX, and Solaris, provide an additional configuration file relevant to DNS clients, */etc/nsswitch.conf*. This name service switch file enables the system administrator to specify which of the various name resolution services are to be consulted when a hostname needs to be translated, as well as the order in which they are called. Here is an example:

```
hosts:    files dns
```

This entry says to consult */etc/hosts* first when attempting to resolve a hostname, and to use DNS if the name is not present in the file.

In fact, the file contains similar entries for many networking functions, as these entries illustrate:

```
passwd:    files nis
services:  files
```

The first entry says to consult the traditional password file when looking for user account information and then to consult the Network Information Service (NIS) if the account is not found in */etc/passwd*. The second entry says to use only the traditional file for definitions of network services.

This sort of construct is also frequently used in *nsswitch.conf*:

```
passwd:    nis [NOTFOUND=return] files
```

This entry says to contact NIS for user account information. If the required information is not found there, the search will stop (the meaning of return), and cause the originating command to fail with an error. The traditional password file is used only when the NIS service is unavailable (e.g., at boot time).

The other operating systems we are considering offer similar facilities. Currently, FreeBSD provides the */etc/host.conf* file, which looks like this:

```
hosts                    FreeBSD 4 resolver order configuration
bind
```

This file says to look in the hosts file first and then to consult DNS. Older versions of Linux also used this file, with a slightly different syntax:

```
order hosts,bind        Linux host.conf syntax
```

AIX uses the */etc/netsvc.conf* file for the same purpose. Here is an example which sets the same order as the preceding:

```
hosts = local, bind     AIX resolver order configuration
```

Finally, Tru64 uses the */etc/svc.conf* file, as in this example:

```
hosts=local,bind        Tru64 resolver order configuration
```

The AIX and Tru64 file also contain entries for other system and network configuration files.

Routing Options

As with hostname resolution, there are a number of options for configuring routing within a network:

- If the LAN consists of a single Ethernet network not connected to any other networks, no explicit routing is usually needed (since all hosts are visible and adjacent to all others). The ifconfig commands used to configure the network interfaces will usually provide them with enough information for them to route packets to their destination.

- *Static routing* may be used for small- to medium-sized networks not characterized by many redundant paths to most destinations. This is set up by explicit route commands that are executed at boot time.

- *Dynamic routing*, in which optimal paths to destinations are determined at packet transmission time, may be used via the routed or gated daemon. They are discussed in "Routing Daemons" in Chapter 8.

Static routing relies on the route command. Here are some examples of its use:

```
# route add 192.168.1.12 192.168.3.100
# route add -net 192.168.2.0 netmask 255.255.255.0 192.168.3.100
```

The first command adds a static route to the host 192.168.1.12, specifying host 192.168.3.100 as the intermediate point (gateway). The second command adds a route to the subnet 192.168.2 (recall that host 0 refers to a network itself), via the same gateway.

The command form is slightly different under FreeBSD, Solaris, and AIX (note the hyphen used with the netmask keyword):

```
# route add -net 192.168.2.0 -netmask 255.255.255.0 192.168.3.100
```

Linux uses a slightly different form for the route command:

```
# route add -net 10.1.2.0 netmask 255.255.240.0 gw 10.1.3.100
```

The gw keyword is required.

The command form route add default is used to define a default gateway. All non-local packets for which there is not an explicit route in the routing table are sent to this host for forwarding.

 For many client systems, defining the default gateway will be all the routing configuration that is necessary.

The command netstat -r may be used to display the routing tables. Here is the output from a Solaris system named *kali*:

```
# netstat -r
Routing Table: IPv4
  Destination    Gateway      Flags  Ref  Use   Interface
------------- --------------- ----- ----- ------ ---------
192.168.9.0   kali            U      1      4   hme0
default       suzanne         UG     1      0
localhost     localhost       UH     3    398   lo0
```

The first line in the output's table of routes specifies the route to the local network, through the local host itself. The second line specifies the default route for all traffic destined beyond the local subnet; here, it is the host named *suzanne*. The final line specifies the route used by the loopback interface to redirect packets to the local host.

Use the -n option to view IP addresses rather than hostnames. This can be useful when there are DNS problems.

To remove a route, replace the add keyword with delete:

```
# route delete -net 192.168.1.0 netmask 255.255.255.0 192.168.2.100
```

The Linux version of the route command will also display the current routing tables when executed without arguments.

The AIX, FreeBSD, Solaris, and Tru64 versions of route also provide a change keyword for modifying existing routes (e.g., to change the gateway). These versions also provide a flush keyword for removing all routes to remote subnets from the routing table in a single operation; HP-UX provides the same functionality with route's -f option.

All the operating systems provide mechanisms for specifying a list of static routes to be set up each time the system boots. The various configuration files are summarized in the sections that follow.

AIX

On AIX systems, static routes are stored in the ODM. You can use the smit mkroute command to add one or simply issue a route command. The results of the latter persist across boots.

FreeBSD

FreeBSD stores static routes in the */etc/rc.conf* and/or */etc/rc.conf.local* configuration files. Here are some examples of its syntax for these entries:

```
defaultrouter="192.168.1.200"
static_routes="r1 r2"
route_r1="-net 192.168.13.0 192.168.1.49"
route_r2="192.168.99.1 192.168.1.22"
```

The first entry specifies the default gateway for the local system. The second line specifies labels of the static routes that should be created at boot time. Each label refers to a route_ entry later in the file. The latter hold the arguments and options to be passed to the route command.

HP-UX

Static routes are defined in */etc/rc.config.d/netconf* on HP-UX systems, via entries like these, which define the default gateway for this system:

```
ROUTE_DESTINATION[0]=default
ROUTE_MASK[0]="255.255.255.0"
ROUTE_GATEWAY[0]=192.168.9.200
ROUTE_COUNT[0]=1                    Total number of static routes.
ROUTE_ARGS[0]=""                    Additional arguments to the route command.
```

Additional static routes can be defined by increasing the value of the route count parameter and adding additional entries to the array (i.e., [1] would indicate the second static route).

Linux

Linux systems generally list the static routes to be created at boot time in a configuration file in or under */etc/sysconfig*. On Red Hat systems, this file is named *static-routes*. Here is an example:

```
#interface  type  destination    gw  ip-address
eth0        net   192.168.13.0   gw  192.168.9.49
any         host  192.168.15.99  gw  192.168.9.100
```

The first line specifies a route to the 192.168.13 network via the gateway 192.168.9. 49, limiting it to the *eth0* interface. The second line specifies a route to the host 192. 168.15.99 via 192.168.9.100 (valid for any network interface).

On Red Hat systems, the default gateway is defined in the *network* configuration file in the same directory:

```
GATEWAY=192.168.9.150
```

SuSE Linux uses the file */etc/sysconfig/network/routes* to define both the default gateway and static routes. It contains the same information as the Red Hat version, but it uses a slightly different syntax:

```
# Destination    Gateway      Netmask          Device
  127.0.0.0       0.0.0.0      255.255.255.0    lo
```

```
192.168.9.0        0.0.0.0          255.255.255.0    eth0
default            192.168.9.150    0.0.0.0          eth0
192.168.13.0       192.168.9.42     255.255.255.0    eth0
```

The first two entries specify the routes for the loopback interface and for the local network (the latter is required on Linux systems, in contrast to most other Unix versions). The third entry specifies the default gateway, and the final entry defines a static route to the 192.168.13 subnet via the gateway 192.168.9.42.

Solaris

Specifying the default gateway under Solaris is very easy. The file */etc/defaultrouter* contains a list of one or more IP addresses (on separate lines) corresponding to systems/devices that serve as default gateways for the local system.

 Be aware that you need to create this file yourself. It is not created as part of the installation process.

There is no built-in mechanism for specifying additional static routes to be added at boot time. However, you can create a script containing the desired commands and place it in (or link it to) the */etc/rc2.d* directory (or *rc3.d* if you prefer).

Tru64

Tru64 lists static routes in the file */etc/routes*. Here is an example:

```
default 192.168.9.150
-net 192.168.13.0 192.168.10.200
```

Each line of the file is passed as the arguments to the route command. The first entry in the example file illustrates the method for specifying the default gateway for the local system.

Network Testing and Troubleshooting

Once network configuration is complete, you will need to test network connectivity and address any problems that may arise. Here is an example testing scheme:

- Verify that the network hardware is working by examining any status lights on the adapter and switch or hub.
- Check basic network connectivity using the ping command. Be sure to use IP addresses instead of hostnames so you are not dependent on DNS.
- Test name resolution using ping with hostnames or nslookup (see "Managing DNS Servers" in Chapter 8).
- Check routing by pinging hosts beyond the local subnet (but inside the firewall).

- Test higher-level protocol connectivity by using telnet to a remote host. If this fails, be sure that inetd is running, that the telnet daemon is enabled, and that the remote host from which you are attempting to connect is allowed to do so (inetd is discussed in Chapter 8).

- If appropriate, verify that other protocols are working. For example, use a browser to test the web server and/or proxy setup. If there are problems, verify that the browser itself is configured properly by attempting to view a local page.

- Test any network servers that are present on the local system (see Chapter 8).

The first step is to test the network setup and connection with the ping command. ping is a simple utility that will tell you whether the connection is working and the basic setup is correct. It takes a remote hostname or IP address as its argument:*

```
$ ping hamlet
PING hamlet: 56 data bytes
64 bytes from 192.0.9.3: icmp_seq=0. time=0. ms
64 bytes from 192.0.9.3: icmp_seq=1. time=0. ms
64 bytes from 192.0.9.3: icmp_seq=4. time=0. ms
...
^C
----hamlet PING Statistics----
8 packets transmitted, 8 packets received, 0% packet loss
round-trip (ms)  min/avg/max = 0/0/0
```

From this output, it is obvious that *hamlet* is receiving the data sent by the local system, and the local system is receiving the data *hamlet* sends. On Solaris systems, ping's output is much simpler, but still answers the same central question: "Is the network working?":

```
$ ping duncan
duncan is alive
```

Use the -s option if you want more detailed output.

Begin by pinging a system in the local subnet. If this succeeds, try testing the network routes by pinging systems that should be reachable via defined gateways.

If pinging any remote system inside the firewall fails,† try pinging *localhost* and then the system's own IP address. If these fail also, check the output of *ifconfig* again to see if the interface has been configured correctly. If so, there may be a problem with the network adapter.

On the other hand, if pinging the local system succeeds, the problem lies either with the route to the remote host or in hardware beyond the local system. Check the routing tables for the former (make sure there is a route to the local subnet), and check

---

* Control-C terminates the command. Entering Control-T while it is running displays intermediate status information.

† If you need to check connectivity beyond the firewall, you need to use the ssh facility or some other higher-level protocol that is not blocked (e.g., http).

the status lights at the hub or switch for the latter. If hardware appears to be the problem, try swapping the network cable. This will either fix the problem or suggest that it lies with the connecting device or port within that device.

Once basic connectivity has been verified, continue testing by moving up the protocol stack, as outlined above.

Another utility that is occasionally useful for network troubleshooting is arp. This command displays and modifies IP-to-MAC address translation tables. Here is an example using its -a option, which displays all entries within the table:

```
# arp -a
mozart (192.168.9.99) at 00:00:F8:71:70:0C [ether] on eth0
bagel (192.168.9.75) at 00:40:95:9A:11:18 [ether] on eth0
lovelace (192.168.9.143) at 00:01:02:ED:FC:91 [ether] on eth0
sharon (192.168.9.4) at 00:50:04:0A:38:00 [ether] on eth0
acrasia (192.168.9.27) at 00:03:BA:0D:A7:EC [ether] on eth0
venus (192.168.9.35) at 00:D0:B7:88:53:8D [ether] on eth0
```

I found arp very useful for diagnosing a duplicate IP address that had been inadvertently assigned. The symptom of the problem was that a new printer worked only intermittently and often experienced long delays when jobs attempted to connect to it. After checking the printer and its configuration several times, it finally occurred to me to check arp. The output revealed another host with the IP address the printer was using. Once the printer's IP address was changed to a unique value, everything was fine.

arp also supports an -n option which bypasses name resolution and displays only IP addresses in the output. This can again be useful when there are DNS problems.

Once networking is configured and working, your next task is to monitor its activity and performance on an ongoing basis. These topics are covered in detail in "Monitoring the Network" in Chapter 8 and "Network Performance" in Chapter 15, respectively.

CHAPTER 6
Managing Users and Groups

User accounts and authentication are two of the most important areas for which a system administrator is responsible. User accounts are the means by which users present themselves to the system, prove that they are who they claim to be, and are granted or denied access to the information and resources on a system. Accordingly, properly setting up and managing user accounts is one of the administrator's chief tasks.

In this chapter we consider Unix user accounts, groups, and user authentication (the means by which the system verifies a user's identity). We will begin by spending a fair amount of time looking at the process of adding a new user. Later sections of the chapter will consider passwords and other aspects of user authentication in detail.

Unix Users and Groups

From the system's point of view, a user isn't necessarily an individual person. Technically, to the operating system, a user is an entity that can execute programs or own files. For example, some user accounts exist only to execute the processes required by a specific subsystem or service (and own the files associated with it); such users are sometimes referred to as *pseudo users*. In most cases, however, a user means a particular individual who can log in, edit files, run programs, and otherwise make use of the system.

Each user has a *username* that identifies him. When adding a new user account to the system, the administrator assigns the username a *user identification number* (UID). Internally, the UID is the system's way of identifying a user. The *username* is just mapped to the UID. The administrator also assigns each new user to one or more *groups*: a named collection of users who generally share a similar function (for example, being members of the same department or working on the same project). Each group has a *group identification number* (GID) that is analogous to the UID: it is the system's internal way of defining and identifying a group. Every user is a member of one or more groups. Taken together, a user's UID and group memberships determine what access rights he has to files and other system resources.

User account information is stored in several ASCII configuration files:

/etc/passwd
> User accounts.

/etc/shadow
> Encoded passwords and password settings. As we'll see, the name and location of this file varies.

/etc/group
> Group definitions and memberships.

/etc/gshadow
> Group passwords and administrators (Linux only).

We'll consider each of these files in turn.

The Password File, /etc/passwd

The file */etc/passwd* is the system's master list of information about users, and every user account has an entry within it. Each entry in the password file is a single line having the following form:

```
username:x:UID:GID:user information:home-directory:login-shell
```

The fields are separated by colons, and blank spaces are legal only within the *user information* field.

The meanings of the fields are as follows:

username
> The username assigned to the user. Since usernames are the basis for communications between users, they are not private or secure information. Most sites generate the usernames for all of their users in the same way: for example, by last name or first initial plus last name. Usernames are generally limited to 8 characters on Unix systems, although some Unix versions support longer ones.

x
> Traditionally, the second field in each password file entry holds the user's encoded password. When a shadow password file is in use (discussed below)—as is the case on most Unix systems—this field is conventionally set to the single character "x". AIX uses an exclamation point (!), and FreeBSD and trusted HP-UX use an asterisk (*).

UID
> The user identification number. Each distinct human user should have a unique UID. Conventionally, UIDs below 100 are used for system accounts (Linux now uses 500 as the cutoff, and FreeBSD uses 1000). Some sites choose to assign UID values according to some coding scheme where ranges of UIDs correspond to projects or departments (for example, 200–299 is used for chemistry department users, 300–399 is used for physics, and so on).

Multiple user accounts with the same UID are the same account from the system's point of view, even when the usernames differ. If you can, it's best to keep UIDs unique across your entire site and to use the same UID for a given user on every system to which he is given access.

GID

The user's primary group membership. This number is usually the identification number assigned to a group in the file */etc/group* (discussed later in this chapter), although technically the GID need not be listed there.[*] This field determines the group ownership of files the user creates. In addition, it gives the user access to files that are available to that group. Conventionally, GIDs below 100 are used for system groups.

user information

Conventionally contains the user's full name and, possibly, other job-related information. This field is also called the GECOS[†] field, after the name of the operating system whose remote login information was originally stored in the field. Additional information, such as office locations and office and home phone numbers, may also be stored here. Up to five distinct items may be placed within it, separated by commas. The interpretations of these five subfields vary substantially from system to system.

home directory

The user's home directory. When the user logs in, this is her initial working directory, and it is also the location where she will store her personal files.

login shell

The program used as the command interpreter for this user. Whenever the user logs in, this program is automatically started. This is usually one of */bin/sh* (Bourne shell), */bin/csh* (C shell), or */bin/ksh* (Korn shell).[‡] There are also alternative shells in wide use, including *bash*, the Bourne-Again shell (a Bourne shell–compatible replacement with many C shell– and Korn shell–like enhancements), and *tcsh*, an enhanced C shell–compatible shell.

On most systems, the */etc/shells* file lists the full pathnames of the programs that may be used as user shells (accounts with an invalid shell are refused login). On AIX systems, the valid shells are listed in the *shells* field in the *usw* stanza of */etc/security/login.cfg*:

```
usw:
 shells = /bin/sh,/bin/csh,/bin/ksh,/usr/bin/tcsh,...
```

---

[*] Except under AIX. No one will be able to log in to an AIX system without a group file; similarly, any user whose password file entry lists a GID not present in */etc/group* will not be able to log in.

[†] Sometimes spelled "GCOS."

[‡] The actual shell programs are seldom, if ever, really stored in */bin*—in fact, many systems don't even have a real */bin* directory—but there are usually links from the real path to this location.

Here is a typical entry in */etc/passwd*:

```
chavez:x:190:100:Rachel Chavez:/home/chavez:/bin/tcsh
```

This entry defines a user whose username is *chavez*. Her UID is 190, her primary group is group 100, her full name is Rachel Chavez, her home directory is */home/ chavez*, and she runs the enhanced C shell as her command interpreter.

Since */etc/passwd* is an ordinary ASCII text file, you can edit the file with any text editor. If you edit the password file manually, it's a good idea to save a copy of the unedited version so you can recover from errors:

```
# cd /etc
# cp passwd passwd.sav      Save a copy of the current file
# chmod go= passwd.sav      Protect the copy (or use a umask that does this)
# emacs passwd
```

If you want to be even more careful, you can copy the password file again, to something like *passwd.new*, and edit the new copy, renaming it */etc/passwd* only when you've successfully exited the editor. This will save you from having to recopy it from *passwd.sav* on those rare occasions when you totally munge the file in the editor.

However, a better tactic is to use the vipw command to facilitate the process, allowing it to be careful for you. vipw invokes an editor on a copy of the password file (traditionally */etc/ptmp* or */etc/opasswd*, but the name varies). The presence of this copy serves as a locking mechanism to prevent simultaneous password-file editing by two different users. The text editor used is selected via the *EDITOR* environment variable (the default is vi).

When you save the file and exit the editor, vipw performs some simple consistency checking. If this is successful, it renames the temporary file to */etc/passwd*. On Linux systems, it also stores a copy of the previous password file as */etc/passwd.OLD* (Red Hat) or */etc/passwd–* (SuSE).

The vipw command also has the advantage that it automatically performs—or reminds you about—other related activities that are required to activate the changes you just made. For example, on Solaris systems, it offers you the chance to edit the shadow password file as well. More importantly, on FreeBSD and Tru64 systems, it automatically runs the binary password database creation command, which turns the text file into the binary format used on those systems (pwd_mkdb and mkpasswd, respectively).

AIX does not provide vipw.

The Shadow Password File, /etc/shadow

Most Unix operating systems support a *shadow password file*: an additional user-account database file designed to store the encrypted passwords. On most systems, the password file must be world-readable in order for any command or service that translates usernames to/from UIDs to function properly. However, a world-readable password file means that it's very easy for the bad guys to get a copy of it. If the encrypted passwords are included there, a password cracking program could be run against them, and potentially discover some poorly chosen ones. A shadow password file has the advantage that it can be protected against anyone accessing it except the superuser, making it harder for anyone to acquire encoded passwords (you can't crack what you can't get).*

Here are the locations of the shadow password file on the various systems we are considering:

AIX	/etc/security/passwd
FreeBSD	/etc/master.passwd
Linux	/etc/shadow
Solaris	/etc/shadow

HP-UX and Tru64 store encoded passwords in the protected password database when enhanced security is installed (as we will see). Tru64 also has the option of using a traditional shadow password file with the enhanced security package.

At present, entries in the shadow password file typically have the following syntax:

```
username:encoded password:changed:minlife:maxlife:warn:inactive:expires:unused
```

username is the name of the user account, and *encoded password* is the encoded user password (often somewhat erroneously referred to as the "encrypted password"). The remaining fields within each entry are *password aging* settings. These items control the conditions under which a user is allowed to and is forced to change his password, as well as an optional account expiration date. We will discuss these items in detail later in this chapter.

The SuSE Linux version of the vipw command accepts a -s option with which to edit the shadow password file instead of the normal password file. On other systems, however, editing the shadow password file by hand is not recommended. The passwd command and related commands are provided to add and modify entries within the file (as we shall see), a task which can also be accomplished via the various graphical user account management tools (discussed later in this chapter).

The FreeBSD /etc/ master.passwd file

FreeBSD uses a different password file, */etc/master.passwd*, which also functions as a shadow password file in that it stores the encoded passwords and is protected from all non-*root* access. FreeBSD also maintains */etc/passwd*.

---

* Don't be too sanguine about this fact or let it make you complacent about user account security. Shadow password files provide another barrier against the bad guys, nothing more, and they are not invulnerable. For example, some network clients and services have had bugs in the past that made them vulnerable to buffer overrun attacks that could cause them to crash during their authentication phase. Encoded passwords from a shadow password file may be present in the resulting core dumps.

Here is a sample entry from *master.passwd*:

```
ng:encoded-pwd:194:100:staff:0:1136005200:J. Ng:/home/ng:/bin/tcsh
```

Entries in this file include three additional fields sandwiched between the GID and user's full name (highlighted in the example entry): a user class (see "FreeBSD user account controls," later in this chapter), the password expiration date, and the account expiration date (the latter are expressed as seconds since midnight on January 1, 1970 GMT). In this case, user *ng* is assigned to the staff user class, has no password expiration date, and has an account expiration date of June 1, 2002. We'll consider these fields in more detail later in this chapter.

The protected password database under HP-UX and Tru64

Systems that must conform to the C2 security level (a U.S. government–defined system security specification) have additional user account requirements. C2 security requires many system features, including per-user password requirements, aging specifications, and nonaccessible encoded passwords. When the optional enhanced security features are installed and enabled on HP-UX and Tru64 systems, a *protected password database* is used in addition to */etc/passwd*. (It is part of the Trusted Computing Base on these systems.)

Under HP-UX, the protected password database consists of a series of files, one per user, stored in the */tcb/files/auth/x* directory hierarchy, where *x* is a lowercase letter. Each user's file is placed in a file named the same as his username, in the subdirectory corresponding to its initial letter: *chavez*'s protected password database entry is */tcb/files/auth/c/chavez*. On Tru64 systems, the data is stored in the binary database */tcb/files/auth.db*.

The HP-UX files are structured as *authcap* entries (just as terminal capabilities are specified via *termcap* entries on some systems), consisting of a series of colon-separated keywords, each of which specifies one particular account attribute (see the *authcap* manual page for details).

All of this is best explained by an excerpt from *chavez*'s file:

```
chavez:u_name=chavez:u_id#190:\
    :u_pwd=*dkIkf,/Jd.:u_lock@:u_pickpw:chkent:
```

The entry begins with the username to which it applies. The *u_name* field again indicates the username and illustrates the format for attributes that take a character string value. The *u_id* field sets the UID and illustrates an attribute with a numerical value; *u_pwd* holds the encoded password. The *u_lock* and *u_pickpw* fields are Boolean attributes, for which true is the default when the name appears alone; a value of false is indicated by a trailing at-sign (@). In this case, the settings indicate that the account is not currently locked and that user *chavez* is allowed to select her password. The *chkent* keyword completes the entry.

Table 6-1 lists the fields in the protected password database. Note that all time periods are stored as seconds, and dates are stored as seconds since the beginning of

Unix time (although the tools for modifying these entries will prompt for days or weeks and actual dates).

Table 6-1. Protected password database fields

Field	Meaning
u_name	Username.
u_id	UID.
u_pwd	Encrypted password.
u_succhg	Date of last successful password change.
u_lock	Whether the account is locked.
u_nullpw	Whether a null password is allowed.
u_minlen	Minimum password length in characters (Tru64 only).
u_maxlen	Maximum password length.
u_minchg	Minimum time between password changes.
u_exp	Time period between forced password changes.
u_life	Amount of time after which account will be locked if password remains unchanged.
u_maxtries	Number of consecutive invalid password attempts after which account will be locked.
u_unlock	Amount of time after which an account locked because of u_maxtries will be unlocked (Tru64 only).
u_expdate	Date account expires (Tru64 only).
u_acct_expire	Account lifetime (HP-UX only).
u_pickpw	Whether user is allowed to select a password.
u_genpw	Whether user is allowed to use the system password generator.
u_restrict	Whether quality of proposed new passwords is checked.
u_policy	Site-specific program used to check proposed password (Tru64 only).
u_retired	Account is retired: no longer in use and locked (Tru64 only).
u_booauth	If > 0, user can boot the system when *d_boot_authenticate* is true in the system default file (HP-UX only).
u_pw_admin_num	Random number that functions as an initial account password.

All of the available fields are documented on the prpwd manual page.

System default values for protected password database fields are stored in */etc/auth/system/default* under Tru64 and */tcb/files/auth/system/default* under HP-UX. The values in users' records hold changes with respect to these settings. In addition, these system-wide defaults may be set in the *default* file:

- Tru64: *d_pw_expire_warning*, the default warning period for about-to-expire passwords.
- HP-UX: *d_boot_authenticate,* which indicates whether the boot command is password-protected or not.

It is not necessary to edit the protected password database files directly. Indeed, the relevant manual pages discourage you from doing so. Instead, you are encouraged to use the graphical utilities that are provided. Doing so is often helpful because these tools describe the various settings in a more understandable form than the corresponding field name alone provides. Nevertheless, there will be times when examining the entry for a particular user is the best way to diagnose a problem with an account, so you'll need to be able to make some sense of these files. We'll consider the most important of them when we discuss password management later in this chapter.

The Group File, /etc/group

Unix groups are a mechanism provided to enable arbitrary collections of users to share files and other system resources. As such, they provide one of the cornerstones of system security.

Groups may be defined in two ways:

- Implicitly, by GID; whenever a new GID appears in the fourth field of the password file, a new group is defined.
- Explicitly, by name and GID, via an entry in the file */etc/group*.

 The best administrative practice is to define *all* groups explicitly in *the /etc/group* file, although this is not required except under AIX.

Each entry in */etc/group* consists of a single line with the following form:

    name:*:GID:additional-users

The meanings of these fields are as follows:

name
> A name identifying the group. For example, a development group working on new simulation software might have the name *simulate*. Names are often restricted to eight characters.

`*` *or* `!`
> The second field is the traditional group password field, but it now holds some sort of placeholder character. Group passwords are no longer stored in the group file (and, in fact, they are used only by Linux systems).

GID
> This is the group's identification number. User groups generally start numbering at 100.*

---

* Usernames and group names are independent of one another, even when the same name is both a username and a group name. Similarly, UIDs and GIDs sharing the same numerical value have no intrinsic relation to one another.

additional-users

This field holds a list of users (and, on some systems, groups) who are members of the group, *in addition* to those users belonging to the group by virtue of */etc/ passwd* (who need not be listed). Names must be separated by commas (but no spaces may appear within the list).

Here are some typical entries from an */etc/group* file:

```
chem:!:200:root,williams,wong,jones
bio:!:300:root,chavez,harvey
genome:!:360:root
```

The first line defines the *chem* group. It assigns the group identification number (GID) 200 to this group. Unix will allow all users in the password file with GID 200 plus the additional users *williams*, *wong*, *jones*, and *root* to access this group's files. The *bio* and *genome* groups are also defined, with GIDs of 300 and 360, respectively. Users *chavez* and *harvey* are members of the *bio* group, and *root* is a member of both groups.

The various administrative tools for managing user accounts generally have facilities for manipulating groups and group memberships. In addition, the group file may be edited directly.

On Linux systems, the vigr command may be used to edit the group file while ensuring proper locking during the process. It works in an analogous way to vipw, creating a temporary copy of the group file for actual editing, and saving a copy of the previous group file when modifications are complete.

If your Linux system has vipw but not vigr, chances are that the latter is supported anyway. Create a symbolic link to vipw named vigr in the same directory location as the former to enable the variant version of the command: ln -s /usr/sbin/vipw /usr/sbin/vigr.

Most Unix systems impose a limit of 16 (or sometimes 32) group memberships per user. Tru64 also limits each line in */etc/group* to 225 characters. However, group definitions can be continued onto multiple lines by repeating the initial three fields.

User-private groups

Red Hat Linux uses a different method, known as *user-private groups* (UPGs), for assigning user primary group membership. In this scheme, every user is the sole member of a group with the same name as his username, whose GID is the same as his UID. Users can then be added as additional members to other groups as needed.

This approach is designed to make project file sharing easier. The goal is to allow a group of users, say *chem*, to share files in a directory, with every group member being able to modify any file. To accomplish this, you change the group ownership of the directory and its files to *chem*, and you turn on the setgid permission mode for the directory (chmod g+s), which causes new files created there to take their group ownership from the directory rather than the user's primary group.

The dilemma for this line of reasoning comes when deciding how group write access should be enabled for files in the shared directory. UPG proponents argue that this needs to be accomplished automatically by using a umask of 002. However, the side-effect of this convenience—users not having to explicitly assign write permission to files they want to share—means that other files the user creates (e.g., ones in his home directory) will also be group-writeable, a very undesirable outcome for security reasons. The "solution" is to make the user's primary group a private group, to which granting write access is benign or irrelevant, since the group is equivalent to the user.

In the end, however, UPGs are deeply embedded within the Red Hat Linux way of doing things, so administrators of Red Hat systems must learn to live with them.

 UPGs are also created by the FreeBSD `adduser` command.

Dynamic Group Memberships

In most cases, Unix does not distinguish between the two ways of establishing group membership; exceptions are the group ownership of new files and accounting data records, both of which generally reflect/record the current primary group membership. In other contexts—for example, file access—a user is simultaneously a member of all of her groups: her primary group and all of the groups for which she is listed as an additional member in */etc/group*.

The groups command displays a user's current group memberships:

```
$ groups
chem bio phys wheel
```

The groups command will also take a username as an argument. In this case, it lists the groups to which the specified user belongs. For example, the following commands lists the groups of which user *chavez* is a member:

```
$ groups chavez
users bio
```

In a few circumstances, the group that is the user's primary group is important. The most common example is accounting systems where resource usage is tracked by project or department in addition to user. In such contexts, the primary group is typically the one that is charged for a user's resource use.[*]

For such cases, a user can temporarily change the group designated as her primary group by using the `newgrp` command:

```
$ newgrp chem
```

---

[*] Solaris provides project-based accounting in another way. See "System V–Style Accounting: AIX, HP-UX, and Solaris" in Chapter 17 for details.

The `newgrp` command creates a new shell for this user, setting the primary group to be *chem*. Without an argument, `newgrp` resets the primary group to the one specified in the password file. The user must be a member of the group specified as the argument to this command.

FreeBSD does not support changing the primary group and so does not provide `newgrp`.

The `id` command can be used to display the currently active primary and secondary group memberships:

```
$ id
uid=190(chavez) gid=200(chem) groups=100(users),300(bio)
```

Current primary group membership is indicated by the "gid=" field in the command output. On Solaris systems, you must include the `-a` option to view the equivalent information.

The Linux group shadow file, /etc/gshadow

On Linux systems, an additional group configuration file is used. The file */etc/gshadow* is the group shadow password file. It contains entries of the form:

```
group-name:encoded password:group-admins:additional-users
```

where *group-name* is the name of the group, and *encoded password* is the encoded version of the group password. *group-admins* is a list of users who are allowed to administer the group by changing its password and modifying memberships within the group (note that being so designated does not make them members of the specified group). *additional-users* is almost always a copy of the additional group members list from */etc/group;* it is used by the `newgrp` command to determine which users can designate this group as their primary group (see below). Both lists are comma-separated and may not contain spaces.

Here are some sample entries from a group shadow file:

```
drama:xxxxxxxxxx:foster:langtree,siddons
bio:*:root:root,chavez,harvey
```

The group *drama* has a group password, and users *langtree* and *siddons* are members of it (as are any users who have it their primary group, as defined in */etc/passwd*). Its group administrator is user *foster* (who may or may not be a member of this group). In contrast, group *bio* has a disabled group password (since an asterisk is not a valid encoding for any password character), *root* is its group administrator, and users *root*, *chavez*, and *harvey* are additional members of the group.

The SuSE version of the `vigr` command accepts a `-s` option in order to edit the shadow group file instead of the normal group file.

On Linux systems, the `newgrp` command works slightly differently, depending on the group's entry in the group password file:

- If the group has no password, `newgrp` fails unless the user is a member of the specified new group, either because it is her primary group or because her username is present in the additional members list in the group shadow password file, */etc/gshadow*.

  Because secondary group memberships for file access purposes are taken from the */etc/group* file, it makes no sense for a user to appear in the group shadow file but not in the main group file. Omitting a secondary user defined in */etc/group* from the shadow group list prevents him from using `newgrp` with that group, which might be desirable in some unusual circumstances.

- If the group has a password defined, any user who knows the password can change to this group with `newgrp` (the command prompts for the group password).

- If the group has a disabled password (indicated by an asterisk in the password field of */etc/gshadow*), no user may change her primary group to that group with `newgrp`.

The HP-UX /etc/logingroup file

If the file */etc/logingroup* exists on an HP-UX system, its contents are used to determine the initial group memberships when a user logs in. In this case, the additional members list in the group file is used to determine which users may change their primary group to a given group with `newgrp`. Common sense dictates that the additional members list in the *logingroup* file be a superset of the list in the corresponding entry in */etc/group*.

AIX group sets

AIX extends the basic Unix groups mechanism to allow a distinction to be made between the groups a user belongs to, which are defined by the password and group files, and those that are currently active. The latter are referred to as the *concurrent group set*; we'll refer to them as the "group set." The current *real group* and group set are used for a variety of accounting and security functions. The real group at login is the user's primary group, as defined in the password file. When a user logs in, the group set is set to the entire list of groups to which the user belongs.

The `setgroups` command is used to change the active group set and designated real group. The desired action is specified via the command's options, which are listed in Table 6-2.

Table 6-2. Options to the AIX setgroups command

Option	Meaning
-a glist	Add the listed groups to the group set.
-d glist	Delete the listed groups from the group set.

Table 6-2. Options to the AIX setgroups command (continued)

Option	Meaning
-s glist	Set the group set to the specified list of groups.
-r group	Set the real group (group owner of new files and processes, etc.).

For example, the following command adds the groups *phys* and *bio* to the user's current group set:

```
$ setgroups -a phys,bio
```

The following command adds *phys* to the current group set (if necessary) and designates it as the real group ID:

```
$ setgroups -r phys
```

The following command deletes the *phys* group from the current group set:

```
$ setgroups -d phys
```

If the *phys* group was also the current real group, the next group in the list (in this case *system*) becomes the real group when *phys* is removed from the current group set. Note that each time a setgroups command is executed, a new shell is created.

Without arguments, setgroups lists the user's defined groups and current group set:

```
$ setgroups
chavez:
user groups = chem,bio,phys,genome,staff
process groups = phys,bio,chem
```

The groups labeled "user groups" are the entire set of groups to which user *chavez* belongs, and the groups labeled "process groups" form the current group set.

User Account Database File Protections

Proper file ownership and protection on the user accounts database files are extremely important to maintaining system security. All of these files must be owned by *root* and a system group such as GID 0. The two shadow files should also prevent access by anyone but their owner. *root* may have write access to any of these files.

Apply the same ownership and protection to any copies of these files you make. For example, here is a long directory listing of the various files from one of our systems:

```
# ls -l /etc/pass* /etc/group* /etc/*shad*
-rw-r--r--   1 root     root         681 Mar 20 16:15 /etc/group
-rw-r--r--   1 root     root         752 Mar 20 16:11 /etc/group-
-r--r--r--   1 root     root         631 Mar  6 12:46 /etc/group.orig
-rw-r--r--   1 root     root        2679 Mar 19 13:15 /etc/passwd
-rw-r--r--   1 root     root        2674 Mar 19 13:15 /etc/passwd-
-rw-------   1 root     shadow      1285 Mar 19 13:11 /etc/shadow
-rw-------   1 root     shadow      1285 Mar 15 08:37 /etc/shadow-
```

We made a copy of the group file (*group.orig*) which we protected against all write access. The files with the hyphens appended to their name are backup files created by the `vipw` and `vigr` utilities. Whatever the specific files present on your system, ensure that all of them are protected properly, and make doubly sure that no shadow file is readable by anyone but the superuser.

Standard Unix Users and Groups

All Unix systems typically predefine many user accounts. With the exception of *root*, these accounts are seldom used for logins. The password file as shipped usually has these accounts disabled. Be sure to check the shadow password file on your system, however. System accounts without passwords are significant security holes that should be plugged right away.

The most common system user accounts are listed in Table 6-3.

Table 6-3. Standard Unix user accounts

Usernames	Description
root	User 0, the superuser. The defining feature of the superuser account is UID 0, not the username *root*; *any* account with UID 0 is a superuser account.
bin, daemon, adm, lp, sync, shutdown, sys	System accounts traditionally used to own system files and/or execute the associated system server processes. However, many Unix versions define these users but never actually use them for file ownership or process execution.
mail, news, ppp	Accounts associated with various subsystems and facilities. Again, these accounts serve to own the corresponding files and to execute the component processes.
postgres, mysql, xfs	Accounts created by optional facilities installed on the system to administer and execute their services. These three examples are accounts associated with Postgres, MySQL, and the X font server, respectively.
tcb	Administrative account that owns the C2-style security-related files and databases on some systems with enhanced security (tcb=trusted computing base).
nobody	Account used by NFS and some other facilities. As defined on BSD systems, *nobody* traditionally has the UID -2, which usually appears in the password file as 65534=$2^{16}-2$ (UIDs are of the unsigned data type: on 64-bit systems, this number may be much larger). System V's *nobody* UID is 60001. Some systems define usernames for both of them. Inexplicably, Red Hat uses 99 as *nobody*'s UID, although it defines other usernames for the traditional values.

Unix systems are similarly shipped with a */etc/group* file containing entries for standard groups. The most important of these are:

- *root, system, wheel,* or *sys*: The group with GID 0. Like the superuser, this group is very powerful and is the group owner of most system files.
- Most systems define a number of system groups, analogous to the similarly named system user accounts: *bin, daemon, sys, adm, tty, disk, lp,* and so on. Traditionally, these groups own various system files (e.g., *tty* often owns all the special files connected to serial lines); however, not all of them are actually used on every Unix system.
- FreeBSD and other BSD-based systems use the *kmem* group as the owner of programs required to read kernel memory.

- *mail*, *news*, *cron*, *uucp*: groups associated with various system facilities.
- *users* or *staff* (often GID 100): Many Unix systems provide a group as the default primary group for ordinary user accounts.

Using Groups Effectively

Effective file permissions are intimately connected to the structure of your system's groups. On many systems, groups are the only method the operating system provides to refer to and operate on arbitrary sets of users. Some sites define the groups on their systems to reflect the organizational divisions of their institution or company: one department becomes one group, for example (assuming a department is a relatively small organizational unit). However, this isn't necessarily what makes the most sense in terms of system security.

Groups should be defined on the basis of the need to share files and, correlatively, the need to protect files from unwanted access. This may involve combining several organizational units into one group or splitting a single organizational unit into several distinct groups. Groups need not mirror "reality" at all if that's not what security considerations call for.

Group divisions are often structured around projects; people who need to work together, using some set of common files and programs, become a group. Users own the files they use most exclusively (or sometimes a group administrator owns all the group's files), common files are protected to allow group access, and all of the group's files can exclude non–group member access without affecting anyone in the group. When someone works on more than one project, then he is made a member of both relevant groups.

When a new project begins, you can create a new group for it and set up some common directories to hold its shared files, protecting them to allow group access (read-execute if members won't need to add or delete files and read-write-execute if they will). Similarly, files will be given appropriate group permissions when they are created based on the access group members will need. New users added to the system for this project can have the new group as their primary group; relevant existing users can be added to it as secondary group members in the group file.

The Unix group mechanism is not a perfect security solution, however. For example, suppose that a user needs access to just one or two files that are owned by a group to which she doesn't belong, and you don't want to make her a member of the second group because it will give her other privileges that you don't want her to have. One solution is to provide a setgid program that allows her to access the needed files; the setuid and setgid access modes are the subject of the next subsection. However, to properly address such a dilemma, you have to go beyond what is offered by the standard Unix group scheme. Access control lists, a mechanism that allows file permissions to be specified on a per-user basis, are the best solution to such problems, and we will consider them in "Protecting Files and the Filesystem" in Chapter 7.

Managing User Accounts

In this section, we will consider the processes of adding, configuring, and removing user accounts on Unix systems.

Adding a New User Account

Adding a new user to the system involves the following tasks:

- Assign the user a username, a user ID number, and a primary group, and decide which other groups she should be a member of (if any). Enter this data into the system user account configuration files.
- Assign a password to the new account.
- Create a home directory for the user.
- Place initialization files in the user's home directory.
- Use chown and/or chgrp to give the new user ownership of his home directory and initialization files.
- Set other user account parameters appropriate for your system (possibly including password aging, account expiration date, resource limits, and system privileges).
- Add the user to any other facilities in use as appropriate (e.g., the disk quota system, mail system, and printing system).
- Grant or deny access to additional system resources as appropriate, using file protections or the resources' own internal mechanisms (e.g., the */etc/ftpusers* file controls access to the ftp facility).
- Perform any other site-specific initialization tasks.
- Test the new account.

We will consider each of these steps in detail in this section. This discussion assumes that you'll be adding a user by hand. Few people actually do this anymore, but it is important to understand the whole process even if you use a tool that automates a lot of it for you. The available tools are discussed later in this chapter.

Defining a New User Account

The process of creating a new user account begins by deciding on its basic settings: the username, UID, primary group, home directory location, login shell, and so on. If you assign UIDs by hand, it is usually easiest to do so according to some scheme. For example, you could choose the next available UID, assign UIDs from each range of 100 by department, or do whatever makes sense at your site. In any case, once these parameters have been chosen, the new account may be entered into the password file.

If you decide to edit the password file directly, keep the entries within it ordered according to user ID. New entries will be easier to add, and you'll be less likely to create unwanted duplicates.

Assigning a Shell

As we've seen, the final field in the password file specifies the login shell for each user. If this field is empty, it usually defaults to */bin/sh*, the Bourne shell.* On Linux systems, this is a link to the Bourne-Again shell bash (usually */usr/bin/bash*).

Users can change their login shell using the chsh command (or a similar command; see Table 6-4), and the system administrator may also use chsh to set or modify this password file field. For example, the following command will change user *chavez*'s login shell to the enhanced C shell:

```
# chsh -s /bin/tcsh chavez
```

For this purpose, the legal shells are defined in the file */etc/shells*; only programs whose pathnames are listed here may be selected as login shells by users other than *root*.† Here is a sample */etc/shells* file:

```
/bin/sh
/bin/csh
/bin/false
/usr/bin/bash
/usr/bin/csh
/usr/bin/ksh
/usr/bin/tcsh
```

Most of these shells are probably familiar to you. The unusual one, */bin/false*, is a shell used to disable access to an account;‡ it results in an immediate logout to any account using it as a login shell.

You may add additional entries to this file, if necessary. Be sure to specify a full pathname (in which no directory component is world-writable).

Table 6-4. Shell and full-name modification commands

Task	Command
Change login shell	Usual: chsh Solaris: passwd -e (*root* use only)
Change full name (GECOS field)	Usual: chfn Solaris: passwd -g (*root* use only)

---

* Or the superficially similar POSIX shell (which more closely resembles the Korn shell).

† This is actually a configuration option of the chsh command, so this restriction may or may not be enforced on your system.

‡ More accurately, the false command always exits immediately, with a return value signifying failure (the value 1). When this command is used as a login shell, the described behavior results.

Captive accounts

Sometimes it is desirable to limit what users can do on the system. For example, when users spend all their time running a single application program, you can make sure that's all they do by making that program their login shell (as defined in the password file). After the user successfully logs in, the program begins executing, and when the user exits from it, they are automatically logged out.

Not all programs can be used this way, however. If interactive input is required, for example, and there is no single correct way to invoke the program, then simply using it as a login shell won't work. Unix provides a *restricted shell* to address such problems.

A restricted shell is a modified version of the Bourne or Korn shell. The name and location of the restricted Bourne shell within the filesystem vary, but it is usually */bin/Rsh* (often a link to */usr/bin/Rsh*). rksh is the restricted Korn shell, and rbash is the restricted Bourne Again shell. These files are hard links to the same disk file as the regular shell, but they operate differently when invoked under the alternate names. AIX and Tru64 provide Rsh, HP-UX and Solaris provide rksh, and Linux systems provide rbash. Some shells let you specify restricted mode with a command-line flag (e.g., bash -restricted).

Restricted shells are suitable for creating *captive accounts*: user accounts that run only an administrator-specified set of actions and that are logged off automatically when they are finished. For example, a captive account might be used for an operator who runs backups via a menu set up by the administrator. Or a captive account might be used to place users directly into an application program at login. A captive account is set up by specifying the restricted shell as the user's login shell and creating a *.profile* file to perform the desired actions.

The restricted shell takes away some of the functionality of the normal shell. Specifically, users of a restricted shell may not:

- Use the *cd* command.
- Set or change the value of the *PATH*, *ENV*, or *SHELL* variables.
- Specify a command or filename containing a slash (/). In other words, only files in the current directory can be used.
- Use output redirection (> or >>).

Given these restrictions, a user running from a captive account must stay in whatever directory the *.profile* file places him. This directory should not be his home directory, to which he probably has write access; if he ended up there, he could replace the *.profile* file that controls his actions. The *PATH* variable should be set as minimally as possible.

A captive account must not be able to write to any of the directories in the defined path. Otherwise, a clever user could substitute his own executable for one of the commands he is allowed to run, allowing him to break free from captivity. What this means in practice is that the user should not be placed in any directory in the path as his final destination, and the current directory should *not* be in the search path if the current directory is writable.

Taking this idea to its logical conclusion, some administrators set up a separate *rbin* directory—often located as a subdirectory of the captive account's home directory—containing hard links to the set of commands the captive user is allowed to run. Then the administrator sets the user's search path to point only there. If you use this approach, however, you need to be careful in choosing the set of commands you give to the user. Many Unix commands have *shell escape* commands: ways of running another Unix command from within the command. For example, in vi you can run a shell command by preceding it with an exclamation point and entering it at the colon prompt (when available, the restricted version, rvi, removes this feature). If a command supports shell escapes, the user can generally run any command, including a unrestricted shell. While the path you set will still be in effect for commands run in this way, the user is not prevented from specifying a full pathname in a shell escape command. Thus, even a command as seemingly innocuous as more can allow a user to break free from a captive account, because a shell command may be run from more (and man) by preceding it with an exclamation point.

Be sure to check the manual pages carefully before deciding to include a command among the restricted set. Unfortunately, shell escapes are occasionally undocumented, although this is most true of game programs. In many cases, shell escapes are performed via an initial exclamation point or tilde-exclamation point (~!).

 In general, you should be wary of commands that allow any other programs to be run within them, even if they do not include explicit shell escapes. For example, a mail program might let a user invoke an editor, and most editors allow shell escapes.

Assigning a Password

Since passwords play a key role in overall system security, every user account should have a password. The passwd command may be used to assign an initial password for a user account. When used for this purpose, it takes the relevant username as its argument. For example, the following command assigns a password for the user *chavez*:

```
# passwd chavez
```

You are prompted for the password twice, and it does not appear on the screen. The same command may also be used to change a user's password, should this ever be necessary (for example, if she forgets it).

Criteria for selecting good passwords and techniques for checking password strength and specifying password lifetimes are discussed later in this chapter, after we have finished our consideration of creating user accounts.

Under AIX, whenever the superuser assigns a password to an account with `passwd` (either manually or indirectly via SMIT), that password is pre-expired, and the user will be required to change it at the next login.

Traditionally, Unix passwords were limited to a maximum length of 8 characters. Recent systems, including FreeBSD and Linux when using the MD5 encoding mechanims, and HP-UX and Tru64 in enhanced security mode, allow much longer ones (at least 128 characters). AIX and Solaris still currently limit passwords to 8 characters.

Creating a Home Directory

After adding a user to the */etc/passwd* file, you must create a home directory for the user. Use the `mkdir` command to create the directory in the appropriate location, and then set the permissions and ownership of the new directory appropriately. For example:

```
# mkdir /home/chavez
# chown chavez.chem /home/chavez
# chmod 755 /home/chavez
```

On Unix systems, user home directories conventionally are located in the */home* directory, but you may place them in any location you like.

User Environment Initialization Files

Next, you should give the user copies of the appropriate initialization files for the shell and graphical environment the account will run (as well as any additional files needed by commonly used facilities on your system).

The various shell initialization files are:

Bourne shell	*.profile*
C shell	*.login*, *.logout*, and *.cshrc*
Bourne-Again shell	*.profile*, *.bash_profile*, *.bash_login*, *.bash_logout*, and *.bashrc*
Enhanced C shell	*.login*, *.logout*, and *.tcshrc* (or *.cshrc*)
Korn shell	*.profile* and any file specified in the *ENV* environment variable (conventionally *.kshrc*)

These files must be located in the user's home directory. They are all shell scripts (each for its respective shell) that are executed in the standard input stream of the login shell, as if they had been invoked with `source` (C shells) or `.` (sh, bash, or ksh). The *.profile*, *.bash_profile*, *.bash_login*, and *.login* initialization files are executed at login.* *.cshrc*, *.tcshrc*, *.bashrc*, and *.kshrc* are executed every time a new shell is spawned. *.logout* and *.bash_logout* are executed when the user logs out.

As administrator, you should create standard initialization files for your system and store them in a standard location. Conventionally, the directory used for this purpose is */etc/skel*, and most Unix versions provide a variety of starter initialization files in this location. These standard initialization files and the entire directory tree in which they are kept should be writable only by *root*.

Here are the locations of the skeleton initialization file directories on the various systems:

AIX	*/etc/security* (contains *.profile* only)
FreeBSD	*/usr/share/skel*
HP-UX	*/etc/skel*
Linux	*/etc/skel*
Solaris	*/etc/skel*
Tru64	*/usr/skel*

In any case, you should copy the relevant file(s) to the user's home directory after you create it. For example:

```
# cp /etc/skel/.bash* /home/chavez
# cp /etc/skel/.log{in,out} /home/chavez
# cp /etc/skel/.tcshrc /home/chavez
# chown chavez.chem /home/chavez/.[a-z]*
```

There are, of course, more clever ways to do this. I tend to copy all the standard initialization files to a new account in case the user wants to use a different shell at some later point. It is up to the user to modify these files to customize her own user environment appropriately.

Depending on how you use your system, several other initialization files may be of interest. For example, many editors have configuration files (e.g., *.emacs*), as do user mail programs. In addition, the Unix graphical environments use various configuration files.

Sample login initialization files

The .*login* or .*profile* files are used to perform tasks that only need to be executed upon login, such as:

- Setting the search path
- Setting the default file protection (with `umask`)
- Setting the terminal type and initializing the terminal

---

* The bash shell executes as many of *.bash_profile*, *.bash_login*, and *.profile* as exist in a user's home directory (in that order).

- Setting other environment variables
- Performing other customization functions necessary at your site

The contents of a simple *.login* file are listed below; it will serve to illustrate some of its potential uses (which we have indicated with comments):

```
# sample .login file
limit coredumpsize 0k          # suppress core files
umask 022                      # set default umask
mesg y                         # enable messages via write
biff y                         # enable new mail messages
# add items to the system path
setenv PATH "$PATH:/usr/local/bin:~/bin:."
setenv PRINTER ps              # default printer
setenv EDITOR emacs            # preferred editor
setenv MORE -c                 # make more always clear screen
# set an application-specific environment variable
setenv ARCH_DIR /home/pubg95/archdir/
# set command prompt to hostname plus current command number
set prompt = '`hostname`-\!> '
# very simple terminal handling
echo -n "Enter terminal type: "; set tt=$<
if ("$tt" == "") then
  set tt="vt100"
endif
setenv TERM $tt
```

We can create a very similar *.profile* file:

```
# sample .profile file
ulimit -c 0
umask 022
mesg y
biff y
PATH=$PATH:usr/local/bin:$HOME/bin:.
PRINTER=ps
EDITOR=emacs
MORE=-c
ARCH_DIR=/home/pubg95/archdir/
PS1="`hostname`-\!> "
export PATH PRINTER EDITOR MORE ARCH_DIR PS1
echo -n "Enter terminal type: "; read tt
if [ "$tt" = "" ]; then
  tt="vt100"
fi
export TERM=$tt
```

The main differences are in the ulimit command, the different syntax for environment variables (including the export commands), and the different mechanism for obtaining and testing user input.

Sample shell initialization files

Shell initialization files are designed to perform tasks that need to be executed whenever a new shell is created. These tasks include setting shell variables (some of which have important functions; others are useful abbreviations) and defining aliases (alternate names for commands). Unlike environment variables such as *TERM*, shell variables and aliases are not automatically passed to new shells; therefore, they need to be established whenever the operating system starts a new shell.

The contents of a simple *.cshrc* file are illustrated by this example:

```
# sample .cshrc file
alias j jobs                    # define some aliases
alias h history
alias l ls -aFx
alias ll ls -aFxl
alias psa "ps aux | head"
# the next alias shows the method for including a replaceable
# command line parameter within an alias definition: \!:1 => $1
alias psg "ps aux | egrep 'PID|\!:1' | more -c"
# set shell variables to specified various features
set history = 100               # remember 100 commands
set savehist = 100              # save 100 commands across logins
set nobeep                      # never beep!
set autologout 60               # logout after 1 hour idle time
set noclobber                   # warn about overwriting files
set ignoreeof                   # don't interpret ^D as logout
set prompt = "`hostname-\!>> " # set prompt
```

If you are using the enhanced C shell, tcsh, you might modify the last two commands and add a couple of others:

```
set correct cmd                 # try to correct mistyped commands
set ignoreeof 2                 # 2 ^D's => logout
set rmstar                      # confirm rm * commands
set prompt="%m:%~-%h>> "        # prompt is: hostname:dir-cmd_num>>
```

The Bourne-Again shell similarly uses *.bashrc* as its shell initialization file. In the Korn shell, a shell initialization file may be defined via the *ENV* environment variable (usually in *.profile*):

```
export ENV=$HOME/.kshrc
```

An alternate shell initialization file can be specified for bash via the *BASH_ENV* environment variable.

Both of these shells define aliases using a slightly variant syntax; an equal sign is included between the alias and its definition:

```
alias l="ls -lxF"
```

Consult the documentation for any of the shells to determine all of the available options and features and the shell variables used enable them.

 Be aware that the Bourne-Again shell (bash) behaves differently depending on whether it is invoked as */bin/sh* or not (if so, it emulates the behavior of the traditional Bourne shell in some areas).

The AIX /etc/security/environ file

AIX provides an additional configuration file where you may set environment variables that are applied to the user's process at login. Here is a sample stanza from that file:

```
chavez:
    userenv = "MAIL=/var/spool/mail/chavez,MAILCHECK=1800"
    sysenv =  "NAME=chavez@dalton"
```

This entry specifies three environment variables for user *chavez*, specifying her mail spool folder, how often to check for new mail (every 30 minutes), and the value of the *NAME* environment variable, respectively. The *userenv* and *sysenv* entries differ in that the latter may not be modified.

If you include an entry named *default* in this file, its settings will be applied to all users who do not have an explicit stanza of their own.

Desktop environment initialization files

System administrators are frequently asked to provide configuration files that initialize a user's graphical environment. These environments are all based on the X window system, and its most commonly used initialization files are named *.xinitrc, .xsession*, and *.Xauthority*. Specific window managers and desktop environments also generally support one or more separate configuration files. For example, the Common Desktop Environment (CDE) uses the *.dtprofile* initialization file, as well as many files below the ~/.dt subdirectory.

Commercial Unix versions generally install CDE as the default windowing system. Unix versions available for free allow users to choose from several offerings, usually at installation time (FreeBSD works this way). On Linux systems, the systemwide X initialization files dynamically choose a desktop environment when X is started.

For example, on Red Hat Linux systems, in the absence of any other configuration, desktop initialization occurs via the file */etc/X11/xinit/xinitrc*, which then runs */etc/X11/xinit/Xclients*. The latter file uses the following process to determine which environment to start:

- If the file */etc/sysconfig/desktop* exists, its contents are compared to the keywords GNOME, KDE, and AnotherLevel (in this order). If a keyword is found within the file, the corresponding environment is started if it is available. If not, the system attempts to start the GNOME desktop environment, falling back to KDE in the event of failure (for example, if GNOME is not installed).

- Next, the file *.wm_style* is searched for in the user's home directory. If it is found and it contains any of the keywords AfterStep, WindowMaker, fvwm95, Mwm or Lesstif (searching in that order and taking only the first match), the corresponding window manager is started if it is available.

- If nothing else has been selected or is present at this point, the fvwm (tried first) or twm simple window manager is started (the latter is available on virtually every Unix system because it is part of the X11 distribution).

As you can see, the default process tries to start a fancy graphical environment first, falling back to various simpler ones if necessary.

What happens on SuSE Linux systems depends on the specifics of how the user account was created:

- In the absence of any *.xinitrc* file in the user's home directory, the default X initialization file (*/usr/lib/X11/xinit/xinitrc*) attempts to start the fvwm2, fvwm, and twm window managers (in that order).

- If the default *.xinitrc* file (contained in */etc/skel*) has been copied to the user's home directory, a different procedure is used. First, the script checks to see whether the environment variable *WINDOWMANAGER* is set. If so, it uses the path specified as its value as the location of the desired window manager.

  If this environment variable is not set, the initialization file attempts to locate the KDE environment files on the system. If these files cannot be located, those for fvwm2 are tried next, followed by all window managers listed in the file */usr/X11/bin/wmlist*.

  The first window manager that is located is set as the value of the *WINDOWMANAGER* environment variable. As the file concludes, this variable is used to initiate the selected graphical environment. In this way, the SuSE scheme differs from that of Red Hat in that it attempts to start only a single window manager.

Systemwide initialization files

For Bourne, Bourne-Again, and Korn shell users, the file */etc/profile* serves as a systemwide initialization file that is executed before the user's personal login initialization file. The *PATH* variable is almost always defined in it; it therefore applies to users without explicit *PATH* variables set in their *.profile*. Sometimes a default umask is also specified here. Here is a simple */etc/profile* file designed for the bash shell, adapted from a Red Hat Linux system; we have annotated it with comments:

```
PATH="$PATH:/usr/X11R6/bin"
PS1="[\u@\h \w]\\$ "          # prompt: [user@host dir]$
ulimit -c 0                   # suppress core files
# set umask, depending on whether UPGs are used or not
alias id=/usr/bin/id          # shorthand to save space
if [ `id -gn` = `id -un` -a `id -u` -gt 99 ]; then
    umask 002                 # UID=GID>99 so it's a UPG
else
    umask 022
fi
```

```
USER=`id -un`
unalias id                    # remove id alias
LOGNAME=$USER
MAIL="/var/spool/mail/$USER"
HOSTNAME=`/bin/hostname`
HISTSIZE=100
HISTFILESIZE=100
export PATH PS1 USER LOGNAME MAIL HOSTNAME HISTSIZE HISTFILESIZE
# execute all executable shell scripts in /etc/profile.d
for i in /etc/profile.d/*.sh ; do
    if [ -x $i ]; then
        . $i
    fi
done
unset i                       # clean up
```

Under Red Hat Linux, the files in the installed */etc/profile.d* directory initialize the user's language environment and also set up various optional facilities. The system administrator may, of course, add scripts to this directory, as desired.

All systemwide initialization files should be writable only by the superuser.

The tcsh shell also has systemwide initialization files: */etc/csh.cshrc*, */etc/csh.login* and */etc/csh.logout*.

AIX supports an additional systemwide initialization file, */etc/environment* (in addition to */etc/security/environ*, mentioned earlier). This file is executed by init and affects all login shells via the environment they inherit from init. It is used to set the initial path and a variety of environment variables.

The best way to customize systemwide initialization files is to create your own scripts that are designed to run after the standard scripts complete. Hooks are sometimes provided for you. For example, on SuSE Linux systems, */etc/profile* automatically calls a script named */etc/profile.local*, if it exists, as its final action. Even if your version of the initialization file does not have such a hook, it is easy enough to add one (via the source or . command, depending on the shell).

This approach is preferable to modifying the vendor-supplied file itself since future operating system upgrades will often replace these files without warning. If all you've added to them is a simple call to your own local, systemwide initialization script, it will be easy to insert the same thing into the new version of the vendor's file. On the other hand, if you do decide to modify the original files, be sure to keep a copy of your modified version in a safe location so that you can restore it or merge it into the new vendor file after the upgrade.

Setting File Ownership

After you copy the appropriate initialization files to the user's home directory, you must make the new user the owner of the home directory and all its files and subdirectories. To do this, execute a command like this one:

```
# chown -R chavez:chem /home/chavez
```

The -R ("recursive") option changes the ownership on the directory and all the files and subdirectories it contains, all the way down. Note that the second component of chown's first parameter should be the user's primary group.

Adding the User to Other System Facilities

The user should also be added to the other facilities in use at your site. Doing so may involve the following activities:

- Adding the user to various security facilities, which may include assigning system privileges. Some of these are discussed later in this chapter.
- Assigning disk quotas (see "Monitoring and Managing Disk Space Usage" in Chapter 15).
- Defining a mail alias and fulfilling any other requirements for the mail system that is in use (see Chapter 9).
- Setting print-queue access (see Chapter 13).

Any other site-specific user account tasks, for local or third-party applications, should ideally be performed as part of the account creation process.

Specifying Other User Account Controls

Many systems provide additional methods for specifying various characteristics of user accounts. The sorts of controls include password change and content, valid login times and locations, and resource limits. Table 6-5 lists the general sorts of account attributes provided by the various Unix flavors.

Table 6-5. Available user account attribute types

	Password lifetimes	Password strength	Login times	Login locations	Resource limits
AIX	yes	yes	yes	yes	yes
FreeBSD	yes	no	yes	yes	yes
HP-UX	yes	yes	yes	no	no
Linux	yes	yes	PAM[a]	PAM[a]	PAM[a]
Solaris	yes	yes	no	no	no
Tru64	yes	yes	yes	no	yes

[a] Functionality is provided by the PAM facility (discussed later in this chapter).

We will defer consideration of password-related account controls until later in this chapter. In this section, we'll consider available controls on when and where logins can occur and how to set user account resource limits in other context of each operating system. We'll also consider other settings related to the login process as appropriate.

AIX user account controls

AIX provides several classes of user account attributes, which are stored in a series of files in */etc/security*:

/etc/security/environ
> Environment variable settings (discussed previously)

/etc/security/group
> Group administrators

/etc/security/limits
> Per-account resource limits

/etc/security/login.cfg
> Per-tty valid login time and system-wide valid login shells

/etc/security/passwd
> User passwords and password change data and flags

/etc/security/user
> Per-user account login controls and attributes

The contents of all of these files may be modified with the chuser command and from SMIT. We'll look at several of these file in this subsection and at */etc/security/ passwd* and the password-related controls in */etc/security/user* later in this chapter.

Here are two sample stanzas from */etc/security/user*:

```
default:
      admin = false              Is an administrative user.
      login = true               Can login locally.
      daemon = true              Can run cron/SRC processes.
      rlogin = true              Can connect with rlogin.
      su = true                  Users can su to this account.
      sugroups = ALL             Groups that can su to this user.
      logintimes = ALL           Valid login times.
      ttys = ALL                 Valid terminal locations.
      umask = 022                Default umask.
      expires = 0                Expiration date (0=never).
      account_locked = false     Account is not locked.
      loginretries = 0           Unlimited tries before account is locked.
   chavez:
      admin = true
      admingroups = chem,bio     Groups she administers.
      expires = 1231013004       Account expires 1:30 A.M. 12/31/04
      loginretries = 5           Lock account after 5 login failures.
      logintimes = 1-5:0800-2000 User can log in M–F, 8 A.M.–6 P.M.
```

The first stanza specifies default values for various settings. These values are used when a user has no specific stanza for her account and when her stanza omits one of these settings. The second stanza sets some characteristics of user *chavez*'s account, including an expiration date and allowed login times.

Here is a sample stanza from */etc/security/limits*, which sets resource limits for user processes:

```
chavez:
    fsize = 2097151
    core = 0
    cpu = -1
    data = 262144
    rss = 65536
    stack = 65536
    nofiles = 2000
```

The *default* stanza specifies default values. Resource limits are discussed in detail in "Monitoring and Controlling Processes" in Chapter 15.

The */etc/security/login.cfg* file contains login-related settings on a per-tty basis. Here is a sample *default* stanza:

```
default:
    logintimes =              Valid login times (blank=all).
    logindisable = 10         Disable terminal after 10 unsuccessful tries.
    logindelay = 5            Wait 5*#tries seconds between login attempts.
    logininterval = 60        Reset failure count after 60 seconds.
    loginreenable = 30        Unlock a locked port after 30 minutes (0=never).
```

This file also contains the list of valid shells in its *usw* stanza (as noted previously).

FreeBSD user account controls

FreeBSD uses two additional configuration files to control user access to the system and to set other user account attributes. The first of these, */etc/login.access*, controls system access by user and/or system and/or tty port. Here are some sample entries:

```
+:chavez:dalton.ahania.com    Chavez can login from dalton.
+:users:.ahania.com           The users group can log in from this domain.
-:ALL EXCEPT wheel:console    Only administrators on the console.
```

The three fields hold + or – (for allow and deny), a list of users and/or groups, and a login origination location, respectively.

The order of entries within this file is important: the first matching entry is used. Thus, the example file would not work properly, because users who are not members of the *wheel* group would still be able to log in on the console due to the second rule. We would need to move the third entry to the beginning of the file to correct this. In general, entries should move from the most specific to the most general.

The */etc/login.conf* is used to specify a wide variety of user account attributes. It does so by defining user classes, consisting of named groups of settings. User accounts are assigned to a class via the fifth field in the */etc/master.passwd* file.

The following example file defines three classes, the *default* class, used for users not assigned to a specific class, and the classes *standard* and *gauss*:

```
default:\
# Initial environment settings
        :copyright=/etc/COPYRIGHT:\
        :welcome=/etc/motd:\
        :nologin=/etc/nologin:\
        :requirehome:\
        :setenv=PRINTER=picasso,EDITOR=emacs:
        :path=/bin /usr/bin /usr/X11R6/bin ...:\
        :umask=022:\
# Login time and origin settings
        :times.allow=MoTuWeThFr0700-1800,Sa0900-1700:\
        :ttys.deny=console:\
        :hosts.allow=*.ahania.com:\
# System resource settings
        :cputime=3600:\
        :maxproc=20:\
        :priority=0:\
# Password settings
        :passwd_format=md5:\
        :minpasswordlen=8:
standard:\
        :tc=default:
gauss:\
        :cputime=unlimited:\
        :coredumpsize=0:\
        :priority=1:\
        :times.allow=:times.deny=:
        :tc=default:
```

The *default* class contains settings related to the initial user environment (login messages file, the location for the *nologin* file, settings for environment variables, and the umask), allowed and/or denied login times, originating ttys and/or hosts (denials take precedence over allows if there are conflicts), system resource settings (see "Monitoring and Controlling Processes" in Chapter 15 for more information) and settings related to password encoding, selection and lifetimes (discussed later in this chapter).

The *standard* class is equivalent to the *default* class since its only attribute is the *tc* capability include directive (used to include the settings from one entry within another). The *gauss* class defines a more generous maximum CPU-usage setting, disables core file creation, sets the default process priority to 1 (one step lower than normal), and allows logins all of the time. Its final attribute also includes the settings from the *default* class. The preceding attributes act as overrides to the default settings since the first instance of an attribute within an entry is the one that is used.

After editing the *login.conf* file, you need to run the cap_mkdb command:

```
# cap_mkdb -v /etc/login.conf
cap_mkdb: 9 capability records
```

Linux user account controls

On Linux systems, the file */etc/login.defs* contains settings related to the general login process and user account creation and modification. The most important entries in this file are described in the following annotated example file:

```
ENV_PATH path                       Search paths for users and root.
ENV_ROOTPATH path
FAIL_DELAY 10                       Wait 10 seconds between login tries.
LOGIN_RETRIES 5                     Maximum number of login attempts.
LOGIN_TIMEOUT 30                    Seconds to wait for a password.
FAILLOG_ENAB yes                    Record login failures in /var/log/faillog.
LOG_UNKFAIL_ENAB yes                Include usernames in the failure log.
LASTLOG_ENAB yes                    Record all logins to /var/log/lastlog.
MOTD_FILE /etc/motd;/etc/motd.1     List of message-of-the-day files.
HUSHLOGIN_FILE .hushlogin           Name of hushlogin file (see below).
DEFAULT_HOME yes                    Allow logins when user's home is inaccessible.
UID_MIN 100                         Minimum/maximum values for UIDs/GIDs
UID_MAX 20000                          (used by the standard user account
GID_MIN 100                            creation tools).
GID_MAX 2000
CHFN_AUTH no                        Don't require a password to use chfn.
CHFN_RESTRICT frw                   Allow changes to full name and office and work phones.
```

The HUSHLOGIN_FILE setting controls whether any message-of-the-day display can be suppressed on a per-user basis. If this parameter is set to a filename without a path (traditionally *.hushlogin*), these messages will not be displayed if a file of that name is present in the user's home directory (the file's contents are irrelevant).

This parameter may also be set to a full pathname, for example, */etc/hushlogin*. In this case, its contents are a list of usernames and/or login shells; when a user logs in, if either the user's login name or shell is listed within this file, the messages will not be displayed.

In addition to the settings listed in the sample file, */etc/login.defs* includes several other settings related to user passwords; we will consider them later in this chapter. See the manual page for *login.defs* for additional information about the contents of this configuration file.

Solaris login process settings

Solaris supports a systemwide login process configuration file, */etc/default/login*. Here are some of the most useful login-related settings within it:

```
CONSOLE=/dev/console        If defined, limits logins on this tty to root.
TIMEOUT=300                 Abandon login attempt after 5 minutes.
SYSLOG=YES                  Log root logins and login failures to syslog.
SLEEPTIME=4                 Wait 4 seconds between failed logins.
SYSLOG_FAILED_LOGINS=1      Generate syslog record at second failure.
```

Specifying login time restrictions under HP-UX and Tru64

HP-UX and Tru64 allow the system administrator to specify when during a day, week, or other time period a user's account may be used. This is done with the *u_tod* attribute in the protected password database. For example, the following entry from an HP-UX system generally allows access on weekdays and during the day (6 A.M. to 6 A.M.) on the weekend but forbids access on any day between 2 A.M. and 5 A.M.:

```
u_tod=Wk0500-2359,Sa0600-1800,Su0600-1800
```

Here is the equivalent setting under Tru64:

```
u_tod=Wk,Sa-Su0600-1800,Never0200-0500
```

The *Never* keyword supported by Tru64 allows for a more compact description of the same restrictions.

Testing the New Account

Minimally, you should try logging in as the new user. A successful login will confirm that the username and password are valid and that the home directory exists and is accessible. Next, verify that the initialization files have executed: for example, look at the environment variables, or try an alias that you expect to be defined. This will determine if the ownership of the initialization files is correct; they won't execute if it isn't. (You should test the initialization files separately before installing them into the skeleton directory.) Try clearing the terminal screen. This will test the terminal type setup section of the initialization file.

Using su to re-create a user's environment

The su command is ideal for some types of testing of newly created accounts. When given a username as an argument, su allows a user to temporarily become another user (*root* is simply the default username to change to when none is specified). Under the default mode of operation, most of the user environment is unchanged by the su command: the current directory does not change, values of most environment variables don't change (including *USER*), and so on. However, the option – (a minus sign alone) may be used to simulate a full login by another user without actually logging out yourself. This option is useful for testing new user accounts and also when you are trying to reproduce a user's problem.

For example, the following command simulates a login session for user *harvey*:

```
# su - harvey
*********************************************************
**       Regular Maintenance from 20:00 - 23:00 today  **
*********************************************************
harvey@phoenix /home/harvey>> clear
```

In addition to its usefulness for new-account testing, such a technique is very handy when users complain about "broken" commands and the like.

Once testing is complete, the new user account is ready to use.

Disabling and Removing User Accounts

Users come and users go, but it isn't always completely clear what to do with their accounts when they leave. For one thing, they sometimes come back. Even when they don't, someone else will probably take their place and may need files related to projects that were in progress when they left.

When someone stops using a particular computer or leaves the organization, it is a good idea to disable their account(s) as soon as you are notified. If the person was dismissed or otherwise left under less than ideal circumstances, it is imperative that you do so. Disabling an account is one task that you can do very quickly: simply add an asterisk to the beginning of the encoded password* in the shadow password file, and they will no longer be able to log in. You can then do whatever else needs to be done to retire or remove their account in whatever haste or leisure is appropriate.

On many systems, you can also lock an account from the command line using the passwd command's -l option. Locking an account via an administrative command generally uses the same strategy of prepending a character to the encoded password.

For example, the following command locks user *chavez*'s account:

```
# passwd -l chavez
```

Disabling or locking an account rather than immediately removing its password file entry prevents file ownership problems that can crop up when a username is deleted. On some systems, the passwd command's -u option may be used to unlock a locked user account; changing the user's password also has the side effect of unlocking the account.

Here are the specifics for the systems we are considering (all commands take the username as their final argument):

System	Lock account	Unlock account
AIX	chuser account_locked=true	chuser account_locked=false
FreeBSD	chpass -e	chpass -e
HP-UX	passwd -l	edit /etc/passwd manually
Linux	passwd -l	passwd -u
Solaris	passwd -l	edit /etc/shadow manually
Tru64	usermod -x administrative_lock_ applied=1	usermod -x administrative_lock_ applied=0

On FreeBSD systems, you can disable an account by setting the account expiration date to a date in the past with chpass -e, or you can edit the shadow password file manually.

---

* By adding an asterisk to the beginning of the password field, you can even restore the account at a later time with its password intact, should that be appropriate. This is an example of the recommended practice of making an action reversible whenever possible and practical.

On HP-UX and Tru64 systems running enhanced security, a user account is locked via the *u_lock* protected password database attribute (where *u_lock* means locked, and *u_lock@* means unlocked), rather than via the password modification mechanism.

When it is clear that the user account is no longer needed, the account can either be *retired* or completely removed from the system (by deleting the user's home directory and changing ownerships of all other files he owned). A retired account continues to exist as a UID within the user account databases,* but no access is allowed through it; its password is set to asterisks and its expiration date is often set to the date the user departed. You will also want to change the login shell to */bin/false* to prevent access via Kerberos or ssh.

Removing a user account

When removing or retiring a user from the system, there are several other things that you might need to do, including the following:

- Change other passwords that the user knew.
- Terminate any running processes belonging to the user (possibly after investigating any that appear strange or suspicious).
- Remove the user from any secondary groups.
- Remove the user's mail spool file (possibly archiving it first).
- Define/redefine a mail alias for the user account in the mail aliases file (*/etc/aliases*) and any include files referenced in it, sending mail to someone else or to the user's new email address, as appropriate. Don't forget to remove the user from any mailing lists.
- Make sure the user hasn't left any cron or at jobs around. If there is any other batch system in use, check those queues too. See if the user has any pending print jobs, and delete them if she does. (I found an enormous, gratuitous one on one occasion.)
- Make a backup of the user's home directory and then delete it, change its ownership, move all or part of it, or leave it alone, as appropriate.
- Search the system for other files owned by the user and handle them as appropriate (find will be helpful here).
- Remove the user from the quota system or set the account's quota to 0.
- Remove the user from any other system facilities where her username may be specified (e.g., printer permissions, */etc/hosts.equiv* and *.rhosts* files if they are in use).
- Perform any other site-specific termination activities that may be necessary.

---

* C2 and higher U.S. government security levels require that accounts be retired rather than removed so that UIDs don't get reused, and system audit, accounting, and other records remain unambiguous.

In most cases, writing a script to perform all of these activities is very helpful and time-saving in the long run.

Administrative Tools for Managing User Accounts

Shell scripts to automate the user account creation process have been common for a long time on Unix systems, and most Unix vendors/environments also provide graphical utilities for the same purpose. The latter tools allow you to make selections from pick lists and radio buttons and type information into blank fields to specify the various user account settings.

The advantage of these tools is that they take care of remembering a lot of the steps in the process for you. They usually add entries to all relevant account configuration files (including ones related to enhanced security, if appropriate), and they make sure that the entries are formatted correctly. They also typically create the user's home directory, copy initialization files to it, and set the correct ownerships and protection. Most of the tools are extremely easy to use, if somewhat tedious and occasionally time-consuming.

All of these tools also suffer from the same disadvantage: their abilities usually end after completing the activities I've already listed. A few of them perform one or two additional activities—adding the user to the mail system is among the most common—but that still leaves a lot to do. The best of these tools allow you to customize the activities that are performed, as well as the default values for available account settings; unfortunately, many of the currently available Unix user account management facilities lack any serious customization capabilities.

The best way to use any of these tools is first to set up defaults that reflect how things are done on your system, to the extent that the tool you've chosen allows you to do so. Doing so will minimize the time it takes to add a new user account to the configuration files. Then write a script that you can run by hand after the tool completes its work to automate the rest of the steps required to fully set up a new account.

In this section, we'll consider the most important and useful command-line utilities and graphical facilities for managing user accounts that are available on the Unix systems we are considering.

Command-Line Utilities

Most systems provide something in the way of command-line utilities for manipulating user accounts and sometimes groups. Note that in most cases, user passwords still need to be set separately using the `passwd` command.

The useradd command: HP-UX, Linux, Solaris, and Tru64

Three commands for managing user accounts are provided on many Unix systems: useradd, for adding new accounts; usermod, for changing the settings of existing accounts; and userdel, for deleting user accounts. HP-UX, Linux, Solaris, and Tru64 support these commands.

The useradd command has two modes: defining a new user and setting systemwide defaults. By default, useradd adds a new user to the system, with the desired username specified as its final argument. Other attributes of the user account are specified using useradd's many options, described in the Table 6-6.

Table 6-6. useradd command options

Option	Meaning
-u *uid*	UID (defaults to next highest unused UID).
-g *group*	Primary group.
-G *groups*	Comma-separated list of secondary groups.
-d *dir*	Home directory full pathname (defaults to *current-base-dir/username*; the current base directory is itself specified with useradd's -D option, and is usually set to */home*). Tru64 also provides the -H option for specifying the home directory base when creating a new user account.
-s *shell*	Full path to login shell.
-c *name*	Full name (GECOS field text).
-m	Create user's home directory and copy the standard initialization files to it.
-k *dir*	Skeleton directory containing initialization files (defaults to */etc/skel*); only valid with -m. Not provided by Tru64.
-e *date*	Account expiration date (default is none); format: *yyyy-mm-dd*.
-f *n*	Number of days the account can be inactive before being disabled automatically.
-p	On Tru64 systems, requests a prompt for the user's initial password. On Linux systems, the option requires the encoded password as its parameter, making it useful in scripts where you are importing user accounts from another Unix system's password file, but it is of little use otherwise. Solaris and HP-UX do not provide this option.
-D	Set option defaults using the -f, -e, -g, and -b options (the last option is -d on Tru64 systems). The -s option may also be used on Linux systems, and the -x skel_dir=*path* option provides the same functionality under Tru64.
-b *dir*	Default base directory for user home directories (for example */home*); only valid with -D. Tru64 uses -d for this function (as well as for its normal role when creating a user account).

Here is the useradd command to create user *chavez*:

```
# useradd -g chem -G bio,phys -s /bin/tcsh -c "Rachel Chavez" -m chavez
```

This command creates user *chavez*, creates the directory */home/chavez* if it doesn't already exist (the home directory's pathname is the concatenation of the base directory and the username), and copies initialization files from */etc/skel* to the new directory. It also places *chavez* in the groups *chem*, *bio*, and *phys* (the first one is her primary group). Her UID will be the next available number on the system.

The Tru64 version of useradd also supports setting some extended attributes using the -x option. For example, the following command sets the valid login hours for user *chavez* to weekdays during normal U.S. business hours:

```
# useradd normal options -x logon_hours=Wk0900-1700 chavez
```

Setting useradd's defaults. The -D option tells useradd to set systemwide default values for various account attributes to be used when creating new users. For example, the following command sets the default group to *chem*, sets the base directory to */abode*, and disables the account inactivity feature.

```
# useradd -D -g chem -b /abode -f -1
```

You can display the current options by executing useradd -D alone or by examining the command's configuration file, */etc/default/useradd*; here is an example file:

```
GROUP=100
HOME=/home
INACTIVE=-1
EXPIRE=2005-01-01
SHELL=/bin/bash
SKEL=/etc/skel
```

Although there is no command option to do so, you can change the default skeleton directory location by editing the SKEL line in the file.

Modifying accounts with usermod. A user's current attributes may be changed with the usermod command, which accepts all useradd options except -k. The -d and -m now refer to the new home directory for the user (and -m now requires -d). In addition, usermod supports a -l option, used to change the username of an existing user. For example, the following command changes *chavez*'s username to *vasquez*, moving her home directory appropriately:

```
# usermod -m -l vasquez chavez
```

In addition to these commands, the normal chsh and chfn commands available to all users may be used by the superuser to quickly change the login shell and user information fields for a user account, respectively (passwd -e and -g under Solaris).

For example, on a Linux system, the following commands change user *harvey*'s login shell to the Korn shell and specify a variety of information to be stored in the user information field of his password file entry:

```
# chsh -s /bin/ksh harvey
# chfn -f "Harvey Thomas" -o 220 -p 555-9876 -h 555-1234 harvey
```

User *harvey*'s password file entry now looks like this:

```
harvey:x:500:502:Harvey Thomas,220,555-9876,555-1234:/home/harvey:/bin/ksh
```

The various items of information stored within the user information field are separated by commas.

 There is no hard-and-fast convention for what the various subfields of the password file user information field should be used for, and different tools use them to hold different information. Accordingly, the format of the chfn command varies somewhat in different Unix versions and even within individual versions. The preceding example was from a Red Hat Linux system; the SuSE Linux version of the command would be:

```
# chfn -f "Harvey Thomas" -r 220 -w 555-9876 \
   -h 555-1234 harvey
```

In the same way, the GUI tools for managing user accounts also divide this field using different schemes.

Removing accounts with userdel. The userdel command is used to remove a user account. For example, the following command removes user *chavez* from the password and shadow password file:

```
# userdel chavez
```

The -r option may be added to remove her home directory and all files within it as well as the account itself.

On Tru64 systems, userdel retires user accounts by default. You must use the -D option to actually delete them.

Commands for managing groups

Similarly, the groupadd and groupmod commands may be used to set up and modify new groups (although not their memberships). For example, the following command adds a new group named *socio*:

```
# groupadd socio
```

The new group is assigned the next available user group GID number (greater than 99); alternatively, a specific GID may be specified by adding the -g option to the command.

The following command renames the *bio* group to *biochem*:

```
# groupmod -n biochem bio
```

A group's GID may also be changed with the -g option to groupmod.

Finally, you can remove unwanted groups in a way analogous to userdel with the groupdel command, which takes the name of the group to be deleted as its argument. Note that this command does not let you remove a group that is serving as the primary group for any user account.

The Linux gpasswd command

Linux systems provide the gpasswd command for adding and removing members of groups and for specifying group administrators. For example, the following command adds user *chavez* to the *drama* group:

```
# gpasswd -a chavez drama
```

In a similar way, the -d option may be used to remove the user from a group.

The -A and -M options are used to specify the list of group administrators and additional group members (allowed to use newgrp) in the group shadow file. For example, the following command designates users *root* and *nielsen* as group administrators for the *bio* group:

```
# gpasswd -A root,nielsen bio
```

The list of users specified as the argument to either option is comma-separated and must not contain any internal spaces. Note that these options replace the current settings in */etc/gshadow*; they do not add additional users to the existing list.

The FreeBSD user account utilities

FreeBSD provides the adduser command for creating new user accounts. It does so by prompting you for all of the required information, as in this example, which creates an account for user *zelda*:

```
# adduser -s
Enter username [a-z0-9_-]: zelda
Enter full name []: Zelda Zelinski
Enter shell csh ... ksh [tcsh]: return
Enter home directory (full path) [/home/zelda]: return
Uid [1021]: return
Enter login class: default []: staff
Login group zelda [zelda]: return
Login group is ``zelda''.
Invite zelda into other groups: chem phys bio no
[no]: chem
Enter password []: not echoed
Enter password again []: not echoed
Name:    zelda
Password: ****
Fullname: Zelda Zelinski
Uid:     1021
Gid:     1021 (zelda)
Class:   staff
Groups:  zelda chem
HOME:    /home/zelda
Shell:   /bin/tcsh
OK? (y/n) [y]: y
Add another user? (y/n) [y]: n
```

The command's -s (silent) option provides a less verbose prompt sequence. The opposite is -v, which prompts for default settings for this session before adding users:

```
# adduser -v
Enter your default shell: csh ... ksh no [sh]: tcsh
Your default shell is: tcsh -> /bin/tcsh
Enter your default HOME partition: [/home]: return
Copy dotfiles from: /usr/share/skel no [/usr/share/skel]: return
Send message from file: /etc/adduser.message no
[/etc/adduser.message]: return
Use passwords (y/n) [y]: return
...
```

Verbose mode also inserts additional prompts for an alternate message file and additional message recipient, and it allows you to add to the generated message before it is sent. The verbose/silent setting for the command is sticky: when neither option is included, it defaults to the last value to which it was set.

Normally, the adduser command generates a mail message for the new user as it creates the account. The default message template is stored in */etc/adduser.message*. Here is the default new user welcome message for our new user *zelda*:

```
To: zelda
Subject: Welcome
Zelda Zelinski,
your account ``zelda'' was created.
Have fun!
See also chpass(1), finger(1), passwd(1)
```

I always modify the standard message file to fix the capitalization error and hideous quoting. This is one case where I don't bother keeping a copy of the original!

adduser's defaults are stored in the */etc/adduser.conf* configuration file. Here is an example:

```
defaultpasswd = yes          Require passwords.
dotdir = "/usr/share/skel"
send_message = "/etc/adduser.message"
logfile = "/var/log/adduser"
home = "/home"
path = ('/bin', '/usr/bin', '/usr/local/bin')
shellpref = ('csh', 'sh', 'bash', 'tcsh', 'ksh', 'no')
defaultshell = "tcsh"
defaultgroup = USER          This setting enables user-private groups.
defaultclass = "users"       Default user class (initially empty).
uid_start = "1000"           Lowest UID assigned.
```

As is noted in the comment, the *defaultclass* variable is initially unassigned. If you want to have a specific login class assigned to new accounts, you'll need to modify this entry in the configuration file (as we have done above). User classes are described in detail later in this chapter.

You can also specify some of these items via adduser options, as in this example:

```
# adduser -dotdir /etc/skel -group chem -home /homes2 \
         -shell /usr/bin/tcsh -class users
```

The chpass command may be used to modify existing user accounts. When invoked, it places you into a form within an editor (selected with the *EDITOR* environment variable), where you may modify the account settings. Here is the form you will edit:

```
#Changing user database information for zelda.
Login: zelda
Password: $1$dGoBvscW$kE7rMy8xCPnrBuxkw//QHO
Uid [#]: 1021
Gid [# or name]: 1021
Change [month day year]: January 1, 2002        Most recent pwd change.
Expire [month day year]: December 31, 2005       Account expiration date.
Class: staff
Home directory: /home/zelda
Shell: /bin/tcsh
Full Name: Zelda Zelinski
Office Location:                                 Additional (optional) GECOS subfields.
Office Phone:
Home Phone:
Other information:
```

Be sure to modify only the settings data, leaving the general structure of the form intact.

The rmuser command may be used to remove a user account, as in this example:

```
# rmuser zelda
Matching password entry:
zelda:*:1021:1021:staff:0:0:Zelda Zelinski:/home/zelda:/bin/tcsh
Is this the entry you wish to remove? y
Remove user's home directory (/home/zelda)? y
```

The command also removes files belonging to the specified users from the various system temporary directories.

The AIX user account utilities

AIX provides the mkuser, chuser, and rmuser commands for creating, modifying, and deleting user accounts, respectively. Their syntax is so verbose, however, that it is usually much easier to use the SMIT tool when adding users interactively.

The mkuser command requires a series of *attribute=value* pairs specifying the account characteristics, followed at last by the username. Here is an example of using mkuser to add a new user account:

```
# mkuser home=/home/chavez gecos="Rachel Chavez" pgrp=chem chavez
```

Of the standard password file fields, we allow mkuser to select the UID and assign the default shell. mkuser uses the settings in */usr/lib/security/mkuser.default* for basic account attribute defaults, as in this example file:

```
user:
        pgrp = staff
        groups = staff
        shell = /usr/bin/ksh
        home = /home/$USER
```

```
admin:
        pgrp = system
        groups = system
        shell = /usr/bin/ksh
        home = /home/$USER
```

The two stanzas specify defaults for normal and administrative users, respectively. You create an administrative user by specifying the -a option on the mkuser command or by specifying the attribute *admin=true* to either mkuser or chuser.

Table 6-7 lists the most useful account attributes which can be specified to mkuser and chuser. Password-related attributed are omitted; they are discussed later in this chapter.

Table 6-7. AIX user account attributes

Attribute	Meaning
id=*UID*	UID
prgp=*group*	Primary group
groups=*list*	Group memberships (should include the primary group)
gecos="*full name*"	GECOS field entry
shell=*path*	Login shell
home=*path*	Home directory
login=*true/false*	Whether local logins are allowed
rlogin=*true/false*	Whether remote logins are allowed
daemon=*true/false*	Whether user can use cron or the SRC
logintimes=*list*	Valid login times
ttys=*list*	Valid tty locations
loginretries=*n*	Number of login failures after which to lock account
expire=*date*	Account expiration date
su=*true/false*	Whether other users can su to this account
sugroups=*list*	Groups allowed to su to this account
admin=*true/false*	Whether account is an administrative account
admgroups=*list*	Groups this account administers
umask=*mask*	Initial umask value
usrenv=*list*	List of initial environment variable assignments (normal user context)
sysenv=*list*	List of initial environment variable assignments (administrative user context)

The mkuser command runs the *mkuser.sys* script in */usr/lib/security* as part of its account creation process. The script is passed four arguments: the home directory, username, group, and shell for the new user account.

This script serves to create the user's home directory and copy one or both of */etc/security/.profile* and an internally generated *.login* file to it. Here is the *.login* file that the script generates:

```
#!/bin/csh
set path = ( /usr/bin /etc /usr/sbin /usr/ucb $HOME/bin ... )
setenv MAIL "/var/spool/mail/$LOGNAME"
setenv MAILMSG "[YOU HAVE NEW MAIL]"
if ( -f "$MAIL" && ! -z "$MAIL") then
     echo "$MAILMSG"
endif
```

It is equivalent to the standard *.profile* file.

You can modify or replace this script to perform more and/or different activities, if desired. For example, you might want to replace the exiting if statement that copies initialization files with commands like these (which use a standard skeleton file directory):

```
if [ -d /etc/skel ]; then
    for f in .profile .login .logout .cshrc .kshrc; do
        if [ -f /etc/skel/$f ] && [ ! -f $1/$f ]; then
            cp /etc/skel/$f $1
            chmod u+rwx,go-w $1/$f
            chown $2 $1/$f
            chgrp $3 $1/$f
        fi
    done
fi
```

These commands ensure that the skeleton directory and the files within it exist before attempting the copy. They also are careful to avoid overwriting any existing files.

Because */usr/lib/security* may be overwritten during an operating system upgrade, you'll need to save a copy of the new version of *mkuser.sys* if you modify it.

Removing user accounts. The rmuser command removes a user account. Include the -p option to remove the corresponding stanzas from all account configuration files rather than just the password file. For example, the following command removes all settings for user *chavez*:

```
# rmuser -p chavez
```

Utilities for managing groups. The mkgroup, chgroup, and rmgroup commands may be used to add, modify, and remove groups under AIX. Once again, the SMIT interface is at least as useful as the raw commands, although these come in handy once in a while. For example, the following command creates a new group named *webart* and assigns users to it (via secondary memberships):

```
# mkgroup users=lasala,yale,cox,dubail  webart
```

Graphical User Account Managers

With the exception of FreeBSD, all of the Unix variations we are considering provide some sort of graphical tool for managing user accounts. Some of them, most notably Linux, offer several tools. We'll consider the most useful of these for each operating system.

Managing users with SMIT under AIX

Figure 6-1 illustrates the SMIT user management facilities. The dialog on the left (and behind) displays the Security and Users submenu, and the dialog on the right displays the user account attributes dialog. In this case, we are adding a new user, but the dialog is the same for modifying a user account. The various fields in the dialog correspond to fields within the password file and the various secondary account configuration files within */etc/security*.

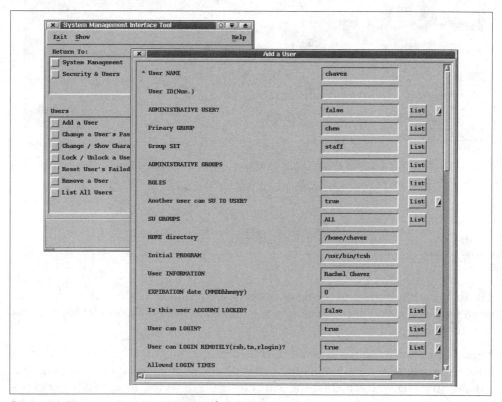

Figure 6-1. User account management with SMIT

The SMIT facility functions as an interface to the mkuser and related commands we considered earlier, and it is quite obvious which attributes the various dialog fields correspond to. SMIT also uses the same default values as mkuser.

Managing users with SAM under HP-UX

Figure 6-2 illustrates the SAM user management facilities on HP-UX systems. The dialog on the left shows the items available by selecting the Accounts for Users and Groups item in SAM's main window. The dialog at the upper left is used to access user account attributes when adding or modifying a user (we are doing the latter here). Its fields correspond to the traditional password file entries.

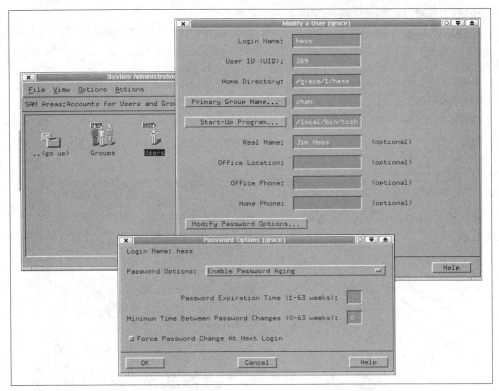

Figure 6-2. User account management with SAM

The dialog at the bottom of the figure appears as a result of clicking the Modify Password Options button in the main user account window. We'll consider its contents later in this chapter.

You can customize the user account creation and removal processes via the Actions → Task Customization menu path from the main user accounts window. This brings up a dialog in which you can enter the paths to scripts to be run before and after creating or removing a user account. The full pathname for the program name must be given to SAM, *root* must own it, it must have a mode of either 500 or 700—in other words, no group or other access and no write access for *root*—and every directory in its pathname must be writable only by *root*. (All of these are excellent security precautions to take for system programs and scripts that you create in general.)

The programs will be invoked as follows:

```
prog_name -l login -u uid -h home_dir -g group -s shell -p password \
        -R real_name -L office -H home_phone -O office_phone
```

SAM also allows you to define user templates: named sets of user account settings that can customize and speed up the account creation process. The Actions → User Templates submenu allows templates to be created, manipulated and activated. When defining or modifying a template, you use dialogs that are essentially identical to the ones used for normal user accounts.

Choose the Actions → User Templates → Select menu item to activate a template (selecting the desired template from the dialog that follows). Once this is done, the template's defaults are used for all new user accounts created in that SAM session until the template is changed or deselected.

Defaults for user accounts created without a template come from the file */usr/sam/lib/C/ug.ui*. Search the file for the string "default"; it should be apparent which ones set account attribute defaults. You can change them with a text editor, and the new values will be in effect the next time you run SAM. Note that some defaults (e.g., the home directory base) appear in more than one place within the file. Obviously, you'll need to be careful when editing this file. Copy the original before you edit so that you'll have a recovery path should something break.

HP-UX account and file exclusion. On HP-UX systems, SAM allows you to specify user accounts and files that it should never remove. The file */etc/sam/rmuser.excl* lists usernames that will not be removable from within SAM (although they may be retired). Similarly, the file *rmfiles.excl* in the same directory lists files that should never be removed from the system, even if the account of the user who owns them is removed. Naturally, these restrictions have no meaning except within SAM.

Linux graphical user managers

There are a plethora of choices for administering user accounts on Linux systems, including these:

- The Linuxconf facility, a distribution-independent system administration tool
- The Ximian Setup Tools' user accounts module
- The KDE User Manager
- The Red Hat User Manager on Red Hat Linux systems
- The YaST menu-based utility and the YaST2 graphical user account editor on SuSE Linux systems

We'll look at three of these here: Linuxconf and the KDE and Red Hat user managers.

Managing users with Linuxconf. The Linuxconf package is a graphical system administration tool designed specifically for Linux and available by default on some Red Hat systems. It includes a module for managing user accounts, which may be accessed from its main navigation tree or executed separately and directly by entering the userconf command. Once you select a user (or choose to add a new account), the User information dialog is displayed (see Figure 6-3).

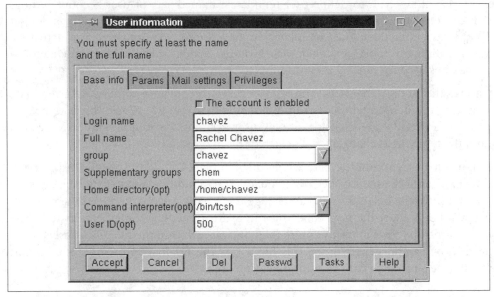

Figure 6-3. Managing user accounts with Linuxconf

The Base info panel allows you to enter information in the traditional password file fields; you may select from predefined lists of groups and login shells to specify those fields. The User ID field is optional; if it is left blank, Linuxconf assigns the next available UID number to a new user account. A user account may also be disabled by deselecting the click box at the top of the form.

On Red Hat systems, this tool automatically creates a user-private group when adding a new user account. It also automatically creates the user's home directory and populates it with the files from */etc/skel*. We will discuss the method for modifying the tool's default behavior later in this section.

The Params panel contains settings related to password aging, and we will consider it later in this chapter. The Mail settings panel sets up the user's email account. The final, rightmost panel, Privileges, contains settings related to this user's ability to use the Linuxconf tool for system administration tasks (discussed in "Role-Based Access Control" in Chapter 7).

Once you have finished entering or modifying a user account, use the buttons at the bottom of the dialog to complete the operation. The Accept button confirms the addition or change, and the Cancel button discards it. The Passwd button may be used to set or change the user's password, and the Del button deletes the current user account.

Deleting a user account is done via the dialog in Figure 6-4. It asks you to confirm the operation and also allows you to specify how to deal with the user's home directory. The first option (Archive the account's data) copies the home directory to a compressed tar file in, e.g., */home/oldaccounts*,with a name like *gomez-2002-04-02-12061.tar.gz*, with the first five components filled in with the username, year, month, day and time; the *oldaccounts* subdirectory is placed under Linuxconf's current default home directory location. After completing this backup operation, the home directory and all of its contents are deleted. The second option simply deletes the home directory and contents without saving them, and the third option leaves the directory and all of its files unchanged.

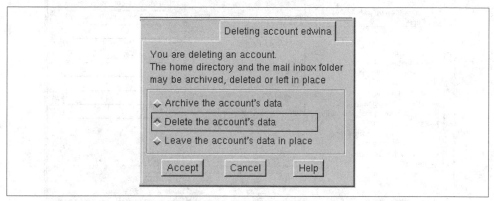

Figure 6-4. Deleting a user with Linuxconf

Linuxconf provides similar facilities for managing groups.

The defaults for various aspects of Linuxconf user account management may be specified via the Config → Users accounts → Policies → Password & account policies menu path. The resulting dialog is illustrated in Figure 6-5.

The lone click box in the dialog specifies whether user-private groups are in use. The next two fields specify the base directory and default permissions mode for user home directories. The next four fields specify scripts to be run when various actions are performed. By default, the first two of these fields are filled in and hold the paths to the scripts that Linuxconf uses when deleting a user account: the first (Delete account command) specifies the script used when a user account and the home directory are simply deleted, and the second (Archive account command) specifies the script used to archive a user home directory and then delete the user account.

I don't recommend modifying or replacing either of these scripts—although examining them can be instructive. Instead, use the next two fields to specify additional scripts to be run when accounts are created and deleted. Note that the account creation script runs after Linuxconf has completed its normal operations, and the account deletion script runs before Linuxconf performs its account deletion operations.

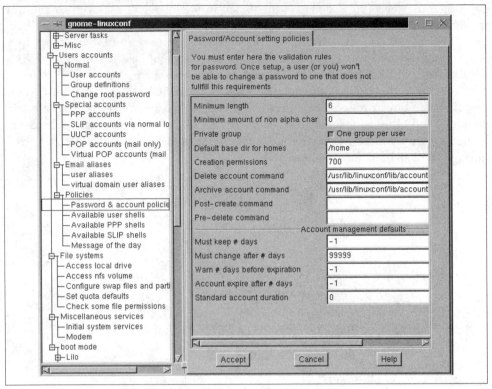

Figure 6-5. Specifying Linuxconf account defaults

The remaining settings in this dialog relate to password aging, and we will consider them later in this chapter.

The KDE User Manager. The KDE User Manager (written by Denis Perchine) is included as part of the KDE desktop environment. You start this facility by selecting the System → User Manager menu path on the KDE main menu or by running the kuser command. Figure 6-6 illustrates the facility's user account properties window.

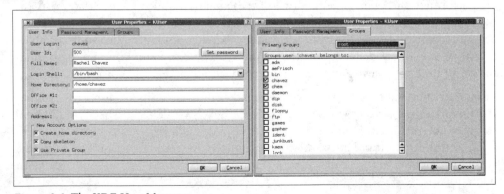

Figure 6-6. The KDE User Manager

The User Info panel (on the left in the figure) is used to set traditional password file fields as well as the password itself. The highlighted portion appears only when adding a new user account, and it allows you optionally to create the user home directory under */home*, copy files from the skeleton directory *(/etc/skel)*, and create a user-private group for the user account. As you can see, the tool also provides an interpretation of the various optional fields of the GECOS field.

The Groups panel displays the user's primary and secondary group memberships.

The third panel in this dialog, labeled Password Management, deals with password aging settings. We will look at it later in this chapter.

The KDE User Manager also provides similar dialog boxes for adding, modifying and deleting groups.

The KDE User Manager has a Preferences panel (reached via the Settings → Preferences menu path) that allows you to specify a different default home directory base and login shell, as well as whether to automatically create the home directory and/or copy files from */etc/skel*. It also specifies whether the user-private groups scheme should be used.

The Red Hat User Manager. Red Hat Linux provides its own user management utility (pictured in Figure 6-7). You can invoke it from the menus of the KDE and Gnome desktops as well as with the `redhat-config-users` command.

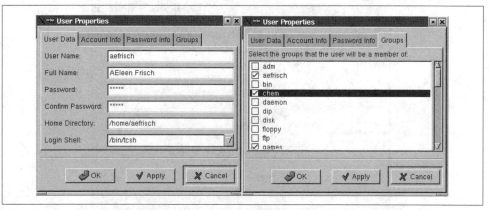

Figure 6-7. The Red Hat User Manager

The User Properties dialog of this tool contains four panels. The User Data panel (displayed on the left in the figure) holds the traditional password file entry fields. The Groups panel lists groups of which the user is a member (display on the right). Note that the primary group is not shown because user-private groups are always used and so the primary group name is always the same as the user account name.

The Account Info panel displays information about whether the user account is locked and any account expiration data which has been assigned. The Password Info panel displays password lifetime data (as we'll see).

Solaris GUI tools for managing user accounts

On Solaris systems, the Sun Management Console may be used to administer user accounts. The relevant module is accessed via the Infrastructure → AdminSuite menu path (and not via the seemingly more obviously named final main menu option). It is illustrated in Figure 6-8.

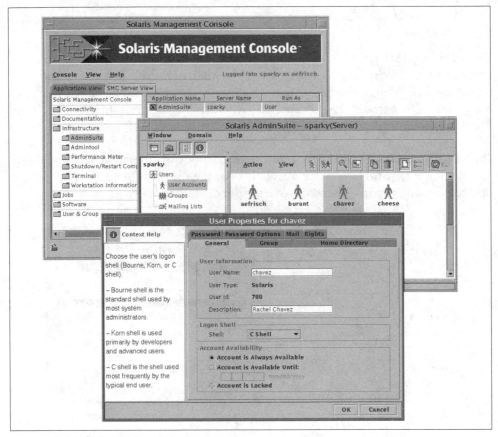

Figure 6-8. The Solaris AdminSuite user manager

The bottom dialog in the figure illustrates the interface for modifying an individual user account. The General panel (pictured) holds some of the traditional password file information as well as account locking and expiration settings. The other panels are Group (group memberships), Home Directory (specifies the home directory server and directory, whether it should be automounted, and its sharing protections), Password (allows you to set a password and force a password change), Password Options (password aging settings, discussed later in this chapter), Mail (email account information), and Rights (assigned roles, discussed in "Role-Based Access Control" in Chapter 7).

Managing user accounts with dxaccounts under Tru64

The Tru64 dxaccounts command starts the user account management facility. It may also be reached via sysman. It is pictured in Figure 6-9.

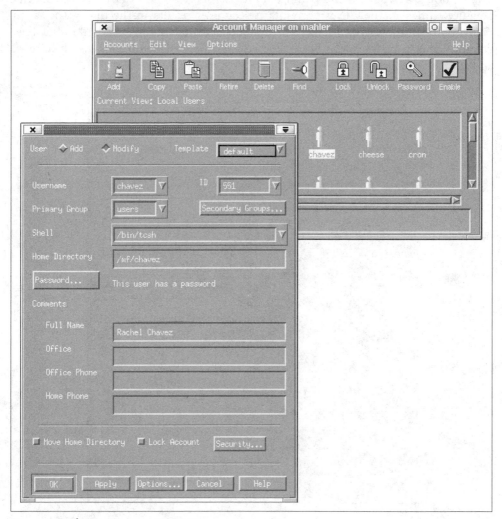

Figure 6-9. The Tru64 Account Manager

The window at the top of the figure displays icons for the user accounts. The buttons under the menu bar may be used to perform various operations on the selected account.

The window at the bottom of the figure displays the main user account dialog (in this case, we are modifying a user account). It holds the usual password file fields, as well as buttons that may be used to assign secondary group memberships and a password. The check boxes in the bottom section of the dialog allow you to change the location of the user's home directory and to lock and unlock the account.

The Security button is present only when enhanced security is activated on the system. We will discuss its use later.

The Options → General menu path from the user icon window allows you to specify default settings for new user accounts. Selecting it results in the dialog shown in Figure 6-10. It allows you to specify minimum and maximum user and group IDs, default primary group, home base directory, shell and skeleton directory locations, and several other settings.

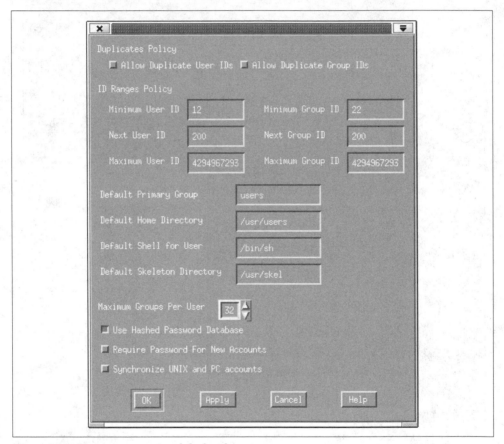

Figure 6-10. Setting user account default values

These default settings are actually stored in the file *$HOME/.sysman/Account_ defaults*. Editing this file often presents a quicker method for setting them.

The Tru64 Account Manager also allows you to define templates for user accounts: named groups of account settings, which can be used as defaults when creating new accounts and which may also be applied to existing accounts as a group. You can view the existing templates via the View → Local Templates menu path from the main window (illustrated in Figure 6-11).

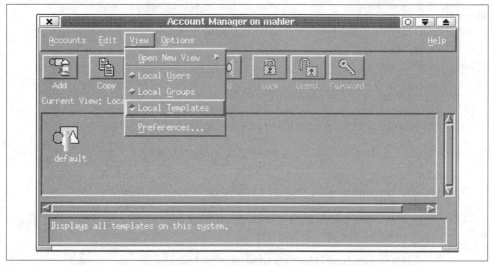

Figure 6-11. Tru64 user account templates

When you create or edit a template, you use dialogs that are essentially identical to those used in the Secuirty section for individual user accounts.

Templates are selected and applied via the Template pull-down menu at the upper left of the main user account dialog (see Figure 6-9). For a new account, selecting a template fills in the various fields in the dialog with the value from the template. When you change the template for an existing account or simply reselect the same template, you apply its current settings to the current account.

Automation You Have to Do Yourself

As we've noted, currently even the most full-featured automated account creation tools don't do everything that needs to be done to fully prepare an account for a new user. However, you can create a script yourself to do whatever the account creation tool you choose omits, and the time you spend on it will undoubtedly be more than made up for in the increased efficiency and decreased frustration with which you thereafter add new users.

The following is one approach to such a script (designed for a Linux system but easily adapted to others). It expects a username as its first argument and then takes any of several options, processing each one in turn and ignoring any it doesn't recognize. For space reasons, this approach contains only minimal error checking (but it doesn't do anything very risky, either):

```
#!/bin/sh
# local_add_user - finish account creation process
```

```
if [ $# -eq 0 ]; then             # no username
  exit
fi
do_mail=1                         # send mail unless told not to
user=$1; shift                    # save username
/usr/bin/chage -d 0 $user         # force password change
while [ $# -gt 0 ]; do            # loop over options
case $1 in                        # process each option
  "-m")                           # don't send mail
    do_mail=0
    ;;
  "-q")                           # turn on disk quotas
    (cd /chem; /usr/sbin/edquota -p proto $user)
    ;;
  "-p")                           # enable LPRng printer use
    # make sure there is a valid local printer group name
    if [ $# -gt 1 ]; then
        val=`/usr/bin/grep -c "ACCEPT .* GROUP=$2" /etc/lpd.perms`
        if [ $val -gt 0 ]; then
            # Add user to that printer group
            /usr/bin/gpasswd -a $user $2
        else
            /bin/echo "Invalid printer group name: $2"
        fi
        shift                     # gobble printer name
    else
        /bin/echo "You must specify a printer group name with -p"
    fi
    ;;
  "-g")                           # set up application program
    /bin/cat /chem/bin/g2k+/login >> /home/$user/.login
    /bin/cat /chem/bin/g2k+/profile >> /home/$user/.profile
    /chem/bin/g2k+/setup $user
    ;;
  *)                              # anything else
    /bin/echo "Garbage in, nothing out: $1"
    ;;
esac
shift                             # drop completed option off list
done
if [ $do_mail -eq 1 ]; then
  /usr/bin/mail -s Welcome $user < /chem/sys/welcome.txt
fi
```

At the discretion of the system administrator, this script can add the user to the disk quota facility (see "Monitoring and Managing Disk Space Usage" in Chapter 15), the LPRng printing subsystem (see "LPRng" in Chapter 13), send a welcoming mail message, and configure the account to use an application program. It also forces the user to change his password at his next login. We will consider user passwords and their administration in detail in the next section.

Administering User Passwords

Because passwords play a central role in overall system security, all user accounts should have passwords.* However, simply having a password is only the first step in making a user account secure. If the password is easy to figure out or guess, it will provide little real protection. In this section, we'll look at characteristics of good and bad passwords. The considerations discussed here apply both to choosing the *root* password (which the system administrator chooses) and to user passwords. In the latter case, your input usually takes the form of educating users about good and bad choices.

Selecting Effective Passwords

The purpose of passwords is to prevent unauthorized people from accessing user accounts and the system in general. The basic selection principle is this: *Passwords should be easy to remember but hard to figure out, guess, or crack.*

The first part of this principle argues against imposing automatically-generated random passwords (except when government or other mandated security policies require it). Many users have a very hard time remembering them, and in my experience, most users will keep a written record of their password for some period of time after they first receive it, even when this is explicitly prohibited.

If users are educated about easier ways to create good passwords, *and* you take advantage of features that Unix systems provide requiring passwords to be a reasonable length, users can select passwords that are just as good as system-generated ones. Allowing users to select their own passwords will make it much more likely that they will choose one that they can remember easily.

In practical terms, the second part of the principle means that passwords should be hard to guess even if someone is willing to go to a fair amount of effort—and there are plenty of people who are. This means that the following items should be avoided as passwords or even as components of passwords:

- Any part of your name or the name of any member of the your extended family (including significant others and pets) and circle of friends. Your maternal grandmother's maiden name is a lot easier to find out than you might think.

- Significant numbers to you or someone close to you: social security numbers, car license plate, phone number, birth dates, etc.

- The name of something that is or was important to you, like your favorite food, recording artist, movie, TV character, place, sports team, hobby, etc. Similarly, if

---

* The only possible exception I see is an isolated, non-networked system with no dial-in modems at a personal residence, but even then you might want to think about the potential risks from repair people, houseguests, neighborhood kids, and so on, before deciding not to use passwords. Every system in a commercial environment, even single-user systems in locked offices, should use passwords.

your thesis was on benzene, don't pick benzene as a password. The same goes for people, places, and things you especially dislike.

- Any names, numbers, people, places, or other items associated with your company or institution or its products.

We could obviously list more such items, but this should illustrate the basic idea.

Passwords should also be as immune as possible to attack by password-cracking programs, which means that the following items should not be selected as passwords:

- English words spelled correctly (because lists of them are so readily available in online dictionaries). You can use the `spell` or similar command to see if a word appears in the standard dictionary:

```
$ echo cerise xyzzy | spell -l
xyzzy
```

In this case, `spell` knows the word cerise (a color) but not xyzzy (although xyzzy is a bad password on other grounds). Note that the standard dictionary is quite limited (although larger ones are available on the web), and with the widespread availability of dictionaries on CD-ROM, virtually all English words ought to be avoided.

- Given the wide and easy accessibility of online dictionaries, this restriction is a good idea even at non-English-speaking sites. If two or more languages are in common use at your site, or in the area in which it's located, words in all of them should be avoided. Words in other kinds of published lists should also be avoided (for example, Klingon words).

- Truncated words spelled correctly should similarly be avoided: "conseque" is just as bad as "consequence." Such strings are just as vulnerable to dictionary-based attacks as is the entire word, and most existing password-cracking programs look specifically for them.

- The names of famous people, places, things, fictional characters, movies, TV shows, songs, slogans, and the like.

- Published password examples.

Avoiding passwords like the items in the first list makes it harder for someone to figure out your password. Avoiding the items in the second list makes it harder for someone to successfully break into an account using a brute-force, trial-and-error method, like a computer program.

If it seems farfetched that someone would go to the trouble of finding out a lot about you just to break into your computer account, keep in mind that hackers roaming around on the Internet looking for a system to break into represent only one kind of security threat. Internal security threats are at least as important for many sites, and insiders have an easier time locating personal information about other users.

In any case, getting on a specific system via any account is often just the first step toward some ultimate destination (or in a random stroll across the Internet); the account that opens the door need not necessarily have any obvious connection to the true goal, which might be elsewhere on the same system or on a completely different computer or site.

Simple modifications of any of these bad passwords, created by adding a single additional character, spelling it backwards, or permuting the letters, are still bad passwords and ought to be avoided. For example, avoid not only "john" but also "nhoj" and "ohnj" and "john2." It doesn't take a password-guessing program very long to try all combinations of adding one character, reversing, and permuting.

Although they are risky themselves, items from the second list can serve as the base for creating a better password (I don't recommend using any personal items in passwords at all). Passwords that use *two or more* of the following modifications to ordinary words are much more likely to be good choices:

- Embedding one or more extra characters, especially symbol and control characters.
- Misspelling it.
- Using unusual capitalization. All lowercase is not unusual; capitalization or inverse capitalization by word is not unusual (e.g., "StarTrek," "sTARtREK"); always capitalizing vowels is not unusual.
- Concatenating two or more words or parts of words.
- Embedding one word in the middle of another word ("kitdogten" embeds "dog" within "kitten").
- Interleaving two or more words: for example, "cdaotg" interleaves "dog" and "cat." With a little practice, some people can do this easily in their heads; others can't. If you need any significant delay between characters as you type in such a password, don't use them.

Table 6-8 illustrates some of these recommendations, using "StarTrek" as a base (although I'd recommend avoiding altogether anything having to do with Star Trek in passwords).

Table 6-8. Creating good passwords from bad ones

Bad	Better	Better Still
StarTrek *(predictable capitalization)*	sTartRek *(unusual capitalization)*	sTarkErT *(unusual capitalization and reversal)*
startrak *(misspelling)*	starTraK *(misspelling and unusual capitalization)*	$TaRTra# *(misspelling, symbols and unusual capitalization)*
StarDrek *(slang)*	jetrekdi *(embedding)*	jetr@kdi *(embedding and symbols)*
trekstar *(word swapping)*	sttraerk *(interleaving)*	sttr@erK *(interleaving, unusual capitalization and symbols)*

Of course, these would all be poor choices now. When selecting passwords and advising users about how to do so, keep in mind that the overall goal is that passwords be hard to guess, for humans and programs, but easy to remember and fast to type.

There are other ways of selecting passwords other than using real words as the base. Here are two popular examples:

- Form a password from the initial letters of each word in a memorable phrase, often a song lyric. Such passwords are easy to remember despite being nonsense strings. Transforming the resulting string results in an even better password. Two examples are given in Table 6-9.

Table 6-9. Forming passwords from memorable phrases

Phrase[a]	Password	Better Password
"Now it's a disco, but not for Lola"	niadbnfl	Ni1db!4L
"I can well recall the first time I ever went to sea"	icwrtftiepts	@cWr1t@eP2c

[a] The lines are from the songs "Copacabana" by Barry Manilow and "Old Admirals" by Al Stewart. Naturally, you wouldn't want to use either of these passwords now.

As the final example illustrates, Unix passwords can be longer than eight characters if you have so configured the system (discussed later in this chapter).

- Form a password by keyboard shifting: select a word or phrase that you can type easily, and then shift your hands on the keyboard in some way before typing it (e.g., up one and over one).[*] You have to be fairly coordinated for this method to be practical for you, but it does generate hard-to-crack passwords since they are essentially random.

---

[*] Some current password-cracking programs can crack words shifted by one position to the left or right, so a more complex shift is required.

Even using these techniques, passwords containing any part of your user account name, your full name, or any other item appearing in your password file entry are fundamentally insecure. Password-cracking programs perform a truly staggering amount of transformations on this information in order to attempt to crack passwords (including simple keyboard shifting!).

Here are some additional general recommendations about passwords and system security:

- There should be no unprotected accounts on the system. This includes accounts without passwords and accounts whose users have left the system but whose passwords remain unchanged. When a user leaves, always disable her account.

- Specify a minimum password length. We recommend setting it to at least eight characters, the traditional Unix maximum password length, which isn't really long enough anyway. Most Unix systems have the ability to use very long passwords; see the section on the PAM facility later in this chapter for details.

- Passwords *must* be changed under any of these (and similar) conditions:

  — Whenever someone other than the user it belongs to learns it, the password needs to be changed.

  — When a user leaves, all passwords that he knew must be changed.

  — When a system administrator leaves, the *root* password and all other site-wide passwords (e.g., dialup passwords) must be changed. Whether to force users to change their passwords is a matter of discretion, but keep in mind that the system administrator had full access to the shadow password file.

  — When a system administrator is fired, every password on the system should be changed since he had access to the list of encrypted passwords.

  — If you have even a suspicion that the shadow password file has been read via the network, the prudent thing is, again, to change every password on the system.

- The *root* password should be changed periodically in any case. Not every site needs to change it religiously once a month, but changing it once in a while when you don't think anyone has learned it errs on the side of caution, just in case you're wrong. Users can be sneaky; if you think someone was paying a bit too much attention to your fingers when you typed in the *root* password, change it.

- Equally important considerations apply to formulating password guidelines for users who have accounts at multiple sites. When we give an account to a new user, we always stress the importance of choosing a brand-new password for our site and not falling back on one of his old favorites, and he is similarly instructed not to use any password in effect at our site in any other context, either concurrently or in the future. Such regulations strike some users as excessively paranoid, but they are really just common sense.

Unix offers options for enforcing password-selection policies; they are discussed later in this section. If you'd like to use a carrot as well as a stick in this regard, see the section on educating users about passwords later in this chapter.

Forcing a password change

Most Unix systems provide commands that allow you to force a user to change her password at the next login. You can use such commands in a script on those (hopefully rare) occasions when everyone must change their password right away.

These are the commands provided by the versions we are considering (they all take a username as their final argument):

AIX	`pwdadm -f ADMCHG`
FreeBSD	`chpass` (interactive, but see below)
HP-UX	`passwd -f`
Linux	`chage -d 0 -M 999` (if not using aging)
Solaris	`passwd -f`
Tru64	`usermod -x password_must_change=1`

The Linux command works by setting the date of the last password change to January 1, 1970, and the maximum password lifetime to 999 days. This is a bit of a kludge, but it gets the job done when password aging is not in effect (you can go back and later remove the maximum password lifetime if desired). However, if you are using password aging, you can omit the `-M` option and allow the normal setting to perform the same function.

On FreeBSD systems, the user account modification utility is interactive and places you into an editor session by default. However, you can use the following script to automate the process of forcing a password change (accomplished by placing a date in the past into the Change field of the form):

```
#!/bin/tcsh
setenv EDITOR ed
/usr/bin/chpass $1 <<END
/Change/
s/:.*$/: 12 31 1999/
w
q
END
```

You can choose any past date that you like.

Managing dozens of passwords

When choosing successive passwords—and especially *root* passwords—try to avoid falling into a *simple* recognizable pattern. For example, if you always capitalize all the vowels, and someone knows this, you effectively lose the value of the unusual capitalization. Similarly, successive passwords are often chosen in the same way; don't always choose names of planets for your passwords. It is especially important to break such patterns when someone with longtime access to the *root* account—and hence well aware of past patterns in passwords—leaves the system or loses *root* access.

That said, it is impossible for most people—even system administrators—to remember all of the *root* passwords that they may need to know across a large enterprise without some scheme for generating/predicting the password for each system.

One approach is to use the same *root* password on all the systems administered by the same person or group of people. This may be effective for some sites, but it has the disadvantage that if the *root* password is compromised on any system, the entire group of systems is then wide open to unauthorized *root*-level access. Sites that have experienced such a break-in tend to give up the convenience of a single *root* password in favor of enhanced security and the ability to contain an intruder should the worst happen.

The solution in this case is to have some scheme (algorithm) for generating root passwords based on some characteristics of the computer system in question. Here is a simple example that indicates how to generate each character of the password in turn:

- First letter of the computer manufacturer
- Number of characters in the hostname
- Last letter of the hostname in uppercase
- First letter of the operating system name
- Operating system version number (first digit)
- The symbol character that is on the same diagonal of the keyboard as the first letter of the hostname (moving up and to the right)

For a Sun system running Solaris 7 named *dalton*, this would yield a password of "s6Ns8r%"; similarly, for an IBM RS/6000 running AIX 4.3 named *venus*, the password would be "i5Sa4&". Although they are too short at only six characters, these are decent passwords in terms of character variety and capitalization, and they are easy to generate mentally as needed with just a little practice.

Another problem that occurs with *root* passwords that are changed on a regular schedule is coordination of changes and getting the new value to everyone involved. Again, this is a case where an algorithm can be of great use. Let's suppose the *root* password must be changed monthly. Successive passwords can be generated from a base component that everyone knows and a varying portion generated from the current month and year. We'll use "xxxx"—a lousy choice, of course—for our base component in a simple example. Each month, we append the month and year to it, adding an additional "x" for months less than 10. In 2000, this would yield the passwords: xxxxx100, xxxxx200, …, xxxx1200.

A real scheme would need to be more complex, of course. This could be done by choosing a more obscure base component and generating the varying portion according to a more complex algorithm: something involving a simple mathematical computation using the month and year as variables, for example.

The advantage of such a system is that any administrator can change the monthly *root* password without inconveniencing other administrators. If someone attempts to use the old *root* password and is unsuccessful, she will realize that the monthly change has occurred and will already know the new password.

In fact, these two separate approaches could be combined. The remaining two (or more) characters of the system information-based password could be used for the varying portion based on the time period.

Educating Users About Selecting Effective Passwords

Helping users use the system more effectively is part of a system administrator's job. Sometimes, this means providing them with the information they need to do something, in this case, choose a good password. There are a variety of ways you might convey information and suggestions about password selection to the users on your systems or at your site:

- A one-page handout (one- or two-sided as appropriate)
- A mail message sent to all new users and, on occasion, to everyone with an account
- A manual page that you create—call it something like *goodpass*—and put into the local manual-page directory
- A script named *passwd* that (perhaps optionally) offers brief advice for selecting good passwords and then calls the real passwd command.

One or more of these suggestions may make sense at your site.

Password advice in the age of the Internet

The Internet and its myriad web sites, many of which now request or require user names and passwords for access, has made advising users on good password usage practices significantly more complicated. As we noted above, users should be prohibited from using their password(s) for the local site in any other context, and especially not on the Internet. But beyond that, users often need to have the risks associated with Internet access and transactions explicitly pointed out from time to time, accompanied by a reminder that the passwords they choose to protect such activities are their only defense against the bad guys.

It is not uncommon for a user to visit several to dozens of such web sites on a regular basis. In theory, the best practice is to use a different password for every one of them. Realistically, however, very few users are capable of remembering that many passwords, especially when some of the sites involved are visited rather infrequently (say, less than once a month). Clearly, we need to modify our usual password selection and usage advice to deal with the realities of the Internet and to be of more genuine help to users.

Treating equally every web site requesting an account name and password merely exacerbates the problem and its inherent combinatorics. Instead, we can divide such Web sites into classes based on the potential losses that might occur if the username and password associated with them was discovered by an unscrupulous person: in other words, by what we have to lose (if anything). There are several general types of such sites:

Information-only sites
These sites merely make information available to their users. They require a password to gain access to that information, but a username and password are available for the asking and have no associated cost. An example of a site would be the technical support area of vendor's web site. Such sites seem to collect user information strictly for marketing purposes and still provide their informational content free of charge. From the user's point of view, the password used at such a site is unimportant, because no loss or other negative consequences would occur even if someone were to discover it.

Fee-based informational sites
These sites make information available to their users upon payment of a fee (usually on a subscription basis, but sometimes on per-visit basis). An example of this kind of site is a magazine's online subscription site, which makes additional information available to its subscribers beyond what it places on its general public web site. The discovery of this kind of password would allow an unauthorized person to gain access to this information, but it would not usually bring any harm to the user himself, provided that the site exercised normal security precautions and did not reveal sensitive information (such as credit card numbers) even to the account holder.

Password-protected purchases, auction bids and other financial transactions
At these sites, a username and password is required to purchase something, but account information related to purchases is not stored. These kinds of sites will allow only registered users to make purchases, but they do not require a full account including billing and shipping addresses, credit card numbers, and so on to be set up and maintained. Rather, they force the user to enter this information for every order (or give the user the option of doing so), without permanently storing the results. Auction sites are similar (from the buyer's point of view): they require bidders to have a registered account, but the actual sale and the corresponding exchange of sensitive information takes place privately between the buyer and seller. The security implications associated with this type of password are more serious than those for information-based sites, but the potential loss from a discovered password is still fairly limited. The bad guy still needs additional information to actually make a purchase (in the case of an auction, he could make a bogus bid while masquerading as the legitimate account holder, but he could not force an actual purchase).

Sites with ongoing purchasing accounts

These sites assign a username and password to registered users and store their complete account information in order to facilitate future purchases, including their billing address, shipping addresses, and multiple credit card numbers. Most online merchants offer such facilities, and in fact you often do not have a choice as to whether an account is set up for you or not if you want to make even one purchase. The unauthorized discovery of the password for such a site can have significant financial consequences, because the bad guy can make purchases using the legitimate user's information and redirect their shipment to any desired location. The choice on the part of such sites to allow such complete access on the basis of a single password clearly favors convenience over security.

Note that sites that store important information about the user or something the user owns or administers also fall into this class. If, for example, the password associated with an account at a site where the official information associated with an Internet domain is stored were to be compromised, the bad guy could modify that information, and the consequences could range from significant inconvenience to all-out havoc.

Sites associated with user finances

These web sites allow account holders to access their bank accounts, stock portfolios, and similar financial instruments, and they obviously pose the greatest risk of immediate financial loss to the user. Some of these are protected only by a username and password; the passwords for such sites must be chosen very carefully indeed.

Note that even the most innocuous sites can change their character over time. For example, a site that now merely provides access to information might at some point in the future add other services; at such time, the password in use there would need to be rethought.

Obviously, the different security needs of the different kinds of sites make different demands on the rigor of password selection. Given that it is seldom practical to have a unique password for every Internet site, we can make the following recommendations:

- Don't use any password from any of your regular computer accounts for any Internet sites, and vice versa. (I can't repeat this often enough).

- Select all passwords for Internet sites using the same good password selection principles as for any other password.

- There is no harm in using the same password for all of the unimportant sites, especially those requiring a (nuisance) password for access to otherwise free information.

- You may also choose to use the same password for fee-based information sites (depending upon the extent to which you wish to protect against unauthorized access to such sites), or you may choose to use a different one, but again there is probably no harm in using the same one for more than one site.

- Consider using a different password at each site where there is anything to lose. Doing so may still result in a large number of passwords to be remembered, and there are many strategies for dealing with this. The most obvious is to write them down. I tend not to prefer this approach; it may be that too many years of system administration have made the mere idea of writing down any password anathema to me, but keeping such a list in a secure location at home is probably an acceptable risk (I wouldn't keep such a list in my wallet or on my PDA).

Another approach is to have a different password at each site but to use a consistent scheme for selecting them. As a simple example, one might generate each password by taking one's favorite woman's name that begins with the same letter as the most important word in the site name, transforming the spelling according to some rule, and appending a favorite number. By constructing passwords in the same way for each site, you can always reconstruct the password for a given site if it is forgotten. Ideally, you would devise a password scheme that generates a deterministic password for a given site and prevents frequent duplicates (the latter is probably not true of this simple example).

Setting Password Restrictions

Users don't like to change their passwords. However, Unix provides mechanisms by which you can force them to do so anyway. You can specify how long a user can keep the same password before being forced to change it (the *maximum password lifetime*), how long he must keep a new password before being allowed to change it again (the *minimum password lifetime*), the minimum password length, and some other related parameters. Setting the minimum and maximum password lifetimes is referred to as specifying *password aging* information.

Before you decide to turn on password aging on your system, you should consider carefully how much password fascism you really need. Forcing users to change their password when they don't want to is one of the least effective system security tactics. Certainly, there are times when passwords must be changed whether users like it or not, such as when an employee with high-level system access is terminated. However, random forced password changes don't ensure that good passwords will be chosen (in fact, the opposite effect is at least as likely). And using a minimum password lifetime to prevent a user from changing her new password right back to what it was before (a password she liked and could remember without writing it down) can also have some unexpected side effects.

One potential problem with a minimum password lifetime comes when a password really needs to be changed—when someone who shouldn't know it does, for example. At such times, a user might be unable to change his password even though he needs to. Of course, the superuser can always change passwords, but then the user will have to hunt down the system administrator, admit what happened, and get it changed. Depending on the security policies and general atmosphere at your site, the user may decide just to wait until the minimum lifetime expires and change it himself, and live with the risk until then. You'll need to decide which is more likely on your system: users attempting to circumvent necessary password aging or users needing to be able to change their passwords at will; either one could be more important for system security in your particular situation.

Many Unix versions also offer other controls related to password selection and related items:

- Minimum password length
- Password selection controls, such as using more than one character class (lowercase letters, uppercase letters, numbers, and symbols) and avoiding personal information and dictionary words
- Password history lists, preventing users from reselecting recent passwords
- Automatic account locking after too many failed login attempts (discussed previously)
- Account expiration dates

Password aging

On most systems, password aging settings for user accounts are stored with the entries in the shadow password file. As we noted earlier, entries in the shadow password file have the following syntax:

```
username:coded password:last_change:minlife:maxlife:warn:inactive:expires:unused
```

where *username* is the name of the user account, and *coded password* is the encoded user password. The remaining fields within each entry control the conditions under which a user is allowed to and is forced to change his password, as well as an optional account expiration date:

last_change
> Stores the date of the last password change, expressed as the number of days since January 1, 1970. Set to 0 to force a password change at the next login (works only when *max_days* is greater than 0 and less than the number of days since 1/1/1970).

maxlife
> Specifies maximum number of days that a user is allowed to keep the same password (traditionally set to a high value such as 9999 to disable this feature).

minlife
> Specifies how long a user must keep a new password before he is allowed to change it again; it is designed to prevent a user from circumventing a forced password change by changing his password and then changing it right back again to the old value (set to zero to disable this feature).

warn
> Indicates how many days in advance the user will be notified of an upcoming password expiration (leave blank to disable this feature).

inactive

Specifies the number of days after the password expires that the account will be automatically disabled if the password has not changed (set to −1 to disable this feature).

expires

Specifies the date on which the account expires and will be automatically disabled (leave blank to disable this feature).

The settings provide a system administrator with considerable control over user password updating practices.

You can edit these fields directly in the shadow password file, or you may use the command provided by the system, usually `passwd` (Linux systems use the `chage` command). The options corresponding to each setting are listed in Table 6-9.

HP-UX and Tru64 systems running enhanced security and AIX provide the same functionality via different mechanisms: the protected password database and the settings in the */etc/security/user* configuration file, respectively. FreeBSD provides an account expiration date via a field in the *master.passwd* file. Table 6-10 also lists the commands for modifying this data.

Table 6-10. Specifying user account password aging settings

Setting	Command
Minimum lifetime	**AIX:** `chuser minage=`*weeks*
	HP-UX: `passwd -n` *days*
	Linux: `chage -m` *days*
	Solaris: `passwd -n` *days*
	Tru64: `usermod -x password_min_change_time=`*days*
Maximum lifetime	**AIX:** `chuser maxage=`*weeks*
	HP-UX: `passwd -x` *days*
	Linux: `chage -M` *days*
	Solaris: `passwd -x` *days*
	Tru64: `usermod -x password_expire_time=`*days*
Warning period	**AIX:** `chuser pwdwarntime=`*days*
	HP-UX: `passwd -w` *days*
	Linux: `chage -W` *days*
	Solaris: `passwd -w` *days*
Inactivity period	**AIX:** `chuser maxexpired=`*weeks*
	Linux: `chage -I` *days*
	Tru64: `usermod -x account_inactive=`*days*
Expiration date	**AIX:** `chuser expires=`*MMDDhhmmyy*
	FreeBSD: `chpass -e` *date*
	Linux: `chage -E` *days*
	Tru64: `usermod -x account_expiration=`*date*

Table 6-10. Specifying user account password aging settings (continued)

Setting	Command
Last change date	**FreeBSD:** chpass (interactive)
	Linux: chage -d *yyyy-mm-dd* (or *days-since-1/1/1970*)
View settings	**AIX:** lsuser -f
	HP-UX: passwd -s
	Linux: chage -l
	Solaris: passwd -s
	Tru64: edauth -g

For example, the following commands set the minimum password age to seven days and the maximum password age to one year for user *chavez*:

```
# passwd -n 7 -x 365 chavez              HP-UX and Solaris
# chage -m 7 -M 365 chavez               Linux
# chuser maxage=52 minage=1 chavez       AIX
# usermod -x password_min_change_time=7 \  Tru64
    password_expire_time=365 chavez
```

Here is the display produced by passwd -s for listing a user's password aging settings:

```
# passwd -s chavez
chavez PS 05/12/2000 0 183 7 -1
```

The second item in the display is the password status, one of PS or P (password defined), NP (no password), or LK or L (account is locked via a password modification). The third item is the date *chavez* last changed her password. The fourth and fifth items indicate the minimum and maximum password lifetimes (in days), and the sixth item shows the number of days prior to password expiration that *chavez* will begin to receive messages to that effect. The final column indicates the inactivity period. In our example, *chavez* must change her password about twice a year, and she will be warned seven days before her password expires; the minimum password age and inactivity periods are not used.

Here is the corresponding display produced by chage under Linux, which is much more informative and self-explanatory:

```
# chage -l harvey
Minimum:        0
Maximum:        99999
Warning:        0
Inactive:       -1
Last Change:              Sep 05, 2002
Password Expires:         Never
Password Inactive:        Never
Account Expires:          Never
```

These settings provide user *harvey* with complete freedom about when (or if) to change his password.

You can also set user account password aging settings with most of the graphical administrative tools we considered earlier. Figure 6-12 illustrates these features.

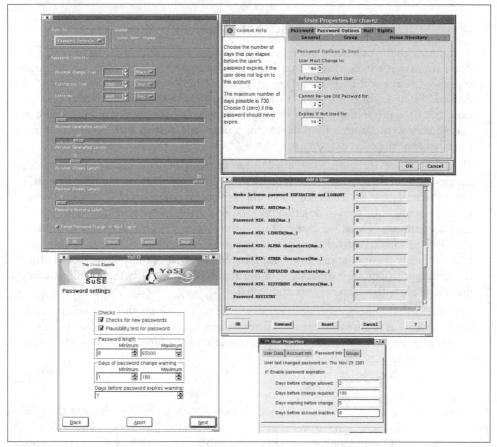

Figure 6-12. Specifying password aging settings

Starting from the upper left and moving clockwise, the figure shows the forms provided by HP-UX's SAM, Solaris' SMC, AIX's SMIT, the Red Hat User Manager, and YaST2. The latter provides a convenient way of setting the system default password aging and length settings (it is reached via the Security → Local security configuration → Predefined security level → Custom settings path from the main panel). Note that three of the four dialogs also include other password-related controls in addition to aging settings. We'll consider them in the next few subsections of this chapter.

Password triviality checks

Security weaknesses arising from user passwords are of two main sorts: poorly chosen passwords are easy to guess or crack, and passwords of any quality may be discovered or inadvertently revealed in a variety of ways. Imposing password aging restrictions represents an attempt to deal with the second sort of risk by admitting up front that sometimes passwords are discovered and by reasoning that changing them periodically will deal with these exigencies.

Fascist or Slave?

Sometimes, that would seem to be the choice that system administrators have. If you don't rule your system with an iron hand and keep users in their place, those same hordes of users will take advantage of you and bury you with their continuous demands. The Local Guru/Unix Wizard role isn't really an alternative to these two extremes; it is just a more benign version of the fascist—the system administrator is still somehow fundamentally different than users and just as inflexible and unapproachable as the overt despot.

Of course, there are alternatives, but I'm not thinking of some sort of stereotypical, happy-medium type solution, as if it really were possible. The solution in this case isn't some shade of gray, but a different color altogether. It is time to think about what other metaphors might be used to describe the relationship of a system administrator to his user community. There are many possibilities—*resource*, *service provider*, *mentor*, *technical attache*, *regent*, *conductor* (as in orchestra, not train or electricity), *catalyst*—and obviously there's not just one right answer. What all of these suggested alternatives attempt to capture is some sense of the interdependence of system administrators and the users with whom they are connected.

Not that defining the system administrator/users role in some other way will be easy. Users, as least as much as system administrators, are comfortable with the familiar, stereotypical ways of thinking about the job, even if they are seldom entirely satisfied with what they yield in practice.

Helping users to choose better, more secure passwords in the first place is the goal of password triviality checking systems (the process is also known as obscurity checking and checking for obviousness). This approach involves checking a new password proposed by a user for various characteristics that will make it easy to crack and rejecting the password if these characteristics are found. Obscurity-checking capabilities are usually integrated into the `passwd` command and may reject passwords of a variety of types, including the following:

- Passwords shorter than some minimum length
- All lowercase or all alphabetic passwords
- Passwords that are the same as the account's username or any of the information in the GECOS field of its password file entry
- Simple transformations of GECOS items: reversals, rotations, doubling
- Passwords or partial passwords that appear in online dictionaries
- Passwords that are simple keyboard patterns—e.g., qwerty or 123456—and thus easily discerned by an observer

Many Unix systems check for the second and third items on the list automatically. Unfortunately, these tests still accept many poor passwords. Some versions allow you to optionally impose additional checks.

Tru64. Tru64 automatically checks that new passwords are not the same as any local username or group name, are not palindromes, and are not recognized by the spell utility (the final test means that the password may not appear in the online dictionary */usr/share/dict/words*, nor be a simple transformation, such as a plural form, of a word within it). Triviality checks are imposed if the user's protected password database file contains the *u_restrict* field, which corresponds to the Triviality checks check box on the Modify Account form.

AIX. AIX provides a different subset of triviality-checking capabilities via these account attributes (stored in */etc/security/user*), which may also be specified using the chuser command:

minalpha
Minimum number of alphabetic characters in the password.

minother
Minimum number of nonalphabetic characters in the new password.

mindiff
Minimum number of characters in the new password that are not present in the old password.

maxrepeats
Maximum number of times any single character can appear in the password.

minlen
Minimum password length. However, if the sum of *minalpha* and *minother* is less than *minlen*, the former is the minimum length that is actually imposed, up to the systemwide maximum of 8.

dictionlist
Comma-separated list of dictionary files containing unacceptable passwords

pwdchecks
List of site-specific loadable program modules for performing additional password preselection checking (see the pwdrestrict_method subroutine manual page).

By default, password triviality checking is not imposed. The *dictionlist* attribute allows site-specific word lists to be added to the standard online dictionary, and the *pwdchecks* attribute provides a hook for whatever checking a site deems appropriate, although developing such a module will take time.

Here are some sample settings that impose a reasonable set of password content restrictions:

```
minalpha=6
minother=2
maxrepeats=2
mindiff=2
```

Linux. Linux systems provide a very simple password obscurity checking facility. It is enabled via the OBSCURE_CHECK_ENAB entry in the */etc/login.defs* configuration file. The facility performs some simple checks on its own and then calls the library provided with the Crack password-cracking package (described later in this chapter). The path to the associated dictionary files can be specified with the CRACKLIB_DICTPATH entry in the same file.

Note that the obscurity checks do not apply when the superuser changes any password, but you can specify whether *root* is warned when a specified password would not pass via the PASS_ALWAYS_WARN setting.

FreeBSD. FreeBSD provides password content controls via user classes; the settings are accordingly specified in */etc/login.conf*. These are the most useful:

minpasswordlen
> Minimum password length.

passwd_format
> Password encoding scheme. The *md5* setting enables passwords longer than 8 characters.

mixpasswordcase
> If set to true, all lowercase passwords are disallowed.

The freely available npasswd command

If you'd like to precheck user passwords but your version of Unix doesn't provide this feature, or if you want to impose more rigorous restrictions on password selection than your system supports, there are freely available programs that you can use for this purpose. For example, the npasswd package (written by Clyde Hoover) is widely available (including all of our systems). It provides a replacement for the normal passwd command that can be configured to check proposed passwords according to a variety of criteria.

Looking at npasswd's configuration file, which is */usr/lib/passwd/passwd.conf* by default, provides a good sense of the kind of checking it does:

```
# npasswd configuration file
# Dictionaries
passwd.dictionaries    /usr/dict/words
passwd.dictionaries    /usr/dict/new_words
passwd.dictionaries    /etc/local_words
# Content controls
passwd.singlecase      no      Disallow single-case passwords.
passwd.alphaonly       no      Disallow all alphabetic passwords.
passwd.charclasses     2       Minimum number of character types in password.
passwd.whitespace      yes     Allow whitespace characters in passwords.
passwd.printableonly   no      Allow nonprinting characters in passwords.
passwd.maxrepeat       2       Only two adjacent characters can be the same.
# Minimum password length
passwd.minpassword     8
```

npasswd performs some simple length and character-type tests on a proposed password and then checks it against the words in the dictionaries specified in the configuration file.

Checking a proposed password against every login name, group name, and so on, on the system—rather than merely against the user's own—seems an unambiguous improvement. It is fairly easy to generate a list of such words. The following script performs a basic version of this task:

```
#!/bin/sh
# mk_local_words - generate local word list file
PATH=/bin:/usr/bin:/usr/ucb; export PATH
umask 077# protect against prying eyes
rm -f /etc/local_words
set `hostname | awk -F. '{print $1,$2,$3,$4,$5,$6,$7}'`
while [ $# -gt 0 ]; do
    echo $1 >> /etc/local_tmp; shift
done
set `domainname | awk -F. '{print $1,$2,$3,$4,$5,$6,$7}'`
while [ $# -gt 0 ]; do
    echo $1 >> /etc/local_tmp; shift
done
# usernames, then GECOS names
cat /etc/passwd | awk -F: '{print $1}' >> /etc/local_tmp
cat /etc/passwd | awk -F: '{print $5}' | \
    awk -F, '{print $1}' | \
    awk '{print tolower($1)};{print tolower($2)}' | \
    grep -v '^$' >> /etc/local_tmp
cat /etc/group | awk -F: '{print $1}' >> /etc/local_tmp
cat /etc/hosts.equiv >> /etc/local_tmp
# add other local stuff to this file (e.g. org name)
if [ -f /etc/local_names ]; then
    chmod 400 /etc/local_names
    cat /etc/local_names >> /etc/local_tmp
fi
sort /etc/local_tmp | uniq > /etc/local_words
rm -f /etc/local_tmp
```

This version can be easily modified or extended to capture the important words on your system. Note that standard awk does not contain the *tolower* function, although both nawk and gawk (GNU awk) do.

Password history lists

Users tend to dislike creating new passwords almost as much as they dislike having to change them in the first place, so it is a common practice for users to oscillate between the same two passwords. Password history records are designed to prevent this. Some number of previous passwords for each user are remembered by the system and cannot be reselected. The HP-UX, Tru64, and AIX password facilities offer this feature. Note that the password history feature is only effective when it is combined with a minimum password lifetime (otherwise, a user can just keep changing his password until the one he wants falls off the list).

Under AIX, the following attributes in *etc/security/user* control how and when previous passwords can be reused:

histexpire
> Number of weeks until a user can reuse an old password (maximum is 260, which is 5 years).

histsize
> The number of old passwords to remember and reject if reselected too soon (maximum is 50).

On Tru64 systems, this feature is enabled when the *u_pwdepth* in a user's protected password database file is nonzero. Its maximum value is 9. It corresponds to the Password History Limit slider on the user account modification screen. The list of old passwords is stored in the *u_pwdict* field, and items cannot be reselected as long as they remain in the history list.

On HP-UX systems, password history settings can be specified on a system-wide basis in the */etc/default/security* file, as in this example:

```
PASSWORD_HISTORY_DEPTH=5        Remember 5 passwords.
```

The maximum setting is 10.

Password settings default values

Default values for password aging settings can be specified on systems using them. These are the default value locations on the systems we are considering:

AIX	The *default* stanza in */etc/security/user*
FreeBSD	The *default* user class in */etc/login.conf* (although this serves as a default only for users not assigned to a specific class)
HP-UX	*/etc/default/security* and */tcb/auth/files/system/default*
Linux	*/etc/login.defs*
Solaris	*/etc/default/passwd* and */etc/default/login*
Tru64	*/etc/auth/system/default*

We've seen examples of most of these already.

Here is an example of the Linux defaults file, */etc/login.defs*:

```
PASS_MAX_DAYS        90                     Must change every 3 months.
PASS_MIN_DAYS        3                      Keep new password 3 days.
PASS_WARN_AGE        7                      Warn 7 days before expiration.
PASS_MIN_LEN         8                      Passwords must be at least 8 chars long.
OBSCURE_CHECKS_ENABLE yes                   Reject very poor passwords.
PASS_CHANGE_TRIES    3                      Users get 3 tries to pick a valid password.
PASS_ALWAYS_WARN     yes                    Warn root of bad passwords (but allow).
PASS_MAX_LEN         8                      Encode this many password characters.
CRACKLIB_DICTPATH /usr/lib/cracklib_dict    Path to dictionary files.
```

Note that some of these settings can interact with the PAM facility used on most Linux systems, so they may not operate exactly as described in this section. PAM is discussed later in this chapter.

The Solaris */etc/default/passwd* file is very similar (although the attribute names are spelled differently):

```
MAXWEEKS=1      Keep new passwords for one week.
MINWEEKS=26     Password expires after 6 months.
PASSLENGTH=6    Minimum password length.
WARNWEEKS=1     Warn user 7 days before expiration.
```

Testing User Passwords for Weaknesses

As we've noted, having users select effective passwords is one of the best ways to protect system security, and educating them about good selection principles can go a long way in this direction. Sometimes, however, you want to be able to assess how well users are doing at this task. Attempting to discern user passwords using a password-cracking program is one way to go about finding out. In this section, we will consider two such programs, crack and john, beginning with the latter, somewhat simpler facility.

It is usually reasonable to test the security of passwords on systems you administer (depending on site policies). However, cautious administrators obtain written permission to run password cracking programs against their own systems.

In contrast, attempting to crack passwords on computers you don't administer is both unethical and (in most cases) illegal. Avoid this temptation and the complications it can bring.

John the Ripper

The John package—its full name is John the Ripper—is an easy-to-use and effective password cracking facility. It is available for all of the Unix systems we are considering.

Once installed, the john command is used to test the passwords contained in the password file given as its argument. The package includes the unshadow command, which can be used to create a traditional Unix password file from *passwd* and *shadow* files.

Here is a simple example of running john:

```
# unshadow /etc/passwd /etc/shadow > /secure/pwdtest
# chmod go= /secure/pwdtest
# john -rules -wordfile:/usr/dict/many_words /secure/pwdtest
```

The first command creates a password file for testing, and the second command protects it from unauthorized access. The final command initiates a john session (which it starts in the background), in this case checking the passwords against the words in the specified dictionary file and many transformations of these words.

As john runs, it periodically writes status information to files in its installation directory (usually */usr/lib/john*); the file *john.pot* holds information about the passwords cracked so far, and the file *restore* contains information necessary for restarting the current session if it is interrupted (the command to do so is simply john -restore). You can specify an alternate restart filename by including the -session:*name* option on the john command line, which takes the desired session name as its argument and names the file accordingly.

The john facility can operate in several distinct password-cracking modes (requested via distinct options to the john command):

Single crack mode (-single*)*
> Passwords are checked against GECOS field information and a multitude of transformations of it.

Wordlist mode (-rules*)*
> Passwords are checked against the words in a dictionary file—a text file containing one word per line—whose location can be specified as an argument to the -wordfile option. The default file is */var/lib/john/password.lst*. The transformations are defined in the facility's configuration file and can be extended and/or customized by the system administrator.

Incremental mode (-incremental[:modename]*)*
> Tries all combinations of characters or a subset of characters in a brute-force attempt to crack passwords. The optional *modename* specifies the character subset to use, as defined in john's configuration file (discussed below). This mode can take an arbitrarily long amount of time to complete.

External mode (-external:modename*)*
> Attempt to crack passwords using an administrator-defined procedure specified in the configuration file (written in a C-like language). The *modename* specifies which procedure to use.

As we noted, John records its progress periodically to its restart file. You can force this information to be written and displayed using commands like these:

```
# kill -HUP pid
# john -status
guesses: 3  time: 0:00:21:52 68% c/s: 46329
```

Similarly, the following command reports the last recorded status information for the session named *urgent*:

```
# john -status:urgent
```

Some aspects of john's functioning are controlled by the facility's configuration file, typically */var/lib/john/john.ini*. Here are some sample entries from that file:

```
# John settings
[Options]
# Wordlist file name, to be used in batch mode
Wordfile = /var/lib/john/password.lst
```

```
# If Y, use idle cycles only
Idle = N
# Crash recovery file saving delay in seconds
Save = 600
# Beep when a password is found (who needs this anyway?)
Beep = N
```

Later sections of this file contain rules/specifications of the procedures for each of the cracking modes.

Using Crack to find poorly chosen passwords

Crack is a freely available package that attempts to determine Unix passwords using the words in an online dictionary as starting points for generating guesses. The package includes a lot of files and may seem somewhat daunting at first, but it generally builds without problems and is actually quite easy to use. These are the most important parts of its directory structure (all relative to its top-level directory, created when the package is unpacked):

Crack
> Crack driver script; edit the first section of the script to configure Crack for your system, and then build the package with the Crack -makeonly command. This same script is used to run the program itself.

Dict
> Subdirectory tree containing dictionary source files (in addition to the standard online dictionary, usually */usr/dict/words*). Dictionary source files are text files containing one word per line, and they are given the extension *.dwg*. You may add files here as desired; placing them into one of the existing subdirectories is the easiest way.

src
> Location of Crack source code.

scripts/mkgecosd
> Rules for generating guesses from GECOS field entries.

conf/rules.*
> Rules for generating guesses from dictionary words.

run/F-merged
> Text file containing clear text form of all cracked passwords. We don't advise keeping this file online except when you are actually running Crack. During a Crack run, several other temporary files are also kept here.

run/Dhost.pid
> Results files for a particular Crack run, including passwords cracked during that run (the hostname and PID filename components are filled in as appropriate).

run/dict
> The compressed Crack dictionaries used during a run are built as needed and stored here.

The entire Crack directory tree should be owned by *root* and should allow no access by anyone but *root*.

Crack also provides a utility to convert the password and shadow password files into a single conventional-style file suitable for use by the program; it is named *shadowmrg.sv* and is stored in the *scripts* subdirectory. It takes the two filenames as its arguments and writes the merged file to standard output.

Here is an example invocation of Crack:

```
# Crack -nice 5 /secure/pwdtest
```

The script builds the compressed dictionary files, if necessary, and then starts the password cracker program in the background. While Crack is running, you can use the *Reporter* script to check on its progress (located in the same directory as the *Crack* script). In this case, Crack runs at lower priority than normal jobs due to the inclusion of -nice.

If you want to stop a Crack run in progress, run the *plaster* script in the *scripts* subdirectory.

Eventually—or quickly, depending on the speed of your CPU and the length of the dictionary files—Crack produces output like the following (in the file Dhost.pid where *host* is the hostname and *pid* is the process ID of the main Crack process):

```
I:968296152:OpenDictStream: status: /ok/ stat=1 look=679 find=679
genset='conf/rules.basic' rule='!?Xc' dgrp='1'
    prog='smartcat run/dict/1.*'
0:968296152:679
I:968296155:LoadDictionary: loaded 130614 words into memory
G:968296209:KHcqrOsvoY8oo:Arcana
```

The general procedure Crack uses is illustrated by this output. It opens each dictionary file in turn and then applies each rule from the various collection of *rules* files in the *run* subdirectory to the words in it, using each transformed word as a guess for every remaining uncracked user password. When it finds a match, it displays the cracked and encoded versions of the password in the output; in this example, the password "Arcana" has just been cracked. Once a rule has been applied to every dictionary word and every password, Crack continues on to the next rule, and eventually on to the next dictionary, until all possibilities have been exhausted or all passwords have been cracked.

Rules specify transformations to apply to a dictionary word and are written using a metalanguage unique to Crack. Here are some example entries illustrating some of its features:

!?Al	Choose only all-alphabetic-character words and convert to lowercase before using as a guess.
!?Ac	Choose only all-alphabetic-character words and capitalize.

>4r	Select words longer than four characters and reverse them. Other transformations are reflection (f) and doubling (d).
>2<8!?A$0	Choose all alphabetic words having 3–7 characters and add a final "0".
>2<8!?A$1	Same as previous but adds a final "1".
>2<7!?A$2$2	Choose all-alphabetic words of 3–6 characters and append "22".
>7!?A1x05$9$9	Choose all-alphabetic words of 8 or more characters, convert to lowercase, extract the first 6 characters, and append "99" (note that character numbering within a word begins at 0).

The installed rules files contain several important types of transformations, and they can be extended and customized as desired.

Once a Crack run has completed, it is important to remove any remaining scratch files, because they may contain clear-text passwords. Running the command make tidy is one way to do so. You will also want to copy the *D** results files and *run/F-merged* file to offline storage and then delete the online copies (restoring the latter the next time you want to run Crack).

 There are several large dictionary files available on the Internet (for example, see *ftp://ftp.ox.ac.uk/pub/wordlists*). Using them to augment the standard Unix dictionary (and any package-provided ones) will make any password cracking program more successful (but it will also take longer to complete).

How well do they do?

We ran Crack and John on a password file containing several poorly chosen passwords. Table 6-11 shows the results we obtained with the standard program options and configurations, using only the standard Unix dictionary with the words "arcana" and "vermillion" added.

Table 6-11. Password-cracking results

Test Password	Crack	John
vermilli	yes	yes
marymary	yes	yes
maryyram	yes	yes
arcana	yes	yes
Arcana	yes	yes
arcana1	yes	yes
arca^Na	no	no
arcana#	no	no
arcana24	no	no

Both of them cracked passwords with simple transformations, but not with special characters or the addition of two numerals. However, adding rules to either facility to handle these cases is very easy.

User Authentication with PAM

Traditionally, with very few exceptions, user authentication on Unix systems occurs at login time. In recent years, however, a new scheme has emerged that allows the authentication process to be performed and customized for a variety of system contexts. This functionality is provided by the PAM facility.

PAM stands for Pluggable Authentication Modules. PAM is a general user authentication facility available under and provided by current versions of FreeBSD, HP-UX, Linux, and Solaris. PAM's goal is to provide a flexible and administrator-configurable mechanism for authenticating users, independent of the various programs and facilities which require authentication services. In this way, programs can be developed independently of any specific user-authentication scheme instead of having one explicitly or implicitly embedded within them. When using this approach, utilities call various authentication modules at runtime to perform the actual user-validation process, and the utilities then act appropriately depending on the results the modules return to them.

There are several components to the PAM facility:

- PAM-aware versions of traditional Unix authentication programs (for example, `login` and `passwd`). Such programs are referred to as *services*.
- Modules to perform various specific authentication tasks. These are implemented as shared libraries (*.so* files), stored in */lib/security* under Linux, */usr/lib/security* under Solaris and HP-UX, and in */usr/lib* under FreeBSD. Each module is responsible for just one small aspect of authentication. After executing, a module returns its result value to the PAM facility, indicating whether it will grant access or deny access to the user in question. A module may also return a neutral value, corresponding to no specific decision (essentially abstaining from the final decision).*
- Configuration data indicating what authentication process should be performed for each supported service, specified via one or more PAM configuration files. On Linux systems, each service has its own configuration file—with the same name as the service itself—in the directory */etc/pam.d* (thus, the configuration file for the login service would be */etc/pam.d/login*). Alternatively, the entire facility may use a single configuration file, conventionally */etc/pam.conf*; this is how the other three systems are set up by default. If both sorts of configuration

---

* For information about available PAM modules, see *http://www.kernel.org/pub/linux/libs/pam/modules.html*. Although this location is part of a Linux site, most PAM modules can be built for other systems, as well.

information are present (and the PAM facility has been compiled to allow multiple configuration sources), the files in */etc/pam.d* take precedence over the contents of */etc/pam.conf*.

- Additional configuration settings required by some of the PAM modules. These configuration files are stored in */etc/security*, and they have the same name as the corresponding service with the extension *.conf* appended.

The best way to understand how PAM works is with an example. Here is a simple PAM configuration file from a Linux system; this file is used by the su service:[*]

```
auth       sufficient   /lib/security/pam_rootok.so
auth       required     /lib/security/pam_wheel.so
auth       required     /lib/security/pam_unix.so shadow nullok
account    required     /lib/security/pam_unix.so
password   required     /lib/security/pam_unix.so
session    required     /lib/security/pam_unix.so
```

As you can see, there are four types of entries that may appear within a PAM configuration file. Auth entries specify procedures for user authentication. Account entries are used to set user account attributes and apply account controls. Password entries are used when a password changes within the context of the current service. Session entries are generally used at present for login purposes to the syslog facility. The group of entries of a particular type are processed in turn and form a stack. In the example file, there is a stack of three auth entries and a single entry of each of the other three types.

The second field in each entry is a keyword that specifies how the results of that particular module affect the outcome of the entire authentication process. In its simplest form,[†] this field consists of one of four keywords:

sufficient
> If this module grants access to the user, skip any remaining modules in the stack and return an authentication success value to the service).

requisite
> If this module denies access, return an authentication failure value to the service and skip any remaining modules in the stack.

required
> This module must grant access in order for the entire authentication process to succeed.

optional
> The result of this module will be used to determine access only if no other module is deterministic.

---

[*] The format for the corresponding */etc/pam.conf* file entries differs only slightly; the service name becomes the first field, with the remaining fields following, as in this example: `su auth sufficient /usr/lib/security/pam_unix.so`.

[†] There is a newer, more complex syntax for the severity field, which we will consider later in this section.

The first two keywords are easy to understand, because they immediately either allow or deny access and terminate the authentication process at that point. The second two indicate whether the module is an essential, integral part of the authentication process. If no module denies or grants access before all of the modules in the stack have executed, authentication success or failure is determined by combining the results of all the required modules. If at least one of them grants access and none of them denies it, authentication is successful. Optional modules are used only when no definitive decision is reached by the required modules.

The third field in each configuration file entry is the path to the desired module (sometimes, only a filename is given, in which case the default library location is assumed). Any required and/or optional arguments used by the module follow its path.

Looking again at the su PAM configuration file, we can now decode the authentication process that it prescribes. When a user enters an su command, three modules are used to determine whether she is allowed to execute it. First, the *pam_rootok* module runs. This module checks whether or not the user is *root* (via the real UID). If so, success is returned, and authentication ends here because of the sufficient keyword (*root* does not need to enter any sort of password in order to use su); if the user is not *root*, authentication continues on to the next module. The *pam_wheel* module checks whether the user is a member of the system group allowed to su to *root*, returning success or failure accordingly (emulating a feature of BSD Unix systems), thereby limiting access to the command to that group. The authentication process then continues with the *pam_unix* module, which requests and verifies the appropriate password for the command being attempted (which depends on the specific user who is the target of su); it returns success or failure depending on whether the correct password is entered. This module is given two arguments in this instance: *shadow* indicates that a shadow password file is in use, and *nullok* says that a null password for the target account is acceptable (omitting this keyword effectively disables accounts without passwords).

The other three entries in the configuration file all call the same module, *pam_unix*. In the account context, this module establishes the status of the target user's account and password, generating an automatic password change if appropriate; the password entry is invoked when such a password change is necessary, and it handles the mechanics of that process. Finally, this session entry generates a syslog entry for this invocation of su.

Many PAM modules allow for quite a bit of configuration. The *pam_wheel* module, for example, allows you to specify which group su access is limited to (via its *group* option). It also allows you to grant access to everyone except members of a specific group (via the *deny* option). Consult the PAM documentation, usually found within the */usr/doc* tree, for full details on the activities and options for available modules.

Here is a more complex configuration file, for the rlogin service, again taken from a Linux system:

```
auth       requisite   /lib/security/pam_securetty.so
auth       requisite   /lib/security/pam_nologin.so
auth       sufficient  /lib/security/pam_rhosts_auth.so
auth       required    /lib/security/pam_unix.so
account    required    /lib/security/pam_unix.so
account    required    /lib/security/pam_time.so
password   required    /lib/security/pam_cracklib.so retry=3 \
                           type=UNIX minlen=10 ocredit=2 \
                           dcredit=2
password   required    /lib/security/pam_unix.so \
                           use_authtok shadow md5
session    required    /lib/security/pam_unix.so
session    optional    /lib/security/pam_motd.so motd=/etc/pmotd
```

When a user attempts to connect to the system via the rlogin service, authentication proceeds as follows: the *pam_securetty* module presents connections to the *root* account via rlogin (if someone attempts to rlogin as *root*, the module returns failure, and authentication ends due to the *requisite* keyword).

Next, the *pam_nologin* module determines whether the file */etc/nologin* exists; if so, its contents are displayed to the user, and authentication fails immediately. When */etc/nologin* is not present, the *pam_rhosts_auth* module determines whether the traditional Unix */etc/hosts.equiv* mechanisms allow access to the system or not; if so, authentication succeeds immediately. In all cases, the *pam_unix* module prompts for a user password (the module uses the same arguments here as in the preceding example).

If authentication succeeds, the account stack comes into play. First, user account and password controls are checked via the *pam_unix* module (which makes sure that the account is not expired and determines whether the password needs to be changed at this time). Next, the *pam_time* module consults its configuration file to determine whether this user is allowed to log in at the current time (discussed below). In order for system access to be granted, neither of these modules must deny access, and at least one of them must explicitly grant it.

When a password change is required, the password stack is used. The first module, *pam_cracklib*, performs several different triviality checks on the new password before allowing it to be chosen. This module is discussed in more detail later in this section.

Finally, the first session entry generates a syslog entry each time the rlogin service is used. The second session entry displays a message-of-the-day at the end of the login process, displaying the contents of the file specified with the *pam_motd*'s *motd* option.

PAM Defaults

The PAM facility also defines an additional service called *other*, which serves as a default authentication scheme for commands and facilities not specifically defined as PAM services. The settings for the other service are used whenever an application requests authentication but has no individual configuration data defined. Here is a typical *other* configuration file:

```
auth      required      pam_warn.so
auth      required      pam_deny.so
```

These entries display a warning to the user that PAM has not been configured for the requested service, and then deny access in all cases.

PAM Modules Under Linux

As these examples have indicated, Linux systems provide a rich variety of PAM modules. Unfortunately, the other systems we are considering are not as well provided for by default, and you will have to build additional modules if you want them.

We will now briefly list the most important Linux PAM modules. Two of the most important are discussed in more detail in subsequent subsections of this chapter. For each module, the stacks in which it may be called are given in parentheses.

pam_deny (account, auth, passwd, session)
pam_permit (account, auth, passwd, session)
> Deny/allow all access by always returning failure/success (respectively). These modules do not log, so stack them with *pam_warn* to log the events.

pam_warn (account, auth, passwd, session)
> Log information about the calling user and host to syslog.

pam_access (account)
> Specify system access based on user account and originating host/domain as in the widely used logdaemon facility. Its configuration file is */etc/security/access.conf*.

pam_unix (account, auth, passwd, session)
pam_pwdb (account, auth, passwd, session)
> Two modules for verifying and changing user passwords. When used in the auth stack, the modules check the entered user password.
>
> When used as an account module, they determine whether a password change is required (based on password aging settings in the shadow password file); if so, they delay access to the system until the password has been changed.
>
> When used as a password component, the modules update the user password. In this context, the *shadow* (use the shadow password file) and *try_first_pass* options are useful; the latter forces the modules to use the password given to a previous module in the stack (rather than generating another, redundant password prompt).

In any of these modes, the *nullok* option is required if you want to allow users to have blank passwords, even as initial passwords to be changed at the first login; otherwise, the modules will return an authorization failure.

pam_cracklib (passwd)

Password triviality checking. Needs to be stacked with *pam_pwdb* or *pam_unix*. See the separate discussion below.

pam_pwcheck (passwd)

Another password-checking module, checking that the proposed password conforms to the settings specified in */etc/login.defs* (discussed previously in this chapter).

pam_env (auth)

Set or unset environment variables with a PAM stack. It uses the configuration file */etc/security/pam_env.conf*.

pam_issue (auth)
pam_motd (session)

Display an issue or message-of-the-day file at login. The issue file (which defaults to */etc/issue*) is displayed before the username prompt, and the message of the day file (defaults to */etc/motd*) is displayed at the end of a successful login process. The location of the displayed file can be changed via an argument to each module.

pam_krb4 (auth, passwd, session)
pam_krb5 (auth, passwd, session)

Interface to Kerberos user authentication.

pam_lastlog (auth)

Adds an entry to the */var/log/lastlog* file, which contains data about each user login session.

pam_limits (session)

Sets user process resource limits (*root* is not affected), as specified in its configuration file, */etc/security/limits.conf* (the file must be readable only by the superuser). This file contains entries of the form:

```
name    hard/soft    resource    limit-value
```

where *name* is a user or group name or an asterisk (indicating the default entry). The second field indicates whether it is a soft limit, which the user can increase if desired, or a hard limit, the upper bound that the user cannot exceed. The final two fields specify the resource in question and the limit assigned to it. The defined resources are:

as

Maximum address space

core

Maximum core file size

cpu
> CPU time, in minutes

data
> Maximum size of data portion of process memory

fsize
> Maximum file size

maxlogins
> Maximum simultaneous login sessions

memlock
> Maximum locked-in memory

nofile
> Maximum number of open files

rss
> Maximum resident set

stack
> Maximum stack portion of address space

All sizes are expressed in kilobytes.

pam_listfile (auth)
> Deny/allow access based on a list of usernames in an external file. This module is best explained by example (assume this is found in the PAM configuration file for the ftp facility):
>
> ```
> auth  required  pam_listfile.so onerr=fail sense=deny \
>               file=/etc/ftpusers item=user
> ```
>
> This entry says that the file */etc/ftpusers* (*file* argument) contains a list of usernames (*item=user*) who should be denied access to ftp (*sense=allow*). If any error occurs, access will be denied (*onerr=fail*). If you want to grant access to a list of users, use the option *sense=allow*. The *item* option indicates the kind of data present in the specified file, one of *user*, *group*, *rhost*, *ruser*, *tty*, and *shell*.

pam_mail (auth, session)
> Displays a message indicating whether the user has mail. The default mail file location (*/var/spool/mail*) can be changed with the *dir* argument.

pam_mkhomedir (session)
> Creates the user's home directory if it does not already exist, copying files from the */etc/skel* directory to the new directory (use the *skel* option to specify a different location). You can use the *umask* option specify a umask to use when the directory is created (e.g., *umask=022*).

pam_nologin (auth)
> Prevents non-*root* logins if the file */etc/nologin* exists, the contents of which are displayed to the user.

pam_rhosts_auth (auth)
> Performs traditional */etc/rhosts* and *~/.rhosts* password-free authentication for remote sessions between networked hosts (see "Network Security" in Chapter 7).

pam_rootok (auth)
> Allows *root* access without a password.

pam_securetty (auth)
> Prevents *root* access unless the current terminal line is listed in the file */etc/securetty*.

pam_time(account)
> Restricts access by time of day, based on user, group, tty, and/or shell. Discussed in more detail later in this chapter.

pam_wheel (auth)
> Designed for the su facility, this module prevents root access by any user who is not a member of a specified group (*group*=name option), which defaults to GID 0. You can reverse the logic of the test to deny *root* access to members of a specific group by using the *deny* option along with *group*.

Checking passwords at selection time

As we've seen, the *pam_cracklib* module can be used to check a proposed user password for strength. By default, the module checks the entered new password against each word in its dictionary, */usr/lib/cracklib_dict*. It also checks that the new password is not a trivial transformation of the current one: not a reversal, palindrome, character case modification, or rotation. The module also checks the password against the module's list of previous passwords for the user, stored in */etc/security/opasswd*.

The arguments to this module specify additional criteria to be used for some of these checks. These are the most important:

retry=n
> Number of tries allowed to successfully choose a new password. The default is 1.

type=string
> Operating system name to use in prompts (defaults to Linux).

minlen=n
> Minimum "length" value for the new password (defaults to 10). This is computed on the basis of the number of characters in the password, along with some weighting for different types of characters (specified by the various *credit* arguments). Due to the character-type credit scheme, this value should be equal to or greater than the desired password length plus one.

*ucredit=*u
*lcredit=*l
*dcredit=*d
*ocredit=*o

> Maximum "length" credits for having uppercase letters, lowercase letters, digits, and other characters (respectively) in proposed passwords (all of them default to 1). If set, characters of each type will add 1 to the "length" value, up to the specified maximum number. For example, *dcredit=2* means that having two or more digits in the new password will add 2 to the number of characters in the password when comparing its "length" to *minlen* (one or zero digits will similarly add 1 or 0 to the "length").

*difok=*n

> The number of characters in the new password that must not be present in the old password (old passwords are stored in */etc/security/opasswd*). The default is 10. Decrease this value when you are using long MD5 passwords.

As an example, consider our previous invocation of *pam_cracklib*:

```
passwordrequiredpam_cracklib.so retry=3 type=Linux \
                    minlen=12 ocredit=2 dcredit=2 difok=3
```

In this case, the user is allowed three tries to select an appropriate password (*retry=3*), and the word "Linux" will be used in the new password prompt rather than Unix (*type=Linux*). Also, the password must have a minimum length-value of 12, where each character in the password counts as 1, and up to two numbers (*dcredit=2*) and two nonalphanumeric characters (*ocredit=2*) can each add an additional 1 to the "length." This effectively forces passwords to be at least seven characters long, and in that case, they must contain two digits and two non-alphanumeric characters (7 characters + 1 alpha + 2 digits + 2 other). Passwords containing only upper- and lowercase letters will have to be at least 10 characters long. The final option specifies that three characters in the new password must not be present in the old password.

Specifying allowed times and locations for system access

The *pam_time* module uses a configuration file, */etc/security/time.conf*, that specifies hours when users may access defined PAM services. Here's an example:

```
#services; ttys; users; times (Mo Tu We Th Fr Sa Su Wk Wd Al)
login;tty*;!root & !harvey & !chavez;Wd0000-2400|Wk0800-2000
games;*;smith|jones|williams|wong|sanchez|ng;!Al0700-2000
```

The first line is a comment indicating the contents of the various fields (note that entries are separated by semicolons). Each entry within this configuration file specifies when access to the indicated services are allowed; the entry applies when *all* of the first three fields match the current situation, and the fourth entry indicates the times when access is allowed.

In our example, the first line specifies that access to the login and rlogin services will be granted to any user except *root*, *harvey*, and *chavez* (the logical NOT is indicated by the initial !) all the time on weekends (*Wd* keyword in the fourth field) and on weekdays between 8:00 A.M. and 6:00 P.M., on any serial-line connected terminal. The second line prohibits access to any PAM-aware game by the listed users between 7:00 A.M. and 8:00 P.M. (again, regardless of tty); it does so by granting access at any time except those noted (again indicated by the initial exclamation point). Note that & and | are used for logical AND and OR, respectively, and that an asterisk may be used as a wildcard (although a bare wildcard is allowed only once within the first three fields).

 As you create entries for this configuration file, keep in mind that you are creating matching rules: use the first three fields to define applicability and the final field to specify allowed or denied access periods. Note that ampersands/ANDs usually join negative (NOT-ed) items, and vertical bars/ORs usually join positive items.

Be aware that this module can provide time-based controls only for initial system access. It does nothing to enforce time limits after users have already logged in; they can stay logged in as long as they like.

MD5 passwords

Linux and some other Unix systems support much longer passwords (up to at least 128 characters) using the MD5 encryption algorithm. Many PAM modules are also compatible with such passwords, and they provide an *md5* option that may be used to indicate they are in use and to request their usage. These include *pam_pwdb*, *pam_unix*, *pam_cracklib*, and *pam_pwcheck*.

If you decided to enable MD5 passwords, you will need to add the *md5* option to all relevant modules in the configuration files for login, rlogin, su, sshd, and passwd services (and perhaps others as well).

 Not all Unix facilities are compatible with MD5 passwords. For example, some ftp client programs always truncate the entered password and so will not send long passwords correctly, thereby preventing ftp access by users with long passwords. Test your environment thoroughly before deciding to enable MD5 passwords.

PAM Modules Provided by Other Unix Systems

As we noted earlier, HP-UX, FreeBSD, and Solaris do not provide nearly as many PAM modules as Linux does by default. Each provides from 8 to 12 modules. All include a version of the basic password-based authentication module, *pam_unix* (named *libpam_unix* on HP-UX systems). There are also a few unique modules provided by these systems, including the following:

System	Module	Description
HP-UX	*libpam_updbe*	This module provides a method for defining user-specific PAM stacks (stored in the */etc/pam_user.conf* configuration file).
Solaris	*pam_projects*	This module succeeds as long as the user belongs to a valid project, and fails otherwise. Solaris projects are discussed in "System V–Style Accounting: AIX, HP-UX, and Solaris" in Chapter 17.
	pam_dial_auth	Perform dialup user authentication using the traditional */etc/dialup* and */etc/d_passwd* files (see "User Authentication Revisited" in Chapter 7).
	pam_roles	Performs authentication when a user tries to assume a new role (see "Role-Based Access Control" in Chapter 7).
FreeBSD	*pam_cleartext_pass_ok*	Accepts authentication performed via cleartext passwords.

More Complex PAM Configuration

The latest versions of PAM introduce a new, more complex syntax for the final severity field:

```
return-val=action [, return-val=action [,...]]
```

where *return-val* is one of approximately fifteen defined values that a module may return, and *action* is a keyword indicating what action should be taken if that return value is received (in other words, if that condition occurs). The available actions are *ok* (grant access), *ignore* (no opinion on access), *bad* (deny access), *die* (immediate deny access), *done* (immediate grant access), and *reset* (ignore the results of all modules processed so far and force the remaining ones in the stack to make the decision). In addition, a positive integer (*n*) may also be specified as the action, which says to skip next *n* modules in the stack, allowing simple conditional authentication schemes to be created.

Here is an example severity field using the new syntax and features:

```
success=ok,open_err=ignore,cred_insufficient=die,\
    acct_expired=die,authtok_expired=die,default=bad
```

This entry says that a success return value from the module grants access; it will still need to be combined with the results of the other modules in order to determine overall authentication success or failure (as usual). A file open error causes the module to be ignored. If the module indicates that the user's credentials are insufficient for access or that his account or authentication token is expired, the entire authentication process fails immediately. The final item in the list specifies a default action to be taken when any other value is returned by the module; in this case, it is set to deny access.

These examples have shown some of the features and flexibility of the PAM facility. Now it is time for you to experiment and explore it further on your own, in the context of the needs of your particular system or site. As always, be careful as you do so, and do some preliminary testing on a noncritical system before making any changes in a production system. Using PAM effectively requires experience, and everyone locks themselves out in some context as they are learning to do so.

LDAP: Using a Directory Service for User Authentication

For several years now, every time anyone put together a list of hot system administration topics, LDAP was sure to be near the top. Many sites are beginning to use LDAP for storing employee information, including user account information, and as a means for performing enterprise-wide user authentication. In this way, LDAP-based account data and authentication can replace separate, per-system logins and network-based authentication schemes like NIS.

In this closing section of the chapter, we'll take a brief look at LDAP—and specifically, the OpenLDAP environment—and consider how it may be used for user authentication.

About LDAP

LDAP, as its fully expanded name—Lightweight Directory Access Protocol—indicates, is a protocol that supports a directory service. The best analogy for a directory service is the phone company's directory assistance. Directory assistance is a mechanism for customers to find information that they need quickly. Traditionally, human operators provided the (hopefully friendly) interface between the user (customer) and the database (the list of phone numbers). Directory assistance is not a means for customers to change their phone number, indicate whether their phone number should be listed or unlisted, or to obtain new telephone service.

A computer-based directory service provides similar functionality. It is a database and means of accessing information within it. Specifically, the directory service database has several specific characteristics that are different from, say, databases used for transaction processing:

- It is optimized for reading (writing may be expensive).
- It provides advanced searching features.
- Its fundamental data structures—collectively known as the schema—can be extended according to local needs.
- It adheres to published standards to ensure interoperability among vendor implementations (specifically, a boatload of RFCs).
- It takes advantage of distributed storage and data-replication techniques.

LDAP's roots are in the X.500 directory service and its DAP protocol. LDAP was designed to be a simpler and more efficient protocol for accessing an X.500

directory. It is "lightweight" in several ways: LDAP runs over the TCP/IP network stack (instead of DAP's full implementation of all seven OSI layers), it provides only the most important small subset of X.500 operations, and data is formatted as simple strings rather than complex data structures. Like DAP itself, LDAP is an access protocol. The actual database services are provided by some other facility, often referred to as the *back end*. LDAP serves a means for efficiently accessing the information stored within it.

In order to emphasize these differences with respect to standard relational databases, different terminology is used for the data stored in a directory. Records are referred to as *entries*, and fields with a record are called *attributes*.

LDAP was first implemented at the University of Michigan in the early 1990s. There are many commercial LDAP servers available. In addition, OpenLDAP is an open source implementation of LDAP based on the work at Michigan (*http://www.openldap.org*). The OpenLDAP package includes daemons, configuration files, startup scripts, libraries, and utilities.

These are the most important OpenLDAP components:

Daemons
> `slapd` is the OpenLDAP daemon, and `slurpd` is the data replication daemon.

A database environment
> OpenLDAP supports the Berkeley DB and the GNU GDBM database engines.

Directory entry-related utilities
> These utilities are `ldapadd` and `ldapmodify` (add/modify directory entries), `ldapdelete` (delete directory entries), `ldapsearch` (search directory for entries matching specified criteria), and `ldappasswd` (change entry password).

Related utilities
> Related utilities include, for example, `slappasswd` (generate encoded passwords).

Configuration files
> Configuration files are stored in */etc/openldap*.

 Unix versions differ in their LDAP support. Some, like Linux and FreeBSD, use OpenLDAP exclusively. Others, like Solaris, provide only client support by default (although Solaris offers an LDAP server as an add-on facility at extra cost). Be sure to check what your version uses if you plan to use the provided facilities. Switching to OpenLDAP is also an option for all of the systems we are considering.

LDAP Directories

LDAP directories are logically tree structures, and they are typically rooted at a construct corresponding to the site's domain name, expressed in a format like this one:

```
dc=ahania,dc=com
```

Each component of the domain name becomes the value for a *dc* (domain component) attribute, and all of them are collected into a comma-separated list. This is known as the directory's base, corresponding in this case to *ahania.com*. Domain names with more than two components would have additional *dc* attributes in the list (e.g., dc=research,dc=ahania,dc=com).

Such a list of *attribute=value* pairs is the method for referring to any location (entry) with the directory. Spaces are not significant between items.

Let's now turn to a sample record from a directory service database:

```
dn: cn=Jerry Carter, ou=MyList, dc=ahania, dc=com
objectClass: person
cn: Jerry Carter
sn: Carter
description: Samba and LDAP expert
telephoneNumber: 22
```

This data format is known as LDIF (LDAP Data Interchange Format). It is organized as a series of attribute and value pairs (colon-separated). For example, the attribute *telephoneNumber* has the value 22.

The first line is special. It specifies the entry's distinguished name (*dn*), which functions as its unique key within the database (I like to think of it as a Borg "designation"). As expected, it is constructed as a comma-separated list of attribute-value pairs. In this case, the entry is for common name "Jerry Carter," organizational unit "MyList" in the example directory for *ahania.com*.

The *objectClass* attribute specifies the type of record: in this case, a *person*. Every entry needs at least one *objectClass* attribute. Valid record types are defined in the directory's schema, and there are a variety of standard record types that have been defined (more on this later). The other attributes in the entry specify the *person*'s surname, description and phone number.

The first component of the *dn* is known as the entry's relative distinguished name (*rdn*). In our example, that would be *cn=Jerry Carter*. It corresponds to the location within the *ou=MyList,dc=ahania,dc=com* subtree where this entry resides. An *rdn* must be unique within its subtree just as the dn is unique within the entire directory.

Here is a simple representation of the directory tree in which successive (deeper) levels are indicated by indentation:

```
dc=ahania,dc=com
    ou=MyList,dc=ahania,dc=com
        cn=Jerry Carter,ou=MyList,dc=ahania,dc=com
        cn=Rachel Chavez,ou=MyList,dc=ahania,dc=com
        more people ...
    ou=HisList,dc=ahania,dc=com
        different people ...
```

The directory is divided into two organization units, each of which has a number of entries under it (corresponding to people).

About schemas

The *schema* is the name given to the collection of object and attribute definitions which define the structure of the entries (records) in an LDAP database. LDAP objects are standardized in order to provide interoperability with a variety of directory-services servers. Schema definitions are stored in files located in the */etc/openldap/schema* subdirectory. The OpenLDAP package provides all of the most common standard schema, and you can add additional definitions, if necessary. You specify the files that are in use via entries in *slapd.conf*, as in these examples:

```
include         /etc/openldap/schema/core.schema
include         /etc/openldap/schema/misc.schema
```

Object definitions in the schema files are fairly easy to understand:[*]

```
objectclass ( 2.5.6.6 NAME 'person' SUP top STRUCTURAL
   MUST ( sn $ cn )
   MAY ( userPassword $ telephoneNumber $ seeAlso $ description ) )
```

This is the definition of the *person* object class. The first line specifies the class name. It also indicates that it is a structural object (the other sort is an auxiliary object, which adds supplemental attributes to its parent object) and that its parent class is *top* (a pseudo-object indicating the top of the hierarchy). The remaining lines specify required and optional attributes for the object.

Attributes are defined in separate stanzas having an even more obscure format. For example, here is the definition of the *sn* (surname) attribute:

```
attributetype ( 2.5.4.4 NAME ( 'sn' 'surname' ) SUP name )
attributetype ( 2.5.4.41 NAME 'name'
   EQUALITY caseIgnoreMatch
   SUBSTR   caseIgnoreSubstringsMatch
   SYNTAX   1.3.6.1.4.1.1466.115.121.1.15{32768} )
```

The *sn* attribute draws its definition from its parent, the *name* attribute. Its definition specifies its syntax and how equality and substring comparisons are to be performed (themselves defined via keywords and values defined elsewhere in the schema).

In general, you can figure out what's going on with most objects by examining the relevant schema files. The website *http://ldap.hklc.com* provides a very convenient interface for exploring standard LDAP schema objects.

Installing and Configuring OpenLDAP: An Overview

Installing OpenLDAP is not difficult, but it can be time-consuming. The first step is to obtain all of the needed software. This includes not only OpenLDAP itself, but also its prerequisites:

---

[*] For those of you familiar with SNMP, LDAP uses ASN.1 syntax for its schemas, and thus its object definitions somewhat resemble SNMP MIB definitions.

- A database manager: GNU gdbm (*http://www.fsf.org*) or BerkeleyDB (*http://www.sleepycat.com*)
- The Transport Layer Security (TLS/SSL) libraries (*http://www.openssl.org*)
- The Cyrus SASL libraries (*http://asg.web.cmu.edu/sasl/*)

Once the prerequisites are met, we can build and install OpenLDAP. The OpenLDAP documentation for doing so is pretty good.

Once the software is installed, the next step is to create a configuration file for the slapd daemon, */etc/openldap/slapd.conf*:

```
# /etc/openldap/slapd.conf
include      /etc/openldap/schema/core.schema
pidfile      /var/run/slapd.pid
argsfile     /var/run/slapd.args
database     ldbm
suffix       "dc=ahania, dc=com"
rootdn       "cn=Manager, dc=ahania, dc=com"
# encode with slappasswd -h '{MD5}' -s <password> -v -u
rootpw       {MD5}Xr4il0zQ4PCOq3aQOqbuaQ==
directory    /var/lib/ldap
```

Additional items may appear in your file. Change any paths that are not correct for your system, and set the correct *dc* components in the *suffix* (directory base) and *rootdn* (database owner) entries (*Manager* is the conventional common name to use for this purpose). Set a password for the root *dn* in the *rootpw* entry. This may be in plain text, or you can use the slappasswd utility to encode it.

Finally, make sure that the specified database directory exists, is owned by *root*, and has mode 700. The configuration file itself should also be readable only by *root*.

Once the configuration file is prepared, you can start slapd manually. On some systems, you can use the provided boot script, as in this example:

```
# /etc/init.d/ldap start
```

If you want the LDAP daemons to be started at boot time, you'll need to ensure that this file is run by the boot scripts.

Next, we create the first directory entries, via a text file in LDIF format (the default LDAP text-based import and export format). For example:

```
# Domain entry
dn: dc=ahania,dc=com
objectclass: dcObject
objectclass: organization
o: Ahania, LLC
dc: ahania.com
# Manager entry
dn: cn=Manager,dc=ahania,dc=com
objectclass: organizationalRole
cn: Manager
```

Use a command like this one to add the entries from the file:

```
# ldapadd -x -D "cn=Manager,dc=ahania,dc=com" -W -f /tmp/entry0
Enter LDAP Password:        Not echoed
adding new entry "dc=ahania,dc=com"
adding new entry "cn=Manager,dc=ahania,dc=com"
```

The -f option to ldapadd specifies the location of the prepared LDIF file. -D specifies the *dn* with which to connect to the server (this process is known as "binding"), and -x and -W say to use simple authentication (more about this later) and to prompt for the password, respectively.

You can verify that everything is working by running the following command to query the directory:

```
# ldapsearch -x -b 'dc=ahania,dc=com' -s base '(objectclass=*)'
version: 2
...
# ahania,dc=com
dn: dc=ahania,dc=com
objectClass: dcObject
objectClass: organization
o: Ahania, LLC
dc: ahania.com
...
```

This command displays the directory's base level (topmost) entry (we'll discuss the command's general syntax in a bit).

At this point, the server is ready to go to work. For more information on installing OpenLDAP, consult Section 2, "Quick Start," of the *OpenLDAP 2.0 Administrator's Guide*.

More about LDAP searching

The full syntax of the ldapsearch command is:

```
ldapsearch options search-criteria [attribute-list]
```

where *options* specify aspects of command functioning, *search-criteria* specify which entries to retrieve, and *attribute-list* specifies which attributes to display (the default is all of them). Search criteria are specified according to the (arcane) LDAP rules, whose simplest format is:

```
(attribute-name=pattern)
```

The pattern can include a literal value or a string containing wildcards. Thus, the criteria *(objectclass=*)* returns entries having any value for the *objectclass* attribute (i.e., all entries).

The following command illustrates some useful options and a more complex search criterion:

```
# ldapsearch -x -b 'dc=ahania,dc=com' -S cn \
    '(&(objectclass=person)(cn=Mike*))' \
    telephoneNumber  description
```

```
dn: cn=Mike Frisch, ou=MyList, dc=ahania, dc=com
telephoneNumber: 18
description: Computational chemist
dn: cn=Mike Loukides, ou=MyList, dc=ahania, dc=com
telephoneNumber: 14
description: Editor and writer
```

The output is (considerably) shortened.

This query returned two entries. The options said to use the simple authentication scheme (-x), to start the search at the entry *dc=ahania,dc=com* (-b), and to sort the entries by the *cn* attribute (-S).

The search criteria specified that the *objectclass* should be *person* and the *cn* should start with "Mike" (illustrating the syntax for an AND condition). The remaining arguments selected the two attributes that should be displayed in addition to the *dn*.

The following command could be used to perform a similar query on a remote host:

```
# ldapsearch -H ldap://bella.ahania.com -x -b 'dc=ahania,dc=com' \
    '(cn=Mike*)'  telephoneNumber description
```

The -H option species the URI for the LDAP server: *bella*.

The search context for LDAP clients can be preset using the *ldap.conf* configuration file (also in */etc/openldap*). Here is an example:

```
# /etc/openldap/ldap.conf
URI  ldap://bella.ahania.com
BASE dc=ahania,dc=com
```

With this configuration file, the previous command could be simplified to:

```
# ldapsearch -x  '(cn=Mike*)'  telephoneNumber description
```

There are a variety of LDAP clients available to make directory-entry viewing and manipulation easier than using LDIF files and command-line utilities. Some common ones are kldap (written by Oliver Jaun, *http://www.mountpoint.ch/oliver/kldap/*), gq (*http://biot.com/gq/*), and web2ldap (*http://web2ldap.de*). The gq utility is pictured in Figures 6-13 and 6-14.

Using OpenLDAP for User Authentication

Enterprise-level user authentication is another appropriate and desirable application for an OpenLDAP-based directory service. Setting up such functionality is not difficult, but the process does require several steps.

Select an appropriate schema

You'll need to incorporate user account and related configuration information conventionally stored in files (or in the NIS facility) into the directory service. Fortunately, there are standard objects for this purpose. In the case of user accounts, the ones to use are *posixAccount* and *shadowAccount* (both defined in the *nis.schema* file). In addition, if you wish to place users into an organizational unit (which is the standard practice, as we'll see), then the *account* object is also used (defined in *cosine.schema*).

Accordingly, we'll add these lines to *slapd.conf*:

```
include  /etc/openldap/schema/cosine.schema
include  /etc/openldap/schema/nis.schema
index    cn,uid       eq
index    uidNumber    eq
index    gidNumber    eq
```

The final three lines create indexes on the specified fields in order to speed up searches.

While you are performing this process, you may also want to enable slapd logging via this configuration file entry:

```
# log connection setup, searches and various stats (8+32+256)
loglevel 296
```

The parameter specifies the desired items to be logged; it is a mask that ANDs bits for the various available items (see the *OpenLDAP Administrator's Guide* for a list). Specify a log level of 0 to disable logging. Log messages are sent to the syslog *local4.debug* facility.

Don't forget to restart slapd after editing its configuration file.

Convert existing user account data

The next step is to transfer the user account data to the directory. The easiest way to do so is to use the open source migration tools provided by PADL software (*http://www.padl.com*). These are a series of Perl scripts that extract the required data from its current location and create corresponding directory entries. Using them goes like this:

- Install the scripts to a convenient location.
- Edit the *migrate_common.ph* file. You will have to modify at least these entries: *DEFAULT_BASE*, *DEFAULT_MAIL_DOMAIN*, *DEFAULT_MAIL_HOST*, and the various sendmail-related entries (if you plan to use OpenLDAP for this purpose as well).

  You should also set *EXTENDED_SCHEMA* to 1 if you want the scripts to create user account entries such as *person*, *organizationalPerson*, and *inetOrgPerson* objects in addition to the account-related objects.

There are two ways to proceed with the migration. First, you can run a script that automatically transfers all of the information to the directory: *migrate_all_online.pl* is used if slapd is running, and *migrate_all_offline.pl* is used otherwise.

I am not brave enough to just go for it; I run the various component scripts by hand so I can examine their work before importing the resulting LDIF files. For example, this command converts the normal and shadow password files to LDIF format:

```
# migrate_passwd.pl  /etc/passwd  passwd.ldif
```

The desired output file is specified as the second parameter.

Here is an example of the conversion process in action. The script takes the following entries from */etc/passwd* and */etc/shadow*:

/etc/passwd	chavez:x:502:100:Rachel Chavez:/home/chavez:/bin/tcsh
/etc/shadow	chavez:zcPv/oXSSS9hJg:11457:0:99999:7:0::

It uses those entries to create the following directory entry:

```
dn: uid=chavez,ou=People,dc=ahania,dc=com
uid: chavez
cn: Rachel Chavez
objectClass: top
objectClass: account
objectClass: posixAccount
objectClass: shadowAccount
uidNumber: 502
gidNumber: 100
gecos: Rachel Chavez
homeDirectory: /home/chavez
loginShell: /bin/tcsh
userPassword: {crypt}zcPv/oXSSS9hJg
shadowLastChange: 11457
shadowMax: 99999
shadowWarning: 7
```

If you choose this route, you will need also to run the *migrate_base.pl* script to create the top-level directory entries corresponding to the *ou*s (e.g., *People* above) in which the scripts place the accounts (and other entities). Another advantage of this method is that you can change the *ou* name if you don't like it, subdivide it, or transform it in other ways, before importing.

Specify the name service search order

Now we are ready to use the directory service for user account operations. In order to do so, we will need two additional packages: *nss_ldap* and *pam_ldap* (both available from *http://www.padl.com*). The first of these provides an interface to the */etc/nsswitch* file. The relevant lines need to be edited to add LDAP as an information source:

```
passwd: files ldap
shadow: files ldap
...
```

These lines tell the operating system to look in the conventional configuration file first for user account information and then to consult the OpenLDAP server.

This module also requires some entries in the *ldap.conf* client configuration file. For example:

```
nss_base_passwd     ou=People,dc=ahania,dc=com
nss_base_shadow     ou=People,dc=ahania,dc=com
nss_base_group      ou=Group,dc=ahania,dc=com
```

These entries specify the directory tree location of the *ou*s holding the user account and group information.

 This configuration file is usually in */etc/openldap*, but it is also possible to place it directly in */etc*, and the latter location takes precedence. If you install the *nss_ldap* package manually, it will probably place an example copy in */etc*. This can cause some trouble and be hard to debug when you don't know that it is there! The *pam_ldap* package does the same thing.

Once things are configured, you can use the following command to view user accounts:

```
# getent passwd
```

In the testing phase, you will want to migrate a few test accounts and then run this command. The migrated accounts will appear twice until you remove them from the configuration files.

Configure PAM to use OpenLDAP. The PAM facility (discussed previously) provides the means for interfacing the OpenLDAP directory data to the user authentication process. Accordingly, you will need the *pam_ldap* package to interface to OpenLDAP.

Once the package is installed, you will need to modify the files in */etc/pam.d* or */etc/pam.conf* to use the LDAP module (examples are provided with the package). For example, here is the modified version of the PAM configuration file for `rlogin` (shown in the format used by per-service PAM configuration files):

```
auth      required     /lib/security/pam_securetty.so
auth      required     /lib/security/pam_nologin.so
auth      sufficient   /lib/security/pam_rhosts_auth.so
auth      sufficient   /lib/security/pam_ldap.so
auth      required     /lib/security/pam_unix.so
auth      required     /lib/security/pam_mail.so
account   sufficient   /lib/security/pam_ldap.so
account   required     /lib/security/pam_unix.so
password  sufficient   /lib/security/pam_ldap.so
password  required     /lib/security/pam_unix.so    strict=false
session   required     /lib/security/pam_unix.so    debug
```

Generally, the *pam_ldap.so* module is just inserted into the stack above *pam_unix.so* (or equivalent module).

There are also several optional PAM-related entries which may be included in *ldap.conf*. For example, the following *ldap.conf* entries restrict user access by host, based on the contents of the user's directory entry:

```
# Specify allowed hosts for each user
pam_check_host_attr  yes
```

The following directory entry illustrates the method for granting user *chavez* access to a list of hosts:

```
dn: uid=chavez,ou=People,dc=ahania,dc=com
objectClass: account                          Parent of hos.t
objectClass: posixAccount                     Unix user account.
...
# List of allowed hosts
host: milton.ahania.com
host: shelley.ahania.com
host: yeats.ahania.com
...
```

Similarly, the following configuration file entries specify a list of allowed users for each host computer:

```
# Limit host access to the specified users
pam_groupdn cn=dalton.ahania.com,dc=ahania,dc=com
pam_member_attribute uniquemember
```

Here is the corresponding entry for a host:

```
# List of allowed users on the local host
dn: cn=dalton.ahania.com,dc=ahania,dc=com
objectClass: device                           Parent of ipHost.
objectClass: ipHost                           Parent of groupOfUniqueNames.
objectClass: groupOfUniqueNames
cn: dalton
cn: dalton.ahania.com
uniqueMember: uid=chavez,ou=People,dc=ahania,dc=com
uniqueMember: uid=carter,ou=People,dc=ahania,dc=com
...
```

Configure directory access control

The final steps in setting things up involves directory access control. The database files themselves are protected against all non-*root* access, so permissions are enforced by the server. Access control information is specified in the server's configuration file, *slapd.conf*, via access control entries like these:

```
# simple access control: read-only except passwords
access to dn=".*,dc=ahania,dc=com" attr=userPassword
    by self write
    by dn=root,ou=People,dc=ahania,dc=com write
    by * auth
access to dn=".*,dc=ahania,dc=com"
    by self write
    by * read
```

The *access to* entry specifies a pattern that the *dn* must match in order for the entry to apply. In the case of multiple entries, the first matching entry is used, and all remaining entries are ignored, so the ordering of multiple entries is very important. The first *access to* entry applies to the *userPassword* attribute of any entry: any *dn* in *dc=ahania,dc=com*. The owner can modify the entry, where the owner is defined as someone binding to the server using that *dn* and its associated password. Everyone else can access it only for authentication/binding purposes; they cannot view it, however. This effect is illustrated in Figure 6-13, which shows user *a2*'s search results for the specified query.

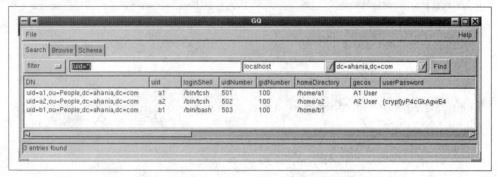

Figure 6-13. The OpenLDAP server prevents unauthorized access

The access control second entry serves as a default for the remainder of the database. Again, the owner can modify an entry, and everyone else can read it, an access level which allows both searching and display. These permissions are often appropriate for a company directory, but they are too lax for user account data. We'll need to examine access control entries in more detail to design something more appropriate.

OpenLDAP access control

An access control entry has the following general form:

```
access to what-data
   by what-users allowed-access
 [by ... ]
```

where *what-data* is an expression for the entries and possibly attributes to which this directive applies, *what-users* specifies who this directive applies to, and *allowed-access* is the access level that they are granted. There can be multiple *by* clauses. All variables can be literal values or include regular expressions.

The defined access levels are the following:

none
    No access.

auth
    Use for authentication only.

compare
> Values are accessible to comparison operations.

search
> Values are accessible to search filters.

read
> Data can be viewed.

write
> Data can be viewed and modified.

The target of the *by* clause has many possibilities, including a *dn* (which may contain wildcards) and the keywords *self* (the entry's owner), *domain* (which takes an expression for a domain as its argument), and *anonymous* (access by users who haven't been authenticated). A single asterisk can be used to signify access by anyone.

Let's look at some examples. The following configuration file directive allows everyone to have read access to the entire specified directory and also allows each entry's owner to modify it:

```
access to dn=".*,dc=ahania,dc=com"
    by self write
    by * read
```

The following example directives allow each entry's owner to read the entire entry but modify only a few attributes:

```
access to dn=".*,dc=ahania,dc=com" attrs="cn,sn,description,gecos"
    by self write
access to dn-".*,dc=ahania,dc=com"
    by self read
```

The following example allows the *uid* of *root* (in any top-level organizational unit) to modify any password attribute in the directory:

```
access to dn=".*,dc=ahania,dc=com" attrs="password"
    by dn="uid=root,ou=[A-Za-z]+,dc=ahania,dc=com" write
```

Note that we are assuming that *ou* names contain only letters.

Finally, this example controls access to the entries under the specified *ou*, limiting read access to members of the local domain:

```
access to dn=".*,ou=People,dc=ahania,dc=com"
    by domain=.*\.ahania\.com read
    by anonymous auth
```

Nonauthenticated users can use the data in this subtree only for LDAP authentication purposes.

You can use constructs like these to implement whatever access control design makes sense for your security objectives and needs. Consult the *OpenLDAP Administrator's Guide* for full details about access control directives.

Securing OpenLDAP Authentication

In all of our examples to this point, we have considered only the simplest method of presenting authentication credentials to the LDAP server: supplying a password associated with a specific distinguished name's password attribute. This is known as simple authentication, and it is the easiest way to bind to the LDAP server. However, since the passwords are sent to the server in the clear, there are significant security problems with this approach.

OpenLDAP supports the common authentication schemes: simple authentication using passwords, Kerberos-based authentication, and using the authentication services provided by the Simple Authentication and Security Layer (SASL). The first two of these are selected by the -x and -k options to the various LDAP client commands, respectively, and the absence of either of them implies SASL should be used. The Kerberos authentication method is deprecated, however, since superior Kerberos functionality is provided by SASL.

SASL was designed to add additional authentication mechanisms to connection-oriented network protocols like LDAP. Unix systems generally use the Cyrus SASL library, which provides the following authentication methods:

ANONYMOUS and PLAIN
> Standard anonymous and simple, plain text password-based binds

DIGEST-MD5
> MD5-encoded passwords

KERBEROS_V4 and GSSAPI
> Kerberos-based authentication for Kerberos 4 and Kerberos 5, respectively

EXTERNAL
> Site-specific authentication modules

Installing and configuring SASL is somewhat complex, and we don't have space to consider it here. Consult *http://asg.web.cmu.edu/sasl/* for more information.

Fortunately, OpenLDAP also provides the means for securing the simple authentication scheme. It uses an interface to the Secure Sockets Layer (SSL) and Transport Layer Security (TLS) networking functions. SSL provides encrypted authentication and data transfer via port 636 (assigned to the ldaps service), while TLS provides this via the standard LDAP port of 389. The advantage of the latter is that both encrypted and unencrypted clients can use the same standard port. However, it is usually best to enable both of them since client support is varied and unpredictable.

In order to use SSL and TLS, you will need to create a certificate for the LDAP server, using a process like this one:

```
# cd /usr/ssl/cert
# openssl req -newkey rsa:1024 -x509 -days 365 \
    keyout slapd_key.pem -out slapd_cert.pem
Using configuration from /usr/ssl/openssl.cnf
Generating a 1024 bit RSA private key
```

```
writing new private key to 'newreq.pem'
Enter PEM pass phrase:        Not echoed.
Verifying password - Enter PEM pass phrase:
-----------------------------------------------------------
You are about to be asked to enter information that
will be incorporated into your certificate request.
Country Name (2 letter code) [AU]:US
State or Province Name (full name) [Some-State]:Connecticut
...
```

First, we change to the SSL certificates directory, and then we run the command that creates the certificate and key files. This process requires you to enter a pass phrase for the private key and to provide many items of information, which are used in creating the certificate. When this process completes, the certificate is located in the file *slapd_cert.pem*, and the key is stored in *slapd_key.pem*.

The next steps consist of removing the pass phrase from the key file (otherwise, you'll need to enter it every time you start slapd), and then setting appropriate ownership and protections for the files:

```
# openssl rsa -in slapd_key.pem -out slapd_key.pem
# chown slapd-user.sldap-group sl*.pem
# chmod 600 sl*.pem
```

Once the certificate files are created, we add entries to *slapd.conf* pointing to the certificate files:

```
# SSL/TLS
TLSCertificateFile /usr/ssl/certs/slapd_cert.pem
TLSCertificateKeyFile /usr/ssl/certs/slapd_key.pem
# Specify ciphers to use -- this is a reasonable default
TLSCipherSuite HIGH:MEDIUM:+SSLv2
```

Finally, we need to modify the boot script that controls slapd so that the startup command lists both normal and secure LDAP as supported protocols. Here is the relevant line:

```
slapd -h "ldap:/// ldaps:///"
```

After you restart the server, you can verify that things are working in several ways. An easy way is to run a search command and watch the associated network traffic as the command runs. For example, you can use the ngrep utility to watch the two LDAP ports and look for unencrypted passwords. In this example, we look for the string "bbb", which is the password used for binding to the server:

```
# ngrep 'bbb' port 636 or port 389
```

Then, in another window, we run an ldapsearch command, which binds to a test entry in the directory (*uid=a2*), specifying the password first with -x and then with -w, using the ldap and ldaps services, respectively. Here is the second command:

```
# ldapsearch -H ldaps://10.0.49.212:636 -w bbb -x \
    -D 'uid=a2,ou=People,dc=ahania,dc=com' 'uid=a*'
```

The search command should return some entries both times, but the `ngrep` command will not find any matching packets for the second search since the password is encrypted.

Alternatively, you can use a client that supports one or both of these facilities. Figure 6-14 illustrates the gq utility's server properties dialog. You can check the appropriate box to use TLS and then run a similar test to the preceding, again searching for the cleartext password (and not finding it when TLS is enabled).

Figure 6-14. Enabling TLS support in the gq client

If you have problems binding to the server, make sure that the password you are using is the correct one for that entry and that the access level for your test entry is sufficient for the operation to succeed. Finally, be sure that you have restarted the `slapd` process and that it has not generated any error messages.

This introduction to OpenLDAP should be sufficient to get you started experimenting with this facility. As with any change of this size and complexity, it is important to test changes in a controlled and limited environment before attempting to apply them to production systems and/or on a large scale.

Wither NIS?

The Network Information Service (NIS) is another distributed database service that allows a single set of system configuration files to be maintained for an entire local network of computers. NIS was created by Sun Microsystems. With NIS, a single password file can be maintained for an entire network of computers almost automatically (you still have to add or modify entries on one copy by hand). This section will provide a brief description of NIS. Consult your system documentation for more details (use man -k nis and man -k yp to get started). In addition, *Managing NFS and NIS*, by Hal Stern, Mike Eisler, and Ricardo Labiaga (O'Reilly & Associates), contains an excellent discussion of NIS.

NIS was designed for a very open environment in which significant trust among all systems is desired (and assumed). As such, many considerations related to protecting systems from the bad guys—outside or inside—were overlooked or ignored in its design. Unfortunately, it isn't an exaggeration to say that NIS is a security nightmare.

If your network has direct connections to other computers outside of your control, or if there are any internal systems that need to be protected from others within the local network, then I'd advise you *not* to use NIS or even NIS+ (which fixes only a few of NIS's most egregious security flaws). Use NIS only when you want an open, mutually trusting security environment across an entire local network that has all its entrances—from the outside world as well as untrusted parts of the same site—protected by very rigorous firewalls.

CHAPTER 7
Security

These days, the phrase "computer security" is most often associated with protecting against break-ins: attempts by an unauthorized person to gain access to a computer system (and the person will bear a strong resemblance to an actor in a movie like *War Games or Hackers*). Such individuals do exist, and they may be motivated by maliciousness or mere mischievousness. However, while external threats are important, security encompasses much more than guarding against outsiders. For example, there are almost as many security issues relating to *authorized* users as to potential intruders.

This chapter will discuss fundamental Unix security issues and techniques, as well as important additional security features offered by some Unix versions. See *Practical Internet and Unix Security* by Simson Garfinkel and Gene Spafford (O'Reilly & Associates) for an excellent, book-length discussion of Unix security.

This chapter will undoubtedly strike some readers as excessively paranoid. The general approach I take to system security grows out of my experiences working with a large manufacturing firm designing its new products entirely on CAD-CAM workstations and experiences working with a variety of fairly small software companies. In all these environments, a significant part of the company's future products and assets existed solely online. Naturally, protecting them was a major focus of system administration and the choices that are appropriate for sites like these may be very different from what makes sense in other contexts. This chapter presents some options for securing a Unix system. It will be up to you and your site to determine what you need.

Security considerations permeate most system administration activities, and security procedures work best when they are integrated with other, normal system activities. Given this reality, discussions of security issues can't really be isolated to a single chapter. Rather, they pop up again and again throughout the book.

Prelude: What's Wrong with This Picture?

Before turning to the specifics of securing and monitoring Unix systems, let's take a brief look at three well-known historical Unix security problems (all of them were fixed years ago):

- The Sendmail package used to include a debug mode designed to allow a system administrator to type in raw commands by hand and observe the effects. Unfortunately, because anyone can run the sendmail program, and because it runs as setuid *root*, a nefarious user could use sendmail to execute commands as *root*. This is an example of a security hole created by a back door in a program: an execution mode that bypasses the program's usual security mechanisms.

- Traditionally, the passwd -f command enabled users to change the information in the GECOS field of their password-file entries. However, as originally implemented, the command simply added the new information to the user's GECOS field without examining it first for characters such as, for example, colons and new lines. This oversight meant that a treacherous user could use the command to add an entry to the password file. This is an example of a program's failure to validate its input. The program simply assumes that the input it receives is valid and harmless without checking that it is in the form and length that is expected.

  Another variation of this problem is called a *buffer overflow*. A buffer overflow occurs when a program receives more input than the maximum amount that it is able to handle. When it later chokes on that input, there can be unexpected side effects, including the ability to run arbitrary commands in the user context of the program (often *root*). Modern programs are usually written to reject input that is too large, but we are still finding and fixing such bugs in programs written in previous years/decades.

- The finger command displays various information about the user you specify as its argument: his full name and other password-file information, as well as the contents of the *.plan* and *.project* files in his home directory. finger is designed to make it easy to find out who is on the system and how to contact them. In the past, however, the command failed to check whether the *.plan* file in a user's home directory was readable by the user running finger before displaying its contents. This meant that an unscrupulous user could create a *.plan* in his own home directory as a link to any file on the system, then run finger on his own account and be able to view the contents of the target file, even when its file protection mode prevented his access. This is an example of a bug that arises from unconscious assumptions about the circumstances and context in which the program will be run.

What do these three items have in common? They all illustrate the fundamental Unix view that the system exists in a trustworthy environment of reasonable people. In all three cases, the programs failed to anticipate or check for unintended uses of their features. Seeing these problems merely as ancient bugs that have been long fixed misses the important point that such a view is inherent in the Unix operating system at a very deep level. This belief is evident even in the rhetoric of Unix commands as simple tools performing one task in a general and optimal way. You can do a lot more with a screwdriver than tightening and loosening screws.

Thinking About Security

Security discussions often begin by considering the kinds of threats facing a system. I'd like to come at this issue from a slightly different angle by focusing first on what needs to be protected. Before you can address any security-related issue on your system, you need to be able to answer the following questions:

- What are you trying to protect?
- What valuable asset might be lost?

If you can answer these questions, you've gone a long way toward identifying and solving potential security problems. One way to approach them is to imagine discovering one morning that your entire computer system/network was stolen during the previous night. Having this happen would upset nearly everyone, but for many different reasons:

- Because of the monetary cost: what is valuable is the computer as a physical object (loss of equipment).
- Because of the loss of sensitive or private data, such as company secrets or information about individuals (one type of loss of data).
- Because you can't conduct business: the computer is essential to manufacturing your product or providing services to your customers (loss of use). In this case, the computer's business or educational role is more important than the hardware per se.

Of course, in addition to outright theft, there are many other causes of all three kinds of losses. For example, data can also be stolen by copying it electronically or by removing the medium on which it is stored, as well as by stealing the computer itself. There is also both physical and electronic vandalism. Physical vandalism can mean broken or damaged equipment (as when thieves break into your office, get annoyed at not finding any money, and pour the cup of coffee left on a desk into the vents on the computer and onto the keyboard). Electronic vandalism can consist of corrupted or removed files or a system overwhelmed by so many garbage processes that it becomes unusable; this sort of attack is called a *denial of service* attack.

Depending on which of these concerns are relevant to you, different kinds of threats need to be forestalled and prepared for. Physical threats include not only theft but also natural disasters (fires, burst pipes, power failures from electrical storms, and so on). Data loss can be caused by malice or accident, ranging from deliberate theft and destruction to user errors to buggy programs wreaking havoc. Thus, preventing data loss means taking into account not only unauthorized users accessing the system and authorized users on the system doing things they're not supposed to do, but also authorized users doing things they're allowed to but didn't really mean or want to do. And occasionally it means cleaning up after yourself.

Once you've identified what needs to be protected and the potential acts and events from which it needs to be protected, you'll be in a much better position to determine what concrete steps to take to secure your system or site.

For example, if theft of the computer itself is your biggest worry, you need to think more about locks than about how often to make users change their passwords. Conversely, if physical security is no problem but data loss is, you need to think about ways to prevent data loss from both accidental and deliberate acts and to recover data quickly should loss occur despite all your precautions.

The final complication is that security inevitably corresponds inversely with convenience: the more secure a system is, the less convenient it is to use, and vice versa. You and your organization will need to find the right set of trade-offs for your situation. For example, isolated systems are easier to make secure than those on networks, but few people want to have to write a tape to transfer files between two local systems.

The key to a well-secured system is a combination of policies that:

- Prevent every possible relevant threat, to the extent that they can be prevented—and they can't always—and the extent that you, your users, and your organization as a whole are willing to accept (or impose) the inconveniences that these security measures entail.

- Plan and prepare for what to do when the worst happens anyway. For example, the best backup plans are made by imagining that tomorrow morning you come in and all your disks have had head crashes. It's helpful to imagine that even the impossible can happen. If it's important that certain people not have access to the *root* account, don't leave *root* logged in on an unattended terminal, not even on the console in the locked machine room where these users can *never* get in. Never is almost always sooner than you think.

Threats can come from a variety of sources. External threats range from electronic joy-riders who stumble into your system more or less at random to crackers who have specifically targeted your system (or another system that can be reached by a route including your system). Internal threats come from legitimate users attempting to do things that they aren't supposed to do, with motivations ranging from curiosity and mischievousness to malice and industrial espionage. You'll need to take different steps depending on which threats are most applicable to your site.

In the end, good security, like successful system administration in general, is largely a matter of planning and habit: designing responses to various scenarios in advance and faithfully and scrupulously carrying out the routine, boring, daily actions required to prevent and recover from the various disasters you've foreseen. Although it may seem at times like pounds, rather than ounces, of prevention are needed, I think you'll find that they are far less burdensome than even grams of cure.

Security Policies and Plans

Many sites find written security policies and plans helpful. By "security policy," I mean a written statement for users of what constitutes appropriate and unacceptable uses of their accounts and the data associated with them. I'll refer to a written description of periodic security-related system administration activities as a "security plan." At some sites, the computer security policy is part of a more comprehensive security policy; similarly, an administrative security plan is often part of a more general disaster-recovery plan.

Security policies

Security policies are most effective when users read, understand, and agree to abide by them at the time they receive their computer accounts, usually by signing some sort of form (retaining a copy of the written policy for future reference). For employees, this usually occurs when they are hired, as part of the security briefing they attend sometime during the first few days of employment. In an educational setting, students can also be required to sign the written security policy when they receive their accounts. During my brief stint in academia, one of my tasks was to create and deliver a BITNET security presentation for students wanting network access; if I were a system administrator at a university now, I'd recommend requiring a general computer security awareness session before a student receives an account for the first time.

A good computer security policy will cover these areas:

- Who is allowed to use the account (generally no one but the user herself). Don't forget to consider spouses, significant others, and children as you formulate this item.

- Password requirements and prohibitions (don't reveal it to anyone, don't use a password here that you have ever used anywhere else and vice versa, etc.). It may also be worth pointing out that no one from the computing/system administration staff will ever ask for it by phone or in person, nor will anyone from a law enforcement agency.

- Proper and improper use of local computers and those accessed via the Internet. This can include not only prohibitions against hacking but also whether personal use of an account is allowed, whether commercial use of a university account is permitted, policies about erotic/pornographic images being kept or displayed online, and the like.

- Conditions under which the user can lose her account. This item can also be somewhat broader and include, for example, when a job might be killed (when the system needs to go down for maintenance, when a job is overwhelming the system, and so on).

- Rules about what kinds of use are allowed on which computers (for example, when and where game-playing is allowed, where large jobs should be run, etc.).

- Consent to monitoring of all aspects of account activity by system administration staff as needed for system/network security, performance optimization, general configuration, and/or accounting purposes.
- Policies concerning how printed output is to be disposed of, whether it can leave the building or site, and similar policies for tapes and other media.

Some sites will need more than one policy for different classes of users. When you formulate or revise a written security policy, it may be appropriate to run it by your organization's legal department.

Security Begins and Ends with People

Getting users to care about security takes time and effort. In the end, a system is only as secure as its most vulnerable part, and it is important not to forget or neglect the system's users. When users cause security problems, there are three main reasons: ignorance, laziness, and malice.

Ignorance is the easiest to address. Developing formal and informal training tactics and procedures is something that happens over time. Users also need to be reminded of things they already know from time to time.

Laziness is always a temptation—for system administrators as well as users—but you'll find it is less of a problem when users have bought in to the system security goals. This requires both support from management—theirs as well as yours—and the organization as a whole and a formal commitment from individual users. In addition, an atmosphere that focuses on solutions rather than on blame is generally more successful than raw intimidation or coercion. When people are worried about getting in trouble, they tend to cover up problems rather than fix them.

Consideration of the third cause, malice, will have to wait. Creating a corporate culture that encourages and fosters employee loyalty and openness rather than deceit and betrayal is the subject of another book, as is recognizing and neutralizing malefactors.

Security plans

Formulating or revising a security plan is often a good way to assess and review the general state of security on a system or network. Such a plan will address some or all of the following issues:

- General computer access policies: the general classes of users present on the system, along with the access and privileges that they are allowed or denied. Describing this will include noting the purpose and scope of the various user groups.
- Optional system security features that are in effect (password aging and other restrictions, user account retirement policies, and so on).

- Preventative measures in effect (for example, the backup schedule, actions to be performed in conjunction with operating system installations and upgrades, and the like).
- What periodic (or continuous) system monitoring is performed and how it is implemented.
- How often complete system security audits are performed and what items they encompass.
- Policies and strategies for actively handling and recovering from security breaches.

Like any policy or procedure, the security plan needs to be reviewed and updated periodically.

Unix Lines of Defense

At an individual system level, Unix offers three basic ways of preventing security problems:

- A variety of network security mechanisms designed to prevent unauthorized connections from being accepted (where unauthorized can be defined based on one or more characteristics: connection source, type of connection, service requested, and the like).
- Passwords are designed to prevent unauthorized users from obtaining any access to the system, even via allowed channels.
- File permissions are designed to allow only designated users access to the various commands, files, programs, and system resources.

In theory, network protection filters out all unauthorized connections, passwords prevent the bad guys from getting on the system in the allowed ways, and proper file permissions prevent normal users from doing things they aren't supposed to do. On a system that is isolated both physically and electronically, theory pretty well matches reality, but the picture becomes much more complicated once you take networking into account. And the various kinds of security mechanisms can interact. For example, network access often bypasses the normal password authentication procedures. For these reasons, in the end, your system is only as secure as the worst-protected system on the network.

Permissions, passwords, and network barriers are useful only as part of an overall security strategy for your system. I find it helpful to think of them in the context of the various "lines of defense" that could potentially be set up to protect your system from the various losses it might experience.

Physical security

The first line of defense is physical access to your computer. The most security-conscious installations protect their computers by eliminating all network and dialup access and strictly limiting who can get physically near the computers. At the far extreme are systems in locked rooms (requiring a password be entered on a keypad in addition to the key for the door lock), isolated in restricted access areas of installations with guarded entrances (usually military or defense-related). To get onto these systems, you have to get into the site, into the right building, past another set of guards in the secure part of that building, and finally into the computer room before you even have to worry about having a valid password on the system. Such an approach effectively keeps out outsiders and unauthorized users; thus, security threats can come only from insiders.

Although this extreme level of physical security is not needed by most sites, all administrators face some physical security issues. Some of the most common include:

- Preventing theft and vandalism by locking the door or locking the equipment to a table or desk. If these are significant threats for you, you might also need to consider other aspects of the computer's physical location. For example, the best locks in the world can be basically worthless if the door has a glass window in it.

- Limiting access to the console and the CPU unit to prevent someone from crashing the system and rebooting it to single-user mode. Even if your system allows you to disable single-user–mode access without a password, there still may be issues here for you. For example, if your system is secured by a key position on its front panel, but you keep the key in the top middle drawer of your desk (right next to your file-cabinet keys) or inserted in the front panel, this level of security is effectively stripped away.

- Controlling environmental factors as much as realistically possible. This concern can include special power systems (backup generators, line conditioners, surge suppressors, and so on) to prevent downtime or loss of data, and fire detection and extinguishing systems to prevent equipment damage. It also includes simple, common-sense policies like not putting open cups of liquid next to a keyboard or on top of a monitor.

- Restricting or monitoring access to other parts of the system, like terminals, workstations, network cables (vulnerable to tapping and eavesdropping), and so on.

- Limiting access to backup tapes. If the security of your data is important to your system, backup tapes need to be protected from theft and damage as well (see Chapter 11). Keep in mind also that backup tapes contain sensitive system configuration data: the password and shadow password file, security key files, and so on.

Firewalls and network filters

Packet filtering and dedicated firewall systems represent an attempt to mitigate the risks associated with placing systems on a network. A firewall is placed between the Internet and the site to be protected; firewalls may also be used within a site or organization to isolate some systems from others (remember that not all threats are external). Packet filtering restricts the sort of network traffic that a system will accept.

We'll look at both of these topics in more detail later in this chapter.

Passwords

When someone gains access to the system, passwords form the next line of defense against unauthorized users and the risks associated with them. As I've said before, *all accounts should have passwords* (or be disabled). The weakness with passwords is that if someone breaks into an account by finding out its password, he has all the rights and privileges granted to that account and can impersonate the legitimate user in any way. File permissions form the next line of defense, against both bad guys who succeeded in breaking into an account and legitimate users trying to do something they're not supposed to. Properly set up file protection can prevent many potential problems. The most vulnerable aspects of file protection are the setuid and setgid access modes, which we'll look at in detail later in this chapter.

Some Unix versions also provide other ways to limit non-*root* users' access to various system resources. Facilities such as disk quotas, system resource limits, and printer and batch queue access restrictions protect computer subsystems from unauthorized use, including attacks by "bacteria" designed specifically to overwhelm systems by completely consuming their resources.*

If someone succeeds in logging in as *root* (or breaks into another account with access to important files or other system resources), system security is irreparably compromised in most cases. When this happens, the administrative focus must shift from prevention to detection: finding out what has been done to the system (and repairing it) and determining how the system was compromised—and plugging that gap. We'll look at both preventing and detecting security breaches in detail in the course of this chapter.

---

* It seems that no new type of security threat is uncovered without acquiring a cute name. *Bacteria*, also known as *rabbits*, are programs whose sole purpose is to reproduce and thereby overwhelm a system, bringing it to a standstill. There are a few other creatures in the security jungle whose names you should know. *Viruses* are programs that insert themselves into other programs, often legitimate ones, producing noxious side effects when their host is later executed. *Worms* are programs that move from system to system over a network, sometimes leaving behind bacteria, viruses, or other nasty programs. *Trojan horses* are programs that pretend to do one thing while doing another. The most common type is a password-stealing program, which mimics a normal login sequence but actually records the password the user types in and then exits. The term is also applied to programs or commands embedded within certain types of files that get executed automatically when the file is processed (PDF files, PostScript files, and attachments to electronic mail messages). *Back doors*, also called *trap doors*, are undocumented, alternative entrances to otherwise legitimate programs which allow a knowledgeable user to bypass security features. *Time bombs* are programs designed to perform particular—usually destructive—actions at a specific date and time. Programs with time bombs may be benign or inactive until the designated moment. In practice, these creatures often work in concert with one another.

Encrypting data

There is one exception to the complete loss of security if the *root* account is compromised. For some types of data files, encryption can form a fourth line of defense, providing protection against *root* and other privileged accounts.

Backups

Backups provide the final line of defense against some kinds of security problems and system disasters. In these cases, a good backup scheme will almost always enable you to restore the system to something near its previous state (or to recreate it on new hardware if some part of the computer itself is damaged). However, if someone steals the data from your system but doesn't alter or destroy it, backups are irrelevant.

Backups provide protection against data loss and filesystem damage only in conjunction with frequent system monitoring, designed to detect security problems quickly. Otherwise, a problem might not be uncovered for a long time. If this occurs, backups would simply save the corrupted system state, making it necessary to go back weeks or months to a known clean state when the problem finally is uncovered and restore or re-create newer versions of files by hand.

Version-Specific Security Facilities

Every commercial Unix version we are considering offers an enhanced security facility of some sort, either as part of the normal operating system or as an optional layered product; we'll consider many of their features in the course of this chapter. The primary commands associated with these facilities are listed below as an aid to your own explorations of what is available on your systems (in other words, check these manual pages first). I've also listed some related facilities available on FreeBSD and SuSE Linux systems:

AIX	chuser, audit, tcbck
FreeBSD	*/etc/periodic/security/**
HP-UX	audsys, swverify
Linux	harden_suse (SuSE)
Solaris	bsmconv, aset, audit
Tru64	prpwd, secsetup

man -k secur (to match "secure" and "security") will also often yield information, as will consulting any security manual or manual chapters in the system documentation.

User Authentication Revisited

We've already looked at the issues surrounding password selection and aging in "Administering User Passwords" in Chapter 6. In this section, we will consider optional user authentication methods and techniques that extend beyond standard password selection and aging. We will also consider another method of securing remote access—the secure shell—later in this chapter.

Smart Cards

The purpose of all user authentication schemes, from passwords on, is to require a prospective user to prove that she really is the person she is claiming to be. The standard Unix login procedure and most secondary authentication programs validate a user's identity based on *something she knows*, like a password, assuming that no one else knows it.

There are other approaches to user authentication. A user can also be validated based on *something she is*, that is, some unique and invariant physical characteristic such a fingerprint* or retina image. Biometric devices validate a person's identity in this way. They are commonly used to protect entrances to secure installations or areas, but they are seldom used just to authenticate users on a computer system.

A third approach is to validate the user based upon *something she has*. That something, known generically as a *token*, can be as simple as a photo ID badge. In the context of login authentication, *smart cards* are used most often. Smart cards are small, ranging in size from more or less credit card–size to about the same size as a small calculator. Some of them operate as a simple token that must be placed into a reader before computer access is granted.

Other smart cards look something like a calculator, with a keypad and a display in which a number appears. Users are required to enter a number from the display in addition to their normal password when they log in to a protected computer. This type of card generally requires the user to enter a personal identification number (PIN) before the card will operate (to provide some protection if the card is lost or stolen). Smart cards are also often designed to stop working if anyone tries take them apart or otherwise gain access to their protected memory.

Once the correct PIN is entered, smart cards can work in several different ways. In the most common mode of operation, the user is presented with a number when he tries to log in, known as a *challenge*. He types that number into his smart card and then types the number the card displays—the *response*—into the computer. The challenge and response values are generated cryptographically.

Under another scheme, the number to give the computer appears automatically after the proper PIN is entered. In this case, the card is synchronized with software running on the target computer; the most elaborate cards of this type can be synchronized with multiple hosts and can also operate in challenge/response mode to access still other computers.

---

* Fingerprints have been recently demonstrated to be quite easy to counterfeit, so they cannot be recommended.

For me, the most convenient type of card is made by RSA Security (*http://www. rsasecurity.com*). These cards automatically generate new numeric passwords every 60 seconds. The cards have an internal clock in addition to their cryptographic functionality, ensuring that they remain synchronized with the server software running on the target system. These cards are most often used as an additional authentication mechanism for dialup and other remote system access.

Smart cards provide an effective and relatively low-cost means of substantially increasing login authentication effectiveness. While they do not replace well-chosen user passwords, the combination of the two can go a long way toward securing a computer system against user account–based attacks.

One-Time Passwords

One-time passwords (OTPs) are another mechanism designed primarily for additional authentication for remote users. As the name implies, such passwords can be used only a single time, after which they become invalid. In addition, successive passwords are not easily predictable. For these reasons, they are a good choice when clear-text passwords are necessary for remote access.

The OPIE package—short for "One-time Passwords in Everything"—is an open source facility for OTPs. It was written by Randall Atkinson, Dan McDonald, and Craig Metz, and was derived from the earlier S/Key package. It is available from *http://www.inner.net/pub/opie/*.

Once OPIE is built and installed, you must replace the login, ftp, su, and/or passwd commands with the versions provided with the package. For example:

```
# cd /bin
# mv login login.save
# ln -s opielogin login
```

Next, you must set up user accounts that you want to have use the OTPs. First, at the system console, you add the user account to the OPIE system:

```
# opiepasswd -c chavez            Must be run on the system console.
Adding chavez:
Using MD5 to compute responses
Enter new secret pass phrase:      not echoed
Again new secret pass phrase:      not echoed
ID chavez OTP key is 123 ab4567
ASKS BARD DID LADY MARK EYES
```

As with any password, the secret pass phrase should be chosen with care.* Make it as long as possible (an entire sentence is good). The *opiepasswd* command displays the user identifying key and the first password.

---

* All OPIE keys and passwords in these examples are simulated.

OPIE stores its information in the file */etc/opiekeys*. This file is thus extremely sensitive and should be protected against all non-*root* access.

The *opiekey* command is used to generate OTPs:

```
$ opiekey 123 ab4567
Using the MD5 algorithm to compute response.
Enter secret pass phrase: not echoed
ASKS BARD DID LADY MARK EYES

$ opiekey -n 3 123 ab4567
Using the MD5 algorithm to compute response.
Enter secret pass phrase: not echoed
121: TELL BRAD HIDE HIS GREY HATS
122: SAYS BILL NOT HERO FROM MARS
123: ASKS BARD DID LADY MARK EYES
```

In the second example, three passwords are generated. They are used in inverse numerical order (highest numbered to lowest numbered). Such a list can be printed for use when traveling, provided that users are aware of the need to keep it secure.

 The opiekey command must not be run over the network, because the secret pass phrase would be transmitted in the clear, defeating the entire OPIE security mechanism. It must be run on the local system.

This is how an OPIE login session looks:

```
login: chavez
otp-md5 123 ab4567 ext
Response: ASKS BARD DID LADY MARK EYES
$
```

The OPIE package includes a PAM module for systems that use PAM. For example, it might be included in an `rlogin` authentication stack as follows:

```
auth    required    pam_securetty.so
auth    required    pam_nologin.so
auth    required    pam_opie.so
auth    required    pam_unix.so
```

This form of the stack uses both OPIE and normal Unix passwords. Alternatively, you could designate the OPIE module as sufficient and remove the *pam_unix* module to replace standard passwords with OTPs.

Note that only users added to the OPIE system with *opiepasswd* will be prompted for OTPs. In general, it is usually best to incorporate all users within the OPIE system, perhaps limiting the package's use to the system that accepts dialup and other remote connections.

When PAM is not in use, you can exempt users from using OPIE with the */etc/opie-access* configuration file. Entries in this file take the form:

```
action    net-or-host/netmask
```

Here are some examples:

```
deny    192.168.20.24/255.255.255.0    Require passwords from this host.
permit  192.168.10.0/255.255.255.0     Exempt this subnet.
```

If this file does not exist, all access uses OPIE. This is the recommended configuration.

Solaris and HP-UX Dialup Passwords

Dialup passwords add another level of user authentication for systems allowing dialup access via modems. When dialup passwords are in use, users are required to provide a dialup password in addition to their username and password before being allowed access to a system over a dialup line. Dialup passwords may also be used as a way to restrict dialup access to certain users (by only giving the password to them).

Dialup passwords are supported by HP-UX and Solaris.

The dialup password facility uses two configuration files: */etc/d_passwd*, the dialup password file (described later in this section), and */etc/dialups* (the file is occasionally named *dial-ups* on a few older systems), which lists the terminal lines that are connected to dial-in modems, one per line:

```
/dev/tty10
/dev/tty11
```

Users who log in through one of these terminal lines must supply a dialup password, as specified in the file */etc/d_passwd*, or they will not be allowed access to the system. If you decide to use dialup passwords, enter *all* the terminal lines connected to modems into this file; even a single unprotected dialup line is a significant security risk.

The file */etc/d_passwd* contains a set of encrypted dialup passwords. The dialup password required depends on the user's login shell.

In the following line, the *d_passwd* file contains three colon-separated fields:

```
shell:encrypted-password:          Final field is left empty
```

shell is the complete pathname of a shell that can be listed in the user's *passwd* entry. The second field is the encrypted password. The final field is always empty, but the second colon is required.

In general, the dialup password file does not provide any support for generating the encrypted password; you must generate it yourself.

On HP-UX systems, you can do this using the -F option to the passwd command. For example:

```
# passwd -F /etc/d_passwd /bin/sh
```

On Solaris systems, encrypted dialup passwords may be generated by changing your own password and then copying the string that appears in the password or shadow password file into */etc/d_passwd*. Be sure to change your password back afterwards.

If you decide to use the same dialup password for all user shells, you should encrypt them using different salts. Their encrypted representation will look different in the file, so it will not be obvious that they are the same password. Changing your own password to the same value a second time will also use a different salt and generate a different encoded string.

Here is a sample dialup password file:

```
/bin/sh:1Ogw4c39EHIAM:
/bin/csh:p9k3tJ6RzSfKQ:
/bin/ksh:9pk36RksieQd3:
/bin/Rsh:*:
```

In this example, there are specific entries for the Bourne shell, Korn shell, and C shell. Dialup access from the restricted Bourne shell (*/bin/Rsh*) is disabled by the asterisk in the password field. Users who use other shells may log in from remote terminals without giving an additional dialup password. However, I recommend that you assign a dialup password to all shells in use at your site (if you need dialup passwords, you need them for everyone).*

Dialup passwords should be changed periodically, even if you don't impose any password-aging restrictions on user passwords. They must be changed whenever anyone who knows the dialup password stops using the system (as part of the general account deactivation procedure), or if there is any hint that an unauthorized user has learned it.

AIX Secondary Authentication Programs

The software supporting smart card numeric passwords is one type of *secondary authentication program*. In general, this term refers to any program that requires additional information from the user before accepting that he is who he claims to be. For example, a program might require the user to answer several questions about their personal preferences ("Which of the following flowers do you prefer?") and compare the responses to those given when the user was initially added to the system (the question may be multiple choice, with the four or five wrong responses chosen randomly from a much larger list). The theory behind this sort of approach is that even if someone discovers or guesses your password, they won't be able to guess your favorite flower, bird, color, and so on, and you won't need to write the answers down to remember them, either, since the questions are multiple choice. It also relies on there being enough questions and choices per question to make blind guessing extremely unlikely to succeed. To be effective, accounts must be automatically disabled after quite a small number of unsuccessful authentications (two or three).

---

* If you decide to use dialup password for PPP access, you will have to modify the chat scripts accordingly to take the additional prompt into account.

AIX provides for an administrator-defined alternative login authentication method, which may be used in addition to or instead of standard passwords. A program is designated an authentication program in the file */etc/security/login.cfg*, via a stanza defining a name for the authentication method (uppercase by convention) and specifying the pathname of the authentication program:

```
LOCALAUTH:
    program = /usr/local/admin/bin/local_auth_prog
```

This stanza defines an authentication method LOCALAUTH using the specified program. Note that the standard AIX password authentication method is named SYSTEM.

Once a method is defined, it may be invoked for a user by including it in the list for the *auth1* user attribute. You can modify this attribute from SMIT, by using the chuser command, or by editing */etc/security/user* directly. For example, the first command below replaces the standard password authentication with the LOCALAUTH method for user *chavez*:

```
# chuser auth1=LOCALAUTH chavez
# chuser auth1=SYSTEM,LOCALAUTH chavez
```

The second command adds LOCALAUTH as an additional authentication method, run after the standard password check for user *chavez*. The program defined in the LOCALAUTH method will be passed the argument "chavez" when user *chavez* tries to log in. Of course, it would be wise to test an additional authentication method thoroughly on a single account before installing it on the system as a whole.

User accounts also have an attribute named *auth2*. This attribute works in the same way that *auth1* does. However, the user does not have to pass the authentication procedure to be allowed onto the system; more technically, the return value from any program specified in the *auth2* list is ignored. Thus, *auth2* is a poor choice for a secondary authentication program, but it will allow a system administrator to specify a program that all users must run at login time.

Better Network Authentication: Kerberos

So far, we've seen several attempts at strengthening user authentication in various ways. The Kerberos system provides another mechanism for securing network authentication operations. Its goal is to allow systems and services to be secure within a network environment controlled by an adversary. Its strategy for accomplishing this is to make sure that no sensitive data is ever sent across the network.

This section provides a very brief introduction to Kerberos Version 5. Figure 7-1 illustrates the basic Kerberos authentication scheme, which relies on *tickets* to authenticate users and authorize access to services. A ticket is just an encrypted network message containing request and/or authentication data and credential expiration data (as we'll see).

In the figure, the data passed between the user workstation (Kerberos client) and the various servers is depicted in the middle column of the drawing, passing between the two relevant computers. The legend describes the layout of this data. Included data is a darker shade, and the key used to encrypt it (if any) is indicated to its left, in the lighter shaded column. The sequence of events follows the circled numbers.

When a user logs in to a Kerberos-enabled workstation and enters his password, a one-way hash is computed from the password (1). This value is used as an encryption key within the Kerberos authentication request (2). The request consists of the unencrypted username and the current time; the time is encrypted using the hash created from the entered password (designated as K_P in the diagram). This is then sent to the Kerberos server, where its authentication function is invoked (3).

The Kerberos server knows the user's correct encoded password (which is not, in fact, stored on the workstation), so it can decrypt the time. If this operation is successful, the time is checked (to avoid replay attacks based on intercepted earlier communications). The server then creates a *session key*: an encryption key to be used for

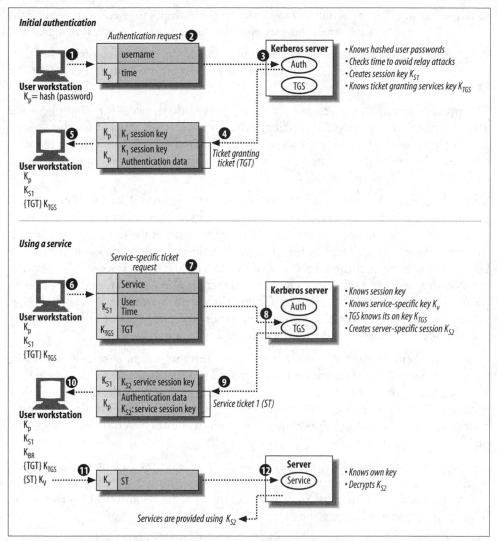

Figure 7-1. Basic Kerberos 5 authentication

communicating with this client during the current session (which typically expires after about 8 hours). This is labeled as K_{S1} in the diagram.

The Kerberos server also knows all the keys corresponding to its own services and services under its control. One of the former is the Kerberos Ticket Granting Service (TGS). Upon successful user authentication, the Kerberos server builds a response for the user (4). This transmission has two sets of data: the session key encrypted with the user password hash K_P, and a ticket-granting ticket (TGT) encrypted with the TGS's own key (designated K_{TGS}). The TGT contains another copy of the session key as well as user authentication data and time-stamps. The TGT will be used to request tickets for the actual services that the client wants to use. It can be thought of as a sort of meta-ticket: an authorization to request and receive actual tickets.

When the workstation receives this response (5), it decrypts the session key and stores it. It also saves the TGT in encrypted form (because it does not know the TGS's key).

The process of requesting access to a specific network service—for example, a file access service—begins at (6). The client builds a request for a ticket for the desired service to be sent to the Kerberos server's TGS. The request (7) contains the name of the desired service (unencrypted), the user information and current time encrypted with the session key, and the TGT.

The TGS can decrypt both parts of the message (8) because it knows both the session key and its own key (K_{TGS}). If the authentication is successful and the ticket's time is within the allowed window, the TGS creates a ticket for the client to use with the actual service (9). As part of this process, it generates another session key for use between the client and the target service (K_{S2}). The second service-specific session key is encrypted using the client's Kerberos server session key, K_{S1}, and the ticket to be supplied to the service is encrypted using the service's own key (designated K_V), which the Kerberos server also knows. The latter ticket consists of another copy of the new session key and user authentication and time-stamp data.

When the client receives this response (10), it decrypts the new session key using K_{S1}, and it stores the service ticket in encrypted form (because it does not know K_V). It presents the latter (11) to the desired server (12). The service decrypts it using its own key (K_V) and in doing so learns the session key to be used for future communication with the client (K_{S2}). Subsequent communications between the two rely solely on the latter session key.

As this description indicates, the Kerberos method assumes an untrustworthy network environment and encrypts all important data. Another nice feature is that it requires no action on the part of the user. All of the requests and ticket presentation happen automatically, triggered by the initial user login.

On the down side, Kerberos relies fundamentally on the security of the Kerberos server. If it is compromised, the security of the entire Kerberos infrastructure is at risk.

Protecting Files and the Filesystem

In general, the goal of every security measure on a system is to prevent people from doing things they shouldn't. Given the all-or-nothing structure of Unix privileges, in practical terms this means you are trying to prevent unauthorized access to the *root* account—it also implies that the *root* account is what the bad guys are trying to gain access to. When they cannot do so directly because the root password has been well chosen, they may try other, indirect routes through the filesystem to gain superuser status.

So, how can you get *root* access from an ordinary, unprivileged user account? One way is to get *root* to execute commands like these:

```
# cp /bin/sh /tmp/.junk
# chmod 4755 /tmp/.junk
```

These commands create a setuid *root* version of the Bourne shell: any user can start a shell with this file, and every command that he runs within it will be executed as if he were *root*. Of course, no reputable system administrator will run these commands on demand, so a cracker will have to trick her into doing it anyway by hiding these commands—or other commands just as deadly—within something that she will execute. One large class of system attack revolves around substituting hacked, pernicious copies of normally benign system entities: Unix command executables, login or other initialization files, and so on. Making sure that the filesystem is protected will prevent many of them from succeeding.

In this section, we'll consider the types of vulnerabilities that come from poorly-chosen filesystem protections and general system disorganization. In the next section, we'll look at ways of finding potential problems and fixing them.

Search Path Issues

It is important to place the current directory and the *bin* subdirectory of the user's home directory at the end of the path list, *after* the standard locations for Unix commands:

```
$ echo $PATH
/usr/ucb:/bin:/usr/bin:/usr/bin/X11:/usr/local/bin:$HOME/bin:.
```

This placement closes a potential security hole associated with search paths. If, for example, the current directory is searched before the standard command locations, it is possible for someone to sneak a file named, say, ls into a seemingly innocuous directory (like */tmp*), which then performs some nefarious action instead of or in addition to giving a directory listing. Similar effects are possible with a user's *bin* subdirectory if it or any of its components is writable.

Most importantly, the current directory should not even appear in *root*'s search path, nor should any relative pathname appear there. In addition, none of the directories in *root*'s search path, nor any of their higher-level components, should be writable by anyone but *root*; otherwise someone could again substitute something else for a standard command, which would be unintentionally run by and as *root*.

 Scripts should always set the search path as their first action (which includes only system directories protected from unauthorized write access). Alternatively, a script can use the full pathname for every command, but it's easy to slip up using the latter approach.

Small Mistakes Compound into Large Holes

It is possible, and probably even common, for large security problems to arise from small mistakes, an effect tangentially related to the one described in the science fiction story "Spell My Name with an S" by Isaac Asimov. Consider these two small file protection errors:

- User *chavez*'s *.login* file is writable by its group owner (*chem*).
- The directory */etc* is writable by its user and group owners (*root* and *system*, respectively).

Suppose user *chavez* is also a member of group *system*: now you have a situation where anyone in the *chem* group has a very good chance of replacing the password file.

How does that work? Since *~chavez/.login* is writable by group *chem*, anyone in that group can edit it, adding commands like:

```
rm -f /etc/passwd
cp /tmp/data526 /etc/passwd
```

Since *chavez* is a member of the *system* group and */etc* is writable by group *system*, both commands will succeed the next time *chavez* logs in (unless she notices that the file has been altered—would you?). Keep in mind how powerful write access to a directory is.

More subtle variations on this theme are what usually happen in practice; */etc* being writable is not really a small mistake. Suppose instead that the system administrator had been careless and had the wrong umask in effect when she installed a new program, xpostit (which creates memo pad windows under X), into */usr/local/bin*, and that file was writable by group *system*. Now the bad guy is able to replace only the xpostit executable. Exploiting this weakness will take more work than in the previous case but is ultimately just as successful: writing a program that merely starts the real xpostit when most users run it but does something else first when *root* runs it. (A smart version would replace itself with the real xpostit after *root* has used it to cover its tracks.)

It usually isn't hard to get *root* to run the doctored xpostit. The system administrator may already use it anyway. If not, and if the bad guy is bold enough, he will walk over to the system administrator's desk and say he's having trouble with it and hope she tries it herself to see if it works. I'm sure you can imagine other ways.

In addition to once again pointing out the importance of the appropriate ownership and protection for all important files and directories on the system, the preceding story highlights several other points:

- Because it is always world-writable, don't use */tmp* as any user's home directory, not even a pseudo-user who should never actually log in.

- Think carefully about which users are supplementary members of group 0 and any other system groups, and make sure that they understand the implications.

- *root*'s umask should be 077 or a more restrictive setting. System administrators should turn on additional access by hand when necessary.

The setuid and setgid Access Modes

The set user ID (setuid) and set group ID (setgid) file access modes provide a way to grant users increased system access for a particular command. However, setuid access especially is a double-edged sword. Used properly, it allows users access to certain system files and resources under controlled circumstances, but if it is misused, there can be serious negative security consequences.

setuid and setgid access are added with chmod's s access code (and they can similarly be recognized in long directory listings):

```
# chmod u+s files          setuid access
# chmod g+s files          setgid access
```

When a file with setuid access is executed, the process' effective UID (EUID) is changed to that of the user owner of the file, and it uses that UID's access rights for subsequent file and resource access. In the same way, when a file with setgid access is executed, the process' effective GID is changed to the group owner of the file, acquiring that group's access rights.

The passwd command is a good example of a command that uses setuid access. The command's executable image, */bin/passwd*, typically has the following permissions:

```
$ ls -lo /bin/passwd
-rwsr-xr-x 3 root 55552 Jan 29 2002 /bin/passwd
```

The file is owned by *root* and has the setuid access mode set, so when someone executes this command, his EUID is changed to *root* while that command is running. setuid access is necessary for passwd, because the command must write the user's new password to the password file, and only *root* has write access to the password file (or the shadow password file).

The various commands to access line printer queues are also usually setuid files. On systems with BSD-style printing subsystems, the printer commands are usually setuid to user *root* because they need to access the printer port */dev/printer* (which is owned by *root*). In the System V scheme, the printing-related commands are sometimes setuid to the special user *lp*. In general, setuid access to a special user is preferable to setuid *root* because it grants fewer unnecessary privileges to the process.

Other common uses of the setuid access mode are the at, batch, and mailer facilities, all of which must write to central spooling directories to which users are normally denied access.

setgid works the same way, but it applies to the group owner of the command file rather than to the user owner. For example, the wall command is setgid to group *tty*, the group owner of the special files used to access user terminals. When a user runs wall, the process' EGID is set to the group owner of */usr/bin/wall*, allowing him to write to all TTY devices.

 As the examples we've considered have illustrated, setuid and setgid access for system files varies quite a bit from system to system (as does file ownership and even directory location). You should familiarize yourself with the setuid and setgid files on your system (finding all of them is discussed later in this chapter).

To be secure, a setuid or setgid command or program must not allow the user to perform any action other than what it was designed to do, including retaining the setuid or setgid status after it completes. The threat is obviously greatest with programs that are setuid to *root*.

Aside from commands that are part of Unix, other setuid and setgid programs should be added to the system with care. If at all possible, get the source code for any new setuid or setgid program being considered and examine it carefully before installing the program. It's not always possible to do so for programs from third-party application vendors, but such programs are usually less risky than free programs. Ideally, the part requiring privileged access will be isolated to a small portion of the package (if it isn't, I'd ask a lot of questions before buying it). Methods to ensure security when creating your own setuid and setgid programs are discussed in the next section.

Writing setuid/setgid programs

Two principles should guide you in those rare instances where you need to write a setuid or setgid program:

Use the minimum privilege required for the job.

Whenever possible, make the program setgid instead of setuid. 99 percent of all problems can be solved by creating a special group (or using an existing one) and making the program setgid. Almost all of the remaining 1 percent can be solved by creating a special user and using setuid to that special user ID. Using setuid to *root* is a bad idea because of the difficulty in foreseeing and preventing every possible complication, system call interaction, or other obscure situation that will turn your nice program into a security hole. Also, if the program doesn't need setuid or setgid access for its entire lifetime, reset its effective UID or GID back to the process' real UID or GID at the appropriate point.

Avoid extra program entrances and exits.

In addition to writing in an explicit back door, this principle rules out many different features and programming practices. For example, the program should not support shell escapes,* which allow a shell command to be executed inside another program. If a setuid program has a shell escape, any shell command executed from within it will be run using the process' effective UID (in other words, as *root* if the program is setuid to *root*). To be completely secure, the program should not call any other programs (if it does so, it inherits the security holes of the secondary program). Thus, if a setuid program lets you call an editor and the editor has shell escapes, it's just as if the first program had shell escapes.

This principle also means that you should avoid system calls that invoke a shell (popen, system, exec{vp,lp,ve}, and so on). These calls are susceptible to attacks by clever users.

Access Control Lists

Access control lists (ACLs) offer a further refinement to the standard Unix file permissions capabilities. ACLs enable you to specify file access for completely arbitrary subsets of users and/or groups. All of our reference operating systems provide ACLs, with the exception of FreeBSD.†

The first part of this section covers AIX ACLs. It also serves as a general introduction to ACLs and should be read by all administrators encountering this topic for the first time. Table 7-1 lists features of the ACL implementations on the systems we are considering.

Table 7-1. ACL features by operating system

Feature	AIX	FreeBSD[a]	HP-UX	Linux	Solaris	Tru64
Follows POSIX standard?	no	yes	no	yes	yes	yes
chmod deletes extended ACEs?	numeric mode only	no	varies[b]	no	no	no
ACL inheritance from parent directory's default ACL?	no	yes	no	yes	yes	yes
NFS support?	yes	no	no	yes	yes	yes
ACL backup/restore support	backup (by inode)	no	fbackup	star[c]	ufsdump	dump

[a] ACL support in FreeBSD is preliminary.
[b] The most recent versions of chmod support the -A option, which retains ACL settings
[c] See *http://www.fokus.gmd.de/research/cc/glone/employees/joerg.schilling/private/star.html*.

Note that the NFS support listed in the table refers to whether NFS file operations respect ACLs for other systems running the same operating system (homogeneous

---

* Strictly speaking, as long as the program ensured that any created child processes did not inherit the parent's setuid or setgid status (by resetting it between the fork and the exec), shell escapes would be OK.

† Actually, POSIX ACL functionality is partially present in current releases of FreeBSD, but the facility is still considered experimental.

NFS, if you will). Heterogeneous NFS support is seldom offered. Even when NFS is supported, there can still be privilege glitches arising from NFS's practice of caching files and their permissions for read purposes in a user-independent manner. Consult the documentation for your systems to determine how such situations are handled.

Introducing access control lists

On an AIX system, an access control list looks like this:

```
attributes:                          Special modes like setuid.
base permissions                     Normal Unix file modes:
   owner(chavez): rw-                 User access.
   group(chem): rw-                   Group access
   others: r--                        Other access.
extended permissions                 More specific permission entries:
   enabled                              Whether they're used or not.
   specify r-- u:harvey               Permissions for user harvey.
   deny -w- g:organic                 Permissions for group organic.
   permit rw- u:hill, g:bio           Permissions for hill when group bio is active.
```

The first line specifies any special attributes on the file (or directory). The possible attribute keywords are SETUID, SETGID, and SVTX (the sticky bit is set on a directory). Multiple attributes are all placed on one line, separated by commas.

The next section of the ACL lists the *base permissions* for the file or directory. These correspond exactly to the Unix file modes. Thus, for the file we're looking at, the owner (who is *chavez*) has read and write access, members of the group *chem* (which is the group owner of the file) also have read and write access, and all others have read access.

The final section specifies *extended permissions* for the file: access information specified by user and group name. The first line in this section is the word *enabled* or *disabled*, indicating whether the extended permissions that follow are actually used to determine file access. In our example, extended permissions are in use.

The rest of the lines in the ACL are *access control entries* (ACEs), which have the following format:

```
operation  access-types  user-and-group-info
```

The *operation* is one of the keywords permit, deny, and specify, which correspond to chmod's +, -, and = operators, respectively. permit says to add the specified permissions to the ones the user already has, based on the base permissions; deny says to take away the specified access; and specify sets the access for the user to the listed value. The *access-types* are the same as those for normal Unix file modes. The *user-and-group-info* consists of a user name (preceded by u:) or one or more group names (each preceded by g:) or both. Multiple items are separated by commas.

Let's look again at the ACEs in our sample ACL:

```
specify  r--  u:harvey            Permissions for user harvey.
deny     -w-  g:organic           Permissions for group organic.
permit   rw-  u:hill, g:bio       Permissions for hill when group bio is active.
```

The first line grants read-only access to user *harvey* on this file. The second line removes write access for the *organic* group from whatever permissions a user in that group already has. The final line adds read and write access to user *hill* while group *bio* is part of the current group set (see "Unix Users and Groups" in Chapter 6). By default, the current group set is all of the groups to which the user belongs.

ACLs that specify a username and group are useful mostly for accounting purposes; the previous ACL ensures that user *hill* has group *bio* active when working with this file. They are also useful if you add a user to a group on a temporary basis, ensuring that the added file access goes away if the user is later removed from the group. In the previous example, user *hill* would no longer have access to the file if she were removed from the *bio* group (unless, of course, the file's base permissions grant it to her).

If more than one item is included in the *user-and-group-info*, all of the items must be true for the entry to be applied to a process (Boolean AND logic). For example, the first ACE below is applied only to users who have both *bio* and *chem* in their group sets (which is often equivalent to "are members of both the *chem* and *bio* groups"):

```
permit   r--  g:chem, g:bio
permit   rw-  u:hill, g:chem, g:bio
```

The second ACE applies to user *hill* only when both groups are in the current group set. If you wanted to grant write access to anyone who was a member of either group *chem* or group *bio*, you would specify two separate entries:

```
permit   rw-  g:bio
permit   rw-  g:chem
```

At this point, it is natural to wonder what happens when more than one entry applies. When a process requests access to a file with extended permissions, the permitted accesses from the base permissions and *all* applicable ACEs—all ACEs that match the user and group identity of the process—are combined with a union operation. The denied accesses from the base permissions and all applicable ACEs are also combined. If the requested access is permitted *and* it is not explicitly denied, then it is granted. Thus, contradictions among ACEs are resolved in the most conservative way: access is denied unless it is both permitted and not denied.

This conservative, least-privilege approach is true for all the ACL implementations we are considering.

For example, consider the ACL below:

```
attributes:
base permissions
    owner(chavez): rw-
    group(chem):   r-
    others:        ---
```

```
extended permissions
   enabled
   specify  r-- u:stein
   permit   rw- g:organic, g:bio
   deny     rwx g:physics
```

Now suppose that the user *stein*, who is a member of both the *organic* and *bio* groups (and not a member of the *chem* group), wants write access to this file. The base permissions clearly grant *stein* no access at all to the file. The ACEs in lines one and two of the extended permissions apply to *stein*. These ACEs grant him read access (lines one and two) and write access (line two). They also deny him write and execute access (implicit in line one). Thus, *stein* will not be given write access, because while the combined ACEs do grant it to him, they also deny write access, and so the request will fail.

Manipulating AIX ACLs

ACLs may be applied and modified with the `acledit` command. `acledit` retrieves the current ACL for the file specified as its argument and opens the ACL for editing, using the text editor specified by the EDITOR environment variable. The use of this variable under AIX is different than in other systems. For one thing, there is no default (most Unix implementations use `vi` when EDITOR is unset). Second, AIX requires that the full pathname to the editor be supplied, */usr/bin/vi*, not just its name. Once in the editor, make any changes to the ACL that you wish. If you are adding extended permissions ACEs, be sure to change *disabled* to *enabled* in the first line of that section. When you are finished, exit from the editor normally. AIX will then print the message:

```
Should the modified ACL be applied? (y)
```

If you wish to discard your changes to the ACL, enter "n"; otherwise, you should press Return. AIX then checks the new ACL and, if it has no errors, applies it to the file. If there are errors in the ACL (misspelled keywords or usernames are the most common), you are placed back in the editor, where you can correct them and try again. AIX puts error messages like this one at the bottom of the file, describing the errors it found:

```
* line number 9: unknown keyword: spceify
* line number 10: unknown user: chavze
```

You don't have to delete the error messages themselves from the ACL.

But this is the slow way of applying an ACL. The `aclget` and `aclput` commands offer alternative ways to display and apply ACLs to files. `aclget` takes a filename as its argument and displays the corresponding ACL on standard output (or to the file specified to its -o option). The `aclput` command is used to read an ACL in from a text file. By default, it takes its input from standard input or from an input file specified with the -i option. Thus, to set the ACL for the file *gold* to the ACL stored in the file *metal.acl*, you could use this command:

```
$ aclput -i metal.acl gold
```

This form of aclput is useful if you use only a few different ACLs, all of which are saved as separate files to be applied as needed.

To copy an ACL from one file to another, put aclget and aclput together in a pipe. For example, the command below copies the ACL from the file *silver* to the file *emerald*:

```
$ aclget silver | aclput emerald
```

To copy an ACL from one file to a group of files, use xargs:

```
$ ls *.dat *.old | xargs -i /bin/sh -c "aclget silver | aclput {}"
```

These commands copy the ACL in *silver* to all the files ending in *.dat* and *.old* in the current directory.

You can use the ls -le command to quickly determine whether a file has an extended permissions set or not:

```
-rw-r-----+ 1 chavez chem  51 Mar 20 13:27 has_acl
-rwxrws---- 2 chavez chem 512 Feb 08 17:58 no_acl
```

The plus sign appended to the normal mode string indicates the presence of extended permissions; a minus sign indicates that there are no extended permissions.

Additional AIX ACL notes:

- The base permissions on a file with an extended access control list may be changed with chmod's symbolic mode, and any changes made in this way will be reflected in the base permissions section of the ACL. However, chmod's numeric mode must not be used for files with extended permissions, because using it automatically removes any existing ACEs.

- Only the backup command in backup-by-inode mode will backup and restore the ACLs along with the files.

Unlike other ACL implementations, files do not inherit their initial ACL from their parent directory. Needless to say, this is a very poor design.

HP-UX ACLs

The lsacl command may be used to view the ACL for a file. For a file with only normal Unix file modes set, the output looks like this:

```
(chavez.%,rw-)(%.chem,r--)(%.%,---) bronze
```

This shows the format an ACL takes under HP-UX. Each parenthesized item is known as an *access control list entry*, although I'm just going to call them "entries." The percent sign is a wildcard within an entry, and the three entries in the previous listing specify the access for user *chavez* as a member of any group, for any user in group *chem*, and for all other users and groups, respectively.

A file can have up to 16 ACL entries: three base entries corresponding to normal file modes and up to 13 optional entries. Here is the ACL for another file (generated this time by lsacl -l):

```
silver:
rwx chavez.%
r-x %.chem
r-x %.phys
r-x hill.bio
rwx harvey.%
--- %.%
```

This ACL grants all access to user *chavez* with any current group membership (she is the file's owner). It grants read and execute access to members of the *chem* and *phys* groups and to user *hill* when a member of group *bio*, and it grants user *harvey* read, write and execute access regardless of his group membership and no access to any other user or group.

Entries within an HP-UX access control list are examined in order of decreasing specificity: entries with a specific user and group are considered first, followed by those with only a specific user, those with only a specific group, and the other entry last of all. Within a class, entries are examined in order. When determining whether to permit file access, the first applicable entry is used. Thus, user *harvey* will be given write access to the file *silver* even if he is a member of the *chem* or *phys* group.

The chacl command is used to modify the ACL for a file. ACLs can be specified to chacl in two distinct forms: as a list of entries or with a chmod-like syntax. By default, chacl adds entries to the current ACL. For example, these two commands both add read access for the *bio* group and read and execute access for user *hill* to the ACL on the file *silver*:

```
$ chacl "(%.bio,r--) (hill.%,r-x)" silver
$ chacl "%.bio = r, hill.% = rx" silver
```

In either format, the ACL must be passed to chacl as a single argument. The second format also includes + and - operators, as in chmod. For example, this command adds read access for group *chem* and user *harvey* and removes write access for group *chem*, adding or modifying ACL entries as needed:

```
$ chacl "%.chem -w+r, harvey.% +r" silver
```

chacl's -r option may be used to replace the current ACL:

```
$ chacl -r "@.% = 7, %.@ = rx, %.bio = r, %.% = " *.dat
```

The @ sign is a shorthand for the current user or group owner, as appropriate, and it also enables user-independent ACLs to be constructed. chacl's -f option may be used to copy an ACL from one file to another file or group of files. This command applies the ACL from the file *silver* to all files with the extension *.dat* in the current directory:

```
$ chacl -f silver *.dat
```

Be careful with this option: it changes the ownership of target files if necessary so that the ACL exactly matches that of the specified file. If you merely want to apply a standard ACL to a set of files, you're better off creating a file containing the desired ACL, using @ characters as appropriate, and then applying it to files in this way:

```
$ chacl -r "`cat acl.metal`" *.dat
```

You can create the initial template file by using lsacl on an existing file and capturing the output.

You can still use chmod to change the base entries of a file with an ACL if you include the -A option. Files with optional entries are marked with a plus sign appended to the mode string in long directory listings:

```
-rw-------+ 1 chavez chem 8684 Jun 20 16:08 has_one
-rw-r--r-- 1 chavez chem 648205 Jun 20 11:12 none_here
```

Some HP-UX ACL notes:

- ACLs for new files are not inherited from the parent directory.
- NFS support for ACLs is not included in the implementation.
- Using any form of the chmod command on a file will remove all ACEs except those for the user owner, group owner, and other access.

POSIX access control lists: Linux, Solaris, and Tru64

Solaris, Linux, and Tru64 all provide a version of POSIX ACLs, and a stable FreeBSD implementation is forthcoming. On Linux systems, ACL support must be added manually (see *http://acl.bestbits.ac*); the same is true for the preliminary FreeBSD version, part of the TrustedBSD project (e.g., see *http://www.freebsd.org/news/status/report-dec-2001-jan-2002.html*, as well as the project's home page at *http://www.trustedbsd.org*). Linux systems also require that the filesystem be mounted with the option -o acl.

Here is what a simple POSIX access control list looks like:

```
u::rwx                    Owner access.
g::rwx                    Group owner access.
o:---                     Other access.
u:chavez:rw-             Access for user chavez.
g:chem:r-x               Access for group chem.
g:bio:rw-                Access for group bio.
g:phys:-w-               Access for group phys.
m:r-x                     Access mask: sets maximum allowed access.
```

The first three items correspond to the usual Unix file modes. The next four entries illustrate the ACEs for specific users and groups; note that only one name can be included in each entry. The final entry specifies a protection mask. This item sets the maximum allowed access level for all but user owner and other access.

In general, if a required permission is not granted within the ACL, the corresponding access will be denied. Let's consider some examples using the preceding ACL.

Suppose that *harvey* is the owner of the file and the group owner is *prog*. The ACL will be applied as follows:

- The user owner, *harvey* in this case, always uses the u:: entry, so *harvey* has rwx access to the file. All group entries are ignored for the user owner.

- Any user with a specific u: entry always uses that entry (and all group entries are ignored for her). Thus, user *chavez* uses the corresponding entry. However, it is subject to the mask entry, so her actual access will be read-only (the assigned write mode is masked out).

- Users without specific entries use any applying group entry. Thus, members of the *prog* group have r-x access, and members of the *bio* group have r-- access (the mask applies in both cases). Under Solaris and Tru64, all applicable group entries are combined (and then the mask is applied). However, on Linux systems, group entries do not accumulate (more on this in a minute).

- Everyone else uses the specified other access. In this case, that means no access to the file is allowed.

On Linux systems, users without specific entries who belong to more than one group specified in the ACL can use all of the entries, but the group entries are not combined prior to application. Consider this partial ACL:

```
g:chem:r--
g:phys:--x
m:rwx
```

The mask is now set to rwx, so the permissions in the ACEs are what will be granted. In this case, the access for users who are members of group *chem* and group *phys* can use either ACE. If this file is a script, they will not be able to execute it because they do not have rx access. If they try to read the file, they will be successful, because the ACE for *chem* gives them read access. However, when they try to execute the file, neither ACE gives them both r and x. The separate permissions in the two ACEs are not combined.

New files are given ACLs derived from the directory in which they reside. However, the directory's own access permission set is not used. Rather, separate ACEs are defined for use with new items. Here are some examples of these default ACEs:

```
d:u::rwx              Default user owner ACE.
d:g::r-x              Default group owner ACE.
d:o:r--               Default other ACE.
d:m:rwx               Default mask.
d:u:chavez:rwx        Default ACE for user chavez.
d:g:chem:r-x          Default ACE for group chem.
```

Each entry begins with d:, indicating that it is a default entry. The desired ACE follows this prefix.

We'll now turn to some examples of ACL-related commands. The following commands apply two access control entries to the file *gold*:

Solaris and Linux
```
# setfacl -m user:harvey:r-x,group:geo:r-- gold
```
Tru64
```
# setacl -u user:harvey:r-x,group:geo:r-- gold
```

The following commands apply the ACL from *gold* to *silver*:

Solaris
```
# getfacl gold > acl; setfacl -f acl silver
```
Linux
```
# getfacl gold > acl; setfacl -S acl silver
```
Tru64
```
# getacl gold > acl; setacl -b -U acl silver
```

As the preceding commands indicate, the getfacl command is used to display an ACL under Solaris and Linux, and getacl is used on Tru64 systems.

The following commands specify the default other ACE for the directory */metals*:

Solaris
```
# setfacl -m d:o:r-x /metals
```
Linux
```
# setfacl -d -m o:r-x /metals
```
Tru64
```
# setacl -d -u o:r-x /metals
```

Table 7-2 lists other useful options for these commands.

Table 7-2. Useful ACL manipulation commands

Operation	Linux	Solaris	Tru64
Add/modify ACEs	setfacl -m *entries* setfacl -M *acl-file*	setfacl -m *entries* setfacl -m -f *acl-file*	setacl -u *entries* setacl -U *acl-file*
Replace ACL	setfacl -s *entries* setfacl -S *acl-file*	setfacl -s *entries* setfacl -s -f *acl-file*	setacl -b -u *entries* setacl -b -U *acl-file*
Remove ACEs	setfacl -x *entries* setfacl -X *acl-file*	setfacl -d *entries*	setacl -x *entries* setacl -X *acl-file*
Remove entire ACL	setfacl -b		setacl -b
Operate on direc-tory default ACL	setfacl -d	setfacl -m d:*entry*	setacl -d
Remove default ACL	setfacl -k		setacl -k
Edit ACL in editor			setacl -E

On Linux systems, you can also backup and restore ACLs using commands like these:

```
# getfacl -R --skip-base / > backup.acl
# setfacl --restore=backup.acl
```

The first command backs up the ACLs from all files into the file *backup.acl*, and the second command restores the ACLs saved in that file.

On Tru64 systems, the acl_mode setting must be enabled in the kernel for ACL support.

Encryption

Encryption provides another method of protection for some types of files. Encryption involves transforming the original file (the *plain* or *clear* text) using a mathematical function or technique. Encryption can potentially protect the data stored in files in several circumstances, including:

- Someone breaking into the *root* account on your system and copying the files (or tampering with them), or an authorized *root* user doing similar things
- Someone stealing your disk or backup tapes (or floppies) or the computer itself in an effort to get the data
- Someone acquiring the files via a network

The common theme here is that encryption can protect the security of your data even if the files themselves somehow fall into the wrong hands. (It can't prevent all mishaps, however, such as an unauthorized *root* user deleting the files, but backups will cover that scenario.)

Most encryption algorithms use some sort of *key* as part of the transformation, and the same key is needed to decrypt the file later. The simplest kinds of encryption algorithms use external keys that function much like passwords; more sophisticated encryption methods use part of the input data as the part of the key.

The crypt command

Most Unix systems provide a simple encryption program, crypt.* The crypt command takes the encryption key as its argument and encrypts standard input to standard output using that key. When decrypting a file, crypt is again used with the same key. It's important to remove the original file after encryption, because having both the clear and encrypted versions makes it very easy for someone to discover the keys used to encrypt the original file.

crypt is a very poor encryption program (it uses the same basic encryption scheme as the World War II Enigma machine, which tells you that, at the very least, it is 50 years out of date). crypt can be made a little more secure by running it multiple times on the same file, for example:

```
$ crypt key1 < clear-file | crypt key2 | crypt key3 > encr-file
$ rm clear-file
```

---

* U.S. government regulations forbid the inclusion of encryption software on systems shipped to foreign sites in many circumstances.

Each successive invocation of crypt is equivalent to adding an additional rotor to an Enigma machine (the real machines had three or four rotors). When the file is decrypted, the keys are specified in the reverse order. Another way to make crypt more secure is to compress the text file before encrypting it (encrypted binary data is somewhat harder to decrypt than encrypted ASCII characters).

In any case, crypt is no match for anyone with any encryption-breaking skills—or access to the *cbw* package.* Nevertheless, it is still useful in some circumstances. I use crypt to encrypt files that I don't want anyone to see accidentally or as a result of snooping around on the system as *root*. My assumption here is that the people I'm protecting the files against might try to look at protected files as *root* but won't bother trying to decrypt them. It's the same philosophy behind many simple automobile protection systems; the sticker on the window or the device on the steering wheel is meant to discourage prospective thieves and to encourage them to spend their energy elsewhere, but it doesn't really place more than a trivial barrier in their way. For cases like these, crypt is fine. If you anticipate any sort of attempt to decode the encrypted files, as would be the case if someone is specifically targeting your system, don't rely on crypt.

Public key encryption: PGP and GnuPG

Another encryption option is to use the free public key encryption packages. The first and best known of these is Pretty Good Privacy (PGP) written by Phil Zimmerman (*http://www.pgpi.com*). More recently, the Gnu Privacy Guard (GnuPG) has been developed to fulfill the same function while avoiding some of the legal and commercial entanglements that affect PGP (see *http://www.gnupg.org*).

In contrast to the simple encoding schemes that use only a single key for both encryption and decryption, *public key encryption* systems use two mathematically-related keys. One key—typically the *public key*, which is available to anyone—is used to encrypt the file or message, but this key cannot be used to decrypt it. Rather, the message can be decrypted only with the other key in the pair: the *private key* that is kept secret from everyone but its owner. For example, someone who wants to send you an encrypted file encrypts it with your public key. When you receive the message, you decrypt it with your private key.

Public keys can be sent to people with whom you want to communicate securely, but the private key remains secret, available only to the user to whom it belongs. The advantage of a two-key system is that public keys can be published and disseminated without any compromise in security, because these keys can be used only to encode messages but not to decode them. There are various public key repositories on the Internet; two of the best known public key servers are *http://pgp.mit.edu* and *http://www.keyserver.net*. The former is illustrated in Figure 7-2.

---

* See, for example, *http://www.jjtc.com/Security/cryptanalysis.htm* for information about various tools and web sites of this general sort.

Both PGP and GnuPG have the following uses:

Encryption

They can be used to secure data against prying eyes.

Validation

Messages and files can be digitally signed to ensure that they actually came from the source that they claim to.

These programs can be used as standalone utilities, and either package can also be integrated with popular mail programs to protect and sign electronic mail messages in an automated way.

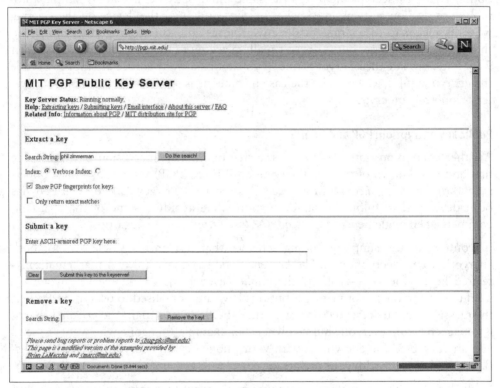

Figure 7-2. Accessing a public key server

Using either package begins with a user creating his key pair:

PGP	*GnuPG*
`$ pgp -kg`	`$ gpg --gen-key`

Each of these commands is followed by a lot of informational messages and several prompts. The most important prompts are the identification string to be associated with the key and the passphrase. The identifier generally has the form:

```
Harvey Thomas <harvey@ahania.com>
```

Sometimes an additional, parenthesized comment item is inserted between the full name and the email address. Pay attention to the prompts when you are asked for this item, because both programs are quite particular about how and when the various parts of it are entered.

The passphrase is a password that identifies the user to the encryption system. Thus, the passphrase functions like a password, and you will need to enter it when performing most PGP or GnuPG functions. The security of your encrypted messages and files relies on selecting a phrase that cannot be broken. Choose something that is at least several words long.

Once your keys have been created, several files will be created in your *$HOME/.pgp* or *$HOME/.gnupg* subdirectory. The most important of these files are *pubring.pgp* (or *.gpg*), which is the user's public key ring, and *secring.pgp* (or *.gpg*), which holds the private key. The public key ring stores the user's public key as well as any other public keys that he acquires.

 All files in this key subdirectory should have the protection mode 600.

When a key has been acquired, either from a public key server or directly from another user, the following commands can be used to add it to a user's public key ring:

PGP
```
$ pgp -ka key-file
```

GnuPG
```
$ gpg --import key-file
```

The following commands extract a user's own public key into a file for transmission to a key server or to another person:

PGP
```
$ pgp -kxa key-file
```

GnuPG
```
$ gpg -a --export -o key-file username
```

Both packages are easy to use for encryption and digital signatures. For example, user *harvey* could use the following commands to encrypt (-e) and digitally sign (-s) a file destined for user *chavez*:

PGP
```
$ pgp -e -s file chavez@ahania.com
```

GnuPG
```
$ gpg -e -s -r chavez@ahania.com file
```

Simply encrypting a file for privacy purposes is much simpler; you just use the -c option with either command:

PGP
```
$ pgp -c file
```

GnuPG
```
$ gpg -c file
```

These commands result in the file being encrypted with a key that you specify, using a conventional symmetric encryption algorithm (i.e., the same key will be used for decryption). Should you decide to use this encryption method, be sure to remove the clear-text file after encrypting. You can have the pgp command do it automatically by adding the -w ("wipe") option.

I don't recommend using your normal passphrase to encrypt files using conventional cryptography. It is all too easy to inadvertently have both the clear text and encrypted versions of a file on the system at the same time. Should such a mistake cause the passphrase to be discovered, using a passphrase that is different from that used for the public key encryption functions will at least contain the damage.

These commands can be used to decrypt a file:

PGP
```
$ pgp encrypted-file
```

GnuPG
```
$ gpg -d encrypted-file
```

If the file was encrypted with your public key, it is automatically decrypted, and both commands also automatically verify the file's digital signature as well, provided that the sender's public key is in your public key ring. If the file was encrypted using the conventional algorithm, you will be prompted for the appropriate passphrase.

Selecting passphrases

For all encryption schemes, the choice of good keys or passphrases is imperative. In general, the same guidelines that apply to passwords apply to encryption keys. As always, longer keys are generally better than shorter ones. Finally, don't use any of your passwords as an encryption key; that's the first thing that someone who breaks into your account will try.

It's also important to make sure that your key is not inadvertently discovered by being displayed to other users on the system. In particular, be careful about the following:

- Clear your terminal screen as soon as possible if a passphrase appears on it.
- Don't use a key as a parameter to a command, script, or program, or it may show up in ps displays (or in lastcomm output).
- Although the crypt command ensures that the key doesn't appear in ps displays, it does nothing about shell command history records. If you use crypt in a shell that has a command history feature, turn history off before using crypt, or run crypt via a script that prompts for it (and accepts input only from */dev/tty*).

Role-Based Access Control

So far, we have considered stronger user authentication and better file protection schemes. The topic we turn to next is a complement to both of these. Role-based access control (RBAC) is a technique for controlling the actions that are permitted to individual users, irrespective of the target of those actions and independent of the permissions on a specific target.

For example, suppose you want to delegate the single task of assigning and resetting user account passwords to user *chavez*. On traditional Unix systems, there are three approaches to granting privileges:

- Tell *chavez* the *root* password. This will give her the ability to perform the task, but it will also allow here to do many other things as well. Adding her to a system group that can perform administrative functions usually has the same drawback.

- Give *chavez* write access to the appropriate user account database file (perhaps via an ACL to extend this access only to her). Unfortunately, doing so will give her access to many other account attributes, which again is more than you want her to have.

- Give her superuser access to just the passwd command via the sudo facility. Once again, however, this is more privilege than she needs: she'll now have the ability to also change the user's shell and GECOS information on many systems.

RBAC can be a means for allowing a user to perform an activity that must traditionally be handled by the superuser. The scheme is based on the concept of *roles*: a definable and bounded subset of administrative privileges that can be assigned to users. Roles allow a user to perform actions that the system security settings would not otherwise permit. In doing so, roles adhere to the principle of least privilege, granting only the exact access that is required to perform the task. As such, roles can be thought of as a way of partitioning the all powerful *root* privilege into discrete components.

Ideally, roles are implemented in the Unix kernel and not just pieced together from the usual file protection facilities, including the setuid and setgid modes. They differ from setuid commands in that their privileges are granted only to users to whom the role has been assigned (rather than to anyone who happens to run the command). In addition, traditional administrative tools need to be made roles-aware so that they perform tasks only when appropriate. Naturally, the design details, implementation specifics, and even terminology vary greatly among the systems that offer RBAC or similar facilities.

We've seen somewhat similar, if more limited, facilities earlier in this book: the sudo command and its *sudoers* configuration file (see "Becoming Superuser" in Chapter 1) and the Linux pam_listfile module (see "User Authentication with PAM" in Chapter 6).

Currently, AIX and Solaris offer role-based privilege facilities. There are also projects for Linux[*] and FreeBSD.[†] The open source projects refer to roles and role based access using the term *capabilities*.

---

[*] The Linux project may or may not be active. The best information is currently at *http://www.kernel.org/pub/linux/libs/security/linux-privs/kernel-2.4/capfaq-0.2.txt*.

[†] See *http://www.trustedbsd.org/components.html*.

AIX Roles

AIX provides a fairly simple roles facility. It is based on a series of predefined *authorizations*, which provide the ability to perform a specific sort of task. Table 7-3 lists the defined authorizations.

Table 7-3. AIX authorizations

Authorization	Meaning
UserAdmin	Add/remove all users, modify any account attributes.
UserAudit	Modify any user account's auditing settings.
GroupAdmin	Manage administrative groups.
PasswdManage	Change passwords for nonadministrative users.
PasswdAdmin	Change passwords for administrative users.
Backup	Perform system backups.
Restore	Restore system backups.
RoleAdmin	Manage role definitions.
ListAuditClasses	Display audit classes.
Diagnostics	Run system diagnostics.

These authorizations are combined into a series of predefined roles; definitions are stored in the file */etc/security/roles*. Here are two stanzas from this file:

```
ManageBasicUsers:                                        Role name
    authorizations=UserAudit,ListAuditClasses            List of authorizations
    rolelist=
    groups=security                                      Users should be a member of this group.
    screens=*                                            Corresponding SMIT screens.
ManageAllUsers:
    authorizations=UserAdmin,RoleAdmin,PasswdAdmin,GroupAdmin
    rolelist=ManageBasicUsers                            Include another role within this one.
```

The ManageBasicUsers role consists of two authorizations related to auditing user account activity. The groups attribute lists a group that the user should be a member of in order to take advantage of the role. In this case, the user should be a member of the *security* group. By itself, this group membership allows a user to manage auditing for nonadministrative user accounts (as well as their other attributes). This role supplements those abilities, extending them to all user accounts, normal and administrative alike.

The ManageAllUsers role consists of four additional authorizations. It also includes the ManageBasicUsers role as part of its capabilities. When a user in group *security* is given ManageAllUsers, he can function as *root* with respect to all user accounts and account attributes.

Table 7-4 summarizes the defined roles under AIX.

Table 7-4. AIX pre-defined roles

Role	Group	Authorizations	Abilities
ManageBasicUsers	*security*	UserAudit ListAuditClasses	Modify audit settings for any user account.
ManageAllUsers	*security*	UserAudit ListAuditClasses UserAdmin RoleAdmin PasswdAdmin GroupAdmin	Add/remove user accounts; modify attributes of any user account.
ManageBasicPasswds	*security*[a]	PasswdManage	Change passwords of all nonadministrative users.
ManageAllPasswds	*security*	PasswdManage PasswdAdmin	Change passwords of all users.
ManageRoles		RoleAdmin	Administer role definitions.
ManageBackup		Backup	Backup any files.
ManageBackupRestore		Backup Restore	Backup or restore any files.
RunDiagnostics		Diagnostics	Run diagnostic utilities; shutdown or reboot the system.
ManageShutdown[b]	*shutdown*		Shutdown or reboot the system.

[a] Membership in group *security* is actually equivalent to ManageBasicPasswd with respect to changing passwords.
[b] This is actually a pseudo-role in that it is defined solely via group membership and does not use any authorizations.

Roles are assigned to user accounts in the file */etc/security/user.roles*. Here is a sample stanza:

```
chavez:
    roles = ManageAllPasswds
```

This stanza assigns user *chavez* the ability to change any user account password.

You can also use SMIT to assign roles (use the chuser fast path), or the chuser command:

```
# chuser roles=ManageAllUsers aefrisch
```

In some cases, the AIX documentation advises additional activities in conjunction with assigning roles. For example, when assigning the ManageBackup or Manage-BackupResore roles, it suggests the following additional steps:

- Create a group called *backup*.
- Assign the ownership of the system backup and restore device to *root* user and group backup with mode 660.
- Place users holding either of the backup related roles to group *backup*.

Check the current AIX documentation for advice related to other roles.

You can administer roles themselves with SMIT or using the `mkrole`, `rmrole`, `lsrole`, and `chrole` commands. You can add new roles to the system as desired, but you are limited to the predefined set of authorizations.

Solaris Role-Based Access Control

The Solaris RBAC facility is also based upon a set of fundamental authorizations. They are listed in the file */etc/security/auth_attr*. Here are some example entries from this file:

```
# authorization name  :::description  ::attributes
solaris.admin.usermgr.:::User Accounts::help=AuthUsermgrHeader.html
solaris.admin.usermgr.pswd:::Change Password::help=AuthUserMgrPswd.html
solaris.admin.usermgr.read:::View Users and Roles::help=AuthUsermgrRead.html
solaris.admin.usermgr.write:::Manage Users::help=AuthUsermgrWrite.html
```

The first field in each entry is the name of the attribute; the naming convention uses a hierarchical format for grouping related authorizations. Many of the fields within the entries are reserved or unused. In general, only the name (first), short description (fourth), and attributes (seventh) fields are used, and the latter field generally holds only the name of the help file corresponding to the authorization (the HTML files are located in the */usr/lib/help/auths/locale/C* directory).

The first entry after the comment introduces a group of authorizations related to user account management. The following three entries list authorizations that allow their holder to change passwords, view user account attributes, and modify user accounts (including creating new ones and deleting them), respectively. Note that this file is merely a list of implement authorizations. You should not alter it.

Authorizations can be assigned to user accounts in three separate ways:

- Directly, as plain authorizations.
- As part of a *profile*, a named group of authorizations.
- Via a *role*, a pseudo-account that users can assume (via the `su` command) to acquire additional privilege. Roles can be assigned authorizations directly or via profiles.

Profiles are named collections of authorizations, defined in */etc/security/prof_attr*. Here are some sample entries (wrapped to fit here):

```
User Management:::Manage users, groups, home directory:
    auths=solaris.profmgr.read,solaris.admin.usermgr.write,
    solaris.admin.usermgr.read;help=RtUserMngmnt.html
User Security:::Manage passwords,clearances:
    auths=solaris.role.*,solaris.profmgr.*,
    solaris.admin.usermgr.*;help=RtUserSecurity.html
```

The entries in this file also have empty fields that are reserved for future use. Those in use hold the profile name (first field), description (field four), and attributes (field five). The final field consists of one or more *keyword=value-list* items, where items in the value list are separated by commas and multiple keyword items are separated by semicolons.

For example, the first entry defines the User Management profile as a set of three authorizations (specified in the auths attribute) and also specifies a help file for the profile (via the help attribute). The profile will allow a user to read profile and user account information and to modify user account attributes (but not passwords, because solaris.admin.usermgr.pswd is not granted).

The second entry specifies a more powerful profile containing all of the user account, profile management, and role management authorizations (indicated by the wild-cards). This profile allows a user to make any user modifications whatsoever.

Solaris defines quite a large number of profiles, and you can create ones of your own as well to implement the local security policy. Table 7-5 lists the most important Solaris profiles. The first four profiles are generic and represent increasing levels of system privilege. The remainder are specific to a single subsystem.

Table 7-5. Solaris RBAC profiles

Profile	Abilities
Basic Solaris User	Default authorizations.
Operator	Perform simple, nonrisky administrative tasks
System Administrator	Perform nonsecurity-related administrative tasks
Primary Administrator	Perform all administrative tasks.
Audit Control	Configure auditing.
Audit Review	Review auditing logs.
Cron Management	Manage at and cron jobs.
Device Management	Manage removable media.
Device Security	Manage devices and the LVM.
DHCP Management	Manage the DHCP service.
Filesystem Management	Mount and share filesystems.
Filesystem Security	Manage filesystem security attributes.
FTP Management	Manage the FTP server.
Mail Management	Manage sendmail and mail queues.
Media Backup	Backup files and filesystems.
Media Restore	Restore files from backups.
Name Service Management	Run nonsecurity-related name service commands.
Name Service Security	Run security-related name service commands.
Network Management	Manage the host and network configuration.
Network Security	Manage network and host security.
Object Access Management	Change file ownership/permissions.
Printer Management	Manage printers, daemons, spooling.
Process Management	Manage processes.

Table 7-5. Solaris RBAC profiles (continued)

Profile	Abilities
Software Installation	Add application software to the system
User Management	Manage users and groups (except passwords).
User Security	Manage all aspects of users and groups.

The */etc/security/exec_attr* configuration file elaborates on profiles definitions by specifying the UID and GID execution context for relevant commands. Here are the entries for the two profiles we are considering in detail:

```
User Management:suser:cmd:::/etc/init.d/utmpd:uid=0;gid=sys
User Management:suser:cmd:::/usr/sbin/grpck:euid=0
User Management:suser:cmd:::/usr/sbin/pwck:euid=0
User Security:suser:cmd:::/usr/bin/passwd:euid=0
User Security:suser:cmd:::/usr/sbin/pwck:euid=0
User Security:suser:cmd:::/usr/sbin/pwconv:euid=0
```

The */etc/user_attr* configuration is where user accounts and profiles and/or authorizations are associated. Here are some sample entries (lines are wrapped to fit):

```
#acct ::::attributes (can include auths;profiles;roles;type;project)
chavez::::type=normal;profiles=System Adminstrator
harvey::::type=normal;profiles=Operator,Printer Management;
    auths=solaris.admin.usermgr.pswd
sofficer::::type=role;profiles=Device Security,File System Security,
    Name Service Security,Network Security,User Security,
    Object Access Management;auths=solaris.admin.usermgr.read
sharon::::type=normal;roles=sofficer
```

The first entry assigns user *chavez* the System Administrator profile. The second entry assigns user *harvey* two profiles and an additional authorization.

The third entry defines a role named *sofficer* (Security Officer), assigning it the listed profiles and authorization. An entry in the password file must exist for *sofficer*, but no one will be allowed to log in using it. Instead, authorized users must use the su command to assume the role. The final entry grants user *sharon* the right to do so.

The final configuration file affecting user roles and profiles is */etc/security/policy.conf*. Here is an example of this file:

```
AUTHS_GRANTED=solaris.device.cdrw
PROFS_GRANTED=Basic Solaris User
```

The two entries specify the authorizations and profiles to be granted to all users.

Users can list their roles, profiles, and authorizations using the roles, profiles, and auths commands, respectively. Here is an example using profiles:

```
$ profiles
Operator
Printer Management
Media Backup
Basic Solaris User
```

Here is an example using the `auths` command, sent to a pipe designed to make its output readable:

```
$ auths | sed 's/,/ /g' | fold -s -w 30 | sort
solaris.admin.printer.delete
solaris.admin.printer.modify
solaris.admin.printer.read
solaris.admin.usermgr.pswd
solaris.admin.usermgr.read
solaris.device.cdrw
solaris.jobs.user
solaris.jobs.users
...
```

Solaris also includes a PAM module, *pam_roles.so*, which determines whether the user has the right to assume a role he is trying take on.

Network Security

We'll now turn our attention beyond the single system and consider security in a network context. As with all types of system security, TCP/IP network security inevitably involves tradeoffs between ease-of-use issues and protection against (usually external) threats. And, as is true all too often with Unix systems, in many cases your options are all or nothing.

Successful network-based attacks result from a variety of problems. These are the most common types:

- Poorly designed services that perform insufficient authentication (or even none at all) or otherwise operate in an inherently insecure way (NFS and X11 are examples of facilities having such weaknesses that have been widely and frequently exploited).

- Software bugs, usually in a network-based facility (for example, sendmail) and sometimes in the Unix kernel, but occasionally, bugs in local facilities can be exploited by crackers via the network.

- Abuses of allowed facilities and mechanisms. For example, a user can create a *.rhosts* file in her home directory that will very efficiently and thoroughly compromise system security (these files are discussed later in this section).

- Exploiting existing mechanisms of trust by generating forged network packets impersonating trusted systems (known as *IP spoofing*).

- User errors of many kinds, ranging from innocent mistakes to deliberately circumventing security mechanisms and policies.

- Problems in the underlying protocol design, usually a failure to anticipate malicious uses. This sort of problem is often what allows a denial-of-service attack to succeed.

Attacks often use several vulnerabilities in combination.

Maintaining a secure system is an ongoing process, requiring a lot of initial effort and a significant amount of work on a permanent basis. One of the most important things you can do with respect to system and network security is to educate yourself about existing threats and what can be done to protect against them. I recommend the following classic papers as good places to start:

- Steven M. Bellovin, "Security Problems in the TCP/IP Protocol Suite." The classic TCP/IP security paper, available at *http://www.research.att.com/~smb/papers/*. Many of his other papers are also useful and interesting.

- Dan Farmer and Wietse Venema, "Improving the Security of Your Site by Breaking Into It," available at *ftp://ftp.porcupine.org/pub/security/index.html*. Another excellent discussion of the risks inherent in Internet connectivity.

We'll discuss TCP/IP network security by looking at how systems on a network were traditionally configured to trust one another and allow each other's users easy access. Then we'll go on to look at some of the ways that you can back off from that position of openness by considering methods and tools for restricting access and assessing the vulnerabilities of your system and network.

Security Alert Mailing Lists

One of the most important ongoing security activities is keeping up with the latest bugs and threats. One way to do so is to read the CERT or CIAC advisories and then *act on them*. Doing so will often be inconvenient—closing a security hole often requires some sort of software update from your vendor—but it is the only sensible course of action.

One of the activities of the Computer Emergency Response Team (CERT) is administering an electronic mailing list to which its security advisories are posted as necessary. These advisories contain a general description of the vulnerability, detailed information about the systems to which it applies, and available fixes. You can add yourself to the CERT mailing list by sending email to *majordomo@cert.org* with "subscribe cert-advisory" in the body of the message. Past advisories and other information are available from the CERT web site, *http://www.cert.org*.

The Computer Incident Advisory Capability (CIAC) performs a similar function, originally for Department of Energy sites. Their excellent web site is at *http://www.ciac.org/ciac/*.

Establishing Trust

Unless special steps are taken, users must enter a password each time they want access to the other hosts on the network. However, users have traditionally found this requirement unacceptably inconvenient, and so a mechanism exists to establish trust between computer systems which then allows remote access without passwords. This trust is also known as *equivalence*.

The first level of equivalence is the host level. The */etc/hosts.equiv* configuration file establishes it. This file is simply a list of hostnames, each on a separate line.* For example, the file for the system *france* might read:

```
spain.ahania.com
italy.ahania.com
france.ahania.com
```

None, any, or all of the hosts in the network may be put in an */etc/hosts.equiv* file. It is convenient to include the host's own name in */etc/hosts.equiv*, thus declaring a host equivalent to itself. When a user from a remote host attempts an access (with rlogin, rsh, or rcp), the local host checks the file */etc/hosts.equiv*. If the host requesting access is listed in */etc/hosts.equiv* and an account with the same username as the remote user exists, remote access is permitted without requiring a password.

If the user is trying to log in under a different username (by using the -l option to rsh or rlogin), the */etc/hosts.equiv* file is not used. The */etc/hosts.equiv* file is also not enough to allow a superuser on one host to log in remotely as *root* on another host.

The second type of equivalence is account-level equivalence, defined in a file named *.rhosts* in a user's home directory. There are various reasons for using account-level instead of host-level equivalence. The most common cases for doing so are when users have different account names on the different hosts or when you want to limit use of the *.rhosts* mechanism to only a few users.

Each line of *.rhosts* consists of a *hostname* and, optionally, a list of *usernames*:

```
hostname [usernames]
```

If *username* is not present, only the same username as the owner of the *.rhosts* file can log in from *hostname*. For example, consider the following *.rhosts* file in the home directory of a user named *wang*:

```
england.ahania.com   guy donald kim
russia.ahania.com    felix
usa.ahania.com       felix
```

The *.rhosts* allows the user *felix* to log in from the host *russia* or *usa*, and users named *guy, donald*, or *kim* to log in from the host *england*.

If remote access is attempted and the access does not pass the host-level equivalence test, the remote host then checks the *.rhosts* file in the home directory of the target account. If it finds the hostname and username of the person making the attempted access, the remote host allows the access to take place without requiring the user to enter a password.

---

* The file may also contain NIS netgroup names in the form: +@*name*. However, the *hosts.equiv* file should *never* contain an entry consisting of a single plus sign, because this will match any remote user having the same login name as one in the local password file (except *root*).

Host-level equivalence is susceptible to spoofing attacks, so it is rarely acceptable anymore. However, it can be used safely in an isolated networking environment if it is set up carefully and in accord with the site's security policy.

Account-level equivalence is a bad idea all the time because the user is free to open up his account to anyone he wants, and it is a disaster when applied to the *root* account. I don't allow it on any of my systems.

The implications of trust

Setting up any sort of trust relationship between computer systems always carries a risk with it. However, the risks go beyond the interaction between those two systems alone. For one thing, trusts operates in a transitive manner (*transitive trust*). If *hamlet* trusts *laertes*, and *laertes* trusts *ophelia*, then *hamlet* trusts *ophelia*, just as effectively as if *ophelia* were listed in *hamlet*'s */etc/hosts.equiv* file (although not as conveniently). This level of transitivity is easy to see for a user who has accounts on all three systems; it also exists for all users on *ophelia* with access to any account on *laertes* that has access to any account on *hamlet*.

There is also no reason that such a chain need stop at three systems. The point here is that *hamlet* trusts *ophelia* despite the fact that *hamlet*'s system administrator has chosen not to set up a trusting relationship between the two systems (by not including *ophelia* in */etc/hosts.equiv*). *hamlet*'s system administrator may have no control over *ophelia* at all, yet his system's security is intimately dependent on *ophelia* remaining secure.

In fact, Dan Farmer and Wietse Venema argue convincingly that an implicit trust exists between *any* two systems that allow users to log in from one to the other. Suppose system *yorick* allows remote logins from *hamlet*, requiring passwords in all cases. If *hamlet* is compromised, *yorick* is at risk as well; for example, some of *hamlet*'s users undoubtedly use the same passwords on both systems—which constitutes users' own form of account-level equivalence—and a *root* account intruder on *hamlet* will have access to the encrypted passwords and most likely be able to crack some of them.

Taken to its logical conclusion, this line of reasoning suggests that any time two systems are connected via a network, their security to some extent becomes intertwined. In the end, your system's security will be no better than that of the least protected system on the network.

The Secure Shell

The secure shell is becoming the accepted mechanism for remote system access. The most widely used version is OpenSSH (see *http://www.openssh.org*). OpenSSH is based on the version originally written by Tatu Ylönen. It is now handled by the OpenBSD team. The secure shell provides an alternative to the traditional clear-text remote sessions using `telnet` or `rlogin` since the entire session is encrypted.

From an administrative point of view, OpenSSH is wonderfully easy to set up, and the default configuration is often quite acceptable in most contexts. The package consists primarily of a daemon, sshd; several user tools (ssh, the remote shell; sftp, an ftp replacement; and scp, an rcp replacement); and some related administrative utilities and servers (e.g., sftp-server).

 Be sure you using a recent version of OpenSSH: some older versions have significant security holes. Also, I recommend using SSH protocol 2 over the earlier protocol 1 as it closes several security holes.

The OpenSSH configuration file are stored in */etc/ssh*. The most important of these is */etc/ssh/sshd_config*. Here is a simple, annotated example of this file:

```
Protocol 2                              Only use SSH protocol 2.
Port 22                                 Use the standard port.
ListenAddress 0.0.0.0                   Only accept IPv4 addresses.
AllowTcpForwarding no                   Don't allow port forwarding.
SyslogFacility auth                     Logging settings.
LogLevel info
Banner /etc/issue                       Display this file before the prompts.

PermitEmptyPasswords no                 Don't accept connections for accounts w/o passwords.
PermitRootLogin no                      No root logins allowed.
LoginGraceTime 600                      Disconnect after 5 minutes if no login occurs.
KeepAlive yes                               Send keep alive message to the client.
X11Forwarding no                        No X11 support.
X11DisplayOffset 10

# sftp subsystem                        Enable the sftp subsystem.
Subsystem sftp  /usr/lib/ssh/sftp-server
```

This file is designed for a server using SSH in its simplest mode: user authentication occurs via normal user passwords (encrypted for transmission). The package also offers stricter authentication, which involves using public key cryptography to ensure that the remote session is originating from a known host. See the documentation for details on these features.

Securing Network Daemons

TCP/IP-related network daemons are started in two distinct ways. Major daemons like named are started at boot time by one of the boot scripts. The second class of daemons are invoked on demand, when a client requests their services. These are handled by the TCP/IP "super daemon," inetd. inetd itself is started at boot time, and it is responsible for starting the other daemons that it controls as needed. Daemons controlled by inetd provide the most common TCP/IP user-oriented services: telnet, ftp, remote login and shells, mail retrieval, and so on.

inetd is configured via the file */etc/inetd.conf*. Here are some sample entries in their conventional form:

```
#service  socket  prot  wait?   user  program arguments
telnet    stream  tcp   nowait  root  /usr/sbin/in.telnetd in.telnetd
tftp      dgram   udp   wait    root  /usr/sbin/in.tftpd in.tftpd -s /tftpboot
```

As indicated in the comment line, the fields hold the service name (as defined in */etc/services*), the socket type, protocol, whether or not to wait for the command to return when it is started, the user who should run the command, and the command to run along with its arguments.

Generally, most common services will already have entries in */etc/inetd.conf*. However, you may need to add entries for some new services that you add (e.g., Samba servers).

TCP Wrappers: Better inetd access control and logging

The free TCP Wrappers facility provides for finer control over which hosts are allowed to access what local network services than that provided by the standard TCP/IP mechanisms (*hosts.equiv* and *.rhosts* files). It also provides for enhanced logging of inetd-based network operations to the syslog facility. The package was written by Wietse Venema, and it is included automatically on most current Unix systems. It is also available from *ftp://ftp.porcupine.org/pub/security/tcp_wrapper_7.6-ipv61.tar.gz* (although the filename will undoubtedly change over time).

The package is centered around tcpd, an additional daemon positioned between inetd and the subdaemons that it manages. It requires that you modify inetd's configuration file, */etc/inetd.conf*, replacing the standard daemons you want the facility to control with tcpd, as in these examples:

```
Before:
#service  socket  protocol  wait?   user  program arguments
shell     stream  tcp       nowait  root  /usr/sbin/rshd rshd
login     stream  tcp       nowait  root  /usr/sbin/rlogind rlogind

After:
#service  socket  protocol  wait?   user  program arguments
shell     stream  tcp       nowait  root  /usr/sbin/tcpd /usr/sbin/rshd
login     stream  tcp       nowait  root  /usr/sbin/tcpd /usr/sbin/rlogind
```

(Note that daemon names and locations vary from system to system). The tcpd program replaces the native program for each service that you want to place under its control. As usual, after modifying *inetd.conf*, you would send a HUP signal to the inetd process.

Once inetd is set up, the next step is to create the files */etc/hosts.allow* and */etc/hosts.deny*, which control what hosts may use which services. When a request for a network service comes in from a remote host, access is determined as follows:

- If */etc/hosts.allow* authorizes that service for that host, the request is accepted and the real daemon is started. The first matching line in */etc/hosts.allow* is used.

- When no line in *hosts.allow* applies, *hosts.deny* is checked next. If that file denies the service to the remote host, the request is denied. Again, the first applicable entry is used.
- In all other cases, the request is granted.

Here are some sample entries from *hosts.allow*:

```
fingerd          : ophelia hamlet laertes yorick lear duncan
rshd, rlogind    : LOCAL EXCEPT hamlet
ftpd             : LOCAL, .ahania.com, 192.168.4
```

The first entry grants access to the remote `finger` service to users on any of the listed hosts (hostnames may be separated by commas and or spaces). The second entry allows `rsh` and `rlogin` access by users from any local host—defined as one whose hostname does not contain a period—except the host *hamlet*. The third entry allows `ftp` access to all local hosts, all hosts in the domain *ahania.com*, and all hosts on the subnet 192.168.4.

Here is the */etc/hosts.deny* file:

```
tftpd : ALL : (/usr/sbin/safe_finger -l @%h | /usr/bin/mail -s %d-%h root) &
ALL : ALL :
```

The first entry denies access to the Trivial FTP facility to all hosts. It illustrates the optional third field in these files: a command to be run whenever a request matches that entry.[*] In this case, the `safe_finger` command is executed (it is provided as part of the package) in an attempt to determine who initiated the `tftp` command, and the results are mailed to *root* (%h expands to the remote hostname from which the request emanated, and %d expands to the name of the daemon for that service). This entry has the effect of intercepting requests to undesirable services (the package's author, Wietse Venema, refers to it as "bugging" that service and as "an early warning system" for possible intruder trouble). Note that the daemon must be active within */etc/inetd.conf* for this to be effective; if you don't need or want such logging, it is better to comment out the corresponding line in */etc/inetd.conf* to disable the service.

The second entry in the example *hosts.deny* file serves as a final stopgap, preventing all access that has not been explicitly permitted.

`tcpd` uses the syslog *daemon* facility, using the *warning* (for denials of service) and *info* (for configuration file syntax errors) severity levels. You will probably want to use the `swatch` facility or a similar tool to sift thought the huge amounts of logging information it will generate (see "Essential Administrative Techniques" in Chapter 3).

---

[*] If you try to place a command into either of these files, you may get errors similar to this one from syslog:
```
error: /etc/hosts.deny, line 3: bad option name or syntax
```
Comment out the following line in the Makefile and rebuild tcpd:
```
#STYLE = -DPROCESS_OPTIONS # Enable language extensions.
```
Alternatively, you can convert the file to the extended version of the access language described on the *hosts_options* manual page.

This section describes basic TCP Wrappers functionality. There is also an extended configuration language available for more fine-grained access control. See the *hosts_options* manual page for details.

xinetd

Red Hat Linux systems provide an alternate version of inetd named xinetd, written by Panos Tsirigotis and Rob Braun. The package is also available for most Unix versions. xinetd provides many more features for access control and logging than the traditional daemon does. Some of its functionality overlaps with TCP Wrappers, although you can also use the two packages in concert. The package's home page is *http://www.xinetd.org*.

xinetd uses the configuration file */etc/xinetd*. Here is an example from a Red Hat system:

```
defaults
{
    log_type                = SYSLOG authpriv
    log_on_success          = HOST PID
    log_on_failure          = HOST
    instances               = 20
}
includedir /etc/xinetd.d
```

The defaults section lists default settings that will apply to all subdaemons controlled by xinetd unless they are specifically overridden. In this case, the file specifies that logging should go to the syslog authpriv facility, and it selects the items to be included in log messages for successful and failing connection attempts. In addition, no server can have more than 20 processes running; this limit affects services that start additional server processes to handle increased request loads.

The final line specifies a directory location where additional configuration files are stored. Each file in the indicated directory will be used by xinetd. This feature allows you to store the settings for individual subdaemons in their own files.

Here is the configuration file for rlogin, which defines the same settings as a traditional */etc/inetd.conf* entry:

```
service rlogin
{
        socket_type             = stream
        protocol                = tcp
        wait                    = no
        user                    = root
        server                  = /usr/sbin/in.rlogind
        server-args             = -l
        log_on_success          += USERID
        log_on_failure          += USERID
        disable                 = no
}
```

The entry specifies items to include in log messages in addition to the defaults (the meaning of +=), and the final item enables the subdaemon.

If you want to use TCP Wrappers with xinetd, you specify tcpd as the server and the subdaemon as a server argument. For example, these configuration entries will cause TCP Wrappers to control the telnetd daemon:[*]

```
flags       = NAMEINARGS
server      = /usr/sbin/tcpd
server_args = /usr/sbin/in.telnetd
```

Here is a sample entry for the imapd daemon that illustrates the use of access control:

```
service imap
{
        socket_type  = stream
        protocol     = tcp
        wait         = no
        user         = root
        server       = /usr/sbin/imapd
        only_from    = 192.168.10.0 localhost
        no_access    = dalton.ahania.com
        access_times = 07:00-20:00
        banner_fail  = /usr/etc/deny_banner
}
```

The only_from entry specifies the hosts that are allowed to use this service; requests from any remote host not on the specified subnet will be refused. The no_access entry performs the opposite function and denies access to the specified host(s).

The access_times entry specifies when the service is available to users who are allowed to use it.

The final entry specifies a file to be displayed whenever a connection is refused (or fails for some other reason).

See the *xinetd.conf* manual page for details on all of the available configuration options.

Disable what you don't need

A better solution to securing some services is to remove then altogether. You can decide to disable some of the TCP/IP daemons in the interest of system security or performance (each places a small but measurable load on the system). There are,

---

[*] Most inetd-controlled daemons take the daemon name as their first argument. xinetd knows this and so automatically passes the command name from the server entry as the first argument when the daemon is started. This is a convenience feature which makes it unnecessary to include the server name in the server_args entry. However, when TCP Wrappers is involved, this process would be incorrect, as the daemon is now specified in server_args rather than server. This flag is designed to handle this case, and it causes the command name from server_args to be inserted into the resulting daemon-starting command in the appropriate location.

naturally, consequences for eliminating certain daemons. If you disable rwhod, then the rwho and ruptime commands won't work.

To disable a daemon like rwhod, comment out the lines that start it in your system initialization files. For example, the following lines are typical of those used to start rwhod:

```
#if [ -f /etc/rwhod ]; then
#   /etc/rwhod; echo -n ' rwhod' > /dev/console
#fi
```

Disabling services managed by the inetd daemon is accomplished by commenting out the corresponding line from *letc/inetd.conf*. For example, these lines disable the tftp and rexd services (both notorious security holes):

```
#service  socket      protocol wait?  user     program arguments
#
#tftp     dgram       udp      nowait nobody   /usr/sbin/tftpdtftpd -n
#rexd     sunrpc_tcp tcp      wait   root     /usr/sbin/rpc.rexd  rexd 100017 1
```

When inetd is running, send it a HUP signal to get it to reread its configuration file.

In general, you should disable inetd services that you are not using. Make it one of your short-term goals to figure out what every entry in its configuration file does and to get rid of the ones you don't need. Some likely candidates for commenting out: tftp and bootps (except for boot servers for diskless workstations), rexd, uucp (seldom has any effect on the real uucp facility), pop-2 and pop-3 (if you are not using these mail-related services), and netstat, systat, and finger (the latter three give away too much gratuitous information that is helpful to crackers—run the command telnet localhost for the first two to see why).

 On AIX systems, use SMIT to remove services that are controlled by the system resource controller.

Port Scanning

Port scanning is the process of searching a network for available network services. The technique is used by potential intruders to find possible points of attack on a system. For this reason, you need to have at least a basic understanding of port-scanning tools.

The nmap utility is one of the most widely used port scanners. Its home page is *http://www.insecure.org/nmap/*.

Here is a sample nmap run that scans ports on host *kali*:

```
# nmap kali
Starting nmap ( www.insecure.org/nmap/ )
Interesting ports on kali.ahania.com (192.168.19.84):
(The 1529 ports scanned but not shown below are in state: closed)
```

```
Port       State      Service
22/tcp     open       ssh
23/tcp     open       telnet
25/tcp     open       smtp
37/tcp     open       time
79/tcp     open       finger
80/tcp     open       http
512/tcp    open       exec
513/tcp    open       login
514/tcp    open       shell
515/tcp    open       printer
4559/tcp   open       hylafax
6000/tcp   open       X11
Nmap run completed -- 1 IP address (1 host up) scanned in 0 seconds
```

This information is quite useful to a system administrator. It reveals that at least one questionable service is running (the finger service). In addition, this one told me that I have forgotten to remove the web server from this system (why anyone would think it is a good idea to enable a web server as part of the operating system installation process is beyond me).

As this example illustrates, running nmap on your own hosts can be a useful security diagnostic tools. Be aware that running it on hosts that you do not control is a serious ethical breach.

There are many utilities that watch for and report port-scanning attempts. I don't have any recent experience with any of them and so can't recommend any particular package. However, a web search for "detect port scan" and similar phrases will yield a wealth of candidates.

Defending the Border: Firewalls and Packet Filtering

Firewall systems represent an attempt to hold on to some of the advantages of a direct Internet connection while mitigating as many of the risks associated with it as possible. A firewall is placed between the greater Internet and the site to be protected; firewalls may also be used within a site or organization to isolate some systems from others (remember that not all threats are external).

The definitive work on firewalls is *Firewalls and Internet Security: Repelling the Wily Hacker* by William R. Cheswick and Steven M. Bellovin (Addison-Wesley). Another excellent work is *Building Internet Firewalls* by Elizabeth D. Zwicky, Simon Cooper, and D. Brent Chapman (O'Reilly & Associates).

Don't underestimate the amount of work it takes to set up and maintain an effective firewall system. The learning curve is substantial, and only careful, continuous monitoring can ensure continuing protection. Don't let your management, colleagues, or users underestimate it either. And contrary to what the many companies in the firewall business will tell you, it's not something you can buy off the shelf.

By being placed between the systems to be protected and those they need to be protected from, a firewall is in a position to stop attacks and intruders before they ever reach their target. Firewalls can use a variety of mechanisms for doing so. Cheswick and Bellovin identify three main types of protection:

Packet filtering

Network packets are examined before being processed, and those requesting access that is not allowed or are suspicious in any way are discarded (or otherwise handled). For example, filtering out packets coming from the external network that claim to be from a host on the internal network will catch and eliminate attempts at IP spoofing.

Packet filtering can be done on a variety of criteria, and it may be performed by a router, a PC with special software, or a Unix system with this capability. The most effective packet filters, whether hardware or software based, will have these characteristics:

- The ability to filter on source system, destination system, protocol, port, flags, and/or message type.
- The ability to filter both when a packet is first received by the device (on input) and when it leaves the device (on output).
- The ability to filter both incoming and outgoing packets.
- The ability to filter based on both the source and destination ports. In general, the more flexibly combinable the filtering criteria are, the better.
- The ability to filter routes learned from external sources.
- The ability to disable source routing.
- The ability to disable reprogramming from the network (or any location other than the console).

 Even if a server is not functioning as a firewall or a router, you may still want to perform packet filtering on it as doing so will circumvent many sorts of attacks. Minimal filtering includes ensuring that outgoing packets have a source address that belongs in your network (this is good-citizen filtering, which detects IP spoofing from within your network), and checking that incoming packets don't claim to have come from inside your network (this thwarts most incoming IP spoofing).

Application-level protection

Firewalls typically offer very little in the way of network services; indeed, one way to set one up initially is remove or disable every network-related application, and then slowly, carefully add a very few of them back in. All nonessential services are removed from a firewall, and the ones that are offered are often replacements for the standard versions, with enhanced authentication, security checking, and logging capabilities.

Substituting an alternate—and most often, much simpler, more straightforward, and less feature-rich—versions of the usual applications has the additional advantage that most cracker attacks will be simply irrelevant, since they are typically aimed at standard network components. The vulnerabilities of, say, `sendmail`, are not as important if you are using something else to move electronic mail messages across the firewall.

Connection relaying for outgoing traffic

Users inside the firewall perimeter can still access the outside world without introducing additional risk if the firewall completes the connection between the inside and outside itself (rather than relying on the standard mechanisms). For example, TCP/IP connections can be relayed by a simple program that passes data between the two discrete networks independently of any TCP/IP protocols.

Most firewalls employ a combination of strategies. (Note that Cheswick and Bellovin discourage the use of packet filtering alone in creating a firewall design.)

The firewall system itself must be secured against attack. Typically, all nonessential operating system commands and features are removed (not just networking-related ones). Extensive logging is conducted at every level of the system, usually with automated monitoring as well (firewall systems need lots of disk space), and probably with some redundancy to a write-only logging host and/or a hardcopy device. The *root* account is usually protected with a smart card or another additional authentication system, and there are few or no other user accounts on the firewall system.

Figure 7-3 illustrates some possible firewall configurations.

Configuration 1 uses a single host connected via separate network adapters to the internal and external network. A router may also be placed in front of the computer in this scheme. Packets are *not* forwarded between the two network interfaces by TCP/IP; rather, they are handled at the application or circuit level. This type of configuration is very tricky to make secure, because the firewall host is physically present on both networks.

Configuration 2, an arrangement referred to as *belt-and-suspenders* from how their interconnections look in diagrams like this one, physically separates the connections to the internal and external networks across two distinct hosts. In a variation of this arrangement, the router between the two hosts is replaced by a direct network connection, using separate network adapters; this firewall mini-network need not even run TCP/IP.

Configuration 3 is a still more paranoid modification of number 2, in which the connection between the two firewall systems is not permanent but is created only on demand, again using a separate mechanism from the network interfaces to the internal and external networks.

Configuration 4 represents the only way you can be absolutely sure that your network is completely protected from external threats (at least those coming in over a network wire).

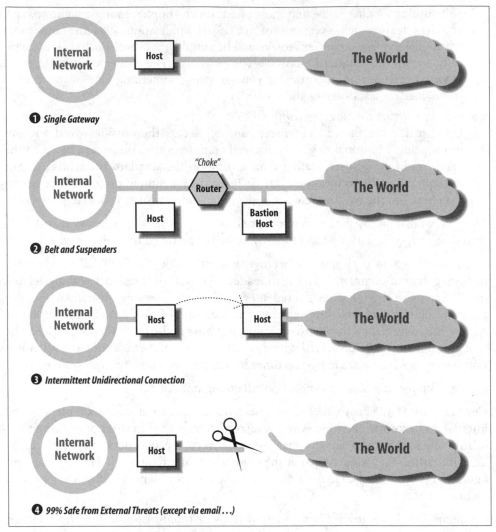

Figure 7-3. Some firewall configuration options

Most Unix systems are suitable for adaptation as firewalls, although using routers for this purpose is more common and generally more secure. However, free operating systems like Linux and FreeBSD systems make decent, low-cost choices when configured with the proper software, and they have the advantage that all the source code for the operating system is readily available.

At its heart, an effective firewall design depends on formulating a very thorough and detailed security policy (including how you plan to deal with potential intruders). You need to be able to state very precisely what sorts of activities and accesses you will and will not permit. Only then will you be in a position to translate these restrictions into actual hardware and software implementations.

Hardening Unix Systems

Throughout this chapter, I've been suggesting that systems ought to provide only the minimum amount of services and access that are needed. This is especially true for important server systems, especially—but not limited to—ones at site boundaries. The process of making a system more secure than the level the default installed operating system provides is known as *hardening the system*.

In this section, we'll look at the general principles of system hardening. Naturally, the actual process is very operating system–specific. Some vendors provide information and/or tools for automating some of the process. There are also some open source and commercial tools related to this topic. Here is a list of helpful websites related to system hardening that are available at this writing (July 2002):

AIX	*http://biss.beckman.uiuc.edu/security/workshops/1999-10/*
FreeBSD	*http://www.trustedbsd.org*
	http://draenor.org/securebsd/
HP-UX	*http://www.interex.org/conference/iworks2001/proceedings/5103/5103.pdf*
	http://www.bastille-linux.org (This tool works under HP-UX as well.)
Linux	*http://www.linux-sec.net/Distro/distro.gwif.html*
	http://www.bastille-linux.org
Solaris	*http://wwws.sun.com/software/security/blueprints/*
	http://www.yassp.org
Tru64	*http://www.maths.usyd.edu.au/u/psz/securedu.html*

 Many operating systems are available in an enhanced security or "trusted" version. This is true of AIX, HP-UX, Solaris, and Tru64. There are several heightened-security Linux distributions and BSD projects with the same goal.

What follows is a discussion of the most important concepts and tasks related to system hardening. Be aware that the order of activities in this discussion is not rigorous, and actual task ordering would need to considered carefully prior to making any changes to a system.

 Hardening activities must be completed before the system is placed on the network for the first time.

Plan Before Acting

Before you begin the hardening process, it's only common sense to plan the steps you plan to take. In addition, it's a good idea to perform the process on a practice system before doing so on a production system. Other important preliminary activities include:

- Plan the filesystem and disk partition layout with security in mind (see below).
- Familiarize yourself with recent security bulletins.
- Sign up for security mailing lists if you have not already done so.
- Download any software packages you will need.

Finally, as you go through the hardening process, take notes to document what you did.

Secure the Physical System

One of the first decisions to make is where to physically locate the server. Important servers should not be in public areas. In addition, consider these other items:

- Secure the physical location with locks and the like.
- Assign a BIOS/RAM/EEPROM password to prevent unauthorized users from modifying setup settings or perform unauthorized boots.
- Attach any equipment identification tags/stickers used by your organization to the computer and its components.

Install the Operating System

It is much easier to harden a system whose operating system you've installed yourself, because you know what it includes. You might want to install only the minimum bootable configuration and then add the additional packages that you need in a separate step. Once you've done the latter, there are some additional tasks:

- Set up disk partitioning (or logical volumes), taking into account any security considerations (see below).
- Apply any operating system patches that have been released since the installation media was created.
- Enable the high-security/trusted operating system version if appropriate.
- Build a custom kernel that supports only the features you need. Remove support for ones you don't need. For systems that are not operating as routers, you should remove the IP forwarding capabilities. Intruders can't exploit features that aren't there.
- Configure automatic so that administrator intervention is not allowed (if appropriate).

Secure Local Filesystems

You'll also need to secure the filesystem. This task includes:

- Looking for inappropriate file and directory permissions and correcting any problems that are found. To review, the most important of these are:
  - Group and/or world writable system executables and directories
  - Setuid and setgid commands
- Decide on mount options for local filesystems. Take advantage of any security features provided by the operating system. For example, Solaris allows you to mount a filesystem with the option nosuid, which disables the setuid bit on every file within it. Isolating nonsystem files into a separate filesystem allows you to apply this option to those files.
- On some systems under some conditions, if */usr* is a separate filesystem, it can be mounted read-only.
- Encrypt sensitive data present on the system.

Securing Services

Securing the system's services represents a large part of the hardening task. In this area, the guiding principle should be to install or enable only the ones the system actually needs.

- Disable all unneeded services. Keep in mind that services are started in several different ways: within */etc/inittab*, from system boot scripts, by inetd. Alternatively, when possible, the software for an unneeded service can be removed from the system completely.
- Use secure versions of daemons when they are available.
- If at all possible, run server processes as a special user created for that purpose and not as *root*.
- Specify the maximum number of instances to run, for each server that lets you specify a maximum, or use xinetd. Doing so can help prevent some denial-of-service attacks.
- Specify access control and logging for all services. Install TCP Wrappers if necessary. Allow only the minimum access necessary. Include an entry in */etc/hosts. deny* that denies access to everyone (so only access allowed in */etc/hosts.allow* will be permitted).
- Use any per-service user level access control that is provided. For example, the cron and at subsystems allow you to restrict which users can use them at all. Some people recommend limiting at and cron to administrators.
- Secure all services, whether they seem security-related or not (e.g., printing).

Restrict root Access

Make sure that only authorized people can use *root* privileges:

- Select a secure *root* password, and plan a schedule for changing it regularly.
- Use sudo or system roles to grant ordinary users limited root privilege.
- Prevent *root* logins except on the system console.

Configure User Authentication and Account Defaults

Decide on and implement user account controls, setting up the default before adding users if possible. Related activities include:

- Set up the shadow password file if necessary.
- Configure PAM as appropriate for the relevant commands.
- Define user account password selection and aging settings.
- Set up other default user account restrictions as appropriate (e.g., resource limits).
- Plan the system's group structure if necessary, as well as other similar items, such as projects.
- Set up default user initialization files in */etc/skel* or elsewhere.
- Ensure that administrative and other accounts to which no one should ever log in have a disabled password and */bin/false* or another nonlogin shell.
- Remove unneeded predefined accounts.

Set up Remote Authentication

- Disable *hosts.equiv* and *.rhosts* passwordless authentication.
- Use ssh for remote user access.
- Configure PAM as appropriate for the relevant commands.

Install and Configure Ongoing Monitoring

Set up ongoing monitoring and auditing, including procedures for checking their results over time.

- Configure the syslog facility. Send/copy syslog messages to a central syslog server for redundancy.
- Enable process accounting.
- Install and configure any necessary software (e.g., swatch) and write any necessary scripts.
- Install Tripwire, configure it, and record system baseline data. Write the data to removable media and then remove it from the system.

Backup

Creating and implementing a backup schedule is an important part of securing a system. In addition, performing a full backup of the system once it is set up is essential:

- Perform the backup and verify the data.
- Creating two copies of the media is a good idea.

Other Activities

Add the new host to the security configuration on other system, in router access control lists, and so on, as necessary.

Detecting Problems

So far, we've looked at lots of ways to prevent security problems. The remainder of this chapter will look at ways to detect and investigate security breaches. We'll consider all of the various monitoring activities that you might want to use as they would be performed manually and in isolation from one another. There are both vendor-supplied and free tools to simplify and automate the process, and you may very well choose to use one of them. However, knowing what to look for and how to find it will help you to evaluate these tools and use them more effectively. The most sophisticated system watchdog package is ultimately only as good as the person reading, interpreting, and acting on the information it produces.

The fundamental prerequisite for effective system monitoring is knowing what normal is, that is, knowing how things ought to be in terms of:

- General system activity levels and how they change over the course of a day and a week.
- Normal activities for all the various users on the system.
- The structure, attributes, and contents of the filesystem itself, key system directories, and important files.
- The proper formats and settings within important system configuration files.

Some of these things can be determined from the current system configuration (and possibly by comparing it to a newly installed system). Others are a matter of familiarity and experience and must be acquired over time.

Password File Issues

It is important to examine the password file regularly for potential account-level security problems, as well as the shadow password file when applicable. In particular, it should be examined for:

- Accounts without passwords.

- UIDs of 0 for accounts other than *root* (which are also superuser accounts).
- GIDs of 0 for accounts other than *root*. Generally, users don't have group 0 as their primary group.
- Accounts added or deleted without your knowledge.
- Other types of invalid or improperly formatted entries.
- The password and shadow files' own ownership and permissions.

On some systems, the pwck command performs some simple syntax checking on the password file and can identify some security problems with it (AIX provides the very similar pwdck command to check its several user account database files). pwck reports on invalid usernames (including null ones), UIDs, and GIDs, null or nonexistent home directories, invalid shells, and entries with the wrong number of fields (often indicating extra or missing colons and other typos). However, it won't find a lot of other, more serious security problems. You'll need to check for those periodically in some other manner. (The grpck command performs similar simple syntax checking for the */etc/group* file.)

You can find accounts without passwords with a simple grep command:

```
# grep '^[^:]*::' /etc/passwd
root::NqI27UZyZoq3.:0:0:SuperUser:/:/bin/csh
demo::7:17:Demo User:/home/demo:/bin/sh
::0:0:::
```

The grep command looks for two consecutive colons that are the first colon characters in the line. This command found three such entries. At first glance, the entry for *root* appears to have a password, but the extra colon creates a user *root* with a nonsense UID and no password; this mistake is probably a typo. The second line is the entry for a predefined account used for demonstration purposes, probably present in the password file as delivered with the system. The third line is one I've found more than once and is a significant security breach. It creates an account with a null username and no password with UID and GID 0: a superuser account. While the login prompt will not accept a null username, some versions of su will:

```
$ su ""
# No password prompt!
```

In the password file examined with grep, the extra colon should be removed from the *root* entry, the *demo* account should be assigned a password (or disabled with an asterisk in the password field in */etc/passwd* or perhaps just deleted), and the null username entry should be removed.

Accounts with UID or GID 0 can also be located with grep:

```
# grep ':00*:' /etc/passwd
root:NqI27UZyZoq3.:0:0:SuperUser:/:/bin/csh
harvey:xyNjgMPtdlx*Q:145:0:Thomas G. Harvey:/home/harvey:/bin/ksh
badguy:mksU/.m7hwkOa:0:203:Bad Guy:/home/bg:/bin/sh
larooti:lso9/.7sJUhhs:000:203:George Larooti:/home/harvey:/bin/csh
```

The final line of output indicates why you should resist using a command like this:

```
# grep ':0:' /etc/passwd | grep -v root        This won't catch everything.
```

Whoever added user *larooti* has been tricky enough to add multiple zeros as the UID and the word "root" in the GECOS field. That person has also attempted to throw suspicion on user *harvey* by including his home directory in this entry. That is one of its two functions; the other is to enable the entry to pass some password file checking programs (including pwck). It seems unlikely, although not impossible, that user *harvey* is actually responsible for the entry; *harvey* could be very devious (or monumentally stupid, which can look very similar). I wouldn't consider the home directory clear evidence either way.

You can find new accounts by scanning the password file manually or by comparing it to a saved version you've squirreled away in an obscure location. The latter is the best way to find missing accounts, because it's easier to notice something new than that something is missing. Here is a sample command:

```
# diff /etc/passwd /usr/local/bin/old/opg
36c36,37
< chavez:9Sl.sd/i7snso:190:20:Rachel Chavez:/home/chavez:/bin/csh
---
> claire:dgJ6GLVsmOtmI:507:302:Theresa Claire:/home/claire:/bin/csh
> chavez:9So9sd/i7snso:190:20:Rachel Chavez:/home/chavez:/bin/csh
38d38
< wang:l9jsTHn7Hg./a:308:302:Rich Wang:/home/wang:/bin/sh
```

The copy of the password file is stored in the directory */usr/local/bin/old* and is named *opg*. It's a good idea to choose a relatively unconventional location and misleading names for security-related data files. For example, if you store the copy of the password file in */etc** or */var/adm* (the standard administrative directory) and name it *passwd.copy*, it won't be hard for an enterprising user to find and alter it when changing the real file. If your copy isn't secure, comparing against it is pointless. The example location given above is also a terrible choice, but it's merely a placeholder. You'll know what good choices are on your system. You might also want to consider keeping the comparison copy encrypted (assuming you have access to an effective encryption program) or storing it on removable media (which are not available in general).

The sample output displayed previously indicates that user *wang* has been added, user *claire* has been deleted, and the entry for user *chavez* has changed since the last time the copy was updated (in this case, her password changed). This command represents the simplest way of comparing the two files (we'll look at more complex ones soon).

Finally, you should regularly check the ownership and permissions of the password file (and any shadow password file in use). In most cases, the password file should be owned by *root* and a system administrative group and be readable by everyone but

---

* There may be copies of the password file in */etc*, but these are for backup rather than security purposes.

writable only by the owner; the shadow password file should not be readable by anyone but *root*. Any backup copies of either file should have the same ownership and permissions:

```
$ cd /etc; ls -l *passwd* *shadow*
-rw-r—r--    1    root    system    2732 Jun 23 12:43    /etc/passwd.sav
-rw-r—r--    1    root    system    2971 Jul 12 09:52    /etc/passwd
-rw-------    1    root    system    1314 Jul 12 09:55    /etc/shadow
-rw-------    1    root    system    1056 Apr 29 18:39    /etc/shadow.old
-rw-------    1    root    system    1276 Jun 23 12:54    /etc/shadow.sav
```

Monitoring the Filesystem

Checking the contents of important configuration files such as */etc/passwd* is one important monitoring activity. However, it is equally important to check the attributes of the file itself and those of the directory where it is stored. Making sure that system file and directory ownerships and protections remain correct over time is vital to ensuring continuing security. This includes:

- Checking the ownership and protection of important system configuration files.
- Checking the ownership and protection on important directories.
- Verifying the integrity of important system binary files.
- Checking for the presence or absence of certain files (for example, */etc/ftpusers* and */.rhosts*, respectively).

Possible ways to approach these tasks are discussed in the following subsections of this chapter. Each one introduces an increased level of cautiousness; you'll need to decide how much monitoring is necessary on your system.

Checking file ownership and protection

Minimally, you should periodically check the ownership and permissions of important system files and directories. The latter are important because if a directory is writable, a user could substitute a new version of an important file for the real one, even if the file itself is protected (as we've seen).

Important system files that need monitoring are listed in Table 7-6 (note that filenames and locations vary somewhat between Unix versions). In general, these files are owned by *root* or another system user; none of them should be world-writable. You should become familiar with all of them and learn their correct ownerships and protections.

Table 7-6. Important files and directories to protect and monitor

File(s)	Purpose
/.cshrc, /.login, /.logout, /.kshrc, /.profile, and so on	*root* account's initialization files (traditional location)
/.forward, /.mailrc	*root*'s mail initialization files

File(s)	Purpose
/.emacs, /.exrc	*root*'s editor initialization files
/.rhosts	Should not exist
~, ~/.cshrc, ~/.login, ~/.profile,	User home directories and initialization files
~/.rhosts	Probably should not exist
~/bin	User binary directory (conventional location)
/dev/*	Special files (the disk and memory devices are the most critical)
/etc/*	Configuration files in */etc* and its subdirectories (use find /etc -type f to find them all)
/sbin/init.d	Boot script location on some systems
/tcb	Enhanced security directory (HP-UX and Tru64)
/var/adm/*	Administrative databases and scripts
/var/spool/*, /usr/spool/*	Spooling directories
/bin, /usr/bin, /usr/ucb, /sbin, /usr/sbin	System (and local) binaries directories
/usr/local/bin, ...	Local binaries directory (as well as any other such locations in use)
/lib/*, /usr/lib/*	System libraries directories; shared libraries (common code that is called at runtime by standard commands) are the most vulnerable
/usr/include	System header (*.h*) files (replacing one of these can introduce altered code the next time a program is built locally)
All setuid and setgid files	Wherever they may be

You should be familiar with the correct ownership and protection for these files (as well as any others of importance to your system). You can facilitate the task of checking them with a script that runs a command like ls -l on each one, saves the output, and compares it to a stored list of the proper ownerships and permissions. Such a script can be very simple:

```
#!/bin/csh
# sys_check - perform basic filesystem security check
umask 077

# Make sure output file is empty.
/usr/bin/cp /dev/null perm.ck
alias ck "/usr/bin/ls -l \!:* >> perm.ck"
ck /.[a-z]*
ck /dev/{,r}disk*
. . .
ck /usr/lib/lib*

/usr/bin/diff /usr/local/bin/old/pm perm.ck > perm.diff
```

This script is a C shell script so that it can define an alias to do the work; you could do the same thing with a Bourne shell function. The script runs the ls -l command on the desired files, saving the output in the file *perm.ck*. Finally, it compares the current output against a saved data file. If the files on your system change a lot, this script will produce a lot of false positives: files that look suspicious because their modification time changed but whose ownership and protection are correct. You can avoid this by making the ls command a bit more complex:[*]

```
ls -l files | awk '{print $1,$3,$4,$NF}' >> perm.ck
```

This command compares only the file modes, user owner, group owner, and filename fields of the ls command.

In addition to checking individual files, it is important to check the protection on all directories that store important files, making sure that they are owned by the proper user and are not world-writable. This includes both directories where Unix commands are stored, administrative directories like */var/adm* and */etc*'s subdirectories, and the spooling directories under */var/spool*. Any other directory containing a setuid or setgid file should also be checked.

Looking for setuid and setgid files

The number of setuid commands on the system should be kept to a minimum. Checking the filesystem for new ones should be part of general system security monitoring. The following command will list all files that have the setuid or setgid access mode set:

```
# find / \( -perm -2000 -o -perm -4000 \) -type f -print
```

You can compare the command's output against a saved list of setuid and setgid files and thereby easily locate any changes to the system. Again, you can do a more comprehensive comparison by running ls -l on each file and comparing that output to a saved list:

```
# find / -type f \( -perm -2000 -o -perm -4000 \) \
        -exec ls -l {} \; | diff - /usr/local/bin/old/fs
2d1
< -rwsr-xr-x 1 root bin 41792 Jun 7 1995 /usr/local/bin/xpostit
```

Any differences uncovered should be investigated right away. The file storing the expected setuid and setgid files' data can be generated initially using the same find command after you have checked all of the setuid and setgid files on the system and know them to be secure. As before, the file itself must be kept secure, and offline copies should exist. The data file and any scripts which use it should be owned by *root* and be protected against all group and other access. Even with these precautions, it's important that you be familiar with the files on your system, in addition to any security monitoring you perform via scripts, rather than relying solely on data files you set up a long time ago.

---

[*] The corresponding alias command is:

```
alias ck "ls -l \!:* | awk '{print "'$1,$3,$4,$NF'"}'" >> perm.ck"
```

The trick is that the quotes in the awk command are needed to insert the argument placeholder characters themselves, rather than their current values, into the alias.

Checking modification dates and inode numbers

If you want to perform more careful monitoring of the system files, you should compare not only file ownership and protection, but also modification dates, inode numbers, and checksums (see the next section). For the first two items, you can use the ls command with the options -lsid for the applicable files and directories. These options display the file's inode number, size (in both blocks and bytes), owners, protection modes, modification date, and name. For example:

```
$ ls -lsid /etc/rc*
690 3 -rwxr-xr-x 1 root root 1325 Mar 20 12:58 /etc/rc0
691 4 -rwxr-xr-x 1 root root 1655 Mar 20 12:58 /etc/rc2
692 1 drwxr-xr-x 2 root root 272 Jul 22 07:33 /etc/rc2.d
704 2 -rwxr-xr-x 1 root root 874 Mar 20 12:58 /etc/rc3
705 1 drwxr-xr-x 2 root root 32 Mar 13 16:14 /etc/rc3.d
```

The -d option allows the information on directories themselves to be displayed, rather than listing their contents.

If you check this data regularly, comparing it against a previously saved file of the expected output, you will catch any changes very quickly, and it will be more difficult for someone to modify any file without detection (although, unfortunately, far from impossible—rigging file modification times is not really very hard). This method inevitably requires that you update the saved data file every time you make a change yourself, or you will have to wade through lots of false positives when examining the output. As always, it is important that the data file be kept in a secure location to prevent it from being modified.

Computing checksums

Checksums are a more sophisticated method for determining whether a file's contents have changed. A *checksum* is a number computed from the binary bytes of the file; the number can then be used to determine whether a file's contents are correct. Checksums are most often used to check files written to disk from tape to be sure there have been no I/O errors, but they may also be used for security purposes to see whether a file's contents change over time.

For example, you can generate checksums for the system commands' executable files and save this data. Then, at a later date, you can recompute the checksums for the same files and compare the results. If they are not identical for a file, that file has changed, and it is possible that someone has substituted something else for the real command.

The cksum command computes checksums; it takes one or more filenames as its arguments and displays the checksum and size in blocks for each file:

```
$ cksum /bin/*
09962 4 /bin/[
05519 69 /bin/adb
...
```

This method is far from foolproof. For example, crackers have been known to pad a smaller file with junk characters to make its checksum match the old value. Unfortunately, cksum computes a very easy-to-simulate file signature. There are even cases of viruses remaining in memory, intercepting directory listing and checksum commands, and returning the correct information (which the virus saved before making alterations to the system).

The GNU md5sum utility is a better checksum choice. It is part of the textutils package, and it is included with some Linux distributions. See *http://www.gnu.org/manual/textutils-2.0/html_node/textutils_21.html* for more information.

In any case. you'll need to take the following precautions when computing and comparing checksums if you suspect the system has been compromised:

- Make sure that you have a copy of the checksum utility that you know to be secure. This means restoring the utility from original operating system distribution media or a post-installation backup you made if there is any doubt about system integrity.
- Compare the current system state with a data file that has been stored offline, because the copy on the disk may have been altered.
- Make the comparisons after rebooting to single-user mode.

Paranoia Is Common Sense

Sooner or later, a recalcitrant user will accuse you of being overly paranoid because she resents some restriction that reasonable security measures impose. There's not really much you can say in response except to explain again why security is important and what you are trying to protect against. In general, cries of "paranoia" are really just a sign that you are performing your job well. After all, it is your job to be at least one level more paranoid than your users think you need to be—and than potential intruders hope you will be.

Run fsck occasionally

It is also possible for modifications to be made on a filesystem if someone succeeds in breaking into a system, usually via the fsdb utility. Running fsck occasionally, even when it is not necessary for filesystem integrity purposes, never hurts. You should also run fsck after rebooting if you think someone has succeeded in breaking into the system.

Automating Security Monitoring

There are a variety of tools available for automating many of the security monitoring activities we have considered so far. We'll look briefly at a few of them in this section.

Trusted computing base checking

A *trusted computing base* (TCB) is a system environment whose security is verifiably trustworthy and that includes the capability of ensuring its continued integrity. The TCB may be present on a computer along with other software, and users interact with the system in a trusted mode via a *trusted path*, which eliminates any untrusted applications and operating system components before allowing access to the TCB. Communication with the TCB is usually initiated by a specific key sequence on such systems; for example, on an AIX system, pressing the Secure Attention Key sequence (CTRL-X CTRL-R by default) accesses the TCB. These facilities are used in systems secured at B1 and higher levels, and the requirements specify that the operating system must be reinstalled in the high security mode (a TCB cannot be added to an existing system).

A full consideration of trusted computing is beyond the scope of this book. However, some of the utilities provided as part of TCB support can still be used for general filesystem monitoring even when the TCB facility is not active. Typically, these utilities compare all important system files and directories against a list of correct attributes that was created at installation time, checking file ownerships, protection modes, sizes, and checksums, and, in some cases, modification dates. TCB-checking utilities and similar programs also usually have the ability to correct any problems that they uncover.

These are the facilities provided by the Unix versions we are considering (their capabilities vary somewhat):

AIX	tcbck
HP-UX	swverify
Solaris	aset
Tru64	fverify

System integrity checking with Tripwire

The Tripwire facility, originally produced by the COAST project of Purdue University, is unquestionably among the finest free software packages in existence. The current home page is *http://www.tripwire.org*.

Tripwire compares the current state of important files and directories with their stored correct attributes according to criteria selected by the system administrator. It can compare all important file properties (more precisely, all inode characteristics), and it includes the ability to compute file signatures in many different ways (nine are included as of this writing). Comparing file checksums computed using two different algorithms makes it extremely difficult for a file to be altered without detection.

Tripwire uses an ASCII database to store file attributes to be used for future comparisons. This database is created the first time you run the `tripwire` command (by including the `-init` option). Ideally, you should use this option after reinstalling the operating system from the original media to eliminate the possibility that the system is already corrupt. `tripwire` creates database entries and makes comparisons to them based on the instructions in its configuration file, *tw.config* by default.

Here is an excerpt from a configuration file:

```
# Pathname            Attributes to Check
/usr/bin              +ugpinsm12-a
/usr/local/bin        R
/usr/lib              R-2
 ...
/usr/bin/at           R+8-2
```

The first entry indicates that the user and group owners, protection, inode number, number of links, inode creation time, and file modification times as well as file signatures 1 and 2 (which correspond to the MD5 and Snefru algorithms) will be checked for the files in */usr/bin*, and that any changes in file access times will be ignored. The second entry performs the same checks for the files in */usr/local/bin*, because *R* is a built-in synonym for the string specified for */usr/bin* (it is also the default). For the files in */usr/lib*, all checks except file signature 2 are performed. The final entry refers to a file rather than a directory, and it substitutes file signature 8 (Haval) for signature 2 for the `at` command executable (overriding the specification it would otherwise have from the first sample entry).

Thus, it is very easy to perform different tests on different parts of the filesystem depending upon their unique security features. The configuration file syntax also includes C preprocessor-style directives to allow a single configuration file to be used on multiple systems.

Once the Tripwire database is created, it is essential to protect it from tampering and unauthorized viewing. As the Tripwire documentation repeatedly states, the best way to do so is to store it on a removable, write-protectable medium like a floppy disk; the locked disk with the database will be placed in the drive only when it is time to run Tripwire. In fact, in most cases, both the database and the executable fit easily onto a single floppy disk. In any case, you will want to make a secure backup copy of both `tripwire` and its related `siggen` utility after building it, so that the online copies can be easily restored in case of trouble.

When you create the initial database for a system, take the time to generate all of the file signatures you might conceivably want. The set you select should include two difficult-to-forge signatures; you may also want to include one quickly computed, lower-quality signature. You don't have to use as time-consuming a procedure on a regular basis—for example, you might use one quick and one good signature for routine checks—but the data will be available should you ever need it.

Here is part of a report produced by running tripwire:

```
changed: -rwsrwsr-x root 40120 Apr 28 14:32:54 2002 /usr/bin/at
deleted: -rwsr-sr-x root 149848 Feb 17 12:09:22 2002
   /usr/local/bin/chost
added: -rwsr-xr-x root 10056 Apr 28 17:32:01 2002 /usr/local/bin/cnet2
changed: -rwsr-xr-x root 155160 Apr 28 15:56:37 2002
   /usr/local/bin/cpeople
...
### Attr Observed (what it is) Expected (what it should be)
###=========== ============================== ==================
/usr/bin/at
  st_mode: 104775 104755
  st_gid: 302 0
  st_ctime: Fri Feb 17 12:09:13 2002 Fri Apr 28 14:32:54 2002
/usr/local/bin/cpeople
  st_size: 155160 439400
  st_mtime: Fri Feb 17 12:10:47 2002 Fri Apr 28 15:56:37 2002
  md5 (sig1): 1Th46QB8YvkFTfiGzhhLsG 2MIGPzGWLxt6aEL.GXrbbM
```

On this system, the chost command executable has been deleted, and a file named
cnet2 has been added (both in */usr/local/bin*). Two other files on the system have
been changed. The at command has had its group owner changed to group 302, and
/usr/bin/at is group-writable. The cpeople executable has been replaced: it is a different size and has a different signature and modification time.

More Administrative Virtues

Security monitoring primarily requires two of the seven administrative virtues: attention to detail and adherence to routine. They are related, of course, and mutually rein-
force one another. Both also depend on that metavirtue, foresight, to keep you on the
right path during those times when it seems like too much trouble.

- Attention to detail. Many large security problems display only tiny symptoms,
  which the inattentive system administrator will miss, but you (and your tools
  and scripts) will not.
- Adherence to routine. The night you decide to forego security monitoring so
  that some other job can run overnight has a much better than average chance of
  being the night the crackers find your system.

Vulnerability scanning

The next step up in monitoring intensity is to actively search for known problems
and vulnerabilities within the system or network. In this section, we'll look at a couple of the packages designed to do this (as well as mentioning several more).

General system security monitoring via COPS. The free Computer Oracle and Password
System (COPS) can automate a variety of security monitoring activities with a single

system. Its capabilities overlap somewhat with Crack and Tripwire, but it offers many unique ones as well. It was written by Dan Farmer, and its home page is *http://dan.drydog.com/cops/software/*.

These are COPS' most important capabilities:

- Checks *root*'s environment by examining the account's initialization files in the root directory for umask and path definition commands (and then checking path components for writable directories and binaries), as well as ownership and protections of the files themselves. Also checks for non-root entries in any */.rhosts* file.

  COPS also performs similar checks of the user environment of each account defined in the password file.

- Checks the permissions of the special files corresponding to entries in the filesystem configuration file, */etc/fstab*.

- Checks whether any commands or files referenced in the system boot scripts are writable.

- Checks whether any commands or files mentioned in crontab entries are writable.

- Checks password file entries for syntax errors, duplicate UID's, non-*root* users with UID 0, and the like. Performs a similar check of the group file.

- Checks the system's anonymous FTP setup (if applicable), as well as the security of the tftp facility and some other facilities.

- Checks the dates of applicable system command binaries against ones noted in CERT advisories to determine whether known vulnerabilities still exist.

- Runs the Kuang program, an expert system that tries to determine if your system can be compromised by its current file and directory ownerships and permissions (see the upcoming example output). It attempts to find indirect routes to *root* access like those we considered earlier in this chapter.

- The COPS facility also has the (optional) ability to check the system for new setuid and setgid files and to compute checksums for files and compare them to stored values. Both the C/shell-script version and the Perl version are initiated via the cops script. You can configure the first version by editing this script as well as the *makefile* before building the COPS binaries. You configure the Perl version, which resides in the *perl* subdirectory of the main COPS directory, by editing the cops script and its configuration file, *cops.cf*. The following output is excerpted from a COPS report. The lines beginning with asterisks denote the script or program within the COPS facility that produced the subsequent output section (use -v to produce this verbose output):

```
**** dev.chk ****              Checks device files for local file systems.
Warning! /dev/sonycd_31a is _World_ readable!
**** rc.chk ****               Checks boot scripts' contents.
Warning! File /etc/mice (inside /etc/rc.local) is _World_writable (*)!
**** passwd.chk ****           Checks password file.
Warning! Passwd file, line 2, user install has uid == 0 and is not root
```

```
install:x:0:0:Installation program:/:/INSTALL/install
Warning! Passwd file, line 8, invalid home directory:
admin:x:10:10:basic admin::
**** user.chk ****               Checks user initialization files.
Warning! /home/chavez/.cshrc is _World_ writable!
**** kuang ****                  Searches for system vulnerabilities.
Success! grant uid -1 replace /home/chavez/.cshrc grant uid 190
    grant gid 0 replace /etc/passwd grant uid 0
```

The final section of output from Kuang requires a bit of explanation. The output here describes chains of actions that will result in obtaining *root* access based on current system permissions. The item here notes that user *nobody*—meaning in this case, anybody at all who wants to—can replace the *.cshrc* file in user *chavez*'s home directory (because it is world-writable), making user 190 (*chavez*) the user owner and group 0 the group owner (possible because *chavez* is a member of the *system* group). Commands in this file can replace the password file (because it is group writable), which means that *root* access can be obtained.

The example output also illustrates that COPS can produce some false positives. For example, the fact that */dev/sonycd_31a* is world-readable is not a problem because the device is used to access the system's CD-ROM drive. The bottom line is that it still takes a human to make sense of the results, however automated obtaining them may be.

Scanning for network vulnerabilities

The are a variety of tools now available for scanning systems for network-based vulnerabilities that might offer opening to potential intruders. One of the best is the Security Administrator's Integrated Network Tool (Saint), also written by Dan Farmer (see *http://www.wwdsi.com/saint/*). It is based on Dan's earlier, now infamous, Satan[*] tool. It is designed to probe a network for a set of known vulnerabilities and security holes, including the following:

- NFS vulnerabilities: exporting filesystems read-write to the world, accepting requests from user (unprivileged) programs, NFS-related portmapper security holes.

- Whether the NIS password file can be retrieved.

- ftp and tftp problems, including whether the *ftp* home directory is writable and whether tftp has access to parts of the filesystem that it should not.

- A + entry in */etc/hosts.equiv*, granting access to any user with the same name as a non-*root* local account on any accessible system.

- The presence of an unprotected modem on the system (which could be used by an intruder for transport to other systems of interest).

- Whether X server access control is enabled.

---

[*] The Security Administrator Tool for Analyzing Networks.

- Whether the rexd facility is enabled (it is so insecure that it should never be used).
- Whether any versions of software with reported vulnerabilities are present. The software is updated for new security vulnerabilities as they are discovered.
- Whether any of the SANS top 20 vulnerabilities is present. See *http://www.sans.org/top20.htm* for the current list (scroll past the very long self-promotional section and you'll find the list).

Saint works by allowing you to select a system or subnetwork for scanning, probing the systems you have designated at one of three levels of enthusiasm, and then reporting its findings back to you. Saint is different from most other security monitoring facilities in that it looks for vulnerabilities on a system from the outside rather than the inside. (This was one of the main sources of the considerable controversy that surrounded Satan at its release, although it was not the first facility to operate in this manner.)

One excellent feature of Saint is that its documentation tells you how to fix the vulnerabilities that it finds. The add-on interfaces also contain many helpful links to articles and CERT advisories related to its probes as well as to software designed to plug some of the holes that it finds.

Figure 7-4 illustrates one of the reports that can be produced from Saint runs using the add-on reporting tool. This one shows a summary of the vulnerabilities that it found categorized by type, and the detail view of the first category is also displayed.

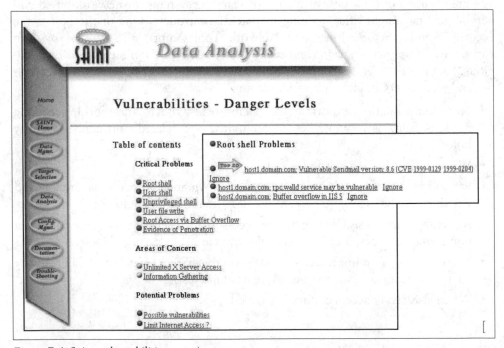

Figure 7-4. Saint vulnerabilities overview report

Renaud Deraison's Nessus package has similar goals to Saint. For more information about it, see *http://www.nessus.org*.

Security and the Media: An Unhelpful Combination

Many well-meaning persons suppose that the discussion respecting the means for baffling the supposed safety of locks offers a premium for dishonesty, by showing others how to be dishonest. This is a fallacy.... Rogues knew a good deal about lockpicking long before locksmiths discussed it among themselves.

—Rudimentary Treatise on the Construction of Locks (1853)
[Quoted in Cheswick and Bellovin (1994)]

Intelligent people disagree about how much detail to include when discussing security problems. Some say never to mention anything that an intruder could use; however, it's difficult for system administrators to evaluate how vulnerable their system is without understanding how potential threats work. Given the sheer volume of security alerts, people need enough details to be both technically and emotionally able to take a problem seriously.

In my view, however, media coverage of emerging security problems is seldom helpful. Any benefit obtained from the quick spread of information is more than offset by the panic that sets in among nontechnical folks based on the incomplete, exaggerated, and often inaccurate reports. Managers all too often overreact to such media reports, especially when open source operating systems are involved. Demands to immediately remove services that are actually needed are all too common. Part of the administrator's job is to attempt to keep things in perspective, with both managers and users.

It is important to keep in mind the media's motives in these instances: capturing viewers and selling newspapers. Security concerns are not the prime motivation behind such stories, and better computer security is not among the benefits that they reap from them.

What to Do if You Find a Problem

If one of the security monitoring tools you use finds a problem, there are two concerns facing you: preventing further damage and correcting whatever the current problem is. How strongly to react depends to a great extent on the security requirements of your site; everyone needs to investigate every unexpected change to the system uncovered in a security check, but how quickly it has to be done and what to do in the meantime will depend on what the problem is and how much of a risk you and your site are willing to assume.

For example, suppose Tripwire finds a single change on the system: the group owner of */usr/local/bin* has been changed from *bin* to *system*. Assuming you've set up an appropriate configuration file and are running Tripwire nightly, you can probably just change the group owner back and find out which system administrator made this silly mistake. At the other extreme, if the one change is a replacement of /etc/ passwd, and you are doing only minimal security monitoring—checking file ownerships, modes, sizes and modification dates—you've got a much bigger problem. You can no longer really trust any file on the system, because the data you have isn't good enough to determine which files have been altered. In such an extreme case, this is the right—if extremely painful—thing to do:

- Disconnect the system from any unsecured network (which is pretty much any network).

- Reboot the system immediately to single-user mode to attempt to get rid of any malignant users or processes. There are more complex strategies for handling an intrusion in progress; however, they are not recommended for the uninitiated or the fainthearted.

- Back up any files that you cannot afford to lose (but be aware that they may already be tainted). Back up all log and accounting files to aid in future investigation of the problem.

- You may want to keep the system down while you investigate. When you are ready to bring the system back online, reinstall the operating system from scratch (including remaking all filesystems). Restore other files manually and check them out carefully in a secure filesystem. Rebuild all executables for which you have the source code.

 If you anticipate ever taking an legal action with respect to the break-in, you must save the original disks in the system unaltered. You will have to replace the hard disks to reinstall the operating system and bring the system back online.

The severity of this cure should emphasize once again the importance of formulating and implementing an effective security monitoring process.

Investigating System Activity

Regularly monitoring the processes running on your system is another way to minimize the likelihood of security breaches. You should do this periodically, perhaps as often as several times during the day. Very shortly, you will have a good sense of what "normal" system activity is: what programs run, how long they run, who runs them, and so on. You'll also be in a reasonably good position to notice any unusual activity: users running different programs than they usually do, processes that remain idle for long periods of time (potential Trojan horses), users logged in at unusual times or from unusual locations, and the like.

As you know, the ps command lists characteristics of system processes. You should be familiar with all of its options. Let's look at some examples of how you might use some of these options. Using the BSD command format, you can use ww to get the entire command run by a user into the display (this output is wrapped):

```
$ ps ax | egrep 'PID|harvey'
241 co R 0:02 rm /home/harvey/newest/g04/1913.exe /home/mar

$ ps axww | egrep 'PID|harvey'
PID TT STAT TIME COMMAND
241 co R 0:02 rm /home/harvey/newest/g04/1913.exe
  /home/harvey/newest/g04-221.chk  /home/harvey/newest/g04-271.int
  /home/harvey/newest/g04-231.rwf  /home/harvey/newest/g04-291.d2e
  /home/harvey/newest/g04-251.scr  /usr/local/src/local_g04
```

In this case, you can see all the files that were deleted by using two w's.

The c option reveals the actual command executed, rather than the one typed in on the command line. This is occasionally useful for discovering programs run via symbolic links:

```
$ ps aux | egrep 'PID|smith'
USER PID %CPU %MEM SZ RSS TT STAT TIME COMMAND
smith 25318 6.7 1.1 1824 544 p4 S 0:00 vi
smith 23888 0.0 1.4 2080 736 p2 I 0:02 -csh (csh)

$ ps -auxc | egrep 'PID|smith'
USER PID %CPU %MEM SZ RSS TT STAT TIME COMMAND
smith 25318 6.7 1.1 1824 544 p4 S 0:00 backgammon
smith 23888 0.0 1.4 2080 736 p2 I 0:02 -csh (csh)
```

User *smith* evidently in his current directory has a file named vi, which is a symbolic link to */usr/games/backgammon*.

The -f option under System V can help you identify processes that have been idle for a long time:

```
$ ps -ef
UID PID PPID C STIME TTY TIME COMMAND
chavez 2387 1123 0 Apr 22 ? 0:05 comp_h2o
```

This process has been around for a long time but has accumulated very little CPU time. For instance, if today is May 5, it's time to look into this process. Hopefully, you'd actually notice it before May 5.

As these examples indicate, creative use of common commands is what's needed in a lot of cases. The more familiar you are with the commands' capabilities, the easier it will be to know what to use in the situations you encounter.

Monitoring unsuccessful login attempts

Repeated unsuccessful login attempts for any user account can indicate someone trying to break into the system. Standard Unix does not keep track of this statistic, but many Unix versions provide facilities that do so.

Under AIX, checking for lots of unsuccessful login attempts is relatively easy. The file */etc/security/user* includes the keyword *unsuccessful_login_count* in the stanza for each user:

```
chavez:
    admin = false
    time_last_login = 679297672
    unsuccessful_login_count = 27
    tty_last_unsuccessful_login = pts/2
    time_last_unsuccessful_login = 680904983
    host_last_unsuccessful_login = hades
```

This is clearly a lot of unsuccessful login attempts. Anything above two or three is probably worth some investigation. The following command displays the username and number of unsuccessful logins when this value is greater than 3:

```
# egrep '^[^*].*:$|gin_coun' /etc/security/user | \
awk '{if (NF>1 && $3>3) {print s,$0}} ; NF==1 {s=$0}'
chavez: unsuccessful_login_count = 27
```

The egrep command prints lines in */etc/security/user* that don't begin with an asterisk and end with a colon (the username lines) and that contain the string "gin_coun" (the unsuccessful login count lines). For each line printed by egrep, the awk command checks whether the value of the third field is greater than 3 when there is more than one field on the line (the username lines have just one field). If it is, it prints the username (saved in the variable *s*) and the current line.

When the user logs in, she gets a message about the number of unsuccessful login attempts, and the field in */etc/security/user* is cleared. However, if you check this file periodically using the cron facility, you can catch most strings of unsuccessful login attempts before they are erased. Users should also be encouraged to report any unexpected unsuccessful login attempts that they are informed of at login time.

Tru64 also keeps track of unsuccessful login attempts in this way, storing the current number in the *u_numunsuclog* field in each user's protected password database file.

su log files

Virtually all Unix implementations provide some mechanism for logging all attempts to become superuser. Such logs can be very useful when trying to track down who did something untoward. Messages from su are typically written to the file */var/adm/sulog*, and they look something like this:

```
SU 07/20 07:27 - ttyp0 chavez-root
SU 07/20 14:00 + ttyp0 chavez-root
SU 07/21 18:36 + ttyp1 harvey-chavez
SU 07/21 18:39 + ttyp1 chavez-root
```

This display lists all uses of the su command, not just those used to su to *root*, as when user *harvey* first su'ed to *chavez* and then to *root*. If you look only at su commands to *root*, you might mistakenly suspect *chavez* of doing something that *harvey* was actually responsible for. On some systems, su log messages are always entered under the real username, ignoring any intermediate su commands.

Here are the locations of the su log file on various systems:

AIX	*/var/adm/sulog*
FreeBSD	Within */var/log/messages*
HP-UX	*/var/adm/sulog*
Linux	Within */var/log/messages*
Tru64	*/var/adm/sialog*
Solaris	Specified in the SULOG setting in */etc/default/su*.
sudo facility	*/var/adm/sudo.log*

History on the root account

A simple way of retaining some information about what's been done as *root* is to give *root* a shell that supports a history mechanism, and in *root*'s initialization file set the number of commands saved across login sessions to a large number. For example, the following commands cause the last 200 commands entered by *root* to be saved:

```
C shell                         Korn shell
set history = 200               export HISTSIZE=200
set savehist = 200              export HISTFILE=/var/adm/.rh
```

Under the C shell, commands are saved in the file */.history* for *root*. Under the Korn shell, commands are written to the file named in the *HISTFILE* environment variable (*$HOME/.sh_history* by default). Of course, a clever user can turn off the history feature before misbehaving with the *root* account, but it can also often be overlooked (especially if you don't put the command number in the prompt string). Alternatively, you can copy the history file to some secure location periodically via the cron facility.

Tracking user activities

There are other utilities you can use to determine what users have been doing on the system, sometimes enabling you to track down the cause of a security problem. These commands are listed in Table 7-7.

Table 7-7. Command summary utilities

Command	Unix versions	Displays information about
last	All	User login sessions
lastcomm	All	All commands executed (by user and TTY)
acctcom	AIX, HP-UX, Solaris, Tru64	All commands executed (by user and TTY)

 These commands draw their information from the system accounting files, the age of which determines the period of time that they cover. Note that accounting must be running on the system for any of them to be available (see Chapter 17).

The last command displays data for each time a user logged into the system. last optionally may be followed by a list of usernames and/or terminal names. If any arguments are distinguished, the report is limited to records pertaining to at least one of them (OR logic):

```
$ last
harvey ttyp1  iago    Fri Sep 16 10:07  still logged in
ng     ttyp6          Fri Sep 16 10:00  10:03 (00:02)
harvey ttyp1  iago    Fri Sep 16 09:57  10:07 (00:09)
chavez ttyp5          Fri Sep 16 09:29  still logged in

$ last chavez
chavez ttyp5          Fri Sep 16 09:29 still logged in
chavez ttypc  duncan  Thu Sep 15 21:46 - 21:50 (00:04)
chavez ttyp9          Thu Sep 15 11:53 - 18:30 (07:23)

$ last dalton console
dump   console        Wed Sep 14 17:06 - 18:56 (01:49)
dalton ttyq4  newton  Wed Sep 14 15:58 - 16:29 (00:31)
dalton ttypc  newton  Tue Sep 13 22:50 - 00:19 (01:28)
dalton console        Tue Sep 13 17:30 - 17:49 (00:19)
ng     console        Tue Sep 13 08:50 - 08:53 (00:02)
```

last lists the username, tty, remote hostname (for remote logins), starting and ending times, and total connect time in hours for each login session. The ending time is replaced by the phrase "still logged in" for current sessions. At the end of each listing, last notes the date of its data file, usually */var/adm/wtmp*, indicating the period covered by the report.

The username *reboot* may be used to list the times of system boots:

```
$ last reboot
reboot ~  Fri Sep 9 17:36
reboot ~  Mon Sep 5 20:04
```

lastcomm displays information on previously executed commands. Its default display is the following:

```
$ lastcomm
lpd       F  root              0.08 secs  Mon Sep 19 15:06
date         harvey   ttyp7    0.02 secs  Mon Sep 19 15:06
sh           smith    ttyp3    0.05 secs  Mon Sep 19 15:04
calculus  D  chavez   ttyq8    0.95 secs  Mon Sep 19 15:09
more      X  ng       ttypf    0.17 secs  Mon Sep 19 15:03
ruptime      harvey   console  0.14 secs  Mon Sep 19 15:03
mail      S  root     ttyp0    0.95 secs  Fri Sep 16 10:46
```

The display lists the command name, flags associated with the process, the username and tty associated with it, the amount of CPU time consumed by its execution, and the time the process exited. The flags may be one or more of:

S   Command was run by the superuser.

F   Command ran after a fork.

D   Command terminated with a core dump.

X   Command was terminated by a signal (often CTRL-C).

The command optionally accepts one or more image or command names, user-names, or terminal names to further limit the display. If more than one item is specified, only lines that contain all of them will be listed (Boolean AND logic). For example, the following command lists entries for user *chavez* executing the image *calculus*:

```
$ lastcomm chavez calculus
calculus  D  chavez   ttyq8   0.95 secs  Mon Sep 19 15:09
calculus     chavez   ttyp3  10.33 secs  Mon Sep 19 22:32
```

Under System V, the acctcom command produces similar information (output is shortened):

```
$ acctcom
COMMAND                           START    END      CPU
NAME      USER      TTYNAME  TIME     TIME     (SECS)
calculus  chavez    ttyq8    15:52:49 16:12:23 0.95
grep      harvey    ttyq3    15:52:51 15:52:55 0.02
rm        root      tty02    15:52:55 15:55:56 0.01
```

acctcom's most useful options are -u and -t, which limit the display to the user or TTY specified as the option's argument (respectively), and -n pattern, which limits the display to lines containing *pattern*. The pattern can be a literal string or a regular expression. This option is often used to limit the display by command name. If more than one option is specified, records must match all of them to be included (AND logic). For example, the following command displays vi commands run by *root*:

```
$ acctcom -u root -n vi
COMMAND                          START    END      CPU
NAME     USER      TTYNAME  TIME     TIME     (SECS)
vi       root      tty01    10:33:12 10:37:44 0.04
vi       root      ttyp2    12:34:29 13:51:47 0.11
vi       root      ttyp5    11:43:28 11:45:38 0.08
```

Unfortunately, acctcom doesn't display the date in each line as lastcomm does, but you can figure it out by knowing when its data file (*/var/adm/pacct*) was created and watching the dates turn over in the display (records are in chronological order). If you're trying to track down a recent event, use the -b option, which displays records in reverse chronological order.

So what can you do with these commands? Suppose you find a new UID 0 account in the password file and you know the file was all right yesterday. After checking its modification time, you can use the su log file to see who became *root* about that time; last will tell you if *root* was logged in directly at that time. Assuming *root* wasn't directly logged in, you can then use lastcomm or acctcom to find out who ran an editor at about the right time. You may not get conclusive proof as to who made the change, but it may help you to narrow the possibilities; you can then talk to those users in person. Of course, there are trickier ways of changing the password file that will evade detection by this method; there's no substitute for limiting access to the *root* account to trustworthy people. This example also illustrates the importance of detecting security problems right away; if you can't accurately narrow down the time that the password file was changed, it will surely be impossible to figure out who did it.

Event-auditing systems

Event-auditing systems are much more sophisticated tools for tracking system activities, and they are accordingly much more useful than the simple tools provided by standard Unix. Auditing is a required part of the U.S. government C2 and higher security levels. All of the commercial Unix versions we are considering have an auditing facility as a standard or optional component.

Auditing systems all work in basically the same way, although the details of the mechanics of setting up and administering auditing are different. Once you understand how one auditing system works, you can work with another one very easily. These are the main steps required to set up event auditing on a system:

- Choose which events you want to keep track of. In general, auditing events are defined at the system call level. Thus, you can track file opens, closes, reads, writes, unlinks (deletions), and so on, but you can't track file edits with vi. Some systems let you define new events, but this is rarely necessary.
- Choose which system objects—for the most part, this means individual files—you want to monitor. Not all auditing systems let you narrow the scope to specific files.
- Group events and/or objects into classes of related items. Sometimes this step is done for you, and you have no choice as to how classes are defined.
- Set the system default audit event (or class) list, and then indicate which events or classes should be audited for the various users on the system. On some systems, you have to do both variations of this task: designate system defaults, including a list of users to be audited, and then specify what to audit for each applicable user.
- Decide where the audit trail data files should be located in the filesystem. Many auditing systems allow or require you to specify a list of audit logging directories (so that the next one is already waiting when one fills up).
- Set any other audit system parameters: how large audit files can get, how often to switch to a new file, what file format to use, and so on.
- Change the system boot scripts so that auditing is started automatically at boot time and terminated before a system shutdown.

Auditing is one case where a well-designed system administration tool is a tremendous help, due to the number of tasks that it includes and the staggering amount of data that an auditing system generates. However, it sometimes takes a bit of time to figure out the mappings between the less than intuitive descriptions of the available events and what you actually want to watch for.

Once auditing is in effect, the next step is figuring out how to generate reports from the data. This will take some time. The best way to learn how to do this is to simulate the kinds of events you want to be able to detect on an idle system: turn auditing on for all events (ensuring that the records will go to a new audit file), do something you want to be able to track (for example, make a trivial change in the password file, delete a file in */tmp*, change the ownership of a file, etc.), and then turn auditing off.* Then look at the audit records you've just generated using the system's report facilities. This will enable you both to recognize what your target act looks like in terms of audit events and to learn the correspondence between audit event and classes and higher-level commands. In some cases, performing different commands as different users will be helpful in sorting things out.

Intruders Can Read

At various points in this chapter, I've said that intruders will go to very great lengths to cover their tracks. The most sophisticated intruders know all the ins and outs of the available types of system protection and monitoring facilities—and all of their vulnerabilities. That is why it is important to have system-checking tools and their associated data files that are beyond the reach of any system intruder.

There are various ways to accomplish this:

- Have backup copies of important utilities, preferably made at the time of their original installation. Depending on the media type, two backup copies might be called for.

- Be cautious in keeping online data files describing the correct system configuration. Storing them on a write-protected diskette, which is accessed only as needed, is one approach (assuming that the database is small enough to fit). Again, redundant copies are probably a good idea. Making a printed copy is another way to protect such data (provided it is in ASCII form).

- System log files—from su, the syslog facility, the auditing subsystem, and so on—also need restrictive permissions online and frequent backing up. Redundant copies are also a possibility here. For example, you can log syslog messages locally and to a secure remote system, and both trails would need to be altered for a cracker to hide an action. Important log files can also be printed out on a regular basis or in real time; those ancient hardcopy system consoles had their uses.

You'll need to be careful about storing these backup copies. Remember that threats don't always come from outsiders.

---

* On some systems, you need to execute a few commands to force the auditing records out to disk; ls -l a few times will usually do the trick.

CHAPTER 8
Managing Network Services

Users have come to expect and rely on a variety of network services: logging in to a remote system, accessing files stored on a remote system, seeing information from various websites, and so on. High level network operations typically use a hostname to specify a network location, an easy and convenient practice for users. Accordingly, at the most basic level, network operations depend on two essential abilities: translating a hostname to an IP address and determining the route to a desired remote destination.

For this reason, configuring and managing services that handle name resolution and routing will take up a large part of this chapter. After considering these topics in detail, we will also consider other important network services, including DHCP, which is responsible for assigning IP addresses, and the service that synchronizes the current time on the various systems within a network. The final section of the chapter will consider software and techniques for monitoring network status over time.

 inetd is another important network service. It controls many application-specific services (such as ftp and telnet). It is discussed in "Network Security" in Chapter 7 in conjunction with the TCP Wrappers package, because its configuration has a large potential effect on system security.

Managing DNS Servers

The Domain Name System (DNS) is the facility that provides name resolution services.* This service consists of two distinct activities: the actual hostname-to-IP address

---

* Actually, to be rigorously technically correct, DNS is the specification for name resolution services. On Unix systems, the actual implementation is called the Berkeley Internet Name Domain (BIND). Other systems, such as Windows NT and its successors, call the implementation DNS as well, conflating this distinction. Unix parlance also frequently uses the designation "DNS" for both the specification and the implementation, as I've done in the text above.

translation process and distribution mechanisms for the underlying translation data. Structurally, DNS is a distributed database whose contents are spread across the entire Internet, with individual DNS servers permanently storing only the subset of data for which they are responsible. Queries into this massively distributed database work because DNS has the ability to forward translation requests to the appropriate server automatically, in a manner that scales extremely well. The total amount of DNS data is also referred to as the DNS *namespace*.

The DNS organizational structure defines the domain name hierarchy familiar to most Internet users (see Figure 8-1). Domain names are arranged within a tree structure rooted at the *root domain*, which is designated by a single dot: ".". Underneath the root domain are a series of *top-level domains* (TLDs) whose names take one of two forms: generic suffixes loosely indicating organization type (gTLDs) or two-character country codes (ccTLDs). The currently defined generic TLDs are summarized in Table 8-1 (see *http://www.icann.org/tlds/* for up-to-the-minute information).

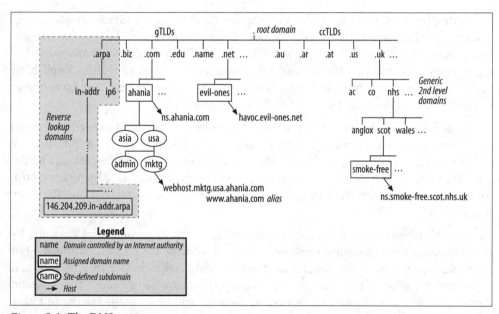

Figure 8-1. The DNS namespace

Table 8-1. Generic TLDs

gTLD	Current use
.com	Commercial entity (used by companies worldwide)
.edu	Degree-granting U.S. higher education institutions (i.e., accredited colleges and universities)
.org	Originally intended for noncommercial entities, but now used generically
.net	Originally intended for Internet infrastructure related organizations (e.g., ISPs), but now used generically
.gov	U.S. government entity

Table 8-1. Generic TLDs (continued)

gTLD	Current use
.mil	U.S. military
.int	"International": organizations established by treaties between nations (e.g., NATO)
.biz	Businesses
.info	"Informational": generic
.name	Individuals
.aero	Air transport industry.
.coop	Cooperative associations/organizations (see *http://www.coop.org* for definitions and more information)
.museum	Museums
.pro	"Professionals": e.g., physicians, attorneys; not yet active as of this writing (early 2002)
.arpa	TLD for *reverse lookup domains* (perform IP address-to-hostname translation); site-specific reverse lookup domains are subdomains of *in-addr.arpa*

Examples of country code TLDs include *.us* (USA),* *.uk* (United Kingdom), *.jp* (Japan), *.fr* (France), *.it* (Italy), *.de* (Germany), *.at* (Austria), *.es* (Spain), *.ar* (Argentina), *.mx* (Mexico), *.fi* (Finland), *.cn* (China), *.pl* (Poland) and *.au* (Australia). As these examples indicate, the country code can derive from either the English or native-language country name (e.g., Japan/*.jp* versus España/*.es*). See *http://www.iana.org/cctld/cctld-whois.htm* for a full list of country code TLDs.

Some of these TLDs are further subdivided before organization-specific domain names are assigned, creating generic second-level domains.† For example, the *.uk* ccTLD includes the *co.uk*, *ac.uk* and *nhs.uk* subdomains for commercial, academic, and National Health Service organizations, respectively (as well as many others; *http://www.ilrt.bris.ac.uk/people/cmdjb/projects/uksites/uk-domains.html* has all the gory details).

Consult *http://www.alldomains.com/alltlds.html* for a list of second-level domains by country code. These domains are sometimes subdivided by the national authority. For example, *scot.nhs.uk* is the domain for the National Health Service in Scotland, and organizations within it are assigned fourth-level domain names (e.g., the Scotland Anti-Smoking Council—a fictitious organization—might be *smoke-free.scot.nhs.uk*).

To obtain your own domain, you must register with the proper authority for the TLD in which you want your domain to be located. See the following websites for lists of accredited registrars:

---

* Formerly reserved for state, regional, local, primary and secondary educational and other public entities, second-level *.us* subdomains are now available to U.S. citizens and U.S.-based organizations.

† You can also say that *co.uk* and the others are subdomains of the TLD *.uk*. In fact, all domains are subdomains, because even TLDs are subdomains of the root domain.

---

gTLDs

    http://www.icann.org/registrars/accredited-list.html

ccTLDs

    Follow the "URL for registration services" link on the appropriate *http://www. iana.org/root-whois/cc.htm* page (where *cc* is the country code). Note that some countries also have other registrars, but you'll probably have to do a web search to find them.

.us subdomains

    http://www.nic.us

Once an organization has obtained a domain name, it can subdivide it further if that makes sense. For example, as illustrated in Figure 8-1, *ahania.com* is divided into two subdomains organized by geographical location, and the *usa.ahania.com* subdomain is subdivided based on organizational function. Each level of a domain can contain both host records and subdomains.

If you follow a branch of the domain tree long enough, you will eventually reach actual hosts. In Figure 8-1, the hosts *ns.smoke-free.scot.nhs.uk* and *webhost.mktg.usa. ahania.com* both reside in fourth-level domains within the overall tree. However, the former is located at the top level of its specific domain, *smoke-free.scot.nhs.uk*, while the latter is within a third-level subdomain of *ahania.com*. Structurally, *havoc.evil-ones.net* is similar to *ns.smoke-free.scot.nhs.uk* in that it also is located at the top of its domain, *evil-ones.com*. We will consider other items within this illustration at various points within this section.

About Domain Names

Domain names are not case-sensitive. Each subdomain component is limited to 63 characters. A fully qualified hostname is limited to 255 characters. Second-level domain names are recommended to be 12 characters or less. Name characters are limited to letters, numbers, and hyphens. The first and last characters cannot be hyphens. Everybody prefers shorter names to longer ones (less typing).

DNS implementations, including the Unix Berkeley Internet Name Domain (BIND), include the following components:

The resolver

    A subroutine library used by commands and user programs (specifically, *gethostbyname* and its relatives). We discussed resolver configuration in "Adding a New Network Host" in Chapter 5.

The name server

    On Unix systems, this is the daemon *named*. This server is configured via a collection of ASCII configuration files. (The daemon's name is pronounced "name-D.")

Zones

Name servers provide name resolution services for a DNS *zone*. A zone is the name given to the collection of hosts within a domain, excluding any subdomains. For example, in Figure 8-1, the *ahania.com* zone consists of all the hosts within *ahania.com* itself, but not those within any of its subdomains or their children. If each subdomain has its own authoritative name server (defined below), the *ahania.com* domain would contain five (forward) zones: *ahania.com*, *usa.ahania.com*, *asia.ahania.com*, *admin.usa.ahania.com*, and *mktg.usa.ahania.com*.

Some zone files hold records that map hostnames to IP address and are used for DNS queries. Others define *reverse lookup* zones and are used to perform the opposite query: mapping an IP address to a host name. Reverse lookup zones are assigned names of the form *c.b.a.in-addr.arpa* where *c*, *b*, and *a* are the third, second, and first components of local network address, respectively. For example, *10.168.192.in-addr.arpa* is the reverse lookup zone for the 192.168.10 subnet. The order of numbers within the network address is reversed in the reverse lookup zone name. The first component, *c*, is omitted when it is not used for the network part of IP addresses: e.g., *1.10.in-addr.arpa* is the reverse lookup zone for the 10.1 subnet.

Every forward zone has at least one corresponding reverse lookup zone. Thus, the *ahania.com* domain in Figure 8-1 would also contain five reverse lookup zones (although their names are not evident from the illustration). The figure does include one reverse lookup zone for illustrative purposes.

Name Server Types

Name servers can operate in many different ways:

- They can perform *recursive* or *nonrecursive* searches in response to queries. Suppose server *tom* has the answer to a query, but you ask server *bill* (who doesn't know the answer). In a recursive query, *bill* will ask *tom* for you and then return the answer to you. In a nonrecursive query, *bill* will reply that he doesn't know and tell you to ask *tom* next. Most Unix clients expect name servers to perform recursive queries, and this is their default mode.

- They can return *authoritative* or *nonauthoritative* answers to a query. Authoritative answers are returned by servers that are designated as the holders of a specific set of data (see below). Nonauthoritative responses come from servers that happen to know the required information as a result of a prior query. Name servers generally retain information they have learned in their *cache* for a period of time (after which it is discarded). The cache is also reinitialized every time the server is restarted. In the BIND versions we are considering, negative query responses are also cached, meaning the name server keeps track of names that it could not resolve and does not try again until the data expires from the cache. The cache timeout values are determined by the server that provided the original information.

- Authoritative servers come in several varieties:

  — *Master name servers* hold the official copy of the DNS data records for a zone. This data is stored in configuration files. Previously, master name servers were called *primary name servers*, and you may also see the term *primary master name server* from time to time.

  — *Slave name servers*, which are also authoritative with respect to the data for their zone. These servers obtain the DNS data records from the zone's master servers. Slave name servers were formerly called *secondary name servers*.

  — *Stub name servers* function like slave name servers, but limit their data to the records corresponding systems that are to name servers.* In other words, ordinary host records are excluded. These name servers are used to make it easy to update the pointers in a parent zone when the name servers in one of its subdomains change.

  — *Distribution name servers* are name servers (usually slave or stub) whose existence is not publicized beyond the local domain. For this reason, they are sometimes called *stealth name servers*. These servers are not really invisible, however. Anyone who knows their IP address can send queries to them.

  Stealth servers can also be created inadvertently when a subdomain's parent name server is not configured correctly. If the parent name server has the wrong server listed as the subdomain's name server, then the real name server for the subdomain won't be able to be found by anyone (since the parent zone's name server will give out the wrong address).

- Servers that hold no official DNS records for any zone are known as *caching-only name servers*, referring to the fact that they retain all information that they learn within their cache (at least for a time).

- *Forwarders* are name servers that have been designated as the target for queries outside the local domain (i.e., off site queries). When a name server is configured to use a forwarder, it always sends queries for hosts it doesn't recognize to the forwarder. If the forwarder cannot provide the answer, the name server will then attempt to determine the answer itself by contacting other name servers that it knows about.

  If a name server is configured to rely completely on designated forwarders, it is known as a *forward-only name server*. In this case, if the forwarder does not return the answer, the query will simply fail.

  The idea behind forwarders is two-fold: to channel most queries into a few designated servers and thereby reduce the load on the other DNS servers. Typically, the requests that get forwarded are addresses beyond the local domain, so local name resolution performance is never impacted by remote operations.

---

* Specifically, they hold only the SOA record, the NS records, and the A records corresponding to the hosts listed in the NS records.

The second advantage of forwarders is that over time they build up a cache with a large amount of data from the remote queries. By having forwarders perform all of these queries, all this data is in one place, and having all remote queries check this server first allows them to take maximum advantage of the results of previous queries (which increases the chances that a desired address will already be known). Contrast this to the situation in which each DNS server performs every query it receives; in this case, the results of previous queries for remote sites will be scattered across the entire local network, and the chances that queries will be unnecessarily repeated are much greater.

We will consider each of the various types of name servers in detail later in this section.

About BIND

The first version of what was to become BIND was written in 1984, and many versions have been released in the years since then. Currently, BIND maintenance and development is handled by the Internet Software Consortium, and you can obtain the current source code from them (*http://www.isc.org/products/BIND/*). As of this writing, the latest version is BIND 9.2.1 (released in May, 2002).

Unfortunately, at the moment, there are three major BIND versions in actual use: BIND 4, BIND 8, and BIND 9 (which, despite the numbering, are consecutive major releases). Vendors are very slow to upgrade their supplied versions of BIND, and BIND security patches are released much more frequently than operating system updates. Table 8-2 lists the versions of BIND shipped with our reference operating systems. Shaded rows indicate releases with significant known security holes that should be upgraded. Note that in some cases more recent versions are available for download from the vendor web site.

Table 8-2. Recommended versus vendor-supplied BIND versions

Environment	Version
ISC recommendations	BIND 4: 4.9.8 (minimum level)
	BIND 8: 8.2.5 (minimum level); 8.3.1 (current revision)
	BIND 9: 9.2.1 (current revision)
AIX 5.1	4.9.3
FreeBSD 4.6	8.3.2
HP-UX 11	4.9.7
HP-UX 11i	9.2.0
Linux:Red Hat 7	9.1.3 or 9.2.0
SuSE 7 or 8	9.1.3

Table 8-2. Recommended versus vendor-supplied BIND versions (continued)

Environment	Version
Solaris 8	8.1.2
Solaris 9	8.2.4
Tru64 5.1	8.2.2-P5 plus security patches

You can determine the BIND version running on a system by checking the system messages file produced by syslog (for the daemon facility) and also with the dig utility (discussed later in this section). If no name server has been configured, you can still find out what version your system includes by starting named manually; it generally starts, reports its version and other information, and then exits when it finds no valid configuration files.

In many cases, the version of BIND shipped by a vendor was the latest available at the time the operating system was released. Security problems with that version were discovered after the release date. As the table indicates, several operating system versions of BIND should be updated from the delivered version (updates are sometimes available at the vendor website).

In the case of AIX and HP-UX 11, the release is so old that I recommend replacing it altogether, with BIND 9 if possible.*

Replacing Vendor-Supplied Software

Some system administrators are hesitant to make major substitutions to the software provided with their systems. Vendors usually discourage you from replacing any part of the operating system that they supply. In fact, they often will not support things if you do so. This reason, along with simple common sense, means that replacing the standard software with something else is not something that you should do lightly.

Nevertheless, there are times when doing so is the best choice, despite these considerations: when the vendor-provided software has security problems, is missing important features that your site needs, or fails to interoperate with related facilities on other systems (it doesn't "play nice"). In these cases, installing better software is the right move. Even so, I install only fully released and tested software on production systems (beta software goes only on my test systems).

Finally, prudence suggests that if you do decide to replace a package, be sure to save all of the components of the original installed version in case you need to rollback.

---

* Some HP-UX versions are incompatible with vanilla BIND 9 and must use BIND 8; see the ISC web site for details. However, you can download HP's port of BIND 9 from *http://www.software.hp.com/cgi-bin/ swdepot_parser.cgi/cgi/displayProductInfo.pl?productNumber=BIND9.2.*

There are significant differences among BIND versions. Table 8-3 summarizes them; most of the features themselves are discussed in the course of this section (although DNS performance is covered in "Network Performance" in Chapter 15).

Table 8-3. Comparing important BIND versions

Feature	BIND 4.9.3[a]	BIND 8.1.2	BIND 9.1.0 and later
Access control	kludge	yes	yes
DNS Security Extensions	no	some	yes
Dynamic updates	no	yes	yes
Forwarding	yes	yes	yes
Forward zones	no	no[b]	yes
Incremental zone transfers	no	no[b]	yes
IPv6 support	no	yes	yes
Multiprocessing (threads)	no	no	yes
Recursion can be disabled	yes	yes	yes
Round robin load balancing	yes	yes	yes
Update notifications	no	yes	yes
Views	no	no	yes

[a] Some features marked "no" were present in experimental form.
[b] Added in BIND 8.2.

We will consider only BIND 8 and 9 in the remainder of our discussion, and the appellation "BIND 8" will refer to BIND 8.2.0 and later versions. BIND 8–specific items will be marked with a ❽; BIND 9 with a ❾.

Configuring named

The named server uses several configuration files. We'll begin by looking at the full list briefly and then go on to consider example configurations for several real-world scenarios. For more information about DNS and BIND, including full details about the various configuration files, consult Paul Albitz and Cricket Liu's excellent book, *DNS and BIND* (O'Reilly & Associates).

 DNS configuration files are prime examples of configuration files that can benefit from a revision control system. These files are very important and also have a somewhat obscure syntax. A revision control system like CVS or RCS not only automatically tracks modifications to these files but also makes it easy to revert to a working version should one of the configuration files become messed up by typos or other errors.

Table 8-4 lists the locations of BIND components on the various operating systems.

Table 8-4. BIND component locations

Component	Location[a]
named main configuration file	**Usual/ISC:** */etc/named.conf* **FreeBSD:** */etc/namedb/named.conf*
named executable	**Usual/ISC:** */usr/sbin/named* **Solaris:** */usr/sbin/in.named* **Tru64:** */sbin/named*
Directory provided for named files	**Usual/ISC:** none **FreeBSD:** */etc/namedb* **Tru64:** */etc/namedb*
Default hints file name	**Usual/ISC:** not specified **FreeBSD:** *named.root* **Linux:** *root.hint*
Boot script that starts named	**Usual/ISC:** */etc/init.d/named* **FreeBSD:** */etc/rc.network* **Solaris:** */etc/init.d/inetsvc* **Tru64:** */sbin/init.d/named*
Boot script configuration file: named-related entries	**ISC:** none **FreeBSD:** */etc/rc.conf* and/or */etc/rc.conf.local*: *named_enable="YES"*, *named_flags="named-args"* **Red Hat:** */etc/sysconfig/named*: *ROOTDIR=dir-for-chroot*; *OPTIONS="named-args"* (don't use -t) **SuSE 7:** */etc/rc.config*: *START_NAMED="yes"* **Solaris:** none used **Tru64:** */etc/rc.config*: *BIND_CONF="YES"*; *BIND_SERVERARGS="named-args"*; *BIND_SERVERTYPE="keyword"*

a AIX and HP-UX are excluded from this table as they provide only BIND 4. In general, the current version of BIND 9 from the ISC is recommended for these systems

The master configuration file: named.conf

The file */etc/named.conf* is the main configuration file for named.[*] It specifies the type of name server that will be run and all of its operating characteristics. Entries in this file have the following general syntax:

```
keyword [argument] {
/* This is a comment */
   item;   // comment
   item;   # another comment
   ...
};
```

---

* Under BIND 4, this file is */etc/named.boot* and it is usually referred to as the *boot file*. The file also has a very different syntax. Note in particular that semicolons no longer mark comments in the new version but instead serve an essential syntactic role within entries.

Note that the keyword section and each item within it must be terminated by a semicolon. As the example illustrates, there are three different valid comment styles. The first, C-style format (/* comment */) can span multiple lines. In addition, statements can continue onto multiple lines without any special demarcation because they are always terminated by a semicolon.

Here is a simple version of the *named.conf* file which illustrates its basic features:

```
options {                              Set global options.
    directory "/var/named";            Directory for other configuration files.
    pid-file "/var/run/named";         Hold the PID of the named process.
};

zone "." {                             Defines zone for the root servers cache.
    type hint;                         Zone type.
    file "named.cache";                File that contains the data records.
};

zone "0.0.127.in-addr.arpa" {          Reverse lookup zone for loopback address.
    type master;                       This is the master server for this zone.
    file "localhost.rev";              File that contains the data record.
    notify no;                         Don't notify slave servers of updates.
};
```

There are three statements within this file. The first one, options, sets global options for this server. In this case, we specify the directory where the remaining configuration files are located and a pathname for the file holding the PID of the named process.

The remaining two statements define zones and their characteristics. The zone name follows the keyword, and the type option in each statement indicates the sort of zone it is. In this example, the first zone statement corresponds to the root domain, and its type is the special type hint. Such zone entries are used to indicate the location of the root hints file, which contains the addresses of the root zone name servers (discussed in the next subsection). Here, the file is specified as */var/named/named.cache*.

The second zone statement defines a zone named *0.0.127.in-addr.arpa*, for which this host is the master name server. This zone is a reverse lookup zone. It is used to map an IP address to a hostname. In this case, its data file will map 127.0.0.1 to *localhost*. The data records for this zone are stored in the file */var/named/localhost. rev*. Zone files are discussed in detail later in this section.

Entries like these two will be present in every *named.conf* file. In fact, the version shown is sufficient for configuring a caching-only name server.

Here are simple zone statements that define a master name server:

```
zone "ahania.com" {
    type master;
    file "ahania.com.db";              Zone file name.
};
```

```
zone "10.168.192.in-addr.arpa" {
   type master;
   file "192.168.10.rev";              Reverse zone file name.
};
```

These two statements are quite similar to the ones we've seen already. They designate this server as a master name server for the *ahania.com* and *10.168.192.in-addr.*
arpa zones, the forward and reverse zones for the same set of hosts. The file option in
each statement specifies the location of the zone file holding the DNS data records
(relative to the default directory). Note that the full *named.conf* file will also contain
an options statement and zone statements for the root hints file and the loopback
reverse lookup zone like those we examined previously.

A slave server is equally easy to configure in its most basic form. It includes a zone
statement like these in addition to the options statement and root hints file and loopback reverse lookup zone definitions:

```
zone "ahania.com" {
   type slave;
   masters { 192.168.10.1; };   # maximum = 10 masters
   file "back/ahania.com.bak";  # make backup file easy to find
};
zone "10.168.192.in-addr.arpa" {
   type slave;
   masters { 192.168.10.1; };
   file "back/192.168.10.bak";
};
```

In these zone statements, the name server type is now slave. The masters statement
takes a list of master name server IP addresses from which this slave should obtain
the zone data. Multiple servers are contacted in the order in which they are listed,
until an answer is received.

If a file option is included, that file is used as a local backup file for the zone data. It
is updated every time the slave name server gets new data from a master name server
and is loaded when the server starts up. When this happens, the slave name server
simply checks to see whether the master name server has more recent data, downloading it only if necessary and thereby providing faster server startup.

A given name server can be a master server for more than one zone and can also be a
master server for some zones and a slave server for others.

 Store up-to-date copies of the zone files on slave servers in a separate
directory. That way, it will be easy to promote a slave name server to a
master name server in a hurry.

Table 8-5 lists the most important statements and options that can appear in the
named configuration file.

Table 8-5. *Important named.conf statements and options*

Statement and purpose	
Basic syntax	**Meaning of option**

options: define global options applying to all zones which do not override them.

```
options {
    [allow-query { list; };]
    [allow-transfer { list; };]
    [allow-notify { list; };]
    [also-notify { list; };]
    [blackhole { list; };]
    [directory "path";]
    [forward only|first;]
    [forwarders { list; };]
    [maintain-ixfr-base yes|no;]❽
    [notify yes|no|explicit❾;]
    [provide-ixfr yes|no;]❾
    [pid-file "name";]
    [request-xfer yes|no;]
    [other-options]
};
```

	Accept queries only from these servers.
	Send zone transfers only to these servers.
	Valid sources for update notifications.
	Send update notices to all slaves plus these.
	Completely ignore these hosts.
	Default directory for relative pathnames.
	Use forwarding exclusively/first.
	Server to which to forward external queries.
	Maintain data for incr. zone transfers.
	Send update notices (explicit=only to list).
	Send incremental zone transfers.
	Path to file holding named process's PID.
	Request incremental zone transfers.

zone: define a zone and its characteristics.

```
zone "name" {
    type keyword;
    [file "path";]
    [masters { list; };]
    [allow-query { list; };]
    [allow-transfer { list; };]
    [allow-update { list; };]
    [allow-update-forwarding { list; };]❾
    [also-notify { list; };]
    [forward only|first;]
    [forwarders { list; };]
    [notify yes|no|explicit❾;]
    [update-policy { rule-list; };]❾
    [other-options]
};
```

	Server type: master, slave, stub, forward, etc.
	Pathname to zone file.
	List of master name server.
	Accept queries only from these servers.
	Send zone transfers only to these servers.
	Valid sources for dynamic updates.
	Valid sources for updates to send to master.
	Send update notices to all slaves plus these.
	Use forwarding exclusively/first.
	Server to which to forward external queries.
	Send update notices (explicit=only to list).
	Specify who can dynamically update what.
	Rules syntax:
	`grant|deny who-key what where [types];`

logging: specify logging behavior.

```
logging {
    channel name {
        syslog facility;
        [severity level;]
    | file "path";
    | null;
    };
    [channel ...]
    [category keywords { channel-list; };]
    [category default { channel-list; };]
};
```

	Define log target.
	Send messages to this syslog facility.
	Specify syslog severity level.
	Send messages to this file.
	Discard messages.
	Send specific types of log data to channel(s).
	Send default message set to channel(s).

server: define how to communicate with a specific name server.

```
server ip-address {
    [provide-ixfr yes|no;]❾
    [request-ixfr yes|no;]❾
    [support-ixfr yes|no;]❽
    [keys { key; };]
};
```

	Provide IXFR to this server.
	Request IXFR from this server.
	This server supports incr. zone transfers.
	Specify TSIG key to use with this server.

Table 8-5. Important named.conf statements and options (continued)

Statement and purpose	
Basic syntax	Meaning of option
acl: define an IP address match list.	
| ```
acl "name" {
  [!] match-string; ... [!] match-string;
};
``` | *Each match string can be an IP or network address or the name of another address list. ! = do not match.* |
| **key**: defines a key (shared secret security). | |
| ```
key "name" {
  algorithm hmac-md5;
  secret "encoded-key";
};
``` | *This is the only supported algorithm. Encode the key using dnskeygen❽ or dnssec-keygen❾.* |
| **view**: defines a BIND 9 view. | |
| ```
view "name" {❾
  match-clients { list; };
  zone "zone-name" { ... };
  [zone ...]
  [other-options]
};
``` | *Hosts that access zone through this view. Zone(s) as defined in this view. Other options to apply to this view.* |
| **controls**: specifies **ndc/rndc** server access. | |
| ```
controls {❾
  inet addr allow { hosts; } keys { keys; };
};
``` | *Allow listed hosts to manage this name server with rndc via specified address (port is optional), using cryptographic keys.* |
| **include**: inserts the contents of an external file. | |
| `include "path";` | *BIND's include file mechanism.* |

We will see examples of most of these statements when we consider the various BIND features. Before we do that, however, we will complete the BIND big picture by looking at the other configuration files.

The root hints file

In addition to any data records for the zones they serve, all name servers also need to have information about the DNS root domain to resolve hostnames beyond the local domain (because a query for a remote site may need to be forwarded there). As we saw, the *named.conf* file contains a zone definition for the root zone having zone type hints. The file specified in this statement is known as the *root hints file*. It contains the IP addresses of the name servers for the root domain. You can select any name you like for this file. Commonly used names are *named.root*, *db.cache* and *root.hint*.

The root hints file has the same form and contents on every DNS name server (at least it should). You can obtain the standard file by retrieving the file */domain/named.root* from *ftp.rs.internic.net* using anonymous FTP.

Here is part of the current version of the file, with additional annotations:

```
; Name server definitions
;Zone           TTL     Class Type  Host
.               3600000  IN     NS    A.ROOT-SERVERS.NET.
```

```
                            3600000  IN    NS    B.ROOT-SERVERS.NET.
;
; Map the hostnames to IP addresses
;Host                    TTL     Class Type  IP Address
A.ROOT-SERVERS.NET.      3600000  IN    A    198.41.0.4
B.ROOT-SERVERS.NET.      3600000  IN    A    128.9.0.107
```

This excerpt defines two name servers for the root zone in its first two entries on lines 3 and 4, after the comments (which are indicated by semicolons). The fields in these two entries hold the zone name, the cache lifetime (time-to-live, or TTL) for this record on remote servers (in seconds), the class (virtually always set to IN for Internet), the record type (here, NS for name server), and the name server hostname.

The final two lines of the file specify the IP addresses corresponding to these name servers. These fields in these entries hold the hostname, the cache TTL, the class, the record type (A for address), and finally the IP address assigned to this host.

The format of the records in this file are the same as those for any DNS zone file. We will discuss their format in detail in the next section. The records in the root hints file are loaded into the name server when it starts, and the file is not consulted thereafter. You will need to obtain the current version of this file from time to time (a few times a year).

Zone files

Zone files hold the actual DNS data records for master name servers. This data is loaded when the server starts up. Entries within a zone file are known as *DNS resource records*, and they have the following general syntax:

```
entity-name [ttl] IN record-type data
```

entity-name is the item that is being defined or specified, *ttl* is an optional time-to-live value (cache lifetime in seconds), IN is the class (Internet), *record-type* is a code string indicating the kind of record this is, and *data* is the value, mapping, or other data being associated with this entity.

Table 8-6 lists the most important types of DNS resource records, along with their basic zone file syntax. We've omitted the optional TTL field in the table.

Table 8-6. Important DNS resource record types

Type and Purpose	Basic Syntax
SOA: Start of authority record, specifying basic parameters for this zone	`@ IN SOA` *hostname admin* `(`
	`s    ;` *serial number (32-bit)*
	`time ;` *slave update check interval*
	`time ;` *failed update retry interval*
time syntax: *n*[s|m|h|d|w]	`time ;` *discard timeout if master is down*
	`time ;` *TTL for negative replies❾ or cached data❽*
	`)`
NS: Name server definition	*zone* `IN NS` *server-hostname*
A: Hostname-to-IP address mapping	*hostname* `IN A` *IP-address*

Table 8-6. Important DNS resource record types (continued)

Type and Purpose	Basic Syntax
CNAME: Host alias definition	*alias* IN CNAME *hostname*
MX: Designate a mail server for a host	*hostname* IN MX *priority mail-server*
PTR: IP address-to-hostname mapping	*host-part-of-address* IN PTR *hostname*
SRV: Advertise an available service	*_service._proto.domain* IN SRV *priority weight port host*
AAAA: IPv6 hostname-to-address mapping	*hostname* IN AAAA *IPv6-address*

There are also a few directives which may be used in a zone file:

```
$TTL time                        Default TTL for cached address mappings.
$ORIGIN domain                   Specify/change default domain context.
$GENERATE range record-template  Automatically generate resource records.
$INCLUDE path                    Insert external file's contents.
```

An initial $TTL directive is required by BIND 9. Its argument is a time period expressed either as a plain number (interpreted as seconds) or as a number followed by a units code letter: s (seconds), m (minutes), h (hours), d (days), or w (weeks). These same code letters can be used in the TTL field of other resource records and within the appropriate start of authority record fields.

We'll now examine excerpts from a forward zone file, which illustrate many of these resource types. Here is the beginning of the file:

```
$TTL 24h                                 Lifetime for cached mappings.
@ SOA IN ns.ahania.com. chavez.dalton.ahania.com. (
    200204010 ; serial                   Indicates the zone file version.
          5h ; refresh (5 hrs)           Slaves check for updates this often.
        1200 ; retry (20 mins)           Retry a failed update after this long.
          4w ; expire (28 days)          Discard zone data if master down this long.
        3600 ; minimum (1 hour)          Cache lifetime for negative answers.
    )
```

The zone file begins with a $TTL directive setting the default timeout period for cached mappings to two hours.

Next comes the SOA record. This one continues over several lines, indicated by the parentheses. The first line specifies the zone (the @ symbol is shorthand for the zone specified in the corresponding zone statement in *named.conf*), record type and class (SOA and IN), the zone's master name server (usually the current host), and the administrative contact's email address. The zone statement referencing this file defines the *ahania.com* zone.

Notice that the latter two fields use a variant of the normal syntax. First, both end with a dot. In DNS resource records, absolute host and domain names end with a dot (which represents the root domain). Names not ending with a dot are assumed to be relative to the current zone. Leaving off a dot when it is needed is the most common error made by beginners, and doing so will cause queries for these names to fail. Secondly, the @ sign usually present in an email address is replaced by a period.

The remaining fields in the SOA record specify various timeout periods. Most of them apply to slave servers for this zone. Their meanings are described in the annotations. However, a few additional points are in order:

- The serial number field should be incremented each time the zone file is modified. It is used by slave servers to determine whether their data is current. Serial numbers need not be consecutive but must always increase. (This is an unsigned 32-bit value.)

  A common practice is to use serial numbers of the form *yyyymmddn* (e.g., 200210243). This allows for up to 10 changes per day, and you can use two *n* digits if you need more than that (and you have my sympathy).

- The final field has different meanings in BIND 8 and BIND 9. In the former, it sets the default record TTL value for both positive and negative query responses. In version 8.2 and higher, it sets only the latter. The default TTL value is set with $TTL in those versions.

- Timeout period recommendations:
  — Refresh periods are generally a few hours, but a shorter or longer period may be appropriate, depending on the volatility of your site (I decrease this value to two hours if DHCP is also used).

  — The data expiration period is typically set to one or two weeks.

  — One to three hours is a good range for the negative query cache lifetime (the latter is the maximum). Positive cache lifetimes tend to be longer; I use one day on my systems.

  — The best retry interval is highly dependent on what tends to cause server outages and how long they tend to last. I chose the value of 20 minutes because that's a good value when a system has crashed due to a power outage caused by an electrical storm, my prime nemesis when it comes to system uptime.

Here is the next section of the file:

```
; Define name servers for this zone.
ahania.com.             IN  NS   ns.ahania.com.
ahania.com.             IN  NS   lyta.ahania.com.

; Specify some name-to-IP address mappings.
ns.ahania.com.          IN  A    192.168.10.1
lyta.ahania.com.        IN  A    192.168.10.10
talia                   IN  A    192.168.10.12
```

The first two records define authoritative name servers for the specified zone, *ahania. com*. The records do not distinguish between master and slave servers; that is done in *named.conf*. Generally, all authoritative name servers for the current zone and all of its subdomains (child zones) are included in the zone file. We'll see examples of the latter further on in this section.

The second section in the preceding zone file excerpt defines three hostname-to-IP address mappings for hosts in this zone. The third entry, for host *talia*, illustrates the use of a relative hostname (without a final dot).

The following records illustrate some zone file shortcut features, as well as several other record types:

```
; Some records for host susan.
susan.ahania.com.      IN  A      192.168.10.11
                       IN  MX     10 susan.ahania.com.
www.ahania.com         IN  CNAME  susan.ahania.com.

; Advertise the FTP service.
_ftp._tcp.ahania.com.   IN  SRV   10 0 21 lyta.ahania.com.
_finger._tcp.ahania.com. IN SRV    0 0 79 .   ; none available
```

The first three records all apply to host *susan*. Because the first field in each of the first two lines is the same, it can be omitted from the second one. The first record is an A record that specifies *susan*'s IP address.

The second record for host *susan* is an MX ("mail exchanger") record. This type of record specifies the host to which mail addressed to *anyone@susan.ahania.com* should be delivered. In this case, it is host *susan* itself. MX records are discussed in detail in "About Electronic Mail" in Chapter 9.

The third line holds a CNAME record that defines an alternate name for host *susan* (more precisely, it maps an alias to the host's *canonical name*). It defines *www.ahania.com* as an alias for *susan.ahania.com*, and queries for the alias will return the IP address that is associated with *susan*.

The final two records in the preceding example are SRV ("server selection") records. This record type is used to advertise the availability of a specific network service within a specified domain.[*] These records are just beginning to be used in the Unix world, but Windows 2000 and its successors make extensive use of them. The first field in the record holds the encoded service specification (*_service._tcp-or-udp.domain*), and the final four fields hold the server's priority (used to select among multiple available servers), weighting value (used to perform primitive load balancing among servers of equal priority), the port number, and the host offering the service. SRV records are described in detail in *DNS and BIND*.

The first SRV record indicates that *lyta* offers the FTP service for the *ahania.com* domain, using the standard FTP port (21/tcp). The second SRV record uses a dot as the server host name, and it will result in negative responses to general DNS queries attempting to locate a finger service in this domain. Service names are those defined in */etc/services*, and the protocol is always _tcp or _udp.

---

[*] Previously, advertising such services relied on defining generic hostnames like *ftp.ahania.com*.

Common Mistakes

Beginning DNS administrators often make these two mistakes: forgetting to update the serial number after editing a zone file and forgetting to include final periods when specifying absolute host names. The first mistake results in secondary servers not being updated when they should be, and the second mistake results in the definition of names like *something.ahania.com.ahania.com*.

Reverse zone files and PTR records. Reverse zone files are very similar to the zone files we've just looked at. For example, here is a file that can be used for the *0.0.127.in-addr.arpa* zone hosted by every name server:

```
$TTL 4w
@ IN SOA ns.ahania.com. chavez.dalton.ahania.com. (
   ...Usual items.
     )

1    IN PTR localhost.
```

Following the SOA record, this file's sole record maps the host address 1 to the hostname *localhost*. The host address is added to the network address specified in the zone name, so this PTR ("pointer") record maps 127.0.0.1 to *localhost*.

Here are the PTR records corresponding to the hosts in the preceding forward zone file for *ahania.com*:

```
1    IN  PTR  ns.ahania.com.
10   IN  PTR  lyta.ahania.com.
11   IN  PTR  susan.ahania.com.
12   IN  PTR  talia.ahania.com.
```

These records would be found in the zone file for the *10.168.192.in-addr.arpa* reverse lookup zone. All of the hostnames are specified in absolute form since the default zone context is the reverse lookup zone (and not the corresponding forward zone).

You can include multiple subnets in the same reverse zone file if appropriate. For example, these records come from the file *168.192.in-addr.arpa*:

```
1.10    IN  PTR  ns.ahania.com.
10.10   IN  PTR  lyta.ahania.com.
11.10   IN  PTR  susan.ahania.com.
12.10   IN  PTR  talia.ahania.com.
1.20    IN  PTR  moonlight.ahania.com.
2.20    IN  PTR  starlight.ahania.com.
```

This file contains PTR records for hosts on the 192.168.10 and 192.168.20 subnets.

IPv6 zone file resource records. The normal A records do not support IPv6 addresses, so an additional resource record type has been defined: AAAA.* Here is an example:

```
six.ahania.com. IN  AAAA  4321:0:1:2:3:4:567:89ab
```

An additional reverse mapping space has been defined for these addresses: *ip6.int*, and it is specified in PTR records for such hosts. Here is the pointer record for the preceding example (wrapped):

```
b.a.9.8.7.6.5.0.4.0.0.0.3.0.0.0.2.0.0.0.1.0.0.0.0.0.0.1.2.3.4.ip6.int. IN PTR six.
ahania.com.
```

Note that all zeros must be included in the reverse address.

Common mistakes to avoid

Here are some mistakes that are commonly made by new DNS administrators that you can avoid:

* Life, and administering DNS, is much easier if you limit hostnames to alphanumeric characters.
* Systems listed in NS records must always use the hosts' actual, fully qualified domain names. Never use a CNAME alias in this context.
* The same point applies to MX records: specify only real, fully qualified domain names as the target hosts.
* Email delivery problems are often caused by improper or missing PTR records for name servers or MX hosts. Be sure that these records exist and that they are correct.
* Do not use wildcards in MX records.

Using subdomains

Defining subdomains is only a bit more complicated than the configuration for single-level domains. Here are the steps for doing so:

* Decide on the subdomain strategy and divisions and assign responsibility to the appropriate administrator(s).
* Create the *named.conf* file and the forward and reverse zone files for the master name servers for the new subdomain.
* Delegate the authority for the new subdomain via NS statements within the parent zone.

---

* Another scheme, using A6 and DNAME resource record types, is also implemented in BIND 9. For a long time, the two schemes competed, and A6 seem likely to win. However, in mid-2002, the proposed standard using them was reclassified to experimental status. As of this writing, the AAAA-based scheme remains a proposed standard. See *http://www.ietf.org/internet-drafts/draft-ietf-dnsext-ipv6-addresses-02.txt* for details.

For example, these resource records define the *asia.ahania.com* subdomain when they appear in the zone file for *ahania.com*:

```
; asia subdomain
asia.ahania.com.        IN  NS   ns.asia.ahania.com.
                        IN  NS   test.asia.ahania.com.
                        IN  NS   atlas.zoas.org.

; glue records
ns.asia.ahania.com.     IN  A    192.168.24.10
test.asia.ahania.com.   IN  A    192.168.24.24
```

The first three records define name servers for the *asia.ahania.com* subdomain, thereby delegating authority for these zones to them. The other two records in the file are normal A records defining the IP addresses of these name servers. These are referred to as *glue records* since they provide the data necessary for the locating the subdomain's name server. Without them, the parent zone's name server would have, for example, no way to resolve the hostname *ns.asia.ahania.com* (it's a chicken and egg problem) and so would not be able to refer or follow queries into the subdomain. Nevertheless, the records are really foreign to the parent zone file. Note that no glue record is needed for the third name server, *atlas.zoas.org*, since its IP address can be determined with a normal DNS query.

Delegating the corresponding reverse lookup zone is simple if the new zone is a distinct subnet and the parent zone is situated one level above it in the hierarchy. In this case, the new zone corresponds to the 192.168.24 subnet. If the *ahania.com* name servers also handle the *168.192.in-addr.arpa* zone, records like these delegate the *24.168.192.in-addr.arpa* zone to the same name servers as for *asia.ahania.com*:

```
; 24.168.192.in-addr.arpa subdomain
24      IN  NS   ns.asia.ahania.com.
24      IN  NS   test.asia.ahania.com.
```

Note that glue records are not needed here, since the name server IP addresses can be determined with an ordinary DNS query.

Reverse zone files with arbitrary subnetting. Standard DNS reverse zone files and PTR records assume that the network-host address separation falls on a byte boundary. If this is not the case, there is a technique to work around this limitation known as the "CNAME hack" (although it has since become official in RFC 2317). It involves creating a series of CNAME records for each numeric host ID along with NS records for the name servers that hold the actual PTR records for each subnet.

For example, suppose our network is 192.168.88.0/27. We have 8 subnets of 30 hosts each. If we want to delegate the PTR records for each subnet to their own name server, we use resource records like these:

```
Zone file for the 192.168.88 domain
$ORIGIN 88.168.192.in-addr.arpa.        Set default domain: append to relative names.
1     IN CNAME  1.sub0                   1.sub0 is an alias for 1.88.168.192.in-addr.arpa
2     IN CNAME  2.sub0
...
```

```
30    IN CNAME   30.sub0
33    IN CNAME   33.sub1
...

sub0 IN NS      ns.zoas.org.              Name servers for the first two subnets.
sub1 IN NS      ns2.essadm.com.
```

Reverse zone file for sub0.88.168.192.in-addr.arpa (on ns.zoas.org)
```
1     IN PTR     spring.zoas.org.
2     IN PTR     charles.zoas.org.
...
30    IN PTR     helen.zoas.org.
```

Reverse zone file for sub1.88.168.192.in-addr.arpa (on ns2.essadm.com)
```
33     IN PTR   monica.essadm.com.
...
```

What happens when the domain's name server receives a translation request for 192. 168.88.2? This is a request for the PTR record corresponding to *2.88.168.192.in-addr.arpa*. The name server recognizes that name and returns the target of the CNAME record, here *2.sub0.88.168.192.in-addr.arpa*, as well as the address of the name server for the corresponding reverse zone, *ns.zoas.org* (we've listed only one, but real files would have at least two per subnet). In this way, a query for an IP address translation is redirected by the CNAME records to the proper name server for the corresponding subnet. When that server is contacted, it can reply with the actual hostname from the PTR record for 192.168.88.2: *spring.zoas.org*.

The effect of this strategy is to insert an additional pseudo-component into the zone structure that can vary by subnet. Here, we've used *sub0*, *sub1*, and so on. In this case, each subnet is actually a different site (as might be common at an ISP).

In actual practice, the subnet component is named after the numeric range of the host part of IP addresses within the subnet. In other words, *sub0* would be 0–31, *sub1* would be 32–63, and so on. In the same way, the resource records applying to host 2 would be:

```
$ORIGIN 88.168.192.in-addr.arpa.
2                               IN  CNAME   2.0-31
2.0-31.88.168.192.in-addr.arpa. IN  NS      ns.zoas.org.
```

As illustrated in the NS record, absolute names are often used in the resource records as well. These sort of names are more descriptive for experienced administrators, but I think the technique is harder to grasp when first presented with names that are this hard to parse.

This technique can produce a very long and tedious zone file. The $GENERATE directive can be used to create the required records quickly, in a single operation. For example, these directives create all of the CNAME records required for the first two subnets in the previous example:

```
$ORIGIN 88.168.192.in-addr.arpa.
$GENERATE 1-30  $ IN CNAME $.0-31
```

```
$GENERATE 33-62 $ IN CNAME $.33-63
0-31  IN NS ns.zoas.org.
32-63 IN NS ns2.essadm.com.
```

The dollar sign within the $GENERATE directive's record template is replaced by each number in the specified range in turn, causing each such directive to create 32 CNAME records.

See *DNS and BIND* for full details on this topic.

Forwarders

So far, we have ignored the nitty gritty details of how DNS queries are performed, but we can do so no longer. When a hostname needs to be resolved to an IP address, a local name server is consulted first. If the local name server does not know its address or the address of a name server in the corresponding domain, the name server consults one of the servers in the root zone. The name server asks the root name server for the address of a name server in the appropriate TLD and then gradually works its way down the domain hierarchy until it arrives at the target domain and obtains the desired IP address.

For example, when trying to resolve *ns.asia.ahania.com* from, say, *four.zoas.org*, the latter host first contacts a local name server. That server may not recognize the target host or even any part of the domain list within the name, so it contacts one of the root name servers. In this case, the local name server may not know *asia.ahania.com* or *ahania.com* or even *.com*, so it has to ask a root name server for help. The root name server provides the local name server with a referral to a name server for *.com*. Things continue in this way, moving down to *ahania.com* and then finally to *asia. ahania.com*, where the desired address is obtained.

When you consider a large, very active site with many connections to foreign sites, it becomes clear that having every name server resolve such hostnames is not the most efficient strategy. For example, clients in two separate subdomains attempting to connect to the same foreign site would both cause their name server to do all the work of resolving the hostname.

Forwarding provides a ways of channeling external name resolution queries through a few designated servers. Doing so has several benefits:

- Identical queries are not repeated during the record's cache lifetime.
- Information gained from one query can be used in others. For example, finding a name server for *.com* needs to be done only once.
- All of the external hostname information can be collected into one or a few locations, making it easily accessible to everyone at the site.
- The load placed on local name servers by queries for remote sites is minimized.

Forwarders are designated by having other name servers point to them rather than via any configuration options on the server itself. For example, the following options configure the server to use designated forwarders for all zones:

```
options
   forwarders { 192.168.10.50; 192.168.24.6; };
   forward first;
};
```

The forwarders option specifies a list of name servers to consult for all external queries that cannot be resolved from its cached translation data. In this example, two name servers are listed. The forward option takes a keyword as its argument. The keyword *first* says that forwarders should be consulted for appropriate external queries (in the order they are listed), but if none of them succeed in resolving the hostname, then the server will attempt to resolve it itself (this is the default). The other possible keyword, *only*, suppresses the server's own name resolution attempt should all of the forwarders fail.

These options may also be specified within a zone statement to limit forwarding to that zone, to define a different forwarders list for that zone, or to specify different forwarding behavior in that zone. In this case, the zone type is usually set to forward:

```
zone "forward.ahania.com" {
   type forward;
   forward only;
   forwarders { 192.168.10.50; 192.168.24.6; };
};
```

Not everyone agrees that using forwarders is always the way to go. One of the book's technical reviewers explains the alternate viewpoint:

> While forwarders do have their place, I personally feel it is much better to limit the number of name servers per physical site. We have two caching-only name servers that service about 90% of our 45K host network. We get really good cache performance because everyone uses them. Giving each network their own name server would just be a waste of resources.

> The one good reason to have forwarders or more caching-only servers is if you have two different physical sites, each with their own ISP link. You don't want to make the usability of one site's link dependent on the other.

Slave name server notifications

As I've already mentioned, slave servers check whether their data needs to be updated whenever they start up. In addition, by default, masters also notify all slave servers they know about whenever the zone data changes, either because the zone file has been edited or due to dynamic updates to its data from DHCP (discussed below). When they receive such DNS notification messages, slave servers compare the master server's serial number with the version they have, retrieving the updated data when appropriate.

Notification is enabled by default, but it can be disabled with the following option to either the options or zone statement:

```
notify no;                              The default is yes.
```

BIND 9 adds a third keyword: explicit. This keyword allows you to limit update notifications to the list of name servers specified in the options statement's allow-notify option. For example:

```
options {
  notify explicit;
  allow-notify { 192.168.10.1; 192.168.20.2; ...; };
};
```

Finally, you can specify additional slave name servers that should be notified of changes with the also-notify substatement, which can be used with either the options or zone statement. This option is needed when there is a slave name server that needs updates but is not listed in an NS record in the zone file, e.g., a slave name server that is only accessible from within the site but needs to receive updates from a name server providing external name resolution of internal names.

Dynamic updates

Using DHCP for client address assignment greatly complicates the original DNS scheme. Traditional servers do not expect hostname mappings to change very often, so the static data files used by traditional DNS are a storage mechanism that works fine. However, when IP addresses are changing on a frequent basis, manual maintenance of DNS records becomes impractical.

BIND can be configured to accept *dynamic updates*: hostname and IP address pairings from DHCP servers as they are assigned. Such updates can add, remove, and/or modify DNS records. Dynamic updates must be sent to an authoritative name server for the zone. Slave name servers that receive them forward them to the master name server (which has the only modifiable copy of the zone data).

 In practice, dynamic updates generally only work when the DHCP server and DNS server are from the same implementation.

Dynamic updates are enabled on a per-zone basis, via the allow-update option to the zone statement. For example, the following statement enables dynamic updates for the *dhcp.ahania.com* zone:

```
zone "dhcp.ahania.com" {
  type master;
  file "dhcp.ahania.com.db";
  allow-update { 192.168.33.3; 192.168.33.5; };
};
```

In this case, dynamic updates will be accepted only from the two listed servers.

You should never add records to a zone that accepts dynamic updates by editing the zone file. Manual and dynamic updates do not mix easily. For this reason, many sites isolate all of their DHCP clients into one or more separate zones.

The allow-update-forwarding option in BIND 9 can be used to specify a list of servers from which a slave name server will forward dynamic updates to the master name server:

```
zone "dhcp.ahania.com" {
   type slave;
   masters { 192.168.33.62; };
   file "back/ahania.com.bak";
   allow update-forwarding { 192.168.33.32/27; };
};
```

As you can see, its syntax is very similar to allow-update. In this case, updates from any system on the specified subnet are allowed.

BIND 9 also provides the update-policy option as an alternative to allow-update. It takes a much more complex dynamic access specification as its argument, consisting of one or more access rules have this general form:

```
grant|deny who-key  what  where  [record-types];
```

who specifies the source of the update via the key name for that entity (keys are discussed in a later subsection). This forces all dynamic updates to be cryptographically signed.

What is a keyword indicating the subset of the next argument to which updates may be made, *where* is the domain or subdomain to be updated, and *record-type* is a list of resource record keyword for the kinds of records to which the rule applies.

The possible values of *what* are:

name
    The update must be to the domain in the *where* field.

subdomain
    The update must be to a subdomain of the domain in the *where* field (within the same zone). In other words, the name to be updated must end in *where*.

wildcard
    The domain to be updated must match the wildcard string in the *where* field.

self
    The update must apply to the entity specified in the *who* field itself. In this case, *where* must still be specified, but it is not used.

Here are some examples:

Allow ns.dhcp.ahania.com to modify domain records via signed updates
```
grant ns.dhcp.ahania.com. name ns.dhcp.ahania.com.;
```

Allow subdomain clients to update only their own address records
```
grant *.dhcp.ahania.com. self dhcp.ahania.com. A;
```

Allow only ns.win2k.ahania.com to modify SRV records in its zone
```
grant ns.win2k.ahania.com. subdomain _udp.win2k.ahania.com. SRV;
grant ns.win2k.ahania.com. subdomain _tcp.win2k.ahania.com. SRV;
deny *.win2k.ahania.com. wildcard *.win2k.ahania.com. SRV;
```

The rule list is specified as the argument to update-policy:

```
zone "dhcp.ahania.com" {
  type master;
  file "dhcp.ahania.com.db";
  update-policy {
    grant *.dhcp.ahania.com. self dhcp.ahania.com. A;
  };
};
```

Note that ordering is important within rule lists, because the first matching rule is used, even when a later rule would be a closer (more explicit) match. As usual, more specific rules generally precede ones that apply more widely.

See *DNS and BIND* for more sophisticated examples of this option.

Incremental zone transfers

When a master name server sends the zone data to a slave name server, the process is known as a *zone transfer*. By default, the entire zone contents are transmitted. However, in some circumstances, the master name server can send only those records that have changed since the last update, via an *incremental zone transfer*. These two types are also known as AXFR and IXFR, respectively (after the query type that is used).

 Incremental zone transfers are incompatible with manual editing of the zone file, so they should only be used for dynamically updated zones.

Incremental zone transfers are enabled in the *named.conf* file, via the options and/or server statements. The latter statement is used to specify how the local server should communicate with specific other name servers. Here are example statements for enabling incremental zone transfers:

BIND 8	*BIND 9*
`options {`	
`  maintain-ixfr-base yes;`	*No global options required.*
`  ...`	
`};`	
`server 192.168.33.62 {`	`server 192.168.33.62 {`
`  support-ixfr yes;`	`  provide-ixfr yes;`
`};`	`  request-ixfr yes;`
	`};`

Under BIND 8, the maintain-ixfr-base option tells the name server to maintain a transaction log from which incremental transfer data can be drawn. The server statement means that IXFR will be used when communicating with the specific server system.

Under BIND 9, incremental zone transfers are enabled by default for all zones that are configured for dynamic updates (and the transaction-based data is always maintained). The two options within the server statement indicate whether the local server will provide or accept incremental zone transfers to the specific system, as appropriate. The provide-ixfr option applies only when communicating with slave name servers, and request-ixfr applies only when communicating with a master name server.

In practice, these options are often used to disable IXFR (with an argument of no), since the default is to use incremental zone transfers. They are also used to identify servers that do and don't support IXFR within a network with name servers using different DNS versions and hence with differing capabilities.

Access control

As we've seen, many BIND statements take a list of addresses as their argument. So far, we have provided only literal lists of IP addresses. There is another possibility, however. The acl statement* is used to define an *address match list*. Here is an example:

```
# Define a list of our name servers.
acl "servers" { 10.1.10.50; 10.1.20.1; 10.1.30.200; };
# Define another list.
acl "sample" {                      List name is "sample."
    10.1.10.1;                      IP address.
  ! 10.1.20.200;                    ! means NOT: exclude this IP address.
    10.1.20/24;                     Specifies a subnet.
    servers;                        Include another address match list.
};
```

As usual, ordering with an address match list is important, because the first match is used (this matters when you are combining positive and negative matches). Note that the exclamation point negation character applies only to the item that it precedes (i.e., it does not "stick"). Address match lists must be defined before they are used. In general, address match lists may be used anywhere that a list of hosts is expected.

BIND provides four predefined address match lists: *none* (matches nothing), *all* (matches any IP address), *localhost* (matches any IP address assigned to the local system), and *localnets* (matches all subnets to which the local system has an interface attached).

---

* Despite its name, this statement does not define a true access control list, but merely a list of IP addresses and patterns to match that can be used in other security-related statements.

Here are some example uses of address match lists:

```
acl "extern" { 192.168.1.100; 192.168.20.200; };
acl "hidden" { 192.168.50.25; 192.168.50.26; };
acl "testers" { 10.20.30.100; 10.20.30.101; };

options {
  directory "/var/named";
  forwarders { extern; };
  also-notify { hidden; 192.168.51.77; };
  allow-query { localnets; };
  ...
};

zone "experiment.zoas.org." {
  type master;
  file "exper.zoas.org";
  allow-query { testers; };
};
```

Various items in the options statement use address match lists to specify the list of forwarders, most of the list of additional servers that should be sent zone file data modification notifications, and the list of hosts that are allowed to query this name server. In addition, an address match list is used to limit the hosts allowed to query this name server for the zone *experiment.zoas.org* to the two specified in the *testers* list.

The allow-query option is one of several that enable you to restrict various types of access to the data on a name server. The complete list is given in Table 8-7. These options may appear in either the options statement or a zone statement.

Table 8-7. DNS server access control options

Option	Description
allow-query	*Meaning*: Allow only these hosts to query this name server.
	Result: Data is not revealed to unauthorized outsiders.
allow-transfer	*Meaning*: Allow only these hosts to request zone transfers.
	Result: Prevents unauthorized zone transfers.
allow-update	*Meaning*: Accept dynamic updates only from these hosts.
	Result: Prevents unauthorized modifications to zone data.
blackhole	*Meaning*: List of hosts to ignore completely.
	Result: Refuses interaction with unwanted partners.
bogus	*Meaning*: List of hosts that should never be queried.
	Result: Prevents invalid/malicious data within your cache.

While address match lists provide ways to limit access to data records, they are not a foolproof mechanism. For example, the source of queries or requests could be impersonated by a bad guy. Cryptographic techniques for securing and authenticating communications are needed for a truly secure DNS environment. The next section will consider the various available options.

Securing DNS communications

Both BIND 8 and 9 can be configured to use transaction signatures for communicating between pairs of name servers. This mechanism, known as TSIG, uses a symmetric encryption scheme (the same key is used to encrypt and decrypt a message) for signing server-to-server queries and responses. In this way, messages purportedly from a specific server can be verified as originating from that server. Note that this scheme simply signs the messages; the transmitted data is not encrypted (because it is not secret). See "Protecting Files and the Filesystem" in Chapter 7 for a detailed discussion of signing and encryption.

You set up name servers to use TSIG via these steps:

- Create a key using a utility provided with BIND on one system.
- Send the key to the other system in some secure way (e.g., via a telephone call, using an sshssh-based copy operation, etc.).
- Define the key with key statements and specify it for use in server and zone statements within the two *named.conf* files. Note that the key must be given the same name on both systems (as well as having the same value).
- Restart both name servers. Subsequent communications between them will then be signed.

Here are the commands for creating a key:

```
# dnskeygen -H 128 -h -n apricot-mango.ahania.com.          BIND 8
# dnssec-keygen -a HMAC-MD5 -b 128 -n HOST \                BIND 9
        apricot-mango.ahania.com.
Kapricot-mango.ahania.com.+157+52961
```

Each command creates the specified key as 128 bits long, type HOST, using the HMAC-MD5 algorithm. Conventionally, key names resemble domain names, with the pair of systems to which they apply specified as the first component (here, *apricot* and *mango*).

The commands create two files beginning with the name displayed in the output, one with the extension *.key* and the other with the extension *.private*. The filename is of the form *Kkey-name+algorithm+fingerprint*, where *algorithm* is the algorithm number, and *fingerprint* is a hash value computed from the key used to identify it (functioning like an instance number).

The actual key is included in both files. For example:

```
# cat Kapricot-mango.ahania.com.+157+52961.private
Private-key-format: v1.2
Algorithm: 157 (HMAC)
Key: QiL+oT+iV9EHxhbYRcdG8g==          This is the string you want.
```

The key must now be transmitted to the other system in some secure way (i.e., other than via a clear network transmission).

Once the files are present on both systems, the servers can be configured to use TSIG communications. Here are some example statements from *named.conf* on the slave name server *mango* that make use of this key:

```
include "keys.list";                    Keys are stored in a separate, non-readable file.

zone paranoia.ahania.com. {
  type slave;
  masters { 192.168.10.214; ... };
};

server 192.168.10.214 {  # apricot
  keys { "apricot-mango.ahania.com." };
};
```

The first statement includes the contents of another file within this configuration file, and the second statement defines a zone. The final statement specifies that zone transfer requests to 192.168.10.214 will be signed with the specified key.

The actual key statement is within the included file (which is also protected from non-owner access):

```
# keys.list
key "apricot-mango.ahania.com." {
  algorithm hmac-md5;
  secret "encoded=string=goes=here";
};
```

On the master name server *apricot*, the key is used in the zone statement to require that zone transfer requests be signed with that key in order to be honored:

```
include "keys.list";                    Same file as on mango.

server 192.168.10.100 { # mango
  keys { apricot-mango.ahania.com.; };
};

zone paranoia.ahania.com. {
  type master;
  file "paranoia.ahania.com";
  allow-transfer { key apricot-mango.ahania.com.; };
};
```

The key *name* construct replaces the address list in the allow-transfer option. Keys may also be specified in the same way within the allow-update and update-policy options in the zone statement.

 Although these strings are referred to as *keys* and as *encoded*, all they really are is 128-bit strings of random bits, expressed in base 64. 24-character ASCII character strings have the same structure, and any such string can be used for this purpose (you don't have to generate it using cryptographic tools). In the end, there is nothing magical about TSIG keys, and they function as simple shared secrets known only to the two servers that use them.

BIND 9 security futures. While the TSIG mechanism works well for communication between pairs of hosts, it does not scale well to large sites with many name servers, due both to the significant amount of work required to configure name servers and periodically generate keys (as with any shared secret, keys should be changed regularly) within even a medium-sized site, and the logistical impossibility of setting up TSIG between every pair of name servers worldwide that might ever want to communicate. The first of these issues can be addressed by automating key generation and distribution.

BIND 9 extends the TSIG facility via the use of the TKEY mechanism. In this scheme, known as the Diffie-Hellman algorithm, the two servers automatically exchange data values that each one has computed from a random number and its key. Using the data from the other server and their own key, they then compute the same shared secret key. TKEY's advantage is that the actual key itself does not need to be sent from one server to the other. Although some of the infrastructure for the TKEY mechanism is present in configuration file options, the named server does not yet support TKEY as of this writing (Version 9.2.0 is latest to be released).

BIND 9 also includes the DNS Security Extensions (DNSSEC) facility, a far more elaborate and sophisticated set of mechanisms and procedures for securing DNS communications using public key cryptography. Asymmetric key pairs are used to create the digital signatures, with the private key used to decrypt what the public key has encrypted (or vice versa; see "Protecting Files and the Filesystem" in Chapter 7). Once again, the data itself is not encrypted.

DNSSEC uses several new resource record types:

- KEY records are used to store the public key for a zone. The keys for a zone must be signed by its parent zone to create a *chain of trust* for DNS communications.

- SIG records are used to store the digital signature produced by the zone's private key for each *resource record set* (the set of all records of a specific type: all A records, all MX records, and so on). This signature is a secure hash performed on the zone data using the private key.

- NXT records are used to specify the next record within the zone when it is placed into its *canonical order* (a hierarchical and alphabetical ordering scheme defined as part of DNSSEC). These records are returned whenever a negative answer to a query—e.g., that host doesn't exist—is required, and they too can be signed (while a null response can't).

At this time, DNSSEC is still considered experimental, and there are several outstanding issues that stand between its present form and its production deployment.

- Vital parts of the infrastructure do not exist (e.g., the ability for zones to be signed by the *.com* domain). DNSSEC can still be used locally, however.

- It takes a significant amount of CPU resources and elapsed time to generate the SIG and NXT records for a zone, and not all current systems running DNS servers would be up to the task. In addition, the time that would be required to sign major TLDs seems to be unrealistic with respect to practical considerations.

- The amount of data within a zone is multiplied by a factor of three or more. This increases DNS network bandwidth requirements significantly.

- Not all functions work when DNSSEC and non-DNSSEC implementations are both used within the same network (e.g., queries from a DNSSEC-aware resolver to a non-DNSSEC forwarder).

In conclusion, while it is probably time to start learning about and experimenting with DNSSEC, it is still fairly far away from production use.

BIND 9 views

I've alluded to the practice of keeping internal DNS data private and inaccessible to external queries while still allowing internal users to resolve external name servers as needed. Such a separation is sometimes referred to as *split DNS*. BIND 9 offers a new feature that makes implementing such a design very easy: views.

Views are a means of varying the properties of a zone depending on who is using it. For example, the zone can appear one way to internal users and another way to external users. Here are some example view statements that illustrate this feature:

```
acl "internal" { 10.1.1.0/24; };        acl statements must be outside views.
acl "external" { any; };                The any keyword matches any address.

view "inside" {                         Zone definition for internal clients.
  match-clients { "internal"; };
  zone "public.zoas.org." {
    type master;
    file "public.zoas.org.zone.internal";
  };
};

view "outside" {                        Zone definition for everyone else.
  match-clients { "external"; };
  recursion no;
  zone "public.zoas.org." {
    type master;
    file "public.zoas.org.zone.external";
  };
};
```

First, we define two address match lists, which are then used with the match-clients options inside the two view statements. As usual, the first match-clients option that applies is used, so view ordering is important (if these two views were reversed, everyone would see only view *outside*).

The same zone, *public.zoas.org*, is defined in each view, but different zone files are used in each case. In addition, recursive queries are disabled in the outside view; if the name server cannot resolve a name, it does not contact any additional servers in an attempt to do so.

One ramification of using views is that there cannot be any independent zone statements in *named.conf*. All zones must be part of a view.

See the excellent article "Supporting Screened Hosts with BIND 9.x Views" by Scott DeJong (*Sys Admin* magazine 11:5, May 2002) for more complex view scenarios.

Securing the named process

Making server-to-server communications and zone data access secure is important, but you also need to ensure that the BIND server itself is not a trouble spot. There are three things you can do to protect it:

- Make sure that named has been patched with all available security fixes. Check your vendor's or the ISC web site regularly to determine if any new fixes have been released, and install them right away. Monitor security news groups and/or mailing lists to ensure that you'll hear about detected problems right away.

- Don't run named as root. Create a special user and group, often called *named*, to run it. Use the named command's -u *username* option to start the server running as the specified user. Grant this user access to the various configuration files by changing their ownership (e.g., for key files) or protection.

- Run named in a chrooted environment. The named command's -t *directory* option can be used to specify the new root directory. Of course, you'll need to set up the required directory structure under the selected root directory and copy all required files there:

  — */etc/named.conf*

  — The named executable, along with any required libraries (BIND 8 only). Alternatively, you can link named statically when you build it to avoid any dependencies.

  — */dev/null* and possibly */dev/random*. Use mknod to create them. Here are example commands from a Linux system:

    ```
    # mknod /named-root/dev/null   c 1 3
    # mknod /named-root/dev/random c 1 8
    ```

  — The major and minor device numbers vary among Unix versions; use ls -l to determine the appropriate values to use.

  — Under BIND 8, a version of the password and group files containing just the named user and group. BIND 9 consults these files before chrooting, so copying them is not necessary. Note that the home directory for the named user should be / in both cases, not the chosen root directory location (because the specified home directory is interpreted from the named process's perspective).

You will also need to modify the default directory location to be / in *named.conf*'s options statement.

Configuring logging

The destination for status and error messages as well as what sorts of messages to save are both highly configurable in BIND. This is done via the logging statement. This statement has two distinct parts: definitions of message *channels* (output destinations) and associations of message *categories* with target channels.

Here is a simple logging statement illustrating these features:

```
logging {
  channel "xfers" {
    file "logs/named.xfers";
  };
  channel "to-syslog" {
    syslog local1;                    Syslog facility.
    severity warning;                 Minimum syslog severity level.
  };
  channel "to-file" { file "logs/named.log"; };

  category xfer-in  { "xfers"; };
  category xfer-out { "xfers"; };
  category security { "to-file"; "to-syslog"; };
};
```

This statement defines three channels: the syslog local1 facility and two files in the *logs* subdirectory of the named default directory.

The three category lines specify what messages actually go to each potential destination. The file *logs/named.xfers* will receive all messages about incoming and outgoing zone transfers, the file *logs/named.log* will receive all security-related messages (approvals and denials of requests), and the security-related messages of level warning and higher will also be logged to the syslog local1 facility (as specified by the severity option in the corresponding channel definition).

There are a few predefined logging channels:

```
default_syslog                 Syslog's daemon facility.
default_debug                  The file named.run in the default directory.
default_stderr                 Send messages to named's standard error.
null                           Discard messages.
```

The default channels all use syslog severity level information (where applicable).

Table 8-8 lists the most important BIND logging categories. In BIND 9, the default logging behavior sends logging category default to the *default_syslog* and *default_debug* channels. BIND 8 also logs a few more messages types to each location as well as panic messages to *default_stderr*.

Table 8-8. Useful BIND logging categories

Category	Associated messages
default	Refers to all messages for which no channel is explicitly specified.
general	Miscellaneous unclassified messages.

Table 8-8. Useful BIND logging categories (continued)

Category	Associated messages
config	Configuration file processing messages.
dnssec	TSIG and DNSSEC-related messages.
lame-servers	Misconfigured remote servers discovered by named when it tried to query them.
network❾	Network operations.
notify	Messages arising from notification messages.
queries	Per-query log messages.
resolver	DNS resolution operations (e.g., recursive lookups for clients).
security	Request approvals and denials.
update	Dynamic updates.
xfer-in	Zone transfers the server is receiving.
xfer-out	Zone transfers the server is sending.
cname❽	CNAME mapping-related messages.
ncache❽	Messages related to negative cache entries.
panic❽	Server panics (fatal errors).
packet❽	Dumps of all packets sent and received.
statistics❽	Summary statistics about name server operations.

Some of the BIND 8–only categories will probably eventually be implemented in a future version of BIND 9. They are ignored (with a warning) in *named.conf*.

Name Server Maintenance and Troubleshooting

Configuring a DNS name server can be a fair amount of work, but even once that is done, there are still additional tasks required to keep it running:

- Add additional name servers if the load on existing ones becomes too great or the topology of your network changes significantly. How you'll handle expected future growth should be part of your name server deployment plan.
- Check for and apply software patches frequently.
- Update the root hints file a few times per year.
- Update zone files as appropriate. Update the reverse zones at the same time, and don't forget to increment the serial number in each file.
- Review DNS logging information on a regular basis.
- Monitor the reliability and performance of your name servers in the context of overall network activity (see "Network Performance" in Chapter 15).

Controlling the named server process

The named process is typically started at boot time by one of the usual boot scripts (often */etc/init.d/named*). On systems with System V–style boot scripts, you can also use the same script to stop or restart the daemon:

```
# /etc/init.d/named restart
```

As we've seen, you can specify the location of the file that holds the daemon's PID; this file is typically */var/run/named.pid*. You can use this information to signal the named process manually, as in this example:

```
# kill `cat /var/run/named.pid`
```

Note that killing the daemon is not recommended in general, and especially not if you are using dynamic updates.

The BIND software distribution also provides a utility to manipulate the name server process. This command is named `ndc` under BIND 8 and `rndc` under BIND 9. Both support several subcommands: `stop` terminates the server process after any pending updates are complete, `halt` stops the server immediately, `reload` causes the server to reload its configuration and zone files (or just one zone if its name is specified as the subcommand's argument), and `dumpdb` and `stats` write the cache contents and server statistics to a log file (by default, *named_dump.db* and *named.stats*, respectively). `ndc` also supports a `restart` subcommand (which does the obvious).

Here are some examples:

```
# rndc reload              Reload configuration and zone file.
# ndc reload
# rndc -s apricot stop      Terminate a remote name server process.
```

`ndc` also supports remote server management, but it is unsecured: any user who can run `ndc` on an allowed remote system can perform any operation on the system's DNS servers. For this reason, I don't recommend using this feature. Under BIND 9, you can use the controls statement in *named.conf* to specify a key with which `rndc` must sign its messages:

```
include "rncd.key";
controls {
  inet * allow { 192.168.10/24; } keys { "rndc-key";};
};
```

The included file contains a key statement defining the specified key in the same manner as we considered earlier.

The `rndc` command also requires that the key be defined in its configuration file, */etc/rndc.conf*:

```
options {
  default-server localhost;        Manage this server by default.
  default-key "rndc-key";          Sign messages with this key by default.
};
```

```
key "rndc-key" {
  algorithm hmac-md5;
  secret "a=whole=lotta=characters";
};
```

You can use command-line options to override both the default server (-s) and the default key (-y).

Using the nslookup and dig utilities

The nslookup command is another utility provided as part of the BIND package. It is used to perform ad hoc DNS queries and is very useful for troubleshooting purposes.

Here is an example of using nslookup in its default mode:

```
$ nslookup                          This command starts an interactive session.
> mango                             Look up this host name (local domain assumed).
Server:         localhost
Address:        127.0.0.1#53

Name:   mango.ahania.com
Address: 192.168.10.100
> set type=PTR                      Query PTR records (the default is A).
> server 10.18.114.44               Use this server for queries.
Default server: freya
Address: 10.18.14.44#53
> 192.168.10.214
Server:         10.18.114.44
Address:        10.18.114.44#53

214.10.168.192.in-addr.arpa  name = apricot.ahania.com.
> exit
```

These commands illustrate using nslookup for forward and reverse queries, including via a different name server.

Examining the SOA record for a zone can be useful at times. It shows the name servers for the zone and the email address for the zone's administrator:

```
$ nslookup
> set type=SOA
> state.ct.us
Server: ns1.worldnet.att.net
Address:  204.127.129.1

Non-authoritative answer:
state.ct.us
        primary name server = info.das.state.ct.us
        responsible mail addr = hostmaster.po.state.ct.us
        serial  = 2002041801
        refresh = 14400 (4 hours)
        retry   = 600 (10 mins)
        expire  = 604800 (7 days)
        default TTL = 604800 (7 days)
state.ct.us     nameserver = info.das.state.ct.us
```

```
state.ct.us          nameserver = dbru.br.ns.els-gms.att.net
info.das.state.ct.us     internet address = 159.247.0.198
dbru.br.ns.els-gms.att.net       internet address = 199.191.128.106
```

You can also use the serial number data in such records to compare the data versions on master and slave servers when you are trying to troubleshoot zone transfer problems.

Setting the type to NS enables you to determine the authoritative name servers for a zone or website. A type of ANY also returns all records associated with a name.

The newer `dig` utility performs the same functions as `nslookup`. It has the following general syntax:

```
dig [@server] name  [type] [options]
```

For example, this command determines the version of BIND that a server is running:

```
$ dig @bonita.ahania.com version.bind txt chaos
...
;; QUESTION SECTION:
;version.bind.                CH      TXT

;; ANSWER SECTION:
version.bind.          0      CH      TXT     "9.1.3"
...
```

The output tells us that this server is running BIND 9.1.3.[*]

Routing Daemons

Having covered the first step in any network operation—finding out the address for the desired host—it is now time to turn to the second prerequisite: determining how to get there. The routing needs of many sites can be handled by installing routers and setting up default gateways and static routes on client systems (as we saw in "Adding a New Network Host" in Chapter 5). However, some situations call for more sophisticated routing services. This section provides an introduction to the daemons that provide them. The processes and algorithms described here are also used by dedicated routers.

Routing daemons dynamically select the best route from among the multiple paths to a given packet's destination. More precisely, what is determined is the best next step along the path toward the destination, because the ultimate target may be far beyond their field of vision.

Routers cache routing information that they learn in the course of their operation, and the routers and daemons within a network use various schemes to exchange routing information.

---

[*] Or at least that it claims to be. In fact, the system administrator can change this string to any value (although most people don't), so the information provided is not always available or reliable.

There are two routing daemons provided by Unix systems: routed and gated. routed (pronounced "route-D") is the older and simpler of the two and is infrequently used these days. gated (pronounced "gate-D") is a general purpose routing daemon, and it is the preferred choice for most sites.

For detailed information about the topics and daemons discussed in this section, see *TCP-IP Network Administration* by Craig Hunt (O'Reilly & Associates).

Routing Concepts and Protocols

As we noted, many sites need only *minimal routing* (specifying a default gateway on every system) or *static routing* (defining some static routes as needed). These approaches work well for networks that are fairly simple (there are not many alternate paths to destinations), are relatively stable (routers do not go down very often), and have ample network bandwidth (routing efficiency is not a major factor in network traffic).

However, complex networks require the use of *dynamic routing*, which includes the following characteristics:

- Selecting the best route among multiple routes to a destination based on current network conditions.
- Maintaining and updating the routing table based on information received via routing protocols.

In other words, both the route selection and the data on which the selection is made are updated continuously to reflect the current network state. The data about what routes exist and are operational are known as *reachability information*.

Routing protocols specify the methods for determining the best route to a destination and the means by which information is exchanged between and distributed among distinct routing daemons. They are subdivided two different ways:

By usage context: interior versus exterior protocols
>   Interior protocols are used for internal routing inside an *autonomous system*: a network under the control of a single administrative entity (typically corresponding to a site). Exterior protocols are designed for routing between autonomous systems.

By algorithm: distance-vector versus link-state protocols
>   Distance-vector protocols use a measure of the distance to a destination to determine the best route (for example, a route with fewer hops is preferred over one requiring more hops). In contrast, link-state protocols compute each possible route based on a current map of the network topology. These maps are continuously maintained and updated by each router based on information it receives from neighboring routers.

Distance-vector protocols are simple and minimize the amount of data that must be exchanged between routers, but they can take an unacceptably long time to adapt to changes in the network (e.g., router availability). Link-state protocols react to changes more quickly, but they require significantly more CPU and memory resources on the router.

There are a variety of routing protocols in use. For interior routing, there are two that predominate, RIP and OSPF.

The Routing Information Protocol (RIP) is a simple distance-vector protocol. Each router periodically broadcasts the contents of its routing table, specifically, the addresses of the destinations it knows about and the number of hops required to get to them. Routing information is also broadcast in response to update requests from other RIP routers and daemons in more recent versions of RIP. A given router or daemon uses the information provided by its neighbors (adjacent routers, one hop away) to determine the cost of each potential route, ultimately selecting the shortest one.

The maximum distance considered is 15 hops; destinations farther away are all considered to be infinitely distant. In addition to this limited range, RIP's other main disadvantage is its *slow convergence* in the face of changing network conditions. Long timeout periods and default update intervals in combination with the algorithm it uses to recompute routes mean that routing information can remain out of date for unacceptably long periods of time (many minutes). While routing information is out of date, affected destination hosts are unreachable. There are extensions to RIP (and the follow-on version, RIP-2) that ameliorate this behavior, but not all RIP implementations include them.

The Open Shortest Path First (OSPF) protocol is a link-state protocol. OSPF routers build and maintain a *link-state database*, which is a directed-graph representation of the entire network from the perspective of that router. This data is then shared with its neighbor routers, and all of their maps are then updated accordingly. OSPF routers choose the best route to a destination by computing the shortest distance route from its current information.

OSPF allows large networks to be subdivided into *areas* to reduce the computational requirements of computing and storing the network topology data. Routing between areas is handled by designated *area border routers*. When areas are in use, the *backbone* is a special area to which all other areas are attached (without areas, the entire site is the backbone).

The routed daemon uses the RIP protocol, while the gated daemon can use several different protocols, including both RIP and OSPF. Note that only one of these daemons should be run at a time.

Configuring routed

Although it runs only RIP, routed is available on almost all Unix systems, and it is extremely simple to administer. This daemon has two modes, server mode and quiet mode, selected with the -s and -q command-line options (respectively). Quiet-mode daemons listen for RIP updates but do not broadcast data themselves. Most systems operate in this manner. Only routers and host systems functioning as routers (via multiple network interfaces) should operate in server mode.

routed can optionally load a list of known gateways from the */etc/gateways* configuration file when it starts up, but this is seldom necessary because the RIP protocol quickly discovers its neighbors. Otherwise, there is no other configuration necessary for routed itself.

The daemon is generally started at boot time in one of the system boot scripts. Here are the specifics for the various operating systems we are considering:

AIX	Started by */etc/rc.tcpip*.
	Enabled by removing # from the commands in *rc.tcpip*.
FreeBSD	Started in */etc/rc.network*.
	Enabled in */etc/rc.conf* and/or */etc/rc.conf.local*:
	`router_enable="YES", router="routed"`
	`router_flags="named-args"`
HP-UX	Not supplied; use gated (see below).
Red Hat Linux	Started in */etc/init.d/routed*.
	Configured in */etc/sysconfig/routed*:
	`SILENT="true-or-false"`
SuSE Linux	Started in */etc/init.d/routed*.
	Enabled in */etc/rc.config* (SuSE 7 only):
	`START_ROUTED="yes"`
Solaris	Started in */etc/init.d/inetinit*.
Tru64	Started in */sbin/init.d/route*.
	Configured in */etc/rc.config*:
	`ROUTED="yes";`
	`ROUTED_FLAGS="args";`

Note that Solaris names this daemon `in.routed`.

Configuring gated

gated is a more sophisticated routing daemon capable of supporting multiple routing protocols (both interior and exterior). It is provided by AIX, HP-UX, and Tru64.

The software was originally free, but it was later taken over by the Merit GateD Consortium, and subsequent versions that it produced were available primarily to consortium members. Current versions are available as commercial software from NextHop Technologies (*http://www.nexthop.com*). The last free[*] version was 3.6, but this is quite adequate for most sites' needs. It is easy to find on the Internet: e.g., *http://freshmeat.net/projects/gated/*.

---

[*] Version 3.6 is free, but making and distributing changes may be technically prohibited (Freshmeat describes the license as "free to use but restricted"). The last unrestricted version seems to be 3.5.10.

gated's configuration file is */etc/gated.conf*. This file has a specified format that must be followed, with this general layout: options, interface definitions, protocol selection and configuration, static route, and route importing and exporting. Here is an example of the first two sections:

```
options syslog upto info ;          Global options.
interfaces {                        Declare an interface for later use.
  interface 192.168.10.150 ;
} ;
router-id 192.168.10.150 ;          Required for OSPF.
```

The options statement specifies that logging should go to the syslog facility and include all messages of info severity and higher. This setting is actually the default and is included only to illustrate the options statement (which is in fact not needed at all in many cases).

The second statement defines a network interface for gated. This is required only if the interface will be referred to later in the configuration file.

Next come the protocol selections and their configuration. For example, the following statement enables the RIP protocol:

```
# enable RIP
rip yes {                           Use RIP.
  nobroadcast ;                     Equivalent to routed -q.
  interface 191.168.10.150 {
    version 2 ;                     Use RIP-2.
    authentication simple "a-password" ;
  } ;
} ;
```

This statement says to use RIP-2 in quiet mode and specifies an authentication password included in and expected for all valid updates. It provides some minimal protection against malicious routing data. MD5 passwords are also supported.

If you wanted to disable RIP, you'd use this statement:

```
rip no ;
```

Here is a simple configuration statement for the OSPF protocol:

```
ospf yes {
  backbone {
    interface 192.168.10.150 {
      priority 5 ;
      authentication simple "another-pass" ;
    } ;
  } ;
} ;
```

This statement enables OSPF. It indicates that the system is part of the backbone area and specifies the interface through which the system is attached, along with an authentication mechanism to use with other routers in this area. The priority value is used when various OSPF routers are trying to select a designated router for an area, where higher values mean less likelihood of being selected (the default is 10).

This statement could contain additional area substatements if the system has multiple interfaces connected to different areas, enabling it to function as an *area border router*. These lines follow the same syntax as the backbone configuration except that they are introduced by a line of the form:

```
area name
```

As we've noted, additional sections of the configuration file define static routes and what route information to advertise to external routers. We won't consider them in this brief introduction.

Vendor specifics. gated is provided by AIX, HP-UX, and Tru64 (presumably, IBM, HP and DEC/Compaq were members of the consortium). Here are the specifics for these systems:

AIX Started by */etc/rc.tcpip*.
Enabled by removing # from the commands in *rc.tcpip*.

HP-UX Started by */sbin/init.d/gated*.

Tru64 Started in */sbin/init.d/gateway*.
Configured in */etc/rc.config*:
```
GATED="yes";
GATED_FLAGS="args";
```

You can obtain or build gated for any of the other systems discussed in this book. For example, there is a FreeBSD version in the ports collection, and many Linux distributions include it as an optional component.

Configuring a DHCP Server

In "Adding a New Network Host" in Chapter 5, we considered the process of configuring a client system to obtain an IP address from a DHCP server. In this section, we complete the picture by discussing DHCP server configuration and management.

DHCP servers vary quite a bit from system to system, but the basic concepts that apply to all of them do not. We'll consider these concepts before diving into the specifics of server configuration on the various Unix systems.

DHCP servers draw the IP addresses that they provide from lists of addresses that they have been given to manage. These lists are known as *scopes*. Unix DHCP servers can manage one or more scopes. For example, suppose we have a network of two subnets, 10.10.1.0/24 and 10.10.20.0/24, and we place a DHCP server on each one. We want to use 101 IP addresses from each subnet for dynamic assignment, hosts 100 through 200. We might divide up the addresses this way:

Subnet 1 DHCP Server	Subnet 2 DHCP Server
10.10.1.100–10.10.1.175	10.10.20.100–10.10.20.175
10.10.20.176–10.10.20.200	10.10.1.176–10.10.1.200

Each server is assigned part of the address range for each subnet. When a client requests an IP address, the DHCP server always assigns one from the appropriate subnet (if none is available, the request fails). Splitting the addresses this way provides for some fault tolerance. If either server goes down, a DHCP relay (see below) can be set up temporarily on its subnet pointing to the other server, and IP address assignment will still take place.

Within a scope, certain IP addresses can be *excluded*, meaning that they are permanently unavailable for assignment (perhaps some server is using one as its static IP address). In addition, certain addresses can be *reserved* for specific hosts, identified by their MAC address (for example, for a laptop that you want to have the same IP address whenever it is connected to a specific subnet but still changes IP addresses as it moves around). When possible, we'll be excluding the address 10.10.1.125 and reserving the address 10.10.1.105 in our configuration examples (both in subnet 1).

Since DHCP operates by broadcasting (see "Adding a New Network Host" in Chapter 5), requests generally only reach a DHCP server on the local subnet. I recommend placing a DHCP server on every subnet, but this is not always feasible. When it is not, DHCP clients can still receive address assignment from a server on another subnet via a *DHCP relay server*. This server forwards DHCP requests from the local subnet to a designated DHCP server.

 Some routers can be configured to forward DHCP-related broadcast packets between subnets. In this case, a DHCP relay server would not be necessary.

Table 8-9 summarizes the DHCP server facilities on the various operating systems we are considering. The remaining parts of this section will discuss DHCP configuration for each operating system.

Table 8-9. DHCP server component locations

Component	DHCP server	DHCP relay
Server executable	**AIX:** */usr/sbin/dhcpsd*	**AIX:** */usr/sbin/dhcprd*
	HP-UX: */usr/lbin/bootpd*	**ISC:** */usr/sbin/dhcrelay*
	ISC: */usr/sbin/dhcpd*	**Solaris:** */usr/lib/inet/in.dhcpd*
	Solaris: */usr/lib/inet/in.dhcpd*	**Tru64:** */usr/sbin/bprelay*
	Tru64: */usr/sbin/joind*	
Configuration file	**ISC:** */etc/dhcpd.conf*	**ISC:** none
	AIX: */etc/dhcpsd.cnf*	**AIX:** */etc/dhcprd.cnf*
	HP-UX: */etc/dhcptab*	**Solaris:** none
	Solaris: */var/dhcp/dhcptab* and network files in */var/dhcp*	**Tru64:** none
	Tru64: */etc/join/server.pcy, /etc/join/nets, /etc/join/dhcpcap*	

Table 8-9. DHCP server component locations (continued)

Component	DHCP server	DHCP relay
Boot script that starts the DHCP server	**ISC:** */etc/init.d/dhcpd* (add manually for FreeBSD) **AIX:** */etc/rc.tcpip* **HP-UX:** none (run by `inetd`) **Solaris:** */etc/init.d/dhcp* **Tru64:** */sbin/init.d/dhcp*	**ISC:** */etc/init.d/dhcrelay* (add manually for FreeBSD) **AIX:** */etc/rc.tcpip* **Solaris:** */etc/init.d/dhcp* **Tru64:** none

Boot script configuration file: DHCP server-related entries	**AIX:** none
	HP-UX: none
	Red Hat: */etc/sysconfig/dhcpd*
	   DHCPDARGS="args"
	SuSE 7: */etc/rc.config*
	   DHCP_INTERFACE="eth0"
	   DHCP_RUN_CHROOTED="yes|no"
	   DHCP_RUN_AS="user"
	SuSE 8: */etc/sysconfig/dhcpd*
	   DHCP_INTERFACE="eth0"
	   DHCP_RUN_CHROOTED
	   DHCP_RUN_AS="user"
	   DHCP_OTHER_ARGS="args"
	Solaris 8: */etc/default/dhcp*
	   RUN_MODE=server PATH=/var/dhcp
	Solaris 9: */etc/inet/dhcpsvc.conf*
	   DAEMON_ENABLED="TRUE"
	Tru64: */etc/rc.config*
	   JOIND="yes"
	   JOIND_FLAGS="args"
		AIX: none
		HP-UX: N/A
		Red Hat: none
		SuSE 7: */etc/rc.config*
		   DHCRELAY_INTERFACES="eth0":
		   DHCRELAY_SERVERS="host"
		SuSE 8: */etc/sysconfig/dhcpd*
		   DHCRELAY_INTERFACES="eth0"
		   DHCRELAY_SERVERS="host"
		Solaris 8: */etc/default/dhcp*
		   RUNMODE=relay
		   RELAY_DESTINATIONS=server
		Solaris 9: */etc/inet/dhcpsvc.conf*
		   DAEMON_ENABLED=TRUE RUN_MODE=relay
		   RELAY_DESTINATIONS=server
		Tru64: none

Leases data files	**ISC:** */var/lib/dhcp/dhcpd.leases* **AIX:** */etc/dhcpsd.ar*, */etc/dhcpsd.cr* **HP-UX:** */var/tmp/bootp.dump* **Solaris:** network files in */var/dhcp* **Tru64:** */var/join/*.btr*	

AIX

The AIX DHCP server is dhcpsd. It is configured via the */etc/dhcpsd.cnf* configuration file. Here is a configuration file that I've annotated:

```
logFileName /var/log/dhcp/dhcpsd.log
logFileSize 1000                    Use four 1000K log files in rotation.
numLogFiles 4
logItem     SYSERR                  Items to log: system, object and protocol errors,
logItem     OBJERR                  and all warnings. Other choices include:
logItem     PROTERR                      EVENT (that occurred), ACTION (taken), INFO
logItem     WARNING                      (misc. information), ACNTING (play-by-play).

leaseTimeDefault  240 minute        Default lease time.
supportBOOTP      No                Don't support remote booting.
supportUnlistedClients Yes          Accept requests from any client.
```

```
network 10.10.0.0 24                              Our network address and length.
{
  subnet 10.10.1.0 10.10.1.100-10.10.1.175        Address range to assign.
  {
    client 1 aa:bb:cc:dd:ee:ff 10.10.1.105        Reservation.
    {
      option 51 36000                             Longer lease time for this client.
    }
    client 0 0 10.10.1.125                         Address exclusion.
    option 3 10.10.1.5                             Subnet-specific option (default gateways).
    option 28 10.10.1.255                          Broadcast address.
  }
  subnet 10.10.20.0 10.10.20.176-10.10.20.200      Address range to assign.
  {
    option 3 10.10.20.88                           Default gateways for this subnet.
    option 48 10.10.20.45                          X font server.
    option 28 10.10.20.255                         Broadcast address.
  }
  option 15 zoas.org                               Global options: domain
  option 1 255.255.255.0                           Netmask
}

# Dynamic DNS update commands
updateDNS "/usr/sbin/dhcpaction '%s' '%s' '%s' '%s' BOTH NONIM >>/tmp/updns.out 2>&1 "
removeDNS "/usr/sbin/dhcpremove '%s' BOTH NONIM >>/tmp/rmdns.out 2>&1 "
```

The subnet statements contain the actual IP address ranges to be assigned by this server. As this file illustrates, AIX uses standard DHCP option numbers to identify options; see the manual page for DHCP_Server (section 4) for translations.

Dynamic DNS updates are triggered when the updateDNS and removeDNS statements are included within the configuration file. Each of them defines the command to use to perform the corresponding update operations. I don't modify these from the settings provided in the delivered configuration file. The DNS server must also be running on the local system.

AIX also provides some tools for managing DHCP server configuration and operation. The dhcpsconf command starts a GUI tool that can be used to create a configuration file and to also to manage the DHCP server. It is illustrated in Figure 8-2.

The main window has three main areas: Option List (list of available DHCP options), Key List (main statement types to add to the configuration file), and DHCP Server File (illustrates the structure of the file so far). You begin a new configuration file by adding a network (select it in the Key List area and then click Add), and then at least one subnet beneath it.

In general, the current selection is placed in a position immediately subordinate to whatever is selected in the right-hand pane. Adding an option when the network is selected makes it a global option for that network, while doing the same thing when a subnet or client is selected limits the option's scope to that entity. In the figure, we are in the process of adding the X font server option to subnet 2. You use the Server → Server Defaults menu path to specify global options and other server characteristics.

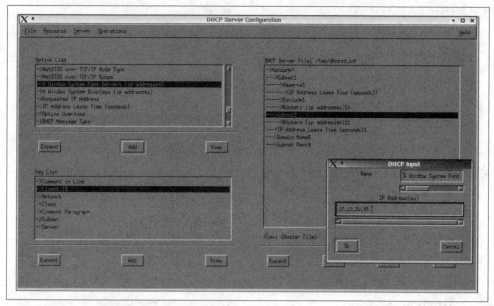

Figure 8-2. The AIX DHCP server configuration utility

The items on the Operations menu control the DHCP server process, and they can be used to Start it, Stop it, obtain its Status, or have it reread its configuration file (Refresh).

AIX also provides the `dadmin` command for querying a DHCP server. For example, the following command queries the DHCP server on *kumquat*, asking about the status of the specified IP address:

```
# dadmin -h kumquat -q 192.168.44.23
PLEASE WAIT....Gathering Information From the Server....
IP Address   Status  Lease Time Start Time  Last Leased Proxy ...
10.10.20.180 Free
```

This IP address is not currently in use.

The AIX DHCP relay server is `dhcprs`, and its configuration file is */etc/dhcprs.cnf*. Here is an example:

```
Log file directives as for the DHCP server
server          10.10.30.1
```

The server statement is the most important in the file, and it specifies which remote DHCP server to forward requests to.

ISC DHCP: FreeBSD and Linux

The open source operating systems all use the DHCP implementation from the Internet Software Consortium (see *http://www.isc.org*). The DHCP server is `dhcpd`. It uses the configuration file */etc/dhcpd.conf*. Here is an example version illustrating its features:

```
    default-lease-time 14400;                      Global options.
    option subnet-mask 255.255.255.0;
    option domain zoas.org;

    subnet 10.10.1.0 netmask 255.255.255.0 {
       range 10.10.1.100 10.10.1.104;              IP addresses available for assignment.
       range 10.10.1.106 10.10.1.124;
       range 10.10.1.126 10.10.1.175;
       option routers 10.10.1.5;                   Options sent to these clients.
       option broadcast-address 10.10.1.255;
    }

    subnet 10.10.20.0 netmask 255.255.255.0 {
       range 10.10.20.176 10.10.20.200;            Another address range.
       option routers 10.10.20.88;                 Options for these clients.
       option broadcast-address 10.10.20.255;
       option font-servers 10.10.20.45;
    }

    host special {                                 A reservation.
       hardware ethernet aa:bb:cc:dd:ee:ff;
       fixed-address 10.10.1.105;
       default-lease-time 36000;                   Longer lease time for this host.
    }
```

This configuration file is very easy to understand. Note that we had to specify exclusions by defining multiple ranges for the 10.10.1.0 subnet (although being able to have more than one range is also a point in this DHCP server's favor).

Fixed IP addresses can also be assigned based on the client ID, which is defined in the client's configuration. This can be useful, for example, when a company has a pool of wireless cards that staff members borrow. Some of them use the client ID option to ensure they get the same address regardless of which card they happen to have borrowed. Include the following option within the host configuration to accomplish this:

```
    option dhcp-client-identifier string;
```

The corresponding client configuration file entry is:

```
    send dhcp-client-identifier string;
```

Before you can run the ISC DHCP server for the first time, you must create its lease file using this command:

```
    # touch /var/lib/dhcp/dhcpd.leases
```

The file must exist before the server will start. The server also creates a backup file in the same location, named *dhcpd.leases~*, which is used while updating the lease file. If this process should ever crash and leave the system without a leases file, you must copy the backup file to the normal filename before restarting the DHCP server. Otherwise, duplicate leases will quickly abound on the affected subnets, and you'll have no end of fun cleaning the mess up.

There is also a DHCP relay server from the ISC, dhcrelay. It requires no configuration file and takes the desired DHCP server as its argument, as in this example:

```
# dhcrelay 10.10.30.1
```

The server is usually started by a boot script. Some systems have options for configuring it other than editing the corresponding script file; see Table 8-9 for details.

There is a graphical utility for configuring the DHCP server available in the KDE desktop environment. It is named kcmdhcpd and written by Karl Backström (*http://www.lysator.liu.se/~backstrom/kcmdhcpd/*), and it is illustrated in Figure 8-3.

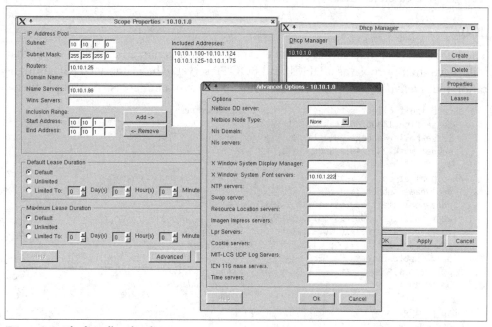

Figure 8-3. The kcmdhcpd utility

In the illustration, the 10.10.1.0 subnet's scope is being set up. The window on the left is used to specify the scope's most important properties. We have also clicked on that window's Advanced button to open the smaller, frontmost window (where we are setting the option for an X font server). The utility's main window appears on the right.

ISC DHCP Version 3 adds support for dynamic DNS updates.[*] This feature is in a preliminary state and may change over time. It currently works only with systems that have only a single network interface. The current implementation also lacks any security features and so should only be used when preventing unauthorized updates is not an issue.

---

[*] As well as a lot of other cool features!

The following configuration file excerpt illustrates the method for enabling dynamic updates:

```
subnet ... {
  normal statements ...
  ddns-domainname "dhcp.zoas.org";
  ddns-rev-domainname "in-addr.arpa";
}
```

The two additional substatements specify the DNS domain and reverse lookup domain that should be added to host names/IP addresses when DNS A and PTR records are created for them (respectively).

HP-UX

The HP-UX DHCP daemon is on the eccentric side. It is named bootpd, a name that reflects its dual purpose as a DHCP and BOOTP server. The primary DHCP configuration file is */etc/dhcptab*, which uses a termcap-like syntax. Here is an example file:

```
dhcp_default_client_settings:\            Global settings.
  lease-time=14400:dn=zoas.org:\
  lease-policy=accept-new-clients:\
  subnet-mask=255.255.255.0:

dhcp_pool_group:\                         Defines a scope and its properties.
  pool-name=subnet1:\
  addr-pool-start-address=10.10.1.100:\
  addr-pool-last-address=10.10.1.175:\
  reserved-for-other=10.10.1.125:\        Exclusion.
  reserved-for-other=10.10.1.105:\        Reservation.
  allow-bootp-clients=FALSE:\
  gw=10.10.1.5:\                          Default gateway.
  ba=10.10.1.255:                         Broadcast address.

dhcp_pool_group:\
  pool-name=subnet2:\
  addr-pool-start-address=10.10.20.100:\
  addr-pool-last-address=10.10.20.200:\
  gw=10.10.20.88:\                        Default gateway.
  ba=10.10.20.255:\                       Broadcast address.
  xf=10.10.20.45:                         X font server.
```

Here, we have defined our usual address ranges for the two subnets, along with their associated options. Note that IP addresses for reservations are included in the exclusion list.

Reservations themselves are handled in another configuration file, */etc/bootptab*. Here is an example entry:

```
pandora:\
        ht=ethernet:\                     Identifier type.
        ha=aabbccddeeff:\                 Hardware address.
        ip=10.10.1.105:\                  IP address to assign.
```

```
         vm=rfc1048:\                      Implementation style.
         sm=255.0.0.0:\                     Subnet mask.
         ba=10.10.1.255                     Broadcast address.
```

The bootpd daemon serves as a DHCP relay agent (in addition to its remote booting functions). Like reservations, relaying is specified in the */etc/bootptab* file, as in this example:

```
     subnet3:\                              Group name from dhcptab.
         ht=ethernet:\
         ha=000000000000:\                  This will match any MAC address.
         hm=000000000000:\
         bp=10.10.2.99  :\                  Relay host IP address.
         th=0:\                             Seconds to wait before relaying.
         hp=4                               Maximum hops.
```

You can also specify relaying for individual hosts by specifying its MAC address as the host address (ha) and using a mask of all ones (hm).

The HP-UX DHCP server supports dynamic updates to the DNS only in Version 11i. They are enabled via options to the pool group definition, as in this example:

```
     dhcp_pool_group:\
       pool-name=subnet2:\
       ...
       pcsn:\                               Use hostname specified by client.
       ddns-address=10.10.1.100:\           DNS server address.
```

In general, you can edit the configuration files by hand, or you can use SAM to control the various settings within it. Note that the relevant SAM areas are labeled with reference to remote booting (i.e., BOOTP), but they can be used to administer DHCP as well; the path from the main menu is Networking and Communications → Bootable Devices.

Solaris

The Solaris DHCP server is named in.dhcpd (following the usual naming convention for Solaris network daemons). Its configuration files reside in */var/dhcp*. It uses two separate files. The first of these, *dhcptab*, defines global and subnet- or client-specific options. Here is an example, which illustrates its termcap-like format:

```
     Locale     m  :UTCoffst=-14400:DNSdname="zoas.org":\
                   :Subnet=255.255.255.0:
     plum       m  :Include=Locale:LeaseTim=14400:LeaseNeg:
     special    m  :Include=Locale:LeaseTim=36000:
     10.10.1.0  m  :Subnet=255.255.255.0:Router=10.10.1.5:\
                   :Broadcst=10.10.1.255:
     10.10.20.0 m  :Subnet=255.255.255.0:Router=10.10.20.88:\
                   :Broadcst=10.10.20.255:XfontSrv=10.10.20.45:
```

This file defines a series of *macros*, named groups of settings. It also illustrates the use of the Include setting, which allows one macro to be incorporated in another macro as a whole. The settings themselves have very easy-to-understand names.

The first two items are used to define global options (note that the first one is included in the second and third entries). The second item, *plum*, will be assigned to most of the IP addresses in the scope, so it functions as a global default (although there is no way to tell this from this configuration file). This item conventionally has the same name as the DHCP server's hostname.

The third item will be used to apply different settings to our reserved IP address. The final two items define settings that apply to the scopes associated with the specified subnets. The initial name field must be the same as the subnet address.

The actual IP addresses to assign are stored in files (known as *network files*) in the same directory, and they are given names created by replacing all of the periods in the subnet address with underscores. For example, here is the file named *10_10_1_0*, corresponding to the 10.10.1.0 subnet:

```
client            flags    IP address      DHCP server      Expires   Macro
00                00       10.10.1.100     10.10.1.50       0         plum
00                00       10.10.1.101     10.10.1.50       0         plum
00                00       10.10.1.102     10.10.1.50       0         plum
00                00       10.10.1.103     10.10.1.50       0         plum
00                00       10.10.1.104     10.10.1.50       0         plum
01AABBCCDDEEFF    02       10.10.1.105     10.10.1.50       0         special
00                00       10.10.1.106     10.10.1.50       0         plum
...
00                01       10.10.1.125     10.10.1.50       0         plum
...
00                00       10.10.1.200     10.10.1.50       0         plum
```

Each line in the file defines an IP address within the scope. The fields in this file contain the client ID that is currently using the IP address (or 00 if it is free), flags applying to that entry (00 for addresses used for normal assignments), the IP address itself, the IP address of the DHCP server that manages it, the lease expiration time (0 if it is unassigned), and the macro within the *dhcptab* file that provides the options for that IP address.

In this case, we are looking at a file before the DHCP service has been started. Thus, all the dynamic fields in the file retain their initial entries.

The reserved address, 10.10.1.105, has a somewhat different format. The client ID is set to the string consisting of 01 (indicating that it is an Ethernet address) followed by the MAC address (sans colons). The flags field is set to 2, indicating that the address is permanently assigned. This entry also uses a different macro from the *dhcptab* file to obtain its longer lease time.

The excluded address, host 125, is assigned a flag value of 1, which indicates that the address is unavailable for assignment.

The Solaris DHCP server does not currently support dynamic updates to the DNS.

in.dhcpd can also function as a DHCP relay server. You specify this behavior via the facility's boot configuration file: */etc/default/dhcp* under Solaris 8 and */etc/inet/dhcpsvc.conf* under Solaris 9. Here are examples illustrating the relevant entries:

```
/etc/default/dhcp (Solaris 8):          /etc/inet/dhcpsvc.conf (Solaris 9):
RUNMODE=relay                           RUNMODE=relay
RELAY_DESTINATIONS=10.10.30.1           RELAY_DESTINATIONS=10.10.30.1
                                        DAEMON_ENABLED=TRUE
```

Solaris provides the DHCP Manager graphical utility for configuring DHCP. It can be started from the administrative area of the desktop or using the dhcpmgr command in */usr/sadm/admin/bin*. Solaris 8 also provides the nongraphical, menu-based utility dhcpconfig for the same purpose (the utility exists under Solaris 9, but this functionality has been removed).

Tru64

The Tru64 DHCP server is named joind. It uses several configuration files in */etc/join*. The first of these is *server.pcy* which is used to specify global server options. Here is a sample version of the file:

```
accept_client_name          Allow clients to specify their own hostnames.
#support_bootp              Don't support BOOTP.
#registered_clients_only    Accept requests from anyone.
send_options_in_offer       Include DHCP options in the initial offer.
use_macaddr_as_id           Use the MAC address to identify special clients.
```

The next file is named *nets*, and it is used to specify the various scopes managed by this DHCP server and the range of available addresses within them:

```
10.10.1.0    10.10.1.22    10.10.1.100-10.10.1.104
                           10.10.1.106-10.10.1.124
                           10.10.1.126-10.10.1.175

10.10.20.0   10.10.1.22    10.10.20.175-10.10.20.200
```

The first scope is for the 10.10.1.0 subnet, and it is defined as three address ranges. The second scope is for the 10.10.20.0 subnet, defined via a single address range. The second field in each line specifies the DHCP server managing the scope. Note that fields which are the same in successive lines do not need to be repeated.

The final configuration file is *dhcpcap*, a termcap-style configuration file used to specify DHCP options. Here are some example entries:

```
special:\
  :ht=ether:ha=aabbccddeeff:\      Identify this client via its MAC address.
  :ip=10.10.1.105:\                Assign this IP address.
  :gw=10.10.1.5:\                  Default gateway.
  :ba=10.10.1.255:\                Broadcast address.
  :sm=255.255.255.0:\              Subnet mask.
  :dn="zoas.org":\                 DNS domain name.
  :lt=36000:                       Lease time.
```

```
subnet1:\
    :nw=10.10.1.0:\                          Network address.
    :gw=10.10.1.5:\                          Default gateway.
    ...Same options as above.
    :lt=14400:                               Lease time.

subnet2:\
    :nw=10.10.20.0:\                         Network address.
    :gw=10.10.20.88:\                        Default gateway.
    :ba=10.10.20.255:\                       Broadcast address.

    ...Same options as above.
    :lt=14400:\                              Lease time.
    :xf=10.10.20.45:                         X font server.
```

Note that many settings must be repeated in each stanza as there is no global section or include mechanism.

These configuration files may be created and modified manually. However, Tru64 also provide the xjoin utility for accomplishing this. It is illustrated in Figure 8-4.

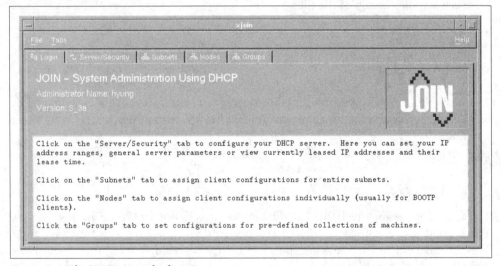

Figure 8-4. The Tru64 xjoin facility

The Tru64 DHCP server does not provide dynamic updates to the DNS.

The DHCP relay server is named bprelay, and it is started by a command of the following form, where the argument is the address of the DHCP server to which to relay:

```
# bprelay 10.10.30.1
```

Note that this server is not started by any boot script. You will have to modify a boot script if you want it to run as a matter of course.

Time Synchronization with NTP

Computers often don't work right when the hosts on a network have differing ideas about what time it is. For example, DNS servers become very upset when the master server's and slave servers' ideas of the current time are significantly different and will not accept zone transfers under such conditions. Also, many security protocols, such as Kerberos, have time-out values that depend on accurate clocks

The Network Time Protocol (NTP) was designed to remedy this situation by automating time synchronization across a network.* The NTP home page is *http://www. ntp.org*. There is also a lot of useful information available at *http://www.eecis.udel. edu/~mills/ntp.htm*.

You may wonder how computer clocks get out of synchronization in the first place. Computers contain a oscillator along with some hardware to interface it to the CPU. However, instability in the oscillator (for example, due to temperature changes) and latencies in computer hardware and software cause errors in the system clock (known as *wander* and *jitter*, respectively). Thus, over time, the clock settings of different computers that were initially set to the same time will diverge since the errors introduced by their respective hardware will be different.

NTP is designed to deal with these realities in a very sophisticated manner. It has been around since 1980 and was designed and written by Professor David L. Mills of the University of Delaware and his students. This protocol provides time synchronization for all of the computers within a network and is constructed to be both fault tolerant and scalable to very large networks. It also includes features for authentication between clients and servers and for collecting and displaying statistics about its operations. The protocol has a target precision of about 232 picoseconds.

How NTP Works

NTP operates in a hierarchical client/server fashion, with authoritative time values moving down from the top-level servers through lower-level servers and then to clients. The entire scheme is based on the availability of what it calls *stratum 1 servers*: servers that receive current time updates from a known-to-be-reliable source, such as an attached reference clock. Servers that receive time values from these servers are known as *stratum 2 servers* (and so on down the server hierarchy).

There are several options for obtaining authoritative time:

- The system can be connected to an external atomic clock.
- You can connect to the National Institute of Standards and Technology (NIST) by modem and receive this data.

---

* An older mechanism uses the `timed` daemon. I recommend replacing it with `ntpd`, which has the advantage of setting all of the clocks to the correct time. `timed` merely sets them all to the same time as the master server and has no mechanism for ensuring that the time is accurate.

What Is Time?

Here we look at time strictly from a standards point of view.

In 1967, a second was defined as "the duration of 9,192,631,770 periods of the radiation corresponding to the transition between the two hyperfine levels of the ground state of the cesium-133 atom." (Cesium atoms keep busy.) Before 1967, the length of a second was tied to the Earth's rotation, and the exact length of a second would get longer each year. The time standard consisting of these 1967 standard seconds is known as TAI (International Atomic Time).

Coordinated Universal Time (UTC) is the official standard for the current time used by NTP. UTC evolved from the previous standard, Greenwich Mean Time (GMT).

Unfortunately, TAI time does not exactly mesh with how long it really takes the earth to rotate on its axis. As a result, leap seconds are inserted into UTC about every 18 months to maintain synchronization with the planet's slightly irregular and slowing rotation. The leap seconds ensure that, on average, the Sun is directly overhead within 0.9 seconds of 12:00:00 UTC on the meridian of Greenwich, U.K.

- You can use a Global Positioning System (GPS)–based device, which can receive time values as well as positioning information from satellite sources.
- You can obtain the authoritative time values for your network from external stratum 1 NTP servers on the Internet. This is in fact the most common practice for Internet-connected organizations that do not require the extreme precision needed for a few real-time applications (e.g., air traffic control).

  The web page *http://www.eecis.udel.edu/~mills/ntp/servers.htm* contains links to lists of Internet-accessible stratum 1 and 2 servers. For most sites, a stratum 2 server is sufficient. Note that some servers require advance permission before you may connect to them, so check the requirements carefully before setting up a connection to an Internet NTP server.

In client mode, NTP makes periodic adjustments to the system clock based on the authoritative time data that it receives from the relevant servers. If the current time on the system differs from the correct time by more than 128 milliseconds, NTP resets the system clock. In its normal mode of operation, however, NTP makes adjustments to the system clock gradually by adjusting its parameters to achieve the needed correction. Over time, the NTP daemon on the system records and analyzes successive time errors—known as *clock drift*—and continues to correct the time automatically based on this data, even when it cannot reach its time server system. This entire process is known as *disciplining* the system clock.

In actual practice, NTP requires multiple sources of authoritative time. This strategy is used to protect against both single points of failure and unreliability of any single server (due to hardware failure, malicious tampering, and so on). In other words,

NTP views all time data with a certain amount of distrust, and its algorithms prefer at least three time sources. Each distinct server is sampled multiple times, and the NTP algorithms determine the best value to use for the current time from all of this data (naturally taking into account the network latency, the amount of time required for the time value to be transmitted from the remote server to the local system). This value is then used to adjust the time on the local system as described above. In a similar manner, client systems may also be configured to request time data from multiple NTP servers.[*]

All in all, NTP functions extremely well, and all the systems within a network can achieve synchronization to within a few milliseconds of one another. This level of accuracy is more than sufficient for most organizations.

Setting Up NTP

The first step for implementing NTP within your network is, as usual, planning. You'll need to decide several things, including how and where to obtain authoritative time values, the placement of NTP servers within the network, and which clients will connect to which servers. To get started, you might connect one or two local servers to three external stratum 2 servers; the local servers will become the top-level NTP servers within your organization. Then you can connect clients to the servers, and time synchronization will begin.

When things are working, you can move to the suggested configuration of three local servers each connected to three external servers and using a total of at least five external servers. Later, if necessary, you can add top-level servers or even another layer of servers within your organization that use the externally-connected ones as their authoritative time source.

Within an individual system, the NTP facility consists of a daemon process, a boot script, a configuration file, several log files, and a few utilities. Installing it is very easy. You can either download and build the package from source code or install it from a package provided by your operating system vendor.

Once the software is installed, the next step is to configure the facility. NTP's configuration file is conventionally */etc/ntp.conf*. Here is a very simple sample file for a client system:

```
server      192.168.15.33
logfile     /var/log/ntp
driftfile   /etc/ntp.drift
```

---

[*] Readers interested in very accurate time will be interested in this comment from one of the book's reviewers: "One of NTP's few shortcomings is its inability to handle asymmetric path delays. The latest versions of NTP mitigate this using the huff 'n' puff filter (see the *tinker* command and *huffpuff* keyword in the 'Miscellaneous Options' documentation)."

The first line specifies a server to use when obtaining time data, and remaining lines specify locations of NTP's log file and drift file respectively (the latter stores data about local clock errors for future time corrections).

The configuration files for servers also include a server entry for their sources of time data. In addition, they may include lines like this one:

```
peer 192.168.15.56 key 7
```

This entry indicates that the indicated server is a peer, a computer with which the local system will exchange—send and receive—time data. Generally, the top-level servers within the organization can be configured as peers, functioning as both clients and servers with respect to one another and as servers with respect to general client systems. The key keyword is used to specify an authentication key for this connection (discussed below).

If a server has a reference clock connected to it, the server entry within its configuration file is somewhat different:

```
server 127.127.8.0 mode 5
```

Reference clocks are usually connected via a serial line, and they are specified with an IP address beginning with 127.127. The final two components of the IP address indicate the type of device (check the device's documentation) and unit number, respectively.

NTP also includes an authentication facility, which enables clients and servers to verify that they are communicating with known and trusted computers. The facility is based upon a private key scheme; keys are conventionally stored in the file */etc/ntp.keys*. This file can contain up to 65,536 32-bit keys. When in use, the facility adds several lines to the configuration file:

```
keys /etc/ntp.keys
trustedkey 1 2 3 4 5 6 7 15
request key 15
control key 15
```

The first line identifies the NTP key file. The second line activates the indicated keys within the file, and the remaining two lines specify which key to use for NTP queries and configuration changes, where the indicated key functions as a password in those contexts (corresponding to the ntpdc and ntpq utilities, respectively). Once specified and enabled, these keys may be used with the key keyword in server and peer entries.

The most recent versions of NTP also include an additional authentication option referred to as the *autokey* mechanism. This scheme was designed for NTP's multicast mode, in which time data is broadcast rather than being explicitly exchanged between clients and servers. Using it, clients can generate session keys that can be used to confirm the authenticity of received data.

Once configured, the NTP daemon must be started at boot time. On System V–style systems, this is accomplished via a boot script within the usual */etc/rcn.d* script hierarchy (included as part of the NTP package); on BSD-style systems, you will have to add the command to one of the boot scripts.

On client machines, at boot time, the system time may be explicitly synchronized to that of its server by running the `ntpdate` utility included with the package. This command takes a form something like the following:

```
ntpdate -bs 192.168.15.56
```

The `-b` option says to set the system time explicitly (rather than adjusting it in the normal manner), and the `-s` option says to send the command output to the syslog facility (rather than standard output). The remaining item on the simple command line is the IP address of a server from which to request the current time. Multiple servers may be specified if desired. Be aware that running `ntpdate` must take place before the NTP daemon is started. In addition, many application programs and their associated server processes react rather badly to substantial clock changes after they have started, so it is a good idea to perform time synchronization activities early enough in the boot process that they precede the starting of other servers that might depend on them.

Eventually, the command `ntpdate` will be retired, as its functionality has been merged into `ntpd` in the most recent versions. The command form `ntpd -g -q` is the equivalent form, and it queries the time and set the clock to it, exiting afterwards. The server to contact is specified, as usual, in the configuration file.

Enabling ntpd under FreeBSD

FreeBSD systems provide `nptd` by default. The daemon is started by the `rc.network` boot script at startup whenever the following variables are set in *rc.conf* or *rc.config. local* in */etc*:

```
xntpd_enable="YES"              Start the ntpd daemon.
ntpdate_enable="YES"            Run the ntpdate command at startup.
ntpdate_flags="-bs 10.1.5.22"   Specify options to ntpdate (e.g., desired host).
```

By default, `ntpd` is disabled.

A Simple Authentic Time Option

For many sites, the usual authentic time options have significant inconveniences associated with them. Reference clocks and GPS devices can be expensive, and using an Internet-based time server can be inconvenient if your connectivity to the Internet is intermittent. At my site, we've found a low-cost and simple solution suitable for our network. It involves using an inexpensive clock that automatically synchronizes to NIST's WWVB time code by receiving its radio transmission.* In my case, the

---

* One reviewer notes, "You can do something similar with a hand-held GPS with a communication port. These usually speak a marine control code, but it is trivial to convert it to RS-232."

specific clock is an Atomic Time PC Desktop Clock (see *http://www.arctime.com* under desktop clocks for details), which retails for about $100 U.S. The device is shown in Figure 8-5.

Figure 8-5. Atomic Time PC Desktop Clock

Devices of this type can be used as reference clocks using the usual NTP facilities, but this model is not supported. However, for my site, this is not a problem. We use a simple Expect script to communicate with the device (which is attached to the computer via a serial port) and to retrieve the current time:

```
#!/usr/bin/expect

set clock /dev/ttyS0
spawn -open [open $clock r+]

# set the serial line characteristics
stty ispeed 300 ospeed 300 parenb -parodd \
  cs7 hupcl -cstopb cread clocal -icrnl \
  -opost -isig -icanon -iexten -echo -noflsh < $clock

send "o"
expect -re "(.)"
send "\r"
expect -re "(.)"
# expect 16 or more characters
expect -re "(...............*)"
exit
```

The script defines a variable pointing to the appropriate serial line, sets the line characteristics using the stty command, and then communicates with the device via a series of send and expect commands. These tell the clock to transmit the current time and the script displays the resulting data on standard output:

```
Mon Oct 07 13:32:22 2002 -0.975372 seconds
```

We then use a Perl script to parse and reconstruct the data into a form required by the date command; for example:

```
date 100713322002.22
```

(Remember that date's argument format is *mmddhhmmyyyy.ss*.) We can then use configuration file entries like the following to set up NTP on that computer:

```
server 127.127.1.1                      # LCL (the local clock)
fudge 127.127.1.1 stratum 12
```

These lines specify the local system clock as the NTP time source. The server then becomes the authoritative source of time information for all the other systems within the network. These other systems use the standard NTP facility for synchronizing to this time source. This level of ultimate time accuracy is perfectly adequate for our simple needs. However, we set the server's stratum to the highest value so that no one else will consider our time authoritative.

An even simpler alternative is to simply define cron jobs on the other servers to update the time from this master server once or twice a day (using ntpdate or ntpd -g -q). This approach would also avoid the latencies introduced by the spawned sub-processes.

Managing Network Daemons under AIX

In general, AIX uses the System Resource Controller to manage daemons, and the ones related to networking are no exception. The startsrc and stopsrc commands are used to manually start and stop server processes within the SRC. The following commands illustrate the facility's use with several common TCP/IP daemons:

```
# stopsrc -g tcpip          Stop all TCP/IP-related daemons.
# stopsrc -s named          Stop the DNS name server.
# startsrc -s inetd         Start the master networking server.
# startsrc -g nfs           Start all NFS-related daemons.
```

As these commands illustrate, the -s and -g options are used to specify the individual server or server group (respectively) to which the command applies. As usual, the lssrc command may be used to display the status of daemons controlled by the SRC, as in this command, which lists the servers within the nfs group:

```
# lssrc -g nfs
Subsystem        Group          PID          Status
biod             nfs            344156       active
rpc.statd        nfs            376926       active
rpc.lockd        nfs            385120       active
nfsd             nfs                         inoperative
rpc.mountd       nfs                         inoperative
```

On this system, the daemons related to accessing remote filesystems are running, while those related to providing remote access to local filesystems are not.

Monitoring the Network

For most of us, networking-related tasks make up a large fraction of our system administration duties. Installing and configuring a network can be a daunting task, especially if you're starting from scratch. However, monitoring and managing the network on an ongoing basis can be no less daunting, especially for very large networks. Fortunately, there are a variety of tools to help with this job, ranging from simple single-host network status utilities to complex network monitoring and management packages. In this section, we'll take a look at representative examples of each type, thereby enabling you to select the approach and software that is appropriate for your site.

Standard Networking Utilities

We'll begin with the standard Unix commands designed for various network monitoring and troubleshooting tasks on the local system. Each command provides a specific type of network information and allows you to probe and monitor various aspects of network functionality. (We've already considered three such tools: ping and arp in "Network Testing and Troubleshooting" in Chapter 5 and nslookup in "Using the nslookup and dig utilities" earlier in this chapter).

The netstat command is the most general of these tools. It is used to monitor a system's TCP/IP network activity. It can provide some basic data about how much and what kind of network activity is currently going on, and also summary information for the recent past.

 The specific output of the netstat command varies somewhat from system to system, although the basic information that it provides is the same. Moving from these generic examples to the format on your systems will be easy.

Without arguments, netstat lists all active network connections with the local host.* In this output, it is often useful to filter out lines containing "localhost" to limit the display to interesting data:

```
# netstat | grep -v localhost
Active Internet connections
Proto Recv-Q Send-Q  Local Address   Foreign Address  (state)
tcp        0    737   hamlet.1018     duncan.shell     ESTABLISHED
tcp        0      0   hamlet.1019     portia.shell     ESTABLISHED
tcp      348      0   hamlet.1020     portia.login     ESTABLISHED
tcp      120      0   hamlet.1021     laertes.login    ESTABLISHED
tcp      484      0   hamlet.1022     lear.login       ESTABLISHED
tcp     1018      0   hamlet.1023     duncan.login     ESTABLISHED
tcp        0      0   hamlet.login    lear.1023        ESTABLISHED
```

On this host, *hamlet*, there are currently two connections each to *portia*, *lear*, and *duncan*, and one connection to *laertes*. All but one of the connections—a connection

---

* Some versions of netstat also include data about Unix domain sockets in this report (omitted from the upcoming example).

to *lear*—are outgoing: the address form of a hostname with a port number appended indicates the originating system for the connection.* The *.login* suffix indicates a connection made with rlogin or with rsh without arguments; the *.shell* appendix indicates a connection servicing a single command.

The Recv-Q and Send-Q columns indicate how much data is currently queued between the two systems via each connection. These numbers indicate current, pending data (in bytes), not the total amount transferred since the connection began. (Some versions of netstat do not provide this information and thus always display zeros in these columns.)

If you include netstat's -a option, the display will also include passive connections: network ports where a service is listening for requests. Here is an example from the output:

```
Proto Recv-Q Send-Q  Local Address  Foreign Address (state)
tcp        0      0  *:imap         *:*             LISTEN
```

Passive connections are characterized by the LISTEN keyword in the state column.

The -i option is used to display a summary of the network interfaces on the system:

```
# netstat -i
Name   Mtu Network      Address    Ipkts     Opkts
lan0  1500 192.168.9.0  greta      2399283   932981
loo   4136 127.0.0.0    loopback   15856     15856
```

This HP-UX system has one Ethernet interface named *lan0*. The output also gives the maximum transmission unit (MTU) size for each interface's local network and a count of the number of incoming and outgoing packets since the last boot. Some versions of this command also give counts of the number of errors as well.

On most systems, you can follow the -i option with a time interval argument (in seconds) to obtain an entirely different display comparing network traffic and error and collision rates (in fact, -i is often optional). On Linux systems, substitute the -w option for -i.

Here is an example of this netstat report:

```
# netstat -i 5 | awk 'NR!=3 {print $0}'
     input   (en0)    output           input   (Total)  output
packets errs  packets errs colls packets errs  packets errs colls
   47     0    66      0    0      47     0    66      0    0
  114     0   180      0    0     114     0   180      0    0
  146     0   227      0    0     146     0   227      0    0
   28     0    52      0    0      28     0    52      0    0
^C
```

---

* Why is this? Connections on the receiving system use the defined port number for that service, and netstat is able to translate them into a service name like *login* or *shell*. The port on the transmitting end is just some arbitrary port without intrinsic meaning and so remains untranslated.

This command displays network statistics every five seconds.[*] This sample output is in two parts: it includes two sets of input and output statistics. The left half of the table (the first five columns) shows the data for the primary network interface; the second half shows total values for all network interfaces on the system. On this system, like many others, there is only one interface, so the two sides of the table are identical.

The input columns show data for incoming network traffic, and the output columns show data for outgoing traffic. The errs columns show the number of errors that occurred while transferring the indicated number of network packets. These numbers should be low, less than one percent of the number of packets. Larger values indicate serious network problems.

The colls column lists the number of collisions. A collision occurs when two hosts on the network try to send a packet within a few milliseconds of one another.[†] When this happens, each host waits a random amount of time before retrying the transmission; this method virtually eliminates repeated collisions by the same hosts. The number of collisions is a measure of how much network traffic there is, because the likelihood of a collision happening is directly proportional to the amount of network activity. Collisions are recorded only by transmitting hosts. On some systems, collision data isn't tracked separately but rather is merged in with the output errors figure.

The collision rate is low on an average, well-behaved network using hubs or coax cable, just a few percent of the total traffic. You should start to become concerned when it rises above about five percent. Network segments using full-duplex switches should not see any collisions at all, and any amount of them indicates that the switch is overloaded.

The -s option displays useful statistics for each network protocol (cumulative since the last boot). Here is an example output section for the TCP protocol:

```
# netstat -s
...
Tcp:
    50 active connections openings
    0 passive connection openings
    0 failed connection attempts
    0 connection resets received
    3 connections established
    45172 segments received
    48365 segments send out
    1 segments retransmitted
    0 bad segments received
    3 resets sent
```

[*] The awk command throws away the first line after the headers, which displays cumulative totals since the last reboot.

[†] Remember that collisions occur only on CSMA/CD Ethernet networks; token ring networks, for example, don't have collisions.

Some versions of netstat provide even more detailed per-protocol information.

netstat can also display the routing tables using its -r option. See "Adding a New Network Host" in Chapter 5 for a discussion of this mode.

Graphical utilities to display similar data are also becoming common. For example, Figure 8-6 illustrates some of the output generated by the ntop command, written by Luca Deri (*http://www.ntop.org*). When it is running, the command generates web pages containing the collected information.

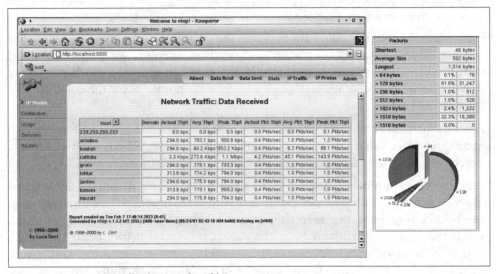

Figure 8-6. Network traffic data produced by ntop

The window on the left in the illustration depicts one of ntop's most useful displays. It shows incoming network traffic for the local system, broken down by origin. The various columns list average and peak data transmission rates for each one. A similar display for outgoing network traffic is also available. This information can be very useful in narrowing down network performance problems to the specific systems that are involved.

ntop provides many other tables and graphs of useful network data. For example, the pie chart on the right side of the figure illustrates the breakdown of network traffic by packet length.

As we've seen, the ping command is useful for basic network connectivity testing. It can also be useful for monitoring network traffic by observing the round trip time between two locations over time. The best way to do this is to tell ping to send a specific number of queries. The command format to do this varies by system:

AIX and HP-UX	ping *host packet-size count*
AIX, FreeBSD, Linux, and Tru-64	ping -c *count* [-s *packet-size*] *host*
Solaris	ping -s *host packet-size count*

Here is an example from an AIX system:

```
# ping beulah 64 5
PING beulah: (192.168.9.84): 56 data bytes
64 bytes from 192.168.9.84: icmp_seq=0 ttl=255 time=1 ms
64 bytes from 192.168.9.84: icmp_seq=1 ttl=255 time=0 ms
64 bytes from 192.168.9.84: icmp_seq=2 ttl=255 time=0 ms
64 bytes from 192.168.9.84: icmp_seq=3 ttl=255 time=0 ms
64 bytes from 192.168.9.84: icmp_seq=4 ttl=255 time=0 ms
----beulah PING Statistics----
5 packets transmitted, 5 packets received, 0% packet loss
round-trip min/avg/max = 5/5/6 ms
```

This command pings *beulah* 5 times, using the default packet size of 64 bytes. The summary at the bottom of the output displays the packet-loss statistics (here, none) and round-trip time statistics. Used in this way, ping can provide a quick measure of network performance, provided that you know what normal is for the connection in question.

You can increase the packet size to a value greater than the MTU to force packet fragmentation (a value above 1500 is usually sufficient for Ethernet networks) and thereby use ping to monitor performance under those conditions.*

The traceroute command (devised by Van Jacobson) is used to determine the route taken by network packets to arrive at their destination. It obtains this route information by a clever scheme that takes advantage of the packet's time-to-live (TTL) field, which specifies the maximum hops the packet can travel before being discarded. This field is automatically decremented by each gateway that the packet passes through. If its value reaches 0, the gateway discards the packet and returns a message back to the originating host (specifically, an ICMP time-exceeded message).

traceroute uses this behavior to identify each location in the route to the destination. It begins with a TTL of 1, so packets are discarded by the first gateway. traceroute then obtains the gateway address from the resulting ICMP message. After a fixed number of packets with TTL 1 (usually 3), the TTL is increased to 2. In the same way, this packet is discarded by the second gateway, whose identity can be determined by the resulting error message. The TTL is gradually increased in this way until a packet reaches the destination.

Here is an example of traceroute in action:

```
# traceroute www.fawc.org
traceroute to fawc.org (64.226.114.72),30 hops max,40 byte packets
 1  route129a.ycp.edu (208.192.129.2) 1.870 ms   1.041 ms   0.976 ms
 2  209.222.29.105 (209.222.29.105) 3.345 ms   3.929 ms   3.524 ms
 3  Serial2-2.GW4.BWI1.ALTER.NET (157.130.25.173) 9.155 ms ...
 4  500.at-0-1-0.XL2.DCA8.ALTER.NET (152.63.42.94)  8.316 ms ...
```

---

* The "ping of death" attacks (1998) consisted of fragmented ping packets that were too large for their memory buffer. When the packet was reassembled and the buffer overflowed, the system crashed.

```
 5  0.so-0-0-0.TL2.DCA6.ALTER.NET (152.63.38.73)  9.931 ms ...
 6  0.so-7-0-0.TL2.ATL5.ALTER.NET (152.63.146.41)  24.248 ms ...
 7  0.so-4-1-0.XL2.ATL5.ALTER.NET (152.63.146.1)  25.320 ms ...
 8  0.so-7-0-0.XR2.ATL5.ALTER.NET (152.63.85.194)  24.330 ms ...
 9  192.ATM7-0.GW5.ATL5.ALTER.NET (152.63.82.13)  26.824 ms ...
10  interland1-gw.customer.alter.net (157.130.255.134) 24.498 ms ...
11  * * *       No messages received from these hosts.
12  * * *
13  64.224.0.67 (64.224.0.67)  24.937 ms  25.155 ms  24.738 ms
14  64.226.114.72 (64.226.114.72)  26.058 ms  24.587 ms  26.677 ms
```

Each numbered line corresponds to a successive gateway in the route, and each line displays the hostname (when available), IP address, and the round-trip times for each of the three packets (I've truncated long lines to fit). This particular route spent quite a bit of time traveling inside *alter.net*.

Sometimes, routers or firewalls drop ICMP packets or fail to send error messages. These situations result in lines like 11 and 12, where three asterisks indicate that the gateway could not be identified. Other lines may also contain asterisks for similar reasons. Occasionally, the successive outgoing packets take different routes to the destination, and different intermediate gateway data is returned. In such cases, all of the gateways are listed.

 Both traceroute and netstat provide a -n option which specifies that output contain IP addresses only (and hostname resolution should not be attempted). These options are useful for determining network information when DNS name resolution is not working or is unavailable.

Packet Sniffers

Packet sniffers provide a means for examining network traffic on an individual packet basis. They can be invaluable for troubleshooting problems related to a specific network operation, such as a client-server application, rather than general network connectivity issues. They can also be abused, of course, and used for eavesdropping purposes. For this reason, they must be run as *root*.

The freel tcpdump utility is the best-known tool of this type (it was originally written by Van Jacobson, Craig Leres, and Steven McCanne and is available from *http://www.tcpdump.org*). It is provided with the operating system by many vendors—all but HP-UX and Solaris in our case—but can be built for these systems as well. (Solaris provides the snoop utility instead, which we'll discuss later in this subsection.)

tcpdump allows you to examine the headers of TCP/IP packets. For example, the following command displays the headers for all traffic involving host *romeo* (some initial and trailing output columns have been stripped off to save space):

```
# tcpdump -e -t host romeo
arp 42: arp who-has spain tell romeo
arp 60: arp reply spain is-at 03:05:f3:a1:74:e3
ip 58: romeo.1014 > spain.login: S 27643873:27643873(0) win 16384
```

```
ip 60: spain.login > romeo.1014: S 19898809:19898809(0) ack
                                           27643874 win 14335
ip 54: romeo.1014 > spain.login: . ack 1 win 15796
ip 55: romeo.1014 > spain.login: P 1:2(1) ack 1 win 15796
ip 60: spain.login > romeo.1014: . ack 2 win 14334
ip 85: romeo.1014 > spain.login: P 2:33(31) ack 1 win 15796
ip 60: spain.login > romeo.1014: . ack 33 win 14303
ip 60: spain.login > romeo.1014: P 1:2(1) ack 33 win 14335
...
ip 60: spain.login > romeo.1014: F 177:177(0) ack 54 win 14335
ip 54: romeo.1014 > spain.login: . ack 178 win 15788
ip 54: romeo.1014 > spain.login: F 54:54(0) ack 178 win 15796
ip 60: spain.login > romeo.1014: . ack 55 win 14334
```

This output displays the protocol and packet length, followed by the source and destination hosts and ports. For TCP packets, this information is followed by the TCP flags (a period or one or more uppercase letters), ack plus the acknowledgement sequence number, and win plus the contents of the TCP window size field. Note that the literal sequence numbers are displayed only in the first packet in each direction; after that, relative numbers are used to improve readability.

So what good is this output? You can monitor the progress of a TCP/IP operation (the packets that are displayed can be specified in a number of ways); here we see the initial connection and final termination of an rlogin connection from *romeo* to *spain*. You can also monitor how network traffic is affecting connections of interest by observing the values in the window field. This field specifies the data window that the sending host will accept in future packets, specifying the maximum number of bytes. The window field also serves as the TCP flow-control mechanism, and a host will reduce the value it places there when the host is congested or overloaded (it can even use a value of 0 to temporarily halt incoming transmissions). In our example, there are no congestion problems on either host.

tcpdump can also be used to display the contents of TCP/IP packets, using its -X option, which displays packet data in hex and ASCII. For example, this command displays the packet data from packets sent from *mozart* to *salieri*:

```
# tcpdump -X -s 0 src mozart and dst salieri
...
0x0000    4510 0053 dd9e 4000 3c06 cbe8 c100 0935    E..S..@.<......5
0x0010    c100 09d8 0201 03fd 1ead 846c c70d c3d6    ...........l....
0x0020    5018 f000 6e99 0000 4672 6920 4d61 7220    P...n...Fri.Mar.
0x0030    2031 2030 393a 3438 3a32 3120 4553 5420    .1.09:48:21.EST.
0x0040    3230 3032 0d0a 6d61 686c 6572 2d32 3032    2002..mozart-202
0x0050    3e3e                                       >>
```

The output shows only one packet. It contains the current date and time and the initial prompt after a successful rlogin command from *salieri* to *mozart*.

The -s 0 option tells tcpdump to increase the number of bytes of data that are dumped from each packet to whatever limit is required to display the entire packet (the default is usually 60 to 80).

We've now seen two examples of the arguments to tcpdump, which consists of an expression specifying the packets to be displayed. In other words, it functions as a filter on incoming packets. A variety of keywords are defined for this purpose, and logical connectors are provided for creating complex conditions, as in this example:

```
# tcpdump src \( mozart or salieri \) and tcp port 21 and not dst vienna
```

The expression in this command selects packets from *mozart* or *salieri* using TCP port 21 (the FTP control port) that are not destined for *vienna*.

 You can save packets to a file rather than displaying them immediately using the -w option. You then use the -r option to read from a file rather than displaying current network traffic.

A few vendor-provided versions of tcpdump have some eccentricities:

- The AIX version does not provide the -X option (although you can dump packets in hex with -x). I recommend replacing it with the latest version from *http://www.tcpdump.org* if you need to examine packet contents.

- Tru64 requires that the kernel be compiled with packet filtering enabled (via the options PACKETFILTER directive). You must also create the *pfilt* device (interface):

```
# cd /dev; MAKEDEV pfilt
```

Finally, you must configure the interface to allow tcpdump to set it to promiscuous mode and to access the frame headers:

```
# pfconfig +p +c network-interface
```

It is often useful to pipe the output of tcpdump to grep to further refine the displayed output. Alternatively, you can use the ngrep command (written by Jordan Ritter, *http://www.packetfactory.net/projects/ngrep/*) which builds grep functionality into a packet filter utility. For an example of using ngrep, see "LDAP: Using a Directory Service for User Authentication" in Chapter 6.

The Solaris snoop command

The Solaris snoop command is essentially equivalent to tcpdump, although I find its output is more convenient and intuitive. Here is an example of its use:

```
# snoop src bagel and dst acrasia and port 23
Using device /dev/eri (promiscuous mode)
        bagel -> acrasia      TELNET C port=32574 a
        bagel -> acrasia      TELNET C port=32574
        bagel -> acrasia      TELNET C port=32574 e
        bagel -> acrasia      TELNET C port=32574
        bagel -> acrasia      TELNET C port=32574 f
        bagel -> acrasia      TELNET C port=32574
        bagel -> acrasia      TELNET C port=32574 r
        bagel -> acrasia      TELNET C port=32574
        bagel -> acrasia      TELNET C port=32574 i
        bagel -> acrasia      TELNET C port=32574
        bagel -> acrasia      TELNET C port=32574 s
```

```
bagel -> acrasia      TELNET C port=32574
bagel -> acrasia      TELNET C port=32574 c
bagel -> acrasia      TELNET C port=32574
bagel -> acrasia      TELNET C port=32574 h
```

As this example illustrates, the snoop command accepts the same expressions as tcpdump for use in filtering the packets to display. This output displays a portion of the login sequence from a telnet session. The data from the packet is displayed to the right of the header information; here we see the login name that was entered.

snoop has several useful options, as illustrated in these examples:

# **snoop -o** *file* **-q**	*Save packets to a file.*
# **snoop -i** *file*	*Read packets from a file.*
# **snoop -v** [**-p** *n*]	*Display packet details (for packet n).*

Packet collecting under AIX and HP-UX

HP-UX's nettl facility and AIX's iptrace and ipreport utilities are general-purpose packet collection packages. They both collect network packet data into a binary file and can display specified information from such files in an easy-to-read format. They have the advantage that data collection is fundamentally decoupled from its display.

The specific data to save is highly configurable, and data collection occurs automatically via a network daemon or cron job. This allows the facilities to gather and accumulate a body of network information which can be used for troubleshooting and performance analysis. In addition, ad hoc filtering can take place afterwards, allowing for much more complex reporting.

The Simple Network Management Protocol

The tools discussed in the previous subsection can be very useful for examining network operations and/or traffic for one or two systems. However, you'll eventually want to examine network traffic and other data in the context of the network as a whole, moving beyond the point of view of any single system. Much more elaborate tools are needed for this task. We will consider several examples of such packages in the next section. To understand how they work, however, we'll need to consider the Simple Network Management Protocol (SNMP), the network service that underlies a large part of the functionality of most network management programs. We'll begin with a brief look at SNMP's fundamental concepts and data structures and then go on to the practicalities of using it on Unix systems. Finally, we'll discuss some security issues that must be resolved when using SNMP.

For a more extended treatment of SNMP, I recommend *Essential SNMP* by Douglas Mauro and Kevin Schmidt (O'Reilly & Associates).

SNMP concepts and constructs

SNMP was designed to be a consistent interface for both gathering data from and seting parameters of various network devices. The managed devices can range from switches and routers to network hosts (computers) running almost any operating system. SNMP succeeds in doing this reasonably well, once you have it configured and running everywhere you need it. The hardest part is getting used to its somewhat counterintuitive terminology, which I'll attempt to decode in this section.

SNMP has been around for a while, and there are many versions of it (including several flavors of Version 2). The ones that are implemented currently are Version 1 and Version 2c. There is also a Version 3 in development as of this writing. We will address version-specific issues when appropriate.

Figure 8-7 illustrates a basic SNMP setup. In this picture, one computer is the Network Management Station (NMS). Its job is to collect and act on information from the various devices being monitored. The latter are grouped on the right side of the figure and include two computers, a router, a network printer, and an environmental monitoring device (these are only a part of the range of devices that support SNMP).

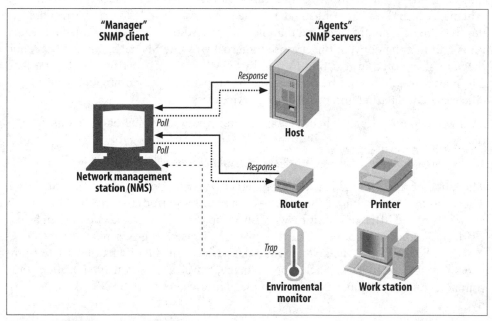

Figure 8-7. SNMP manager and agents

In the simplest case, the NMS periodically polls the devices it is managing, sending queries for the devices' current status information. The devices respond by transmitting the requested data. In addition, monitored devices can also send traps: unsolicited messages to the NMS, usually generated when the value of some monitored parameter falls out of the acceptable range. For example, an environmental monitoring device may send a trap when the temperature or humidity is too low or too high.

The term *manager* is used to refer both to the monitoring software running on the NMS as well as the computer (or other device) running the software. Similarly, the term *agent* refers to the software used by the monitored devices to generate and transmit their status data, but it is also used more loosely to refer to the device being monitored. Clearly, SNMP is a client-server protocol, but its usage of "client" and "server" is reversed from the typical usage: the local manager functions as the client, and the remote agents function as servers. This is similar to the terms' usage in the X Window system: X clients on remote hosts are displayed by the X server on the local host. SNMP messages use TCP and UDP ports 161, and traps use TCP and UDP ports 162. Some vendors use additional ports for traps (e.g., Cisco uses TCP and UDP ports 1993).

For an SNMP manager to communicate with an agent, the manager must be aware of the various data values that the agent keeps track of. The names and contents of these data values are defined in one or more Management Information Bases (MIBs). A MIB is just a collection of value/property definitions whose names are arranged into a standard hierarchy (tree structure). A MIB is not a database but rather a schema. A MIB does not hold any data values; it is simply a definition of the data values that are being monitored and that may be queried or modified. These data definitions and naming conventions are used internally by the SNMP agent software, and they are also stored in text files for use by SNMP managers. MIBs may be standard and may be implemented by every agent, or proprietary, describing data values specific to a manufacturer and possibly to a device class.

This will become clearer when we look at an actual data value name. Consider this one:

> *iso.org.dod.internet.mgmt.mib-2.system.sysLocation* = "Dabney Alley 6 Closet"

The name of this data value is the long, italicized string on the left of the equal sign. The various components of the name—separated by periods—correspond to different levels of the MIB tree (starting with *iso* at the top). Thus, *sysLocation* is eight levels deep within the hierarchy. The tree structure is used to group related data values together. For example, the *system* group defines various data items that relate to the overall system (or device), including its name, physical location (*sysLocation*), and primary contact person. As this example indicates, not all SNMP data need be dynamic.

Figure 8-8 illustrates the overall SNMP namespace hierarchy. The top levels of the tree exist mainly for historical reasons, and most data resides in the *mgmt.mib-2* and *private.enterprises* subtrees. The former implements what is now the standard MIB, named MIB II (it is an enhancement to the original standard), and it has a large number of items under it. Only two of its direct children are included in the illustration: system, which holds general information about the device, and host, which holds data related to computer systems. Other important children of *mib-2* are *interfaces* (network interfaces); *ip*, *tcp*, and *udp* (protocol-specific data); and *snmp* (SNMP traffic data). Note that all names within the MIB are case-sensitive. Clearly, not all parts of the hierarchy apply to all devices, and only the relevant portions are implemented by most agents.

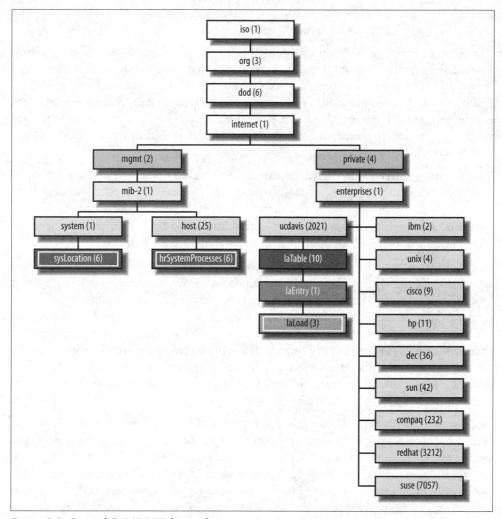

Figure 8-8. General SNMP MIB hierarchy

The highlighted items in the figure are leaf nodes that actually contain data values. Here, we see the system location description, the current number of processes on the system, and the system load average (moving from left to right).

Each of the points with the MIB hierarchy has both a name and a number associated with it. The numbers for each item are also given in the figure. You can refer to a data point by either name or number. For example, *iso.org.dod.internet.mgmt.mib-2.system.sysLocation* can also be referred to as 1.3.6.1.2.1.1.6. Similarly, the *laLoad* data item can be specified as *iso.org.dod.internet.private.enterprises.ucdavis.laTable.laEntry.laLoad* and as 1.3.6.1.4.1.2021.10.1.3. Each of these name types is known generically as an OID (object ID). Usually, only the name of the final node—*sysLocation* or *laLoad*—is needed to refer to a data point, but occasionally the full version of the OID must be specified (as we'll see).

The *private.enterprises* portion of the MIB tree contains vendor-specific data definitions. Each organization that has applied for one is assigned a unique identifier under this mode; the ones corresponding to the vendors of our operating systems, U.C. Davis, and Cisco are pictured. For a listing of all assigned numbers, see *ftp://ftp.isi.edu/in-notes/iana/assignments/enterprise-numbers/*. You can request a number for your organization from the Internet Assigned Numbers Authority (IANA) at *http://www.iana.org/cgi-bin/enterprise.pl*.

The *ucdavis* subtree is important for Linux and FreeBSD systems, because the open source Net-SNMP package is what is used on these systems. This package was developed by U.C. Davis for a long time (and Carnegie Mellon University before that), and this is the enterprise-specific subtree that applies to open source SNMP agents. This package is available for all the operating systems we are considering.

Another important MIB is the remote monitoring MIB, RMON. This MIB defines a set of generic network statistics. It is designed to allow data collection from a series of autonomous probes positioned around the network which ultimately transmit summary data to a central manager. Probe capabilities are supported by many current routers, switches and other network devices. Placing probes at strategic points throughout a WAN can greatly reduce the network traffic required to monitor the performance across the entire network by limiting the raw data collection to the probes and minimizing communication with a distant NMS by reducing it to summary form.

Access to SNMP data is controlled by passwords called *community names* (or strings). There are generally separate community names for the agent's read-only and read-write modes, as well as an additional name used with traps. Each SNMP agent knows its name (i.e., password) for each mode and will not answer queries which specify anything else. Community names can be up to 32 characters long and should be chosen using the same security considerations as *root* passwords. We'll discuss other security implications of community names in a bit later.

Unfortunately, many devices are delivered with SNMP enabled, using the default read-only community string *public* and sometimes the default read-write community string *private*. It is imperative that you change these values *before* the device is placed on the network (or that you disable SNMP for the device). Otherwise, you immediately place the device at risk for easy attack for hijacking and tampering by hackers, and its can vulnerability can put other parts of your network at risk.

The procedure for changing this value varies by device. For hosts, you change it in the configuration file associated with the SNMP agent. For other types of devices, such as routers, consult the documentation provided by the manufacturer.

In contrast to the relative complexity of the data definitions, the set of SNMP operations that monitor and manage devices is quite limited, consisting of *get* (to request a value from device), *set* (to specify the value of a modifiable device parameter), and *trap* (to send a trap message to a specified manager). In addition, there are a few variations on these basic operations, such as *get-next*, which requests the next data item in the MIB hierarchy. We'll see the operations in action in the next subsection.

SNMP implementations

The commercial Unix operating systems we are considering all provide an SNMP agent, implemented as a single daemon or a series of daemons. In addition, the Net-SNMP package provides SNMP functionality for Linux, FreeBSD, and other free operating systems. It can also be used with commercial Unix systems that do not provide SNMP support.

AIX and Net-SNMP also provide some simple utilities for performing client operations. The utilities from the latter may also be built and used for systems providing their own SNMP agent.

Table 8-10 lists the various components of the SNMP packages provided by and available to the various operating systems we are considering.

Table 8-10. SNMP components

Component	Location
Insecure agent running after initial OS install?	**AIX:** yes **HP-UX:** yes **Net-SNMP[a]:** no **Solaris:** yes **Tru64:** yes
Primary agent daemon	**AIX:** */usr/sbin/snmpd* **HP-UX:** */usr/sbin/snmpdm* **Net-SNMP:** */usr/local/sbin/snmpd /usr/sbin/snmpd* (SuSE Linux) **Solaris:** */usr/lib/snmp/snmpdx* **Tru64:** */usr/sbin/snmpd*
Agent configuration file(s)	**AIX:** */etc/snmpd.conf* **HP-UX:** */etc/SnmpAgent.d/snmpd.conf* **Net-SNMP:** */usr/local/share/snmp/snmpd.conf /usr/share/snmp/snmpd.conf* (SuSE Linux) **Solaris:** */etc/snmp/conf/snmpdx.** and */etc/snmp/conf/snmpd.conf* **Tru64:** */etc/snmpd.conf*
MIB files	**AIX:** */etc/mib.defs* **HP-UX:** */etc/SnmpAgent.d/snmpinfo.dat /opt/OV/snmp_mibs/** (OpenView) **Net-SNMP:** */usr/share/snmp/mibs/** **Solaris:** */var/snmp/mib/** **Tru64:** */usr/examples/esnmp/**

Table 8-10. SNMP components (continued)

Component	Location
Enterprise number(s)	**AIX:** 2 (*ibm*), 4 (*unix*)
	HP-UX: 11 (*hp*)
	Net-SNMP: 2021 (*ucdavis*)
	Linux: Red Hat: 3212; SuSE: 7057
	Solaris: 42 (*sun*)
	Tru64: 36 (*dec*), 232 (*compaq*)
Management/monitoring package	**AIX:** Tivoli
	HP-UX: OpenView
	Solaris: Solstice Enterprise Manager
Boot script that starts the SNMP agent(s)	**AIX:** */etc/rc.tcpip*
	FreeBSD: */etc/rc* (add command manually)
	HP-UX: */sbin/init.d/Snmp**
	Linux: */etc/init.d/snmpd*
	Solaris: */etc/init.d/init.snmpdx*
	Tru64: */sbin/init.d/snmpd*
Boot script config. file: relevant entries	**Usual:** none used
	HP-UX: */etc/rc.config.d/Snmp*: SNMP_*_START=1*
	Linux: SuSE 7: */etc/rc.config: START_SNMPD="yes"*

^a Net-SNMP is used on FreeBSD and Linux systems.

We'll consider some of the specifics for the various operating systems a bit later in this section.

Net-SNMP client utilities

Unlike most implementations, the Net-SNMP package includes several useful utilities that can be used to query SNMP devices. You can build these tools for most operating systems even when they provide their own SNMP agent, so we'll consider them in some detail in this section. In addition, reading these examples will provide you with a greater understanding of how SNMP works, regardless of the specific implementation.

The first tool we'll consider is `snmptranslate`, which provides information about the MIB structure and its entities (but does not display any actual data). Table 8-11 lists the most useful `snmptranslate` commands.

Table 8-11. Useful snmptranslate commands

Purpose	Command
Display MIB subtree	`snmptranslate -Tp .oid`[a]
Text description for OID	`snmptranslate -Td .oid`[a]
Show full OID name (*mib-2* subtree only)	`snmptranslate -IR -On name`

Table 8-11. Useful snmptranslate commands (continued)

Purpose	Command
Translate OID name to number	snmptranslate -IR *name*
Translate OID number to name	snmptranslate -On .*number*[†]

[a] Absolute OIDs (numeric or text) are preceded by a period.

As an example, we'll define an alias (using the C shell) which takes a terminal leaf entry name (in the *mib-2* tree) as its argument and then displays the definition for that item, including its full OID string and numeric equivalent. Here is the alias definition:

```
% alias snmpwhat 'snmptranslate -Td `snmptranslate -IR -On \!:1`'
```

The alias uses two snmptranslate commands. The one in back quotes finds the full OID for the specified name (substituted in via !:1). Its output becomes the argument of the second command, which displays the description for this data item.

Here is an example using the alias which shows the description for the *sysLocation* item we considered earlier:

```
% snmpwhat sysLocation
.1.3.6.1.2.1.1.6
sysLocation OBJECT-TYPE
  -- FROM        SNMPv2-MIB, RFC1213-MIB
  -- TEXTUAL CONVENTION DisplayString
  SYNTAX        OCTET STRING (0..255)
  DISPLAY-HINT  "255a"
  MAX-ACCESS    read-write
  STATUS        current
  DESCRIPTION   "The physical location of this node (e.g.,
                'telephone closet, 3rd floor'). If the location is
                 is unknown, the value is the zero-length string."
::={iso(1) org(3) dod(6) internet(1) mgmt(2) mib-2(1) system(1) 6}
```

Other forms of the snmptranslate command provide related information.

The snmpget command retrieves data from an SNMP agent. For example, the following command displays the value of *sysLocation* from the agent on *beulah*, specifying the community string as *somethingsecure*:

```
# snmpget beulah somethingsecure sysLocation.0
system.sysLocation.0 = "Receptionist Printer"
```

The specified data location is followed by an *instance* number, which is used to specify the row number within tables of data. For values not in tables—scalars—it is always 0.

For tabular data, indicated by an entry named *somethingTable* within the OID, the instance number is the desired table element. For example, this command retrieves the 5-minute load average value, because the 1-, 5-, and 15-minute load averages are stored in the successive rows of the *enterprises.ucdavis.laTable* (as defined in the MIB):

```
# snmpget beulah somethingsecure laLoad.2
enterprises.ucdavis.laTable.laEntry.laLoad.2 = 1.22
```

The snmpwalk command displays the entire subtree underneath a specified node. For example, this command displays all data values under *iso.org.dod.internet.mgmt.mib-2.host.hrSystem*:

```
# snmpwalk beulah somethingsecure host.hrSystem
host.hrSystem.hrSystemUptime.0 = Timeticks: (31861126)
                           3 days, 16:30:11.26
host.hrSystem.hrSystemDate.0 = 2002-2-8,11:5:4.0,-5:0
host.hrSystem.hrSystemInitialLoadDevice.0 = 1536
host.hrSystem.hrSystemInitialLoadParameters.0 =
  "auto BOOT_IMAGE=linux ro root=2107
   BOOT_FILE=/boot/vmlinuz enableapic vga=0x0314."
host.hrSystem.hrSystemNumUsers.0 = Gauge32: 1
host.hrSystem.hrSystemProcesses.0 = Gauge32: 205
host.hrSystem.hrSystemMaxProcesses.0 = 0
```

The format of each output line is:

```
OID = [datatype:] value
```

If you're curious what all these items are, use snmptranslate to get their full descriptions.

Finally, the snmpset command can be used to modify writable data values, as in this command, which changes the device's primary contact (the s parameter indicates a string data type):

```
# snmpset beulah somethingelse sysContact.0 s "chavez@ahania.com"
system.sysContact.0 = chavez@ahania.com
```

Other useful data types are i for integer, d for decimal, and a for IP address (see the manual page for the entire list).

Generating traps. The Net-SNMP package includes the snmptrap command for manually generating traps. Here is an example of its use, which also illustrates the general characteristics of traps:

```
# snmptrap -v2c dalton anothername '' .1.3.6.1.6.3.1.1.5.3 \
     ifIndex i 2 ifAdminStatus i 1 ifOperStatus i 1
```

The -v2c option indicates that an SNMP version 2c trap is to be sent (technically, version 2 traps are called *notifications*).The next two arguments are the destination (manager) and community name. The next argument is the device uptime, and it is required for all traps. Here, we specify a null string, which defaults to the current uptime. The final argument in the first line is the trap OID; these OIDs are defined in one of the MIBs used by the device. This one corresponds to the *linkDown* (as defined in the IF-MIB), defined as a network interface changing state.

The remainder of the arguments (starting with ifIndex) are determined by the specific trap being sent. This one requires the interface number and its administrative and operational statuses, each specified via a keyword–data type–value triple (these particular data types are all integer). In this case, the trap specifies interface 2. A status value of 1 indicates that the interface is up, so this trap is a notification that it has come back online after being down.

Here is the syslog message that might be generated by this trap:

```
Feb 25 11:44:21 beulah snmptrapd[8675]: beulah.local[192.168.9.8]:
Trap system.sysUpTime.0 = Timeticks:(144235905) 6 days, 06:39:19,
.iso.org.dod.internet.snmpV2.snmpModules.snmpMIB.snmpMIBObjects.
  snmpTrap.snmpTrapOID.0 = OID: 1.1.5.3,
interfaces.ifTable.ifEntry.ifIndex = 2,
interfaces.ifTable.ifEntry.ifAdminStatus = up(1),
interfaces.ifTable.ifEntry.ifOperStatus = up(1)
```

SNMP-managed devices generally come with predefined traps that you can sometimes enable/disable during configuration. Some agents are also extensible and allow you to define additional traps.

AIX and Tru64 clients. AIX also provides an SNMP client utility, snmpinfo. Here is an example of its use:

```
# snmpinfo -c somethingsecure -h beulah -m get sysLocation.0
system.sysLocation.0 = "Receptionist Printer"
```

The -c and -h options specify the community name and host for the operation, respectively. The -m option specifies the SNMP operation to be performed—here, get—and other options are next and set.

Here is the equivalent command as it would be run on a Tru64 system:

```
# snmp_request beulah somethingsecure get 1.3.6.1.2.1.1.6.0
```

Yes, it really does require the full OID. The third argument specifies the SNMP operation, and other keywords used there are getnext, getbulk and set.

Configuring SNMP agents

In this section, we'll look at the configuration file for each of the operating systems.

Net-SNMP snmpd daemon (FreeBSD and Linux). FreeBSD and Linux systems use the Net-SNMP package (*http://www.net-snmp.org*), also previously known as UCD-SNMP. The package provides both a Unix host agent (the snmpd daemon) and a series of client utilities.

On Linux systems, this daemon is started with the */etc/init.d/snmp* boot script and uses the */usr/local/share/snmp/snmpd.conf* configuration file by default.* On FreeBSD systems, you must add a command like the following to one of the system boot scripts (e.g., */etc/rc*):

```
/usr/local/sbin/snmpd -L -A
```

The options tell the daemon to send log messages to standard output and standard error instead of to a file. You can also specify an alternate configuration file using the -c option.

Here is a sample Net-SNMP snmpd.conf file:

```
# snmpd.conf
rocommunity     somethingsecure
rwcommunity     somethingelse
trapcommunity   anothername
trapsink        dalton.ahania.com
trap2sink       dalton.ahania.com

syslocation   "Building 2 Main Machine Room"
syscontact    "chavez@ahania.com"

# Net-SNMP-specific items: conditions for error flags
#keyw [args] limit(s)
load  5.0 6.0 7.0              1,5,15 load average maximums.
disk  / 3%                     root filesystem below 3% free.
proc  portmap 1 1              Must be exactly one portmap process running.
proc  cron  1 1                Require exactly one cron process.
proc  sendmail                 Require at least one sendmail process.
```

The first three lines of the file specify the community name for accessing the agent in read-only and read-write mode and the name that will be used when it sends traps (which need not be a distinct value as above). The next two lines specify the trap destination for SNMP version 1 and version 2 traps; here it is host *dalton*.

The next section specifies the values of two MIB II variables, describing the location of the device and its primary contact. They are both located under *mib-2.system*.

The final section defines some Net-SNMP–specific monitoring items. These items check for a 1-, 5-, or 15-minute load average above 5.0, 6.0, or 7.0 (respectively), whether the free space in the root filesystem has dropped below 3%, and whether the portmap, cron, and sendmail daemons are running. When the corresponding value falls outside of the allowed range, the SNMP daemon sets the corresponding error flag data value under *enterprises.ucdavis* for the table row corresponding to the specified monitoring item: *laTable.laEntry.laErrorFlag*, *dskTable.dskEntry.dskErrorFlag*, and *prTable.prEntry.prErrorFlag*, respectively. Note that traps are not generated.

---

* Be aware that the RPMs provided with recent SuSE operating systems use the */etc/ucdsnmpd.conf* configuration file instead, although you can change this by editing the boot script. The canonical configuration file location under SuSE is also different: */usr/share/snmp*.

You can also use the command snmpconf -g to configure a *snmpd.conf* file. Add the -i option if you want the command to automatically install the new file into the proper directory (rather than placing it in the current directory).

Net-SNMP access control. The community definition entries introduced above also have a more complex form in which they accept additional parameters to specify access control. For example, the following command defines the read-write community as *localonly* for the 192.168.10.0 subnet:

```
rwcommunity localonly 192.168.10.0/24
```

The subnet to which the entry applies is specified by the second parameter.

Similarly, the following command specifies a read-only community name *secureread* for host *callisto* and limits access from that host to the *mib-2.hosts* subtree.

```
rocommunity secureread callisto .1.3.6.1.2.1.25
```

The starting point for allowed access is specified as the entry's third parameter.

This syntax is really a compact form of the general Net-SNMP access control directives com2sec, view, group, and access. The first two are the most straightforward:

```
#com2sec  name      origin          community
com2sec   localnet  192.168.10.0/24 somethinggood
com2sec   canwrite  192.168.10.22   somethingbetter

#view  name   in or out  subtree        [mask]
view   mibii  included   .1.3.6.1.2.1
view   sys    included   .1.3.6.1.2.1.1
```

The com2sec directive defines a named query source–community name pair; this item is known as a *security name*. In our example, we define the name *localnet* for queries originating in the 193.0.10 subnet using the community name *somethinggood*.

The view directive assigns a name to a specific subtree; here we give the *mib-2* subtree the label *mibii* and the name *sys* to the *system* subtree. The second parameter indicates whether the specified subtree is included or excluded from the specified view (more than one view directive can be used with the same view name). The optional mask field takes a hexadecimal number, which is interpreted as a mask further limiting access within the given subtree, for example, to specific rows within a table (see the manual page for details).

The group directive associates a security name (from com2sec) with a security model (corresponding to an SNMP version level). For example, the following entries define the group *local* as the *localnet* security name with each of the available security models:

```
#group  grp name  model  sec. name
group   local     v1     localnet
group   local     v2c    localnet
group   local     usm    localnet              usm means version 3.
group   admin     v2c    canwrite
```

The final entry defines the group *admin* as the *canwrite* security name with SNMP Version 3.

Finally, the access entry brings all of these items together to define specific access:

```
#        group                            read  write notify
#access  name   context model level match view  view  view
access   local  ""      any   noauth exact mibii none  none
access   admin  ""      v2c   noauth exact all   sys   all
```

The first entry allows queries of the *mib-2* subtree from the 192.168.10 subnet using the community string *somethinggood* while rejecting all other operations (access happens via the *mibii* view). The second entry allows any query and notification from 193.0.10.22 and also allows set operations within the *system* subtree from this source using SNMP version 2c clients, all using the *somethingbetter* community name.

See the *snmpd.conf* manual page for full details on these directives.

The Net-SNMP trap daemon. The Net-SNMP package also includes the `snmptrapd` daemon for handling traps that are received. You can start the daemon manually by entering the `snmptrapd -s` command, which says to send trap messages to the `syslog` Local0 facility (warning level). If you want it to be started at boot time, you'll need to add this command to the */etc/init.d/snmp* boot script.

The daemon can also be configured by the */usr/share/snmp/snmptrapd.conf* file. Entries in this file have the following format:

```
traphandle OID|default program [arguments]
```

`traphandle` is a keyword, the second field holds the trap's OID or the keyword `default`, and the remaining items specify a program to be run when that trap is received, along with any arguments. A variety of data is passed to the program when it is invoked, including the device's hostname and IP address and the trap OID and variables. See the documentation for full details.

Note that `snmptrapd` is a very simple trap-handler. It is useful if you want to record or handle traps on a system without a manager as well as for experimentation and learning purposes. However, in the long run, you'll want a more sophisticated manager. We'll consider some of these later in this section.

Configuring SNMP nder HP-UX. HP-UX uses a series of SNMP daemons (*subagents*), all controlled by the SNMP master agent, `snmpdm`. The daemons are started by scripts in the */sbin/init.d* subdirectory. The *SnmpMaster* script starts the master agent.

The subagents are:

- The HP-UX subagent (*/usr/sbin/hp_unixagt*), started by the *SnmpHpunix* script.
- The MIB2 subagent (*/usr/sbin/mib2agt*), started by the *SnmpMib2* script.
- The trap destination subagent (*/usr/sbin/trapdestagt*), started by the *SnmpTrpDst* script.

HP-UX also provides the */usr/lib/snmp/snmpd* script for starting all the daemons in a single operation.

The main configuration file is */etc/SnmpAgent.d/snmpd.conf*. Here is an example of this file:

```
get-community-name:  somethingsecure
set-community-name:  somethingelse
max-trap-dest:       10                    Max. number of trap destinations.
trap-dest:           dalton.ahania.com
location:            "machine room"
contact:             "chavez@ahania.com"
```

There are also more complex versions of the community name definition entries which allow you to specify access control on a per-host basis, as in this example:

```
get-community-name: somethingsecure \
  IP: 192.168.10.22 192.168.10.222 \
  VIEW: mib-2 enterprises -host           Use -name to exclude a subtree.
default-mibVIEW: internet                 Default accessible subtree.
```

The first entry (continued across three lines) allows two hosts from the 192.168.10 subnet to access the *mib-2* and *enterprises* subtrees (except the former's *host* subtree) in read-only mode, using the *somethingsecure* community name. The second entry defines the default MIB access; it is applied to queries from hosts for which no specific view has been specified.

 HP-UX's SNMP facility is designed to be used as part of its OpenView network management facility, a very elaborate package which allows you to manage many aspects of computers and other network devices from a central control station. In the absence of this package, the SNMP implementation is fairly minimal.

Configuring SNMP under Solaris. Solaris' SNMP agent is the snmpdx daemon.[*] It controls a number of subagents. The most important of these is mibiisa, which responds to standard SNMP queries within the *mib-2* and *enterprises.sun* subtrees (although MIB II is only partially implemented).

The daemons use configuration files in */etc/snmp/conf*. The primary settings are contained in *snmpd.conf*. Here is an example:

```
# set some system values
sysdescr    "old Sparc used as a router"
syscontact "chavez@ahania.com"
syslocation "Ricketts basement"

# default communities and trap destination
read-community    hardtoguess
```

---

[*] Solaris also supports the Desktop Management Interface (DMI) network management standard, and its daemons can interact with snmpdx on these systems.

```
write-community    hardertoguess
trap-community     usedintraps
trap               dalton.ahania.com        Maximum of 5 destinations.

# hosts allowed to query (5/line, max=32)
manager localhost dalton.ahania.com hogarth.ahania.com
manager blake.ahania.com
```

Be aware of the difference between the community definition entries in the preceding example and those named system-read|write-community; the latter allow access to the *system* subtree only.

The *snmpdx.acl* configuration file may be used to define more complex access control, via entries like these:

```
acl = {
      {
          communities = somethinggreat
          access = read-write
          managers = localhost, dalton.ahania.com
      }
      {
          communities = somethinggood
          access = read-only
          managers = iago.ahania.com, hamlet.ahania.com, ...
      }
}
```

This access control entry defines the access levels and associated community strings for two lists of hosts: the local system and *dalton* receive read-write access using the *somethinggreat* community name, and the second list of hosts receives read-only access using the *somethinggood* community name.

The AIX snmpd daemon. AIX's snmpd agent is configured via the */etc/snmpd.conf* configuration file. Here is an example:

```
# what to log and where to log it
logging  file=/usr/tmp/snmpd.log  enabled
logging  size=0  level=0

# agent information
syscontact   "chavez@ahania.com"
syslocation  "Main machine room"

#community name    [IP-address    netmask        [access   [view]]]
community  something
community  differs  127.0.0.1    255.255.255.255 readWrite
community  sysonly  127.0.0.1    255.255.255.255 readWrite  1.17.2
community  netset   192.168.10.2 255.255.255.0   readWrite  1.3.6.1

#view   name     [subtree(s)]
view    1.17.2   system enterprises
view    1.3.6.1  internet
```

```
#trap    community  destination  view     mask
trap     trapcomm   dalton       1.3.6.1  fe
```

This file illustrates both general server configuration and access control. The latter is accomplished via the community entries, which not only define a community name, but also optionally limit its use to a host and potentially an access type (read-only or read-write) and a MIB subtree. The latter are defined in view directives. Here we define one view consisting of the *system* and *enterprises* subtrees and another consisting of the entire *internet* subtree. Note that the view names must consist of an OID-like string in dotted notation.

The Tru64 snmpd daemon. The Tru64 snmpd agent is also configured via the */etc/snmpd. conf* configuration file. Here is an example:

```
sysLocation   "Machine Room"
sysContact    "chavez@ahania.com"

#community  name       IP-address    access
community   something  0.0.0.0       read      Applies to all hosts.
community   another    192.168.10.2  write

#trap  [version]  community   destination[:port]
trap              trapcomm    192.168.10.22
trap   v2c        trap2comm   192.168.10.212
```

The first section of the file specifies the usual MIB variables describing this agent. The second section defines community names; the arguments specify the name, the host to which it applies (0.0.0.0 means all hosts), and the type of access. The final section defines trap destinations for all traps and for version 2c traps.

SNMP and security

As with any network service, SNMP has a variety of associated security concerns and tradeoffs. At the time of this writing (early 2002), a major SNMP vulnerability was uncovered and its existence widely publicized (see *http://www.cert.org/advisories/CA-2002-03.html*). Interestingly, Net-SNMP was one of the few implementations that did not include the problem, while all of the commercial network management packages were affected.

In truth, prior to Version 3, SNMP is not very secure. Unfortunately, many devices do not yet support this version, which is still in development and is a draft standard, not a final one. One major problem is that community names are sent in the clear over the network. Poor coding practices in SNMP agents also mean that some devices are vulnerable to takeover via buffer overflow attacks, at least until their vendors provide patches. Thus, a decision to use SNMP involves balancing security needs with the functionality and convenience that it provides. Along these lines, I can make the following recommendations:

- Disable SNMP on devices where you are not using it. Under Linux, remove any links to */etc/init.d/snmp* in the *rcn.d* subdirectories.

- Choose good community names.

- Change the default community names before devices are added to the network.

- Use SNMP Version 3 clients whenever possible to avoid compromising your well-chosen community names.

- Block external access to the SNMP ports: TCP and UDP ports 161 and 162, as well as any additional vendor-specific ports (e.g., TCP and UDP port 1993 for Cisco). You may also want to do so for some parts of the internal network.

- Configure agents to reject requests from any but a small list of origins (whenever possible).

- If you must use SNMP operations across the Internet (e.g., from home), do so via a virtual private network or access the data from a web browser using SSL. Some applications that display SNMP data are discussed in the next section of this chapter.

- If your internal network is not secure and SNMP Version 3 is not an option, consider adding a separate administrative network for SNMP traffic. However, this is an expensive option, and it does not scale well.

As I've hinted above, SNMP Version 3 goes a long way toward fixing the most egregious SNMP security problems and limitations. In particular, it sends community strings only in cryptographically encoded form. It also provides optional user-based authenticated access control for SNMP operations. All in all, learning about and migrating to SNMP Version 3 is a very good use of your time.

Network Management Packages

Network management tools are designed to monitor resources and other system status metrics on groups of computer systems and other network devices: printers, routers, UPS devices, and so on. In some cases, performance data can be monitored as well. The current data is made available for immediate display, usually via a web interface, and the software updates and refreshes the display frequently.

Some programs are also designed to be proactive and actively look for problems: situations in which a system or service is unusable (basic connectivity tests fail) or the value of some metric has moved outside the acceptable range (e.g., the load average on a computer system rises above some preset level, indicating that CPU resources are becoming scarce). The network monitor will then notify the system administrator about the potential problem, allowing her to intervene before the situation becomes critical. The most sophisticated programs can also begin fixing some problems themselves when they are detected.

Standard Unix operating systems provide very little in the way of status monitoring tools, and those utilities that are included are generally limited to examining the local system and its own network context. For example, you can determine current CPU usage with the uptime command, memory usage with the vmstat command, and various aspects of network connectivity and usage via the ping, traceroute and netstat commands (and their GUI-based equivalents).

In recent years, a variety of more flexible utilities have appeared. These tools allow you to examine basic system status data for group of computers from a single monitoring program on one system. For example, Figure 8-9 illustrates some simple output from the Angel Network Monitor program, written by Marco Paganini (*http://www.paganini.net/angel/*). The image has been converted to black and white from the full-color original.

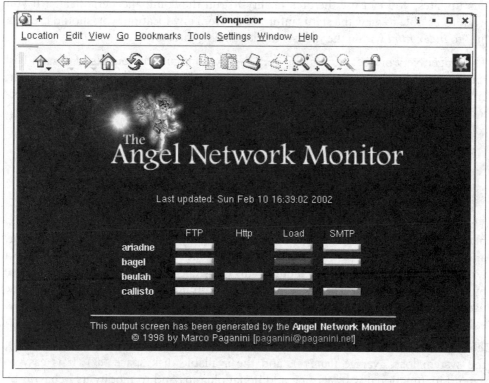

Figure 8-9. The Angel Network Monitor

The display produced by this package consists of a matrix of systems and monitored items, and it provides an easy-to-understand summary display of the current status for each valid combination. Each row of the table corresponds to the specified computer system, and the various columns represent a different network service or other system characteristic that is being monitored. In this case, we are monitoring the status of the FTP facility, the web server service, the system load average, and the electronic mail protocol, although not every item is monitored for every system.

In its color mode, the tools uses green bars to indicate that everything is OK (white in the figure), yellow bars for a warning condition, red bars for a critical condition (gray in the figure), and black bars to indicate that data collection failed (black in the figure). A missing bar means that the data item is not being collected for the system in question.

In this case, system *callisto* is having problems with its load average (it's probably too high), and its SMTP service (probably not responding). In addition, the load average probe to system *bagel* failed. Everything else is currently working properly.

The angel command is designed to be run manually. Once it is finished, a file named *index.html* appears in the package's *html* subdirectory, containing the display we just examined. The page is updated each time the command is run. If you want continuous updates, you can use the cron facility to run the command periodically. If you want to be able to view the status information from any location, you should create a link to *index.html* within the web server documents directory.

The Angel Network Monitor is also very easy to configure. It consists of a main Perl script (angel) and several plug-ins, auxiliary scripts that perform the actual data gathering. The facility uses two configuration files, which are stored in the *conf* subdirectory of the package's top-level directory. I had to modify only one of them, *hosts. conf*, to start viewing status data.

Here is a sample entry from that file:

```
#label :plug-in  :args        :column:images
#                       host!port   critical!warning   !failure
ariadne:Check_tcp:ariadne!ftp:FTP:alertred!alertyellow!alertblack
```

The (colon-separated) fields hold the label for the entry (which appears in the display), the plug-in to run, its arguments (separated by !'s), the table column header, and the graphics to display when the retrieved value indicates a critical condition, a warning condition, or a plug-in failure. This entry checks the FTP service on *ariadne* by attempting to connect to its standard port (a numeric port number can also be used) and uses the standard red, yellow, and black bars for the three states (the OK state is always green).

The other provided plug-ins allow you to check whether a device is alive (via ping), the system load average (uptime), and the available disk space (df). It is easy to extend its functionality by writing additional plug-ins and to modify its behavior by editing its main configuration file.

The Angel Network Monitor performs well at the job it was designed for: providing a simple status display for a group of hosts. In doing so, it operates from the point of view of the local system, monitoring those items that can be determined easily by external probes, such as connecting to ports on a remote system or running simple commands via rsh or ssh. While its functionality can be extended, more complex monitoring needs are often better met by a more sophisticated package.

Proactive network monitoring

There is no shortage of packages that provide more complex monitoring and event-handling capabilities. While these packages can be very powerful tools for information gathering, their installation and configuration complexity scales at least linearly with their features. There are several commercial programs that provide this functionality, including Computer Associates' Unicenter and Hewlett-Packard's OpenView (see the cover article in the January 2000 issue of *Server-Workstation Expert* magazine for an excellent overview, available at *http://swexpert.com/F/SE.F1. JAN.00.pdf*). There are also many free and open source programs and projects, including OpenNMS (*http://www.opennms.com*), Sean MacGuire's Big Brother (free for non-commercial uses, *http://www.bb4.com*) and Thomas Aeby's Big Sister (*http:// bigsister.graeff.com*). We'll be looking at the widely-used NetSaint package, written by Ethan Galstad (*http://netsaint.org*).

NetSaint. NetSaint is a full-featured network monitoring package which can not only provide information about system/resource status across an entire network but can also be configured to send alerts and perform other actions when problems are detected.

 NetSaint's continuing development is taking place under a new name, Nagios, with a new web site (*http://www.nagios.com*). As of this writing, the new package is still in an alpha version, so we'll discuss Net-Saint here. Nagios should be 100% backward compatible with NetSaint as it develops toward Version 1.0.

Installing NetSaint is straightforward. Like most of these packages, it has several prerequisites (including MySQL and the `mping` command).[*] These are the most important NetSaint components:

- The `netsaint` daemon, which continually collects data, updates displays, and generates and handles alerts. The daemon is usually started at boot time via a link to the *netsaint* script in */etc/init.d*.
- Plug-in programs, which perform the actual device and resource probing.
- Configuration files, which define devices and services to monitor.
- CGI programs, which support web access to the displays.

Figure 8-10 displays NetSaint's Tactical Overview display. It provides summary information about the current state of everything being monitored. In this case, we are monitoring 20 hosts, of which 4 currently have problems. We are also monitoring 40 services, 5 of which have reached their critical or warning state. The display shows an abnormally high number of failures to make the discussion more interesting.

Figure 8-10 also shows the NetSaint menu bar in the window's left frame. The items under Monitoring select various status displays. Figure 8-11 is a composite illustration showing selected items corresponding to the second and third menu choices.

---

[*] Recent SuSE Linux distributions include NetSaint (although it installs the package in nonstandard locations).

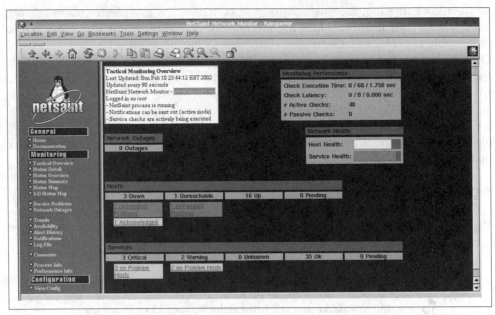

Figure 8-10. The NetSaint Network Monitor

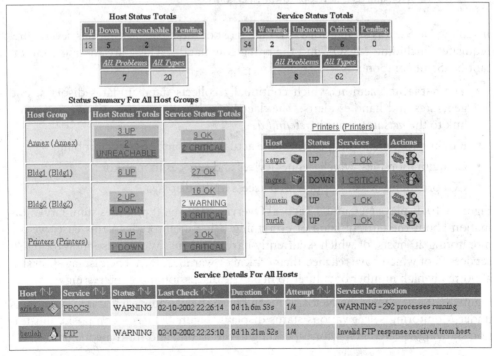

Figure 8-11. NetSaint status summaries

The two tables at the top of the figure present the overall status figures in tabular form. The items in the middle row of the illustration provide a breakdown of host and service status by computer location (on the left) as well as the details for each device in the Printers host group. In this way, the location of trouble can be determined quickly.

NetSaint provides links within each table to more detailed information. If you click on the "2 WARNING" text in Bldg2's Service Status item, the table at the bottom of the figure is displayed. This table provides details about the two warning-level conditions: the FTP service is not responding as expected to queries, and there are 292 processes running (which is above the warning threshold).

Figure 8-12 illustrates NetSaint's individual host-level reports (which we've reformatted slightly to save space). This report is for a host named *leah*, a Windows system (if the user-defined icon is to be believed). Earlier, this system was down for over 2 hours. In fact, it has been up only half the time during the periods during which it was monitored.

The Host State Information table displays a variety of specific information about the host's recent monitoring history and its current monitoring configuration. The comment displayed at the bottom of the figure was entered by the system administrator, and it provides a reason for the system's recent outage.

The Host Commands area enables the administrator to change many aspects of this host's monitoring configuration, including enabling/disabling monitoring and/or alert notifications, adding/modifying scheduled downtime for the host (during which monitoring ceases and alerts are not sent), and forcing all defined checks to be run immediately (rather than waiting for their next scheduled instance).

The second menu item allows you to acknowledge any current problem. Acknowledging simply means "I know about the problem, and it is being handled." NetSaint marks the corresponding event as such, and future alerts are suppressed until the item returns to its normal state. This process also allows you to enter a comment explaining the situation, an action that is very helpful when more than one administrator examines the monitoring data.

Table 8-12 lists the locations of the various NetSaint components.

Table 8-12. NetSaint components

Item	Standard[a]	SuSE RPM
Daemon	*bin/netsaint*	*/usr/sbin/netsaint*
Configuration files	*etc*	*/etc/netsaint*
Plug-ins	*libexec*	*/usr/lib/netsaint/plugins*
Generated HTML pages	*share/images*	*/usr/share/netsaint/images*
Web interface	*sbin*	*/usr/lib/netsaint/cgi*

Table 8-12. NetSaint components (continued)

Item	Standard[a]	SuSE RPM
Logs and comments	*var/log*	*/var/log/netsaint*
Documentation	none	*/usr/share/netsaint/doc*

[a] Relative to */usr/local/netsaint*.

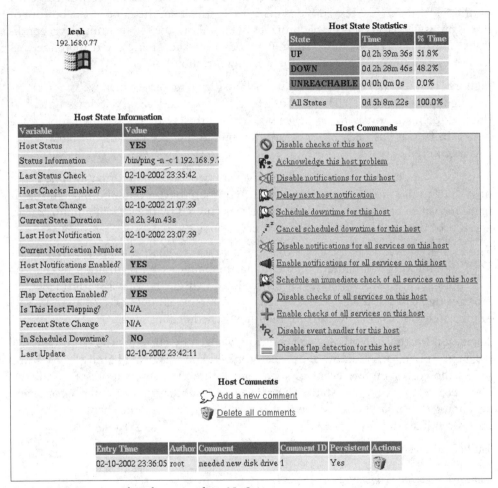

Figure 8-12. Host-specific information from NetSaint

Configuring NetSaint can seem daunting at first, but it is actually relatively straightforward once you understand all of the pieces. It has several configuration files:

netsaint.cfg
  Defines directory locations for the package's various components, the user and group context for the netsaint daemon, what items to log, log file rotation settings, various timeouts and other performance-related settings, and additional

items related to some of the package's advanced features (e.g., enabling event handling and defining global event handlers).

commands.cfg and hosts.cfg
> Define host and service test commands and specify which hosts and services are monitored. These two files hold the same sorts of entries, and they exist as separate files simply for the sake of convenience.

nscgi.cfg
> Holds settings related to the NetSaint displays, including paths to web page items and scripts, and per-item icon and sound selections. The file also defines allowed access to NetSaint's data and commands.

resource.cfg
> Defines macros that may be used within other settings for clarity and security purposes (e.g., to hide passwords from view).

We will briefly consider entries in the second class of files here. The file holds several different kinds of entries, including the following:

command
> Define a monitoring task and its associated command. These entries are also used to define commands used for other purposes such as sending alerts and event handlers.

host
> Define a host/device to be monitored.

hostgroup
> Create a list of hosts to be grouped together in displays.

service
> Define an item on a host/device to be checked periodically.

contact
> Specify a list of recipients for alerts.

timeperiod
> Assign a name to a specified time period.

Here are some example command definitions:

```
command[do_ping]=/bin/ping -c 1 $HOSTADDRESS$
command[check_telnet]=/usr/local/netsaint/libexec/check_tcp -H $HOSTADDRESS$ -p 23
```

The first entry defines a command named do_ping, which runs the ping command to send a single ICMP packet to a host. When this command appears in a service entry, the corresponding host is automatically substituted for the built-in NetSaint macro $HOSTADDRESS$.

The second entry defines the check_telnet command, which runs the plug-in named check_tcp, which attempts to connect to the TCP port specified by -p on the indicated host.

It is also possible to define commands with arguments that are replaced at execution time using macros of the form $ARG*n*$, as in this example:

```
command[check_tcp]=/usr/local/netsaint/libexec/check_tcp -H $HOSTADDRESS$ -p $ARG1$
```

The entry defines the `check_tcp` command and calls the same plug-in, but it uses the first argument as the desired port number.

Many plug-ins use the `-w` and `-c` options to define value ranges that should generate warning- and critical-level alerts, respectively. Somewhat counterintuitively, these options expect the range of acceptable values as their argument. For example, the following entry defines the command `snmp_load5` and sets the warning level to values over 150:

```
command[snmp_load5]=/usr/local/netsaint/libexec/check_snmp
  -H $HOSTADDRESS$ -C $ARG1$ -o .1.3.6.1.4.1.2021.10.1.5.2
  -w 0:150 -c :300 -l load5            Output is wrapped here.
```

It calls the `check_snmp` command provided with the package for the current host, using the first command argument as the SNMP community name, and retrieves the 5-minute load average value (in 3-digit form), labeling the data as "label5." The value will trigger a warning alert if it is over 150; `-w 0:150` means that values between 0 and 150 are not in the warning range. It will also trigger a critical alert if it is over 300, i.e., not in the range 0 (optional) to 300. If both are triggered, critical wins.

The following entries illustrate the definitions for hosts:

```
#host[label]=descr.; IP address;parent;check command
host[ishtar]=ishtar;192.168.76.98;taurus;check-printer-alive;10;120;24x7;1;1;1;
host[callisto]=callisto;192.168.22.124;;check-host-alive;10;120;24x7;1;1;1;
```

Let's take these entries apart, field by field (they are separated by semicolons). The first one is the most complicated and has the following syntax: `host[*name*]=*description*`, where *label* is the label to be used in status displays and *description* is a (possibly longer) phrase describing the device (we've used the same text for both). The next field holds the device's IP address, which is the item which actually identifies the desired device (the preceding items are just arbitrary labels).

The third field specifies the parent device for the item: a list of one or more labels for intermediate devices located between the current system and this one. For example, to reach *ishtar*, we must go through the router named *taurus*, so *taurus* is specified as its parent. The fourth field specifies the command NetSaint should use to determine whether the host is accessible ("alive"), and the fifth field indicates how many checks must fail before the host is assumed to be down (10 in our example). The parent is optional, and the entry for *callisto* does not use it.

The remaining fields in the example entries relate to alert notifications. They hold the time interval between alerts when a host remains down, in minutes (here, two hours), the time period during which alerts should be sent, and three flags indicating whether to send notifications when the host recovers after being down, when the host goes down, and when the host is unreachable due to a failure of an intermediate device, respectively (where 0 means no and 1 means yes). The time period is defined elsewhere in the configuration file. This one, named 24x7, is included in the default file and means "all the time." It's a convenient choice when you are getting started using NetSaint. All the flags are set to yes in our examples.

Now that we have both commands and hosts entries, we are ready to define specific items that NetSaint should monitor. These items are known as *services*. Here are some sample entries:

```
#service[host]  =label;;  when;;;;    notify;;;;;;        check-command
service[callisto]=TELNET;0;24x7;4;5;1;admins;960;24x7;0;0;0;;check_telnet
service[callisto]=PROCS;0;24x7;4;5;1;admins;960;24x7;0;0;0;;snmp_nproc!commune!250!400
service[ingres]=HPJD;0;24x7;4;5;1;localhost;960;24x7;0;0;0;;check_hpjd
```

The most important fields in these entries are the first, third, sixth, and final ones, which hold the following settings:

- The service definition (field 1), using the syntax service[*host-label*]=*service-label*. For example, the first example entry defines a service named TELNET for the host entry named *callisto*.

- The name of the time period during which this check should be performed (field 3), again defined in a timeperiod entry.

- The contact name (field 7): this item holds the name of a contact entry defined elsewhere in the file. The latter entry type is used to specify lists of users to be contacted when alerts are generated.

- The command to run to perform the check (final field), defined via a command entry elsewhere in the configuration file. Arguments to the command are specified as separate !-separated subfields with the command.

The other fields hold the volatility flag (field 2), maximum number of checks before a service is considered down (4), number of minutes between normal checks and failure rechecks (5 and 6), number of minutes between failure alerts while the service remains down (8), time period during which to send alerts (8), and three alert flags corresponding to service recovery and whether or not to send critical alerts and warning alerts, respectively. The penultimate field holds the command name for the event handler for this service (see below); no event handler is specified in these cases. The default values, used in the examples, are good starting points.

As we saw in Figure 8-11, NetSaint displays can summarize status information for a group of devices. You specify this by defining host group. For example, the following configuration file entry defines the Printers host group (as displayed in the right table in the middle row in the illustration):

```
hostgroup[Printers]=Printers;localhost;ingres,lomein,turtle,catprt
```

The syntax is simple:

```
hostgroup[label]=description;contact-group;list-of-host-names
```

Keep in mind that the host labels refer to the names of host definitions within the NetSaint configuration file (and not necessarily to literal hostnames). The members of the specified contact group will be notified whenever there is any problem with any device in the list.

In addition to sending alert messages, NetSaint also provides support for event handlers: commands to be performed when a service check fails. In this way, you can begin dealing with a problem before you even know about it. Here are the entries corresponding to a simple event handler:

```
#event handler for disk full failures
command[clean]=/usr/local/netsaint/local/clean $STATETYPE$
service[beulah]=DISK;0;24x7;4;5;1;localhost;960;24x7;0;0;0;clean;check_disk!/!15!5
```

First, we define a command named clean, which specifies a script to run. Its sole argument is the value of the $STATETYPE$ NetSaint macro, which is set to HARD for critical failures and SOFT for warnings. The clean command is then specified as the event handler for the DISK service on *beulah*. The script uses the find command to delete junk files within the filesystem and uses the argument value to decide how aggressive to be. In this case, the warning level means that the disk is 85% full and critical alerts correspond to 95% full, values specified via the final two parameters to the service monitoring command named check_disk (defined elsewhere), whose first argument is the filesystem to check.

NetSaint has a few other nice features which we'll consider very briefly. First of all, it can save data between runs (and it does so under the default configuration). You can also specify whether to display the saved status information when the NetSaint page is first opened. The following *netsaint.cfg* entries control this feature:

```
retain_state_information=1
retention_update_interval=60
use_retained_program_state=1
```

You can also save the data produced by the status commands for future use outside of NetSaint, using these main configuration file entries:

```
process_performance_data=1
service_perfdata_command=process-service-perfdata
```

The command specified in the second entry must be defined in *hosts.cfg* or another configuration file. Typically, this command simply writes the command's output to an external file: e.g., echo $OUTPUT$ >> *file*. The $OUTPUT$ macro expands to the full output returned by the monitoring command. You can also specify a separate processing command for host status monitoring commands. The data in the file can be analyzed, sent to a database (see the next section), or processed in any other way that you like.

So far, we have considered NetSaint in the context of a single monitoring location. In other words, all monitoring commands are issued from a single master system. However, the NetSaint daemon can also be configured to accept data sent from outside sources. It refers to this option as passive mode, which may be enabled via the check_external_commands main configuration file directive.

As we noted earlier, access to NetSaint is defined in the *nscgi.cfg* configuration file. Here are some example entries from that file:

```
use_authentication=1
authorized_for_configuration_information=netsaintadmin,root,chavez
authorized_for_all_services=netsaintadmin,root,chavez,maresca
hostextinfo[bagel]=;redhat.gif;;redhat.gd2;;168,36;,,;
```

The first entry enables the access control mechanism. The next two entries specify users who are allowed to view NetSaint configuration information and services status information (respectively). Note that all users also must be authenticated to the web server using the Apache htpasswd mechanism.

The final entry specifies extended attributes for the host defined in the entry labeled *bagel*. The filenames in this example specify images files for the host in status tables (GIF format) and in the status map (GD2 format), and the two numeric values specify the device's location within the status map. NetSaint status maps provide a quick way of accessing information about individual devices. A sample status map is displayed in Figure 8-13. The illustration shows the saintmap utility written by David Kmoch (*http://www.netsaint.org/download/*), which provides a convenient way of creating status maps. In this case, we have grouped devices by their physical location (although we haven't bothered to label the groups). The lines from *taurus* to each device in the bottom group illustrate the fact that *taurus* is the gateway to this location. When used by NetSaint, each icon will have a status indication—up or down—added to it, enabling an administrator to get an overall view of things right away, even when the network is very large and complex.

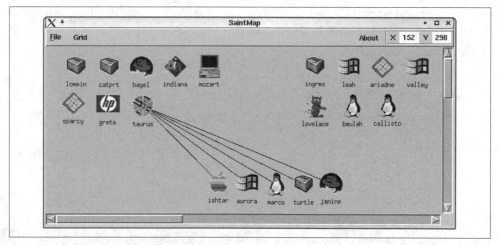

Figure 8-13. Using netsaint to create a status map

Identifying trends over time

NetSaint is very good about providing up-to-the-minute status information, but there are also times when it is helpful to compare the current situation to conditions in the past. Accordingly, we now turn to tools that track status and performance data over time, thereby providing the sort of historical usage data that is essential to performance tuning and capacity planning.

MRTG and RRDtool. One of the best-known packages of this type is the Multi-Router Traffic Grapher (MRTG), written by Tobias Oetiker and Dave Rand. It collects data over time and automatically produces graphs of it over various time periods (see *http://www.mrtg.org*). As its name suggests, it was first designed to track the ongoing performance of the routers in a network, but it can be used for a wide variety of data (even ranging beyond the computer realm). The general term for this type of data is "time series data," and it consists of any value that can be tracked over time.

More recently, MRTG has been supplanted by Oetiker's newer package, RRDtool (*http://people.ee.ethz.ch/~oetiker/webtools/rrdtool/*). RRDtool has much more powerful—and configurable—graphing facilities, although it requires a separate data collection script or package (the web site contains a list of some of the latter).

Both these tools work by storing only the data needed to produce the various graph types. Instead of saving every data point, they store a collection of the most recent ones, as well as summary values collected over various time periods. When new data comes in, it replaces the oldest point in the current collection of raw values, and the relevant summary data values are updated as appropriate. This strategy results in small, fixed-size databases nevertheless offering a wealth of important information.

We'll now look briefly at the RRDtool package and then consider a popular data collection front-end named Cricket. We'll begin by creating a simple database, using the RRDtool command provided by the package:

```
# rrdtool create ping.rrd \
   --step 300 \                          Interval is 5 minutes.
   DS:trip:GAUGE:600:U:U \
   DS:lost:GAUGE:600:U:U \
   RRA:AVERAGE:0.5:1:600 \               600 5-minute averages.
   RRA:AVERAGE:0.5:6:700 \               700 30-minute averages.
   RRA:AVERAGE:0.5:24:775 \              775 2-hour averages.
   RRA:AVERAGE:0.5:288:750 \             750 daily averages.
   RRA:MAX:0.5:1:600 \
   RRA:MAX:0.5:6:700 \
   RRA:MAX:0.5:24:775 \
   RRA:MAX:0.5:288:797
```

This command creates a database named *ping.rrd* consisting of two fields, trip and lost, defined by the two DS lines (DS for "data set"). They will hold the round-trip travel time for ICMP packets and the percentage of lost packets resulting from running the ping command. Both are of type GAUGE, meaning that the data for these fields should be interpreted as a distinct value. The other data types refer to counters of various sorts, and their values are interpreted as changes with respect to the preceding value; they include COUNTER for monotonically increasing data and DERIVE for data that can vary up or down.

The fourth field in each DS line is the time period between data samples, in seconds (here 10 minutes), and the final two fields hold the valid range of the data. A setting of U stands for unknown, and two U's together have the effect of allowing the data itself to define the valid range (i.e., accept any value).

The remaining lines of the command, labeled RRA, create round-robin archive data within the database. Each RRA applies to every defined DA in the file. The second RRA field indicates the kind of aggregate value to compute; here, we compute averages and maximum. The remaining fields specify the maximum percentage of the required sampled data that can be missing, the number of raw values to combine, and the number of data points of this type to store.

Those final two fields can be confusing at first. Let's consider a simple example: values of 6 and 100 would mean that the average (or other function) of 6 raw values will be computed, and the most recent 100 averages will be saved. If the time period between data points is 300 seconds (the default value and also specified via the --step option), this will be a 30-minute average value (6*5 minutes), and we will have 30-minute averages going back for 50 hours (100*6*5). Note that the aggregate periods do not overlap; the 30-minute values are for the preceding 30 minutes, the 30 minutes before that, and so on. In addition, aggregate definitions always start from the present moment.*

Thus, in our example database, we are creating 5-minute (--step 300) averages and maximums, 30-minute values of each type (5*6=30), 2-hour values (5*24=120) and daily values (5*288=1440=24 hours). Eventually, we will have data going back for over 2 years. At any given time, we'll have 50 hours worth of 5-minute averages (600*5 minutes), about 14.5 days of 30-minute averages, about 64.5 days of 2-hour averages, and 750 days of daily averages. We'll also have the maximum value data for each point.

There are many ways to add data to an RRDtool database. Here is a script illustrating one of the simplest, using rrdtool's update keyword:

```
#!/bin/csh
ping -w 30 -c 10 $1 > /tmp/ping_$1
set trip=`tail -1 /tmp/ping_$1 | awk -F= '{print $2}' | \
        awk -F/ '{print $2}'`
set lost=`grep transmitted /tmp/ping_$1 | awk -F, '{print $3}' \
        | awk -F% '{print $1}'`
rm -f /tmp/ping_$1
rrdtool update ping.rrd "N:"$trip":"$lost
```

---

* In other words, contrary to how MRTG works, they do not begin where the preceding one left off.

We use the `ping` command to generate the data, then we take apart the output, and finally we use `rrdtool` update to enter it into our database. The final argument to the command is a colon-separated list of data values, beginning with the time to be associated with the data (`N` means now) followed by the value for each defined data field, in order. In this case, we use normal Unix commands to obtain the data we need, but we could also have used SNMP as the sources.

Once we've accumulated data for awhile, we can create graphs, again using `rrdtool`. For example, the following command (taken from a script) creates a simple graph of the data from the previous 24 hours:

```
rrdtool graph ping.gif \
  --title "Packet Trip Times" \
  DEF:time=ping.rrd:trip:AVERAGE \
  LINE2:time\#0000FF
```

This command defines a graph of a single value, specified via the DEF (definition) line. The graphed variable is named *time*, and it comes from the stored averages of the trip field in the *ping.rrd* database (raw values cannot be graphed). The LINE2 line is what actually graphs its values. This line refers to a 2-point line of the defined variable time, displayed in the color corresponding to the RGB value #0000FF (blue). The backslash before the number sign is required to protect it from the shell; it is not part of the command syntax. The resulting output file, named *ping.gif*, is displayed in Figure 8-14 (although the blue line appears black in this version).

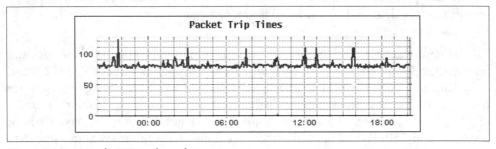

Figure 8-14. A simple RRDtool graph

In the graph, time flows forward from left to right, and the current time is at the extreme right (here, about 8:00 P.M.).

You can display more than one value per graph. Consider Figure 8-15, which displays the values of the 5-minute load average (black line) and number of processes (gray line) for a system.

The upper graph displays the values in their normal ranges. In this case, we cannot see much detail in the load average line because its values are too small with respect to the number of processes. In the bottom graph, we correct this by multiplying the load average by 10 to bring the two data sets within the same general numerical range. Since load averages are a somewhat arbitrary metric anyway, this does not distort the data (because only relative load average values are really meaningful).

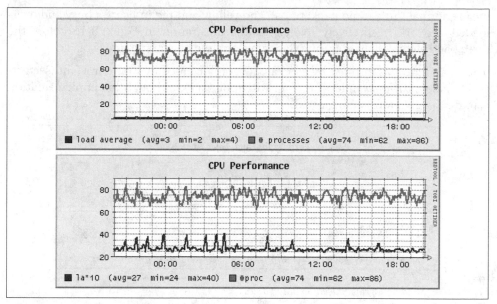

Figure 8-15. Graphing two values

Here is the command from the script that created the bottom graph:

```
rrdtool graph cpu.gif \
   --title "CPU Performance" \
  DEF:la=cpu.rrd:la5:AVERAGE \
  CDEF:xla=la,10,* \
  DEF:np=cpu.rrd:nproc:AVERAGE \
  LINE2:xla\#0000FF:"la*10" \
 'GPRINT:la:AVERAGE:(avg=%.0lf' \
 'GPRINT:la:MIN:min=%.0lf' \
 'GPRINT:la:MAX:max=%.0lf)' \
  LINE2:np\#FF0000:"# procs" \
 'GPRINT:np:AVERAGE:(avg=%.0lf' \
 'GPRINT:np:MIN:min=%.0lf' \
 'GPRINT:np:MAX:max=%.0lf)'
```

The CDEF (computed definition) command is used to create a new graph variable based on an expression. In this case, we define the variable *xla* by multiplying the *la* variable by 10. The expression is specified in Reverse Polish Notation (RPN; see the RRDtool documentation if this is unfamiliar). Both variables are graphed by LINE2 subcommands, and these examples use the optional third field to set a label for the line. In addition, the parenthesized summary data for each variable shown at the bottom of the graph is created via the GPRINT subcommands (enclosed in quotation marks to protect special characters from the shell).

As a final graph example, consider Figure 8-16. In this graph, we again display data from *ping.rrd*. The average round-trip time is again a blue line, but this time the background is shaded to indicate whether the packet loss was significant: green means normal (little or no packet loss), and yellow and red indicate a busy and over-loaded network, respectively. Note that the illustration in Figure 8-16 colors the three bands white, light gray, and dark gray, and the blue graph line is black.

This technique was inspired by an example graph created by Brandon Gant (see *gallery/brandon_01.html* under the main RRDtool page), although his implementation is undoubtedly more sophisticated.

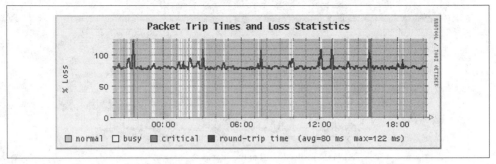

Figure 8-16. Shading a graph based on data values

Here is the command section that created the shaded bands:

```
DEF:stat=ping.rrd:lost:AVERAGE \
CDEF:band0=stat,0,GE,m,13,LT,+,2,EQ,INF,0,IF \
CDEF:band1=stat,13,GE,m,27,LT,+,2,EQ,INF,0,IF \
CDEF:band2=stat,27,GE,m,1000,LT,+,2,EQ,INF,0,IF \
AREA:band0\#00FF00:"normal" \
...
```

We define the variable *stat* as the lost field from *ping.rrd*. Next, we create three more variables, named *band0*, *band1*, and *band2*, via a complex conditional expression that sets the variable's value to infinity (INF) if it is true and 0 otherwise. For example, the first RPN expression is equivalent to 0 <= *stat* < 13. As defined above, the AREA subcommand generates a green area plot labeled "normal," which in this case consists of a series of vertical green lines and white spaces (since the variable is 0 or infinite). There are two additional AREA lines for the other two bands in the full command. Since each value of *stat* is placed into one of the three bands, the entire graph background is filled in.

Creating graphs like these can be tedious, but fortunately, there is a utility named RRGrapher which automates the process. This CGI script, written by Dave Plonka (*http://net.doit.wisc.edu/~plonka/RRGrapher/*), is illustrated in Figure 8-17.

You can use this tool to create graphs that draw data from multiple RRD databases. In this example, we are plotting values from two databases over a specified time period. The latter is one of RRGrapher's most convenient features, since rrdtool requires times to be expressed in standard Unix format (seconds since 1/1/1970) but you can enter them here in a readable format.

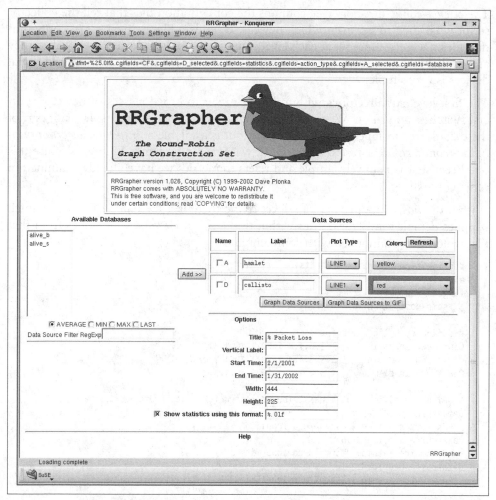

Figure 8-17. The RRGrapher utility

Using Cricket to feed RRDtool. To use RRDtool to gather and present data from more than a few sources, you will need some sort of front-end package to automate the process. The Cricket package is an excellent choice for this purpose. It was written by Jeff Allen (*http://www.afn.org/~jam/software/cricket/*). Cricket is written in Perl, and it requires a very large number of modules to function (plan on several visits to CPAN), so installing it may take a bit of time. Once it is up and running, these are its most important components:

- The *cricket-config* subdirectory tree, containing specifications for each device to be monitored (see below).

- The collector script, run periodically from cron (usually every five minutes).

- The grapher.cgi script, used to display Cricket graphs within a web browser.

The *cricket-config* directory tree contains the configuration files that tell the collector script what data to get from which devices. It holds a hierarchical set of configuration files. Default values set at each level continue to apply to lower levels unless they are explicitly overridden. Once the initial setup is completed, adding additional devices is very simple.

The first-level subdirectories within this tree refer to broad classes of devices: routers, switches, and so on. We will be examining the device class hosts. It is not part of the default tree installed with the package, but is available at *http://www.certaintysolutions.com/tech-advice/cricket-contrib/* (it was created by James Moore). We use this one because it is relatively simple and refers to metrics we have already examined in other contexts.

Within the *hosts* subdirectory of *cricket-config* there is a file named *Defaults*, which supplies default values for entries within this subtree. Here are some lines from that file, which we've annotated with comment lines:

```
# cricket-config/hosts/Defaults
# device specification
target --default--
   snmp-host = %server%

# define symbolic names for some SNMP OIDs
OID    ucd_load1min       1.3.6.1.4.1.2021.10.1.3.1
OID    ucd_load5min       1.3.6.1.4.1.2021.10.1.3.2
OID    ucd_load15min      1.3.6.1.4.1.2021.10.1.3.3

# define specific data values to be collected (RRD data sources)
datasource ucd_load1min
   ds-source = snmp://%snmp%/ucd_load1min
datasource ucd_load5min
   ds-source = snmp://%snmp%/ucd_load5min
datasource ucd_load15min
   ds-source = snmp://%snmp%/ucd_load15min

# define a data source group named ucd_System
targetType    ucd_System
   ds    =    "ucd_cpuUser, ucd_cpuSystem, ucd_cpuIdle,
             ucd_memrealAvail, ucd_memswapAvail,
             ucd_memtotalAvail, ucd_load1min, ucd_load5min,
             ucd_load15min"

# define 3 subgroups of ucd_System for graphing purposes
   view   =    "cpu: ucd_cpuUser ucd_cpuSystem ucd_cpuIdle,
              Memory: ucd_memrealAvail ucd_memswapAvail
              ucd_memtotalAvail, Load: ucd_load1min ucd_
              load5min ucd_load15min"

# define graphs to be generated
graph   ucd_load5min
   legend   =   "5 Min Load Av"
   si-units=   false
```

```
graph   ucd_memrealAvail
   legend   =   "Used RAM"
   scale    =   1024,*
   bytes    =   true
   units    =   "Bytes"
```

These entries are all quite intuitive. We can see the underlying RRD database structure used for this data, but using Cricket means that we don't have to worry about it. The entries following the data source definitions relate to the Cricket reporting structure (as we'll see).

Specific hosts to be monitored are generally defined in files named *Targets*. Each host has a subdirectory under *hosts* in which such a file lives. Here are some excerpts from the file for host *callisto*:

```
# cricket-config/hosts/callisto/Targets
Target --default--
   server           =   callisto
   snmp-community =   somethingsecure
# Specify data source groups to collect
target ucd_sys
   target-type    =   ucd_System
   short-desc     =   "CPU, Memory, and Load"
target boot
   target-type    =   ucd_Storage
   inst           =   1
   short-desc     =   "Bytes used on /boot"
   max-size       =   19487
   storage        =   boot
```

This file instructs Cricket to collect values for all of the items defined in the ucd_System and ucd_Storage groups. Each target will appear as an option within the Cricket web interface for this host.

Figure 8-18 illustrates some Cricket output. The upper-left window lists the first-level menu; each of its items corresponds to a top-level subdirectory under *cricket-config*. The lower-right graph shows the page corresponding the ucd_sys target for host *callisto*. It begins with a summary of the current data and then displays one or more graphs showing the data over time (you can select which ones appear via the links in the right-hand cell in the Summary table).

In this case, we have chosen the weekly graph. It shows clearly that *callisto* generally used very little of its CPU resources in the past seven days, but there was an exceptional period on the previous Sunday (although even then the load average was never very high). Graphs like these can be very helpful in determining what the normal range of behavior is for the various devices for which you are responsible. When you understand the normal status and variation, you are in a much better position to recognize and understand the significance of anomalies that do turn up.

As we've seen, network monitoring software can be a powerful tool for keeping track of system status, both at the current moment and over the long haul. However, don't

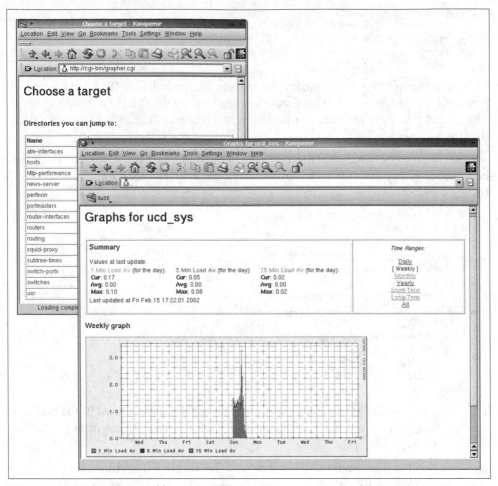

Figure 8-18. Cricket status and history reports

underestimate the time it will take to implement a monitoring strategy for a real-world environment. As with most things, careful planning can minimize the amount of time that this will require, but putting a monitoring strategy in place is always a big job. You need to consider not only the installation and configuration issues but also the performance impact on your network and the security ramifications of the daemons and protocols you are enabling. While this can be a daunting task and cannot be rushed, in the end it is worth the effort.

## CHAPTER 9

Electronic Mail

Making sure that electronic mail gets sent out and delivered is one of the system administrator's most important jobs, and it's also one that becomes extremely visible should things go wrong. Administering email is inevitably time-consuming and frustrating, at least intermittently. It also is comprised of a set of tasks that can seem rather daunting to the newcomer. However, don't let any initial feelings of confusion discourage or overwhelm you; in a surprisingly short time, you'll be in control and complaining with the best of them about the mail system's eccentricities and shortcomings.

About Electronic Mail

As with regular postal mail, a properly functioning electronic-mail system depends on a series of distinct and often geographically-separated facilities and processes working together. Typically, each of these parts is handled by one or more programs specifically designed to perform the corresponding tasks.

In general, on Unix systems, the electronic mail facility is composed of the following components:

Programs that allow users to read and write mail messages
> In the jargon, such programs are known as *mail user agents*. There are a variety of such programs available, ranging from the traditional (and primitive) mail command to character-based, menu-driven programs such as elm, mutt, pine, and the mh family, to Internet-integrated packages such as Netscape (some users also prefer the mail facilities embedded within their favorite editor, such as emacs). These programs require only a little administrative time and attention, usually consisting of setting system-wide defaults for the various packages.

Programs that accept outgoing email (submission agents), send it along its way, and begin the delivery process
> Delivering mail to its final destination is the responsibility of *mail transport agents*, which relay mail messages within a site or out onto the Internet toward their final destinations. Transport agents run as daemons, and they generally use the directory */var/spool/mqueue* as a work queue to hold messages waiting for processing.

sendmail is the traditional Unix transport agent. sendmail usually functions as the submission agent as well, although some mail programs (user agents) now incorporate this capability themselves. Current estimates indicate that sendmail handles about 75% of all email. Other available transport agents include Postfix, qmail, and smail. At present, transport agents most often use the Simple Mail Transfer Protocol (SMTP) to exchange data, although other transport protocols are seen occasionally (e.g., UUCP).

Programs that transfer messages to the user's mailbox

Once mail arrives at its destination, the transport agent hands it off to a *delivery agent* that actually places messages into the appropriate user's mailbox (among other tasks). User mailboxes are located in */var/mail* (*/var/spool/mail* under AIX, FreeBSD, and Tru64) and consist of text files named for the corresponding user account.

There may be different delivery agents for the various classes of messages (e.g., local versus remote) and different transport protocols (e.g., SMTP versus UUCP). Commonly used delivery agents include procmail, mail, rmail, and mail.local (the latter is part of the sendmail package).

Programs that retrieve stored messages from an ISP or other holding location

When a user or organization has only an intermittent connection to the Internet, incoming remote messages are usually stored on their ISP's server until they are ready to collect them. Periodically, such users/sites must establish a connection to the ISP and send out all new messages and retrieve those waiting for them. The program that performs these actions might be termed a *retrieval agent*,* and fetchmail is the most common. Once messages have been downloaded, they are usually handed off to a transport agent for local routing and delivery.

Programs to access delivered messages from a different computer

Some organizations and individual users choose to access email from a computer other than the one where their mailbox is located (the target location for the delivery agents). For example, a user at a site with a central mail server may prefer to read his mail on his own workstation rather than on the designated server. Such schemes use a *message store* to hold accumulated messages. They may be stored in traditional user mailboxes—files within the designated mail spool director—or as records in a database. The user agent must connect to the message store to view, access, manipulate, and potentially download the messages. When doing so, the user agent is functioning as an *access agent*. The message retrieval processes uses the Post Office Protocol (POP3) or Internet Message Access Protocol (IMAP) for communication.

Figure 9-1 illustrates some of these components and concepts via a sample mail message sent from Hamlet (user account *hamlet* at *uwitt.edu*) to his friend Ophelia (*ophe624@elsinore.gov*).

---

* What I'm calling a retrieval agent can also be thought of as a type of access agent (see the following paragraph).

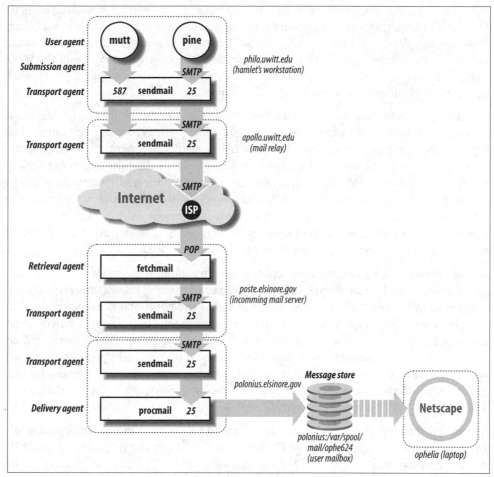

User agent — mutt · pine

philo.uwitt.edu
(hamlet's workstation)

Submission agent — SMTP

Transport agent — 587 sendmail 25

SMTP

Transport agent — sendmail 25

apollo.uwitt.edu
(mail relay)

SMTP

Internet ISP

POP

Retrieval agent — fetchmail

SMTP

poste.elsinore.gov
(incomming mail server)

Transport agent — sendmail 25

SMTP

Transport agent — sendmail 25

Message store

polonius.elsinore.gov

Delivery agent — procmail 25 → Netscape

polonius:/var/spool/
mail/ophe624
(user mailbox)

ophelia (laptop)

Figure 9-1. Example email configuration

Hamlet composes his message to Ophelia using a mailer program like pine or mutt on one of the workstations in his department (hostname *philo*). Depending on his user agent and its exact configuration, it may forward the message to the local sendmail process using port 587, allowing sendmail to submit it to the mail facility, or it may do the submission operation itself, communicating with sendmail via SMTP on port 25 (the transport agent standard port). In our example, pine has been configured to function as a submission agent as well as a user agent, while mutt relies on sendmail for mail submission.

At this site, all outgoing mail is funneled through a single mail relay host named *apollo*, so the sendmail process on *philo* passes the message along to the corresponding process on *apollo*, which in turns relays it to the Internet. From there, the message will eventually be sent to *ophe624@elsinore.gov*, which is redirected (via DNS MX records) to some system at the ISP used by the *elsinore.gov* site.

When convenient, the incoming mail server at *elsinore.gov*, named *poste*, connects to the ISP and uses the fetchmail program to retrieve waiting messages. fetchmail then forwards the data to sendmail, using the SMTP protocol and port 25, thereby simulating normal incoming TCP/IP mail. The sendmail process on *poste* sends the messages for user *ophe624* to the sendmail process on *polonius*, where the procmail program places it in the correct mailbox, */var/spool/mail/ophe624*.

From the point of view of the sendmail transport agent, the mail is now delivered. However, Ophelia still hasn't seen the message. She typically reads her mail on her laptop. To do so, she has configured Netscape's email component to connect to the message store—in this case, her mailbox on *polonius* (providing the appropriate username and password for authentication). Once she's connected, Netscape displays information about the messages in her mailbox, showing her the actual message when requested, retrieving all data via the IMAP protocol. At her option, Ophelia can delete the message, download it to her laptop, or file it away into one of her mail folders on *polonius* (or even leave it in her incoming mailbox).

If *elsinore.gov* had a direct Internet connection, the initial delivery of mail messages to their site would be somewhat different. Instead of using fetchmail to retrieve messages from a remote ISP site, mail would arrive at the computer designated for that domain via DNS MX records. Most often, this means the site's firewall, where some extra precautions are taken. Instead of running sendmail on the firewall, which involves significant security risks, the firewall can run a much simpler, unprivileged daemon that forwards SMTP packets to a designated host inside the firewall (in our example, *poste* could again be used for the latter at *elsinore.gov*). Such a daemon is known as an *SMTP proxy*.

For added security, this function can be split into two noncommunicating processes. In fact, the most widely used SMTP proxy facility is the combination of smtpd to receive and store incoming SMTP data and smtpfwdd to forward SMTP data to the incoming mail server (available from *http://www.obtuse.com*). The smtpd daemon simply accepts SMTP packets, constructs mail messages, and writes them into a spool directory on disk (e.g., */var/spool/smtpd*). Sometime later, smtpfwdd reads messages from that location and invokes a program to submit them to the mail system. Usually, this program is sendmail, and it forwards the messages to a transport agent inside the firewall. On the firewall system, however, sendmail does not run as a daemon and is configured to accept mail only from smtpfwdd. This configuration is illustrated in Figure 9-2.

Both daemons implement only the minimal set of SMTP commands to perform their tasks. By limiting the proxy processes' functions to simple reading and writing, any potential troubles arising from malicious SMTP commands are avoided. In addition, smtpd can optionally filter messages based on a variety of access control settings, and smtpfwdd can filter messages based on content.

smtpd is designed to be invoked on demand by inetd, so adding an entry for it to the */etc/inetd.conf* configuration file is part of the installation process. smtpfwdd runs as a

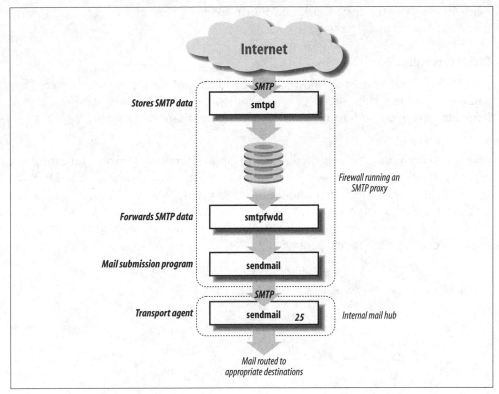

Figure 9-2. An SMTP proxy at a firewall

daemon and is, accordingly, started at boot time. Consult the accompanying documentation for more information about these programs.

Mail Addressing and Delivery

So far, we have considered only the most straightforward mail addressing case: a message is addressed to a user at a particular site. However, several complications can arise, making real-world delivery of actual mail messages much more complex:

- DNS MX records can redirect a message to a host other than the one to which it was directed.

- Name-mapping functions in the transport agent can map public email addresses to local user accounts and/or hosts (e.g., *Rachel_Chavez@ahania.com* to *chavez@dalton*).

- Email aliases can redirect incoming messages for a user to a different host and/or user (or even to a group of users).

- Mail-forwarding mechanisms can also redirect mail to a different destination address, a facility typically used for users who are away from their home site for an extended period (e.g., on vacation) or who have left an organization altogether.

We will consider the first, third, and fourth items in this section. Transport agent name mapping is discussed later in this chapter.

DNS MX records

DNS MX records specify the host(s) that handle email for a given computer. They cause email addressed to that host to be sent to a new destination system rather than being delivered on that host itself. MX records have the general format:

```
host [ttl] IN MX n destination
```

host is the computer to which the record applies, *n* is a number indicating the record's priority level (lower numbers indicate higher priority), and *destination* is the name of the host to which mail should be (re)directed. Note that the destination can be the same as the host itself, and it often is. The hostname specified must be the one used in the corresponding A record; CNAMEs are not allowed. (*ttl* is the usual, optional caching time-to-live parameter.)

Here are some examples for the domain *ahania.com*:

```
dalton       IN  MX  10  dalton
             IN  MX  20  postal
             IN  MX  90  remote.ahania.com.

newton       IN  MX  10  apple
             IN  MX  20  postal

ahania.com.  IN  MX  10  granada.ahania.com.
             IN  MX  20  laguna.ahania.com.
```

Host *dalton* normally receives its own mail since it is listed as its own highest-priority destination host. That is, mail addressed to *someone@dalton* or *someone@dalton.ahania.com* is delivered to host *dalton*. If *dalton* is unavailable, mail is redirected first to host *postal* (i.e., *postal.ahania.com*) and then to host *remote.ahania.com*, if *postal* is also down.

In contrast, email destined for host *newton* is redirected to host *apple* under normal circumstances. In other words, mail to *someone@newton* or *someone@newton.ahania.com* is actually delivered to host *apple*. If *apple* is unavailable, mail goes to *postal* instead. Thus, in this example, *postal* serves as a backup mail server for both hosts.

The final two lines specify a default mail destination system for mail addresses of the form *somebody@ahania.com*. By default, mail addressed to a user at this site—without including any hostname in the address—is routed to the system *granada*, which serves as the incoming mail server for that site. System *laguna* is specified as a backup mail destination.

Mail aliases

Mail aliases are another way of rerouting email. In contrast to DNS MX records, these operate on a per-user basis. Mail aliases are usually defined in the file */etc/aliases* (or occasionally */etc/mail/aliases*); this facility is provided by the transport agent. These aliases are automatically applied to the local recipients of incoming mail. Names specified in email message addresses are compared against the entries in the aliases file and are translated according to its directives.*

 Some mailer programs also allow users to define personal mail aliases, but these apply only to outgoing messages created by that specific user, and they won't be considered here since they are expanded *before* the message enters the larger mail system.

Entries in the aliases file have the following format:

```
local-name: user [, user ...]
```

Aliases may be continued onto as many lines as needed by indenting the second and subsequent lines. This line has the affect of translating the specified *local-name* into its corresponding expansion (whatever follows the colon) whenever it is encountered as an email address by the transport agent on the local system.

Here are some example entries:

```
eve:       ewood
ewood:     ewood@altos
ike:       \issac@newton

chem:      enzo, nadia, vala
phys:
  ike,
  enzo,
  kip
science:   chem, phys, max
vala:      vala@zoas.com
```

The first three entries illustrate user account aliases. In this case, mail for *eve* is redirected to *ewood*. The name *ewood* is itself an alias, and it expands to *ewood@altos*, so mail coming to this system for *eve* would go to *ewood@altos* (at least to start with). Aliases continue to be expanded up to ten levels deep. In the same way, the third entry defines an alias for *ike*: *\issac@newton*. This is a *terminal alias*: the initial backslash prevents any further expansion on the local system, including via *.forward* files (see below).

The next three sample entries are used to define some local mailing lists. The first two lists have three members each. The third list, *science*, has two other mailing lists as its members (along with *max*). Any duplicates in the resulting list are automatically removed by sendmail (user *enzo* in our example). Note also that entry order is irrelevant in the aliases file. Thus, the alias defining *vala* does not need to precede its use in the *chem* mailing list.

---

* This is true for the most common mail system configurations. If NIS or LDAP is in use, the situation can be a bit more complicated. This issue is covered in detail in the discussion of transport agents later in this chapter.

The component email addresses for mailing lists may also be listed in an external file; the alias itself is then defined via an include directive in the aliases file, as in this example:

```
curry: :include:/usr/local/mail_lists/curry_lovers.list
```

The full path to the include file must be specified (the directory location in the example is arbitrary). In this case, *curry_lovers.list* is a text file containing the list of email addresses for this mailing list. You will also see aliases such as owner-curry and similar names, which are used for mailing list administration.

Names encountered in email addresses which are not defined in the aliases file are assumed to be usernames on the local system under normal circumstances. You can also configure some transport agents to perform other kinds of address lookups (as we'll see). Similarly, unqualified names (i.e., without an *@host* part) in alias definitions within the aliases file are also interpreted as local usernames.

The sendmail facility and other transport agents do not access the aliases file directly. Instead, they use binary random access databases to speed up the alias expansion process. Whenever you edit the aliases file, you must update these binary files by running the newaliases command (no arguments required).* However, newaliases does not need to be run when you edit a list file specified with an include directive.

Aliases may also be used to redirect mail messages to a file or a program, via entries like the following:

```
help:  help-list, /data/help/incoming
info:  "|/usr/local/admin/send_info"
```

The first alias directs mail addressed to *help* to *help-list* and also appends it to the file */data/help/incoming*. The second alias pipes mail messages to the specified program.

Any file specified in an aliases file entry must already exist. For sendmail, the file must also be writable by the package's default user (a configuration option discussed later in this chapter), and it must be setuid to owner but not be executable (i.e., chmod -x,u+s). This unusual permission requirement makes it quite unlikely that any file will be accidentally overwritten. Postfix also requires the file to be writable by its default user.

Defining a pipe as an alias sends mail messages to the standard input of the specified program. The program runs as the transport agent's default user, and the program's working directory is set to the mail queue directory (usually */var/spool/mqueue*). By default, the program is executed by /bin/sh for sendmail, although you can (and should) specify a different shell for security reasons (discussed later). Postfix attempts to run the program directly but falls back to /bin/sh if necessary.

---

* newaliases is equivalent to sendmail -bi, which may be used in those rare cases in which no newaliases command is provided.

Use a Single Aliases File

Using a single aliases file has a number of advantages, including limiting alias administration to a single point and preventing some sorts of mail bouncing problems. Such a file lists every user at the site and defines an alias for each that points to the system where he receives or collects email. This master aliases file can be distributed using one of the methods described in Chapter 14.

Mail forwarding

Mail forwarding is the third mail redirection mechanism we will consider. Mail forwarding for specific users can be specified at the site level using features of the transport agent, or it can be accomplished by an individual user himself. Mail redirection using sendmail and other transport agents is usually performed when a user has permanently left an organization. We will discuss these facilities when we consider sendmail and Postfix in detail, later in this chapter.

User-specified mail forwarding uses the same basic idea as mail aliases. A user can cause his mail to be automatically forwarded to a different address by creating a file named *.forward* in his home directory.[*] This file contains one or more email addresses to which email should be forwarded (the simplest format is to put each address on a separate line). For example, if the *.forward* file in user *chavez*'s home directory contained the single line *rachelc@zoas.org*, her email would be forwarded to the specified address. If she wanted to keep a local copy of the mail as well, she could use this *.forward* file:

```
rachelc@zoas.org, "/home/chavez/mail_pile"
```

This file would forward the mail to the same address and also place a copy of each forwarded message into the file *mail_pile* in her home directory. The target file must already exist and be owned by user *chavez*, and common sense dictates that it should be writable only by the user herself, as should every component subdirectory of the directory tree in which it resides.

In some configurations/versions, sendmail enforces these file protection requirements and will not append mail to files that are group- or world-writable or are placed in an insecure directory location. Postfix has similar requirements.

With sendmail, forwarding messages to pipes or files also requires that the user's login shell be listed in the */etc/shells* file. If this file is not used (e.g., under AIX), you must create it manually (or rely on the internal default list of */bin/sh* and */bin/csh*). You can disable this requirement by including the following line within the shells file:

```
/SENDMAIL/ANY/SHELL/
```

---

[*] Actually, the mail-forwarding file path is a configurable list within the transport agent.

Such an entry is necessary to enable forwarding for users whose shell prevents logging in to the mail server (e.g., having `nologin` as their shell).

Putting it all together

So how do all of these separate pieces interact to deliver mail? First, the MX records are examined to see whether email is rerouted at the DNS level. If so, the mail is sent to the same user at the new host.

If no MX record causes the mail to go to another host, the address is processed for aliasing via the aliases file and then the forwarding mechanism. Either of these has the potential to redirect the mail to a different user and/or host. If the host changes, the message is routed to the specified host (where MX record checking begins again). On the other hand, if the aliasing does not redirect the message to a different host, the message is delivered to the appropriate user on the local system.

Let's consider an example (illustrated in Figure 9-3).[*] Consider a message addressed to *jane_smith@ahania.com* (arriving from some remote sender). The message is directed first to the incoming mail server, *poffice.ahania.com*, the destination designated by the MX record for the domain *ahania.com*.

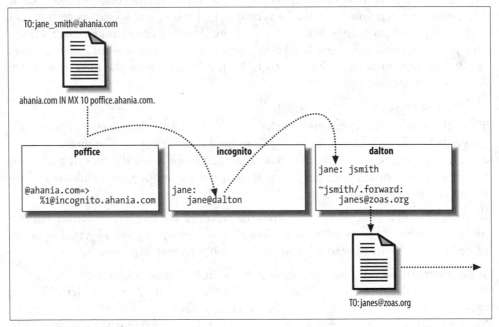

Figure 9-3. Mail redirection

---

[*] To illustrate the various mail redirection possibilities, this example violates many design principles for an effective and efficient email system: a central aliases file, a logical and well-ordered set of DNS MX records, and so on.

The sendmail configuration on *poffice* specifies that all incoming mail addressed to *ahania.com* be sent to the same user at host *incognito*. On *incognito*, an alias for *jane* on *incognito* points to *jane@dalton*. Finally, on *dalton*, *jane* is aliased to *jsmith*, a local user account. However, user *jsmith* has a *.forward* file in her home directory consisting of the entry *janes@zoas.org*. So the mail is readdressed accordingly, and the mail system in the *ahania.com* domain sends the message back out onto the Internet. When the message arrives at the *zoas.org* domain, the entire process begins again.

Electronic Mail Policies

Electronic mail frequently raises as many social issues as it does technical ones. Part of the system administrator's job is to educate users about using email properly and its risks. Many sites implement an email policy to specify appropriate and inappropriate uses of user email accounts, as well as to inform users about their rights (and limitations to them).

The following is a list of items you should consider including in an educational or policy document about email:

- Reminders to keep email brief and to-the-point and to strive for the same level of politeness one would use in verbal communications (avoid "flaming"). Wait a day or so before replying to or sending an emotionally charged message (in the latter case, having someone else read the message before you send it is also a good idea).

- Limit a message's recipients as much as possible. In other words, be conservative about copying (CCing) to additional people. When replying, send your response only to the message's author or at least remove extraneous recipients from the list. Avoid making Reply All the default in your mailer program.

- Any policy your site has with respect to blind copying (BCCs).

- Any forbidden uses of email at your site: e.g., commercial ventures not related to your organization, chain letters, spam, and so on.

- Any policies you have made with respect to mail attachments (e.g., quarantining ones possibly containing viruses).

- Email should not be considered private, so confidential information should not be sent via email. You should also mention any organizational policy on users' email ownership and privacy (i.e., whether management reserves the right to examine any email message).

- Politeness dictates that email messages not be forwarded to third parties without the original sender's approval.

- Email is not considered legal notification in most instances. Use written communication (a memo or letter) instead of or in addition to email when you need to officially/legally convey information.

- Email can be forged, so trust your instincts about suspicious messages and investigate them before taking any action.

Email Ethics for System Administrators

Anyone with root access on a system can obviously read any file on it, including users' electronic mail. However, system administrators should obviously not do so in general, and they should make every effort to avoid looking at actual messages even when they must debug the mail system. Most times, test messages can be sent to simulate actual mail traffic. Even if you do need to examine real mail messages, examining the mail headers is sufficient in almost all cases.

Configuring User Mail Programs

As we've noted, there are a variety of mailer programs available for use as user agents. Some of the most popular are listed in Table 9-1. Some of them—pine, the mh family, and Netscape—can also be configured to function as direct mail submission agents; the others rely on the transport agent for this task.

Table 9-1. Mail programs provided by Unix systems

	AIX	FreeBSD	HP-UX	Linux	Solaris	Tru64
System V mail			✓		✓	✓
BSD mail	✓	✓	✓	✓	✓ ᵃ	✓ ᵃ
elm (*ftp://ftp.virginia.edu/pub/elm/*)	■	✓	✓ ᵃ	✓	■	■
mutt (*http://www.mutt.org*)	■	✓	■	✓	■	■
pine (*http://www.washington.edu/pine/*)	■	✓	■	✓	✓	■
Netscape (*http://www.netscape.com*)	✓	✓	■	✓	✓	✓
mh and variants (*http://www.mhost.com/nmh/*)	✓	✓	■	✓	✓	✓
Emacs internal mailer rmail (*http://www.gnu.org*)	■	✓	■	✓	✓	✓

ᵃ The corresponding command is mailx.

In Table 9-1, ✓ indicates that the program is installed with the operating system or provided as an optional package within installation media. A program marked with ■ is available by Internet download.

Selecting a mailer program is generally a matter of personal preference. As such, we won't discuss their ordinary features here. Instead, we will focus on system administrator configuration issues for three of the most popular mailers: BSD mail, mutt, and pine. However, there are two points with regard to other mailer agents that you should be aware of:

- elm (by David Taylor) is still in wide use as a mailer program, but its functionality has been pretty well superceded by mutt. mutt's interface is almost identical to elm's, and it is a considerably more powerful program (especially compared to vanilla elm, without the many separately available modifications installed). Users who like elm might be encouraged to try mutt.

- The mh family (mh, nmh, xmh, exmh) uses a mailbox format that is substantially different from the ones used by other user agents. The most widely used mailbox format on Unix systems is the *mbox* format, in which all messages are stored within a single file, separated by lines beginning with "From " (i.e., followed by a space and no colon). For this reason, this format is sometime referred to as the *From_* format.

  In contrast, the mh mailbox is a directory in which individual mail messages are stored as separate files, with the message number as the filename. Deleted messages have names of the form *,n*: the original name prepended with a comma. Some other mailer programs (e.g., mutt) can be configured to read mh mailboxes.

The one task user agents always require of system administrators is configuration of systemwide default settings. Additionally, users may require help to set up some of these programs' advanced features. In the remainder of this section, we will look at the configuration files for the BSD mail program, mutt, and pine. We will then consider how to set up the latter two programs to use PGP for encrypting email messages.

Table 9-2 lists the user-specific and systemwide configuration files associated with these three user agents. Note that systemwide configuration files are applied before the user's own file, so systemwide settings can be overridden by individual users. The table also lists the command form that can be used to bypass the system configuration file entirely. However, pine does have the capability of imposing systemwide settings on users (as we will see).

Table 9-2. Mailer configuration files and options

Mailer	System file	User file	Option to bypass system configuration file
BSD mail	/etc/mail.rc	~/.mailrc	mail -n
mutt	/etc/Muttrc	~/.muttrc	mutt -n
pine	/usr/lib/pine.conf and /usr/lib/pine.conf.fixed[a]	~/.pinerc	pine -P /dev/null

[a] These configuration files are sometimes stored in /usr/local/lib instead.

Here is a sample *mail.rc* configuration file for the mail program (annotated):

```
set append            Append messages to mailbox (versus prepend).
set asksub askcc      Prompt for subject and CC list.
set autoprint         Print next message after a delete command.
set metoo             Don't remove sender from group lists.
set nosave            Don't save cancelled messages to dead.letter.
set Replyall          Make the r command = reply to sender only.
ignore Received Message-Id Resent-Message-Id Status Mail-From Via
```

The first five entries set some useful mail options and are generally self-explanatory. The *Replyall* option causes mail's r reply command to default to replying only to the sender of the letter, rather than to the entire recipient list. In other words, it interchanges the functions of mail's r and R subcommands. Setting this will cut down on a lot of unnecessary mail traffic, and it may even prevent some embarrassment on the part of new mail users. However, you may need to inform experienced users of such a change if you make it on an existing system.

The remaining lines in the configuration file tell mail to ignore the listed mail header lines when determining to whom a reply should go.

Users sometime want to change the text editor used by the mail program's e command (used to edit a message). mail uses whatever editor is specified in the *EDITOR* environment variable in this context.

mutt (written by Michael Elkins and others) comes with an excellent template configuration file that lists and describes all the available options. Here is an annotated sample of a systemwide *Muttrc* file:

```
# System configuration file for Mutt
# ignore certain headers when determining reply recipient
ignore "from " received content- mime-version status sender
ignore references return-path lines x-status message-id
# set some options
set abort_nosubject=ask-yes        Prompt to abort if no subject (default=yes).
set askcc=yes                      Prompt for CC list.
set askbcc=no                      Don't prompt for BCC list.

set beep=no                        Turn off beeping!
set beep_new=no                    Even on new message arrival.

set confirmappend=no               Don't prompt for confirmation when appending
set confirmcreate=yes                 to a mail folder, but do confirm folder creations.

set header=no                      Don't include headers in quoted messages.
set mail_check=300                 Check for new mail every 5 minutes.
set mime_forward=no                Include replied-to message as text (rather
                                      than as a MIME attachment).
```

This file lists some useful options for mutt. Note that mutt also automatically uses the text editor specified in the *EDITOR* environment variable as the internal editor for creating new mail messages.

pine (written at the University of Washington) supports two systemwide configuration files: *pine.conf* and *pine.conf.fixed*. The latter file contains mandatory settings that cannot be overridden by the user in any way (they are applied last, after all other configuration files and command-line options). The two files are otherwise indistinguishable in format and directory location.

Template configuration files can be created with the pine -conf command. The resulting template file, which includes all major settings with descriptions, is sent to standard output. You can also set configuration file options using the program's internal configuration facilities (choose s and then c from the main menu).

Here is an annotated pine configuration file:

```
# pine configuration file
editor=/usr/bin/jove                          Specify editor for mail messages; the default
                                              is pico (included in the pine package).


# set some options
feature-list=enable-suspend,                  Let pine sessions be suspended with ^Z.
# start editor immediately when composing mail message
   enable-alternate-editor-implicitly,
# Make quoted messages in replies as short as possible
   no-include-header-in-reply,                Strip off headers.
   no-include-attachments-in-reply,           Attachments too.
   strip-from-sigdashes-on-reply,             And signatures.

   enable-bounce-command,                     Allow message bounce (resend) command.
   enable-full-headers-cmd,                   Allow users to optionally view all headers.
   enable-jump-shortcut,                      Entering a number jumps to that message.
   enable-tab-completion,                     Tab key file completion turned on.
   quell-status-message-beeping,              No beeping!
   quit-without-confirm,                      Suppress confirmation at exit.
   save-will-advance                          Go on to next message after message save.

# show these fields when creating a new mail message
default-composer-hdrs=To:,Subject:,Cc:
```

Unlike the other mailers we've considered, pine does not respect the setting of the *EDITOR* environment variable. Rather, users must use the program's own *editor* setting to specify an alternate message composition editor. The *enable-alternate-editor-implicitly* setting causes the specified editor to be invoked immediately when entering the body of a new message (rather than having to enter pine's ^_ command). The other entries in this configuration file are easy to understand.

Automated Email Message Encryption

The PGP facility may be used to encrypt and decrypt email messages as well as regular files; indeed, this is one of its most common uses. While users may perform these processes manually (as described in Chapter 7), most prefer that it be handled within their mailer program. Both mutt and pine can provide this functionality (PGP must be installed on the local system and be in the search path).

mutt must have been compiled with PGP support in order to use this feature. You can check the build options using the mutt -v command; check for the *HAVE_PGP* option.

Configuring mutt to incorporate PGP requires adding some entries to one of its configuration files. Fortunately, the package provides the exact entries that you need in some sample configuration files (named *pgp*.rc*). Here are a few lines from the file for PGP version 6, which illustrate the nature of the entire set of additional entries:

```
# -*-muttrc-*-
# PGP command formats for PGP 6.
```

```
# decrypt a pgp/mime attachment
set pgp_decrypt_command="PGPPASSFD=0; export PGPPASSFD; cat - %f |
  pgp6 +compatible +verbose=0 +batchmode -f"

# create a pgp/mime signed attachment
set pgp_sign_command="PGPPASSFD=0; export PGPPASSFD; cat - %f |
  pgp6 +compatible +batchmode -abfst %?a? -u %a?"
...
```

As this listing indicates, mutt runs external processes to perform PGP operations on mail messages, and the actual commands to run are defined in entries like these.

To use PGP with mutt to sign or encrypt an outgoing message, you enter the p command before sending it. This invokes the PGP menu; its most important items are e (encrypt message), s (sign message), b (do both), and f (forget it—cancel). Selecting items from this menu merely flags the desired PGP operations for the message. They are actually carried out when the send command (y) is given. At this point, you will be prompted for the key to use and the corresponding passphrase.

PGP decryption in mutt is even more automated. When an encrypted and/or signed message is opened, the relevant PGP operations are performed automatically once mutt has prompted for the PGP passphrase.

mutt creates encrypted mail messages as MIME attachments with content type "application/pgp-encrypted", not as inline text. It can also decrypt only messages in this format.

pine also supports PGP encryption and decryption, via add-on utilities. One of the most widely-used is pgp4pine (by Holger Lamm; *http://pgp4pine.flatline.de*). pine places the encrypted text within the main text of the email message, surrounded by header lines; it does not handle MIME attachments.

Once pgp4pine is installed, you must specify two configuration file settings to be able to call it from within pine:

```
# Programs that message text is piped into prior to display
display-filters=_BEGINNING("-----BEGIN PGP")_ /usr/bin/pgp4pine -d -i TMPFILE
# Programs that message text is piped into prior to sending
sending-filters=/usr/bin/pgp4pine -e -i TMPFILE -r RECIPIENTS
```

The first entry defines a pattern to search for in incoming mail messages: in this case, the text "-----BEGIN PGP", followed by the command with which to process it (to decrypt it, in this case). Once defined, mail messages containing PGP-encrypted text within their body are automatically decrypted (after the passphrase is entered).

The second entry is used to define a series of filters that can optionally be applied to outgoing mail messages. It defines a single filter that performs PGP encryption and/or signing.

To create an encrypted mail message, you must select a filter after issuing the pine send command; using this configuration, the key sequence Ctrl-X Ctrl-N initiates a send and selects the first filter, pgp4pine, resulting in the following menu:

```
You may:
a) Sign and encrypt the message
b) Sign the message
c) Encrypt the message
d) Send it unmodified
q) Abort and Quit
```

If you select any of the first three options, you will be prompted for the passphrase. Note that a key corresponding to the recipient's email address must be present on your key ring (you cannot select a key if pine cannot determine which key to use).

If you want to use PGP as a matter of course for mail messages, add the *compose-send-offers-first-filter* to the *feature-list* in one of the pine configuration files.

The pgp4pine facility also has its own configuration file, *~/.pgp4pinerc*. In general, the supplied file works well without modification. However, you will want to verify the settings specifying the name of the PGP main command for your version of PGP. For example, here is the setting that corresponds to PGP Version 6:

```
profile_pgp6_pgp6bin=pgp
```

This entry says that the pgp command is the one to use. Verify that all entries whose names begin with "profile_pgp*n*" are correct for the corresponding version of PGP.

 One disadvantage of pgp4pine is that it uses a predictable name for its temporary file. Users should ensure that any such files lingering after crashes are deleted (although this happens only very rarely).

Configuring Access Agents

There are several administrative tasks associated with using message stores for some or all email recipients:

- Selecting and designating a mail server for the message store. For large sites, this task expands to designing and deploying a scheme in which several servers divide this task.

- Configuring daemons to run POP and/or IMAP on the mail servers.

- Setting up user mail programs to access the message store instead of or in addition to the default local mailbox.

The first item is intimately related to the overall network architecture and capacity planning, and this issue is discussed in this context in Chapter 15.

The second item deals with providing server-side support for remote email clients wishing to access and retrieve messages. There are two main protocols used for this purpose: the Post Office Protocol Version 3 (POP3, or just POP) and the Internet Message Access Protocol Version 4 (IMAP4, or just IMAP).

POP is the older of the protocols, and it is also simpler than IMAP. It was designed for "offline" mail processing; the user's mail program connects to the mail server and downloads any new mail messages to the local system (usually deleting them from the server after doing so). In this scheme, the remote server functions purely as a temporary remote storage site. Although POP clients can be configured to automatically poll the mail server periodically, POP remains a manual transfer method at heart.

IMAP implements an interactive client-server model of interaction between the mail server and the client software. Mail can be downloaded to the local system as with POP, but an IMAP client can also be used to access and manage a centrally located mailbox from any remote location. When an IMAP client accesses a remote mailbox, it can perform operations on the messages stored there without necessarily having to download any of them. By default, only mail headers are transferred to the client (to save bandwidth). The body of the message is downloaded only when a message is selected for viewing, and it is not deleted from the server. Messages can be marked with various status flags (e.g., read vs. unread), and this data is stored along with the message (and accordingly appears during subsequent IMAP sessions). An IMAP client can also access multiple mailboxes and mailboxes shared among a group of users.

The functional differences between the two protocols will become clear with an example. Suppose that user *chavez*'s mail is delivered to a system named *poffice*. If her mail program supports POP, *chavez* can transfer messages that arrive on *poffice* to a different system, most likely her usual workstation. Under this POP configuration, *chavez*'s mailbox on *poffice* serves as a message store, and the mailbox on her local system is her "real" one. She can choose to retain or delete the downloaded messages on the server (via a configuration option). If she chooses the latter, the next time she connects to the message store, only messages that arrived since her previous access will be present in the mailbox.

The POP approach can be beneficial for retrieving mail from remote dialup locations, because it minimizes the time you must be connected to the mail server.

In contrast, with IMAP, user *chavez*'s "real" mailbox is on *poffice* itself, and she can access it from any system within the network. When she connects to it via a mail program running IMAP, she will see all of the messages in her mailbox. She will be able to distinguish new messages from those she's already read (she may even have some messages that are marked as deleted but haven't yet been actually discarded). She can also save messages from her default mailbox—known as her "inbox"—to other mail folders that she has created (which frequently reside in the directory tree under *~chavez/Mail* on the server).

There are many sources of POP and IMAP daemons, and many Unix vendors provide one with the operating system (or as a optional package). The following list gives the paths to the daemons provided by various Unix versions we are considering:

| AIX | */usr/sbin/pop3d* and */usr/sbin/imapd* |
| FreeBSD | several provided in the ports collection |

HP-UX	none provided
Red Hat Linux	*/usr/sbin/ipop3d* and */usr/sbin/imapd*
SuSE Linux	*/usr/sbin/pop3d* and */usr/sbin/imapd*
Solaris	*/opt/sfw/sbin/ipop3d* and */opt/sfw/sbin/imapd*
Tru64	*/usr/sbin/pop3d* and */usr/sbin/imapd*

In addition, there is a widely used POP/IMAP server package available for free from the University of Washington (*http://www.washington.edu/imap/*). In fact, some of the vendor-provided versions are simply this package.

Usually, both POP and IMAP daemons are controlled by inetd, using */etc/inetd.conf* configuration file entries like these:

```
pop-3  stream  tcp  nowait  root  /usr/sbin/tcpd  ipop3d
imap   stream  tcp  nowait  root  /usr/sbin/tcpd  imapd
```

Both daemons should use tcpwrappers for access control. There may be other POP- and IMAP-related entries in some inetd configuration files, corresponding to other versions/configurations of the protocols.

The services corresponding to these protocols are defined in */etc/services* with entries like these:

```
pop3   110/tcp          # Post Office Protocol - Version 3
pop3   110/udp          # Post Office Protocol - Version 3
imap   143/tcp  imap2   # Internet Message Access Protocol
imap   143/udp  imap2   # Internet Message Access Protocol
```

You may also find entries for POP2 (generally port 109) and IMAP version 3 (port 220), which is no longer in wide use, as well as some SSL-enabled variants. The latter are preferable to avoid sending plain-text passwords across the network.

If you add POP or IMAP daemons to a system, don't forget to verify that the required entries in */etc/services* and */etc/inetd.conf* are present and active (i.e., not commented out). You may also need to modify the entries in some cases (most often true for the inetd configuration entries).

Ordinarily, both POP and IMAP rely on passwords for user authentication. Some particularly poorly implemented clients require the password to be reentered for each IMAP operation, which can be very tedious. In these cases, it may be preferable to use host-level equivalence (*hosts.equiv*-type) authentication. Most IMAP daemons can configured to do this by creating a link from the IMAP server file to */etc/rimapd*. See "Network Security" in Chapter 7 for more information about inetd, */etc/services*, and host-level equivalence authentication.

Carnegie Mellon University has developed a much more sophisticated IMAP daemon facility known as Cyrus. This package is designed to be efficient and secure even for very large sites. Cyrus has a number of interesting characteristics:

- Users are not allowed to log in to mail server systems. The actual files are directly accessible only to the Cyrus processes, via a special user account created for the facility. Users can access mailboxes only via mailer programs implementing IMAP (or POP).

- The mailbox format is nonstandard and designed for scalability. Individual messages are stored in discrete files. In addition, user mailboxes are protected with access control lists.
- User authentication can be performed in any of several ways: standard Unix passwords, Kerberos, PAM.
- Disk-use quotas can be imposed on user mailboxes, if desired.

For more information about IMAP in general and the Cyrus package, see the book *Managing IMAP* by Dianna Mullet and Kevin Mullet (O'Reilly & Associates).

Setting Up User Agents to Use POP and IMAP

Many mailer programs support POP and IMAP access to remote mailboxes, among them mutt, pine, the mh family, and Netscape. In this section, we will briefly consider how to configure some of them to use a remote mailbox. Unlike the settings for PGP and mail encryption, settings for POP and IMAP are user-specific and thus typically reside in the user-specific configuration file.

mutt support for POP and IMAP must be selected at compile time (use the -v option and look for *USE_POP* and *USE_IMAP*). The following configuration file entries set up mutt as a POP client.

```
set pop_host=poffice
set pop_user=chavez
set pop_pass=xxx
set pop_delete=yes                Delete messages on server after downloading.
```

In this case, this user connects to host *poffice* via POP as user *chavez* (her mailbox is in the usual location), using the specified password for authentication (obviously, including this third entry requires care with the configuration file permissions). Once a message is downloaded from the server, it is deleted from the mailbox. mutt's G command is used to initiate mail retrieval via POP.

Here are the entries needed to connect to the same server as the same user using IMAP:

```
set spoolfile={poffice}INBOX      Where new messages arrive.
set folder={poffice}Mail          Saved mail directory.
set imap_user=chavez              Connect as this user…
set imap_pass=xxx                 …with this password.
set imap_checkinterval=900        Check for new mail every 15 minutes.
set imap_passive=no               Open new IMAP connections as required.
```

The first entry specifies the mail spool file as the usual user mailbox on the specified server (the meaning of the keyword *INBOX*). The second entry defines another mail location—a *namespace*, in IMAP parlance—as *~/Mail* (where ~ refers to the user account used for access, specified here as *chavez* in line 3).

pine also uses very simple configuration file entries for these purposes. Only one entry is needed to configure the POP client:

```
inbox-path={poffice/pop3}
```

This makes the default mailbox for pine the user's remote mailbox on the *poffice* system (accessed with the POP3 protocol), using the same username as on the local system.

The entries for an IMAP server are very similar:

```
inbox-path={poffice/user=chavez}inbox
folder-collections={poffice/user=chavez}Mail/[]
```

The first entry specifies the user's default mailbox as the mailbox corresponding to user *chavez* on system *poffice* (no protocol is specified because IMAP is the default). The second entry defines the mail folder collection to be the directory *poffice: ~chavez/Mail*.

Netscape can also be configured to use POP or IMAP to retrieve or access mail on a remote system, and it is a very popular choice for PC and Macintosh users. The relevant settings are reached by selecting the Edit → Preferences menu path and then clicking on the Mail Servers item under Mail & Newsgroups. The Incoming Mail Servers area of the resulting dialog lists any configured remote mail servers. You can set one up by clicking the Add or Edit button as appropriate.

Figure 9-4 illustrates the dialog used to configure a POP server.

Figure 9-4. Configuring Netscape to use POP

The fields in this dialog are generally self-explanatory. The Server Type field allows you to select the protocol for remote mail access (POP is chosen here). The POP tab lets you specify whether to leave messages on the server or delete them after downloading.

The corresponding dialogs for an IMAP server are illustrated in Figure 9-5. The General tab again lists the server name, protocol, username, password retention setting, and mail check interval (if any).

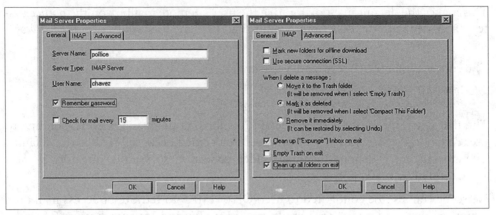

Figure 9-5. Configuring a Netscape IMAP Server

The IMAP panel, shown on the right in the figure, includes settings related to offline downloads, using an SSL-secured session, and handling of deleted messages. When a message is deleted with IMAP, the message is marked as such, but it is retained on the server by default; it actually goes away when the mail folder is "cleaned up" (known as "expunging"). With these options, a user can select how deleted messages are treated and whether/when folders are automatically expunged.

The dialog's Advanced tab lets you specify IMAP namespaces to be accessed on this server. It comes into play only when namespaces other than the defaults are in use.

Configuring the Transport Agent

Setting up the transport agent is perhaps the most crucial mail-related job presented to the system administrator. There are a variety of transport agents available on Unix systems, but sendmail is by far the most widely used. According to current estimates, sendmail handles over 75% of *all* Internet mail traffic (Unix and non-Unix alike). Other transport agents used on Unix systems include Postfix, smail, qmail, and exim. We will consider sendmail and Postfix here.

sendmail

Eric Allman's sendmail package is a very powerful facility, capable of handling email from the moment a user submits a message from a mailer program, transporting it across a LAN or the Internet to the proper destination system, and then finally handing it off to the delivery agent, which actually places the message in the user's mailbox. In fact, because the package includes a delivery agent program, the facility as a whole can handle every aspect of electronic mail except composing and reading messages and retrieving them from message stores. sendmail is also a well-proven facility, and, at this point, is quite secure, provided that it is configured properly.

 There are commercial and free versions of sendmail. The commercial versions, developed and sold by Sendmail, Inc., include additional features as well as easy-to-use graphical interfaces, integration with other related commercial products (e.g., virus-scanning software), and technical support. Vendor-supplied versions of sendmail are created from the free package.

sendmail is available from *http://www.sendmail.org*; see also *http://www.sendmail.net*, which is Sendmail, Inc.'s site for the free version. For information about commercial sendmail products, see *http://www.sendmail.com*.

The current sendmail version series is 8.12.3 (circa April, 2002). sendmail's major version number—8—refers to the extensive rewrite of sendmail done in 1993 by its author, Eric Allman. The other numbers are revisions within that series.[*] Unfortunately, vendor-included versions of sendmail tend to lag behind the current version to varying degrees, with free operating systems remaining closest to the current version and commercial operating systems quite a bit further behind. (At the moment, sendmail versions included with commercial operating systems range from 8.8 to 8.10 for the Unix flavors we are considering.)

You can identify which version of sendmail is running on a system by running the following command:

```
$ echo | sendmail -bt -d0
Version 8.11.3
Compiled with: LDAPMAP MAP_REGEX LOG MATCHGECOS MIME7TO8 MIME8TO7
               NAMED_BIND NETINET NETUNIX NEWDB NIS QUEUE SASL
               SCANF SMTP USERDB

============ SYSTEM IDENTITY (after readcf) ============
      (short domain name) $w = poffice
  (canonical domain name) $j = poffice.ahania.com
        (subdomain name) $m = ahania.com
             (node name) $k = poffice.ahania.com
========================================================
ADDRESS TEST MODE (ruleset 3 NOT automatically invoked)
Enter <ruleset> <address>
```

This sendmail command runs the facility in its interactive address-testing mode, with some additional debugging output enabled; in this case, the input is taken from standard input, which is null, thereby terminating the session after the initial messages are displayed (*/dev/null* could also be used as the input source).

---

[*] sendmail Version 9 is in development as of this writing.

The resulting output indicates the sendmail version information and the set of compilation options with which it was built. For example, this version includes support for interfacing with an LDAP database (indicated by the first keyword in the list). The second section of the output displays information about the local system and its DNS domain environment. The final lines pertain to email address translation and can thus be ignored here.

If you want to find out the sendmail version running on a remote system, telnet to port 25 (specified as telnet's second parameter):

```
$ telnet pauling 25
Trying 192.168.9.220...
Connected to pauling.
Escape character is `^]'.
220 pauling ESMTP Sendmail 8.11.0/8.11.0; Sun, 4 Mar 2001 ...
^]
telnet> quit
```

Taking the last couple of years as the norm, upgrades to sendmail appear very frequently—every 2–3 months, barring major bugs or security holes. Ideally, hosts that relay mail into and out of your site should be kept up-to-date with the latest version of sendmail since these are your most vulnerable security points. Other hosts, which usually rely on a central mail server for mail transport, can probably make do with the version that came with the operating system (unless a major security problem is discovered). In any case, check security sites and mailing lists (as well as the sendmail home page) regularly for notices of newly discovered sendmail vulnerabilities and appropriate fixes.

The sendmail facility consists of many components: the sendmail daemon, some related commands and programs, several configuration files and databases, and configuration-file building tools. These files will be located in standard locations only if you install sendmail yourself from source code. Table 9-3 lists sendmail's major components, along with their directory locations for the various Unix operating systems.

Table 9-3. Where to find the components of the sendmail package

sendmail component	Location
sendmail binary	**Usual:** */usr/sbin*
	Solaris: */usr/lib*
Boot script that starts sendmail	**AIX:** */etc/rc.tcpip*
	FreeBSD: */etc/rc*
	HP-UX: */sbin/init.d/sendmail*
	Linux: */etc/init.d/sendmail*
	Solaris: */etc/init.d/sendmail*
	Tru64: */sbin/init.d/sendmail*

sendmail component	Location
Boot script configuration file (and `sendmail`-enabling entry)	**AIX:** none used
	FreeBSD: */etc/defaults/rc.conf, /etc/rc.conf*[a] *(sendmail_enable="YES")*
	HP-UX: */etc/rc.config.d/mailservs*[a] *(export SENDMAIL_SERVER=1)*
	Linux: */etc/sysconfig/sendmail*[b] */etc/rc.config.d/sendmail.rc.config*[a] *(SuSE 7) (START_SENDMAIL="yes")*
	Solaris: */etc/default/sendmail*[a] *(DAEMON=yes)*
	Tru64: */etc/rc.config.** (set arguments only)
`vacation` utility	**Usual:** */usr/bin*
	Linux: not provided by standard Red Hat
`newaliases` and `mailq` commands	**Usual:** */usr/bin*
	AIX: */usr/sbin*
	Tru64: */usr/sbin*
`smrsh` restricted shell (for piping to commands in mail aliases)	**AIX:** not provided
	FreeBSD: */usr/libexec*
	HP-UX: */usr/sbin*
	Linux: */usr/sbin* (Red Hat) */usr/lib/sendmail.d/bin* (SuSE)
	Solaris: */usr/lib*
	Tru64: not provided
`mail.local` (local delivery agent)	**AIX:** not provided
	FreeBSD: */usr/libexec*
	HP-UX: not provided
	Linux: */usr/bin* (Red Hat) */usr/lib/sendmail.d/bin* (SuSE)
	Solaris: */usr/lib*
	Tru64: not provided
aliases file	**Usual:** */etc*
	FreeBSD: */etc/mail*
	HP-UX: */etc/mail*
	Tru64: */var/adm/sendmail*
sendmail.cf (primary config. file)	**Usual:** */etc/mail*
	AIX: */etc*
	Linux: */etc*
	Tru64: */var/adm/sendmail*
Additional config. files	**Usual:** */etc/mail*
	AIX: */etc*
	Tru64: */var/adm/sendmail*

Table 9-3. *Where to find the components of the sendmail package (continued)*

sendmail component	Location
Configuration file build area (i.e., location of Build script)	**AIX:** */usr/samples/tcpip/sendmail/cf* **FreeBSD:** */usr/share/sendmail/cf/cf* **HP-UX:** */usr/newconfig/etc/mail/cf/cf* **Linux:** */usr/share/sendmail-cf/cf/cf* (Red Hat)[c] */usr/share/sendmail/cf* (SuSE) **Solaris:** */usr/lib/mail/cf* **Tru64:** not provided[d]
sendmail.pid (contains PID of sendmail process)	**AIX:** */etc* **FreeBSD:** */var/run* **HP-UX:** */etc/mail* **Linux:** */var/run* **Solaris:** */etc/mail* **Tru64:** */var/run*
syslog *mail* facility messages	**AIX:** *not configured* **FreeBSD:** */var/adm/messages* **HP-UX:** */var/adm/syslog/mail.log* **Linux:** */var/log/maillog* (Red Hat) */var/log/mail* (SuSE) **Solaris:** */var/adm/messages* **Tru64:** */var/adm/syslog.dated/*/mail.log*

[a] Other features can also be specified in these files (e.g., daemon options).
[b] The /etc/sysconfig/sendmail file does not exist by default and must be created if desired.
[c] On Red Hat systems, you must install the separate sendmail-cf package if you want to modify your sendmail configuration.
[d] The Mail section of the sysman utility offers a prompt-based *sendmail.cf* setup facility (the direct command is mailsetup). I ignore it and use the real thing.

sendmail's functioning is controlled by the sendmail daemon, and all the other components work under its direction. The daemon is generally started at boot time with a command like the following:

```
sendmail -bd -q30m
```

This command runs sendmail as a background daemon and checks its work queue every 30 minutes. In boot scripts, starting the daemon is generally preceded by commands that remove lingering junk files from sendmail's queue directory.

On systems with System V–style boot scripts, you can start or restart the sendmail daemon with a command like this one:

```
# /sbin/init.d/sendmail restart
```

See Table 9-3 to determine the configuration file location on your system.

On AIX systems, you use these commands to direct the System Resource Controller to start or restart the daemon:

```
# startsrc -s sendmail
# refresh -s sendmail
```

Configuring sendmail

Previously, configuring sendmail was something of a black art; it took a long time to learn how, and even then the process remained at least somewhat mysterious to all but the true gurus. However, since the sendmail configuration process began using the m4 macro preprocessor facility to create *sendmail.cf* configuration files, the job has become much, much easier. The discussion that follows presents an introduction to sendmail configuration; of necessity, some of sendmail's complexity is glossed over at times.

When you create a sendmail configuration file, you tell sendmail about the specifics of mail submission and delivery on the local computer system. sendmail is highly configurable, allowing you to specify desired behavior in detail and to modify almost any of its default settings. Fortunately, however, these defaults are well-chosen, and configuring sendmail is quite simple for the most commonly used mail scenarios.

sendmail's main configuration file, *sendmail.cf*, is created by running a much simpler source file through the m4 macro processor. To build a custom configuration, you must create this second file, process it, install the resulting file into the proper directory, and notify the daemon to reread it.

The configuration file build directory varies for different Linux distributions (see Table 9-3). The main directory contains a variety of sample configuration source files (their extension is *.mc*), and you can usually begin a new configuration by copying and then modifying one of them. In their simplest form, these files contain three main types of entries:

Macro invocations
> These entries are predefined macros that expand to the items necessary to enable a particular sendmail feature or setting. Macro names are conventionally in uppercase letters, and their arguments are specified as a parenthesized, comma-separated list. The most commonly used macro is FEATURE, which selects the sendmail feature corresponding to its argument. Feature names are keywords with lowercase names: e.g., FEATURE(`smrsh'). Features are defined in files named *../feature/name.m4*, and you can examine these files to see what a given FEATURE macro really does.

Additional macro definitions
> These macros are performed via the m4 *define* command, which has the form:
>
>   define(`NAME_OF_ITEM',`value')
>
> Item names are in uppercase (e.g., MASQUERADE_AS). Such defines are used both to enable sendmail features and to set the values of various sendmail parameters. The latter have names beginning with conf (e.g., confALIAS_FILE).

Comments
> Source files usually begin with a block of comments, delimited by divert(-1) and divert(0) commands (these tell the preprocessor to ignore all lines between

them). Additional comments may appear elsewhere in the file following the string "dnl".[*]

As the examples illustrated, character strings specified as macro arguments are enclosed with an initial backquote and a closing single quote:

`string'   *Note the odd quotes.*

You can find information about all of sendmail's m4-based configuration options in the *README* file in top-level *sendmail.cf* build directory (i.e., ../ relative to the directory listed in Table 9-3); this document is titled "Sendmail Configuration Files" and is also available on the sendmail websites. For the goriest of details, consult the book *sendmail* by Brian Costales with Eric Allman (O'Reilly & Associates).

Getting started: A sample mail client configuration

The listing below illustrates the use of these various items within a sendmail source file. This file is used on the client systems of a site that uses a designated mail hub for all nonlocal outgoing mail; in other words, mail submitted on a client system destined for any local system is delivered directly, but all mail destined for systems outside the local domain gets forwarded to the mail hub. This configuration assumes that the aliases file on each system defines the ultimate email destination for all users in the domain.

```
divert(-1)
#####################################################

    If you modify this file, you will have
    to regenerate /etc/sendmail.cf (run ./Build)


#####################################################
divert(0)
VERSIONID(`Config file for Red Hat Linux')
OSTYPE(`linux')
FEATURE(`smrsh')
define(`PROCMAIL_MAILER_PATH',`/usr/bin/procmail')
FEATURE(`local_procmail')
define(`SMART_HOST',`poffice.ahania.com. ')
define(`STATUS_FILE',`/var/log/mail.stats')
MAILER(`smtp')
MAILER(`procmail')
```

As usual, the source file begins with comments. The first macro in the file, VERSIONID, specifies a version string identifying this particular version of the source file; often, the value of this macro is a source control system ID string,[†] although in our case it is simply a few words of description.

---

[*] You may also see this string at the end of some configuration file lines. The dnl macro is an m4 construct that says to discard everything following it until the newline character when processing the file.

[†] In other words, "Id" within the source file, which is filled in with a verbose and ugly version string when you check the file out.

The next macro, OSTYPE, specifies the operating system type of the target system; in this case, Linux is selected. This macro causes another, OS-specific source file to be included within this source file. The various defined *ostypes* and their associated source files are located in the *../ostype* subdirectory (relative to the build directory). You should select—and examine—the one corresponding to your operating system. Looking at the file is important so that you are aware of predefined defaults set there.

The next three macros select two sendmail features: the first FEATURE macro, smrsh, says that sendmail's smrsh program should be used as the shell through which mail is sent to files and programs. The second feature, local_procmail, says to make procmail the default local delivery agent. The intervening line defines the path to the procmail program (the default is */usr/local/bin/procmail*).

The next two lines use the define macro to indicate the system that is the outgoing mail hub for mail outside the local domain (*poffice*) and to specify an alternate location for the sendmail status/statistics file (usually */etc/mail/statistics*). The final two lines of the file use the MAILER macro to specify that SMTP and procmail local mailers (delivery agents) are in use on this system.

Note that the order of items within this file is important. This is the general structure of an *.mc* source file:

```
VERSIONID
OSTYPE
DOMAIN              Domain-wide configuration file
FEATURE
define
MAILER              First "smtp", then "local", then others
LOCAL_RULE_*        Local rewriting rules (advanced feature)
LOCAL_RULESET
```

Thus, FEATUREs generally precede defines. However, if a setting related to a feature is specified in a define macro, that define should precede the corresponding FEATURE. We saw an example of the latter with the local_procmail feature in our example.

The DOMAIN macro may be used to specify a domain-wide configuration file holding settings desired on every host (or across a group of hosts), as in this example which selects the *generic* domain:

```
DOMAIN(`generic')
```

The name specified as its argument is taken as the name of an *.m4* file in *../domain* relative to the build directory (i.e., *../domain/generic.m4* in this example).

Occasionally, you may want to ensure that some feature is disabled. The undefine macro is used in these cases, as in this example, which disables alias expansion:

```
undefine(`ALIAS_FILE')
```

Building sendmail.cf

The *Build* script in the build subdirectory is used to create a configuration file from a *.mc* source file. I also tend to be a bit cautious in installing the new file, so I use a process like this:

```
# cd build-dir
# emacs test.mc
# ./Build test.cf
# cp /etc/mail/sendmail.cf /etc/mail/sendmail.cf.save
# cp test.cf /etc/mail/sendmail.cf
# chmod 444 /etc/mail/sendmail.cf
```

Whenever you change your sendmail configuration, you must send the running daemon a HUP signal:

```
# kill -HUP `head -1 /location/sendmail.pid`
```

The *sendmail.pid* file stores the process ID of the sendmail daemon (on its first line), along with the command used to initiate it (line two).

Some systems do not provide a *Build* script. In these cases, use one of the following commands (executed in the build directory):

```
# make test.cf
# m4 ../m4/cf.m4 test.mc > test.cf
```

The first command is used when there is a *Makefile* present in the build directory, and the second is the vanilla invocation of the m4 macro processor. In the latter case, the command explicitly prepends the standard sendmail m4 include file to the source file; this step is taken care of for you by the *Build* script or *Makefile*.

Configuring the mail hub

Here is a source file that might be used to build the *sendmail.cf* file for the mail hub computer system (the initial comment block and VERSIONID and OSTYPE macros have been omitted):

```
FEATURE(`use_cw_file')
dnl Send out all mail as user@ahania.com
MASQUERADE_AS(`ahania.com')
FEATURE(`masquerade_envelope')
FEATURE(`allmasquerade')
MAILER(`smtp')
MAILER(`local')
```

The first feature specifies that an external configuration file will be used to specify a list of hosts and domains for which this system will accept and deliver mail locally (traditionally known as the *cw file*, after sendmail's internal "class w"). The default file for this purpose is */etc/mail/local-host-names*, an ordinary text file containing one name per line. At a minimum, this should contain all the aliases for the local hostname. You will also need to include the local domain within the file in order to support local delivery of addresses of the form *user@local-domain* (i.e., *user@ahania.com*, in our example).

This macro is actually included by default in most sendmail configurations. Therefore, mail client systems also use this file (it is enabled within one of the m4 include files), and you should configure it on such systems as well.

The three lines following the comment enable masquerading on this host. Masquerading presents a single, common source location for all outgoing mail. For example, it can be used to make all email appear to be coming from a single system, regardless of where it was actually submitted. It can also be used to make all local sender addresses conform to a particular form (often *user@site*),

In this case, the MASQUERADE_AS macro causes all mail leaving the site to appear to be coming from the user at *ahania.com*, and all references to any local computer are removed. The masquerade_envelope feature causes masquerading to occur within the message's envelope* as well as the standard mail headers, and allmasquerade says to masquerade recipient names as well as sender names (the latter is useful when the recipient list includes both local and nonlocal people).

You can exclude some hosts and/or domains from masquerading using the MASQUERADE_EXCEPTION macro, which takes as its argument the host or domain to be excluded.

A related feature is always_add_domain, which appends the local domain to unqualified usernames (although many mailers also do this). It also respects the setting of MASQUERADE_AS. Including this feature is virtually always safe.

If you decide to use masquerading, you may want to exclude some usernames from the translation process. This is the purpose of the EXPOSED_USER macro. For example, the following macro excludes *root* from masquerading:

```
EXPOSED_USER(`root')
```

Other system-related mail addresses should also be so excluded, including *Mailer-Daemon*, *postmaster*, and so on.

We will consider additional masquerading-related features in the "Virtual Hosting" section later in this chapter.

Selecting mailers

The final two lines of the example mail hub configuration file—the MAILER macros—activate various delivery agents: in this case, SMTP and the default local delivery agent.

---

* The envelope is additional data wrapped around the actual message headers and content. It contains the actual delivery addresses, and it is built from the message's mail headers by the mailer (delivery agent).

`sendmail` has many defined mailers, including the following:

local
> Local mail delivery (using default or defined programs)

smtp
> SMTP mail transport

procmail
> Delivery via procmail

cyrus
> Delivery to the Cyrus facility

fax
> Delivery to HylaFAX (by Sam Leffler; see *http://www.hylafax.org*)

qpage
> Delivery to the QuickPage paging facility (*http://www.qpage.org*)

usenet
> Usenet news delivery

uucp
> UUCP mail transport

Once again, order matters among the selected mailers. You will be safe if you place *smtp* first, follow it with *local*, and then list any other mailers. Note that the mailers *local* and *procmail* are made equivalent when you include `FEATURE(`local_procmail')`.

 Best practice is to include `MAILER` macros only for those mailers that your site actually uses.

Each of these defined mailers has some associated parameters that can be defined, including *mailer*`_MAILER_PATH` and *mailer*`_MAILER_ARGS`, which specify the executable path and desired command arguments, respectively (where *mailer* is replaced by the uppercase mailer name). We'll look at an example in a bit.

The program used for local mail delivery—`MAILER(local)`—varies quite a bit from Unix version to version:

AIX	*/bin/bellmail*
FreeBSD	*/usr/libexec/mail.local*
HP-UX	*/usr/bin/rmail*
Linux	*/usr/bin/procmail*
Solaris	*/usr/lib/mail.local*
Try64	*/bin/mail*

In general, you can determine the default local mailer by running a command like the following (the location of the configuration file will vary):

```
$ grep Mlocal /etc/sendmail.cf
Mlocal,          P=/usr/bin/procmail, ...
```

The path following "P=" indicates the local delivery agent. There are many delivery agents in use on Unix systems: `mail`, `rmail`, `deliver`, `mail.local` (part of the sendmail package), `procmail`, and `uux` with `rmail` (for UUCP-transported mail).

The default local delivery agent is */bin/mail* for mail messages and */bin/sh* for mail messages piped to files or programs. You can override these programs and/or locations with `define` macros such as these:

```
define(`LOCAL_MAILER_PATH', `/usr/bin/rmail')
define(`LOCAL_MAILER_ARGS', `rmail -d $u')
define(`LOCAL_SHELL_PATH', `/usr/bin/sh')
define(`LOCAL_SHELL_ARGS',`sh -c $u')
```

These entries define the local delivery agent to be */usr/bin/rmail* and specify an alternate location for the shell. The `_ARGS` parameters specify the command to run in each case: `rmail` will use the `-d` option followed by the delivery address ($u, which resolves to the appropriate username), and piped email will be processed with `sh -c` *address* (where $u will again expand to the delivery address—in this case, the command specified as the alias translation).

If you want to use `sendmail`'s `mail.local` program as the local delivery agent, you can simply include this macro in your configuration source file:

```
FEATURE(`local_lmtp',`path-to-mail.local')
```

The second argument is optional and defaults to */usr/libexec/mail.local.*[*]

As with the local delivery agent, you can determine which program is used for piped mail messages using a command such as `grep Mprog /etc/sendmail.cf`. Since piped email is a traditional security hole, many administrators choose to replace `sh` with a more restricted shell. The `smrsh` shell included with sendmail fits the bill nicely (it's pronounced "smursh," but it stands for "sendmail restricted shell").

As we've seen, `smrsh` may be selected using the following `FEATURE` macro:

```
FEATURE(`smrsh',`path')
```

The second argument is again optional and defaults to */usr/libexec/smrsh*.

Like other restricted shells (see Chapter 7), `smrsh` ignores all I/O redirection within commands, strips all initial paths from command names, and restricts allowable commands to those stored in its executables directory, usually */usr/lib/sendmail.d/bin*. The administrator then places permitted (safe) commands (e.g., `vacation`) in that

---

[*] An alternate default directory for `mail.local` and `smrsh` can be set by defining the `confEBINDIR` parameter.

directory, usually via symbolic links, taking care to exclude unsafe commands, such as shells (other than smrsh itself), command interpreters (e.g., Perl, Python), and programs offering shell escapes. Neither the directory nor the files within it should be group- or world-writable.

 procmail can spawn a subshell, so it should probably not be included in smrsh's set of allowed commands (although it is often included anyway). An alternative method for allowing users to run procmail is to make it the local mailer (as is the default on Linux systems). You'll have to decide which tradeoff is the lesser evil on your system if users need procmail and you want to make them use smrsh for piped email.

More about pipes to files and programs. Normally, pipes to files can be made to ordinary files, devices, and other filesystem entities. You may want to limit them to ordinary files (to prohibit device access and prevent inadvertent errors, such as overwriting directories) by defining confSAFE_FILE_ENV:

```
define(`confSAFE_FILE_ENV',`/')
```

If you further want to limit the allowed locations for writes to files, specify the root of the desired directory as the second parameter. For example, the following entry restricts such writes to files under *home*:

```
define(`confSAFE_FILE_ENV',`/home')
```

Finally, you can disable mail message relaying to files and programs by removing the / and | characters from the list of flags given to the local mailer:

```
MODIFY_MAILER_FLAGS(`LOCAL',`-|/')
```

Some client and mail hub variations

In this section, we look briefly at a potpourri of additional features related to general client or hub configuration.

An isolated internal network. A non-Internet-connected LAN can easily rely on a single host to serve as its conduit to the outside world. The client systems in such a network use an additional feature: nocanonify. This feature tells sendmail not to expand email addresses to their fully qualified form on the local system. Instead, it will be done on the mail hub. Delaying it until then saves some unnecessary or redundant DNS lookups locally even for hosts with connections to the Internet. Moreover, it is essential to include this feature when clients with limited or no DNS access will be sending messages to arbitrary Internet destinations that they may not be able to resolve.

On the mail hub, the relay_entire_domain feature allows that system to accept mail for forwarding from any host in the local domain. Relaying is discussed in more detail when we consider sendmail's anti-spam features later in this section.

A null client. It is possible to define an even more minimal client system than the one we examined earlier. sendmail offers the option of a "null client" system in which all mail is sent to another host for processing. It uses a minimal configuration file, consisting of merely the OSTYPE macro and one FEATURE macro:

```
FEATURE(`nullclient',`poffice')
```

This example specifies the target host—the system to which to forward outgoing mail—as *poffice*. This feature also automatically turns off all address aliasing and forwarding features.[*]

If you decide to set up a null client system, you should examine the corresponding operating system–specific include file (in *../ostype*) to ensure that no unwanted features are enabled there. In addition, there is no need to run the sendmail daemon on such a client system (user agents will invoke it themselves when necessary).

Mailer-specific and other local relays. More complex mail transport schemes can also be implemented in addition to what is provided by the SMART_HOST feature (which specifies a host to handle mail addressed to hosts outside the local domain). For example, different mailers can each have a specified relay host for forwarding mail traffic using the corresponding protocol. For example, the following macro defines *oldmail* as the relay host for UUCP-based mail:

```
define(`UUCP_RELAY',`oldmail')
```

Mailer-specific relay settings take precedence over SMART_HOST.

The MAIL_HUB feature routes *all* outgoing mail to a specified host, as in this example:

```
define(`MAIL_HUB',`poffice')
```

Alternatively, LOCAL_RELAY can be defined to route unqualified mail addresses to a specific host:

```
define(`LOCAL_RELAY',`poste')
LOCAL_USER(`root admin')
```

These macros cause all mail addressed to just a username to be routed to *poste* for processing, although mail to *root* and to *admin* is excepted. The entries in the aliases file are not used for such rerouted addresses.[†]

Here is a summary of the various mail hub specification macros:

SMART_HOST
> Handles mail going outside domain

---

[*] You can disable aliasing and/or forwarding with the macros undefine(`ALIAS_FILE') and define(`confFORWARD_PATH',`'), respectively.

[†] If you use both MAIL_HUB and LOCAL_RELAY, MAIL_HUB wins, unless you also include the stickyhost feature. In the latter case, mail to unqualified usernames goes to the LOCAL_RELAY destination, and all other local outgoing mail goes to the MAIL_HUB destination.

```
MAIL_HUB
    Handles local domain mail
LOCAL_RELAY
    Handles local unqualified addresses
```

More addressing options

sendmail supports several ways of implementing aliasing of various sorts, including
NIS/NIS+, LDAP, and lookup tables (databases, actually), in addition to the aliases
file and forwarding mechanisms. In this section, we consider some of these aliasing
methods, along with some related issues.

Sender aliasing. sendmail supports lookup table–based aliasing in addition to the standard mechanisms; the databases used for these lookups are generically known as
"maps." The genericstable feature selects map lookup for outgoing sender
addresses. You enable it with configuration source file entries like the following:

```
FEATURE(`genericstable',`hash /etc/mail/senders')
GENERICS_DOMAIN_FILE(`/etc/mail/local-host-names')
```

The first entry selects the generics table feature and specifies the database as the
hash-type Berkeley DB file */etc/mail/senders.db* (the argument's syntax is thus *db-type
path*). The default is *hash /etc/mail/genericstable*.

The second macro specifies that the file listing the domains to which the map should
be applied is */etc/mail/local-host-names* (the same file listing hosts and domains to be
considered as local). Alternatively, a different file could be specified, or the GENERICS_
DOMAIN macro could be used to list the local domains explicitly.

Obviously, the associated database file must also be created. The process for doing
so is simple:

- Create a text file containing entries of the following format:

    ```
    sender-address desired-translation
    ```

    For example:

    ```
    chavez     rachel_chavez@ahania.com
    carr       steve_carr@zoas.org
    ewood      eve_wood@ahania.com
    ```

    Names in the left column implicitly have the local domain appended to them,
    because only fully qualified sender names are translated by the generics table fea-
    ture. (More complex entries are also supported; see the sendmail documentation
    for details.)

- Create a database file from the text file using the makemap command. For exam-
    ple, to create a database from the file *senders.txt*, you would generally use this
    command, which creates the file */etc/mail/senders.db*:

    ```
    # cd /etc/mail; makemap hash senders < senders.txt
    ```

sendmail supports several database formats. The hash variation of the Berkeley DB database used above is generally preferred, and it is supported by all the systems we are considering, except AIX. On AIX systems, use the *dbm* file type.[*] Note also that database support is selected at compile time; verify that the list of compiler options includes NEWDB (indicating Berkeley DB support) and/or NDBM (DBM support).

So what happens when someone replies to one of these genericized email addresses? The aliasing mechanisms in the local domain need to recognize and translate the address accordingly (e.g., via an aliases file entry) for the mail to be delivered to the proper recipient. You can also use the virtual user table feature for the reverse translations (discussed under "Virtual hosting," a little later in this section).

A few more points: first, it is often a good idea to include the always_add_domain feature when using a generics table to ensure that all names are fully qualified. Second, the generics_entire_domain feature can be used to apply generics table translation to senders from subdomains of the domains using the feature. Finally, be aware that map translations are not recursive; only a single lookup operation is performed.

Using LDAP for incoming mail addresses. Another option for address aliasing is to use an LDAP database to store the associated information. Recent versions of sendmail include the capability to issue LDAP queries (provided it is selected at compile-time; check the options for LDAPMAP). The following configuration source file macros enable LDAP support for our example domain:

```
FEATURE(`ldap_routing')
LDAP_ROUTE_DOMAIN(`ahania.com')
define(`confLDAP_DEFAULT_SPEC', `-h orwell.ahania.com -b ou=People,dc=ahania,dc=com')
```

The first feature enables LDAP support, and the second macro specifies the domain to which it applies. The final macro specifies the LDAP server and the base distinguished name at which to begin the search (see Chapter 6 for a detailed discussion of LDAP).

Once enabled, sendmail uses the following LDAP attributes of the *inetLocalMailRecipient* object class:[†]

mailLocalAddress
Incoming mail address

mailRoutingAddress
Local address to which to deliver mail

mailHost
Host to which to route mail (not often used)

---

[*] Under AIX, you must also build the makemap utility from the sendmail source distribution; it is not provided.

[†] You can change this class and other LDAP-related defaults using optional arguments to the ldap_routing feature.

Here are some example LDAP records:

```
dn: uid=chavez,ou=People,dc=ahania,dc=com
uid: chavez
objectClass: posixAccount
objectClass: inetLocalMailRecipient
mailLocalAddress: rachel_chavez@ahania.com
mailRoutingAddress: chavez@dalton.ahania.com

dn: uid=nadia,ou=People,dc=ahania,dc=com
uid: nadia
objectClass: posixAccount
objectClass: inetLocalMailRecipient
mailLocalAddress: nadia_rega@ahania.com
mailRoutingAddress: nrega

dn: uid=scarr,ou=People,dc=ahania,dc=com
uid: scarr
objectClass: posixAccount
objectClass: inetLocalMailRecipient
mailLocalAddress: steve_carr@ahania.com
mailRoutingAddress: scarr@zoas.org
mailHost: oldmail.ahania.com
```

(Note that only the relevant attributes are shown; in actual practice, these entries would probably contain additional object classes and their associated attributes.)

The first two examples translate generic incoming addresses: a fully qualified address and a (local) alias, respectively. The final example performs a similar translation, this time introducing a different domain in the target address. In addition, the mail will be routed to the host *oldmail* (as specified in the `mailHost` attribute). In other words, incoming messages addressed to *steve_carr@ahania.com* will be routed to host *oldmail*, which will deliver them to *scarr@zoas.org*.

The redirect feature. sendmail offers a very convenient way to deal with email that comes to people who have left an organization: its redirect feature. When this is included in the configuration source file, mail addressed to any recipient of the form *someone@anywhere.REDIRECT* is returned to the sender with the message:

```
551 User has moved; please try someone@anywhere
```

To use the feature, you must define aliases of the proper form for users who have left. For example, this alias will notify anyone who sends a message to *erika* that her mail should now go to *eps@essadm.com*:

```
erika:   eps@essadm.com.REDIRECT
```

Virtual hosting

We saw a simple example of address masquerading when we considered the example mail hub configuration earlier. Many times, however, a mail host needs to provide mail services for several distinct domains (often in the context of website hosting). This process is known as *virtual hosting*, and sendmail provides several features to support it. The most important of these is the virtual user table, which translates incoming addresses according to a map that you set up.

Here are some sample configuration file entries using this feature:

```
FEATURE(`virtusertable',`hash /etc/mail/vuser')
VIRTUSER_DOMAIN_FILE(`/etc/mail/local-host-names')
```

As you can see, the virtual user table entries are quite similar to those used with the generics table feature.

The format of the source file for the virtual user map is:

```
incoming-address desired-local-recipient
```

The entries in this file typically include not only individual user address translations but also blanket transformations of the addresses for entire domains. Here are some examples (assume *ahania.com* is the local domain):

```
rachel_chavez@ahania.com   chavez@dalton.ahania.com
erika@ahania.com           erikap@mango.essadm.com
help@ahania.com            error:No such user
@essadm.com                czarina@essadm.com
@zoas.org                  %1@ahania.com
```

The first two entries translate addresses to different users within the same and a different domain, respectively. The third entry returns an error to the sender for any message addressed to *help* in the local domain.

The final two entries match any address in the specified domain. The entry for *essadm.com* sends all messages to any user at that domain to the user *czarina*. The final line maps all addresses of the form *user@zoas.com* to the same username in the local domain. Note that more complex constructs are possible; see the sendmail documentation for details about the entry syntax.

Once again, the makemap command is used to create the database file. For example:

```
# cd /etc/mail; makemap hash vuser < vuser.txt
```

By default, the map is used only for fully qualified addresses in the local domain. The virtuser_entire_domain feature can be used to apply virtual user table translation to addresses referring to subdomains of the associated domain(s).

Virtual hosting requires that the DNS setup for the hosted domains match the setup specified to sendmail. In particular, the MX records for these domains should point to the appropriate system in the host domain.

The services switch file

The order of various name-lookup services is controlled, as usual, by the network services switch file, which is */etc/nsswitch.conf* on Linux and Solaris systems (more specifically, it is controlled by the *aliases* entry). For example, the following entry specifies that the standard aliases file should be used for aliases, followed by any NIS, and then the NIS+ maps:

```
aliases: files nis nisplus
```

For systems not supporting the services switch file, sendmail provides similar functionality via the confSERVICE_SWITCH_FILE setting:

```
define(`confSERVICE_SWITCH_FILE',`/etc/mail/service.switch')
```

The file above selects the usual name and location for this file (although the setting isn't configured at all on many systems). The file has a slightly different format, omitting the colon following the initial keyword:

```
aliases     files nis nisplus
hosts       files dns nis nisplus
```

As this example indicates, the sendmail services switch file can contain entries for both *aliases* and *hosts*, providing search orders for mail addresses and hostnames, respectively. See "Adding a New Network Host" in Chapter 5 for more information about the network services switch file.

Spam suppression

sendmail offers several features designed for dealing with spam, the electronic equivalent of junk mail.* These features can be grouped into four areas:

Message relaying
> Current versions of sendmail disable relaying, the passing on of received messages that are not destined for any local user. Doing so prevents the bad guys from using your mail server as a conduit for generating spam traffic, consuming (stealing) your resources in the process. Accordingly, this item is related more to general spam prevention than to eliminating spam locally.

Verifying sender data
> By default, sendmail rejects mail coming from a DNS domain whose name cannot be resolved and from senders without fully qualified mail addresses (there are features to override these defaults). Such messages are very likely to have forged headers and to be spam. You can use the access database to define exceptions to these tests if you need to (see the next item).

Address-based mail filtering via an access database and public blacklists
> Mail from various users and/or sites can be rejected. These features are highly configurable to allow both limited relaying and specification of mail sources whose messages you want to ignore or reject.

---

* The official technojargon term for spam is unsolicited commercial email, or UCE; it is also occasionally referred to as unsolicited bulk email (UBE).

Mail header checking

sendmail can apply a series of administrator-defined checks to mail headers to determine whether the mail should be accepted. See the sendmail documentation and the file *knetch.mc* (ostensibly from Eric Allman's own system), which is usually included in the build directory, for more information and examples.

We will consider the first and third items in more detail in the remainder of this section. For a different approach to detecting and processing spam, see the section on procmail later in this chapter.

Message relaying. Prior to sendmail Version 8.9, the transport agent operated in a friendly mode, relaying any mail that was presented to it. This is known as "promiscuous relaying." Unfortunately, systems that allow such relaying—referred to as "open relays"—have been misused by spammers, who send messages through systems that allow relaying, thus disguising or erasing the true origin of the messages. This is a problem for the relay system because the spammers are consuming bandwidth and system resources on the relay host. For example, all of the DNS lookups needed to deliver, say, 10,000 spam email messages are happening on your system rather than theirs.

As a result, all relaying is turned off by default in recent sendmail versions. However, sendmail does include options to turn on relaying only as needed, in limited and controlled ways. We've already seen one example of this in the relay_entire_domain feature. Also, when you use the cw file for the domain lists for the generics and/or virtual user tables, you effectively turn on relaying for the included domains.

The RELAY_DOMAIN and RELAY_DOMAIN_FILE macros can be used to specify additional domains for relaying. These macros take a domain list and filename (containing the domain list) as arguments, respectively. You can also use the access database to specify allowed relay domains and hosts (see the next section).

You may also want to reject mail addressed to nonexistent local addresses. The LUSER_RELAY macro specifies how such messages should be handled. For example:

```
define(`LUSER_RELAY',`tundra.ahania.com')
define(`LUSER_RELAY',`local:trashman')
define(`LUSER_RELAY',`error:wrong number bozo')
```

The first example reroutes such messages to the host *tundra*. The second sends them to a local address (via the LOCAL mailer); this address can be an alias pointing anywhere you want. Finally, the third example returns such messages with the indicated error message (which may not be appropriate for use at your site).

If you are using limited relaying, the best practice is to undefine the relay settings for mailers you are not using in order to minimize your site's vulnerability to misuse by spammers. For example:

```
undefine(`UUCP_RELAY')
```

and similarly for other unused mailers (e.g., DECNET, BITNET and so on).

Some people advise rejecting all mail with any variation of UUCP-style addresses using this macro:

```
FEATURE(`nouucp',`reject')
```

This advice arose from the fact that spammers used to occasionally use such addresses in an attempt to trick sendmail. However, doing this will reject all legitimate email from sites that happen to still use UUCP (and there are more of them than you think). All in all, this feature has no appreciable effect on spam and can block real electronic mail. For this reason, I strongly discourage you from using it.

Public blacklists and the access database

We now turn to two features related to stopping spam at the incoming mail host, preventing it from ever reaching user mailboxes.

The first of these is the ability to reject mail from any site included in one of the public lists of known spammers and open relays:

```
FEATURE(`dnsbl')
```

This feature tells sendmail to check senders against such a list. Such facilities use standard DNS facilities to take advantage of the normally unused IP address 127.0.0. 2; the facilities set up an otherwise normal DNS server that returns this address for all sites (IP addresses) in their list. Transport agents can choose to interpret the address as marking a bad site, and sendmail rejects mail from these sites when this feature is enabled.*

The default list to check is the Realtime Blackhole List run by the Paul Vixie and coworkers' Mail Abuse Prevention System (MAPS) project (see *http://maps.vix.com* for more information; the actual server is *rbl.maps.vix.com*). You can specify a different server to query via the second argument to the macro, and you may include the feature multiple times. MAPS provides other lists as well, as do several other organizations (e.g., the Open Relay Behaviour-modification System (ORBS); see *http:// www.orbs.org*).

There is always a small possibility of rejecting legitimate mail messages using this feature. If this occurs, you can use the access database to make exceptions without disabling the entire feature.

You enable use of an access database (map) using the following features:

```
FEATURE(`access_db', `hash /etc/mail/access')
FEATURE(`blacklist_recipients')
```

The access_db feature's arguments specify the type and pathname for the database file (as for the generics and virtual user tables); the default file type and location are given in the example.

---

* You can also consult these lists via the procmail mail filtering program and have more options for handling the corresponding messages (see the discussion of this facility later in this chapter).

The second feature is optional. The `blacklist_recipients` feature allows you to include access database entries blocking incoming messages for local mail recipients and hosts.

You create the access database file using the `makemap` command:

```
# cd /etc/mail; makemap hash access < access.txt
```

The entry format for access database entries is the following:

item action

where *item* is a username, host, domain, or network, and *action* is a keyword indicating how to treat email from that source. The available keywords include:

OK
> Accept email even if it fails other tests.

RELAY
> Relay messages from this source.

REJECT
> Reject messages from this source.

ERROR
> Reject messages with a specified error message (see examples).

DISCARD
> Silently ignore messages from this source.

In addition, if a site's entry in the access database specifies mail rejection in any of its variations, outbound mail directed there will also be prohibited.

Here are some examples:

```
bad-guys.org                    REJECT
evil-ones.net                   ERROR:"550 No spam accepted"
mole.bad-guys.org               OK
zoas.org                        RELAY
10.0.22                         RELAY
something4nothing@notaol.org    DISCARD
mybadguy@                       REJECT
fortress.ahania.com             ERROR:"550 No mail allowed"
```

The first two entries reject mail from the specified domains, using the default and specified error message, respectively. Note that error messages that you specify must begin with the 550 error code. The third entry defines an exception to the preceding rejection of mail from the *bad-guys.org* domain, allowing mail from host *mole* to get through.

The fourth and fifth entries allow relaying of mail originating from the *zoas.org* domain and any host on the 10.0.22 subnet. The following two entries apply to specific mail accounts, discarding any mail received from sender *something4nothing* in the *notaol.org* domain and rejecting incoming mail addressed to *mybadguy* in the local domain. The final entry rejects mail addressed to anyone on host *fortress* in the local domain.

Note that the last two entries, which apply to local recipients rather than remote senders, require the `blacklist_recipients` feature in order to be valid.

If finer-grained access control is desired, the access database also supports a slightly modified syntax variation allowing separate entries for senders, recipients, and connections at a site. It consists of prepending one of *From:*, *Connect:*, and *To:* to the simpler entry. For example, the following entry rejects mail from the specified address but allows outgoing messages addressed to it:

```
From:spammer@notaol.org       REJECT
```

Similarly, the following entries reject mail to and from *evil-ones.org* but define an exception for one sender and another recipient:

```
From:evil-ones.org            REJECT
To:evil-ones.org              REJECT
From:myguy@evil-ones.org      OK
To:mygal@evil-ones.org        OK
```

You can also use the access database to implement unidirectional relaying. For example, this entry relays messages from *zoas.org* but does not relay messages from other sources to it:

```
Connect:zoas.org              RELAY
```

Note that *Connect:* is used, not *From:*. Use *To:* to allow relaying to a specified destination.

 Access control entries allowing access from specific sites or senders cannot protect against address spoofing.

The entries in the access database are used by three distinct `sendmail` message examination phases.[*] Messages are checked first for allowed relaying (based on the client hostname and address), then for an allowed sender, and finally for an allowed recipient. If a message is rejected in one phase, it cannot be restored later. This means that the preceding syntax does not allow for certain kinds of exceptions to be defined. For example, you cannot allow email to a specific user always to get through regardless of its origin, because the local addresses checks are downstream from the message source checks.

However, you can use the `delay_checks` feature to reverse the order of the three test phases. In this mode, recipient-level access controls have the highest precedence, rather than the lowest.

---

[*] To be more technically accurate, the entries are used by three different sendmail "rulesets": *check_relay*, *check_mail*, and *check_rcpt*.

In addition, if you add the `friend` argument when you invoke the delay_checks feature, you can define local addresses that are exceptions to all access checks, using the following syntax:

```
To:rubbish@ahania.com        SPAMFRIEND
```

This entry exempts all mail addressed to *rubbish* in the local domain from access control tests, causing it to be accepted regardless of its origin. (Thus, "spamfriend" is used to mark recipients who don't mind getting spam.)

sendmail security

In this section, we take up several topics related to `sendmail` security. We'll begin by considering the ownerships and permissions of the various `sendmail`-related files and directories, to which I've already alluded several times in the course of this discussion. There are several points to keep in mind:

- The directory locations of all `sendmail`-related files—executables, configuration files, spool directory, and so on—should be safe: *root* should own each subdirectory in the path (along with the appropriate group), and no component of any path should be world-writable.

- The configuration files themselves should not be world-writable either. This includes *sendmail.cf* and any other configuration files you are using (usually located in */etc/mail*).

- Ideally, the spool directory should be protected against all but *root*[*] access, using a mode of 700. However, restricting access in this way prevents ordinary users from listing the queue contents with `mailq`. If this is a problem, you have the choice of relaxing the permissions with a less restrictive mode or using a privacy option to allow certain users to view the queue despite the protection (discussed below).

The sendmail default user. Although it is a SETUID *root* program, the `sendmail` process always tries to reduce its privilege to the minimum required to perform a task by giving up its *root* privilege for some other user context appropriate to the task at hand. For example, it takes on the identity of the recipient user when performing certain mail forwarding tasks.

The `confDEF_USER_ID` parameter specifies the user/group combination to use when `sendmail` wants to reduce its privilege but there is no specific user identity to take on. Here is an example:

```
define(`confDEF_USER_ID',`mailnull:mailngrp')
```

---

[*] Or another user specified via the `confRunAsUser` parameter.

The macro sets the user and group identities that `sendmail` assumes to the user and group named *mailnull* and *mailngrp*, respectively. The *mailnull* user should be defined with a password file entry like this one:

```
mailnull:***:9947:9947:sendmail default:/not/real:/dev/null
```

The user's home directory should not exist, and no valid login shell should be specified. The password for this account should also be set to an asterisk or other invalid character (either here or in the shadow password file when in use).

The group is set up similarly, for example:

```
mailngrp:*:9947:
```

The actual UID and GID do not matter, but this user and group should not own any files or be used for any other purpose. As a result, the *nobody* user should not be used as the default user.

Privacy options. `sendmail` provides a number of options for restricting or eliminating various sensitive tasks via the `confPRIVACY_FLAGS` parameter:

```
define(`confPRIVACY_FLAGS',`flag-list')
```

The second argument is a comma-separated list of flags that you want to enable. There are several flags you should consider including:

- `authwarnings` is the default setting for this parameter. It causes `sendmail` to add authentication warning headers to suspicious mail messages (see the `sendmail` documentation for details on these checks).

- `noexpn` and `novrfy` prevent responses to the SMTP EXPN and VRFY commands, respectively. These commands are designed to expand aliases and verify mail addresses, but they are often misused by spammers (to discover legitimate email addresses) and other bad guys. You may also prefer to use `goaway`, which disables all SMTP verification and status queries.

- `restrictmailq` restricts the use of the `mailq` command to users in the group that owns the */var/spool/mqueue* directory. In addition, it permits group members to view the queue even when the directory permissions do not allow file access, allowing you to use a protection mode of 700 without breaking the `mailq` command.

- `restrictqrun` prevents anyone but the user owner of the queue directory (usually *root*) from processing the queue.

- `noreceipts` causes `sendmail` to ignore return-receipt requests (eliminating the associated bandwidth wastage).

SASL authentication. The Simple Authentication and Security Layer (SASL) provides authentication capabilities to connection-based network communications (for more information, see *http://asg.web.cmu.edu/sasl/*). SASL authentication can be performed using a variety of mechanisms, and the communications partners can also negotiate a protection method (e.g., encryption) for future messages. A variety of network facilities use SASL, including OpenLDAP and sendmail.

Authentication for SMTP connections via SASL is supported starting in sendmail Version 8.10 using the Cyrus SASL facility (*http://asg.web.cmu.edu/cyrus/*), and Version 8.11 adds support for encryption via TLS (the Transport Layer Security protocol, designed to replace SSL; see *http://www.openssl.org*). SASL support must be enabled at compile time (check for the SASL option).

sendmail provides macros that allow you to specify:

* Allowed authentication mechanisms, as well as those acceptable for relaying
* Authentication requirements and authentication data (or location) for the local server
* Authentication and encryption requirements on a per-domain or host level via entries in the normal access map

To use these features, you must install the Cyrus SASL library (see *http://asg.web.cmu.edu/cyrus/*), compile sendmail with SASL support, and then configure it appropriately. For more information, consult the following:

* The "STARTTLS" and "SMTP Authentication" sections of the sendmail configuration *README* file
* The *auth.html* and *starttls.html* pages at *http://www.sendmail.org/~ca/email/* and the *sysadmin.html* page in the *cyrus* subdirectory at the same location

Reducing the sendmail daemon's privileges. In the past, the fact that sendmail runs setuid *root* has been one of the factors allowing for security breaches. As a result, suggestions for reducing the daemon's privilege level appear frequently. One method for doing so is to use the chroot facility (see Chapter 3). This approach retains the setuid status but limits the daemon's functioning to a minimal, isolated filesystem.

Version 8.12 provides a different technique for addressing this issue. It separates sendmail into two daemons, one operating as the transport agent and another operating a mail submission agent that handles mail from mailer programs that require message submission services. Their characteristics are described in Table 9-4.

Table 9-4. Dividing the sendmail daemon

	Transport agent	Submission program
Name	sm-mta	sendmail
Owners (user, group)	*root*, GID 0	*sm-msp, sm-msp*
File Protection	550 (not SETUID)	555 + SETGID
Run as daemon?	yes	no
Work queue	*/var/spool/mqueue*	*/var/spool/clientmqueue*
Configuration file	*sendmail.cf*	*submit.cf*

The binaries for the two files are copies of the same executable with different ownerships and permissions. The sm-mta program is a drop-in replacement for the current sendmail daemon. It requires changing the name of the program in the system startup files and adding the -L sm-mta option to the startup command. For example:

```
/usr/sbin/sm-mta -L sm-mta -bd -q30m
```

The other program is owned by a new user and group and is setgid to that group. Its work queue must be also be owned by this user and group and have the mode 660. It is not run as a daemon and has a separate configuration file, called *submit.cf* above. The latter includes the msp feature:

```
FEATURE(`msp')
```

The feature enables and sets the various mail submission program–related parameters (e.g., the work queue directory).

Check the documentation for the latest version of sendmail for current information about these features.

Monitoring ongoing operation

sendmail provides several utilities for monitoring its ongoing operation. The most important of these is mailq (equivalent to sendmail -bp), which lists the contents of sendmail's work queue (*/var/spool/mqueue*):

```
# mailq
f3FHZeIO8989     1240 Sun Apr 15 13:35 chavez
           (Deferred: Connection refused by dalton.ahania.com.)
                       jones@dalton.ahania.com
```

This display lists only a single entry. The first line indicates the name of the message file in the work queue directory along with its submission time and sender. The second line in this entry indicates the message status; in this case, the remote host to which the message is addressed is not answering. The final line lists the recipient address.

Several different types of files may be present in the work queue directory; all have names consisting of a prefix plus the message ID. The prefix indicates the file content type:

qf Control file (includes message headers)

df Data file (message text)

xf Holds mailer error messages ("transcript file")

Qf Indicates a bounced message

tf Temporary file used as scratch when the *qf* file is being updated

Tf Message processing has generated 32 or more locking failures

There are a couple of situations in which you may have to deal with the contents of the mail work queue:

- If the queue becomes seriously overloaded, sendmail and/or system performance can be strained. In such cases, the best response is to temporarily stop the sendmail daemon, move the files to an alternate directory (or rename and recreate *mqueue*, making sure to set the ownerships and protections properly: *root* and 700), and restart the daemon. Then you can run sendmail manually on the saved files at a more convenient time without affecting any more incoming mail. To do so, use a command like the following, where *save_queue* is the location of the moved files:

  ```
  # sendmail -oQ/var/spool/save_queue -q
  ```

- Check the queue occasionally for files that will never be successfully processed. For example, from time to time you will encounter orphaned *df* files, messages without any control file (which are therefore undeliverable). You can archive or delete these files as you see fit.

You can also examine sendmail operations by looking at the statistics file contents with the mailstats command, a separate utility included in the sendmail package (the statistics file location is set by defining *STATUS_FILE* and defaults to */etc/mail/ statistics*). Here is an example of running mailstats:

```
# mailstats
Statistics from Sun Apr  8 14:38:37 2001
msgsfr bytes_from  msgsto bytes_to msgsrej msgsdis  Mailer
    53        378K       5     12K       0       0  local
  1231       7425K       0      0K       0       0  relay
-----------------------------------------------------------------
T 1284       7803K       5     12K       0       0
C 1284                   5              0
```

(The first column, which shows mailer numbers, is omitted to save space.) The columns show the number of messages received (*msgsfr*), sent (*msgsto*), rejected (*msgsrej*), and discarded (*msgsdis*), as well as the number of bytes received (*bytes_ from*) and sent (*bytes_to*), broken down by mailer. This output is from a system that holds very few user mailboxes, so the local traffic is quite limited. Most messages are relayed to a mail hub for processing. The final two lines in the output show the totals for the each column and the connection totals. Much larger numbers and additional mailers will probably appear in the output from typical systems at your site.

sendmail includes the ability to keep track of hosts to which delivery has failed and to use that data to prioritize future work. The following macro enables this feature using the conventional directory location:

```
define(`confHOST_STATUS_DIRECTORY',`/var/spool/mqueue/.hoststat')
```

You can view the current status data using the hoststat command (equivalent to sendmail -bh):

```
# hoststat
---Hostname-------------How long ago----------Results---------
dalton.ahania.com           00:00:30  Deferred: Connection refu
newton.ahania.com           01:47:03  250 2.0.0 f32Hl3720131 Me
```

The entries indicate the time and results of the last connection attempt for each host. You can reset all host connection data by issuing the purgestat command (equivalent to sendmail -bH).

Performance

In this section, we look at some of the parameters that sendmail provides for optimizing its performance.

Mail queues can get very large when a great deal of mail arrives at the same time. The mail queue can get large at other times as well. For example, as we've seen, mail messages are held in the work queue when the first attempt to deliver them fails. This can cause two types of performance bottlenecks. First, disk I/O itself can simply overwhelm its I/O capacity. In addition, very large queue directories suffer from the Unix operating systems' degrading directory-lookup performance (which becomes prohibitive at about 2000 files for typical nonlogged Unix filesystems).

One solution to both types of I/O bottlenecks is to use multiple queue directories, ideally each placed on a different physical disk. The following macro configures sendmail to use multiple work queues:

```
define(`QUEUE_DIR',`/var/spool/mqueue/q*')
```

The macro tells sendmail to use all subdirectories with names starting with "q" under the usual directory as its work queues (sendmail picks the queue for each message at random). The directories can be local subdirectories or (better) symbolic links to actual directories on different disks. Multiple queue directories can also allow mail message processing to proceed in parallel across each work location. Files can be moved between queue directories on the same system, because the algorithm used to generate their names is guaranteed not to repeat for 60 years.

Here are some additional settings that may be useful in some situations. Most of them define parameters that serve to throttle back the workload when things get overloaded:

define(`confMAX_DAEMON_CHILDREN',n)
> When needed, the main sendmail daemon will create additional child processes to help. This sets the maximum number of additional processes; additional connections will be refused when the maximum is reached. The default is no limit.

define(`confFALLBACK_MX',`host')
> The fallback host to which to send bounced messages and messages with bogus addresses for further processing. Defining this can reduce the load somewhat on the local server. This setting is undefined by default.

define(`CONNECTION_RATE_THROTTLE',n)
> The rate at which connections are accepted as n per second (the default is no limit). Additional connections are delayed. This setting can be useful for both smoothing out spikes in mail traffic and regulating the general flow rate.

```
define(`confMIN_QUEUE_AGE',`time')
```
Minimum time a message must wait in the queue before processing. This can be useful on a busy server as a way to process only a part of the queue at a time, as each queue run will skip jobs younger than this. The time is specified as a number followed by s (seconds), m (minutes) or h (hours): e.g., 5m. The default is 0, meaning no delay.

```
define(`confQUEUE_LA',nq)
define(`confREFUSE_LA',nr)
```
Load averages at which to queue all incoming mail (suppressing attempts at immediate delivery) and at which to refuse additional connections (they default to 8 times and 12 times the number of CPUs, respectively). These may need to be lowered somewhat on very busy systems with slower CPUs.

```
define(`confMIN_FREE_BLOCKS',n)
```
The number of blocks of free space that must be present in the work queue's filesystem for additional mail to be accepted. The default is 100. This parameter provides a way to reserve a portion of disk space that (greedy) sendmail cannot use.

```
define(`confMAX_MESSAGE_SIZE',bytes)
define(`mailer_MAILER_MAX',bytes)
```
The maximum size of acceptable messages (larger ones are rejected). The first macro sets the limits for the system; the second form specifies a limit for an individual mailer.

```
define(`confCON_EXPENSIVE',`True')
define(`SMTP_MAILER_FLAGS',`e')
```
These two macros can be used to queue outgoing SMTP mail without further processing. They can be useful for a very busy system with an intermittent ISP connection where just letting the mail accumulate in the queue is too much of a performance hit.

```
define(`confTO_parameter',n)
```
sendmail provides a plethora of configurable timeout parameters for each phase of message processing. In most cases, the defaults are fine, but you may want to decrease some of them on very busy servers.

Debugging techniques

There are several distinct sources of information that can be useful for debugging sendmail configurations and operations. See the book *sendmail*, by Brian Costales with Eric Allman (O'Reilly & Associates), for full information about all of the debugging features discussed in this section.

The first of these is the facility's log file. Here are some sample entries (which we have wrapped to fit the page):

```
Apr 15 12:44:12 kevin sendmail[25907]: f3FGhti25833:
to=chavez@newton.ahania.com, ctladdr=jones (133/78),
```

```
delay=00:00:17, xdelay=00:00:00, mailer= esmtp, pri=210301,
relay=newton.ahania.com., dsn=4.0.0,
stat=Deferred: Connection refused by newton.ahania.com.

Apr 15 12:49:49 kevin sendmail[25927]: f3FGnmd25925:
to=ahania@newton.ahania.com, ctladdr=root (0/0),
delay=00:00:01, xdelay=00:00:01, mailer=esmtp, pri=30056,
relay=newton.ahania.com. [192.168.9.216], dsn=5.1.1,
stat=User unknown

Apr 15 16:22:35 kevin sendmail[20388]: f36KK5h20388:
ruleset=check_mail, arg1=<someone@zoas.org>,
relay=IDENT:root@[10.0.19.223],
reject=451 4.1.8 <someone@zoas.org>...
Domain of sender address someone@zoas.org does not resolve
```

All three of these entries clearly indicate specific mail delivery problems. The first entry indicates that host *newton* is not currently answering SMTP queries, and so this message from local user *jones* (UID 133, GID 78) has been sent to the work queue. The second entry indicates that the user *ahania* is unknown on host *newton*. Finally, the third entry indicates that the domain name in the sender address cannot be resolved via DNS.

You can also use the telnet command to see the results for various senders and recipients by connecting to port 25. In these example, system *kevin* plays postman for the local domain. In this mode, you enter actual SMTP commands manually.

Here is the initial connection command:

```
# telnet kevin 25
Trying 10.0.19.223...
Connected to kevin.
Escape character is `^]'.
220 kevin.ahania.com ESMTP Sendmail 8.11.0/8.11.0; Mon, 16 Apr 2001 11:22:54 -0400
HELO zebra
250 kevin.ahania.com Hello zebra [10.0.19.184], pleased to meet you
```

(Throughout this output, we've wrapped lines as necessary.)

The test session begins by issuing a HELO[*] command, which begins an SMTP session and gives the connecting hostname as its argument. Next, we set up a test mail message by specifying the sender:

```
MAIL From: luc@bad-guys.org
550 5.7.1 luc@bad-guys.org... Access denied
```

Access from this sender is denied, as specified by the access map. We clear the message state and try another test message:

```
RSET
250 2.0.0 Reset state
MAIL From: bill@zoas.org
```

---

[*] The ESMTP version is EHLO.

```
250 2.1.0 bill@zoas.org... Sender ok
RCPT To: mybadguy
550 5.7.1 mybadguy... Access denied
```

The failure this time occurs because the recipient is prohibited by the access map from receiving mail. Here is our next attempt:

```
RSET
250 2.0.0 Reset state
MAIL From: bond@mole.bad-guys.org
250 2.1.0 bond@mole.bad-guys.org... Sender ok
RCPT To: chavez
250 2.1.5 chavez... Recipient ok
DATA
354 Enter mail, end with "." on a line by itself
This is a test message.
.
250 2.0.0 f3GFOD728166 Message accepted for delivery
QUIT
221 2.0.0 kevin.ahania.com closing connection
Connection closed by foreign host.
```

The message succeeds, and we enter the message text with the SMTP DATA command (although there is no need to do so if testing the addressing is what we are after). After the message is sent, we end the telnet session.

Properly interpreting the output from such test sessions requires a knowledge of the local sendmail configuration. For example, if the local configuration uses the delay_ checks feature, then the output of the first attempt would be different:

```
MAIL From: luc@bad-guys.org
250 2.1.0 luc@bad-guys.org... Sender ok
RCPT To: chavez
550 5.7.1 chavez... Access denied
```

In this case, the prohibited address seems to pass, and recipient *chavez* seems to be the problem, but this is simply the result of delaying the sender check until after the recipient check; the "Access denied" message appears after the recipient but applies to the sender.

Another useful SMTP command is ETRN, which tells the sendmail daemon to process the queue for the host given as its argument:

```
ETRN zebra.ahania.com
250 2.0.0 Queuing for node zebra.ahania.com started
```

Such commands can be used to retrieve messages manually from a remote source such as an ISP.

You can see sendmail perform the SMTP transactions for a message by using its verbose option, -v, as in this example:

```
# sendmail -v chavez@ahania.com < /dev/null
```

sendmail's verify mode (-bv) can be used to verify a recipient address, as in this example, which checks the address *chavez*:

```
# sendmail -bv chavez
chavez@newton.ahania.com... deliverable:
mailer relay, host kevin, user chavez@newton.ahania.com
```

The output indicates that the address is deliverable: it will be relayed to user *chavez* on host *newton* in the local domain via relay system *kevin*.

Another useful sendmail feature is its address translation mode (-bt). Traditionally, this mode was used to verify and debug the complex address rewriting rules needed in earlier versions of sendmail, and it can still be used for this task. Over the years, however, many other useful internal commands have been added. Several useful ones are illustrated in the following annotated session:

```
# sendmail -bt
ADDRESS TEST MODE (ruleset 3 NOT automatically invoked)
Enter <ruleset> <address>
> /mx zebra                               List MX records for host.
getmxrr(zebra) returns 2 value(s):
        zebra.ahania.com.
        bella.ahania.com.ahania.com.
> $m                                      Display value of internal variable.
ahania.com
> $=w                                     Display member of a class (here, local hosts).
[192.168.9.220]
kevin
localhost
[127.0.0.1]
ahania.com
> .Cwsalk                                 Add a member to class w (local hosts): salk.
> /map virtuser rachel_chavez@ahania.com
map_lookup:                               Translate an address using the virtual user map.
virtuser (rachel_chavez@ahania.com)
returns chavez@ahania.com                 This is the translation (local address).
> /try smtp chavez                        Show address translation for mailer/recipient.
Trying envelope recipient address chavez for mailer smtp
canonify        returns: chavez           Output shortened!
PseudoToReal    returns: chavez
MasqSMTP        returns: chavez < @ LOCAL >
EnvToSMTP       returns: chavez < @ kevin . ahania . com . >
final           returns: chavez @ kevin . ahania . com
Rcode = 0, addr = chavez@kevin.ahania.com
> /tryflags S                             The /try command now applies to senders.
> /try smtp chavez                        Show address translation for mailer/sender.
Trying envelope sender address chavez for mailer smtp
...
Rcode = 0, addr = rachel_chavez@ahania.com
> ^D
```

The two /try subcommands indicate that incoming SMTP-transported mail to recipient *chavez* goes to *chavez* on host *kevin* (where is it relayed to its final destination, as we've seen), and that outgoing SMTP-transported messages from user *chavez* will have *rachel_chavez@ahania.com* as the sender (the same information was also given by the earlier /map subcommand).

Other useful subcommands include =M, which lists defined mailers, and -d*n*.*m*, which turns on the specified debugging level , a topic to which we now turn.

sendmail also offers an exhaustive debugging mode, selected with the command's -d option. The option takes a debugging level and optional sublevel as its argument— the syntax is -d*level*.*sublevel*—where the level indicates the general area of output information and the sublevel indicates the verbosity level (the default for the latter is 1, the least detailed level). Multiple level specifications can be given, separated by commas.

Table 9-5 lists the most useful debugging options. Note that these options appear on normal sendmail commands: most often, sending a test message, but sometimes using -q to process the work queue. In some cases, you need to include -v to make the debugging output appear.

Table 9-5. Useful sendmail debugging options

Option	Result
-d0	Show sendmail version, compile flags, and host and domain information.
-d0.15	Also display defined mailers, with flags ("F=").
-d8.7	Show DNS name resolution process.
-d11.2	Trace the delivery process.
-d17	Show MX hosts.
-d27	Show alias translation, including forwarding.
-d34.11	Trace header generation (including skipped ones).
-d35.9	Display internal macro values (e.g., $k).
-d37	Display options as they are set.
-d37.8	Also show each item added to class lists (e.g., class w, which holds local hosts/domains).
-d40	Watch queue processing.
-d44.5	Show all file open attempts (useful primarily for file opening–related failures).
-d60	Display map lookup operations.

Here is an example displaying the delivery process for local recipient *trucks*:

```
# sendmail -v -d11.2 trucks < /dev/null
trucks... aliased to trucks@zebra.ahania.com
openmailer: procmail -Y -a  -d trucks
trucks... Connecting to local...
openmailer: openmailer: running as r/euid=371/0, r/egid=0/0
MCI@80efaf0: flags=2<TEMP>,
        errno=0, herrno=0, exitstat=0, state=2, pid=13143,
        maxsize=0, phase=NULL, mailer=local,
```

```
        status=NULL, rstatus=NULL,
        host=NULL, lastuse=Wed Dec 31 19:00:00 1969
trucks... Sent
giveresponse: status=0, dsn=2.0.0, e->e_message=<NULL>
```

Here we see that the local mailer is procmail, as well as a great deal of information about the process that delivers the mail.

Similarly, the following command shows the alias translation process for user *lilith* on host *dalton* (output is shortened):

```
# /usr/sbin/sendmail -d27 lilith < /dev/null
alias(lilith)
lilith (, lilith) aliased to ldonna
alias(ldonna)
ldonna (, ldonna) aliased to lcapri
alias(lcapri)
lcapri (, lcapri) aliased to lmc2499@dalton.ahania.com
forward(lmc2499)
alias(lil)
lil (, lil) aliased to lil@garden.ahania.com
```

This output traces a somewhat lengthy chain of aliases that ultimately translates *lilith* to *lil@garden.ahania.com*.

Macro summary

We will end our consideration of sendmail with Table 9-6, which lists all the macros we have discussed in this section (ordered alphabetically by the name of the most significant component).

Table 9-6. Essential sendmail macros

Macro	Meaning and use
define(`ALIAS_FILE',`path')	Location of aliases file.
undefine(`ALIAS_FILE')	Disable aliases file.
define(`confCON_EXPENSIVE',`True')	Hold (don't transport) mail for expensive mailers.
define(`confDEF_USER_ID',`user:group')	Default user and group.
define(`confEBINDIR',`path')	Location of smrsh and mail.local.
define(`confFALLBACK_MX',`host')	Send bounced/bogus mail here.
define(`confFORWARD_FILE',`path[:path...]')	Path to search for forward files ($z = ~).
define(`confLDAP_DEFAULT_SPEC', `-h ldap-host -b root-key')	Specify the LDAP server and root key.
define(`confMAX_DAEMON_CHILDREN',n)	Maximum child processes.
define(`confMAX_MESSAGE_SIZE',bytes)	Largest acceptable message.
define(`confMIN_FREE_BLOCKS',blocks)	Required filesystem free space.
define(`confMIN_QUEUE_AGE',`time')	Messages stay in queue at least this long.
define(`confPRIVACY_FLAGS',`flag-list')	SMTP privacy options.

Table 9-6. Essential sendmail macros (continued)

Macro	Meaning and use
define(`confQUEUE_LA',*load-average*)	Queue all incoming mail when load average is above this level.
define(`confREFUSE_LA',*load-average*)	Refuse connections when load average is above this level.
define(`confSAFE_FILE_ENV',`*path*')	Pipe mail only to regular files under the specified path.
define(`confSERVICE_SWITCH_FILE',`*path*')	Location of network services switch file (when not provided by the operating system).
define(`confTO_parameter',*n*)	Set timeout length.
define(`CONNECTION_RATE_THROTTLE',*n*)	Accept only *n* connections per second.
define(`LOCAL_MAILER_ARGS',`*command*')	How to run the local mailer program.
define(`LOCAL_MAILER_PATH',`*path*')	Path to the local mailer program executable.
define(`LOCAL_RELAY',`*host*')	Send mail to unqualified names here.
FEATURE(`stickyhost')	Do so even if the MAIL_HUB feature is also used.
define(`LOCAL_SHELL_ARGS',`*command*')	How to run mailer for piped messages.
define(`LOCAL_SHELL_PATH',`*path*')	Path to the shell program.
define(`MAIL_HUB',`*host*')	Send local mail to a different host.
define(`*mailer*_MAILER_ARGS',`*command*')	How to run the specified mailer's program.
define(`*mailer*_MAILER_FLAGS',`*addl-flags*')	Add flags to the usual set for the specified mailer.
define(`*mailer*_MAILER_MAX',*bytes*)	Maximum message size for the specified mailer.
define(`*mailer*_MAILER_PATH',`*path*')	Path to the executable for the specified mailer.
define(`*mailer*_RELAY',`*host*')	Use this to relay mail for the specified mailer.
define(`PROCMAIL_MAILER_PATH',`*path*')	Path to procmail.
define(`SMART_HOST',`*host*')	Send all nonlocal mail to this host.
define(`SMTP_MAILER_FLAGS',`e')	Make the SMTP mailer "expensive."
define(`STATUS_FILE',`*path*')	Location of statistics file.
DOMAIN(`*name*')	Include the *../domain/name.m4* file.
EXPOSED_USER(`*user*')	Exclude user from masquerading.
FEATURE(`access_db', `*dbtype path*')	Use the specified access database.
FEATURE(`allmasquerade')	Masquerade recipients, too.
FEATURE(`always_add_domain')	Add domain to unqualified names.
FEATURE(`blacklist_recipients')	Allow incoming address entries in the access map.
FEATURE(`delay_checks'[, `friend'])	Reverse the order of access checks. If the argument is included, enable the SPAMFRIEND feature (overrides checks).
FEATURE(`dnsbl'[,`*server*'])	Use the Internet blacklist on the specified server.
FEATURE(`generics_entire_domain')	Use the generics table for hosts in subdomains of any relevant domain.

Table 9-6. Essential sendmail macros (continued)

Macro	Meaning and use
`FEATURE(`genericstable',`dbtype path')`	Use the specified generics table map for rewriting outgoing sender addresses.
`FEATURE(`ldap_routing')`	Use LDAP for mail routing.
`FEATURE(`local_lmtp'[,`path-to-mail.local'])`	Use `mail.local` as the local mailer for pipes to files and programs (specifying the path to the executable if necessary).
`FEATURE(`local_procmail')`	Use `procmail` as the local mailer.
`FEATURE(`masquerade_envelope')`	Masquerade envelope as well as headers.
`FEATURE(`msp')`	Use separate MTA and MSA processes.
`FEATURE(`nocanonify')`	Defer DNS lookups (usually to mail hub).
`FEATURE(`nouucp',`reject')`	Reject UUCP-style mail addresses.
`FEATURE(`nullclient',`mailhub')`	Send all mail to the specified server for processing.
`FEATURE(`redirect')`	Enable *.REDIRECT* alias suffix support for users who have left the organization.
`FEATURE(`relay_entire_domain')`	Perform relaying for any host in a local domain.
`FEATURE(`smrsh'[,`path-to-smrsh'])`	Use `smrsh` for piped email messages.
`FEATURE(`use_cw_file')`	Define local hosts and domains in a file.
`define(`confCW_FILE',`path')`	Specify the path to the file.
`FEATURE(`virtuser_entire_domain')`	Use the virtual user table for hosts in subdomains of any relevant domain.
`FEATURE(`virtusertable',`dbtype path')`	Use the specified virtual user table map for routing incoming addresses.
`GENERICS_DOMAIN(`domain')` `GENERICS_DOMAIN_FILE(`path')`	Use the generics table for the specified domain or domains listed in the specified file.
`LDAP_ROUTE_DOMAIN(`ldap-domain')` `LDAP_ROUTE_DOMAIN_FILE(`path')`	Use LDAP routing for the specified domain or the domains listed in the specified file.
`LOCAL_USER(`name')`	Exclude user from the effect of `LOCAL_RELAY`.
`LUSER_RELAY(`host, address, or error')`	Destination/error for invalid local addresses.
`MASQUERADE_AS(`domain')`	Make all messages appear to be coming from the specified domain.
`MASQUERADE_EXCEPTION(`host or domain')`	Don't apply masquerading to this host or domain.
`MODIFY_MAILER_FLAGS(`mailer',`+|-flags')`	Add/remove the specified flags from the default list for the indicated mailer.
`OSTYPE(`name')`	Specify operating system.
`RELAY_DOMAIN(`domain')` `RELAY_DOMAIN_FILE(`path')`	Relay messages for the specified domain or the domains listed in the specified file.
`VERSIONID(`string')`	Identify the version of the configuration source file.
`VIRTUSER_DOMAIN(`domain')` `VIRTUSER_DOMAIN_FILE(`path')`	Use the virtual user table for the specified domain or the domains listed in the specified file.

Postfix

Postfix is an alternative mail transport agent that has received quite a bit of attention in the past couple of years. It is the work of Wietse Venema; he wrote the initial version while spending a sabbatical year at IBM's Thomas J. Watson Research Center (where the program was named VMailer). The first production-quality version of Postfix was released in 1999, and it is still a work in progress. The package's home page is *http://www.postfix.org*.

 This discussion is based on the Postfix version current at the time of this writing (20010228 Patchlevel 01). Fortunately for its users but unfortunately for writers, the package is evolving rapidly. This discussion also assumes familiarity with common electronic mail facility concepts. See the earlier discussion of sendmail if you need such information (even if you don't plan on using sendmail).

Postfix was designed as a sendmail replacement with several goals in mind:

High security
> Mail processing activities are divided among several distinct processes to insulate them (and there are no parent/child relationships among the various processes). This separation means that there is no direct path from the Internet to the most privileged parts of the facility. In addition, none of the components are SETUID, and most of the pieces can be optionally run in chrooted environment.

Performance under high loads
> The documentation states that Postfix can process and deliver over 1,000,000 mail message a day on a desktop PC (configuration not specified). Postfix includes a considerable number of settings that you can use to optimize its functioning in your specific environment.

Easy configuration and administration
> Postfix configuration files are simple, and you can get even a fairly complex configuration up and running in a matter of minutes.

Compatibility with existing mail setups
> Postfix provides several commands for compatibility with existing habits and scripts, including sendmail, newaliases, and mailq, and it supports the usual mail aliasing and forwarding mechanisms.

Figure 9-6 illustrates the basic Postfix mail transport process. As it indicates, the package's design is modular, separating the various processes from each other and allowing you to easily disable features you don't need to use. In the diagram, each of the rounded rectangles represents a daemon. The shaded rectangles indicate the message-flow path through the facility, and the white rectangles provide specific auxiliary services.

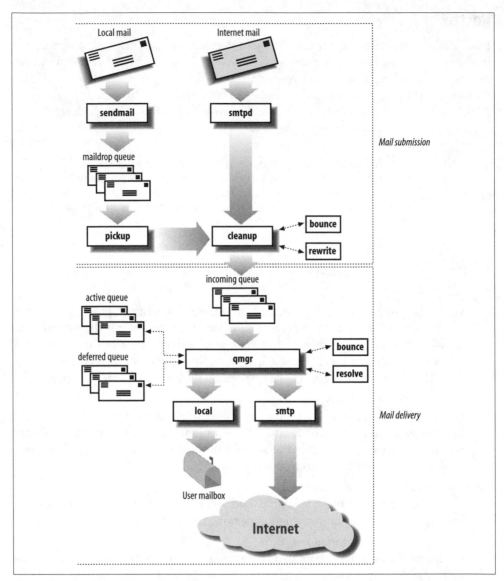

Figure 9-6. Postfix mail processing

The left part of the diagram depicts how Postfix receives incoming mail. Mail created on the local system is handled by a component named sendmail, which sends it to the *maildrop* queue to await processing. This queue is processed by the pickup daemon, which feeds messages to the cleanup daemon. Incoming mail from outside sources is handled by the smtpd daemon, which similarly sends it to the cleanup daemon.

The cleanup daemon prepares messages for delivery, adding any required headers, optionally transforming addresses, bouncing invalid and acceptable messages, and so on. The rewrite (address rewriting) and bounce daemons aid in these processes.

When finished, cleanup sends the message to the *incoming* queue to await delivery (packaged as a single file).

With the incoming queue, the Postfix delivery process begins. The queue manager process (qmgr) oversees and controls the delivery process. Jobs from the *incoming* queue are moved to the *active* queue and then either delivered or sent to the *deferred* queue. Whenever space opens up in the *active* queue, one job each is moved from *incoming* and *deferred*. Jobs waiting in the *deferred* queue are scheduled via an "exponential backup" algorithm: each delivery failure results in a longer wait period before the next attempt.

Within the *active* queue, jobs are selected using a round-robin selection method based on their final destination (to prevent any one site from consuming a disproportionate share of resources). An unreachable destination list is maintained and used to optimize the selection process.

The bounce and resolve daemons aid the queue manager in its work. Ultimately, qmgr hands messages off to a delivery agent. Two of these are illustrated in the figure: local, which places messages in local user mailboxes, and smtp, which typically routes outgoing messages to the Internet.

A few pieces of the package are not shown in the diagram. The most important of these is the master daemon, which serves as the supervisor for the entire facility and is the only daemon that is always running. In addition, there are two other mailers: the error mailer for creating and handling mail resulting from errors, and the pipe mailer, which handles mail destined for other transport protocols (currently UUCP).

Table 9-7 lists the standard locations for the various Postfix components.

Table 9-7. Postfix components and their locations

Postfix component	Location
Command binaries	**Usual:** */usr/sbin*[a]
Daemon binaries	**Usual:** */usr/libexec/postfix*
	Linux: */usr/lib/postfix* (SuSE)
Queue directory	**Usual:** */var/spool/postfix*
Configuration files	**Usual:** */etc/postfix*
Boot script that starts Postfix	**AIX:** Modify */etc/rc.tcpip*
	FreeBSD: */etc/rc*
	HP-UX: Create */sbin/init.d/postfix*[b]
	Linux: */etc/init.d/postfix* provided in RPMs[b]
	Solaris: Create */etc/init.d/postfix*[b]
	Tru64: Create */sbin/init.d/postfix*[b]
Boot script configuration file	**Usual:** None used
	Linux: */etc/rc.config.d/postfix.rc.config* (SuSE 7)
	Make sure *POSTFIX_CREATECF="no"*
	/etc/sysconfig/postfix (SuSE 8)

Table 9-7. Postfix components and their locations (continued)

Postfix component	Location
syslog mail-facility messages	**AIX:** Not configured
	FreeBSD: */var/log/maillog*
	HP-UX: */var/adm/syslog/mail.log*
	Linux: */var/log/maillog* (Red Hat)
	* /var/log/mail* (SuSE)
	Solaris: */var/adm/messages*
	Tru64: */var/adm/syslog.dated/*/mail.log*

ª The FreeBSD ports collection installs Postfix under */usr/local* by default.
ᵇ You must create/verify links to desired S and K files.

In addition to the daemons, the Postfix facility includes several administrative utilities. The most important of these are postfix (used to start and stop the facility and similar actions) and postmap (creates Postfix lookup maps). We will see examples of their use later in this section. Other commands include:

postalias
> Maintains the aliases database (used by newaliases)

postconf
> Displays Postfix configuration parameters

postsuper
> Maintains/cleans up Postfix queues

postcat
> Displays the contents of queue files

postdrop
> Submits mail to the *maildrop* queue when the queue is not world-writable

postkick, postlock, *and* postlog
> Scriptable interfaces to Postfix features

Finally, Postfix configuration files reside in */etc/postfix*. The only exception to this is the *aliases* file, which is typically located in */etc*.

Installing Postfix

Installing Postfix is not difficult, but it does require some care. It is possible to use both Postfix and sendmail on the same system, and the procedures for doing so are discussed in the *INSTALL* file in the Postfix source distribution. In this discussion, we will assume that Postfix is replacing sendmail.

These are the steps required to install Postfix:

- Back up your current sendmail installation. Make sure that you save all components of the package: binaries, configuration files, and the build directory, map source files, and so on.

- Make sure that all sendmail queues are empty (flush them if necessary). Then stop the daemon and disable the associated boot script commands/files.

- Remove all sendmail components except the *aliases* file and the directory it resides in. Alternatively, you can copy the *aliases* file to */etc* if this is not its standard location (see Table 9-3).

  On systems with a package manager, you can use the appropriate utility to remove the corresponding package(s) (see "Essential Administrative Techniques" in Chapter 3). On Linux systems, you will need to include the --nodeps option on the rpm -e command to successfully remove the sendmail RPMs. This is safe because the components that other programs depend on are all included with Postfix and so will remain available once it is installed.

- Install Postfix, either from a binary package (currently, these are available for Linux and FreeBSD) or from source code.

- Set up the Postfix configuration files. Run the newaliases command to ensure that the alias file's binary database has been generated.

- Modify or create the required scripts to start Postfix at boot time (see Table 9-7). At a minimum, you'll need to run the postfix start command.

- Start Postfix, and test the new mail system.

I recommend trying this process for the first time on a test system, rather than your central mail hub!

Configuring Postfix

Postfix configuration files reside in the */etc/postfix* directory. This location is assumed in the discussion that follows.

Postfix's primary configuration file is *main.cf*. The Postfix package includes a sample version of *main.cf*, which describes most of its possible entries. The package also provides a number of smaller sample files illustrating features related to a single purpose (named *sample-*.cf*).

The *main.cf* file often begins with entries specifying the package's file and directory locations. These sample entries list the default settings:*

```
config_directory = /etc/postfix
queue_directory = /var/spool/postfix
daemon_directory = /usr/libexec/postfix
command_directory = /usr/sbin
```

These entries also illustrate the general entry format: *setting = value*. When *value* is a list, the individual items are separated with spaces and optional commas. Entries in

---

* If the daemon and command locations are the same, the *program_directory* entry may be present instead of the two separate ones in this example.

the configuration file may continue onto as many lines as needed by beginning the second and subsequent lines with whitespace.

There are several related settings you should be aware of (but for which the default values are often correct):

```
myhostname = garden.ahania.com
mydomain = ahania.com
mydestination = $myhostname, localhost.$mydomain
```

These entries specify the local hostname, the local domain (defaults to the domain part of *myhostname*), and a list of destinations that should be considered local (the local host), respectively. Note that parameter settings may be used in other entries by preceding the parameter name with a dollar sign.

 On SuSE 7 Linux systems, the SuSEconfig automated system configuration facility will write over your *main.cf* file every time it is run unless you disable this in the */etc/sysconfig/postfix* configuration file (or in */etc/rc.config.d/postfix.rc.config* on system running SuSE 7):

```
POSTFIX_CREATECF="no"
```

Notifying the daemon. Whenever you modify the Postfix configuration, you will need to notify the master daemon with this command:

```
# postfix reload
```

This command tells the process to reread its configuration files.

Client systems. Next, we consider some settings relevant to mail client systems. For a minimal client configuration, only two additional entries are needed:

```
relayhost = poffice.ahania.com
mynetworks_class = host
```

The first entry specifies a destination for all nonlocal mail, and the second prevents Postfix from relaying mail for any computer except the local host.

You can also specify a host to handle all unknown local users. This example redirects mail for unknown local users to the same user on system *poffice*:

```
luser_relay = $user@poffice.ahania.com
```

Finally, if you want to define a null client system, which forwards even seemingly local mail to a mail server, define a *relayhost* and comment out the entries for *smtp unix* and *local unix* in the *master.cf* configuration file.

The mail hub. The configuration file on the mail hub typically has some additional entries. Here are some annotated examples:

```
# add the domain to list of local destinations
mydestination = $myhostname, localhost.$mydomain, $mydomain
# relay mail from these origins: any host in the domain
relay_domains = $mydestination, $mydomain
```

In both cases, *mydomain* is added to the parameter's default list. In agreement with current security recommendations, relaying is disabled by default in Postfix.

By default, Postfix relays mail for all hosts in the domains listed in *relay_domains*. It also relays for hosts from any subnet the local host trusts, as defined by the *mynetworks* parameter:

```
mynetworks = 10.0.19.0/24, 10.0.13.0/24, 127.0.0.0/8
```

In this case, Postfix will trust any host on the 10.0.19 and 10.0.13 subnets, as well as the local host. It is important to specify the setting for *mynetworks* correctly. It should consist of only trusted local subnets (and not the entire class A, B, or C address).* If this parameter is not explicitly defined, the list defaults to the local subnet and 127.0.0.0.

Postfix can also automatically rewrite all local sender addresses on outgoing mail to the *user@domain* form by including these entries:

```
masquerade_domains = $mydomain
masquerade_exceptions = root, postmaster
```

The first entry sets the domain used for address masquerading, and the second entry lists users whose addresses should be excluded from the operation

The local delivery agent. By default, Postfix uses its own local daemon for local mail delivery. You can specify a different program with the *mailbox_command* parameter. For example, this entry makes procmail the local delivery agent:

```
mailbox_command = /usr/bin/procmail
```

If you choose to use procmail this way, you must define an alias for *root*, or mail for the superuser will be lost.

The *mail_spool_directory* parameter may be used to specify an alternate directory for user mailboxes, as in this example:

```
mail_spool_directory = /var/newmail
```

Systems with intermittent Internet connections. On mail hubs having only intermittent Internet connections (for example, via a dialup ISP), you can use these entries to accumulate messages between connections:

```
relayhost = ISP-host          Relay external mail to this host.
defer_transports = smtp       Hold outgoing mail transported via SMTP.
disable_dns_lookups = yes     Don't perform DNS name resolution tests.
```

The final entry is necessary to avoid mail being rejected because of name resolution failures. It may be used on any system that lacks external DNS lookup capabilities.

---

* How this list is interpreted is determined by the *mynetworks_style* parameter, whose default setting is *subnet*.

Postfix also includes a feature designed to optimize the process of delivering mail to an intermittently connected site; the daemon that provides this functionality is known as the *flush* daemon. It is configured via the *fast_flush_domains* parameter:

```
fast_flush_domains = $relay_domains
```

This entry causes fast flush service to be used for all domains for which this server relays mail. When the connection to one of these locations is made,* this service causes Postfix to attempt to deliver only the mail destined for that specified destination rather than flushing the entire queue. Obviously, this is much more efficient for both the client and the mail server.

Address transformations. Postfix can perform a variety of address-transformation operations on sender and recipient addresses. The simplest of these is to append the local domain to nonqualified outgoing sender addresses, using the *myorigin* parameter:

```
myorigin = $mydomain
```

This entry is often included on both the mail hub and client systems.

Like sendmail, Postfix can use binary lookup tables—called maps—to perform various sorts of address translations and for other purposes, such as access control. Maps are created from a text source file with the postmap command.

Outgoing mail address mapping—e.g., to a standard form like *first.last@domain*—is done via the *canonical* map, which is specified via this configuration file entry:

```
canonical_maps = hash:/etc/postfix/canonical.db
```

This example specifies that the file *canonical.db* in the Postfix configuration directory should be used as the canonical address map, and that the file is a hash-type database.

Here are some example entries from the map's source file:

```
chavez      rachel_chavez@ahania.com
carr        steve_carr@zoas.org
ewood       eve_wood@ahania.com
```

When this map is used, the sender name in the left column is translated to the form given in the right column.

The following command may be used to create the *canonical.db* map from a source file named *canonical*:

```
# postmap hash:canonical
```

The *hash:* prefix specifies the database type (a hash is the default, so the prefix is actually optional here). Use the postconf -m command to list the database types supported on your system; the list of possibilities includes *hash*, *dbm*, and *btree*.

---

* More specifically, when the connecting system issues an SMTP ETRN command (described in the discussion of fetchmail later in thus chapter),

The default *canonical* map is applied to both senders and recipients within the message and the envelope. Alternatively, you can specify a map used only for sender addresses or recipient addresses via these configuration file parameters:

```
sender_canonical_maps = hash:/etc/postfix/sender_canonical
recipient_canonical_maps = hash:/etc/postfix/recipient_canonical
```

These maps are applied before the general *canonical* map when it is also enabled.

 Postfix Address Maps

Postfix can similarly perform map lookup–based transformations on incoming recipient addresses using its *virtual* map (discussed later in this section).

Postfix also offers a map for generating mail messages indicating the new address for departed users. This is called the *relocated* map. Here are the associated configuration file entries:

```
relocated_maps = hash:/etc/postfix/relocated
local_recipient_maps = $relocated_maps, $alias_maps,
                       unix:passwd.byname
```

The first entry specifies the type and file location for the map file, as usual. The second entry adds the *relocated* map to the front of the list of items to use for looking up incoming mail recipients. In this case, the *relocated* map is checked first, followed by the *aliases* database and the password file.

Entries in the *relocated* map consist of the local username and the new email address. Here is an example:

```
erika      eps@essadm.com
```

Virtual domains. Postfix can be configured to support virtual domains, using its *virtual* map facility. Here is an example configuration file entry enabling this feature using the *virtual.db* map file:

```
virtual_maps = hash:/etc/postfix/virtual
```

The map file performs two functions: enabling virtual domain support for listed domains and specifying incoming recipient address translations. Here are some example entries from the *virtual* map source file (assume the local domain is *ahania. com*):

```
zoas.org                    whatever
essadm.com                  whatever

webmaster@essadm.com        czarina@lecarre.ahania.com
smith@zoas.org              hayes@oldwest.ahania.com
jones@zoas.org              kidcurry@oldwest.ahania.com
@zoas.org                   @ahania.com
rachel_chavez@ahania.com    chavez@dalton.ahania.com
```

The first two entries enable virtual hosting for the *zoas.org* and *essadm.com* domains; the text in the second column for such entries is ignored. The third entry redirects mail for *webmaster@essadm.com* to a specific local user. The fourth and fifth entries specify local recipients for users *smith* and *jones* at *zoas.org*. The sixth entry, for *@zoas.org*, will be used for any other recipient in that domain; in this case, mail will be redirected to the same user in *ahania.com*, the local domain. The final entry illustrates that this map may also be used for general incoming recipient address translation unrelated to virtual hosting, in this case translating the address *rachel_chavez@ahania.com* to the appropriate, fully qualified recipient address.

As usual, the *virtual* map database is created with `postmap`. For example, this command would create the hash-type database *virtual.db* from the source file *virtual*:

```
# postmap virtual
```

Postfix handles virtual domains somewhat differently than `sendmail` users may be used to. In particular, usernames that exist in the local domain are not recognized in virtual domains by default. In other words, if *chavez* is a user in *ahania.com*, *essadm.com* is a hosted virtual domain, and there is no virtual map entry for *chavez@essadm.com*, mail to that address will bounce. In contrast, `sendmail`-style virtual domains attempt to deliver such mail to *chavez@ahania.com* (bouncing it when no identically named user exists).

You can implement `sendmail`-style virtual domains by making two modifications to the Postfix configuration:

- Remove the virtual domain entry from the *virtual* map.
- Add the virtual domain name to the *mydestination* list.

LDAP lookups. Postfix can also be configured to use LDAP for local recipient address translations. This capability must be selected at compile time. You can determine whether your installation supports it via the `postconf -m` command.

Here are some example configuration file entries:

```
alias_maps = hash:/etc/aliases, ldap:ldapsource
ldapaliases_server_host = orwell.ahania.com
ldapaliases_search_base = dc=ahania,dc=com
ldapaliases_query_filter = (mailacceptinggeneralid=%s)
ldapaliases_result_attribute = maildrop
```

The first entry adds LDAP the list of items to use for address translation, checking it after the *aliases* file. The remaining entries specify the LDAP server to connect to, the root of the tree to search, the query that should be run, and the record field to return to Postfix (respectively). In this case, the LDAP database is queried by searching the *mailacceptinggeneralid* field for the address; the contents of the *maildrop* field from matching record(s) are used as the new address.

Here is a sample LDAP entry using these default attributes:

```
dn: cn=some-object, dc=ahania, dc=com
...
mailacceptinggeneralid: help@zoas.org
mailacceptinggeneralid: oliviav@essadm.com
maildrop:               vargas@dalton.ahania.com
```

This example illustrates the use of multiple key fields, any of which will translate to the local mail address *vargas@dalton.ahania.com*. Of course, you can use any object type, key field, and return field that makes sense in the context of the local LDAP schema.

Access control and spam suppression

Postfix includes an access control facility that can be used for both security-related and spam-suppression purposes. Postfix allows you to specify incoming mail restrictions based on the connecting system (the "client"), the sender, and/or the recipient, via the *smtpd_client_restrictions*, *smtpd_sender_restrictions*, and *smtpd_recipient_restrictions* configuration file entries, respectively. It also provides the *smtpd_helo_restrictions* and *smtpd_etrn_restrictions* parameters for specifying restrictions for hosts attempting to use the SMTP HELO/EHLO commands (to initiate an SMTP session) and the SMTP ETRN command (to request that pending mail be transferred).

The setting for any of these parameters is a list of items, which can include Postfix keywords and/or a *type:file* specification for an external map. The most important keywords are listed in Table 9-8.

Table 9-8. Postfix access control keywords

Keyword	Meaning
reject_unknown_client *reject_unknown_sender_domain* *reject_unknown_recipient_domain*	Reject if DNS cannot resolve the connecting system's/sender's/ recipient's address (respectively).
reject_non_fqdn_hostname *reject_non_fqdn_sender* *reject_non_fqdn_recipient*	Reject if the connecting system's/ sender's/recipient's hostname is not fully qualified.
permit_mynetworks	Accept if the connecting system is a member of a trusted network
check_relay_domains	Accept if the client system is a member of one of the domains listed in *relay_domains*.
reject_unauth_destination *permit_auth_destination*	Reject/accept if the destination address is in *relay_domains* or *my_destinations*.
reject_maps_rbl	Reject blacklisted sites, as defined by the *maps_rbl_domains* parameter.
reject_unauth_pipelining	Prevent unverified SMTP pipelining (exploited by some bulk mailers).
reject_unknown_hostname	Reject SMTP HELO/EHLO commands from client systems whose hostnames cannot be resolved.
reject_invalid_hostname	Reject if the hostname in the SMPT HELO/EHLO command uses invalid syntax.

Table 9-8. Postfix access control keywords (continued)

Keyword	Meaning
check_client_access type:map check_sender_access type:map check_recipient_access type:map check_helo_access type:map	Determine access by looking up the specified item in the indicated access map.[a]
permit	Permit the access (unconditionally).
reject	Reject the access (unconditionally).

[a] The keyword is optional when used in the corresponding restrictions parameter. Thus, *check_sender_access* is optional in *smtpd_sender_restrictions*, and a bare *type:file* list item will interpreted as the sender access map.

Here are some examples, which also introduce a couple more related parameters:

```
smtpd_sender_restrictions: hash:/etc/postfix/senders,
    reject_non_fqdn_sender, reject_unknown_client
    reject_unknown_sender_domain, reject_unauth_destination,
    reject_unauth_pipelining, reject_maps_rbl
maps_rbl_domains = blackholes.mail-abuse.org, rbl.maps.vix.com
smtpd_recipient_restrictions: hash:/etc/postfix/no-mail, permit
smtpd_helo_restrictions = reject_maps_rbl, reject_invalid_hostname
smtpd_helo_required = yes
smtpd_etrn_restrictions = permit_mynetworks
```

This configuration is fairly restrictive. Messages from unknown clients and unknown senders are rejected, as are ones from or sent by blacklisted domains (lines 1–3), defined as the two sites in the second entry (line 4). Likewise, messages to nonlocal destinations are also rejected (line 2). Senders (line 1) and recipients (line 6) are checked against access maps. Recipients are accepted provided they pass all the restrictions in the access map (line 5). Blacklisted sites are not allowed to connect to this server, and connections using malformed SMTP HELO/EHLO commands are also rejected (line 6), although this command is required for a successful connection (line 7). Finally, only systems in the local networks may use the SMTP ETRN command to retrieve their mail (line 8).

The recipients entry illustrates the use of the generic *permit* keyword, which simply makes the entry's effect evident; in other words, all lines end with an implicit *permit* unless you include an explicit *reject*. When access is determined, list items are applied in order.

Access map source files consist of user and/or domain names, followed by the desired action. At the moment, actions consist of rejection, specifiable in two forms (as illustrated in the examples below), acceptance, and any of the restriction keywords. Here is an example that might be part of a sender access map:

```
bad-guys.org            REJECT
evil-ones.net           550 No spam allowed.
zoas.org                OK
mybadguy@               permit_mynetworks
```

These entries reject all mail from anyone at *bad-guys.org* and *evil-ones.net* (using the indicated error code and message in the latter case). Mail from *zoas.org* is accepted. When a user named *mybadguy* sends a message, it is rejected unless the client system is a member of one of the local networks.

You create the binary form of the map using the postmap command as usual:

```
# cd /etc/postfix; postmap senders
```

 Access control entries allowing access from specific sites and/or senders cannot protect against addressing spoofing.

Postfix also allows you to define "restriction classes": named groups of keywords that can be used within access maps. In fact, if you want to use a reference to an access map within an access map entry, you must do so via a restriction class,[*] as in this example:

```
main.cf:
smtpd_restriction_classes = no_unknown, check_sender, accept_iffy
no_unknown = reject_unknown_sender_domain, reject_unknown_client,
             reject_non_fqdn_sender, reject_non_fqdn_hostname
check_sender =  check_sender_access hash:/etc/postfix/senders
accept_iffy = check_sender_access hash:/etc/postfix/iffy
smtpd_recipient_restrictions = /etc/postfix/our-mail

/etc/postfix/senders:
bad-guys.org               REJECT

/etc/postfix/iffy:
mole@bad-guys.org          OK
weasel@bad-guys.org        OK
ferret@bad-guys.org        OK
bad-guys.org               REJECT

/etc/postfix/our-mail:
chavez@ahania.com          OK
ahania.com                 no_unknown
essadm.org                 check_sender
zoas.org                   accept_iffy
```

This configuration defines three restriction classes: *non_unknown*, which rejects mail from unknown sources; *check_sender*, which looks up the sender in an access map named *senders*; and *accept_iffy*, which looks up the sender in a different access map, *iffy*. In addition, recipients are checked against the *our-mail* access map. This setup allows recipients in different local domains to have different checks applied to their incoming mail.

---

[*] This is required because the corresponding map files need to be open already when the access map is processed, which is one of the effects of defining the restriction class in the main Postfix configuration file.

These restriction classes are actually applied in the recipients map, *our-mail*. Messages to *chavez* are accepted without further checking. Messages to other users in the *ahania.com* domain are checked for unknown client and sender addresses before being accepted for delivery. Messages to users in the *essadm.org* domain are rejected if they come from a sender at *bad-guys.org* (via the sole entry in the *senders* map). Finally, messages to users in *zoas.org* are usually rejected if they come from someone at *bad-guys.org*, but they are accepted from the three *bad-guy.org* users listed in the *iffy* map.

Postfix can also accept or reject mail based on the contents of either the message headers or body contents, using these configuration file entries:

```
header_checks = regexp:/etc/postfix/header_checks
body_checks = regexp:/etc/postfix/body_checks
```

These examples define the pathname for the map used to specify the desired header/body checks. They use a map type of *regexp*, indicating that the specified file is a regular expression map, another of the supported map types (which may be used for any map file throughout the Postfix facility). The map source file looks like this:

```
/viagra/                    REJECT
/^Subject: [-A-Z0-9! ]*$/    REJECT
/^To: .*@bad-guys.org/       REJECT
/[%!@].*[%!@]/               550 Sender-specified routing rejected
```

This map, designed to be used to check mail message headers, rejects mail that contains "viagra" anywhere in the mail headers, has a subject that contains only uppercase letters, numbers, dashes, exclamation points and spaces, is addressed to any user *@garden.ahania.com*, or contains explicit routing within the address. In the latter case, the message is restricted and results in the specified error code and message text.

As usual, the binary map file must be created from this source file using the `postmap` command.

In addition to this regular expression–based filtering, Postfix also includes full content-filtering hooks (à la `procmail`). See the *FILTER_README* file in the top-level directory of the Postfix source tree for details.

Postfix security

Postfix is designed to be very secure. In this section, we'll cover various odds and ends related to Postfix security, beginning with these two configuration file parameters:

```
mail_owner = postfix
default_privs = nobody
```

These entries specify the owner of the Postfix processes and queue directory and the user identity that Postfix assumes when delivering messages to a file or program and there is no associated user context (respectively). The *postfix* user account should have a unique UID and group (typically also named *postfix*).

As with any administrative facility, you will need to ensure that the Postfix files and directories have the proper ownerships and permissions. The `postfix check` command can be used to examine the installation for these problems, and it should be run periodically.

Warning: Programs that "fix" sendmail permissions

The Postfix file and directory permissions can get changed on Linux systems by the automated system configuration utilities: From the Postfix FAQ:

> Unfortunately, some Linux systems have a helpful utility called `linuxconf` that automatically 'fixes' file permissions to what they are supposed to be for Sendmail's `sendmail` command. Even when you reset the SETUID bit on the Postfix `sendmail` executable file, `linuxconf` will happily turn it on again for you.

There is at present no way to prevent `linuxconf` from doing this.

On some older SuSE systems, the `SuSEconfig` facility does the same thing. However, you can override this by adding the following line to */etc/permissions.local*:

```
/usr/sbin/sendmail root.root 755
```

You will also want to check these entries in */etc/sysconfig/security* (or in */etc/rc.config* on pre–Version 8 systems):

```
CHECK_PERMISSIONS=set              Fix incorrect permissions
PERMISSION_SECURITY="secure local" Permission spec. file list
```

Permission correction happens only when the first entry has the value *set*. The second entry indicates which files contain the correct file ownerships and permissions; the list of items is used as extensions to files of the form */etc/permissions.**. Note also that if your system is set to *easy* rather than *secure*, you should consider changing it (see Chapter 7).

As I've noted before, Postfix gives you two configuration options with respect to the *maildrop* queue: the queue directory can be world-writable (via `chmod o+t`), or it can be only group-writable. In the latter case, Postfix uses a SETGID program for local mail submission (owned by the *postfix* user and group). The non-SETGID configuration is the default. To switch to the second option, you must:

- Assign the proper ownership and protection to the *maildrop* queue directory.
- Run the *INSTALL.sh* script (located in the root of the Postfix source tree), specifying this group at the SETGID privilege prompt.

Finally, many administrators choose to run Postfix in a chrooted environment (with */var/spool/postfix* serving as the root directory). This is easy to configure, but it is not the default. The *examples/chroot-setup* subdirectory of the source tree contains example scripts showing the required steps for converting to such a setup for various operating systems. For example, here are the files for a FreeBSD and an AIX system:

```
FreeBSD:
umask 022
mkdir /var/spool/postfix/etc
chmod 755 /var/spool/postfix/etc
cd /etc
cp host.conf localtime services resolv.conf /var/spool/postfix/etc

AIX:
umask 022
mkdir /var/spool/postfix/etc
chmod 755 /var/spool/postfix/etc
for file in /etc/environment /etc/netsvc.conf /etc/localtime
do
    test -e $file && cp $file /var/spool/postfix/etc
done
cp /etc/services /etc/resolv.conf /var/spool/postfix/etc
mkdir /var/spool/postfix/dev
chmod 755 /var/spool/postfix/dev
mknod /var/spool/postfix/dev/null c 2 2
chmod 666 /var/spool/postfix/dev/null
```

FreeBSD requires only that a few files from */etc* exist in the chroot jail. The script for AIX conditionally copies a list of files (i.e., if they exist), copies two files that it knows it will need, and creates a */dev/null* device in the jail (using the mknod command). Note that both scripts are careful to set the umask appropriately and to set the ownership and permissions for any subdirectories they create.

Monitoring and performance

As with any system facility, Postfix requires some amount of ongoing monitoring and occasional maintenance. In this section, we look at some of the features related to monitoring and performance optimization.

We've seen the postfix command several times already. Three of its most important options are *start* and *stop*, which start and stop the facility, and *flush*, which may be used to force processing of the mail queue. These commands may be used to take care of common facility-wide failures and backlogs.

Postfix also allows you to configure what sorts of errors should be reported to *postmaster*:

```
notify_classes = list
```

The item list consists of one or more keywords: *bounce* (copies message), *2bounce* (for double bounces), *delay* (sends headers only), *policy* (UCE restriction rejections), *protocol* (protocol errors), *resource* (shortages/problems), and *software* (problems causing failed deliveries). The default list is *resource, software*.

Postfix also provides many resource usage and performance-related settings that can be used to optimize its configuration on your system. The most important of these are listed in Table 9-9.

Table 9-9. Some Postfix resource usage and performance parameters

Parameter	Meaning
default_destination_concurrency_limit	Number of parallel deliveries to the same destination. The default of 10 can be lowered if some site(s) are a bottleneck for delivering other mail.
default_destination_recipient_limit	Maximum number of recipients per message delivery (more are batched). The default is 50.
minimal_backoff_time	Amount of time to wait after the first failed delivery attempt. The default is *1000s* (the units must be specified), about 17 minutes.
maximal_backoff_time	Maximum amount of time to wait after a failed delivery attempt (waiting time increases with each failure to this limit). The default is *4000s* (about 67 minutes).
queue_run_delay	Second between qmgr attempts to process the queue. The default is *1000s*.
bounce_size_limit	Maximum size in bytes of the body text that is included in a bounced message. The default is 50000.
default_process_limit	Maximum number of child processes for each Postfix subsystem.
message_size_limit	Maximum size of a message in bytes. The default is 1,024,000 (a pseudo MB).
qmgr_message_active_limit	Maximum number of entries in the *active* queue.
queue_minfree	Amount of free space that must remain available in the filesystem containing the queue directories (the default is 0).

Debugging

There are three main sources of troubleshooting information available with Postfix: syslog entries, verbose command modes, and system call tracing. We will consider each of these in turn.

Normally, Postfix sends status and error messages to the syslog facility. You can configure the minimum severity level for which you want messages reported in the usual way, using the */etc/syslog.conf* configuration file.

You can enable verbose logging for the various Postfix daemons by adding the -v option to the command corresponding specifications in */etc/postfix/master.cf* (in the final column). For example, this modification enables verbose mode for the smtpd daemon:

```
smtp   inet   n   -   n   -   -   smtpd -v
```

The final source of debugging information comes from system call tracing. Be aware, however, that this data is extremely verbose and often obscure. You can enable tracing in this way:

- Add -D to smtpd line in *master.cf*.
- Configure the debugger_command in the *main.cf* configuration file:

```
debugger_command =
    PATH=/usr/bin:/usr/X11/bin
    strace -p $process_id -o /tmp/pfx_$process_id & sleep 5
```

This entry is from a Linux system. strace may need to be replaced by trace, ktrace, truss, or some other command on your system.

Once the daemon is invoked, system call tracing output goes to the specified file in the */tmp* directory. You can examine this file as it runs and use the same command to stop the trace operation when appropriate.

It is also possible to run Postfix daemons under a symbolic debugger. See the documentation for details about how to accomplish this.

Retrieving Mail Messages

As we've already seen, sites that connect intermittently to the Internet can complicate mail relaying and delivery. The central issue for such sites is the method for forcing mail to be sent and retrieved periodically in some automated way. Basically, the local queue needs to be flushed (e.g., via sendmail -q or postfix flush) when the connection is made, and mail for local users needs to be retrieved. (Of course, these two processes can be handled by different servers and so need not happen at the same time). Sending local mail is easily handled by adding the appropriate command to the connection script (or creating a script that activates the connection, flushes the queue, and then terminates the connection).

Retrieving mail can be performed manually via the SMTP ETRN command on remote servers that allow SMTP connections and support the enhanced SMTP protocol. Here is an example:

```
# telnet kevin.ahania.com 25
Trying 10.0.19.223...
Connected to kevin.
Escape character is `^]'.
220 kevin.ahania.com ESMTP Sendmail 8.11.0/8.11.0;
Mon, 16 Apr 2001 11:22:54 -0400
EHLO astarte
250 kevin.ahania.com Hello astarte
...
ETRN mailhost.zoas.org
```

The final command requests mail for the specified host.

The fetchmail program, written by Eric Raymond, provides automated mail retrieval capabilities. It is a powerful program that supports a variety of transport protocols and authentication mechanisms. It operates by retrieving messages from a remote mail server and sending them on to SMTP port 25 on the local system (or a specified remote system). As a result, to the transport agent, they look like normal incoming mail messages.

 You will often need to ensure that *localhost* is included in the transport agent's list of allowed relay hosts for fetchmail to function properly.

The `fetchmail` command is the heart of the package. It is generally started at boot time via a command like this one:

```
fetchmail -d 900
```

This command starts the program in daemon mode and specifies that it will poll each remote mail server every 900 seconds (four times an hour). When the daemon is running, the `fetchmail` command (without arguments) wakes up the daemon and forces an immediate poll of all servers defined in the configuration file. Alternatively, you can specify hosts to poll by listing their names as arguments, as in this example:

```
# fetchmail mailer.notaol.com
```

This command polls the specified host immediately, determining connection information from its configuration file entry (discussed below). Alternatively, you can specify various connection parameters via command-line options (which override settings in the configuration file entry).

The `fetchmail --quit` command form kills the running daemon. You can also include -v or -v -v for verbose/ultra verbose output.

`fetchmail`'s default configuration file is ~/.fetchmailrc (i.e., located in the home directory of the user who issues the `fetchmail` command, typically *root*). An alternate location may be specified with the *FETCHMAILHOME* environment variable or the -f command-line option. The configuration file must have the protection mode 600.

Table 9-10 lists the most important `fetchmail` configuration parameters, giving both the configuration file and command-line option forms.

Table 9-10. Important fetchmail parameters

Keyword	Meaning	Command-line option
set daemon *seconds*	Set the polling interval in seconds when `fetchmail` is run as a daemon.	-d
set logfile *path*	Enable logging to the specified file.	-L
set syslog set nosyslog	Use/don't use `syslog` for messages (`fetchmail` logs to the *mail* facility, using the *info*, *alert*, and *err* severity levels).	--syslog --nosyslog
defaults *settings*	Specify defaults for various settings.	
poll *host*	Define a remote mail server.	
proto *protocol*	Connection protocol to use (e.g., *pop3*, *imap*, *etrn*).	-p
user *username*[a]	User account on the remote server.	-u
is *user(s)*[a] to *user(s)*[a]	Corresponding local user account (the two keywords are synonymous).	
password *string*[a]	Password for the remote account.	
auth *scheme*	Specify the authorization scheme in use: e.g., *password*, *kerberos*, *kerberos_v5*, *ntlm*, *ssh*, *any* (try various in turn).	-A
localdomains *list*	Domains to treat as local.	

Table 9-10. Important fetchmail parameters (continued)

Keyword	Meaning	Command-line option
smtphost *host(s)*[a]	Send incoming mail to this host (or the first available host when the argument is a list). Hostname(s) may include an optional port number: *host/port* (the default is port 25).	-S *host*
limit *bytes*[a]	Limit message to this size (ignored by the ETRN protocol).	-l
keep[a] nokeep[a]	Retain/don't retain downloaded messages on the server (using ETRN implies *nokeep*).	-k -K
flush[a]	Delete old messages from the server before fetching new ones (valid for POP3/IMAP protocols only).	-F
folder *path(s)*[a]	Specify remote mailbox path (valid for IMAP only).	-r *path*
preconnect *command*[a]	Run this command before connecting.	
postconnect *command*[a]	Run this command after connecting.	
plugin *command*	Use this command to make the server connection.	--plugin
skip *host*	Poll this host only when it is explicitly listed on the command line (e.g. fetchmail [*options*] *host*).	
via *host*	Poll this DNS name; when used, the string following *poll* is treated just as a label.	
interval *n*	Poll this site only on every *n*th poll (i.e., less frequently than normal).	

[a] These are user-related options, which must follow all server-related options (unmarked) in configuration file entries.

Here is a sample *.fetchmailrc* file:

```
set logfile /var/log/fetchmail.logset syslog
defaults proto pop3 user "ispuser"

poll pop.essadm.org pass "password"
poll mailer.notaol.org proto imap
    user "rjchavez24" there has password "another-password"
    and is chavez here
poll getmail via pop.essadm.org proto etrn
poll poffice.ahanai.com proto imap auth ssh
    plugin "ssh %h /usr/sbin/imapd"
```

The first section of this configuration file defines some global settings and provides defaults for some parameters for the entries that follow. In this case, logging messages go to the specified log file and also to the syslog facility. The default connection protocol is POP3, and the default user is *ispuser*.

The first *poll* entry defines a POP3 connection to *pop.essadm.org*, and the entry specifies the password for the *ispuser* account on the remote system.

The second *poll* entry defines an IMAP mail server (at *mailer.notaol.org*), to which the local host connects as user *rjchavez24* (with the indicated password), corresponding to the local user *chavez*. In other words, this entry retrieves the mail for *rjchavez24* from the specified server and delivers it to user *chavez*. Note that you can use multiple *user* keywords with an entry to retrieve mail for multiple users in a single operation.

The third *poll* entry also retrieves mail from *pop.essadm.org* (as did the first *poll* entry). Here the target is specified as *getmail*, which functions simply as an entry label (which can be referenced on the fetchmail command line), and the host to which to connect follows the *via* keyword. This entry specifies the ETRN protocol, so it will cause *fetchmail* to issue an SMTP ETRN command to the remote server on behalf of the local host.

The final entry illustrates the method for using ssh to connect to a remote mail server, in this case *poffice.ahania.com*.

In fetchmail configuration files, you will sometimes see entries like this one, which is designed to retrieve mail for multiple local users from a common ("multidrop") mailbox on the mail server:

```
poll pop.essadm.org proto pop3 localdomains zoas.org ahania.com
    user "ispuser" pass "password" to trucks * here
```

This entry polls to *pop.essadm.org* using the POP3 protocol, mapping the remote user *ispuser* to the local user *trucks* and passing through all other users' mail to the local host (specified by the asterisk as the final entry in the *to* user list). However, you should be aware that this approach is prone to many sorts of problems: mail to mailing lists can end up being delivered to the account running fetchmail instead of local subscribed users, mail destined for blind-carbon-copied recipients may be lost, mail loops can arise—the list goes on. The fetchmail documentation recommends that you use the ETRN protocol instead in such circumstances.

There are quite a few other fetchmail features that space constraints preclude discussing in detail. Consult Table 9-10 and the fetchmail documentation for more information.

The fetchmail package also includes a graphical configuration tool, fetchmailconf, which can make setting up configuration file entries easier for new fetchmail users. Figure 9-7 illustrates its novice-mode configuration dialogs; these specific settings would create entries similar to some that we looked at earlier.

The program also has an advanced configuration mode, which lets you set up entries that are as complex as you need them to be.

Mail Filtering with procmail

Previously, we've considered spam suppression features in both sendmail and Postfix. These features can be very effective at blocking some spam before it ever enters your site. The procmail program, written by Stephen van den Berg, offers a different method for accomplishing this task. The package's homepage is *http://www.procmail.org*.

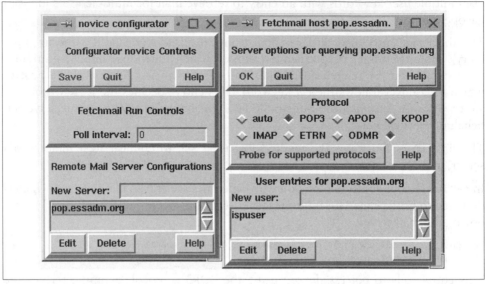

Figure 9-7. The fetchmail configuration utility

In fact, procmail is a very powerful, general-purpose mail filtering facility. Its capabilities are not limited to removing spam; procmail can be used for several different purposes:

- To identify spam messages, which can then be discarded or set aside for later examination.

- To scan mail for security problems, such as viruses, macros within mail attachments, and so on, allowing you to discard or quarantine suspicious messages.

- To sort incoming mail messages by sender, subject area, or any other scheme that makes sense to you.

- To reject mail from specific users or sites or with specific characteristics or content (as defined locally); again, such mail can either be discarded or set aside as appropriate.

In fact, procmail is the mail filtering tool of choice for most users on Unix systems.

procmail can be applied to incoming mail in two main ways:* by using it as the local delivery agent (the program to which the transport agent hands off local messages for actual delivery), or by piping incoming mail for individual users to it, usually in the *.forward* file, as in this canonical example:

```
"|IFS=' ' && exec /usr/bin/procmail -Yf- || exit 75 #username"
```

---

* procmail can also be used to process an existing mailbox; see the "Notes" section of the man page for an example script, or use a command like cat *file* | formail -s procmail. Be very careful when using this technique with a mail spool file: it is very easy to create infinite loops that continuously generate new mail messages.

This example first sets the shell's interfield separator character to a space (see Chapter 3) and execs procmail, specifying -Y (assume BSD mailbox format) and -f- (which tells the program to update the timestamp in the leading *From* header). You may need to modify the path to one appropriate to your system. If you want to be extra cautious, you can use an entry like this one:

```
"|IFS=' ' && p=/usr/bin/procmail && test -f $p
         && exec $p -Yf- || exit 75 #username"
```

This version tests for the existence of the procmail executable before running it. The output is wrapped here, but it is a single line in the *.forward* file.

In any case, if the procmail program fails, the process returns an exit code of 75. The final item is a shell comment, but it is required. As the procmail man page explains it, this item "is not actually a parameter that is required by procmail; in fact, it will be discarded by sh before procmail ever sees it; it is however a necessary kludge against overoptimizing sendmail programs." Whatever.

> The individual user *.forward* file entries are not needed—and should not be used—when procmail is the local delivery agent.

Configuring procmail

procmail gets its instructions about which mail filtering operations to perform in a configuration file. The systemwide configuration file is */etc/procmailrc*. The user-specific procmail configuration file is *~/.procmailrc*. The systemwide configuration file is also invoked when individual users run procmail unless its -p option is included or the configuration file to use is explicitly specified as the command's final argument.

> When procmail is being used only on a per-user basis, it is best to leave the global configuration file empty. Actions specified in the global configuration file are run in the *root* account context, and you have to set up this file very carefully in order to avoid security risks.

procmail examines each successive mail message it receives and applies the various filters defined in the configuration file (known as "recipes") in turn. The first recipe that results in a destination or other disposition for the message causes all further processing to stop. If all of the recipes are applied without effect—in other words, if the message passes unaffected through all the filters—the mail is appended to the user's normal mailbox (which can be defined via the procmail *DEFAULT* variable).

procmail configuration file entries have this general format:

:0 [*flags*]	*Indicates the start of a new recipe.*
* *condition*	*Zero or more lines of regular expressions.*
disposition	*Destination/treatment of matching messages.*

Let's begin with some simple examples:

```
# Define variables
PATH=/bin:/usr/bin:/usr/local/bin:$HOME/bin:/usr/sbin
MAILDIR=$HOME/Mail
DEFAULT=$MAILDIR/unseen

# Discard message from this user.
:0
* ^From.*jerk@bad-guys.org
/dev/null

# Copy all mail messages into my message archive file.
:0c:
archive
```

The initial section of the configuration file defines some procmail variables: the search path, the mail directory, and the default message destination for messages not redirected or discarded by any recipe.

The first recipe filters out mail from user *jerk* at *bad-guys.org* by redirecting it to */dev/null*. Note that the condition is a regular expression against which incoming message text is matched. Contrary to expectations, however, pattern matching is not case-sensitive by default.

The second recipe unconditionally copies all incoming messages to the file *~/Mail/archive*—relative pathnames are interpreted with respect to *MAILDIR*—while retaining the original message in the input stream. Since there is no condition specified, all messages will match and be processed by the recipe.

Copying occurs because the c flag (clone the message) is included in the start line. As this recipe indicates, the start line can potentially include a variety of items. The 0 can be followed by one or more code letters (flags specifying message-handling variations), and the entire string can be followed by another colon, which causes procmail to use a lock file when processing a message with this recipe. The lock file serves to prevent multiple procmail processes, handling different mail messages (as might be generated by the transport agent when mail is arriving rapidly), from trying to write to the same file simultaneously. The terminal colon can optionally be followed by a lock-file name. In most cases, the filename is left blank (as it was here), allowing procmail to generate the name itself.

If this was the entire *.procmailrc* configuration file, all messages not discarded by the first recipe would end up in the location specified by the *DEFAULT* variable: *~/Mail/unseen*.

Similar recipes can be used to direct procmail to sort incoming mail into bins:

```
# Set directory for relative pathnames
HOME=/home/aefrisch/Mail

# Sort and transfer various types of messages
:0:
```

```
* ^From: (patti_singleton|craig_stone|todd_stone)@notaol\.org
new-family

:0c:
* ^TO_help@zoas\.org
support/archive

:0:
* ^TO_help@zoas\.org
* ^Subject: Case.*[GVPM][0-9][0-9][0-9]+
support/existing
:0:
* ^TO_help@zoas\.org
support/incoming
```

The first recipe sends mail from various users at *notaol.org* to the indicated mail folder (they are some of my siblings). The remaining three recipes copy all messages addressed to *help* into the file *archive* in the indicated directory and sort the messages into two other mail folders. The third recipe directs messages whose subject line begins with "Case" and contains one of the indicated letters followed by three or more consecutive digits into the *existing* file, and all other messages go into the *incoming* file (both in my ~/*support* subdirectory).

The ordering of configuration-file recipes can be important. For example, mail to *help* from one of my siblings will still go into the *new-family* file, not one of the ~/ *Mail/support* files.

The ^*TO_* component used in some of the preceding recipes is actually a procmail keyword, and it causes the program to check all recipient-related headers for the specified pattern.

You can specify more than one condition by including multiple asterisk lines:

```
# Define a FROM header set
FROM="^(From[    ]|(Resent-)?(From|Reply-To|Sender):)"
# Discard some junk
:0H
* $ $(FROM).*@bad-guys\.org
* ^Subject: .*what a deal
/dev/null

:0
* ^Subject:.*last chance|\
  ^Subject:.*viagra|\
  ^Subject:.*??
/dev/null
```

The first recipe discards mail from anyone in the indicated domain that contains the indicated string in the subject line. Note that conditions are joined with AND logic. If you want to use OR logic, you must construct a single condition using the regular expression | construct. The second recipe provides an example of doing so. Its search expression could be written more succinctly, but this way it is easier to read.

This recipe also illustrates the use of configuration-file variables. We define one named *FROM*, which matches a variety of headers indicating a message's sender/origin (the square brackets contain a space and a tab character). The variable is then used in the first condition, and the initial dollar sign is required to force variable dereferencing within the pattern.

Other procmail disposition options

You can also use a pipe as the destination by including a vertical bar as the first character in the line:

```
# Run message (except from root and cron) through a script
:0
* !^From: (root|cron)
| $HOME/bin/chomp_mail.pl
```

This recipe sends all mail not from *root* or *cron* (the exclamation mark indicates a negative test) to the indicated Perl script. We don't use procmail locking here; if the script does any writing to files, it will need to do its own locking (procmail locking is not recommended for this purpose).

 Be aware that procmail assumes that commands will be executed in the context of the Bourne (sh) shell at a very deep level. If your login shell is a C shell variant, place the following command at the top of your procmail configuration file to avoid unwanted weirdness:

```
$SHELL=/bin/sh
```

In these next examples, we forward mail to another user and generate and send a mail message within procmail recipes:

```
# Distribute CCL mail list messages related to Gaussian
:0
* ^Subject: CCL:.*g(aussian|9)
! ccl_gauss,ccl_all

# Distribute remaining CCL mailing list messages
:0
* ^Subject: CCL:
! ccl_all

# Send rejection message to this guy
:0
* ^From:.*persistent@bad-guys\.org
* !X-Loop: chavez@ahania.com
| ( formail -r -a "X-Loop: chavez@ahania.com"; \
    echo "This is an auto-generated reply."; \
    echo "Mail rejected; it will never be read." ) \
  | sendmail -t -oi
```

The first recipe distributes selected items from a mailing list to a group of local users. Messages from the mailing list are identifiable by the beginning of their subject lines, and the recipe selects messages with either "gaussian" or "g9" anywhere in the subject line. The selected messages are forwarded to the two indicated local users, which are actually aliases expanding to a list of users.

The second recipe sends all the remaining messages from the same list to the *ccl_all* alias. The users in this internal list want to receive the entire mailing list, and the combination of recipes 1 and 2 produces that result.

The final recipe sends a reply to any mail messages from the specified user. It uses the `formail` utility, which is part of the `procmail` package. The `formail -r` command creates a reply to the mail message the command receives as input, discarding existing message headers and the message body. The new body text is created via the two echo commands which follow, and the completed message is piped to `sendmail` for submission to the mail facility. `sendmail`'s -t option tells the program to determine the recipients from the message headers, and -oi causes it not to treat a line containing a sole period as the end of input (only rarely needed, but traditionally included just to be safe).

This message also illustrates a technique for avoiding mail loops with `procmail`. The `formail` command adds an *X-Loop* header to the outgoing mail message (via the -a option). The conditions also check for the presence of this header, bypassing the message when it is found. In this way, this recipe prevents `procmail` from processing the generated message should it bounce.

Table 9-11 lists some useful `formail` options.

Table 9-11. Useful formail options

Option	Meaning
-r	Generate a reply, deleting existing headers and body.
-X *header:*	Extract/retain the named message header.
-k	Keep the message body also when using -r or -X.
-a *header:text*	Append the specified header if it is not already present.
-A *header:text*	Append the specified header in any case.rr
-i *header:text*	Append the specified header, prepending *Old-* to the name of the existing header (if any).
-I *header:text*	Replace the existing header line.
-u *header:*	Keep only the first occurrence of the named header.
-U *header:*	Keep only the final occurrence of the named header.
-x *header:*	Just extract the named header .
-z	Ensure that there is whitespace following every header field name, and remove (zap) headers without contents. If used with -x, it also trims initial and final whitespace from the resulting output.

`procmail` recipes can also be used to transform incoming mail messages. Here is a nice example by Tony Nugent (slightly modified):

```
# --- Strip out PGP stuff ---
:0fBbw
```

```
* (BEGIN|END) PGP (SIG(NATURE|NED MESSAGE)|PUBLIC KEY BLOCK)
| sed -e 's+^- -+-+' \
    -e '/BEGIN PGP SIGNED MESSAGE/d' \
    -e '/BEGIN PGP SIGNATURE/,/END PGP SIGNATURE/d' \
    -e '/BEGIN PGP PUBLIC KEY BLOCK/,/END PGP PUBLIC KEY BLOCK/d'

# Add (or replace) an X-PGP header
:0Afhw
| formail -I "X-PGP: PGP Signature stripped"
```

These recipes introduce several new procmail flags. The set in the first recipe, Bfw, tells procmail to search the message body only (B) (the default is the entire message), that the recipe is a filter (f) and messages should continue to be processed by later configuration file entries after it completes, and that the program should wait for the filter program to complete before proceeding to the next recipe in the configuration file (w).

The sed command in the disposition searches for various PGP-related strings within the message body (b flag). When found, it edits the message, replacing two space-separated hyphens at the beginning of a line with a single hyphen and removing various PGP-related text, signature blocks and public key blocks (accomplishing the last two operations by using sed's text section–removal feature).

The next recipe will be applied only to messages that matched the conditions in the previous recipe (the A flag), operating as a filter (f) on the message headers only (h) and waiting for the filter program to complete before continuing with the remainder of the configuration file (w). The disposition causes the message to be piped to formail, where an *X-PGP* header is added to the message or an existing header of this type is replaced (-I option).

Table 9-12 lists the most important procmail start-line flags.

Table 9-12. procmail Flags

Flag	Meaning
H[a]	Search the message headers.
B[a]	Search the message body.
h[a]	Process the message header.
b[a]	Process the message body.
c	Perform the operation on a copy of the message.
D	Perform case-sensitive regular expression matching.
f	Recipe is a filter only; matching messages remain in the input stream.
A	Chain this recipe to the immediately preceding one, executing only when a message has matched the patterns in the preceding recipe (which will have included the f flag).
a	Process this recipe only when the preceding one was successful.
e	Process this recipe only when the preceding one failed.

Table 9-12. procmail Flags (continued)

Flag	Meaning
E	Process this recipe only when the preceding recipe's conditions did not match the current message (i.e., create an ELSE condition).
w	Wait for the filter program to complete and check its exit code before continuing on to the next recipe. The W form does the same thing while suppressing any "Program failure" messages.

a The default actions when none of the relevant flags are specified are H and bh. However, H alone implies B is off (search headers only), b without h says to process only the message body, and so on.

Using procmail to discard spam

procmail can be very useful in identifying and removing spam messages. For it to be successful, you must be able to describe common patterns in the messages you want to treat as spam and write recipes accordingly.

In this section, we will look at a variety of recipes that may be useful as starting points for dealing with spam. They happen to come from my own .procmailrc file, and so are applied only to my mail. As an administrator, you can choose to deal with spam at several levels: via the transport agent (e.g., checking against blacklists), at the system level, and/or on a per-user basis. In the case of procmail-based filtering, anti-spam recipes can be used in a systemwide *procmailrc* file or made available to users wanting to filter their own mail.

The following recipe is useful at the beginning of any procmail configuration file, because it formats mail headers into a predictable format:

```
# Make sure there's a space after header names
:0fwh
|formail -z
```

The next two recipes provide simple examples of one approach to handling spam:

```
# Mail from mailing lists I subscribe to
:0:
* ^From: RISKS List Owner|\
  ^From: Mark Russinovich
to-read

# Any other mail not addressed to me is spam
# Warning: may discard BCC's to me
:0
* !To: .*aefrisch
/dev/null
```

Spam is discarded by the second recipe, which defines spam as mail not addressed to me. The first recipe saves mail from a couple of specific senders to the file *to-read*. It serves to define exceptions to the second recipe, because it saves messages from these two senders regardless of who they are addressed to. This recipe is included because I want to retain the mail from the mailing lists corresponding to these senders, but it does not arrive addressed to me.

In fact, there are other recipes which fall between these two, because there are a lot of exceptions to be handled before I can discard every message not addressed to me. Here are two of them:

```
# Mail not addressed to me that I know I want
:0:
* !To: .*aefrisch
* ^From: .*oreilly\.com|\
  ^From: .*marj@zoas\.org|\
  ^From: aefrisch
$DEFAULT

# Keep these just in case
:0:
* ^To: .*undisclosed.*recipients
spam
```

The first recipe saves mail sent from the specified domain and the remote user *marj@zoas.org* via the first two condition lines. I include this recipe because I receive mail from these sources which is not addressed to me—and thus can resemble spam—because of the way their mailer programs handle personal mailing lists. I also retain messages from myself, which result from a CC or BCC on an outgoing message.

The second recipe saves files addressed to any variant of "Undisclosed Recipients" to a file called *spam*. Such mail is almost always spam, but once in a while I discover a new exception.

The next few recipes in my configuration file handle mail that is addressed to me but is still spam. This recipe discards mail with any of the specified strings anywhere in the message headers:

```
# Vendors who won't let me unsubscribe
:0H
* cdw buyer|spiegel|ebizmart|bluefly gifts|examcram
/dev/null
```

Such messages are spam sent by vendors from which I did once buy something and who ignore my requests to stop sending me email.

The next two recipes identify other spam messages based on the *Subject:* header:

```
# Assume screaming headers are spam
:0D
* ^Subject: [-A-Z0-9\?!._ ]*$
/dev/null

# More spam patterns
:0
* ^Subject: .*(\?\?|!!|\$\$|viagra|make.*money|out.*debt)
/dev/null
```

The first recipe discards messages whose subjects consist entirely of uppercase letters, numbers, and a few other characters. The second message discards messages whose subject lines contain two consecutive exclamation marks, question marks or dollar signs, the word "viagra," "make" followed by "money," or "out" followed by "debt" (with any intervening text in the latter two cases).

It is also possible to check mail senders against the contents of an external file containing spam addresses, partial addresses, or any other patterns to be matched:

```
# Check my blacklist (a la Timo Salmi)
:0
* ? formail -x"From" -x"From:" -x"Sender:" -x"X-Sender:" \
           -x"Reply-To:" -x"Return-Path" -x"To:" | \
    egrep -i -f $HOME/.spammers
/dev/null
```

This recipe is slightly simplified from one by Timo Salmi. It uses `formail` to extract just the text from selected headers and pipes the resulting output into the `egrep` command, taking the patterns to match from the file specified to its `-f` option (`-i` makes matches case insensitive).

My spam identification techniques are very simple and therefore quite aggressive. Some circumstances call for more restraint than I am inclined to use. There are several ways of tempering such a drastic approach. The most obvious is to save spam messages to a file rather than simply discarding them. Another is to write more detailed and nuanced recipes for identifying spam. Here is an example:

```
# Discard if From:=To:
SENTBY=`formail -z -x"From:"`
:0
* ! ^To: aefrisch
* ? ^To: .*$SENTBY
/dev/null
```

This recipe discards messages where the sender and recipient addresses are the same—a classic spam characteristic—and are different from my address. The contents of the *From:* header are extracted to the *SENTBY* variable via the backquoted `formail` command. This variable is used in the second condition, which examines the *To:* header for the same string. More complex versions of such a test are also possible (e.g., one could examine more headers other than just *From:*).

There are also a myriad of existing spam recipes that people have created available on the web.

Using procmail for security scanning

`procmail`'s pattern-matching and message-disposition features can also be used to scan incoming mail messages for security purposes: for viruses, unsafe macros, and so on. You can create your own recipes to do so, or you can take advantage of the ones that other people have written and generously made available. In this brief section, we will look at Bjarni Einarsson's Anomy Sanitizer (see *http://mailtools.anomy. net/sanitizer.html*). This package is written in Perl and requires a basic knowledge of

Perl regular expressions to configure.* Once configured, you can run the program via procmail using a recipe like this one:

```
:0fw
|/usr/local/bin/sanitizer.pl /etc/sanitizer.cfg
```

This recipe uses the *sanitizer.pl* script as a filter on all messages (run synchronously), using the configuration file given as the script's argument.

The package's configuration file, conventionally */etc/sanitizer.cfg*, contains two types of entries: general parameters indicating desired features and program behavior, and definitions of file/attachment types and the way they should be examined and modified.

Here are some examples of the first sort of configuration file entries:

```
# Global parameters
feat_log_inline = 1     # Append log to modified messages.
feat_log_stderr = 0     # Don't log to standard error also.
feat_verbose = 0        # Keep logging brief.
feat_scripts = 1        # Sanitize incoming shell scripts.
feat_html = 1           # Sanitize active HTML content.
feat_forwards = 1       # Sanitize forwarded messages.


# Template for saved file names
file_name_tpl       = /var/quarantine/saved-$F-$T.$$
```

The first group of entries specify various aspects of *sanitize.pl*'s behavior, including level of detail and destinations for its log messages as well as whether certain types of message content should be "sanitized": examined and potentially transformed to avoid security problems. The final entry specifies the location of the package's quarantine area: the directory location where potentially dangerous parts of mail messages are stored after being removed.

The next set of entries enables scanning based on file/attachment-extension and specifies the number of groups of extensions that will be defined and default actions for all other types:

```
feat_files = 1                        # Use type-based scanning.
file_list_rules = 3                   # We will define 3 groups.
# Set defaults for all other types
file_default_policy = defang          # Rewrite risky constructs.
file_default_filename = unnamed.file  # Use if no file name given.
```

A sanitizer policy indicates how a mail part/attachment will be treated when it is encountered. These are the most important defined policies:

mangle
 Rewrite the file name to avoid reference to a potentially dangerous extension (e.g., rewrite to something of the form *DEFANGED-nnnnn*).

---

* The program also requires that its library file and those from the MIME:Base64 module that it uses be available within the Perl tree. See the installation instructions for details.

defang

Rewrite the file contents and rename it to eliminate potentially dangerous items. For example, Java Scripts in HTML attachments are neutralized by rewriting their opening line:

```
<DEFANGED_SCRIPT language=JavaScript>
```

accept

Accept the attachment as is.

drop

Delete the attachment without saving it.

save

Remove the attachment, but save it to the quarantine directory.

We'll now turn to some example file-type definitions. This set of entries defines the first file type as the filename *winmail.dat* (the composite mail message and attachment archive generated by some Microsoft mailers) and all files with extensions *.exe*, *.vbs*, *.vbe*, *.com.* *,chm*, *.bat*, *.sys* or *.scr*:

```
# Always quarantine these file types
file_list_1_scanner = 0
file_list_1_policy  = save
file_list_1         = (?i)(winmail\.dat
file_list_1        += |\.(exe|vb[es]|c(om|hm)|bat|s(ys|cr))*)$
```

Notice that the *file_list_1* parameter defines the list of filenames and extensions using Perl regular expression syntax. The policy for this group of files is *save*, meaning that files of these types are always removed from the mail message and saved to the quarantine area. The attachment is replaced by some explanatory text within the modified mail message:

```
NOTE:  An attachment was deleted from this part of the message,
because it failed one or more checks by the virus scanning system.
The file has been quarantined on the mail server, with the following file name:

    saved-Putty.exe-3af65504.4R
```

This message is a bit inaccurate, since in this case the attachment was not actually scanned for viruses but merely identified by its file type, but the information that the user will need is included.

 Clearly, it will be necessary to inform users about any attachment removal and/or scanning policies that you institute. It will also be helpful to provide them with alternative methods for receiving files of prohibited types that they may actually need. For example, they can be taught to send and receive word-processing documents as Rich Text Format files rather than, say, Word documents.

Here are two more examples of file group definitions:

```
# Allow these file types through: images, music, sound, etc.
file_list_2_scanner = 0
file_list_2_policy  = accept
file_list_2         = (?i)\.(jpe?g|pn[mg]
file_list_2      += |x[pb]m|dvi|e?ps|p(df|cx)|bmp
file_list_2      += |mp[32]|wav|au|ram?
file_list_2      += |avi|mov|mpe?g)*$

# Scan these file types for macros, viruses
file_list_3_scanner = 0:1:2:builtin 25
file_list_3_policy  = accept:save:save:defang
file_list_3         = (?i)\.(xls|d(at|oc|ot)|p(pt|1)|rtf
file_list_3      += |ar[cj]|lha|[tr]ar|rpm|deb|slp|tgz
file_list_3      += |(\.g?z|\.bz\d?))*$
```

The first section of entries defines some file types that can be passed through unexamined (via the *accept* policy). The second group defines some extensions for which we want to perform explicit content scanning for dangerous items, including viruses and embedded macros in Microsoft documents. The *file_list_3* extension list includes extensions corresponding to various Microsoft document and template files (e.g., *.doc*, *.xls*, *.dot*, *.ppt* and so on) and a variety of popular archive extensions.

The scanner and policy parameters for this file group now contain four entries. The *file_list_3_scanner* parameter's four colon-separated subfields define four sets of return values for the specified scanning program: the values 0, 1, and 2 and all other return values resulting from running the *builtin* program. The final subfield specifies the program to run—here it is a keyword requesting *sanitizer.pl*'s built-in scanning routines with the argument 25—and serves as a placeholder for all other possible return values that are not explicitly named in earlier subfields (each subfield can hold a single or comma-separated list of return values).

The subfields of the *file_list_policy_3* parameter define the policy to be applied when each return value is received. In this case, we have the following behavior:

Return value	Action
0	Accept the attachment.
1 and 2	Remove and save the attachment.[a]
all others	Modify the attachment to munge any dangerous constructs.

[a] Why two values here? The tool's virus-scanning features require four return codes, so four must be defined for the other features as well.

By default, the *sanitizer.pl* script checks macros in Microsoft documents for dangerous operations (e.g., attempting to modify the system registry or the Normal template). However, I want to be more conservative and quarantine all documents containing any macros. To do so, I must modify the script's source code. Here is a quick and dirty solution to my problem, which consists of adding a single line to the script:

```
# Lots of while loops here - we replace the leading \000 boundary
# with 'x' characters to ensure this eventually completes.
#
$score += 99 while ($buff =~ s/\000Macro recorded/x$1/i);
$score += 99 while ($buff =~ s/\000(VirusProtection)/x$1/i);
```

The line in bold is added. It detects within the document macros that have been recorded by the user. The solution is not an ideal one, because there are other methods of creating macros which would not be detected by this string, but it illustrates what is involved in extending this script, if needed.

Debugging procmail

Setting up `procmail` configuration files can be both addictive and time-consuming. To make debugging easier, `procmail` provides some logging capabilities, specified with these configuration file entries:

```
LOGFILE=path
LOGABSTRACT=all
```

These variables set the path to the log file and specify that all messages directed to files be logged. If you would like even more information, including a recipe-by-recipe summary for each incoming message, add this entry as well:

```
VERBOSE=yes
```

Here are some additional hints for debugging procmail recipes:

- Isolate everything you can from the real mail system. Use a test directory as *MAILDIR* when developing new recipes to avoid clobbering any real mail, and place the recipes in a separate configuration file. Similarly, use a test file of messages rather than any real mail by using a command like this one:

    ```
    cat file | formail -s procmail rcfile
    ```

    This command allows you to use the prepared message file and also to specify the alternate configuration file.

- When testing spam-related recipes, send messages to a file while you are debugging, rather than to */dev/null*.

- If you are trying to test the matching-conditions part of a recipe, use a simple, uniquely-named file as the destination, and incorporate the possibly more complex destination expression only when you have verified that the conditions are constructed correctly.

You can also run the *sanitizer.pl* script to test your configuration with a command like this one:

```
# cat mail-file | /path/sanitizer.pl config-file
```

You will also want to include this line within the configuration file:

```
feat_verbose = 1        # Produce maximum detail in log messages.
```

Additional information

Here are some other useful procmail-related web pages:

http://www.ii.com/internet/robots/procmail/qs/
Nancy McGough/Infinite Ink's "Procmail Quick Start"

http://www.uwasa.fi/~ts/info/proctips.html
Timo Salmi's wonderful "Procmail Tips and Recipes" page

http://www.iki.fi/era/procmail/mini-faq.html
The official procmail FAQ

http://www.ling.Helsinki.fi/users/reriksso/procmail/links.html
A very large collection of procmail-related links

A Few Final Tools

We'll end this chapter on electronic mail by looking at a few related tools and utilities.

You should be aware of the vacation program (included with the sendmail package). It is a utility for automatically sending a predefined reply to all arriving mail while a user is away from email access. To use it, the user creates a file named *.vacation.msg* in his home directory and creates a *.forward* file containing an entry like the following:

```
\username, "|/usr/bin/vacation username"
```

This sends each mail message to the user's usual mailbox and pipes it to the vacation program, giving the username as its argument. The slash is needed before the username to create a terminal mail destination and avoid an infinite loop.

Finally, the user activates the service with the following command:

```
$ vacation -I
```

To disable vacation, simply move or remove the *.forward* file.

 Running the vacation command without any arguments triggers an automated setup process. First, a message file is created and started in a text editor (selected via the *EDITOR* environment variable). The program then automatically creates a *.forward* file and runs vacation -I. As a side effect, any existing *.forward* file is lost.

Next, you might find useful these commands that notify users that they have received new mail: biff, xbiff, and coolmail (a prettier xbiff written by Byron C. Darrah and Randall K. Sharpe; I found it on the Internet at *http://www.redhat.com/swr/src/coolmail-1.3-9.src_dl.html*, but it builds easily on other systems). The oldest of these, biff, requires the comsat network service, which is managed by inetd. These days, however, it is often disabled by default in */etc/inetd.conf* because the graphical utilities have usually replaced biff. To enable the comsat service, uncomment the corresponding line in *inetd.conf* and kill -HUP the inetd process.

Postfix also sends `comsat`-based messages directly, and this feature is enabled by default. To disable the comsat client code in the Postfix delivery agent, include the following parameter in */etc/postfix/main.cf*:

```
biff = no
```

HP-UX, FreeBSD, and Solaris all offer a neat utility called `from`. This program displays the header lines from all mail messages in your mailbox, as in this example:

```
$ from
From uunet!modusmedia.com!palm Thu Mar  1 23:04:39 2001
From uunet!ccsilver.com!sales Fri Mar  2 20:16:38 2001
From uunet!suse.de!isupport Fri Mar  2 17:16:39 2001
```

Finally, grepmail is a utility for searching mail folders; it was written by David Coppit and is available free of charge at *http://grepmail.sourceforge.net*). It searches the headers and/or message text for a specified regular expression and displays matching messages. It has many options; Table 9-13 lists the most useful.

Table 9-13. grepmail options

Option	Meaning
-R	Recurse subdirectories.
-b	Body must match the expression
-h	Header must match the expression.
-i	Make the search case-insensitive.
-v	Display nonmatching messages.
-l	Display only the names of files with a matching message.
-d *date*	Limit search to messages on the specified date (one format is *mm/dd/yy*). You can also use the forms before *date*, after *date*, and between *date* and *date* as this option's argument. See the manual page for details.
-m	Add a *X-Mailfolder:* header to displayed messages.
-M	Don't search nontext MIME attachments.

Here are a couple of examples of using grepmail:

```
$ grepmail -R -i -l hilton ~/Mail
Mail/conf/acs_w01

$ grepmail -i hilton ~/Mail/conf/acs_w01 | grep -i telephone
Telephone:  619-231-4040
```

The first command searches for the string "hilton" (in any mix of cases) in all the mail files in the user's mail directory tree, specifying that only the filename for matching files be displayed. The second command searches the file found by the first command for the same string, this time displaying the entire matching message. In this case, the output of grepmail is piped to grep to search for the string "telephone". The resulting command returns one matching line. Of course, the two grepmail command could also be combined, but I have separated them to illustrate several command options.

CHAPTER 10
Filesystems and Disks

Managing Unix filesystems is one of the system administrator's most important tasks. You are responsible for ensuring that users have access to the files they need and that these files remain uncorrupted and secure. Administering a filesystem includes tasks such as:

- Making local and remote files available to users
- Monitoring and managing the system's disk resources
- Protecting against file corruption, hardware failures, and user errors via a well-planned backup schedule
- Ensuring data confidentiality by limiting file and system access
- Checking for and correcting filesystem corruption
- Connecting and configuring new storage devices when needed

Some of these tasks—such as checking for and correcting filesystem corruption—are usually done automatically at boot time, as part of the initial system startup. Others—like monitoring disk space usage and backups—are often done manually, on a periodic or as-needed basis.

This chapter describes how Unix handles disks and filesystems. It covers such topics as mounting and dismounting local and remote filesystems, the filesystem configuration file, making local filesystems available to remote Unix and Windows users, checking local filesystem integrity with the fsck utility, and adding new disks to the system. It also looks at some optional filesystem features offered in some Unix implementations.

 We looked at file ownership and protection in "Files" in Chapter 2. This chapter considers filesystem protection for network shared filesystems. Other related topics considered elsewhere in this book include the discussions in Chapter 15 of managing disk space with disk quotas ("Monitoring and Managing Disk Space Usage"), disk I/O performance ("Disk I/O Performance Issues"), and planning for swap space ("Managing Memory"), and the discussion of planning and performing backups in Chapter 11.

Filesystem Types

Before any disk partition can be used, a filesystem must be built on it. When a filesystem is made, certain data structures are written to disk that will be used to access and organize the physical disk space into files (see "From Disks to Filesystems," later in this chapter).

Table 10-1 lists the most important filesystem types available on the various systems we are considering.

Table 10-1. Important filesystem types

Use	AIX	FreeBSD	HP-UX	Linux	Solaris	Tru64
Default local	jfs or jfs2	ufs	vxfs[a]	ext3, reiserfs	ufs	ufs or advfs
NFS	nfs	nfs	nfs	nfs	nfs	nfs
CD-ROM	cdrfs	cd9660	cdfs	iso9660	hsfs	cdfs
Swap	not needed	swap	swap, swapfs	swap	swap	not needed
DOS	not supported	msdos	not supported	msdos	pcfs	pcfs
/proc	procfs	procfs	not supported	procfs	procfs	procfs
RAM-based	not supported	mfs[b]	not supported	ramfs, tmpfs	tmpfs	mfs
Other		union	hfs	ext2	cachefs	

[a] HP-UX defines the default filesystem type in */etc/default/fs's LOCAL* variable.
[b] This feature is deprecated and will be replaced by the md facility in Version 5.

About Unix Filesystems: Moments from History

In the beginning was the System V filesystem. Well, not really, but that's where we'll start. This filesystem type once dominated System V–based operating systems.[*]

The superblock of standard System V filesystems contained information about currently available free space in the filesystem in addition to information about how the space in the filesystem is allocated. It held the number of free inodes and data blocks, the first 50 free inode numbers, and the addresses of the first 100 free disk blocks. After the superblock came the inodes, followed by the data blocks.

The System V filesystem was designed for storage efficiency. It generally used a small filesystem block size: 2K bytes or less (minuscule, in fact, by modern standards). Traditionally, a block is the basic unit of disk storage;[†] all files consume space in multiples of the block size, and any excess space in the last block cannot be used by other files and is therefore wasted. If a filesystem has a lot of small files, a small block size

---

[*] The filesystem that came to be known as the System V filesystem (s5fs) actually predates System V.

[†] This block is not related to the blocks used in the default output from commands like df and du. Use -k with either command to avoid having to worry about units.

minimizes waste. However, small block sizes are much less efficient when transferring large files.

The System V filesystem type is obsolete at this point. It is still supported on some systems for backward compatibility purposes only.

The BSD Fast File System (FFS) was designed to remedy the performance limitations of the System V filesystem. It supports filesystem block sizes of up to 64 KB. Because merely increasing the block size to this level would have had a horrendous effect on the amount of wasted space, the designers introduced a subunit to the block: the *fragment*. While the block remains the I/O transfer unit, the fragment becomes the disk storage unit (although only the final chunk of a file can be a fragment). Each block may be divided into one, two, four, or eight fragments.

Whatever its absolute performance status, the BSD filesystem is an unequivocal improvement over System V. For this reason, it was included in the System V.4 standard as the UFS filesystem type. This is its name on Solaris and Tru64 systems (as well as under FreeBSD). For a while, this filesystem dominated in the Unix arena.

In addition to performance advantages, the BSD filesystem introduced reliability improvements. For example, it replicates the superblock at various points in the filesystem (which are all kept synchronized). If the primary superblock is damaged, an alternate one may be used to access the filesystem (instead of it becoming unreadable). The utilities that create new filesystems report where the spare superblocks are located. In addition, the FFS spreads the inodes throughout the filesystem rather than storing them all at the start of the partition.

The BSD filesystem format has a more complex organizational structure as well. It is organized around *cylinder groups*: logical subcylinders of the total partition space. Each cylinder group has a copy of the superblock, a cylinder group map recording block use in its domain, and a fraction of the inodes for that filesystem (as well as data blocks). The data structures are placed at a different offset into each cylinder group to ensure that they land on different platters. Thus, in the event of limited disk damage, a copy of the superblock will still exist somewhere on the disk, as well as a substantial portion of the inodes, enabling significant amounts of data to be potentially recoverable. In contrast, if all of the vital information is in a single location on the disk, damage at that location effectively destroys the entire disk.

The Berkeley Fast File System is an excellent filesystem, but it suffers from one significant drawback: fsck performance. Not only does the filesystem usually need to be checked at every boot, the fsck process is also very slow. In fact, on current large disks, it can take hours.

Journaled filesystems

As a result, a different filesystem strategy was developed: journaled filesystems. Many operating systems now use such filesystems by default. Indeed, the current Solaris UFS filesystem type is a journaled version of FFS. In these filesystems, filesystem structure integrity is maintained using techniques from real-time transaction processing. They use a *transaction log* which is stored either in a designated location within the filesystem or in a separate disk partition set aside for this purpose.

As the filesystem changes, all metadata changes are recorded to the log, and writing entries to the log always precedes writing the actual buffers to disk.[*] In the case of a system crash, the entries in the log are replayed, which ensures that the filesystem is in a consistent state. This operation is very fast, and so the filesystem is available for essentially immediate use. Note that this mechanism is exactly equivalent to traditional `fsck` in terms of ensuring filesystem integrity. Like `fsck`, it has no effect on the integrity of the data.

Journaled filesystems can also be more efficient than traditional filesystems. For example, the actual disk writes for multiple changes to the same metadata can be combined into a single operation. For example, when several files are added to a directory, then each one causes an entry to be written to the log, but all four of them can be combined in a single write to disk of the block containing the directory.

BSD soft updates

In the BSD world, development of the FFS continues. The current version offers a feature called *soft updates* designed to make filesystems available immediately at boot time.[†]

The usual FFS writes blocks to disk in a synchronous manner: in order, and waiting for each write operation to complete before stating the next one. In contrast, the soft updates method uses a delayed, asynchronous approach by maintaining a write-back cache for metadata blocks (a technique referred to as *delayed writes*). This often produces significant performance improvements in that many modifications to metadata can take place in memory rather than each one having to be performed on disk. For example, consider a directory tree removal. With soft updates, the metadata changes for the entire delete operation might be made in only a single write, a great savings compared to the traditional approach.

---

[*] Writes to the log itself can be synchronous (forced to disk immediately) or buffered (written to disk only when the buffer fills up).

[†] For technical details about soft updates, see the articles "Metadata Update Performance in File Systems" by Gregory Ganger and Yale Patt, published in the *USENIX Symposium on Operating Systems Design and Implementation* (1994; available in an expanded version online at *http://www.ece.cmu.edu/~ganger/papers/CSE-TR-243-95.pdf*) and "Soft Updates: A Technique for Eliminating Most Synchronous Writes in the Fast Filesystem" by Marshall Kirk McKusick and Gregory R. Ganger, published in the *Proceedings of 1999 USENIX Annual Technical Conference* (available online at *http://www.usenix.org/publications/library/proceedings/usenix1999/mckusick.html*). For a comparison of FFS with soft updates to journaled filesystems, see the paper "Journaling versus Soft Updates: Asynchronous Meta-data Protection in File Systems" by Margo I. Seltzer, Gregory R. Ganger, M. Kirk McKusick, Keith A. Smith, Craig A. N. Soules, and Christopher A. Stein, published in the *Proceedings of 2000 USENIX Annual Technical Conference* (available online at *http://www.usenix.org/publications/library/proceedings/usenix2000/general/seltzer.html*).

Of course, overlapping changes to metadata can also occur. To account for these situations, the soft updates facility maintains *dependency* data specifying the other metadata changes that a given update assumes have already taken place.

Blocks are selected for writing to disk according to an algorithm designed for overall filesystem efficiency. When it is time to write a metadata block to disk, soft updates reviews the dependencies associated with the selected block. If there are any dependencies that assume that other pending blocks will have been written first, the changes creating the dependencies are temporarily undone (*rolled back*). This allows the block to be written to disk while ensuring that the filesystem remains consistent. After the write operation completes, the rolled back updates to the block are restored, ensuring that the in-memory version contains the current data state. The system also removes dependency list entries that have been fulfilled by writing out that block.[*]

Soft updates have the advantage that the only filesystem inconsistencies that can be caused by a crash are inodes and data blocks marked as in use that are actually free (consult the papers listed in the earlier footnote to see why this is true). Because these errors are benign, the filesystem can be made available for immediate use after rebooting. A background process similar to fsck is used to locate and correct these errors.

Default Local Filesystems

Table 10-2 lists the characteristics of the default local filesystem types for the various Unix versions.

Table 10-2. Default local filesystem characteristics

Item	AIX	FreeBSD	HP-UX	Linux (Red Hat)	Linux (SuSE)	Solaris	Tru64	Tru64
Type	jfs	ufs	vxfs	ext3	reiserfs	ufs	ufs	advfs
Journaled	yes	soft updates	yes	yes	yes	yes	no	yes
64 bit (files>2 GB)	yes	yes	yes	yes	yes	yes	yes	yes
Dynamic resizing	yes	yes	yes	yes	yes	yes[a]	no	yes[b]
Sparse file support	yes	yes	yes	no	yes	yes	yes	yes

[*] Occasionally, soft updates require more write operations than the traditional method. Specifically, block roll forwards immediately make the block dirty again. If the block doesn't change again before it gets flushed to disk, an extra write operation occurs that would not otherwise have been necessary. The block selection algorithm attempts to minimize the number of rollbacks in order to avoid these situations.

Table 10-2. Default local filesystem characteristics (continued)

Item	AIX	FreeBSD	HP-UX	Linux (Red Hat)	Linux (SuSE)	Solaris	Tru64	Tru64
NFSv3 support	yes	yes	yes	yes	yes	yes	yes	yes
dump version provided	yes	yes	yes	yes	no	yes	yes	yes

^a Solaris 9 only
^b Requires the AdvFS utilities (additional cost option)

Managing Filesystems

This section covers such topics as mounting and dismounting local and remote filesystems, the filesystem configuration file, and checking local filesystem integrity with the fsck utility: in other words, the nitty gritty details of managing filesystems.

Mounting and Dismounting Filesystems

Mounting is the process that makes a filesystem's contents available to the system, merging it into the system directory tree. A filesystem can be mounted or dismounted: that is, it can be connected to or disconnected from the overall Unix filesystem. The only exception is the root filesystem, which is always mounted on the root directory while the system is up and cannot be dismounted.

Thus, in contrast to some other operating systems, mounting a Unix filesystem does more than merely make its data available. Figure 10-1 illustrates the relationship between a system's disk partitions (and their corresponding special files) and its overall filesystem. On this system, the root filesystem—the filesystem stored on the first partition of the root disk (disk 0)—contains the standard Unix subdirectories */bin*, */etc*, and so on. It also contains the empty directories */home*, */var*, and */chem*, which serve as *mount points* for other filesystems. This filesystem is accessed via the special file */dev/dsk/c1d0s0*.

The figure also shows several other filesystems. One of them, accessed via the special file */dev/dsk/c1d0s8* (partition 8 of the root disk), contains the files and directories under */var*. A third filesystem—partition 9 on disk 1—is accessed via the special file */dev/dsk/c1d1s9* and contains users' home directories, located under */home*.

Another filesystem on this system is stored on partition 2 of disk 1 and is accessed via the special file */dev/dsk/c1d1s2*. Its own root directory contains the subdirectories *./organic* and *./inorganic* and their contents. We'll call this the */chem* filesystem, after its mount point within the system's directory tree. When */dev/dsk/c1d1s2* is mounted, these directories will become subdirectories of */chem*.

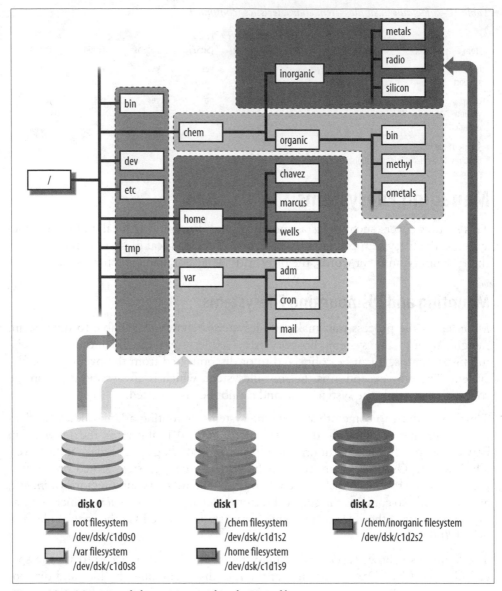

Figure 10-1. Mounting disk partitions within the Unix filesystem

One of the directories in the */chem* filesystem, *./inorganic*, is empty and is to be used as the mount point for yet another filesystem. The files in this fifth filesystem, on partition 2 on disk 2 and corresponding to the special file */dev/dsk/c1d2s2*, become a subtree of the */chem* filesystem when mounted.

The files in the root directory and its system subdirectories all come from disk 0, as do the empty directories */chem*, */home*, and */var* before filesystems are mounted on them. Figure 10-1 illustrates the fact that the contents of the */chem* directory tree come from two different physical disks.

In most cases, there is no necessary connection between a given filesystem and a particular disk partition (and its associated special file), for example, between the */chem* filesystem and the special file */dev/dsk/c1d1s2*. The collection of files on a disk partition can be mounted on *any* directory in the filesystem. After it is mounted, its top-level directory is accessed via the directory path where it is mounted, and it is often referred to by that directory's name.

At the same time, the root directory of the mounted filesystem replaces the directory where the filesystem is mounted. As a side effect, any files that were originally in the mount directory—in this example, any files that might have been in */chem* prior to mounting the new filesystem—disappear when the new filesystem is mounted and thus cannot be accessed; they will reappear once the filesystem is dismounted.

To illustrate this phenomenon, let's watch a filesystem being mounted:

```
# ls -saC /chem                                /chem's contents before mount.
total 20
4 .              4 ..           12 README
# mount /dev/dsk/c1d1s2 /chem                  Mount partition 2 on disk 1.
# ls -saC /chem                                /chem's contents after mount.
total 48
4 .              4 ..            4 inorganic       32 lost+found
4 organic
# du -s /chem                                  /chem is much bigger.
587432 /chem
```

Before the filesystem is mounted, there is just one ordinary file in */chem*: *README*. After */dev/dsk/c1d1s2* is mounted, *README* disappears. It's still on the root disk, but it can't be accessed while the */chem* filesystem is mounted. However, it will reappear when the filesystem is dismounted. After the filesystem is mounted, the subdirectories *organic* and *inorganic* appear, along with their contents (reflected in the larger amount of data under */chem*).

 On most Unix systems, a filesystem can only be mounted in one place at one time (Linux is an exception).

Disk Special File Naming Conventions

We looked at disk special filenames in detail in "Devices" in Chapter 2. The following list reviews the disk special file naming conventions for a SCSI disk under the various operating systems we are considering by listing the special file used for a partition on the third SCSI disk (SCSI ID 4) on the first SCSI controller (accessed in raw mode):*

AIX	*/dev/hdisk2* (refers to the entire disk)
FreeBSD	*/dev/da0s1e* (short form: */dev/da1c*)
HP-UX	*dev/rdsk/c0t4d0*
Linux	*/dev/sdc1*
Solaris	*/dev/rdsk/c0t4d0s7*
Tru64	*/dev/rdisk/dsk2c*

The mount and umount Commands

To mount a filesystem manually, use the `mount` command as follows:

```
# mount [-o options] block-special-file  mount-point
```

This command mounts the filesystem located on the specified disk partition. The root directory on this filesystem will be attached at *mount-point* within the overall Unix filesystem. This directory must already exist before the `mount` command is executed.

For example, the commands:

```
# mkdir /users2
# mount /dev/dsk/c1t4d0s7 /users2
```

create the directory */users2* and mount the filesystem located on the disk partition */dev/dsk/c1t4d0s7* on it. On some systems, mount's -r option may be used to mount a filesystem read-only. For example:

```
# mount -r /dev/dsk/c1t4d0s7 /mnt
```

Use mount without options to display a list of currently mounted filesystems.

The `mount` command can also be used to mount remote filesystems via NFS. We'll consider this use later in this chapter.

The umount command may be used to dismount filesystems:

```
# umount name
```

This command dismounts the filesystem specified by *name*, where *name* is either the name of the filesystem's block special file or the name of the mount point where this filesystem is mounted. The -f option may be used to force an dismount operation in some cases (e.g., when there are open files), but it should be used with caution.

This section has illustrated only the simplest uses of `mount` and `umount`. We'll look at many more examples in the course of this chapter.

---

* Under FreeBSD 4, the block and raw devices are equivalent. Character devices are vestigial in Version 4 and are slated to be removed in FreeBSD Version 5.

Figuring Out Who's Using a File

Filesystems must be inactive before they can be dismounted. If any user has one of a filesystem's directories as her current directory or has any file within the filesystem open, you'll get an error message something like this one if you try to unmount that filesystem:

```
umount: /dev/hdb1: device is busy
```

The fuser command may be used to determine which files within a filesystem are currently in use and to identify the processes and users that are using them. If fuser is given a filename as its argument, it reports on that file alone. If it is given a disk special filename as its argument, it reports on all files within the corresponding filesystem. The -u option tells fuser to display user ID's as well as PID's in its output.

For example, the following command displays all processes and their associated users that are using files on the specified disk on an HP-UX system:

```
$ fuser -u /dev/dsk/c1t1d0
```

Under Linux, including the -m option will allow you to specify the filesystem by name; the -c option performs the same function under Solaris.

Here is an example of fuser's output:

```
/chem: 3119c(chavez) 3229(chavez)  3532(harvey)  3233e(wang)
```

Four processes are using the *chem* filesystem at this moment. Users *chavez* and *harvey* have open files, indicated by the second and third process IDs, which appear without a final code letter. User *chavez* also has her current working directory within this filesystem (indicated by the c code after the first PID), and user *wang* is running a program whose executable resides within the filesystem (indicated by the e code after the final PID).

fuser's -k option may be used to kill all of the processes using the specified file or filesystem.

The lsof command performs a similar function on FreeBSD systems (and is also available for the other operating systems as well). Its output is a great deal more detailed. Here is a small part of its output (shortened to fit):

```
COMMAND PID    USER     FD    TYPE    DEVICE    NAME
vi      74808 aefrisch cwd   VDIR 116,131072   /usr/home/aefrisch
vi      74808 aefrisch rtd   VDIR 116,131072   /
vi      74808 aefrisch txt   VREG 116,131072   /usr/bin/vi
vi      74808 aefrisch txt   VREG 116,131072   /usr/libexec/ld-elf.so.1
vi      74808 aefrisch txt   VREG 116,131072   /usr/lib/libncurses.so.5
vi      74808 aefrisch txt   VREG 116,131072   /usr/lib/libc.so.4
vi      74808 aefrisch   0   VCHR      0,0     /dev/ttyp0
vi      74808 aefrisch   1   VCHR      0,0     /dev/ttyp0
vi      74808 aefrisch   2   VCHR      0,0     /dev/ttyp0
vi      74808 aefrisch 3-W   VREG 116,131072   /usr/home/aefrisch/.login
vi      74808 aefrisch   4   VREG 116,131072   /var/tmp/vi.recover/vi.CJ6cay
vi      74808 aefrisch   5   VREG 116,131072   / (/dev/ad0s1a)
```

These are the entries generated by a vi process editing this user's *.login* file. Note that this file is opened for writing, indicated by the W following the file descriptor number (column FD).

FreeBSD also provides the fstat command, which performs a similar function.

The Filesystem Configuration File

Mounting filesystems by hand every time they are needed would quickly become tedious, so the required mount commands are generally executed automatically at boot time. The filesystem configuration file typically contains information about all of the system's filesystems, for use by mount and other commands.[*]

/etc/fstab is the standard Unix filesystem configuration file. It generally has the following format:

```
special-file  mount-dir  fs-type  options  dump-freq  fsck-pass
```

The fields have the following meanings:

special-file
> The name of the special file on which the filesystem resides. This must be a block device name.

mount-dir
> The directory on which to mount the filesystem. If the partition will be used for swapping, / is sometimes used for this field.

fs-type
> The filesystem type. The value for local filesystems is highly version-dependent. Common type values are nfs for volumes mounted remotely via NFS, swap or sw for swap partitions (although Tru64 uses UFS for these as well, and HP-UX also has the swapfs type for paging to a file within the filesystem), and ignore, which tells mount to ignore the line. Available filesystem types for the various Unix versions are listed later in this chapter.

options
> This field consists of one or more options, separated by commas. The *fs-type* field, above, determines which options are allowed for any given kind of filesystem. For *ignore* type entries, this field is ignored.
>
> Multiple options are separated by commas, without intervening spaces. On many systems, the keyword defaults may be placed into this field if no options are needed. Table 10-3 lists commonly used options for local filesystems and paging/swap spaces.

---

[*] This section covers only local disks. We'll look at entries for remote disks later in this chapter.

dump-freq

A decimal number indicating the frequency with which this filesystem should be backed up by the dump utility. A value of 1 means backup should occur every day, 2 means every other day, and so on. A value of 0 means that the device is not to be backed up (for example, swap devices). Not all systems actually use this field.

fsck-pass

A decimal number indicating the order in which fsck should check the filesystems. A value of 1 indicates that the filesystem should be checked first, 2 indicates that the filesystem should be checked second, and so on. The root and/or boot filesystems generally have the value 1. All other filesystems generally have higher pass numbers. For optimal performance, two filesystems that are on the same disk drive should have different pass numbers; however, filesystems on different drives may have the same pass number, letting fsck check the two filesystems in parallel. fsck will usually be fastest if all filesystems checked on the same pass are roughly the same size. This field should be 0 for swap devices (0 disables checking by fsck).

Table 10-3. Commonly used filesystem options

Option	Meaning
rw	Read-write filesystem (default for read-write devices).
ro	Read-only filesystem (default for read-only media such as CDs).
nosuid	The SetUID access mode is ignored within this filesystem; suid is the default.
noauto	Don't automatically mount this filesystem at boot time; auto is the default (Linux, FreeBSD).
noexec	Prevent binary programs from executing; exec is the default (Linux, FreeBSD, Tru64).
nodev	Prevent device access via special files (AIX, Linux, FreeBSD, Tru64).
user	Allow ordinary users to mount this filesystem (Linux).
nogrpid	Use System V–style group ownership inheritance for new files (i.e., the owner's primary group); BSD-style is the default (Linux, Tru64).
resuid=*n* resgid=*n*	Set the UID/GID that has access to the reserved blocks with the filesystem (Linux ext2/ext3).
largefiles	Support files larger than 2 GB (HP-UX VxFS, Solaris).
logging	Maintain a transaction log (Solaris). The default is nologging.
delaylog	Delay writing log entries slightly to improve performance, increasing risk of loss slightly. (HP-UX VxFS)
writeback	Write out log metadata and filesystem blocks in either order, for a slight performance improvement and increased risk of loss in the event of a crash (Linux ext3).
nolog	Don't use a transaction log (HP-UX VxFS).
nologging	Don't use a transaction log (Solaris).
forcedirectio	Use direct I/O to this filesystem: i.e., no buffering (Solaris). Useful for certain applications such as databases.
notail	Disable default behavior of storing small files directly within the hash tree (Linux ReiserFS).
resize=*n*	Resize the filesystem to *n* blocks on mounting (Linux ReiserFS).

Table 10-3. Commonly used filesystem options (continued)

Option	Meaning
rq	Mount read-write and enable disk quotas (Tru64).
quota	Enable disk quotas (HP-UX, Solaris).
userquota groupquota	Enable user/group disk quotas (FreeBSD).
usrquota grpquota	Enable user/group disk quotas (Linux).
pri=n	Set swap space priority (0 to 32767). Under Linux, higher numbers indicated more favored areas, which are used first; HP-UX favors lower priority areas.
xx	Ignore this entry (FreeBSD).

Here are some typical */etc/fstab* entries, defining one or more local filesystems, a CD-ROM drive, and a swap partition:

```
# FreeBSD
# device       mount     type      options        dump fsck
/dev/ad0s1a    /         ufs       rw               1 1
/dev/cd0c      /cdrom    cd9660    ro,noauto        0 0
/dev/ad0s2b    none      swap      sw               0 0

# Linux
# device       mount     type      options        dump fsck
/dev/sda2      /         reiserfs  defaults         1 1
/dev/sda1      /boot     ext2      defaults         1 2
/dev/cdrom     /cdrom    auto      ro,noauto,user   0 0
/dev/sda3      swap      swap      pri=42           0 0

# HP-UX
# device       mount     type      options        dump fsck
/dev/vg00/lvol3 /        vxfs      defaults         0 1
/dev/vg00/lvol1 /stand   hfs       defaults         0 1
/dev/dsk/c1t2d0 /cdrom   cdfs      defaults         0 0
/dev/vg01/swap ...       swap      pri=0            0 0

# Tru64
# device       mount     type      options        dump fsck
root_domain#root /       advfs     rw               0 1
/dev/disk/cdrom0c /cdrom cdfs      ro               0 2
# swap partition is defined in /etc/sysconfigtab
```

 HP-UX and Tru64 use a logical volume manager by default for all local disks. Accordingly, the devices specified in */etc/fstab* refer to logical volumes rather than actual disk partitions. Hence the rather strange device names in their examples. Logical volume managers are discussed later in this chapter.

Tru64 specifies swap partitions via the following stanza in the */etc/sysconfigtab* file:

```
vm:
    swapdevice = /dev/disk/dsk0b
```

Solaris: /etc/vfstab

Solaris uses a different filesystem configuration file, */etc/vfstab*, which has a somewhat different format:

```
block-special-file char-special-file  mount-dir fs-type fsck-pass auto-mount? options
```

The ordering of the normal *fstab* fields is changed somewhat, and there are two additional ones. The second field holds the character device corresponding to the block device in the first field (which is used by the fsck command). The sixth field specifies whether the filesystem should be mounted automatically at boot time (note that the root filesystem is set to no).

Here is an example file:

```
# Solaris
# mount          fsck
# device         device             mount  type fsck auto? options
/dev/dsk/c0t3d0s2 /dev/rdsk/c0t3d0s0 /      ufs  1    no    rw
/dev/dsk/c0t3d0s0 /dev/rdsk/c0t3d0s0 /home  ufs  2    yes   rw,logging
/dev/dsk/c0t3d0s1 -                  -      swap -    no    -
```

Note that hyphens are placed in unused fields.

AIX: /etc/filesystems and /etc/swapspaces

The filesystem configuration file under AIX is */etc/filesystems*. This file is updated automatically by various AIX filesystem manipulation commands, including crfs, chfs, and rmfs. */etc/filesystems* contains all the information in */etc/fstab* and some additional data as well, arranged in a stanza-based format. Here are some example entries:

```
/:
        dev     = /dev/hd4           Disk device.
        vol     = "root"            Descriptive label.
        vfs     = jfs2              Filesystem type.
        mount   = automatic         Mount automatically with mount -a.
        check   = true              Check with fsck if needed.
        log     = /dev/hd8          Device to use for filesystem log.

/chem:
        dev     = /dev/us00         Logical volume.
        vol     = "chem"           Descriptive label.
        vfs     = jfs2              Filesystem type.
        log     = /dev/loglv01      Device to use for filesystem log.
        mount   = true              Mount automatically with mount -a.
        check   = 2                 Sets the fsck pass.
        options = rw,nosuid         Mount options.
        quota   = userquota         Enable user disk quotas.
```

Each mount point in the overall filesystem has its own stanza, specifying which logical volume (equivalent to a disk partition for this purpose) is to be mounted there. Like HP-UX and Tru64, AIX uses a logical volume manager by default (discussed later in this chapter).

Under AIX, paging logical volumes are listed in *letc/swapspaces*, rather than in the filesystem configuration file. That file is maintained by paging space administration commands such as mkps, chps, and rmps, and its format is very simple:

```
hd6:
     dev = /dev/hd6

paging00:
     dev = /dev/paging00
```

This sample file lists two paging areas.

Automatic Filesystem Mounting

Regardless of its form, once the filesystem configuration file is set up, mounting may take place automatically. mount's -a option may be used to mount all filesystems that the filesystem configuration file says should be mounted on most systems. In addition, if a filesystem is included in the filesystem configuration file, the mount and umount commands will now require only the mount point or the special file name as their argument. For example, the command:

```
# mount /chem
```

looks up */chem* in the filesystem configuration file to determine what special file is used to access it and then constructs and performs the proper mount operation. Similarly, the following command dismounts the filesystem on special file /dev/disk1d.:

```
# umount /dev/disk1d
```

umount also has a -a option to dismount all filesystems.

Both mount and umount have options to specify the type of filesystem being mounted or dismounted. Generally, this option is -t, but HP-UX and Solaris use -F, and AIX uses -v. This option may be combined with -a to operate on all filesystems of a given type. For example, the following command mounts all local filesystems under Tru64:

```
# mount -a -t advfs
```

FreeBSD, Tru64, and Linux also allow a type keyword to be preceded with no, causing the command to operate on all filesystem types except those listed. For example, this Linux command mounts all filesystems except DOS filesystems and remote (NFS) filesystems:

```
# mount -tnomsdos,nfs -a
```

Finally, under FreeBSD, Tru64, and Solaris, umount has a -h option that unmounts all remote filesystems from a specified host. For example, this command unmounts all filesystems from *dalton*:

```
# umount -h dalton
```

Under AIX, the -n option performs the same function.

Using fsck to Validate a Filesystem

A number of problems, ranging from operator errors to hardware failures, can corrupt a filesystem. The fsck utility ("filesystem check") checks the filesystem's consistency, reports any problems it finds, and optionally repairs them. Only under very rare circumstances will these repairs cause even minor data loss.

 The equivalent utility for Tru64 AdvFS filesystems is verify (located in */sbin/advfs*).

fsck can find the following filesystem problems:

- One block belonging to several files (inodes).
- Blocks marked as free but in use.
- Blocks marked as used but free.
- Incorrect link counts in inodes (indicating missing or excess directory entries).
- Inconsistencies between inode size values and the number of data blocks referenced in address fields.
- Illegal blocks (e.g., system tables) within files.
- Inconsistent data in the filesystem's tables.
- Lost files (nonempty inodes not listed in any directory). fsck places these files in the directory named *lost+found* in the filesystem's top-level directory.
- Illegal or unallocated inode numbers in directories.

Basically, fsck performs a consistency check on the filesystem, comparing such items as the block free list against the disk addresses stored in the inodes (and indirect address blocks) and the inode free list against inodes in directory entries. It is important to understand that fsck's scope is limited to repairing the *structure* of the filesystem and its component data structures. The utility can do nothing about corrupted *data* within structurally intact files.

On older BSD-style systems, the fsck command is run automatically on boots and reboots. Under the System V scheme, fsck is run at boot time on filesystems only if they were not dismounted cleanly (e.g., if the system crashed). System administrators rarely need to run this utility manually: on boots when it finds serious problems (because fsck's automatic mode isn't authorized to repair all problems), after creating a new filesystem, and under a few other circumstances. Nevertheless, you need to understand how fsck works so that you'll be able to verify that the system boots correctly and to quickly recognize abnormal situations.

fsck has the following syntax:

```
# fsck [options] device
```

device is the special file for the filesystem. fsck runs faster on a character special file. If the device is omitted—as it is at boot time—all filesystems listed in the filesystem configuration file will be checked (all filesystems whose *check* attribute is not false will be checked under AIX).

 On all systems except FreeBSD and Linux, the block device must be specified for the root filesystem in order to check it with fsck.

If fsck finds any problems, it asks whether or not to fix them. The example below shows a fsck report giving details about several filesystem errors and prompting for input as to what action to take:

```
# fsck /dev/rdisk1e
/dev/rdisk1e
** Phase 1--Check Blocks and Sizes
POSSIBLE FILE SIZE ERROR I = 478
** Phase 2--Check Pathnames
** Phase 3--Check Connectivity
** Phase 4--Check Reference Counts
UNREF FILE I = 478  OWNER = 190  MODE = 140664
SIZE = 0  MTIME = Sept 18 14:27 1990
CLEAR? y

FREE INODE COUNT WRONG IN SUPERBLOCK
FIX? y

** Phase 5--Check Cylinder Groups
1243 files   28347 blocks  2430 free
*** FILE SYSTEM WAS MODIFIED ***
```

fsck found an unreferenced inode—an inode marked as in use but not listed in any directory. fsck's output indicates its inode number, owner UID, and mode. From this information, we can figure out that the file is owned by user *chavez* and is a socket. The mode is interpreted as illustrated in Figure 10-2.

The first one or two digits of the mode indicate the file type: in this case, a socket that can be safely removed.

The available options for fsck allow automatic correction of the filesystem to take place (or be prevented):

-p Preen the filesystem; automatically perform repairs that don't change any file's contents.

-n Answer no to all prompts: list but don't repair any problems found.

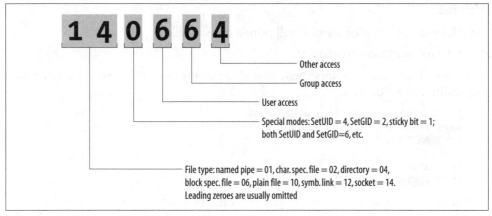

Figure 10-2. Interpreting fsck output

-y   Answer yes to all prompts: repair all damage regardless of severity. Use this option with caution.*

-P   Preen the filesystem only if it is dirty (Tru64).

-f   Force a check even if the filesystem is clean (Linux).

-b *n*
      Use an alternate superblock located at block *n* (BSD-style syntax). 32 is always an alternate superblock.

fsck is normally run with the -p option. In this mode, the following problems are silently fixed:

- Lost files will be placed in the filesystem's *lost+found* directory, named for their inode number.
- Link counts in inodes too large.
- Missing blocks in the free list.
- Blocks in the free list also in files.
- Incorrect counts in the filesystem's tables.
- Unreferenced zero-length files are deleted.

More serious errors will be handled with prompts as in the previous example.

For UFS filesystems under Solaris, the BSD-style options are specified as arguments to the -o option (the filesystem type-specific options flag). For example, the following command checks the UFS filesystem on */dev/dsk/c0t3d0s2* and makes necessary nondestructive corrections without prompting:

```
# fsck -F ufs -o p /dev/dsk/c0t3d0s2
```

---

* At the same time, it's not clear what alternatives you have. You can't mount a damaged filesystem, and, unless you're a real wizard regarding filesystem internals, fsck is the only tool available for fixing the filesystem.

After fsck

If `fsck` modifies any filesystem, it will print a message like:

```
*** FILE SYSTEM WAS MODIFIED ***
```

If the root filesystem was modified, an additional message will also appear, indicating additional action needed:

BSD-style if the automatic filesystem remount fails:
```
mount reload of /dev/device failed:
*** REBOOT NOW ***
```

System V-style:
```
***** REMOUNTING ROOT FILE SYSTEM *****
```

If this occurs as part of a normal boot process, the remount or reboot will be initiated automatically. If `fsck` has been run manually on the root filesystem on a BSD system, the rebooting command needs to be entered by hand. Use the reboot command with the -n option:

```
# reboot -n
```

The -n option is very important. It prevents the `sync` command from being run, which flushes the output buffers and might very well recorrupt the filesystem. This is the only time when rebooting should occur without syncing the disks.

From Disks to Filesystems

As we've seen, the basic Unix file storage unit is the disk partition. Filesystems are created on disk partitions, and all of the separate filesystems are combined into a single directory tree. The initial parts of this section discuss the process by which a physical disk becomes one or more filesystems on a Unix system, treating the topic at a conceptual level. Later subsections discuss the mechanics of adding a new disk to the various operating systems we are considering.

Defining Disk Partitions

Traditionally, the Unix operating system organizes disks into fixed-size partitions, whose sizes and locations are determined when the disk is first prepared (as we'll see). Unix treats disk partitions as logically independent devices, each of which is accessed as if it were a physically separate disk. For example, one physical disk may be divided into four partitions, each of which holds a separate filesystem. Alternatively, a physical disk may be configured to contain only one partition comprising its entire capacity.

Many Unix implementations allow several physical disks to be combined into a single logical device or partition upon which you can build a filesystem. Systems offering a *logical volume manager* carry this trend to its logical conclusion, allowing multiple physical disks to be combined into a single logical disk, which can then be divided into logical partitions. AIX uses only an LVM and does not use traditional partitions at all.

Physically, a disk consists of a vertical stack of equally spaced circular platters. Reading and writing is done by a stack of heads that move in and out along the radius as the platters spin around at high speed. The basic idea is not so different from an audio turntable—I hope you've seen one—although both sides of the platters can be accessed at once.[*]

Partitions consist of subcylinders[†] of the disk: specific ranges of distance from the spindle (the vertical center of the stack of platters): e.g., from one inch to two inches, to make up an arbitrary example. Thus, a disk partition uses the same sized and located circular section on all the platters in the disk drive. In this way, disks are divided vertically, through the platters, not horizontally.

Partitions can be defined as part of adding a new disk. In some versions of Unix, default disk partitions are defined in advance by the operating system. These default definitions provide some amount of flexibility by defining more than one division scheme for the physical disk.

Figure 10-3 depicts a BSD-style partition scheme. Each drawing corresponds to a different disk layout: one way of dividing up the disk. The various cylinders graphically represent each partition's location on the disk. The solid black area at the center of each disk indicates the part of the disk that cannot be accessed, containing the bad block list and other disk data.

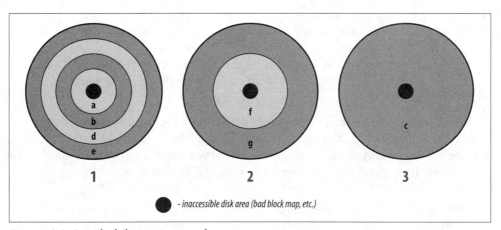

Figure 10-3. Sample disk partitioning scheme

---

[*] Also, the disk tracks are concentric, not continuous, as they are on an LP. If you don't know what an LP is, think of it as a really wide CD (about 12" diameter) with data on both sides.

[†] I'm using this term in a descriptive sense only. Technically, a disk *cylinder* consists of the same set of tracks on all the platters that make up the disk (where a *track* is the portion of the platter surface that can be accessed from one of the discrete radial positions that the head can take as its moves along the radius).

Readers who prefer numeric to graphical representations can consider the numeric partitioning scheme in Table 10-4, which illustrates the same point.

Table 10-4. Sample disk partitioning scheme

Partition	Start	End
a	655360	671739
b	327680	655359
c	0	671739
d	163840	327679
e	0	163839
f	327680	671739
g	0	327679

Seven different partitions are defined for the disk, named by letters from *a* to *g*. Three drawings are needed to display all seven partitions because some of them are defined to occupy the same disk locations.

Traditionally, the *c* partition comprised the entire disk, including the forbidden area; this is why the *c* partition was never used under standard BSD. However, on most current systems using this sort of naming convention, you can use the *c* partition to build a filesystem that uses the entire disk. Check the documentation if you're unsure about the conventions on your system.

The other six defined partitions are *a*, *b*, and *d* through *g*. However, it is not possible to use them all at one time, because some of them include the same physical areas of the disk. Partitions *d* and *e* occupy the same space as partition *g* in the sample layout. Hence, a disk will use either partitions *d* and *e*, or partition *g*, but not both. Similarly, the *a* and *b* partitions use the same area of the disk as partition *f*, and partitions *f* and *g* use the same area as partition *c*.

This disk layout, then, offers three different ways of using the disk, divided into one, two, or four partitions, each of which may hold a filesystem or be used as a swap partition. Some disk partitioning schemes offer even more alternative layouts of the disk. Flexibility is designed in to meet the needs of different systems.

 This flexibility also has the following consequence: nothing prevents you from using a disk drive inconsistently. For example, nothing prevents you from mounting */dev/disk2d* and */dev/disk2g* from the same disk. However, this will have catastrophic consequences, because these two partitions overlap. Best practice is to modify partitions in a standard layout that you will not be using so that they have zero length (or delete them).

These days, the following partition naming conventions generally apply:

- The partition holding the root (or boot) filesystem is the first one on the disk and is named partition *a* or slice 0.
- The primary swap partition is normally partition *b*/slice 1.
- Partition *c* and slice 2 refer to the entire disk.

Adding Disks

In this section, we'll begin by examining the general process of adding a disk to a Unix system and then go on to consider the commands and procedures for the various operating systems. The following list outlines the steps needed to make a new disk accessible to users:

- The disk must be physically attached to the computer system. Consult the manufacturer's instructions and your own system's hardware documentation for the procedure.
- A suitable device driver for the disk's controller must be present in the operating system. If the new disk is being added to an existing controller, or you're also adding a new controller that is among those supported by the operating system, this is not a problem. Otherwise, you'll need to build a new kernel or load the appropriate kernel module (see Chapter 16).
- The disk must be low-level formatted.* These days, this is always done by the manufacturer.
- One or more partitions must be defined on the disk.
- The special files required to access the disk's partitions must exist or be created.
- A Unix filesystem must be created on each of the disk partitions to be used for user files.
- The new filesystem should be checked with fsck.
- The new filesystem should be entered into the filesystem configuration file.
- The filesystem can be mounted (perhaps after creating a new directory for its mount point).
- Any site-specific activities must be performed (such as configuring backups and installing disk quotas).

The processes used to handle these activities will be discussed in the sections that follow.

---

* What I'm referring to here is not what is meant when one "formats" a diskette or disk on a PC system. In general, microcomputer operating systems like Windows use the term *format* differently than Unix does. Formatting a disk on these systems is equivalent to making a filesystem under Unix (and most other operating systems). Unix disk formatting is equivalent to what Windows calls a *low-level format*. This step is almost never needed in either environment.

As usual, planning should precede implementation. Before performing any of these operations, the system administrator must decide how the disk will be used: which partitions will have filesystems created on them and what files (types of files) will be stored in them. The layout of your filesystems can influence your system's performance significantly. You should therefore take some care in planning the structure of your filesystem.

For best performance, heavily used filesystems should each have their own disk drive, and they should not share a disk with a swap partition. Preferably, heavily used filesystems should be located on drives attached to different controllers. This setup balances the load between disk drives and disk controllers. These issues are discussed in more detail in "Disk I/O Performance Issues" in Chapter 15. Coming up with the optimal layout may require consulting with other people: the database administrator, software developers, and so on.

We now turn to the mechanics of adding a new disk. We'll begin by considering aspects of the process that are common to all systems. The subsequent subsections discuss adding a new SCSI disk to each of the various Unix versions we are considering.

Finding a Hardware/Software Balance

Some system administrators love tinkering with hardware; the most hard-core of them consider reseating the CPU boards as the first response to any system glitch. At the other extreme are system administrators who can program their way out of any emergency but throw up their hands when they have to install a new disk drive.

A good system administrator will be able to hold her own in both the hardware and software arenas. Most of us tend to prefer one to the other, but we can all become proficient in both areas in the long run. The best way to improve your skills in whatever areas you feel least comfortable is to find a safe test system where you can learn, experiment, play, and make mistakes in private and without risk. In time, you may even find that you actually enjoy doing jobs that used to bore, disgust, or intimidate you.

Preparing and connecting the disk

There are two main types of disks in wide use today: IDE disks and SCSI disks. IDE* disks are low cost devices developed for the microcomputer market, and they are generally used on PC-based Unix systems. SCSI disks are generally used on (non-Intel) Unix workstations and servers from the major hardware vendors. IDE disks

---

* IDE expands to Integrated Drive Electronics. These disks are also known as ATA disks (AT Attachment). Current IDE disks are virtually always EIDE: extended IDE, a follow-on to the original standard. SCSI expands to Small Computer System Interface.

generally do not perform as well as SCSI disks (claims made by ATA-2 drive vendors notwithstanding).

IDE disks are easy to attach to the system, and the manufacturer's instructions are generally good. When you add a second disk drive to an IDE controller, you will usually need to perform some minor reconfiguration for both the existing and new disks. One disk must be designated as the master device and the other as the slave device; generally, the existing disk becomes the master and the new disk is the slave.

The master/slave setting for a disk is specified by means of a jumper on the disk drive itself, and it is almost always located on the same face of the disk as the bus and power connector sockets. Consult the documentation for the disk you are using to determine the jumper location and proper setting. Doing so on the new drive is easy because you can do it before you install the disk. Remember to check the existing drive's configuration as well, because single drives are often left unjumpered by the manufacturer. Note that the master/slave setting is not an operational definition; the two disks are treated equally by the operating system.

SCSI disks are in wide use in both PC-based systems and traditional Unix computers. When performance counts, use SCSI disks, because high-end SCSI subsystems are many times faster than the best EIDE-based ones. The SCSI subsystems are also more expensive than the best EIDE-based ones.

SCSI disks may be internal or external. These disks are designated by a number ranging from 0 to 6 known as their SCSI ID (the SCSI ID 7 is used by the controller itself). Normal SCSI adapters thus support up to seven devices, each of which must be assigned a unique SCSI ID; wide SCSI controllers support up to 15 devices (ID 7 is still used for the controller). SCSI IDs are generally set via jumpers on internal devices and via a thumbwheel or push button counter on external devices. Keep in mind that when you change the ID setting of a SCSI disk, the device must generally be power-cycled before the change will take effect.

On rare occasions, the ID display setting on an external SCSI disk will not match what is actually being set. When this happens, the counter is either attached incorrectly (backwards) or faulty (the SCSI ID does not change even though the counter does). When you are initially configuring a device, check the controller's power-on message to determine whether all devices are being recognized and to determine the actual SCSI ID assignments being used. Once again, these problems are rare, but I have seen two examples of the former and one example of the latter in my career.

SCSI disks come in many varieties; the current offerings are summarized in Table 10-5. You should be aware of the distinction between normal and *differential* SCSI devices. In the latter type, there are two physical wires for each signal within the bus, and such devices use the voltage difference between the two wires as the signal value. This design reduces noise on the bus and allows for longer total cable lengths. Special cables and terminators are needed for such SCSI devices (as well as adapter support), and you cannot mix differential and normal devices. Differential signaling has used two forms over the years, high voltage differential (HVD) and low voltage differential (LVD); the two forms cannot be mixed. The most recent standards employ the latter exclusively.

Table 10-5. SCSI versions

Version name	Single-ended	Bus width	Maximum total cable length Differential	Maximum speed
SCSI-1, SCSI-2	5 MB/s	8 bits	6 m	25 m (HVD)
Fast SCSI	10 MB/s	8 bits	3 m	25 m (HVD)
Fast Wide SCSI	20 MB/s	16 bits	3 m	25 m (HVD)
Ultra SCSI	20 MB/s	8 bits	1.5 m	25 m (HVD)
Wide Ultra SCSI	40 MB/s	16 bits	1.5 m	25 m (HVD)
Ultra2 SCSI	40 MB/s	8 bits	n/a	12 m (HVD), 25 m (LVD)
Wide Ultra-2 SCSI	80 MB/s	16 bits	n/a	12 m (HVD), 25 m (LVD)
Ultra3 SCSI (a.k.a. Ultra160 SCSI)	160 MB/s	16 bits	n/a	12 m (LVD)
Ultra320 SCSI	320 MB/s	16 bits	n/a	12 m (LVD)

Table 10-5 can also serve as a simple history of SCSI. It shows the progressively faster speeds these devices have been able to obtain. Speed-ups come from a combination of a faster bus speed and using more bits for the bus (the "wide" devices). The most recent SCSI standards are all 16 bits, and the term "wide" has been dropped from the name because there are no "narrow" devices from which they need to be distinguished.

 The maximum total cable length in the table refers to a chain consisting entirely of devices of that type. If you are using different (compatible) device types in the same chain, the maximum length is the minimum allowed for the various device types. Lowest common denominator wins in this case.

There are a variety of connectors that you will encounter on SCSI devices. These are the most common:

- DB-25 connectors are 25-pin connectors that resemble those on serial cables. They have 25 rounded pins positioned in two rows about 1/8" apart. For example, these connectors are used on external SCSI Zip drives.

- 50-pin Centronics connectors were once the most common sort of SCSI connector. The pins on the connector are attached to the top and bottom of a narrow flat plastic bar about 2" long, and the connector is secured to the device by wire clips on each end.

- 50-pin micro connectors (also known as mini-micro connectors or SCSI II connectors) are distinguished by their flat, very closely spaced pins, also placed in two rows. This connector is much narrower than the others at about 1.5" in width.
- 68-pin connectors (also known as SCSI III connectors) are a 68-pin version of micro connectors designed for wide SCSI devices.

Figure 10-4 illustrates these connector types (shown in the external versions).

Figure 10-4. SCSI connectors

From left to right, Figure 10-4 shows a Centronics connector, two versions of the 50-pin mini-micro connector, and a DB-25 connector. 68-pin connectors look very similar to these 50-pin mini-micro connectors; they are simply wider. Figure 10-5 depicts the pin numbering schemes for these connectors.

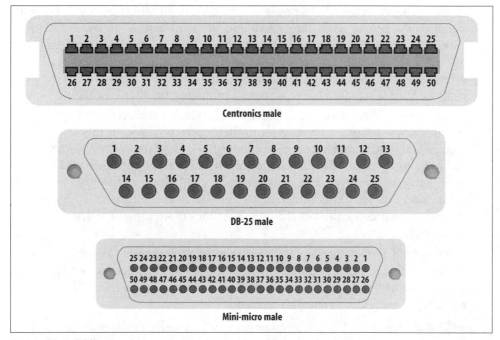

Figure 10-5. SCSI connector pinouts

You can purchase cables that use any combination of these connectors and adapters to convert between them.

The various SCSI devices on a system are connected in a daisy chain (i.e., serially, in a single line). The first and last devices in the SCSI chain must be terminated for proper operation. For example, when the SCSI chain is entirely external, the final device will have a terminator attached and the SCSI adapter itself will usually provide termination for the beginning of the chain (check its documentation to determine whether this feature must be enabled or not). Similarly, when the chain is composed of both internal and external devices, the first device on the internal portion of the SCSI bus will have termination enabled (for example, via a jumper on an internal disk), and the final external device will again have a terminator attached.

Termination consists of regulating the voltages across the various lines comprising the SCSI bus. Terminators prevent the signal reflection that would occur on an open end. There are several different types of SCSI terminators:

- *Passive* terminators are constructed from resistors. They attempt to ensure that the line voltages in the SCSI chain remain within their proper operating ranges. This type of termination is the least expensive, but it tends to work well only when there are just one or two devices in the SCSI chain and activity on the bus is minimal.

- *Active* terminators use voltage regulators and resistors to force the line voltages to their proper ranges. While passive terminators simply reduce the incoming signal to the proper level (thus remaining susceptible to all power fluctuations within it), active terminators use a voltage regulator to ensure a steady standard for use in producing the target voltages. Active terminators are only slightly more expensive than passive terminators, and they are always more reliable. In fact, the SCSI II standard calls for active termination for all SCSI chains.

- *Forced perfect termination (FPT)* uses a more complex and accurate voltage regulation scheme to force line voltages to their correct values. In this scheme, the voltage standard is taken from the output of two regulated voltages, and diodes are used to eliminate fluctuations within it. This results in increased stability over active termination. FPT will generally eliminate any flakiness in a SCSI chain, and you should consider it any time your chain consists of more than three devices (despite the fact that it is 2–3 times more expensive than active termination).

- Some hybrid terminators are also available. In such devices, key lines are controlled via forced perfect termination, and the remaining lines are regulated with active termination. Such devices tend to be almost as expensive as FPT terminators and so are seldom preferable to them.

A few SCSI devices have built-in terminators that you select or deselect via a switch. External boxes containing multiple SCSI disks also often include termination. Check the device characteristics for your devices to determine if such features are present.

Be aware that filesystems on SCSI disks are not guaranteed to survive a change of controller model (although they usually will); the standard does not specify that they must be interoperable. Thus, if you move a SCSI disk containing data from one system to another system with a different kind of SCSI controller, there's a chance you will not be able to access the existing data on the disk and will have to reformat it. Similarly, if you need to change the SCSI adapter in a computer, it is safest to replace it with another of the same model.

Having said this, I will note that I do move SCSI disks around fairly often, and I've only seen one failure of this kind. It's rare, but it does happen.

Once the disk is attached to the system, you are ready to configure it. The discussion that follows assumes that the new disk to be added is connected to the computer and is ready to accept partitions. These days, disks seldom if ever require low-level formatting, so we won't pay much attention to this process.

Before turning to the specific procedures for various operating systems, we'll look at the general issue of creating special files.

Making special files

Before filesystems can be created on a disk, the special files for the desired disk partitions must exist. Sometimes, they are already on the system when you go to look for them. On many systems, the boot process automatically creates the appropriate special files when it detects new hardware.

Otherwise, you'll have to create them yourself. Special files are created with the mknod command. mknod has the following syntax:

```
# mknod name | major minor
```

The first argument is the filename, and the second argument is the letter c or b, depending on whether you're making the character or block special file. The other two arguments are the major and minor device numbers for the device. These numbers serve to identify the proper device driver to the kernel. The major device number indicates the general device type (disk, serial line, etc.), and the minor device number indicates the specific member within that class.

These numbers are highly implementation-specific. To determine the numbers you need, use the ls -l command on some existing special files for disk partitions; the major and minor device numbers will appear in the size field. For example:

```
$ cd /dev/dsk; ls -l c1d*          Major, minor device numbers.
brw-------   1 rootroot0,144 Mar 13 19:14 c1d1s0
brw-------   1 rootroot0,145 Mar 13 19:14 c1d1s1
brw-------   1 rootroot0,146 Mar 13 19:14 c1d1s2
...
brw-------   1 rootroot0,150 Mar 13 19:14 c1d1s6
brw-------   1 rootroot0,151 Mar 13 19:14 c1d1s7
brw-------   1 rootroot0,160 Mar 13 19:14 c1d2s0
```

```
brw-------    1 rootroot0,161 Mar 13 19:14 c1d2s1
...
$ cd /dev/rdsk; ls -l c1d1*
crw-------    1 rootroot3,144 Mar 13 19:14 c1d1s0
crw-------    1 rootroot3,145 Mar 13 19:14 c1d1s1
...
```

In this example, the numbering pattern is pretty clear: block special files for disks on controller 1 have major device number 0; the corresponding character special files have major device number 3. The minor device number of the same partition of successive disks differs by 16. So if you want to make the special files for partition 2 on disk 3, its minor device number would be 162+16 = 178, and you'd use the following mknod commands:

```
# mknod /dev/dsk/c1d3s2  b 0 178
# mknod /dev/rdsk/c1d3s2 c 3 178
```

Except on Linux and FreeBSD systems, be sure to make both the block and character special files.

On many systems, the /dev directory includes a shell script named MAKEDEV which automates running mknod. It takes the base name of the new device as an argument and creates the character and block special files defined for it. For example, the following command creates the special files for a SCSI disk under Linux:

```
# cd /dev
# ./MAKEDEV sdb
```

The command creates the special files /dev/sdb0 through /dev/sdb16.

FreeBSD

The first step is to attach the disk to the system and then reboot.* FreeBSD should detect the new disk. You can check the boot messages or the output of the dmesg command to ensure that it has:

```
da1 at adv0 bus 0 target 2 lun 0
da1: <SEAGATE ST15150N 0017> Fixed Direct Access SCSI-2 device
da1: 10.000MB/s transfers (10.000MHz, offset 15), Tagged Queueing Enabled
da1: 4095MB (8388315 512 byte sectors: 255H 63S/T 522C)
```

 On Intel-based systems, disk ordering happens at boot time, so adding a new SCSI disk with a lower SCSI ID than an existing disk will cause special files to be reassigned† and probably break your /etc/fstab setup. Try to assign SCSI IDs in order if you anticipate adding additional devices later.

---

* If the system has hot swappable SCSI disks, you can use the cancontrol rescan *bus* command to detect them without rebooting.

† This can happen at other times as well. For example, changes to fiber channel configurations such as switch reconfigurations might lead to unexpected device reassignments, because the operating system gets information on hardware addressing from the programmable switch.

FreeBSD disk partitioning is a bit more complex than for the other operating systems we are considering. It is a two-part process. First, the disk is divided into physical partitions, which BSD calls *slices*. One or more of these is assigned to FreeBSD. The FreeBSD slice is then itself subdivided into partitions. The latter are where filesystems actually get built.

The fdisk utility is used to divide a disk into slices. Here we create a single slice comprising the entire disk:

```
# fdisk -i /dev/da1
******* Working on device /dev/da1 *******
...
Information from DOS bootblock is:
The data for partition 1 is:
<UNUSED>
Do you want to change it? [n] y
Supply a decimal value for "sysid (165=FreeBSD)" [0] 165
Supply a decimal value for "start" [0]
Supply a decimal value for "size" [0] 19152
Explicitly specify beg/end address ? [n] n
sysid 165,(FreeBSD/NetBSD/386BSD)
    start 0, size 19152 (9 Meg), flag 0
        beg: cyl 0/ head 0/ sector 1;
        end: cyl 18/ head 15/ sector 63
Are we happy with this entry? [n] y
The data for partition 2 is:
<UNUSED>
Do you want to change it? [n] n
...
Do you want to change the active partition? [n] n
Should we write new partition table? [n] y
```

 Unless you want to create multiple slices, this step is required only on the boot disk on an Intel-based system. However, if you're using a slice other than the first one, you'll need to create the special files to access it:

```
# cd /dev; ./MAKEDEV /dev/da1s2a
```

The disklabel command creates FreeBSD partitions within the FreeBSD slice:

```
# disklabel -r -w da1 auto
```

The auto parameter says to create a default layout for the slice. You can preview what disklabel will do by adding the -n option.

Once you have created a default label (division), you can edit it by running disklabel -e. This command starts a editor session from which you can modify the partitioning (using the editor specified in the *EDITOR* environment variable).

disklabel is a very cranky utility, and often fails with the message:

```
disklabel: No space left on device
```

The message is completely spurious. This happens more often with larger disks than with smaller ones. If you encounter this problem, try running sysinstall, and select the Configure→Label menu path. This form of the utility can usually be coaxed to work, but even it will not accept all valid partition sizes. Caveat emptor.

Once you have made partitions, you create filesystems using the newfs command, as in this example:

```
# newfs /dev/da1a
/dev/da1a: 19152 sectors in 5 cylinders of 1 tracks, 4096 sectors
  9.4MB in 1 cyl groups (106 c/g, 212.00MB/g, 1280 i/g)
super-block backups (for fsck -b #) at:
 32
```

The following options can be used to customize the newfs operation:

-U Enable soft updates (recommended).

-b *size*
> Filesystem block size in bytes (the default is 16384; value must be a power of 2).

-f *size*
> Filesystem fragment size: the smallest allocatable unit of disk space. The default is 2048 bytes. This parameter determines the minimum file size, among other things. It must be a power of 2 less than or equal to the filesystem block size and no smaller than one eighth of the filesystem block size. Experts recommend always making this value one eighth of the filesystem block size.

-i *bytes*
> Number of bytes per inode (the default is 4 times the fragment size: 8192 with the default fragment size). This setting controls how many inodes are created for the new filesystem (number of inodes equals filesystem size divided by byte per inode). The default value generally works well.

-m *free*
> Percentage of free space reserved. The default is 8%; you can usually safely decrease it to about 5% or even less for a very large disk.

-o speed | space
> Set the optimization preference. speed means that the filesystem will attempt to minimize the time spent allocating disk blocks, while space means that it will try to minimize disk fragmentation. The default is space if the minimum free space percentage is less than 8%, and speed otherwise. Hence, speed is the default with the default free space percentage.

The tunefs command can be used to modify the values of -m and -o for an existing filesystem (using the same option letters). Similarly, -n can be used to enable/disable soft updates for an existing filesystem (it takes enable or disable as its argument).

Finally, we run fsck on the new filesystem:

```
# fsck /dev/da1a
** /dev/da1a
** Last Mounted on
** Phase 1 - Check Blocks and Sizes
** Phase 2 - Check Pathnames
** Phase 3 - Check Connectivity
** Phase 4 - Check Reference Counts
** Phase 5 - Check Cyl groups
1 files, 1 used, 4682 free (18 frags, 583 blocks, 0.4% fragmentation)
```

In this instance, fsck finishes very quickly.

 If you use the menu-driven version of disklabel in the sysinstall utility, the newfs and mount commands can be run for you automatically (and the utility does so by default).

The growfs command can be used to increase the size of an existing filesystem, as in this example:

```
# growfs /dev/da1a
```

By default, the filesystem is increased to the size of the underlying partition. You can specify a specific new size with the -s option if you want to.

Linux

After attaching the disk to the system, it should be detected when the system is booted. You can use the dmesg command to display boot messages. Here are some sample messages from a very old, but still working, Intel-based Linux system:

```
scsi0 : at 0x0388 irq 10 options CAN_QUEUE=32 CMD_PER_LUN=2 ...
scsi0 : Pro Audio Spectrum-16 SCSI
scsi : 1 host.
Detected scsi disk sda at scsi0, id 2, lun 0
scsi : detected 1 SCSI disk total.
```

The messages indicate that this disk is designated as *sda*.

 On Intel-based systems, disk ordering happens at boot time, so adding a new SCSI disk with a lower SCSI ID than an existing disk will cause special files to be reassigned* and probably break your */etc/fstab* setup. Try to assign SCSI IDs in order if you anticipate adding additional devices later.

---

* This can happen at other times as well. For example, changes to fiber channel configurations such as switch reconfigurations might lead to unexpected device reassignments because the operating system gets information on hardware addressing from the programmable switch.

If necessary, create the device special files for the disk (needed only when you have many, many disks). For example, these commands create the special files used to access the sixteenth SCSI disk:

```
# cd /dev; ./MAKEDEV sdp
```

Assuming we have our special files all in order, we will use fdisk or cfdisk (a screen-oriented version) to divide the disk into partitions (we'll be creating two partitions). The following commands will start these utilities:

```
# fdisk /dev/sda
# cfdisk /dev/sda
```

The available subcommands for these utilities are listed in Table 10-6.

Table 10-6. Linux partitioning utility subcommands

Action	fdisk	cfdisk
Create new partition.	N	N
Change partition type.	T	T
Make partition active (bootable).	A	B
Write partition table to disk.	W	W
Change display/entry size units.	U	U
Display partition table.	P	Always visible
List available subcommands.	m	At dialog bottom

cfdisk is often more convenient to use because the partition table is displayed continuously, and we'll use it here. cfdisk subcommands always operate on the current (highlighted) partition. Thus, in order to create a new partition, move the highlight to the line corresponding to Free Space and press n.

You first need to select either a primary or a logical (extended) partition. PC disk partitions are of two types: *primary* and *extended*. A disk may contain up to four partitions. Both partition types are a physical subset of the total disk. Extended partitions may be further subdivided into units known as *logical* partitions (or drives) and thereby provide a means for dividing a physical disk into more than four pieces.

Next, cfdisk prompts for the partition information:

```
Primary or logical [pl]: p
Size (in MB): 110
```

If you'd rather enter the size in a different set of units, use the u subcommand (units cycle among MB, sectors, and cylinders). Once these prompts are answered, you will be asked if you want the partition placed at the beginning or the end of the free space (if there is a choice).

Use the same procedure to create a second partition, and then activate the first partition with the b subcommand. Then, use the t subcommand to change the partition types of the two partitions. The most commonly needed type codes are 6 for Windows FAT16, 82 for a Linux swap partition, and 83 for a regular Linux partition.

Here is the final partition table (output has been simplified):

```
                           cfdisk 2.11i

                      Disk Drive: /dev/hde
                      Size: 3228696576 bytes
          Heads: 128    Sectors per Track: 63    Cylinders: 782

      Name        Flags       Part Type     FS Type       Size (MB)
      --------------------------------------------------------------
      /dev/sda1   Boot        Primary       Linux           110.0
      /dev/sda2               Primary       Linux            52.5
                              Pri/Log       Free Space        0.5
```

(Yes, those sizes are small; I told you it was an old system.)

At this point, I reboot the system. In general, when I've changed the partition layout of the disk—in other words, done anything other than change the types assigned to the various partitions—I always reboot PC-based systems. Friends and colleagues accuse me of being mired in an obsolete Windows superstition by doing so and argue that this is not really necessary. However, many Linux utility writers (see fdisk) and filesystem designers (see mkreiserfs) agree with me.

Next, use the mkfs command to create a filesystem on the Linux partition. mkfs has been streamlined in the Linux version and requires little input:

```
# mkfs -t ext3 -j /dev/sda1
```

This command[*] creates a journaled ext3 filesystem, the current default filesystem type for many Linux distributions. The ext3 filesystem is a journaled version of the ext2 filesystem, which was used on Linux systems for several years and is still in wide use. In fact, ext3 filesystems are backward-compatible and can be mounted in ext2 mode.

If you want to customize mkfs's operation, the following options can be used:

-b *bytes*

Set filesystem block size in bytes (the default is 1024).

-c

Check the disk partition for bad blocks before making the filesystem.

-i *n*

Specify bytes/inode value: create one inode for each *n* bytes. The default value of 4096 usually creates more than you'll ever need, but probably isn't worth changing.

---

[*] Actually, the fsck, mkfs, mount, and other commands are front ends to filesystem-specific versions. In this case, mkfs runs mke2fs.

-m *percent*

Specify the percentage of filesystem space to reserve (accessible only by *root* and group 0). The default is 5% (half of what is typical on other Unix systems). In these days of multigigabyte disks, even this percentage may be worth rethinking.

-J *device*

Specify a separate device for the filesystem log.

Once the filesystem is built, run fsck:

```
# fsck -f -y /dev/sda1
```

The -f option is necessary to force fsck to run even though the filesystem is clean. The new filesystem may now be mounted and entered into */etc/fstab*.

The tune2fs command may be used to list and alter fields within the superblock of an ext2 filesystem. Here is an example of its display output (shortened):

```
# tune2fs -l /dev/sdb1
Filesystem magic number:  0xEF53
Filesystem revision #:    1 (dynamic)
Filesystem features:      filetype sparse_super
Filesystem state:         not clean
Errors behavior:          Continue
Filesystem OS type:       Linux
Inode count:              253952
Block count:              507016
Reserved block count:     25350
Free blocks:              30043
Free inodes:              89915
First block:              0
Block size:               4096
Last mount time:          Thu Apr  4 11:28:19 2002
Last write time:          Wed May 22 10:00:36 2002
Mount count:              1
Maximum mount count:      20
Last checked:             Thu Apr  4 11:28:01 2002
Check interval:           15552000 (6 months)
Next check after:         Tue Oct  1 12:28:01 2002
Reserved blocks uid:      0 (user root)
Reserved blocks gid:      0 (group root)
```

The check-related items in the list indicate when fsck will check the filesystem even if it is clean (they appear fifth to third from last). The Linux version of fsck for ext3 filesystems checks the filesystem if either the maximum number of mounts without a check has been exceeded or the maximum time interval between checks has expired (20 times and 6 months in the preceding output; the check interval is given in seconds).

tune2fs's -i option may be used to specify the maximum time interval between checks in days, and the -c option may be used to specify the maximum number of mounts between checks. For example, the following command disables the time-between-checks function and sets the maximum number of mounts to 25:

```
# tune2fs -i 0 -c 25 /dev/sdb1
Setting maximal mount count to 25
Setting interval between check 0 seconds
```

Another useful option to tune2fs is -m, which allows you to change the percentage of filesystem space held in reserve. The -u and -g options allow you to specify the user and group ID (respectively) allowed to access the reserved space.

You can convert an ext2 filesystem to ext3 with a command like this one:

```
# tune2fs -j /dev/sdb2
```

Existing ext2 and ext3 filesystems can be resized using the resize2fs command, which takes the filesystem and new size (in 512-byte blocks) as parameters. For example, the following commands will change the size of the specified filesystem to 200,000 blocks:

```
# umount /dev/sdc1
# e2fsck -f /dev/sdc1
e2fsck 1.23, 15-Aug-2001 for EXT2 FS 0.5b, 95/08/09
Pass 1: Checking inodes, blocks, and sizes
Pass 2: Checking directory structure
Pass 3: Checking directory connectivity
Pass 4: Checking reference counts
Pass 5: Checking group summary information
/1: 11/247296 files (0.0% non-contiguous), 15979/493998 blocks
# resize2fs -p /dev/sdc1 200000
resize2fs 1.23 (15-Aug-2001)
Begin pass 1 (max = 1)
Extending the inode table     XXXXXXXXXXXXXXXXXXXXXXXXXXXXXXXXXXXXXXXX
Begin pass 3 (max = 10)
Scanning inode table          XXXXXXXXXXXXXXXXXXXXXXXXXXXXXXXXXXXXXXXX
The filesystem on /dev/sdc1 is now 200000 blocks long.
```

The -p option says to display a progress bar as the operation runs. Naturally, the size of the underlying disk partition or logical volume (discussed later in this chapter) will need to be increased beforehand.

Increasing the size of a filesystem is always safe. If you want the new size to be the same as the size of the underlying disk partition—as is virtually always the case—you can omit the size parameters from the resize2fs command. To decrease the size of a filesystem, perform the resize2fs operation first, and then use fdisk or cfdisk to decrease the size of the underlying partition. Note that data loss is always possible, even likely, when decreasing the size of a filesystem, because no effort is made to migrate data within the filesystem prior to shortening it.

The Reiser filesystem. Some Linux distributions also offer the Reiser filesystem, designed by Hans Reiser (see *http://www.reiserfs.org*).[*] The commands to create a Reiser filesystem are very similar:

```
# mkreiserfs /dev/sdb3
<-------------mkreiserfs, 2001------------->
reiserfsprogs 3.x.0k-pre9
mkreiserfs: Guessing about desired format..
mkreiserfs: Kernel 2.4.10-4GB is running.
13107k will be used
Block 16 (0x2142) contains super block of format 3.5 with standard journal
Block count: 76860
Bitmap number: 3
Blocksize: 4096
Free blocks: 68646
Root block: 8211
Tree height: 2
Hash function used to sort names: "r5"
Objectid map size 2, max 1004
Journal parameters:
        Device [0x0]
        Magic [0x18bbe6ba]
        Size 8193 (including journal header) (first block 18)
        Max transaction length 1024
        Max batch size 900
        Max commit age 30
Space reserved by journal: 0
Correctness checked after mount 1
Fsck field 0x0
ATTENTION: YOU SHOULD REBOOT AFTER FDISK!
        ALL DATA WILL BE LOST ON '/dev/hdf2'!
Continue (y/n):y
Initializing journal - 0%....20%....40%....60%....80%....100%
Syncing..ok
ReiserFS core development sponsored by SuSE Labs (suse.com)
Journaling sponsored by MP3.com.
To learn about the programmers and ReiserFS, please go to
http://namesys.com
Have fun.
# reiserfsck -x /dev/sdb3
<-------------reiserfsck, 2001------------->
reiserfsprogs 3.x.0k-pre9
Will read-only check consistency of the filesystem on /dev/hdf2
        Will fix what can be fixed w/o --rebuild-tree
Will put log info to 'stdout'
Do you want to run this program?[N/Yes] (note need to type Yes):Yes
13107k will be used
##########
reiserfsck --check started at Wed May 22 11:36:07 2002
##########
```

---

[*] The name is pronounced like the word riser (as in stairs) and rhymes with sizer and miser.

```
Replaying journal..
No transactions found
Checking S+tree..ok
Comparing bitmaps..ok
Checking Semantic tree...ok
No corruptions found
There are on the filesystem:
        Leaves 1
        Internal nodes 0
        Directories 1
        Other files 0
        Data block pointers 0 (zero of them 0)
###########
reiserfsck finished at Wed May 22 11:36:19 2002
###########
```

Reiser filesystems may be resized with the resize_reiserfs -s command. They can also be resized when they are mounted. The latter operation uses a command like the following:

```
# mount -o remount,resize=200000 /dev/sdc1
```

This command changes the size of the specified filesystem to 200,000 blocks. Once again, increasing the size of a filesystem is always safe, while decreasing it requires great care to avoid data loss.

Solaris

In this section, we add a SCSI disk (SCSI ID 2) to a Solaris system.

After attaching the device, boot the system with boot -r, which tells the operating system to look for new devices and create the associated special files and links into the */devices* tree.[*] The new disk should be detected when the system is booted (output simplified):

```
sd2 at esp0: target 2 lun 0
   corrupt label - wrong magic number
   Vendor 'QUANTUM', product 'CTS160S', 333936 512 byte blocks
```

The warning message about a corrupt label comes because no valid Sun label (a vendor-specific disk header block that Sun uses) has been written to the disk yet. If you miss the messages during the boot, use the dmesg command.

We now label the disk and then create partitions on it (which Solaris sometimes calls *slices*). Solaris uses the format utility for these tasks.[†] Previously, it was often necessary to tell format about the characteristics of your disk. These days, however, the utility knows about most kinds of disks, which makes adding a new disk much simpler.

---

[*] You should verify that these steps are done correctly after the boot. If not, you can create the */devices* entries and links in */dev* by running the drvconfig and disks commands. Neither requires any arguments.

[†] Solaris also contains a version of the fdisk utility designed for operating system installations. This is not what you should use to prepare a new disk.

Here is the command used to start format and write a generic label to the disk (if it is unlabeled):

```
# format /dev/rdsk/c0t2d0s2              Partition 2 = the entire disk.
selecting /dev/rdsk/c0t2d0s2
[disk formatted, no defect list found]

FORMAT MENU:
...Menu is printed here.
format> label                            Write generic disk label.
Ready to label disk, continue? y
```

Once the disk label is written, we can set up partitions. We'll be dividing this disk into two equal partitions. We use the partition subcommand to define them:

```
format> partition
PARTITION MENU:
        0       - change `0' partition
        1       - change `1' partition
        ...
        7       - change `7' partition
        select - select a predefined table
        modify - modify a predefined partition table
        name   - name the current table
        print  - display the current table
        label  - write partition map and label to the disk
        quit
partition>                               Redefine partition 0
Enter partition id tag[unassigned]: root  Specifies partition use.
Enter partition permission flags[wm]: wm  Read-write, mountable.
Enter new starting cyl[0]:
Enter partition size[0b, 0c, 0e, 0.00mb, 0.00gb]: 5.00gb
...
partition> 1
Enter partition id tag[unassigned]:
Enter partition permission flags[wm]: wm
Enter new starting cyl[0]: 10403
Enter partition size[0b, 0c, 0e, 0.00mb, 0.00gb]: 7257c
...
partition> print                         Print partition table.
Current partition table (unnamed):
Total disk cylinders available: 17660 + 2 (reserved cylinders)
```

Part	Tag	Flag	Cylinders	Size	Blocks	
0	root	wm	0 - 10402	5.00GB	(10403/0/0)	10486224
1	unassigned	wm	10403 - 17659	3.49GB	(7257/0/0)	7315056
2	unassigned	wm	0	0	(0/0/0)	0
...						
7	unassigned	wm	0	0	(0/0/0)	0

We define two partitions here, 0 and 1. In the first case, we specify a starting cylinder number of 0 and the partition size in GB. In the second case, we specify a starting cylinder and the length in cylinders. We took a look at the partition table between issuing these two commands to find these numbers.

The partition ID tag is a label specifying the intended use of the partition. Partition 0 will be used for the root filesystem and is labeled accordingly.

The permission flags are usually one of wm (read-write and mountable) and wu (read-write and not mountable). The latter is used for swap partitions.

Once the partitions are defined, we write a label to the disk using the label subcommand:

```
partition> label
Ready to label disk, continue? y
partition> quit
format> quit
```

The partition submenu also has a name subcommand, which allows a custom partition table to be named and saved; it can be applied to a new disk with the select subcommand on the same menu.

Now, we create filesystems on the new disk partitions with the newfs command:

```
# newfs /dev/rdsk/c0t2d0s0
newfs: construct a new file system /dev/rdsk/c0t2d0s3: (y/n)? y
/dev/rdsk/c0t0d0s3: 10486224 sectors in 10403 cylinders
                    of 16 tracks, 63 sectors
5120.2MB in 119 cyl groups (88 c/g, 43.31MB/g, 5504 i/g)
super-block backups (for fsck -F ufs -o b=#) at:
 32, 88800, 177568, 266336, 355104, 443872, 532640, 621408, 710176, ...
```

The prudent course of action is to print out this list and store it somewhere for safe keeping, in case both the primary superblock and the one at address 32 get corrupted.*

Finally, we run fsck on the new filesystem:

```
# fsck -y /dev/rdsk/c0t2d0s0
** /dev/rdsk/c0t0d0s3
** Last Mounted on
** Phase 1 - Check Blocks and Sizes
** Phase 2 - Check Pathnames
** Phase 3 - Check Connectivity
** Phase 4 - Check Reference Counts
** Phase 5 - Check Cyl groups
2 files, 9 used, 5159309 free (13 frags, 644912 blocks,  0.0% fragmentation)
```

This process is repeated for the other disk partition.

You can customize the parameters for the new filesystem using these options to newfs:

-b size

Filesystem block size in bytes (the default is 8192; value must be a power of 2 from 4096 to 8192).

---

* A tip from one of the book's technical reviewers: "If you lose your list of backup superblocks, make a filesystem on a device of the same size and read the locations of the superblocks when you newfs that new partition."

-f *size*

    Filesystem fragment size: the smallest allocateable unit of disk space. The default is 1024 bytes (must be a power of 2 in the range of 1024 to 8192). This parameter determines the minimum file size, among other things. It must be less than or equal to the filesystem block size and no smaller than one eighth the filesystem block size.

-i *bytes*

    Number of bytes per inode (the default is 2048). This setting controls how many inodes are created for the new filesystem (number of inodes equals filesystem size divided by bytes per inode). The default value of 2048 usually creates more than you'll ever need except for filesystems with many, many tiny files. You can usually increase this to 4098 without risk.

-m *free*

    Percentage of free space reserved. The default is 10%; you can usually safely decrease it to about 5% or even less for a very large disk.

The -N option to newfs may be used to have the command display all of the parameters it would pass to mkfs—the utility that does the actual work—without building the filesystem.

 Logging is enabled for Solaris UFS filesystems at mount time, via the logging mount option.

AIX, HP-UX, and Tru64

These operating systems use a logical volume manager (LVM) by default. Adding disks to these systems is considered during the LVM discussion later in this chapter.

Remaking an existing filesystem

Occasionally, it may be necessary to reconfigure a disk. For example, you might want to select another layout, using a different set of partitions. You might want to change the value of a filesystem parameter, such as its block size. Or you might want to add an additional swap partition or get rid of an unneeded one. Sometimes, these operations require that you recreate the existing filesystems.

Recreating a filesystem will destroy all the existing data in the filesystem, so it is essential to perform a full backup first (and to verify that the tapes are readable; see Chapter 11). For example, the following commands may be used to reconfigure a filesystem with a 4K block size under Linux:

```
# umount /chem                    Dismount filesystem.
# dump 0 /dev/sda1                 Backup.
# restore -t                       Check tape is OK!
# mke2fs -b 4096 -j /dev/sda1      Remake filesystem.
```

```
# mount /chem                          Mount new filesystem.
# cd /chem; restore -r                 Restore files.
```

A very cautious administrator would make two copies of the backup tape.

Logical Volume Managers

This section looks at *logical volume managers* (LVMs). The LVM is the only disk management facility under AIX, and the corresponding facilities are also used by default under HP-UX and Tru64. Linux and Solaris 9 also offer LVM facilities. As usual, we'll begin this section with a conceptual overview of logical volume managers and then move on to the specifics for the various operating systems.

When dealing with an LVM, you will do well to forget everything you know about disk partitions under Unix. Not only is a completely different vocabulary employed, but some Unix terms—like partition—also are used with completely different meanings. However, once you get past the initial obstacles, the LVM point of view is very clear and sensible, and it is superior to the standard Unix approach to handling disks. A willing suspension of disbelief will come in very handy at first.

In general, an LVM brings the following benefits:

• Filesystems and individual files can be larger than a single physical disk.

• Filesystems may be dynamically extended in size without having to be rebuilt.

• Software disk mirroring and RAID are often supported (for data protection and continued system availability even in the face of disk failures).

• Software disk striping is often provided as part of an LVM for improved I/O performance.

Disks, volume groups, and logical volumes

To begin at the beginning, there are *disks*: real, material, solid objects that hurt your toe if they fall on it. However, such disks must be initialized and made into *physical volumes* before they may be used by the LVM. When they are made part of a volume group (defined in a moment), these disks are divided into allocable units of space known as *physical partitions* (AIX) or *physical extents* (HP-UX and Tru64). The default size for these units is generally 4 MB. Note that these partitions/extents are units of disk storage only; they have nothing to do with traditional Unix disk partitions.

A *volume group* is a named collection of disks. Volume groups can also include collections of disks accessed as a single hardware unit (e.g., a RAID array). Volume groups allow filesystems to span physical disks (although it is not required that they do so). Paradoxically, the volume group is the LVM equivalent of the Unix physical disk: that entity which can be split into subunits called *logical volumes*, each of which holds a single filesystem. Unlike Unix disk partitions, volume groups are infinitely flexible in how they may be divided into filesystems.

HP-UX allows volume groups to be subdivided into sets of disks called *physical volume groups* (PVGs). These groups of disks are accessed through separate controllers and/or buses, and the facility is designed to support high-availability systems by reducing the number of potential single points of hardware failure.

Logical volumes are the entities on which filesystems reside; they may also be used as swap devices, as dump devices, for storing boot programs, and by application programs in raw mode (analogously to a raw-mode disk partition). They consist of some number of fixed physical partitions (disk chunks) generally located arbitrarily within a volume group (although some implementations optionally allow specific physical volumes to be requested when a logical volume is created or extended). Hence, logical volumes may be any size that is a multiple of the physical partition size for their volume group. They may be easily increased in size after creation while the operating system is running. Logical volumes may also be shrunk (although not without consequences to any filesystem they may contain).

Logical volumes are composed of *logical partitions* (AIX) or *logical extents* (HP-UX). Many times, physical and logical partitions are identical (or at least map one-to-one). However, logical volumes have the capability of storing redundant copies of all data, if desired; from one to two additional copies of each data block may be stored. When only a single copy of the data is stored, one logical partition corresponds to one physical partition. If two copies are stored, one logical partition corresponds to two physical partitions: one original and one mirror. Similarly, in a doubly mirrored logical volume, each logical partition corresponds to three physical partitions.

The main LVM data storage entities are illustrated in Figure 10-6 (representing an AIX system). The figure shows how three physical disks are combined into a single volume group (named *chemvg*). The separate disks composing it are suggested via shading.

Three user logical volumes are then defined from *chemvg*.* Two of them—*chome* and *cdata*—store a single copy of their data using physical partitions from three separate disks. *cdata* is a striped logical volume, writing data to all three disks in parallel. It uses identically sized sections from each physical disk. *chome* illustrates the way that a filesystem can be spread across multiple physical disks, even noncontiguously in the case of *hdisk3*.

The other logical volume, *qsar*, is a mirrored logical volume. It contains an equal number of physical partitions from all three disks; it stores three copies of its data (each on a separate disk), and one physical partition per disk is used for each of its logical partitions.

Once a logical volume exists, you can build a filesystem on it and mount it normally. At any point in its lifetime, a filesystem's size may be increased as long as there are

---

* In addition to the logging volume group required by AIX for the jfs journaled filesystem type.

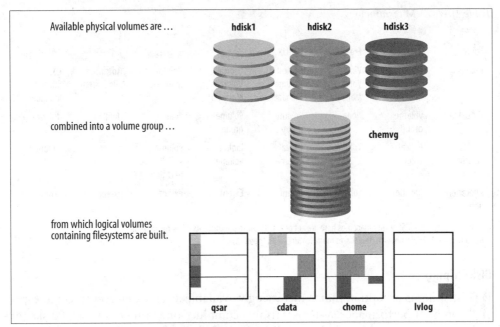

Available physical volumes are ...   hdisk1   hdisk2   hdisk3

combined into a volume group ...   chemvg

from which logical volumes
containing filesystems are built.

qsar   cdata   chome   lvlog

Figure 10-6. Logical volume managers illustrated

free physical partitions within its volume group. There need not initially be any free logical partitions within its logical volume. Generally, both the logical volume and filesystem are resized using a single command.

Some operating systems can also reduce the size of an existing logical volume. If this operation is performed on a mounted filesystem, and the new size of the logical volume is still at least a little larger than the existing filesystem, it can be accomplished without losing any data. Under any other conditions, data loss is very, very likely indeed. This technique is not for the fainthearted.

Currently, there is no easy way to decrease the size of a filesystem under AIX or FreeBSD, even if there is unused space within the filesystem. If you want to make a filesystem smaller, you need to back up the current files (and verify that the tape is readable!), delete the filesystem and its logical volume, create a new, smaller logical volume and filesystem, and then restore the files. The freed logical partitions can then be allocated as desired within their volume group; they can be added to an existing logical volume, used to make a new logical volume and filesystem, used in a new or existing paging space, or held in reserve.

Table 10-7 lists the LVM-related terminology used by the various Unix operating systems.

Table 10-7. LVM terminology

Item	AIX	FreeBSD[a]	HP-UX	Linux	Solaris	Tru64 AdvFS[b]	Tru64 LSM
Facility	Logical Volume Manager	Vinum Volume Manager	Logical Volume Manager	Logical Volume Manager	Volume Manager	Advanced File System	Logical Storage Manager
Virtual disk	volume group	None	volume group	volume group	volume	domain	disk group
Logical volume	logical volume	Volume	logical volume	logical volume	volume, soft partition	fileset	volume
Allocation unit	partition	Subdisk	extent	Extent	extent	extent	extent

[a] As we'll see, the FreeBSD entity mappings here are not precise because the concepts are somewhat different.
[b] Not a true LVM, AdvFS nevertheless shares many features with them.

Disk striping

Disk striping is an option that is increasingly available as an extension to Unix, especially on high-performance systems. Striping combines one or more physical disks (or disk partitions) into a single logical disk, viewed like any other filesystem device by the rest of Unix. Disk striping is used to increase I/O performance at least as often as it is used to create very large filesystems spanning more than one physical disk. Striped disks split I/O operations across the physical disks in the stripe, performing them in parallel, and are thus able to achieve significant performance improvements over a single disk (although not always the nearly linear speedups that are sometimes claimed). Striping is especially effective for single-process transfer rates to a very large file and for processes performing a large number of I/O operations. Disk striping performance is discussed in detail in "Disk I/O Performance Issues" in Chapter 15.

Special-purpose striped-disk devices are available from many vendors. In addition, many Unix systems offer software disk-striping. They provide utilities for configuring physical disks into a striped device, and the striping itself is done by the operating system, at the cost of some additional overhead.

The following general considerations apply to software striped-disk configurations:

- For maximum performance, the individual disks in the striped filesystem should be on separate disk controllers. However, it is permissible to place different disks on a given controller into separate stripe sets.

- Some operating systems require that the individual disks be identical devices: the same size, the same partition layout, and often the same brand. If the layouts are different, the size of the smallest disk is often what is used for the filesystem and any additional space on the other disks will be unusable and wasted.

- In general, disks used for striping should not be used for any purpose other than the I/O whose performance you want to optimize. Placing ordinary user files on striped disks seldom makes sense. Similarly, striping swap space makes sense only if paging performance is the most significant disk I/O performance factor on the system.

- In no case should the device containing the root filesystem be used for disk striping. This is really a corollary of the previous item.

- The stripe size selected for a striped filesystem is important. The optimal value depends on the typical data transfer characteristics and requirements for the application programs for which the filesystem is intended. Some experimentation with different stripe sizes will probably be necessary. Provided that processes using the striped filesystem perform large enough I/O operations, a larger stripe size will generally result in better I/O performance. However, the tradeoff is that larger stripe sizes mean a larger filesystem block size and, accordingly, less efficient allocation of available disk space.

- Software disk striping is really designed for two to four disks. In most cases, any additional performance gains are generally quite modest.

- SCSI disks make the most sense when you're using software striping for performance.

Software disk-striping is generally accomplished via the LVM or similar facility.

Disk mirroring and RAID

Another approach to combining multiple disks into a single logical device is RAID (or *Redundant Array of Inexpensive* Disks). In general, RAID devices are designed for increased data integrity and availability (via redundant copies), not for improved performance (RAID 0 is an exception).

There are at least 6 defined RAID levels that differ in how the multiple disks within the unit are organized. Most available hardware RAID devices support some combination of the following levels (level 2 is not used in practice). Table 10-8 summarizes the available RAID levels.

Table 10-8. Commonly used RAID levels

Level	Description	Advantages/Disadvantages
0	Disk striping only.	+ Best I/O performance for large transfers.
		+ Largest storage capacity.
		− No data redundancy.
1	Disk mirroring: every disk drive is duplicated for 100% data redundancy.	+ Most complete data redundancy.
		+ Good performance on small transfers.
		− Largest disk requirements for fault tolerance.

* Some acronym expansions put "Independent" here.

Table 10-8. Commonly used RAID levels (continued)

Level	Description	Advantages/Disadvantages
3	Disk striping with a parity disk; data is split across component disks on a byte-to-byte basis; the parity disk enables reconstruction of all data if a drive fails.	+ Data redundancy with minimal overhead. + Decent I/O performance for reads. − Parity disk is a bottleneck for writes. − Significant operating system overhead.
4	Disk striping with a parity disk; data is split across component disks on a per-block basis; the parity disk enables reconstruction of all data if a drive fails.	+ Data redundancy with minimal overhead. + Better than level 3 for large sequential writes. − Parity disk is a bottleneck for small writes. − Significant operating system overhead.
5	Same as level 3 except that the parity information is split across multiple component disks, in an attempt to prevent the parity disk from becoming an I/O bottleneck.	+ Data redundancy with minimal overhead. + Best performance for writes. − Not as fast as level 3 or 4 for reads. − Significant operating system overhead.

Figure 10-7 illustrates RAID 5 in action, using 5 disks.

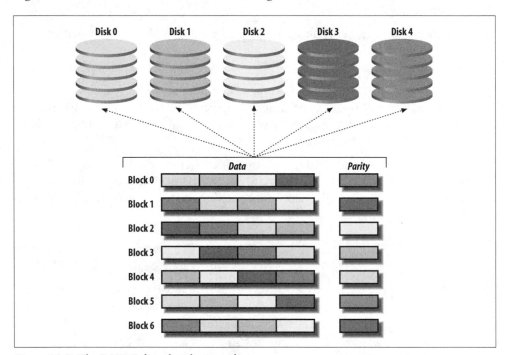

Figure 10-7. The RAID 5 data distribution scheme

There are also some hybrid RAID levels:

- RAID 0+1: Mirroring of striped disks. Two striped sets are mirrors of one another. Data is striped across each stripe set, and the same data is sent to both stripes. Thus, this RAID variation provides both I/O performance advantages and fault tolerance.

- RAID 1+0 (sometimes called RAID 10): Striping across mirror sets. Similar in intent to RAID 0+1, it provides equivalent performance advantages and slightly better fault tolerance in that it is easier to rebuild the RAID device after a single disk failure (since the data on only one mirror set is affected).

Both these levels use a minimum of four disks.

Most hardware RAID devices connect to standard SCSI or SCSI-2 controllers.[*] Many systems also offer software RAID facilities within their LVM (as we shall see).

The following considerations apply to all software RAID implementations:

- Be careful not to overload disk controllers when using software RAID, because this will significantly degrade performance for all RAID levels. Putting disks on separate controllers is almost always beneficial.

- As with plain disk striping, the stripe size chosen for RAID 5 can effect performance. The optimum value to choose is very highly dependent on the typical I/O operation type.

- The sad fact is that if you want both high performance and fault tolerance, software RAID, and especially RAID 5, is likely to be a poor choice. RAID 1 works reasonably (with two-way mirroring), although it does add some overhead to the system. The additional overhead that RAID 5 places on the operating system is considerable, about 23% more than required for normal I/O operations. The bottom line for RAID 5 is to spend the money to get a hardware solution, and use software RAID 5 only if you can't afford anything better. Having said that, software RAID 5 often works well on a dedicated file server with a lot of CPU horsepower, some fast SCSI disks, and very few write operations.

AIX

AIX defines the root volume group, *rootvg*, automatically when the operating system is installed. Here is a typical setup:

```
# lsvg rootvg              Display volume group attributes.
VOLUME GROUP:   rootvg          VG IDENTIFIER:  0000018900004c0...
VG STATE:       active          PP SIZE:        32 megabyte(s)
VG PERMISSION:  read/write      TOTAL PPs:      542 (17344 MB)
MAX LVs:        256             FREE PPs:       69 (2208 MB)
LVs:            11              USED PPs:       473 (15136 MB)
OPEN LVs:       10              QUORUM:         2
TOTAL PVs:      1               VG DESCRIPTORS: 2
STALE PVs:      0               STALE PPs:      0
ACTIVE PVs:     1               AUTO ON:        yes
```

---

[*] A small minority use fiber channel.

```
MAX PPs per PV: 1016                    MAX PVs:        32
LTG size:       128 kilobyte(s)         AUTO SYNC:      no
HOT SPARE:      no
# lsvg -l rootvg                 List logical volumes in a volume group.
rootvg:
LV NAME             TYPE      LPs   PPs   PVs   LV STATE       MOUNT POINT
hd5                 boot      1     1     1     closed/syncd   N/A
hd6                 paging    16    16    1     open/syncd     N/A
hd8                 jfs2log   1     1     1     open/syncd     N/A
hd4                 jfs2      1     1     1     open/syncd     /
hd2                 jfs2      49    49    1     open/syncd     /usr
hd9var              jfs2      3     3     1     open/syncd     /var
hd3                 jfs2      1     1     1     open/syncd     /tmp
hd1                 jfs2      1     1     1     open/syncd     /home
hd10opt             jfs2      1     1     1     open/syncd     /opt
lg_dumplv           sysdump   32    32    1     open/syncd     N/A
```

Adding a new disk under AIX follows the same basic steps as for other Unix systems, although the commands used to perform them are quite different. Once you've attached the device to the system, reboot it. Usually, AIX will discover new devices at boot time and automatically create special files for them. Defined disks have special filenames like */dev/hdisk1*. The cfgmgr command may be used to search for new devices between boots; it has no arguments.

The lsdev command will list the disks present on the system:

```
$ lsdev -C -c disk
hdisk0 Available 00-00-0S-0,0 1.0 GB SCSI Disk Drive
hdisk1 Available 00-00-0S-2,0 Other SCSI Disk Drive
...
```

The new disk must then be made part of a volume group. To create a new volume group, use the mkvg command:

```
# mkvg -y "chemvg" hdisk5 hdisk6
```

This command creates a volume group named *chemvg* consisting of the disks *hdisk5* and *hdisk6*. mkvg's -s option can be used to specify the physical partition size in MB: from 1 to 1024 (4 is the default). The value must be a power of 2.*

After a volume group is created, it must be activated with the varyonvg command:

```
# varyonvg chemvg
```

Thereafter, the volume group will be activated automatically at each boot time. Volume groups are deactivated with varyoffvg; all of their filesystems must be dismounted first.

---

* You will need to increase this parameter for disks larger than 4 GB (1016 * 4 MB), because the maximum number of physical partitions is 1016. You can increase the latter limit using the -t option to mkvg and chvg. The new maximum will be this option's value times 1016. This can be necessary when adding a large (18 GB or more) disk to an existing volume group containing significantly smaller disks. It may also eventually be necessary for future very, very large disks.

A new disk may be added to an existing volume group with the extendvg command. For example, the following command adds the disk *hdisk4* to the volume group named *chemvg*:

```
# extendvg chemvg hdisk4
```

The following other commands operate on volume groups:

chvg

Change volume group characteristics.

reducevg

Remove a disk from a volume group (removing all disks deletes the volume group).

importvg

Add an existing volume group to the system (used to move disks between systems and to activate existing volume groups after replacing the root disk).

exportvg

Remove a volume group from the system device database but don't alter it (used to move disks to another system).

Logical volumes are created with the mklv command, which has the following basic syntax:

```
mklv -y "lvname" volgrp n [disks]
```

lvname is the name of the logical volume, *volgrp* is the volume group name, and *n* is the number of logical partitions. For example, the command:

```
# mklv -y "chome" chemvg 64
```

makes a logical volume in the *chemvg* volume group consisting of 64 logical partitions (256 MB) named *chome*. The special files */dev/chome* and */dev/rchome* will automatically be created by mklv.

The mklv command has many other options, which allow the administrator as much control over how the logical volume maps to physical disks as desired, down to the specific physical partition level. However, the default settings work very well for most applications.

The following commands operate on logical volumes:

extendlv

Increase the size of a logical volume.

chlv

Change the characteristics of a logical volume.

mklvcopy

Increase the number of data copies in a logical volume.

rmlv

Delete a logical volume.

A small logical volume in each volume group is used for logging and other disk management purposes. Such logical volumes are created automatically by AIX and have names like *lvlog00*.

Once the logical volumes have been created, you can build filesystems on them. AIX has a version of `mkfs`, but `crfs` is a much more useful command for creating filesystems. There are two ways to create a filesystem:

- Create a logical volume and then create a filesystem on it. The filesystem will occupy the entire logical volume.
- Create a filesystem and let AIX create a logical volume for you automatically.

The second way is faster, but the logical volume name AIX chooses is quite generic (*lv00* for the first one so created, and so on), and the size must be specified in 512-byte blocks rather than in logical partitions (which default to 4 MB units).

The `crfs` command is used to create a filesystem. The following basic form may be used to create a filesystem:

```
crfs -v jfs2 -g vgname -a size=n -m mt-pt -A yesno -p prm
```

The options have the following meanings:

-v jfs2
: The filesystem type is jfs2 ("enhanced journaled filesystem," using the logging logical volume in its volume group), the recommended local filesystem type.

-g *vgname*
: Volume group name.

-a size=*n*
: Size of the filesystem, in 512-byte blocks.

-m *mt-pt*
: Mount point for the filesystem (created if necessary).

-A *yesno*
: Whether the filesystem is mounted by `mount -a` commands.

-a frag=*n*
: Use a fragment size of *n* bytes for the filesystem. This value can range from 512 to 4096, in powers of 2, and it defaults to 4096. Smaller sizes will allocate disk space more efficiently for usage patterns consisting of many small files.

-a nbpi=*n*
: Specify *n* as the number of bytes per inode. This setting controls how many inodes are created for the new filesystem (number of inodes equals filesystem size divided by bytes per inode). The default value of 4096 usually creates more than you'll ever need except for filesystems with many, many tiny files. The maximum value is 16384.

-a compress=LZ
: Use transparent LZ compression on the files in the filesystem (this option is disabled by default).

For example, the following command creates a new filesystem in the *chemvg* volume group:

```
# crfs -v jfs2 -g chemvg -a size=50000 -a frag=1024 -m /organic2 -A yes
# mount /organic2
```

The new filesystem will be mounted at */organic2* (automatically at boot time), is 25 MB in size, and uses a fragment size of 1024 bytes. A new logical volume will be created automatically, and the filesystem will be entered into */etc/filesystems*. The initial mount must be done by hand.

The -d option is used to create a filesystem on an existing logical volume:

```
# crfs -v jfs2 -d chome -m /inorganic2 -A yes
```

This command creates a filesystem on the logical volume we created earlier. The size and volume group options are not needed in this case.

The chfs command may be used to increase the size of a filesystem. For example, the following command increases the size of the */inorganic2* filesystem (and of its logical volume *chm00*) created above:

```
# chfs -a size=+50000 /inorganic
```

An absolute or relative size may be specified for the size parameter (in 512-byte blocks). The size of a logical volume may be increased with the extendlv command, but it has no effect on filesystem size.

The following commands operate on AIX jfs and jfs2 filesystems:

chfs
> Change filesystem characteristics.

rmfs
> Remove a filesystem, its associated logical volume, and its entry in */etc/filesystems*.

Replacing a failed disk. When you need to remove a disk from the system, most likely due to a hardware failure, there are two considerations to keep in mind:

- If possible, perform the steps to remove a damaged non-root disk from the LVM configuration *before* letting field service replace it (otherwise, it will take some persistence to get the system to forget about the old disk).
- Items must be removed in the reverse order from the way they were created: filesystems, then logical volumes, then volume groups.

The following commands remove *hdisk4* from the LVM configuration (the volume group *chemvg2* and the logical volume *chlv2* holding the */chem2* filesystem are used as an example):

```
# umount /chem2              Unmount filesystem.
# rmfs /chem2               Repeat for all affected filesystems.
# rmlvcopy chlv2 2 hdisk4   Remove mirrors on hdisk4.
```

```
# chps -a n paging02          Don't activate paging space at next boot.
# shutdown -r now             Reboot the system.
# chpv -v r hdisk4            Make physical disk unavailable.
# reducevg chemvg2 hdisk4     Remove disk from volume group.
# rmdev -l hdisk4 -d          Remove definition of disk.
```

When the replacement disk is added to the system, it will be detected, and devices will be created for it automatically.

Getting information from the LVM. AIX provides many commands and options for listing information about LVM entities. Table 10-9 attempts to make it easier to figure out which one to use for a given task.

Table 10-9. AIX LVM informational commands

If you want to see:	Use this command:
All disks on the system	lspv
All volume groups	lsvg
All logical volumes	lsvg -l 'lsvg'
All filesystems	lsfs
All filesystems of a given type	lsfs -v *type*
What logical volumes are in a volume group	lsvg -l *vgname*
What filesystems are in a volume group	lsvgfs *vgname*
What disks are in a volume group	lsvg -p *vgname*
Which volume group a disk is in	lsvg -n hdisk*n*
Disk characteristics and settings	lspv hdisk*n*
Volume group settings	lsvg *vgname*
Logical volume characteristics	lslv *lvname*
Size of an unmounted local filesystem (in blocks)	lsfs *file-system*
Whether there is any unused space on a logical volume already containing a filesystem (compare lv size and fs size)	lsfs -q *file-system*
Disk usage summary map by region	lspv -p hdisk*n*
Locations of the free physical partitions on a disk broken down by region	lspv hdisk*n*
Locations of all free physical partitions in a volume group, by disk and disk region	lsvg -p *vgname*
Which logical volumes use a given disk, broken down by disk region	lspv -l hdisk*n*
What disks a logical volume is stored on, including disk region distribution	lslv -l *lvname*
Table showing the physical-to-logical partition mapping for a logical volume	lslv -m *lvname*
Table showing physical partition usage for a disk by logical volume	lspv -M hdisk*n*

Disk striping and disk mirroring. A striped logical volume is created by specifying mklv's -S option, indicating the stripe size, which must be a power of 2 from 4K to 128K. For example, this command creates a 500 MB logical volume striped across two disks consisting of a total of 125 logical partitions, each 4 MB in size:

```
# mklv -y cdata -S 64K chemvg 125 hdisk5 hdisk6
```

Note that the disk names are required on the `mklv` command when creating a striped logical volume.

Multiple data copies—mirroring—may be specified with the -c option, which takes the number of copies as its argument (the default is 1). For example, the following command creates a two-way mirror logical volume:

```
# mklv -c 2 -s s -w y biovg 500 hdisk2 hdisk3
```

The command specifies two copies, a super strict allocation policy (forces each mirror to a separate physical disk, which are listed), and specifies that write synchronization take place during each I/O operation (which reduces I/O performance but guarantees data synchronization).

An entire volume group can also be mirrored. This is configured using the `mirrorvg` command.

Finally, the -a option is used to request placement of the new logical volume within a general region of the disk. For example, this command requests that the logical volume be placed in the center portion of the disk to as great an extent as possible:

```
# mklv -y chome -ac chemvg 64
```

Disks are divided into five regions named as follows (beginning at the outer edge): *edge*, *middle*, *center*, *inner-middle*, and *inner-edge*. The *middle* region is the default, and the other available arguments to -a are accordingly e, im, and ie.

AIX does not provide general software RAID, although one can use mirrors and stripes to achieve the same functionality as RAID 0, 1, and 1+0.

HP-UX

HP-UX provides another version of a LVM that is used by default. The *vg00* volume group holds the system files, which are divided into several logical volumes:

```
# vgdisplay vg00                        Display volume group attributes.
--- Volume groups ---                   Output shortened.
VG Name                 /dev/vg00
VG Write Access         read/write
VG Status               available
Max LV                  255
Cur LV                  8
Open LV                 8
Max PV                  16
Cur PV                  1
Act PV                  1
Max PE per PV           2500
PE Size (Mbytes)        4
Total PE                2169
Alloc PE                1613
Free PE                 556
Total Spare PVs         0
Total Spare PVs in use  0
```

```
# bdf                                    Output shows mounted logical volumes.
Filesystem            kbytes     used    avail %used Mounted on
/dev/vg00/lvol3       143360    22288   113567   16% /
/dev/vg00/lvol1        83733    32027    43332   42% /stand
/dev/vg00/lvol7      2097152   419675  1572833   21% /var
/dev/vg00/lvol6      1048576   515524   499746   51% /usr
/dev/vg00/lvol5        65536     1128    60386    2% /tmp
/dev/vg00/lvol4      2097152   632916  1372729   32% /opt
/dev/vg00/lvol8        20480     1388    17900    7% /home
```

The process of creating a volume group begins by designating the component disks (or disk partitions) as physical volumes, using the pvcreate command:

```
# pvcreate /dev/rdsk/c2t0d0
```

Next, a directory and character special file must be created in /dev for the volume group:

```
# mkdir /dev/vg01
# mknod /dev/vg01/group c 64 0x010000
```

The major number is always 64, and the minor number is of the form $0x0n0000$, where n varies from 0 to 9 and must be unique across all volume groups (I assign them in order).

The volume group may now be created with the vgcreate command, which takes the volume group directory in /dev and the component disks as its arguments:

```
# vgcreate /dev/vg01 /dev/dsk/c2t0d0
```

vgcreate's -s option may be used to specify an alternate physical extent size (in megabytes). The default of 4 may be too small for large disks. You can add an additional volume to an existing volume group with the vgextend command.

The vgcreate and vgextend commands also have a -g option, which allows you to define named subsets of the disks in the volume group, known as *physical volume groups*, as in this example that creates two physical volume groups in the *vg01* volume group:

```
# vgcreate /dev/vg01 -g groupa /dev/dsk/c2t2d0 /dev/dsk/c2t4d0
# vgextend /dev/vg01 -g groupb /dev/dsk/c1t0d0 /dev/dsk/c1t1d0
```

The file /etc/lvmpvg holds the physical volume group data, and it may be edited directly rather than running vgcreate:

```
VG      /dev/vg01
PVG     groupa
/dev/dsk/c2t0d0
/dev/dsk/c2t4d0
PVG     groupb
/dev/dsk/c1t0d0
/dev/dsk/c1t1d0
```

Once the volume group is created, the lvcreate command may be used to create a logical volume. For example, the following command creates a 200 MB logical volume named *chemvg*:

```
# lvcreate -n chemvg -L 200 /dev/vg01
```

If the specified size is not an even multiple of the extent size (4 MB), the size is rounded up to the nearest multiple.

If the new logical volume is to be used for the root or boot filesystem or as a swap space, you must run the lvlnboot command with its -r, -b, or -s option (respectively). The command takes the logical volume device as its argument:

```
# lvlnboot -r -s /dev/vg01/swaplv
```

The -r option will create a combined boot/root volume if the specified logical volume is the first one on the physical volume.

Once a logical volume is built, a filesystem may be built upon it. For example:

```
# newfs /dev/vg01/rchemvg
```

The logical volume name is concatenated to the volume group directory in */dev* to form the special filenames referring to the logical volume; note that newfs uses the raw device. The new filesystem may then be mounted and entered into the filesystem configuration file.

You can customize the parameters for a new VxFS filesystem using these options to newfs:

-b *size*
> Filesystem block size in bytes. The default is 1024 for filesystems smaller than 8 GB, 2048 for ones up to 16 GB, 4096 for ones less than 32 GB, and 8192 for larger ones. The value must be a power of 2 from 4096 to 8192 (or to 65536 on 700 series systems using disk striping, which is discussed later in this chapter).

-l
> Enable files larger than 2 GB.

Other commands that operate on LVM entities are listed below:

vgextend
> Add disk to volume group.

vgreduce
> Remove disk from volume group.

vgremove
> Remove a volume group.

lvextend
> Add physical extents or mirrored copies to a logical volume.

lvreduce
> Remove physical extents or mirrored copies from a logical volume.

Lvremove
> Remove a logical volume from a volume group.

Displaying LVM information. The following commands display information about LVM entities:

pvdisplay *disk*
> Summary information about the disk drive.

pvdisplay -v *disk*
> Mapping of physical extents to logical extents.

vgdisplay *vg*
> Summary information about the volume group.

vgdisplay -v *vg*
> Brief information about all logical volumes within the volume group.

lvdisplay *lv*
> Summary information about the logical volume.

lvdisplay -v *lv*
> Mapping of logical to physical extents for the logical volume.

Disk striping and mirroring. The LVM is also used to perform disk striping and disk mirroring on HP-UX systems. For example, the following command creates a 200 MB logical volume named *cdata* with one mirrored copy:

```
# lvcreate -n cdata -L 200 -m 1 -s g /dev/vg01
```

The -s g option specifies that the mirrors must be placed into different physical volume groups.

Under HP-UX, disk striping occurs at the logical volume level. The following command creates an 800 MB four-way striped logical volume, using a striped width of 64 KB:

```
# lvcreate -n tyger -L 400 -i 4 -I 64 /dev/vg01
```

The -i option specifies the number of stripes (disks) and can be no larger than the total number of disks in the volume group; -I specifies the stripe size in KB, and its valid range is powers of 2 from 4 to 64.

Most HP-UX version do not provide software RAID.*

Tru64

Tru64 provides two facilities which have many of the characteristics of a logical volume manager:

- The Advanced File System (AdvFS), whose name is something of a misnomer, as it is actually both a filesystem type and a simple logical volume manager. The

---

* Software RAID is provided under HP-UX with VxVM (the Veritas Volume Manager, which supports software RAID 5, 0+1, and 1+0). HP began shipping VxVM with HP-UX 11i.

filesystem is included with the operating system, but there is also an add-on product containing additional AdvFS utilities.

- The Logical Storage Manager (LSM) facility is an advanced LVM facility. It adds an additional layer to the structure usually found in logical volume managers. This is an add-on product.

We'll consider each of them in separate subsections.

AdvFS. The AdvFS defines the following entities:

- A *volume* is a logical entity that can correspond to a disk partition, an entire disk, an LSM volume (see below), or even an external storage device such as a hardware RAID array.
- A *domain* is a set of one or more volumes.
- A *fileset* is a directory tree that can be mounted within the filesystem. Domains can contains multiple filesets.

Unlike other LVMs, under the AdvFS, domains and filesets—physical storage and directory trees—are independent, and either one can be modified without affecting the other (as we'll see).

The AdvFS facility is used by default on Tru64 systems. It defines two domains and several filesets:

```
# showfdmn root_domain                    Describe this domain.
             Id                Date Created  LogPgs  Version  Domain Name
3a535b22.000c47c0  Wed Jan  3 12:02:26 2001    512       4   root_domain

   Vol   512-Blks        Free  % Used  Cmode  Rblks  Wblks  Vol Name
    1L     524288       95680     82%     on    256    256  /dev/disk/dsk0a
# mountlist -v                            List mounted filesets.
        root_domain#root                  Root filesystem.
        usr_domain#usr                    Mounted at /usr.
        usr_domain#var                    Mounted at /var.
# showfsets usr_domain                    List filesets in a domain.
usr
        Id          : 3a535b27.0005a120.1.8001
        Files       :    43049, SLim=        0,  HLim=        0
        Blocks (512) : 1983812, SLim=        0,  HLim=        0
        Quota Status : user=off group=off Output shortened.
var
        Id          : 3a535b27.0005a120.2.8001
        Files       :     1800, SLim=        0,  HLim=        0
        Blocks (512) :   34954, SLim=        0,  HLim=        0
        Quota Status : user=off group=off
```

You can create a new domain with the mkfdmn command:

```
# mkfdmn /dev/disk/dsk1c chem_domain
```

This command creates the *chem_domain* domain consisting of the specified volume (here, a disk partition). If you have the AdvFS Utilities installed, you can add volumes to a domain with the addvol command, as in this example, which adds a second disk partition to the *chem_domain* domain:

```
# addvol /dev/disk/dsk2c chem_domain
# balance chem_domain
```

You can similarly remove a volume from a domain with the rmvol command. The balance command is typically run after either one; it has the effect of balancing disk space usage among the various volumes in the domain to improve performance.

Once a domain has been created, you can create filesets within it. This process creates an entity which is effectively a relocateable filesystem; a fileset is ready to accept files as soon as it is created (no mkfs step is required), and its contents can be moved to a different physical disk location in its domain if required.

The following commands create two filesets with our domain, and mount them into two existing directories immediately afterward:

```
# mkfset chem_domain bronze
# mkfset chem_domain silver
# mount chem_domain#bronze /bronze
# mount chem_domain#silver /silver
```

The fileset is referred to by appending its name to the domain name, separated by a number sign (#). Note that we don't have to specify any actual disk locations (and indeed we cannot do so). These matters are handled by the AdvFS itself.

The rmfset command may be used to remove a fileset from a domain. The renamefset command may be used to change the name of a fileset, as in this example:

```
# renamefset chem_domain lead gold
```

The AdvFS offers some limited disk striping facilities as part of its optional utilities package. A file can be striped by creating it with the stripe command:

```
# stripe -n 2 sulfur
```

This command creates the file *sulfur* as a two-way striped file. The file must created before any data is placed into it. More complex striping of entire volumes can be done with the Logical Storage Manager described in the next subsection.

LSM. The Tru64 Logical Storage Manager is designed to support advanced disk features such as disk striping and fault tolerance. It is a layered product which must be added to the basic Tru64 operating system.

Under the LSM, a whole new set of terminology comes into play:

Disk group
    A named collection of disks using a common LSM database. This roughly corresponds to a volume group.

Plex

The primary data storage entity. A plex can be *concatenated*, meaning that the discrete subdisks are simply combined sequentially, or *striped*, where data is striped across subdisks for higher performance. Software RAID 5 plexes can also be created.

Subdisk

A group of contiguous physical disk blocks. Subdisks are defined to force plexes to specific physical disk locations.

Volume

A collection of one or more plexes, conceptually performing the same function as a logical volume. Filefilesystemssystems are built upon volumes. The innovation introduced by the LSM is that the component plexes in a mirrored volume need not be identical. For example, one plex might be made up of three subdisks, and another one could be composed of four subdisks of the same total size.

For the most common cases, you need only worry about disk groups and volumes; plexes are taken care of automatically by the LSM. In the remainder of this section, we'll look briefly at some simple examples of LSM configuration. Consult the documentation for full details.

The voldiskadd command is used to create new disk group.* This command takes the disks to be added to the group as its arguments:

```
# voldiskadd dsk3 dsk4 ...
```

It is an interactive tool which will prompt you for the additional information it needs, including the disk group name (we'll use *dg1* in our examples) and the use for each disk (data or spare).

If you later want to place additional disks into a disk group, you use the voldg command, as in this example, which adds several more disks to *dg1*:

```
# voldg -g dg1 adddisk dsk9 dsk10 dsk11
```

Volumes are generally created with the volassist command. For example, the following command creates a volume consisting of a concatenated plex named *chemvol*, essentially a logical volume comprised of space from multiple disks on which a filesystem can be built:

```
# volassist -g dg1 make chemvol 2g dsk3 dsk4
```

The volume is created using the *dg1* disk group, using the specified disks (the disk list is optional). Its size is 2 GB.

---

* This discussion assumes that the LSM has been initialized by creating the root disk group. This is done with the volsetup command, which takes two or more disks as its arguments. The vold and voliod daemons should also be running (which happens automatically during a successful LSM installation).

We'll go on to make this a mirrored plex, using these commands:

```
# volassist -g dg1 mirror chemvol init=active layout=nolog dsk5 dsk6
# volassist addlog chemvol dsk7
```

The first command adds a mirror to the *chemvol* volume (we've again chosen to specify which disks to use). The second command adds the required logging area to the volume.

 The same technique could be used to mirror a single disk by using only one disk in each volassist command.

We can create a striped plex in a similar way:

```
# volassist -g dg1 make stripevol 2g layout=stripe nstripe=2 dsk3 dsk4
```

This command creates a two-way striped volume named *stripevol*.[*]

The following command will create a 3 GB RAID 5 volume:

```
# volassist -g dg1 make raidvol 3g layout=raid5 nstripe=5 disks
```

For both striped and RAID 5 volumes, you can also use the stripeunit attribute (following nstripe) to specify the stripe size.

Disk groups containing mirrored or RAID 5 volumes should include designated hot spare disks. The following commands designate *dsk9* as a hot spare for our disk group:

```
# voledit -g dg1 set spare=on dsk9
# volwatch -s lsmadmin@ahania.com
```

The volwatch command enables automatic hot spare replacement (-s), and its argument is the email address to which to send notifications when these events occur.

Once an LSM volume is created, it can be placed within an AdvFS domain and used for creating filesets.

The following commands are useful in obtaining information about LSM entities:

voldg -g *dg* free
> Display free space in a disk group.

voldisk list
> List all component disks used by the LSM.

volprint -v
> List all volumes.

---

[*] For more complex striped and RAID 5 plexes, you may need to define subdisks to force the various stripes to specific disks (e.g., to spread them across multiple controllers) as the default assignments made by the LSM often do not do so.

```
volprint -ht volume
```
Display information about a specific volume.

```
volprint -pt
```
List all plexes.

```
volprint -lp plex
```
Display information about a specific plex.

```
volprint -st
```
List all subdisks.

```
volprint -l subdisk
```
Display information about a specific subdisk.

Finally, the volsave command is used to save the LSM metadata to a disk file, which can then be backed up. The default location for these files is */usr/var/lsm*/db, but you can specify an alternate location using the command's -d option. The files themselves are given names of the form *LSM.n.host*, where *n* is a 14 digit encoding of the date and time. The volrestore command will restore the saved data should it ever be necessary.

Solaris

Solaris 9 introduces a logical volume manager as part of the standard operating system. This facility was available as an add-on product with earlier versions of Solaris (although there have been some changes with respect to previous versions—see the documentation for details).

The Solaris Volume Manager supports striping, mirroring, RAID 5, *soft partitions* (the ability to divide any disk into more than four partitions), and some other features. The Volume Manager must be initialized before its first use, using commands like these:

```
# metadb -a -f c0t0d0s7        Create initial state database replicas.
# metadb -a -c 2 c1t3d0s2       Add replicas on this slice.
```

We are now ready to create volumes. We will look briefly at some simple examples in the remainder of this section.

The Solaris Volume Manager uses fixed names for volumes of the form *dn*, where *n* is an integer from 0 to 127. Thus, the maximum number of volumes is 128. The metainit command does most of the work of creating and configuring volumes.

The following command will create a *concatenated* volume consisting of three disks:

```
# metainit d1 3 1 c1t1d0s2 1 c1t2d0s2 1 c1t3d0s2
```

The parameters are the volume name, the number of components (always greater than one for a concatenated volume), and then three pairs consisting of the number of component disks (always 1 here) followed by desired disk(s). When the command completes, the volume *d1* can be treated as if it were a single disk partition.

You can expand an existing filesystem using a similar command, as in this example, which expands the */docs* filesystem (originally on *c0t0d0s6*):

```
# umount /docs
# metainit d10 2 1 c0t0d0s6 1 c2t3d0s2   Add additional disk space.
# vi /etc/vfstab                          Change the filesystem's devices to /dev/md/[r]dsk/md10.
# mount /docs
# growfs -M /dev/md/rdsk/d10              Increase the filesystem size to the volume size.
```

The following command will create a striped volume:

```
# metainit d2 1 2 c1t1d0s2 c2t2d0s2 -i 64k
```

The parameters following the volume name indicate that we are creating a single striped volume with two component disks, using a stripe size (*interlace* value) of 64 KB (-i).

You can mirror volumes using metainit's -m option, followed by the metattach command, as in this example:

```
# metainit d20 -f 1 1 c0t3d0s2      Create the volume to be mirrored.
# umount /dev/dsk/c0t3d0s2
# metainit d21 1 1 c2t1d0s2         Create a volume to be used as the mirror.
# metainit d22 -m d20               Specify the volume to be mirrored.
# vi /etc/vfstab                    Modify entry to point to the mirror volume (d22).
# mount /dev/md/dsk/d22             Remount filesystem.
# metattach d22 d21                 Add a mirror.
```

In this case, we add a mirror to an existing filesystem. We use the -f option on the first metainit command to force a volume to be created from an existing filesystem.

 If we were mirroring the root filesystem, we would run the metaroot command (specifying the mirror volume as its argument) and then reboot the system, rather than ummounting and remounting the filesystem.

Other volume types can also be mirrored—concatenated, striped, etc.—using just the final two commands.

You can specify the read and write policies for mirrored volumes using the metaparam command, as in this example:

```
# metaparam -r geometric -w parallel d22
```

The -r option specifies the read policy, one of roundrobin (successive read operations go to each disk in turn, which is the default), first (all reads go to the first disk), and geometric (read operations are divided between the component disks by assigning specific disk regions to each one). The geometric read policy can minimize seek times by confining disk head movement to a subset of the disk, which can produce measurable performance improvements for I/O that is seek time–limited (e.g., randomly accessed data, such as a database).

The -w parameter specifies the write policy, one of parallel (write to all disks at the same time, which is the default) and serial. The latter might be used to improve performance when both mirrors are on the same busy disk controller.

The following command will create a RAID 5 volume:

```
# metainit d30 -r disks -i 96k
```

This creates a RAID 5 volume using a stripe size of 96 KB. The default stripe size is 16 KB, and it must range from 8 KB to 100 KB.

 Don't try to access a RAID 5 volume until it has finished initializing. This can take a while. You can check its status with the metastat command.

You can replace a failed RAID 5 component volume using the metareplace command, as in this example:

```
# metareplace -e d30 c2t5d0s2
```

Alternatively, you can define a *hot spare pool* from which disks can be taken as needed for all RAID 5 devices. For example, these commands create a pool named *hsp001** and designate it for use with RAID 5 device *d30*:

```
# metainit hsp001 c3t1d0s2 c3t2d0s2
# metaparam -h hsp001 d30
```

You can modify the disks in a hot space pool using the metahs command and its -a (add), -r (replace), and -d (delete) options.

The last Volume Manager feature we'll consider is soft partitions. Soft partitions are simply logical partitions (subsets) of a disk. For example, the following command creates a volume consisting of 2 GB from the specified disk:

```
# metainit d7 -p c2t6d0s2 2g
```

When used with a new disk, you can add the -e option to the command. This causes the disk to be repartitioned so that all but 4 MB is in slice 0 (the 4 MB is in slice 7 and is used to hold a state database replica). For example, this command performs that repartitioning and then assigns 3 GB of slice 0 to volume *d8*:

```
# metainit d8 -p -e c2t5d0s2 3g
```

Once volumes are created, you can create a UFS filesystem on them using newfs as usual. You can also remove any volume with the metaclear command, which takes the desired volume as its argument. Naturally, any data on the volume will be lost.

---

* Hot spare pool names must be of the form *hspnnn*, where *nnn* ranges from 000 to 999. Why you would need 1000 hot space pools for 128 volumes is a good question.

The following commands are useful for obtaining information about the Volume Manager and individual volumes:

metadb
> List all state database replicas.

metadb -I
> Show status of state database replicas.

metastat *dn*
> Show volume status.

metaparam *dn*
> Show volume settings.

Linux

Linux systems can use both a logical volume manager and software disk striping and RAID, although the two facilities are separate. They are compatible, however; for example, RAID volumes can be used as components in the logical volume manager.

The Linux Logical Volume Manager (LVM) project has been in existence for several years (its homepage is *http://www.sistina.com/products_lvm.htm*), and support for the LVM is merged into the Linux 2.4 kernel. Conceptually, the LVM allows you to combine and divide physical disk partitions in a completely flexible manner. The resulting filesystems are dynamically resizable. The current version of the LVM supports up to 99 volume groups and 256 logical volumes. The maximum logical volume size is currently 256 GB.

The logical volume manager is included in some recent Linux distributions (for example, SuSE Linux 6.4 and later). If it is not included in yours, installing it is quite straightforward:

- Download the LVM package and the appropriate kernel patch for your system.
- Unpack and build the LVM package.
- If necessary, patch the kernel source code and build a new kernel, enabling LVM support during the kernel configuration process. One way to do this is to use the make xconfig command. Use the Block Devices button from the main menu.
- If you have selected modular support for the LVM, add entries to */etc/modules. conf* to enable the modprobe command to load the LVM module at boot time. Here are the needed entries:

      alias block-major-58 lvm-mod
      alias char-major-109 lvm-mod

- Install the new kernel into the boot directory, and enable its use with LILO or GRUB.

- Modify the system startup and shutdown scripts to activate and deactivate the LVM configuration. Add these commands to the startup scripts:

```
vgscan                       # Search for volume groups
vgchange -a y                # Activate all volume groups
```

Add this command to the *shutdown* script:

```
vgchange -a n                # Deactivate all volume groups
```

- Reboot the system using the new kernel.

The LVM package includes a large number of administrative utilities, each of which is designed to create or manipulate a specific type of LVM entity. For example, the commands vgcreate, vgdisplay, vgchange, and vgremove create, display information about, modify the characteristics of, and delete a volume group (respectively). You can also backup and restore the volume group configurations with vgcfgbackup and vgcfgrestore, change the size of a volume group with vgextend (increase its size by adding disk space to it) and vgreduce (decrease its size), divide and combine volume groups (vgsplit and vgmerge), move a volume group between computer systems (vgexport and vgimport), search all local disks for volume groups (vgscan), and rename a volume group (vgrename). (Many of these commands are similar to the HP-UX equivalents.)

There are similar commands for other LVM entities:

Physical volumes
   pvcreate, pvdisplay, pvchange, pvmove, and pvscan.

Logical volumes
   lvcreate, lvdisplay, lvchange, lvremove, lvreduce, lvextend, lvscan, and lvrename.

Let's look at some of these commands in action as we create a volume group and some logical volumes and then build filesystems on them.

The first step is to set the partition type of the desired disk partitions to 0x8E. We use fdisk for this task; here is the process for the first disk partition:

```
# fdisk /dev/sdb1
Command (m for help): t
Partition number (1-4): 1
Hex code (type L to list codes): 8e
Command (m for help): w
```

The first time we use the LVM, we need to run vgscan to initialize the facility (among other things, it creates the */etc/lvmtab* file). Next, we designate the disk partitions as physical volumes by specifying the desired disk partitions as command arguments to the pvcreate command (*/dev/sdc2* is the second partition we will be using in our volume group):

```
# pvcreate /dev/sdb1 /dev/sdc2
pvcreate -- reinitializing physical volume
pvcreate -- physical volume "/dev/sdb1" successfully created
...
```

We are now ready to create a volume group, which we will name *vg1*:

```
# vgcreate vg1 /dev/sdb1 /dev/sdc2
vgcreate -- INFO: using default physical extent size 4 MB
vgcreate -- INFO: maximum logical volume size is 255.99 Gigabyte
vgcreate -- doing automatic backup of volume group "vg1"
vgcreate -- volume group "vg1" successfully created and activated
```

This command creates the *vg1* volume group using the two specified disk partitions. In doing so, it creates/updates the ASCII configuration file */etc/lvmtab* (which holds the names of the system's volume groups) and places a binary configuration file into two subdirectories of */etc*: *lvmtab.d/vg1* and *lvmconf/vg1.conf* (the latter directory will also store old binary configuration files for this volume group, reflecting changes to its characteristics and components).

The vgcreate command also creates the special file */dev/vg1/group*, which can be used to refer to the volume group as a device.

Now we can create two 800 MB logical volumes:

```
# lvcreate -L 800M -n chem_lv vg1
lvcreate -- doing automatic backup of "vg1"
lvcreate -- logical volume "/dev/vg1/chem_lv" successfully created
# lvcreate -L 800M -n bio_lv -r 8 -C y vg1
lvcreate -- doing automatic backup of "vg1"
lvcreate -- logical volume "/dev/vg1/bio_lv" successfully created
```

We set the sizes of both logical volumes via the lvcreate command's -L option. In the case of the second logical volume, *bio_lv*, we also specify that the read-ahead mode chunk size is 8 sectors via -r (the amount of data returned at a time during sequential access) and specify that a contiguous logical volume be created (via the -C y option).

Once again, two new special files are created, each named after the corresponding logical volume and located under the volume group directory in */dev* (here, */dev/vg1*).

We can now create filesystems using the ordinary mke2fs command, specifying the logical volume as the device on which to build the new filesystem. For example, the following command creates an ext3 filesystem on the *bio_lv* logical volume:

```
# mke2fs -j /dev/vg1/bio_lv
```

Once built, this filesystem may be mounted as usual. You can also build a Reiser filesystem on a logical volume.

In addition to the previously mentioned commands, the LVM provides the e2fsadmin command, which can be used to increase the size of a logical volume and the ext2 or ext3 filesystem it contains a single, nondestructive operation. This utility requires the resize2fs utility (originally developed by PowerQuest as part of its PartitionMagic product and now available under the GPL at *http://e2fsprogs.sourceforge.net*).

Here is an example of its use; the following command adds 100 MB to the *bio_lv* logical volume and the filesystem that it contains:

```
# umount /dev/vg1/bio_lv
# e2fsadm /dev/vg1/bio_lv -L+100M
e2fsck 1.18, 11-Nov-1999 for EXT2 FS 0.5b, 95/08/09
Pass 1: Checking inodes, blocks, and sizes
Pass 2: Checking directory structure
Pass 3: Checking directory connectivity
Pass 4: Checking reference counts
Pass 5: Checking group summary information
/dev/vg1/bio_lv: 11/51200 files (0.0% non-contiguous), 6476/819200 blocks
lvextend -- extending logical volume "/dev/vg1/bio_lv" to 900 MB
lvextend -- doing automatic backup of volume group "vg1"
lvextend -- logical volume "/dev/vg1/bio_lv" successfully extended

resize2fs 1.19 (13-Jul-2000)
Begin pass 1 (max = 5)
Extending the inode table       XXXXXXXXXXXXXXXXXXXXXXXXXXXXXXXXXXXXXXXXXX
Begin pass 3 (max = 25)
Scanning inode table            XXXXXXXXXXXXXXXXXXXXXXXXXXXXXXXXXXXXXXXXXX
The filesystem on /dev/vg1/bio_lv is now 921600 blocks long.

e2fsadm -- ext2fs in logical volume "/dev/vg1/bio_lv"
successfully extended to 900 MB
```

Note that the filesystem must be unmounted in order to increase its size.

To use the Linux software RAID facility, you must install the component disks, enable RAID support in the kernel and then set up the RAID configuration. You can perform the second task using a utility like make xconfig and selecting the Block Devices category from the main menu. The Multiple devices driver support item is the one that must be enabled to access all of the other RAID-related items. I recommend enabling all of them.

RAID devices use special files of the form */dev/mdn* (where *n* is an integer), and they are defined in the */etc/raidtab* configuration file. Once defined, you can create them using the mkraid command and start and stop them with the raidstart and raidstop commands. Alternatively, you can define them with the *persistent superblock* options, which enables automatic detection and mounting/dismounting of RAID devices by the kernel. In my view, the latter is always the best choice.

The best way to understand the */etc/raidtab* file is to examine some sample entries. Here is an entry corresponding to a striped disk using two component disks, which I have annotated:

```
raiddev /dev/md0              Defines RAID device 0.
raid-level 0                  RAID level.
nr-raid-disks 2               Number of component disks.
chunk-size 64                 Stripe size (in KB).
persistent-superblock 1       Enable the persistent superblock feature.
device /dev/sdc1              Specify the first component disk ...
```

```
raid-disk 0                                and number it.
device /dev/sdd1                           Same for all remaining component disks.
raid-disk 1
```

If we had wanted to define a two-way mirror set instead of a stripe set, using the same disks, we would omit the chunk-size parameter and change the raid-level parameter from 0 to 1 in the first section, and the rest of the entry would remain the same.

We can set up a RAID 0+1 disk, a mirrored striped disk, in this way:

```
raiddev /dev/md0
...Set up the first striped disk.
raiddev /dev/md1
...Set up the second striped disk.

raiddev /dev/md2
raid-level 1
nr-raid-disks 2
persistent-superblock 1
device /dev/md0                            The component disks are also md devices.
raid-disk 0
device /dev/md1
raid-disk 1
```

The following entry defines a RAID 5 disk containing 5 component disks, as well as a spare disk to be automatically used should any of the active disks fail:

```
raiddev /dev/md0
raid-level 5                               Use RAID level 5.
nr-raid-disks 5                            Number of active disks in the device.
persistent-superblock 1
device /dev/sdc1                           Specify the 5 component disks.
raid-disk 0
device /dev/sdd1
raid-disk 1
device /dev/sde1
raid-disk 2
device /dev/sdf1
raid-disk 3
device /dev/sdg1
raid-disk 4
device /dev/sdh1                           Specify a spare disk.
spare-disk 0
```

You can use multiple spare disks if you want to.

RAID devices can be used with the logical volume manager if desired.

FreeBSD

FreeBSD provides the Vinum Volume Manager. It uses somewhat different concepts than other LVMs. Under Vinum, a *drive* is a physical disk partition. Disk space is allocated from drives in user-specified chunks known as *subdisks*. Subdisks in turn are used to define *plexes*, and one or more plexes makes up a Vinum *volume*. Multiple plexes within a volume constitute mirrors.

 Be prepared to be very patient when learning Vinum. It is quite inflexible in how it wants operations to be performed. Plan to learn the procedures on a safe test system.

In addition, be aware that the facility is still under development. As of this writing, only the most basic functionality is present.

To use a disk partition with Vinum, it must be prepared as follows:

- Create one or more slices on it using `fdisk`.
- Create an initial disk label using `disklabel` or `sysinstall`. I prefer the latter. If you choose to use `sysinstall`, create a single swap partition in each slice that you want to use with Vinum. Ignore the messages about it being unable to start the swap partition (you don't want it to anyway).
- Modify the disk label using `disklabel -e`. Only the partition list at the bottom will need to be changed. It must look like this when you are done:

```
#         size  offset   fstype  [fsize bsize bps/cpg]
c: 11741184        0     unused          # (Cyl.    0 - 11647)
e: 117411184       0     vinum
```

If you used `sysinstall` to create the initial disk label, all you have to do is add the final line.

Partition *e* is somewhat arbitrary, but it works. Note that partition *c* cannot be used with Vinum.

Once the drives are prepared, the best way to proceed is to create a description file that defines the Vinum entities that you want to create. Here is a file that defines a volume named *big*:

```
drive d1 device /dev/da1s1e        Define drives.
drive d2 device /dev/da2s1e
volume big                         Define volume big.
  plex org concat                  Create a concatenated plex.
    sd length 500m drive d1        First 500 MB subdisk from drive d1.
    sd length 200m drive d2        Second 200 MB subdisk from drive d2.
```

The file first defines the drives to be used, naming them *d1* and *d2*. Note that this operation needs to be performed only once for a given partition. Future example configurations will omit drive definitions.

The second section of the file defines the volume *big* as one concatenated plex (org concat). It consists of two subdisks: 500 MB of space from */dev/da1s1e* and 200 MB of space from */dev/da2s1e*. This disk space will be treated as a single unit.

You can create these entities using the following command:

```
# vinum create /etc/vinum.big.conf
```

The final argument specifies the location of the description file.

Once the volume is created, you can create a filesystem on it:

```
# newfs -v /dev/vinum/big
```

The device is specified via the file in */dev/vinum* named for the volume. The -v option tells newfs not to look for partitions on the specified device. Once newfs completes, the filesystem may be mounted. For it to be detected properly at boot time, however, the following line must be present in */etc/rc.conf*:

```
start_vinum="YES"
```

This causes the Vinum kernel module to be loaded on boots.

Here is a description file that defines a striped (RAID 1) volume:

```
volume fast
  plex org striped 1024k
    sd length 0 drive d1
    sd length 0 drive d2
```

This stripe set consists of two components. The plex line has an additional entry, the stripe size. This value must be a multiple of 512 bytes. The subdisk definitions specify a length of 0; this corresponds to all available space in the device. The actual volume can be created using the vinum create command as before.

If both of these volumes were created, then different areas of the various disk partitions would be used by each one. Vinum drives can be subdivided among different volumes. You can specify the location with the drive when the subdisk is created (see the *vinum(8)* manual page for details).

The following configuration file creates a mirrored volume by defining two plexes:

```
volume mirror
  plex org concat               First mirror.
    sd length 1000m drive d1
  plex org concat               Second mirror.
    sd length 1000m drive d2
```

Creating and activating the mirrored volume requires several vinum commands (the output is not shown):

```
# vinum create file            Create the volume.
# vinum init mirror.p1         Initialize the subdisk.
Wait for command to finish.
# vinum start mirror.p1        Activate the mirror.
```

When you first create a mirrored volume, the state of the second plex appears in status listings as faulty, and its component subdisk has a status of empty. The vinum init command initializes all of the component subdisks of plex *mirror.p1*, and the vinum start command regenerates the mirror (actually, creates it for the first time). Both of these commands start background processes to do the actual work, and you must wait for the initialization to finish before running the regeneration. You can check on their status using this command:

```
# vinum list
```

Once both of these commands have completed, you can build a filesystem and mount it.

The following description file created a RAID 5 volume named *safe*:

```
volume safe
  plex org raid5 1024k
    sd length 0 drive d1
    sd length 0 drive d2
    sd length 0 drive d3
    sd length 0 drive d4
    sd length 0 drive d5
```

This volume consists of a single plex containing five subdisks. The following commands can be used to create and activate the volume:

```
# vinum create file              Create the volume.
# vinum init safe.p0             Initialize the subdisks.
```

Once again, the initialization process runs in the background, and you must wait for it to finish before creating a filesystem.

As a final example, consider this description file:

```
volume zebra
  plex org striped 1024k
    sd length 200m drive d1
    sd length 200m drive d2
  plex org striped 1024k
    sd length 200m drive d3
    sd length 200m drive d4
```

This file defines a volume named *zebra*, which is a striped mirrored volume (RAID 0+1). The volume consists of two striped plexes which become mirrors. The following commands are required to create and activate this volume:

```
# vinum create file              Create the volume.
# vinum init zebra.p0 zebra.p1   Initialize subdisks.
# vinum start zebra.p1           Regenerate the mirror.
```

The following commands are useful for displaying Vinum information:

vinum list
   Display information about all Vinum entities.

vinum ld
   List drives, including current free space.

vinum lv
   List volumes.

```
vinum ls
```
List subdisks.

```
vinum ls -v
```
Display subdisk details, including the plex they are part of and their component drives.

```
vinum lp
```
List plexes.

```
vinum lp -v
```
Display plex details, including the volume they belong to.

You can follow any of these commands with the name of a specific item to limit the display to its characteristics.

Here is an example of the vinum `list` command:

```
4 drives:
D d1                State: up        Device /dev/ad1s1e      Avail: 2799/2999 MB (93%)
D d2                State: up        Device /dev/ad1s2e      Avail: 2799/2999 MB (93%)
D d3                State: up        Device /dev/ad1s3e      Avail: 2799/2999 MB (93%)
D d4                State: up        Device /dev/ad1s4e      Avail: 532/732 MB (72%)

1 volumes:
V zebra             State: up        Plexes:      2 Size:        400 MB

2 plexes:
P zebra.p0      S State: up          Subdisks:    2 Size:        400 MB
P zebra.p1      S State: faulty      Subdisks:    2 Size:        400 MB

4 subdisks:
S zebra.p0.s0       State: up        P0:        0  B Size:       200 MB
S zebra.p0.s1       State: up        P0:     1024 kB Size:       200 MB
S zebra.p1.s0       State: R 16%     P0:        0  B Size:       200 MB
S zebra.p1.s1       State: R 16%     P0:     1024 kB Size:       200 MB
```

This display shows the *zebra* volume we defined earlier. The subdisk initialization has completed. At this moment, the regeneration operation is 16% complete.

Floppy Disks

On systems with floppy disk drives, Unix filesystems may also be created on floppy disks. (Before they can be used, floppy disks must, of course, be formatted.) But why bother? These days, it is usually much more convenient to use floppy disks in one of the following ways:

- Mounted as a DOS-type filesystem whose files can then be accessed with standard utilities like cp and ls.

- Using special utilities designed to read and write files to and from DOS disks (we'll look at specific examples in a minute).

Floppy disk special files

Floppy disks are accessed using the following special files (the default refers to a 1.44 MB 3.5-inch diskette):

AIX	*/dev/fd0*
FreeBSD	*/dev/fd0*
HP-UX	*/dev/dsk/c0t1d0* (Normal disk naming convention)
Linux	*/dev/fd0*
Solaris	*/dev/diskette*
Tru64	*/dev/fd0*

Floppy disk special files are only occasionally needed on Solaris systems, because these devices are managed by the media handling daemon (discussed later in this chapter).

Using DOS disks on Unix systems

Methods for accessing DOS disks vary widely from system to system. In this section, we'll look at formatting diskettes in DOS format and copying files to and from them on each system.

Under HP-UX, the following commands format a DOS floppy disk:

```
$ mediainit -v -i2 -f16 /dev/rdsk/c0t1d0
$ newfs -n /dev/rdsk/c0t1d0 ibm1440
```

The -n option on the newfs command prevents boot information from being written to the diskette.

HP-UX provides a number of utilities to access files on DOS diskettes: doscp, dosdf, doschmod, dosls, dosll, dosmkdir, dosrm, and dosrmdir. Here is an example using doscp:

```
$ doscp /dev/rdsk/c0d1s0:paper.txt paper.new
```

This command copies the file *paper.txt* from the diskette to the current HP-UX directory.

On Linux and FreeBSD systems, a similar process is used. These commands format a DOS floppy and write files to it:

```
Linux                              FreeBSD
# fdformat /dev/fd0                # fdformat /dev/fd0
# mkfs -t msdos /dev/fd0           # newfs_msdos /dev/fd0
# mount /dev/fd0 /mnt              # mount /dev/fd0 /mnt
# cp prop2.txt /mnt                # cp prop2.txt /mnt
# umount /mnt                      # umount /mnt
```

The Mtools utilities are also available on Linux and FreeBSD systems (described in the next section).

AIX also provides several utilities for accessing DOS disks: `dosformat`, `dosread`, `doswrite`, `dosdir`, and `dosdel`. However, they provide only minimal functionality—for example, there is no wildcard support—so you'll be much happier and work more efficiently if you use the Mtools utilities.

On Solaris systems, diskettes are controlled by the volume management system and its `vold` daemon. This facility merges the diskette as transparently as possible within the normal Solaris filesystem.

These commands could be used to format a diskette and create a DOS filesystem on it:

```
$ volcheck
$ fdformat -d -b g04
```

The `volcheck` command tells the volume management system to look for new media in the devices that it controls. The `fdformat` command formats the diskette, giving it a label of *g04*.

The following commands illustrate the method for copying files to and from diskette:

```
$ volcheck
$ cp ~/proposals/prop2.txt /floppy/g96
$ cp /floppy/g96/drug888.dat ./data
$ eject
```

The diskette is mounted in a subdirectory of */floppy* named for its label (or in */floppy/ unnamed_floppy* if it does not have a label). Configuration of `vold` is discussed later in this chapter.

Tru64 provides no support for DOS diskettes, so you'll need to use the Mtools utilities, to which we will now turn.

The Mtools utilities

The Mtools package is available for all the Unix versions we are considering. It is currently maintained by David Niemi and Alain Knaff (see *http://mtools.linux.lu*).

The package contains a series of utilities for accessing DOS diskettes and their files, modeled after their similarly named DOS counterparts:

`mformat`
> Format a diskette in DOS format.

`mlabel`
> Label a DOS diskette.

`mcd`
> Change the current directory location on the diskette.

`mdir`
> List the contents of a directory on a DOS diskette.

`mtype`
> Display the contents of a DOS file.

mcopy

    Copy files between a DOS diskette and Unix.

mdel

    Delete file(s) on a DOS diskette.

mren

    Rename a file on a DOS diskette.

mmd

    Create a subdirectory on a DOS diskette.

mrd

    Remove a subdirectory from a DOS diskette.

mattrib

    Change DOS file attributes.

Here are some examples of using the Mtools utilities:

```
$ mdir
Volume in drive A is GIAO24
Directory for A:/
SILVERDAT79    1-29-95   9:36p
PROP43_1 TXT2304    1-29-95   9:33p
REFCARD  DOC73216    1-13-95   5:28p
3 File(s)    1381376 bytes free
$ mren prop43_1.txt prop43_1.old
$ mcopy a:refcard.doc .
Copying REFCARD.DOC
$ mcopy proposal.txt a:
Copying PROPOSAL.TXT
$ mmd data2
$ mcopy gold* a:data2
Copying GOLD.DAT
Copying GOLD1.DAT
$ mcopy "a:\data\*.dat" ./data
Copying NA.DAT
Copying HG.DAT
$ mdel silver.dat
```

As these examples illustrate, the Mtools utilities are designed to make accessing diskettes as painless as possible. For example, it generally assumes that files being referred to are on the floppy disk. The only time that you have to refer explicitly to the diskette—via the *a*: construct—is with the mcopy command, which makes sense because there is no other way to know which direction the copy is taking place. Note also that filenames on diskette are not case-sensitive.

Stupid DOS partition tricks

On PC-based Unix systems, hard-disk DOS partitions can also be mounted within the Unix filesystem. This allows not only for copying files between Unix and the other operating systems, but also for handling the entire partition using Unix utilities. For example, suppose you decide to change the partitioning scheme on your boot disk, decreasing the size of the DOS partition (without affecting the Unix partitions). The following commands will let you do so without reinstalling DOS, Windows, or *any* installed software:

```
# mount -t msdos /dev/hdal /mnt          Linux is used as an example.
# cd /mnt
# tar -c -f /tmp/dos.tar *
# unmount /mnt
Mess with partitions and/or filesystems.
# mount -t msdos /dev/hda1 /mnt
# cd /mnt
# tar -x -f /tmp/dos.tar
# cd /; umount /mnt
```

You could restore only some of the files from the `tar` archive if that is what made sense. Many other operations along these lines are also possible: for example, moving the DOS partition from the first hard drive to the second one, copying a DOS partition between systems or across a network, and so on. There are, of course, other ways of accomplishing these same tasks, but this procedure is often much faster.

 When the partition in question is the Windows boot partition, this procedure works very well with older and simpler Windows versions such as Windows 98 and Windows ME. For Windows NT and later, you may have to alter the *Boot.Ini* file to get the system to boot.

CD-ROM Devices

CD-ROM drives are also generally treated in a manner similar to disks. The following special files are used to access SCSI CD-ROM devices:

AIX	*/dev/cd0*
FreeBSD	*/dev/cd0c* or */dev/acd0c* (SCSI or ATAPI)
Linux	*/dev/cdrom*
Solaris	*/dev/dsk/c0tnd0s02* (Normal disk naming conventions)
HP-UX	*/dev/dsk/cmtnd0* (Normal disk naming conventions)
Tru64	*/dev/disk/cdrom0c*

The following example commands all mount a CD on the various systems:

```
mount -o ro -v cdrfs /dev/cd0 /mnt          AIX
mount -r -t cd9660 /dev/cd0c /mnt           FreeBSD
mount -o ro -F cdfs /dev/dsk/c1t2d0 /mnt    HP-UX
mount -r -t iso9660 /dev/sonycd_31a /mnt    Linux
mount -o ro -t hsfs /dev/c0t2d0s0 /mnt      Solaris
mount -r -t cdfs /dev/disk/cdrom0c /mnt     Tru64
```

Entries can also be added to the filesystem configuration file for CD-ROM filesystems.

CD-ROM drives under AIX

On AIX systems, if you add a CD-ROM drive to an existing system, you'll need to create a device for it in this manner:

```
# mkdev -c cdrom -r cdrom1 -s scsi -p scsi0 -w 5,0
cd0 available
```

This command adds a CD-ROM device using SCSI ID 5.

Individual CDs are usually mounted via predefined mount points. For example, the following commands create a generic CD-ROM filesystem to be mounted on */cdrom*:

```
# mkdir /cdrom
# crfs -v cdrfs -p ro -d cd0 -m /cdrom -A no
```

This filesystem will be mounted read-only and will not automatically be mounted when the system boots. A CD may now be mounted with the `mount /cdrom` command.

The `lsfs` command may be used to list all defined CD-ROM filesystems:

```
$ lsfs -v cdrfs
Name       Nodename  Mount Pt        VFS    Size  Options  Auto  Acct
/dev/cd0   --        /cdrom          cdrfs  --    ro       no    no
```

The Solaris media-handling daemon

Solaris has a similar media handling facility implemented by the `vold` daemon. It generally mounts CDs and diskettes in directory trees rooted at */cdrom* and */floppy*, respectively, creating a subdirectory named for the label on the current media (or *unnamed_cdrom* and *unnamed_floppy* for unlabeled ones).

There are two configuration files associated with the volume management facility. */etc/vold.conf* specifies the devices that it controls and the filesystem types it supports:

```
# Volume Daemon Configuration file
#

# Database to use (must be first)
db db_mem.so

# Labels supported
label dos label_dos.so floppy
label cdrom label_cdrom.so cdrom
label sun label_sun.so floppy

# Devices to use
use cdrom drive /dev/dsk/c0t6 dev_cdrom.so cdrom0
use floppy drive /dev/diskette dev_floppy.so floppy0

# Actions
insert /vol*/dev/diskette[0-9]/* user=root /usr/sbin/rmmount
insert /vol*/dev/dsk/* user=root /usr/sbin/rmmount
```

```
eject /vol*/dev/diskette[0-9]/* user=root /usr/sbin/rmmount
eject /vol*/dev/dsk/* user=root /usr/sbin/rmmount
notify /vol*/rdsk/* group=tty /usr/lib/vold/volmissing -c

# List of file system types unsafe to eject
unsafe ufs hsfs pcfs
```

The section labeled Actions indicates commands to be run when various events occur—media is inserted or removed, for example. The final section lists filesystem types that must be unmounted before being removed and hence will require the user to issue an eject command.

If you want to share mounted CDs via the network, you'll need to add an entry to /etc/rmmount.conf:

```
# Removable Media Mounter configuration file.
#

# File system identification
ident hsfs ident_hsfs.so cdrom
ident ufs ident_ufs.so cdrom floppy
ident pcfs ident_pcfs.so floppy

# Actions
action -premount floppy action_wabi.so.1
action cdrom action_filemgr.so
action floppy action_filemgr.so

# File System Sharing
share cdrom*
share solaris_2.x* -o ro:phys
```

File-sharing entries are in the final section of this file. An entry is provided for sharing standard CD-ROM filesystems (mounted at /cdrom/cdrom*). The -o in the second entry in this section passes options to the share command, in this case limiting access. You can modify the provided entry for CD-ROMs if appropriate. Shared CD-ROM filesystems can be mounted by other systems using the mount command and entered into their /etc/vfstab files.

 Tru64 also has a vold daemon. However, it is part of its Logical Storage Manager facility and thus performs a completely different function.

Sharing Filesystems

In the final section of this chapter, we consider sharing local filesystems with other systems, including Windows systems. It covers the most common Unix filesystem sharing facility, NFS, and the Samba facility, which makes Unix filesystems available to Windows systems.

More information about NFS is available in *NFS and NIS* by Hal Stern, Mike Eisler and Ricardo Labiaga (O'Reilly & Associates). More information about Samba is available in the books *Teach Yourself Samba in 24 Hours by* Gerald Carter with Richard Sharpe (SAMS) and *Using Samba* by Robert Eckstein, David Collier-Brown, and Peter Kelly (O'Reilly & Associates).

NFS

The Network File System (NFS) enables filesystems physically residing on one computer system to be used by other computers in the network, appearing to users on the remote host as just another local disk.[*] NFS is universally available on Unix systems.

The following configuration files are used by NFS:

/etc/fstab (*/etc/vfstab* under Solaris)
> Remote filesystems are entered into the filesystem configuration file, using only a slightly varied syntax from regular entries.

/etc/exports
> This file controls which filesystems on the local system can be mounted by remote hosts and under what conditions and restrictions. On Solaris systems, this file is not used, but the file */etc/dfs/dfstab* performs an analogous function.

Table 10-10 lists the daemons used by NFS and the files that start them in the various Unix versions.

Table 10-10. NFS daemons[a]

Item	AIX	FreeBSD	HP-UX	Linux	Solaris	Tru64
Main NFS daemon	nfsd	nfsd	nfsd	rpc.nfsd	nfsd	nfsd
Handles mount requests	mountd	mountd	mountd	rpc. mountd	mountd	mountd
Block/asynch. I/O	biod	nfsiod	biod			nfsiod
File locking	rpc.lockd	rpc.lockd	rpc.lockd	rpc.lockd	lockd	Rpc.lockd
Network status monitor	rpc.statd	rpc.statd	rpc.statd	rpc.statd	statd	Rpc.statd
RPC port mapper	portmap	portmap	portmap	portmap	rpcbind	portmap
Boot script(s)[a]	/etc/rc.nfs	/etc/rc.net-work	/sbin/init.d/ nfs.*	/etc/init.d/ nfs*	/etc/init.d/nfs.*	/etc/init.d/ nfs*

[a] The portmap daemon is started by a different file, as part of general TCP/IP initialization.

---

[*] However, NFS assumes that users will have accounts with the same UID on both systems.

A few remarks about some of these daemons are in order:

- The nfsd daemon handles filesystem exporting and file access requests from remote systems. An NFS server—any system that makes its filesystems available to other computers—runs multiple instances of this daemon.
- The biod daemon performs NFS (block) I/O operations for client processes. Multiple instances of this daemon typically run on NFS clients.
- The mountd daemon handles mount requests from remote systems.
- The rpc.lockd daemon manages file locking on both server and client systems.
- The rpc.statd daemon handles lock, crash, and recovery services (client and server).
- The portmap daemon facilitates initial connection between local and remote servers (not strictly an NFS daemon but required for the NFS server facility to function).

As Table 10-10 indicates, the names of these daemons vary on some systems.

Mounting remote directories

As we've noted, remote filesystems may be entered into the filesystem configuration file in order to allow them to be automatically mounted at boot time. The format for an NFS entry is:

```
host:pathname mount-pt nfs options 0 0
```

where the first field is a concatenation of the remote hostname and the pathname to the mount point of the desired filesystem on the remote host, joined with a colon. For example, to designate the filesystem mounted at */organic* on host *duncan*, use *duncan:/organic*. The filesystem type field is set to nfs, and the remaining fields have their usual meanings. Note that the dump frequency and fsck pass fields should be zero.

Here is an example:

```
# device          mount            type  options  dump fsck
duncan:/organic   /duncan/organic  nfs   bg,intr    0  0
```

On Solaris systems, the */etc/vfstab* entries look like this:

```
# mount           fsck
# device          dev   mount           type  pass  auto?  options
duncan:/organic   -     /remote/organic nfs   -     yes    bg,intr
```

In addition to options for local filesystems, there are many other options available for remote filesystems. The most important are summarized in Table 10-11.

Table 10-11. Important NFS-specific mounting options

Option	Meaning
bg	If the NFS mount of this filesystem fails on the first try, continue retrying in the background. This speeds up booting when remote filesystems are unavailable.
retry=*n*	Number of mount retries before giving up (100,000 is the default).
timeo=*n*	Set the timeout—the length of time to wait for the first try of each individual NFS request before giving up—to the specified number of tenths of seconds. Each subsequent retry doubles the previous timeout value.
retrans=*n*	Retransmit a request *n* times before giving up (the default is 3).
soft, hard	Quit or continue trying to connect even after the retrans value is met.
intr	Allow an interrupt to kill a hung process.
rsize=*n* wsize=*n*	The size of the read or write buffer in bytes. Tuning these sizes can have a significant impact of NFS performance on some systems.

The soft and hard options are worth special mention. They define the action taken when a remote filesystem becomes unavailable. If a remote filesystem is mounted as hard, NFS will try to complete any pending I/O requests forever, even after the maximum number of retransmissions is reached; if it is mounted soft, an error will occur and NFS will cancel the request.

If a remote filesystem is mounted hard and intr is not specified, the process will block (be hung) until the remote filesystem reappears. For an interactive process especially, this can be quite annoying. If intr is specified, sending an interrupt signal to the process will kill it. This can be done interactively by typing Ctrl-C (although it won't die instantly; you'll still have to wait for the timeout period). For a background process, sending an INT (2) or QUIT (3) signal will usually work (again not necessarily instantaneously):

```
# kill -QUIT 34216
```

Sending a KILL signal (–9) will not kill a hung NFS process.

It would seem that mounting filesystems soft would get around the process-hanging problem. This is fine for filesystems mounted read-only. However, for a read-write filesystem, a pending request could be a write request, and so simply giving up could result in corrupted files on the remote filesystem. Therefore, read-write remote filesystems should always be mounted hard, and the intr option should be specified to allow users to make their own decisions about hung processes.

Here are some additional example */etc/fstab* entries for remote filesystems:

```
duncan:/benzene    /rings    nfs rw,bg,hard,intr,retrans=5 0  0
portia:/propel     /peptides nfs ro,soft,bg,nosuid          0  0
```

The first command mounts the filesystem mounted at */benzene* on the host *duncan* under */rings* on the local system. It is mounted read-write, hard, with interrupts enabled. The second command mounts the */propel* filesystem on the host *portia* under */peptides*; this filesystem is mounted read-only, and the SetUID status of any of its files is ignored on the local host.

Under AIX, remote filesystems have stanzas in */etc/filesystems* like local ones, with some additional keywords:

```
/rings:  Local mount point.
    dev      = /benzene           Remote filesystem.
    vfs      = nfs                Type is NFS.
    nodename = duncan             Remote host.
    mount    = true               Mount on boot.
    options  = bg,hard,intr       Mount options.
```

Once defined in the filesystem configuration file, the short form of the mount command may be used to mount the filesystem. For example, the following command mounts the proper remote filesystem at */rings*:

```
# mount /rings
```

The mount command may also be used to mount remote filesystems on an ad hoc basis, for example:

```
# mount -t nfs -o rw,hard,bg,intr duncan:/ether /mnt
```

This command mounts the */ether* filesystem from *duncan* under */mnt* on the local system. Note that the option that specifies the filesystem type varies on some systems. In fact, the filesystem type is usually superfluous.

Exporting local filesystems

The */etc/exports* file controls the accessibility of local filesystems to network access (except on Solaris systems; see below). Its traditional form consists of a series of lines containing a local filesystem mount point and followed by one or more hostnames:

```
/organic    spain canada
/inorganic
```

This export configuration file allows the hosts *spain* and *canada* to mount the */organic* filesystem and any remote host to remotely mount the */inorganic* filesystem.

The preceding examples present only the simplest examples of filesystem export options. In fact, any filesystem, directory, or file can be exported, not just the entire filesystem. And there is greater control over the type of access allowed. Entries in */etc/exports* consist of lines of the form:

```
pathname -option,option...
```

pathname is the name of the file or directory to which network access will be allowed. If *pathname* is a directory, all of the files and directories below it within the same local filesystem are also exported, but not any filesystems mounted within it. The second field in the entry consists of options specifying the type of access to be given and to whom.

A filesystem should be exported only once to a given host. Exporting two different directories within the same filesystem to the same host doesn't work in general.

Here are some sample entries from */etc/exports* (note that only the first option in the list is preceded by a hyphen):

```
/organic   -rw=spain,access=brazil:canada,anon=-1
/metal/3   -access=duncan:iago,root=duncan
/inorganic -ro
```

This file allows the host *spain* to mount */organic* for reading and writing and the hosts *brazil* and *canada* to mount it read-only, and it maps *anonymous* users—usernames from other hosts that do not exist on the local system and the *root* user from any remote system—to the UID –1. This corresponds to the *nobody* account, and it tells NFS not to allow such a user access to anything. On some systems, the UID –2 may be used to allow anonymous users access only to world-readable files. The `-rw` option exports the directory read-write to the hosts specified as its argument and read-only to all other allowed hosts; this access is referred to as *read-mostly*.

 Note that hosts within a list are separated by colons.

The second entry grants read-write access to */metal/3* to the hosts *duncan* and *iago*, and allows *root* users on *duncan* to retain that status and its access rights when using this filesystem. The third entry exports */inorganic* read-only to any host that wants to use it.

Table 10-12 lists the most useful *exports* file options.

Table 10-12. Useful exports file options

Option	Meaning
rw=*list* ro=*list*	Read-write and read-only access lists. rw is the default.
root=*list*	List of hosts where *root* status may be retained for this filesystem.
anon=*n*	Map remote root access to this UID.
maproot=*n*	Map remote root access to this UID (FreeBSD).
mapall=*n*	Map all remote users to this UID (FreeBSD).
root_squash	Map UID 0 and GID 0 values to the anonymous values (under Linux, to those specified in the anonuid and anongid options). This is the default.
anonuid=*n* anongid=*n*	UID/GID to which to map incoming *root*/group 0 access (Linux).
noaccess	Prohibits access to the specified directory and its subdirectories (Linux). This option is used to prevent access to part of a tree that has already been exported.
secure	Require access to be via the normal privileged NFS port (Linux). This is the default. I do not recommend ever using the insecure option.

If you modify */etc/exports*, the `exportfs` command must be run to put the new access restrictions into effect. The following command puts all of the access information in */etc/exports* into effect:

```
# exportfs -a
```

FreeBSD does not provide the `exportfs` command. You can use this command instead:

```
# kill -HUP `cat /var/run/mountd.pid`
```

Tru64 also does not have `exportfs`. The NFS `mountd` daemon detects changes to the file automatically.

The `showmount` command may be used to list exported filesystems (using its -e option) or other hosts that have remotely mounted local filesystems (-a). For example, the following command shows that the hosts *spain* and *brazil* have mounted the */organic* filesystem:

```
# showmount -a
brazil:/organic
spain:/organic
```

This data is stored in the file */etc/rmtab*. This file is saved across boots, so the information in it can get quite old. You may want to reset it from time to time by copying */dev/null* onto it (the system boot scripts take care of this automatically when NFS is started).

 If you're having trouble allowing other systems to mount the local filesystems from some particular system, the first thing to check is that the NFS server daemons are running. These daemons are often not started by default. If they are not running, you can start them manually, using the boot script listed in Table 10-10.

Exporting directories under Linux. The *exports* file has a slightly different format on Linux systems; options are included in parentheses at the end of the entry:

```
/organic     spain(rw) brazil(ro) canada(ro)
/metal/3     *.ahania.com(rw,root_squash)
/inorganic   (ro)
```

Based on this file, */organic* is exported read-write to *spain* and read-only to *brazil* and *canada*. */metal/3* is exported read-write to any host in the domain *ahania.com*, with UID 0 access mapped to the *nobody* account. */inorganic* is exported read-only to the world.

Exporting filesystems under Solaris. On Solaris systems, filesystem exporting is done via the */etc/dfs/dfstab* configuration file, which stores the `share` commands needed to export filesystems. The following *dfstab* file is equivalent to the *exports* file we looked at previously:

```
share -F nfs -o rw=spain,access=brazil:canada,anon=-1 /organic
share -F nfs -o access=duncan:iago,root=duncan /metal/3
share -F nfs -o ro /inorganic
```

For example, the first line exports the *organic* filesystem: it allows *spain* to mount it for reading and writing and *brazil* and *canada* to mount it read-only. Requests from usernames without accounts on the local system are denied.

These same commands need to be executed manually to put these access restrictions into effect prior to the next reboot (be sure that mountd is running).

The NFS Automounter

Once a network has even a moderate number of systems in it, trying to cross-mount even one or two filesystems from each system can quickly become a nightmare. The NFS automounter facility is designed to handle such situations by providing a means by which remote directories are mounted only when they are needed: when a user or process uses or refers to a file or subdirectory located within the remote directory. Directories that have not been used in a while are also unmounted automatically.

Using the automounter has the potential for simplifying remote directory management. The filesystem configuration file is made more straightforward because it lists only local filesystems and perhaps one or two statically mounted remote filesystems or directories. Booting is faster because NFS mounts are done later. Systems can also be shut down unexpectedly with fewer ill effects and hung processes.

The automounter works by detecting attempted access to any part of the remote directories under its control. When such an event occurs, the automounter generally mounts the remote filesystem into a directory known as its *staging area*—usually */tmp_mnt*—and creates a (pseudo) symbolic link to the mount location expected by the user. For example, if a user attempts to copy the file */data/organic/strained/propell.com*, and */organic* is a directory on host *spain*, the automounter will mount that remote directory on */tmp_mnt* and create a link to the local mount point, */data/organic*. To the user, the file will look like it really is located in */data/organic/strained*; however, if he changes to the directory */data/organic* and issues a pwd command, the real mount point will be visible (confusion is also likely if he uses a command like cd .. after moving to an automounted directory until he gets used to how the automounter works).

The automounter uses configuration files known as *maps*, which are of two types:

- Direct maps hold entries for remote directories to be mounted on demand by the automounter. These entries are really just abbreviated versions of traditional NFS /etc/fstab entries.

- Indirect maps are used for local directories whose subdirectories are each NFS-mounted, most likely from different remote hosts. For example, user home directories are usually managed with an indirect map. They are all automounted at a standard location within the filesystem on every system within a network, even though every one of them may be physically located on a separate system.

Indirect maps are used far more frequently than direct ones.

Direct maps are conventionally stored in */etc/map.direct*. Here is a sample entry from a direct map:

```
/metal/3     -intr    dalton:/metal/3
```

This entry places the directory */metal/3* on host *dalton* under automounter control. The directory will be mounted when needed at */metal/3* on the local system; directories controlled by direct maps do not use the automounter staging area. The second field in the entry holds options for the mount command.

Indirect maps are generally named for the local directory whose (potential) contents they specify. Here is a short version of the indirect map */etc/auto.homes*, which is used to configure the local directory */homes*; its entries specify the remote locations of the various subdirectories of */homes*:

```
chavez-rw,intr   dalton:/home/chavez
harvey-rw,intr   iago:/home/harvey
wang-rw,intr     portia:/u/wang
stein-rw,intr    hamlet:/home/stein4
```

The format is very similar to that for direct maps. In this case, the first field is the name of the subdirectory of */homes* from which the remote directory will be accessed locally. Note that we have set up automounting at */homes*, not in the usual location of */home*, because it is illegal to mix local and automounted subdirectories within the same local directory.

Once the automounter is configured in this way on every system, user home directories will be invariant to the system the user happens to be using. No matter where he is, his home directory will always have the same files within it.

The automounting facility uses the automount daemon, which may be started with a command like this one:

```
# automount -tl 600 /homes /etc/auto.homes /- /etc/auto.direct
```

The -tl option specifies how long a directory must be idle before it is automatically unmounted (in seconds; five minutes is the default). The next two arguments illustrate the method for specifying a local directory for automounter control and its corresponding indirect map. The final two arguments illustrate how a direct map is specified; the local directory is always specified as /- for a direct map. A command like the previous needs to be added to (or uncommented out within) the system initialization scripts for the automounter to be started at boot time.

If you want to stop the automounter process for some reason, use the kill command without any signal option; this will send the process a TERM signal and allow it to terminate gracefully and clean up after itself. For example:

```
# kill `ps -ea | grep automoun | awk '{print $1}'`
```

If you kill it with -9, hung processes and undeletable phantom files are the almost certain result.

Samba

The free Samba facility allows Unix filesystems to be shared with Windows systems. Samba does so by supporting the Server Message Block (SMB) protocol,* the native resource sharing protocol for Microsoft networks. It is available for all of the Unix versions we are considering.

With Samba, you can make Unix filesystems look like shared Windows filesystems, allowing them to be accessed using the normal Windows facilities and commands such as net use. Linux systems can also mount Windows filesystems within the Unix filesystem using a related facility.

Installing Samba is quite simple. The books I mentioned earlier have excellent discussions of the procedure. Once you have built Samba, the next step is to create the Samba configuration file, *smb.conf*, usually stored in the *lib* subdirectory of the main Samba directory or in */etc/samba*.

Here is a simple version of this file:

```
[global]                                 Global settings applying to all exports.
hosts allow = vala, pele
hosts deny = lilith
valid users = dagmar, @chem, @phys, @bio, @geo
invalid users = root, admin, administrator
max log size = 2000                      Log size in KB.
[chemdir]                                Define a directory (share) for export.
path = /chem/data/new                    Local (Unix) path to be shared.
comment = New Data                       Description of the filesystem.
read only = no                           Filesystem is not read-only.
case sensitive = yes                     Filenames are case sensitive.
force group = chemists                   Map all user access to this Unix group.
read list = dagmar, @chem, @phys         Users/groups allowed read access.
write list = @chem                       Users/groups allowed write access.
```

The first section of the configuration file, introduced by the [global] line, specifies global Samba settings that apply to all filesystems exported via the facility. Its first two lines specify remote systems that are allowed to access Samba filesystems and those that are forbidden from doing so, respectively. The next two lines similarly specify Unix users and groups that are allowed and denied access (note that group names are prefixed by an at sign: *@chem*). The final line of this first section specifies the maximum size of the Samba log file in KB.

The second section of the sample Samba configuration file defines a filesystem for exporting (i.e., a share). In this case, it consists of the local path */chem/data/new*, and it will be accessed by remote systems using the share name *chemdir* (defined in the section's header line). This exported filesystem is exported read-write and uses case-sensitive filenames. All incoming access to the filesystem will take place as if the user

---

* Also known as the Common Internet File System, CIFS (this week...).

were a member of the local Unix *chemists* group. Windows user *dagmar* and groups *chem* and *phys* are allowed read access to the filesystem, and members of Windows group *chem* are also given write access. Whether an individual file may be read or written will still be determined by its Unix file permissions.

User home directories are exported in a slightly different way via configuration file entries like these:

```
[homes]                              Create the special homes share.
comment = Home directories
writeable = yes
valid users = %S                     %S expands to the share name (here = username).
```

These entries create a share for each local Unix user home directory (as defined in the password file). These shares are actually created on the fly as they are accessed. For example, if user *chavez* attempts to access the share *india**home* (where *india* is the Unix system), the share *india**chavez* will be created and presented to her. Only she will be able to access this share due to the valid users line in the homes share definition; all other users will be denied access. User *chavez* can access the share as either *india**homes* or as *india**chavez*.

You can use the `testparm` command to verify the syntax of a Samba configuration file before you install it. See the Samba documentation for full details on configuration file entries.

Another useful Samba feature is the username mapping file, specified via a configuration file entry like the following:

```
username map = /etc/samba/smbusers
```

Entries within the file look like this:

```
# Unix = Windows
chavez = rachel
root = Administrator admin          Multiple names are allowed.
quigley = "Filbert Quigley"         Quote names with spaces.
```

Map files can have some unexpected effects. For one thing, when a password is required by the Unix system before access is granted, it is that password for the Unix account that will be needed. This can be confusing if the mapping sends a user to an account that is different from the one he usually uses. Secondly, home share names will again reflect the mapped Unix username.

The `smbstatus` command may be used to display current remote users of local filesystems on the Unix system:

```
$ smbstatus
Samba version 1.9.16
Service uid     gid      pid    machine
-------------------------------------------
chemdir nobody  chemists 14810 vala (192.168.13.34) Jul 14 11:51:07
No locked files
```

Samba authentication

In general, Samba prompts the user for a password when required. By default, these passwords are sent across the network in unencrypted form (i.e., as clear text). This is an insecure practice that most sites will find unacceptable. Samba can be modified to use only encoded passwords as follows:

- Add the following entries to the global section of the Samba configuration file:

  ```
  encrypt passwords = yes
  security = user
  ```

- Use the mksmbpasswd.sh script included with the Samba package source code to create the initial Samba password file. For example:

  ```
  # cat /etc/passwd | mksmbpasswd.sh > /etc/samba/private/smbpasswd
  ```

  The *smbpasswd* file should be owned by *root* and have the permissions mode 600. The subdirectory in which it resides should be protected 500.

Once encrypted passwords are enabled, users must use the smbpasswd command in order to set their Samba passwords.

You can use a single Unix server to authenticate all Samba passwords by using these configuration file entries:

```
security = server
password server = host
encrypt passwords = yes
```

You can authenticate Samba using a Windows domain controller with these configuration file entries:

```
security = domain
workgroup = domain
password server = domain-controllers
encrypt passwords = yes
```

See the Samba documentation and the previously cited books for more details about this topic (including how to use a Samba server as a Windows domain controller).

Mounting Windows filesystems under Linux and FreeBSD. The Samba package includes the smbclient utility in order to access remote SMB-based shares from the Unix system. It uses an interface similar to the FTP facility.

A much better approach is provided on Linux systems via the built-in smbfs filesystem type. For example, the following command mounts the *depot* share on *vala* as the local directory */win_stuff*:

```
# mount -t smbfs -o username=user,password=xxx //vala/depot /win_stuff
```

This command makes the connection as the specified user account on the Windows system using the specified password. If the password option is omitted, you will be prompted for the proper password. If you do include a password in the */etc/fstab* file, be sure to protect the file from ordinary users. In general, you should not use the

Administrator password. Create an unprivileged user account to use for the mount process instead.

A similar facility is available under FreeBSD Version 4.5 and later. For example:

```
# mount_smbfs -I vala //chavez@vala/depot /mnt
Password:                           Not echoed.
```

Passwords can be stored in a file named *$HOME/.nsmbrc*. In this case, add the -N option to the command to suppress the password prompt. Here is a sample file:

```
[VALA:CHAVEZ:DEPOT]                 server:user:share
password=xxxxxxxx
```

Yes, the first line really does have to be in uppercase (ugh!).

You can also enter such filesystems into */etc/fstab* on either system, using entries like these:

```
# remote share      mount point  type  options
//chavez@vala/depot  /depot/vala  smbfs  noauto 0 0                          FreeBSD
//vala/depot         /depot/vala  smbfs  noauto,username=chavez,password=x 0 0  Linux
```

Under FreeBSD, you'll need to specify the password in the *.nsmbrc* file if you want to remote share to mounted automatically.

CHAPTER 11

Backup and Restore

Every user of any computer figures out sooner or later that files are occasionally lost. These losses have many causes: users may delete their own files accidentally, a bug can cause a program to corrupt its data file, a hardware failure may ruin an entire disk, and so on. The damage resulting from these losses can range from minor to expansive and can be very time-consuming to fix. To ensure against loss, one primary responsibility of a system administrator is planning and implementing a backup system that periodically copies all files on the system to some other location. It is also the administrator's responsibility to see that backups are performed in a timely manner and that backup tapes (and other media) are stored safely and securely. This chapter will begin by discussing backup strategies and options and then turn to the tools that Unix systems provide for making them.

An excellent reference work about backups on Unix systems is *Unix Backup and Recovery* by W. Curtis Preston (O'Reilly & Associates). It covers the topics we are discussing here in complete detail and also covers material beyond the scope of this book (e.g., backing up and restoring databases).

Planning for Disasters and Everyday Needs

Developing an effective backup strategy is an ongoing process. You usually inherit something when you take over an existing system and start out doing the same thing you've always done when you get a new system. This may work for a while, but I've seen companies try to retain their centralized, hordes-of-operators–based backup policies after they switched from a computer room full of mainframes to a building full of workstations. Such an attempt is ultimately as comical as it is heroic, but it all too often ends up only in despair, with no viable policy ever replacing the outdated one. The time to develop a good backup strategy is right now, starting from however you are approaching things at the moment.

Basically, backups are insurance. They represent time expended in an effort to prevent future losses. The time required for any backup strategy must be weighed against the decrease in productivity, schedule slippage, and so on if the files are needed but are not available. The overall requirement of any backup plan is that it be able to restore the entire system—or group of systems—within an acceptable amount of time in the event of a large-scale failure. At the same time, a backup plan should not sacrifice too much in the way of convenience, either in what it takes to get the backup done or how easy it is to restore one or two files when a user deletes them accidentally. The approaches one might take when considering only disaster recovery or only day-to-day convenience in isolation are often very different, and the final backup plan will need to take both of them into account (and will accordingly reflect the tension between them).

There are many factors to consider in developing a backup plan. The following questions are among the most important:

What files need to be backed up? The simplest answer is, of course, *everything*, and while everything but scratch files and directories needs to be saved somewhere, it doesn't all have to be saved as part of the system backups. For example, when the operating system has been delivered on CD-ROM, there is really no need to back up the system files, although you may choose do so anyway for reasons of convenience.

Where are these files? This question involves both where the important files are within the filesystem and which systems hold the most important data.

Who will back up the files? The answer may depend on where the files are. For example, many sites assign the backup responsibility for server systems to the system administrator(s) but make users responsible for files that they keep on their workstation's local disks. This may or may not be a good idea, depending on whether or not all of the important files really get backed up.

Where, when, and under what conditions should backups be performed? Where refers to the computer system on which the backup will be performed; this need not necessarily be the same as the system where the files are physically located. Similarly, in an ideal world, all backups would be performed after hours on unmounted filesystems. That's not always practical in the real world, however.

How often do these files change? This information will help you decide both when and how often to perform backups and the type of schedule to implement. For example, if your system supports a large, ongoing development project, the files on it are likely to change very frequently and will need to be backed up at least daily and probably after hours. On the other hand, if the only volatile file on your system is a large database, its filesystem might need to backed up several times every day while the other filesystems on the same system would be backed up only once a week.[*]

---

[*] In actual fact, a database is often backed up using a facility provided by the software vendor, but you get the idea here.

How quickly does an important missing or damaged file need to be restored? Since backups protect against both widespread and isolated file loss, the timeframe in which key files need to be back online needs to be taken into account. The number of key files, how widely spread they are throughout a filesystem (or network), and how large they are will also influence matters. Your system may only have one irreplaceable file, but you'll need to plan very differently depending on whether it is 1 KB or 1 GB in size. Note that losing even a single 1 KB file can wreak havoc if it's the license file without which the central application program won't run.

How long do we need to retain this data? Backups protect current data from accidents. As such, they are normally needed—or useful—only for a relatively short period (months or a year or two) In contrast, most sites also need to create permanent archives of important "point-in-time" data, for example, the software and data used to prepare a tax return. These need to be saved for an indefinite period: many years or even decades. While the requirements are similar, the goals are different enough that you are unlikely to be able to rely on your regular backups for archival purposes. Thinking about this kind of data and how to create and store it must be part of every effective backup plan.

Where should the backup media be stored? Recent backups are generally kept close to the computer for quick restoration. Long-term backups and archives should be stored in a secure offsite location.

Where will the data be restored? Will the backup files be used only on the system from which they were made, or is there an expectation that they could be restored to a different system in an emergency? If multisystem compatibility is ever important, it needs to be taken into account in designing the backup and recovery plan. For example, you might need to ensure that any compression scheme in use on one system can be decoded by the other target systems (or avoid using any vendor-specific formats). Other examples of this sort of issue include access control list data that might be backed up along with files and backups of a filesystem from a system that is larger than the maximum filesystem size on the target system.

Backing up Active Filesystems

Virtually all Unix documentation recommends that filesystems be unmounted before a backup is performed (except for the root filesystem). This recommendation is rarely followed, and in practice, backups can be performed on mounted filesystems. However, you need to make users aware that open files are not always backed up correctly. It is also true that there are circumstances in which events in an active filesystem can cause some files or even the entire backup archive itself to be corrupt. We will consider those that are relevant to the various available backup programs as we discuss them.

Backup Capacity Planning

Once you have gathered all the data about what needs to be backed up and the resources available for doing so, a procedure like the following can be used to develop the detailed backup plan itself:

1. Begin by specifying an ideal backup schedule without considering any of the constraints imposed by your actual situation. List what data you would like to be backed up, how often it needs to be backed up, and what subdivisions of the total amount make sense.

2. Now compare that ideal schedule to what is actually possible in your environment, taking the following points into consideration:

   - When the data is available to be backed up: backing up open files is always problematic—the best you can hope for is to get an uncorrupted snapshot of the state of the file at the instant that the backup is made—so, ideally, backups should be performed on idle systems. This usually translates to after normal working hours.

   - How many tape drives (or other backup devices) are available to perform backups at those times and their maximum capacities and transfer rates: in order to determine the latter, you can start with the manufacturer's specifications for the device, but you will also want to run some timing tests of your own under actual conditions to determine realistic transfer rates that take into account the system loads, network I/O rates, and other factors in your environment. You will also need to take into account whether all the data is accessible to every backup device or not.

At this point (as with any aspect of capacity planning), there is no substitute for doing the math. Let's consider a simple example: a site has 180 GB of data that all needs to be backed up once a week, and there are 3 tape drives available for backups (assume that all of the data is accessible to every drive). Ideally, backups should be performed only on week nights between midnight and 6 A.M. In order to get everything done, each tape drive will have to back up 60 GB of data in the 30 hours that the data is available. That means that each tape drive must write 2 GB of data per hour (333 KB/sec) to tape.

This is within the capabilities of current tape drives when writing local data.* However, much of the data in our example is distributed across a network, so there is a chance that data might not be available at a fast enough rate to sustain the tape drive's top speed. Some backup programs also pause when they encounter an open file, giving it a chance to close (30 seconds is a typical wait period); when there are a lot of open files in a backup set, this can substantially increase how long the backup takes to complete.

---

* In practice, of course, you would also need an auto loading tape device (or someone to change tapes in the middle of the night).

In addition, we have not made any allowances for performing incremental backups (discussed below) between full backups. Thus, this example situation seems to strain the available resources.

3. Make modifications to the plan to take into account the constraints of your environment. Our example site is cutting things a bit too close for comfort, but they have several options for addressing this:

   - Adding additional backup hardware, in this case, a fourth tape drive.

   - Decreasing the amount of data to be backed up or the backup frequency: for example, they could perform full backups only every two weeks for some or all of the data.

   - Increasing the amount of time available/used for backups (for example, performing some backups on weekends or doing incremental backups during the early evening hours).

   - Staging backups to disk. This scheme writes the backup archives to a dedicated storage area. The files can then be written to tape at any subsequent time. Disks are also faster than tape drives, so this method also takes less time than directly writing to tape. It does, of course, require that sufficient disk space be available to store the archives.

4. Test and refine the backup plan. Actually trying it out will frequently reveal factors that your on-paper planning has failed to consider.

5. Review the backup plan on a periodic basis to determine if it is still the best solution to your site's backup needs.

Backup Strategies

The simplest and most thorough backup scheme is to copy all the files on a system to tape or other backup media. A *full backup* does just that, including every file within a designated set of files, often defined as those on a single computer system or a single disk partition.*

Full backups are time-consuming and can be unwieldy; restoring a single file from a large backup spanning multiple tapes is often inconvenient, and when files are not changing very often, the time taken to complete a full backup may not be justified by the number of new files that are actually being saved. On the other hand, if files are changing very rapidly, and 50 users will be unable to work if some of them are lost, or when the amount of time a backup takes to complete is not an issue, then a full backup might be reasonable even every day.

---

* For the purposes of this discussion, I'll focus on per-disk partition backups, but keep in mind that this is not the only reasonable way of organizing things. I'll also refer to "backup tapes" most of the time in this chapter. In most cases, however, what I'll be saying will apply equally well to other backup media.

Incremental backups are usually done more frequently. In an incremental backup, the system copies only those files that have been changed since some previous backup. Incrementals are used when full backups are large and only a small amount of the data changes within the course of, say, one day. In such cases, backing up only the changed files saves a noticeable amount of time over performing a full backup.

Some Unix backup programs use the concept of a *backup level* to distinguish different kinds of backups. Each backup type has a level number assigned to it; by definition, a full backup is level 0. Backing up the system at any level means saving all the files that have changed since the last backup at the previous level. Thus, a level 1 backup saves all the files that have changed since the last full (level 0) backup; a level 2 backup saves all the files that have been changed since the last level 1 backup, and so on.*

A typical backup strategy using multiple levels is to perform a full backup at the beginning of each week, and then perform a level 1 backup (all files that have changed since the full backup) each day. The following weekly backup schedule summarizes one implementation of this plan:

> *Monday:* Level 0 (full)
> *Tuesday–Friday:* Level 1 (incremental)

A seven-day version of this approach is easy to construct.

The primary advantage of this plan is that only two sets of backup media are needed to restore the complete filesystem (the full backup and the incremental). Its main disadvantage is that the daily backups will gradually grow and, if the system is very active, may approach the size of the full backup set by the end of the week.

A popular monthly plan for sites with very active systems might look something like this:

> *First Monday:* Level 0 (full)
> *All other Mondays:* Level 1 (weekly incremental to previous Level 0)
> *Tuesday–Friday:* Level 2 (daily incremental to previous Level 1)

This plan will require three sets of backup media to do a complete restore (the most recent backup of each type).

In deciding on a backup plan, take into account how the system is used. The most heavily used portions of the filesystem may need to be backed up more often than the other parts (such as the root filesystem, which contains standard Unix programs and files and which therefore rarely changes). A few parts of the system (like */tmp*) need never be backed up. You may want to create some additional filesystems that

---

* Not all backup commands explicitly use level numbers, but the concept is valid for and can be implemented with any of the available tools, provided you are willing to do some of the record keeping yourself (by hand or by script).

will never be backed up; anyone using them would be responsible for backing up his own files.

You should also consider performing a full backup—whether the schedule calls for it or not—before you make significant changes to the system, such as building a new kernel, adding a new application package, or installing a new version of the operating system. This may be one of the few times that the root filesystem gets backed up, but if you ever have a problem with your system disk, you will find it well worth the effort when you can avoid a significant amount of reconfiguration.

Unattended backups

The worst part of doing backups is sitting around waiting for them to finish. Unattended backups solve this problem for some sites. If the backup will fit on a single tape, one approach is to leave a tape in the drive when you leave for the day, have the backup command run automatically by cron during the night, and pick up the tape the next morning.

Sometimes, however, unattended backups can be a security risk; don't use them if untrusted users have physical access to the tape drive or other backup device and thus could steal the media itself. Backups needed to be protected as strongly as the most secure file on the system.

Similarly, don't do unattended backups when you can't trust users not to accidentally or deliberately write over the tape or other rewriteable media (ejecting the tape after the backup is completed sometimes prevents this, but not always). You also won't be able to use them if the backup device is in heavy use and can't be tied up by the backup for the entire night.

Data verification

In many cases, backups can simply be written to media, and the media can go directly to its designated storage location. This practice is fine as long as you are 100% confident in the reliability of your backup devices and media. In other cases, data verification is a good idea.

Data verification consists of a second pass through the backed-up data, in which each file is compared to the version on disk, ensuring that the file was backed up correctly. It also verifies that the media itself is readable.

Some sites will choose to verify the data on all backups. All sites should perform verification operations on at least a periodic basis for all of their backup devices. In addition, as they age and wear out, many devices begin to produce media that can only be successfully read in the drive that produced it. If you need backups that will be readable by devices or systems other than the one that originally wrote on the physical media, you should also periodically verify the backups' readability by examining them on the target devices and systems.

Storing backup media

Properly storing the backup tapes, diskettes, or other media once you've written them is an important part of any backup plan. Here are some things to keep in mind when deciding where to store your backup media:

Know where things are. Having designated storage locations for backups makes finding the right one quickly much more likely. It is also important that anyone who might need to do a restore knows where the media are kept (you will want to take a vacation occasionally). Installation CDs, bootable recovery tapes, boot diskettes, and the like also ought to be kept in a specific location known to those people who may need them. I can assure you from personal experience that a system failure is much more unpleasant when you have to dig through boxes of tapes or piles of CDs looking for the right one before you can even attempt to fix whatever's wrong with the system.

Another aspect of knowing where things are concerns figuring out what tape holds the file that you need to restore. Planning for this involves making records of backup contents, which is discussed later in this chapter.

Make routine restorations easy. Backups should be stored close enough to the computer so that you can quickly restore a lost file, and tapes should be labeled sufficiently well so that you can find the ones you need.

Ideally, you should have a full set of tapes for each distinct operation in your backup schedule. For example, if you do a backup every day, it's best to have five sets of tapes that you reuse each week; if you can afford it, you might even have 20 sets that you rotate through every four weeks. Using a single set of tapes over and over again is inviting disaster.

Labeling tapes clearly is also a great help in finding the right one quickly later. Color-coded labels are favored by many sites as an easy yet effective way to distinguish the different sets of tapes. At the other extreme, I visited a site where the backup system they developed prints a detailed label for the tape at the conclusion of each backup.

Write-protect backup media. This prevents backup media from being accidentally overwritten. The mechanism for write-protection varies with different media types, but most mechanisms involve physically moving a plastic dial or tab to some designated position. The position that is the unwriteable one varies: floppy disks, optical disks and DAT (4mm) tapes are writeable when the tabbed opening is closed, while 8mm tapes and removable disks are writeable when it is open.

Consider the environment. Most backup media like it cool, dry, and dark. High humidity is probably the most damaging environment, especially for cartridge-enclosed media, which are easily ruined by the moisture condensation that accompanies temperature drops in humid conditions. Direct sunlight should also be avoided, especially for floppy disks, since most plastic materials will deform when subjected to the temperature within the trunk of a car or the enclosed passenger compartment on a hot summer day. Dust can also be a problem for most backup media. I've had lint make floppy disks unreadable after taking them home in my coat pocket (now I put them in a zip-top plastic bag first).

The fact that backup media prefer the same environment used for many computer rooms does not necessarily mean that any or all backup media should be stored in the same room as the computer. Doing so runs the risk that a major problem will destroy both the computer and the backups. Backup tapes are actually more sensitive to some types of problems than some computer components. For example, if a pipe bursts above the computer room, the computer may suffer only minor damage, but your backup tapes will usually all be ruined if they get wet.

If the tape storage area differs in temperature from the computer area by more than a few degrees, allow the tapes to acclimate to the computer temperature before writing to them.

Magnetic interference is also something to think about. One of this book's technical reviewers relayed a story about "an entire backup library that kept getting wiped out on a nearly daily basis. Turns out that the tapes were in a secure location but placed against a wall that was shared with a freight elevator. The magnetic fields and such caused by the moving lift caused all that nice magnetic tape storage to become erased. Funny but cautionary."

Handle media properly.   Some media have special requirements that you'll need to take into account. For example, floppy disks and zip disks ideally should be stored upright, resting on a thin edge rather than stacked on top of one another. Similarly, cartridge tapes like to be stored with the spools vertical (perpendicular to the ground, like a car's tires) with the edge that contacts the drive heads down (so gravity pulls tape away from the spools). When you're counting on media to preserve important data, humor them and orient them the way they prefer.

Take security into account.   In every location where you store backup tapes, the usual physical security considerations apply: the tapes should be protected from theft, vandalism, and environmental disasters as much as is possible.

Off-site and long-term storage

Off-site backups are the last barrier between your system and total annihilation. They are full backup sets that are kept in a locked, fireproof, environmentally-controlled location completely off site. Such backups should be performed on unmounted filesystems if at all possible.

Preparing backups for off-site storage is also one of the few times when simply making a backup is not enough.* In these cases, you also need to verify that the backup

---

* Another such time is when you are rebuilding a filesystem.

tape or diskette is readable. This is done by using an appropriate restore command to list the contents of the tape or diskette. While this will not guarantee that every file is completely readable, it will improve the odds of it considerably. Some backup utilities provide a full verification facility in which the entire content of each file in a backup set is compared with the corresponding file on disk; this is the preferred method of checking critical backups. In any case, backups should be verified in the best way available whenever the integrity of the backup is essential.

Permanent Backups

For data meant for permanent archiving, you should create and verify two sets of backup media with the idea that the redundant copy can be used should the first one fail. The media should also be checked periodically (annually or possibly biannually). When a particular media item fails—and they all will eventually—a new copy should be made from the other one to replace it.

You should also make sure that you have at least one working drive of the type that you are using for permanent storage media. For example, if you have an archive of 8 mm tapes, you will need to always have working 8 mm tape drives to read them. This will continue to be true if your primary backup medium changes. Similarly, you must maintain whatever software programs and other running environment is required to use the data for it to be of any use.

Finally, tapes should be rewound or retensioned regularly (perhaps twice a year) to maintain readability. Given this requirement, tapes are being superceded by CDs as permanent storage media.

When Being Compulsive is Good

It's very easy to put off doing backups, especially when you are responsible only for your own files. However, performing backups regularly is vital. Basically, it's a good idea to assume that the next time you sit down at the computer, all your disks will have had head crashes. Keeping such a catastrophe in mind will make it obvious what needs to be backed up and how often. Backups are convenient for restoring accidentally deleted files, but they are also essential in the event of serious hardware failures or other disasters. Catastrophes *will* happen. All hardware has a finite lifetime, and eventually something will fail.

Given this reality, it is obvious why an almost drone-like adherence to routine is an important attribute for an effective system administrator. Planning for worst-case scenarios is part of the job. Let them call you compulsive if they want to; one day, your compulsiveness—also known to many as carefulness—will save them, or at least their files.

Backup Media

When I first started working as a system administrator, 9-track tape was the only medium you'd consider using for a backup.* That's certainly no longer true. Today, there are many different media suitable for storing backed-up data. This section provides a quick summary of the available choices. This list includes most of the drives and media types which are in common use. The backup strategy for any particular system will often involve more than one media type.

Up-to-the-minute information about available backup devices and media may be obtained from *http://www.storagemountain.com*. There is also an excellent discussion in *Unix Backup and Recovery*.

Magnetic tape

Magnetic tape of one sort or another has been the traditional backup medium for decades. Over the years, it has taken on a variety of sizes and forms, beginning with 7-track and then 9-track tape: 1/2-inch wide tape wound around a circular reel. The introduction of plastic cartridges containing the tape and both reels was a major step forward in terms of reducing the space requirements of backup media. The first tape of this type was 1/4-inch cartridge tape (also known as QIC tape), which for a while was the medium of choice for most workstations; these tapes are still occasionally used.

Around 20 years ago, higher-capacity tapes in formats originally developed for other markets became available. 8 mm tape drives became popular in the late 1980s and are still in wide use. Originally designed for video uses, the tapes are about the size of an audio cassette. 4 mm digital audio tapes (commonly called DAT tapes although the data storage scheme is technically known as DDS) are also in wide use. DAT cartridges are about 25% smaller than 8 mm tapes.

 8 mm and 4 mm tapes come in two grades, one designed for video and audio recording (respectively), and a better, more expensive grade designed for data. Be sure to purchase only data-quality tapes. Although lower-quality tapes will sometimes appear to work fine, in my experience they are much, much less reliable about retaining data (despite urban legends to the contrary).

Both of these tape types are in use today, although DAT is far more prevalent than 8 mm. Both types of tape come in a variety of lengths and corresponding data capacities. Currently, the largest ordinary 8 mm tapes are 160 meters long and hold up to

---

* The only other possibilities were punch cards and paper tape.

7 GB of data,* although there are also tapes that hold 1.2 GB (54 m) and 2.4 GB (112 m). DAT tapes correspond to various DDS levels:

DDS-1
2 and 3 GB tapes (60 and 90 m

DDS-2
4 GB tapes (120 m)

DDS-3
12 GB tapes (125 m)

DDS-4
20 GB tapes (150 m)

DDS-3 and DDS-4 use a different technology than the earlier versions.

Be aware that only the newest tape drives can support the largest tapes, but most drives provide read-only backward compatibility.

There are also several newer magnetic tape technologies. Exabyte's Mammoth-2† and Sony's Advanced Intelligent Tape (AIT) technologies take 8 mm tapes to much higher capacities: 20, 40, or 60 GB and 35 or 50 GB, respectively. They both use the Advanced Metal Evaporative (AME) cartridge developed by Sony (a new 8 mm format). Some Mammoth-2 drives can also read earlier 8 mm tapes, but they require an extensive clearing procedure to be performed after each instance. These are also among the fastest tape drives, with transfer rates of up to 12 MB/s for Mammoth-2 drives and 6 MB/s for AIT drives.

The Digital Linear Tape (DLT) technology was initially developed by Digital Equipment Corporation, but they later sold it to Quantum Corporation. This format uses cartridges similar to DEC's old TK family, which have proven themselves to be extremely reliable and long-lived. It is also a fast format, with transfer rates of up to 10 MB/s.

The high capacity of magnetic tapes make them ideal for unattended backups: you can put a tape in at night, start a shell script that puts several filesystems on one tape, and go home.

Tapes also have some disadvantages:

- They are extremely sensitive to heat and electromagnetic fields and fail quite easily when they are mishandled. Electromagnetic fields are produced by a variety of common devices found near computers, including UPS power supplies, external peripheral devices containing their own power supplies, monitors, and

---

* That is, 7 GB of bits. The amount of "data" written may be much more if the original files are compressed before or as they are written to tape. Tape drive and media manufacturers love to inflate their products' capacities by quoting maximum compressed data numbers.

† This was preceded by the Mammoth technology, which was notoriously unreliable. Mammoth-2 initially seems to be better.

---

speakers. Moreover, simply reading a magnetic tape also contributes to data degradation.

- They are sequential storage devices. In order to reach a given file on a tape, you have to wind the tape to the proper point. This is more of a problem for older tapes drives; current high-end drives can reach an arbitrary point on a tape in seconds.

Magneto-optical disks

Magneto-optical disks have the same width and length as floppy disks but are about twice as thick and hold a lot more data. Magneto-optical disks also come in 3.5-inch and 5.25-inch versions,* and their current capacity ranges up to 9.1 GB. Optical disks are purported to be much more stable than any of the purely magnetic media; the stability comes from the fact that they are written magnetically but are read optically, so reading the disk has no degrading effect on the stored data. In addition, the media can also be erased and rewritten as needed. Finally, magneto-optical disks also have the advantage of being random access devices. Transfer rates for these devices peak at about 5 MB/s.

Current drives are still quite expensive—over $2000—as are the disks themselves, but they are nevertheless very popular. As I noted in the previous edition of this book (circa 1995), "a rewriteable medium that can permanently store over a gigabyte of data in the space of a couple floppy disks probably has a future." Now it's gigabytes of data and a definite future.

There are also other optical formats used or in development by a few manufacturers.

CDs and DVDs

Writeable CDs and DVDs have become viable backup media due to the substantial price reductions for both drives and media. There are two types of writeable CDs, referred to as CD-R (write-once CDs) and CD-RW (rewriteable CDs). Both come in 640 MB capacity, and recently 700 MB CD-R media have become available.

Writeable DVD technology is just emerging into the general marketplace at this writing. In fact, there are several DVD recording formats:

DVD-RAM
    The first available format, it is now falling out of use since it cannot be read in ordinary DVD drives.

---

* You might wonder what is so magical about 3.5 and 5.25 inches. Devices of this size fit easily into the standard device bays found in PCs as well as into available storage boxes.

DVD-R

Write-once DVDs (also an aging technology).

DVD-RW

Rewriteable DVDs that can be read by ordinary DVD drives.

DVD+RW

An emerging technology devised by a coalition of drive manufacturers. These drives can produce ordinary (sequential) DVDs as well as random access disks. The former are readable by ordinary DVD players (but not by recorders of the other types), although some older models may require firmware updates. DVD+RW media can hold up to 4.7 GB per side.

As of this writing, Hewlett-Packard has recently released a low-cost DVD+RW writer suitable for use on PC-based systems, so this may become a popular backup device in that market in time.

Removable disks: Zip and Jaz

Removable disks are fully enclosed disk units that are inserted into a drive as needed. They tend to be significantly more reliable than either tapes or floppy disks. On Unix systems, they generally behave like a hard disk, but it is also possible to treat them as a giant floppy disk. They are suitable as backup media in some environments and circumstances.

There have been a variety of removable disk technologies over the years. The Zip and Jaz drives by Iomega have come to dominate this market. Zip drives—which come in 100 MB and 250 MB sizes—can be used with most Unix systems. Jaz drives, which have capacities of 1 GB or 2 GB, can also be used. I had a great deal of trouble with early Jaz drives, which were designed for infrequent, intermittent backup use and consistently failed when used on even a semi-continuous basis. More recent drives are said to be better. Both drive types are available with various I/O interfaces: SCSI, USB, IDE.

Floppy disks

Floppy disk drives are still found on most PC-based computer systems,* and they do have some limited backup uses. For example, PC-based Unix versions (as well as a few running on larger systems) often use floppy disks for emergency boot devices. In addition, floppy disks can be useful for inherently limited backup tasks, such as saving customized system configuration files from the root filesystem. Standard floppy disks hold 1.44 MB, and some Unix workstations include drives that double that capacity to 2.8 MB. Occasionally, you will come across a floppy drive that also supports Super disks: media that look like floppy disks but hold 120 MB.

---

* Although this will probably no longer be true in a couple of years.

Hard disks

Given the low prices of hard disks these days, they may also be a viable backup target device in some circumstances. For example, some sites provide a large backup disk on the local network where users can make periodic copies of key files that they are working on. Large disks can also be used for scratch purposes, for temporary data repositories and data holding areas, and similar purposes. They can also be used as a staging area where backups are stored temporarily on the way to being written to tape or other media.

Stackers, jukeboxes, and similar devices

There are a variety of devices designed to make media handling more automated, as well as to store and make available large numbers of media units. For example, there are auto-loading tape drives—also known as *stackers*—which can feed tapes automatically from a stack of 10 or so. Early stackers could access the component tapes only in order, but many current devices can retrieve any desired tape.

Another type of device puts multiple drive units into a box that looks to users like a single tape drive with the combined capacity of all of its components. Alternatively, such a device can be used to make multiple identical tapes simultaneously.

Still other units combine both multiple drives and tape auto-loading capabilities. These devices are known as *jukeboxes* or *libraries*.* The most sophisticated of them can retrieve a specific tape and place it into the desired drive. Some of these devices include integrated bar-code readers so that tapes can be identified by their physical label rather than storage location or electronic label. Similar devices also exist for optical disks and writeable CD-ROMs.

Media Lifetime

From time to time, you also need to think about the reasonable expected lifetime of your backup media. Stored under the right conditions, tapes can last for years, but unfortunately you cannot count on this. Some manufacturers recommend replacing tapes every year. This is certainly a good idea if you can afford to do so. The way that tapes and diskettes are stored also affects their lifetime: sunlight, heat, and humidity can all significantly shorten it. I always replace tapes that have had read errors or other failures more than once, regardless of their age; for some people and situations, a single failure is enough. I always throw away diskettes and Zip disks at the first hint of trouble.

---

* Very large libraries (greater than 500 volumes) are known as *silos*. The two types of devices used to be distinguished by whether or not multiple hosts could be connected, but some libraries now have this capability. Separate silos are also able to pass tapes between them.

Even so-called permanent media like CDs actually have a finite lifetime. For example, CDs begin to fail after about 5 years (and sometimes even sooner). Accordingly, creating two copies of important data and checking them periodically is the only prudent course.

Given these considerations, your site may want to consider alternative media for off-site and archival backups. For example, manufacturers of optical disks claim a lifetime of 15 years for this media (this is based on accelerated aging tests; as of this writing, we won't know for about 8–9 years whether this is really true).

Comparing Backup Media

Table 11-1 lists the most important characteristics of a variety of backup media. The largest media capacity for each item shown is the biggest that was available as of this writing. These size values refer to raw data capacity: the actual amount of data that can be written to the media.

The drive price is the lowest generally available price at this time and can be assumed to use the least expensive I/O interface; you can expect SCSI versions of many devices that are also available in IDE form to cost at least 15% more (and sometimes much more). Similarly, at about $100, a USB floppy drive costs 10 times that of an ordinary one.

The media prices are the lowest commonly available when the media is purchased in large quantities (e.g., 50–100 for CDs) and in no-frills packaging (e.g., on a spindle for CDs rather than in individual jewel cases). All prices are domestic prices in the United States, in U.S. dollars, as of mid-2002.

The minimum lifetime column gives an approximate rule-of-thumb time period when you can expect some media to begin failing. Of course, individual media will fail even sooner in some cases.

Table 11-1. Popular backup devices and media

Type	Media capacity	Drive price[a]	Media price[a]	Minimum lifetime
Floppy disk	1.44 MB[b]	$10	$0.25	2 years
Super disk	120 MB	$120	$8	2–3 years
Zip Disk	100 MB	$70	$5	3–5 years
	250 MB	$140	$12	3–5 years
Jaz Disk	1 GB	$300	$80	4–5 years
	2 GB	$340	$100	4–5 years
CD-R	700 MB (80 minutes)	$150	$0.85	5 years
CD-RW	640 MB (74 minutes)	$150	$1	5 years
DVD-R	4.7 GB (single-sided)	$700	$8	5 years?
	9.4 GB (double-sided)	$700	$40	5 years?

Table 11-1. Popular backup devices and media (continued)

Type	Media capacity	Drive price[a]	Media price[a]	Minimum lifetime
DVD+RW	4.7 GB	$600	$8	5 years?
DAT tape 4 mm DDS	4 GB (120 m DDS-2)	$550	$6	3–4 years
	12 GB (125 m DDS-3)	$700	$12.50	3–4 years
	20 GB (150 m DDS-4)	$1200	$26	3–4 years
8 mm tape	7 GB (160 m)	$1200	$6	2–4 years
Mammoth-2 (AME)	20 GB	$2500	$36	3–4 years?
	60 GB	$3700	$45	3–4 years?
AIT tape	35 GB	$900	$79	3–4 years?
	50 GB	$2600	$85	3–4 years?
	100 GB	$3900	$105	3–4 years?
DLT	40 GB	$4000	$70	10 years
SuperDLT	110 GB	$6000	$150	10 years
Magneto-optical (RW)	5.2 GB	$2300	$65	15 years?
	9.1 GB	$2700	$93	15 years?
Hard disk	100 GB (IDE)	N/A	$2–3/GB	5–7 years
	180 GB (SCSI)	N/A	$10/GB	5–7 years

[a] Approximate minimum price in U.S. dollars.
[b] A few floppy drives provided by Unix vendors increase the maximum capacity to 2.8 MB.

Tape Special Files

Traditionally, special files used to access tape drives had names of the form */dev/rmt*n or */dev/rmt/*n, where *n* indicates the drive number. Tape drives are virtually always accessed via the character (raw) special file. Currently, special file names usually include other characters as prefixes and/or suffixes, which indicate the way the device is to be accessed: the density setting to use, whether to use the drive's built-in hardware compression, whether to rewind the tape after the operation is completed, and so on.

AIX systems also use suffixes to select whether the tape should be retensioned before use. Retensioning refers to equalizing the tension on a tape, and it consists of moving the tape to the beginning, then the end, and then rewinding back to the beginning; it's even slower than it sounds. The idea is to eliminate any latent slackness in the tape, but it is seldom necessary in practice.

Table 11-2 lists the current tape special file naming conventions for the various operating systems we are considering.

Table 11-2. Tape special file names

Unix version	Format and examples[a]	Prefixes/suffixes	man page
AIX	/dev/rmtn[.m] /dev/rmt0.1 /dev/rmt0.5 **Note**: Compression is enabled and disabled with the chdev command.	m: none=rewind, no retension, low density 1=no rewind, no retension, low density 2=rewind, retension, low density 3=no rewind, retension, low density 4=rewind, no retension, high density 5=no rewind, no retension, high density 6=rewind, retension, high density 7=no rewind, retension, high density	rmt(4)
FreeBSD	/dev/[n]rastn /dev/[e|n]rsan /dev/nrast0 /dev/nrsa0	n=no rewind e=eject tape on close (Density and compression are chosen with the mt utility.)	ast sa(4)
HP-UX	/dev/rmt/citjd0TYPE[b][n] /dev/c0t3d0DDSbn /dev/c0t3d0BESTbn	i=controller j=SCSI ID n=no rewind b=use BSD-style error control TYPE=keyword indicating tape type and/or density (e.g., *BEST*, *DDS*)	mt(7)
Linux	/dev/[n]stnx /dev/nst0 /dev/nst0m	n=no rewind x: none=default density l=low density m=medium density a=autoselect density	st
Solaris	/dev/rmt/nx[b][n] /dev/rmt/0lbn /dev/rmt/0hbn	b=use BSD-style error control n=no rewind x: none=default density l=low density m=medium density h=high density c=use hardware compression	st
Tru64[b]	/dev/[n]rmt/tapen_dm /dev/nrmt/tape0_d2 /dev/nrmt/tape0_d3	m: 0=low density, use compression 1=high density, use compression 2=low density, no compression 3=high density, no compression (values 4–7 are also defined for some drives)	tz

[a] In all cases, n refers to the tape drive number. The examples are all for a non-rewinding tape device with hardware compression disabled using the lowest and highest density (as available).

[b] Older Tru64 systems use the now-obsolete device names of the form */dev/tz** and */dev/ta**.

Some systems provide simpler names as links to commonly-used tape devices. You can figure out which device they refer to by looking at a long directory listing. Here is an example from an HP-UX system:

```
crw-rw-rw-  2 bin bin 205 0x003000 Oct 7 1999 0m
crw-rw-rw-  2 bin     bin   205 0x003080 Oct  7  1999 0mb
crw-rw-rw-  2 bin     bin   205 0x003040 Oct  7  1999 0mn
crw-rw-rw-  2 bin     bin   205 0x0030c0 Oct  7  1999 0mnb
crw-rw-rw-  2 bin     bin   205 0x003000 Oct  7  1999 c0t3d0BEST
crw-rw-rw-  2 bin     bin   205 0x003080 Oct  7  1999 c0t3d0BESTb
crw-rw-rw-  2 bin     bin   205 0x003040 Oct  7  1999 c0t3d0BESTn
crw-rw-rw-  2 bin     bin   205 0x0030c0 Oct  7  1999 c0t3d0BESTnb
crw-rw-rw-  1 bin     bin   205 0x003001 Oct  7  1999 c0t3d0DDS
crw-rw-rw-  1 bin     bin   205 0x003081 Oct  7  1999 c0t3d0DDSb
crw-rw-rw-  1 bin     bin   205 0x003041 Oct  7  1999 c0t3d0DDSn
crw-rw-rw-  1 bin     bin   205 0x0030c1 Oct  7  1999 c0t3d0DDSnb
```

In this case, *0m* and *c0t3d0BEST* refer to the same tape drive and access mode (as do their corresponding suffixed forms).

The default tape drive on a system is usually the first drive in its default (rewinding) mode:

AIX	*/dev/rmt0*
FreeBSD	*/dev/rsa0*
HP-UX	*/dev/rmt/0m*
Linux	*/dev/st0*
Solaris	*/dev/rmt/0*
Tru64	*/dev/rmt/tape0_d0*

On Linux systems (and some others), the device */dev/tape* is a link to the default tape device on the system. You can make the link point to whatever drive you want to by recreating the link. On FreeBSD systems, some commands use the *TAPE* environment variable to locate the default tape drive.

AIX tape device attributes

On AIX systems, you can use the `lsattr` command to view the attributes of a tape drive:

```
$ lsattr -E -H -l rmt0
attribute      value description                       user_settable

block_size     1024  BLOCK size (0=variable length)    True
compress       yes   Use data COMPRESSION              True
density_set_1  140   DENSITY setting #1                True
density_set_2  20    DENSITY setting #2                True
extfm          yes   Use EXTENDED file marks           True
mode           yes   Use DEVICE BUFFERS during writes  True
```

This 8 mm tape drive will use data compression and a block size of 1024 by default.

You must use the chdev command to change the many attributes of a tape drive (rather than having these selections encoded into the special file name as with other systems). For example, the following command changes the block size to 1024 and turns off compression and retensioning for drive 1:

```
# chdev -l rmt0 -a block_size=1024 -a compress=no -a ret=no
```

Backing Up Files and Filesystems

Most systems offer a variety of utilities for performing backups, ranging from general-purpose archiving programs like tar and cpio to programs designed for implementing multilevel incremental backup schemes on a per-filesystem basis. When the largest tapes held only a couple hundred megabytes, choosing the right utility for system backups was easy. tar and cpio were used for small and ad hoc backups and other data transfer needs, and the more sophisticated utilities specifically designed for the task were used for system backups, because their specialized abilities—the ability to span tapes and to automatically perform incremental backups—were essential to getting the job done.

This distinction breaks down to a great extent when a single tape can hold gigabytes of data. For example, incrementals are less important when you can fit all the important data on a system onto one or two tapes—and you have the time to do so. Large tapes also make it practical to back up a system in logically grouped chunks of files, which may be spread arbitrarily throughout the physical filesystem. A successful system backup process can be built around whatever utilities make sense for your system.

 One dubious piece of advice about backups that is frequently given is that you should limit filesystem size to the maximum backup media capacity available on the system. In this view, multi-tape backup sets are simply too much trouble, and the backup process is simplified if all of the data from a filesystem will fit onto a single tape.

While being able to back up a filesystem with a single tape is certainly convenient, I think it is a mistake to let current media capacity dictate filesystem planning to such a degree. Breaking disks into more, smaller filesystems limits flexibility in allocating their resources, a concern that is almost always far more important than reducing the complexity of backing them up. Designing the filesystem needs to take *all* of the factors affecting the system and its efficient use into account. If tape-sized backup sets are what is desired, it's easy enough to write scripts to do so when overall circumstances dictate that some individual filesystems need to be bigger.

When tar or cpio Is Enough

In some cases, especially single-user systems, an elaborate backup process is not needed. Rather, since the administrator and the user are one and the same person, it will be obvious which files are important, how often they change, and so on. In cases like this, the simpler tape commands, tar and cpio, may be sufficient to periodically save important files to tape (or other media).

While the canonical model for this situation is Unix running on a workstation, these utilities may also be sufficient for systems with relatively small amounts of critical data. tar and cpio also have the advantage that they will back up both local and remote filesystems mounted via NFS.

The tar command

We'll begin with a simple example. The following tar command saves all files under */home* to the default tape drive:

```
$ tar -c /home
```

-c says to create a backup archive.

tar's -C option (big C) is useful for gathering files from various parts of the filesystem into a single archive. This option causes the current directory to be set to the location specified as its argument before tar processes any subsequent pathname arguments. Multiple -C options may be used on the same command. For example, the following tar commands save all the files under the directories */home*, */home2*, and */chem/public*:

```
$ tar -cf /dev/rmt1 /home /home2 /chem/public
$ tar -cf /dev/rmt1 -C /home . -C /home2 . -C /chem public
```

The two commands differ in this respect: the first command saves all of the files using absolute pathnames: */home/chavez/.login*, for example. The second command saves files using relative pathnames: *./chavez/.login*. The file from the first archive would always be restored to the same filesystem location, while the file from the second archive would be restored relative to the current directory (in other words, relative to the directory from which the restore command was given).

It is a good idea to use absolute pathnames in the arguments to -C. Relative pathnames specified to -C are interpreted with respect to the current directory at the time that option is processed rather than with respect to the initial current directory from which the tar command was issued. In other words, successive -C options accumulate, and tar commands using several of them as well as relative pathnames can become virtually uninterpretable.

Traditionally, all tar options were placed in a single group immediately following the command verb, and a preceding hyphen was not needed. The POSIX standard specifies a more traditional Unix syntax, preferring the second form to the first one for this command:

```
$ tar xpfb /dev/rmt1 1024 ...
$ tar -x -p -f /dev/rmt1 -b 1024 ...
```

The versions of tar on current operating systems usually accept both formats, but an initial hyphen may become be a requirement at some point in the future.

tar archives are often compressed, so it is very common to see compressed tar archives with names like *file.tar.Z*, *file.tar.gz* or *file.tgz* (the latter two files are compressed with the GNU gzip utility).

Solaris enhancements to the tar command. The Solaris version of tar offers enhancements that make the command more suitable for system-level backups. They allow all or part of the list of files and directories to be backed up to be placed in one or more text files (with one item per line). These files are included in the file list given to tar, preceded by -I, as in this example:

```
$ tar cvfX /dev/rst0 Dont_Save /home -I Other_User_Files -I Misc
```

This command backs up the files and directories in the two include files, as well as those in */home*. The command also illustrates the use of the -X option, which specifies the name of an exclusion file listing the names of files and directories that should be skipped if encountered by tar. Note that wildcards are not permitted in either include or exclusion files. In case of conflicts, exclusion takes precedence over inclusion.

The -I and -X options may also be used in restore operations performed with the tar command.

On Solaris and a variety of other System V systems, the file */etc/default/tar* may be used to customize the mappings of the default archive destinations specified with tar's single-digit code characters (for example, the command tar 1c creates an archive on drive 1). Here is a version from a Solaris system:

#	Block	#
#Archive=Device	Size	Blocks
#		
archive0=/dev/rmt/0	20	0
archive1=/dev/rmt/0n	20	0
archive2=/dev/rmt/1	20	0
archive3=/dev/rmt/1n	20	0
archive4=/dev/rmt/0	126	0
archive5=/dev/rmt/0n	126	0

```
archive6=/dev/rmt/1          126    0
archive7=/dev/rmt/1n         126    0
```

The first entry specifies the device that will be used when `tar 0` is specified. In this case, it is the first tape drive in its default modes. The second entry defines archive 1 as the first tape drive in non-rewinding mode. The remaining two fields are optional; they specify the block size for the device and its total capacity (which may be set to zero to have the command simply detect the end-of-media marker).

The GNU tar utility: Linux and FreeBSD. Linux distributions and FreeBSD provide the GNU version of the `tar` command. It supports `tar`'s customary features and contains some enhancements to them, including the ability to optionally span media volumes (`-M`) and to use `gzip` compression (`-z`). For example, the following command will extract the contents of the specified compressed `tar` archive:

```
$ tar xfz funsoftware.tgz
```

The cpio command

cpio can also be used to make backups. It has several advantages:

* It is designed to easily back up completely arbitrary sets of files; `tar` is easiest to use with directory subtrees.
* It packs data on tape much more efficiently than `tar`. If fitting all your data on one tape is an issue, `cpio` may be preferable.
* On restores, it skips over bad spots on the tape, while `tar` just dies.
* It can span tapes, while many versions of `tar` are limited to a single volume.

Using its `-o` option, `cpio` copies the files whose pathnames are passed to it via standard input (often by `ls` or `find`) to standard output; you redirect standard output to use `cpio` to write to floppy disk or tape. The following examples illustrate some typical backup uses of `cpio`:

```
$ find /home -print | cpio -o >/dev/rmt0
$ find /home -cpio /dev/rmt0
```

The first command copies all files in *home* and its subdirectories to the tape in drive 0. The second command performs the identical backup via a version of `find` that offers a `-cpio` option.

Incremental backups with tar and cpio

Combining `find` with `tar` or `cpio` is one easy way to perform incremental backups, especially when only two or three distinct backup levels are needed. For example, the following commands both copy all files under *home* which have been modified today into an archive on *dev/rmt1*, excluding any object (*.o*) files:

```
$ find /home -mtime -1 ! -name \*.o -print | cpio -o >/dev/rmt1
$ tar c1 `find /home -mtime -1 ! -name '*.o' ! -type d -print`
```

The find command used with tar needs to exclude directories, because tar will automatically archive *every* file underneath any directory named in the file list, and all directories in which *any* file has changed will appear in the output from find.

You can also use find's -newer option to perform an incremental backup in this way:

```
$ touch /backup/home_full
$ find /home -print | cpio -o > /dev/rmt0
A day later...
$ touch /backup/home_incr_1
$ find /home -newer /backup/home_full -print | cpio -o > /dev/rmt0
```

The first command timestamps the file */backup/home_full* using the touch command (*/backup* is a directory created for such backup time records), and the second command performs a full backup of */home*. Some time later, the second two commands could be used to archive all files that whose data has changed since the first backup and to record when it began. Timestamping the record files before this backup begins ensures that any files that are modified while it is being written will be backed up during a subsequent incremental, regardless of whether such files have been included in the current backup or not.

pax: Detente between tar and cpio

The pax command attempts to bridge the gap between tar and cpio by providing a single general-purpose archiving utility.* It can read and write archives in either format (by default, it writes tar archives), and offers enhancements over both of them, making it an excellent utility for system backups in many environments. pax is available for all of the Unix versions we are considering. Like cpio, pax archives may span multiple media volumes.

pax's general syntax is:

```
pax [mode_option] other_options files_to_backup
```

The *mode_option* indicates whether files are being written to or extracted from an archive, where -w says to write to an archive, -r says to read and extract from an archive, and -rw indicates a pass-through mode in which files are copied to an alternate directory on disk (as with cpio -p); pax's default mode when no *mode_option* is given is to list the contents of an archive.

The following commands illustrate pax file archiving modes of operation:

```
$ pax -w -f /dev/rmt0 /home /chem
$ find /home /chem -mtime -1 -print | pax -w -f /dev/rmt0
$ pax -w -X -f /dev/rmt0 /
```

---

* Indeed, on systems offering pax, cpio and tar are often just links to it. pax's syntax is an amalgamation of the two, which is not surprising for a peace imposed by POSIX (although the name purportedly stands for *portable archive exchange*).

The first two commands perform a full and incremental backup of the files in */home* and */chem* to the default tape drive in each case. The third command saves all of the files in the disk partition corresponding to the root directory; the -X option tells pax not to cross filesystem boundaries.

AIX prefers pax over vanilla tar and cpio. The command has been enhanced to support large files (over 2 GB).

Getting Users to Do Backups

At some sites, certain backup responsibilities are left to individual users: when a site has far too many workstations to make backing up all of their local disks practical, when important data resides on non-Unix systems like PCs (especially if they are not connected to the local area network), and so on.

However, even when you're not actually performing the backups yourself, you will probably still be responsible for providing technical support and, more often than not, reminders to the users who will be performing the backups. Here are some approaches I've tried to facilitate this:

- Make a habit of encouraging users rather than threatening them (threats don't work anyway).
- Use peer pressure to your advantage. Setting up a central backup storage location that you look after can make it obvious who is and isn't doing the backups they are supposed to. Note that this idea is inappropriate if data sensitivity is an issue.
- Create tools that automate the backup process as much as possible for users. Everyone has time to drop in a tape and start a script before they leave for the day.
- Provide a central repository for key files that get backed up as part of the system/ site procedure. Users can copy key files and know they will be backed up when they're really in a jam and really don't have time to do a backup themselves.

Backing Up Individual Filesystems with dump

The BSD dump utility represents the next level of sophistication for backup systems under Unix. It selectively backs up all of the files within a filesystem (single disk partition), doing so by copying the data corresponding to each inode to the archive on the backup device. It also has the advantage of being able to back up any type of file, including device special files and sparse files. Although there are slight variations among different versions of this command, the discussion here applies to the following Unix implementations of this command:

AIX	backup
FreeBSD	dump

HP-UX	dump and vxdump
Linux	dump (but the package is not usually installed by default)
Solaris	ufsdump
Tru64	dump and vdump

On systems supporting multiple filesystem types, dump may be limited to UFS (BSD-type) filesystems; on Linux systems, it is currently limited to ext2/ext3 filesystems, although the XFS filesystem provides the similar xfsdump utility. Under HP-UX, vxdump and vxrestore support VxFS filesystems. Tru64 provides vdump for AdvFS filesystems.

dump keeps track of when it last backed up each filesystem and the level at which it was saved. This information is stored in the file */etc/dumpdates* (except on HP-UX systems, which use */var/adm/dumpdates*). A typical entry in this file looks like this:

```
/dev/disk2e      2 Sun Feb  5 13:14:56 1995
```

This entry indicates that the filesystem */dev/disk2e* was last backed up on Sunday, February 5 during a level 2 backup. If dump does not find a filesystem in this list, it assumes that it has never been backed up.

If *dumpdates* doesn't exist, the following command will create it:

```
# touch /path/dumpdates
```

The *dumpdates* file must be owned by the user *root*. If it does not exist, dump will not create it and won't record when filesystem backups occur, so create the file before running dump for the first time.

The dump command takes two general forms:

```
$ dump options-with-arguments filesystem
$ dump option-letters corresponding-arguments filesystem
```

where *filesystem* is the block special file corresponding to the filesystem to be backed up or the corresponding mount point from the filesystem configuration file. In the first, newer form, the first item is the list of options to be used for this backup, with their arguments immediately following the option letters in the normal way (e.g., -f /dev/tape).

In the second, older form, *option-letters* is a list of argument letters corresponding to the desired options, and *corresponding-arguments* are the values associated with each argument, in the same order. This syntax is still the only one available under Solaris and HP-UX.

Although not all options require arguments, the list of arguments must correspond *exactly*, in order and in number, to the options requiring arguments. For example, consider the set of options 0sd. The s and d options require arguments; 0 does not. Thus, a dump command specifying these options must have the form:

```
$ dump 0sd s-argument d-argument filesystem
```

Failing to observe this rule can have painful consequences if you are running the command as *root*, including destroying the filesystem if you swap the argument to the f option and dump's final argument when you are running the command as *root*. You'll get no argument from me if you want to assert that this is a design defect that ought to have been fixed long before now. When you use dump, just make sure an argument is supplied for each option requiring one. To avoid operator errors, you may want to create shell scripts that automatically invoke dump with the proper options.

dump's most important options are the following (we will use the newer form):

-0, ..., -9

These options indicate the level of the dump this command will perform. Given any level *n*, dump will search *dumpdates* for an entry reporting the last time this filesystem was dumped at level *n–1* or lower. dump then backs up all files that have been changed since this date. If *n* is zero, dump will back up the entire filesystem. If there is no record of a backup for this filesystem for level *n–1* or lower, dump will also back up the entire filesystem. If no level option is specified, it defaults to -9. This option does not require any argument.

Older versions of dump not supporting hyphenated options require that the level option be the first option letter.

-u

If dump finishes successfully, this option updates its history file, *dumpdates*. It does not require an argument.

-f *device*

This option states that you want to send the dump to something other than the default tape drive (i.e., to a file or to another device). The defaults used by various Unix versions were listed previously. If you use this option, it must have an argument, and this argument must precede the filesystem being dumped. A value of "-" (a single hyphen) for its argument indicates standard output.

-W

Display only what will be backed up when the indicated command is invoked, but don't perform the actual backup operation.

-s *feet* -d *dens*

These options were needed on older versions of dump to determine the capacity of the backup media. Recent versions of dump generally don't need them as they keep writing until they detect an end-of-media mark.

If you do need to use them to lie to dump about the tape length because your version uses a default capacity limit suitable for ancient 9-track tapes, -s specifies the *size* of the backup tape, in feet; -d specifies the density of the backup tape, in bits per inch. Since dump will respect end-of-media marks that it encounters before it has reached this limit, the fix for such situations is to set the capacity to something far above the actual limit. For example, the options -d 50000 -s 90000 define a tape capacity somewhat over 4 GB.

-b *factor*
> Specifies the block size to use on the tape, in units of 1024-byte (or sometimes 512-byte) blocks.

Here is a typical use of the dump command:

```
$ dump -1 -u -f /dev/tape /chem
```

The second command performs a level 1 incremental backup on the */chem* filesystem using the tape drive linked to */dev/tape*; dump will update the file the *dumpdates* file upon completion.

dump notifies the user whenever it requires some interaction. Most often, dump will have filled the tape currently in use and ask for another. It will also ask whether to take corrective actions if problems arise. In addition, dump prints many messages describing what it is doing, how many tapes it thinks it will need, and the like.

The HP-UX fbackup utility

HP-UX provides the fbackup and frecover utilities designed to perform system backups. One significant advantage that they have over the standard Unix utilities is that they can save and restore HP-UX access control lists along with other file metadata.

fbackup provides for nine levels of incremental backups, just like dump. fbackup stores backup records in the file */var/adm/fbackupfiles/dates*, which the system administrator must create before using fbackup.

The following examples illustrate how fbackup might be used for system backup operations:

```
# fbackup -0u -f /dev/rmt/1m -i /chem
# fbackup -1u -i /chem -i /bio -e /bio/med
# fbackup -1u -f /dev/rmt/0m -f /dev/rmt/1m -i /chem
# fbackup -0u -g /backup/chemists.graph -I /backup/chemists.TOC
```

The first command performs a full backup of */chem* to tape drive 1, updating the fbackup database. The second command does a level 1 backup of */chem* and */bio*, excluding the directory */bio/med* (as many -i and -e options as you need can be included). The third command performs a level 1 backup of */chem* using multiple tape drives in sequence.

The final command performs a full backup as specified by the graph file */backup/chemists.graph*, writing an index of the backup to the file */backup/chemists.TOC*. A graph file is a text file with the following format:

```
c    path
```

where *c* is a code indicating whether *path* is to be included (i) or excluded (e) from the backup.

Related Tape Utilities

There are two other Unix tape utilities you should know about, which are also of use in performing backups from time to time.

Data copying and conversion with dd

The dd utility transfers raw data between devices. It is useful for converting data between systems and for reading and writing tapes from and to non-Unix systems. It takes a number of *option=value* pairs as its arguments. Some of the most useful options are:

if   Input file: source for data.

of   Output file: destination for data.

ibs
> Input block size, in bytes (the default is 512).

obs
> Output block size, in bytes (the default is 512).

fskip
> Skip tape files before transferring data (not available in all implementations).

count
> The amount of data (number of blocks) to transfer.

conv
> Keyword(s) specifying desired conversion of input data before outputting: swab means swap bytes, and it is the most used conversion type. lcase and ucase mean convert to lower- and uppercase, respectively, and ascii and ebcdic mean convert to ASCII or EBCDIC.

For example, the following command processes the third file on the tape in drive 0, using an input block size of 1024 bytes and swapping bytes in all data; the command writes the converted output to the file */chem/data/c70.dat*:

```
$ dd if=/dev/rmt0 of=/chem/data/c70.dat \
     ibs=1024 fskip=2 conv=swab
```

 As always, be careful to specify the appropriate devices for if and of; transposing them can have disastrous consequences.

Tape manipulation with mt

Unix provides the mt command for direct manipulation of tapes. It can be used to position tapes (to skip past backup save sets, for example), to rewind tapes, and to perform other basic tape operations. Its syntax is:

```
$ mt [-f tape-device] command
```

where *tape-device* specifies which tape drive to use, and *command* is a keyword indicating the desired action. Useful keywords include `rewind` (to rewind the tape), `status` (display device status—you can see whether it is in use, for example), `fsf` *n* (skip the next *n* files), and `bsf` *n* (skip back *n* files).

For example, to rewind the tape in the second tape drive, you might use a command like:

```
$ mt -f /dev/rmt1 rewind
```

The Solaris version of `mt` includes an `asf` subcommand, which moves the tape to the *n*th file on the tape (where *n* is given as `asf`'s argument), regardless of the tape's current position.

Under FreeBSD, the `mt` command is used to set the tape drive density and compression:

```
$ mt -f /dev/nrsa0 comp on density 0x26
```

AIX also includes the `tctl` utility (to which `mt` is really a link). `tctl` has the same syntax as `mt` and offers a few additional seldom-wanted subcommands.

Restoring Files from Backups

All of the backup facilities described in the previous sections have corresponding file restoration facilities. We'll look at each of them in turn in this section.

Restores from tar and cpio Archives

Individual files or entire subtrees can be restored easily from `tar` and `cpio` archives. For example, the following pairs of commands restore the file */home/chavez/freeway/quake95.data* and user *harvey*'s home directory (respectively) from an archive made of */home* located on the tape in the default tape drive (here, we use */dev/rmt0* for as the example location):

```
$ tar -xp /home/chavez/freeway/quake95.data
$ cpio -im '*quake95.data' < /dev/rmt0
$ tar -xp /home/harvey
$ cpio -imd '/home/harvey*' < /dev/rmt0
```

The `-p` option to `tar` and `-m` option to `cpio` ensure that all file attributes are restored along with the file. `cpio`'s `-d` option creates subdirectories as necessary when restoring a directory subtree (`tar` does so by default).[*]

---

[*] The second `cpio` command also assumes that there is no file or directory in */home* that begins with "harvey" other than user *harvey*'s home directory.

Restores with pax are similar. For example, the first of the following commands lists the files on the tape in drive 0, and the remaining commands extract various files from it:

```
$ pax -f /dev/rmt0 -v          –v gives a more detailed/verbose listing.
$ pax -r '/h95/*.exe'          Select files via a regular expression.
$ pax -r /home/chavez          Restore chavez's home directory.
$ pax -r -f my_archive -c '*.o'  Restore everything except object files.
# pax -r -pe -f /dev/rmt0      Restore files incl. owner, mode & mod. time.
```

pax's coolest feature has to be its -s option, which allows you to massage filenames as files are written to, extracted from, or even just listed from an archive. It takes a substitution command as used in ed or sed as its argument (which will usually need to be enclosed in single quotation marks) indicating how filenames should be transformed. For example, the following command changes the second-level directory name of each file from *chavez* to *harvey* as files are read from the archive, changing their target location on disk:

```
$ pax -r -s ',^/home/chavez/,/home/harvey/,' \
     -f /dev/rmt0 /home/chavez
```

The substitution clause searches for */home/chavez* at the beginning of the pathname of each file to be restored and changes it to */home/harvey*, using commas as the field separator within the substitution string.

Here are some additional -s clauses for specific kinds of transformations:

```
-s ',^/home/chavez/,,'    Remove partial directory component.
-s ',^.*//*,,'            Remove entire directory component.
-s ',^//*,,'              Make pathnames relative to current directory.
```

Multiple -s options are allowed, but only the first matching one is used for any given filename.

 Be aware that pax is not without its eccentricities. One of the most annoying is the following: in some versions of pax, directories matched via wildcards in the pattern list during restore operations are not extracted in their entirety; only explicitly listed ones are. Note that this is the opposite of the way cpio works and also counter to the way tar operates. I'd be positive this was a bug except that it happens in more than one vendor's version, although not in every vendor's version. With pax, *caveat emptor* would appear to be the watchword.

Restoring from dump Archives

The restore utility retrieves files from backup tapes made with the dump utility. It is supported by those systems supporting a version of dump. Solaris calls its version ufsrestore in keeping with the name of its version of dump. HP-UX and Tru64 provide vxrestore and vrestore commands for their default filesystem types. All of these commands have the same syntax and options. The commands can restore single files, directories, or entire filesystems.

To restore an entire filesystem, you must restore the most recent backup tapes from *each* backup level: the most recent full dump (0), the most recent level 1 dump, and so on. You must restore each level in numerical order, beginning with level 0. restore places the files it retrieves in the current working directory. Therefore, to restore a filesystem as a whole, you may wish to create and mount a clean, empty filesystem, make the current working directory the directory in which this filesystem is mounted, and then use restore to read the backup tapes into this directory. Note that such restore operations will have the side effect of recreating deleted files.

After a full restore, you need to do a full (level 0) backup. The reason for this is that dump backs up files by their inode number internally, so the tape from which you just restored from won't match the inodes in the new filesystem since they were assigned sequentially as files were restored.

In general, the restore command has the following forms (similar to dump's):

```
$ restore options-with-arguments [files-and-directories]
$ restore option-letters corresponding-arguments [files-and-directories]
```

where *files-and-directories* is a list of files and directories for restore to retrieve from the backup tape. If no files are listed, the entire tape will be restored.

In the first, newer form, the first item is the list of options to be used for this backup with their arguments immediately following the option letters in the normal way (e.g., -f /dev/tape). In the second, older form, *option-letters* is a list of argument letters for the desired options, and *corresponding-arguments* are the values associated with each argument, in the same order. This syntax is still the only one available under AIX and Solaris.

Most options to restore do not have any arguments. However, as with dump, it is important that any arguments appear in the same order as the options requiring them.

restore places the files that it retrieves in the current working directory. When a directory is selected for restoration, restore restores the directory and all the files within it, unless you have specified the -h option.

restore's most important options are the following:

-r

> *Read* and restore the entire tape. This is a very powerful command; it should be used only to restore an entire filesystem located on one or more tapes. The filesystem into which the tape is read should be newly created and completely empty. This option can also be used to restore a complete incremental dump on top of a newly restored filesystem. That is, after using the -r option to restore the most recent full dump, you use it again to restore successive incremental dumps until the filesystem has been completely restored.

-x

Extract all files and directories listed and restore them in the current directory. Each filename to be extracted must be a complete pathname *relative* to the root directory of the filesystem being restored. For example, to restore the file */chem/pub/old/gold.dat* from a dump of the */chem* filesystem, you must specify the filename as *pub/old/gold.dat*. You should be in */chem* when you execute the restore command if you want the file to be restored to its original location.

-t

Type the names of the listed files and directories if they appear on the backup tape. This option lets you find out whether a given file is on a particular tape more quickly than reading the entire tape. When used without a file list, it verifies that a dump tape is readable.

-f *file*

The corresponding argument is the name of the file or device holding the dump. If this option is omitted, restore assumes that the dump tape is mounted on your default tape drive. Use a hyphen for *file* to specify standard input.

-s *n*

The value *n* indicates which file on tape is to be used for the restore. For example, -s 3 says to use the third tape file.

-i

Enter *interactive* mode. This is almost always the most convenient method for restoring a small group of files. It is described in detail in the next section.

A typical usage of the restore command is:

```
# cd /home
# restore -x -f /dev/rmt1 chavez/mystuff others/myprogram
```

This restores the directory */home/chavez/mystuff* and the file called */home/others/myprogram* from a backup tape (assuming that */home* is the filesystem in the archive). The directories *chavez* and *others* are assumed to be in the current directory (and created if necessary), and the specified subdirectory and file are restored under them. These both originally resided within the */home* directory. Note, however, that the mount point name is not used in the restore command. The command must be executed from */home* to restore the files to their original locations.

On Solaris and HP-UX systems, the corresponding options would be:

```
xf /dev/rmt1 chavez/mystuff others/myprogram
```

dump and restore both save files independently of where the filesystem happens to be mounted at the time; that is, the pathnames used by these commands are relative to their position in their *own* filesystem, not in the overall system filesystem. This makes sense, because the filesystem could potentially be mounted anywhere in the overall directory tree, and files should still be able to be restored to their correct location relative to the current mount point for their filesystem.

If you need to restore some files that have been destroyed by accident, your most difficult problems will be determining which set of backup tapes contains these files and waiting for the system to read through one or more full backup tapes. If you do incremental backups, knowing when a file was last modified will help you to find the correct backup tape. Creating online table-of-contents files is also very useful (this topic is discussed later in this chapter).

The restore utility's interactive mode

The interactive mode is entered with restore's -i option. Once there, the contents of a tape can be scanned and files chosen for extraction. This mode's use is illustrated in this sample session:

```
$ restore -i -f /dev/rmt1          Initiate restore's interactive mode.
restore > help
Available commands are:
    ls [arg] - list directory
    cd arg - change directory
    add [arg] - add `arg' to list of files to be extracted
    delete [arg] - delete `arg' from list of files to be extracted
    extract - extract requested files
...
If no `arg' is supplied, the current directory is used
restore > ls                       List directory on tape.
chavez/    harvey/    /ng
restore > cd chavez/vp             Change tape current directory.
restore > ls
v_a.c      v_a1.c     v_b3.c       v_d23.c     v_early
restore > add v_a1.c               Select (mark) files to be restored.
restore > add v_early
restore > ls
v_a.c      *v_a1.c    v_b3.c       v_d23.c     *v_early
restore > delete v_early           Remove a file from the extract list..
restore > extract                  Write selected files to current directory.
You have not read any tapes yet.
Unless you know which volume your file(s) are on you should start
with the last volume and work towards the first.
Specify next volume #: 1           Tape number if known.
set owner/mode for '.'? [yn] n     Don't change ./'s ownership or protection.
restore > quit                     End the restore interactive session.
```

The final prompt from restore asks whether to change the ownership and protection of the current directory to match that of the root directory on the tape. Answer yes only if you are restoring an entire filesystem.

Combining Several Backups onto a Single Tape

If you want to place several archives onto the same tape, all you need to do is rewind the tape (if necessary) before writing the first archive and then use a nonrewinding device for all subsequent backup operations.

To retrieve files from a multiarchive tape, you must position the tape at the proper location before issuing the restoration command. `restore` can do this automatically using its `-s` option, which takes the tape file number you want to use as its argument.

For all other backup types, position the tape with the `mt` command. For example, the following commands position the tape just after the second archive on the tape:

```
$ mt -f /dev/rmt0 rewind      If necessary
$ mt -f /dev/nrmt0 fsf 2
```

Again, you will need to use the nonrewinding form of the tape device; otherwise, the tape will be rewound to the beginning after positioning. Once at the desired point, you can write an additional backup archive to the tape or perform a restore operation using the next archive on the tape, as appropriate.

The HP-UX frecover utility

The HP-UX `frecover` utility restores files archived by `fbackup`, using a very similar syntax. For example, the first of the following commands restores the */chem/fullerenes* subdirectory tree:

```
# frecover -x -i /chem/fullerenes
# frecover -r -f /dev/rmt/1m
```

The second command restores all files on the tape in drive 1. `frecover` also accepts the `-i`, `-e`, and `-g` options. Other useful options include the following:

- `-X` and `-F` restore all retrieved files relative to the current directory (converting absolute pathnames to relative ones) or into the current directory (stripping off all paths), respectively.

- `-o` says to overwrite files on disk that are newer than the file in the backup set.

- `-N` says to read the backup media without restoring any files. It is useful for verifying the integrity of a backup and for creating table-of-contents files.

Moving Data Between Systems

In general, `tar`, `cpio`, and `dump` write archives that are readable on many different computer systems. However, sometimes you will run into problems reading a tape on a system other than the one on which it was written. There are four major causes for such problems:

Block size differences

The simplest cause of tape reading problems is a difference in the block size with which the archive was written and the block size expected by the drive on which you're trying to read it. Some tape drives assume specific fixed block sizes. You can specify the block size to backup and restore utilities (-b is often the relevant option), and on many systems you can set the characteristics of the drive itself. The most commonly used block sizes are 512 and 1024.

Archive format incompatibilities

The backup utilities provided by early versions of Unix differed from those in use today, so very old computer systems may not be able to read tapes written on a current machine. The modern versions of most utilities include backward-compatibility options that allow you to write tapes in the old format if you need to read them on an ancient system.

Byte order differences

Whether a computer system is *big endian* or *little endian* determines how it interprets the individual bytes within larger data units, such as words. Big-endian systems consider the byte with the lowest address as the most significant; little-endian systems consider it to be the least significant. Tape archives, like all other data on a computer system, reflect this fundamental attribute of the hardware. When you want to read a tape produced by a computer of one type on a different computer of the other type, you'll need to swap the bytes before utilities like tar can make sense of the archive.

For example, you could use this AIX command to list the contents of a tape written on an IRIX system:

```
$ dd if=/dev/rmt1 conv=swab | tar tvf -
```

The dd command reads the tape file and swaps the bytes, passing the converted archive to the tar command, which lists the archive it finds on standard input. You could construct the equivalent reversed pipe to produce a byte-swapped archive on tape.

Compressed archives

If you write a tape on a drive that performs automatic data compression, you won't be able to read it on a drive that lacks this feature. In order to write tapes that will be readable on drives without compression, you'll need to specify the noncompressing special file to the backup utility (refer to the discussion of special files earlier in this chapter, as well as the relevant manual pages for your systems, for details).

Making Table of Contents Files

It is often convenient to have online listings of the contents of system backup tapes. For one thing, they make it much easier to figure out which tape has the file you need to restore, especially when multiple levels of incremental backups are in use. It is quite easy to create such files at the time the backup is performed.

If you're using `tar` or `cpio` for backup, you can take advantage of the `-v` option to create a listing of the tape's contents as it is written, as in these examples:

```
$ today='date +%d%b%Y'
$ tar -cv /home > /backup/home_full_$today.TOC
                    or
$ tar -cv /home | tee /backup/home_full_$today.TOC
```

Both `tar` commands archive the contents of */home*, generating a long, directory-like listing as it does so and saving it to a file with a name like */backup/home_full_21mar1995.TOC*. The second command also displays the same output on the screen.

`cpio` sends the file list to standard error, so it must be captured slightly differently:

```
$ toc='date +/backup/home_full_%d%b%y.TOC'
$ find /home -print |  cpio -ov > /dev/rmt0 2> $toc
```

If you want to use the C shell, the commands are a little different:

```
% set toc='date +/backup/home_full_%d%b%y.TOC'
% (find /home -print | cpio -ov > /dev/rmt0) >& $toc
```

The file lists produced by `cpio` commands like these contain only the pathnames of the files in the archive. If you want a more detailed listing, you can generate it with a second `cpio` command or a more complex pipe leading up to the `cpio` backup command:

```
$ cpio -itv < /dev/rmt0 > $toc
$ find /home | cpio -o | tee /dev/rmt0 | cpio -t -i -v > $toc
```

The first command lists the files in the archive on tape. The second command avoids having to reread the backup tape by using the `find` command to generate a list of files, which `cpio` makes into an archive. This archive is then sent both the the tape drive and to another `cpio` command. The latter lists the archive contents and writes it to the specified table-of-contents file.

Making a table of contents file for a `dump` tape requires a subsequent `restore` command. For example, here is a script that performs a backup with `dump` and then creates a table-of-contents file with `restore`:

```
#!/bin/csh
# bkup+toc - perform dump and verify tape/make TOC file
# $1 = filesystem
# $2 = dump level (default=0)
#
if ($#argv < 1) then
  echo "do_backup: filesystem [dump-level]"
  exit 1
endif

set lev=0
if ("$2" != "") set lev=$2
dump -${lev} -u -f /dev/rmt1 $1
if ($status) then
```

```
      echo "do_backup: dump failed"
      exit 1
endif
restore -t -v -f /dev/rmt1 > /backup/`date +$1:t_%m-%d-%Y.$lev`
```

This script runs the dump command on the filesystem given as its first argument, using the backup level specified as its second argument (or level 0 by default). If the dump command exits normally, the restore command is used to verify the backup and write its contents to a file. The file's name contains the disk name and the month, day, and year when the backup was done, and its extension is the backup level: e.g., *chem_06-24-2001.2* would be the filename for a level 2 backup of */chem* made on June 24, 2001.

On an HP-UX system, you can use this frecover command to create a table-of-content file:

```
# frecover -r -Nv -f /dev/rmt/0m > $toc
```

Network Backup Systems

So far, we've considered only backups and restores of disks on a local computer system. However, many organizations need to take a more unified and comprehensive approach to their total backup needs. We will consider various available solutions for this problem in this section.

Remote Backups and Restores

The simplest way to move beyond the single-system backup view is to consider remote backup and restores. It is very common to want to perform a backup over the network. The reasons are varied: your system may not have a tape drive at all since not all systems come with one by default any more, there may be a better (faster, higher capacity) tape drive on another system, and so on.

Most versions of dump and restore can perform network-based operations (Tru64 requires you to use the separate rdump and rrestore commands). This is accomplished by specifying a device name of the form *host:local_device* as an argument to the -f option. The hostname may also optionally be preceded by a username and at-sign; for example, -f chavez@hamlet:/dev/rmt1 performs the operation on device */dev/rmt1* on host *hamlet* as user *chavez*.

This capability uses the same network services as the rsh and rcp commands. Remote backup facilities depend on the daemon */usr/sbin/rmt* (which is often linked to */etc/rmt*).[*] To be allowed access on the remote system, there needs to be a *.rhosts* in its root directory, containing at least the name of the (local) host from which the data will come. This file must be owned by *root*, and its mode must not allow any

---

[*] On a few older systems, you'll need to create the link yourself.

access by group or other users (for example, 400). This mechanism has the mechanism's usual negative security implications (see "Network Security" in Chapter 7).

 Some versions of the tar command can also use the rmt remote tape facility.

The HP-UX fbackup and frestore utilities accept remote tape drives as arguments to the normal -f option. For example:

```
# fbackup -0u -f backuphost:/dev/rmt/1m -i /chem
```

The Amanda Facility

Amanda is the Advanced Maryland Automated Network Disk Archiver. It was developed at the University of Maryland (James da Silva was the initial author). The project's home page is *http://www.amanda.org*, where it can be obtained free of charge. This section provides an overview of Amanda. Consult Chapter 4 of *Unix Backup and Recovery* for a very detailed discussion of all of Amanda's features (this chapter is also available on the Amanda home page).

About Amanda

Amanda allows backups from a network of clients to be sent to a single designated backup server. The package operates by functioning as a wrapper around native backup software like GNU tar and dump. It can also back up files from Windows clients via the Samba facility (smbtar). It has a number of nice features:

- It uses its own network protocols and thus does not suffer from the security problems inherent in the rmt approach.

- It supports many common tape and other backup devices (including stackers and jukeboxes).

- It can perform full and incremental backups and decide the backup level automatically based on specified configuration parameters.

- It can take advantage of hardware compression features, or it can compress archives prior to writing them to tape (or other media) when the former is not available. Software compression may be performed either by the main server or by the client system.

- It provides excellent protection against accidental media overwriting.

- It can use holding disks as intermediate storage for backup archives to maximize tape write performance and to ensure that data is backed up in spite of tape errors (allowing the backup set to be written to backup media at a later time).

- It can use Kerberos-based authentication in addition to providing its own authentication scheme. Kerberos encryption can also be used to protect the data as it is transmitted across the network.

At present, Amanda does have a couple of annoying limitations:

- It cannot split a backup archive across multiple tapes. When it encounters an end-of-tape mark while saving a backup archive, it begins writing the archive from the beginning on the next tape.

- It cannot produce individual backup archives larger than a single tape. This is a consequence of the first limitation.

- Only a single backup server is supported.

How Amanda works

Amanda uses a combination of full and incremental backups to save all of the data for which it is responsible, using the smallest possible daily backup set that can do so. Its scheme first computes the total amount of data to be backed up. It uses this total, along with a couple of parameters defined by the system administrator, to figure out what to do in the current run. These are the key parameters:

The number of runs in a backup cycle
At a rate of one Amanda run per day, this corresponds to the desired number of days between full backups.

The percentage of data that changes between Amanda runs
In the single run per day case, this is the percentage of the data that changes each day.

Amanda's overall strategy is twofold: to complete a full backup of the data within each cycle and to be sure that all changed data has been backed up between full dumps. The traditional method of doing this is to perform the full backup followed by incrementals on the days between them. Amanda operates differently.

Each run (night), Amanda performs a full backup of part of the data, specifically, the fraction that is required to back up the entire data set in the course of a complete backup cycle. For example, if the cycle is 7 days long (with one run per day), 1/7 of the data must be backed up each day to complete a full backup in 7 days. In addition to this "partial" full backup, Amanda also performs incremental backups for all data that has changed since its own last full backup.

Figure 11-1 illustrates an Amanda backup cycle lasting 4 days, in which 15% of the data changes from day to day. The box at the top of the figure stands for the complete set of data for which Amanda is responsible; we have divided it into four segments to represent the part of the data that gets a full backup at the same time.

The contents of the nightly backups are shown at the bottom of the figure. The first three days represent a start-up period. On the first night, the first quarter of the data is fully backed up. On the second night, the second quarter is fully backed up, and the 15% of the data from the previous night that changed during day 2 is also saved. On day 3, the third quarter of the total data is fully backed up, as well as the changed 15% of day 2's backup. In addition, 15% of the portion backed up on the first night

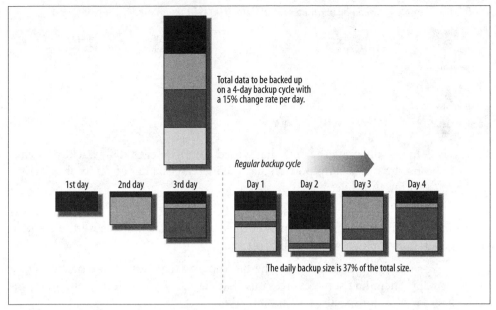

Figure 11-1. The Amanda backup scheme

is written for each of the intervening nights since its full backup: in other words, 30% of that quarter of the total data.

By day 4, the normal schedule is in force. Each night, one quarter of the total data is backed up in full, and incrementals are performed for each of the other quarters as appropriate to the time that has passed since their last full backup.

 This example uses only first-level incremental backups. In actual practice, Amanda uses multiple levels of incremental backups to minimize backup storage requirements.

To restore files from an Amanda backup, you may need one complete cycle of media.

Let's now consider a numeric example. Suppose we have 100 GB of data that we need to back up. Table 11-3 illustrates four Amanda backup schedules based on differing cycle lengths and per-day change percentages.

Table 11-3. Sample Amanda backup sizes (total data=100 GB)

	3-day cycle 10% change	5-day cycle 10% change	7-day cycle 10% change	7-day cycle 15% change
Full portion	33.3	20.0	14.3	14.3
1st previous day	3.4	2.0	1.4	2.2
2nd previous day	6.8	4.0	2.8	4.4
3rd previous day		6.0	4.2	6.6

Table 11-3. Sample Amanda backup sizes (total data=100 GB) (continued)

	3-day cycle 10% change	5-day cycle 10% change	7-day cycle 10% change	7-day cycle 15% change
4th previous day		8.0	5.6	8.8
5th previous day			7.0	11.0
6th previous day			8.4	13.2
Daily size (GB)	**43.5**	**40.0**	**43.7**	**60.5**

The table columns illustrate the data that would comprise each daily backup, breaking it down by the full backup portion and the incremental data from each previous full backup within the cycle.

Note that Amanda computes what should be backed up every time it is run, so it is not as static as the preceding examples suggest, but the examples nevertheless provide a general picture of how the facility operates.

In the next section, we consider how the backup size depends on the backup cycle more formally, including some expressions that can be used to decide on an appropriate backup cycle for specific conditions.

Estimating the Daily Change Rate

You can use the find command to help estimate the daily change rate:

```
$ find dir -newer /var/adm/yesterday -ls | \
    awk '{sum+=$7}; END {print "diff =",sum}'
```

Repeat the command as needed to cover all the data to be backed up. Use touch to update the time for the file */var/adm/yesterday* after all the find commands are run.

Then, divide this value by the total used space (e.g., taken from df output). Repeat the process for several days or weeks to determine an average rate.

Doing the math

Next, we consider some expressions that can be used to compute starting parameters for Amanda (which can be fine-tuned over time, based on actual use). If this sort of mathematical analysis is of no interest to you, just skip this section.

We will use the following variables:

T = total amount of data
p = percentage change between runs (in decimal form: e.g. 12%=0.12)
n = number of runs in a complete cycle (often days)
S = amount of data that must be backed up every run (day)
F = fraction of the total data that must be backed up every run (day): S/T

To compute per-run amount of data that must be backed up, use this expression for S:

$$S = \frac{T}{n} + \frac{Tp(n-1)}{2}$$

For example, 70 GB of data that changes by 10% per day using a 1 week backup cycle requires that 31 GB be backed up every night ($70/7 + 70 \times 0.1 \times 6/2 = 10 + 42/2 = 10 + 21 = 31$). If 31 GB is larger than the maximum capacity that you have in the available time, you'll need to adjust the other parameters (see below).

Alternatively, if you have a fixed amount of backup capacity per run, you can figure out the required cycle length. Refer to the discussion of capacity planning earlier in this chapter for information on determining how much capacity you have.

To compute n for a given nightly capacity, use this expression:

$$n = \frac{x \pm \sqrt{x^2 - 2p}}{p}$$

where

$$x = \left(\frac{p}{2} + \frac{S}{T} \right)$$

We have introduced the variable x to make the expression for n simpler. Suppose that you have a nightly backup capacity of 40 GB for the same scenario (70 GB total data, changing at 10% per day). Then $x = 0.1/2 + 40/70 = 0.05 + 0.57 = 0.62$. We can now compute n: $(0.62 \pm \sqrt{0.38 - 0.2}) / 0.1 = (0.62 \pm \sqrt{0.18}) / 0.1 = (0.62 \pm 0.42) / 0.1 = 6.2 \pm 4.2$.

This calculation yields solutions of 2 and 11 (rounding to integers). We can either do full backups of about half the data every night or use a much longer 11-day cycle and still be able to get the backups all done. Note that these values take maximum advantage of the available capacity.

Now suppose that you have a nightly backup capacity of only 20 GB for the same scenario (70 GB total data, changing at 10% per day). Then $x = 0.1/2 + 40/70 = 0.05 + 0.29 = 0.34$. We can now compute n: $(0.34 \pm \sqrt{0.12 - 0.2}) / 0.1$. The square-root term is now imaginary (since 0.12–0.20 is negative), indicating that this proposed configuration will not work in practice.[*] The available capacity is simply too small.

In general, you can compute the minimum per-run capacity for a given per-run percentage change (p) with this expression (which introduces F as the fraction of the total data that must be backed up):

$$F_{minimum\ for\ fixed\ p} = 2\sqrt{\frac{p}{2} - \frac{p}{2}} \text{ (where } F = \frac{S}{T}\text{)}; \quad \therefore S_{minimum} = FT$$

---

[*] Mathematically, there are no real solutions to the underlying quadratic equation.

F indicates the fraction of that data that must be backed up each run in order for the system to succeed. So, in our case of a 10% change rate, $F = 2 \times \sqrt{0.1/2} - (0.1/2) = 2 \times \sqrt{0.05} - 0.05 = 2 \times 0.22 - 0.05 = 0.44 - 0.05 = 0.39 \approx 40\%$. Note that this expression is independent of T (the total backup data); whenever the data changes by about 10% per run, you must be able to back up at least 40% of the total data every run for success. In our case, this corresponds to a minimum nightly capacity of $0.4 \times 70 = 29$ GB.

Alternatively, you can compute the run cycle n that is required to minimize F (and thus S) for a given value of p with this expression:[*]

$$n_{minimum\ S} = \sqrt{\frac{2}{p}}$$

In our case, the cycle period which minimizes the amount of data to be backed up is $\sqrt{2/0.01} = \sqrt{20} = 4.47 \approx 5$ days. Again, this value is independent of the amount of data. In our case, when the data is changing by 10% per day, a cycle time of 5 days will minimize the amount of data that must be backed up every night. This is the most efficient cycle length with the minimum nightly backup capacity.

Thus, both the minimum time cycle and per-run fraction of data to back up are determined only by the rate at which the data is changing, and the actual per-run backup size for a given amount of total backup data can be easily computed from them. Thus, having an accurate estimate for p is vital to rational planning.

 This discussion ignores compression in analyzing backup procedures. If your tape drive can compress data, or if you decide to compress it with software before writing it to tape, you will need to take the expected compression factor into account in your computations.

Configuring Amanda

Building and installing Amanda is generally straightforward, and the process is well-documented, so we will not consider it here.

The Amanda system includes the following components:

- Client programs, of which amandad is the most important. This daemon communicates with the Amanda server during backup runs, calling other client programs as appropriate: selfcheck (verify local Amanda configuration), sendsize (estimate backup size), sendbackup (perform backup operations), and amcheck (verify Amanda setup). These programs are part of the Amanda client system; on the Amanda server, these programs are found with the package's other helper programs, in */usr/local/lib/amanda* or */usr/lib/amanda*.

---

[*] Mathematically, the value of n where $\partial F / \partial n = 0$. In this specific example, the mathematical region around the minimum is quite flat.

- Server programs to perform the various phases of the actual backup operations. The amdump program is the one that initiates an Amanda run, and it is usually run periodically from cron. It controls a number of other programs, including planner (determine what to backup), driver (interface to device), dumper (communicate with client amandad processes), taper (write data to media), and amreport (prepare report for an Amanda run).

- Administrative utilities to perform related tasks. They include amcheck (verify Amanda configuration is valid and the facility is ready to run), amlabel (prepare media for use with Amanda), amcleanup (clean up after an aborted run or system crash), amflush (force data from the holding area to backup media), and amadmin (perform various administrative functions).

- Configuration files that specify Amanda operations, such as what to back up and how often to do so, as well as the locations and characteristics of the tape device. These files are *amanda.conf* and *disklist*, and they reside in a subdirectory of the main Amanda directory (canonically, this location is */usr/local/etc/amanda*, but it can be */etc/amanda* when the package is preinstalled). A typical name is *Daily*. Each subdirectory corresponds to an Amanda "configuration," a distinct set of settings and options referred to by the directory name.

- The amrestore utility, which can be used to restore data from Amanda backups. In addition, the amrecover utility supports interactive file restoration. It relies on a couple of daemons to do its job: amindexd and amidxtaped.

Setting up an Amanda client. Once you have installed the Amanda software on a client system, there are a few additional steps to take. First, you must add entries to the */etc/inetd.conf* and */etc/services* files to enable support for the Amanda network services:

```
/etc/services:
amanda      10080/udp
```

```
/etc/inetd.conf:
amanda  dgram   udp   wait   amanda   /path/amandad   amandad
```

The Amanda daemon runs as user *amanda* in this example; you should use whatever username you specified when you installed the Amanda software.

In addition, you'll need to ensure that all the data that you want to be backed up is readable by the Amanda user and group. Similarly, the file */etc/dumpdates* must exist and be writeable by the Amanda group.

Finally, you must set up the authorization scheme that amandad will use. This is usually selected at compile time. You may use normal *.rhosts*-based authentication, Kerberos authentication (see below) or a separate *.amandahosts* (the default mechanism). The *.amandahosts* file is similar to a *.rhosts* file, but it applies only to the Amanda facility and so does not carry the same level of risk. Consult the Amanda documentation for full information about authentication options.

Selecting an Amanda server. Selecting an appropriate system as the Amanda server is crucial to good performance. You should keep the following items in mind:

- The system should have the best tape drives (or other backup devices) possible.
- The system should have sufficient network bandwidth for the estimated data flow.
- The system should have sufficient disk space for the holding area. A good size is at least twice the size of the largest per-run dump size.
- If the server will be performing software compression on the data, a fast CPU is necessary.
- Large amounts of memory will have little effect on backup performance, so there is no reason to overconfigure the system with memory.

Setting up the Amanda server. There are several steps necessary to configure the Amanda server once the software is installed. First of all, you must add entries to the same network configuration files as those for Amanda clients:

```
/etc/services:
amanda        10080/udp
amandaidx     10082/tcp
amidxtape     10083/tcp


/etc/inetd.conf:
amandaidx  stream  tcp  nowait  amanda /path/amindexd   amindexd
amidxtape  stream  tcp  nowait  amanda /path/amidxtaped amidxtaped
```

Next, you must configure Amanda by creating the required configuration files. Create a new subdirectory under *etc/amanda* in the top-level Amanda directory (i.e., */usr/local* or */*), if necessary. We will use *Daily* as our example. Then, create and modify *amanda.conf* and *disklist* configuration files in this subdirectory (the Amanda package contains example files that can be used as a starting point).

We will begin with *amanda.conf* and consider its contents in groups of related entries. We will examine an annotated sample *amanda.conf* file.

The initial entries in the file typically specify information about the local site and locations of important files:

```
org "ahania.com"              Organization name for reports.
mailto "amanda-rep"           Mail reports to this user.
dumpuser "amanda"             Amanda user account.
printer "tlabels"             Printer for tape labels.
logdir "/var/log/amanda"      Put log files here.
indexdir "/var/adm/amindex"   Store backup set index data here.
```

The next few entries specify the basic parameters for the backup procedure:

```
# fundamental parameters
dumpcycle 7 days    Length of the backup cycle (default=10 days).
runspercycle 5      Amanda runs per cycle (if < 1/day).
```

```
# network-related resource settings
netusage 400 kps      Maximum network bandwidth (default=300).
inparallel 20         Max. simultaneous backups (default=10).
ctimeout 120          Client timeout period (default=30 seconds).

# incremental level bump parameters
bumpsize 20 mb        Min. savings for level 2 incrs. (default=10).
bumpdays 1            Required # days at each level (default=2).
bumpmult 2            Multiply bumpsize by this for each higher incremental level (default=1.5).
```

The incremental bump level parameters specify when Amanda should increase the incremental backup level in order to make the backup set size smaller. Using these settings, Amanda will switch from level 1 incrementals to level 2 incrementals whenever it will save at least 20 MB of space. The multiplication factor has the effect of requiring additional savings to move to each higher incremental level. The threshold for each level is this factor times the saving required for the previous level, i.e., 40 for levels 2 to 3, 80 for levels 3 to 4, and so on. This strategy is designed to ensure that the added complexity of multiple levels of incremental backups also bring significant savings in the size of the backup set.

These next entries specify information about the tape drive and media to use:

```
# number of tapes in use     Set to at least # tapes required for one full cycle
tapecycle 25                     plus a few spares (default=15).
labelstr "Daily[0-9][0-9]*"  Format of the table labels (regular expression).

tapedev "/dev/rmt/0"
tapetype "DLT"

#changerdev "/dev/whatever"
#tpchanger "script-path"     Script to change to next tape (supplied).
#runtapes 4                  Maximum number of tapes per run.
```

The first two entries specify the number of tapes in use and the pattern used by their electronic labels. Note that tapes must be prepared with amlabel prior to use (discussed below).

The next two entries specify the location of the tape drive and its type. The final three entries are used with tape changers and are commented out in this example. Only one of *tapedev* and *tpchanger* must be used.

Tape types are defined elsewhere in the configuration file with stanzas like this:

```
define tapetype DLT {
    comment "DLT with 10 GB tapes"
    length 12500 mb      Tape capacity (takes compression into account).
    speed 1536 kps       Drive speed.
    lbl-templ "file"     PostScript template file for printed labels.
}
```

The example configuration file includes many defined tape types. The *length* and *speed* parameters are used only for estimation purposes (e.g., how many tapes will be required). When performing the actual data transfer to tape, Amanda will keep writing until it encounters an end-of-tape mark.

The following entry and *holdingdisk* stanza defines a disk holding area:

```
# When media is unavailable, save this % of holding space
# for degraded-mode incremental backups.
reserve 50                 Default is 100%.

holdingdisk amhold0 {      Name is amhold0.
   comment "Primary holding disk"
   directory "/scratch/amanda"
# amount of space to use (+) or save (-); 0=use all (default)
   use -2 Gb               Always leave this much space.
}
```

More than one holding disk may be defined.

The final task to be done in the configuration file is to define various dump types: generalized backup actions having specific characteristics (but independent of the data to be backed up). Here is an example for the *normal* backup type (you can choose any names you like):

```
define dumptype normal {
   comment "Ordinary backup"
   holdingdisk yes      Use a holding disk.
   index yes            Maintain index info on contents.
   program "DUMP"       Backup command.
   priority medium      Specify backup relative priority.
# use 24-hour clock without punctuation
   starttime 2000       Don't begin backup before this time (8 P.M. here).
}
```

This dump type uses a holding disk, creates an index for the backup set contents for interactive restoration and uses the dump program to perform the actual backup. It runs at medium priority compared to other backups (the possibilities are *low* (0), *medium* (1), *high* (2) and an arbitrary integer, with higher numbers meaning the backup will be performed sooner). Backups using this method will not begin before 8 pm regardless of when the amdump command is issued.

Amanda provides several pre-defined dump types in the example *amanda.conf* file which can be used or customized as desired.

Here are some other parameters that are useful in dump type definitions:

```
program "GNUTAR"          Use the GNU tar program for backups.
                          This is also the value to use for Samba backups.
exclude ".exclude"        GNU tar exclusion file (located in top-level
                          of the filesystem to be backed up).
compress server "fast"    Use software compression on server using the
                          fastest compression method. Other keywords are
                          "client" and "best".
auth "krb4"               Use Kerberos 4 user authentication.
kencrypt yes              Encrypt transmitted data.
ignore yes                Do not run this backup type.
```

Amanda's *disklist* configuration file specifies the actual filesystems to be backed up. Here are some sample entries:

```
# host    partition    dumptype    spindle
hamlet    sd1a         normal      -1
hamlet    sd2a         normal      -1
dalton    /chem        srv_comp    -1
leda      //leda/e     samba       -1    # Win2K system
astarte   /data1       normal       1
astarte   /data2       normal       1
astarte   /home        normal       2    # dump all alone
```

The columns in this file hold the hostname, disk partition (specified by file in */dev*, full special file name, or mount point), the dump type, and a spindle parameter. The latter serves to control which backups can be done at the same time on a host. A value of -1 says to ignore this parameter. Other values define backup groups within a host; Amanda will only run backups from the same group in parallel. For example, on host *astarte*, the */home* filesystem must be backed up separately from the other two (the latter may be backed up simultaneously if Amanda so wishes).

There are a few final steps that are needed to complete the Amanda server setup:

- Prepare media with the `amlabel` command. For example, the following command will prepare a tape labeled "DAILY05" for use with the Amanda configuration named *Daily*:

    ```
    $ amlabel Daily DAILY05
    ```

    Similarly, the following command will prepare the tape in slot 5 of the associated tape device as "CHEM101" for use with the *Chem* configuration:

    ```
    $ amlabel Chem CHEM101 slot 5
    ```

- Use the amcheck command to check and verify the Amanda configuration.
- Create a cron job for the Amanda user to run the `amdump` command on a regular basis (e.g., nightly). This command takes the desired configuration as its argument.

Amanda expects the proper tape to be in the tape drive when the backup process begins. You can determine the next tape needed for the *Daily* configuration by running the following command:

```
# amadmin Daily tape
```

The Amanda system will need some ongoing administration, including tuning and cleanup. The latter is accomplished via the `amflush` and `amcleanup` commands. `amflush` is used to force the data in the holding disk to backup media, and it is typically required after a media failure occurs during an Amanda run. In such cases, the backup data is still written to the holding disk. The `amcleanup` command needs to be run after an Amanda run aborts or after a system crash.

Finally, you can temporarily disable an Amanda configuration by creating a file named *hold* in the corresponding subdirectory. While this file exists, the Amanda system will pause. This can be used to keep the configuration information intact in the event of a hardware failure on the backup device or a device being temporarily needed for another task.

Amanda reports and logs

The Amanda system produces a report for each backup run and sends it by electronic mail to the user specified in the *amanda.conf* configuration file. The reports are quite detailed and contain the following sections:

- The dump date and time and estimated media requirements:

```
These dumps were to tape DAILY05.
Tonight's dumps should go onto one tape: DAILY05.
```

- A summary of errors and other aberrations encountered during the run:

```
FAILURE AND STRANGE DUMP SUMMARY:
dalton.ahania.com /chem lev 0 FAILED [request ... timed out.]
```

Host *dalton* was down so the backup failed.

- Statistics about the run, including data sizes and write rates (output has been shortened):

```
STATISTICS:
                            Total      Full      Daily
                          --------   --------   --------
Dump Time (hrs:min)         2:48       2:21       0:27
Output Size (meg)          9344.3     7221.1     2123.2
Original Size (meg)        9344.3     7221.1     2123.2
Avg Compressed Size (%)      --         --         --
Tape Used (%)               93.4       72.2       21.2
Filesystems Dumped           10          2          8
Avg Dump Rate (k/s)        1032.1     1322.7      398.1
Avg Tp Write Rate (k/s)    1234.6     1556.2     1123.8
```

- Additional information about some of the errors/aberrations, when available.

- Informative messages from the various subprograms called by amdump:

```
NOTES:
    planner: Adding new disk hamlet.ahania.com:/sda2
    taper: tape DAILY05 9568563 kb fm 1 [OK]
```

- A summary table listing the data that was backed up and related information:

```
DUMP SUMMARY:
                          DUMPER STATS            TAPER STATS
HOST    DISK   L ORIG-KB OUT-KB COMP% MMM:SS  KB/s MMM:SS  KB/s
        ------------------------------------------------------------
hamlet  sd1a   1   28255  28255   --    2:36 180.3  0:21 1321.1
hamlet  sd2a   0  466523 466523   --   36:51 211.1  5:33 1400.8
dalton  /chem  1   FAILED-----------------------------------------
ada     /home  1   39781  39781   --    5:16 125.7  0:29 1356.7
...
```

You should examine the reports regularly, especially the sections related to errors and performance.

Amanda also produces log files for each run, *amdump.n*, and *log.date.n*, located in the designated log file directory. These are more verbose versions of the email report, and they can be helpful in tracking some sorts of problems.

Restoring files from an Amanda backup

Amanda provides the interactive amrecover utility for restoring files from Amanda backups. It requires that backup sets be indexed (using the *index yes* setting) and that the two indexing daemons mentioned previously be enabled. The utility must be run as *root* from the appropriate client system.

Here is a sample session:

```
# amrecover Daily
AMRECOVER Version 2.4.2. Contacting server on depot.ahania.com ...
...
Setting restore date to today (2001-08-12)
200 Working date set to 2001-08-14.
200 Config set to Daily.
200 Dump host set to astarte.ahania.com.
$CWD '/home/chavez/data' is on disk '/home' mounted at '/home'.
200 Disk set to /home.
amrecover> cd chavez/data
/home/chavez/data
amrecover> add jetfuel.jpg
Added /chavez/data/jetfuel.jpg
amrecover> extract
Extracting files using tape drive /dev/rmt0 on host depot...
The following tapes are needed: DAILY02
Restoring files into directory /home
Continue? [Y/n]: y
Load tape DAILY02 now
Continue? [Y/n]: y
warning: ./chavez: File exists
Warning: ./chavez/data: File exists
Set owner/mode for '.'? [yn]: n
amrecover> quit
```

In this case, the amrecover command is very similar to the standard restore command in its interactive mode.

The amrestore command can also be used to restore data from an Amanda backup. It is designed to restore entire images from Amanda tapes. See its manual page or the discussion in *Unix Backup and Restore* for details on its use.

Commercial Backup Packages

There are several excellent commercial backup facilities available. An up-to-date list of current packages can be obtained from *http://www.storagemountain.com*. We won't consider any particular package here but, rather, briefly summarize the important features of a general-purpose backup package, which can potentially serve as criteria for comparing and evaluating any products your site is considering.

You should expect the following features from a high-end commercial backup software package suitable for medium-sized and larger networks:

- The ability to define backups sets as arbitrary lists of files that can be saved and reloaded into the utility as needed.
- A capability for defining and saving the characteristics and data comprising standard backup operations.
- A facility for exclusion lists, allowing you to create, save, and load lists of files and directories to exclude from a backup operation (including wildcard specifications).
- An automated backup scheduling facility accessed and controlled from within the backup utility itself.
- The ability to specify default settings for backup and restore operations.
- The ability to back up all important file types (e.g., device files, sparse files) and attributes (e.g., access control lists).
- The ability to back up open files or to skip them entirely without pausing (at your option).
- The ability to define and initiate remote backup and restore operations.
- Support for multiple backup servers.
- Support for high-end backup devices, such as stackers, jukeboxes, libraries and silos.
- Support for tape RAID devices, in which multiple physical tapes are combined into a single high-performance logical unit via parallel write operations.
- Support for non-tape backup devices, such as removable disks.
- The capability to perform multiple operations to distinct tape devices simultaneously.
- Support for multiplexed backup operations in which multiple data streams are backed up to a single tape device at the same time.
- Support for clients running all of the operating systems in use at your site.
- Compatibility with the standard backup utilities, which may be important to some sites (so that saved files can be restored to any system).
- Facilities for automatic archiving of inactive files to alternate online storage devices (for example, jukeboxes of optical disks) to conserve disk space and reduce backup requirements.
- Inclusion of some kind of database manager so that you (and the backup software) can perform queries to find the media needed to restore files.

See Chapter 5 of *Unix Backup and Recovery* for an extended discussion of commercial backup package features.

Backing Up and Restoring
the System Filesystems

This final section covers backing up and restoring the filesystem containing the operating system itself, including the case of a system disk failure. Recovering from such a disaster has come to be known as "bare metal recovery" in recent years. *Unix Backup and Restore* includes detailed chapters describing these techniques and procedures for several Unix varieties.

Filesystems containing operating system files such as / and */usr* pose few problems when all you need to restore is the occasional accidentally deleted or otherwise lost file. When the file in question is an unmodified system file, you can usually restore it from the operating system installation media, provided you have it and that it is readable under normal system conditions. If either of these conditions is not true, you should do a full backup of all system filesystems from time to time.

Files that you modify in the system partitions should be backed up regularly. In Chapter 14, we looked at a script that saves all modified configuration and other files to a user filesystem, allowing them to be backed up regularly and automatically via the system backup procedures. Alternatively, the script could save them directly to the backup media (even to a diskette if the archive is small enough).

When system filesystems need to be completely restored (usually due to hardware problems), some special considerations come into play. There are often two distinct approaches that can be taken:

- Reinstalling from the original operating system installation tapes or CDs and then restoring files you have modified. This approach may also involve reconfiguring some subsystems.

- Booting from alternate media and then restoring the filesystems from full backups that you have made.

Which alternative is preferable depends a lot on the characteristics of your particular system: how many files have been customized and how widely they are spread across the various system filesystems, how much device and other reconfiguration needs to be redone, and similar considerations. If you have to restore multiple partitions, it is usually faster to reinstall the operating system from scratch unless unsaved data in another partition on the same disk will be lost using the standard installation procedures.

If you decide to take the second route, booting from alternate media and then restoring from a backup, you will need to make reliable full backups of the system whenever it changes significantly. Because you are depending on them for a system restoration in an emergency, these backups should be verified or even made in duplicate.

In either case, you will sometimes also need to consult records of the disk partitions and associated filesystem layouts, as well as the logical volume configuration, when a logical volume manager is in use. This is vital when the system disk has been damaged and must be replaced to restore the system to its previous configuration. Be sure to keep records of this data (see below).

Here is a general procedure for restoring a key filesystem from a backup (some of the individual steps are discussed in detail Chapter 10):

- Boot off alternate media, either an installation tape or CD, or a special bootable diskette or tape (discussed in a bit). At this point, you will be running off an in-memory filesystem (RAM disk) or one based on the boot medium.
- Create device files for the disks, disk partitions, and/or tape drive that you will need to access, if necessary. They may already have been provided for you if you used a system utility to create the bootable tape or diskette.
- Prepare the hard disk as necessary. This may include formatting (rarely) or partitioning it. Be sure to do anything required to make the disk bootable.
- Create a new filesystem on the appropriate partition, if necessary.
- Mount the system filesystem (*/mnt* is the conventional location).
- Change the current directory to the mount point. Restore the files from the backup tape. Afterwards, change back to the root directory and dismount the restored filesystem.
- Repeat the process for any additional filesystem and then reboot the system.

There is one additional point to consider when using this approach—or planning to rely on it. The filesystem provided by emergency boot tapes or diskettes is very limited, and only a small subset of the normal system commands are available. You will need to verify that the restoration utility you need is available after booting from alternate media. For example, if the boot diskette provides only cpio, the backup of the root filesystem had better not be a tar archive or you will be in trouble. You should also ensure that any shared libraries needed by your desired utility are present. Be sure to verify this before the disaster occurs.

We will now look at this process on each of our Unix operating systems individually.

AIX: mksysb and savevg

AIX provides the mksysb utility for creating bootable backup tapes of the actual live system, which are self-restoring in the event of a failure. It saves all of the filesystems in the root volume group, generally /, */usr*, */var*, */home* (unless you've moved it), and */tmp*, plus any paging spaces in *rootvg*. mksysb is invoked as follows:

```
# mksysb -i /dev/rmt0
```

mksysb relies on a data file that records various system configuration information. It is updated by including mksysb's -i option. Use the -m option instead if you wish to restore the exact disk locations of the filesystems in the root volume group as well as their contents (-m says to save the logical volume maps as well as the other configuration information).

To restore the root volume group, boot from the mksysb tape and select the appropriate option from the resulting menu. The system will then be restored from the mksysb tape.

You can use a similar technique to clone a system from a mksysb tape made on a different system. If all the devices are identical, the only restriction is that you should not install a kernel from a multiprocessor system onto a single CPU system or vice versa.

When devices differ between the source and target system, a slightly modified technique is used. First, you boot off the install media, and then you select the option for restoring from a mksysb tape. In this mode, the operating system will automatically substitute drivers from the installation media when the ones on the mksysb tape are not correct for the target system. Note that this method will work only if the target system has the correct drives for accommodating both the mksysb and installation media simultaneously.

Restoring individual files from a mksysb tape

mksysb tapes can also serve as nonemergency backups of the root volume group. It is very easy to restore individual files from it. These tapes contain four distinct (tape) files, and the disk files from the root volume group are in the fourth file, which consists of a restore archive.

Thus, you could use the following command to restore the file */usr/bin/csh* and the subdirectory */etc/mf* from a mksysb backup tape:

```
# restore -s 4 -x -q -f /dev/rmt0 ./bin/csh ./etc/mf
```

The -s option indicates which tape file to use, and the -q option suppresses the initial prompt asking you to press the Enter key after you have mounted the first volume. Use restore's -T option to list the contents of the archive.

Saving and restoring AIX user volume groups

The savevg command may be used to back up an entire user volume group, just as mksysb does for the root volume group. For example, the following command saves all of the files in the *chemvg* volume group to tape drive 1:

```
# savevg -i chemvg /dev/rmt1
```

The -i option creates the configuration file needed to save and restore the volume group; using -m instead also saves the logical volume maps, allowing their physical locations on disk to be reproduced.

savevg also has a -e option, which says to exclude the files and directories listed in the file */etc/exclude.vgname* from the save set.* Wildcards are not permitted in exclusion lists.

All of the logical volumes and filesystems and the files within them in a volume group can be restored from a savevg tape; the restvg utility performs this operation. For example, these commands restore the *chemvg* volume group we just saved:

```
# restvg -q -f /dev/rmt1
# restvg -q -s -f /dev/rmt1 hdisk4 hdisk5
```

The first command restores the volume group to its original disks, beginning immediately and without prompting for the first tape volume. The second command restores the structure and contents of the *chemvg* volume group to disks 4 and 5, shrinking all logical volumes to the minimum size necessary to hold the files within them (-s).

The tape made by savevg is a restore archive, so it is easy to extract individual files from it, as in this example:

```
# restore -f /dev/rmt1 -T -q
# restore -f /dev/rmt1 -x -q -d ./chem/src/h95
```

The first command lists the contents of the archive, and the second command restores the */chem/src/h95* subtree, creating any necessary subdirectories (-d).

FreeBSD

FreeBSD provides a several options for restoring system files, but all of them require that you have a complete backup of the filesystem from which to restore.

In the event of a system disk or boot failure, you must boot from alternate media (CD-ROM or a boot floppy). Then select the Fixit option from the main menu that appears. At this point, you can choose to boot from the second installation CD (which will function as a live filesystem) or a fixit floppy, or you can start a limited shell. The first two options tend to be the most useful.

The fixit floppy is a limited FreeBSD operating system containing enough tools to restore from a backup. It includes support for the tar and restore commands and tape devices. You create a fixit floppy by mounting the first installation CD and using a command like this one:

```
# dd if=/cdrom/floppies/fixit of=/dev/rfd0c bs=36b
```

This floppy can be customized after creation for your specific needs.

In order to save the disk partition layouts on a FreeBSD system, use the fdisk -s and disklabel commands. Along with */etc/fstab*, this information will allow you to reconstruct the disk partitions and filesystem layout. The disklabel command can also be used to write a boot block to a replacement system disk.

---

* The mksysb command also recognizes -e, and its exclusion file is */etc/exclude.rootvg*.

HP-UX: make_recovery

HP-UX provides the make_recovery facility for creating bootable recovery tapes as part of the Ignite-UX package (the utility is stored in */opt/ignite/bin*). A common method of using this utility is the following:

```
# make_recovery -p -A -d /dev/rmt/1mn
# emacs /var/opt/ignite/recovery/arch.include
# make_recovery -r -A -d /dev/rmt/1mn -C
```

First, we run the command in preview mode (-p). This command does not write any data to tape, but instead creates the file */var/opt/ignite/recovery/arch.include* which consists of a list of the items to be included. Here, we are choosing to save the entire root filesystem via -A; the default is to save only the subset of files that are part of the HP-UX operating system.

Once this command completes, we check the */var/opt/ignite/logs/makrec.log1* log file for any errors or warnings. If any are present, we must take any corrective action necessary and then rerun the first command.

Once any warnings are dealt with, the *arch.include* file can be edited to add or remove items, and then make_recovery can be run again in resume (-r) mode.[*] The -C option tells the command to update the stored data of the most recent make_recovery procedure.

This process must be repeated after each significant system change. The check_recovery command can be used to determine if make_recovery needs to be run.

Although these tapes are not intended to replace normal backups, it is possible to retrieve individual files from them. To do so, you must manually position the tape to the second file and then extract the desired items with tar:

```
# cd /
# mt -t /dev/rmt/1mn fsf 1
# tar xvf /dev/rmt/1m relative-pathname(s)
```

The file list should be specified as relative pathnames (e.g., *etc/hosts*, not */etc/hosts*).

 The most recent versions of the HP Ignite-UX package also provide make_tape_recovery (creates tape recovery images on the client system itself and from the Ignite-UX server) and make_net_recovery (write a recovery image to the disk drive of the Ignite-UX server across the network). See the documentation for details

---

[*] In some cases, additional considerations apply when some system files reside outside the root volume group; see the manual page for details.

Linux

On Linux systems, you can create a boot floppy of the current kernel with this command:

```
# dd if=/boot/file of=/dev/fd0
```

Simply copying the compressed kernel to diskette is all that is required, because the Linux kernel is structured so that it is the image of a bootable floppy disk (and it is loadable by either the DOS boot loader or lilo).

This procedure will enable you to boot your system should there be some problem booting from the hard disk. However, if your system disk is damaged and the root filesystem there is inaccessible, you will need a true recovery system to restore things. In such circumstances, you can boot using a *rescue disk*, which is created with the installation CD mounted with a command like this one:

```
# dd if=/cdrom/disks/rescue of=/dev/fd0 bs=18k
```

The rescue floppy contains tools needed to restore a saved backup, including tape devices and the tar command.

To record the disk partitioning information, use the fdisk -l command. Along with */etc/fstab*, this information will allow you to reconstruct the disk partitions and filesystem layout, and you can use lilo to create a boot block on a replacement system disk. Note that its -r option will prove very useful when the new root partition is mounted at some other point (e.g., */mnt*) within the rescue filesystem.

 Recent versions of Red Hat Linux also provide a system rescue option when booting from the installation CD.

Solaris

Solaris provides little in the way of tools for system backup and recovery. You should make full backups of the root filesystem. You can then boot off alternate media to create a minimally working system and restore from your backup.

The prtvtoc command along with */etc/checklist* will provide the information required to recreate the disk partitioning and filesystem layout scheme. You can use the installboot command to write a boot block to the system disk. Note that boot images are stored within the installed filesystem at */usr/platform/model/lib/fs/ufs/bootblk*, where *model* is a string corresponding to your specific Sun hardware model (e.g., *SUNW-Sun-Blade-100*).

Tru64: btcreate

Tru64 provides the btcreate command for creating a bootable backup tape for the operating system. The tape consists of a bootable miniature operating system and a complete backup of the system files.

Running btcreate is very easy in that it will prompt you for all of the information that it requires. The default (suggested) answers are almost always correct. A restore from a btcreate tape will recreate the logical volume configuration from the original system in addition to restoring all of the system files.

On Tru64 systems, you can use the disklabel -r command to record disk partitioning information and recreate them if necessary.

## CHAPTER 12

Serial Lines and Devices

This chapter discusses how to work with serial lines on Unix systems. Traditionally, this meant configuring terminals and modems, but now the topic's scope has grown to include related facilities as well, such as fax services and USB.

This chapter begins by considering traditional serial lines. First, we'll look at the special files used for serial lines and other terminal sessions. Next, we will discuss how to set the characteristics of individual terminals and generic terminal types. We then go on to consider terminal line configuration issues, including how to add and troubleshoot new terminals and modems. We'll conclude with a brief look at the HylaFAX fax service package and USB devices.

 Celeste Stokely's website, at *http://www.stokely.com/unix.serial.port. resources*, is an invaluable guide to all aspects of using serial ports on Unix systems.

About Serial Lines

Serial lines were first used for connecting terminals to computers. As time went on, however, many other devices have been connected via serial lines as well: modems, printers, digital cameras, and MP3 players, to name just a few. While serial lines are not fast communications channels, they do provide a straightforward, standardized way of sending data to or from a computer. In traditional contexts, serial lines use the RS-232 communications standard. We will consider this standard in some detail later in this chapter, after we've discussed some more practical aspects of administering serial lines and devices.

Device Files for Serial Lines

The special files for serial ports vary between systems, but they traditionally have names of the form */dev/tty*n, where *n* is a one- or two-digit number corresponding to the serial line number (System V and BSD style, respectively); numbering begins at 0 or 00. For example, */dev/tty2* and */dev/tty16* correspond to the third and seventeenth serial lines on a system, respectively (BSD-style systems always use two digits: */dev/tty02*). Terminals, modems, and other serial devices are accessed via these special files.

On more recent System V–based systems, special files for direct terminal lines are stored in the directory */dev/term* and have names that are their line number: */dev/term/14*, for example. There are often links to the older names.

The file */dev/tty* (no suffix) serves a special purpose. It is a synonym for each process's controlling TTY. It can be used to ensure output goes to the terminal, regardless of any I/O redirection.

The special file */dev/console* always refers to the system console device. On many workstation systems, */dev/console* is redefined depending on how the workstation is being used. */dev/console* refers to the system CRT display when the system is being used in a nongraphical mode. When a windowing session is running, however, */dev/console* may become one of its windows (rather than the device as a whole).

Systems may have other terminal special files corresponding to devices that they support. For example, under AIX, the special file */dev/lft* is used for the physical workstation console. It comes into play most often when the console is used as an ordinary character terminal (i.e., its nongraphical, command-line login mode). It is also the device to which the X server attaches when the workstation is running in its normal graphical mode.

There are also other terminal devices in */dev* used for indirect login sessions via a network or windowing system; these are the *pseudo-terminal* devices. Each pseudo-terminal consists of two parts:

- The *master* or *control* pseudo-terminal, which usually has a device name of the form */dev/pty[p-s]n* or */dev/ptc/n* (BSD and System V, respectively). Many systems support both naming formats.
- The *slave* pseudo-terminal (also called a *virtual terminal*), which has a device name of the form */dev/tty[p-s]n* or */dev/pts/n*. It emulates an ordinary serial line terminal for command output.

n is usually a single hexadecimal digit in both cases. The slave pseudo-terminals provide a TTY-like interface to user processes. The two parts work in pairs, with the same device number *n*. Output appears in the virtual terminal, and this device is also what is listed by commands like ps. On recent System V–based systems, only a single master pseudo-terminal is used for all of the virtual terminals (true for the System V names under AIX, HP-UX and Solaris; Tru64 has merged the control functionality into the slave device, thus eliminating use of a master pseudo-terminal special file).

Table 12-1 lists the special files for serial lines and pseudo-terminals on the various systems we are considering. The special files for the first serial line and the first pseudo-terminal are listed in each case.

Table 12-1. *Serial line special files*

Version	Serial line	Dial-out form	Pseudo-terminal Control	Slave
AIX[a]	/dev/tty0	/dev/tty0	/dev/ptc	/dev/pts/0
FreeBSD	/dev/ttyd0	/dev/cuaa0	/dev/ptyp0	/dev/ttyp0
HP-UX[a]	/dev/tty0p0	/dev/cua0p0, /dev/ttyd0p0[b]	/dev/ptmx	/dev/pts/0
Linux	/dev/ttyS0	/dev/ttyS0	/dev/ptyp0	/dev/ttyp0
Solaris[a]	/dev/term/a	/dev/cua/0	/dev/ptmx	/dev/pts/0
Tru64	/dev/tty00	/dev/tty00	(not used)	/dev/pts/0

[a] Also provides the BSD-style pseudo-terminal special filenames.
[b] This form is used for dial-in modems.

As the table indicates, dial-out modems sometimes use a different special file than terminals do. For example, under Solaris, the special file */dev/cua/0* refers to the first serial line in dial-out mode. Similarly, under HP-UX, */dev/cua0p0* and */dev/ttyd0p0* both refer to the same serial line and are used for dial-out and dial-in modems, respectively.

The two special files differ only in their *minor device numbers* (their subtype within their device class), which are offset by 128. You can use the ls -1 command to find the major and minor device numbers for a special file; they appear in the size field:

```
crw-rw-rw-   1 bin    bin    1 0x000201 Feb  1 06:59 cua0p2
crw-rw-rw-   1 bin    bin    1 0x000201 Feb  1 06:59 cul0p2
crw--w--w-   1 bin    bin    1 0x000200 Jan 15 15:52 tty0p2
crw--w----   1 uucp   bin    1 0x000202 Feb  1 06:59 ttyd0p2
```

These four devices all refer to the same physical serial port, accessed in different modes: as a dial-out modem, as a direct serial connection to another computer, as a terminal line, and as a dial-in modem.

You could use the MAKEDEV or mknod command if you needed to create any of these special files for a serial line. The first is preferred if it is available because it is much easier to use:

```
# cd /dev
# ./MAKEDEV tty4
```

This command will create all the special files associated with the fifth serial line.

On systems without MAKEDEV, you must run the mknod command. For example, the following commands may be used to create the additional outgoing special files for a bidirectional modem on the fifth terminal line (which is usually named */dev/tty0p4*):

```
# mknod /dev/cul0p4 c 1 0x401
# mknod /dev/cua0p4 c 1 0x401
```

These commands both create character special files (the *c* code letter) for device class 1 (serial lines). You can then use these device files for configuring the serial line in the various contexts (as we'll see). Alternatively, you can use SAM to create any required special files, via its Peripheral Devices → Terminals and Modems → Actions → Add Terminal or Add Modem menu path.

The tty Command

The tty command displays what special file is being used for a login session. For example:

```
$ hostname
hamlet
$ tty
/dev/tty12
$ rlogin duncan
AIX Version 5
(C) Copyrights by IBM and by others 1982, 2000.
$ tty
/dev/pts/4
```

This user is directly logged in to the 13th terminal line on *hamlet*. On *duncan*, his remote session is using pseudo-terminal 4.

Specifying Terminal Characteristics

Unix programs are generally written to be terminal-independent: they don't know about or rely on the specific characteristics of any particular kind of terminal, but rather, they call a standard screen manipulation library that is responsible for interfacing to actual terminals. Such libraries serve to map general terminal characteristics and functions (e.g., clearing the screen) to the specific character sequences required to perform them on any specific terminal.

Terminal definitions are stored in databases on the system, and users indicate what kind of terminal they are using by setting the *TERM* environment variable (usually at login time). These databases are handled differently under BSD and System V and are the subject of the next section.

termcap and terminfo

Programs use the name specified in the *TERM* environment variable as a key into the system terminal definitions database. Under the BSD scheme, terminal definitions are stored in the file */etc/termcap*; under System V, they are stored in the subdirectories of the *terminfo* top-level subdirectory. Some systems provide both facilities:

AIX	*/usr/lib/terminfo*
FreeBSD	*/etc/termcap* (a link to */usr/share/misc/termcap*)
Linux	*/etc/termcap* and */usr/share/terminfo*
HP-UX	*/usr/lib/terminfo* (a link to */usr/share/lib/terminfo*)

Solaris	*/etc/termcap* and */usr/share/lib/terminfo*
Tru64	*/usr/share/lib/termcap* and */usr/lib/terminfo*

This section provides a brief overview of *termcap* and *terminfo* entries. See the Nutshell Handbook *termcap & terminfo*, by John Strang, Linda Mui, and Tim O'Reilly (O'Reilly & Associates), for detailed information about the Unix terminal definition databases and modifying or writing entries.

termcap entries

The BSD *termcap* database is a text file consisting of a series of entries that describe how different terminals function. Here is a sample entry for a VT100 terminal:

```
d0|vt100|vt100am|dec vt100:\
  :co#80:li#24:am:ho=\E[H:\
  :ku=\EOA:kd=\EOB:
```

This sample entry is much shorter than an actual entry, but it will serve to illustrate the features of *termcap* entries. The first line is a series of aliases for the terminal type. Any entry without a space can be used as the value of the *TERM* environment variable. The remainder of the entry is a colon-separated series of capability codes and values. There are several kinds of capabilities. They can specify:

Data about the terminal
> In the sample entry, the *co* code tells how many columns the terminal screen has (80), the *li* code indicates how many lines it has (24), and the *am* code says that the terminal can automatically wrap long output strings onto multiple lines on the terminal screen.

The sequence of characters sent to the terminal to get it to perform some action
> In the sample entry, the *ho* code indicates the character sequence required to move the cursor "home" (the upper left corner of the screen). In these sequences, the ESCAPE character is abbreviated \E. Thus, to get a VT100 to move the cursor to its upper left corner, you send it the sequence "ESCAPE [H."[*]

The character sequence emitted when a special key is pressed
> In the sample entry, the *ku* code holds the sequence for the up arrow key; on a VT100, the terminal emits "ESCAPE O A" when you press this key. Similarly, the *kd* code specifies the sequence emitted by the down arrow key.

On FreeBSD systems, you must run the following command after modifying the termcap file:

```
# cap_mkdb /usr/share/misc/termcap
```

---

[*] This doesn't mean that if you type this sequence, the cursor will move. This discussion refers to sequences sent to the terminal *as a device*, before any hardware interpretation.

---

terminfo entries

The System V *terminfo* database is a series of binary files describing terminal capabilities. Each entry is a separate file in the subdirectory of the main *terminfo* location that is named for the first letter of its name: e.g., the *terminfo* entry for a VT100 is stored in the file *terminfo/v/vt100*. *terminfo* entries are compiled from source code vaguely similar to *termcap*. Here is the equivalent *terminfo* source code for the sample *termcap* entry for the VT100:

```
vt100|vt100am|dec vt100,
    am, cols#80, lines#24, home=\E[H,
    kcud1=\EOB, kcuu1=\EOA,
```

The following commands are available for manipulating *terminfo* entries:

tic
> Compile *terminfo* source.

infocmp
> List source for a compiled *terminfo* entry. The -C option says to list the equivalent *termcap* entry for a compiled *terminfo* entry (i.e., translate from *terminfo* to *termcap*).

captoinfo
> Translate a *termcap* entry into *terminfo* source.

Modifying entries

If you need to change a *termcap* entry, you just have to edit */etc/termcap*; to change a *terminfo* entry, list its source with infocmp, edit the source, and then recompile it with tic. In either case, it's wise to test the new entry by installing it under a slightly different name (*vt100t* for example) rather than merely replacing the old one. The easiest way to create a new entry is usually to find an existing one for a similar device and then rename and modify it for the new terminal type.

The *terminfo* commands listed previously are useful not only for modifying *terminfo* entries or creating new ones but also whenever you need to convert an entry from one format to the other. For example, I wanted to use an old terminal I had on an AIX system, but the system had no *terminfo* entry for it. However, I was able to find a *termcap* entry for it on a BSD system, so all I had to do was extract the entry into a separate file, ship it to the AIX system, run captoinfo on it, and then compile the result with tic.

Users can specify an alternate *termcap* or *terminfo* database with the *TERMCAP* and *TERMINFO* environment variables. If their value is a filename, that file (*TERMCAP*) or directory (*TERMINFO*) will be used instead of the usual location. In the latter case, the named directory must contain subdirectories named for the first letter of the entries they hold, just as the standard location does. Thus, if *TERMINFO* is set *to* */home/chavez/terminfo* and *TERM* is set to *etchasketch*, the file */home/chavez/terminfo/e/etchasketch* must be a compiled *terminfo* entry for that device type.

The *TERMCAP* environment variable can also be used to pre-retrieve a *termcap* entry; this feature is discussed in the next subsection.

The tset Command

Once a user has set the terminal type with the TERM environment variable, the tset command can be used to initialize the terminal. Without arguments, tset sets basic terminal properties to common default values, including setting the erase, kill, and interrupt characters, and sending any appropriate initialization sequences for that terminal type. tset is traditionally included in default user initialization files when the user's default login location is a terminal.

Although it's most often used without options, tset is actually a very versatile utility. For example, it can prompt for the terminal type if desired by using its -m option. For example, the following command prompts the user for the terminal type, supplying *vt100* as a default, and then initializes the terminal:

```
$ tset -m ":?vt100"
TERM = (vt100)
```

If the user enters a carriage return, tset will use *vt100* as the terminal type; otherwise, it will use whatever type the user enters. In either case, tset will then initialize the terminal accordingly. Instead of *vt100*, you can enter any terminal type that your system supports.

You can use tset to prompt for and set the *TERM* variable by including its hyphen option, which directs tset to echo the terminal type to standard output:

```
$ TERM=`tset - -Q -m ":?vt100"`          Bourne and Korn shells
$ export TERM

% setenv TERM `tset - -Q -m ":?vt100"`      C shell
```

The -Q option suppresses the normal messages tset prints out.

On BSD-based systems, tset can also be used to set the *TERMCAP* environment variable. When used this way, the entire *termcap* entry corresponding to the type named in the *TERM* variable becomes the value of the *TERMCAP* variable. Setting *TERMCAP* allows programs to start up more quickly, since they don't need to search the *termcap* database file.

tset's -s option generates the shell commands necessary to set the *TERM* and *TERMCAP* environment variables (commands are generated for the shell specified in the *SHELL* environment variable). There are many ways of executing them; one common way is to use the eval command:

```
$ eval `tset -sQ -m ":?vt100"`
```

The tset command in back quotes is executed first. It prompts for the terminal type, initializes the terminal, and then emits the commands necessary to set *TERM* and

TERMCAP, which are executed by eval. These are the commands tset produces for the Bourne shell:

```
export TERMCAP TERM;
TERM=vt100;
TERMCAP=`d0|vt100:co#80:li#24:am:ho=\E[H: . . .';
```

Another way to execute the emitted commands is to capture them in a file, which is then source'd (in the C shell):*

```
tset -sQ -m ":?vt100" >! ~/.tmpfile
source ~/.tmpfile
rm ~/.tmpfile
```

These are the commands as they might appear in a user initialization file. They can also be kept in a separate file, to be source'd whenever it is necessary to change the terminal type. The first command prompts for the terminal type and initializes the terminal. The remaining commands generate and execute setenv commands for TERM and TERMCAP, and then finally delete the temporary file.

What's in the temporary file? Assuming that the user selects the terminal type vt100 (i.e., assuming that she selects the default that tset suggests), *~/.tmpfile* will look like this:

```
set noglob;
setenv TERM vt100;
setenv TERMCAP 'd0|vt100:co#80:li#24:am:ho=\E[H: ... ';
unset noglob;
```

The set noglob command turns off shell interpretation for the special characters (asterisks and so on) that are commonly used in *termcap* entries. Note that if something goes wrong with this sequence of commands, unsetnoglob will never be executed, and the user will get a shell in which shell wildcards don't work. This is rare, but it's certainly confusing.

The stty Command

While tset performs type-specific terminal initialization, the stty command can be used to specify generic terminal and terminal line characteristics (such as parity). Its general syntax is:

$ **stty** *option* [*value*]

Not all options require values. stty's options are not preceded by hyphens, although some options have a hyphen as the first character of their name. Options often come in pairs—like echo and -echo—where the second form means the negative of the first (in this case "no echo").

---

* If you're wondering what the exclamation point after the output redirection sign is for, it overrides the shell's *noclobber* variable, which prevents files from being accidentally overwritten. With the exclamation point, any existing file will be overwritten anyway.

stty has a large number of options; the most useful are listed in Table 12-2.

Table 12-2. Commonly used stty options

Option	Meaning	Example
n	Baud rate.	38400
rows *n*	Lines on the screen.	rows 36
columns *n*	Columns on the screen.	columns 80
echo	Echo typed characters on the screen.	-echo
erase *c*	Delete the previous character.	erase ^H
kill *c*	Erase entire command line.	kill ^U
intr *c*	Interrupt the foreground command.	intr ^C
eof *c*	End-of-file signal.	eof ^D
susp *c*	Suspend the foreground command.	susp ^Z
lnext *c*	Interpret the next character literally (used to insert control characters into the command line).	lnext ^V
werase *c*	Erase the previous word.	werase ^W
rprnt *c*	Reprint the pending command line.	rprnt ^R
stop *c*	Pause terminal input and output.	stop ^S
start *c*	Restart paused terminal.	start ^Q
flush *c*	Discard all pending (undisplayed) output.	flush ^O
quit *c*	Kill foreground command and dump core.	quit ^\
oddp	Enable odd parity.	oddp
evenp	Enable even parity.	evenp
-parity	No parity is generated or detected.	-parity
cstopb	Use two stop bits.	cstopb
-cstopb	Use one stop bit.	-cstopb
clocal	Use hard carrier (-clocal means soft).	-clocal
sane	Reset many options to reasonable settings.	sane

For example, the werase option tells stty which character, when typed, should erase the previous word. By default, it's Ctrl-W. (Try it; many Unix users aren't even aware that this feature exists.[*]) Likewise, the reprint option tells stty which character, when typed, will make the system reprint the line you're currently typing. The sane option just might help you to restore normal functioning if you accidentally do something that confuses your terminal.

---

[*] Some C shell versions change its behavior. The line bindkey "^W" backward-delete-word in the *.cshrc* file will fix it.

Among the most useful stty options is erase, which defines the control sequence that erases the previous character (performed by the Delete or Backspace key). If the key is echoed as ^H or ^? instead of removing the previous character:

```
$ grpe^H^H
```

A command like the following will fix it:

```
$ stty erase ^h
```

This command sets the erase character to Ctrl-H, the sequence emitted by the Backspace key. You can type the desired keystroke in as erase's argument or use the symbolic form: the caret character followed by the appropriate letter for that control sequence. Case does not matter, and this symbolic form may be used for any stty option requiring a character as its value. The code for the Delete key is ^?.

When a terminal has become hopelessly messed up and won't respond to anything, the following command sequence may help:

```
^J^Jstty sane^J
```

This has the effect of clearing out any junk remaining around in the terminal's buffer and then resetting the terminal to a set of safe settings.

The stty -a command may be used to display the current terminal settings:

```
$ stty -a
speed 38400 baud; rows 40; columns 80; line = 0;
intr = ^C; quit = ^\; erase = ^?; kill = ^U; eof = ^D;
eol = <undef>; eol2 = <undef>; start = ^Q; stop = ^S; susp = ^Z;
rprnt = ^R; werase = ^W; lnext = ^V; flush = ^O; min = 1;
time = 0; -parenb -parodd cs8 -hupcl -cstopb cread -clocal
-crtscts -ignbrk brkint -ignpar -parmrk -inpck -istrip -inlcr
-igncr icrnl ixon -ixoff -iuclc -ixany imaxbel opost -olcuc
-ocrnl onlcr -onocr -onlret -ofill -ofdel nl0 cr0 tab0 bs0 vt0
ff0 isig icanon iexten echo echoe echok -echonl -noflsh -xcase
-tostop -echoprt echoctl echoke
```

stty and the terminal characteristics databases provide complementary information. *termcap* and *terminfo* provide generic information about all terminals of a given type, while stty -a provides information about the current setting of options that are, for the most part, supported by many terminals. For example, the *vt100* entries provide fairly complete information about the features specific to VT100 terminals. However, by themselves, *termcap*, *terminfo*, and tset do not support users who like or require particular terminal options—for example, users who like "#" as an erase character (a feature of very, very old Unix systems) or whose modem only runs at 9600 baud.* stty controls the TTY device driver, and thus it allows a user to specify

---

* This term follows colloquial usage, which falsely equates the term baud with bits/sec. The former is properly defined as "symbols per second, where a symbol encodes one or more bits. Such a definition is only correctly applicable to the analogue data stream between two modems. For example, a V.32 modem provides 9600 bps at 2400 baud, using 16 different symbols (points in amplitude/phase space), each encoding 4 bits." (Thanks to Peter Jeremy for that one.)

options like these. It can be particularly useful when a user logs in to another system remotely; in this situation, the properties of the remote connection often don't correspond exactly to the default settings and must be explicitly changed.

Adding a New Serial Device

To add a new serial device to the system, you must perform the following steps:

- Physically connect the terminal or modem to the computer.
- Determine the special file in */dev* that communicates with the serial line.
- In the case of terminals, make sure a *termcap* or *terminfo* entry exists for the kind of terminal you are adding. If none exists, you will have to create one.
- Add or modify an entry in the relevant configuration files (which files to use depends on the desired use: login, dial-up, dial-out, and so on).
- If appropriate, force init to reread the terminal configuration information.

Each of these steps will be considered in turn.

Making the Physical Connection

This section discusses issues related to making the physical connection between a terminal or modem and the computer. It is condensed from the Nutshell Handbook *Managing uucp and Usenet*, by Grace Todino and Tim O'Reilly (O'Reilly & Associates), with some additions and slight alterations.

The serial cables used to connect computers or terminals to modems are commonly called RS-232 cables; technically, they conform—more or less—to the Electronic Industries Association (EIA) RS-232C or the more recent RS-232D standard. By extension (really by bending, if not breaking, the standard), RS-232 cables have come to be used to connect computers to all kinds of serial devices—terminals, printers, and ports on other computers, as well as modems.

Full RS-232 cables consist of up to 25 wires, each with a specific function and each intended to carry a different signal. Only two of the wires are commonly used for data transmission; the rest are used for various kinds of control signals. In fact, many of the signals defined by the RS-232 standard are rarely used. Table 12-3 lists the RS-232 signals typically used for serial devices. Accordingly, current devices virtually always use only a subset of the 25 pins, and smaller connectors containing only the relevant pins are much more common than ones with the full set.

Table 12-3. RS-232 signals and their functions

Pin Number	Function	Direction (DTE DCE)
1	Frame Ground (FG)	↔
2	Transmit Data (TD)	→

Table 12-3. RS-232 signals and their functions (continued)

Pin Number	Function	Direction (DTE DCE)
3	Receive Data (RD)	←
4	Request to Send (RTS)	→
5	Clear to Send (CTS)	←
6	Data Set Ready (DSR)	←
7	Signal Ground (GND)	↔
8	Data Carrier Detect (DCD)	←
20	Data Terminal Ready (DTR)	→

In general, serial communication works as follows. A piece of equipment (a computer or a modem) sends a signal across the cable by applying a small positive or negative voltage to a specific pin in the cable's end connector. The signal is carried across the wires in the cable to the corresponding pin at the other end, where it is detected by another piece of equipment. The voltage either may be held high (positive) as a go-ahead signal or may pulse quickly to convey data, with the sequence of negative and positive voltages being interpreted as binary values.

As Table 12-3 indicates, only two of the 25 pins—pins 2 and 3—are actually used for data transmission. These two lines are used differently by computers and modems. The RS-232 standard defines two types of equipment: Data Terminal Equipment (DTE) and Data Communications Equipment (DCE). Most (but not all) computers are DTE; modems are always DCE. DTE uses pin 2 to transmit data and pin 3 to receive it; DCE does the reverse.

To connect a terminal or computer to a modem or printer (DTE↔DCE), you want to make the connection *straight through*: all the pins on the first device are connected to the corresponding pin on the second device (see Figure 12-1). To make a connection between two computers (DTE↔DTE) or between a terminal and a computer, you need a cable with lines 2 and 3 crossed. The latter is known as a *null-modem* cable. Modems use straight-through cables, not null-modem cables.

 If you do not know whether a device is DTE or DCE, you can always tell by measuring the voltage on pins 2 and 3. The transmitter should always have a negative voltage, even when idle. If pin 2 is negative, the device is DTE. If pin 3 is negative, the device is DCE.

Hardware handshaking and flow control

Pin 7 is the signal ground. It provides the reference against which other signals are measured. A pin is said to be *asserted* when a voltage greater than ±5 volts (relative to signal ground) is present on the pin. On the data lines, a voltage more negative than −5 volts is considered a binary 1, and a voltage more positive than +5 volts is considered a binary 0.

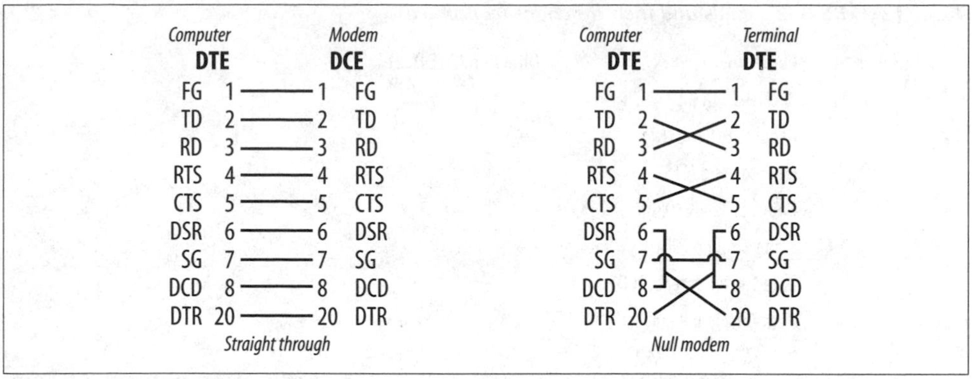

```
   Computer        Modem              Computer         Terminal
     DTE            DCE                 DTE               DTE
   FG   1 ———— 1   FG              FG   1 ———— 1   FG
   TD   2 ———— 2   TD              TD   2  ⤬   2   TD
   RD   3 ———— 3   RD              RD   3  ⤬   3   RD
   RTS  4 ———— 4   RTS             RTS  4  ⤬   4   RTS
   CTS  5 ———— 5   CTS             CTS  5  ⤬   5   CTS
   DSR  6 ———— 6   DSR             DSR  6 ┐  ┌ 6   DSR
   SG   7 ———— 7   SG              SG   7 ┤⤬ ├ 7   SG
   DCD  8 ———— 8   DCD             DCD  8 ┘  └ 8   DCD
   DTR 20 ———— 20  DTR             DTR 20     20   DTR
       Straight through                 Null modem
```

Figure 12-1. Pin assignments for serial cables

On the control lines, a positive voltage is considered the "on" state and a negative voltage is considered off. This is the direct opposite of the case for the data lines.

The remainder of the RS-232 lines shown in Chapter 11 are control lines. Most types of equipment (including modems) are not happy just to receive a stream of data. They need more control through a process called *handshaking*. In handshaking, some preliminary communication between the two pieces of equipment must take place before data can be sent.

Let's consider what type of handshaking might be necessary between a computer and a modem in order to dial up another computer system.

First of all, on an outgoing call, the computer needs to know that the modem is available to make the call. Then the modem needs to tell the computer that it has made a connection.

A computer (DTE) asserts pin 20 (Data Terminal Ready) to show that it is ready. A modem (DCE) asserts pin 6 (Data Set Ready). When the modem makes a connection with another modem on the other end, it asserts pin 8 (Data Carrier Detect) to let the computer know that a connection has actually been established. Most Unix systems in the U.S.A. ignore DSR and simply rely on DCD alone for this type of handshaking (although European systems may use DSR). DTR is asserted when a program such as getty opens the device with an *open* system call. The *open* sleeps on the line until DCD is asserted by the modem or terminal on the other end of the line. These voltages usually remain high during the entire transmission.*

If the voltage on pin 20 drops, it tells the modem that the computer is unable to continue transmission, perhaps because it is down. The modem will hang up the phone

---

* Modern Unix computers often use a scheme known as *soft carrier*, in which DCD is assumed always to be asserted (and the actual line is not checked). Under this approach, only 3 pins are needed for communication: transmit (2), receive (3), and signal ground (7). Some cables contain only these three pins. You can enable soft carrier for a terminal line using the stty command's -clocal option or via settings in a configuration file.

if a call is in progress. If the voltage on pin 8 drops, it tells the computer that the modem no longer has a connection. In both cases, these pins give a simple yes/no report on the state of the transmission. This form of handshaking is sometimes referred to as *modem control*.

There is a further level of handshaking that is used to control the rate of data transmission. Particularly when transmitting large amounts of data at high speed, it is possible that one end of a link may try to send data faster than the other end can receive it. To keep this from happening, there is a *flow-control handshake* that allows either end to prevent the other from sending any more data until the slower end catches up.

RTS/CTS is used as a kind of throttle. Whenever a DTE device is able to *send* data, it asserts pin 4, Request to Send. If the DCE is ready to *accept* data, it asserts pin 5, Clear to Send. If the voltage on RTS or CTS drops at any time, this tells the sending system that the receiver is not ready for more data: "Whoa! Hold on till I get my buffers cleared." Since this flow control handshake is implemented in the serial port hardware, it is considerably more efficient and reliable than the Ctrl-S/Ctrl-Q (XON/XOFF) handshake that can be performed in software.

Table 12-4 provides an example of a conversation between computer and modem that illustrates these principles in action (the plus and minus signs signify raised and lowered voltage, respectively).

Table 12-4. Computer-modem communications

Device	Signal	Meaning
Computer	DTR +	*I want to call another system. Are you ready?*
Modem	DSR +	*I'm ready. Go ahead and dial.*
Modem	DCD +	*I've got your party.*
Computer	RTS +	*Can I send data now?*
Modem	CTS +	*Sure. Go ahead.*
Computer	TD ...	*Data sent out.*
Modem	... RD	*Data received.*
Modem	CTS -	*Hold on for a moment!*
Modem	CTS +	*I'm OK again. Go ahead!*
The previous four steps may be repeated, with either device in the sending role, and either device using flow control.		
Computer	DTR -	*I'm done. Please hang up.*
Modem	DCD -	*Whatever you say.*

The function of pins 6, 8, and 20 is asymmetrical between DTE and DCE (in the same way as pins 2 and 3). A DTE device (a computer or terminal) asserts DTR (pin 20) and expects to receive DSR (pin 6) and DCD (pin 8). Therefore, a null-modem cable must cross these control lines as well as the data lines, allowing DTR (pin 20) on each DTE interface to drive both DSR (pin 6) and pin 8 (DCD) on the other. That is, whenever either side asserts DTR, the other side thinks it is getting DSR and DCD.

 Some publications suggest that you can fake out pins 4 and 5 by tying them together at each end of the cable. As a result, whenever the computer looks for a go-ahead signal, it gets it—from itself. This is really a poor practice. It will generally work if you are simply connecting terminals, since people cannot type fast enough ever to require the computer to "cry uncle." Nevertheless, there can be problems. For example, a function key programmed to send a long string of characters—or a PC trying to upload a file—can send too fast for a loaded system to capture all the characters. Dropped characters can result, unless the system can rely on the flow-control handshake.

For similar reasons, pins 4 and 5 are also crossed in null modem cables. Figure 12-1, earlier in the chapter, illustrates the pin assignments for a straight through and a null modem cable.

Now that we've considered how they work, it's time to consider actual serial cables. There are several varieties you may encounter, illustrated in Figure 12-2.* The cables pictured are the following, from left to right:

- USB Type-B and Type-A connectors (both male). USB is discussed in the final section of this chapter.
- DB-9 connector (female), a 9-pin cable commonly used for connecting devices to computer serial ports.
- DB-25 connector (male), containing the full 25 pins.
- 8-pin mini DIN connector (male), a connector type used for serial ports on older Macintosh systems.
- RJ-12 modular plug containing 6 wires. RJ-45 (8-wire) plugs are also used for serial devices (as well as for network cables).

Figure 12-2. Serial cables

The latter two connector types are less frequently used these days.

Figure 12-3 displays the pin numbering schemes for the four traditional serial connectors (looking at the front of the connector).

* http://www.cablestogo.com/resources/connector_guide.asp is a very useful guide to cable connectors and contains excellent illustrations of the full range of cable types for computer devices.

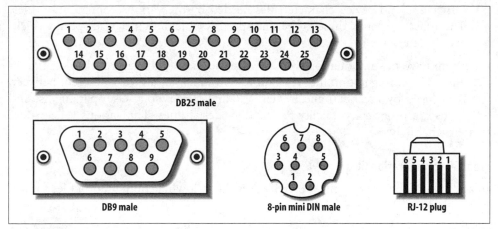

Figure 12-3. Serial cable pin assignments

Table 12-5 lists the pin equivalencies for three cable types.

Table 12-5. Serial cable pin correspondences

Signal	DB25	DB9	Mini DIN
FG	1	*none*	*none*
TD	2	3	3
RD	3	2	5
RTS	4	7	6
CTS	5	8	2
DSR	6	6	*none*
SG	7	5	4, 8
DCD	8	1	7
DTR	20	4	1

Finally, the RS-232C standard limits the maximum length for RS-232 cables to 50 feet. In practice, however, they can be used over much larger distances (many hundreds of feet), especially at lower baud rates.

Terminal Line Configuration

Once you've physically connected the device to the computer, you need to assemble the information necessary to configure the line:

- The appropriate special file.
- If the device is a terminal, the name of the corresponding *termcap* or *terminfo* entry.

- Other line and device characteristics needed by the various configuration files. The most crucial of these is the line speed (or maximum device speed, whichever is determinant).

Once you have this information, you are ready to modify the appropriate configuration files. The configuration files relevant to terminal lines are very different between the BSD (used by FreeBSD) and System V (almost everybody else) paradigms, and Solaris uses a proprietary* facility for handling serial lines. The various versions are treated separately.

FreeBSD configuration files

In addition to the *termcap* file, FreeBSD uses the following configuration files for terminal lines:

/etc/ttys
> Lists serial lines in use and their characteristics

/etc/gettytab
> Holds generic serial line definitions

/etc/ttys must contain an entry for each terminal-related device to be used, including serial lines used for other purposes (e.g., printers) and pseudo-terminals. Each entry in the */etc/ttys* file has four fields:

```
port  command  type [flags]
```

Fields are separated by one or more spaces or tab characters. Comments begin with a number sign and may be placed at the end of an entry or on separate lines. The fields have the following meanings:

port
> Special filename in */dev* that communicates with this serial line.

command
> The command that init should execute to monitor this terminal line. For terminals and modems, the program used is getty. If init should not create a process to monitor this line, this field should contain the keyword *none*. This is the case for pseudo terminals and for serial lines where no one will log in: printers, terminals used purely as displays, and the like. Use a full pathname for all commands, and enclose commands containing spaces in quotation marks.

type
> For serial lines that support user logins, the name of a terminal type described in */etc/termcap*. If a terminal type is included, the *TERM* variable will be set to this value at login. Alternatively, the field can contain the keyword network (for

---

* Not that anyone else would want it…

pseudo terminals) or `dialin` (for dial-up modems); such keywords can be used by user initialization files or the `tset` command.*

flags

Zero or more keywords, separated by spaces. The following keywords are supported:

`on`

Line is enabled, and command will be run by `init`.

`off`

Line is disabled, and the entry is ignored. No getty process is created.

`secure`

Allow root logins.

`window=`*cmd*

`init` should run *cmd* before the one in field 2.

`group=`*name*

Used to define named groups of teminal for use the */etc/login.conf* file (see "Managing User Accounts" in Chapter 6).

`off` status is used for lines that are down, not in use, or for which no getty command should be run (e.g., a line connected to a dial-out modem). Multiple keywords should not be enclosed in quotation marks, even though they are separated by spaces. For pseudo-terminals, the status field should be blank (not on).

Here are some sample entries:

```
# dev   command                     type      flags
ttyd0   "/usr/libexec/getty std.9600"   vt100     on secure
ttyd1   "/usr/libexec/getty std.38400"  dialup    off  # 555-1111
ttyv0   "/usr/libexec/getty Pc"         cons25    on secure
ttyp0   none                            network   off
```

The first entry describes the terminal on the first terminal line. This terminal has type *vt100*, corresponding to a VT100 terminal. Whenever the terminal line is idle (i.e., whenever a user logs out or when the system enters multiuser mode), `init` runs the specified getty command, using the *std.9600*entry in */etc/gettytab* to provide information about the terminal line (discussed below). This terminal is enabled, and it is secure, meaning that users may use it to log in as *root*.

The second entry describes a dialup modem on the second serial line (the baud speed serves only a descriptive function since the line is off). The third line defines a virtual

---

* What I'm calling *keywords* have *termcap* entries like the following:

```
sa|network:\
  :tc=unknown:
```

This entry defines a terminal type of *network* whose only characteristic equivalences it to the *unknown* terminal type.

terminal session for a directly connected terminal (or the console), and the final line illustrates the entry form for virtual terminal devices for network use.

Secure terminal lines. If you wish to allow people to log in as *root* on a specific terminal, place the keyword secure in the status field for its terminal line. Conversely, you can prevent users from logging in as *root* by omitting or deleting the keyword secure from this field. For security reasons, secure status should only be granted to the system console and possibly to one or more directly connected terminals. Denying it to pseudo-terminals means that anyone wanting to become *root* via a network session will need to log in initially as a normal user and then become *root*. Thus, such users will need to know both a user account password and the *root* password.

The /etc/gettytab file. The command field in */etc/ttys* usually contains a getty command, which has the following syntax:

```
"getty gettytab-entry"
```

gettytab-entry identifies a particular entry in the file */etc/gettytab*, specifying the characteristics of this terminal line. This file is similar in form to */etc/termcap*. The first line of each entry identifies one or more synonymous names that identify the entry; any name not containing spaces can be used as a valid argument to getty. Subsequent lines describe various line characteristics. Here are some sample lines:

```
# /etc/gettytab
default:\
    :cb:ce:ck:lc:fd#1000:im=\r\n%s/%m (%h) (%t)\r\n\r\n:\
    :sp#1200:if=/etc/issue:
cons8:\
    :p8:sp#9600:
2|std.9600|9600-baud:\
    :sp#9600:
g|std.19200|19200-baud:\
    :sp#19200:
std.38400|38400-baud:\
    :sp#38400:
```

The names *std.n* are traditionally used for standard terminal lines, running at *n* baud. Thus, *std.9600* in the previous example refers to terminal lines at 9600 baud. Autobaud modems are set to the type corresponding to their maximum speed. These entries frequently set only the *sp* (line speed) characteristic.

The *default* entry sets defaults for all entries; characteristics set in individual entries override them.

System V configuration files

System V also uses the getty program to handle terminal lines, but it is started in a different way. In addition to the *terminfo* and/or *termcap* databases, the System V–style terminal configuration files are the following:

/etc/inittab
> System initialization configuration file

/etc/gettydefs
> Terminal line definition file

The lines in */etc/inittab* to start getty processes look like this:

AIX	`cons:0123456789:respawn:/usr/sbin/getty /dev/console`
	`t1:234:respawn:/usr/sbin/getty /dev/tty0`
HP-UX	`cons:123456:respawn:/usr/sbin/getty console console`
	`t1:234:respawn:/usr/sbin/getty -h tty0p1 57600`
Linux	`1:2345:respawn:/sbin/mingetty --noclear tty1`
	`t1:234:respawn:/sbin/mgetty -D -i /etc/issue -s 57600 ttyS1`
Tru64	`cons:1234:respawn:/usr/sbin/getty console console vt100`
	`t1:234:respawn:/usr/sbin/getty /dev/tty00 57600 vt100`

Starting at the left, the fields are the *inittab* identifier, the run levels to which the entry applies, the action to take, and the process to initiate: in this case, getty. The action field for terminal line entries holds either *off* (for lines not in use) or *respawn*, which says to start another getty process whenever one exits.

The getty command's syntax varies among these four Unix versions. The preceding examples included the entries for the console device and a modem on the first serial line. In general, the System V–style getty command takes two arguments: the TTY name, corresponding to the name part of the special filename (i.e., without */dev/*), and a label to look up in *the /etc/gettydefs* file, which holds generic line definitions. The label is often the same as the line speed.

Here are a few version-specific comments:

- The AIX version of getty does not use the *gettydefs* or the second getty parameter (configuration data is stored in the ODM database). It requires the full pathname to the special file as its sole argument.

- The -h option on the HP-UX version tells getty not to force a hang up on the terminal line before initializing it.

- Linux systems do not define a console device in the usual way. Instead, one or more virtual console sessions are defined for use when the console is used as a terminal (rather than as a graphical workstation). The --noclear option to the mingetty command says not to clear the screen before issuing a login prompt. This command is a minimal implementation of getty used only in this context.

- Linux offers several getty-type commands for use with terminal lines and modems. I prefer mgetty, and recent Red Hat and SuSE distributions finally agree with me. Its -D option says the line is a data line, i.e., there is no fax machine on the line (-F says the opposite). The -i option specifies an alternate, shorter text file to be displayed before the login prompt, a step always appreciated by users of slower modems. Finally, -s specifies the line speed. The final command line item is mgetty's required parameter: the name part of the device file.

- The Tru64 getty command uses a third parameter specifying the terminal type for that terminal line.

When adding a new device, you'll need to add a new line to */etc/inittab* (or modify an existing one). There must be a separate entry in the *inittab* file for every terminal line on which someone can log in.

The */etc/gettydefs* file. The */etc/gettydefs* file is used on HP-UX and Tru64 systems. Here are some sample entries from an HP-UX system:

```
console # B9600 SANE CLOCAL CS8 ISTRIP IXANY TAB3 HUPCL
        # B9600 SANE CLOCAL CS8 ISTRIP IXANY TAB3 HUPCL
        #Console Login: #console

19200 fixed baud entry
19200 # B19200 CS8 CLOCAL
      # B19200 SANE -ISTRIP CLOCAL
      #@S login: #19200

Modem cycle with hardware flow control
28800 # B28800 CS8 CRTSCTS
      # B28800 SANE -ISTRIP HUPCL CRTSCTS
      #@S login: #14400

14400 # B14400 CS8 CRTSCTS
      # B14400 SANE -ISTRIP HUPCL CRTSCTS
      #@S login: #9600

9600  # B9600 CS8 CRTSCTS
      # B9600 SANE -ISTRIP HUPCL CRTSCTS
      #@S login: #28800
```

Each entry in */etc/gettydefs* describes one operating mode. Distinct entries are separated by blank lines. The fields in each entry are as follows:

```
label # initial flags
      # final flags
      # login prompt #next label
```

The *label* is used to refer to the entry on the getty command. The initial and final flags are set on the device during the periods before and after login is executed, respectively. Commonly used flags are:

B*n*
    Baud rate of *n* baud.

CLOCAL
    Local directly connected line.

HUPCL
   Hang up on close (useful for modems).

TAB3
   Tabs are sent to the terminal as spaces.

SANE
   Set various parameters to reasonable values (as in stty).

The fourth field in the *gettydefs* file holds the login prompt used on that line.

The *nextlabel* field indicates which label should be used next if a break character is received on the line. It is designed to enable cycling through various baud rates on dialup lines. If the *next label* is the same as the *label*, no such cycling will occur; this is how hard-wired lines are set up. In our example file, the *19200* entry is hardwired at that speed, and the remaining three entries form a small cycle.

Setting terminal line types under HP-UX. On HP-UX systems, the default terminal type for each terminal line may be specified in the */etc/ttytype* file. It has entries of the form:

```
terminal-type line-name
```

terminal-type is the name of a *terminfo* entry, and *line-name* is again the name part of the special filename. For example, the following entry sets the default terminal type to *vt100* for the fourth terminal line:

```
vt100 tty0p3    HP-UX
vt100 tty03     Tru64
```

The Linux mgetty configuration files. mgetty uses several configuration files stored in */etc/mgetty+sendfax*:

mgetty.config
   Main mgetty configuration file (entries common to data and fax lines).

login.config
   Specifies programs to be run by connection type. The default version of this file is usually quite adequate; simply uncomment the entries applying to the types of connections you will support. The /bin/login entry is typically used for dial-up lines.

dialin.config
   Accept/reject incoming calls based on Caller ID.

/etc/nologin.ttyxx
   If this file exists, the corresponding line is disabled.

Configuring terminal lines under AIX. As we've noted, AIX uses *inittab* but not *gettydefs*. Terminal line characteristics are stored in the ODM and may be set or changed with the chdev command. For example, the following command enables logins on */dev/tty0*, setting the line speed to 19200 baud; setting the stty modes before a login to hupcl, cread, and tab3 (hang up on close, enable received, and expand tabs to spaces); and setting the stty modes after login is executed to cread, echoe, and cs8 (enable receiver, echo erase characters as backspace-space-backspace, and use 8-bit characters):

```
$ chdev -l tty0 -a login=enable -a speed=19200 -a term=vt100 \
        -a runmodes='hupcl,cread,table3' \
        -a logmodes='cread,echoe,cs8'
```

Any stty options may be used for the initial and final flags, set with the *runmodes* and *logmodes* attributes (respectively).

The *login* terminal line attribute indicates how the line will be used. When it is given a value of *share*, connections may take place in both directions (as for a bidirectional model):

```
# chdev -l tty0 -a login=share ...
```

A value of *disable* configures a line for dial-out only, and *enable* is the correct value for a dial-in–only line.

Starting the Terminal Line

The final step in installing a new serial device is (re)starting its line. To start up a terminal line, you must force init to reread the terminal line initialization information. When it does, init becomes aware that the device has been added and takes the appropriate action (usually starting a getty process for it).

Under FreeBSD, the following command sends a hang-up (HUP) signal to init (process 1):

```
# kill -HUP 1
```

init catches this signal and interprets it as a command to reread initialization information without interrupting the system's activity; kill is being used in its generic, signal-sending capacity rather than to terminate a process. Therefore, by modifying the configuration files and executing the command kill -HUP 1, you add a new terminal without rebooting the system or otherwise interrupting the system's normal operation.

On most System V–based systems, the telinit q command performs the same function. Under HP-UX and Tru64, use init q instead (unless you've created a link named telinit).

After you execute this command, check the new terminal. It should have a login prompt and allow you to log in normally. Sorting out terminal line problems is the topic of the next section.

Terminal Handling Under Solaris

With Solaris, terminal lines are handled in a very different manner. The Service Access Facility (SAF) controls terminal lines and remote printing under Solaris (it is derived from the System V.4 standard). The seeming complexity of the SAF can be somewhat intimidating initially, but it is more verbose than truly complicated. The SAF has the potential to manage vast areas of system capabilities, but in fact, in its present form, what it does is really quite limited. We'll attempt to demystify its workings here.

 Solaris provides a graphical tool for interfacing with the SAF. It does make setting things up a lot easier and more automated. However, in this section, we'll be looking at the underlying commands first, so that the concepts and procedures are clear.

Structure of the Service Access Facility

The Service Access Facility (SAF) is organized in the following hierarchy:

- At the top level is the *Service Access Controller* (SAC), which oversees the entire facility. The sac daemon is started in */etc/inittab* by an entry like this one:

      sc:234:respawn:/usr/lib/saf/sac -t 300

  The -t option to the sac command specifies how often the daemon polls the port monitors it controls (in seconds).

- The SAC starts and controls various *port monitors*: processes responsible for monitoring one or more ports and connecting requests that arrive on them with the proper system process. sac starts all of the port monitors listed in its configuration file, */etc/saf/_sactab*, when it begins executing.

  Currently, there are two different port monitors: ttymon, which is responsible for terminal lines, and listen. The latter was designed to be responsible for managing general network services, but it is really capable of handling only remote printing in the present implementation.* On many systems, it is not used at all.

- Port monitors connect requests to local system *services*. For example, ttymon connects incoming requests on serial lines to the login service and the login program.

Multiple instances of a port monitor may be present. For example, there will be one ttymon process on the system for each serial port managed by the SAF.

---

* An amusing comment in */etc/init.d/inetsvc* attests to this fact when it explains why the main TCP/IP networking daemon, inetd, is started with the -s option:

```
# Run inetd in "standalone" mode (-s flag) so that it doesn't have
# to submit to the will of SAF. Why did we ever let them change inetd?
# /usr/sbin/inetd -s
```

The following commands are used to configure the SAF and its serial port monitors:

sacadm
    High level SAF configuration: add, delete, enable, disable, start, and stop port monitors.

pmadm
    Configure port monitor services (and associated processes) for individual ports.

ttyadm
    Helper utility formats input to pmadm for serial ports.

sttydefs
    Create and modify entries in */etc/ttydefs* describing terminal line characteristics.

Port monitors

The sacadm -1 command lists port monitors currently administered by the sac daemon:

```
# sacadm -1
PMTAG    PMTYPE   FLGS RCNT  STATUS    COMMAND
zsmon    ttymon    -    0    ENABLED   /usr/lib/saf/ttymon #
```

This output illustrates more of the structure implicit in the SAF. The PMTAG field shows the name assigned to a particular defined instance of a port monitor. If that sounds like gibberish, the following may help. The term "port monitor" is used somewhat promiscuously in the Solaris documentation. There are three kinds of entities that might be referred to as port monitors, depending on the context:

- *Port monitor types*, of which there are only two: *ttymon* and *listen*. The fact that these are also the names of the executable commands for individual port monitor processes is one major source of confusion.

- *Port monitor tags* (PMTAG), which define groups of one or more actual port monitor processes (whether or not they are all actually running at any given time). By default, there is only one defined tag per port monitor type: *zsmon* for ttymon (named for the Zilog serial ports used on Sun CPU boards), and *tcp* for listen (in the United States, anyway). However, it is possible to have more than one PMTAG per port monitor type; we'll look at how one might be created shortly.

- *Actual port monitor processes*, each handling a single port (or request source in the case of network printing requests). The port monitor processes for a given port monitor tag are defined in the file */etc/saf/pmtag/_pmtab* (for example, */etc/saf/zsmon/_pmtab*), which is maintained by the pmadm command. *ttymon* port monitors run the ttymon command, and *listen* port monitors run the listen command. Individual port monitors are identified by *service tags* (SVCTAG).

Sun recommends creating a PMTAG for each block of serial ports with its own separate controller. The `sacadm` command may be used to create a new PMTAG. For example, this command creates *mux0* as a `ttymon`-type port monitor:

```
# sacadm -a -p mux0 -t ttymon -c /usr/lib/saf/ttymon \
        -v `ttyadm -V` -y "MUX 0 ttymon" -n 9999
```

The options to `sacadm` used in the preceding example have the following meanings:

-a   Add a port monitor.

-t   Specify port monitor type (`ttymon` or `listen`).

-p   Specify PMTAG.

-c   Specify command to run for associated port monitor processes.

-v   Specify version number (returned by the command `ttyadm -V`).

-y   Description for *pmtab* entry.

-n   Number of times to restart port monitor if it dies.

The command creates a subdirectory of */etc/saf* named *mux0*; the `pmadm` command would be used to create actual port monitors associated with this PMTAG.

The `pmadm -l` command may be used to list all port monitors for a given PMTAG:[*]

```
$ pmadm -l -p zsmon        Use -L for a compact format.
PMTAG  PMTYPE  SVCTAG FLGS ID   <PMSPECIFIC>
zsmon  ttymon  ttya   u    root /dev/term/a I - /usr/bin/login
- 38400 ldterm,ttcompat ttya login: - tvi925 n  # Bidir. Modem
zsmon  ttymon  ttyb   u    root /dev/term/b - - /usr/bin/login
- 9600 - ttyb login: - tvi925 -                 # Terminal
```

On this system, the *zsmon* PMTAG includes two *ttymon* port monitors: *ttya* and *ttyb*, controlling */dev/term/a* and */dev/term/b*, respectively. *ttya* is used for a bidirectional (dial-in/dial-out) modem, and *ttyb* controls a terminal.

Creating port monitors with pmadm

The following `pmadm` command could be used to create the port monitor for */dev/term/b*:

```
# pmadm -a -p zsmon -s ttyb -i root -f u -v `ttyadm -V` \
        -m "`ttyadm -d /dev/term/b -T vt100 -s /usr/bin/login \
        -l 57600 -p \"ttyb login: \"`"
```

Since `pmadm` is a complicated and completely general port monitor administration utility, Solaris provides some auxiliary commands to help generate its required input. The auxiliary command for serial lines is `ttyadm`.

---

[*] The -t and -s options may be used with `pmadm -l` to list port monitors of a given type or with a specified SVCTAG, respectively.

Let's take the preceding command apart:

`pmadm -a`	*Add a port monitor.*
`-p zsmon`	*Port monitor tag.*
`-s ttyb`	*Service tag (conventional name is shown).*
`-i root`	*Run service (specified below) as this user (root).*
`-f u`	*Create utmp entry for port (required by login).*
``-v `ttyadm -V` ``	*Version (determined/returned by ttyadm).*
``-m "`ttyadm ...`"``	*Port monitor-specific data, formatted by ttyadm:*
`ttyadm -d /dev/term/b`	*Special file for port.*
`-T vt100`	*Terminal type (defined in the terminfo database).*
`-s /usr/bin/login`	*Service program.*
`-l 57600`	*Line type (entry label in /etc/ttydefs).*
`-p \"ttyb login: \"`	*Login prompt (protect quotes with backslashes).*

This command adds (`-a`) the port controlled by the special file */dev/term/b* (`-d` to ttyadm) to the port monitor zsmon's control (`-p`). The `pmadm` command uses the `ttyadm` command twice to format its input correctly: the output of `ttyadm` is placed into the `pmadm` command via back quotes. The second `ttyadm` command does most of the work. It specifies that the */usr/bin/login* service will execute at that port when connection is requested (`ttyadm -s`); the login prompt will be:

```
ttyb login:
```

The terminal line's configuration corresponds to the entry labeled *57600* in the */etc/ttydefs* file (`ttyadm -l`).

The command for a bidirectional modem line is similar (the changes are in boldface):

```
# pmadm -a -p zsmon -s ttya -i root -f u -v `ttyadm -V` \
       -m "`ttyadm -d /dev/term/a -T vt100 -s /usr/bin/login \
       -l 57600E -p \" login: \" \
       -b -S n -t 30 -m ldterm,ttcompat`"
```

The second `ttyadm` command uses these additional options:

`-b`
: Designates a bidirectional modem line.

`-S n`
: Set software carrier off.

`-t 30`
: Login timeout period (seconds).

`-m ldterm,ttcompat`
: Additional STREAMS modules to load (required for modems).

To change a port monitor definition, you must remove the old one first, using `pmadm -r`, and then use `pmadm -a` to add a correctly configured one.

The ttydefs file

The configuration file used by `ttymon` is */etc/ttydefs*. It is viewed and maintained by the `sttydefs` command. `ttydefs` holds essentially the same data as `gettydefs`; the sttydefs interface is an attempt to provide continuity across any future file format changes.

Here are some sample entries from */etc/ttydefs*:

```
57600E:57600 hupcl:57600 hupcl::57600E

57600:57600 hupcl evenp:57600 evenp::38400
38400:38400 hupcl evenp:38400 evenp::19200
19200:19200 hupcl evenp:19200 evenp::57600
```

The first entry specifies a line fixed at 57600 baud. The remaining lines form a cycle for an autobaud modem (the *hupcl* attribute tells the line to hang up when a connection terminates and the *evenp* attribute select even parity).

The sttydefs -l command may also be used to view the available line definitions. Here is the output corresponding to the first sample entry above:

```
$ sttydefs -l 57600E
---------------------------------------------
57600E:57600 hupcl evenp:57600 evenp::57600E
---------------------------------------------

ttylabel:        57600E
initial flags:   57600 hupcl evenp
final flags:     57600 evenp
autobaud:        no
nextlabel:       57600E
```

The sttydefs command has two other main options, -a and -r, which add and remove entries from the */etc/ttydefs* file, respectively. When adding an entry, the following additional options are available:

-n   Next label.

-i   Initial flags.

-f   Final flags.

-b   Set autobaud on terminal line.

The next label, initial flags (terminal settings set prior to login), and final flags (terminal settings after login) have the same meanings as they do in the */etc/ttydefs* file, but their use has been greatly expanded. Any flags accepted by the stty command are accepted in this field, separated by spaces. The -a and -r options require and the -l option accepts a label for the */etc/ttytab* entry.

For example, the following commands add a new entry named *57600i* and delete an entry named *1200* from the */etc/ttydefs* file:

```
# sttydefs -a 57600i -n 57600i -i "57600 erase ^h" \
          -f "57600 sane crt erase ^?"
# sttydefs -r 1200
```

Using admintool to configure serial lines

admintool can be used to perform the same configuration steps we have just done manually. Figure 12-4 illustrates the dialog it provides for performing this task.

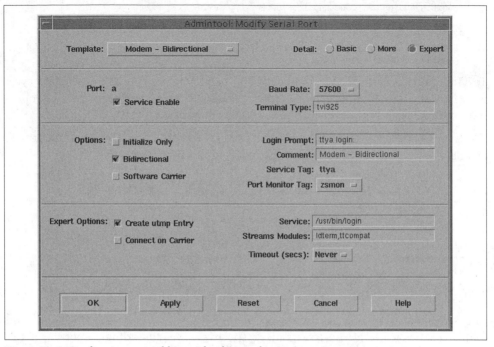

Figure 12-4. Configuring a serial line with admintool

The tool provides three configuration modes—basic, more, and expert—which provide access to successively more attributes. It also provides a series of templates: predefined collections of settings designed for specific purposes. The figure illustrates those designed for a bidirectional modem.

Most of the fields are self-explanatory. The only tricky one is labeled Baud Rate. It is used to select an entry within */etc/gettydefs,* rather than specifying a literal baud rate.

Troubleshooting Terminal Problems

Messed-up terminals are an occasional problem that system administrators have to deal with. When a terminal is hung (when it won't respond to any input) or seems to have gone crazy, here are some things to try that address the most common causes:

- If the user knows what she did last, try to undo it. For example, if she was experimenting with stty options, try a stty sane command.

- If the terminal doesn't respond at all, the user might have accidentally hit Ctrl-S, the pause key, the hold screen key, or something else that temporarily stops output. Try entering Ctrl-Q and then these other keys to see if things get going again.

- Check the terminal settings via its setup menu. In particular, is its baud rate set correctly?

- Try entering the reset command. If it doesn't work, try preceding and following it with a line feed (Ctrl-J if the terminal has no line feed key):

    ```
    ^Jreset^J
    ```

  Substituting stty sane in place of reset can also work. Running either command twice in succession is frequently necessary.

- If the user has turned the power off and back on, check other settings like the emulation mode. If the user hasn't cycled power, try this yourself; there are some conditions that only cycling the power will clear. Leave the terminal off for about 10 seconds to allow the internal capacitors to discharge completely.

- Next, go to another terminal and try to kill the program that was running on the hung terminal. It may be that the program—and not the terminal—is hung. Try a variety of signals in an attempt to neutralize the process—TERM (kill's default), KILL, INT, QUIT, STOP—use kill -l to list the available signals or consult */usr/include/sys/signal.h*.

  Use the ps command with its -t option to limit the display to the desired terminal. -t takes the device name as its argument, in the same form in which it appears in the TTY column of ps's output. For example, the following command displays the processes for */dev/tty15*:

    ```
    $ ps -t15
    ```

  If nothing else works, trying killing the user's login shell. If the terminal doesn't come back after a few seconds, try cycling the power again.

- If cycling the power and killing everything in sight doesn't bring the terminal back, check the connections. Has the connector fallen off the back, for example? (In some cases, you'll want to check this first.) If a cable is loose, it will eventually fall due to gravity alone, even if the terminal hasn't moved an inch in months.

For a new terminal, try checking these items:

- Is the terminal plugged into the correct RS-232 connector on the back of the system? It is easy to lose track of a cable between the terminal and the computer. Good record keeping and labeling will help eliminate this problem.

- Is the cable functioning properly? You can verify this by testing it on another cable or swapping it with a cable known to be working.

- Are the brightness and contrast settings turned all the way down? Verify that the display is in fact visible.

- Is the terminal port enabled and does it specify an appropriate way to call getty?

- Is the getty process running? Use ps piped to grep to count the number of getty processes and verify that the right number are present. Did you remember to signal init?

- Are you using the right kind of cable (null modem versus straight through)? If not, a command like the following will hang:

  ```
  # cat file > /dev/ttyn
  ```

  Don't forget to kill the process once you've verified that it is hung.

 A device called a breakout box can be invaluable for troubleshooting difficult cable problems, especially if you are trying to build your own cables. You can usually pick one up at any electronics supply store for a reasonable price (under $50 U.S.). The breakout box includes LEDs that display which signals are actually active at any point. Better models also allow you to easily rearrange the wires in a cable or assert the proper voltage on individual pins for testing purposes.

Controlling Access to Serial Lines

Most Unix versions provide some mechanism for limiting direct *root* logins to certain terminal lines. Note that these mechanisms have no effect on the ability of a user to gain *root* access via the su command. We'll consider the ones offered by each operating system in turn.

As we've seen earlier in this chapter, FreeBSD allows you to state explicitly whether direct *root* logins may take place on a line-by-line basis via the *secure* keyword in */etc/ttys*. For example, these entries allow *root* logins on the terminal connected to the first serial line, but not on the terminal connected to the second serial line:

```
# name   getty                      type    flags
ttyd0    "/usr/libexec/getty std.9600"  vt100   on secure
ttyd1    "/usr/libexec/getty std.9600"  vt100   on
```

FreeBSD also provides general user class–based terminal restrictions via the *ttys.allow* and *ttys.deny* attributes in */etc/login.conf*. See "Managing User Accounts" in Chapter 6 for details.

Under Solaris, if the file */etc/default/login* contains a *CONSOLE* entry, direct *root* logins are limited to that device. For example, this entry limits *root* logins to the system console:

```
CONSOLE=/dev/console
```

On HP-UX systems, the file */etc/securetty* lists devices where *root* is allowed to log in. Here are some sample entries:

```
console
tty00
tty01
```

Note that */dev/* is not included in the line designation. The HP-UX file restricts access to the listed terminal lines to privileged users, rather than applying only to *root*.

Tru64 uses the file */etc/securettys* in a similar manner:

```
/dev/console    # console
:0              # X display
local:0
```

Note that the full special filename is included in the Digital Unix file. The second and third entries are also typically found in these files and refer to X-based sessions.

Linux systems can restrict terminal access via the PAM facility. The *pam_securetty* module provides support for a HP-UX style */etc/securetty* file, and the *pam_time* module allows you to specify terminal access by user, group, PAM service and/or day and time. See "User Authentication with PAM" in Chapter 6 for details.

Under AIX, the lsuser command can be used to determine the terminals on which *root* is allowed to log in directly:

```
# lsuser -fa ttys rlogin root
root:
    ttys=ALL
    rlogin=true
```

This command also indicates whether direct *root* logins can come in over the network. The following command will disable network-based *root* logins and limit *root* logins to the console device and the terminal on the first serial port:

```
# chuser ttys="/dev/lft,/dev/tty0" rlogin=false root
```

The *ttys* attribute takes a comma-separated list of TTY special files, indicating the terminals upon which the specified user may log in—note that this mechanism is available for all users, not just *root*. The keyword *ALL* applies to all terminal lines (including network connections), and prefacing any special filename with an exclamation point excludes that terminal. For example, this command prevents direct *root* logins on serial lines 0 and 1:

```
# chuser ttys="!/dev/tty0,!/dev/tty1" rlogin=false root
```

This mechanism is an interface to the *ttys* attribute in *root*'s stanza in */etc/security/ user*. It may be used to set up restrictions for any user, as well as a default terminal list via the *default* stanza. The file may also be edited directly.

HP-UX and Tru64 Terminal Line Attributes

Under HP-UX and Tru64, the enhanced security facility provides a mechanism for specifying several security-related terminal line attributes. Default values applying to all terminals without explicitly set overrides are found in the *t_* fields of the *default* file, stored in */etc/auth/system* under Tru64 and */tcb/files/auth/system* under HP-UX.

Here is an example from a Tru64 system:

```
default:\
        :d_name=default:\
        …
        :t_logdelay#2:t_maxtries#10:t_unlock#0:\
        :t_login_timeout#15:chkent:
```

These are the settable terminal line attribute fields, which may be used in the *default* file and in the *ttys* file; the latter contains entries for each terminal line on the system and is located in */etc/auth/system* under Tru64 (in binary form, as *ttys.db*) and in */tcb/files/auth/system* under HP-UX:

t_maxtries
> Terminal will be automatically locked after *t_maxtries*+1 consecutive login failures.

t_logdelay
> Indicates the number of seconds to wait after an unsuccessful login attempt before giving the next prompt.

t_lock
> Indicates that the terminal line is locked (t_lock@ means unlocked).

t_login_timeout
> Number of seconds after which to abort an incomplete login.

t_unlock
> Number of seconds after which to unlock a terminal locked due to too many unsuccessful login attempts (Tru64 only). A value of 0 means that the terminal line must be explicitly unlocked by the system administrator.

Here is an example *ttys* entry:

```
tty02:t_devname=tty02:t_uid=root:t_logtime#791659419:\
    :t_unsucuid=wang:t_unsuctime#793396080:t_prevuid=chavez:\
    :t_prevtime#791659434:t_failures#4:t_maxtries#8:t_logdelay#5:\
    :t_login_timeout#20:chkent:
```

In addition to the specific security attributes, the entry also holds information about recent login activity on that terminal line: the UID and time of the most recent successful login, last unsuccessful login attempt, and most recent logout from this terminal; and the number of consecutive login failures (this is reset to 0 after a successful login). See the ttys manual page for details on all terminal line-related attributes.

In addition, the *v_users* attribute in the *devassign* file can specify a comma-separated list of users who may access each device on the system; see the devassign manual page for more information.

The HylaFAX Fax Service

Many current Unix operating systems provide some sort of fax support. In this section, we'll consider the free HylaFAX package, originally written by Sam Leffler while at Silicon Graphics,* because it is the most widely used and is available for many different Unix versions. HylaFAX is capable of sending and receiving faxes on the local system, and accepting fax jobs from other hosts on the network. Outgoing faxes are queued as necessary. An interface to electronic mail is also available. The package's home page is *http://www.hylafax.org*.

Fax services are provided by three daemons:

faxq
> The queuing agent, which prepares fax files, and schedules and initiates outgoing fax transmissions.

hfaxd
> The fax server daemon, which provides local and remote fax submission support, access control and other management functions.

faxgetty
> A getty implementation which handles incoming faxes.

The package also includes a variety of utilities, many of which we'll consider here; the corresponding binary files are mainly stored in */usr/local/bin* and */usr/local/sbin*, although a few are in */var/spool/hylafax/bin* (if you use the default installation directories).

Actual fax images are stored in the subdirectories *docq* (outgoing) and *recvq* (incoming) under */var/spool/hylafax*. Other important subdirectories of this main HylaFAX spooling location are *sendq* (outgoing job control files), *log* (contains log files for each fax session), *config* (modem type definitions), and *etc* (most HylaFAX configuration files).

HylaFAX installs easily on most systems, and the documentation provides lots of information about the process, so we won't spend time considering it here. Once the software is installed, you use the faxsetup script to perform initial configuration. The script asks you a series of questions about your system setup and desired package usage, and automatically generates configuration files based upon that information.

The faxaddmodem script is used to configure a modem within the HylaFAX system, and it is called by faxsetup during the initial setup process. You can also use it to change the settings for an existing modem.

---

* The latter is evidenced by the default fax cover sheet still distributed with the package: it includes the SGI logo.

Be sure to specify the outgoing serial line device to these scripts on systems that use multiple device special files to refer to the same serial line: e.g., */dev/cuaa0*, */dev/cua0p0*, and */dev/cua/0* under FreeBSD, HP-UX, and Solaris (respectively).

Once the faxsetup script has completed, there are still a few items to deal with:

- Make sure that HylaFAX daemons are started when the system boots. On systems with System V–style initialization files, ensure that the initialization file (*hylafax*) included with the package is copied into the *init.d* subdirectory and linked to the proper *rcn.d* subdirectory. On FreeBSD and AIX systems, you may have to add a command executing it to one of the system initialization files.

 Regardless of the system, this script is the best way to start, stop and restart the HylaFAX daemons.

- Configure the serial line to run the HylaFAX faxgetty program if you plan to receive faxes. This will be done in */etc/inittab* or in */etc/ttys* under FreeBSD. Here is a sample *inittab* entry from a Linux system:

```
fax:2345:respawn:/usr/local/sbin/faxgetty ttyS0
```

The command requires only the desired serial line as its argument. On Solaris systems, you must perform this step and also make sure that no ttymon monitor is assigned to the fax serial port.

- Set up cron jobs to perform periodic maintenance on the HylaFAX spooling area. The faxqclean command will automatically purge files related to completed jobs and older failed jobs. How often to run it depends on the amount of fax traffic and the available disk space on the system. If you just send/receive the occasional fax, running it once a week is probably fine; on the other hand, if the system functions as a full-time fax server, then the current documentation recommends running it once an hour.

The faxcron command will automatically purge files related to completed jobs and older failed jobs as well as create some useful fax service reports. The command is designed to run daily. For most sites, the default settings work fine, but you can customize faxcron as needed. Current modifiable parameters include how long to retain old received faxes, log entries, temporary files, and the like.

Here are some sample *crontab* entries:

```
0 * * * *   /usr/local/sbin/faxqclean
0 3 * * *   /usr/local/sbin/faxcron | mail faxadm
```

The output of faxcron is mailed to the fax administrator since it contains useful reports. Note that faxcron is a bash script. If your system does not have bash, then you must explicitly run the command with sh:

```
0 3 * * *   /bin/sh /usr/local/sbin/faxcron | mail faxadm
```

Sending Faxes

The HylaFAX package provides the `sendfax` utility for submitting faxes. The following example briefly illustrates its features and use:

```
$ sendfax -s na-let \              Use letter size images (use a4 for A4).
  -T 5 -t 2 \                      Dial call up to 5 times; attempt to transmit twice.
  -f "Erika Plantagenet" \         Fax sender name.
  -r "Sales Data" \                Contents of Re: field (subject).
  -c "Call if any questions." \    Comments.
  -P high \                        Priority (vs. bulk or normal).
  -h dalton.ahania.com \           Send to HylaFAX server on this host.
  -a 20:05 \                       Transmit fax at 8:05 P.M.
  -d "Amy Ng@1.293.555.1212" \     Recipient name and phone number.
  letter.txt graph.tif             Files to transmit.
```

A few notes:

- The `-d` option must follow all other options which apply to that fax. It may also appear more than once in order to send the fax to multiple recipients. Other options which appear between instances of `-d` apply to the subsequent fax. For example, in this command, the fax to Amy is sent at high priority and the one to Sam is sent at bulk priority:

    ```
    $ sendfax -P bulk -d "Sam@5551212" -P high -d "Amy@5552121" fax.txt
    ```

- HylaFAX can handle ASCII text, PDF, PostScript and TIFF image files as fax content.

- Users can specify a default fax server via the *FAXSERVER* environment variable.

- Support for remote faxing must be set up on the server system (see below).

- Many of the options refer to information used on the fax cover sheet. Not all items will work with all cover templates (include the default provided with the package). The default template file is */usr/lib/fax/faxcover.ps*.

Don't Be Afraid to Say No

I try to avoid being a prima donna as much as possible, but setting up fax cover templates for HylaFAX is one place where I draw the line, pointing to my job description as I refuse to help. Don't get suckered into doing this or you'll be ensnared in an infinite time sink. These files must be in PostScript format and use the dictionary mechanism for passing fax-specific parameters (e.g., the sender and recipient names). There is no easy way to generate them, and I'm no PostScript hacker. I leave creating one as an exercise for the fax user (and fortunately no one has ever ordered me to do otherwise).

The key point to make with users is that they can always create a cover sheet as the first page of the fax file that they create. Using the sendfax command's `-n` option will suppress the HylaFAX cover page, as will setting AutoCoverPage to no (see below).

Managing Faxes

HylaFAX provides several utilities for monitoring the fax facility and manipulating fax jobs. For example, the faxstat command displays information about fax jobs, as in these examples:

```
# faxstat -s -l                                    List faxes to send.
HylaFAX scheduler on dalton.ahania.com: Running
Modem ttyS0 (1.293.555.9988): Sending job 4

JID  Pri S  Owner   Number      Pages  Dials TTS Status
4    127 R  chavez  2032390846  0:2    0:12
5    127 B  jones   2032390846  0:0    0:12      Blocked

# faxstat -r -l                                    List faxes that have been received.
HylaFAX scheduler on dalton.ahania.com: Running
Modem ttyS0 (1.293.555.9988): Sending job 4

Protect Page  Owner    Sender/TSI  Recvd@  Filename
-rw----   1   14       2935551122  19:52   fax00012.tif
```

This system is currently sending a fax, has one more job waiting to send and has recently received one as well. The xferfaxstats command may be used to produce a summary report of all fax activity, broken down by sending user.

Several other utilities are provided for manipulating individual fax jobs, which are referred to by job ID (listed in the first column in the faxstat -s output). The faxrm and faxabort commands can be used to remove/terminate fax jobs, as in these examples:

```
$ faxrm 4                                          Remove pending fax (abort if sending).
Job 4 removed.

$ faxrm -a -h mahler 28                            Remove fax job on another host as fax admin.
Password:                                          Fax administration password (see below).
Job 28 removed.
```

A user removes a fax job on the local system in the first example. Another user removes a job from a remote host in the second command by specifying the proper HylaFAX administrative password.

 Contrary to most job manipulation commands of this type, the superuser cannot use faxrm to remove a user's fax job. Rather, *root* must use a command like the following:

```
# su chavez -c "faxrm 4"
```

The quotation marks are necessary for the argument to be passed to the faxrm command.

The `faxalter` command may be used to modify the characteristics of a pending fax job. For example, the following command sets job 24 to be released for transmission at 9:00 P.M. and sets its priority to bulk (low):

```
$ faxalter -p bulk -a 21:00 24
```

As we've seen, the `faxstat` command also lists the status of faxes that have been received, including the files where they are stored. The `faxabort` command may be used to abort a current incoming fax. The `faxinfo` command may be used to view the characteristics of a received fax:

```
# faxinfo fax00027.tif
/var/spool/fax/recvq/fax00027.tif:
    Sender: +12935557778
     Pages: 3
   Quality: Normal
      Page: North American Letter
  Received: 2002:02:02 11:23:21
TimeToRecv: 0:24
SignalRate: 38400 bit/s
DataFormat: 2-D MR
```

Incoming faxes are saved in TIFF format. They may be viewed with any TIFF viewer, or you may use the `fax2ps` command to convert them to PostScript format.

Ideally, I'd like to be able to route incoming faxes to their recipient automatically. However, current fax technology doesn't provide a general way to specify a recipient electronically.[*] Beyond the fax data itself, all an incoming fax includes is the originating phone number, the incoming phone number and/or transmitting station identifier (TSI), a string associated with the sending fax machine (or modem).

HylaFAX can route faxes based on any of these. In practical terms, the most useful routing items are the originating phone number (which must be obtained via caller ID) and the incoming phone number. In the latter case, HylaFAX has the ability to route on the direct inward dial (DID) or direct number identification service (DNIS) telephone number. DID and DNIS are services offered by the telephone company in which a block of virtual telephone numbers are all routed to one or more real phone lines.[†] Using either of them, various employees in a company can each be assigned their own, unique fax number, but all incoming faxes actually go to one or more phone lines managed by the HylaFAX server. The DID/DNIS number of the incoming call is passed to HylaFAX which can use it as a key for determining where to route the fax.

---

[*] HylaFAX developers and partisans take extreme exception to this opinion.

[†] DNIS is also used in other contexts (e.g., for routing voice calls to the correct person based upon the which of several 800 telephone numbers was dialed). Similarly, DID is also used, for example, to route incoming phone calls to employee extensions without requiring an operator. Both services are expensive. DNIS typically uses a T1 line, and its monthly costs start at around $100–200 U.S. In my area (Connecticut, U.S.A.), DID currently costs about $100 U.S. per month for 20 virtual numbers and also requires a startup fee of about $750 U.S. (as of July 2002).

Processing of received faxes is handled automatically by the */var/spool/hylafax/bin/ faxrcvd* script. In its delivered form, it calls a script named FaxDispatch in */var/spool/ hylafax/etc* via the shell's dot command. This script has the responsibility for setting the SENDTO and FILETYPE environment variables. They specify the mail recipient and file type to be used for routing the file, which default to FaxMaster and ps, respectively.

This file must be a valid sh script. The HylaFAX documentation suggests a from like the one is this simple version:

```
case "$DEVICE" in                Attempt to match the incoming modem line.
ttyS4)
    SENDTO=amy_ng
    ;;
ttyS5)
    SENDTO=sam_wood
    ;;
esac

case "$SENDER" in                Attempt to match originating phone number in TLS.
12935551212)
    SENDTO=chavez
    ;;
esac

case "$CIDNUMBER" in             Attempt to match the DNIS or caller ID number.
8985551212)
    SENDTO=harvey
    FILETYPE=tif
    ;;
*41255512*)
    SENDTO=mktg
    ;;
esac
```

If *FaxDispatch* finds a match, it resets the value of SENDTO and possibly FILETYPE which were initialized in faxrcvd. Ultimately, faxrcvd sends the fax in a mail message to the SENDTO user, converting it to the format specified in FILETYPE (PostScript format by default); the converted fax is included in the message as a MIME attachment. Note that the CIDNUMBER variable is used for both Caller ID and DID/DNIS numbers (based on which of them is in use).

In general, the order of statements in FaxDispatch will be significant. Using the logic in the preceding example, the final matching entry will prevail over any previous ones.[*]

Unfortunately, this routing feature is not of any practical use at my site because we don't have DID, and users at my site cannot predict who is going to send them faxes.

---

[*] Since FaxDispatch is a shell script, it can in fact be made to perform any desired function, provided you have the time to write the appropriate script.

In such cases, however, you can modify the faxrcvd script to perform whatever actions you want for an incoming fax rather than always generating email. For example, we replace most of its logic with a simple command that just prints each incoming fax, something like this:

```
/usr/bin/fax2ps -S $1 | lpr -P $FAX_PRINTER
```

Faxes are then delivered the old fashioned way, via sneakernet.

HylaFAX Configuration Files

The HylaFAX package uses a number of configuration files. These are the most important:

/usr/local/lib/fax/hfaxd.conf
Configuration file for hfaxd, containing the locations of important configuration files, entry format for various status display lines, basic timeout settings and other fundamental parameters. It seldom needs to be altered.

/usr/local/lib/fax/hyla.conf
Settings for sendfax and other client commands. Users can define their own versions of these settings via the file *~/.hylarc*. The system-wide version must be created by the system administrator. Here is a simple example:

```
AutoCoverPage: no
Cover-From-Company: Ahania, LLC
Cover-From-Voice: 1-293-555-1212
Cover-From-Fax: 1-293-555-1213
```

/var/spool/hylafax/etc/config
General settings for the local site. Here is an example version of this file:

```
LogFacility:        daemon          Syslog facility for messages.
CountryCode:        1
AreaCode:           293
LongDistancePrefix: 1
InternationalPrefix: 011
DialStringRules:    etc/dialrules
ServerTracing:      1               Log all server actions.
MaxConcurrentJobs:  1               Should be £ total modems.
MaxSendPages:       20              Maximum fax sizes.
MaxRecvPages:       50
MaxDials:           12              Total number of phone call attempts.
MaxTries:           3               Maximum transmission attempts (after connect).
```

Most of these settings define items needed to dial telephone numbers properly. The final settings specify the maximum lengths for faxes (including any cover page) and the maximum number of phone calls and transmission attempts that will be made to send each fax.

/var/spool/hylafax/etc/config/config.line
Per-modem configuration files, containing a variety of communications-related settings as well as overrides to the settings in the main *config* file. These files

have an extension named for the serial line to which they apply. On systems using subdirectories of */dev* for serial device files, the extension is constructed as *subdirectory_device*: e.g., */dev/cua/0* would use *config.cua_0* under Solaris.

Controlling Access to HylaFAX

Host and user-based access control to the local HylaFAX facility is defined in the */var/spool/hylafax/etc/hosts.hfaxd* file. Entries in this file have the following form:

```
sender:map-to-uid:send-password:admin-password
```

where *sender* is a regular expression against which potential fax senders are compared. It can contain patterns to match the username and/or host name. The second field, *map-to-uid*, is the local UID to which matched senders should be mapped for permissions and accounting purposes (if desired). *send-password* is an optional encoded password to be used for validation prior to accepting a fax, and *admin-password* is an encoded password which must be entered in order for matching users to perform administrative functions (e.g., modifying or removing other users' faxes).

The order of entries within the file is important since the first matching entry is used. If no entry matches, access is denied. Thus, entries are generally ordered from most to least specific.

Here is a sample *hosts.hfaxd* file:

```
^chavez@.*ahania\.com$:::xxxxx       chavez can administer from anywhere in domain.
!^s_king@                            User s_king uses too much paper: deny access.
ahania\.com$::::                     Users in the domain can send (no password).
zoas\.org$:1234:yyy:                 zoas.org's users need password (UID mapped).
192.168.10.33                        All users on this host can fax.
```

As the second entry indicates, a leading exclamation point indicates an access denial entry.

The HylaFAX package provides the `faxadduser` and `faxdeluser` commands for adding and removing entries to this file. However, they are required only when you need to generate an encoded password; in other cases, it is just as easy to edit the file directly.

Here is a `faxadduser` command which creates an entry allowing user *mercury* to administer the fax system:

```
# faxadduser -a olympus mercury
```

This is the resulting entry:

```
mercury:::UiB7EkUrafx7I
```

This is actually too broad, since any user from any FQDN containing "mercury" would also match. However, once the encoded password is created, it is easy to edit manually. Alternatively, you could use a `faxadduser` command like this one:

```
# faxadduser -a olympus 'mercury@.*ahania\.com'
```

Be aware that `faxadduser` does not check to see if an existing entry like the one you are adding already exists; it simply blindly adds what you specify to the file.

 HylaFAX also has many other useful features--such as an email-to-fax gateway, faxing to pages, bulk faxing (horrors!), and the ability to reject junk faxes--which space limitations don't permit us to consider. However, the basic ones discussed here are sufficient for many environments.

USB Devices

The Universal Serial Bus (USB) was designed by a consortium of hardware and software vendors—Compaq, Intel, Microsoft and NEC—beginning in 1994. It was conceived to provide a standardized way of connecting a wide range of peripheral devices to a computer (read "personal computer") and to correct some of the limitations of traditional serial and parallel lines.

USB has the following advantages:

- Up to 127 devices can be connected.
- Devices can be added and removed while the system is running.
- Connectors have been standardized across all device types.
- It is much faster. The theoretical bandwidth of a USB bus is 12 Mbs/sec; however, actual throughput is more like 8–8.5 Mbs/sec, and devices seldom achieve more than about 2 Mbs/sec.

USB cables contain only four wires: power, ground, send, and receive. Communication is handled in a hierarchical manner, under the control of a master; attached devices all function as slaves, thereby eliminating issues such as avoiding collisions. USB cable connectors are illustrated on the far left in Figure 12-2, and Figure 12-5 illustrates their corresponding pinouts.

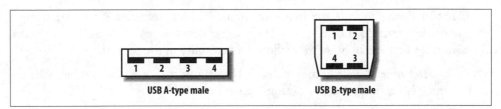

Figure 12-5. USB connectors

B-type connectors are used for the USB port on the device, and A-type connectors are used for the port on the hub or computer system.

FreeBSD, HP-UX, Linux, Solaris, and Tru64 all support USB devices to some extent, although the support under HP-UX and Tru64 is limited to the USB keyboards and mice that come with the system (and are accordingly preconfigured by the operating system).

We will consider configuring three sample USB devices—a mouse, a Zip drive, and a printer—on the other three systems in the remainder of this section.

Table 12-6 summarizes the device files used for some USB devices on these systems.

Table 12-6. Example USB device special files

Device	FreeBSD	Linux	Solaris
mouse	/dev/ums0	/dev/input/mouse0, /dev/input/mice	/dev/usbms
Zip drive	/dev/da0s4	/dev/sda4	/dev/dsk/c1t0d0s0:c
printer	/dev/ulpt0	/dev/usblp0	/dev/usbprn0

FreeBSD USB Support

FreeBSD provides good support for USB devices, although some of it is in the experimental stage. See the FreeBSD USB project's home page, *http://www.etal.net/~n_hibma/usb/*, for details on the current status.

Before you can use USB devices, you must configure support in the kernel. The following kernel configuration file lines relate to USB support:

```
device      uhci        General USB support modules.
device      usb
device      ugen
device      ohic        Alternate USB chipset support.
device      uhid
device      ukbd        Keyboard.
device      ulpt        Printer.
device      umass       Mass storage: Zip drive.
device      umodem      Modem.
device      ums         Mouse.
device      uscanner    Scanner.
```

You should always include the first four items. Include *uhid* also if you are using a mouse or keyboard. Include as many of the other items as makes sense for your configuration (or include all of them to allow for flexibility in the future).

You can determine if your kernel includes USB support that is compatible with the USB controller on the system by examining the output of dmesg:

```
# dmesg | grep usb
usb0: OHCI version 1.0, legacy support
usb0: <OHCI (generic) USB controller> on ohci0
usb0: USB revision 1.0
```

This kernel is configured for USB support, and it successfully detected the controller.

You can load the USB kernel module manually via the kldload usb command. Alternatively, you can set the appropriate modules to load automatically in the */boot/*

loader.conf file. Here we load general USB support and the modules for the mouse, keyboard, printer and Zip drive:

```
usb_load="YES"
ums_load="YES"
ukdb_load="YES"
umass_load="YES"
ulpt_load="YES"
```

See Chapter 16 for information about building FreeBSD kernels and modules.

You can list the current USB devices with the usbdevs command:

```
# usbdevs
addr 1: OHCI root hub, (unknown)
    addr 2: Genius USB Wheel Mouse, KYE
    addr 3: TUSB2046 hub, Texas Instruments
        addr 4: Espon Stylus Photo 1280
        addr 5: USB Zip 250, Iomega
```

This system has a USB mouse in one of the system's USB ports and a USB hub in the other. The secondary hub has a printer and a Zip 250 drive attached to it.

Some USB devices are configured automatically when they are detected, via the usbd daemon; the actions performed are specified in its configuration file, */etc/usbd.conf*. This is the case for the printer, the Zip drive, and the USB mouse used in the system console's text mode.

Using the mouse under X as well requires an additional step, however. You must edit the *XF86Config* file to make X aware of the USB mouse (this file is usually in */etc*). Under XFree86 Version 3.3, you modify the Pointer section as follows:

```
Section "Pointer"
   Device   "/dev/sysmouse"
   Protocol "MouseSystems"
EndSection
```

A USB printer is also easy to configure. You can set it up like any other printer within the LPD facility, using the special file */dev/ulpt0* to refer to the printer.

A Zip drive is accessed via the USB mass storage driver. Via sleight of hand, it manages to trick the standard SCSI driver into servicing a USB disk. Accordingly, the kernel must also provide SCSI support in order to use such USB devices, and SCSI disk special files will be used to refer to them.

For example, the following command can be used to mount the disk in a Zip drive at */zip*:

```
# mount -t msdos /dev/da0s4 /zip
```

The DOS partition on a Zip disk appears as the fourth slice to FreeBSD.

Alternatively, you can create a UFS filesystem on a Zip disk using the usual commands (see "From Disks to Filesystems" in Chapter 10):

```
# disklabel -w -r da0 zip250
# newfs /dev/da0c
# mount -t ufs /dev/da0c /somewhere
```

Linux USB Support

Linux also provides good support for USB devices. Once again, support for them must be enabled in the kernel. Figure 12-6 illustrates `make xconfig`'s USB menu.

We show only part of this very long parameter list (the gap indicates omitted selections). The items are divided into sections of related settings, beginning with general USB support and then support for hubs and devices classes, followed later by choices corresponding to specific USB devices. The ones required for our three devices are highlighted. I recommend selecting module-based support whenever possible.

You will also want to install the *usbutils* package and possibly the *usbview* package, as well (the latter provides a graphical USB device display command of the same name). We'll use tools from the former in this section.

You can view the currently attached USB devices with `lsusb`:

```
# lsusb | grep Bus
Bus 001 Device 001: ID 0000:0000
Bus 001 Device 002: ID 0458:0003 KYE Systems Corp.(Mouse Systems)
Bus 001 Device 003: ID 0451:2046 Texas Instruments TUSB2046 Hub
Bus 001 Device 004: ID 059b:0030 Iomega Corp. Zip 250
```

USB device attributes are also available within the */proc* filesystem, in files named like */proc/bus/usb/bus#/dev#*. For example, the usbmodules command can be used to list the device-specific modules used by a USB device:

```
# usbmodules --device /proc/bus/usb/001/002
usbmouse
hid
```

As with FreeBSD, using a USB mouse in the system console does not require configuration. If you want to use one under X, however, you must edit the *XF86Config* file, usually found in */etc/X11* (we are assuming Version 4 here). In order to use a USB mouse instead of the usual mouse type, add an InputDevice section like this one:

```
Section "InputDevice"
    Identifier "USB Mouse"
    Driver "mouse"
    Option "Protocol" "IMPS/2"
    Option "Device" "/dev/input/mice"
EndSection
```

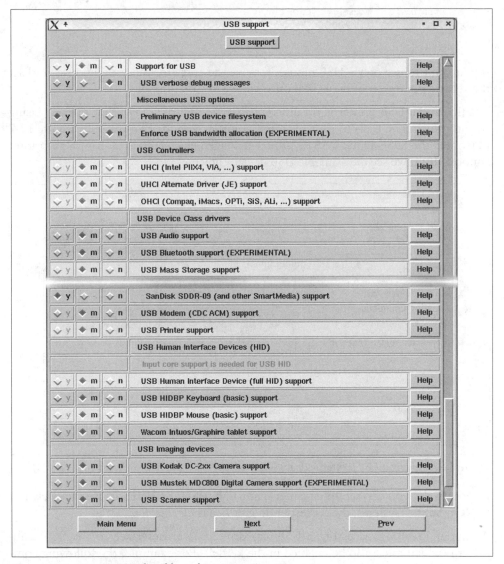

Figure 12-6. Linux USB-related kernel parameters

The special file mentioned in this example, *mice*, refers to any and all USB mice present on the system. If you want to specify just the first USB mouse, substitute */dev/input/mouse0*.

In addition, you must designate the mouse to the X server via an InputDevice directive in the ServerLayout section. For example, these entries allow you to use both a normal and a USB mouse:

```
Section "ServerLayout"
    Identifier   "Layout[all]"
```

```
        InputDevice  "Mouse[1]" "CorePointer"
        InputDevice  "USB Mouse" "SendCoreEvents"
        ...
    EndSection
```

If you want to use only a USB mouse, remove the entry for the usual mouse, and set the second parameter of the USB mouse's entry to CorePointer.

Configuring a USB printer is no different than configuring any other printer. Using the administrative tools to do so is often a quick method. For example, Figure 12-7 illustrates the SuSE Linux YAST2 printer management facility's built-in USB printer support. In it, we see the available USB device choices.

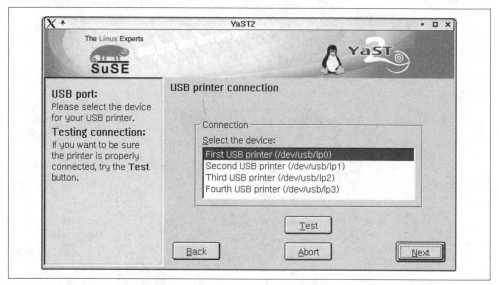

Figure 12-7. Adding a USB printer with YAST2

Alternatively, you can set up a printer manually, using the same device file, */dev/usb/lp0*. On SuSE 7 systems, the corresponding device is */dev/usblp0*.

As under FreeBSD, accessing a USB Zip drive uses an interface to the SCSI subsystem (which must also be enabled in the kernel). For example, the following command could be used to mount a Zip disk at */zip*:

```
# mount -t vfat /dev/sda4 /zip
```

The Zip disk's DOS partition is interpreted as partition 4 on the disk. You can also build other filesystem types on Zip disks, if you like.

For more information about the Linux USB project, see *http://www.linux-usb.org*.

Solaris USB Support

Solaris also provides support for USB devices. In fact, some Sun systems, like my Sun Blade, come with USB keyboards and mice standard, and no additional configuration is required to use them.

You can also use the system's USB ports for other sorts of devices. I tried using the same devices on my Sun as for the other two operating systems. The Zip drive worked fine. I used the following command to mount it:

```
# mount -F pcfs /dev/dsk/c1t0d0s0:c /zip
```

Like the other systems, the Solaris USB mass storage driver interfaces to the SCSI drive, and so the Zip drive's special filename is of the usual SCSI form. The DOS partition corresponds to the *c* slice.

Solaris offers support only for a very few USB printers, accessed via the */dev/usbprn** device files or via the usual */dev/printers/** files.

Keeping Up to Date

Serial lines and terminal handling is an area in which tremendous changes have taken place in recent years. Thus, it illustrates one of the occupational hazards of any technically-oriented profession: having one's expertise become outdated and stale. Here are some simple things you can do to avoid having this happen to you:

- Attend system administration-related technical conferences, such as LISA (see *http://www.usenix.org/events/*), or those put on by hardware vendors. I try to attend at least one a year.

- Regularly monitor administrative and security-related websites, mailing lists or newgroups. Late breaking news often first appears in these forums. This is especially important for administrators of open source operating systems.

- Subscribe to—and read—periodicals (at least a few of the articles or columns) devoted to the types of systems that you administer. I subscribe to *SysAdmin* magazine (see *http://www.samag.com*) as well as some operating system–specific publications.

- Reread all of the manual pages on the system every six months. I have a friend who does this religiously, and it's his recommendation. I must admit that I don't really have time to do this, but I do try to read all of the administrative (1m) manual pages about once a year. (Even this is a lot to do when you administer 10 different kinds of systems.)

CHAPTER 13
Printers and the Spooling Subsystem

Despite years of hype about the coming paperless office, printing has become more frequent and more complex as time has passed, not less so. Ordinary users now routinely print tens or even hundreds of pages a week, often including the sort of high-quality graphics formerly done only rarely, on expensive, special-purpose devices.

This chapter discusses the printing subsystems of the various Unix versions we are considering. Nowhere is there more variation than in accessing printing devices and spooling jobs. The FreeBSD, Linux,* and Tru64 operating systems use the BSD spooling system, HP-UX and Solaris use the System V spooling system, and AIX uses its own spooling system. Each of them is discussed individually.

In this chapter, I'll talk almost exclusively about "print" jobs, but the general discussion applies equally well to related hardcopy devices such as plotters. In fact, the Unix spooling subsystems are flexible enough to be used for purposes unrelated to printing: archiving data, running programs in batch mode, and playing music, among others.†

A spooling system typically includes the following components:

Printers
> Current output devices include laser printers and inkjet printers, as well as special-purposes devices such as label printers. Printing can be done by a printer attached to the local computer via a serial, parallel, or USB port; by a printer on a remote system; or by a standalone device connected directly to the local area network.

User commands to initiate printing
> The user specifies the file to print, which device to print it on (if there is more than one possibility), and any other necessary instructions. BSD calls them print jobs, while System V and AIX refer to them as print requests.

---

* Linux distributions also offer the LPRng system, discussed later in this chapter. In some cases, this is now the default.

† The spooling system can also be used to send faxes, a topic discussed in Chapter 12 (and placed there because most of the administrative tasks related to faxing concern interfacing to serial lines and modems).

Queues

Queues store and sequentially process print jobs. Conceptually, a queue is basically a line waiting to use a specific device.

Spooling directories

Spooling directories hold pending jobs. Under BSD, the entire file to be printed is copied to a spooling directory. Under AIX and System V, by default only a small request file is generated, and the file is accessed in its original location at the proper time.

Server processes

Server processes accept print requests, set up and store the files associated with them, and transfer the resulting jobs from the spooling directory to the actual devices.

Filters

Filters transform the files to be printed into the internal formats required by the printer. Filters are programs which the print server runs automatically for each print job.

Administrative commands

These commands start and stop the entire subsystem or specific printers and manage queues and individual print jobs. In addition, configuration files are usually used to specify the various characteristics and desired settings for each printing device. They are typically modified automatically by the various administrative commands, but some files need to be edited manually.

Remote printing support

These days, remote printing is at least as common as local printing. A system that lets users on other hosts send jobs to some or all of its printers is referred to as a *print server*, and the remote systems from which jobs originate are thus its *clients*. We will consider remote printing in the context of each of the three spooling subsystems.

 An excellent reference for all aspects of Unix printing is the book *Network Printing* by Todd Radermacher and Matthew Gast (O'Reilly & Associates). Despite its title, it discusses both the local and network-related aspects of print spooling, including a extended section on print filters.

Table 13-1 presents a summary of the spooling subsystem components for the various Unix versions.

Table 13-1. Print system components

Component	Location
Version	**BSD:** FreeBSD, Linux, Tru64
	System V: HP-UX, Solaris
	Proprietary: AIX

Table 13-1. Print system components (continued)

Component	Location
Spool directories	**BSD:** */var/spool/lpd/**
	System V: */var/spool/lp/request/**
	AIX: */var/spool/lpd/qdir* and */var/spool/qdaemon*
	FreeBSD: */var/spool/output/lpd/**
	Solaris: */var/spool/lp/requests/**
Configuration file(s)	**BSD:** */etc/printcap*
	System V: */etc/lp/**
	AIX: */etc/qconfig*
	Solaris: */etc/printers.conf* in addition
First serial port device	**AIX:** */dev/tty0*
	FreeBSD: */dev/ttyd0*
	HP-UX: */dev/ttyp0*
	Linux: */dev/ttyS0*
	Solaris: */dev/term/a*
	Tru64: */dev/tty00*
First parallel port device	**Usual:** */dev/lp0*
	FreeBSD: */dev/lpt0*
	HP-UX: */dev/lp*
	Solaris: */dev/ecpp0*
	Linux: */dev/parport0*, but a module usually maps this to */dev/lp0*
Boot script (starts the spooling daemon)	**AIX:** */etc/inittab* and */etc/rc.tcpip*
	FreeBSD: */etc/rc*
	HP-UX: */sbin/init.d/lp*
	Linux: */etc/init.d/lpd*
	Solaris: */etc/init.d/lp*
	Tru64: */sbin/init.d/lpd*
Boot script configuration	**FreeBSD:** *lpd_enable="YES"* (and others) in */etc/rc.conf* or */etc/rc.conf.local*
	HP-UX: *LP=1* in */etc/rc.config.d/lp*
	SuSE: *START_LPD="yes"* and *DEFAULT_PRINTER* in */etc/rc.config* (SuSE 7)
	DEFAULT_PRINTER in */etcsysconfig/printer* (SuSE 8)
Remote printing support	**Usual:** incoming and outgoing BSD-based
	AIX: BSD, AIX, outgoing System V
	HP-UX: incoming and outgoing BSD and HP-UX

We will conclude this section by considering some useful and often requested user commands related to printing beyond those required to submit and manipulate print jobs. We describe each of the briefly, and Table 13-2 gives their availability by operating system.

a2ps *or* enscript

> Commands to convert text files to PostScript. Many systems provide both of these (as well as other, similar commands).

mpage

> A command to print text or PostScript files with multiple page images appearing on each sheet of paper. The default is to print 4 pages per sheet. The utility can print up to 8 pages per sheet.

lptest *and* pmbpage

> Utilities to generate test output for printers. The first command produces the standard line-printer ripple pattern: a long string consisting of all available characters, which is offset by one character in each successive printed line. The second command produces an image that may be used to determine the boundaries of the printable area on a physical page.

pr

> A utility that can format text files as a series of columns across the page (among other things). In this mode, it can be useful for preprocessing certain kinds of text files prior to printing them. Note that pr in its more general form is also used by various traditional print filtering mechanisms.

ghostview, gv *and similar commands*

> Utilities that allow you to preview PostScript files on screen. They rely upon the Ghostscript PostScript facility.

ghostscript

> A command that allows a PostScript file to be printed to a non-PostScript printer.

Screen capture utilities

> Most versions of the X Windows system provide the xwd command for creating an image file from a window. More sophisticated screen capturing facilities are included as part of the gimp graphics editing package.

Table 13-2. Available user printing-related utilities[a]

Command	AIX	FreeBSD	HP-UX	Linux	Solaris	Tru64
a2ps and/or enscript	✓	✓	✓	✓	✓	✓
mpage	✓	✓	✓	✓	✓	✓
lptest	✓	✓		✓	✓	✓
pmbpage		✓		✓		
pr	a	✓	a	✓	✓	a
ghostview and/or gv	a	✓	a	✓	✓	✓
xwd	✓	✓	✓	✓	✓	
gimp	a	✓ or a	a	✓	✓	a

a A check (✓) means that the item is provided with the operating system or included among its optional components. The letter *a* indicates that the item can be obtained for that operating system, typically by downloading source code from the Internet and then building the program, although sometimes in prebuilt form via one of the public software archives.

The BSD Spooling Facility

The BSD printing subsystem is often referred to by the name of the spooling daemon, lpd. We will so designate it from now on. It can maintain multiple printers, printers at local and remote sites, and multiple print queues. This system can be adapted to support laser printers, raster printers, and other types of devices. As shipped, the spooling system is usually configured to support only a standard line printer.

User Commands

The LPD spooling system provides several commands allowing users to submit and manage their print jobs:

lpr

   Submits a job for printing. When a job is submitted, the lpd daemon assigns it a job ID number, which is used to refer to it in any subsequent commands.

lpq

   Lists jobs that are currently in a print queue.

lprm

   Removes jobs from the print queues. By default, users can remove only their own jobs, but *root* can delete any job.

Each of these commands includes a -P option for specifying the desired printer. If it is omitted, the default printer is used, which is specified by setting the *PRINTER* environment variable to the name of the printer to be used by default. If this variable is not set and -P is not included on a command, the first printer defined in the */etc/ printcap* configuration file (discussed below) is used (although some older LPD subsystem implementations default to the printer named *lp*).

The LPD user commands are also supported for compatibility purposes by AIX and Solaris.

Manipulating Print Jobs

The system administrator is often called upon to manage and manipulate individual print jobs. We will consider the basic techniques for doing so in this section.

Use the lpq command to list the contents of a print queue. For example, the following command lists the jobs in the queue for printer *ps*:

```
$ lpq -P ps
Rank    Owner   Job   Files    Total Size
1st     chavez  15    11726.f  74578 bytes
2nd     harvey  16    fpppp.F  12394 bytes
```

lprm can be used to remove individual print jobs. Its syntax is:

```
# lprm -P printer jobs-to-remove
```

The jobs to be removed may be specified in various ways: as a list of job IDs and/or usernames (in the latter case, all jobs belonging to the specified users will be removed), or with a single hyphen, in which case all jobs will be removed when the command is run by *root*. So, to remove job 15 from the queue *ps*, use the command:

```
# lprm -P ps 15
```

Similarly, to remove all jobs from the *plot* queue, use this command:

```
# lprm -P plot -
```

Finally, you can use the lpc administrative utility (which we'll discuss in more detail very shortly) to reorder jobs within a queue. For example, to move a job within its print queue, use lpc's topq subcommand. This command moves job 12 to the top of the *ps* queue:

```
# lpc topq ps 12
```

The final parameter is the list of jobs to move. It may be specified as a list of job IDs and/or usernames (the latter select all jobs belonging to those users). topq will move the specified jobs to the top of the queue for the specified printer. If more than one job is specified, the jobs take on the order in which they are listed on the command line: at the end, the job listed first will be at the top of the queue.

Managing Queues

The lpc utility is used to perform most administrative tasks connected with the spooling system under BSD, including shutting down a printer for maintenance, displaying a printer's status, and manipulating jobs in print queues (as we've just seen). The command to invoke the line printer control utility is simply lpc:

```
# lpc
lpc>
```

lpc is now running and issues its own prompt. lpc has several internal subcommands:

status *printer*
> Display status of the line printer daemon and the specified print queue.

stop *printer*
> Stops all printing on *printer* after the current job has finished. Users can still use lpr to add new jobs to the queue, but they won't be printed until the printer is started again. This command lets you stop the printer in a clean way, and it is usually used when you need to add supplies or perform routine maintenance.

abort *printer*
> Terminates any printing in progress immediately and disables all printing on the specified printer. It does not remove any jobs from the queue; any jobs currently in the queue will be printed when the printer is restarted. To restart the printer,

use the start command. abort is useful when the spooling system reports that a daemon is present but nothing appears to be happening. abort is an immediate version of stop.

clean *printer*
> Remove all jobs from the printer's queue. The current job will still complete.

start *printer*
> Restarts printing on the printer after an abort or stop command.

disable *printer*
> Prevents users from adding new jobs to the specified queue. The superuser can still add jobs to the queue, and printing will continue. Disabling its queue, waiting for all pending jobs to finish, and then stopping the printer is the most graceful way to turn off a printer.

enable *printer*
> Allows users to spool jobs to the queue again. enable restores normal operation after the disable command.

down *printer*
> Stops printing and disables the queue for printer. Thus, down is equivalent to disable plus stop.

up *printer*
> Enables the queue and starts printing on printer. Thus, up is equivalent to enable plus start.

For all of the lpc subcommands, the keyword *all* can be substituted for the printer name to act on every printer on the system. lpc also provides a help subcommand that can be used to obtain the list of available subcommands or a description of any individual subcommand.

Here are some examples using lpc:

```
# lpc
lpc> status ps
ps:
    queuing is enabled          Info about the ps queue and device.
    printing enabled
    5 entries in spool area
    daemon started              The lpd daemon is running.
lpc> disable ps                 Block new job submissions to ps.
ps:
    queuing disabled
lpc> stop ps                    Stop printing on device ps.
ps:
    printing disabled
lpc> quit
```

Single lpc internal commands can also be executed from the command line by specifying it as lpc's arguments:

```
# lpc up ps
```

The Spooling Daemon

The BSD spooling daemon is usually located at */usr/sbin/lpd*. It is started by a system initialization script at boot time (see Table 13-1), using commands like the following:

```
if [ -f /usr/sbin/lpd ]; then
    rm -f /dev/printer /var/spool/lpd.lock
    /usr/sbin/lpd; echo -n 'lpd' >/dev/console
fi
```

If the server program is readable, the boot script removes the old socket and old lock file (the latter is designed to ensure that only one instance of the daemon is running at any time), and then the script starts the daemon. The new daemon will automatically recreate its lock file and communications interface as part of its initialization tasks.

Occasionally, the spooling daemon gets hung. The main symptom of this is a queue with jobs in it but nothing printing. In this case, you should kill the old daemon and start a new one manually:

```
# ps aux | grep lpd
root   5990  2.2  0.8  1408  352  p0   S   0:00   grep lpd
root    208  0.0  0.2  1536   32   ?   I   0:00   lpd
# kill -9 208
# rm -f /dev/printer /var/spool/lpd.lock
# /usr/lib/lpd
```

Note that you also need to remember to remove the old socket and lock files.

The same actions can be accomplished by invoking the *lpd* boot script (when available). For example:

```
# /etc/init.d/lpd restart
```

Configuring Queues: The printcap File

The file */etc/printcap* lists all output devices supported by the spooling system.* In other words, the entries in the printcap file define the available printers on the system.

Here is a sample printcap entry for a simple line-oriented printer (a rather rare item these days):

```
# line printer--system default printer
lp|lpt1|Machine Room Line Printer:\
    :sd=/var/spool/lpd/lpt1:\        Spool directory
    :lp=/dev/lp0:\                   Printer's physical device
    :lf=/var/adm/lpd-errs:\          Path to printer's error log file
    :pl#66:pw#132:                   Set page length and width
```

---

* Unlike the similarly named and constructed *termcap* file, the *printcap* file is not merely a printer characteristics database. On the contrary, it is a required configuration file.

The first line is a comment (indicated by the number sign). The second line provides names for this entry and its associated queue and printer, separated by vertical bar characters. Specifying several names, as we've done here, is typical: a short name for common use and additional names indicating the printer type and/or location.

Fields within a printcap entry are separated by and surrounded by colons, and entries may extend beyond one line by escaping the newline character with a backslash and including a tab at the beginning of each continuation line. Setting names are typically two characters and are usually followed by an assignment character and the desired value.

We've annotated the remaining lines in the preceding printcap entry. These settings are fairly self-explanatory. The only tricky part is the two settings on the final line. These are numeric settings specifying the page length and width (in lines and characters, respectively) for this printer, and the assignment character is a number sign instead of an equal sign.

Here is a more complex printcap entry for a laser printer:

```
# laser printer
ps|ps3a|hp4000|3rd Floor Laser Printer:\
    :sd=/var/spool/lpd/ps3a:\              Spool directory
    :lp=/dev/lp0:\                         Printer's physical device
    :lf=/var/adm/lperr/ps-errs:\           Error log file
    :pl#66:pw#0:\                          Page length/width
    :mx#500:hl:\                           Max. file size=500 blocks; print burst page last
    :if=/usr/lbin/pcfof +Chp4000tn.pcf:\   Filter specifications
    :vf=/usr/lbin/psrast:\
    :af=/var/adm/lpacct:                   Accounting file
```

The entry begins as before with a comment and a line specifying several names for this printer. The next four lines define the same settings as in our first example, and the following line defines the maximum number of pages that a job may send to this printer (here set to 1000 blocks) and also specifies that the banner/burst page be printed after each job rather than before. This setting, *hl*, is a Boolean setting; specifying its name turns it on, and appending an at sign to the name turns it off: *hl@*.

The next two fields specify filters to be used with this printer: *if* specifies a program that prepares the input for printing, and *vf* specifies a program that processes input consisting of raster images. The many filter settings that can be specified are listed in Table 13-3. Multiple filters are piped together as specified in the *printcap* manual page; see the same source for the calling arguments that are used with filter programs. General filter programs are often provided by the operating system vendor, and manufacturers also can supply ones customized for their printer devices.

The final line in the laser printer entry specifies the accounting file to be used with this printer. This file will eventually be processed by the pac utility, described in Chapter 17. Accounting records are not generated automatically by the LPR subsystem but must be explicitly created by one of the filter programs. Traditionally, this is handled by the *if* filter. We'll look at a sample filter program later in this section.

Table 13-3 lists the most important printcap entry fields.

Table 13-3. Useful printcap entry settings

Field	Default	Meaning
General Settings		
br	none	Baud rate for serial line printers.
mc	none	Maximum number of copies that can be requested (FreeBSD only).
mj	1 million	Maximum number of jobs in queue (not available under FreeBSD and some Linux).
mx	0	Maximum file size (0=no limit).
pc	200	Price per page/foot (units=$0.0001).
pl, pw	66,132	Page length in lines, width in characters (used for accounting).
px, py	0, 0	Page width/length in pixels.
rg	none	Restrict printing to members of this group (not always implemented).
rw	off	Open output device read-write.
Printer Operations		
hl	off	Print burst page after job.
sb	off	Use a one-line banner only.
sc	off	Suppress multiple copy requests.
sf	off	Suppress form feeds.
sh	off	Suppress burst (header) pages.
File/Directory Locations		
*f	none	Filters, where the initial character defines the filter type: *if*=input and accounting, *of*=general output, *cf*=cifplot, *df*=dvi/TEX, *ff*=Fortran (AKA formfeed), *gf*=plot, *nf*=ditroff, *tf*=troff, *vf*=raster image, *xf*=pass-through (for preformatted output).
af	none	Accounting file pathname.
lf	*/dev/console*	Error log file pathname.
lo	*lock*	Lock filename.
lp	*/dev/lp*	Device special file.
sd	*/usr/spool/lp*	Spooling directory.
st	*status*	Status filename.
Remote Printing		
rm	none	Remote host.
rp	lp	Remote queue name.
rs	off	Require remote users to have a local account.

See the manual page for full details on all printcap entry fields.

Spooling directories

As we've noted, a spooling directory holds files destined for a particular printer until the daemon, lpd, can print them. Spooling directories are conventionally located under */var/spool/lpd*. Each printer generally has its own spooling directory.

All spooling directories must be owned by the special user *daemon* and the group *daemon* and have access mode 755 (read and execute access for everyone; read, execute, and write access for user). This protection scheme gives the spooling system sole write access to files that have been spooled, forcing users to use the spooling system and preventing anyone from deleting someone else's pending files or otherwise misbehaving.

To create a new spooling directory called */var/spool/lpd/newps*, execute the following commands:

```
# cd /var/spool/lpd
# mkdir newps
# chown daemon.daemon newps
# chmod 755 newps
# ls -ld newps
drwxr-xr-x  2 daemon    daemon    2048 Apr  8 09:44 newps
```

You will have to create new spooling directories when you add additional printers.

Restricting printer access

The printcap variable *rg* can be used to restrict a print queue to the members of a specified group. For example, *rg=chem* will restrict the printer to members of the *chem* group. Not all implementations of the LPD spooling service support this feature (for example, Tru64 does not).

We'll look at the access restriction scheme for remote printing later in this section.

A filter program

Here is a simple printer filtering program that illustrates the general techniques used in such programs, including accounting record creation (we have removed all of the code testing for invalid input, missing/empty files, and the like to make the basic structure clear):

```
#!/bin/sh
# Filter for PostScript files to an HP DeskJet

# Obtain and process program options.
while getopts a:c:h:m:n:p:q:r option; do
   ...
done
acct_file="$1"          # Real filter tests for not null
```

```
# Set parameter defaults.
MODEL=""
RESOLUTION="600"
QUALITY="normal"

# Let user override defaults if desired.
. $HOME/config.hp      # Real filter checks if file exists

# Create option for model if defined
if [ '' != "$MODEL" ]; then
  MODEL="-sModel=$MODEL"
fi

# Reset printer, prevent stair step and print
printf '\033E\033&k2G\033&s0C'
gs -q -sDEVICE=hpdj $MODEL -r"$RESOLUTION" \
    -sPrintQuality="$QUALITY" \
    -sPagecountFile="./_pages_$randstring" \
    -sOutputFile=- $PSCONFIGFILE -
printf '\033E'          # Printer reset/final page eject

# Write accounting record
pages=`cat ./_pages_$randstring`
printf '%7.2f\t%s:%s\n' "$pages" "$host" "$user" >> "$acct_file"
rm -f ./_pages_$randstring
```

The program first parses its options (not shown) and then stores the name of the printing accounting file given as its final argument. It then sets the default values for some printer specification parameters—printer model, print resolution, and print quality—and then reads in a user-specific configuration file that can change some of these values. Next, the script defines the *MODEL* variable as the option that will be used on the subsequent print command if the user has specified a specific printer model (by default, no model is specified).

The final two sections of the script perform the real work. First, the printer is sent an appropriate reset string (this script is designed for Hewlett-Packard DeskJet series printers) via the printf command. Then the gs command invokes the Ghostscript facility to process the files to be printed (they are assumed to be PostScript files). Finally, the printer is sent a simple reset code to restore its default settings and eject the final page (if necessary).

The last action of the script is creating and writing the accounting record. It relies on the page count provided by the Ghostscript facility via an external file, specified on the gs command line and here (we won't worry about how the *randstring* variable is created). Once the page count is read, the script writes a properly formatted record to the accounting file and removes the scratch file.

Remote Printing

The BSD printing facility can also send files to printers on remote hosts or directly attached to the network, provided that the remote printers also support the LPD spooling protocol. Here is a sample printcap entry for a remote printer:

```
# Remote printer entry
remlp|hamlq|hamlet's letter quality printer|:\
    :lp=:\
    :rm=hamlet:rp=lp2:\
    :lf=/var/adm/lpd_rem_errs:\       Include a log file if you need debugging info.
    :sd=/var/spool/lpd/remlp:
```

This entry specifies the properties of a printer named *remlp*. The empty *lp* field shows that this entry describes a remote printer, and the *rm* field indicates the destination system for remote printing (in this case, the host *hamlet*). The *rp* field holds the name of the target printer on the destination host. Thus, in this example, sending a file to the printer *remlp* will result in its being printed by printer *lp2* on system *hamlet*. Although this entry does not contain any specific details about the remote printer, the printcap entry can include filter, accounting file, and other settings as well. Alternatively, these items can be defined in the remote system's own *printcap* file. Of course, the local printcap entry will need to define all appropriate printer settings for network-attached printers that support LPD.

Accepting incoming remote print jobs also requires minimal additional configuration. In order for a system to allow a remote system to send jobs to it, the remote system's hostname must be listed in the file */etc/hosts.lpd* or */etc/hosts.equiv*. If the first file exists, the hostname must appear in it, or remote printing requests will be refused. If */etc/hosts.lpd* does not exist, the */etc/hosts.equiv* file is checked (see "Network Security" in Chapter 7 for more on the */etc/hosts.equiv* file).

Finally, if a printer's *printcap* entry contains the *rs* characteristic, only remote users with accounts on the local system (defined as an account having the same UID on the local and remote systems) will be allowed to send remote jobs to that printer.

Adding a New Printer

To add a new printer to a system using the BSD spooling facility, you must:

- Physically connect the printer to the computer (if applicable). Follow the manufacturer's instructions regarding cable selection and general procedures.

- For serial line printers, make sure that the line is disabled (in other words, no getty process should be started for it). See Chapter 12 for details.

- If this is the first printer on the system, verify that the lpd server will be started at boot time: make sure the relevant boot scripts are present, the lines relating to lpd are not commented out, and any configuration variables in use are set properly.

- Add an entry for the printer to */etc/printcap*. If you are adding a new printer of the same type as an existing one, you can copy and modify the existing entry, changing the name, special file, spool directory, accounting file, error log file, and any other relevant characteristics as appropriate for the new printer. Printer manufacturers also sometimes provide *printcap* entries for their printers.

- Create a spooling directory for the printer.
- Create the printer's accounting file (defined in the *af* field of their printcap entry) with the touch command; for example:

```
# touch /var/adm/lp_acct/ps3
# chown daemon /var/adm/lp_acct/ps3
# chmod 755 /var/adm/lp_acct/ps3
```

As in this example, printer accounting files are typically stored under */var/adm*, and must be owned by user *daemon*, and *daemon* requires write access to the file.

- Start the printer and its queue:

```
# lpc up ps3
```

- Test the new printer by spooling a small file.

Troubleshooting hints are discussed in the final section of this chapter.

LPD Variations

We close this section by looking briefly at some of the features of the LPD spooling system in the various operating system environments.

FreeBSD

In addition to the commands we've considered so far, FreeBSD also provides the chkprintcap command, which performs some primitive verification of printcap entries. Its most useful form is with its -d option. In this mode, it will ensure that no two printers are sharing a spool directory and will also create any missing spool directories referenced in the printcap file.

FreeBSD's lptcontrol command is also occasionally useful. It can be used to change the state of a parallel port among the following: standard, extended, polled, and interrupt-driven (see the manual page for details). Note that lptcontrol will need to be run at boot time in order to retain the desired setting.

Tru64

Tru64 provides an excellent printer configuration utility named printconfig, illustrated in Figure 13-1.

Its main window is in the upper left in the illustration. Here, you can add a new printer, choosing from a large list of predefined types in the upper scroll box, or you can modify one of the existing printers listed in the lower box. You can also designate any printer to be the system default printer (the tool automatically assigns *lp* as one of its names and reorders printcap entries appropriately).

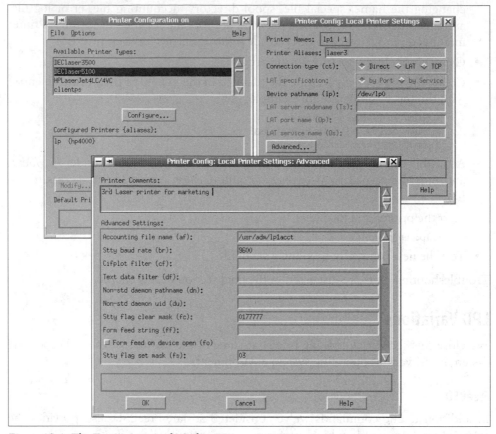

Figure 13-1. The Tru64 printconfig utility

The windows in the upper right and bottom center of the illustration show the process of adding a new printer (here named *laser3*). The most important printcap entry fields are included on the former, while all of the remaining possible settings are accessible via the scrolling list in the latter. The utility fills in default values for many fields based on the printer type you initially selected, including the paths to many filter programs (provided with the operating system).

Tru64 also provides an older text-based, menu driven utility named lprsetup. This brief session will give you a sample of its general flavor:

```
# /usr/sbin/lprsetup

Tru64 UNIX Printer Setup Program
Command  < add modify delete exit view quit help >: view

lp|lp0|0|hp4000:\
        :af=/usr/adm/lpacct:\
        :if=/usr/lbin/pcfof +Chp4000tn.pcf:\
        :lf=/usr/adm/lperr:\
```

```
        :lp=/dev/lp:\
        ...

    Command < add modify delete exit view quit help >: quit
```

Linux

Linux systems also provide GUI interfaces for creating printcap entries. For example, the linuxconf tool can be used to configure printers. Similarly, SuSE's yast2 tool can do the same job; the appropriate module is reached by selecting Hardware → Printer from the main window. The resulting dialogs are illustrated in Figure 13-2.

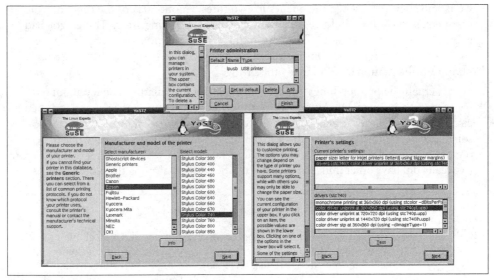

Figure 13-2. SuSE Linux yast2 printer configuration

The main window for this module (at the top in the figure) lists configured printers and also allows you to add a new one. The two other windows in the illustration are from the series of dialogs that follow during the add printer process. The one on the left specifies the specific printer model you are adding, and the one on the right allows you to specify characteristics of that particular printer. In this case, we specify letter-size paper and color printing at a resolution of 360×360 dpi. Later dialogs request other general information required by the printcap entry, and the tool creates the entry automatically once the process completes.

System V Printing

The System V printing system is used on a wide range of Unix systems, from microcomputers with a single printer to high-end mainframes with many printers. Among the operating systems we are considering, the System V printing facility is used by HP-UX and Solaris.

Traditionally, System V printing command options did not allow a space between the option letter and its argument. Although some implementations are more flexible today, we retain the older syntax here.

User Commands

The System V spooling subsystem provides several user commands for submitting and managing print jobs:

lp

Initiate print requests. When a user submits a print job, it is assigned a unique *request ID*, which is used to identify it thereafter, usually consisting of the printer name and a number: "ps-102" for example. The lp user command is also supported for compatibility purposes by FreeBSD.

lpstat

List queue contents and configuration. This command is discussed later in this subsection.

cancel

Cancel a pending request. By default, users can remove only their own jobs, but *root* can delete any job.

All of these commands are supported by AIX as an alternate interface to its own queuing system.

The system default printer

The lp command includes a -d option for specifying the desired destination: printer or printer class (see below). If it is omitted, the destination designated in the *LPDEST* environment variable is used. If this variable is not set and -d is not included on a command, the system default printer is used. This is set by the system administrator using the lpadmin command, as in this example which makes *PS2* the default destination:

```
# lpadmin -dPS2
```

The lpstat command's -d option may be used to list the system default destination:

```
$ lpstat -d
system default destination: PS2
```

Device classes

When initiated by the lp command, print requests are sent to the queue for a *destination*. Destinations may be either a specific printer (or other device) or a *deviceclass*, which provides a mechanism to group similar devices and declares them to be equivalent to and substitutable for one another.[*] For example, all of the laser printers can be grouped into a class *laser*, users may then spool a print request to destination *laser*, and it will be printed on the first available device in that class. All devices within a device class share a single queue.

The lp command places a print request into a queue, either for a specific device or a class containing several devices. Sometime later, the print service daemon, lpsched, actually sends the job to the printing device. We'll discuss how to place specific printers into device classes later in this section.

Getting status information

The lpstat command can provide status information about current printing queues and devices. Table 13-4 lists lpstat's most useful options.

Table 13-4. Options to lpstat

Option	Meaning
-a*list*	Indicate whether the queues for the printers in *list* are accepting jobs or not.
-c*list*	Display the members of the listed classes.
-o*list*	List print requests. In this case, *list* may include request IDs, printer names, and class names. In the latter case, all requests for these printers and classes will be displayed.

[*] In other operating systems, this construct is called a *printer pool*.

Table 13-4. Options to lpstat (continued)

Option	Meaning
-p*list*	Display the current status of the specified printers.
-u*list*	Display the status of all jobs belonging to the specified users.
-v*list*	Display the special file used by the specified printers.
-s	Provide a summary: list all classes and their members and all printers and their associated devices.
-t	Display all status information
-d	Display the system default destination.

All lists are comma-separated; enclose them in quotes if they contain special characters that have meaning to the shell. For all options, if the list is omitted, all entities of the specified type are assumed. For example, the command

```
# lpstat -uchavez,jones
```

lists all jobs belonging to users *chavez* and *jones*, while lpstat -u lists all jobs belonging to all users. Similarly, lpstat -c may be used to list the members of all defined classes.

Without any options, lpstat displays all requests that were submitted by the user executing the lpstat command (it is thus equivalent to lpstat -u$USER).

For example, the following command lists all jobs in the queue for printer *PS*:

```
$ lpstat -oPS
PS-1139    chavez    89427    May 25 07:19 on PS
PS-1140    harvey   302052    May 25 07:21
PS-1141    stein     58357    May 25 07:26
PS-1142    stein      9846    May 25 07:26
```

The following command displays the current status of destinations *PS* and *PS2*:

```
$ lpstat -pPS,LP2
printer PS now printing PS-1139. enabled since May 13 22:12
printer LP2 is idle. enabled since May 13 22:12
```

The following command indicates whether the queue for device class *laser* is accepting new jobs or not:

```
$ lpstat -alaser
laser accepting requests since Jan 23 17:52
```

The following command displays the special file used as an interface for *PS*:

```
$ lpstat -vPS
device for PS: /dev/tty0
```

Manipulating Individual Print Requests

Under System V, the system administrator may cancel any pending job using the cancel command, which takes either the request IDs of the jobs to be cancelled or a list of one or more printers as its argument. In the first case, the specified requests are cancelled, even if they are currently printing; in the second case, whatever request is currently printing on each indicated printer is terminated.

Other useful options to cancel in conjunction with a printer list allow you to remove multiple requests via a single operation: -a removes all requests belonging to the user who executes the command for the listed printer, and -e (for everything) removes every job in the queue. The -i option limits the operation to local print jobs, and the -u option limits the operation to requests belonging to the user specified as its argument. The -u option may be specified multiple times to select more than one user.

For example, the following command cancels all jobs belonging to users *chavez* and *harvey* on printers *PS2* and *PS3*:

```
# cancel PS2 PS3 -uchavez -uharvey
```

Pending print jobs may also be moved between print queues with the lpmove command, which has the following syntax:

```
# lpmove request-IDs new_dest
# lpmove old_dest new_dest
```

The first form moves the specified jobs to the new destination designated as the command's final argument; the second form moves all jobs currently queued for *old_dest* to *new_dest* (useful when a printer has gone down and an alternate is available). Note that if *old_dest* and *new_dest* are printers in the same class, then an lpmove is not necessary: since the same queue feeds both devices, jobs will automatically be routed to the second printer if the first one goes down.

On the other hand, if *old_dest* is currently up and running, the lpmove command has the side effect of disabling that queue as well as moving all jobs within it.

In many implementations (including HP-UX but not Solaris), lpmove can only be used when the printing service is shut down (how to do so is discussed later in this section).

Managing Queues

In the System V printing subsystem, queues are controlled via two pairs of commands: accept and reject, and enable and disable.

The accept and reject commands may be used to permit and inhibit spooling to a print queue; both take a list of destinations as their argument. With its -r option, reject may also specify a reason for denying requests, which will be displayed to users attempting to send jobs to that queue. For example, the following commands close and then reopen the queue associated with the printer *PS*:

```
# reject PS
# accept PS
```

The following command closes the queue for the destination class *laser*:

```
# reject -r"There is no paper in the entire building..." laser
```

accept and reject don't affect whether pending jobs continue to print or not.

The enable and disable commands are used to control the status of a particular printing device. They both take a list of printers as their arguments; in this case, since actual devices are being controlled, destination classes are not valid arguments. disable also has a -r option to allow an administrator to specify a reason that a printer is going down. It also has a -c option, which automatically cancels any jobs that are currently printing on the specified device(s). By default, jobs printing when the disable command is executed will be reprinted on another printer in the same class (if any) or when the device comes back up. For example, the following commands disable and then reenable the device *PS*:

```
# disable -r"Changing toner cartridge; back by 11" PS
# lpstat -pPS
Printer PS disabled since May 24 10:53 -
Changing toner cartridge; back by 11
# enable PS
```

Starting and Stopping the Print Service

Print requests are actually handled by the lpsched daemon, which is started automatically at system boot time. The commands look something like these:

```
if [ "$LP" -eq 1 -a -s /var/spool/lp/pstatus ]; then
    ps -ef | grep lpsched | grep -iv grep > /dev/null 2>&1
    if [ $? = 0 ]; then
        /usr/sbin/lpshut > /dev/null 2>&1
    fi
    rm -f /var/spool/lp/SCHEDLOCK
    /usr/sbin/lpsched && echo line printer scheduler started
fi
```

These commands first verify that the printing subsystem is enabled in the startup configuration files (*LP* is set to 1 for this HP-UX system) and that the subsystem's status file exists and is not empty. Then the process list is examined to determine whether lpsched is already running; if it is, the lpshut command is used to terminate it gracefully. Check to make sure the server startup and shutdown programs are available. Next, lpsched's lock file is deleted (this file ensures that only one instance of lpsched is running at a time), and then the new daemon is started (which will create its own lock file). If lpsched starts successfully, a message is printed to standard output.

The -r option to lpstat may be used to determine if the print scheduling daemon is running:

```
$ lpstat -r
scheduler is running
```

As we've seen, the printing service may be shut down with the lpshut command. This command disables all devices but does not prevent requests from being added

---

to queues. The print service may be restarted by rerunning the appropriate boot script, as in this HP-UX example:

```
# lpshut
# /sbin/init.d/lp start
```

If you kill *lpsched* using any other method, or if it crashes, you may need to remove its lock file manually (*/var/spool/lp/SCHEDLOCK*) if the boot script does not do this for you.

As we've seen, the administrative commands for the System V spooling system generally reside in */usr/sbin*.

Managing Printers and Destination Classes

The `lpadmin` command is used to define and modify the characteristics of printer devices and classes. It should only be used for such purposes when `lpsched` has been stopped with `lpshut`.

The `-p` option is used to specify the printer to be affected by the `lpadmin` command. `-p` may be used on every `lpadmin` command. `lpadmin` also has many other options designed to perform various administrative functions within the spooling system.

Defining or modifying a printer

In its most basic form, the `lpadmin` command defines a printer by specifying its device file and model definition:

```
lpadmin -pprinter -vspecial-file interface-option
```

where *printer* is the name for the printer and *special-file* is the pathname to the special file through which the system communicates with the printer. If the specified printer already exists, its definition is modified; otherwise, a new printer is created.

The interface option has one of the following forms:

-e*printer*
  Copy an existing printer's interface.

-m*model*
  Specify printer by model type by specifying the appropriate filename in */var/spool/lp/model*.[*]

-i*interface-path*
  Specify the full path to a printer interface program.

---

[*] This conventional location is often a link. Under HP-UX 10, it is a link to */etc/lp/model*, and on Solaris systems, it is a link to */usr/lib/lp/model*. Indeed, both operating systems keep most of the spooling subsystem-related configuration data in subdirectories under */etc/lp* (with links to the "standard" locations).

The purpose of these options is to specify which printer interface program is to be used with the new printer. A printer interface is a shell script that performs the various tasks necessary to prepare the printer for printing and then spools the desired files to the device. When a printer is defined, its interface program is copied to the directory */var/spool/lp/interface* into a file having the same name as the printer.

The easiest option to use is -e, which says to use the same interface as an existing printer. For example, the following command defines a new printer *PS4*, attached via */dev/ttd2*; it is the same model as the existing printer *PS3*:

```
$ lpadmin -pPS4 -ePS3 -v/dev/ttd2
```

For a new printer type, you may find an appropriate interface program already on the system since modern operating systems usually provide many of them (stored in */var/spool/lp/model*). Interface programs are also often available from the manufacturer of the printer.

The -m option specifies the filename of an interface program stored in */var/spool/lp/model*. For example, the following command defines a new printer named *Workhorse*, which will use the interface program named *laserjet4* and is attached to the computer via */dev/ttd5*:

```
$ lpadmin -pWorkhorse -v/dev/ttd5 -mlaserjet4
```

This command will create a copy of */var/spool/lp/model/laserjet4* as */var/spool/lp/interface/Workhorse*.

Finally, the -i option may be used to specify the path to the desired interface program explicitly.

Deleting printers

The -x option to lpadmin removes the definition of a printer from the system. For example, this command removes the printer *Slow* from the system:

```
# lpadmin -xSlow
```

Managing device classes

The -c option to lpadmin is used to place a printer into a class. For example, the command:

```
# lpadmin -pPS2 -claser
```

will add the printer *PS2* to the class *laser*, creating the class if it does not already exist.

Similarly, the -r option may be used to remove a printer from a class. For example, the following command removes the printer *PS1* from the class *laser*:

```
# lpadmin -pPS1 -rlaser
```

You can also place the printer into a destination class as you create it:

```
# lpadmin -pPS7 -v/dev/ttd2 -mpostscript -claser
```

Even when a printer has been placed into a class, users can still spool print jobs to its individual queue.

This command creates a printer *PS7*, a PostScript printer accessed via */dev/ttd2*, and adds it to the class *laser*.

When removing a printer from a class or from the system with -**r** or -x, if the specified printer is the only member of its class, that class is also removed as a side effect.

Defining Printer Classes

It is important to ensure that all of the printers within a class are functionally equivalent to one another. If they're not the same make and model, they should at least have identical capabilities and produce identical output for a given print job.

In-queue priorities

Print requests in destination queues are assigned priority numbers that determine the order in which requests get printed (the default is their order of submission). The standard System V scheme is to use priority numbers ranging from 0 to 39, with lower numbers designating higher priorities (meaning printed sooner). Solaris uses this system, but HP-UX uses a different system with priorities running from 0 to 7, with 7 being the highest priority level. The two operating systems also differ in the commands they provide for setting and modifying job priorities.

Priorities under HP-UX. HP-UX provides the -g option to lpadmin to define a default priority level for each printer. For example, this command sets the default priority level for printer *PS0* to 2:

```
# lpadmin -pPS0 -g2
```

The default priority level is 0 (the lowest level). In the case of a printer class, the default priority for jobs placed in the queue is the highest default priority among printers in the class.

Priority levels for pending jobs can be modified with the lpalt command (which can also alter some other job characteristics such as the title and number of copies). For example, this command changes the priority level for the specified job to 7:

```
# lpalt -p7 PS0-21
```

We'll look at other options to lpalt later in this section.

The lpfence command provides the final mechanism for managing printing via priorities. It sets a minimum priority level—called the *fence*—for a job to be allowed to print. This characteristic is specified for an individual print queue (printer or class). For example, the following commands modify the queue *PS1*, setting its default priority to 1 and its fence to 4:

```
# lpadmin -pPS1 -g1
# lpfence PS1 4
```

In this configuration, new jobs without explicit priorities will be assigned priority 1, but only jobs with a priority of 4 or more will be printed. As with lpadmin, lpfence can only be executed when lpsched is not running.

When a user initiates a print request with the lp command, he can specify a priority level using the -p option. At the moment, there is no way to limit the priority level that an individual user can specify, so any priority system you implement can be circumvented by a knowledgeable user.

Priorities under Solaris. Solaris provides the lpusers command to set the system-wide default printing priority level and to specify priority limits on a user-by-user basis.

The -d option is used to set the system default priority: the priority level a request will be assigned when no explicit priority is set on the lp command. For example, the following command sets the system default priority to 15:

```
# lpusers -d15
```

The priority of an individual print request may be specified with the -q option to lp:

```
$ lp -dlaser -q25 long_file
```

This user has lowered the priority of this print request by setting the priority level to 25. Similarly, the following command queues a print request at higher than normal priority (by specifying a lower priority level):

```
$ lp -dlaser -q10 imp_file
```

The system administrator can set limits on how much a user can lower the priority level for his requests. These limits, in combination with the system default printing priority, can effectively set different printing priorities for different classes of users.

The -q option to the lpusers command specifies priority level limits. The -u option specifies one or more users to whom the specified limit applies. If no users are specified, -q sets the default priority limit; this limit is for users who do not have a specific value assigned. If -u is used without -q (i.e., no priority is specified), the limits for the specified users are reset to the system default priority limit. Here are some examples:

```
# lpusers -d15                  System default priority level.
# lpusers -q10                  System default priority limit.
# lpusers -q5 -uchavez,wang     Users chavez and wang' limit is 5.
# lpusers -q0 -uharvey          User harvey's limit is 0.
# lpusers -ustein               User stein's limit is 10.
```

First, the system default priority level and limit are set to 15 and 10, respectively. For this system, unprioritized jobs are given a priority level of 15, and in general, users may increase their priority by specifying a priority level as low as 10. However, the users *chavez* and *wang* may specify a level as low as 5, and user *harvey* may specify one as low as 0, effectively granting him almost immediate access to a printer if desired. Finally, the priority limit for user *stein* is set to the system default of 10.

The system administrator may change the priority of a pending print request using lp -q in conjunction with the -i option, which specifies a request ID. For example, the following command lowers the priority setting to 2 for print job PS-313:

```
# lp -iPS-313 -q2
```

This option may be used to rearrange jobs within a print queue.

The -H option to lp allows a fast method to move a job to the head of a queue. By specifying the immediate keyword as its argument, the specified job advances at once to the top of the queue:

```
# lp -iPS-314 -Himmediate
```

Two successive jobs sent to the top of the queue in this manner will print in reverse chronological order: the job sent most recently will print first.

If you want a job to start printing immediately, without even waiting for the current job to finish, the current job may be suspended with the hold keyword. For example, the following commands start up request PS-314 as soon as possible:

```
# lp -iPS-314 -Himmediate
# lp -iPS-209 -Hhold
```

Many printers, especially PostScript printers, can sometimes retain a printing state across jobs. How killing a job in this way will affect them is indeterminate. It's usually better to let the printing job finish.

If you do suspend a printing job, you can restart it later by specifying the resume keyword to lp -H:

```
# lp -iPS-209 -Hresume
```

Printer interface programs

We conclude this subsection with a brief look at printer interface programs. These programs may range from very simple to quite complex. By convention, an interface script takes the following arguments:

```
program-name request-ID username job-title #copies printer-options file(s)
$0              $1         $2       $3       $4      $5              $6
```

Here is a simple interface program:[*]

```
#!/bin/sh

job=$1; user=$2; title=$3; copies=$4; do_banner=$5
printer=`basename $0`
```

---

[*] Actually, the simplest possible interface program is:

```
#!/bin/sh
cat $6 2>&1
```

It ignores most of its arguments and can print only one file at a time.

```
star="**************************************************"

# Construct the banner page unless suppressed
if [ "$do_banner" != "no" ]; then
    echo "\004\c"
    echo "\n\n\n$star"
    banner $title
    echo "\n\n\nUser: $user"
    echo "Job: $job"
    echo "Printer: $printer"
    echo "Date: `date`"
    echo "\004\c"
fi

# Print the files
shift;shift;shift;shift;shift      Discard all arguments except the file list.
files="$*"
while [ $copies -gt 0 ]; do
    for file in $files
    do
        cat "$file" 2>&1
        echo "\004\c"
    done
    copies=`expr $copies - 1`
done
```

When this program is invoked, standard output from the script will go to the printer. This script first prints a banner page (unless the user didn't want one), using the print job's title and including other data including the username, printer name, and date. It then sends the appropriate number of copies of each file to the printer, placing a form feed after each one.

If there is no interface program for your printer, you can try writing one yourself. The simplest way to do so is to use one of the existing programs as a starting point.

Remote Printing

Remote printing is far less standard under the System V spooling system than for the LPD spooling system. Thus, we will consider each system separately.

HP-UX remote printing

HP-UX supports outgoing printing to other HP-UX systems and to remote LPD-based systems by providing the *rmodel* printer model, which can be specified in a normal lpadmin command to create a print queue. Here is a sample command, which creates a local queue named *hamlas* (-p) for printing on the printer named *laser* (-orp) located on host *hamlet* (-orm):

```
# lpadmin -phamlas -v/dev/null -mrmodel -ob3 -ormhamlet -orplaser
```

The -ob3 option enables support for BSD-style print request numbering. Note also that the printer device is specified as */dev/null* (-v).

HP-UX will also accept incoming print jobs from other HP-UX systems and LPD-based systems. It provides the rlpdaemon server for this purpose, generally controlled by inetd (see "Network Security" in Chapter 7) via a configuration entry like this one:

```
printer stream tcp nowait root /usr/sbin/rlpdaemon rlpdaemon -i
```

The -i option tells rlpdaemon to exit after processing the request that invoked it, and it should only be used when the server is controlled by inetd. Don't forget to tell inetd to reread its configuration file after activating this line. In addition, the corresponding service must be defined in */etc/services*:

```
printer   515/tcp    spooler # remote print spooling
```

If a system will be receiving more than an occasional remote print job, rlpdaemon should be started at boot time instead (you can modify the *lp* boot script to accomplish this), and the */etc/inetd.conf* entry should be commented out. You can also use SAM to set up remote printing.

 HP-UX also provides the HP Distributed Print Service (HPDPS) as part of the Distributed Computing Environment (DCE). We will not consider it here.

Solaris remote printing

The Solaris version of lpadmin includes a -s option, which can be used to define a remote LPD-based printer. Its argument is the remote host and queue in the format: *host*!*queue*. Here is an example:

```
# lpadmin -pColor -shamlet\!dj200
```

This command adds a queue named *Color*, which sends jobs to the queue *dj200* on host *hamlet*. No model or device specification options are required in this case. Note that the exclamation mark must be escaped to protect it from the shell.

If the name of the remote queue is the same as the one you are specifying for the local queue, only the hostname need be given to -s:

```
# lpadmin -pdj200 -shamlet
```

The Solaris version of lpadmin can also send print jobs directly to a remote printer device (i.e., network attached) in raw mode (in which job data is not interpreted) by using the *netstandard* model, as in this example:

```
# lpadmin -php4k -v/dev/null -mnetstandard -o protocol=tcp \
        -o dest=engprt
```

A port number can be added to the remote hostname using a colon as the separator character.

Solaris provides the in.lpd daemon for servicing incoming print requests from LPD-based systems. It is controlled by inetd via the following configuration file entry:

```
printer stream  tcp6  nowait  root  /usr/lib/print/in.lpd  in.lpd
```

You can comment/uncomment this entry to enable/disable this facility. The daemon interfaces to the rest of the Solaris printing system as needed in order to fulfill incoming print requests.

Adding a New Printer

Now that we've looked at all of the pieces, we're ready to add a new printer to the system. To add a new local printer to a System V system, you must:

- Physically connect the printer to the computer.
- For serial line printers, set the run level field for the port's entry in */etc/inittab* to *off*.
- If this is the first printer on the system, make sure that there is a link from the *init.d/lp* boot script to an S-file and a K-file file in the appropriate boot subdirectories.
- Shut down the printing service with lpshut. Then add the new printer to the system with lpadmin.
- Add the printer to a device class, if appropriate.
- Restart the lpsched system. Then, start the printer and its queue; for example:

      # accept PS3; enable PS3
      printer "PS3" now accepting requests
      printer "PS3" now enabled

- Test the new printer by printing a small file. Troubleshooting hints are discussed in the final section of this chapter.

System V Spooling System Variations

As we've noted before, System V spooling system implementations vary quite a bit. In this section, we will look at some additional operating system–specific characteristics on our two operating systems.

Solaris: Additional configuration files

On Solaris systems, the lpadmin command maintains a printer configuration file, */etc/printers.conf*. This is an ordinary text file, but it is better not to edit it manually as it is only a summary of printer configuration. Printer configurations may also be stored in one of the available directory services (e.g., NIS, NIS+, LDAP, and so on).

There is also a user-specific configuration file feature. A user can create a file named *.printers* in her home directory containing her desired default printer, desired options for various printers, aliases for print commands, and the like. See the *printers* manual page for details.

The lpset and lpget commands are also provided for maintaining both of these printer configuration databases.

Solaris: Controlling printer access

Solaris provides the -u option to lpadmin for managing user access to printers and classes. By default, all users are allowed to use any destination. With the -u option, the system administrator can specify who can use each destination by defining an allow list or a deny list.

For any destination, if the allow list exists, only users whose usernames appear in it will be allowed access to it. If there is a deny list, those users appearing on the list will be denied access to the printer. An allow list precludes the existence of a deny list. Allow and deny lists do not affect *root* or the special user *lp*.

Usernames are specified in the form:

> *host*!*username*

where *host* is a hostname and *username* indicates a user on that host. Either part is optional. Either part may also be replaced by the keyword all, which acts as a wild-card for that component. A missing *host* corresponds to the local system. Here are some examples:

!chavez	*User chavez on the local system.*
hamlet!chavez	*User chavez on hamlet.*
chavez	*User chavez on any system.*
hamlet!all	*All users from hamlet.*
!all	*All local users.*

For example, the following command allows only users on *hamlet* and *duncan* to use destination *PS1*:

```
# lpadmin -pPS1 -uallow:duncan\!all,hamlet\!all
```

The following command prevents user *harvey* on the local system and user *wang* on any system from using destination *laser*:

```
# lpadmin -plaser -udeny:\!harvey,wang
```

You can remove a user from an allow list by using a deny list and vice versa. For example, this command removes user *wang* from the list of denied users for *laser*:

```
# lpadmin -plaser -uallow:wang
```

Now suppose we want to remove user *duncan!idaho* from the allow list on *PS1* that we set up earlier. If we execute this command:

```
# lpadmin -pPS1 -udeny:duncan\!idaho
```

the result will be removing the *duncan!all* entry from the allow list (this makes sense if you think about it).

Finally, be aware that consecutive additions to the allow list or deny list are additive: the lists keep getting bigger rather than being replaced. If you need to start over in constructing either list, use the -uallow:all option to clear all current entries.

Solaris: Forms and filters

Solaris extends the lpadmin command in many ways. Here are some of the most useful additional options:

-D*string*
> Create a description of the printer for use in status displays.

-I*type*
> Define the types of jobs the printer can handle.

-f*name*
> Specify allowed forms for a printer or class.

-o*name*=*value*
> Specify additional printer characteristics.

The first option is self-explanatory, and it is extremely useful at sites where there are a lot of printers. The remaining options serve to define the variations that are possible for a single printer (or destination class). For example, the -f option is used to specify forms that are allowed or not allowed on a destination device. *Forms* are alternate print media supported by the same device, for example, different sizes of paper, labels, or printed forms such as invoices or checks. Forms are defined via the lpforms command and are stored in */etc/lp/forms*.

The -I option is used to define the types of files that can be printed at the destination. -I is designed to enable fully automated printing. Ideally, once all destinations are configured with -I, the print service will have the ability to figure out where to print a request based upon the file's characteristics—known as its *content type*—without the user having to specify a destination at all (the user can specify the file's content type with the -T option to lp). Programs known as *filters* are provided to convert different content types; the lpfilter command installs and manages these filter programs (which are stored in */etc/lp/fd*). See the lp, lpfilter, and lpadmin manual pages for details on content types and filters in the Solaris spooling system.

Here is an example illustrating some of these options:

```
# lpadmin -p exp2 -v /dev/term/b -c exper \
        -I "simple,fortran,pcl,postscript" \
        -f "allow:plain,invoice,labels,secret" -o width=14i \
        -D "WhizBang Model 2883/XX2 Printer"
```

This command defines a printer, attached via */dev/term/b*, named *exp2*, and described as a "WhizBang Model 2883/XX2 Printer". It is part of the class *exper*. The printer can handle plain ASCII files, text files with Fortran carriage control information, and PCL and PostScript output. The allowed forms on this device are *invoice*, *plain*, *labels*, and *secret*. The -o option specifies that the printer has a width of 14 inches. Note that we've added a space between options and their argument for readability (since Solaris allows it).

HP-UX: Altering pending print jobs

We introduced the lpalt command earlier in this section in the context of changing the priority of a pending job (via its -p option). The command can also be used to change other aspects of pending jobs. These are its most useful options:

-n*n*

> Change the number of copies to be printed to *n*. This can be useful for preventing printer abuse before it happens.

-t*title*

> Change the job title.

-d*queue*

> Move the job to new queue. A new request ID will be generated. This option has an advantage over lpmove in that the scheduler can remain running in this case.

-o*name=val*

> Change other job option (specified with lp -o).

The following command illustrates some of these options:

```
# lpalt -n1 -p7 -dPS6 laser-23
request id is PS6-78 (1 file)
```

This command moves the specified job to the queue *PS6*, setting the number of copies to 1 and its in-queue priority to 7. The job is assigned a new request ID when it enters the new queue.

HP-UX: Analyzing printer usage

HP-UX also provides a utility for analyzing spooling subsystem usage data: lpana. In order for data to be collected, lpsched must be run with the -a option. You will need to modify */sbin/init.d/lp* if you want this to be the default mode. The lpana command supports a -d option to specify the printer or class in which you are interested (otherwise, all destinations are included).

Here is an example of the report produced by this utility:

```
# lpana
performance analysis is done from Aug.18 '01 10:00 through Aug.18 '01 11:03
---printers    ----wait----   ---print---    ---bytes---    -sum- num_of
    /classes--    AV    SD    AV    SD    AV      SD     KB requests
PS1            2'11   111   0'19    13   9029    4387    150      17
test           0'13     1   0'44    22  41462  154801   2875      71
```

This report provides data for two printers, *PS1* and *test*, for a one-hour period on August 18, 2001. The data about total printer traffic is at the extreme right of the report, in the last two columns. The final column lists the number of jobs handled during the report period, and the penultimate column gives their collective size in kilobytes.

Columns two through four list the average wait time, print time, and size in bytes for each printer, as well as the standard deviation of each figure. Times are given in the format: *minutes'seconds*. From this report, we can see that the printer *test* not only printed far more jobs than *PS1*, and although the jobs were larger on average (almost five times as large), they printed much more quickly (in about 44 seconds, on average). Jobs queued to *test* also waited much less time before printing than did ones to *PS1*.

Graphical administration tools

Both HP-UX and Solaris provide graphical tools for administering the printing subsystem. In both cases, the tools can be used both to manipulate print jobs and queues and to configure printers. We will focus on the latter.

Under HP-UX, the SAM facility's printing area is reached via Printers and Plotters → LP Spooler from the main window. The resulting window is the uppermost one in Figure 13-3.

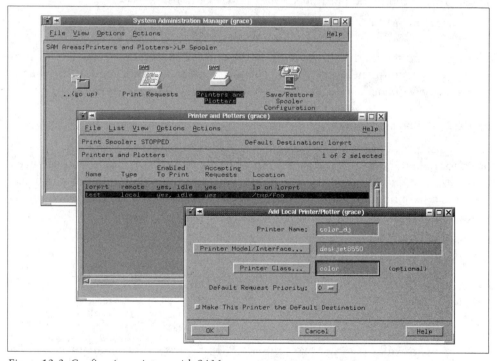

Figure 13-3. Configuring printers with SAM

Selecting Printers and Plotters brings up a list of configured print destinations (shown in the middle window). The bottom window illustrates part of the process of adding a new printer. Here we are adding a printer named *color_dj*. We have selected the model from a pop-up list (by clicking on the Printer Model/Interface button), in this case *deskjet8550*. We are also placing the printer into the class *color*.

On Solaris systems, the Print Manager module of the admintool facility can be similarly used to configure a new print destination. It is illustrated in Figure 13-4.

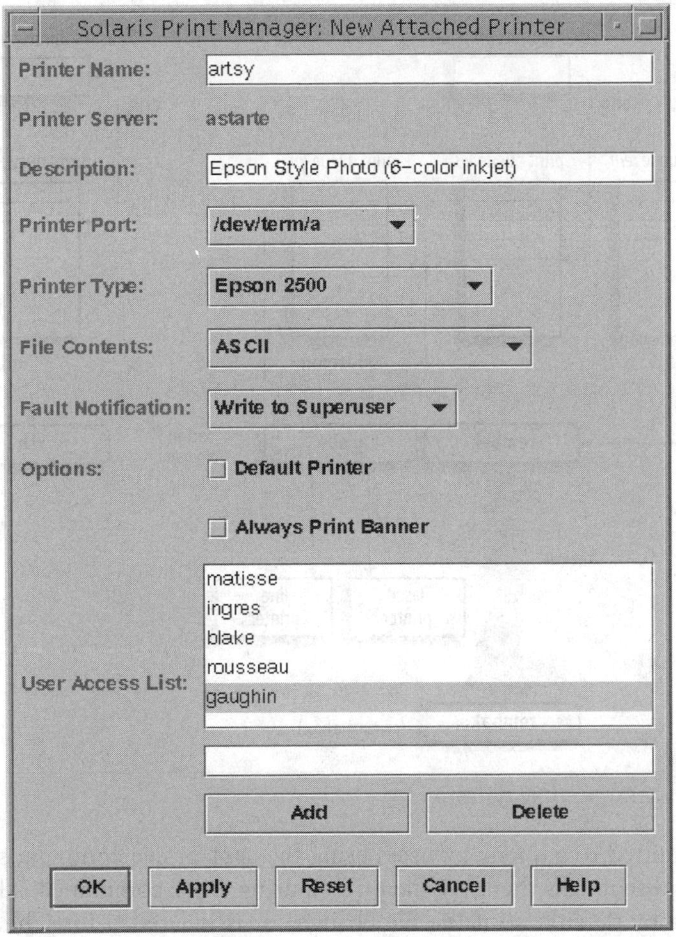

Figure 13-4. Configuring a printer with the Solaris Print Manager

The figure shows the main dialog used to configure a local printer. We have specified a name and description for this printer and selected its special file, model, supported content, and the desired error notification method via pop-up menus. Finally, we have used the unlabeled field and the Add button at the bottom of the form to construct the list of users who are allowed to use this printer. Thus, while this form does not present every option which can be configured via lpadmin, it does make basic configuration tasks quick and straightforward.

The AIX Spooling Facility

AIX offers a third approach to printing and spooling. It is based on AIX's general queueing system; printing is just one predefined way to use it. The queueing system's general operation is illustrated in Figure 13-5.

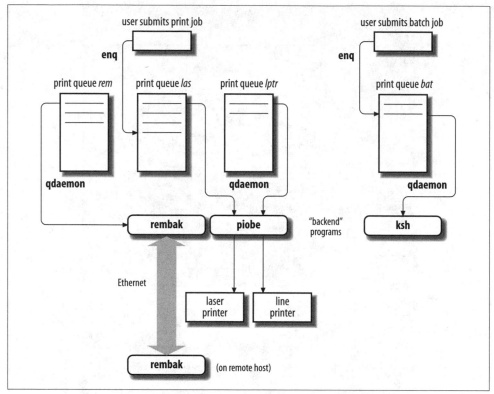

Figure 13-5. The AIX queueing system

Jobs are submitted to a queue by users using the qprt or enq commands (or another user command that calls them). A file printed using these commands is linked to the spooling area by default, so if the file changes or is deleted before the job actually prints, the output will be affected (the -c option may be used to copy the file to the spooling area with either command). Print requests are stored in */var/spool/lpd/qdir*, and any spooled files are stored in */var/spool/qdaemon*.

 AIX also supports the BSD and System V user print commands for ease-of-use purposes: lp, cancel, lpstat, lpr, lpq, and lprm.

The queues are monitored by the qdaemon daemon, which schedules and initiates jobs. When it is time for a job to execute, qdaemon sends the corresponding file to the queue's *backend* program for processing. In the case of printing on the local system, the program is */usr/lib/lpd/piobe*, but in theory, any program may be used as a backend (this is discussed further later in this section). The output of the backend program is then sent to a specified physical device in the case of local printing. It may also be directed to a file.

SMIT provides an excellent interface to the queueing system, and it is usually the easiest way to create and configure queues and their associated devices. In this section, we will look at all of the components of the queuing system individually so that you will understand how the system works, even if you choose to use SMIT to make administering it easier. The SMIT fastpaths mkpq and chpq will take you directly to the forms to create and modify queues and their associated printing devices.

Manipulating Print Jobs

The enq command is the main interface to the printing system. It can be used by users to initiate print requests and by the system administrator to alter the status of print jobs and queues. AIX also provides a series of more intuitively named utilities, which are effectively aliases to subsets of enq's functionality: qprt (print), qcan (cancel a job), qchk (check the status of a job or queue), qmov (move jobs from one queue to another), qadm (administer the subsystem), and others. Their options work the same as the corresponding enq options.

Job numbers

Each print job is assigned a unique job number within the queueing system, by which it may be referred to in subsequent commands. Unfortunately, it is often not displayed by default. However, the print submission commands enq -j, lpr -j, and qprt -#j will all display the job number assigned to a print job at the time it is submitted. lp displays job numbers by default. Alternatively, the job number may be determined via the qchk command (described in a bit).

The default print queue under AIX

On all AIX printing-related commands, the -P option is used to specify the desired queue; if it is omitted, then the system default queue—the first one listed in */etc/qconfig*—will be used. Users can set their own default printer via the *PRINTER* or *LPDEST* environment variables. Note that the latter always takes precedence over the former, even when the BSD-compatible lpr command is used to submit the print job.

Displaying job and queue status information

The qchk command display status information about print jobs and queues. Its -q option may be used to display the status of a specified queue. For example, the following command lists the status of the queue *laser3*:

```
$ qchk -q -P laser3
Queue   Dev     Status    Job  Files   User      PP  %   Blks Cp Rnk
-------  -----   --------  ---  ------  --------  --- --  ----- -- ---
laser3  dlas3   RUNNING   30   1213.f  chavez    10  43   324  1   1
                QUEUED    31   hpppp   harvey              41  1   2
                QUEUED    32   fpppp   harvey              83  1   3
                QUEUED    33   x27j.c  king               239  1   4
```

The columns in the report hold the queue name and device (which are not repeated on subsequent lines), the job status, job number, file to be printed, submitting user, pages printed so far, percentage of the job printed so far, job size in blocks, number of copies requested, and rank within the queue for each job in the queue.

When a queue is down, the first line of the display will look like this:

```
laser3 dlas3   DOWN
```

Other useful options to qchk for listing queue contents are -A (replaces -q to list all queues), -L (for a long listing format), and -u followed by a list of users to limit the display to jobs submitted by those users. For systems with large numbers of print jobs, where three-digit job numbers are not sufficient, add -W to the qchk command to display the full job numbers.

Deleting print jobs

To delete a job in a print queue, use the qcan command:

```
# qcan -x job-number
```

where *job-number* is the number of the job to be removed; since job numbers are unique across the entire queueing system, the queue name isn't needed. All jobs in a queue may be deleted with the -X option:

```
# qcan -P laser -X
```

When run as the administrator, this command removes all jobs from queue *laser*. If the specified queue is used for remote printing (described later in this section), the command will affect only jobs that haven't yet been transferred to the remote system.

Moving jobs between queues

Pending print jobs may be moved between print queues using the qmov utility. Here are some examples using qmov:

```
# qmov -m laser -# 8
# qmov -m laser -P inkjet
# qmov -m laser -P inkjet -u chavez
```

The first qmov command moves job 8 from its present queue to the *laser* queue. The second command moves all jobs currently in the *inkjet* queue to the *laser* queue. The third command moves all of user *chavez*'s jobs in the queue *inkjet* to the queue *laser*. qmov will not move a currently printing job, and you'll get an error if there are no jobs matching your specifications in the source queue.

Suspending print jobs

The qhld command holds and releases jobs in print queues. For example, this command places print job 8 on hold:

```
# qhld -# 8
```

This command places all jobs currently waiting in the queue *laser* on hold:

```
# qhld -P laser
```

qhld's -r option releases a previously held job:

```
# qhld -r -# 8
# qhld -r -P laser
```

The qprt -#h and enq -H commands may be used to submit a job to a queue in an initial held status.

Print job priorities

Jobs are assigned priorities within the queue. Together with the queue discipline parameter (described below), these priorities determine the order of printing. Priorities range from 0 to 20 for ordinary users (the default is 15); users in the group *system* may use priorities up to 30. Any user may alter the values for his own jobs; the system level (21-30) is the only way for an administrator to guarantee that a job she moves up will stay above the others. Higher-numbered jobs print sooner.

Users can assign a priority to a job when they submit it with qprt's -R option. To change the priority of a pending job, use the enq -R command:

```
# enq -# job-number -R new-priority
```

For example, the following command changes the priority of job number 45 to 22:

```
# enq -# 45 -R 22
```

Managing Queues and Devices

AIX makes a distinction between queues and devices and requires them to be configured and managed as separate objects. Each queue has one or more associated *devices*, which are the entities that map one-to-one with physical printers. Similarly, a printing device can have more than one queue feeding it.

The following qadm options control individual device status:

-D *dev*
: Designate a device as down; no more jobs will be sent to it, but current jobs will finish.

-U *dev*
: Bring a device back up.

-K *dev*
: Same as -D, but current jobs are killed.

If a queue has only one device associated with it, the queue name alone will suffice to designate the device. If more than one device is controlled by the queue, you must specify which one you want by appending its name to the queue name, using a colon as separator. For example, the following command brings the *lp0* device of the queue *laser* down:

```
# qadm -D laser:lp0
```

Jobs can still be sent to the queue even when its device(s) are down. An entire queue may be disabled by changing its *up* attribute in */etc/qconfig* to *FALSE*, a task that can be accomplished with the chque command. For example, the following command disables the queue *laser*:

```
# chque -q laser -a "up = FALSE"
```

The spaces around the equal sign, the quotation marks, and the uppercase letters on the keyword are all required.

When a queue has been disabled, its devices are automatically taken down; they will need to be brought back up (with qadm -U) when the queue is reenabled.

 Current AIX documentation still states that the queueing system should be shut down before changes like disabling a queue are performed, using these commands:

```
# chgsys -s qdaemon -O     Turn off autorestarting
# enq -G                   Stop the queueing subsystem
```

However, these commands no longer seem to be effective under AIX 5, and the qdaemon process is immediately restarted anyway. Nevertheless, it is only prudent to wait to make major configuration changes to a print queue until current jobs have completed, pending jobs have been deleted or moved, and the associated device(s) have been disabled with qadm -D.

The qdaemon Server Process

The qdaemon server is managed by the System Resource Controller. It is started from the *inittab* file via an entry like this one:

```
qdaemon:23456789:wait:/usr/bin/startsrc -sqdaemon
```

You can check its status with the following command:

```
# lssrc -s qdaemon
Subsystem        Group          PID       Status
qdaemon          spooler        311412    active
```

Configuring Queues: The /etc/qconfig File

Queues are defined in the */etc/qconfig* file. Each queue has one or more associated *devices*, which are the entities that map one-to-one with physical printers. The linked pair of a queue and a device is sometimes referred to as a *virtual printer*. We'll begin by looking at the structure of the queue configuration file and then go on to consider the commands that are typically used to manipulate it.

 The queue configuration file is an ordinary text file, but it should be edited directly only with great caution and by administrators who are intimately familiar with the entire qdaemon subsystem. Very minor setting changes are usually safe to make, but adding new queues and devices should be done with the commands provided or with SMIT, as they create or modify entries in the ODM which are not easy to perform manually.

In general, a print queue definition has the following form:

```
queue-name:
    device = qdev1[,qdev2 ...]
    attribute = value
    ...
qdev1:
    backend = /usr/lpd/piobe
    attribute = value
    ...
[qdev2:
    backend = /usr/lib/lpd/piobe
    attribute = value
    ...]
```

Here are two sample print queue entries from */etc/qconfig*:

```
lpt:                          A queue named lpt
    device = lp0
lp0:                          Its associated device
    file = /dev/lp0
    header = never
    trailer = never
    access = both
    backend = /usr/lib/lpd/piobe

laser:                        A queue named laser
    device = lp0,lp1          Queue laser's two devices
    acctfile = /var/adm/qacct
lp0:
    file = /dev/lp0           The first device, listed again
    header = always
    trailer = never
    access = both
    backend = /usr/lib/lpd/piobe
lp1:                          The second device
    file = /dev/lp1
    header = never
    trailer = never
    access = both
    backend = /usr/lib/lpd/piobe
```

Each full definition has several parts. The first is the queue definition, beginning with a header line consisting of the queue name followed by a colon. In the example, *lpt* and *laser* are the two queue header lines. Next, indented with respect to the header, are queue attribute definitions. The queue *lpt* has only one attribute defined: its device, *lp0*. *laser*'s stanza specifies two devices, *lp0* and *lp1*, and defines a file in which to place accounting data.

The definitions for a queue's device(s) must immediately follow the queue definition. Hence, *lp0* is defined after *lpt*, and *lp0* and *lp1* are defined after *laser*. Although both queues use device *lp0*, its definition must still be repeated in each queue definition. In fact, as in our example, the settings for the device may differ, and each set will apply only to jobs printed on that device from the corresponding queue.

When a queue has multiple associated queue devices, it is used to feed jobs to all the devices, which are assumed to be equivalent. When it is time for a job to be spooled, qdaemon will send it to the first available device for its queue. When more than one queue services the same device, as in the preceding example, then the spooler alternates among them, regardless of the relative sizes, priorities and age of the jobs within them (such characteristics are compared only among jobs in the same queue to determine printing order, not across queues).

The most important queue and device attributes are listed in Table 13-5.

Table 13-5. Important AIX queue and device attributes

Attribute	Meaning
Queue attributes	
acctfile	Accounting file pathname (the default is not to use any accounting file).
device	List of associated device names.
discipline	Job selection algorithm: *fcfs* for first come, first served or *sjn* for shortest job next (the default is *fcfs*).
up	Set to *TRUE* or *FALSE*, depending on whether the queue is enabled or disabled.
Device attributes	
access	Available access to printer device: one of *write* (meaning only write access) or *both* (read-write access). The latter is the default.
align	Whether to send a form feed before starting a job if the printer is idle (default = *TRUE*).
backend	Path to the backend program.
file	Special file associated with the device as defined in the ODM (which is not the same as the raw port's special file).
header	When a header page should be placed before a job. Valid keywords are: *never* (the default setting), *always*, and *group* (print header only once for multifile print jobs).
trailer	When a trailer page should be sent (same keywords and default value as for header).

The easiest way to view the attributes of a queue or queue device is to view the queue configuration file.

If you'd like all of the gory details about a printer, use the following command:

```
# lsvirprt -q queue -d device | more
```

Creating and modifying print queues

SMIT provides the easiest method for creating and modifying print queues. Its use is illustrated in Figure 13-6.

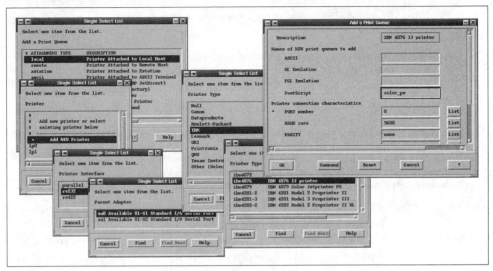

Figure 13-6. Creating a print queue with SMIT

If you follow the stack of dialogs from the bottommost (at the top left) to topmost (top right), you will see the successive prompts generated by SMIT to obtain the information necessary to create a new printer device and queue(s) to feed it. Here we add a new local printer, attached via a serial port (specifically, port 0 attached to the sa0 adapter). The printer is an IBM 4076 inkjet printer, and we create a queue for PostScript jobs named *color_ps*. Optionally, we could have created several different queues for this printer, each designed to handle a different type of print job. The final dialog also allows you to configure various serial line settings.

AIX provides several commands that may be used to create and configure printer devices and queues in a similar manner. For example, the following command may be used to create a queue and device similar to what we just accomplished with SMIT (in this case, we add a generic type printer):

```
# /usr/lib/lpd/pio/etc/piomkpq \
    -A local \                    A local printer
    -p generic \                  Generic printer type
    -v osp \                      ODM data type (list with lsdev -P -c printer)
    -s rs232 -r sa0 -w 0 \        Uses the specified serial adapter and port
    -D asc -q text1 \             A queue for ASCII data
    -D ps -q ps1                  Another queue for PostScript data
```

Printer type definitions are stored in */usr/lib/lpd/pio/predef*. The entire collection might not be included in the operating system installation and often must be installed manually later.

Here is the command for adding a similar printer attached to a parallel port:

```
# /usr/lib/lpd/pio/etc/piomkpq -A local -p generic -v osp \
    -s parallel -r ppa0 -w 0     Parallel port information
    -D asc -q text2
```

The following command adds an additional, previously defined device to an existing queue:

```
# /usr/lib/lpd/pio/etc/piomkpq -A local -p generic \
    -d lp2 -D asc -Q text0     Both the device and the queue already exist.
```

The device options are replaced by -d, and the queue is specified with -Q rather than -q.

The chque and chquedev commands may be used to change the attributes of queues and devices, respectively, as in these examples:

```
# chque -q laser -a "discipline = sjn"
# chquedev -q laser -d lp0 -a "header = never"
```

The first command changes the *discipline* attribute for queue *laser* to *sjn* (shortest job next). The spaces around the equal sign are required. The second command changes the *header* attribute for the *laser* queue's device *lp0* to the value *never*. Be aware that this change will affect the printer on that device only when it is accessed from queue *laser*.

The rmquedev and rmque commands may be used to remove devices and queues (respectively):

```
# rmquedev -q tek -d lp2
# rmque -q tek
```

These commands remove the device for the queue *tek* and then the queue itself (queues can be deleted with rmque only after all their devices are gone). However, the device *lp2* is still defined in the ODM. If you should ever need to remove it, you can verify its existence and then remove it with these commands:

```
# lsdev -C -l lp2
lp2 Available 01-S3-00-00 Other serial printer
# rmdev -l lp2 -d
```

These commands should be used with caution and only when no queue is referencing device *lp2*.

 If you use SMIT to remove a queue and its device(s), the ODM objects are removed as well.

Remote Printing

The following queue form in *etc/qconfig* is used to define a queue for a printer on another host:

```
rem0:
device = @laertes
host = laertes
up = TRUE
s_statfilter = /usr/lib/lpd/aixshort
l_statfilter = /usr/lib/lpd/aixlong
rq = laser
@laertes:
backend = /usr/lib/lpd/rembak
```

The *rem0* queue will send remote print jobs to the queue *laser* on the system *laertes*. The backend program for remote printing is */usr/lib/lpd/rembak*. If the remote system is a BSD system, the filters */usr/lib/lpd/bsdshort* and */usr/lib/lpd/bsdlong* should be substituted for the AIX filters in the queue definition, and the filters */usr/lpd/att{short,long}* are used for System V systems supporting remote printing (i.e., serving as print servers).

For incoming LPD-based print jobs, AIX runs the BSD lpd daemon and uses the normal */etc/hosts.lpd* (or */etc/hosts.equiv*) file to allow remote BSD systems to send print jobs to its queues, as described previously in the BSD section of this chapter. However, you may need to start the lpd daemon manually:

```
# startsrc -s lpd
```

Incoming jobs also require the writesrv service to be running. It is usually started from */etc/inittab*, but you can verify that it is running with lssrc.

Adding a New Printer

To add a printer to the queueing system, these steps must be taken:

- Physically connect the device to the system.
- Make a device and queue for that printer. I find it's easiest to use SMIT for this step. Enter the command smit mkpq to perform this process. Choose the correct printer type from the list; then specify the controller and line to which the printer is attached.
- Test the printer. Printer troubleshooting tips are discussed later in this chapter.

Using the Queueing System as a Batch Service

The printing system represents but one use of the AIX queueing system. Since potentially any program may be used as a queue backend program, many other uses are possible, such as a simple batch system. Here is a sample configuration:

```
batch:
    device = batdev
```

```
          discipline = fcfs
batdev:
backend = /bin/csh
```

With a shell specified as the backend program, users may submit shell scripts to the queue. The qdaemon will manage this queue, sending one script at a time to be processed by the shell. Shell scripts could be used to run any desired program. For example, the following script could be used to run a program bigmodel:

```
#!/bin/csh
ln -s ~chavez/output/bm.scr fort.8
ln -s ~chavez/output/bm.out fort.6
bigmodel <<END &> ~chavez/output/bm.log
140000
C6H6N6
Na
Hg
END
```

This file illustrates several important features about running programs from shell scripts (in this case, a Fortran program):

- The symbolic links set up at the beginning of the file are used to associate Fortran unit number and files. By default, I/O to unit *n* uses a file named *fort.n*. Symbolic links allow a user to specify any desired paths.

- The form <<END is used to place standard input for a command or program within the shell script. All subsequent lines prior to one containing just the string specified after the << are interpreted as input to the command or program.

- The queueing system has no provision for saving job output, so the script must handle this itself.

Once set up, the enq command may be used as an interface to such a batch queue, allowing users to submit jobs to the queue and the administrator to delete them, alter their priority, and manage the status of the batch queue in the same manner as for print queues.

Troubleshooting Printers

This section contains strategies and suggestions for approaching various printing problems.

The first step is to narrow down the problem as precisely as possible. Which printers are affected? Are all users affected or just the one with the problem? Once you've determined where the problem is, you can set about dealing with it.

If you've installed a printer but nothing prints on it, check the following items:

- Make sure you're using the right kind of cable. Check the printer's documentation for the manufacturer's recommendations.

- Make sure the connections are good and that you've specified the right port in the configuration file or commands. If you're using a serial line, make sure the line has been deactivated in */etc/ttytab*, */etc/ttys*, or */etc/inittab*. Signal init to reread its configuration file. Kill the getty process watching that line, if necessary.
- Verify that its queue is set up correctly. Send a file to it and then make sure something appears in the spool directory (use the -c option on the printing command under System V and AIX). If it doesn't, the protection on the spooling directories or files may be wrong. In particular, *root* may own something it shouldn't.

  On System V systems, the spool directories located under */var/spool/lp/request* are usually owned by the user *lp* and are protected 755 (write access only for the owner) or sometimes 770. The files in the spool directories are owned by group and user *lp* and are protected 440.

  Under BSD, the spool directories are traditionally owned by user *daemon* or *lp* and group *lp* and also protected 755 (or more stringently).

  Under AIX, pending requests are stored in */var/spool/lpd/qdir*, owned by user *root* and group *printq* and protected 660, and spooled files are stored in */var/spool/qdaemon*, owned by user *bin* and group *printq*, and protected 660.

- Removing and recreating the queue will sometimes fix things. This works when the queue configuration looks okay but is actually messed up by an invisible control character or another junk character somewhere. It also works when you remember something you forgot the first time when you recreate the queue.
- When all else fails, check the log files. Error messages can appear in several places: the general syslog error log, the syslog *lpr* facility error log, and the queue's own log file (when supported). Of course, if any of these are not defined, error messages sent there will be lost.

If a printer suddenly stops working and its configuration hasn't changed, try the following:

- Is the daemon still running? If not, restart it. If it is, it may still be worth stopping and restarting it if no other jobs are printing:

  ```
  # kill -9 pid-of-lpd-process      BSD
  # /usr/lib/lpd

  # lpshut                          System V
  # /etc/init.d/lp start

  # enq -G                          AIX
  ```

- Has someone spooled a huge job? A very large bitmap may take over half an hour to print on some slow PostScript printers. PostScript printers can also take a very long time to print any complex graphics. If the Processing light is flashing, things are probably still OK; when a job finally overwhelms the printer, the printer usually prints an error page rather than just getting hung. Of course, your patience and that of other waiting users may run out well before then.

- Aborting the current job may clear up the problem (the colloquial term for such a job is *wedged*).
- Power-cycling the device will clear most device hang-ups, although you will often lose the job that was printing at the time.

For problems with remote printing, try the following:

- Determine whether the printer is working locally.
- You can test remote job connectivity by creating a queue to a file and seeing if it is spooled properly. In this way, you can determine if the problem is network communications generally or something specifically related to the device. For example, network delays can cause a queue or printer to time out.
- If the preceding test fails, try connecting to the remote server's port 515 with telnet. You should get a connection. You may then get an error message about an improper "from address." The latter is from the lpd process and is not significant.

  Network printers also generally support telnet for configuration purposes. Try connecting to the printer with telnet (no port number needed). You can then verify that the printer is accessible and also check its various settings for misconfiguration.

- Check the log file for further information. Note that you may need to check the various log file locations on both the remote and local host, because the relevant information can appear in any one of them depending on the particular problem.

Sharing Printers with Windows Systems

In this section, we'll consider printing to and from Windows systems.

Printing to a Windows Printer from a Unix System

Like most System V–based Unix operating systems, Windows NT and Windows 2000 systems provide an LPD service to handle incoming remote print jobs from non-Windows systems. The queues on the client Unix systems can be set up as normal for outgoing printing to a remote LPD server (as discussed earlier in this chapter). On the Windows server, you will need to do the following:

- Install the LPD printing support software, if necessary. This is part of the Windows TCP/IP implementation, but it is not selected by default at initial operating system installation. Under Windows NT 4, you can do this via the Services tab of the Network Properties dialog.

Under Windows 2000, start the Add/Remove Programs control panel applet, click Add/Remove Windows Components, and then select Other Network File and Print Services. Click the Details button, and then choose Print Services for Unix.

- Start the LPD service. Under Windows NT 4, execute the `net start lpdsvc` command to start the incoming print job server. You may want to add this command to the *AutoExNT.Bat* file if you have installed that facility.

Under Windows 2000, navigate to the Services and Applications → Services object in the Computer Management application. Then select the TCP/IP Print Server entry and change the start up method to Automatic (as illustrated in Figure 13-7).

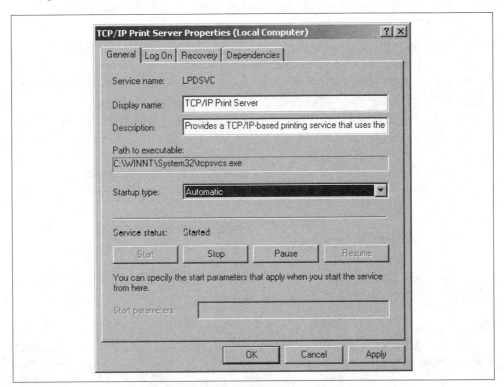

Figure 13-7. Modifying the Windows 2000 LPD service

Accepting Incoming Windows Print Jobs via Samba

The Samba facility can be used to make Unix printers visible to Windows clients as normal shared printers (for Samba basics, see "Sharing Filesystems" in Chapter 10).

Sharing a printer can be accomplished in two ways: by creating a share entry for a specific printer or by sharing all of the printers within a printcap file. Here is a Samba configuration file entry corresponding to the first approach. It creates a share named *laser4*:

```
[laser4]
    printable = yes             Entry is a printer.
    comment = LW on dalton      Browse description.
    public = yes
    postscript = yes            Jobs will send PostScript files.
    printer name = laz4         Local printer queue name.
    printer driver = Windows-name   Official Windows designation
```

The final field specifies the driver to be used on the Windows system when printing to this printer. It must be set to the string that appears in the Add Printer Wizard's printer selection dialog's Printers list, in other words, the descriptive name by which Microsoft refers to it (e.g., "Apple LaserWriter II NTX-J v50.5"). This field does not hold the path to the driver file.

If you want to store the printer driver files locally (rather than requiring them to be on the Windows system), you can use the *printer driver location* setting as well and set up a local share to hold them. This technique is discussed in detail in the *Network Printing* book cited earlier.

Here are some sample entries that illustrate the second approach to sharing printers with Samba:

```
[global]                              Add these to the global section.
    load printers = yes               Share all printers in the printcap file.
    printcap name = /usr/local/samba/lib/printcap
    printing = bsd|sysv|aix|hpux|lprng   Specify local print spooler type.

[printers]                            One entry for all printers.
    comment = Exported printers
    path = /var/spool/smb-print
    printable = yes
    guest ok = yes
    guest account = samba
    auto services = david monet       Browseable printers.
```

This approach requires specifying several settings with the *global* section of the Samba configuration file. In this example, they direct the Samba system to create shares for all of the printers listed in the designated printcap file and also specify the spooling system in use on the local system.

The *printers* entry completes the process of sharing printers. Our example specifies a path used for scratch space and a list of printers to appear in browse lists.

Two observations are worth making at this point:

- You must define printers for export within a printcap-style file even if the local spooling system is not LPD-based.

- Be aware that the *auto services* entry merely adds printer names to the browse list. Any printer defined in the specified printcap file will be available to users that know its name. Use a separate printcap file (as above) to make only a subset of the system's printers available via Samba.

Creating queues for the Samba printers under Windows

On the Windows system, you must create a queue for such remote printers, using the Add Printer wizard as usual. Specify the printer type as local (not remote), and then create an LPR port for it (if one doesn't already exist); select New Port, provide a port name, and then choose the LPR port type (illustrated in Figure 13-8). Then enter the name of the remote system and printer into the resulting dialog, and go on to complete the remainder of the Add Printer process as normal.

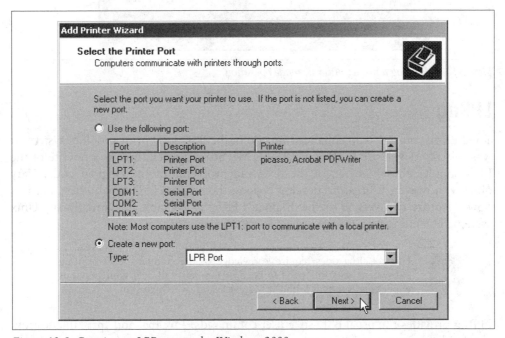

Figure 13-8. Creating an LPR port under Windows 2000

On Windows NT 4 systems, there can be occasional problems where PostScript or PCL files are printed as text rather than having their instructions interpreted by the printers as a program to be run. This happens because the job has somehow been marked as text data rather than as raw data.

You can configure the printer to treat all jobs as raw data by accessing its Properties and then choosing the Advanced tab and then the Print Processor button. In the resulting dialog, choose the RAW setting (illustrated in Figure 13-9).

You can make this setting apply to the print spooler as a whole by setting the HKEY_LOCAL_MACHINE\System\CurrentControlSet\Services\LPDSVC\Parameters\SimulatePassThrough registry key to 1.

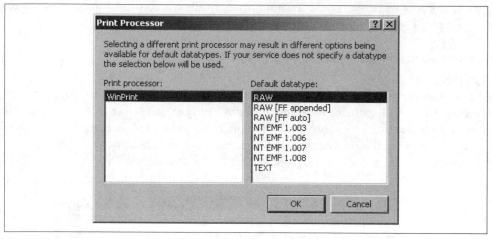

Figure 13-9. Forcing a printer into raw mode operation

LPRng

The LPRng package is an enhanced version of the BSD LPD print spooling system. It was initially developed in the early 1990s by Patrick Powell, first as a rewrite of the LPD spooler that was free of the licensing problems of the original code. Very quickly, however, it began to develop beyond the original LPD capabilities, and it is now a feature-rich version of the original. LPRng is available for virtually any Unix system. The home page for the project is *http://www.lprng.com*.

 Using LPRng does require knowledge of the standard BSD printing subsystem, so you'll need to become familiar with it if your previous experience is mostly with the System V and/or AIX version.

LPRng provides the usual BSD-style user commands: lpr, lpq, and lprm. In addition, it provides versions of lp, lpstat, and cancel for compatibility. It uses the conventional top-level spool directory, */var/spool/lpd*.

The LPRng version of lpr is quite a bit smarter than the standard version. It is capable of submitting print jobs directly to a remote system, so there is no longer any need to run the lpd daemon on hosts that are not also print servers themselves (eliminating its modest system load).

Here is an lpr example, which spools a print job directly to the *matisse* queue on system *painters*:

```
$ lpr -Pmatisse@painters files
```

Another nice feature of LPRng is that lpd may optionally be run as the *daemon* user rather than *root*.

Installing LPRng is straightforward and well documented in both the *LPRng-HOWTO* document and in the *Network Printing* book mentioned earlier, so I'll simply outline the steps here:

- Disable all queues, wait for any current jobs to finish, and stop the current print daemon.
- Back up all current print subsystem components: configuration files, command binaries, and so on.
- Rename or remove the old printing items.
- Install the LPRng package (building the software from source code in most cases). If you want to run a less privileged lpd server, uncomment the *--disable-setuid* setting in the *configure.custom* script and run that rather than the usual *configure* script.
- Modify system startup scripts to support LPRng.
- Configure printers and queues within the new printing subsystem.
- Verify the new configuration with the package's checkpc -f command, which verifies printcap file entries, creates any needed spool directories, log files, accounting files, and the like.
- Start the spool daemon, and test everything thoroughly.
- Give users access to the print queues.

The LPRng package provides scripts for some operating systems, which can accomplish some of these tasks. They have names of the form *preremove.*.sh* (to shut down the printing subsystem before removing it), *preinstall.*.sh* (remove old printing system components), *postremove.*.sh* (performs actions needed after the old printing system is removed), and *postinstall.*.sh* (runs after the LPRng software is built and installed; sets up initial configuration files, spooling directories and the like). The middle component of each script name is the operating system name: e.g., *solaris*, *linux*, etc. Check the LPRng package directory and the documentation for the scripts applicable to your systems.

Enhancements to the lpc Command

The LPRng version of lpc provides many new subcommands. The most important are summarized in Table 13-6.

Table 13-6. LPRng enhancements to the lpc command

Subcommand	Purpose
hold *queue* [*ids*]	Places the specified job or all jobs in the queue into a hold state, preventing them from printing.
release *queue* [*ids*]	Allow the specified held print job(s) to print.
holdall *queue*	Place all new jobs entering the queue into the held state. Use noholdall to terminate this behavior (held jobs will still need to be explicitly released).

Table 13-6. LPRng enhancements to the lpc command (continued)

Subcommand	Purpose
move `old-queue ids new-queue`	Transfer the specified print jobs between queues.
redirect `old-queue new-queue`	Redirect jobs spooled to the old queue to the new queue. Specify `off` for the latter to turn off redirection.
redo `queue [id]`	Reprint the specified job.
kill `queue`	Equivalent to `abort` plus `start`: kill the current job, and then restart the queue.
active `printer[@host]`	Determine whether the specified spool daemon is active or not.
reread `printer[@host]`	Forces the specified spool daemon to reread its configuration files.
class `queue class-list`	Limit printing from the specified queue to jobs in the specified class(es), where *class* is usually a comma-separated list of one or more class letters (see below). The keyword `off` removes any current class restrictions in effect.[a]

a This parameter may also be used for pattern matching against print job characteristics (see the `lpc` manual page for details).

In most cases, you can substitute the keyword `all` for a queue name in these `lpc` sub-commands to apply the command to all print queues.

Print classes and job priorities

LPRng implements a very simple print job priority scheme. It is combined with its support for print job classes: print jobs have a shared set of characteristics that require specific special handling and/or printer capabilities. The most common use for classes is for jobs requiring special paper.

A user can place a job into a specific class when submitting it using the `-C` option:

```
$ lpr -Ccheck -Plaser2 January
```

This job is placed into the class *check* on printer *laser2*.

The uppercased first letter of the class name is also used as the in-queue priority for the job. Priorities levels run from A (high) to Z. Thus, the preceding job would be assigned a priority level of C. The default value for jobs not specifying a specific class is class and priority level A.

By default, a print queue allows jobs of any class to print, printing them in accord with the priority scheme. To limit printing to a specific class, use an `lpc` command like this one:

```
# lpc class laser check
```

This will allow only jobs in class *check* to print; all others will be held. To allow any job to print, use this command:

```
# lpc class laser off
```

Using classes can be a bit tricky. For example, if you alternate between printing checks and regular output on a printer, you probably don't want to turn off class *check* after all the checks are printed. Rather, you want check jobs to be held until the proper paper is again in place in the printer. In this case, the following command will be more effective:

```
# lpc class laser A
```

This sets the allowed class to class *A* (the default), so jobs spooled in class *check* will be held as desired.

Configuring LPRng

LPRng uses three configuration files (stored in */etc*): *printcap*, *lpd.conf*, and *lpd.perms*, which hold queue configuration, global spooler configuration and printer access rules, respectively. The first of these is a modified version of the standard LPD print-cap file. It uses a relaxed syntax: all fields use an equal sign to assign values rather than having datatype-specific assignment characters (although the form *name@* is still used to turn off Boolean flags), multiple line entries do not require final back-slash characters, and no terminal colon is needed to designate field boundaries.

Here are two simple entries from *printcap*:

```
hp:                                     Example local printer.
  :lp=/dev/lp0
  :cm=HP Laser Jet printer              Description for lpq command.
  :lf=/var/log/lpd.log
  :af=/var/adm/pacct
  :filter=/usr/local/lib/filters/ifhp
  :tc=.common                           Include the .common section.

laser:                                  Example remote printer.
  :lp=painters@matisse
  :tc=.common                           Include the .common section.

.common:                                Named group of items.
  :sd=/var/spool/lpd/%P
  :mx=0
```

The first entry is for a local printer named *hp* on the first parallel port. This printcap entry specifies a description for the printer, the name of its log and accounting files, and a filter with which to process jobs. The final field, *tc*, provides an "include" feature within printcap entries. It takes a list of names as its argument. In this case, the field says to include the settings in the printcap entry called *.common* within the current entry. Thus, it has the effect of removing any length limits on print jobs to printer *hp* and of specifying its spool directory as */var/spool/lpd/hp*.

The second printcap entry creates a queue for a remote printer, *matisse* on host *painters*, which also has no job length limits and uses the spool directory */var/spool/lpd/laser*. The last two items are again set using the *tc* include field.

The LPRng printcap file allows for variable expansion within printcap entries. We saw an example of this in the *sd* field in the preceding example. The following variables are supported:

%P   Printer name

%Q   Queue name

%h   Simple hostname

%H   Fully-qualified hostname

%R   Remote print queue name

%M   Remote computer hostname

%D   Current date

We will now go on to consider additional LPRng features and the printcap settings that support them.

Separate client and server entries

By default, printcap entries apply both to spooling system clients—user programs like lpr—and servers—the lpd daemon. However, you can specify that an entry apply only to one of these contexts, as in these example entries:

```
laser:server            Entry applies to the lpd daemon.
  :lp=/dev/lp0

laser:                  Entry applies to client programs.
  :lp=matisse@painters
```

The first entry defines the printer *laser* as the device on the first parallel port. The *server* field indicates that the entry is active only when lpd is using the printcap file (and not when it is accessed by programs like lpr). The second entry defines the printer *laser* for client programs as a remote printer (*matisse* on *painters*). Clients will be able to send jobs directly to this remote printer.

In this next example, clients are required to use the local print daemon in order to print to the printer *laser2*:

```
laser2:force_localhost   Force clients to use the local server.
laser2:server
  :lp=/dev/lp0
  :sd=/var/spool/lpd/%P
```

The *force_localhost* setting (a Boolean, which is off by default) tells clients accessing this printcap entry to funnel jobs through the local lpd server process.

Using a common printcap file for many hosts

One of LPRng's most powerful capabilities is the built-in features for constructing a single central printcap file which can be copied to or shared among many hosts. This flexibility comes from the *on* setting (for "on host"). Here is an example:

```
laser:
  :oh=*.ahania.com,!astarte.ahania.com
  :lp=/dev/lp0
```

This entry defines a printer named *laser* on every host in the domain *ahania.com* except *astarte*. The printer will always be located on the first parallel port.

The following entry will define a printer named *color* on every host in the 10.0.0 subnet. For most hosts, the printer points to the *color* queue on 10.0.0.4, while for 10.0. 0.4 itself, it points to the device on the first parallel port.

```
color:
  :oh=10.0.0.0/24,!10.0.0.4      Host specification by IP address.
  :lp=%P@10.0.0.4
  :tc=.common

color:
  :oh=10.0.0.4
  :lp=/dev/lp0
  ...
```

The *%P* construct in the first entry's *lp* setting is not really necessary here, but it would be useful if this setting occurred in a named group of settings, as in this example:

```
color:tc=.common
laser:tc=.common
draft:tc=.common


.common:
  :oh=*.ahania.com,!astarte.ahania.com
  :lp=%P@astarte.ahania.com
```

These entries define the printers *color*, *laser*, and *draft* on every host in *ahania.com* except *astarte* as the corresponding queue on *astarte* (which are defined elsewhere in the printcap file).

Special-purpose queues

In this section, we examine how to set up queues for several more complex printing scenarios.

Bounce queues. Here is a printcap entry for a simple store-and-forward queue (as we've seen before):

```
laser:server
  :lp=matisse@painters
  :sd=/var/spool/lpd/%P
```

The queue *laser* collects jobs and sends them on to the queue *matisse* on host *painters* as is. However, it is sometimes useful to process the jobs locally before sending them on to be printed. This is accomplished via a *bounce* queue, as in this example:

```
blots:server
  :sd=/var/spool/lpd/%P
```

```
:filter=path and arguments
:bq_format=l                          Binary jobs will be sent on.
:bq=picasso@painters
```

This queue named *blots* accepts jobs, runs them through program specified in the *filter* setting, and then sends them to queue *picasso* on host *painters* for printing.

Printer pools. LPRng allows you create a printer pool: a queue that feeds several printing devices, as in this example:

```
scribes:server
:sd=/var/spool/lpd/%P
:sv=lp1,lp2,lp3
```

Here, the queue *scribes* sends jobs to queues *lp1*, *lp2*, and *lp3* (which must be defined elsewhere in the printcap file), as each queue becomes free (which, of course, occurs when the associated device is free). This mechanism provides a very simple form of load balancing.

Here is part of the printcap entry for *lp1*:

```
lp1:
:sd=/var/spool/lpd/%P
:ss=scribes
```

The *ss* setting specifies the controlling queue for this printer. Note that it does not prevent jobs from being sent directly to queue *lp1*; the only effect of this setting seems to be to make queue status listings more readable.

Print job destinations can also be determined on a dynamic basis. Here is an example:

```
smart:
:sd=/var/spool/lpd/%P
:destinations=matisse@printers,degas@france,laser
:router=/usr/local/sbin/pick_printer
```

The program specified in the *router* setting is responsible for determining the destination for each submitted print job. The router program is a standard print filter program. Its exit status determines what happens to the job (0 means print, 37 means hold, and any other value says to delete the job), and it must write the queue destination and other information to standard output (where lpd obtains it). See the *LPRng-HOWTO* document for full details on dynamic print job routing.

Filters

As we've noted before, print jobs are processed by filter programs before they are sent to the printer device. Filters are responsible for initializing the device to a known initial state, transforming the output into a form that it understood by the printer, and ensuring that all output has been sent to the printer at the end of the job. The first and third tasks are typically accomplished by adding internal printer commands to the beginning and end of the print job. Filter programs are also responsible for creating printer accounting records.

As the examples we've looked at have shown, LPRng provides the *filter* printcap setting for specifying a default filter for all jobs in a particular queue. In addition, it supports many of the various output type–specific filter variables used in traditional printcap entries (i.e., the **f* settings).

The LPRng package often uses the ifhp filter program also written by Patrick Powell. It is suitable for use with a wide variety of current printers. The characteristics of the various supported printers are stored in its configuration file, *ifhp.conf* (usually stored in */etc*). The following printcap entry illustrates settings related to its use:

```
lp:
  :sd=/var/spool/lpd/%P
  :filter=/usr/local/libexec/filters/ifhp
  :ifhp=model=default
```

The *filter* setting specifies the path to ifhp, and the *ifhp* setting specifies the appropriate printer definition with its configuration file. In this case, we are using the default settings, which work well with a wide variety of printers.

Sample Accounting Script

The LPRng facility includes an excellent Perl script that demonstrates the method for getting page count information from modern printers. It is called *accounting.pl* and is included with the source distribution.

Other printcap entry options

It is also possible to store printcap entries in forms other than a flat text file. For example, they could be stored in an LDAP directory. LPRng allows for such possibilities by allowing printcap entries to be fetched or created dynamically as needed. This is accomplished by setting the *printcap_path* in the *lpd.conf* configuration file as a pipe to a program rather than a path to a printcap file:

```
printcap_path=|program
```

Such an entry causes LPRng to execute the specified program whenever it needs a printcap entry (the desired entry is passed to the program as its standard input). For example, such a program could retrieve printcap information from an LDAP directory. See Chapter 11 of *Network Printing* for details and extended examples.

Global Print Spooler Settings

The *lpd.conf* configuration file holds a variety of settings relating to the print spooler service. Among the most important are ones related to printer connection and timeouts and to print job logging. Some of the most commonly used are listed in the example configuration file below:

```
# communication-related settings
connect_grace=3                    Wait period between jobs (default=0).
network_connect_grace=3
connect_timeout=600                Cancel job after this interval (default=0).
```

```
send_try=2                              Maximum number of retries (default is no limit).
max_servers_active=10                   Max. # lpd child processes (default is half the
                                             system process limit).

# logging settings
max_log_file_size=256                   Maximum file sizes in KB (default is no limit).
max_status_size=256
min_log_file_size=128                   Keep this much data when the files are too big
min_status_size=64                           (default is 25%).
max_status_line=80                      Truncate entries to this length (default=no limit).

# central logging server
logger_destination=scribe               Destination for log file entries.
logger_pathname=/tmp/lprng.tmp          Local temporary file to use.
logger_max_size=1024                    Max. size of the temporary file (default=no limit).
logger_timeout=600                      Wait time between connections to the remote
                                             server (default is whenever data is generated).
```

Printer Access Control

The third LPRng configuration file, *lpd.perms*, is used to control access to the print service and its printers. Each entry in the file provides a set of characteristics against which potential print jobs are matched and also indicates whether such jobs should be accepted. The first entry that applies to a specific print job will be used to determine its access. Accordingly, the order of entries within the file is important.

The syntax of the *lpd.perms* file is explained best by examining some examples. For example, these entries allow users to remove their own print jobs and *root* to remove any print job:

```
ACCEPT SERVICE=M SAMEUSER
ACCEPT SERVICE=M SERVER REMOTEUSER=root
REJECT SERVICE=M
```

The first keyword in an entry is always *ACCEPT* or *REJECT*, indicating whether matching requests are to be performed. These entries all apply to the M service, which corresponds to removing jobs with lprm. The various entries allow the command to succeed if the user executing and the user owning the print jobs are the same (*SAMEUSER*), or if the user executing it is *root* (*REMOTEUSER=root*) on the local system (*SERVER*). All other lprm requests are rejected.

Available *SERVICE* codes include C (control jobs with lpc), R (spool jobs with lpr), M (remove jobs with lprm), Q (get status info with lpq), X (make connection to lpd), and P (general printing). More than one code letter can be specified to *SERVICE*.

There are several keywords that are compared against the characteristics of the print job and the command execution context:

USER, GROUP, HOST, PRINTER
> These items are compared to the ownership and other characteristics of the print job to which the desired command will be applied. In addition, the *SERVER* keyword requires that the command be executed on the local server.

REMOTEUSER, REMOTEGROUP, REMOTEHOST

These items are compared to the user, group, and host where or with whom the desired command originated. Note that the "remote" part of the name can be misleading, because it need not refer to a remote user or host at all.

The preceding keywords all take a string or list of strings as their arguments. These items are interpreted as patterns to be compared to the print job or command characteristics.

SAMEUSER, SAMEHOST

These keywords require that *USER* be the same as *REMOTEUSER* and *HOST* be the same as *REMOTEHOST*, respectively. For example, the following entry limits use of the lprm command to users' own jobs and requires that the command be run on the same host from which the print job was submitted:

```
ACCEPT SERVICE=M SAMEUSER SAMEHOST
```

We'll now examine some additional *lpd.perms* entries. The following entry rejects all connections to the lpd server that originate outside the *ahania.com* domain or from the hosts *dalton* and *hamlet*:

```
REJECT SERVICE=X NOT REMOTEHOST=*.ahania.com
REJECT SERVICE=X REMOTEHOST=dalton,hamlet
```

Note that these entries could not be formulated as *ACCEPTs*. Hosts may be specified by hostname or by IP address.

The following entries allow only members of the group *padmin* to use the lpc command on the local host:

```
ACCEPT SERVICE=C SERVER REMOTEGROUP=padmin
REJECT SERVICE=C
```

The *LPC* keyword can be used to limit the lpc subcommands that can be executed. For example, the following entry allows members of group *printop* to hold and release individual print jobs and move them around within a queue:

```
ACCEPT SERVICE=C SERVER REMOTEGROUP=printop LPC=topq,hold,release
```

The following entries prevent anyone from printing to the printer *test* except user *chavez*:

```
ACCEPT SERVICE=R,M,C REMOTEUSER=chavez PRINTER=test
REJECT SERVICE=* PRINTER=test
```

User *chavez* can also remove jobs from the queue and use lpc to control it.

The following command prevents print job forwarding on the local server:

```
REJECT SERVICE=R,C,M FORWARD
```

The *DEFAULT* keyword is used to specify a default action for all requests not matching any other configuration file entry:

```
# All everything that is not explicitly forbidden.
DEFAULT ACCEPT
```

The default access permissions in the absence of an *lpd.perms* file is to accept all requests.

Other LPRng capabilities

LPRng has quite a few additional capabilities which space constraints prevent us from considering, including the ability for more sophisticated user authentication using a variety of mechanisms, including PGP and Kerberos. Consult the LPRng documentation for full details.

CUPS

The Common Unix Printing System (CUPS) is another project aimed at improving, and ultimately superceding, the traditional printing subsystems. CUPS is distinguished by the fact that it was designed to address printing within a networking environment from the beginning, rather than being focused on printing within a single system. Accordingly, it has features designed to support both local and remote printing, as well as printers directly attached to the network. We will take a brief look at CUPS in this section. The homepage for the project is *http://www.cups.org*.

CUPS is implemented via the Internet Printing Protocol (IPP). This protocol is supported by most current printer manufacturers and operating systems. IPP is implemented as a layer on top of HTTP, and it includes support for security-related features such as access control, user authentication, and encryption. Given this structure, CUPS requires a web server on printer server systems.

Architecturally, CUPS separates the print job handling and device spooling functions into distinct modules. Print jobs are given a identifier number and also have a number of associated attributes: their destination, priority, media type, number of copies, and so on. As with other spooling subsystems, filters may be specified for print queues and/or devices in order to process print jobs. The CUPS system provides many of them. Finally, backend programs are responsible for sending print jobs to the actual printing devices.

CUPS also supports printer classes: groups of equivalent printers fed by a single queue (we've previously also referred to such entities as printer pools). CUPS extends this construct by introducing what it calls "implicit classes." Whenever distinct printers and/or queues on different servers are given the same name, the CUPS system treats the collection as a class, controlling the relevant entities as such. In other words, multiple servers can send jobs to the same group of equivalent printers. In this way, implicit classes may be used to prevent any individual printing device or server system from becoming a single point of failure. Classes may be nested: a class can been a member of another class.

Printer Administration

CUPS supports the lpr, lpq, and lprm commands and the lp, lpstat, and cancel commands from the BSD and System V printing systems, respectively. For queue and printer administration, it offers two options: command-line utilities, including a version of the System V lpadmin command, or a web-based interface. The latter is accessed by pointing a browser at port 631: for example, *http://localhost:631* for the local system.

The following commands are available for managing and configuring print queues. Note that all of them except lpinfo specify the desired printer as the argument to the -p option:

lpstat
> View queue status.

accept *and* reject
> Allow/prevent jobs from being sent to the associated printing device.

enable *and* disable
> Allow/prevent new print jobs from being submitted to the specified queue.

lpinfo
> Display information about available printers (-v) or drivers (-m).

lpadmin
> Configure print queues.

Here is an example lpadmin command, which adds a new printer:

```
# lpadmin -plj4 -D"Finance LaserJet" -L"Room 2143-A" \
        -vsocket://192.168.9.23 -mlaserjet.ppd
```

This command add a printer named *lj4* located on the network using the indicated IP address. The printer driver to be used is *laserjet.ppd* (several are provided with the CUPS software). The -D and -L options provide descriptions of the printer and its location, respectively.

In general, the -v option specifies the printing device as well as the method used to communicate with it. Its argument consists of two colon-separated parts: a connection-type keyword (which selects the appropriate backend module), followed by a location address. Here are some syntax forms:

parallel:/dev/*device*	*Local parallel port*
serial:/dev/*device*	*Local serial port*
usb:/dev/usb/*device*	*Local USB port*
ipp://*address*/*port*	*IPP-based network printer*
lpd://*address*/*DEVICE*	*LPD-based network printer*
socket://*address*[:*port*]	*Network printer using another protocol (e.g., JetDirect)*

The CUPS version of lpadmin has several other useful options: -d to specify a system default printer (as under System V), -c and -r to add/remove a printer from a class, and -x to remove the print queue itself.

Under CUPS, printers need only be configured on the server(s) where the associated queues are located. All clients on the local subnet will be able to see them once CUPS is installed and running on each system.

CUPS configuration files

CUPS maintains several configuration files, stored in the */etc/cups* directory. Most of them are maintained by lpadmin or the web-based administrative interface. The one exception, which you may need to modify manually, is the server's main configuration file, *cupsd.conf*.

Here are some sample annotated entries (all non-system-specific values are the defaults):

`ServerName painters.ahania.com`	*Server name.*
`ServerAdmin root@ahania.com`	*CUPS administrator's email address.*
`ErrorLog /var/log/cups/error_log`	*Log file locations.*
`AccessLog /var/log/cups/access_log`	
`PageLog /var/log/cups/page_log`	*Printer accounting data.*
`LogLevel info`	*Log detail (other levels: debug, warn, error).*
`MaxLogSize 1048571`	*Rotate log files when current is bigger than this.*
`PreserveJobFiles No`	*Don't keep files after print job completes.*
`RequestRoot /var/spool/cups`	*Spool directory.*
`User lp`	*Server user and group owners.*
`Group sys`	
`TempDir /var/spool/cups/tmp`	*CUPS temporary directory.*
`MaxClients 100`	*Maximum client connections to this server.*
`Timeout 300`	*Printing timeout period in seconds.*
`Browsing On`	*Let clients browse for printers.*
`ImplicitClasses On`	*Implicit classes are enabled.*

 Readers familiar with the Apache facility will notice many similarities to its main configuration file (*httpd.conf*).

Access control and authentication

Printer access control, user authentication, and encryption are also enabled and configured in the *cupsd.conf* configuration file.[*]

Encryption is controlled by the *Encryption* entry:

```
Encryption IfRequested
```

The entry indicates whether or not to encrypt print requests (in order to use encryption, the OpenSSL library must be linked into the CUPS facility). The default is to encrypt files if the server requests it; other values are *Always* and *Never*. Additional keywords may be added as other encryption methods become available.

---

[*] These features are somewhat in flux as of this writing, so there may be additional capabilities in your version of CUPS. Consult the CUPS documentation for details on the current state of things.

There are two main entries related to user authentication:

AuthType

> Source of authentication data, one of: *None*, *Basic* (use data in the Unix password and group file, transmitted Base64-encoded), and *Digest* (use the file *passwd.md5* in */etc/cupsd* for authentication data). The last method offers a medium level of security against network sniffing. The CUPS system provides the lppasswd command for maintaining the *passwd.md5* file.

AuthClass

> Method of authentication. The default is *Anonymous* (perform no authentication). Other options are *User* (valid username and password are required), *System* (user must also belong to the system group, which can be defined using the *SystemGroup* entry), and *Group* (user must also belong to the group specified in the *AuthGroupName* entry).

The encryption- and user authentication–related entries are used to specify requirements for specific printers or printer classes. These are defined via stanzas like the following in the configuration file:

```
<Location /item>
[Encryption entry]              The ordering here is not significant.
[Authentication entries]
[Access control entries]
</Location>
```

The pseudo-HTML directives delimit the stanza, and the item specified in the opening tag indicates the entities to which the stanza applies.* It can take one of the following forms:

```
/                    Defaults for the CUPS system.
/printers            Applies to all non-specified printers.
/printers/name       Applies to a specific printer.
/classes             Applies to all non-specified classes.
/classes/name        Applies to the specified class.
/admin               Applies to CUPS administrative functions.
```

Here a some example stanzas (which also introduce the access control directives):

```
<Location />              System defaults.
Order Deny,Allow          Interpret Allow list as overrides to Deny list.
Deny From All             Deny all access…
Allow From 127.0.0.1      …except from the local host.
</Location>

<Location /printers>
Order Allow,Deny          Interpret Deny list as exceptions to Allow list.
Allow From .ahania.com    Allow access from these domains…
Allow From .essadm.com
```

---

* Again, note the similarity to the Apache configuration file syntax.

```
Deny From 192.168.9.0/24          ...but exclude this subnet.
</Location>

<Location /classes/checks>        Applies to class named checks.
Encryption Always                 Always encrypt.
AuthType Digest                   Require valid user account and password.
AuthClass Group                   Restrict to members of the finance group.
AuthGroupName finance
Order Deny,Allow
Deny From All                     Deny all access...
Allow From 10.100.67.0/24         ...except from this subnet.
</Location>

<Location /admin>                 Access for administrative functions.
AuthType Digest                   Require valid user account and password.
AuthClass System                  Limit to system group members.
Order Deny,Allow
Deny From All                     Restrict access to the local domain.
Allow From .ahania.com
</Location>
```

Consult the CUPS documentation for information about the facility's other features as well as its installation procedure.

Font Management Under X

On most current Unix systems, fonts are made available to applications via the X Window system (although some application packages manage their own font information). In this section, we will consider the main administrative tasks related to managing fonts.

 In an ideal world, fonts would be something that users took care of themselves. However, in this world, font handling under X is cumbersome enough that the system administrator often needs to get involved.

In this section, we consider font management using the standard X11R6 tools, and we refer to directory locations as defined by the normal installation of the package. These facilities and locations are often significantly altered (and broken) in some vendors' implementations.

Font Basics

When you think of a font, you probably think of something like Times or Helvetica. These names actually referred to font *families* containing a number of different typefaces: for example, regular Times, italic Times, bold Times, bold italic Times, and so on. At the moment, there are quite a few different formats for font files. The most important distinction among them is between bitmap fonts and outline fonts. Bitmap fonts store the information about the characters in a font as bitmap images, while outline fonts define the characters in a font as a series of lines and curves, comprising in this way mathematical representations of the component characters.

From a practical point of view, the main difference between these two font types is scalability. Outline fonts can be scaled up or down any arbitrary amount and look equally good at all sizes. In contrast, bitmap fonts do not scale well, and they look extremely jagged and primitive as they get larger. For this reason, outline fonts are generally preferred to bitmap fonts.

To further complicate matters, there are two competing formats for outline fonts: Adobe Type 1 and TrueType. In technical terms, the chief difference between them consists of the kind of curves used to represent the characters: Bezier curves and b-splines, respectively. The other major difference between the two formats is price, with Type 1 fonts generally being significantly more expensive than TrueType fonts.

All of these different types of fonts are generally present under X. The most important formats are listed in Table 13-7, along with their corresponding file extensions.

Table 13-7. Common font file formats

Format	Bitmap/outline	Extension(s)
Portable Compiled Font	bitmap	*.PCF.gz*
Speedo	bitmap	*.spd*
Ghostscript font	outline	*.gsf*
Type 1	outline	*.pfa, .pfb, .afm*
TrueType	outline	*.ttf*

The PCF fonts are bitmap fonts (generally stored in compressed format) that come as part of the XFree86 system, typically located in directories under */usr/X11R6/lib/X11/ fonts* or */usr/lib/X11/fonts*. The Speedo fonts were donated to the X Window system by Bitstream and are located in the same place. The Ghostscript fonts are Type 1 fonts installed with that facility (using a slight variation in format). In addition, there may be Type 1 and/or TrueType fonts present on the system.

Type 1 fonts consist of multiple files. The *.pfa* and *.pfb* files contain the actual font outline representation, in ASCII and binary format, respectively, and the *.afm* file contains font metrics information in ASCII format. Type 1 fonts on Unix systems generally use the binary *.pfb* files (probably because they are smaller in size), but *.pfa* files may also be used. The corresponding *.afm* file is also required in order to print.

The X window system uses a somewhat arcane naming convention for referring to fonts. Here is its general syntax and an example for a font in the Octavian family:

```
-foundry-family-weight-slant-stretch-style-pixel-points-xres-yres-spacing-avgwidth-registry-encoding
-monotype-octavian mt-medium-i-normal--0-0-0-0-p-0-iso8859-1
```

The components have the following meanings. The *foundry*[*] is the organization (often a commercial entity) that provided/sold the font, Monotype in our example. The *family* indicates the overall grouping of typefaces to which this particular item belongs (for example, Times or Helvetica); our example is from the Octavian MT family (note that spaces commonly appear within the family name). The next few items indicate which member of the family this one is: *weight* is a keyword indicating the relative darkness of this typefaces with respect to other family members (medium, bold, light, black and so on), *slant* is a single character indicating whether this typeface is upright (r for roman, i for italic or o for oblique), *stretch* is a keyword indicating whether the typeface is expanded or compressed with respect to normal lettering (normal, condensed, expanded and so on), and *style* is a keyword indicating any additional typographic style information relevant to this typeface (e.g., expert, ornaments, oldstylefigures, etc.). Our example typeface is Octavian Italic (not bold, not condensed/expanded, and no additional style designation).

The remaining fields specify the default point size (*points*), the body size in pixels at that point size (*pixels*), the typeface's default horizontal and vertical resolution (*xres* and *yres*), its spacing class (*spacing*: one of m for monospace/fixed width, c for character cell and p for proportional), a measure of the average width of the glyphs in the font (*avgwidth*), and the character set use for coding the font (*registry* and *encoding*). Most of the numeric fields tend to be set to zero for outline fonts, indicating the font's default value should be used—as they are in our example—and the three remaining fields are generally set to the values shown in the example as well.

In most instances, you'll never need to construct one of these names by hand. Instead, you can use utilities which create them for you automatically for various contexts. However, if you ever do need to generate one yourself, you can find all the essential information by running the strings command on the (binary) font file and looking at the information displayed at the beginning of its output (if you have an ASCII font file, you can look at that file's contents directly).

For more general information about fonts, consult the FAQ from the *comp.fonts* newsgroup (version 2.1.5, dated August 1996, is the most recent, available at *www. nwalsh.com/comp.fonts/FAQ*). For additional information about TrueType fonts, consult the TrueType HowTo (available on the web at *pobox.com/~brion/linux/ TrueType-HOWTO.html*).

Managing Fonts under X

We now turn to the question of how X applications locate fonts they need. As we noted previously, the fonts that come with the X window system conventionally reside under */usr/X11R6/lib/X11/fonts*. In fact, though, when an application needs a

---

[*] As one of the technical reviewers noted, this term comes "from the days of moveable set type where a iron working foundry was responsible for manufacturing the type sets."

font to display on the screen, it checks the current font path to find it. Traditionally, the default font path is defined in the *XF86Config* configuration file (generally located in */etc* or */etc/X11*, with several links to other places) via *FontPath* lines in the Files section:

```
Section "Files"
    RgbPath       "/usr/X11R6/lib/X11/rgb"
    FontPath      "/usr/X11R6/lib/X11/fonts/misc"
    FontPath      "/usr/X11R6/lib/X11/fonts/75dpi"
    ...
EndSection
```

Each successive *FontPath* entry adds an additional directory to the font path.

On more recent systems, these lines have been replaced by one like this:

```
FontPath      "tcp/localhost:7100"
```

This indicates that a font server is in use, listening for font requests on TCP port 7100 on the local machine.[*] Additional *FontPath* entries may again be present, specifying either local directories or ports on other computers. The introduction of the font server in X11R5 made life easier since it allowed files to be shared between systems. The font server process actually runs the xfs program.[†]

However the default font path is set up, and individual user can always modify it via the xset command, using its fp option.

Adding Fonts to X

Adding fonts for use in screen display by the X Window system is very easy. For Type 1 fonts, the procedure is as follows:

- Create a directory to hold the new fonts (if necessary) and copy the font files there. Generally, you will need to put in both the *.pfa* or *.pfb* file and the *.afm* file there.

- Generate the required configuration files, named *fonts.dir* and *fonts.scale* (although, in fact, these two files are identical for the case of Type 1 fonts). This can be done manually, or you can use a utility to do it for you; some versions of the standard X mkfontdir command work well for this task, and the type1inst

---

[*] Note that on some systems running RedHat Linux, the entry appears like one of these:

```
FontPath "unix/:-1"
FontPath "unix/:7100"
```

This format indicates that the system is using the Red Hat–modified version of the X font server from which networking capabilities have been removed.

[†] The font server may be enabled on any of the systems we are considering (it is often installed by default). Doing so consists of installing the software, setting up its configuration file (discussed in brief a bit later), and modifying the system boot scripts so that the server process is started automatically.

command is very reliable (available at *http://sunsite.unc.edu/pub/Linux/X11/xutils/*). Both of them are run from within the directory holding the new fonts.

The entry in the files corresponding to our Octavian Italic typeface looks like this (we've wrapped it to fit):

```
oci_____.pfb      -monotype-octavian mt-medium-i-normal--0-0-0-0-p-0-iso8859-1
```

The first item is the filename dictating the Type 1 font (*oci_____.pfb* in this case), and the second item is the standard X typeface designation.

- If you created a new font directory, add it to the font path. If you are not using a font server, this is done by adding another *FontPath* entry to the *XF86Config* file. If you are using a font server, then you must edit an entry in its configuration file. The xfs font server typically stores its configuration file as */etc/X11/fs/config*. You'll need to an additional component to the catalogue list:

```
catalogue = /usr/share/fonts/ISO8859-7/Type1,
            /usr/share/fonts/default/Type1,
            /usr/X11R6/lib/X11/fonts/misc,
            /usr/X11R6/lib/X11/fonts/Type1,
            /usr/X11R6/lib/X11/fonts/Speedo,
            /more/fonts/type1
```

Here we have added the */more/fonts/type* directory as the final component of the catalogue. Note that the various catalogue entries are separated by commas.

- Restart the font server (e.g., a command like /etc/init.d/xfs restart). Also restart any current X session.

Once this is all complete, the new fonts should be available to any application that uses the standard X font facilities. You can verify that the fonts are installed correctly using the X commands xfontsel and xfd; the gimp application provides another very pleasant way of exploring the new fonts. The first two commands can also be useful for exploring what fonts are available on the system and displaying all the characters within a given typeface. However, the latter job is better handled by the freely-available gfontview utility, whose output is displayed in Figure 13-10. This facility allows you to view a single character, a short string, or a palette containing every character within it (in the example display, I've been somewhat self-absorbed in my choice of test character and character string). You can get this utility at *http://gfontview.sourceforge.net*.

Printing support

Printing the newly installed fonts introduces a few additional wrinkles. In order to be printed, Type 1 fonts must be rendered (technically, rasterized). Under X, this is usually handled by the Ghostscript facility (*http://www.ghostscript.org*), which must be configured for any new fonts.

Ghostscript font configuration occurs via its *Fontmap* configuration file, located in the */usr/share/ghostscript/*n.nn directory, where the final component of the path corresponds to the package version (under FreeBSD, the path begins at */usr/local/share*).

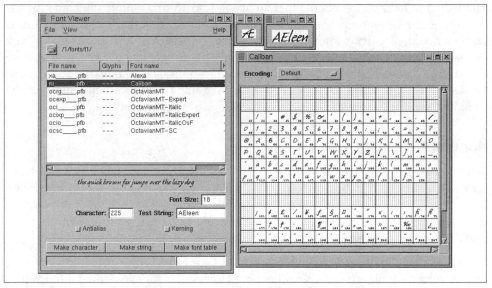

Figure 13-10. The gfontview font display utility

Here are some sample entries from this file:

```
/NimbusRomNo9L-Regu        (n021003l.pfb)  ;
/NimbusRomNo9L-ReguItal    (n021023l.pfb)  ;
/Times-Roman               /NimbusRomNo9L-Regu      ;
/Times-Italic              /NimbusRomNo9L-ReguItal  ;
```

Each line contains three fields: a name preceded by a slash, a filename enclosed in parentheses or another name, and finally a semicolon; spaces and/or tabs separate the fields from one another. If the second field is a filename, print requests for the correspondingly named font will use this font file. If the second field is another name (indicated by an initial slash), then the first field becomes an alias—an alternate name—for the same typeface. For example, the preceding entries will result in the file *n021003I.pfb* being used when someone wants to print the Times-Roman font.[*]

In order to print our Octavian typeface, we need to add a line like the following to this file:

```
/OctavianMT-Italic         (oci_____.pfb)  ;
```

The type1inst utility mentioned earlier creates a *Fontmap* file within the current directory along with the *fonts.dir* and *fonts.scale* files, making it easy to add the required entries to the actual Ghostscript font configuration file.

---

[*] Occasionally, you will need to create aliases for fonts in order to get them to print properly. The most common example occurs with "regular" typefaces that do not have "Roman" in their name. This can confuse some environments and applications. In such cases, creating an alias in the expected format will often do the trick. For example:

```
/OctavianMT-Roman /OctavianMT ;
```

The filename field may contain either an absolute path or a simple file name. In the latter case, the Ghostscript font path will be searched for that file. The default path is set up when the facility is compiled and typically consists of subdirectories under */usr/share/fonts/default* (e.g., *ghostscript* and *Type1*). You can make fonts available to Ghostscript by adding them to these existing locations (and modifying the current *fonts.dir* and *fonts.scale* files accordingly), or by using a new location, which can be added to the Ghostscript path by setting the *GS_LIB* environment variable.

Handling TrueType Fonts

With TrueType fonts, the fun really begins. Basically, the X font facilities and Ghostscript were designed around bitmap and Type 1 fonts and PostScript printing. However, users tend to have access to lots of TrueType fonts, and they naturally want to use them on Unix systems. Fortunately, support for TrueType fonts within traditional X facilities has become available.

The main facility that needs to understand TrueType fonts is the font server. Unfortunately, many vanilla xfs programs do not. However, TrueType compatibility font servers have been merged into the main XFree86 distribution as modules. See the "Fonts in Xfree86" document at *http://www.xfree.org* for full details (currently, *http://www.xfree86.org/4.0.3/fonts.html*) as well as the X TrueType Server Project home page, *http://x-tt.dsl.gr.jp*, and the FreeType Project homepage, *http://www.freetype.org*.

The module based on the excellent xfsft server can be included by editing the *Modules* section of the *XF86Config* file and adding a *Load* entry for the module *freetype*.

Once you have a TrueType-capable font server, the procedure for adding new TrueType fonts is almost identical to that for adding Type 1 fonts. The difference lies in using the ttmkfdir utility instead of type1inst (available at *http://www.joerg-pommnitz.de/TrueType/xfsft.html*; click on the link in the paragraph referring to the "tool that creates the *fonts.scale* file").

Here are three *fonts.dir* entries for TrueType fonts, Eras Light and Eras Bold:

```
eraslght.ttf    -itc-Eras Light ITC-medium-r-normal--0-0-0-0-p-0-iso8859-1
erasbd.ttf      -itc-Eras Bold ITC-medium-r-normal--0-0-0-0-p-0-iso8859-1
:2:mincho.ttc   -misc-mincho-...
```

The final entry shows the method for referring to individual fonts with a TrueType Collection file.

For printing TrueType fonts from general X applications the best option is to use a version of Ghostscript which has been compiled with *ttfont* option, enabling TrueType support with the facility (it must be a version 5 revision of Ghostscript). In this case, you simply add entries as usual to the *Fontmap* file pointing to the TrueType font files.

## CHAPTER 14

Automating Administrative Tasks

Although extensive programming experience is seldom a requirement for a system administration position, writing shell scripts and other sorts of programs is nevertheless an important part of a system administrator's job. There are two main types of programs and scripts that you will be called upon to create:

- Those designed to make system administration easier or more efficient, often by automating some process or job.
- Those that provide users with necessary or helpful tools that are not otherwise available to them.

This chapter discusses scripts intended for both contexts.

In general, automation offers many advantages over performing such tasks by hand, including the following:

Greater reliability
Tasks are performed in the same (correct) way every time. Once you have automated a task, its correct and complete performance no longer depends on how alert you are or your memory.

Guaranteed regularity
Tasks can be performed according to whatever schedule seems appropriate and need not depend on your availability or even your presence.

Enhanced system efficiency
Time-consuming or resource-intensive tasks can be performed during off hours, freeing the system for users during their normal work hours.

We've already considered the cron facility, which runs commands and scripts according to a preset schedule (see "Essential Administrative Techniques" in Chapter 3). In this chapter, we'll begin by looking at some example shell scripts and then consider some additional programming/scripting languages and other automation tools.

Creating Effective Shell Scripts

In this section, we'll consider several different routine system administration tasks as examples of creating and using administrative shell scripts. The discussions are meant to consider not only these tasks in themselves but also the process of writing scripts. Most of the shell script examples use the Bourne shell, but you can use any shell you choose; it's merely a Unix prejudice that "real shell programmers use the Bourne/Korn/zsh shell," however prevalent that attitude/article of faith may be.*

Password File Security

We discussed the various security issues surrounding the password file in "Detecting Problems" in Chapter 7 and "Unix Users and Groups" in Chapter 6. The various commands used to check it and its contents could be combined easily in a shell script. Here is one version (named ckpwd):

```
#!/bin/sh
# ckpwd - check password file (run as root)
#
# requires a saved password file to compare against:
#      /usr/local/admin/old/opg
#
umask 077
PATH="/bin:/usr/bin"; export PATH

cd /usr/local/admin/old          # stored passwd file location
echo ">>> Password file check for `date`"; echo ""

echo "*** Accounts without passwords:"
grep '^[^:]*::' /etc/passwd
```

---

* Once upon a time, the C shell had bugs that made writing administrative C shell scripts somewhat dicey. Although the versions of the C shell in current operating systems have fixed these bugs, the attitude that the C shell is unreliable persists. In addition, the C shell is considered poorly designed by many scripting gurus.

```
if [ $? -eq 1 ]                     # grep found no matches
then
    echo "None found."
fi
echo ""

# Look for extra system accounts
echo "*** Non-root UID=0 or GID=0 accounts:"
grep ':00*:' /etc/passwd | \
awk -F: 'BEGIN        {n=0}
         $1!="root"   {print $0 ; n=1}
         END          {if (n==0) print "None found."}'
echo ""

sort </etc/passwd >tmp1
sort <opg >tmp2                     # opg is the previously saved copy
echo "*** Accounts added:"
comm -23 tmp[1-2]                   # lines only in /etc/passwd
echo ""
echo "*** Accounts deleted:"
comm -13 tmp[1-2]                   # lines only in ./opg
echo ""
rm -f tmp[1-2]

echo "*** Password file protection:"
echo "-rw-r--r--  1 root    wheel>>> correct values"
ls -l /etc/passwd

echo ""; echo ">>> End of report."; echo ""
```

The script surrounds each checking operation with echo and other commands designed to make the output more readable so that it can be scanned quickly for problems. For example, the grep command that looks for non-*root* UID 0 accounts is preceded by an echo command that outputs a descriptive header. Similarly, the grep command's output is piped to an awk command that removes the *root* entry from its output and displays the remaining accounts or the string "None found" if no other UID or GID 0 accounts are present.

Instead of using diff to compare the current password file with the saved version, the script uses comm twice, to present the added and deleted lines separately (entries that have changed appear in both lists). The script ends with a simple ls command; the administrator must manually compare its output to the string displayed by the preceding echo command. However, this comparison also could be automated by piping ls's output to awk and explicitly comparing the relevant fields to their correct values. (I'll leave the implementation of the latter as an exercise for the reader.)

Here is some sample output from ckpwd:

```
>>> Password file check for Fri Jun 14 15:48:26 EDT 2002
*** Accounts without passwords:
None found.
*** Non-root UID=0 or GID=0 accounts:
badboy:lso9/.7sJUhhs:000:203:Bad Boy:/home/bb:/bin/csh
```

```
*** Accounts added:
chavez:9Sl.sd/i7snso:190:20:Rachel Chavez:/home/chavez:/bin/csh
wang:l9jsTHn7Hg./a:308:302:Rick Wang:/home/wang:/bin/sh
*** Accounts deleted:
chavez:Al9ddmL.3qX9o:190:20:Rachel Chavez:/home/chavez:/bin/csh
*** Password file protection:
-rw-r--r--  1 root     system      >>> correct values
-rw-r--r--  1 root     system      1847 Jun 11 22:38 /etc/passwd
>>> End of report.
```

If you don't like all the bells and whistles, the script needn't be this fancy. For example, its two sort, two comm, and five other commands in the section comparing the current and saved password files could easily be replaced by the diff command we looked at in "Detecting Problems" in Chapter 7 (and possibly one echo command to print a header). In the extreme case, the entire script could consist of just the four commands we looked at previously:

```
#!/bin/sh
# minimalist version of ckpwd
/usr/bin/grep '^[^:]*::' /etc/passwd
/usr/bin/grep ':00*:' /etc/passwd
/usr/bin/diff /etc/passwd /usr/local/admin/old/opg
/usr/bin/ls -l /etc/passwd
```

How much complexity is used depends on your own taste and free time. More complexity usually means it takes longer to debug.

Whatever approach you take, ckpwd needs to be run regularly to be effective (probably by cron).

Monitoring Disk Usage

It seems that no matter how much disk storage a system has, the users' needs (or wants) will eventually exceed it. As we discuss in "Monitoring and Managing Disk Space Usage" in Chapter 15, keeping an eye on disk space is a very important part of system management, and this monitoring task is well suited to automation via shell scripts.

The script we'll consider in this section—ckdsk—is designed to compare current disk use with what it was yesterday and to save today's data for comparison tomorrow. We'll build the script up gradually, starting with this simple version:

```
#!/bin/sh
# ckdsk: compares current and saved disk usage
# saved data is created with du_init script
#
PATH="/bin:/usr/bin"; export PATH

cd /usr/local/admin/ckdsk
if [ ! -s du.sav ] ; then
    echo "ckdsk: Can't find old data file du.sav."
    echo "       Recreate it with du_init and try again."
```

```
    exit 1
fi
du -k /iago/home/harvey > du.log
cat du.log | xargs -n2 ../bin/cmp_size 40 100 du.sav
mv -f du.log du.sav
```

After making sure yesterday's data is available, this script checks the disk usage under the directory *iago/home/harvey* using du, saving the output to the file *du.log*. Each line of *du.log* is fed by xargs to another script, cmp_size[*], which does the actual comparison, passing it the arguments 40, 100, and "du.sav," as well as the line from the du command. Thus, the first invocation of cmp_size would look something like this:

```
cmp_size 40 100 du.sav    876 /iago/home/harvey/bin
                          Output from du begins with argument 4.
```

ckdsk ends by replacing the old data file with the saved output from today's du command, in preparation for being run again tomorrow.

This simple version of the ckdsk script is not very general because it works only on a single directory. After looking at cmp_size in detail, we'll consider ways of expanding ckdsk's usefulness. Here is cmp_size:

```
#!/bin/sh
# cmp_size - compare old and new directory size
#     $1 (limit)=min. size for new dirs to be included in report
#     $2 (dlimit)=min. size change for old dirs to be included
#     $3 (sfile)=pathname for file with yesterday's data
#     $4 (csize)=current directory size
#     $5 (file)=pathname of directory
#     osize=previous size (extracted from sfile)
#     diff=size difference between yesterday & today
PATH="/bin:/usr/bin"; export PATH

if [ $# -lt 5 ] ; then
    echo "Usage: cmp_size newlim oldlim data_file size dir"
    exit 1
fi

# save initial parameters
limit=$1; dlimit=$2; sfile=$3; csize=$4; file=$5;

# get yesterday's data
osize=`grep "$file\$" $sfile | awk '{print \$1}'`
if [ -z "$osize" ] ; then            # it's a new directory
    if [ $csize -ge $limit ] ; then  # report if size >= limit
        echo "new\t$csize\t$file"
    fi

    exit 0
```

---

[*] On some systems, cmp_size could be a function defined in ckdsk; on others, however, xargs won't accept a function as the command to run.

```
fi
# compute the size change from yesterday
if [ $osize -eq $csize ]
then
    exit 0
elif [ $osize -gt $csize ]
then
    diff=`expr $osize - $csize`
else
    diff=`expr $csize - $osize`
fi

# report the size change if large enough
if [ $diff -ge $dlimit ] ; then
    echo "$osize\t$csize\t$file"
fi
```

cmp_size first checks to see that it was passed the right number of arguments. Then it assigns its arguments to shell variables for readability. The first two parameters are cutoff values for new and existing directories, respectively. These parameters allow you to tell cmp_size how much of a change is too small to be interesting (because you don't necessarily care about minor disk usage changes). If the size of the directory specified as the script's fifth parameter has changed by an amount greater than the cutoff value, cmp_size prints the directory name and old and new sizes; otherwise, cmp_size returns silently.

cmp_size finds yesterday's size by greping for the directory name in the data file specified as its third parameter (*du.sav* is what ckdsk passes it). If grep didn't find the directory in the data file, it's a new one, and cmp_size then compares its size to the new directory cutoff (passed in as its first argument) displaying its name and size if it is large enough.

If grep returns anything, cmp_size then computes the size change for the directory by subtracting the smaller of the old size (from the file and stored in the variable *osize*) and the current size (passed in as the fourth parameter and stored in *csize*) from the larger. cmp_size then compares the size difference to the old directory cutoff (passed in as its second argument), and displays the old and new sizes if it is large enough.

cmp_size reports on directories that either increased or decreased in size by the amount of the cutoff. If you are only interested in size increases, you could replace the if statement that computes the value of the *diff* variable with a much simpler one:

```
if [ $osize -le $csize ]
then
    exit 0                          # only care if it's bigger
else
    diff=`expr $osize - $csize`
fi
```

Unlike the simple version of ckdsk, cmp_size is fairly general; it could also be used, for example, to process output from the quot command.

One way to make ckdsk more useful is to enable it to check more than one starting directory, with different cutoffs for each one. Here is a version that can do that:

```
#!/bin/sh
# chkdsk2 - multiple directories & per-directory cutoffs
PATH="/bin:/usr/bin"; export PATH

du_it( )
{
# $1 = cutoff in blocks for new directories
# $2 = cutoff as block change for old directories
# $3 = starting directory
# $4 = flags to du
abin="/usr/local/admin/bin"

du $4 $3 > du.tmp
cat du.tmp | xargs -n2 $abin/cmp_size $1 $2 du.sav
cat du.tmp >> du.log; rm du.tmp
}

umask 077
cd /usr/local/admin/ckdsk
rm -f du.log du.tmp 2>&1 >/dev/null
if [ ! -s du.sav ] ; then
    echo "run_cmp: can't find old data file; run du_init."
    exit 1
fi

echo "Daily disk usage report for `date`"; echo ''
df
echo ''; echo "Old\tNew"
echo "Size\tSize\tDirectory Name"
echo "-----------------------------------------------------------"
du_it 40  100 /iago/home/harvey
du_it 1    1 /usr/lib
du_it 1 1000 /home/\* -s
echo "-----------------------------------------------------------"
echo ''
mv -f du.log du.sav
exit 0
```

This script uses a function named *du_it* to perform the du command and pass its output to cmp_size using xargs. The function takes four arguments: the cutoffs for old and new directories (for cmp_size), the starting directory for the du command, and any additional flags to pass to du (optional).

du_it saves du's output into a temporary file, *du.tmp*, which it appends to the file *du.log* afterwards; *du.log* thus accumulates the data from multiple directory checks and eventually becomes the new saved data file, replacing yesterday's version.

The script proper begins by removing any old temporary files from previous runs and making sure its data file (still hardwired as *du.sav*) is available. It then runs df and prints some header lines for the output from cmp_size. This version of the script then calls *du_it* three times:

```
du_it 40  100 /iago/home/harvey
du_it 1     1 /usr/lib
du_it 1 1000 /home/\* -s
```

It will run du and compare its output to the saved data for the directories */iago/home/ harvey*, */usr/lib*, and all of the subdirectories of */home*, passing the du command the -s option in the last case. In the third command, the wildcard is passed through to the actual du command line by quoting it to *du_it*. Different cutoffs are used for each call. When checking */usr/lib*, this version asks to be told about any change in the size of any directory (size or size change greater than or equal to one). In contrast, when checking the users' home directories under */home*, the report includes new directories of any size but only existing directories that changed size by at least 1000 blocks.

ckdsk ends by moving the accumulated output file, *du.log*, on to the saved data file, *du.sav*, saving the current data for future comparisons.

Here is some sample output from ckdsk:

```
Daily disk usage report for Tue Jun 11 09:52:46 EDT 2002

File system       Kbytes     used   avail  capacity  Mounted-on
/dev/dsk/c1d1s0    81952    68848   13104    84%      /
/dev/dsk/c1d1s2   373568   354632   18936    94%      /home
/dev/dsk/c1d2s8   667883   438943  228940    66%      /genome

Old    New
Size   Size   Directory Name
-------------------------------------------------------
348    48     /iago/home/harvey/g02
new    52     /iago/home/harvey/test
2000   1012   /iago/home/harvey
new    912    /usr/lib/acct/bio
355    356    /usr/lib/spell
34823  32797  /home/chavez
9834   3214   /home/ng
new    300    /home/park
-------------------------------------------------------
```

The echo commands set off the output from cmp_size and make it easy to scan.

This version of ckdsk requires new du_it commands to be added by hand. The script could be refined further by allowing this information to be external as well, replacing the explicit du_it commands with a loop over the directories and parameters listed in a data file:

```
cat du.dirs |
while read dir old new opts; do
# default old and new cutoffs to 1
if [ "$old" = "" ]; then
    old=1; fi
```

```
if [ "$new" = "" ]; then
    new=1; fi
if [ -n "$dir" ]; then                # ignore blank lines
    du_it $new $old $dir $opts
fi
done
```

This version also assigns default values to the cutoff parameters if they are omitted from an entry in the data file.

Similarly, the script currently checks all users' home directories. If only some of them need to be checked, the final du_it command could be replaced by a loop like this one:

```
for user in chavez havel harvey ng smith tedesco ; do
    du_it 1 1000 /home/$user -s
done
```

Alternatively, the user list could be read in from an external configuration file. We'll look at obtaining data from files in an upcoming example.

The cron facility is also the most sensible way to run ckdsk.

Root Filesystem Backups and System Snapshots

Backing up the root filesystem is a task for which the benefits don't always seem worth the trouble. Still, re-creating all of the changed system configuration files is also very time-consuming, and can be very frustrating when you don't immediately recall which files you changed.

An alternative to backing up the entire root filesystem—and other separate system filesystems like /usr and /var—is to write a script to copy only the few files that have actually changed since the operating system was installed to a user filesystem, allowing the changed files to be backed up as part of the regular system backup schedule without any further effort on your part. Creating such a script is also a good way to become thoroughly acquainted with all the configuration files on the system. When selecting files to copy, include anything you might ever conceivably change, and err on the side of too many rather than too few files.

Here is a C shell script that performs such a copy:

```
#!/bin/csh
# bkup_sys - backup changed files from system partitions
unset path; setenv PATH "/bin:/usr/bin"

umask 077
if ("$1" != "") then
    set SAVE_DIR="$1"
else
    set SAVE_DIR="/save/`hostname`/sys_save"
endif
```

```
set dir_list=`cat /etc/bkup_dirs`
foreach dir ($dir_list)
  echo "Working on $dir ..."
  if (! -d $SAVE_DIR/$dir) mkdir -p $SAVE_DIR/$dir
  set files=`file $dir/{,.[a-zA-Z]}* | \
            egrep 'text|data' | awk -F: '{print $1}'`
  if ("$files" != "") cp -p $files $SAVE_DIR/$dir:t
end

echo "Backing up individual files ..."
foreach file (`cat /usr/local/admin/sysback/bkup_files`)
   if ("$file:h" == "$file:t") continue      # not a full pathname
   if ("$file:t" == "") continue             # no filename present
   if (! -d $SAVE_DIR/$file:h) mkdir -p $SAVE_DIR/$file:h
   cp -p $file $SAVE_DIR/$file:h
end
echo "All done."
```

This script performs the backup in two parts. First, it copies all text and binary data files from a list of directories to a designated directory; file types are identified by the file command, and the grep command selects ones likely to be configuration files (some extra files will get copied, but this is better than missing something). The default destination location is named for the current host and has a form like */save/hamlet/sys_save*; this location can be overridden by including an alternate location on the bkup_sys command line. The directory list comes from the file */etc/bkup_dirs*, which would contain entries like */, /etc, /etc/defaults, /etc/mail, /var/cron*, and so on.

The final section of the script copies the files listed in */usr/local/admin/sysback/bkup_files*, which holds the names of individual files that need to be saved (residing in directories from which you don't want to save every text and data file). It uses the C shell :h and :t modifiers, which extract the head (directory portion) and tail (filename and extension), respectively, from the filename in the specified variable. The first two lines in this section make sure that the entry looks reasonable before the copy command is attempted.

In both cases, files are stored in the same relative location under the destination directory as they are in the real filesystem (this makes them easy to restore to their proper locations). Subdirectories are created as necessary under the destination directory. The script uses cp -p to copy the files, which reproduces file ownership, protections, and access and modification times.

Copying files in this way is a protection against serious damage to a system filesystem (as well as against accidentally deleting or otherwise losing one of them). However, in order to completely restore the system, in the worst case, you'll need to reproduce the structure as well as the contents of damaged filesystems. To do the latter, you will need to know what the original configuration was. You can write a script to document how a system is set up.

Here is an example from a FreeBSD system:

```
#!/bin/csh
# doc_sys - document system configuration--FreeBSD version
unset path; setenv PATH "/sbin:/usr/sbin:/bin:/usr/bin"

if ("$1" != "") then
    set outfile="$1"                                # alternate output file
else
    set outfile="`hostname`_system.doc"
endif

echo "System Layout Documentation for `hostname`" > $outfile
date >> $outfile
echo "" >> $outfile

echo ">>>Physical Disks" >> $outfile
grep "ata[0-9]+-" /var/run/dmegs.boot >> $outfile      # Assumes IDE disks.
echo "" >> $outfile

echo ">>>Paging Space Data" >> $outfile
pstat -s >> $outfile

echo "" >> $outfile
echo ">>>Links in /" >> $outfile
file /{,.[a-zA-Z]}* | grep link >> $outfile
echo "" >> $outfile

echo ">>>System Parameter Settings" >> $outfile
sysctl -a
```

The purpose of this script is to capture information that you would not otherwise have (or have easy access to). Thus, commands such as df, which give information easily obtained from configuration files, are not included (although they could be in your version if you would find such data helpful). You may want to consider periodically printing out the results from such a script for every system you administer and placing the resulting pages into a notebook.

As this script illustrates, the commands you need to include tend to be very operating-system-specific. Here is a version for an AIX system (the common sections have been replaced with comments):

```
#!/bin/csh
# doc_sys - document system configuration--AIX version
unset path; setenv PATH "/usr/sbin:/bin:/usr/bin"
```

set output file and write header line

```
echo ">>>Physical Disks" >> $outfile
lspv >> $outfile
echo "" >> $outfile

echo ">>>Paging Space Data" >> $outfile
```

```
lsps -a >> $outfile

echo "" >> $outfile
echo ">>>Volume Group Info" >> $outfile
# loop over volume groups
foreach vg (`lsvg`)
    lsvg $vg >> $outfile
    echo "===Component logical volumes:" >> $outfile
    lsvg -l $vg | grep -v ":" >> $outfile
    echo "" >> $outfile
end
echo "" >> $outfile

echo ">>>Logical Volume Details" >> $outfile
# loop over volume groups and then over the component LVs
foreach vg (`lsvg`)
foreach lv (`lsvg -l $vg | egrep -v ":|NAME" | awk '{print $1}'`)
        lslv $lv >> $outfile
        echo "===Physical Drive Placement" >> $outfile
        lslv -l $lv >> $outfile echo "" >> $outfile
    end
end
echo "" >> $outfile

echo ">>>Defined File systems" >> $outfile
lsfs >> $outfile echo "" >> $outfile
```

links in / listed here

```
echo ">>>System Parameter Settings" >> $outfile
lsattr -E -H -l sys0 >> $outfile
lslicense >> $outfile                    # number of licensed users
```

This version of the script also provides information about the volume group and logical volume layout on the system.

Table 14-1 lists commands that will provide similar information for the Unix versions we are considering:

Table 14-1. System information commands

Version	Disk data	Swap space data	System parameters
AIX	lspv	lsps -a	lsattr -E -H -l sys0
FreeBSD	grep *pat* 'dmesg'	pstat -s	sysctl -a
HP-UX	ioscan -f -n -C disk	swapinfo -t -a -m	/usr/lbin/sysadm/system_prep -s system
Linux	fdisk -l	cat /proc/swaps	cat /proc/sys/kernel/* (see script below)
Solaris	getdev	swap -l	cat /etc/system
Tru64	dsfmgr -s	swapon -s	sysconfig (see script below)

See "From Disks to Filesystems" in Chapter 10 for the Logical Volume Manager commands for the various systems.

Sometimes more than just a simple command is needed to complete one of these tasks. For example, the following script displays all the system parameters under Tru64:

```
#!/bin/csh
foreach s ( `/sbin/sysconfig -m | /usr/bin/awk -F: '{print $1}'` )
    /sbin/sysconfig -q $s
    echo "-----------------------------------"
    end
exit 0
```

Similarly, the following script records the current Linux system parameters.

```
#!/bin/csh
foreach f (`find /proc/sys/kernel -type f`)
  echo "$f":
  cat $f
  echo ""
  end
exit 0
```

A Few More Tricks

The following script illustrates a couple of other useful tricks when writing shell scripts. It polls various sites with which the local system communicates to exchange mail and runs a few times a day via the cron facility:

```
#!/bin/sh
# mail.hourly
PATH="/usr/bin:/bin"

cd /usr/local/admin/mail
for sys in (`cat ./mail_list`); do
    if [ ! -f /etc/.no_$sys ]; then
        echo polling $sys
        exchange mail ...
        touch last_$sys
    else
        echo skipping $sys
    fi
done
exit 0
```

This script loops over the list of hosts in the file *mail_list* in the current directory. Let's consider how it works when the current host is *lucia*. The if statement determines whether the file */etc/.no_lucia* exists. If it does, the host *lucia* is not polled. Using a file in this way is a very easy mechanism for creating script features that can be turned on or off easily without having to change the script itself, the way it is called from another script, any *crontab* entries using it, and so on. When I don't want *lucia* to be polled (usually because its owner has turned it off during an out-oftown trip, and I hate seeing dozens of failure messages piling up), I simply run the command touch /etc/.no_lucia. Deleting the same file reinstates polling on a regular basis.

The second technique consists of using an empty file's modification time to store a date. In this script, the touch command in the if loop records when the most recent poll of system *lucia* took place. The date it occurred can be quickly determined by running:

```
$ ls -l /usr/local/admin/mail/last_lucia
```

Such time-stamp files can be used in a variety of contexts:

Backups

> If you create a time-stamp file at the beginning of a backup operation, you can use a -newer clause on a find command to find all files modified since then for a subsequent backup.

Testing

> When you want to find out what files a particular program modifies, create a time-stamp file in */tmp*, run the program, and then find files newer than the time-stamp file once the program finishes (this assumes you are on an otherwise idle system).

Files modified since an operating system installation or upgrade

> Creating a time-stamp file at the end of an operating system installation or upgrade will enable you easily to determine which files you have modified with respect to the versions on the distribution media.

Testing and Debugging Scripts

The following list describes strategies for testing and debugging scripts:

Build the script up gradually. Start by getting a simple version running—without arguments and handling only the easiest case—and then add the bells and whistles. We've seen this strategy in action several times in this chapter already.

Test and debug the logic independently of the functionality if possible. One way to do this is to place an "echo" in front of every substantive command in the script, as in this fragment:

```
if [ some condition ]; then
    echo rm -rf /
else
    echo cp /tmp/junk /unix
fi
```

This will allow you to see what the script does in various cases in a completely safe way. Similarly, you can *replace entire functions* with an echo command:

```
go_on
{
echo running function go_on
```

```
    return
}
```

In general, inserting an echo command is a good way to see where you are in a script, to track variable values, and so on. In some cases, a construct like the following will be helpful:

```
echo "===${variable}==="
```

This sort of technique is useful when you are having trouble with a variable that may contain internal white space.

Use the shell's -v option. This option displays each script line as it is executed, and it will sometimes indicate how the flow of a script is proceeding.

Perform testing and debugging on local copies of system files. The script will modify the copied files rather than the real ones. For example, if the script you are writing alters */etc/passwd*, develop the script using a local copy of */etc/passwd* rather than the real thing.

Use small cases for initial tests. Operate on a single item at first, even if the script is designed to work on a large collection of items. Once that version is working, alter it to work for multiple items.

Don't forget to test boundary conditions. For example, if a script is designed to alter several user accounts, make sure it works for one user account, two user accounts, zero user accounts, and many, many user accounts.

Assume things will go wrong. In general, include as much error-checking code in the script as possible, making sure that the script does something reasonable when errors occur.

Write for the general case. Not only will this give you more powerful tools and meta-tools that you can use over and over, but it is also no harder than coming up with a solution for one specific problem. In fact, if you take a little time to step back from the specifics to consider the general task, it is often easier.

Perl: An Alternate Administrative Language

Perl[*] is a free programming language created by Larry Wall and currently developed and maintained by a core group of talented programmers (see *http://www.perl.org*, *http://www.perl.com* and *http://www.cpan.org* for more information). Perl has become quite popular in recent years. It contains many features that make it very well suited to writing scripts for system administrative tasks, including the following:

- It combines the short development time of traditional shell programming with some of the best aspects of high-level languages such as C. For example, Perl

---

[*] The name has various meanings, official and otherwise. Two frequently cited by its author are Practical Extraction and Report Language and Pathologically Eclectic Rubbish Lister.

contains well-implemented arrays (unlike any shell) and an impressive range of built-in functions, and it also includes the ability easily to run standard Unix commands and use filename wildcards (as in a shell).

- It provides things that are missing from most or all shells, including string functions, built-in arithmetic, and general regular expression support.

- Handling many simultaneous open files is a breeze.

- It offers enhanced security features over standard shells.

Perl features come from a variety of sources, including standard shells, C, Fortran, Basic, Pascal, awk, and sed. I don't think Larry's managed to use any COBOL features yet, but I've been wrong before.

To get started using Perl, I recommend the following books:

- *Learning Perl*, by Randall L. Schwartz and Tom Phoenix (O'Reilly & Associates), and *Effective Perl Programming*, by Joseph N. Hall with Randal L. Schwartz (Addison-Wesley).

- If you are interested in incorporating a graphical interface into Perl scripts, consult *Learning Perl/Tk* by Nancy Walsh (O'Reilly & Associates).

- For examples of using Perl for system administration tasks, see *Perl for System Administration* by David N. Blank-Edelman (O'Reilly & Associates).

A Quick Introduction

The best way to see what Perl has to offer is to look at a few Perl programs. We'll begin with dr, a Perl script I wrote to make the AIX dosread command worth using. By default, dosread copies a single file from a DOS diskette, and it requires that you specify both the DOS filename and the local filename (and not just a target directory). Of course, what one often wants to do is to copy everything on a diskette; this Perl script copies all the files on a diskette to the current directory, translating the destination filenames to lowercase:[*]

```
#!/usr/bin/perl -w Executable location varies.
# dr - copy all the files on a DOS diskette

# store the list of files on the diskette
@files = `dosdir | egrep -v "^(Free|There)"`;

foreach $f (@files) {                         # loop over files
    chop $f;                                  # remove newline char
    $g = $f;
    $g =~ tr/A-Z/a-z/;                        # translate to lowercase
    print $f,"*",$g,"\n";
    system("dosread -a -v $f ./$g");
    }
```

---

[*] One technical reviewer comments: "chomp is better. chop is so Perl 4."

The first command looks almost like a C shell command. It runs the command in back quotes and stores the output in the array *@files* (the AIX dosdir command lists the files on a diskette, and the egrep command throws away the summary line). Names of numerically indexed arrays begin with an @ sign when the entire array is referenced as a whole. Note also that Perl statements end with a semicolon.

Perl scalar variable names always begin with a dollar sign, as the next few commands illustrate; no special syntax is needed to dereference them. The remainder of the script is a foreach loop; the commands within the loop are enclosed in curly braces (as in C). The loop variable is *$f*, and *$g* eventually holds a lowercase version of the name in *$f*.

The final two commands do the actual work. The print command displays a string like the following for each file on the diskette:

```
PROPOSAL.TXT*proposal.txt
```

The purpose of this display is mostly to provide that warm-and-comfortable feeling while AIX's excruciatingly slow diskette commands run. The system command is used to run a Unix command from Perl, in this case dosread.

This version of dr is leisurely paced and is designed to emphasize the similarities between Perl and other languages. However, a native speaker might write it more like this:

```
#!/usr/bin/perl
# dr - terse version
foreach (`dosdir | egrep -v "Free|Total"`) {
chop;
system("dosread @ARGV $_ \L$_");
    }
```

The foreach statement is still intelligible, but the other commands require some explanation. Perl provides a default variable that is used in commands where a variable is needed but none is specified; the name of this variable is *$_* (dollar-underscore). *$_* is being used as the loop variable and as the argument to chop.

The \L construct in the system command translates *$_* to lowercase. This system command is more general than the one in the previous version. It passes any arguments specified to the script—stored in the array *@ARGV*—on to dosread and uses *$_* as both of dosread's arguments; filenames on diskette aren't case-sensitive, so this works fine.

The two versions of dr illustrate an important Perl principle: *there's more than one way to do it* (the Perl slogan).

A Walking Tour of Perl

wgrep is a tool I wrote for some users still longing for the VMS Search command they used years previously. wgrep stands for *windowed grep*, and the command searches files for regular expression patterns, optionally displaying several lines of context around each matching line. Like the command it was designed to imitate, some of its options will strike some purists as excessive, but it will also demonstrate many of Perl's features in a more complex and extended context.

Here is the usage message for wgrep:

```
Usage: wgrep [-n] [-w[b][:a] | -W] [-d] [-p] [-s] [-m] regexp file(s)
-n    = include line numbers
-s    = indicate matched lines with stars
-wb:a = display b lines before and a lines after each matched
              line (both default to 3)
-W    = suppress window; equivalent to -w0:0
-d    = suppress separation lines between file sections
-m    = suppress file name header lines
-p    = plain mode; equivalent to -W -d
-h    = print this help message and exit
Note: If present, -h prevails; otherwise, the rightmost option wins
      in the case of contradictions.
```

Here is a sample of wgrep's most baroque output format, including line numbers and asterisks indicating matched lines, in addition to headers indicating each file containing matches and separators between noncontiguous groups of lines within each file:

```
wgrep -n -s -w1:1 chavez /etc/passwd /etc/group
********** /etc/passwd **********
  00023 carnot:x:231:20:Hilda Carnot:/home/carnot:/bin/bash
* 00024 chavez:x:190:20:Rachel Chavez:/home/chavez:/bin/csh
  00025 claire:x:507:302:Theresa Claire:/home/claire:/bin/csh
********** /etc/group **********
* 00001 wheel:*:0:chavez,wang,wilson
  00002 other:*:1:
**********
  00014 genome:*:202:
* 00015 dna:*:203:chavez
* 00016 mktg:*:490:chavez
  00017 sales:*:513:
```

After initializing several variables related to output formats, wgrep begins by dealing with any options that the user has specified:

```
#!/usr/bin/perl -w
# wgrep - windowed grep utility

$before = 3; $after = 3;              # default window size
$show_stars = 0;
$show_nums = 0;
$sep = "**********\n";
$show_fname = 1;
$show_sep = 1;
# loop until an argument doesn't begin with a "-"

while ($ARGV[0] =~ /^-(\w)(.*)/) {
    $arg = $1;                        # $arg holds the option letter
```

This while statement tests whether the first element of @ARGV (referred to as $ARGV[0] because array element references begin with a $ sign)—the array holding the command-line arguments—matches the pattern contained between the forward slashes: ^-(\w)(.*). Most of the elements of the pattern are standard regular expression constructs; \w is a shorthand form for [a-zA-Z0-9_]. Within a regular expression, parentheses set off sections of the matched text that can be referred to later using the variables $1 (for the first matched section), $2, and so on. The next line copies the first matched section—the option letter—to the variable $arg.

The next portion of wgrep forms the remainder of the body of the while loop and processes the available options:[*]

```
if ($arg eq "s") { $show_stars = 1; }
elsif ($arg eq "n") { $show_nums = 1; }
elsif ($arg eq "m") { $show_fname = 0; }
elsif ($arg eq "d") { $show_sep = 0; }
elsif ($arg eq "w") {
    # parse 2nd matched section at colon into default array @_
    split(/:/,$2);
    $before = $_[0] if $_[0] ne '';
    $after = $_[1] if $_[1] ne '';
    }
elsif ($arg eq "p") {
    $before = 0;
    $after = 0;
    $show_sep = 0; }
elsif ($arg eq "W") {
    $before = 0;
    $after = 0;
    }
elsif ($arg eq "h") { &usage(""); }
else { &usage("wgrep: invalid option: $ARGV[0]");
                    }                  # end of if command
            shift;                     # go on to next argument
                    }                  # end of foreach loop
```

The foreach loop contains a long if-then-else-if construct, illustrating Perl's eclectic nature. In general, conditions are enclosed in parentheses (as in the C shell), and they are formed via Bourne shell–like operators (among other methods). No "then" keyword is required because the commands comprising the if body are enclosed in curly braces (even when there is just a single command). Most of the clauses in this if statement set various flags and variables appropriately for the specified options. The clause that processes the -w option illustrates a very nice Perl feature, conditional assignment statements:

```
split(/:/,$2);
$before = $_[0] if $_[0] ne '';
```

---

[*] There are easier ways to parse lettered command options, but the point of this form is to illustrate some simple Perl. The Getopt module is one popular choice for this task.

The split command breaks the second matched section of the option—indicated by
$2—into fields using a colon as a separator character (remember the syntax is, for
example, -w2:5), storing successive fields into the elements of the default array @_.
The following line sets the value of $before to the first element, provided that it is
not null: in other words, provided that the user specified a value for the window preceding a matched line.

The final else clause calls the usage subroutine when an unrecognized option is
encountered (the ampersand indicates a subroutine call). The shift command following the if statement works just as it does in standard shell, sliding the elements
of @ARGV down one position in the array.

The next section of wgrep processes the expression to search for:

```
&usage("missing regular expression") if ! $ARGV[0];
$regexp = $ARGV[0];
shift;
$regexp =~ s,/,\\/,g;                        # "/" --> "\/"

# if no files are specified, use standard input
if (! $ARGV[0]) { $ARGV[0] = "STDIN"; }
```

If @ARGV is empty after processing the command options, the usage subroutine is
called again. Otherwise, its first element is assigned to the variable $regexp, and
another shift command is executed. The second assignment statement for $regexp
places backslashes in front of any forward slashes that the regular expression contains (since the forward slashes are the usual Perl pattern delimiter characters), using
a syntax like that of sed or ex.

After processing the regular expression, wgrep handles the case where no filenames
are specified on the command line (using standard input instead). The next part of
the script forms wgrep's main loop:

```
LOOP:
foreach $file (@ARGV) {                      # Loop over file list

    if ($file ne "STDIN" && ! open(NEWFILE,$file)) {
        print STDERR "Can't open file $file; skipping it.\n";
        next LOOP;                           # Jump to LOOP label
    }
$fhandle = $file eq "STDIN" ? STDIN : NEWFILE;
$lnum = "00000";
$nbef = 0; $naft = 0;
$matched = 0; $matched2 = 0;
&clear_buf(0) if $before > 0;
```

This foreach loop runs over the remaining elements of @ARGV, and it begins by
attempting to open the first file to be searched. The open command opens the file
specified as its second argument, defining the *file handle*—a variable that can be
used to refer to that file in subsequent commands—specified as its first argument
(file handles are conventionally given uppercase names). open returns a nonzero value

on success. If the open fails, wgrep prints an error message to standard error (STDIN and STDERR are the file handles for standard input and standard error, respectively) and the file is simply skipped.

The variable *$fhandle* is set to "STDIN" or "NEWFILE", depending on the value of *$file*, using a C-style conditional expression statement (if the condition is true, the value following the question mark is used; otherwise, the value following the colon is used). This technique allows the user to specify STDIN on the command line anywhere within the file list.

Following a successful file open, some other variables are initialized, and the clear_buf subroutine is called to initialize the array that will be used to hold the lines preceding a matched line. The call to clear_buf illustrates an alternate form of the if statement:

```
&clear_buf(0) if $before > 0;
```

The file is actually searched using a while loop. It may be helpful to look at its logic in the abstract before examining the code:

```
while there are lines in the file
    if we've found a match already
        if the current line matches too
            print it and reset the after window counter
        but if the current line doesn't match
            if we are still in the after window
                print the line anyway
            otherwise
                we're finally out of the match window, so reset all flags
                and save the current line in the before buffer

    otherwise we are still looking for a matching line
        if the current line matches
            print separators and the before window
            print the current line
            set the match flag
        but if the current line doesn't match
            save it in the before buffer
at the end of the file, continue on to the next file
```

Here is the part of the while loop that is executed once a matching line has been found. The construct <$fhandle> returns each line in turn from the file corresponding to the specified file handle:

```
while (<$fhandle>) {             # loop over the lines in the file
    ++$lnum;                     # increment line number
    if ($matched) {              # we're printing the match window
        if ($_ =~ /$regexp/) {   # if current line matches pattern
            $naft = 0;           #   reset the after window count,
            &print_info(1);      #   print preliminary stuff,
            print $_;            #   and print the line
        }
        else {                   # current line does not match
```

```
            if ($after > 0 && ++$naft <= $after) {
                # print line anyway if still in the after window
                &print_info(0); print $_;
            }
            else {                          # after window is done
                $matched = 0;               # no longer in a match
                $naft = 0;                  # reset the after window count
                # save line in before buffer for future matches
                push(@line_buf, $_); $nbef++;
            }                               # end else not in after window
        }                                   # end else curr. line not a match
    }                                       # end if we're in a match
```

The while loop runs over the lines in the file corresponding to the file handle in the *$fhandle* variable; each line is processed in turn and is accessed using the *$_* variable. This section of the loop is executed when we're in the midst of processing a match: after a matching line has been found and before the window following the match has been finished. This *after window* is printed after the final matched line that is found within the window; in other words, if another matching line is found while the after window is being displayed, it gets pushed down, past the new match. The *$naft* variable holds the current line number within the after window; when it reaches the value of *$after*, the window is complete.

The print_info subroutine prints any stars and/or line numbers preceding lines from the file (or nothing if neither one is requested); an argument of 1 to print_info indicates a matching line, and 0 indicates a nonmatching line.

Here is the rest of the while loop, which is executed when we are still looking for a matching line (and therefore no lines are being printed):

```
        else {                              # we're still looking for a match
            if ($_ =~ /$regexp/) {          # we found one
                $matched = 1;               # so set match flag
                # print file and/or section separator(s)
                print $sep if $matched2 && $nbef > $before && $show_sep && $show_fname;
                print "********** $file **********\n" if ! $matched2++ && $show_fname;
                # print and clear out before buffer and reset before counter
                &clear_buf(1) if $before > 0; $nbef = 0;
                &print_info(1);
                print $_;                   # print current line
            }
            elsif ($before > 0) {
                # pop off oldest line in before buffer & add current line
                shift(@line_buf) if $nbef >= $before;
                push(@line_buf,$_); $nbef++;
            }                               # end elseif before window is nonzero
        }                                   # end else not in a match
    }                                       # end while loop over lines in this file
}                                           # end foreach loop over list of files
exit;                                       # end of script proper
```

Several of the print commands illustrate compound conditions in Perl. In this section of the script, the variable *$nbef* holds the number of the current line within the before window; by comparing it to *$before*, we can determine whether the buffer holding saved lines for the before window is full (there's no point in saving more lines than we need to print once a match is found). The array *@line_buf* holds these saved lines, and the push command (which we saw earlier as well) adds an element to the end of it. The immediately preceding shift(@line_buf) command shifts the elements of this array down, pushing off the oldest saved line, making room for the current line (stored in $_).

Here is the subroutine print_info, which illustrates the basic structure of a Perl subroutine:

```
sub print_info {
    print $_[0] ? "* " : "   " if $show_stars;
    print $lnum," " if $show_nums;
}
```

Any arguments passed to a subroutine are accessible via the default array @_. This subroutine expects a zero or one as its argument, telling it whether the current line is a match or not—and hence whether to print a star or all spaces at the beginning of the line when *$show_stars* is true. The subroutine's second statement prints line numbers if appropriate.*

Subroutine clear_buf is responsible for printing the before window and clearing the associated array, *@line_buf*:

```
sub clear_buf {
# argument says whether to print before window or not
    $print_flag = $_[0];
    $i = 0; $j = 0;
    if ($print_flag) {
        # if we're printing line numbers, fiddle with the counter to
        # account for the before window
        if ($show_nums) {
            $target = $lnum - ($#line_buf + 1);
        }
        $lnum = "00000";
        # yes, we're really counting back up to the right number
        # to keep correct number format -- cycles are cheap
        while ($i++ < $target) { ++$lnum; } }
        while ($j <= $#line_buf) {        # print before window
            &print_info(0);
            print $line_buf[$j++];
            $lnum++ if $show_nums;
        }                                 # end while
    }                                     # end if print_flag
    @line_buf = ();                       # clear line_buf array
}                                         # end of subroutine
```

---

* Yes, this is an ugly kludge from my early Perl days. A more elegant solution is left as an exercise for the reader. But don't miss the lesson that scripts don't have to be perfect to be effective.

The final subroutine is usage. Its first line prints the error message passed to it as its single argument (if any), and the remaining lines print the standard usage message and then cause wgrep to terminate:

```
sub usage {
    print STDERR $_[0],"\n" if $_[0];
    print STDERR "Usage: wgrep [-n] ..."
    many more print commands
    exit;
}
```

Perl Reports

Besides being a powerful programming language, Perl can also be used to generate attractive reports. Here is a fairly simple example:

```
                                Disk
Username (UID)    Home Directory  Space    Security
----------------------------------------------------------
lpd (104)         /               skipped
sanders (464)     /home/sanders   725980K
stein (0)         /chem/1/stein     4982K  ** UID=0
swenson (508)     /chem/1/Swenson deleted
vega (515)        /home/vega         100K  ** CK PASS
...
```

This report was produced using format specifiers, which state how records written with the write command are to look. Here are the ones used for this report:

```
#!/usr/bin/perl -w
# mon_users - monitor user accounts

# header at the top of each page of the report
format top =

                                Disk
Username (UID)    Home Directory  Space    Security
----------------------------------------------------------
.
# format for each line written to file handle STDOUT
format STDOUT =
@<<<<<<<<<<<<<    @<<<<<<<<<<<<<<<<  @>>>>>>   @<<<<<<<<<
$uname,          $home_dir         $disk,    $warn
.
```

The first format statement is the header printed at the top of each page, and the second format statement is used for the lines of the report. Format specifications are terminated with a single period on a line. The second format statement indicates that the variables $uname, $home_dir, $disk, and $warn will be written on each output line, in that order (the variables are defined elsewhere in the script). The line containing the strings of greater-than and less-than signs indicates the starting positions, lengths, and internal justification of the report's fields (text within a field is justified the way the angle bracket points).

Here is the rest of the script used to produce the report:

```perl
open (PASSWD, "/etc/passwd") || die "Can't open passwd: $!\n";

USER:
while (<PASSWD>) {                      # loop over passwd file lines
    chop;
    # lists are enclosed in parentheses
    ($uname,$pass,$uid,$gid,$junk,$home_dir,$junk) = split(/:/);
    # remove newline, parse line, throw out uninteresting entries
    if ($uname eq "root" || $uname eq "nobody" ||
        substr($uname,0,2) eq "uu" ||
        ($uid <= 100 && $uid > 0)) {    # Change UID cutoff if needed
            next USER;
            }
    # set flags on potential security problems
    $warn = ($uid == 0 && $uname ne "root") ? "** UID=0" : "";
    $warn = ($pass ne "!" && $pass ne "*") ? "** CK PASS" : $warn;
    # .= means string concatenation
    $uname .= " ($uid)";                # add UID to username string
    # run du on home directory & extract total size from output
    if (-d $home_dir && $home_dir ne "/") {
        $du = `du -s -k $home_dir`; chop($du);
        ($disk,$junk) = split(/\t/,$du); $disk .= "K";
        }
    else {
        $disk = $home_dir eq "/" ? "skipped" : "deleted";
        }
    write;                              # write out formatted line
    }
exit;
```

This script introduces a couple of new Perl constructs which are explained in its comments.

Graphical Interfaces with Perl

Users greatly prefer graphical interfaces to traditional, text-based ones. Fortunately, it is very easy to produce them with Perl using the Tk module. Here is a simple script that illustrates the general method:

```perl
#!/usr/bin/perl -w
use Tk;                                 # Use the Tk module.

# Read message-of-the-day file.
open MOTD, "/usr/local/admin/motd.txt" || exit;
$first_line=1;
while (<MOTD>) {
    if ($first_line) {                  # Extract the date from line 1.
        chop;
        ($date,@junk)=split();
        $first_line=0;
        }
```

```
    else { $text_block .= $_; }           # Concatenate into $text_block.
    }

my $main = new MainWindow;               # Create a window.
# Window title.
$label=$main->Label(-text => "Message of the Day");
$label->pack;

# Window's text area.
$text=$main->Scrolled('Text', -relief => "sunken",
                       -borderwidth => 2, -setgrid => "true");
$text->insert("1.0", "$text_block");
$text->pack(-side=>"top", -expand=>1, -fill=>"both");

# Window's status area (bottom).
$status = $main->Label(-text=>"Last updated on $date",
                       -relief=>"sunken", -borderwidth=>2,
                       -anchor=>"w");
$status->pack(-side=>"top", -fill=>"x");
# Add a Close button.

$button=$main->Button(-text => "Close Window",
                      # exit when button is pushed:
                      -command => sub{exit});
$button->pack;

MainLoop;                                 # Main event loop: wait for user input.
```

The script has three main parts: processing the text file, creating and configuring the window, and the event loop. The first section reads the text file containing the message of the day, extracts the first field from the first line (assumed to hold the data the file was last modified), and concatenates the rest of its contents into the variable *$text_block*.

The next section first creates a new window (via the new MainWindow function call) and then creates a label for it (assigning text to it), a text area in which text will be automatically filled, a button (labeled "Close Window"), and a status area (again, text is assigned to it). Each of these components is activated using the pack method (function).

Finally, the third section, consisting only of the MainLoop command, displays the window and waits for user input. When the user presses the button, the routine specified to the button's command attribute is called; here, it is the Perl exit command, so the script exits when the button is pushed.

Figure 14-1 illustrates the resulting window.

Note that the fill algorithm used for a simple text area is imperfect.

More complex Perl/Tk programs, including ones accepting user input, are not fundamentally different from this one.

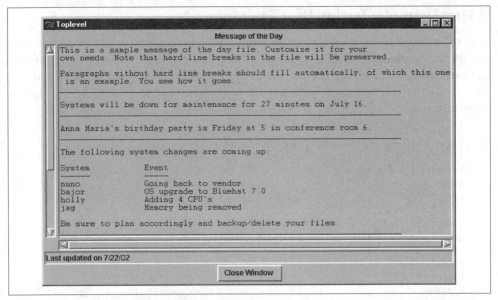

Figure 14-1. Example Perl/Tk output

Expect: Automating Interactive Programs

Don Libes describes his Expect package as "a software suite for automating interactive tools." Expect lets you drive interactive programs from a script. The shell lets you do that too, but only to a very limited extent and not in any general way. Expect lets a script feed input to commands and programs that demand their input from the terminal—meaning */dev/tty*. It also allows different things to happen depending on the output it gets back, which goes far beyond what the shell offers. If this doesn't sound like any big deal—and it didn't to me, at first—read on and consider some of the examples in this section. Expect is actually quite addictive once you begin to figure out what it's good for.

For more information on Expect, see its home page at *http://expect.nist.gov*. The book *Exploring Expect*, by Don Libes (O'Reilly & Associates) is also very helpful.

Conceptually, Expect is a chat script* generalized to the entire Unix universe. Structurally, Expect is actually an extension to another programming language called Tcl. This means that Expect adds commands—and functionality—to the Tcl language. It also means that to build and use Expect, you must also obtain and build Tcl.

---

* Traditionally, a chat script defines the login conversation that occurs between two computers when they connect, and it is made up of a series of expect-send pairs, as in this example:

    ogin: remote ssword: guesswho

This one means, "Wait for the string 'ogin:', then send 'remote', then wait for 'ssword:', then send 'guess-who'."

A First Example: Testing User Environments

The following Expect script illustrates many of the facility's basic features. It is used to run the */usr/local/sbin/test_user* script from a user's account. This shell script tests various security-related features of the user's runtime environment, and it needs to be run as the relevant user. This Expect script allows it to be run by the system administrator:

```
#!/usr/local/bin/expect            Executable location may vary.
# run_test_user - check security of user acct

set user [lindex $argv 0]                # set user to first argument
spawn /bin/sh                            # start a conversation
expect "#"
send "su - $user\r"
expect -re "..* $"
send "/usr/local/sbin/test_user >> /tmp/results\r"
expect -re "..* $"
send "exit\r"
expect "#"
close                                    # end the conversation
```

The first command stores the username specified as the Expect script's argument in the variable *user*. Arguments are stored automatically in the array *argv*, and the lindex Tcl function extracts the first element from the array (numbering begins at zero). In Tcl, square brackets are used to evaluate a function or command and use its return value in another command.

The spawn command begins a conversation; the command specified as its argument is started in a subshell—in this case, the command itself is just a shell—and the Expect script interacts with it via expect and send commands.

expect commands search the output of the spawned command for the first match of a pattern or a regular expression (the latter is indicated by its -re option). When a match is found, the script goes on to the next command; put another way, the script blocks until the desired string is encountered.

send commands provide input to a spawned process (enclosed in quotation marks and usually ending with \r, indicating a carriage return). send commands can include dereferenced variables (as in the first one in the preceding script, whose string contains *$user*).

Thus, the first expect command waits for a sharp sign (#) to appear (the root prompt, since the script will be run by *root*). The following send command transmits a command like su - chavez to the spawned shell. Similarly, the next expect command waits for at least one character and then the end of the output (the latter is denoted by the dollar sign), and the following send command runs the script. Once the next prompt is received, the script sends an exit command to the shell created by the su command; when the root prompt reappears, indicating that the sub-subshell has exited, the script executes the close command, which terminates the spawned command.

This sort of staged conversation represents the simplest use of Expect, although this script also illustrates that Expect can allow you to automate activities that are possible in no other way. Once an Expect script exists, it can be called from a normal shell script just like any other command. For example, this C shell script could be used to automate the testing of a group of user accounts:

```
#!/bin/csh
# test_em_all - security-check user accounts
unset path; setenv PATH "/usr/bin:/bin"

foreach u (`cat /usr/local/admin/check_users`)
    /usr/local/sbin/run_test_user $u
end
```

A Timed Prompt

Here is a timed prompt function. It displays a prompt and waits for user input. If no input is received within a set period of time, the function returns some default value:

```
#!/usr/local/bin/expect
# timed_prompt - prompt with timeout
# args: [prompt [default [timeout]]]

# process arguments
set prompt [lindex $argv 0]
set response [lindex $argv 1]
set tout [lindex $argv 2]
if {"$prompt" == ""} {set prompt "Enter response"}
if {"$tout" == ""} {set tout 5}

set clean_up 1
send_tty "$prompt: "
set timeout $tout
expect "\n" {
    set response [string trimright "$expect_out(buffer)" "\n"]
    set clean_up 0
    }
if {$clean_up == 1} {send_tty "\n"}
send "$response"
```

The first section of the script processes it arguments, assigning them to variables and applying default values. This section of the script is pure Tcl, and it illustrates the language's if statement—everything goes in curly braces. Both these if statements have only a single command in their body, but we'll see more complex examples a bit later. The second if statement also illustrates one of the nicest features of Tcl: the complete equivalence of integers and strings.

The second part of the script does the actual prompting. The send_tty command displays a string on the screen (regardless of any other current conversations), in this case, the prompt string. The set timeout command specifies a timeout period for subsequent expect commands (in seconds, with –1 indicating no timeout).

Given that Expect has built-in timeouts, all the expect command has to look for is a newline (indicating that the user has pressed the return key, ending her input). If a newline is found before the timeout period expires, the *response* variable is assigned the value that the user typed in, minus the final carriage return (via the string Tcl function); if not, then response retains its previous value (the default value specified as the script's second argument). The final command transmits the response (or default value) to the calling script.

The *clean_up* variable is used to keep track of whether a response was entered; if not, a newline is sent to the screen after the expect command times out to avoid a Unix prompt running into the lingering script prompt in an ugly way.

Here is how timed_prompt might be used within a shell script:

```
ishell=`timed_prompt "Enter desired shell [/bin/sh]" "/bin/sh" 10`
```

Repeating a Command Over and Over

In this section, we'll look at another task that is possible in a shell program but is much easier in Expect. This script, loop, runs a command continuously until any character is entered at the keyboard (in a shell script version, you'd have to use CTRL-C to exit). Such a command is very useful for real-time monitoring of any system phenomenon (general system performance, watching a particular process, following some security-related event, and so on).

Here is the script, loop:

```
#!/usr/local/bin/expect
# loop - repeat command until a key is pressed
# args: command [timeout]

set cmd [lindex $argv 0]
set timeo [lindex $argv 1]
if {"$cmd" == ""} {
    send "Usage: loop <command> \[interval]\n"
    exit
    }
if {"$timeo" == ""} {set timeo 3}

set timeout $timeo
set done ""
while {"$done" == ""} {
    system /usr/bin/clear        # run the Unix clear command
    system /usr/bin/$cmd         # run the specified command
    stty raw                     # put terminal in raw mode
    expect "?" {                 # wait for a character
        set done 1
        }
```

```
        stty -raw                        # restore terminal to normal mode
    }
exit
```

The first section of the script again processes command-line arguments and sets the timeout period to the default value of three seconds if necessary. In this case, this means that the desired command will be run once every three seconds.

The second section of the script uses a `while` loop to run the command; as with the `if` command, the condition and body of the loop are both enclosed in curly braces. The first two lines within the loop use the `system` command to run a Unix command without starting a conversation (in contrast to `spawn`), in this case, the `clear` command, followed by the desired command. The latter command is assumed to be in */usr/bin*, but you could modify the script to allow any command to be run. However, should you choose to do so, make sure that a full pathname is included for the command.

The `stty raw` command puts the terminal in raw mode, so that the subsequent expect command will be able to match any single character. When a match is found, the variable *done* is assigned the value 1, which causes the `while` loop to terminate after the terminal has been restored to its normal mode (contrast this with placing the exit command in the body of the expect statement).

Automating Configuration File Distribution

The script we'll look at in this section will illustrate Expect's ability to take different actions depending on what is "said" in the course of a conversation. This script distributes the */etc/hosts* and */etc/shosts.equiv* files to the systems specified as the script's command line arguments.[*]

Here is the first part of the script, which obtains the *root* password:

```
#!/usr/local/bin/expect
# hostdist - distribute hosts and shosts.equiv files

set timeout -1
# get the root password (once!)
stty -echo                          # turn off echoing
send_user "# "                      # prompt for password
expect_user -re "(.*)\n"            # get and remember it
# assign password to variable
send_user "\n"
set passwd $expect_out(1,string)
stty echo                           # turn echo back on
```

---

[*] This script executes in an isolated and trusted network. The actions it performs may or may not make sense in your environment. However, the Expect concepts will still be useful to you. Note that you could also use the rdist facility to perform this function.

The first command turns off expect timeouts, and then the stty command disables echoing while the root password is entered. The expect command, which consumes the entered password, places parentheses around part of the regular expression. These have no effect on whether it is matched in this case, but it does allow whatever matches the enclosed portion of the regular expression to be accessed as a unit later on. This is done two lines later, in the set command, which assigns the saved password to the variable passwd (expect_out is an array that contains the results from the most recent expect command). Once the root password has been obtained, echoing is turned back on.

The next section of the script sets up a loop over the hosts to be updated:

```
set num [llength $argv]                    # number of hosts
incr num -1                                # account for 0-based counting
for {set index 0} {$index <= $num} {incr index} {
    set host [lindex $argv $index]
    spawn /usr/bin/ssh $host
    expect {
       -re "(timed out)|(timeout)" {       # ssh failed
          continue                         # just go on to next host
          }
       -re ".*> *$" {}                     # got a prompt
       }
```

The llength Tcl function returns the length of a list—in this case, this is equivalent to the number of elements in the array *argv*, and the incr command adds a number to a variable (by default, 1), so after the first two commands, the variable *num* holds one less than the number of hosts specified on the command line.

The for loop that begins on the next line makes up the better part of the hostdist script. A Tcl for command has the following general form:

```
for {initialize} {condition} {update} {
    body of the loop
    }
```

(Its structure is very like the C for loop.) The *initialize* clause holds commands to be run before the loop's first iteration, and it usually serves to initialize the loop variable (as it does in our example). The *condition* clause contains a test that determines whether the loop should continue with the next iteration; the *update* clause is run after each loop iteration (and before the next test of the *condition*) and is used to increment the loop variable *index* in our loop.

The first few commands within the body of the loop assign the next hostname in *argv* to the variable host and then execute a spawn command running rlogin to that host. The subsequent expect command is a bit more complex than those we've seen before in that it contains two patterns rather than just one (all enclosed within a pair of curly braces). The first pattern looks for a TCP/IP timeout error message, which would indicate that the ssh command failed; in this case, the continue command causes the script to jump immediately to the next loop iteration. The second pattern searches for a prompt string, which is assumed to end with a greater-than sign (as is true on my systems).

When multiple patterns are included within a single expect command in this way, the first one that matches is used. If more than one pattern matches, the one that occurs earliest in the list is used.

The next section of the script copies the two files from system *iago* to */tmp* on the current remote host. These commands are executed as the user running hostdist because the systems don't trust remote *root* users:

```
# copy the files
send "/usr/bin/rcp iago:/etc/hosts /tmp\r"
expect -re ".*> *$"                        # wait for prompt
send "/usr/bin/rcp iago:/etc/shosts.equiv /tmp\r"
expect -re ".*> *$"                        # wait for prompt
send "/bin/su\r"
expect "assword:"
send "$passwd\r"
```

Once the two rcp commands complete, an su command is given, and the saved *root* password is sent in response to the password prompt.

The next expect command handles commands that are executed as *root*:

```
expect {
    -re "# $" {                            # got a root prompt
        # install new files
        send "/usr/bin/cp /tmp/hosts /etc/hosts\r"
        expect "# $"
        send "/usr/bin/cp /tmp/shosts.equiv /etc/shosts.equiv\r"
        expect "# $"
        send "/usr/bin/chmod 644 /etc/shosts.equiv\r"
        expect "# $"
        send "/usr/bin/rm -f /tmp/hosts /tmp/shosts.equiv\r"
        expect "# $"
        send "exit\r"                      # exit su shell
        expect ".*> *$"                    # wait for prompt
    }

    -re ".*> *$" {}                        # regular prompt: su failed
}
```

The first pattern will match a normal root prompt. When this is received, the script runs the commands that copy the files in */tmp* to */etc*, set their permissions correctly, and remove the originals from */tmp* are executed. Afterwards, the script uses an exit command to end the su shell.

The second pattern in the first expect command matches the normal shell prompt. If it is matched, the su command failed for some reason, and no action is taken (indicated by the empty curly braces following the pattern).

Here is the remainder of the script:

```
    send "logout\r"    # all done with this host
    expect "?"         # accept anything
    close              # terminate spawn command
    }                  # end for loop
exit
```

Once the su shell has terminated (if it ever started), the script sends a logout command to the ssh shell, waits for its output, and terminates the current conversation via the close command.

Keep Trying Until It Works

As our final Expect example, we'll consider a script that repeatedly attempts an operation until it succeeds—a canonical use of Expect. In this case, the operation is to repeatedly dial an electronic mail forwarding service until a successful connection is made.

Here is the script, pester:

```
#!/usr/local/bin/expect
# pester - keep calling until we get through

set done 0                      # did we get through yet?
for {set index 1} {$index <= 2000} {incr index} {
    system "call-command"       # call ISP
    while {$done == 0} {         # continuously check status
        spawn /usr/local/admin/isp_stat
        expect {                # branch depending on results
            -re "(SENDING)|(RECEIVING)" {
                set done 1       # success, so set done to 1
                }
            -re "NO DEV" {
                sleep 120        # line in use; wait a bit
                break
                }
            -re "FAILED" {
                break            # poll failed so try again
                }
            }                    # end expect
        }                        # end while

    if {$done == 1} {break}
    # if we succeeded, end the for loop
    }                            # end for
exit
```

This script actually calls the ISP site only 2000 times before giving up, which is a bit of a hack, but it offers another example of a for loop. The system command executes the appropriate command to initiate the connection, and the subsequent while loop runs a status script—which provides a snapshot of current activity—continuously until a connection is established. The expect command contains three slightly complex regular expressions designed to match the different possible output that the status script can produce (it functions similarly to a case construct).

The break command breaks out of the innermost construct in which it is embedded (i.e., currently in effect). Thus, the break commands in the expect command bodies jump out of the while loop, while the final break command (making up the if body) ends the for loop.

When Only C Will Do

There are some system administrative tasks that cannot be done from a shell script or even from Perl. In such cases, it will be necessary to write a program in a programming language such as C (or whatever you like). However, many of the programming principles we've considered so far still apply.

As a first example, consider this small program, which is a version of the yes command created for a system that lacks it:

```
/* yes.c */
#include <stdio.h>

main(argc,argv)
int argc;
char *argv[];
{
while(1)                    /* repeat forever */
   if(argc>=2)              /* if there was an argument */
      puts(argv[1]);        /* repeat it */
   else
      puts(argv[0]);        /* otherwise use command's name */
}
```

This command works a little differently than the standard yes command in that if no argument is given to the command, it repeats the name it was invoked under rather than "y" by default (if an argument is given, that argument is repeated indefinitely). This allows multiple hard links to be made to the same executable file: yes and no, for example. In virtually every case, repeating "yes" is equivalent to repeating "y".

This version of yes illustrates that C programming need not be incredibly complex and time-consuming, and the program made users on this system quite happy. This program could have been written in Perl, but C is actually easier and more straightforward.

The next C program, designed for an AIX system, illustrates an operation that is best performed in C. This program, setp, assigns a fixed (unvarying) priority to a process (why you might want to do so is discussed in "Monitoring and Controlling Processes" in Chapter 15). Here is a simple version, suitable for a single system administrator's own use:

```
/* setp.c - assign process a fixed priority */
#include <sys/sched.h>
#include <stdio.h>

main(argc,argv)
char *argv[];
int argc;
{
    pid_t pid;
    int p;

    pid=(pid_t)(atoi(*++argv));/* 1st arg is the PID */
    p=atoi(*++argv);/* 2nd arg is the priority */
    setpri(pid,p);/* set it */
    printf("Setting priority of process %d to %d.\n",(int)pid,p);
}
```

The program converts its two arguments to integers with the atoi function and then invokes the AIX setpri system call to actually set the priority. The final print statement is really superfluous in this minimalist version.

The preceding version of setp is fine as an ad hoc tool created by a system administrator for herself. However, if she wants to share it with other members of the system administration staff, it is a little sloppy. Here is a better version (the most important changes are highlighted):

```
/* set_fprio - more careful fixed priority setting utility */
#include <sys/sched.h>
#include <stdio.h>

#include <sys/types.h>
#include <unistd.h>
main(argc,argv)
char *argv[];
int argc;
{
pid_t pid;
int p, old;
/* make sure root is running this */
if (getuid( ) != (uid_t)0) {
    printf("You must be root to run setp.\n");
    exit(1);
    }

/* check for the right number of arguments */
if (argc < 3) {
    printf("Usage: setp pid new-priority\n");
    exit(1);
    }

/* convert arguments to integers */
pid=(pid_t)(atoi(*++argv));
p=atoi(*++argv);
```

```
    old=setpri(pid,p);    /* save and check return value */
    if (old==-1) {
        printf("Priority reset failed for process %d.\n",(int)pid);
        exit(1);
        }
    else {
        printf("Changing priority of process %d from %d to %d.\n", (int)pid,old,p);
        exit(0);
        }
    }
```

These are the most important changes:

- The program first verifies that it is being run by *root*, because the setpri system call only works for *root*. It displays an error message and then exits if someone else tries to use it.

- The program makes sure that it has the proper number of arguments (by determining whether *argc* is less than three or not), again printing an error and exiting if one or both of them is missing.

- The program saves the return value of the setpri system call into the variable *old*. The purpose of this is not to use it in the final print statement—although it is included there—but to determine whether the system call succeeded or not, which is done by the *if* statement. Depending on setpri's return value, an appropriate message is displayed, and the program terminates with a meaningful exit value.

This is the level of care that needs to be taken when writing programs for general or even limited system use. It is not difficult or tremendously time-consuming to do things this way, but it is a bit boring.

Automating Complex Configuration Tasks with Cfengine

Cfengine is a wonderful tool for configuring and maintaining Unix computer systems. Mark Burgess, the author of Cfengine, describes it as follows:

> Cfengine, or the *configuration engine*, is an autonomous agent and a middle to high level policy language for building expert systems which administrate and configure large computer networks. Cfengine uses the idea of classes and a primitive intelligence to define and automate the configuration and maintenance of system state, for small to huge configurations.

What'd he say? Using Cfengine means that you'll have to get used to some unfamiliar jargon, but it's worth it. Basically, what Mark is saying is that Cfengine is a standalone tool (set of tools) that administers and configures computers according to the instructions in its configuration files. The configuration files describe the desired characteristics of various system components using a high-level language which is easy to learn and use (and involves no programming). In this way, Cfengine can automatically bring one or a very large number of systems into line with each one's individually defined configuration specifications. It can also make sure they stay that way by monitoring them and correcting them as needed on an ongoing basis.

In more practical terms, the following list will give you some idea of the breadth of administration and configuration tasks that Cfengine can automate:

- Configure the network interface.
- Edit system configuration files and other text files.
- Create symbolic links.
- Check and correct the permissions and ownership of files.
- Delete unwanted files.
- Compress selected files.
- Distribute files within a network in a correct and secure manner.
- Automatically mount NFS filesystems.
- Verify the presence and integrity of important files and filesystems.
- Execute commands and scripts.
- Manage processes.
- Apply security-related patches and similar corrections.

Cfengine's home page is *http://www.cfengine.org*.

About Cfengine

Cfengine includes the following components:

cfagent
> The main utility that applies a configuration file to the local system.

cfrun
> A utility that applies a configuration file to remote systems

cfservd
> A server process that supports cfrun; it enables the Cfengine agent functionality to be invoked from a remote system

cfexecd
> Another daemon that automates job scheduling and reporting

cfenvd
> An anomaly-detection daemon

cfkey
> A security key-generation utility

Cfengine uses several configuration files (generally stored in */var/cfengine/inputs*). The central configuration file is *cfagent.conf*, which specifies the characteristics of the system that Cfengine is to establish and maintain. Note that in genera,l *cfagent.conf* defines the final desired state of the system; it does not define the steps to take to achieve it.

The best way to introduce this file is with a simple example:

```
control:
    domain = ( ahania.com )          Specify local domain.
    access = ( chavez  root )        Who can run cfagent.
    actionsequence = ( links tidy )  Actions to carry out, in this order.
    maxage = ( 7 )                   Define a variable for later use.

groups:                              Define a list of hosts.
    HaveNoBin = ( blake yeats bogan toi robin )

tidy:                                Action: remove unwanted files.
   /tmp    pattern=*   age=$(maxage) recurse=inf
   /home   pattern=*~  recurse=inf

links:                               Action: maintain symbolic links.
   /logs -> /var/log                 Create this link if needed.

HaveNoBin::                          Create this link only on these hosts.
     /bin -> /usr/bin
```

This file contains four sections, each headed by a keyword followed by a colon. The first section, control, is used to specify general settings for the file, to define variables, and for other similar purposes. In this case, it specifies a list of users who are allowed to run cfagent using this file as input, specifies the sequence of actions that should be carried out when the file is invoked, and defines a variable named maxage, setting its value to 7.

Assignment statements use the syntax illustrated in the example, using parentheses as delimiters:

```
name = ( value )
```

Actions are operations that Cfengine knows how to perform, and they are referred to by keywords. Here, we specify that the tidy action be performed first, followed by the links action. Each referenced action must have a section defining it somewhere in the configuration file.

The next section, groups, defines a list of groups which we've named HaveNoBin. This list will be used in the links section.

The next section in the file is the tidy section, which specifies unwanted files that Cfengine is to remove. These entries have the following general syntax:

```
start-dir [pattern=pattern] [recurse=n] options
```

start-dir is the directory in which to start searching, *pattern* is a pattern against which to match filenames (possibly containing wildcards), *n* indicates how many levels of recursion are wanted (inf means infinite), and *options* are additional options further specifying the files to be selected for removal.

In this case, files under */home* ending with a tilde (and not starting with a period) are chosen (emacs backup files), as are files under */tmp* last modified more than seven days ago. Note that the parameter to the age option is specified using the *maxage* variable.

The final section in the file is the links section, which specifies symbolic links that Cfengine is to maintain. In this case, two such links are listed, using the format:

```
link -> target
```

Here, we specify that the */var/log* directory should be linked to */logs* and also that */bin* should be a link to */usr/bin*. When run, Cfengine checks whether these links exist, creating them if necessary. However, the latter link applies only to hosts in the list HaveNoBin. This is specified by preceding the link specification with a *class* designation (indicated by the double colons). In this case, the class is defined by the host group name, but much more complex classes are possible (as we'll see).

 Actions are performed in the order specified in actionsequence; the ordering of their sections within the configuration file has no effect on their execution order. Thus, in this case, tidy will still be carried out after links even though its section precedes the links section in the configuration file.

Table 14-2 lists the most important Cfengine actions. We'll look at examples of several of them in the next subsection.

Table 14-2. Useful Cfengine actions

Action	Purpose
links	Create/maintain symbolic and hard links.
tidy	Remove unwanted files.
files	Set file ownership and protection, and/or check for modification.
directories	Set directory ownership, protection.
disks	Verify that filesystems are available and contain sufficient free space.
disable	Rename undesirable files to *name.cfengine*.
copy	Copy local or remote files to the local system.
editfiles	Edit ASCII text files.
binservers mailserver homeservers	Specify servers for automatic NFS filesystem mounting by Cfengine.
mountables	Specify local filesystems available for NFS mounting by Cfengine.

Table 14-2. Useful Cfengine actions (continued)

Action	Purpose
miscmounts 1unmount	Specify filesystems to mount or unmount by Cfengine.
processes	Verify the existence of and control processes.
interfaces	Specify characteristics of network interfaces.
resolve	Maintain */etc/resolv.conf*.
defaultroute	Specify the static default gateway.
shellcommands	Execute arbitrary shell commands from within Cfengine.
module:*name*	Use an add-on module.

Actions

We'll begin with a slightly more complicated tidy example:

```
control:
    split = ( " " )
    dirlist = ( "tmp var/tmp 1/scratch 2/scratch" )

tidy:
    /$(dirlist) pattern=* age=3 recurse=inf
```

The control section specifies the list separator character and then defines the variable *dirlist* as a list of four directories. This variable is then used in the tidy specification, and the three options apply to each directory in turn.

The files action is used to specify various desired characteristics and corrective actions for files. Here is an example section:

```
files:
    /etc/security mode=600 owner=root group=0 recurse=inf action=fixall
    /home recurse=inf include=*.dat action=compress
    /var/log/messages owner=root mode=644 action=create
```

The first entry specifies the required ownership and protection of the directory */etc/security* and everything under it. By default, Cfengine checks whether the current settings conform to these specifications. Here, however, action=fixall tells Cfengine to modify the current settings if necessary to match the specified ones.

The second entry causes all files with an extension of *.dat* under */home* to be compressed. The third entry creates the file */var/log/messages* if it does not exist.

The files action can also be used to verify the integrity of system executables in */usr/bin*:

```
control:
    ChecksumDatabase = ( /usr/local/admin/cfengine/cksums )

files:
    /usr/bin checksum=md5 exclude=*.sav action=warnall
```

The database file used to store the correct checksums for files is specified in the control section, and the checksum option in the `files` entry specifies that the comparison be made. A warning will be issued for each incorrect checksum.

On Solaris systems, Cfengine can also specify ACLs for files:

```
acl:                                    Define an ACL.
    { secure1
        method:overwrite                Replace current ACL (default is "append").
        fstype:posix
        default_user:*:=rwx
        default_group:chem:=rwx
        default_other:*:=
        user:chavez:=rwx
        user:mark:+rx
        user:toreo:=r
        mask:*:rwx
    }
files:
    /private acl=secure1 action=fixall
```

The `acl` section defines one or more named ACLs, which can then be specified for files (see "Protecting Files and the Filesystem" in Chapter 7 for more information about access control lists).

The `disable` action causes Cfengine to rename files which ought not to be present on this system:

```
disable:
    /etc/hosts.equiv
    home/.rhosts  inform=true
    /var/log/messages rotate=6
```

The first two entries cause Cfengine to rename the indicated files if they exist, adding the extension *.cfengine*. In the second case, the special directory keyword home is used to refer to all user home directories. In this case, Cfengine also issues a warning message when such files are found.

The third entry illustrates another use for the `disable` section: log file rotation. The entry tells Cfengine to maintain six old copies of *the /var/log/messages* file. As with other log rotation facilities, the saved files are given the extensions *.1* through *.6*.

The following actions specify the default gateway and name server list for the system:

```
defaultroute:                   Specify default gateway.
    192.168.20.44
resolve:                        Name server list.
    192.168.1.1
    192.168.10.24
```

Cfengine adds a static route for the specified default gateway if one does not already exist. Similarly, the servers listed in the resolve section are added to */etc/resolv.conf* if necessary, and the resulting server list are ordered as indicated in the resolve section of *cfagent.conf*.

The processes action may be used to tell Cfengine to verify that important processes are running, restarting them if necessary, as well as to have Cfengine signal processes:

```
processes:
    "sendmail" restart "/usr/sbin/sendmail" useshell=false inform=true
    "inetd" signal=hup
    "kudzu" signal=kill
    "g02" matches<=2 signal=suspend action=bymatch inform=true
```

The first field in each entry is a pattern that is matched against the output of the ps command.* In general, Cfengine will apply the entry's specifications to each matching process.

The first entry causes Cfengine to determine if there is a sendmail daemon running. If not, one is started using the specified command. The useshell options says not to use a subshell when restarting the daemon (see the Cfengine documentation for the rationale and implementation details).

The next two entries specify signals to be sent to the inetd and kudzu processes if they are present.

The final entry causes Cfengine to search for processes matching the string "g02", and it will count the number of such processes. The entry specifies that the desired system state include no more than two such processes. The action=bymatch option tells Cfengine to correct the situation when this condition is not met, according to the directives of the other options. In this case, if there are more than two such processes—i.e., if the desired condition specified by matches=<2 is not met—it suspends all of them (signal=suspend) and outputs a message indicating this.

The editfiles action can be used to make changes to ASCII text files. It is very useful for maintaining certain system configuration files. For example, the following section tells Cfengine to disable some inetd-based unwanted services:

```
editfiles:
    { /etc/inetd.conf
        HashCommentLinesContaining "rlogin"
        HashCommentLinesContaining "rexec"
        HashCommentLinesContaining "finger"
        HashCommentLinesContaining "tftp"
    }
```

Similarly, the following section tells Cfengine to add a line to existing user *.login* scripts if it is not already present:

```
editfiles:
    { home/.login
        AppendIfNoSuchLine  "/usr/local/bin/motd.pl"
    }
```

---

* More specifically, ps aux on BSD-like systems, and ps -ef on System V–based systems.

See the Cfengine documentation for full details on the capabilities of this action.

The copy action is used to tell Cfengine to copy local or remote files to the local system, as in these simple examples:

```
copy:
    /aux/save/etc/ntp.drift dest=/etc/ntp.drift mode=644
    /aux/save/etc/shells dest=/etc/shells mode=644
    /masterfiles/etc/hosts.deny serverfilemaster
        dest=/etc/hosts.deny owner=root group=0 mode=644
```

The first two entries specify local files to be copied from the source—the first field—to the destination location (dest= option). The third entry causes a file to be copied from *filemaster:/masterfiles/etc/hosts.deny* to */etc/hosts.deny* on the local system. The copied file will be assigned the specified ownership and file protection mode.

Classes

Here is a more complex copy section, which also reintroduces Cfengine classes:

```
copy:
    linux::
        $(masteretc)/rc.config dest=/etc/rc.config o=root mode=644

    ShadowHosts::
        $(masteretc)/passwd server=$(pwdmaster) dest=/etc/passwd
            owner=0 group=0 mode=644 trustkey=true
        $(masteretc)/shadow server=$(pwdmaster) dest=/etc/shadow
            owner=0 group=0 mode=600 trustkey=true encrypt=true
```

The first copy operation will occur only on Linux systems, and it consists of copying the file *rc.config* from the location specified in the *masteretc* variable (defined elsewhere in the configuration file) to */etc* and assigning the specified ownership and protection.

The second subsection applies only to the host group ShadowHosts, and it contains two copy specifications. They tell Cfengine to update */etc/passwd* and */etc/shadow* from master copies located on a remote host, specifying the required ownership and permissions. In both cases, the copy operation must use the Cfengine trusted key security mechanism (to ensure that the data is really coming from the source it purports to), and the shadow password file is transmitted in encrypted form.

The cfkey utility is used to set up trusted keys on systems using Cfengine. It must be run before these features can be used.

 cfkey requires a large amount of random data to function properly. If your system does not provide */dev/random* (or it does not work effectively), you must run the cfenvd daemon for a week before you install Cfengine to give it enough time to collect the required random data. cfkey will fail with the error message "error: PRNG not seeded" unless a sufficient amount of random data is available.

Cfengine classes are made up of one or more of the following components:

- An operating system keyword. These include: hpux, aix, solaris, freebsd, linux, osf, and NT. The `cfagent -p -v` command shows keywords defined for the current system.
- A host name.
- A host group name (as defined in the groups section)
- A name of a day of the week.
- An hour of the day, in the format H*nn*: Hr14 for 2:00 P.M.
- A minute of the hour, in the format Min*nn*: Min33 for 33 past the hour.
- A 5-minute interval, in the format Min*n_n+5*: Min00_05 for the first five minutes of the hour. Note that *n* must be divisible by 5.
- A quarter hour, in the format Q*n*: Q2 for the second quarter hour. This construct can also be combined with an hour: e.g., Hr02_Q3 for 2:30–2:44 P.M.
- A day of the month, in the format Day*n*: Day1 for the first.
- A month name.
- A year, in the format Y*rnnnn*: Yr2001 for 2001.
- A locally defined class name:

      control:
              addclasses = (myclass)

The default class is any, which matches any host at any time. Unspecified time and date classes default to all. Multiple classes are joined by periods (AND logic) or vertical bars (OR logic).

Here are some examples:

Class specification	Matches ...
solaris.Monday.Hr01::	*Solaris systems on Mondays at 1:00 A.M.*
aix|hp-ux::	*AIX and HP-UX systems.*
aix.!vader::	*AIX systems except host vader.*
December.Day31.Friday::	*December 31 if it is a Friday.*
Monday.$(fourtimes)::	*Four specified each hour times on Monday.*

The final example uses a list of times defined earlier:

    control:
        fourtimes = (Min03 Min18 Min34 Min49)

If both AND and OR joins are used, ANDs are evaluated first:

Class specification	Matches ...
solaris|aix.Monday.Hr01::	*Solaris systems always;*
	AIX systems on Mondays at 1:00 A.M.
(solaris|aix).Monday.Hr01::	*Solaris and AIX systems on Mondays at 1:00 A.M.*

Classes can be used in any context within the configuration file. In this example, they are used to define a variable differently for different operating systems:

```
control:
   linux::    swaptest = ( /usr/bin/free -m -o )
   aix::      swaptest = ( /usr/sbin/lsps -a )
...
shellcommands:
   $(swaptest) > $(reportdir)/swap_report.out
```

Cfengine interprets unknown class names as hostnames. If no such host exists, the class is ignored. This fact can be used to temporarily disable a section's classes by altering the associated class name (or adding one):

```
Xlinux::
Xany::
```

Real *cfagent.conf* files can become very large, so you may want to use the include file mechanism, the import action. For example, the following configuration file consists entirely of included files whose divisions are used to make each individual file more manageable:

```
import:
   cf.groupdefs                     Always include these files.
   cf.common

   hpux: cf.hpux                     Operating system specific includes.
   aix: cf.aix
   linux: cf.linux
   and so on
```

Configuring cfservd

The Cfengine server has its own configuration file. Here is a simple example:

```
# cfservd.conf
control:
   domain = ahania.com
   cfrunCommand = ( "/var/cfengine/bin/cfagent" )
   IfElapsed = ( 1 )
   ExpireAfter = ( 15 )
   MaxConnections = ( 50 )
   MultipleConnections = ( true )
   LogAllConnections = ( true )
   TrustKeysFrom = ( 192.168.10/24 )
   DynamicAddresses = ( 192.168.10.100-200 )
   topdir = ( /aux/crengine/masterfiles )

grant:                              Grant access to files.
   $(topdir)/outgoing    *.ahania.com

deny:                               Deny access to files.
   $(topdir)/outgoing    maverick.ahania.com
```

The daemon also requires an addition to *etc/services*:

```
cfengine    5308/tcp
```

Finally, you must start the daemon at boot time by adding it to one of the system boot scripts.

Running Cfengine

Once set up, Cfengine may be run manually on the local system with the `cfagent` command. It has the following useful options:

-f *file*

> Specify an alternate configuration file (the default configuration file is */var/cfengine/inputs/cfagent.conf*).

-v

> Verbose output mode.

-n

> Preview a Cfengine run: indicate what would be done, but don't actually perform any actions.

-N *class*

> Disable the specified user-defined class.

The `cfrun` utility is used to initiate Cfengine runs on remote systems. It has the following syntax:

```
cfrun [host-list] [local-options] [-- remote-options] [-- classes]
```

For example, the following command runs Cfengine on hosts *smiley*, *toby*, and *percy* and provides verbose output on the local system:

```
# cfrun smiley toby percy
```

The following command runs Cfengine on all hosts listed in the *cfrun.conf* configuration file (see the documentation for details), although execution will occur only on remote Linux and Solaris systems:

```
# cfrun -v -- -- linux solaris
```

To automate Cfengine runs, use the `cfexecd` daemon (which you must also add to the system startup scripts). Once it is running, you can configure when Cfengine runs via a *cfagent.conf* entry like this one:

```
control:
    schedule = ( Min00_05 Min15_20 Min30_35 Min45_50 )
```

This example will cause Cfengine to run four times an hour.

Stem: Simplified Creation of Client-Server Applications

In this section, we'll look at Stem, a package that makes it very easy to create sophisticated client-server applications for administrative services. Stem is a relatively new open source package developed by Uri Guttman. The project's home page is *http://www.stemsystems.com*. Stem can be used to create a variety of useful client-server applications, including ones that are network-based. In essence, Stem allows you to create complex applications with only script-level effort.

 Running the Stem demonstration programs is a good way to get used to Stem's capabilities. The ones discussed in this section are available from my website (*http://www.aeleen.com*).

Installing Stem is straightforward. Once installed, Stem provides you with the ability to create communicating processes via simple configuration files and ordinary Unix commands (or scripts). Stem handles all interprocess communication for you transparently. As we'll see, Stem can be used to create entirely new applications and can also serve as the conduit that allows existing commands and programs to communicate regardless of their individual interfaces.

To understand some Stem examples, we first need to define a few terms:

- A *hub* is a Stem daemon running on a computer system. Stem applications consist of one or more interconnected hubs.

- A Stem *cell* is an object within a Stem hub. Cells provide the various parts of the applications functionality. Stem cells are objects.[*] As such, they have unique names, a list of attributes that can be set, and some defined methods (functions that perform various operations on them).

  Stem defines three kinds of cells: a *class* cell (a defined cell type), an *object* cell (an actual instance of some class cell making up part of a hub), and a *cloned* cell (the second and later instances of a cell type that allows for multiple cells to be created from it).

- The communications between cells are called *messages*. Messages can consist of any kind of data. Messages are addressed by a triple of *hub:cell:target*, where *hub* and *cell* are the names of the hub and cell to which the message should be sent, and *target* is sometimes used to further specify the message's destination in some cells.

---

[*] Stem uses many terms from object-oriented programming.

Let's look at a simple Stem application which illustrates these items. It is shown in Figure 14-2. This application creates a three-way chat. The three windows in the figure each represent one of the chatters. I've numbered the various lines in the chat to indicate the order in which they were entered. If you look at the figure closely, you'll notice that this chat is somewhat unusual in that not all messages go to every window. In fact, messages from both A and C go only to the sender himself and to B, while messages from B go to everyone..

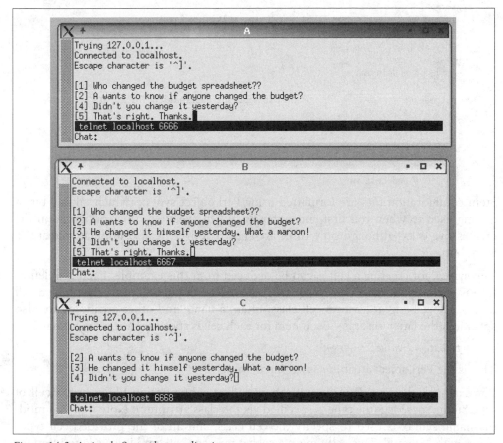

Figure 14-2. A simple Stem chat application

This application was created without any programming. The main part of it is created using this Stem configuration file, named *chat1.stem* (*.stem* is the extension used for Stem configuration files):

```
# simple chat
[
class => 'Stem::SockMsg',
name  => 'A',
args  => [
   port       => 6666,          # communications port for this cell
```

```
    server   => 1,              # listen for connections
    cell_attr => [
        'data_addr' => ':sw:x'  # send input to cell to this address
        ], # end cell_attr
    ],      # end args
],          # end cell A
```
Cells B and C created here, using ports 6667 and 6668, and targets of y and z (respectively).
```
class => 'Stem::Switch',
name  => 'sw',
args  => [
    in_map => [                 # input map: multiplex input
        x => [ qw( x y ) ],
        y => [ qw( x y z ) ],
        z => [ qw( y z ) ],
        ], # end in_map

    out_map => [                # output map: set destination for inputs
        x => 'A',
        y => 'B',
        z => 'C',
        ], # end out_map
    ],      # end args
],          # end cell sw
```

Stem configuration files are formatted using Perl object syntax (which takes a bit of getting used to when you first encounter it). When executed, this configuration file creates five cells (although only three are shown above). It also implicitly creates a Stem hub.

The syntax for creating a cell is can be deduced from this example. Each cell definition is enclosed within a pair of square brackets located in column 1. Defining a cell involves specifying at least its cell class; often, a name and other attributes are also specified (the latter via args). Each item for each cell is specified using the format:

> *attribute => value,*

This is the Perl object attribute assignment syntax.

For example, the first definition in the preceding configuration file creates a cell of type Stem::SockMsg (the type is specified via the class attribute). Note that Perl module name syntax is used to specify the cell class, and all of the provided cell types begin with "Stem::". This cell type is a socket message cell, and it is used to interface external programs to Stem. In this case, we will use it to interface a window to the Stem hub. This cell is given the name A, and several attributes are defined via the args list (enclosed in square brackets). The communications port the cell will use is set, the cell is specified as a server (meaning that it will listen for communications on the port), and the address for messages is specified via the data_addr attribute of the cell_info element in the args list; note that each subordinate list is always enclosed in square brackets. The address given here specifies the current hub (indicated by the empty first field), the cell named *sw*, and the target *x* within that cell. Thus, all input received by this cell will be sent to target *x* in cell *sw*.

The actual configuration file contains two more SockMsg cell specifications, for the B and C chat windows. They are defined similarly, although they have different port numbers and message addresses.

The final cell defined in the configuration file is a switch cell (class Stem::Switch) named *sw*. This type of cell receives messages from other cells and routes them to other cells based on the instructions in its two maps. The maps are specified using its two arguments. The input map defines a list of targets that incoming messages can reference. For each one, the map also defines the list of targets to which messages designated for it should be sent. This is done via another Perl square-bracketed list. The target names included in the list must be quoted, and the Perl qw function is used to do so.

In this case, we see that messages coming in for target *x* will be sent to targets *x* and *y*, those for target *y* will go to all three targets, and those for target *z* will go to targets *y* and *z*.

The output map associates switch targets with other cells. In this case, target *x* is associated with cell A, *y* with B, and *z* with C (as expected). Taken with the input map, this mapping results in the message display behavior we saw in the actual application (see Figure 14-2).

Once the cells are defined, all that remains is to start the Stem process and attach user processes to the ports to which the cells are listening. Here are the commands to do so:

```
xterm -T Chat -n Chat -geometry 80x40+500+0 -e run_stem chat1
xterm -T A -n A -geometry 80x10+0+0 -e ssfe -prompt Chat: telnet localhost 6666
xterm -T B -n B -geometry 80x10+0+175 -e ssfe -prompt Chat: telnet localhost 6667
xterm -T C -n C -geometry 80x10+0+350 -e ssfe -prompt Chat: telnet localhost 6668
```

We use four xterm windows for this simple demonstration application. The first one runs the *run_stem* script included with the Stem package. This creates a Stem hub using the specified configuration file (here, *chat1.stem*). The other three commands run ssfe, a program which provides an input prompt at the bottom of the window while running a specified command (ssfe is included with Stem). Here, we use the telnet command to attach to the ports we specified when creating the socket message cells.

Note that I omitted the Stem hub windows from the previous figure. In fact, that window is also active, and the addition of one additional cell to the configuration file will allow you to interact directly with the hub:

```
[
class  => 'Stem::TtyMsg',
args   => [ ],
],
```

This cell is a TTY message cell, and it creates a command interface to a Stem hub. For this cell, the args attribute is set to an empty list. You can use this command interface to modify the functioning of the running application. For example, you can redefine the switch maps on the fly.

The next logical step is to create a chat program where chatters can be on different computer systems. This will involve a Stem hub on each system where someone is chatting. This is the configuration file that could be used on a client system:

```
# chat_cli.stem
[
class      =>      'Stem::Hub',
name       =>      'chat_client2',
args       =>      [ ],
],

# create a portal for communicating with other hubs
[
class      =>      'Stem::Portal',
args       =>      [ ],
],

[
class      =>      'Stem::SockMsg',
name       =>      'B',
args       =>      [
port              => 6668,
    server            => 1,
    cell_attr         => [
        'data_addr'       => 'chat_server:sw:z'
        ],  # end cell_attr
    ],       # end args
],           # end cell B
```

In this example configuration file, we explicitly create the Stem hub, naming it *chat_client1*. The second cell definition creates a *portal*: an object used for communication between distinct hubs. In this case, this hub will use it to send messages to the Stem hub running the chat server. The final cell definition creates a cell named C, and it uses port 6668 on the local host for communication, and specifies it message destination address as sw:z (target *z* in cell *sw* on hub *chat_server*).

The following commands can be used to start the client application, including the required windows:

```
xterm -T Chat -n Chat -geometry 80x40+500+0 -e run_stem chat_cli
xterm -T C -n C -geometry 80x10+0+350 -e ssfe -prompt Chat: telnet localhost 6668
```

These commands will create the hub process and one chat window.

Here is the configuration file for the chat server:

```
# chat_serv.stem
[
class => 'Stem::Hub',
name => 'chat_server',
args => [ ],
],
```

```
[
class => 'Stem::Portal',
args  => [
   'server' => 1,     # listen for messages from other hubs
   'host' => ''       # accept messages from any host
   ],
],

[
class => 'Stem::SockMsg',
name  => 'A',
args  => [
   port            => 6666,
   server          => 1,
   cell_attr       => [
      'data_addr'     => ':sw:x'
      ],
   ],
],

[
 class    =>      'Stem::Switch',
 name     =>      'sw',
 args     =>      [
   in_map => [  # everybody sees everything
      x => [ qw( x y z ) ],
      y => [ qw( x y z ) ],
      z => [ qw( x y z ) ],
      ],

   out_map => [
      x => 'chat_server:A',
      y => 'chat_client1:B',
      z => 'chat_client2:B',
      ],
   ],
],
```

The first two definitions create the hub (named *chat_server*) and a server portal that will listen for messages from other hubs from any host (the latter is indicated by the null host attribute). The next definition creates a chat cell on the local host (named A), and the final definition defines a switch cell. In this case, all input received from any target will be sent to every target.

The following commands will start the Stem processes used for the chat server:

```
xterm -T Chat -n Chat -geometry 80x40+500+0 -e run_stem chat_serv
xterm -T A -n A -geometry 80x10+0+0 -e ssfe -prompt Chat: telnet localhost 6666
```

Note that we do not have to specify the host names where the Stem hubs are running anywhere in this configuration. Stem automatically handles that for us.

Lots of different kinds of tasks can be performed using this same basic structure. For example, we'll now consider a simple monitoring application that is very similar in stucture to the preceding chat application. Here is the client configuration file:

```
# mon_cli.stem
[
class => 'Stem::Hub',
name  => 'collecting',
args  => [ ],
],
[
class => 'Stem::Portal',
args  => [ ],
],

[
class => 'Stem::Proc',
name  => 'do_it',
args  => [
    path              => '/usr/local/sbin/my_mon',
    cell_attr         => [
        'data_addr'        => 'monitoring:A:A',
        'send_data_on_close'  => 1,
        ],
    ],
],
```

The first three cell definitions create the hub and portal. The final section of the configuration file creates a process cell named *do_it*. Process cells can create and control processes. The path attribute specifies the path to the command or program to be run. In this case, a simple system monitoring script is selected. The cell_attr attribute once again specifies the message destination address where all input received by the cell will be sent. In this case, the cell's input consists of the output from the created process. The final attribute, send_data_on_close, tells the cell to transmit all remaining input when the process ends. It is used to avoid message delays due to data buffering on the local host.

The server portion of the application is created using this configuration file:

```
# mon_serv
[
class => 'Stem::Hub',
name  => 'monitoring',
args  => [ ],
],
[
class => 'Stem::Portal',
args  => ['server' => 1, 'host' => '' ],
],
[
class => 'Stem::SockMsg',
name  => 'A',
```

```
    args => [
       port     => 6666,
       server   => 1,
       cell_attr => [
          'data_addr' => 'monitoring:A:A',
          ],
       ],
    ],
```

Note the similarities to the chat server configuration file. This file creates a hub, portal (as a server portal), a TTY interface to the hub, and a single socket message cell. No switch is needed in this case, as we just want the monitoring output from the client hub to be displayed in a window by the server hub.

So how does this work? The following commands will start the required processes:

On the client
```
xterm -T Client -n Client -geometry 80x40+500+0 -e run_stem mon_cli
```

On the server
```
xterm -T Trigger -n Trigger -geometry 80x40+500+0 -e run_stem mon_serv
xterm -T Monitor -n Monitor -geometry 80x10+0+0 -e telnet localhost 6666
```

Then, in the Stem hub window on the server (Trigger), enter the command:

```
Stem> collecting:do_it cell_trigger
```

This will cause the process cell *do_it* on the client hub to be triggered.* It will then run its associated process and return the appropriate message(s) to the server hub. The messages will then be displayed in the window labeled Monitor. Each one will look like the following:

```
date: Wed Jul 24 01:33:40 EDT 2002
load average: 5.07
total processes: 294
free memory: 4404
-------------------------------------------------
```

This is the output of the script *my_mon*. Note that a similar command to the server hub could be used to perform the same task on a different client system.

This application can easily be made more automated. For example, this implementation assumes that the Stem client processes are already running on the client. However, the *boot_stem* script which is part of the Stem package can be used instead to start the remote client processes instead. In addition, the triggering command to the Stem server hub can also be automated via a script. More complex monitoring applications are also possible with a little more work.

Stem includes a variety of useful predefined cell types. Some of the most useful are listed below:

---

* Technically, this command initiates a message that causes the *do_it* cell's cell_trigger method to be invoked.

Stem::Log

Writes to and manages external log files. Entry formats can be specified via the cell attributes, and the data can be filtered according to a variety of criteria.

Stem::Log::Tail

Monitors external log files for additions. Newly found data can be sent into the Stem application on demand or according to a schedule.

Stem::Cron

Creates and manages scheduled messages transmissions. We've considered only information messages in this section, but in fact Stem messages are actually much more powerful than that. They can be used to initiate any valid operation within any Stem cell.

Stem::AsyncIO

Manages buffered I/O for other cells.

We'll return to the chat application for our final example, which will illustrate creating a simple custom Stem cell type. We will create a cell which receives input, prepends a label to it, and then sends it on to another cell. We will interpose this cell between the chat socket message cells and the switch cell in order to label chat text with its originating window.

Stem cell classes are defined in Perl modules. Here is the Perl code that corresponds to the new cell type (stored as *Stem/ChatLabel.pm* with respect to the location of the chat configuration files):

```
package Stem::ChatLabel;
use strict;

# define cell attributes
my $attr_spec = [
    { 'name' => 'sw_addr', },                  # target switch cell
    { 'name' => 'hub_addr', 'default' => '', },   # target hub
    { 'name' => 'sbefore', 'default' => '', },    # label string
    ];

# called when the cell is created (boilerplate code)
sub new {
    my( $class ) = shift ;
    my $self = Stem::Class::parse_args($attr_spec, @_);
    return $self unless ref $self ;
    return $self ;
    }

# called whenever data is received by the cell
sub data_in {
    my ($self, $msg) = @_;
    # get message data
    my $data = $msg->data();

    # add the label prefix to the current message (if any)
```

```
substr($$data, 0, 0, $msg->from_cell() . ': ') ;
substr($$data, 0, 0, $self->{'sbefore'} . '_') if $self->{'sbefore'};

# create and send modified message
$msg->data($data) ;
$msg->to_cell($self->{'sw_addr'}) ;
$msg->to_hub($self->{'hub_addr'}) if $self->{'hub_addr'};
$msg->dispatch() ;
}

1 ;   # module exit
```

After the initial module definition and use strict statements, the file defines the attributes this cell class will use (in addition to ones used by all cells). This is accomplished by defining $attr_spec. This cell will have three additional attributes: the name of the switch cell where the modified messages should be sent, the hub name where that switch is located (default to the current hub), and the string that should be prepended to the message text (defaults to a null string, but see below).

The next section of the file defines the new() method for this cell. This is the constructor method called when a cell of this type is created. The code here is that typically used for Stem cells, and it was simply copied from the module for another cell.

The final function creates the data_in method for this cell type. This method is invoked whenever a cell of this type receives a message. In this case, the function extracts the current string using the message's data() method. Next, it adds the prefix string if one was defined, using the originating cell name if none was specified in the configuration file. Finally, the data_in method modifies the message's address, substituting its own hub and switch selections for the current ones, and then the message is dispatched.

Here are the relevant portions of the client configuration file showing how this cell can be used:

```
[
class => 'Stem::SockMsg',
name  => 'A',
args  => [
    port      => 6666,
    server    => 1,
    cell_attr => [
      'data_addr' => ':lab:a'  # destination cell = ChatLabel cell
], ], ],

[
class   =>      'Stem::ChatLabel',
name    =>      'lab',
args    =>      [
    sw_addr  => 'sw',          # switch cell name
    hub_addr => 'chat_srv',    # chat server hub name
], ],
```

The socket message cell's message destination cell is changed to the label cell. The label cell itself specifies the server hub name and the switch cell name on that hub. The rest of the configuration file is unchanged.

In this case, messages will be labeled with the name of the socket message cell that received them (since no message prefix attribute was specified for the ChatLabel cell), as in this example:

```
A: Pizza is ok for lunch as long as it is vegetarian.
```

This overview has introduced you only to Stem's most basic capabilities. For more information about Stem and what it can do, consult the package documentation and its home page. As I said before, experimenting with its demo programs and these examples is a good way to become familiar with the package and how it works.

Adding Local man Pages

There's an old and somewhat scatological saying about a job not being finished until the paperwork is done.* In the case of creating scripts and programs, this means writing some sort of documentation. Tools you create can be documented in many different ways, but the usual Unix practice is to produce an online manual page. We'll conclude this chapter with a brief look at creating manual pages for the tools you develop.

Manual-page files are named for the command or utility that they describe, and they are given an extension that matches the number or letter of the *man* subdirectory in which they reside. For example, a manual-page file for the wgrep command placed into *man1* subdirectory would be named *wgrep.1*.†

The simplest possible manual page is just a text file describing a command or topic. However, if you'd like to create something a bit more elaborate, and more like the other manual pages typically found on Unix systems, it is very easy to do so. Manual-page source files are designed for the nroff text formatting system,‡ and they combine the text of the manual page with nroff directives specifying how to format the text. (Not all Unix versions provide the text formatting utilities by default or at all.)

The best way to figure out what the various nroff directives do is to see them in context. In general, they are placed at the beginning of a line and start with a period. Here is a brief manual page source file for the wgrep command, which can also serve as a template for manual pages you might create:

---

* Imagine how it applies to writing a book.

† Perl programs are traditionally documented with POD, a scheme for embedding the documentation in the Perl source. Ugh.

‡ Or the GNU equivalent, groff.

```
.TH wgrep 1
.SH NAME
wgrep - windowed grep utility
.SH SYNOPSIS
wgrep [options] regexp file(s)
.SH DESCRIPTION
.B wgrep
is a
.B grep
utility which prints a window of lines surrounding
each matching line that it finds in the list of files.
By default, the window is three lines before and after
each matching line.
.PP
.B wgrep
has many options which control how its output looks.
It can range from plain to painfully excessive.
.SH OPTIONS
.TP 5
.B -w
Specifies the window size in the form
.B before:after Either one can be omitted.
.TP 5
.B -n
Include line numbers before each printed line.
.TP 5
.B -s
Include asterisks in front of matching lines.
.PP
.SH BUGS
None of course.
.SH SEE ALSO
egrep(1), VMS SEARCH command
```

Here is how the formatted version might look:

wgrep(1)   wgrep(1)
NAME
        wgrep - windowed grep utility

SYNOPSIS
        wgrep [options] regexp file(s)

DESCRIPTION
        wgrep is a **grep** utility which prints a window of lines surrounding each
        matching line that it finds in the list of files. By default, the window is
        three lines before and after each matching line.
        wgrep has many options which control how its output looks. It can range from
        plain to painfully excessive.

OPTIONS
        -w   Specifies the window size in the form **before:after**.
                Either one can be omitted.
        -n   Include line numbers before each printed line.
        -s   Include asterisks in front of matching lines.

BUGS

      `None, of course.`

SEE ALSO

      `egrep(1), VMS SEARCH command`

Table 14-3 lists the `nroff` directives used in the sample manual page along with other related and useful directives.

Table 14-3. Useful nroff constructs

Directive	Explanation
`.TH` *name section*	Title heading.
`.SH` *NAME*	Section heading (names are uppercase by convention).
`.TP` *[n]*	Tagged paragraph: use hanging indent (of *n* spaces if specified).
`.PP`	Start new filled paragraph.
`.IP`	Indented paragraph.
`.nf`	Stop text filling (adjusting words on lines).
`.fi`	Start text filling.
`.B` *text*	Use bold type for text given as its argument.
`.I` *text*	Italicize text given as its argument.
`.R` *text*	Use roman type for text given as its argument.

You can simulate a `man` command for a manual page you are developing with a command like this one:

```
$ nroff -man file | more
```

If you want a printed version of this (or any other) manual page, you'll need to use the `troff` command as well as other printing-related typesetting utilities provided on the system.

## CHAPTER 15

Managing System Resources

This chapter describes the tools and facilities Unix offers for monitoring and managing the system's CPU, memory, disk and network resources, including some of the limitations inherent in the Unix approach. The first part of the chapter provides an overview of system performance considerations and then discusses Unix processes. The chapter then goes on to consider managing the various sytem resources—CPU, memory, local and network I/O, disk space—in detail.

A large part of managing any system resource is knowing how to measure and interpret its current state, and so we'll spend some time looking at ways to monitor resources and to track their use over time.

This chapter provides a detailed introduction to performance monitoring and tuning. For more detailed information about tuning Unix systems, I recommend these books:

- *System Performance Tuning* by Gian-Paolo D. Musameci and Mike Loukides (O'Reilly). This work focuses on Solaris and Linux systems.
- *AIX Performance Tuning* by Frank Waters (Prentice Hall).
- *HP-UX Tuning and Performance* by Robert F. Sauers and Peter S. Weygant (Hewlett-Packard Professional Books).
- *Solaris Internals* by Jim Mauro and Richard McDougall (Prentice Hall).
- *NFS and NIS* by Hal Stern, Mike Eisler, and Ricardo Labiaga (O'Reilly).

Thinking About System Performance

Why is the system so slow? is probably second on any system administrator's things-I-least-want-to-hear list (right after *Why did the system crash again?!*). Like system reliability, system performance is a topic that comes up only when there is a problem. Unfortunately, no one is likely to compliment or thank you for getting the most out of the system's resources.

System performance–related complaints can take on a variety of forms, ranging from sluggish interactive response time, to a job that takes too long to complete or is unable to run at all because of insufficient resources.

In general, system performance depends on how efficiently a system's resources are applied to the current demand for them by various jobs in the system. The most important system resources from a performance perspective are CPU, memory, and disk and network I/O, although sometimes other device I/O can also be relevant. How well a system performs at any given moment is the result of both the total demand for the various system resources and how well the competition among processes* for them is being managed. Accordingly, performance problems can arise from a number of causes, including both a lack of needed resources and ineffective control over them. Addressing a performance problem involves identifying what these resources are and figuring out how to manage them more effectively.

 Know What Normal Is

As with most of life, performance tuning is much harder when you have to guess what normal is. If you don't know what the various system performance metrics usually show when performance is acceptable, it will be very hard to figure out what is wrong when performance degrades. Accordingly, it is essential to do routine system monitoring and to maintain records of performance-related statistics over time.

When the lack of a critical resource is the source of a performance problem, there are a limited number of approaches to improving the situation. Put simply, when you don't have enough of something, there are only a few options: get more, use less, eliminate inefficiency and waste to make the most of what you have, or ration what you have. In the case of a system resource, this can mean obtaining more of it (if that is possible), reducing job or system requirements to desire less of it, having its various consumers share the amount that is available by dividing it between them, having them take turns using it, or otherwise changing the way it is allocated or controlled.

For example, if your system is short of CPU resources, your options for improving things may include some or all of the following:

- Adding more CPU capacity by upgrading the processor.
- Adding additional processors to allow different parts of the work load to proceed in parallel.
- Taking advantage of currently unused CPU capacity by scheduling some jobs to run during times when the CPU is lightly loaded or even idle.

---

* On many modern systems, processes have been replaced by threads as the fundamental execution entity. However, in uniprocessor environments at least, threads and processes are conceptually similar at a system administration level, so I will continue to speak of "processes" throughout this chapter.

- Reducing demands for CPU cycles by eliminating some of the jobs that are contending for them (or moving them to another computer).
- Using process priorities to allocate CPU time explicitly among processes that want it, favoring some over the others.
- Employing a batch system to ensure that only a reasonable number of jobs run at the same time, making others wait.
- Changing the behavior of the operating system's job scheduler to affect how the CPU is divided among multiple jobs.

Naturally, not all potential solutions will necessarily be possible on any given computer system or within any given operating system.

It is often necessary to distinguish between raw system resources like CPU and memory and the control mechanisms by which they are accessed and allocated. For example, in the case of the system's CPU, you don't have the ability to allocate or control this resource as such (unless you count taking the system down). Rather, you must use features like nice numbers and scheduler parameters to control usage.

Table 15-1 lists the most important control mechanisms associated with CPU, memory, and disk and network I/O performance.

Table 15-1. system resource control mechanisms

Resource	Control mechanisms
CPU	Nice numbers
	Process priorities
	Batch queues
	Scheduler parameters
Memory	Process resource limits
	Memory management-related parameters
	Paging (swap) space
Disk I/O	Filesystem organization across physical
	disks and controllers
	File placement on disk
	I/O-related parameters
Network I/O	Network memory buffers
	Network-related parameters
	Network infrastructure

The Tuning Process

The following process offers the most effective approach to addressing system performance issues.

1. Define the problem in as much detail as you can.

The more specific you can be about what is wrong (or less than optimal) with the way things are currently, the more likely it is you can find ways to improve them. Ideally, you'd like to move from an initial problem description like this one:

System response time is slow.

to one like this:

Interactive users running X experience significant delays opening new windows and switching between windows.

A good description of the current performance issues will also implicitly state your performance goals. For example, in this case, the performance goal is clearly to improve interactive response time for users running under X. It is important to understand such goals clearly, even if it is not always possible to reach them (in which case, they are really wishes more than goals).

2. Determine what's causing the problem.

To do so, you'll need to answer questions like these:

- What is running on the system (or, when the performance of a single job or process is the issue, what else is running)? You may also need to consider the sources of the other processes (for example, local users, remote users, the *cron* subsystem, and so on).

- When or under what conditions does the problem occur? For example, does it only occur at certain, predictable times of the day or when remote NFS mounts of local disks have reached a certain level? Are all users affected or only some or even one of them?

- Has anything about the system changed that could have introduced or exacerbated the problem?

- What is the critical resource that is adversely affecting performance? Answering this question will involve finding the performance bottleneck for the job(s) in which you are interested (or for this type of system workload). Later sections of this chapter will discuss tools and utilities that enable you to determine this.

For example, if we examined the system with the X windows performance problems, we might find that the response-time problems occurred only when more than one simulation job and/or large compilation job is running. By watching what happens when a user tries to switch windows under those conditions, we could also figure out that the critical resource is system memory and that the system is paging (we'll have more to say about this later in this chapter).

3. Formulate explicit performance improvement goals.

This step involves transforming the implicit goals (wishes) that were part of the problem description into concrete, measurable goals. Again, being as precise and detailed as possible will make your job easier.

In many cases, tuning goals will need to be developed in conjunction with the users affected by the performance problems, and possibly with other users and management personnel as well. System performance is almost always a matter of compromises and tradeoffs, because it inevitably involves deciding how to apply and apportion the finite available resources. Tuning is easiest and most successful where there is a clear agreement about the relative priority and importance of the various competing activities on the system.

To continue with our example, setting achievable tuning goals will be difficult unless it is decided whose performance is more important. In other words, it is probably necessary to choose between snappy interactive response time for X users and fast completeion times for simulation and compilation jobs (remember that the status quo has already been demonstrated not to work). Decided one way, the tuning goal could become something like this:

> Improve interactive response time for X users as much as possible without making simulation jobs take any longer to complete. Compilations can be delayed somewhat in order to keep the system from paging.

 Not all performance goals that can be formulated can be met. You often must choose between the alternatives that are actually possible. Thus, in the preceding example, you will not be able to meet all three CPU requirements simultaneously on the current system.

4. Design and implement modifications to the system and applications to achieve those goals.

Figuring out what to do is, of course, the trickiest part of tuning a system. We'll look at what the options are for various types of problems in the upcoming sections of this chapter.

It is important to tune the system as a whole. Focusing only on part of the system workload will give you a distorted picture of the problem, because system performance is ultimately the result of the interactions among everything on the system.

5. Monitor the system to determine how well the changes worked.

The purpose here is to evaluate the system status after the change is made and determine whether or not the change has improved things as expected or desired. The most successful tuning method introduces small changes to the system, one at a time, allowing you to thoroughly test each one and judge its effectiveness—and to back it out again if it makes things worse instead of better.

6. Return to the first step and begin again.

System performance tuning is inevitably an iterative process, because even a successful change will often reveal new interactions to understand and new problems to address. Similarly, once the bottleneck caused by one system resource is relieved, a new one centered around a different resource may very well arise. In fact, the initial performance problem can often be just a secondary symptom of the real, more serious underlying problem (e.g., a CPU shortage can be a symptom of serious memory shortfalls).

 Spend Money If You Have It, but Spend Wisely
Not all problems in life can be solved with money, but many performance issues can. If you have *definitively* identified the resource that is in short supply and you can afford to buy more of it (or upgrade it), do so. This approach is often the best and fastest way to address a performance problem. On the other hand, buying hardware in the hope that will alleviate a performance problem is likely to be both wasteful and frustrating.

Most operating systems provide specialized tools for performance tuning. These are the primary tuning tools and procedures for each of the various operating systems we are considering:

AIX	schedtune, vmtune, no
FreeBSD	sysctl, /etc/sysctl.conf
HP-UX	ndd, kmtune
Linux	files under */proc/sys*
Solaris	dispadmin, ndd, */etc/system*
Tru64	sysconfig, */etc/sysconfigtab*, dxkerneltuner

We'll discuss using these tools at the appropriate points within this chapter.

Some systems also provide additional performance monitoring and tuning tools as add-on packages.

Some Tuning Caveats

I'll close this section with two important notes about system performance tuning.

First, be aware of the *experimenter effect*. The term refers to the realization that merely watching something happen can change the thing that is happening in significant ways. In anthropology, this means that the a researcher observing the customs and behaviors of another culture inevitably has an effect on what is observed; people behave differently when they know they are being watched, especially by outsiders. For performance monitoring, running the monitoring tools can also have an effect on the system, and this fact needs to be taken into account when interpreting the data they collect. Ideally, performance data collection should be decoupled from data analysis (and the latter can take place on a different system).

Second, consider this advice from IBM's *AIX Versions 3.2 and 4.1 Performance Tuning Guide*:

> The analyst must resist the temptation to tune what is measurable rather than what is important.

Its overly formal language aside, this maxim reminds us that the tools Unix provides for observing system behavior offer one way of looking at the system, but not the only way. What is actually important to watch and tune on your system may or may not be trivially accessible to either monitoring or modification.

At the same time, it is also necessary to keep this important corollary in mind:

> Resist the temptation to tune something just because it is tunable.

This is, of course, really just another way of saying:

> If it ain't broke, don't fix it.

Monitoring and Controlling Processes

Unix provides the ability to monitor process execution and, to a limited extent, specify execution priorities. By doing so, you can control how CPU time is allocated and (indirectly) how memory is used. For example, you can expedite certain jobs at the expense of all others, or you can maintain interactive response times by forcing large jobs to run at lowered priority. This section discusses Unix processes and the tools available for monitoring and controlling process execution.

The uptime command gives you a rough estimate of the system load:

```
% uptime
3:24pm up 2 days, 2:41, 16 users, load average: 1.90, 1.43, 1.33
```

uptime reports the current time, how long the system has been up, and three load average figures. The load average is a rough measure of CPU use. These three figures report the average number of processes active during the last minute, the last five minutes, and the last 15 minutes. High load averages usually mean that the system is being used heavily and the response time is correspondingly slow. Note that the system's load average does not take into account the priorities of the processes that are running.

What's high? As usual, that depends on your system. Ideally, you'd like a load average under about 3–5 (per CPU), but that's not always possible given the workload that some systems are required to handle. Ultimately, "high" means high enough that you don't need uptime to tell you that the system is overloaded—you can tell from its response time.

Furthermore, different systems behave differently under the same load average. For example, on some workstations, running a single CPU-bound background job at the same time as X Windows will bring interactive response to a crawl even though the load average remains quite low. A low load average is no guarantee of a fast response time, because CPU availability is just one factor affecting overall system performance. You can generally expect to see higher typical load averages on server systems than on single-user workstations.

The ps Command

The ps command gives a more complete picture of system activity. This utility produces a report summarizing execution statistics for current processes. The command's options control which processes are listed and what information is displayed about each one. The format of the command differs considerably between the BSD and System V forms.

To obtain an overall view of current system activity, the most useful form of the BSD-style command is ps aux, which produces a table of all processes, arranged in order of decreasing CPU usage at the moment when the ps command was executed.* It is often useful to pipe this output to head, which displays the most active processes:

```
% ps aux | head -5
USER      PID  %CPU %MEM   SZ   RSS  TTY STAT  TIME COMMAND
harvey  12923  74.2 22.5  223   376  p5  R     2:12 f77 -o test test.F
chavez  16725  10.9 50.8 1146  1826  p6  R N  56:04 g04 Hg0.dat
wang    17026   3.5  1.2  354   240  co  I     0:19 vi benzene.txt
marj     7997   0.2  0.3  142    46  p3  S     0:04 csh
```

The meanings of the fields in this output (as well as others displayed by the -l option to ps) are given in Table 15-2.

The first line in the previous example shows that user *harvey* is running a Fortran compilation. This process has PID 12923 and is currently running or runnable. User *chavez*'s process (PID 16725), executing the program *g04*, is also running or runnable, though at a lowered priority. From this display, it's obvious who is using the most system resources at this instant: *harvey* and *chavez* have about 85% of the CPU and 73% of the memory between them. However, although it does display total CPU time, ps does not average the %CPU or %MEM values over time in any way.†

---

* Linux, FreeBSD, AIX, and Tru64 provide the BSD form of ps. Under AIX and Tru64, the ps command supports both BSD and System V options. The BSD options are not preceded by a hyphen (which is a legal syntax variation under BSD), and the System V options do include a hyphen. Thus, for these Unix versions, ps -au does not equal ps au.

Even in this mode, however, the AIX command is the System V version, even if its output is displayed with BSD column headings. Thus, ps aux output is displayed in PID rather than %CPU order. Solaris also provides a somewhat BSD-like ps command in */usr/ucb* (which uses System V column headings).

† This describes the true BSD definition for these fields. However, many System V–based operating systems fudge them even when they provide a BSD-compatible ps command. Under Linux, AIX, and Solaris, the %CPU column has a different meaning: it indicates the ratio of CPU time to elapsed time for the entire lifetime of each process, a very different statistic than current CPU usage.

Table 15-2. ps command output

Column	Contents
USER (BSD) UID (System V)	Username of process owner.
PID	Process ID.
%CPU	Estimated fraction of CPU consumed (FreeBSD and Tru64); CPUtime/elapsed time (AIX, Solaris, and Linux)
%MEM	Estimated fraction of system memory consumed (BSD-style); the estimates are sometimes quite poor
SZ	Virtual memory used in KB (BSD) or pages (System V)
RSS	Physical memory used (in same units as SZ)
TT, TTY	TTY associated with process.
STAT (BSD) S (System V)	Current process state; one (or more, under BSD) of the following:
	R Running or runnable.
	S Sleeping
	I Idle (BSD); Intermediate state (System V)
	T Stopped
	Z Zombie process
	D (BSD) Disk wait
	X (System V) Growing: waiting for memory
	K (AIX) Available kernel process
	W (BSD) Swapped out
	N (BSD) Niced: execution priority lowered
	< (BSD) Niced: execution priority artificially raised
	TIME Total CPU time used
COMMAND	Command line being executed (truncated).
STIME (System V) STARTED (BSD)	Time or date process started.
F	Flags associated with process (see the ps manual page).
PPID	Parent's PID.
NI	Process nice number.
C (System V) CP (BSD)	Short term CPU-use factor; used by scheduler for computing the execution priority (PRI).
PRI	Actual execution priority (recomputed dynamically).
WCHAN	Specifies the event the process is waiting for.

A vaguely similar listing is produced by the System V ps -ef command:

```
$ ps -ef
UID        PID  PPID  C STIME     TTY      TIME CMD
root         0     0  0 09:36:35  ?        0:00 sched
root         1     0  0 09:36:35  ?        0:02 /etc/init
...
marj      7997     1 10 09:49:32  ttyp3    0:04 csh
harvey   12923 11324  9 10:19:49  ttyp5   56:12 f77 -o test test.F
```

```
chavez   16725 16652  15 17:02:43 ttyp6    10:04 g04 Hg0.dat
wang     17026 17012  14 17:23:12 console  0:19 vi benzene.txt
```

The columns hold the username, process ID, parent's PID (the PID of the process that created it), the current scheduler value, the time the process started, its associated terminal, its accumulated CPU time, and the command it is running. Note that the ordering is by PID, not resource usage. This form of ps is supported under Solaris, HP-UX, AIX, and Tru64. ps is also useful in pipes; a common use is:

```
% ps aux | grep chavez
```

This command lists the processes user *chavez* currently has running.

You can use the sort command in conjunction with the System V version of ps to extract performance-related data from its process listings. For example, the following command finds processes using large amounts of memory (shown in the SZ field):

```
$ ps -el | head -1 ; ps -el | sort -nkr10 | head -5
    F S UID    PID   PPID  C PRI NI SZ      ... TIME  CMD
240001 A 603 630828 483460 240 120 20 9711568 29530:42  1703.exe
240001 A 603 573616 540786 240 120 20 9710404 29516:30  1802.exe
240001 A   0 221240 139322   0  60 20 6140      25:50  X
240001 A   0 303204 270428   0  60 20 2004       0:32  sendmail
240001 A   0 458898 270428   0  60 20 1996       0:07  IBM.Errmd
```

Some columns have been removed from this output for space reasons.

Other Process Listing Utilities

There are several useful, free system monitoring tools. In this section, we'll look at pstree and top.

pstree displays system processes in a tree-like structure, and it is accordingly useful for illuminating the relationships between processes and for a quick, pictorial snapshot of what is running on the system. pstree was written by Werner Almesberger. It can be found by itself on many network sites and as part of the psmisc package (*ftp://sunsite.unc.edu/pub/Linux/system/status/ps*). It is included by default on Linux, and FreeBSD includes it among the additional packages on the installation CDs.[*]

Here is an example of its output:

```
$ pstree
init-+-alarmd
     |-anacron
     |-apmd
     |-atd
     |-crond
     |-gpm
```

---

[*] Solaris has a vaguely similar utility named ptree.

```
  |-inetd-+-in.rlogind---bash---vi                              Two remote users.
  |       `-in.rlogind---bash---mkps---gbmat-+-grops
  |                                          |-gtbl
  |                                          `-gtroff
  |-kapm-idled
  |-7*[kdeinit]
  |-kdeinit-+-kdeinitKDE clients.
  |           `-kdeinit---bash-+-pstree
  |                            |-xclock
  |                            |-xterm---tcsh---ls
  |                            `-2*[xterm---rlogin]
  |-kdeinit---cat
  |-keventd
  |-khubd
  |-kjournald
  |-klogd
  |-login---bash---startx---xinit-+-X          X windows main processes.
  |                               `-startkde---ksmserver
  |-mdrecoveryd
  |-5*[mingetty]
  |-portmap
  |-rpc.statd
  |-sendmail
  |-sshd
  |-syslogd
  |-vmware-guestd
  |-xfs
  `-xinetd---fam
```

In general, all processes are listed by command name, and child processes appear to
the right of their parent process. Thus, init appears at the extreme left of the display,
appropriately, because it is the ultimate parent of every other process. The
notation:

   n*[command]

indicates that there are n processes running command. The sample output shows five
mingetty processes.

On this system, there are three groups of user processes:

- A local user running X and several clients: the KDE window manager, xclock;
  two xterm windows onto remote systems, and a local xterm window running the
  tcsh shell. These processes are displayed on the second and third annotated
  groups of lines in the output.

- A remote user running the bash shell and this pstree command (the annotated
  line headed by "inetd").

- Another remote user running three GNU text processing utilities (the three lines
  making up the second branch "in.rlogind" under "inetd").

The remainder of the lines in the display are the usual system processes.

The top utility provides a continuous display of the system status and most active processes, which it automatically updates every few seconds. Versions of top are included with FreeBSD, HP-UX, Linux, and Tru64. The utility was written by William LeFebvre and is available from *http://www.groupsys.com/top/*.

Here is a snapshot of the display from a Linux system:

```
 6:19pm  up 13 days, 23:42,  1 user,  load average: 0.03, 0.03, 0.00
28 processes: 27 sleeping, 1 running, 0 zombie, 0 stopped
CPU states: 7.7% user, 14.7% system,  0.0% nice, 77.6% idle
Mem: 6952K av, 6480K used,   472K free, 3996K shrd, 2368K buff
Swap: 16468K av,  2064K used, 14404K free
 PID USER    PRI  NI  SIZE RSS  SHARE STAT %CPU %MEM  TIME COMMAND
1215 chavez   14   0  8908 8908 7940 S     1.1  9.4  0:03 kdeinit
1106 chavez   14  -1 12748 9420 1692 S <   0.9  9.9  0:14 X
1262 chavez   16   0  1040 1040  836 R     0.9  1.1  0:00 top
1201 chavez    9   0 10096 9.9M 9024 S     0.1 10.6  0:02 kdeinit
   1 root      8   0   520  520  452 S     0.0  0.5  0:04 init
   2 root      9   0     0    0    0 SW    0.0  0.0  0:00 keventd
 ...
```

The first five lines give general system information: uptime statistics, overall number of processes statistics, and current CPU, memory, and swap space usage. The rest of the display consists of output similar to that provided by various options to ps (with similar column headings), arranged in order of decreasing current CPU usage. In *top* displays, the %CPU column indicates very recent CPU consumption for each process (over the last minute or less of elapsed time).

The HP-UX version of top is display-only. By default, the top display is updated every five seconds. You can change that interval using these command forms:

FreeBSD	top -s 8
Linux	top d8
HP-UX	top -s 8
Tru64	top -s 8

All of these examples set the update interval to eight seconds. top runs continuously until you press the *q* key.

Most versions of top also allow you to interact with the processes that are being displayed. Pressing the *k* and *r* keys allow you to kill and renice a process, respectively (these actions are discussed in detail later in this chapter). In both cases, top will prompt you for the PID of the process that you want to affect.

The /proc Filesystem

All of the Unix versions we are considering except HP-UX support the */proc* filesystem. This is a pseudo filesystem whose files are actually views into parts of kernel memory and its data structures.

On most systems, the *proc* filesystem consists entirely of numbered files or subdirectories under *proc*, each named for the corresponding process's PID. When these items are subdirectories, the available information about each process is divided among several files located within it. Here is an example from a Linux system:

```
$ ls /proc/1234
cmdline cwd environ exe fd maps mem root stat statm status
```

The per-process information contained in the *proc* filesystem is generally available in other ways (e.g., via the ps command).

Linux systems extend the *proc* filesystem to include many other files and subdirectories that hold a great many system settings and current system data. For example, the *cpuinfo* file contains information about the processor on the computer:

```
$ cat /proc/cpuinfo
processor       : 0
vendor_id       : GenuineIntel
cpu family      : 6
model           : 7
model name      : Pentium III (Katmai)
stepping        : 3
cpu MHz         : 497.847
cache size      : 512 KB
fdiv_bug        : no
hlt_bug         : no
f00f_bug        : no
coma_bug        : no
fpu             : yes
fpu_exception   : yes
cpuid level     : 2
wp              : yes
flags           : fpu vme de pse tsc msr pae mce cx8 apic sep
                  mtrr pge mca cmov pat pse36 mmx fxsr sse
bogomips        : 992.87
```

These are some of the most useful files under *proc*:

devices
　　Major and minor device number.

filesystems
　　Filesystems supported by the current kernel.

meminfo
　　Memory usage and configuration statistics.

modules
　　Loaded kernel modules.

pci
　　List of detected PCI devices and their configurations.

scsi/scsi

> List of detected SCSI devices and their configurations.

version

> Linux version of the currently running kernel (long version). The file */proc/sys/ kernel/oslevel* lists only the numeric Linux kernel version string.

There are many, many more files in the */proc* tree. However, I consider many of them to be of marginal use to those who are not programmers or script writers, because their information is available in a more convenient, prettier form via standard Unix commands.

In addition, the *sys* subdirectory tree provides access to kernel variables. Some of these files can be modified to change the corresponding system value. For example, the file *kernel/panic* holds the number of seconds to wait before rebooting after a kernel panic. These commands change the default value of 0 (immediately) to 60 seconds:

```
# cd /proc/sys/kernel
# cat panic
0
# echo "60" > panic
```

 Changing kernel variables always carries associated risk. Experiment on nonproduction systems.

Such changes do not persist across boots, so you'll need to place such commands into a boot script to make them permanent.

Kernel Idle Processes

Occasionally, you may see processes that seem to have accumulated a staggering amount of both CPU time and short-term CPU usage, as in these examples:

```
AIX
USER PID  %CPU %MEM  SZ RSS  TTY STAT STIME      TIME COMMAND
root 516  99.2  0.0  20 20   -   A    Mar 18  6028:47 kproc

Tru64
USER PID  %CPU %MEM   SZ RSS  TTY STAT STIME      TIME COMMAND
root   0   0.0  7.7 396M 17M  ??  R    Jan 23  49:46.53 [kernel idle]
```

Both listed processes are kernel idle processes, which indicate how much idle time—available CPU cycles that went unused—has accumulated since the last system reboot. On AIX systems, there are usually multiple kproc processes (and not all of them are necessarily idle). In any case, such processes are no cause for concern.

Process Resource Limits

Unix provides very simple process resource limits. These are the limits that may be defined:

- Total accumulated CPU time
- Largest file that may be created (whether created from scratch or by extending an existing file)
- Maximum size of the data segment of the process
- Maximum size of the stack segment of the process
- Maximum size of a core file (created when a program bombs)
- Maximum amount of memory that may be used by the process

Resource limits are divided into two types: soft and hard. *Soft limits* are resource use limits currently applied by default when a new process is created. A user may increase these values up to the systemwide *hard limits*, beyond which only the superuser may extend them. Hard limits are thus defined as absolute ceilings on resource use.

The C shell and tcsh have two built-in commands for displaying and setting resource limits. The limit command displays current resource limits. The hard limits may be displayed by including the -h option on the limit command:

```
% limit                            % limit -h
cputime       1:00:00              cputime       unlimited
filesize      1048575 kbytes       filesize      unlimited
datasize      65536 kbytes         datasize      3686336 kbytes
stacksize     4096 kbytes          stacksize     262144 kbytes
coredumpsize  1024 kbytes          coredumpsize  unlimited
memoryuse     32768 kbytes         memoryuse     54528 kbytes
```

The bash and ksh equivalent command is ulimit (also supported in some Bourne shells). The -a and -Ha options will display the current soft and hard limits respectively; for example:

```
$ ulimit -a                        $ ulimit -Ha
time(seconds)    3600              time(seconds)    unlimited
file(blocks)     2097151           file(blocks)     2097151
data(kbytes)     65536             data(kbytes)     257532
stack(kbytes)    4096              stack(kbytes)    196092
memory(kbytes)   32768             memory(kbytes)   unlimited
coredump(blocks) 1024              coredump(blocks) unlimited
```

Table 15-3 lists the commands that set the values of resource limits. They would usually be placed in users' login initialization files.[*]

---

[*] There is also a PAM module for setting limits.

Table 15-3. Setting per-process resource limits

Resource	csh and tcsh	bash and ksh
CPU time	limit cputime *secs*	ulimit -t *secs*
Maximum file size	limit filesize *KB*	ulimit -f *KB*
Maximum process data segment	limit datasize *KB*	ulimit -d *KB*
Maximum process stack size	limit stacksize *KB*	ulimit -s *KB*
Maximum amount of physical memory	limit memory *KB*	ulimit -m *KB*
Maximum core file size	limit coredumpsize *KB*	ulimit -c *KB*
Maximum number of processes[a]		ulimit -u *n*
Maximum amount of virtual memory[a]		ulimit -v *KB*

[a] bash only.

For example, the following commands increase the current CPU time limit to its maximum value and increase the memory use limit to 64 MB:

bash and ksh	*C shell and tcsh*
`$ ulimit -t unlimited`	`% limit cputime unlimited`
`$ ulimit -m 65536`	`% limit memory 65536`

Now for the bad news. On most Unix systems, resource limits are poorly implemented from an administrative standpoint, for several reasons. First, the hard limits are often hard-wired into the kernel and cannot be changed by the system administrator. Second, users can always change their own soft limits. All an administrator can do is place the desired commands into users' *.profile* or *.cshrc* files and hope. Third, the limits are on a per-process basis. Unfortunately, many real jobs consist of many processes, not just one. There is currently no way to impose limits on a parent process and all its children. Finally, in many cases, limits are not even enforced; this is most often true of the ones you probably care about the most: CPU time and memory use. You'll need to experiment to find out which ones are enforced on your system.

 FreeBSD is an exception, and limits can be effectively set via login classes (*/etc/login.conf*). See "Managing User Accounts" in Chapter 6 for details.

However, one limit which it is often worth setting in user login initialization files is the core file size limit. If the users on your system will have little use for core files, set the limit to 0, preventing their creation.

Process Resource Limits Under AIX

AIX includes the structure for a more elaborate version of these limits, via the file */etc/security/limits* (which may be modified directly or by the chuser command). It has stanzas of the form:

```
chavez:
   fsize = 2097151          Maximum file size.
   core = 0                 Maximum core file size.
   cpu = 3600               Maximum CPU seconds.
   data = 131072            Maximum process data segment.
   rss = 65536              Maximum amount of physical memory.
   stack = 8192             Maximum process stack size.
```

Each stanza specifies the resource usage limits for the username that labels the stanza. These settings specify absolute limits on resource usage, and they cannot be overridden by the user.

To change *chavez*'s memory use limit, use a command like this one:

```
# chuser rss=102400 chavez
```

This command sets *chavez*'s default memory use limit to 100 MB by modifying or adding the *rss* line for *chavez* in */etc/security/limits*. As usual, the limits set in the *default* stanza are applied for any user without specific settings of her own. Setting a limit to a value of −1 will allow unlimited use of that system resource.

You can also use SMIT to specify user per-process resource limits. The dialog is illustrated in Figure 15-1, and it displays the appropriate fields from the user account addition/modification screen.

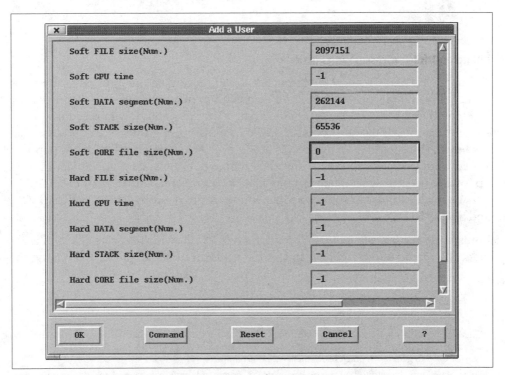

Figure 15-1. Setting per-process Resource Limits with SMIT

Signaling and Killing Processes

Sometimes it's necessary to eliminate a process entirely; this is the purpose of the `kill` command. The syntax of the `kill` command, which is actually a general purpose process signaling utility, is as follows:

```
# kill [-signal] pids
```

pid is the process's identification number (or a space-separated list of process numbers), and *signal* is the (optional) signal to send to the process. The default signal is number 15, the TERM signal, which asks the process to terminate.[*] In general, either the signal number or its symbolic name may be used (although on a few older System V systems, the signal must be specified numerically). You must be the superuser in order to kill someone else's process.

Sometimes, a process may still exist after a `kill` command. If this happens, execute the `kill` command with the -9 option, which sends the process signal number 9, appropriately named KILL. This almost always guarantees that the process will be destroyed. However, it does not allow the dying process to clean up before terminating and therefore may leave the process' files in an inconsistent state.

 Suspended processes must be resumed before they can be killed.

Killing multiple processes with killall

Although you can use the `kill` command to kill more than one process at the same time, many systems provide a `killall` command to make this process slightly easier. This command began life as part of the System V system shutdown procedures. In its simplest form, it kills all processes in the same process group as the process that invoked it (but not the calling process itself); thus, when invoked by `init` as part of a system shutdown, it will kill all processes running on the system. Like `kill`, `killall` optionally takes a signal name or number as its argument. This form of `killall` may also be useful in administrative scripts, and it is provided by Tru64, AIX, HP-UX, and Solaris.[†]

Linux and FreeBSD offer an enhanced form of `killall`, which accepts a second argument: the name of a command. In this form, `killall` kills all processes running the

---

[*] This signal number happens to be the same in System V and BSD. Be aware that this is not always the case. Signals are defined in the */usr/include/signal.h* file (or */usr/include/sys/signal.h*), and the command `kill -l` may be used to generate a quick list of their symbolic names.

[†] Some older Unix operating systems also have a `killall` command, but it has a completely different function. Check the manual page to be safe before using it under an unfamiliar operating system.

---

specified command. For example, the following command sends a KILL signal to all processes running the find command:

```
# killall -KILL find
```

Processes that won't die

Occasionally, processes will not die even after being sent the KILL signal. The vast majority of such processes fall into one of three categories:

- A process in the *zombie* state (displayed as Z status in BSD ps displays and as <defunct> under System V). When a process is exiting, the kernel informs its parent, and the latter must respond to that message. A zombie process results when the parent process does not respond. Usually, init handles terminating such processes when the parent is gone, but on occasion this fails to happen. Zombies are always cleared the next time the system is booted and rarely affect system performance adversely.

- Processes waiting for unavailable NFS resources (for example, trying to write to a remote file on a system that has crashed) will not die if sent a KILL signal. Use the QUIT signal (3) or the INT (interrupt) signal (2) to kill such processes. See "Sharing Filesystems" in Chapter 10 for full details.

- Processes waiting for a device to complete an I/O operation before exiting may not die even when sent a KILL signal. For example, a process might be waiting for a tape to finish rewinding.

Pausing and restarting processes

The signals STOP and CONT may be used to suspend and then resume a running process. They use the same mechanism as the Ctrl-Z facility within user shells, but these signals may be sent by the superuser to any running process.

Managing CPU Resources

CPU usage is usually the first factor that I consider when I am tracking down a performance problem or just trying to assess the current system state in general.[*]

Nice Numbers and Process Priorities

Most Unix systems use a *priority-based round-robin scheduling* algorithm to distribute CPU resources among multiple competing processes. All processes have an *execution priority* assigned to them, an integer value that is dynamically computed and

---

[*] Some people recommend checking memory use first, because CPU shortages are occasionally secondary effects of memory shortages.

updated on the basis of several factors. Whenever the CPU is free, the scheduler selects the most favored process to begin or resume executing; this usually corresponds to the process with the lowest priority number, because lower numbers are defined as more favored than higher ones in typical implementations.

Although there may be a multitude of processes simultaneously present on the system, only one process actually uses the CPU processor at any given time (assuming the system has only a single CPU). Once a process begins running, it continues to execute until it needs to wait for an I/O operation to complete, receives an interrupt from the kernel, or otherwise gives up control of the CPU, or until it exhausts the maximum execution *time slice* (or *quantum*) defined on that system (10 milliseconds is a common value). Once the current process stops executing, the scheduler again selects the most favored process on the system and starts or resumes it. The process of changing the current running process is called a *context switch*.

Multiple runnable processes at the same priority level are placed into the *run queue* for that priority level. Whenever the CPU is free, the scheduler starts the processes at the head of the lowest-numbered, nonempty run queue. When the process at the top of a run queue stops executing, it goes to the end of the line, and the next process moves to the front.

A Unix process has two priority numbers associated with it:

- Its *nice number*, which is its requested execution priority with respect to other processes. This value is settable by the process' owner and by *root*. The nice number appears in the NI column in `ps -l` listings.

- Its current (actual) execution priority, which is computed and dynamically updated by the operating system (in a system-dependent way), often taking into account factors such as the process's nice number, how much CPU time it has had recently, what other processes are runnable and their priorities, and other factors. This value appears in the PRI column in `ps -l` listings.[*]

Under BSD, nice numbers range from –20 and 20, with –20 the most favored priority (the default priority is 0); under System V, nice numbers range from 0 to 39 (the default is 20), with lower numbers again indicating higher priority and more rapid execution. For Unix, less is truly more. Interactive shells usually run at the default level (0 for BSD and 20 for System V). Only the superuser can specify nice numbers lower than the default.

Many systems provide a special nice number that can be assigned to processes that you want to run only when nothing else wants the CPU. On Solaris systems, this number is 19, and on Tru64, HP-UX, and Linux systems, it is 20.

---

[*] See the section on the AIX scheduler later in this chapter for a concrete example of how process priorities are calculated.

On AIX systems, a similar effect can be accomplished by setting a process to the fixed priority level 121 (using the `setpri` system call—see "When Only C Will Do" in Chapter 14 for a sample program calling this function). Because varying priorities always remain at or below 120, a job in the priority range of 121 to 126 will run only when no lower-priority process wants the CPU. Note that once you have assigned a process a fixed priority, it cannot return to having a varying priority.

Any user can be nice and decrease the priority of a process he owns by increasing its nice number. Only the superuser can decrease the nice number of a process. This prevents users from increasing their own priorities and thereby using more than their share of the system's resources.

There are several ways to specify a job's execution priority. First, there are two commands to initiate a process at lowered priority: the `nice` command, built into some shells, and the general Unix command `nice`, usually stored in */bin* or */usr/bin*. These commands both work the same way, but have slightly different syntaxes:

```
% nice [+|- n] command
$ /bin/nice - [[-] n] command
```

In the built-in C shell version of `nice`, if an explicitly signed number is given as its first argument, it specifies the amount the command's priority will differ from the default nice number; if no number is specified, the default offset is +4. With */bin/nice*, the offset from the default nice number is specified as its argument and so is preceded by a hyphen; the default offset is +10, and positive numbers need not include a plus sign. Thus, the following commands are equivalent, despite looking very different:

```
% nice +6 bigjob
$ /bin/nice -6 bigjob
```

Both commands result in `bigjob` having a nice number of 6 under BSD and 26 under System V. Similarly, the following commands both raise `bigjob`'s priority five steps above the default level (to –5 under BSD and 15 under System V):

```
# nice -5 bigjob
# /bin/nice --5 bigjob
```

Thus, BSD and System V nice numbers always differ by 20, but identical commands have equivalent effects on the two systems.

The -1 option to `ps` (either format—the output varies only slightly) may be used to display a process's nice number and current execution priority. Here is some example output from a Linux system:

```
% ps l
    F  UID   PID PPID  PRI  NI   VSZ    RSS WCHAN       COMMAND
 8201  371  8390 8219    1   0  3233    672 wait4   ... rlogin iago
 8201  371  8391 8219    3   4  3487   1196 do_sig  ... big_cmd
 8201    0  8394    1   15  -5  2134   1400 -       ... imp_cmd
```

The column headed NI displays each process's nice number. The column to its immediate left, labeled PRI, shows the process's current actual execution priority.

 Some Unix implementations automatically reduce the priority of processes that consume more than 10 minutes of user CPU time. Because the ps command reports total CPU time (user time plus system time), its display often indicates a total CPU time of more than 10 minutes at the moment this occurs.

Processes inherit the priority of their parent when they are created. However, changing the priority of the parent process does not change the priorities of its children. Therefore, increasing a process's priority number may have no effect if this process has created one or more subprocesses. Accordingly, if the parent process spends most of its time waiting for its children, changing the parent's priority will have little or no effect on the system's performance.

Monitoring CPU Usage

There are many ways of obtaining a quick snapshot of current overall CPU activity. For example, the vmstat command includes CPU activity among the many system statistics that it displays. Its most useful mode uses this syntax:

```
$ vmstat interval [count]
```

where *interval* is the number of seconds between reports, and *count* is the total number of reports to generate. If *count* is omitted, vmstat runs until you terminate it.

Here is an example of the output[*] from vmstat:

```
$ vmstat 5 4
procs     memory            page                  disk          faults       cpu
r b w   avm  fre  re at pi po fr de sr d0 d1 d2 d3  in  sy  cs  us  sy  id
1 0 0 61312 9280  0  0 24  1  2  0  0  4  1  1 12  35  66  16  63  11  26
3 2 0 71936 3616  3  0 96  0  0  0  2 18  0  0  0  23  89  34  72  28   0
5 1 0 76320 3424  0  0  0  0  0  0  0 26  0  0  0  24  92  39  63  37   0
4 1 0 63616 3008  1  1  0  0  0  0  0 21  0  0  0  23  80  33  78  22   0
```

The first line of every vmstat report displays average values for each statistic since boot time; it should be ignored. If you forget this, you can be misled by vmstat's output. At the moment, we are interested in these columns of the report:

r   Number of runnable processes that are waiting for the CPU

cs Number of context switches

us Percentage of CPU cycles spent as user time (i.e., running the heart of user applications)

---

[*] vmstat's output varies somewhat from system to system.

sy   Percentage of CPU cycles spent as system time, both as part of the overhead involved in running user programs (e.g. handling I/O requests) and in providing general operating system services

id   Idle time: percentage of CPU cycles that went unused during the interval

During the period covered by the vmstat report, this system's CPU was used to capacity: there was no idle time at all.* You'll need to use ps in conjunction with vmstat to determine the specific jobs that are consuming the system's CPU resources. Under AIX, the tprof command can also be used for this purpose.

Recognizing a CPU shortage

High levels of CPU usage are not a bad thing in themselves (quite the contrary, in fact: they might mean that the system is accomplishing a lot of useful work). However, if you are tracking down a system performance problem, and you see such levels of CPU use consistently over a significant period of time, a shortage of CPU cycles is one factor that might be contributing to that problem (it may not be the total problem, however, as we'll see).

   Short-term CPU usage spikes are normal.

In general, one or more of the following symptoms may suggest a shortage of CPU resources when they appear regularly and/or persist for a significant period of time:

- Higher than normal load averages.
- Total processor usage (us+sy) that is higher than normal. You might start thinking about future CPU requirements when the total load increases over time and exceeds 80%–90%.
- A large number of waiting runnable processes (r). This indicates that these processes are ready to run but can't get any CPU cycles. I start looking into things when this value gets above about 3–6 (per CPU).
- Ideally, most of the CPU usage should be spent in user time—performing actual work—and not in system time. Sustained abnormally high levels of system time, especially in conjunction with a large number of context switches, can indicate too many processes contending for the CPU,† even when the total CPU usage is not an issue. I like the system time to be a fraction of the user time, about a third or less (applies only when the total time used is nontrivial).

---

* The method for determining whether a single job is CPU-limited or not is somewhat different. When there is a significant difference between the CPU time and the elapsed time taken for a job to complete on an otherwise idle system, some factor(s) other than a lack of CPU cycles are degrading its performance.

† A high system time percentage can also indicate a memory shortage, as we'll see.

- When an overcommitment of CPU resources is the source of a performance bottleneck, there are several options for addressing the situation:
  - If you want to favor some jobs over others, you can explicitly divide up the CPU resources via process priorities.
  - If there is simply more demand for the CPU resources than can be met, you'll need to reduce consumption in some way: move some of the load to a different (presumably less heavily loaded) system, execute some jobs at a later time (during off-hours via a batch system, for example), and the like.*
  - If the operating system supports it, you can change its scheduling procedure to allocate CPU resources to those jobs and in the manner that you deem appropriate.

We'll look at each of these options in turn in the remainder of this section.

Changing a Process's Nice Number

When the system's load is high, you may wish to force CPU-intensive processes to run at a lower priority. This reduces the CPU contention for interactive jobs such as editing, and generally keeps users happy. Alternatively, you may wish to devote most of the system's time to a few critical processes, letting others finish when they will. The renice command may be used to change the priority of running processes. Introduced in BSD, renice is now also supported on most System V systems. Only root may use renice to increase the priority of a process (i.e., lower its nice number).

renice's traditional syntax is:

```
# renice new-nice-number pid
```

new-nice-number is a valid nice number, and *pid* is a process identification number. For example, the following command sets the nice number of process 8201 to 5, lowering its priority by five steps.

```
# renice 5 8201
```

 Giving a process an extremely high priority may interfere with the operating system's own operation. Let common sense reign.

renice under AIX, HP-UX, and Tru64

AIX and HP-UX use a modified form of the renice command. This form requires that the -n option precede the new nice number, as in this example:

```
$ renice -n 12 8201
```

---

* It is also possible to reduce CPU consumption by making the application programs themselves more efficient. Such techniques are beyond the scope of this book; consult *High Performance Computing* by Kevin Dowd (O'Reilly & Associates) for detailed information about the code tuning process.

Tru64 supports both forms of the renice command.

Note that AIX uses the System V–style priority system, running from 0 (high) to 40 (low). For renice under AIX, the new nice number is still specified on a scale from –20 to 20; it is translated internally into the 0–40 scheme actually used. This can make for some slightly strange output at times:

```
# renice -n 10 3769
3769: old priority 0, new priority 10
# ps -l -p 3769
F     S UID  PID PPID C PRI NI ADDR SZ  WCHAN    TTY  TIMECMD
200801 S 371 3769 8570 0  70 30 2aca 84 1d79098 pts/1  0:00 c12
```

The renice command reports its action in terms of BSD nice numbers, but the ps display shows the real nice number.

Changing process priorities under Solaris

System V.4 changed the standard System V priority scheme as part of its support for real-time processes. By default, V.4, and hence Solaris, internally use time-sharing priority numbers ranging from –20 to 20, with 20 as the highest priority (the default is 0). V.4 also supports the BSD renice command, mapping BSD nice numbers to the corresponding time-sharing priority number; similarly, the ps command continues to display nice numbers in the V.3 format. Solaris has incorporated this scheme as part of its V.4 base.

Solaris also uses another command to modify process priorities (again, primarily intended for real-time processes): priocntl. The priocntl form to change the priority for a single process is:

```
# priocntl -s -p new-pri -i pid proc-id
```

where *new-pri* is the new priority for the process and *proc-id* is the process ID of the desired process. For example, the following command sets the priority level for process 8733 to –5:

```
# priocntl -s -p -5 -i pid 8733
```

The following form may be used to set the priority (nice number) for every process created by a given parent process:

```
# priocntl -s -p -5 -i ppid 8720
```

This command sets the priority of process 8720 and all of its children.

The priocntl command has many other capabilities and uses, as we'll see in the course of this chapter (you may also want to consult its manual page).

Setting a user's default nice numbers under Tru64

Tru64 allows you to specify the default nice number for a user's login shell (which will be inherited by all processes that she subsequently creates), via the *u_priority* field in the user's protected password database entry. This field takes a numeric value and defaults to 0 (the usual default nice number). For example, the following form would set the user's nice value to 5:

```
u_priority#5
```

A systemwide default nice value may also be set in */etc/auth/system/default*.

Configuring the System Scheduler

AIX and Solaris provide substantial facilities for configuring the functioning of the system scheduler. Tru64 also offers a few relevant kernel parameters. We'll consider these facilities in this section. The other operating systems offer little of practical use for CPU performance tuning.

 These operations require care and thought and should initially be tried on nonproduction systems.

The AIX scheduler

On AIX systems, dynamic process priorities range from 0 to 127, with lower numbers more favorable. The current value for each process appears in the column labeled *PRI* in ps -1 displays. Normally, process execution priorities change over time (in contrast to nice numbers), according to the following formula:

$$new\_priority = min + nice + (frac * recent)$$

min is the minimum process priority level, normally 40; *nice* is the process' nice number; *recent* is a number indicating how much CPU time the process has received recently (it is displayed in the column labeled *C* in ps -1 output). By default, the parameter *frac* is 0.5; it specifies how much of the recent CPU usage is taken into account (how large the penalty for recent CPU cycles is).

For a new process, *recent* starts out at 0; it can reach a maximum value of 120. By default, at the end of each 10-millisecond time slice (equivalent to one clock tick), the scheduler increases *recent* by one for the process currently in control of the CPU. In addition, once a second, the scheduler reduces *recent* for all processes, multiplying it by a reduction factor that defaults to 0.5 (i.e., *recent* is divided by 2 by default). The effect of this procedure is to penalize processes that have received CPU resources most recently by increasing their execution priority value, and gradually lowering the execution priority value for processes that have had to wait, to the minimum level arising from their nice number.

The result of this scheduling policy is that CPU resources are more or less evenly divided among (compute-bound) jobs at the same nice level. When there are jobs ready to run at both normal and raised nice levels, the normal-priority jobs will get more time than the others, but even the niced jobs will get some CPU time. For long-running processes, the distinction between normal priority and niced processes eventually becomes quite blurred because normal priority processes that have gotten a significant amount of CPU time can easily rise in priority above that of waiting niced processes.

The schedtune utility is used to modify scheduler and other operating system parameters. The schedtune executable is provided in */usr/samples/kernel*.

For normal processes, you can alter two scheduler parameters with this utility: the fraction of the short-term CPU usage value used in computing the current execution priority (-r) and how much the short-term CPU usage number is reduced at the end of each one second interval (-d). Each value is divided by 32 to compute the actual multiplier that is used (e.g., *frac* in the preceding equation is equal to -r/32). Both values default to 16, resulting in factors of one half in both cases.

For example, the following command makes slight alterations to these two parameters:

```
# schedtune -r 15 -d 15
```

The -r option determines how quickly recent CPU usage raises a process's execution priority (lowering its likelihood of resumed execution). For example, giving -r a value of 10 causes the respective priorities of normal and niced processes to equalize more slowly than under the default conditions, allocating a large fraction of the total CPU capacity to the more favored jobs.

Decreasing the value even more intensifies this effect; if the option is set to 4, for example, only one eighth of the recent CPU usage number will be used in calculating the execution priority (instead of one half). This means that this component will never contribute more than 15 to the execution priority (120 * 4/32), so a process that has a nice number greater than 15 will never interfere with the running of a normal process.

Setting -r to 0 makes nice numbers the sole determinant of process execution priorities by removing recent CPU usage from the calculation (literally, multiplying it by 0). Under these conditions, process execution priorities will remain static over time for all processes (unless they are explicitly reniced by hand).

Setting the -d option to a value other than 16 changes what constitutes recent CPU usage. A smaller value means that CPU usage affects the execution priority less than under the default conditions, effectively making the definition of "recent" shorter. On the other hand, a larger value causes CPU usage to affect execution priorities for a longer period of time. In the extreme case, -d 32 means that CPU usage simply accumulates (the divisor every second is 1), so long-running processes will always be less favored than ones that have used less CPU time because every process's recent CPU usage number will eventually rise to the maximum value of 120 and stay there (provided they run long enough). Newer processes will always be favored over those that have already received at least 120 time slices. Their relative nice numbers will determine the execution order for all processes over this threshold, and one at the same nice level will take turns via the usual run queue mechanism.

schedtune's -t option may be used to change the length of the maximum time slice allotted to a process. This option takes the number of 10-millisecond clock ticks by which to *increase* the length of the default time slice as its argument. For example, this command doubles the length of the time slice, setting it to 20 milliseconds:

```
# schedtune -t 1
```

Note that this change applies only to fixed-priority processes (the priority must be set with the setpri system call). Such processes' priority do not change over time (as described above), but rather remain fixed for their entire lifetimes.

schedtune's modifications to the scheduling parameters remain in effect only until the system is rebooted; you'll need to place the appropriate command in one of the system initialization scripts or in */etc/inittab* if you decide that a permanent change is desirable. schedtune -D may be used to restore the default values for *all* parameters managed by this utility at any point (including ones unrelated to the system scheduler). Executing the command without any options will display the current values of all tunable parameters, and the -? option will display a manual page for the command (use a backslash before the question mark in the C shell).

The Solaris scheduler

System V.4 also introduced administrator-configurable process scheduling, which is now part of Solaris. One purpose of this facility is to support *real-time processes*: processes designed to work in application areas where nearly immediate responses to events are required (say, processing raw radar data in a vehicle in motion, controlling a manufacturing process making extensive use of robotics, or starting up the backup cooling system on a nuclear reactor). Operating systems handle such needs by defining a class of processes as real-time processes, giving them virtually complete access to all system resources when they are running. Under such instances, normal time-sharing processes will receive little or no CPU time. Solaris allows a system to be configured to allow both normal time-sharing and real-time processes (although actual real-time systems using other operating systems have seldom actually done this). Alternatively, a system may be configured without real-time processes.

This section serves as an introductory overview to this facility. Obviously, the process scheduler facility is something to play with on a test system first, not something to try on your main production system three days before an important deadline.

Solaris defines various process classes: real-time, time-sharing, interactive, system and interrupts. The latter class is used for kernel processes (such as the paging daemon). For scheduling table definition purposes, each process class has its own set of priority numbers. For example, real-time process priorities run from 0 to 59 (higher is better). Time-sharing processes use priority numbers from 0 to 59 by default.

However, these priority number sets are all mapped to a single set of internal priority numbers running from 0 to 169, as defined in Table 15-4.

Table 15-4. Solaris priority classes

Class	Relative priorities	Absolute priorities
Time-sharing/interactive	0–59	0–59
Kernel	0–39	60–99
Real-time	0–59	100–159
Interrupt	0–9	160–169[a]

[a] The interrupt class uses 100–109 if the real time class is not in use.

As the table indicates, a real-time process will always run before either a system or time-sharing process, because real-time process global priorities—which are actually used by the process scheduler—are all greater than system and time-sharing global priorities. The definitions of each real-time and time-sharing global priority level are stored in the kernel and, if they have been customized, are usually located by one of the system initialization scripts at boot time. The current definitions may be retrieved with the dispadmin -g command. Here is an example:

```
$ dispadmin -g -c TS
# Time Sharing Dispatcher Configuration
RES=1000
# ts_quantum ts_tqexp ts_slpret ts_maxwait ts_lwait PRIORITY LEVEL
    1000         0        10          5         10      #     0
    1000         0        11          5         11      #     1
    1000         1        12          5         12      #     2
    1000         1        13          5         13      #     3
    ...
     100        47        58          5         58      #    57
     100        48        59          5         59      #    58
     100        49        59          5         59      #    59
```

Each line of the table defines the characteristics of a different priority level, numbered consecutively from 0. The *RES=* line defines the time units used in the table. It says how many parts each second is divided into; each defined fraction of a second becomes one unit. Thus, in this file, the time units are milliseconds.

The fields have the following meanings:

ts_quantum
> The maximum amount of time that a process at this priority level can run without interruption.

ts_tqexp
> New priority given to a process running at this priority level that gets the entire maximum run interval. In the preceding example, this has the effect of lowering its priority.

ts_slpret

New priority given to a process at this priority level when it returns from a sleep.

ts_maxwait

Maximum amount of time a process at this level can remain runnable without actually executing before having its priority changed to the value in the *ts_lwait* column. This setting affects processes that are ready to run but aren't getting any CPU time. After this interval, their priority will be increased with the preceding scheduler table.

ts_lwait

New priority given to a process that is runnable and whose maximum wait time has expired. In the preceding example, this usually increases its priority somewhat.

All text after number signs is ignored. Thus, the PRIORITY LEVEL columns are really comments designed to make the table easier to read.

From the preceding example, it is evident how process priorities would change under various circumstances. For example, consider a level 57 process (2 steps short of the most favored priority). If a process at this level runs for its full 100 milliseconds, it will then drop down to priority level 47, giving up the CPU to any higher priority processes. If, on the other hand, it waits for 5 milliseconds after being ready to run, its priority level is raised to 58, making it more likely to be executed sooner.

Here is a rather different time sharing scheduling table:

```
# Time Sharing Dispatcher Configuration
RES=1000
# ts_quantum ts_tqexp ts_slpret ts_maxwait ts_lwait PRIORITY LEVEL
      200        0        59        0        50      #    0
      200        0        59        0        50      #    1
      200        0        59        0        50      #    2
      200        0        59        0        50      #    3
      ...
      160        0        59        0        51      #   10
      160        1        59        0        51      #   11
      ...
      120       10        59        0        52      #   20
      120       11        59        0        52      #   21
      ...
       80       20        59        0        53      #   30
       80       21        59        0        53      #   31
      ...
       40       30        59        0        55      #   40
      ...
       40       47        59        0        59      #   57
       40       48        59        0        59      #   58
       40       49        59        0        59      #   59
```

This table has the effect of conflating the large number of processes down to a few distinct values when processes have to wait to gain access to the CPU. Because *ts_maxwait* is always 0 and *ts_lwait* ranges only between 50 and 59, any runnable process that has to wait gets its priority changed to a value in this range. In addition, when a process returns from a sleep, its priority is set to 59, the highest available value. Note also that processes with high priorities get short time slices compared to the previous table (as little as 40 milliseconds).

You can dynamically install a new scheduler table with the dispadmin command's -s option. For example, this command installs the table contained in the file /etc/ts_ sched.new into memory:

```
# dispadmin -c TS -s /etc/ts_sched.new
```

The table format in the specified file must be the same as that displayed by dispadmin -g, and it must contain the same number of priority levels as the one currently in use. Permanent changes may be made by running such a command at boot time or by creating a loadable module with a new scheduler table (see the ts_dptbl manual page for the latter procedure).

The priocntl command allows a priority level ceiling to be imposed upon a time-sharing process, which specifies the maximum priority level it can attain. This prevents a low priority process from becoming runnable and eventually marching up to the top priority level (as would happen under the first scheduler table we looked at) when you really want that process to run only when nothing else is around. Setting a limit can keep it below the range of normal processes. For example, the following command sets the maximum priority for process 27163 to −5:

```
# priocntl -s -m -5 27163
```

Note that the command uses external priority numbers (not the scheduler table values).

Tru64

Tru64 provides many kernel parameters that control various aspects of the kernel's functioning. On Tru64 systems, kernel parameters may be altered using the sysconfig and dxkerneltuner utilities (text-based and GUI, respectively), although most values are alterable only at boot time.

sysconfig can also be used to display the current and configured values of kernel variables. For example, the following commands display information about the autonice_penalty parameter:

```
# sysconfig -m proc                     Is the proc subsystem static or dynamic?
proc: static
# sysconfig -q proc autonice_penalty    Display current value.
proc:
autonice_penalty = 4
# sysconfig -Q proc autonice_penalty    Display parameter attributes.
proc:
autonice_penalty -       type=INT op=CQ min_val=0 max_val=20
```

The command takes a subsystem name and (optionally) a parameter name as its arguments.

The following command form will modify a current value:

```
# sysconfig -r proc autonice_penalty=6
```

Another useful sysconfig argument is -d; it displays the values set in the kernel initialization file, */etc/sysconfigtab*, which are set at boot time. The majority of this file specifies device configuration; local modifications to standard kernel parameter values come at the end.

Here are some sample entries from this file:

```
generic:                                   General settings.
        memberid = 0
        new_vers_high = 14456554803859776064
        new_vers_low = 51480
ipc:
        shm_max = 67108864                  Max. shared memory (default: 4 MB).
        shm_mni = 1024                      Max. shared regions (default: 128).
        shm_seg = 256                       Max. regions/process (default: 32).
proc:                                       CPU-related settings.
        max_per_proc_stack_size = 41943040
        autonice = 1
        autonice_penalty = 10
```

Each stanza is introduced by the subsystem name. In this example, we configure the generic (general), ipc shared memory* and proc (CPU/process) subsystems.

The proc subsystem is the most relevant to CPU performance. The following parameters may be useful in some circumstances:

- max_per_proc_address_space and max_per_process_data_size may need to be increased from their defaults of 4 GB and 1 GB (respectively) to accommodate very large jobs.

- By default, the Tru64 scheduler gives a priority boost to jobs returning from a block I/O wait (in an effort to expedite interactive response). You can disable this by setting give_boost to 0.

- The scheduler can be configured to automatically nice processes that have used more than 600 seconds of CPU time (this is disabled by default). Setting autonice to 1 enables it, and you can specify the amount to nice by with the autonice_penalty parameter (the default is 4).

- The round_robin_switch_rate can be used to modify the time slice. It does so in an indirect manner. Its default value is 0, which is also equivalent to its maximum value of 100. This setting specifies how many time-slice expiration context switches occur in a second, and the time slice is computed by dividing the CPU clock rate by this value. Thus, setting it to 50 has the effect of doubling the time slice length (because the divisor changes from 100 to 50). Such a modification

---

* These example settings are useful for running large jobs on multiprocessor systems.

should be considered only for systems designed for running long jobs, with little or no interactive activity (or where you've decided to favor computation over interactive activity).

Unix Batch-Processing Facilities

Manually monitoring and altering processes' execution priorities is a crude way to handle CPU time allocation, but unfortunately it's the only method that standard Unix offers. It is adequate for the conditions under which Unix was developed: systems with lots of small interactive jobs. But if a system runs some large jobs as well, it quickly breaks down.

Another way of dividing the available CPU resources on a busy system among multiple competing processes is to run jobs at different times, including some at times when the system would otherwise be idle. Standard Unix has a limited facility for doing so via the at and batch commands. Under the default configuration, at allows a command to be executed at a specified time, and batch provides a queue from which jobs may be run sequentially in a batch-like mode. For example, if all large jobs are run via *batch* from its default queue, it can ensure that only one is ever running at a time (provided users cooperate, of course).

In most implementations, system administrators may define additional queues in the *queuedefs* file, found in various locations on different systems:

AIX	*/var/adm/cron*
FreeBSD	not used
HP-UX	*/var/adm/cron*
Linux	not used
Solaris	*/etc/cron.d*
Tru64	*/var/adm/cron*

This file defines queues whose names consist of a single letter (either case is valid). Conventionally, queue *a* is used for at, queue *b* is used for batch, and on many newer systems, queue *c* is used by cron. Tru64 and AIX define queues *e* and *f* for at jobs using the Korn shell and C shell, respectively (submitted using the at command's -k and -c options).

Queues are defined by lines in this format:

```
q.xjynzw
```

q is a letter, *x* indicates the number of simultaneous jobs that may run from that queue, *y* specifies the nice value for processes started from that queue, and *z* says how long to wait before trying to start a new job when the maximum number for that queue or the facility are already running. The default values are 100 jobs, a nice value of 2 (where 0 is the default nice number), and 60 seconds.

The first two of the following *queuedefs* entries show typical definitions for the at and batch queues. The third entry defines the *h* queue, which can run one or two simultaneous jobs, niced to level 10, and waits for five minutes between job initiation attempts after starting one has failed:

```
a.4j1n
b.2j2n90w
h.2j10n300w
```

The desired queue is selected with the -q option to the at command. Jobs waiting in the facility's queues may be listed and removed from a queue using the -l and -r options, respectively.*

If simple batch-processing facilities like these are sufficient for your system's needs, at and batch may be of some use, but if any sort of queue priority features are required, these commands will probably prove insufficient. The manual page for at found on many Linux systems is the most honest about its deficiencies:

> at and batch as presently implemented are not suitable when users are competing for resources.

A true batch system supports multiple queues; queues that receive jobs from and send jobs to a configurable set of network hosts, including the ability to select hosts based on load-leveling criteria and to allow the administrator to set in-queue priorities (for ordering pending jobs within a queue); queue execution priorities and resource limits (the priority and limits automatically assigned to jobs started from that queue); queue permissions (which users can submit jobs to each queue); and other parameters on a queue-by-queue basis. AIX has adapted its print-spooling subsystem to provide a very simple batch system (see "The AIX Spooling Facility" in Chapter 13), allowing for different job priorities within a queue and multiple batch queues, but it is still missing most important features of a modern batch system. Some vendors offer batch-processing features as an optional feature at additional cost.

There are also a variety of open source queueing systems, including:

- Distributed Queueing System (DQS): *http://www.scri.fsu.edu/~pasko/dqs.html*
- Portable Batch System: *http://pbs.mrj.com*

Managing Memory

Memory resources have at least as much effect on overall system performance as the distribution of CPU resources. To perform well, a system needs to have adequate

---

* The BSD form of the at facility provided the atq and atrm commands for these functions, but they are obsolete forms. Also, only the implementations found on FreeBSD and Linux systems continue to require that the atrun command be executed periodically from within cron to enable the at facility (every 10 minutes was a typical interval).

memory not just for the largest jobs it will run, but also for the overall mix of jobs typical of its everyday use. For example, the amount of memory that is sufficient for the one or two big jobs that run overnight might provide only a mediocre response time under the heavy daytime interactive use. On the other hand, an amount of memory that supports a system's normal interactive use might result in quite poor performance when larger jobs are run. Thus, both sets of needs should be taken into consideration when planning for and evaluating system memory requirements.

Paging and swapping are the means by which Unix distributes available memory among current processes when their total memory needs exceed the amount of physical memory. Technically, *swapping* refers to writing an entire process to disk, thereby freeing all of the physical memory it had occupied. A swapped-out process must then be reread into memory when execution resumes. *Paging* involves moving sections of a process's memory—in units called *pages*—to disk, to free up physical memory needed by some process. A *page fault* occurs when a process needs a page of memory that is not resident and must be (re)read in from disk. On virtual memory systems, true swapping occurs rarely if at all* and usually indicates a serious memory shortage, so the two terms are used synonymously by most people.

Despite the strong negative connotations the term has acquired, paging is not always a bad thing. In the most general sense, paging is what makes virtual memory possible, allowing a process' memory requirements to greatly exceed the actual amount of physical memory. A process' total memory requirement includes the sum of the size of its executable image† (known as its *text segment*) and the amount of memory it uses for data.

To run on systems without virtual memory, the process requires an amount of physical memory equal to its current text and data requirements. Virtual memory systems take advantage of the fact that most of this memory isn't actually needed all the time. Pieces of the process image on disk are read in only as needed. The system automatically maps their *virtual addresses* (relative address with respect to the beginning of the process's image) to real physical memory locations. When the process accesses a part of its executable image or its data that is not currently in physical memory, the kernel reads in—*pages in*—what is needed from disk, sometimes replacing other pages that the process no longer needs.

For a large program that spends most of its time in two routines, for example, only the part of its executable image containing the routines needs to be in memory while they are running, freeing up for other uses the memory the rest of the program's text

---

* Some systems swap out idle processes to free memory. The swapping I refer to here is the forced swapping of active processes due to a memory shortage.

† An exception occurs for executables that can be partially or totally shared by more than one process. In this case, only one copy of the image is in memory regardless of how many processes are executing it. The total memory used by the shared portions in these cases is divided among all processes using them in the output from commands like ps.

segment would occupy on a nonvirtual memory computer. This is true whether the two routines are close together or far apart in the process' virtual address space. Similarly, if a program uses a very large data area, all of it needn't be resident in memory simultaneously if the program doesn't access it all at once. On many modern systems, program execution also always begins with a page fault as the operating system takes advantage of the kernel's virtual memory management facility to read enough of the executable image to get it started.

The problem with paging comes when there is not enough physical memory on the system for all of the processes currently running. In this case, the kernel will apportion the total memory among them dynamically. When a process needs a new page read in and there are no free or reusable pages, the operating system must steal a page that is being used by some other process. In this case, an existing page in memory is *paged out*. For volatile data, this results in the page being written to a paging area on disk; for executable pages or unmodified pages read in from file, the page is simply freed. In either case, however, when that page is again required, it must be paged back in, possibly forcing out another page.

When available physical memory is low, an appreciable portion of the available CPU time can be spent handling page faulting, and all processes will execute much less efficiently. In the worst kind of such *thrashing* conditions, the system spends all of its time managing virtual memory, and no real work gets done at all (no CPU cycles are actually used to advance the execution of any process). Accordingly, total CPU usage can remain low under these conditions.

You might think that changing the execution priorities for some of the jobs would solve a thrashing problem. Unfortunately, this isn't always the case. For example, consider two large processes on a system with only a modest amount of physical memory. If the jobs have the same execution priority, they will probably cause each other to page continuously if they run at the same time. This is a case where swapping is actually preferable to paging. If one job is swapped out, the other might run without page faulting, and after some amount of time, the situation can be reversed. Both jobs finish much sooner this way than they do under continuous paging.

Logically, lowering the priority of one of the jobs should cause it to wait to execute until the other one pauses (e.g., for an I/O operation) or completes. However, except for the special, low-priority levels we considered earlier, low-priority processes do occasionally get some execution time even when higher-priority processes are runnable. This happens to prevent a low-priority process from monopolizing a critical resource and thereby creating an overall system bottleneck or deadlock (this concern is indicative of a scheduling algorithm designed for lots of small interactive jobs). Thus, running both jobs at once, regardless of their priorities, will result in some execution degradation (even for the higher priority job) due to paging. In such cases, you need to either buy more memory or not run both jobs at the same time.

In fact, the virtual memory managers in modern operating systems work very hard to prevent such situations from occurring by using techniques for using memory efficiently. They also try to keep a certain amount of free memory all the time to minimize the risk of thrashing. These are some of the most common practices used to maximize the efficiency of the system's memory resources:

Demand paging

Pages are loaded into memory only when a page fault occurs. When a page is read in, a few pages surrounding the faulted page are typically loaded as well in the same I/O operation in an effort to head off future page faults.

Copy-on-write page protection

Whenever possible, only a single copy of identical pages in use by multiple processes is kept in memory. Duplicate, process-private copies of a page are created only if one of the processes modifies it.

Page reclaims

When memory is short, the virtual memory manager takes memory pages being used by current processes. However, such pages are simply initially marked as free and are not replaced with new data until the last possible moment. In this way, the owning process can *reclaim* them without a disk read operation if their original contents are still in memory when the pages are required again.

The next section discusses commands you can use to monitor memory use and paging activity on your system and get a picture of how well the system is performing. Later sections discuss managing the system paging areas.

Monitoring Memory Use and Paging Activity

The vmstat command is the best tool for monitoring system memory use; it is available on all of the systems we are considering. The most important statistics in this context are the number of running processes and the number of page-outs[*] and swaps. You can use this information to determine whether the system is paging excessively. As you gather data with these commands, you'll also need to run the ps command so that you know what programs are causing the memory behavior you're seeing.

The following sections discuss the memory monitoring commands and show how to interpret their output. They provide examples of output from systems under heavy loads. It's important to keep in mind, though, that all systems from time to time have memory shortages and consequent increases in paging activity. Thus, you can expect to see similar output on your system periodically. Such activity is significant only if it is persistent. Some deviation from what is normal for your system is to be expected, but consistent and sustained paging activity does indicate a memory shortage that you'll need to deal with.

---

[*] Because of the way that AIX keeps its paging statistics, page-ins are better indicators, because a page-in always means that a page was previously paged out.

Determining the amount of physical memory

The following commands can be used to quickly determine the amount of physical memory on a system:

AIX	`lsattr -HE -l sys0 -a realmem`
FreeBSD	`grep memory /var/run/dmesg.boot`
HP-UX	`dmesg | grep Phys`
Linux	`free`
Solaris	`dmesg | grep mem`
Tru64	`vmstat -P | grep '^Total'`

Some Unix versions (including FreeBSD, AIX, Solaris, and Tru64) also support the pagesize command, which displays the size of a memory page:

```
$ pagesize
4096
```

Typical values are 4 KB and 8 KB.

Monitoring memory use

Overall memory usage levels are very useful indicators of the general state of the virtual memory subsystem. They can be obtained from many sources, including the top command we considered earlier. Here is the relevant part of the output:

```
CPU states:  3.5% user,  9.4% system, 13.0% nice, 87.0% idle
Mem:   63212K av,  62440K used,   772K free, 21924K shrd,   316K buff
Swap: 98748K av,   6060K used, 92688K free                 2612K cached
```

Graphical system state monitors can also provide overall memory use data. Figure 15-2 illustrates the KDE System Guard (`ksysguard`) utility's display. It presents both a graphical view of ongoing CPU and memory usage, as well as the current numerical data in the status area at the bottom of the window.

Linux also provides the free command, which lists current memory usage statistics:

```
$ free -m -o
         total     used     free   shared   buffers   cached
Mem:       249      231       18        0        11       75
Swap:      255        2      252
```

The command's options specify display units of MB (-m) and to omit buffer cache data (-o).

The most detailed memory subsystem data is given by vmstat. As we've seen, vmstat provides a number of statistics about current CPU and memory use. vmstat output varies somewhat between implementations. Here is an example of typical vmstat output:*

---

* vmstat's output varies somewhat from system to system, as we'll see.

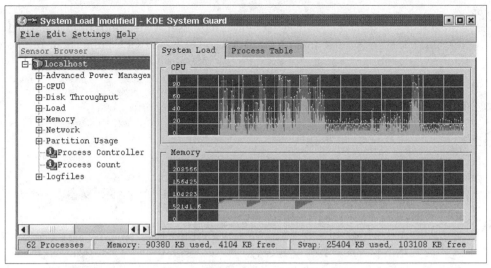

Figure 15-2. Overall system performance statistics

```
$ vmstat 5 4
procs      memory              page                 disk          faults       cpu
r b w   swap   free  re  mf pi po fr de sr s0 s6 s7 s8   in   sy  cs us sy id
0 0 0 1642648 759600 98 257 212 10 10  0  0  0  0  1  4  199  121  92  8  3 88
0 0 0 1484544 695816  0   1  0  0  0  0  0  0  0  0  0  113   35  46  0  1 99
0 0 0 1484544 695816  0   0  0  0  0  0  0  0  0  0  0  113   65  45  0  1 99
0 0 0 1484544 695816  0   0  0  0  0  0  0  0  0  0  0  111   72  44  0  1 99
```

The first line of every `vmstat` report is an average since boot time; it can be ignored for our purposes, and I'll be omitting it from future displays.*

The report is organized into sections as follows:

procs or kthr
> Statistics about active processes. Together, the first three columns tell you how many processes are currently active.

memory
> Memory use and availability data.

page or swap
> Paging activity.

io or disk
> Per-device I/O operations.

faults or system or intr
> Overall system interrupt and context switching rates.

---

* You can define an alias to take care of this automatically. Here's an example for the C shell:
  `alias vm "/usr/bin/vmstat \!:* | awk 'NR!=4'"`

cpu

> Percentage of CPU devoted to system time, user time, and time the CPU remained idle. AIX adds an additional column showing CPU time spent in idle mode while jobs are waiting for pending I/O operations.

Not all versions of vmstat contain all sections.

Table 15-5 lists the most important columns in vmstat's report.

Table 15-5. vmstat report contents

Label(s)	Meaning
r	Number of runnable processes.
b	Number of *blocked* processes (idle because they are waiting for I/O).
w	Number of swapped-out runnable processes (should be 0).
avm, act, swpd	Number of active virtual memory pages (a snapshot at the current instant). For vmstat, a page is usually 1 KB, regardless of the system's actual page size. However, under AIX and HP-UX, a vmstat page is 4 KB.
fre, free	Number of memory pages on the free list.
re	Number of page reclaims: pages placed on the free list but reclaimed by their owner before the page was actually reused.
pi, si, pin	Number of pages paged in (usually includes process startup).
po, so, pout	Number of pages paged out (if greater than zero, the system is paging).
fr	Memory pages freed by the virtual memory management facility during this interval.
dn	Disk operations per second on disk *n*. Sometimes, the columns are named for the various disk devices rather than in this generic way (e.g., *adn* under FreeBSD). Not all versions of vmstat include disk data.
cs	Number of context switches.
us	Percentage of total CPU time spent on user processes.
sy	Percentage of total CPU time spent as system overhead.
id	Idle time percentage (percentage of CPU time not used).

Here are examples of the output format for each of our systems:

```
AIX
kthr     memory             page                   faults       cpu
-----  -------------  ----------------------  -------------  -----------
 r  b   avm    fre  re pi po fr sr cy  in   sy   cs us sy id wa
 0  0 149367 847219  0  0  0  0  0  0 109  258   11 18  7 72  3

HP-UX
      procs          memory         page                              faults       cpu
  r  b  w     avm     free   re  at pi po   fr  de   sr     in  sy    cs  us sy id
  2  0  0  228488  120499    1   0  0  0   10   0    0   1021  44    29  14  1 86

Linux
      procs               memory       swap        io    system       cpu
  r  b  w   swpd   free  buff  cache  si  so    bi   bo   in   cs  us  sy  id
  1  0  0      0   4280  5960  48296   0   0     5    1  101  123   1   0  99
```

FreeBSD

procs			memory		page								disks		faults			cpu		
r	b	w	avm	fre	flt	re	pi	po	fr	sr	ad0	ad1	in	sy	cs	us	sy	id
0	0	0	5392	32500	1	0	0	0	1	0	0	0	229	9	3	0	1	99

Solaris

kthr			memory		page								disk			faults		cpu		
r	b	w	swap	free	re	mf	pi	po	fr	de	sr	dd	f0	s0	--	in	sy	cs	us	sy	id
0	0	0	695496	187920	0	1	1	0	0	0	1	0	0	0	0	402	34	45	0	0	100

Tru64
Virtual Memory Statistics: (pagesize = 8192)

procs			memory		pages							intr			cpu		
r	w	u	act	free	wire	fault	cow	zero	react	pin	pout	in	sy	cs	us	sy	id
3	135	31	15K	10K	5439	110M	8M	52M	637K	42M	63K	4	953	1K	2	0	98

Note that some versions have additional columns.

We'll look at interpreting vmstat output in the next subsection.

Recognizing memory problems

You can expect memory usage to vary quite a lot in the course of normal system operations. Short-term memory usage spikes are normal and to be expected. In general, one or more of the following symptoms may suggest a significant shortage of memory resources when they appear regularly and/or persist for a significant period of time:

- Available memory drops below some acceptable threshold. On an interactive system this may be 5%–15%. However, on a system designed for computation, a steady free memory amount of 5% may be fine.

- Significant paging activity. The most significant metrics in this case are writes to the page file (page-outs) and reads from the page file (although most systems don't provide the latter statistic).

- The system regularly thrashes, even if only for short periods of time.

- The page file gradually increases in size or remains at a high usage level under normal operations. This can indicate that additional paging space is needed or that memory itself is in low supply.

In practical terms, let's consider specific parts of the vmstat output:

- In general, the number in the *w* column should be 0, indicating no runnable swapped-out processes; if it isn't, the system has a serious memory shortage.

- The *po* column is the most important in terms of paging: it indicates the number of page-outs and should ideally be very close to zero. If it isn't, processes are contending for the available memory and the system is paging. Paging activity is also reflected in significant decreases in the amount of free memory (*fre*) and in the number of page reclaims (*re*)—memory pages taken away from one process because another one needs them even though the first process needs them too.

- High numbers in the page-ins column (*pi*) are not always significant because starting up a process involves paging in its executable image and data.* When a new process starts, this column will jump up but then quickly level off again.

The following is an example of the effect mentioned in the final bullet:

```
$ vmstat 5                                    Output is edited.
procs        memory          page
r b w     avm    fre   re    pi  po
0 1 0   81152  17864    0     0   0
1 1 0   98496  15624    0   192   0
2 0 0   84160  11648    0   320   0
2 0 0   74784   9600    0   320   0
2 0 0   74464   5984    0    64   0
2 0 0   78688   5472    0     0   0
1 1 0   60480  16032    0     0   0
^C
```

At the second data line, a compile job starts executing. There is a jump in the number of page-ins, and the available memory (*fre*) drops sharply. Once the job gets going, the page-ins drop back to zero, although the free list size stays small. When the job ends, its memory returns to the free list (final line). Check your system's documentation to determine whether process startup paging is included in vmstat's paging data.

Here is some output from a system briefly under distress:

```
$ vmstat 5                              Some columns omitted.
procs        memory          page    ...     cpu
r b w     avm    fre   re    pi  po        us sy id
1 1 0   43232  31296    0     0   0         3  0 97
1 2 0   46560  32512    0     0   0         5  0 95
5 0 0   82496   2848    2   384 608         5 37 58
2 3 0   81568   2304    2   384 448         4 63 43
4 1 0   72480   2144    0    96  96         6 71 23
5 1 0   72640   2112    0    64  32        12 76 12
4 1 0   73280   3328    0     0   0        23 26 51
2 1 0   54176  19552    0    32   0        34  1 65
^C
```

At the beginning of this report, this system was running well, with no paging activity at all. Then several new processes start up (line 5), both page-in and page-out activity increases, and the free list shrinks. This system doesn't have enough memory for all the jobs that want to run at this point, which is also reflected in the size of the free list. By the end of this report, however, things are beginning to calm down again as these processes finish.

---

* The AIX version of vmstat limits *pi* to page-ins from paging space.

The filesystem cache

Most current Unix implementations use any free memory as a data cache for disk I/O operations in an effort to maximize I/O performance. Recently accessed data is kept in memory for a time in case it is needed again, as long as there is sufficient memory to do so. However, this is the first memory to be freed if more memory is needed. This tactic improves the performance of local processes and network system access operations. However, on systems designed for computation, such memory may be better used for user jobs.

On many systems, you can configure the amount of memory that is used in this way, as we'll see.

Configuring the Virtual Memory Manager

Some Unix variations allow you to specify some of the parameters that control the way the virtual memory manager operates. We consider each Unix version individually in the sections that follow.

 These operations require care and thought and should be initially tried on nonproduction systems. Recklessness and carelessness will be punished.

AIX

AIX provides commands for customizing some aspects of the Virtual Memory Manager. You need to be cautious when modifying any of the system parameters discussed in this section, because it is quite possible to make the system unusable or even crash if you give invalid values. Fortunately, changes made with the commands in the section last only until the system is rebooted.

AIX's schedtune command (introduced in the previous section of this chapter) can be used to set the values of various Virtual Memory Manager (VMM) parameters that control how the VMM responds to thrashing conditions. In general, its goal is to detect such conditions and deal with them before they get completely out of hand (for example, a temporary spike in memory usage can result in thrashing for many minutes if nothing is done about it).

The VMM decides that the system is thrashing when the fraction of page steals (pages grabbed while they were still in use) that are actually paged out to disk[*] exceeds some threshold value. When this happens, the VMM begins suspending processes until thrashing stops.[†] It tries to select processes to suspend that are both having an effect

---

[*] Computed as *po/fr*, using the vmstat display fields.
[†] Suspended processes still consume memory, but they stop paging.

on memory performance and whose absence will actually cause conditions to improve. It chooses processes based on their own repage rates: when the fraction of its page faults are for pages that have been previously paged out rises above a certain value—by default, one fourth—a process becomes a candidate for suspension. Suspended processes are resumed once system conditions have improved and remained stable for a certain period of time (by default, 1 second).

Without any arguments, schedtune displays the current values of all of the parameters under its control, including those related to memory load management. Here is an example of its output:

```
# schedtune
         THRASH              SUSP      FORK          SCHED
 -h    -p    -m     -w    -e    -f      -d      -r      -t       -s
 SYS  PROC  MULTI  WAIT  GRACE  TICKS  SCHED_D  SCHED_R  TIMESLICE  MAXSPIN
  0    4     2      1     2     10      16       16         1        16384


 CLOCK    SCHED_FIFO2   IDLE MIGRATION   FIXED_PRI
  -c          -a            -b              -F
%usDELTA  AFFINITY_LIM  BARRIER/16        GLOBAL
  100         7             4                0
```

Table 15-6 summarizes the meanings of the thrashing-related parameters.

Table 15-6. AIX VMM parameters

Option	Label	Meaning
-h	SYS	Memory is defined as overcommitted when page writes/total page steals > 1/-h. Setting this value to 0 disables the thrash recovery mechanisms (which is the default).
-p	PROC	A process may be suspended during thrashing conditions when its repages/page faults > 1/-p. This parameter defines when an individual process is thrashing. The default is 4.
-m	MULTI	Minimum number of processes to remain running even when the system is thrashing. The default is 2.
-w	WAIT	Number of seconds to wait after thrashing ends (as defined by -h) before any reactivating suspended processes. The default is 1.
-e	GRACE	Number of seconds after reactivation before a process may be suspended again. The default is 2.

Currently, the AIX thrashing recovery mechanisms are disabled by default. In general, it is better to prevent memory overuse problems than to recover from them. However, this is not always possible, so you may find this feature useful on very busy, heavily loaded systems. To enable it, set the value of -h to 6 (the previous AIX default value).

For most systems, it is not necessary to change the default values of the other thrashing control parameters. However, if you have clear evidence that the VMM is systematically behaving either too aggressively or not aggressively enough in deciding whether memory has become overcommitted, you might want to experiment with small changes, beginning with -h or -p. In some cases, increasing the value of -w may be beneficial on systems running a large number of processes. I don't recommend changing the value of -m.

The vmtune command allows the system administrator to customize some aspects of the behavior of the VMM's page replacement algorithm. vmtune is located in the same directory as schedtune: */usr/samples/kernel*. Without options, the command displays the values of various memory management parameters:

```
# vmtune
vmtune:  current values:
  -p        -P        -r         -R         -f       -F        -N         -W
minperm  maxperm  minpgahead maxpgahead minfree maxfree pd_npages maxrandwrt
209507    838028       2          8         120     128      524288        0

   -M        -w        -k        -c        -b         -B           -u        -l       -d
maxpin npswarn npskill numclust numfsbufs hd_pbuf_cnt lvm_bufcnt lrubucket defps
838849    4096     1024        1       196        192          9       131072      1

            -s               -n        -S        -L          -g           -h
sync_release_ilock  nokilluid v_pinshm lgpg_regions lgpg_size strict_maxperm
            0                0         0          0           0           0

  -t
maxclient
 838028

number of valid memory pages = 1048561   maxperm=79.9% of real memory
maximum pinable=80.0% of real memory     minperm=20.0% of real memory
number of file memory pages = 42582      numperm=4.1% of real memory
number of compressed memory pages = 0    compressed=0.0% of real memory
number of client memory pages = 46950    numclient=4.5% of real memory
# of remote pgs sched-pageout = 0        maxclient=79.9% of real memory
```

These are *vmtune*'s most useful options for memory management:

-f *minfree*

Minimum size of the free list—a set of memory pages set aside for new pages required by processes (used to satisfy page faults). When the free list falls below this threshold, the VMM must steal pages from running processes to replenish the free list. The default is 120 pages.

-F *maxfree*

Page stealing stops when the free list reaches or exceeds this size. The default is 128 pages.

-p *minperm*

Threshold value that forces both computational and file pages to be stolen (expressed as a percentage of the system's total physical memory). The default is 18%–20% (depending on memory size).

-P *maxperm*

Threshold value that forces only file pages to be stolen (expressed as a percentage of the system's total physical memory). The default is 75%–80%.

The second pair of parameters determine to a certain extent which sorts of memory pages are stolen when the free list needs to be replenished. AIX distinguishes between *computational* memory pages, which consist of program working storage (non-file-based data) and program text segments (the executable's in-memory image). *File* pages are all other kinds of memory pages (all of which are backed by disk files). By default, the VMM attempts to slightly favor computational pages over file pages when selecting pages to steal, according to the following scheme:

Both types
    %file < *minperm* OR file-repaging ≥ computational-repaging

File pages only
    (*minperm* < %file < *maxperm* AND file-repaging < computational-repaging) OR %file > *maxperm*

%file is the percentage of pages which are file pages. Repage rates are the fraction of page faults that reference stolen or replaced memory pages rather than new pages (determined from the VMM's limited history of pages that have recently been present in memory). It may make sense to reduce *maxperm* on computationally-oriented systems.

FreeBSD

On FreeBSD systems, kernel variables may be displayed and modified with the sysctl command (and set at boot time via its configuration file */etc/sysctl.conf*). For example, the following commands display and then reduce the value for the maximum number of simultaneous processes allowed per user:

```
# sysctl kern.maxprocperuid
kern.maxprocperuid: 531
# sysctl kern.maxprocperuid=64
kern.maxprocperuid: 531 -> 64
```

Such a step might make sense on systems where users need to be prevented from overusing/abusing system resources (although, in itself, this step would not solve such a problem).

The following line in */etc/sysctl.conf* performs the same function:

```
kern.maxprocperuid=64
```

Figure 15-3 lists the kernel variables related to paging activity and the interrelationships among them.

Normally, the memory manager tries to maintain at least *vm.v_free_target* free pages. The pageout daemon, which suspends processes when memory is short, wakes up when free memory drops below the level specified by *vm.v_free_reserved* (it sleeps otherwise). When it runs, it tries to achieve the total number of free pages specified by vm.v_inactive_target.

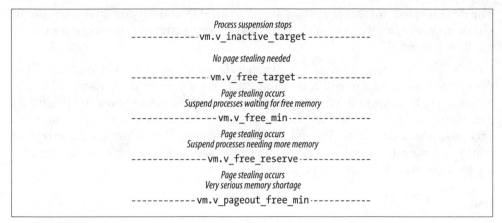

Figure 15-3. FreeBSD memory management levels

The default values of these parameters depend on the amount of physical memory in the system. On a 98 MB system, they have the following settings:

```
vm.v_inactive_target: 1524          Units are pages.
vm.v_free_target: 1016
vm.v_free_min: 226
vm.v_free_reserved: 112
vm.v_pageout_free_min: 34
```

Finally, the variables *vm.v_cache_min* and *vm.v_cache_max* specify the minimum and maximum sizes of the filesystem buffer cache (the defaults are 1016 and 2032 pages, respectively, on a 98 MB system). The cache can grow dynamically between these limits if free memory permits. If the cache size falls significantly below the minimum size, the pageout daemon is awakened. You may decide to increase one or both of these values if you want to favor the cache over user processes in memory allocation. Increase the maximum first; changing the minimum level requires great care and understanding of the memory manager internals.

HP-UX

On HP-UX systems, kernel parameters are set with the kmtune command.

Paging is controlled by three variables, in the following way:

free memory ≥ lotsfree
: Page stealing stops.

desfree ≤ free memory < lotsfree
: Page stealing occurs.

minfree ≤ free memory < desfree
: Anti-thrashing measures taken, including process deactivation (in addition to page stealing).

The default values for these variables are set by HP-UX and depend on the amount of physical memory in the system (in pages). The documentation strongly discourages modifying them.

HP-UX can use either a statically or dynamically sized buffer cache (the latter is the default and is recommended). A dynamic cache is used when the variables *nbuf* and *bufpages* are both set to 0. In this case, you can specify the minimum and maximum percentage of memory used for the cache via the variables *dbc_min_pct* and *dbc_max_pct*, which default to 5% and 50%, respectively. Depending on the extent to which you want to favor the cache or user processes in allocating memory, modifying the maximum value may make sense.

Linux

On Linux systems, modifying kernel parameters is done by changing the values within files in */proc/sys* and its subdirectories (as we've seen previously). For memory management, the relevant files are located in the *vm* subdirectory. These are the most important of them:

freepages

This file contains three values specifying a minimum free page level, a low free page level, and a desired free page level. When there are fewer than the minimum number, user processes are denied additional memory. Between the minimum and low levels, aggressive paging (page stealing) takes place, while between the low and desired levels, "gentle" paging occurs. Above the desired (highest) level, page stealing stops.

The default values (in pages) depend on the amount of physical memory in the system, but they scale as x, $2x$, and $3x$ (more or less). Successfully modifying these values requires a thorough knowledge of both the Linux memory subsystem and the system workload, and doing so is not recommended for the faint of heart.

buffermem

Specifies the amount of memory to be used for the filesystem buffer cache. The three values specify the minimum amount, the borrow percentage, and the maximum amount. They default to 2%, 10%, and 60%, respectively. When memory is short and the size of the buffer cache exceeds the borrow percentage level, pages will be stolen from the buffer cache until its size drops below this size.

If you want to favor the buffer cache over processes in allocating memory, increasing the borrow and/or maximum levels may make sense. On the other hand, if you want to favor processes, reducing the maximum and setting the borrow level close to it makes more sense.

overcommit_memory

Setting the value in this file to 1 allows processes to allocate amounts of memory larger than can actually be accommodated (the default is 0). Some application programs allocate huge amounts of memory that they never actually use, and they may run successfully if this setting is enabled.

Changing parameter values is accomplished by modifying the values in these values. For example, the following command changes the settings related to the buffer cache:

```
# echo "5  33  80" > /proc/sys/vm/buffermem
```

Solaris

On Solaris systems, you can view the values of system parameters via the kstat command. For example, the following command displays system parameters related to paging behavior, including their default values on a system with 1 GB of physical memory:

```
# kstat -m unix -n system_pages | grep 'free '
     cachefree     1966              Units are pages.
     lotsfree      1966
     desfree        983
     minfree        491
     ...
```

Figure 15-4 illustrates the meanings and interrelationships of these memory levels.

Figure 15-4. Solaris paging and swapping memory lLevels

As the figure indicates, setting *cachefree* to a value greater than *lotsfree* provides a way of favoring processes' memory over the buffer cache (by default, no distinction is made between them because *lotsfree* is equal to *cachefree*). In order to do so, you should decrease *lotsfree* to some point between its current level and *desfree* (rather than increasing *cachefree*).

 Solaris 9 has changed its virtual memory manager and has eliminated the *cachefree* variable.

Tru64

Tru64 memory management is controlled by parameters in the *sysconfig* vm subsystem. These are the most useful parameters:

- *vm_aggressive_swap*: Enable/disable aggressive swapping out of idle processes (0 by default). Enabling this can provide some memory management improvements on heavily loaded systems, but it is not a substitute for reducing excess consumption.

- There are several parameters that control the conditions under which the memory manager steals pages from active processes and/or swaps out idle processes in an effort to maintain sufficient free memory. They are listed in Figure 15-5 along with their interrelationships and effects.

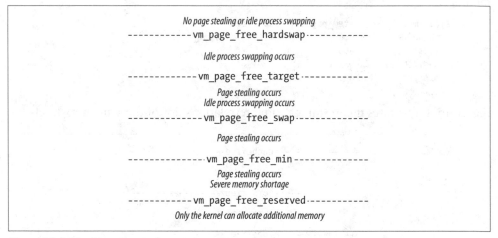

Figure 15-5. Tru64 paging and swapping memory levels

- The default for *vm_page_free_min* is 20 pages. The value of *vm_page_free_target* varies with the memory size; for a system with 1 GB of physical memory, it defaults to 512 pages. The reserved value is always 10 pages.

  The other variables are computed from these values. *vm_page_free_swap* (and the equivalent *vm_page_free_optimal*) is set to the point halfway between the minimum and the target, and *vm_page_free_hardswap* is set to about 16 times the target value.

- Several parameters relate to the size of the buffer cache. *vm_minpercent* specifies the percentage of memory initially used for the buffer cache (the default is 10%). The buffer cache size will increase if memory is available. The parameter ubc_maxpercent specifies the maximum amount of memory that it may use (the default is 100%). When memory is short and the size of the cache corresponds to *ubc_borrowpercent* or larger, pages will be returned to the general pool until the cache drops below this level (and process memory page stealing does not occur). The default for the borrow level is 20% of physical memory.

On file servers, it will often make sense to increase one or both of the minimum and borrow percentages (to favor the cache over local processes in memory allocation). On a database server, though, you will probably want to reduce these sizes.

Managing Paging Space

Specially designated areas of disk are used for paging. On most Unix systems, distinct, dedicated disk partitions—called *swap partitions*—are used to hold pages written out from memory. In some recent Unix implementations, paging can also go to special *page files* stored in a regular Unix filesystem.[*]

 Many discussions of setting up paging space advise using multiple paging areas, spread across different physical disk drives. Paging I/O performance will generally improve the closer you come to this ideal.

However, regular disk I/O also benefits from careful disk placement. It is not always possible to separate both paging space and important filesystems. Before you decide which to do, you must determine which kind of I/O you want to favor and then provide the improvements appropriate for that kind.

In my experience, paging I/O is best avoided rather than optimized, and other kinds of disk I/O deserve far more attention than paging space placement.

How much paging space?

There are as many answers to this question as there are people to ask. The correct answer is, of course, "It depends." What it depends on is the type of jobs your system typically executes. A single-user workstation might find a paging area of one to two times the size of physical memory adequate if all the system is used for is editing and small compilations. On the other hand, real production environments running programs with very large memory requirements might need two or even three times the amount of physical memory. Keep in mind that some processes will be killed if all available paging space is ever exhausted (and new processes will not be able to start).

One factor that can have a large effect on paging space requirements is the way that the operating system assigns paging space to virtual memory pages implicitly created when programs allocate large amounts of memory (which may not all be needed in

---

[*] Despite their names, both swap partitions and page files can be used for paging and for swapping (on systems supporting virtual memory).

any individual run). Many recent systems don't allocate paging space for such pages until each page is actually accessed; this practice tends to minimize per-process memory requirements and stretch a given amount of physical memory as far as possible. However, other systems assign paging space to the entire block of memory as soon as it is allocated. Obviously, under the latter scheme, the system will need more page file space than under the former.

Other factors that will tend to increase your page file space needs include:

- Jobs requiring large amounts of memory, especially if the system must run more than one at a time.
- Jobs with virtual address spaces significantly larger than the amount of physical memory.
- Programs that are themselves very large (i.e., have large executables). This often implies the item above, but not vice versa.
- A very, very large number of simultaneously running jobs, even if each individual job is fairly small.

Listing paging areas

Most systems provide commands to determine the locations of paging areas and how much of the total space is currently in use:

	List paging areas	*Show current usage*
AIX	lsps -a	lsps -a
FreeBSD	pstat -s	pstat -s
HP-UX	swapinfo -t -a -m	swapinfo -t -a -m
Linux	cat /proc/swaps	swapon -s or free -m -o
Solaris	swap -l	swap -l or -s
Tru64	swapon -s	swapon -s

Here is some output from a Solaris system:

```
swapfile            dev   swaplo blocks    free
/dev/dsk/c0t0d0s1   136,1     16 1049312   1049312
```

The Solaris swap command also has a -s option, which lists statistics about current overall paging space usage:

```
total: 22240k bytes allocated + 6728k reserved = 28968k used,
       691568k available
```

Under AIX, the command to list the paging space information is lsps -a:

```
$ lsps -a
Page Space   Phys. Volume   Volume Group   Size    %Used   Active   Auto
hd6          hdisk0         rootvg         200MB   76      yes      yes
paging00     hdisk3         uservg         128MB   34      yes      yes
```

The output lists the paging space name, the physical disk it resides on, the volume group it is part of, its size, how much of it is currently in use, whether it is currently active, and whether it is activated automatically at boot time. This system has two paging spaces totaling about 328 MB; total system swap space is currently about 60% full.

Here is some output from an HP-UX system:

```
# swapinfo -tam
                Mb      Mb      Mb   PCT  START/       Mb
TYPE         AVAIL    USED    FREE  USED  LIMIT RESERVE  PRI  NAME
dev            192      34     158   18%      0       -    1  /dev/vg00/lvol2
reserve          -      98     -98
memory          65      32      33   49%
total          257     164      93   64%      -       0    -
```

The first three lines of the output provide details about the system swap configuration. The first line (dev) shows that 34 MB is currently in use within the paging area at */dev/vg00/lvol2* (its total size is 192 MB). The next line indicates that another 98 MB has been reserved within this paging area but is not yet in use.

The third line of the display is present when pseudo-swap has been enabled on the system. This is accomplished by setting the *swapmem_on* kernel variable to 1 (in fact, this is the default). Pseudo-swap allows applications to reserve more swap space than physically exists on the system. It is important to emphasize that pseudo-swap does not itself take up any memory, up to a limit of seven eighths of physical memory. Line 3 indicates that there is 164 MB of memory overcommitment capacity remaining for applications to use (32 MB is in use).

The final line (total) is a summary line. In this case, it indicates that there is 257 MB of total swap space on this system. 164 MB of it is currently either reserved or allocated: the 34 MB allocated from the paging area plus 98 MB reserved in the paging area plus 32 MB of the pseudo-swap capacity.

Activating paging areas

Normally, paging areas are activated automatically at boot time. On many systems, swap partitions are listed in the filesystem configuration file, usually */etc/fstab*. The format of the filesystem configuration file is discussed in detail in "Managing Filesystems" in Chapter 10, although some example entries will be given here:

```
/dev/ad0s2b      none    swap    sw          0 0    FreeBSD
/dev/vg01/swap   ...     swap    pri=0       0 0    HP-UX
/dev/hda1        swap    swap    defaults    0 0    Linux
```

This entry says that the first partition on disk 1 is a swap partition. This basic form is used for all swap partitions.

Solaris systems similarly place swap areas into */etc/vfstab*:

```
/dev/dsk/c0t0d0s1  -  -  swap  -  no  -
```

Tru64 systems lists swap areas within the vm section of */etc/sysconfigtab*:

```
vm:
      swapdevice = /dev/disk/dsk0b
```

On FreeBSD, HP-UX, Tru64, and Linux systems, all defined swap partitions are activated automatically at boot time with a command like the following:

```
swapon -a > /dev/console 2>&1
```

The swapon -a command says to activate all swap partitions. This command may also be issued manually when adding a new partition. Solaris provides the *swapadd* tool to perform the same function during boots.

Under AIX, paging areas are listed in the file */etc/swapspaces*:

```
hd6:
      dev = /dev/hd6
paging00:
      dev = /dev/paging00
```

Each stanza lists the name of the paging space and its associated special file (the stanza name and the filename in */dev* are always the same). All paging logical volumes listed in */etc/swapspaces* are activated at boot time by a swapon -a command in */etc/rc*. Paging logical volumes can also be activated when they are created or by manually executing the swapon -a command.

Creating new paging areas

As we've noted, paging requires dedicated disk space, which is used to store paged-out data. Making a new swap partition on an existing disk without free space is a painful process, involving these steps:

- Performing a full backup of all filesystems currently on the device and verifying that the tapes are readable.
- Restructuring the physical disk organization (partition sizes and layout), if necessary.
- Creating new filesystems on the disk. At this point, you are treating the old disk as if it were a brand new one.
- Restoring files to the new filesystems.
- Activating the new swapping area and adding it to the appropriate configuration files.

Most of these steps are covered in detail in other chapters. A better approach is the subject of the next subsection.

Filesystem paging

Many modern Unix operating systems offer a great deal more flexibility by supporting *filesystem paging*—paging to designated files within normal filesystems. Page files

---

can be created or deleted as needs change, albeit at a modest increase in paging operating system overhead.

Under Solaris, the `mkfile` command creates new page files. For example, the following command will create the file */chem/page_1* as a 50 MB file:

```
# mkfile 50m /chem/page_1
# swap -a /chem/page_1 0 102400
```

The `mkfile` command creates a 50 MB page file with the specified pathname. The argument specifying the size of the file is interpreted as bytes unless a k (KB) or m (MB) suffix is appended to it. The regular `swap` command is then used to designate an existing file as a page file by substituting its pathname for the special filename.

On HP-UX systems, filesystem paging is initiated by designating a directory as the swap device to the `swapon` command. In this mode, it has the following basic syntax:

```
swapon [-m min] [-l limit] [-r reserve] dir
```

min is the minimum number of filesystem blocks to be used for paging (the block size is as defined when the filesystem was created: 4096 or 8192), *limit* is the maximum number of filesystem blocks to be used for paging space, and *reserve* is the amount of space reserved for files beyond that currently in use which may never be used for paging space. For example, the following command initiates paging to the */chem* filesystem, limiting the size of the page file to 5000 blocks and reserving 10000 blocks for future filesystem expansion:

```
# swapon -l 5000 -r 10000 /chem
```

You can also create a new logical volume as an additional paging space under HP-UX. For example, the following commands create and activate a 125 MB swap logical volume named *swap2*:

```
# lvcreate -l 125 -n swap2 -C y -r n  /dev/vg01
# swapon /dev/vg01/swap2
```

The logical volume uses a contiguous allocation policy and has bad block relocation disabled (-C and -r, respectively). Note that no filesystem is built on the logical volume.

On Linux systems, a page file may be created with commands like these:

```
# dd if=/dev/zero of=/swap1 bs=1024 count=8192    Create 8MB file.
# mkswap /swap1 8192                              Make file a swap device.
# sync; sync
# swapon /swap1                                   Activate page file.
```

On FreeBSD systems, a page file is created as follows:

```
# dd if=/dev/zero of=/swap1 bs=1024 count=8192    Create 8MB file.
# vnconfig -e vnc0 /swap1 swap                    Create pseudo disk /dev/vn0c
                                                  and enable swapping.
```

The `vnconfig` command configures the paging area and activates it.

Under AIX, paging space is organized as special paging logical volumes. Like normal logical volumes, paging spaces may be increased in size as desired as long as there are unallocated logical partitions in their volume group.

You can use the mkps command to create a new paging space or the chps command to enlarge an existing one. For example, the following command creates a 200 MB paging space in the volume group *chemvg*:

```
# mkps -a -n -s 50 chemvg
```

The paging space will be assigned a name like *pagingnn* where *nn* is a number: *paging01*, for example. The -a option says to activate the paging space automatically on system boots (its name is entered into */etc/swapspaces*). The -n option says to activate the paging space immediately after it is created. The -s option specifies the paging space's size, in logical partitions (whose default size is 4 MB). The volume group name appears as the final item on the command line.

The size of an existing paging space may be increased with the chps command. Here the -s option specifies the number of additional logical partitions to be added:

```
# chps -s 10 paging01
```

This command adds 40 MB to the size of paging space *paging01*.

 FreeBSD does not support filesystem paging, although you can use a logical volume for swapping in either environment. The latter makes it much easier to add an additional paging space without adding a new disk.

Linux and HP-UX paging space priorities

HP-UX and Linux allow you to specify a preferred usage order for multiple paging spaces via a priority system. The -p option to swapon may be used to assign a priority number to a swap partition or other paging area when it is activated. Priority numbers run from 0 to 10 under HP-UX, with lower numbered areas being used first; the default value is 1.

On Linux systems, priorities go from 0 to 32767, with higher numbered areas being used first, and they default to 0. It is usually preferable to give dedicated swap partitions a higher usage priority than filesystem paging areas.

Removing paging areas

Paging spaces may be removed if they are no longer needed, unless they're on the root disk. To remove a swap partition or filesystem page file in a BSD-style implementation—FreeBSD, Linux, HP-UX, and Tru64—remove the corresponding line from the appropriate system configuration file. Once the system is rebooted, the swap partition will be deactivated (rebooting is necessary to ensure that there are no active references to the partition or page file). Page files may then be removed normally with rm.

Under Solaris, the `-d` option to the `swap` command deactivates a swap area. Here are some examples:

```
# swap -d /dev/dsk/c1d1s1 0
# swap -d /chem/page_1 0
```

Once the `swap -d` command is executed, no new paging will be done to that area, and the kernel will attempt to free areas in it that are still in use, if possible. However, the file will not actually be removed until no processes are using it.

Under AIX, paging spaces may be removed with `rmps` once they are deactivated:

```
# chps -a n paging01
# rmps paging01
```

The `chps` command removes *paging01* from the list to be activated at boot time (in */etc/swapspaces*). The `rmps` command actually removes the paging space.

Administrative Virtues: Persistence

Monitoring system activity levels and tuning system performance both rely on the same system administrative virtue: persistence. These tasks naturally must be performed over an extended period of time, and they are also inherently cyclical (or even recursive). You'll need persistence most at two points:

- When you are just getting started and don't have any idea what is wrong with the system and what to try to improve the situation.
- After the euphoria from your early successes has worn off and you have to spend more time to achieve smaller improvements.

System performance tuning—and system performance itself—both follow the 80/20 rule: getting the last 20% done takes 80% of the time. (System administration itself often follows another variation of the rule: 20% of the people do 80% of the work.) Keep in mind the law of diminishing returns, and don't waste any time trying to eke out that last 5% or 10%.

Disk I/O Performance Issues

Disk I/O is the third major performance bottleneck that can affect a system or individual job. This section will look first at the tools for monitoring disk I/O and then consider some of the factors that can affect disk I/O performance.

Monitoring Disk I/O Performance

Unfortunately, Unix tools for monitoring disk I/O data are few and rather poor. BSD-like systems provide the `iostat` command (all but Linux have some version of it). Here is an example of its output from a FreeBSD system experiencing moderate usage on one of its two disks:

```
$ iostat 6
          tty            ad0            ad1            cd0            cpu
  tin tout  KB/t tps  MB/s   KB/t tps  MB/s   KB/t tps  MB/s  us ni sy in id
    0   13 31.10  71  2.16   0.00   0  0.00   0.00   0  0.00   0  0 11  2 87
    0   13 62.67  46  2.80   0.00   0  0.00   0.00   0  0.00   0  0 10  2 88
    0   13  9.03  64  0.56   0.00   0  0.00   0.00   0  0.00   1  0  7  1 91
    0   13  1.91  63  0.12   0.00   0  0.00   0.00   0  0.00   2  0  4  2 92
    0   13  2.29  64  0.14   0.00   0  0.00   0.00   0  0.00   2  0  5  1 92
```

The command parameter specifies the interval between reports (and we've omitted the first, summary one, as usual). The columns headed by disk names are the most useful for our present purposes. They show current disk usage as the number of transfers/sec (tps) and MB/sec.

System V–based systems offer the sar command, and it can be used to monitor disk I/O. Its syntax in this mode is:

```
$ sar -d interval [count]
```

interval is the number of seconds between reports, and *count* is the total number of reports to produce (the default is one). In general, sar's options specify what data to include in its report. sar is available for AIX, HP-UX, Linux, and Solaris. However, it requires that process accounting be set up before it will return any data.

This report shows the current disk usage on a Linux system:

```
$ sar -d 5 10
Linux 2.4.7-10 (dalton)        05/29/2002

07:59:34 PM       DEV      tps    blks/s
07:59:39 PM     dev3-0     9.00     70.80
07:59:39 PM    dev22-0     0.40      1.60

07:59:39 PM       DEV      tps    blks/s
07:59:44 PM     dev3-0    61.80    494.40
07:59:44 PM    dev22-0    10.80     43.20

07:59:44 PM       DEV      tps    blks/s
07:59:49 PM     dev3-0    96.60    772.80
07:59:49 PM    dev22-0     0.00      0.00

Average:          DEV      tps    blks/s
Average:        dev3-0    78.90    671.80
Average:       dev22-0     1.12      4.48
```

The first column of every sar report is a time-stamp. The other columns give the transfer operations per second and blocks transferred per second for each disk. Note that devices are specified by their major and minor device numbers; in this case, we are examining two hard disks.

Getting the Most From the Disk Subsystem

Disk performance is something that more effectively results from installation-time planning and configuration than from after-the-fact tuning. Different techniques are most effective for optimizing different kinds of I/O. This means that you'll need to understand the I/O performed by the applications/typical workload on the system.

There are two sorts of disk I/O:

Sequential access
> Data from disk is read in disk block order, one block after another. After the initial seek (head movement) to the starting point, the speed of this sort of I/O is limited by disk transfer rates.

Random access
> Data is read in no particular order. This means that the disk head will have to move frequently to reach the proper data. In this case, seek time is an important factor in overall I/O performance, and you will want to minimize it to the extent possible.

Three major factors affect disk I/O performance in general:

* Disk hardware
* Data distribution across the system's disks
* Data placement on the physical disk

Disk hardware

In general, the best advice is to choose the best hardware you can afford when disk I/O performance is an important consideration. Remember that the best SCSI disks are many times faster than the fastest EIDE ones, and also many times more expensive.

These are some other points to keep in mind:

* When evaluating the performance of individual disks, consider factors such as its local cache in addition to quoted peak transfer rates.

* Be aware that actual disk throughput will seldom if ever achieve the advertised peak transfer rates. Consider the latter merely as relative numbers useful in comparing different disks.

* Musameci and Loukides suggest using the following formula to estimate actual disk speeds: (sectors-per-track * RPM * 512)/60,000,000. This yields an estimate of the disk's internal transfer rate in MB. However, even this rate will only be achievable via sequential access (and rarely even then).

    When random access performance is important, you can estimate the number of I/O operations per second as 1000/(average-seek-time + 30000/rpm)

* Don't neglect to consider the disk controller speed and other characteristics when choosing hardware. Fast disks won't perform as well on a mediocre controller.

- Don't overload disk controllers. Placing disks on multiple disk controllers is one way to improve I/O throughput rates. In configuring a system, be sure to compare the maximum transfer rate for each disk adapter with the sum of the maximum transfer rates for all the disks it will control; obviously, placing too large a load on a disk controller will do nothing but degrade performance. A more conservative view states that you should limit total maximum disk transfer rates to 85%–90% of the top controller speed.

  Similarly, don't overload system busses. For example, a 32-bit/33MHz PCI bus has a peak transfer rate of 132 MB/sec, less than what an Ultra3 SCSI controller is capable of.

Distributing the data among the available disks

The next issue to consider after a system's hardware configuration is planning data distribution among the available disks: in other words, what files will go on which disk. The basic principle to take into account in such planning is to distribute the anticipated disk I/O across controllers and disks as evenly as possible (in an attempt to prevent any one resource from becoming a performance bottleneck). In its simplest form, this means spreading the files with the highest activity across two or more disks.

Here are some example scenarios that illustrate this principle:

- If you expect most of a system's I/O to come from user processes, distributing the files they are likely to use across multiple disks usually works better than putting everything on a single disk.

- A system intended to support multiple processes with large I/O requirements will benefit from placing the data for different programs or jobs on different disks (and ideally on separate controllers). This minimizes the extent to which the jobs interfere with one another.

- For a system running a large transaction-oriented database, ideally you will want to place each of the following item pairs on different disks:
  - Tables and their indexes.
  - Database data and transaction logs.
  - Large, heavily used tables accessed simultaneously.

  Given the constraints of an actual system, you may have to decide which of these separations is the most important.

Of course, placing heavily accessed files on network rather than local drives is almost always a guarantee of poor performance. Finally, it is also almost always a good idea to use a separate disk for the operating system filesystem(s) (provided you can afford to do so) to isolate the effects of the operating system's own I/O operations from user processes.

Data placement on disk

The final disk I/O performance factor that we will consider is the physical placement of files on disk. The following general considerations apply to the relationship between file access patterns, physical disk location, and disk I/O performance:

- Sequential access of large files (i.e., reading or writing, starting at the beginning and moving steadily toward the end) is most efficient when the files are contiguous: made up of a single, continuous chunk of space on disk. Again, it may be necessary to rebuild a filesystem to create a large amount of contiguous disk space.* Sequential access performance is highest at the outer edge of the disk (i.e., beginning at 0) because the platter is the widest at that point (head movement is minimized).

- Disk I/O to large sequential files also benefits from software disk striping, provided an appropriate stripe size is selected (see "From Disks to Filesystems" in Chapter 10). Ideally, each read should result in one I/O operation (or less) to the striped disk.

- Placing large, randomly accessed files in the center portions of disk drives (rather than out at the edges) will yield the best performance. Random data access is dominated by seek times—the time taken to move the disk heads to the correct location—and seek times are minimized when the data is in the middle of the disk and increases at the inner and outer edges. AIX allows you to specify the preferred on-disk location when you create a logical volume (see "From Disks to Filesystems" in Chapter 10). With other Unix versions, you accomplish this by defining physical disk partitions appropriately.

- Disk striping is also effective for processes performing a large number of I/O operations.

- Filesystem fragmentation degrades I/O performance. Fragmentation results when the free space within a filesystem is made of many small chunks of space (rather than fewer large ones of the same aggregate size). This means that files themselves become fragmented (noncontiguous), and access times to reach them become correspondingly longer. If you observe degrading I/O performance on a very full filesystem, fragmentation may be the cause.

  Filesystem fragmentation tends to increase over time. Eventually, it may be necessary or desirable to use a defragmenting utility. If none is available, you will need to rebuild the filesystem to reduce fragmentation; the procedure for doing so is discussed in "From Disks to Filesystems" in Chapter 10.

---

* Unfortunately, some disks are too smart for their own good. Disks are free to do all kinds of remapping to improve their concept of disk organization and to mask bad blocks. Thus, there is no guarantee that what look like sequential blocks to the operating system are actually sequential on the disk.

Tuning Disk I/O Performance

Some systems offer a few hooks for tuning disk I/O performance. We'll look at the most useful of them in this subsection.

Sequential read-ahead

Some operating systems attempt to determine when a process is accessing data files in a sequential manner. When it decides that this is the access pattern being used, it attempts to aid the process by performing *read-ahead* operations: reading more pages from the file than the process has actually requested. For example, it might begin by retrieving two pages instead of one. As long as sequential access of the file continues, the operating system might double the number of pages read with each operation before settling at some maximum value.

The advantage of this heuristic is that data has often already been read in from disk at the time the process asks for it, and so much of the process's I/O wait time is eliminated because no physical disk operation need take place.

AIX. AIX provides this functionality. You can alter the default threshold value of 2 and 8 pages using these vmtune options:

-r *minpgahead*
> Starting number of pages for sequential read aheads.

-R *maxpgahead*
> Maximum number of pages to read ahead. You will want to increase this parameter for striped filesystems. Good values to try are 8–16 times the number of component drives.

Both parameters must be a power of 2.

Linux. Linux provides some kernel parameters related to read-ahead behavior. They may be accessed via these files in */proc/sys/vm*:

page-cluster
> Determines the number of pages read in by a single read operation. The actual number is computed as 2 raised to this power. The default setting is 4, resulting in a page cluster size of 16. Large sequential I/O operations may benefit from increasing this value.

min-readahead and max-readahead
> Specify the minimum and maximum pages used for read-ahead. They default to 3 and 31, respectively.

Finally, the Linux Logical Volume Manager allows you to specify the read-ahead size when you create a logical volume with lvcreate, via its -r option. For example, this command specifies a read-ahead size of 8 sectors and also creates a contiguous logical volume:

```
# lvcreate -L 800M -n bio_lv -r 8 -C y vg1
```

The valid range for -r is 2 to 120.

Disk I/O pacing

AIX also provides a facility designed to prevent general system interactive performance from being adversely affected by large I/O operations. By default, write requests are serviced by the operating system in the order in which they are made (queued). A very large I/O operation can generate many pending I/O requests, and users needing disk access can be forced to wait for them to complete. This occurs most frequently when an application computes a large amount of new data to be written to disk (rather than processing a data set by reading it in and then writing it back out).

You can experience this effect by copying a large file—32MB or more—in the background and then running an ls command on any random directory you have not accessed recently on the same physical disk. You'll notice an appreciable wait time before the ls output appears.

Disk I/O pacing is designed to prevent large I/O operations from degrading interactive performance. It is disabled by default. Consider enabling it only under circumstances like those described.

This feature may be activated by changing the values of the *minpout* and *maxpout* system parameters using the chdev command. When these parameters are nonzero, if a process tries to write to a file for which there are already *maxpout* or more pending write operations, the process is suspended until the number of pending requests falls below *minpout*.

maxpout must be one more than a multiple of 4: 5, 9, 13, and so on (i.e., of the form $4x+1$). *minpout* must be a multiple of 4 and at least 4 less than *maxpout*. The AIX documentation suggests starting with values of 33 and 16, respectively, and observing the effects. The following command will set them to these values:

```
# chdev -l sys0 -a maxpout=33 -a minpout=16
```

If interactive performance is still not as rapid as you want it to be, try decreasing these parameters; on the other hand, if the performance of the job doing the large write operation suffers more than you want it to, increase them. Note that their values do persist across boot because they are stored in the ODM.

Monitoring and Managing Disk Space Usage

This section looks at the tools available to monitor and track disk space usage. It then goes on to discuss ways of approaching a perennial administrative challenge: getting users to reduce their disk use.

Where Did It All Go?

The `df -k` command produces a report that describes all the filesystems, their total capacities, and the amount of free space available on each one (reporting sizes in KB). Here is the output from a Linux system:

```
File system   Kbytes   used    avail   capacity   Mounted on
/dev/sd0a     7608     6369    478     93%        /
/dev/sd0g     49155    45224   0       102%       /corp
```

This output reports the status of two filesystems: */dev/sd0a*, the root disk, and */dev/sd0g*, the disk mounted at *corp* (containing all files and subdirectories underneath */corp*). Each line of the report shows the filesystem's name, the total number of kilobytes on the disk, the number of kilobytes in use, the number of kilobytes available, and the percentage of the filesystem's storage that is in use. It is evident that both filesystems are heavily used. In fact, the */corp* filesystem appears to be overfull.

As we've noted earlier, the operating system generally holds back some amount of space in each filesystem, allocatable only by the superuser (usually 10%, although Linux uses 5% by default). A filesystem may appear to use over 100% of the available space when it has tapped into this reserve.

The `du -k` command reports the amount of disk space used by all files and subdirectories underneath one or more specified directories, listed on a per-subdirectory basis (amounts are given in KB).

A typical du report looks like this:

```
$ du -k /home/chavez
50     /home/chavez/bin
114    /home/chavez/src
...
34823 /home/chavez
```

This report states that in the directory */home/chavez*, the subdirectory *bin* occupies 50 blocks of disk space, and the subdirectory *src* occupies 114 blocks. Using the *du* command on users' home directories and on directories where ongoing development is taking place is one way to determine who is using the system's disk space.

The report from du can be inordinately long and tedious. By using the `-s` option, you eliminate most of the data; du `-s` reports the total amount of disk space that a directory and its contents occupies, but it does not report the storage requirements of each subdirectory. For example:

```
$ du -k -s /home/chavez
34823 /home/chavez
```

In many cases, this may be all the information you care about.

To generate a list of the system's directories in order of size, execute the command:

```
$ du -k / | sort -rn
```

This command starts at the root filesystem, lists the storage required for each directory, and pipes its output to sort. With the -rn options (reverse sort order, sort by numeric first field), sort orders these directories according to the amount of storage they occupy, placing the largest first.

If the directory specified as its parameter is large or has a large number of subdirectories, du can take quite a while to execute. It is thus a prime candidate for automation via scripts and after-hours execution via cron.

The quot command breaks down disk space usage within a single filesystem by user. This command is available on all of the systems we are considering except Linux.[*] quot has the following syntax:

```
# quot file-system
```

quot reports the number of kilobytes used by each user in the specified filesystem. It is run as *root* (to access the disk special files). Here's a typical example:

```
# quot /
/dev/sd0a (/):
6472    root
5234    bin
62      sys
2       adm
```

This report indicates that on the root disk, 6472 kilobytes are owned by the user *root*, 5234 kilobytes are owned by user *bin*, and so on. This command can help you spot users who are consuming excessive amounts of disk space, especially in areas other than their home directories. Like du, quot must access the entire disk and so can take an appreciable amount of time to execute.

Handling Disk Shortage Problems

The commands and scripts we've just looked at will let you know when you have a disk space shortage and where the available space went, but you'll still have to solve the problem and free up the needed space somehow. There is a large range of approaches to solving disk space problems, including the following:

- Buy another disk. This is the ideal solution, but it's not always practical.
- Mount a remote disk that has some free space on it. This solution assumes that such a disk is available, that mounting it on your system presents no security problems, and that adding additional data to it won't cause problems on its home system.
- Eliminate unnecessary files. For example, in a pinch, you can remove the preformatted versions of the manual pages provided that the source files are also available on your system.

---

[*] Linux does provide it for xfs filesystems.

- Compress large, infrequently accessed files.

- Convince or cajole users into deleting unneeded files and backing up and then deleting old files they are no longer using. If you are successful, a great deal of free disk space usually results. At the same time, you should check the system for log files that can be reduced in size (discussed later in this section).

  When gentle pressure on users doesn't work, sometimes peer pressure will. The system administrator on one system I worked on used to mail a list of the top five "disk hogs"—essentially the output of the quot command—whenever disk space was short. I recommend this approach only if you have both a thick skin and a good-natured user community.

- Some sites automatically archive and then delete user files that haven't been accessed in a certain period of time (often two or three months). If a user wants a file back, he can send a message to the system administration staff, who will restore it. This approach is the most brutal and should only be taken when absolutely necessary. It is fairly common in university environments, but rarely used elsewhere. It's also easy to circumvent by touching all your files every month, and performing system backups may also reset access times on inactive files.

These, then, are some of the alternatives.* In most cases, though, when you can't add any disks to the system, the most effective way to solve a disk space problem is to convince users to reduce their storage requirements by deleting old, useless, and seldom (if ever) used files (after backing them up first). Junk files abound on all systems. For example, many text editors create checkpoint and backup files as protection against a user error or a system failure. If these accumulate, they can consume a lot of disk space. In addition, users often keep many versions of files around (noticed most often in the case of program source files), frequently not even remembering what the differences are between them.

The system scratch directory /tmp also needs to be cleared out periodically (as well as any other directories serving a similar function). If your system doesn't get rebooted very often, you'll need to do this by hand. You should also keep an eye on the various system spooling directories under /usr/spool or /var/spool because files can often become stagnant there.

Unix itself has a number of accounting and logging files that, if left unattended, will grow without bound. As administrator, you are responsible for extracting the relevant data from these files periodically and then truncating them. We'll look at dealing with these sources of wasted space in the following sections.

---

* There is another way to limit users' disk usage on some systems: disk quotas (discussed later in this section). However, quotas won't help you once the disks are already too full.

Under some circumstances, a filesystem's performance can begin to degrade when a filesystem is more than 80%–90% full. Therefore, it is a good idea to take any corrective action before your filesystems reach this level, rather than waiting until they are completely full.

Using find to locate or remove wasted space

The find command may be used to locate potential candidates for archival and deletion (or just deletion) in the event of a disk space shortage. For example, the following command prints all files with names beginning with *.BAK.* or ending with a tilde, the formats for backup files from two popular text editors:

```
$ find / -name ".BAK.*" -o -name "*~" -print
```

As we've seen, find can also delete files automatically. For example, the following command deletes all editor backup files over one week old:

```
# find / /bio /corp -atime +7 \( -name ".BAK.*" \
    -o -name "*~" \) -type f -xdev -exec rm -f {} \;
```

When using find for automatic deletion, it pays to be cautious. That is why the previous command includes the -type and -xdev options and lists each filesystem separately. With the cron facility, you can use find to produce a list of files subject to deletion nightly (or to delete them automatically).

Another tactic is to search the filesystem for duplicate files. This will require writing a script, but you'll be amazed at how many you'll find.

Limiting the growth of log files

The system administrator is responsible for reaping any data needed from log files and keeping them to a reasonable size. The major offenders include these files:

- The various system log files in *usr/adm* or *var/adm*, which may include *sulog*, *messages*, and other files set up via */etc/syslog.conf*.

- Accounting files in *usr/adm* or *var/adm*, especially *wtmp* and *acct* (BSD) or *pacct* (System V). Also, under System V, the space consumed by the cumulative summary files and ASCII reports in */var/adm/acct/sum* and */var/adm/acct/fiscal* are worth monitoring.

- Subsystem log files: many Unix facilities, such as cron, the mail system, and the printing system, keep their own log files.

- Under AIX, the files *smit.log* and *smit.script* in users' home directories are appended to every time someone runs SMIT. They become large very quickly. You should watch the ones in your own and *root*'s home directories (if you su to *root*, the files still go into your own home directory). Alternatively, you could run the smit command with the -l and -s options (which specify the log and script filenames respectively) and set both filenames to */dev/null*. Defining an alias is the easy way to do so:

```
alias smit="smit -l /dev/null -s /dev/null"       bash/ksh
alias smit "smit -l /dev/null -s /dev/null"       csh/tcsh
```

There are several approaches to controlling the growth of system log files. The easiest is to truncate them by hand when they become large. This is advisable only for ASCII (text) log files. To reduce a file to zero length, use a command such as:

```
# cat /dev/null > /var/adm/sulog
```

Copying from the null device into the file is preferable to deleting the file, because in some cases the subsystem won't recreate the log file if it doesn't exist. It's also preferable to rm followed by touch because the file ownerships and permissions remain correct and also because it releases the disk space immediately.

To retain a small part of the current logging information, use tail, as in this example:

```
# cd /var/adm
# tail -100 sulog >tmp
# cat tmp > sulog
```

A third approach is to keep several old versions of a log file on the system by periodically deleting the oldest one, renaming the current one, and then recreating it. This technique is described in "Essential Administrative Techniques" in Chapter 3.

AIX provides the skulker script (stored in */usr/sbin*) to perform some of these filesystem cleanup operations, including the following:

- Clearing the queueing system spooling areas of old, junk files.
- Clearing */tmp* and */var/tmp* of all files over one day old.
- Deleting old news files (over 45 days old).
- Deleting a variety of editor backup files, core dump files, and random executables (named *a.out*). You may want to add to the list of file types.

The system comes set up to run skulker every day at 3 A.M. via cron, but the crontab entry is commented out. If you want to run skulker, you'll need to remove the comment character from the skulker line in *root*'s crontab file.

Controlling Disk Usage with Disk Quotas

Disk space shortages are a perennial problem on all computers. For systems where direct control over how much disk space each user uses is essential, disk quotas may provide a solution.

The disk quota system allows an administrator to limit the amount of filesystem storage that any user can consume. If quotas are enabled, the operating system will maintain separate quotas for each user's disk space and inode consumption (equivalent to the total number of files he owns) on each filesystem.

There are two distinct kinds of quota: a *hard limit* and a *soft limit*. A user is never allowed to exceed his hard limit, under any circumstances. When a user reaches his hard limit, he'll get a message that he has exceeded his quota, and the operating system will refuse to allocate any more storage. A user may exceed the soft limit for a limited period of time; in such cases, he gets a warning message, and the operating system grants the request for additional storage. If his disk usage still exceeds this soft limit at the next login, the message will be repeated. He'll continue to receive warnings at each successive login until either:

- He reduces his disk usage to below the soft limit, or
- He's been warned a fixed number of times (or for a specified period of time, depending on the implementation). At this point, the operating system will refuse to allocate any more storage until the user deletes enough files that his disk usage again falls below his soft limit.

The disk quota system has been designed to let users have large temporary files, provided that in the long term, they obey a much stricter limit. For example, consider a user with a hard limit of 15,000 blocks and a soft limit of 10,000 blocks. If this user's storage *ever* exceeds 15,000 blocks, the operating system will refuse to allocate any more storage immediately; he will need to free some storage before he can save any more files. If this user's storage exceeds 10,000 blocks, he'll get a warning but requests for more disk space will still be honored. However, if this user does not reduce his storage below 10,000 blocks, the operating system will eventually refuse to allocate any additional storage until it does fall below 10,000 blocks.

If you decide to implement a quota system, you must determine which filesystems need quotas. In most situations, the filesystems containing user home directories are appropriate candidates for quotas. Filesystems that are reserved for public files (for example, the *root* filesystem) probably shouldn't use quotas. The */tmp* filesystem doesn't usually have quotas because it's designed to provide temporary scratch space.

 Many operating systems require quotas to be enabled in the kernel, and many kernels do not include them by default. Check your kernel configuration before attempting to use quotas.

Preparing filesystems for quotas

After deciding which filesystems will have quotas, you'll need to edit the filesystem entries in the filesystem configuration file (usually */etc/fstab*) to indicate that quotas are in use by editing the options field, as in these examples:[*]

```
FreeBSD
/dev/ad1s1a     /1   ufs      rw,userquota    1 1
```

---

[*] There are two versions of the Linux disk quota facility. This discussion describes Version 1 because Version 2 is relatively new.

Linux
```
/dev/sdb2        /1   reiserfs  usrquota,grpquota 1 1
```

HP-UX
```
/dev/vg01/lvol3  /1   vxfs      rw,quota          0 1
```

Tru64
```
chem_domain#one  /1   advfs     rq                0 1
```

Solaris
```
/dev/dsk/c0t3d0s0 ... /1 ufs  2  yes  rw,logging,quota
```

See "Managing Filesystems" in Chapter 10 for full details on the filesystem configuration file on the various systems.

On AIX systems, add a line like the following to the filesystem's stanza in */etc/filesystems*:

```
quota = userquota,groupquota
```

Include the *userquota* keyword for standard disk quotas and the *groupquota* keyword for group-based disk quotas (described in the final part of this section).

Next, make sure that there is a file named *quotas* in the top-level directory of each filesystem for which you want to establish quotas. If the file does not exist, create it with the touch command:[*]

```
# cd /chem
# touch quotas
# chmod 600 quotas
```

The file must be writable by *root* and no one else.

Setting users' quota limits

Use the edquota command to establish filesystem quotas for individual users. This command can be invoked to edit the quotas for a single user:

```
# edquota username(s)
```

When you execute this command, edquota creates a temporary file containing the hard and soft limits on each filesystem for each user. After creating the file, edquota invokes an editor so you can modify it (by default, vi; you can use the environment variable *EDITOR* to specify your favorite editor). Each line in this file describes one filesystem. The format varies somewhat; here is an example:

```
/chem: blocks in use: 13420, limits (soft=20000, hard=30000)
       inodes in use: 824, limits (soft=0, hard=0)
```

This entry specifies quotas for the */chem* filesystem; by editing it, you can add hard and soft limits for this user's total disk space and inode space (total number of files).

---

[*] This is not always required by recent quota system implementations, but it won't hurt either.

Setting a quota to 0 disables that quota. The example specifies a soft quota of 20,000 disk blocks, a hard quota of 30,000 disk blocks, and no quotas on inodes. Note that the entry in the temporary file does not indicate anything about the user(s) to which these quotas apply; quotas apply to the user specified when you execute the edquota command. When you list more than one user on the command line, you will edit a file for each one of them in turn.

After you save the temporary quota file and exit the editor (using whatever commands are appropriate for the editor you are using), edquota modifies the *quotas* files themselves. These files cannot be edited directly.

The -p option to edquota lets you copy quota settings between users. For example, the following command applies *chavez*'s quota settings to users *wang* and *harvey*:

```
# edquota -p chavez wang harvey
```

Setting the soft limit expiration period

edquota's -t option is used to specify the system-wide time limit for soft quotas. Executing edquota -t also starts an editor session something like this one:

```
Time units may be: days, hours, minutes, or seconds
Grace period before enforcing soft limits for groups:
/chem: block grace period: 3 days, file grace period: 0 days
```

A value of zero days indicates the default value is in effect (usually seven days). You can specify the time period in other units by changing *days* to one of the other listed keywords. Some implementations allow you to specify the grace period in months as well, but then one would have to start to wonder what the point of using disk quotas was in the first place.

Enabling quota checking

The quotaon command is used to activate the quota system and enable quota checking:

```
# quotaon filesystem
# quotaon -a
```

The first command enables the quota system for the specified filesystem. The latter enables quotas on all filesystems listed with quotas in the filesystem configuration file. For example, the following command enables quotas for the */chem* filesystem:

```
# quotaon /chem
```

Similarly, the command quotaoff disables quotas. It can be used with the -a option to disable all quotas, or with a list of filesystem names.

Quota consistency checking

The quotacheck command checks the consistency of the *quotas* file for the filesystem specified as its argument. It verifies that the quota files are consistent with current actual disk usage. This command should be executed after you install or modify the quota system. If used with the option -a, quotacheck checks all filesystems designated as using quotas in the filesystem configuration file.

quotacheck -a and quotaon -a also need to be run at boot time (in this order). You may need to add them to one of the system boot scripts on AIX systems. The other Unix versions run them automatically, via these boot scripts:

FreeBSD	*/etc/rc* (if check_quotas="yes" in */etc/rc.conf*)
HP-UX	*/sbin/init.d/localmount*
Linux	*/etc/init.d/quota*
	(SuSE 7: if START_QUOTA="yes" in */etc/rc.config*)
Solaris	*/etc/init.d/MOUNTFS* and *ufs_quota*
Tru64	*/sbin/init.d/quota* if QUOTA_CONFIG="yes" in */etc/rc.config*

Disk quota reports

The repquota command reports the current quotas for one or more specified filesystem(s). Here is an example of the reports generated by *repquota*:

```
# repquota -v /chem
*** Report for user quotas on /chem (/dev/sd1d)
                     Block limits                File limits
User          used    soft    hard   grace    used   soft   hard   grace
chavez  --   13420   20000   25000            824      0      0
chen    +-    2436    2000    3000   2days       8      0      0
```

The plus sign in the entry for user *chen* indicates that he has exceeded his disk quota.

Users can use the quota command to determine where their current disk usage falls with respect to their disk quotas.

Group-based quotas (AIX, FreeBSD, Tru64 and Linux)

AIX, FreeBSD, Tru64, and Linux extend standard disk quotas to Unix groups as well as individual users. Specifying the -g option to edquota causes names on the command line to be interpreted as group names rather than as usernames. Similarly, edquota -t -g allows you to specify the soft limit timeout period for group quotas.

By default, the quotaon, quotaoff, quotacheck, and repquota commands operate on both user and group quotas. You can specify the -u and -g options to limit their scope to only user quotas or only group quotas, respectively. Users must use the following form of the quota command to determine the current status of group quotas:

```
$ quota -g chem
```

For example, this command will report the disk quota status for group *chem*. Users may query the disk quota status only for groups of which they are a member.

Network Performance

This section concludes our look at performance monitoring and tuning on Unix systems. It contains a brief introduction to network performance, a very large topic whose full treatment is beyond the scope of this book. Consult the work by Musameci and Loukides for further information.

Basic Network Performance Monitoring

The netstat -s command is a good place to start when examining network performance. It displays network statistics. You can limit the display to a single network protocol via the -p option, as in this example from an HP-UX system:

```
$ netstat -s -p tcp                    Output shortened.
tcp:
    178182 packets sent
        111822 data packets (35681757 bytes)
        30 data packets (3836 bytes) retransmitted
        66363 ack-only packets (4332 delayed)
    337753 packets received
        89709 acks (for 35680557 bytes)
        349 duplicate acks
        0 acks for unsent data
        284726 packets (287618947 bytes) received in-sequence
        0 completely duplicate packets (0 bytes)
        3 packets with some dup, data (832 bytes duped)
        11 out of order packets (544 bytes)
        5 packets received after close
        11 out of order packets (544 bytes)
```

The output gives statistics since the last boot.[*]

Network operations are proceeding nicely on this system. The highlighted lines are among those that would indicate transmission problems if the values in them rose to appreciable percentages of the total network traffic.

More detailed network performance data can be determined via the various network monitoring tools we considered in "Monitoring the Network" in Chapter 8.

General TCP/IP Network Performance Principles

Good network performance depends on a combination of several components working properly and efficiently. Performance problems can arise in many places and take many forms. These are among the most common:

- Network interface problems, including insufficient speed and high error rates due to failing or misconfigured hardware. This sort of problem shows up as poor performance and/or many errors on a particular host.

---

[*] Or most recent counter reset, if supported.

Network adapters, hubs, switches, and network devices in general seldom fail all at once, but rather produce increasing error rates and/or degrading performance over time. These metrics should be monitored regularly to spot problems before they become severe. Degradation can also occur due to aging drop cables.

Hardware device setup errors, including half/full duplex mismatches, cause high error and collision rates and result in hideous performance.

- Overloaded servers can also produce poor network response. Servers can have several kinds of shortfalls: too much traffic for its interface to handle, too little memory for the network workload (or an incorrect configuration), and insufficient disk I/O bandwidth. The server's performance will need to be investigated to determine which of these are relevant (and hence where the most attention to the problem should be paid).

- Insufficient network bandwidth for the workload. You can recognize such situations by the presence of slow response and/or significant timeouts on systems throughout the local network, which is not alleviated by the addition of another server system. The best solution to such problems is to use high-performance switches. If this is not possible, another, much less desirable, solution is to divide the network into multiple subnets that separate systems requiring distinct network resources from one another.

All of these problem types are best addressed via by correcting or replacing hardware and/or reallocating resources rather than configuration-level tuning.

Two TCP parameters

TCP operations are controlled by a very large number of parameters. Most of them should not be modified by nonexperts. In this subsection, we'll consider two that are most likely to produce significant improvements with little risk.

- The maximum segment size (MSS) determines the largest "packet" size that the TCP protocol will transmit across the network. (The actual size will be 40 bytes larger due to the IP and TCP headers.) Larger segments result in fewer transmissions to transfer a given amount of data and usually provide correspondingly better performance on Ethernet networks.[*] For Ethernet networks, the maximum allowed size, 1460 bytes (1500 minus 40), is usually appropriate.[†]

---

[*] Note that this will often not be the case for slow network links, especially for applications that are very sensitive to network transmission latencies.

[†] When is it inappropriate? When the headers are larger than the minimum and using a size this large causes packet fragmentation and its resultant overhead. For example, a value of 1200–1300 is more appropriate when, say, the PPP over Ethernet protocol is used, as would be the case on a web server accessed by cable modem users.

- Socket buffer sizes. When an application sends data across the network via the TCP protocol, it is first placed in a buffer. From there, the protocol will divide it as needed and create segments for transmission. Once the buffer is full, the application generally must wait for the entire buffer to be transmitted and acknowledged before it is allowed to queue additional data.

  On faster networks, a larger buffer size can improve application performance. The tradeoff here is that each buffer consumes memory, so the system must have sufficient available memory resources to accommodate all of the buffers for (at least) the usual network load. For example, using read and write socket buffers of 32 KB for each of 500 network connections would require approximately 32 MB of memory on the network server ($32 \times 2 \times 500$). This would not be a problem on a dedicated network server but might be an issue on busy, general-purpose systems.

  On current systems with reasonable memory sizes and no other applications with significant memory requirements, socket buffer sizes of 48 to 64 KB are usually reasonable.

Table 15-7 lists the relevant parameters for each of our Unix versions, along with the commands that may be used to modify them.

Table 15-7. Important TCP parameters

Version	Command	Socket Buffers [default in KB]	MSS [default in bytes]
AIX	`no -o param=value`	tcp_sendspace [16] tcp_recvspace [16]	tcp_mssdflt [512]
FreeBSD	`sysctl param=value` *(also /etc/sysctl.conf)*	net.inet.tcp.sendspace [32] net.inet.tcp.recvspace [64]	net.inet.tcp.mssdflt [512]
HP-UX	`ndd -set /dev/tcp param value` *(also /etc/rc.config.d/nddconf)*	tcp_recv_hiwater_def [32] tcp_xmit_hiwater_def [32]	tcp_mss_def [536]

Linux 2.4 kernel	`echo "value" >`
	`    /proc/sys/net/core/file`
	`echo "values" >`
	`    /proc/sys/net/ipv4/file`
	(holds 3 values: min, default, max)
		rmem_max [64]
		wmem_max [64]
		tcp_rmem [~85]
		tcp_wmem [16]
			not tunable

Solaris	`ndd -set /dev/tcp param value`	tcp_recv_hiwat [48] rcp_xmit_hiwat [48]	tcp_mss_def_ipv4 [512]
Tru64	`sysconfig -r inet param=value` *(also /etc/sysconfigtab)*	tcp_sendspace [60] tcp_recvspace [60]	tcp_mssdflt [536]

The remaining sections will consider performance issues associated with two important network subsystems: DNS and NFS.

DNS Performance

DNS performance is another item that is easiest to affect at the planning stage. The key issues with DNS are:

- Sufficient server capacity to service all of the clients
- Balancing the load among the available servers

At the moment, the latter is best accomplished by specifying different name server orderings within the */etc/resolv.conf* files on groups of client systems. It is also helpful to provide at least one DNS server on each side of slow links.

Careful placement of forwarders can also be beneficial. At larger sites, a two-tiered forwarding hierarchy may help to channel external queries through specific hosts and reduce the load on other internal servers.

Finally, use separate servers for handling internal and external DNS queries. Not only will there be performance benefits for internal users, it is also the best security practice.

DNS itself can also provide a very crude sort of load balancing via the use of multiple A records in a zone file, as in this example:

```
docsrv    IN    A    192.168.10.1
          IN    A    192.168.10.2
          IN    A    192.168.10.3
```

These records define three servers with the hostname *docsrv*. Successive queries for this name will receive each IP address in turn.[*]

This technique is most effective when the operations that are requested from the servers are all essentially equivalent, and so a simple round robin distribution of them is appropriate. It will be less successful when requests can vary greatly in size or resource requirements. In such cases, manual assigning servers to the various clients will work better. You can do so by editing the nameserver entries in */etc/resolv.conf*.

NFS Performance

The Network File System is a very important Unix network service, so we'll complete our discussion of performance by considering some of its performance issues.

Monitoring NFS-specific network traffic and performance is done via the `nfsstat` command. For example, the following command lists NFS client statistics:

```
$ nfsstat -rc

Client rpc:
```

---

[*] Actually, each query will receive each IP address as the first entry in the list that is returned. Most clients pay attention only to the top entry.

```
tcp:        calls    badxids   badverfs   timeouts   newcreds
              0         0          0          0          0
            ...
udp:        calls    badxids   badverfs   timeouts   newcreds    retrans
            302241      7          0          3          0          0
          badcalls    timers     waits
              7         22          0
```

This system performs NFS operations using the UDP protocol (the traditional method), so the TCP values are all 0. The most important items to consider in this report are the following:

timeouts

Operations that failed because the server failed to respond in time. Such operations must be repeated.

badxids

Duplicate replies received for operations that were retransmitted (indicating a "false positive" timeout).

If either of these values is appreciable, there is probably an NFS bottleneck somewhere. If *badxids* is within a factor of, say, 6–7 of timeouts, the responsiveness the remote NFS server is the source of the client's performance problems. On the other hand, if there are many more *timeouts* than *badxids*, then general network congestion is to blame.

The nfsstat command's -s option is used to obtain NFS server statistics:

```
$ nfsstat -s

Server nfs:
        calls   badcalls   badprog   badproc   badvers   badargs
        59077      0          0         0         0         0
    unprivport  weakauth
        0          0


Server nfs V2: (54231 out of 59077 calls)
        null       getattr     setattr        root     lookup    readlink        read
     0   0%     30   0%     12   0%      0   0%    68   0%     0   0% 30223   55%
      wrcache       write       create      remove     rename        link     symlink
     0   0% 23776  43%      4   0%      4   0%     0   0%     0   0%     0   0%
       mkdir        rmdir      readdir      statfs
     1   0%      0   0%     42   0%     71   0%


Server nfs V3: (4846 out of 59077 calls)
        null       getattr     setattr      lookup      access    readlink        read
     0   0%    366   7%      0   0%   3096  63%   711  14%     0   0%     0   0%
       write       create        mkdir     symlink       mknod      remove       rmdir
     0   0%      0   0%      0   0%      0   0%     0   0%     0   0%     0   0%
      rename         link      readdir    readdir+       fsstat      fsinfo    pathconf
     0   0%      0   0%     47   0%    345   7%   166   3%    12   0%   103   2%
      commit
     0   0%
```

The first section of the report gives overall NFS server statistics. The remainder of the report serves to break down NFS operations by type. This server supports both NFS Versions 2 and 3, so we see values in both of the final two sections of the report.

NFS Version 3 performance improvements

Many Unix systems are now providing NFS Version 3 instead of or in addition to Version 2. NFS Version 3 has many benefits in several areas; reliability, security, performance are among them. The following are the most important improvements provided by NFS Version 3:

- TCP versus UDP: Traditionally, NFS uses the UDP transport protocol. NFS Version 3 uses TCP as its default transport protocol.* Doing so provides NFS operations with both flow control and packet-level retransmission. By contrast, when using UDP, any network failure requires that the entire operation be repeated. Thus, using TCP often results in smaller performance hits when there are problems.

- Two-phase writes: Previously, NFS write operations were performed synchronously, meaning that a client had to wait for each write operation to be completed before starting another one. Under NFS Version 3, write operations are performed in two parts:

  — The client queues a write request, which the server acknowledges immediately. Additional write operations can be queued once the acknowledgement is received.

  — The client commits the write operation (possibly after some intermediate modifications), and the server commits it to disk (or requests its retransmission if the data is no longer available (e.g., if there was an intervening system crash).

- The maximum data block size is increased (the previous limit was 8 KB). The actual maximum value is determined by transport protocol; for TCP, it is 32 KB. In addition to reducing the number of packets, a larger block size can result in fewer disks seeks and faster sequential file access. The effect is especially noticeable with high-speed networks.

NFS performance principles

The following points are important to keep in mind with respect to NFS server performance, especially in the planning stages:

- Mounting NFS filesystems in the background (i.e., with the bg option) will speed up boots.

---

* Some NFS Version 2 implementations can also optionally use TCP instead of UDP.

- Use an appropriate number of NFS daemon processes. The rule of thumb is 2 per expected simultaneous client process. In contrast, if there are idle NFS daemons on a server, you can reduce the number and release their (albeit small) memory resources.

- Very busy NFS servers will benefit from a multiprocessor computer. CPU resources are almost never an issue for NFS, but the context switches generated by very large numbers of clients can be significant.

- Don't neglect the usual system memory and disk I/O performance considerations, including the size of the buffer cache, filesystem fragmentation, and data distribution across disks.

- NFS searches remote directories sequentially, entry by entry, so avoid remote directories with large numbers of files.

- Remember that not every task is appropriate for remote files. For example, compiling a program such that the object files are written to a remote filesystem will run very slowly indeed. In general, source files may be remote, but object files and executables should be created on the local system. In general, for best network performance, avoid writing large amounts of data to remote files (although you may to sacrifice disk and network I/O performance in order to use the CPU resources of a fast remote system).

Resources for You

After all of this discussion of system resources, it's worth spending a little time considering ones for yourself. Resources for system administrators come in many varieties: books and magazines, web sites and news groups, conferences and professional organizations, and humor and fun (all work and no play won't do anything positive for your performance).

Here are some of my favorites:

- An excellent Unix internals book: *UNIX Internals: The New Frontier* by Uresh Vahalia (Prentice-Hall).
- Sys Admin magazine, *http://www.sysadminmag.com*
- Useful web sites: *http://www.ugu.com*, *http://www.lwn.net*, *http://www.slashdot.com* (the last for news and rumors).
- LISA: an annual conference for system administrators run by Usenix and Sage (see *http://www.usenix.org/events*).
- *UNIX Hater's Handbook*, ed. Simson Garfinkel, Daniel Weise, and Steve Strassmann (IDG Books) This is still the funniest book I've read in a long time. You can expect to waste a few hours at work if you start reading it there because you won't be able to put it down.

CHAPTER 16
Configuring and Building Kernels

As we've noted many times before, the kernel is the heart of the Unix operating system. It is the core program, always running while the operating system is up, providing and overseeing the system environment. The kernel is responsible for all aspects of system functioning, including:

- Process creation, termination and scheduling
- Virtual memory management (including paging)
- Device I/O (via interfaces with *device drivers*: modules that perform the actual low-level communication with physical devices such as disk controllers, serial ports, and network adapters)
- Interprocess communication (both local and network)
- Enforcing access control and other security mechanisms

Traditionally, the Unix kernel is a single, monolithic program. On more recent systems, however, the trend has been toward *modularized* kernels: small core executable programs to which additional, separate object or executable files—*modules*—can be loaded and/or unloaded as needed. Modules provide a convenient way to provide support for a new device type or add specific new functionality to an existing kernel.

In many instances, the standard kernel program provided with the operating system works perfectly well for the system's needs. There are a few circumstances, however, where it is necessary to create a custom kernel (or perform equivalent customization activities) to meet the special needs of a particular system or environment. Some of the most common are:

- To add capabilities to the kernel (e.g., support for disk quotas or a new filesystem type)
- To add support for new devices

- To remove unwanted capabilities/features from the kernel to reduce its size and resource consumption (mostly memory) and thereby presumably improve system performance
- To change the values of hardwired kernel parameters that cannot be modified dynamically

How often you have to build a new kernel depends greatly on which system you are administering. On some older systems (mid-1990s versions of SCO Unix come to mind), you had to build a new kernel any time you added even the smallest, most insignificant new device or capability to the system. On most current systems, such as FreeBSD and Tru64, you build a kernel only when you want to significantly alter the system configuration. And on a few systems, like Solaris and especially AIX, you may never have to do so.

In this chapter, we'll look at the process of building a customized kernel, and we'll also examine administering kernel modules. There are many reasons you might want to alter the standard kernel: addressing performance issues, supporting a device and subsystem, removing features the system doesn't use (in an effort to make the kernel smaller), adjusting the operating system's behavior and resource limits, and so on. We won't be able to go into every possible change you might make on each of the systems we are considering. Instead, we'll look at the general process you go through to make a kernel, including how to install it and boot from it and how to back out your changes should they prove unsatisfactory.

 Custom kernel building and reconfiguration is not for the faint-hearted, the careless or the ignorant. Know what you're doing, and why, to avoid inadvertently making your system unusable.

In general, building a custom kernel consists of these steps:

- Installing the kernel source code package (if necessary)
- Applying any patches, adding new device driver code, and/or making any other source code changes you may require
- Saving the current kernel and its associated configuration files
- Modifying the current system configuration as needed
- Building a new kernel executable image
- Building any associated kernel modules (if applicable)
- Installing and testing the new kernel

Table 16-1 lists the kernel locations and kernel build directories for the operating systems we are considering.

Table 16-1. Standard kernel image and build directory locations

	Kernel	Configuration or build directory
AIX	*/unix*	none
FreeBSD	*/kernel*	*/usr/src/sys/i386/conf[a]*
HP-UX	*/stand/vmunix*	*/stand/build*
Linux	*/boot/vmlinuz*	*/usr/src/linux*
Solaris	*/kernel/unix* (or *genunix[b]*)	none
Tru64	*/vmunix* or */genvmunix[b]*	*/usr/sys/conf*

[a] This component is architecture-specific; i386 is the generic subdirectory for Intel-based PCs. If you're running on a more recent CPU type, building a kernel for that specific processor may improve the operating system's performance.

[b] The *gen* forms are the generic, hardware-independent versions of the kernel.

We'll begin with the kernel build process on FreeBSD and Tru64 systems (which are very similar) and then consider each of the other environments in turn. In each case, we will also consider other mechanisms for configuring the kernel and/or kernel modules that are available.

 It is possible on many systems to change some kernel parameters while the system is running. We'll look at those mechanisms in this chapter as well. You will also want to review the discussion of the */proc* filesystem in "Monitoring and Controlling Processes" in Chapter 15.

FreeBSD and Tru64

Tru64 and FreeBSD use an almost identical process for building a customized kernel. They rely on a configuration file for specifying which capabilities to include within the kernel and setting the values of various system parameters. The configuration file is located in */usr/sys/conf* on Tru64 systems and in */usr/src/sys/arch/conf* under FreeBSD, where *arch* is an architecture-specific subdirectory (we'll use *i386* as an example).

Configuration filenames are conventionally all uppercase, and the directory typically contains several different configuration files. The one used to build the current kernel is usually indicated in the */etc/motd* file. For example, the *GENERIC* file was used to build the kernel on this FreeBSD system:

```
FreeBSD 4.3-RELEASE (GENERIC) #0: Sat Apr 21 10:54:49 GMT 2001
```

Default Tru64 configuration files are often named *GENERIC* or sometimes *ALPHA*.

On FreeBSD systems, you will first need to install the kernel sources if you have not already done so:

```
FreeBSD
# cd /
# mkdir -p /usr/src/sys          If not already present.
# mount /cdrom
# cat /cdrom/src/ssys.[a-d]* | tar xzvf -
```

To add a device to a Tru64 system, you must boot the generic kernel, */genvmunix*, to force the system to recognize and create configuration information for the new device:

```
Tru64
# shutdown -r now
...
>>> boot -fi /genvmunix
...
# bcheckrc or lsmbstartup
# sizer -n NEWDEVS
```

On both systems, the first step in configuring and building a kernel is to save a copy of the old configuration file and then make any necessary changes to it:

```
FreeBSD                            Tru64
# cd /usr/src/sys/i386/conf        # cd /usr/sys/conf
# cp GENERIC NEWKERN               # cp GENERIC NEWKERN
# chmod +w NEWKERN                 # chmod +w NEWKERN
# emacs NEWKERN                    # emacs NEWKERN [/tmp/NEWDEVS]
```

The *GENERIC* configuration file is the standard, hardware-independent version provided with the operating system. If you have already customized the kernel, you would start with the corresponding configuration file instead.

While editing the new configuration file, add (or activate) lines for new devices or features, disable or comment out lines for services you don't want to include, and specify the values for any applicable kernel parameters. In general, it's unlikely that you'll need to modify the contents of hardware device–related entries. The one exception is the *ident* entry, which assigns a name to the configuration. You should change it so its value corresponds to the name you have selected:

```
ident NEWKERN
```

You may also occasionally remove unneeded subsystems by commenting out the corresponding option's entry, as in this example, which disables disk quotas:

```
#options QUOTA        Tru64
```

On Tru64 systems, you will need to merge in any new device lines from the file created by the `sizer` command (placed into */tmp*), indicated by the optional second parameter to the Tru64 `emacs` command above. One way to locate these device lines is to `diff` that file against your current kernel configuration file or the *GENERIC* file.

The FreeBSD configuration file contains a large number of settings, most of them corresponding to hardware devices and their characteristics. In addition, there are several entries specifying the values of various kernel parameters that might need to be altered in some circumstances. For example:

```
FreeBSD
options    MAXCONS=4
options    MAXDSIZ="(256*1024*1024)"
device         usb                 USB device support.
device         ugen
```

```
device          ohci
device          uhci
device          uhid               Human interface support (needed for mouse).
device          ums                USB mouse.
```

These entries specify the maximum number of virtual consoles and the maximum individual process address space and also select support for a USB mouse. (Note that these lines come from various points in the configuration file.)[*]

You can examine the *LINT* or *NOTES* configuration file for documentation on most available parameters.

The next step in the kernel build process is to run the command that creates a custom build area for the new configuration:

```
FreeBSD                              Tru64
# config NEWKERN                     # doconfig -c NEWKERN
# cd ../../compile/NEWKERN           # cd ../NEWKERN
# make depend                        # make depend
# make                               # make vmunix
# mv /kernel /kernel.save            # mv /vmunix /vmunix.save
# make install                       # cp ./vmunix /
```

doconfig and config create the *NEWKERN* subdirectory, where the new kernel is actually built. Once the make commands complete, the new kernel may be installed in the root directory and tested.

If there are problems building the new kernel, you can boot the saved version with these commands:

```
FreeBSD                              Tru64
disk1s1a:> unload                    >>> boot -fi vmunix.save
disk1s1a:> load kernel.save
disk1s1a:> boot
```

Changing FreeBSD Kernel Parameters

FreeBSD also allows many kernel parameters to be changed dynamically. The sysctl command can be used to list all kernel parameters along with their current values:

```
# sysctl -a
kern.ostype: FreeBSD
kern.osrelease: 4.3-RELEASE
kern.osrevision: 199506
kern.maxvnodes: 6322
kern.maxproc: 532
kern.maxfiles: 1066
...
```

---

[*] Many kernel parameters can also be modified via the sysctl command and its initialization file (see "Managing Memory" in Chapter 15).

The sysctl manual page indicates which parameters may be modified.

You can use this command form to modify a parameter value:

```
# sysctl kern.maxfiles=1066
kern.maxfiles: 1064 -> 1066
```

Such changes do not persist across boots, so they must be repeated each time your system starts. You can also place the desired settings—the string given to -w—into the file */etc/sysctl.conf* to have them automatically applied at boot time. Alternatively, you can rebuild the kernel after setting the corresponding options in the kernel configuration files.

FreeBSD Kernel Modules

FreeBSD also provides support for kernel modules; you can compile them via the corresponding subdirectories in */usr/src/sys/modules*. The `kldstat -v` command displays a list of currently-loaded kernel modules. Virtually all are used for supporting devices or filesystem types. You can load and unload kernel modules manually with the `kldload` and `kldunload` commands.

The file */boot/loader.conf* specifies modules that should be loaded at boot time:

```
userconfig_script_load="YES"    Line created by sysinstall.
usb_load="YES"                  Load USB modules.
ums_load="YES"
umass_load="YES"
```

Of course, you need to create the required modules before they can be autoloaded.

Installing the FreeBSD Boot Loader

Generally, the FreeBSD boot loader is installed by default in the Master Boot Record (MBR) of the system disk. However, should you ever need to, you can install it manually with this command:

```
# boot0cfg -B /dev/ad0
```

The -B option says to leave the partition table unaltered.

You can also use this command's -m option to prevent certain partitions from appearing in the boot menu. This option takes a hexadecimal integer as its argument. The value is interpreted as a bit mask that includes (bit is on) or excludes (bit is off) each partition from the menu (provided that it is a BSD partition in the first place). The ones bit in the mask corresponds to the first partition, and so on.

For example, the following command enables only partition 3 to be listed in the menu:

```
# boot0cfg -B -m 0x4 /dev/ad0
```

The `disklabel -B` command can be used to install the boot program into the boot portion of a FreeBSD subpartition within a physical disk partition, as in this example, which installs the boot program into the first subpartition in the first partition:

```
# disklabel -B /dev/ad0s1
```

Tru64 Dynamic Kernel Configuration

Tru64 also supports two sorts of kernel reconfiguration without needing to build a new kernel: subsystem loading and unloading and kernel parameter modifications.

A very few subsystems may be dynamically loaded and unloaded into the Tru64 kernel. You can list all configured subsystems using the `sysconfig` command:

```
# sysconfig -s
cm: loaded and configured
hs: loaded and configured
ksm: loaded and configured
...
```

Subsystems can be loaded or unloaded. The `-m` option displays whether each one is dynamic (loadable and unloadable with a running kernel) or static:

```
# sysconfig -m | grep dynamic
hwautoconfig: dynamic
envmon: dynamic
lat: dynamic
```

On this system, only three subsystems are dynamic. For these modules, you can use the `sysconfig -c` and `-u` options to load and unload them, respectively.

Static and dynamic subsystems can also have settable kernel parameters associated with them. You can view the list of available parameters with a command like this one:

```
# sysconfig -Q lsm        Parameters for the Logical Storage Manager
lsm:
Module_Name -             type=STRING op=Q min_len=3 max_len=30
lsm_rootdev_is_volume -   type=INT op=CQ min_val=0 max_val=2
Enable_LSM_Stats -        type=INT op=CRQ min_val=0 max_val=1
```

The display lists the parameter name, its data type, allowed operations, and valid range of values. The operations are specified via a series of code letters: *Q* means can be queried, *C* means the change occurs after reboot, *R* means the change occurs on a running system.

In our example, the first parameter (the name of the module) can be queried but not modified; the second parameter (whether the root filesystem is a logical volume) can be modified, but the new value won't take effect until the system reboots; and the third parameter (whether subsystem statistics are recorded) takes effect as soon as it is changed.

You use the -q option to display the current value of a parameter and the -r option to change its value:

```
# sysconfig -q lsm Enable_LSM_Stats
lsm:
Enable_LSM_Stats = 0
# sysconfig -r lsm Enable_LSM_Stats=1
Enable_LSM_Stats: reconfigured
```

The */etc/sysconfigtab* file can be used to set kernel parameters at boot time (see "Managing Memory" in Chapter 15).

If you prefer a graphical interface, the dxkerneltuner utility can also be used to view and modify the values of kernel parameters. The sys_attrs manual page provides descriptions of kernel parameters and their meanings.

HP-UX

SAM is still the easiest way to build a new kernel under HP-UX. However, you can build one manually if you prefer:[*]

```
# cd /stand                                    Move to kernel directory.
# mv vmunix vmunix.save                        Save current kernel.
# cd build                                     Move to build subdirectory.
# /usr/lbin/sysadm/system_prep -v -s system    Extract system file.
# kmtune -s var=value -S /stand/build/system   Modify kernel parameters.
  ...
# mk_kernel -s ./system -o ./vmunix_new        Build new kernel.
# kmupdate /stand/build/vmunix_new             Schedule  kernel install.
# mv /stand/system /stand/system.prev          Save old system file.
# mv /stand/build/system /stand/system         Install new system file.
```

The system_prep script creates a new *system* configuration file by extracting the information from the running kernel. The kmtune command(s) specify the values of kernel variables for the new kernel.

The mk_kernel script calls the config command and initiates the make process automatically. Once the kernel is built, you use the kmupdate command to schedule its installation at the next reboot. You can then reboot to activate it.

If there is a problem with the new kernel, you can boot the saved kernel with a command like the following:

```
ISL> hpux /stand/vmunix.save
```

To determine what kernel object files are available, use the following command to list the contents of the */stand* directory:

```
ISL> hpux ll /stand
```

---

[*] This command is also useful for simply listing the modified variables in the current kernel.

The *system* file contains information about system devices and settings for various kernel parameters. Here are some examples of the latter:

```
maxfiles_lim   1024    Maximum open files per process.
maxusers        250    Number of users/processes to assume when sizing kernel data structures.
nproc           512
```

You can also use SAM to configure these parameters and then rebuild the kernel. Figure 16-1 illustrates using SAM to modify a kernel parameter (in this case, the length of the time slice: the maximum period for which a process can execute before being interrupted by the scheduler).

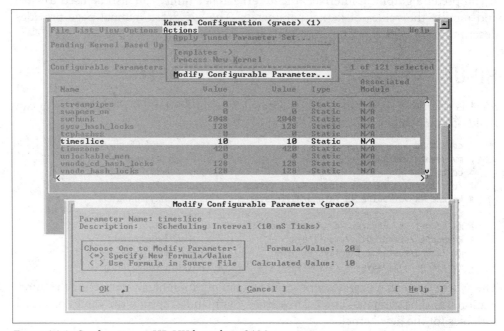

Figure 16-1. Configuring an HP-UX kernel via SAM

The SAM interface also provides descriptions of the available parameters (illustrated in Figure 16-2).

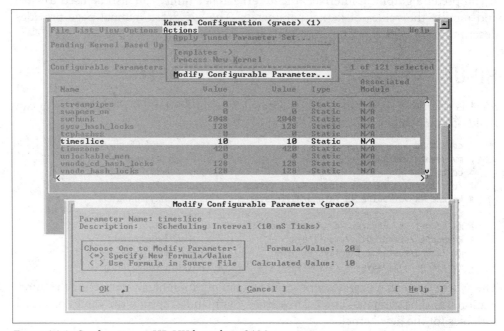

Figure 16-2. SAM Help for kernel parameters

You can build the new kernel by selecting the Actions → Process New Kernel menu option.

HP also provides various sets of kernel parameters for specific system uses. You can access them via the Actions → Apply Tuned Parameter Set menu option. Selecting it results in a list of available sets. For example, the CAE/ME/General Eng. Workstation 64-Bit Kernel is a good choice for any systems whose workload will be dominated by high-performance, compute-intensive 64-bit applications. Once you have selected a set, you can modify the parameters further or simply build a new kernel.

A few kernel parameters can be modified dynamically, most easily via SAM. You can also use the sysdef command to view the system parameters:

```
# sysdef
NAME            VALUE    BOOT    MIN-MAX          UNITS   FLAGS
acctresume          4    -       -100-100                 -
acctsuspend         2    -       -100-100                 -
maxdsiz        503808    -          0-655360     Pages    -
maxfiles         1024    -         30-2048                -
maxuprc            75    -          3-                     -
nbuf           262598    -          0-                     -
timeslice          10    -         -1-2147483648 Ticks    -
```

(This output includes only selected parameters.) The output columns display the parameter name, current value, the value when the system was booted (only if the value has been altered since then), the valid range of values, the units in which the value was measured, and a flag indicating whether the parameter can be modified on a running system (*M* means it is modifiable).

Linux

There was a time when changes to the Linux kernel came out on a daily basis, and the hardest part about building a Linux kernel was knowing how to stop. These days, the production kernel tree is much more stable, but there are still significant kernel updates released on a regular basis.

One way to take advantage of these updates is to download and install the kernel update packages made available in conjunction with the Linux distribution you are using. The advantage of this method is that the changes are merged into the actual distribution's kernel source code—in other words, the source code as modified by the distribution's creators—a process that can be daunting and difficult for anyone else.

However, you may still decide to build your own custom kernel, probably beginning from a standard source-code package. If you decide to go this route, be sure that you understand any changes that may be required to support distribution-specific features that you may be using.

The following commands illustrate the basic procedure for building a Linux kernel (the conservative way, not the kernel hacker's way). By way of illustration, they apply patches to bring the source code package to the current revision level before building the kernel.

The first steps are to save the old kernel and unpack the kernel source code, if necessary:

```
# cp /boot/vmlinuz /boot/vmlinuz.save          Save current kernel.
# cd /usr/src                                  Change to source code area.
# bzip2 -dc linux-2.4.x.tar.bz2 | tar xvf -    Unpack starting kernel.
```

You may choose to install a source-code RPM from your distribution instead of the standard tar archive (the latter is available from *http://www.kernel.org*).

Once you have the Linux kernel source code installed, you start the process here:

```
# for p in patch-list; do                      Apply any patches to kernel.
> bzip2 -dc /tmp/patch$p.bz2 | patch -p0
> done
# cd /usr/src/linux                            Change to build directory.
# cp arch/i386/config.in{,.save}               Save configuration file.
# cp .config .config.save                      If it exists.
# make mrproper                                Clean build area.
# make xconfig                                 Select kernel options.
```

The final command starts an X-based kernel configuration editor (illustrated in Figure 16-3). This utility allows you to specify a huge number of kernel parameters and select the features that you want to include.

The utility divides the available settings into a series of categories accessible from its main window (uppermost in the figure). In the bottom window, we see the settings related to filesystem support, and we have just enabled support for disk quotas by clicking the *y* button in the first item. In this case, we can choose only whether to enable or disable support for the item, and the capability will be included in or excluded from the kernel according to our choice. For other items, however, there is a third option, corresponding to the middle check mark (labeled *m:*), which is used to enable support for the feature via a loadable module. In our example, kernel support for the automounter is provided in this way.

If you are not running X, you may use a text-based menu configuration utility by running `make menuconfig` instead. In the last resort, you may run the `make config` command, which allows you to specify kernel parameters and other settings by answering a series of (seemingly) hundreds of prompts.

 On SuSE Linux systems, the configuration of the currently running kernel can be found in */proc/config.gz*. This functionality is not available in the standard Linux kernel but was added by SuSE for convenience.

Figure 16-3. The Linux make xconfig utility

After completing the kernel configuration, we next verify that certain include-file directory links are present and point to the correct places: the *asm* and *linux* include subdirectories of */usr/include* point to the source tree, and the source tree's *include/ asm* subdirectory points to the correct architecture-specific subdirectory:

```
# ls -ld /usr/include/{linux,asm}
lrwxrwxrwx 1 root system 26   Apr 25 16:03    /usr/include/asm ->
                                         /usr/src/linux/include/asm
lrwxrwxrwx 1 root system 26   Dec 23 21:01   /usr/include/linux ->
                                         /usr/src/linux/include/linux

# ls -ld include
include/:
total 10
lrwxrwxrwx 1 root system 8    Mar  8 17:40   asm -> asm-i386
drwxr-xr-x 2 root system 1024 Apr 25 16:01   asm-alpha
drwxr-xr-x 2 root system 1024 Dec 29 02:04   asm-generic
drwxr-xr-x 2 root system 1024 Apr 25 16:01   asm-i386
drwxr-xr-x 2 root system 1024 Dec  6 04:47   asm-m68k
drwxr-xr-x 2 root system 1024 Apr 25 16:01   asm-mips
```

```
drwxr-xr-x 2 root system 1024 Apr 25 16:01  asm-ppc
drwxr-xr-x 2 root system 1024 Apr 25 16:01  asm-sparc
...
```

Next, we perform some additional preparatory steps:

```
# make dep
# make clean
# emacs Makefile
```

The purpose of editing the *Makefile* is simply to specify a name for this configuration by modifying the *EXTRAVERSION* line near the top:

```
EXTRAVERSION="-new_2-4-666"
```

This variable specifies a suffix that is added to the new kernel executable image file and related file (e.g., *vmlinuz-new_2-4-666* in the example above).

Now, we are ready to begin the actual build process:

```
# make bzImage
# make install
```

The final command installs the kernel and associated files into the proper locations.

If you are using kernel modules (discussed in a bit), you must run these commands as well:

```
# make modules
# make modules_install
```

If you are using a SCSI adapter, you will also need to update the initial RAM disk image used to load the appropriate module:

```
# mkinitrd /boot/initrd-suffix suffix
```

suffix is the suffix you defined to identify the new kernel; in this case, it also identifies the subdirectory of */lib/modules* to use in building the new *initrd* file.

The final step of the build process is to reconfigure and update the Linux boot loader, lilo, which is the subject of the next section. Alternatively, you can use the newer grub loader (which is discussed after lilo) for which reconfiguration is optional.

Using lilo

As we noted in Chapter 4, the boot process on a microcomputer has three stages: the system's master boot record (MBR) contains the primary boot program that starts the boot process and loads a secondary boot program from the boot blocks of the active partition; this second boot program is what loads the actual kernel.

For Intel-based systems, Linux provides lilo, the *Linux Loader*, and most distributions install lilo into the MBR when Linux is installed. You can also install it manually with a command like this one:

```
# lilo -C /etc/lilo.conf
```

The -C option specifies the location of lilo's configuration file; the location in the preceding command is in fact the default location, so this -C clause is redundant.

The *lilo.conf* file specifies lilo's behavior for certain aspects of the boot process and also defines the kernels and operating systems that it can boot. The following sample *lilo.config* file lists the most important entries and the ones that you are most likely to want or need to modify:

```
# global parameters section: apply to all choices
prompt                              Allow user to enter a boot command.
timeout=100                         Wait 10 seconds, then boot default entry.
install=/boot/boot.b                Second stage boot loader.
boot=/dev/hda                       Where to install lilo (no partition=>MBR).
message = /boot/boot.message        Text file displayed before boot prompt.
default = linux                     Default image label.

# first boot selection
image = /boot/vmlinuz               Path to kernel.
label = linux                       Boot prompt response to boot this entry.
root = /dev/hda2                    Partition holding the root directory.
read-only                           Initial mount is read-only.
# kernel argument for ancient Sony CD-ROM
append = "cdu31a=0x340,0,"          Specifies parameters to pass to kernel
                                    (changes device's compiled-in I/O address).

# another Linux boot selection
image = /boot/vmlinuz-safe          An alternate Linux kernel.
label = safe                        Corresponding prompt response.
alias = aok                         Another label for this entry.
root = /dev/hda2
read-only

# a Windows 2000 selection
other = /dev/hda3                   Some other operating system.
label = win2k
table = /dev/hda                    Use this partition table.
```

Generally, lilo gets installed into the MBR area of the system disk using a *boot* configuration file entry like the one above, which references only the disk as a whole (here, */dev/hda*), not any specific partition. However, you can also install the utility into the boot sector of a single disk partition by running a lilo command using the same configuration file and its -b option (which replaces the boot entry in the configuration file). For example, this command loads lilo into the boot sector of the first partition on the first hard disk:

```
# lilo -b /dev/hda1 -C /etc/lilo.conf
```

I tend to install lilo in both the MBR and the Linux partition for maximum flexibility. This way, if I decide to remove lilo from the MBR, I'll be all set to switch over to the Linux partition version.

Booting a Linux partition on the second hard drive is handled in the same basic way. For this to work, lilo must be installed in the MBR of the system's boot disk, as well as in the boot sector of the Linux partition itself on the second disk.

You will need to rerun the lilo command to reinstall it *every* time you rebuild the kernel or change any relevant aspect of the disk partitioning scheme, because it relies on this information when booting. If you forget to do this, the system will not boot and you'll have to boot from a floppy. You will also need to rerun lilo if you change the text of the *boot.message* file.

Using a graphical message screen

Recent versions of lilo provide support for a graphical boot menu screen. The most recent versions of SuSE Linux use this feature, which is defined via configuration file entries like these:

```
message=/boot/message              Image file location.
menu-title="Linux System"
menu-scheme=Wg:kw:Wg:wg            Menu lettering color scheme.
```

The binary image file is created with the mkbootmsg utility (it is part of the gfxboot-devel package). The colon-separated subfields of the *menu-scheme* entry specify colors for the menu's text, highlight bar, border and title text; see the *lilo.conf* manual page for details on specify colors.

lilo and Windows

The final section (stanza) of the sample *lilo.conf* file illustrates the format for booting a Windows partition on the first hard disk. The entry for a Windows operating system on the second hard drive (i.e., *D:*) is more complicated and looks something like this:

```
other = /dev/hdb1        A different operating system.
map-drive=0x80           "Swap" C: and D:.
        to=0x81
map-drive=0x81
        to=0x80
table = /dev/hdb         Use this partition table.
label = w2ksrv           Corresponding prompt response.
```

The *map-drive* commands tricks the BIOS thinking the second disk is the system (*C:*) drive.

You can also boot Linux from the Windows 2000/XP boot menu. You need to be sure that lilo is installed into the *partition* boot sector. Then you need to extract that boot sector by booting off alternate media and running a dd command like this one:

```
# dd if=/dev/hda2 of=linux.ldr bs=512 count=1
```

Then copy the output file to the Windows system disk's root directory and add an entry like the following to the *Boot.Ini* file:

```
multi(0)disk(0)rdisk(0)partition(1)\linux.ldr="Linux"
```

The specified path is to the Windows partition. This causes the Windows boot loader to start the Linux boot loader from its root directory, and the latter is configured to boot Linux from the proper partition.

More complex booting scenarios

It is also possible to boot a Linux partition on each of two disks. The procedure for doing so is the following:

- Decide which partition will be the usual Linux boot partition and set up lilo to boot it and any other non-Linux operating systems on both disks. Create an entry like the following for the second Linux partition:

```
other = /dev/hdb2
label=eviltwin
unsafe
```

- Create a *boot.message* file that tells you which Linux will be booted when you select the default option. Install this configuration into the MBR on the *C:* drive.

- Create (or retain) another lilo configuration to be used on the Linux partition on the second disk. Make sure that this partition's *boot.message* file also lets you know where you are. Install this configuration into the *Linux partition only*; make sure that the *boot* entry specifies the partition and *not* the disk as a whole. (If you want, you can also include an *unsafe* entry for the Linux partition on the first disk within this second *lilo.conf* file. lilo must be installed into that partition's boot sector as well for this to work).

To summarize, we have configuration 1 installed into the MBR on the first hard disk (and possibly into the boot sector of the Linux partition as well), and we have configuration 2 installed in the boot sector of the Linux partition on the second hard disk.

The boot sequence might then go something like this:

```
Welcome to gallant.
Boot choices: linux (default; on C:),
              win2k,
              eviltwin (Linux on D:),

boot: eviltwin

Welcome to goofus.
Boot choices: test (default; on D:),
              goodtwin (Linux on C:)

boot: Return
Loading test...
```

Given these selections, Linux will boot from the *D:* drive. The lilo from the MBR on drive *C:* has run first, and it has then started the boot program on the Linux partition on the *D:* drive—which is again lilo. That (second) lilo then loads the kernel from the *D:* drive. (Note that if you wanted to, you could just keep popping back and forth between the lilo programs on *C:* and *D:* ad infinitum.)

If you think this is pretty silly, omit the *prompt* keyword from the lilo configuration file for the *D:* drive (as well as its *image* section for the Linux partition on the *C:* drive), resulting in a simple *lilo.conf* file on the *D:* drive:

```
install=/boot/boot.b
boot=/dev/hdb2
root=/dev/hdb2
map=/boot/map
image=/boot/vmlinuz
label=linux
```

Once this is installed, selecting eviltwin at the initial boot prompt immediately boots the Linux partition on the second hard disk.

lilo's -r option

Sometimes it is useful to be able to run lilo for a disk partition mounted somewhere other than /. For example, if you have another Linux root filesystem mounted at */mnt*, you might want to run *lilo* to install the kernel (currently) at */mnt/boot/vmlinuz*, using the configuration file */mnt/etc/lilo.conf*. lilo's -r option is designed for such a purpose. It sets the root directory location for the lilo operation to the directory specified as its argument and looks for all files relative to that point. Thus, for the scenario we've been discussing, the correct command is:

```
# lilo -r /mnt
```

The boot.message file

The *boot.message* file is displayed before the boot prompt is issued. Here is an example *boot.message* file:

```
Welcome to JAG
Property of the Linc Guerrilla Hackers Association
Computational science is not for the faint hearted!

Our current boot offerings include:
  * linux (smaller test kernel--2.4.666 currently)
  * safe (SuSE distribution 2.4.something)
  * hacked (do you feel lucky?)
  * windog - guess what ... (on D:)
```

An effective file will list all the defined choices (but it needn't be this eccentric).

The Grub Boot Loader

grub is the Grand Unified Bootloader (*sic*) from the GNU project (see *http://www. gnu.org/software/grub/*), originally written by Erich Boleyn and currently maintained by Gordon Matzigkeit and Okuji Yoshinori. It is designed to be operating system–independent and more flexible than previous programs of this type. Among its advantages is that it functions as a boot-time shell from which you can type any boot commands that may be appropriate, allowing you to specify a different configuration or kernel without prior preparation.

When it starts, grub displays an initial splash screen and a menu of boot choices. You can customize both of these items via its configuration file, *grub.conf*, usually stored in */boot/grub* under Linux.

Here is an annotated example configuration file, illustrating methods for booting a variety of operating systems. We begin with the general section, which applies to all entries:

```
# general section
splashimage (hd0,0)/grub/splash.xpm.gz
default 0              Default boot entry (numbering starts at 0).
timeout 30             Menu timeout period in seconds.
password -md5 xxxxxxx  Use the grub-md5-crypt command to encode.
```

grub uses a simple method for referring to disks and partitions: (hd$n$,m) refers to partition m on disk n, where both sets of numbers start at 0. Thus, the image file displayed behind the menu is located in the *grub* subdirectory on the first partition on the first disk.

Here are entries used to boot Linux:

```
title Linux                        Boot menu label.
root (hd0,0)                       Base partition for future references.
kernel /vmlinuz ro root=/dev/hda2
initrd /initrd.img


title Test-Linux                   Second selection.
root (hd1,1)                       Different base partition.
kernel /boot/vmlinuz-test ro root=/dev/hdb2
initrd /boot/initrd.img-test
```

The first entry is used to boot a Linux installation whose root directory is the second partition on the first disk (indicated via the root kernel parameter) but whose kernel image and associated files are stored in a separate */boot* partition (the first partition on the first disk). The second entry boots a Linux installation on the second hard disk whose root and boot partitions are both on the second partition on that disk.

The following entries could be used to boot a Windows operating system on the third partition of the first and second hard disk, respectively:

```
title Win2K
root (hd0,2)            Specify partition.
makeactive              Activate it.
chainloader +1          Hand off to local boot loader.


title WinXP
map (hd0) (hd1)         "Swap" the two drives.
map (hd1) (hd0)
root (hd0,2)
```

```
makeactive
chainloader +1
```

Here is an entry which may be used to boot FreeBSD:

```
title  FreeBSD
# use the 1st BSD subpartition in disk 1 partition 3
root   (hd0,2,a)
kernel /boot/loader
```

This entry follows the documentation's recommendation to boot FreeBSD using the FreeBSD final-stage boot loader rather than directly invoking the FreeBSD kernel.

grub also has the nice feature of remembering what you booted each time and making it the default for the next time. To enable this capability, set the *default* entry to *saved* and add a *savedefault* directive to the end of each stanza:

```
default saved

title Linux
...
savedefault
```

Installing grub itself is straightforward. Once you have built it, you can use the grub-install program to install it, as in these examples:

```
# grub-install '(hd0)'
# grub-install -root-directory /boot '(hd0)'
```

The first example installs grub into the MBR on the first hard disk. The second command does the same thing, but it lets grub know that the kernel images are in a separate partition mounted at */boot*.

Booting a Linux System with syslinux

Once in a while, you'll run across a system where lilo just will not work. These systems have unusual hardware configurations that are basically not supported by this boot loader. At the moment, I have one such system. It is an older, Intel-based PC with two IDE controllers on the motherboard, one of which does not work. To compensate, the vendor installed another standalone IDE controller into a PCI slot. (No, I didn't know this when I accepted delivery).

The CD-ROM and Zip drive are connected to the motherboard controller, and the system disk uses the separate secondary controller. This is the only configuration that works at all (I've tried all the others), but it confuses every operating system I've wanted to run on this computer. In the case of Linux, lilo just balks at the configuration and hangs on boots.

A good solution for unusual cases like these is to use syslinux, a simple boot loader that runs off a floppy disk (FAT format). To create such a boot floppy, use commands like these:

```
#  mount -t msdos /dev/fd0 /floppy        Mount floppy.
# cp /boot/vmlinuz /floppy                Copy kernel.
```

```
# rdev /floppy/vmlinuz /dev/hda2          Set kernel root directory.
# umount /floppy
# syslinux /dev/fd0                       Add loader program to floppy.
```

Finally, you must create a configuration file for the boot floppy named *syslinux.cfg*. Here is a simple one:

```
label linux
kernel vmlinuz
```

This file specifies the path to the kernel on the floppy and a label for the entry. If required, you can specify kernel parameters (the append keyword), an initial RAM disk (initrd), and other items. Consult the package's documentation for information about all the available configuration-file features.

Once you have finished, booting from this floppy disk automatically boots the kernel on it, using */dev/hda2* as the root partition.

Restoring the DOS Master Boot Program

Should you ever need to, here is the procedure for restoring the standard ("DOS") master boot program:

1. Boot from a bootable DOS floppy.
2. Run the command fdisk /MBR.

You can also perform the same task under Windows 2000 (and follow-ons):

1. Boot into the Recovery Console, either from the distribution CD-ROM or from disk if you installed it.
2. Run its fixmbr command.

Booting Alpha Linux Systems

Alpha Linux systems have different BIOSes than Intel-based systems, and the boot process differs. There are three boot loaders in use at the moment: the MILO boot loaders (used with ARC firmware), the APB boot loader (used with UP1000 systems), and the ABOOT boot loader (used with SRM console systems).

Compaq Alpha systems generally use the latter. As we saw in Chapter 4, commands like these can be used to initiate a boot:

```
aboot> p 2                    Select the second partition to boot from.
aboot> 0                      Boot predefined configuration 0.
```

The following command can be used to boot Linux from the second hard disk partition:

```
aboot> 2/vmlinux.gz root=/dev/hda2
```

You can configure the ABOOT loader using the */etc/aboot.conf* configuration file.

The swriteboot command is used to install a configuration. Here is a sample entry from this file:

```
0:2/vmlinux.gz ro root=/dev/hda2
```

The boot command is preceded by a configuration number and a colon. Thus, this entry defines configuration 0.

To boot from CD-ROM, first use the show dev command to determine the device name for the CD-ROM drive, then enter a command like this one:

```
> boot dqb1 -fl 0
```

The first argument is the device name for the CD-ROM drive.

Linux Loadable Modules

The Linux kernel has supported loadable modules since Version 1.2. In this scheme, you build a minimal kernel and dynamically load modules providing additional functionality as required. Such an approach has the advantage that many types of system changes no longer require a kernel rebuild; it also has the potential to significantly decrease the size of the kernel executable. The *modutils* package provides utilities for building, installing and loading kernel modules.

Running make modules after building a kernel creates the loadable modules files, and make modules_install installs them into a subdirectory of */lib/modules* whose name corresponds to the kernel release level and/or any assigned build suffix.

The lsmod command lists currently loaded modules:

```
Module              Size  Used by
sg                 21216    0  (autoclean) (unused)
smbfs              32144    2  (autoclean)
nls_iso8859-1       2848    1  (autoclean)
ipv6              117744   -1  (autoclean)
mousedev            3968    0  (unused)
hid                11744    0  (unused)
input               3104    0  [mousedev hid]
printer             4832    0  (unused)
usb-uhci           21712    0  (unused)
usbcore            46480    1  [hid printer usb-uhci]
3c59x              22912    1  (autoclean)
```

The output shows the module name, size, number of current users, and other modules that use it. For example, we see that the *smbfs* module (Samba-based support for mounting remote filesystems) has a current use count of 2.

You can get information about a specific module with the modinfo command:

```
# modinfo -d 3c59x                        Description
3Com 3c59x/3c90x/3c575 series Vortex/Boomerang/Cyclone driver
# modinfo -a 3c59x                        Author
Donald Becker <becker@scyld.com>
```

```
# modinfo -n 3c59x                    Corresponding file
/lib/modules/2.4.2-2/kernel/drivers/net/3c59x.o
```

The configuration file *letc/modules.conf* lists various configuration parameters for installed modules. Here are some sample entries to illustrate the type of information stored in this file:

```
# map generic Ethernet interface to the specific device type
alias eth0 3c59x
alias eth1 off                              Disabled.

# set options for the parallel port (passed when loaded)
options parport_pc io=0x378 irq=none,none

# sound subsystem configuration
alias sound-slot-0 es1371
# command to run after insertion/activation
post-install sound-slot-0 /bin/aumix-minimal
    -f /etc/.aumixrc -L  >/dev/null 2>&1 || :
# command to run before removal/deactivation
pre-remove sound-slot-0 /bin/aumix-minimal
    -f /etc/.aumixrc -S >/dev/null 2>&1 || :
```

These days, the modules facility is well integrated into general Linux development, and most packages perform any module configuration and bookkeeping activities themselves, so editing this file is seldom necessary.

Similarly, manual loading or unloading of modules is a rare event because these actions generally occur on demand. However, the following utilities can be used to manually manipulate modules:

depmod

> Determines dependencies among modules. The command creates the file *modules.dep* in the relevant subdirectory of */lib/modules*. This utility may be run automatically at boot time; you may occasionally need to execute it manually after building modules.

modprobe

> Loads a module as well as all modules that it depends on (usually used to load modules automatically at boot time). It can also be used to generate a *modules. conf* file from the current system configuration (use the -c option).

lsmod

> Lists the currently loaded modules.

insmod

> Loads a module interactively.

rmmod

> Unloads a loaded module from the kernel (provided the module is not in use).

Solaris

The Solaris kernel is stored in */kernel/unix*. It is structured around loadable modules: executables that add capabilities and functionality to the system. Modules add flexibility in that they can be installed and uninstalled as needed. The operating system probes the hardware each time the system boots and loads the needed modules. Modules are stored in the subdirectories of */kernel*.

The following commands display information about the current system configuration (in voluminous quantities):

modinfo
> Display loadable modules.

prtconf
> Show system hardware configuration (peripheral devices).

sysdef
> Display loadable modules, hardware configuration, and the values of some tunable kernel parameters.

In general, little kernel configuration is required on Solaris systems, other than adding modules or drivers to support new devices when they are installed.

Vendors generally provide installation instructions and associated drivers along with their hardware. Device drivers can also be manually loaded and unloaded with add_drv and rem_drv, respectively, and other modules can be loaded and unloaded with modload and modunload.

The */etc/system* configuration file allows you to specify what modules are and are not loaded and to specify the values of system parameters. The latter occurs in the section headed by these comment lines:

```
* set: Set an integer variable in the kernel or a module
*       to a new value.
*
set scsi_options=0x58
set TS:ts_maxupri=69
set TS:ts_maxkmdpri=39
```

The sample *set* entries illustrate the format for specifying parameter values. The first command sets a flag for the SCSI subsystem. The following two commands set parameters within the TS module (corresponding to the time-sharing scheduler table), specifying the sizes of the user and kernel priority portions of the general scheduler table. These parameters must be specified when you install a custom scheduler table that is a different size than the default table.[*]

---

[*] The ts_dptbl manual page details the process for doing this, which involves creating a source file, *ts_dptbl.c*, compiling and linking, and installing the resulting module *in /kernel/sched*.

Exercise care in editing */etc/system* because it is possible to create a file that leaves the system unbootable (and always save a copy of the current, working file before modifying it). For such cases, Solaris systems provide an interactive boot mode in which you are prompted for the paths to the *system* and kernel files. The following command may be used to boot interactively:

```
> b -a
```

AIX System Parameters

On AIX systems, you never need to rebuild a kernel because system parameters may be changed on a running system. The current values of AIX system parameters may be displayed with the `lsattr` command:

```
# lsattr -EHl sys0              Final option letter is a lowercase L.
attribute     value       description                    user_settable

keylock       normal      State of system keylock at boot time    False
maxbuf        20          Maximum pages in block I/O BUFFER CACHE True
maxmbuf       2048        Maximum KB real memory allowed for MBUFSTrue
maxuproc      400         Maximum # PROCESSES allowed per user    True
autorestart   false       Automatically REBOOT after a crash      True
iostat        false       Continuously maintain DISK I/O history  True
realmem       65536       Amount of usable physical memory (KB)   False
conslogin     enable      System Console Login                    False
fwversion     IBM,SPH01184   Firmware version,revision levels     False
maxpout       0           HIGH water mark pending write I/Os/file True
minpout       0           LOW water mark pending write I/Os/file  True
fullcore      false       Enable full CORE dump                   True
pre430core    false       Use pre-430 style CORE dump             True
ncargs        6           ARG/ENV list size in 4KB blocks         True
rtasversion   1           Open Firmware RTAS version              False
modelname     IBM,7044-270   Machine name                         False
systemid      IBM,011000189  Hardware system identifier           False
boottype      disk        N/A                                     False
SW_dist_intr  false       Enable SW distribution of interrupts    True
cpuguard      disable     CPU Guard                               True
frequency     93750000 System Bus Frequency                       False
```

The list includes parameters that can be modified and ones that can't. Being able to see, for example, the amount of physical memory present on the system and the current setting of the front panel key (keylock) can be useful and convenient. The latter item is especially useful when the CPU unit is positioned so that the physical key position not readily visible.

The `chdev` command may be used to change many of these parameters. For example, the following command raises the maximum number of simultaneous processes that a user may run to 500:

```
# chdev -l sys0 -a maxuproc=500
```

You can also use the `smit chgsys` command to modify several settings at the same time.

Table 16-2 lists the most important AIX system parameters, along with their associated attribute names.

Table 16-2. AIX system parameters

Parameter	Meaning
Maximum user processes (*maxuproc*)	Maximum number of processes that any user can have at one time (the default is 200). Does not apply to *root*. Increasing *maxuproc* takes immediate effect, but decreases wait until the system is rebooted.
Block I/O buffer cache size (*maxbuf*)	Size of the buffer cache for reads/writes to block special files. Normal file I/O doesn't use the buffer cache (nearly all physical memory is used as an I/O cache under AIX), so leave this one at its default of 20 4K-pages. (I/O to a raw device—in other words, to a logical volume without a filesystem—does use the buffer cache.)
Maximum memory used for MBUFS (*maxmbuf*)	Maximum amount of memory to be used for MBUFS (TCP/IP and NFS in-memory data structures). This parameter is the same as the *wall* attribute tunable with the no command (the default is 2048 KB).
Automatic reboot status (*autorestart*)	Whether or not to reboot the system automatically after a crash (the default is false).
Disk I/O history (*iostat*)	Whether or not to keep records of the I/O activity to the various disks on the system since boot time (if available, this information is displayed as the first report from the `iostat` command). This generally useless data is no loss, so turning off this parameter does no harm, but it has little effect on system performance either way (default is on).
Disk I/O pacing parameters (*minpout* and *maxpout*)	Pending I/O operation watermarks (the I/O pacing facility is discussed in $PERF). The defaults are both 0, which disables the facility.
Full core dump (*fullcore*)	Whether to include all of memory in a crash dump (by default, some types of data are excluded).
Use pre-430 style CORE dump (*pre430core*)	Whether to use the core file format used by AIX version 4.2 and earlier (the default is not to).
ARG/ENV list size in 4 KB blocks (*ncargs*)	Maximum size of the argument list and environment variables for executables, in units of 4 KB. The default is 6 and the maximum is 128. Increase this value only if commands/applications have failed because of the default limitations.

## CHAPTER 17

Accounting

Virtually all current Unix systems provide some form of user-based process accounting: the operating system tracks system usage by recording statistics about each process that is run, including its UID. In addition, records are kept of the image that was run by the process and the system resources (such as memory, CPU time, and I/O operations) that it used.

The accounting system is designed for tracking system resource usage, primarily so that users can be charged money. The data collected by the accounting system can also be used for some types of system performance monitoring and security investigations (see Chapter 15 and Chapter 7).

There are two distinct accounting systems in use, originating from the traditional vanilla BSD and System V environments. Although they are quite different, they are based on the same raw data. Hence, the sort of information that may be gleaned from them is essentially identical, although output methods and formats are not. They also suffer from the same limitations; for example, neither system provides for project-based accounting in any straightforward way.

As with all accounting systems, the Unix accounting software places a small but detectable load on the system. BSD-style accounting used to be enabled in new systems but is generally disabled these days; the process for enabling it is described later in this chapter. System V–style accounting is always initially disabled and must be set up by the system administrator.

On many systems, the accounting utilities are packaged as a separately installable module that the system administrator may include or not, as appropriate. Since the accounting system is also an important component of performance and system security monitoring, I recommend always installing it, even if you don't need accounting features, because the disk requirements are quite modest.

Accounting capabilities also need to be present in the Unix kernel, and many systems make this configurable as well (although they are usually present in default kernels).

Table 17-1 summarizes the main components of the accounting system for the Unix versions we are considering.

Table 17-1. Unix accounting system components

Accounting component	Location
Accounting system variant	**BSD:** FreeBSD, Linux (extended); AIX, Tru64 (commands only) **System V:** AIX, HP-UX, Solaris, Tru64
Primary accounting data file (default/conventional location shown)	**AIX:** */var/adm/pacct* **FreeBSD:** */var/account/acct* **HP-UX:** */var/adm/acct/pacct* **Linux:** */var/log/pacct* (Red Hat); */usr/account/pacct* (SuSE) **Solaris:** */var/adm/pacct* **Tru64:** */var/adm/pacct*
wtmp data file location	**Usual:** */var/adm* **FreeBSD:** */var/log* **Linux:** */var/log* **Solaris:** */var/adm/wtmpx*
utmp data file location	**Usual:** */etc* **FreeBSD:** */var/run* **Linux:** */var/run* **Solaris:** */var/adm/utmpx* **Tru64:** */var/adm*
lastlog data file location	**Usual:** */var/log* **AIX:** */etc/security* **HP-UX:** not used **Tru64:** */var/adm*
Accounting supplemental utilities directory	**AIX:** */usr/sbin/acct, /usr/lib/sa* **FreeBSD:** none **HP-UX:** */usr/sbin/acct* **Linux:** */usr/lib/sa* **Solaris:** */usr/lib/acct* **Tru64:** */usr/sbin/acct*
Boot script that starts accounting	**AIX:** Edit */etc/rc* or other boot script **FreeBSD:** */etc/rc* **HP-UX:** */sbin/init.d/acct* **Linux:** none provided (Red Hat); */etc/init.d/acct* (SuSE) **Solaris:** */etc/init.d/acct* **Tru64:** */sbin/init.d/acct*
Boot script configuration file (and accounting-enabling entry)	**Usual:** none used **FreeBSD:** */etc/defaults/rc.conf* or */etc/rc.conf* (*accounting_enable="YES"*) **HP-UX:** */etc/rc.config.d/acct* (*START_ACCT=1*) **Linux:** */etc/rc.config* (SuSE 7) (*START_ACCT="yes"*) **Tru64:** */etc/rc.config* (*ACCOUNTING="YES"*)

Table 17-1. Unix accounting system components (continued)

Accounting component	Location
Available printer accounting	**AIX:** /usr/sbin/pac
	FreeBSD: /usr/sbin/pac
	HP-UX: none provided
	Linux: lprng accounting.pl (Red Hat); /usr/sbin/pac (SuSE)
	Solaris: none provided
	Tru64: /usr/sbin/pac

 A couple of the utilities we considered in the context of security monitoring, lastcomm and lastlog (in Chapter 7), are also useful for producing accounting reports. See the earlier discussion for details.

Standard Accounting Files

When accounting is enabled, the Unix kernel writes a record to a binary data file as each process terminates. These files are traditionally stored in the home directory of the standard user *adm* (*/var/adm* on most recent systems), although some current systems no longer use that account and simply run the accounting software as *root*. Nevertheless, for sentimental reasons, the examples in this chapter generally use */var/adm* as the location of the accounting data files.

Records written to the raw accounting file by the System V and BSD accounting systems contain the same data. It is only the ordering of the fields within each record that varies between the flavors (consult the */usr/include/sys/acct.h* file for details).[*] Accounting records contain the following data about each process that runs on the system:

- Image name (for example, *grep*)
- CPU time used (separated into user and system time)
- Elapsed time taken for the process to complete (sometimes called "wall clock time")
- Time the process began
- Associated user and group IDs
- Lifetime memory usage (in BSD, the average use of the process' lifetime; in System V, the aggregate sum of the memory in use at each clock tick)
- Number of characters read and written
- Number of disk I/O blocks read and written
- Initiating TTY

---

[*] Linux uses a slight variation on the BSD form.

- Accounting flags associated with the process
- Process' exit status

Other binary data files store additional accounting data:

utmp
> Contains data about each currently logged-in user. `login` enters a record for each successful login, which is then cleared by `init` at logout.

wtmp
> Logs each login and logout to/from the system.

lastlog
> Records the date and time of the last login for each user.

A Thankless Job

There will be days when this tired old saying about system administration will seem one thousand percent correct. On days like those, you'll be battered from encounters with the cynics among your users — the ones who *know the price of everything but the value of nothing*. Don't let them get you down. Having one's worth be undervalued may be an occupational hazard for a system administrator, but you don't have to fall into that particular trap yourself. Just keep in mind that anyone who can put up with the Unix accounting system (in either variety) is worth their weight in gold.

BSD-Style Accounting: FreeBSD, Linux, and AIX

Administering BSD-style accounting involves several tasks:

- Enabling the accounting system and arranging for it to be started automatically at boot time.
- Periodically merging raw accounting records into the summary data files.
- Running accounting reports.

As indicated, BSD-style accounting uses some additional accounting summary files, located in the same directory as the primary accounting file. These files store processed, summarized versions of the accumulated raw accounting data. They are maintained by the `sa` command and are useful in keeping the size of the accounting file to a manageable level:

savacct
> The standard accounting summary file

usracct
> The user-based accounting summary file

Enabling and Disabling Accounting

The accton command controls the current state of a BSD-style accounting facility. The command enables accounting when an accounting file is specified as its argument (its location in the filesystem varies). Without an argument, the command disables accounting. Once the command is executed, accounting records will be written automatically to the accounting file.

The one tricky aspect of accton is that any raw accounting data file you specify must already exist, because the command will not create it. Accordingly, commands such as the following are used to start the accounting system from one of the system boot scripts:

```
return="done"
echo -n "Starting process accounting: "
test -e /var/account/pacct || touch /var/adm/pacct
/usr/sbin/accton /var/adm/pacct || return="failed"
echo "$return"
```

These commands first check that the raw accounting data file exists, creating it if necessary, and then start the accounting system via accton.

Once accounting is installed on FreeBSD and SuSE Linux systems, you can automatically activate it at boot time by editing the appropriate setting in the system's boot script configuration file, as described in Table 17-1.

The current Red Hat Linux version of the accounting package does not include a boot script. However, it is easy to create one from a boot script template (see Chapter 4), using the commands above as a model for the script's *start* function and the bare accton command for the *stop* function. Once you've written the script, you will need to place it into */etc/init.d* and create links to the appropriate *rcn.d* directory for it to be run at boot time.

Merging Accounting Records into the Summary Files

The accounting file will grow without bounds if allowed to do so. Its contents are designed to be processed and merged into the accumulated accounting summary files with the sa command. When invoked with its -s option, the sa command processes raw accounting records and places condensed summary information into the summary files. Here is an example of its use:

```
# cd /var/adm                        Move to accounting directory.
# /usr/sbin/accton                   Briefly disable accounting.
# mv pacct pacct.sav                 Rename raw accounting file.
# cat /dev/null > pacct              Recreate raw accounting file.
# /usr/sbin/accton pacct             Restart accounting.
# sa -s pacct.sav > /dev/null        Merge data into standard summary file.
# rm -f pacct.sav                    Delete saved accounting records.
```

The accounting file is renamed prior to invoking sa so that processes that terminate during processing are recorded. The output from sa is piped to */dev/null* to discard the report it generates. Alternatively, it could be sent to a file.

A script could be created to run these commands, so that they could be executed as needed by the system administrator or automatically via the cron facility.

After a Crash

The accounting system is designed to handle system shutdowns and boots automatically. However, special steps must be taken in the event of a system crash. For the accounting system to process data for processes that were running when a system crash occurred, the administrator must manually close their outstanding accounting records. These records must be closed *before* accounting is started. If accounting is started automatically in the system boot scripts (as it usually is), closing incomplete accounting records needs to occur before the accounting startup scripts are executed. The easy way to accomplish this is to boot to single-user mode after the crash.

The accounting file may be saved by renaming it using a mv command, as in the following example:

```
# mv /var/adm/acct /var/adm/acct.sav
# touch /var/adm/acct
```

The second command recreates the accounting file, readying it for new records when accounting is started in */etc/rc*.

At this point, the system may be booted multiuser. Once booting is complete, the following commands close the accounting records that were pending at the time of the crash:

```
# sa -s /var/adm/acct.sav >/dev/null
# rm -f /var/adm/acct.sav
```

These commands update the summary files and then delete the saved accounting file.

Image-Based Resource Use Reporting: sa

The sa utility produces system usage reports based on the image (command) that was executed. That is, in most cases, its statistics are organized and presented by image name, rather than by user or project. sa reads the raw accounting file and its summary file (*savacct*) to accumulate its data. Without any options, sa produces a report like the following (output has been shortened):

```
# sa
11238    412355.91re   5017.62cp    14avio   148k   login
4299       1782.32re   1000.28cp   122avio    73k   ld
12648      1335.62re    639.28cp    12avio    26k   as
6489       1121.66re    541.82cp    50avio    10k   makemake.c
4           627.93re    258.43cp     3avio     0k   splice
225        6623.90re    248.56cp  2545avio     8k   find
```

In this default output, the image name appears in the final (rightmost) column. The numerical fields in sa's output are identified by their suffixes, which have the following meanings:

none
> Number of times called

cp, cpu
> CPU time (system + user) in minutes

re
> Elapsed time in minutes

avio
> Average number of I/O operations per execution

k
> CPU time-averaged memory use in KB

k*sec
> Aggregate memory use in KB-seconds

tio
> Total I/O operations for all executions

s
> System CPU time in minutes

u
> User CPU time in minutes

Not all data items appear in every report. The first five items appear in the default output. The other items appear in reports generated by some of sa's many options.

sa's output may be sorted in a number of different ways by selecting an appropriate option:

-b   Average total CPU time per execution

-d   Average number of disk I/O operations

-D   Total number of disk I/O operations

-k   CPU time-averaged memory usage

-K   CPU-storage integral

-n   Number of calls

-r   Reverse sorting order

The -D option produces a report containing the total I/O use by the command; lines are sorted according to this total:

```
# sa -D
225        6623.90re    248.56cp   572608tio   8k   find
4299       1782.32re   1000.28cp   522580tio   73k  ld
9205      58785.98re    188.08cp   497421tio   9k   makenv
```

```
56          9610.25re    80.79cp 495507tio  18k  buildsystem
20            50.27re    14.79cp 369163tio  11k  ncheck
```

Here is the output from the -b option, which sorts by average CPU time:

```
# sa -b -r
3           3843.47re     7.91cp 47323avio   1k  update*
2              8.75re     7.39cp  1055avio   2k  code
11           294.67re    50.19cp  5961avio  14k  fsck
4           6680.53re   162.02cp    26avio  20k  timed*
4            627.93re   258.43cp     3avio   0k  splice
```

As illustrated, the -r option may be used to reverse the order of the sort (low to high instead of high to low).

The -m option produces a listing of the total number of processes and CPU time for each user:

```
# sa -m
root    247648  19318.90cpu 7698005tio  3793802k*sec
chavez       2      3.67cpu       0tio  1013391k*sec
harvey       4      7.33cpu       0tio  2024939k*sec
daemon    7799   2742.86cpu 1616886tio   488234k*sec
wang         6   2956.44cpu 1067648tio   406004k*sec
```

Use the -u option to dump out all accounting records in a user-based format.

The -l option may be used to separate user and system time in sa's output:

```
# sa -l
11238   412355.91re 4691.13u   326.49s 14avio 148k  ccom7
4299      1782.32re  861.52u   138.76s 122avio 73k  ld
12648     1335.62re  567.13u    72.15s 12avio  26k  as
4          627.93re  252.13u     6.30s  3avio   0k  splice
```

Include -c to show times as percentages of the total rather than raw values.

You can limit sa's output to the most frequently run commands using its -v and -f options. For example, the report from the following sa command will include only those commands executed more that 100 times:

```
# sa -f -v 100
```

Alternate summary files may be specified with the -S and -U options, where -S indicates an alternative to *savacct*, and -U specifies an alternative to the per-user summary file *usracct*; both should be followed by a pathname. sa's reports may be limited to the raw accounting file with the -i option.

The Linux version of sa provides a few additional options. The most useful adds an additional data sorting capability: --sort-real-time. This option sorts records based on the elapsed time field.

Connect Time Reporting: ac

The ac utility reports on user connect time. It gets its data from the *wtmp* file, containing records on user logins and logouts. Without any options, ac displays the total connect time (in hours) for all users for the lifetime of the *wtmp* file:

```
# ac
        total  5501.06
```

The command may also be followed by one or more usernames, in which case the total for those users is displayed:

```
# ac chavez wang fine
        total  1588.65
```

The -p option breaks down connect time by user:

```
# ac -p
        ng        30.61
        chavez   685.25
        harvey     0.04
        wang     170.77
        sysadmin  44.84
        fine     732.78
```

Usernames may be specified with -p to limit ac's scope:

```
# ac -p chavez wang fine
        chavez   685.25
        wang     170.77
        fine     732.78
        total   1588.79
```

The -d option breaks down the connect time by date, summed over all specified users (the default is everyone):

```
# ac -d
Sep  1  total    77.32
Sep  2  total   228.78
Sep  3  total   260.82
# ac -d chavez wang fine
Sep  1  total    11.83
Sep  2  total    20.36
Sep  3  total    41.00
```

Using -d and -p together produces a summary of login activity, broken down by user and by date; from an accounting point of view, this is likely to be ac's only useful mode:

```
# ac -d -p chavez wang
        chavez    16.07
        wang       4.55
Sep  1  total     20.62
        chavez    15.87
        wang      20.15
Sep  2  total     36.01
        chavez    22.82
```

```
          wang      17.68
   Sep  3  total     40.50
```

ac -d -p would produce a similar listing, including all users.

Connect times for an individual user might exceed 24 hours in a single day; this is easily accounted for by the fact that users may be logged on more than once simultaneously, via multiple windows, terminal sessions, and the like. Indeed, the ubiquitous prevalence of such practices makes connect-time accounting all but useless.

The Linux version of ac tries to be more careful about reconstructing connect-time data when the raw records include orphan records caused by system crashes or reboots, flaky data (which does occur from time to time), and the like. It provides the --compatibility option, which causes the command to revert to the standard dubious behavior.

System V–Style Accounting: AIX, HP-UX, and Solaris

The System V–style accounting scheme is much more elaborate than the BSD-style variant. It is used by AIX, HP-UX, and Solaris systems.

This facility is a complex system of commands, shell scripts, and C programs, called by one another in long sequences, all purported to be totally automated and requiring little or no intervention. In reality, it's a design only a fervent partisan could love (although, to be fair, it does generally get the job done on stable systems). Older versions of the manual pages alternated between assuring the reader that the system was robust, reliable, and trouble-free and describing convoluted procedures for patching corrupted accounting data files. Most of the latter has been edited out at this point, but be forewarned.

The main accounting file is named *pacct*, usually found in */var/adm*. Other key subdirectories used by the system are found under */var/adm/acct*:

fiscal
> Reports by fiscal period (usually month) and old binary fiscal period summary files

nite
> Daily binary summary file; daily processed accounting record; raw disk accounting records; and status, error log, and lock files

sum
> Binary daily and current fiscal period cumulative summary files and daily reports

On AIX systems, these subdirectories have to be created by hand:

```
# cd /var/adm/acct
# mkdir -m 755 fiscal nite sum
# chown adm.adm fiscal nite sum
```

In addition to the *wtmp* and *pacct* files discussed previously, there are some other raw data files generated by this accounting system:

/var/adm/acct/nite/diskacct
Raw disk usage data.

/var/adm/fee
Administrator-entered additional charge records, using the `chargefee` command. `chargefee` allows an administrator to record charges for special services not covered by the accounting system; these charges will automatically be incorporated into the accounting system. It takes two arguments: a username and the number of units to be charged to that user. For example, the following command charges user *chavez* 10 units:

```
# chargefee chavez 10
```

Figure 17-1 illustrates the general flow of data in the System V accounting system, beginning with the raw data files discussed previously. Commands and the operating system enter data into the raw data files, which are processed by a series of utilities, producing several intermediate binary summary files and culminating in ASCII reports suitable for use by the system administrator. All of this processing is handled automatically by cron once accounting is set up.

 On Tru64 systems, the files and subdirectories in */var/adm* are context-dependent symbolic links (see "Files" in Chapter 2). Keep this in mind if you need to create or recreate any accounting system components.

Setting Up Accounting

While accounting is not enabled by default under System V, it is, to a large extent, already set up. The following steps are necessary to enable accounting:

- Verify that a script to start the accounting system is run at boot time. On HP-UX and Solaris systems, you need to verify that the *init.d/acct* script is linked to files in the appropriate *rcn.d* or */etc/rc3.d* subdirectory. On AIX systems, you need to add a command like the following to one of the system startup scripts (the same one called on the other systems):

```
/bin/su - adm -c /usr/sbin/acct/startup
```

The `startup` script calls the `accton` command to initiate accounting.

The following command shuts down accounting:

```
/usr/lib/acct/shutacct
```

Under AIX, this command is included in */etc/shutdown* by default.

- Add cron entries for various accounting utilities. Add the following entries (or a variation of them) to the *crontab* file for user *adm*:

```
# control accounting file size (3:30 a.m. daily)
0  *  *  *      /usr/sbin/acct/ckpacct
# process accounting raw data (4:30 a.m. daily)
```

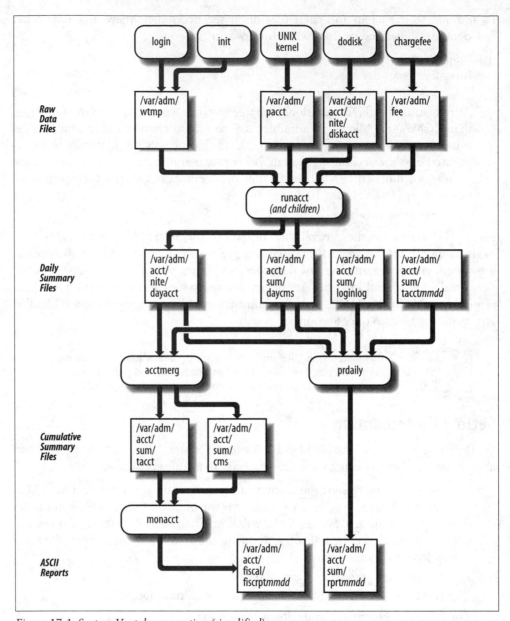

Figure 17-1. System V–style accounting (simplified)

```
30 4  *  *  *    /usr/sbin/acct/runacct 2>
                        /var/adm/acct/nite/fd2log
# generate monthly reports (5:30 a.m. on the first)
30 5  1  *  *    /usr/sbin/acct/monacct
```

Note that the second entry is wrapped to fit the page.

Similar entries may already be present on the system in an active or commented-out form. Note that the accounting utilities directory is */usr/lib/acct* on Solaris systems.

- Add an entry like the following to the *crontab* file for *root*:

```
        # generate disk usage raw data
        # (10:30 p.m. on Saturdays and the 29th)
30 22 29  *  7  /usr/sbin/acct/dodisk
```

- Edit the */etc/acct/holidays* data file to reflect prime and nonprime hours and holidays—days where all day is considered nonprime—at your site. Here is an example of this file:

```
* Prime/Nonprime Table for Accounting System
*
* Curr  Prime  Non-Prime
* Year  Start  Start
2001    0900   2100
*
* Day of  Calendar     Holiday
* Year    Date
    1     Jan 1        New Year's Day
   15     Jan 15       Martin Luther King Day
  149     May 29       Memorial Day
...
```

The first section consists of a single active line (comments are indicated by the initial asterisk) listing the current year, the time at which prime (full price) time starts and when it ends, using a 24-hour clock. The second section lists holidays to be recognized by the accounting system. The fields in each line are the numerical day of the year (Julian date), conventionally followed by a readable date and a description; the accounting system uses only the first field.

- On AIX systems, you must enable accounting for each filesystem for which you want to collect disk accounting data with chfs command, as in this example:

```
# chfs -a accounting=true /chem
```

The resulting entry in */etc/filesystems* will now look something like this:

```
/chem:
    dev= /dev/us00
    vfs= jfs
    log= /dev/logus00
    mount= true
    check= true
    options= rw
    account= true     Accounting is enabled.
```

Once these steps are completed, accounting will begin at the next boot. It may be started manually instead:

```
# /bin/su - adm -c /usr/sbin/acct/startup
```

The startup script is located in */usr/lib/acct* on Solaris systems.

Accounting Reports

Daily accounting reports are stored in files in the *sum* subdirectory, with names of the form *rprtmmdd*, where *mm* and *dd* are the month and day, respectively. Each report file contains five separate reports, covering these areas:

- Per-user usage
- Last login time for each user
- Command use, for the previous day and the previous month
- Terminal/pseudo-terminal activity

Here is a sample of the daily per-user usage report, the most useful section of the daily report file from an accounting perspective:

```
March  7 10:43 2001   DAILY USAGE REPORT FOR hamlet                          Page 1

      LOGIN CPU  (MINS) KCORE-MINS   CONNECT(MINS) DISK  # OF   # OF  # DISK   FEE
 UID  NAME  PRIME NPRIME PRIME NPRIME PRIME NPRIME BLOCKS PROCS  SESS  SAMPLES
  0   TOTAL 40    101    9     34     393   124    0      1186   19    0        0
  0   root  5     10     2     11     102   12     0      1129   10    0        0
 473  wang  35    91     7     23     291   112    0      57     9     0        0
```

The resources used during prime and nonprime hours (as defined in the *holidays* file) are totaled separately by the accounting system (to allow for different charge rates).

The first line of the report is a total line, giving total system usage. After that, there is one line per UID. The fields have the following meanings:

UID
   User's UID.

LOGIN NAME
   Username.

CPU (MINS)
   Total CPU time for all of the user's processes in minutes.

KCORE-MINS
   Total memory used by running processes, in kilobyte-minutes. Basically, this field relates to the product of the memory used times the length of use, summed over all the user's processes. It is an indication of how much memory the user's processes consumed, but it has little to do with the amount of memory that was actually used.

CONNECT (MINS)
   Total connect time (how long the user was logged in).

DISK BLOCKS
   Average total amount of disk space used by the user.

 # OF PROCS
   Total number of processes belonging to this user.

OF SESS

Number of distinct login sessions.

DISK SAMPLES

Number of times dodisk was run during the accounting period, giving a measure of how many values the *DISK BLOCKS* field is averaged over. If dodisk has not been run, this field and the *DISK BLOCKS* field will contain a 0.

FEE

Total fees entered with chargefee.

The daily and monthly command-use reports in the same report file show system resource usage by command name, including the number of times each command was run and the total CPU time, memory use, and I/O transactions it consumed. The terminal activity report shows the percentage of time each terminal line or pseudo-terminal was in use over the accounting period, the total connect time accumulated on it, and the number of distinct login sessions (not that useful a report anymore). The last login report displays the date of the last login for each UID defined in the password file.

The monthly accounting reports are stored in files named *fiscrptmm*, where *mm* indicates the month. They are very similar to the daily reports just described.

Solaris Project-Based Extended Accounting

Solaris provides *extended accounting* for keeping track of system resource usage by project. This facility is independent of the standard System V accounting system also provided by Solaris.

Projects are defined in the */etc/project* configuration file. Solaris provides several utilities for defining projects and assigning users and groups to them, as illustrated in the following examples.

The following command creates a new project called *animate*, assigns it a project ID of 105, and assigns user *chavez* and groups *grarts* and *design* to it:

```
# projadd -c "Animation Project" -U chavez -G grarts,design -p 105 animate
```

Similarly, the following command creates the *cad* project without assigning any members and lets the system assign the next highest project ID:

```
# projadd cad
```

The following commands replace the user list for the *animate* project and rename the *cad* project to *cae*:

```
# projmod -U chavez,wong animate
# projmod -l cae cad
```

The following command removes the *y2k* project:

```
# projdel y2k
```

Here are the */etc/project* file entries corresponding to the two projects we just created:

```
animate:105:Animation Project:chavez,wong:grarts,design:
cad:110::::
```

The contents of each field are obvious, with the exception of the last field, which can be used to define project-specific attributes.

The projects command lists the projects to which the current user or a specified user belongs:

```
# projects chavez
default chemdev animate
```

The -v option lists project descriptions and their names.

At login, the user is placed into the *default* project or, if there is not *default* project, into the first project of which she is a member. She can change the current project by executing the newtask command:

```
$ newtask -p animate
```

The command also optionally takes a command as its final argument, allowing a user to execute a single command for another project. The command also supports a -F option to start a *finalized* task, one from which another task may not be started.

The new project option (-p) is not required. If it is omitted, a new task in the current project is started. Extended accounting data can be collected on a per-task and/or per-process basis. The newtask command would be used to delimit tasks if the former is desired.

You enable collection of the additional accounting data (project and task settings) using the acctadm command, as in these examples:

```
# acctadm -e extended,host,mstate -f /var/adm/exact/task task
# acctadm -e extended,host,mstate -f /var/adm/exact/pacct process
```

The two commands enable task-based (i.e., based on invocations of newtask) and per-process accounting by project (the type is indicated by the final keyword). The -e option specifies the data to be collected (we have enabled everything here), and the -f option specifies the path to the raw accounting data file where records should be written.

Without options, the acctadm command displays the current state of the extended accounting system:

```
# acctadm
            Task accounting: active
       Task accounting file: /var/adm/exacct/task
    Tracked task resources: extended,host,mstate
  Untracked task resources: none
         Process accounting: active
    Process accounting file: /var/adm/exacct/pacct
 Tracked process resources: extended,host,mstate
Untracked process resources: none
```

You must provide your own methods and tools for managing these raw accounting files and processing the records within them.

The upacct Package

The upacct package, written by D. J. Nixon and available free of charge, provides a way to merge the System V–style accounting data from multiple hosts into a single repository. It provides a variety of commands and scripts related to these functions. We will focus on a few of them here.

The upacct command is used to create host-based accounting data summary files and to merge multiple such files together. For example, the following command creates a host-based data file from the standard raw accounting data file:

```
# upacct cmds.hamlet -p /var/adm/pact
```

This command creates the file *cmds.hamlet* in the current directory.

The following command merges several host-based data files into the file *cmds.0*:

```
# upacct cmds.0 cmds.hamlet cmds.dalton cmds.garden
```

The command's first argument indicates the output file. Additional data filenames refer to files to be merged, and the -p option points to any raw accounting data file to be included as well.

Conventionally, the host-based data files are given names of the form *cmds.nnnn* where the extension is a four-digit number. However, you can use any names you like, provided you modify the package's shell scripts to reflect your choice.

The package includes two shell scripts that are useful for reporting on the collected data: *ucomm.sh* and *wcomm.sh*. Both need to be edited prior to their initial use to specify the path to the host-based data files on your system (and to reflect any non-standard file name conventions). Here is an example of running *ucomm.sh*, which takes a username whose data is to be retrieved as its argument:

```
# ucomm.sh chavez
1510.exe    --    176.45 secs    aurora    Tue May 15 15:18:50 2001
    tail    --    270.12 secs    hamlet    Tue May 15 15:11:34 2001
     top    --     11.14 secs    garden    Tue May 15 15:11:21 2001
```

The fields in the display hold the command name, accounting flags, CPU time (in seconds), host, and command start time (respectively). Given this sort of data, it is quite easy to generate reports on per-user and per-system usage levels. We saw an example script of this sort in Chapter 14.

The *wcomm.sh* command is very similar, differing only in that it takes a command name as its argument and displays the username in the first column of its output.

Printing Accounting

Unix systems which use the BSD/lpd-style spooling subsystem also usually offer printing accounting via the pac utility. Printer accounting is enabled with the *af* field in its */etc/printcap* entry. For example, this entry designates */var/adm/ps1_acct* as the accounting file for this printer:

```
laser|postscript|ps1:\
      :lp=/dev/lp:sd=/var/spool/ps1:if=/usr/local/sbin/filt:\
      :mx#0:af=/var/adm/ps1_acct:pw#132:pl#66:pc#100:\
      ...
```

For text printers, the *pw* and *pl* fields (page width and length, in characters and lines, respectively) are used to generate accounting data. For other printer types, a more sophisticated approach is required.

Under AIX, printing accounting is enabled by adding an *acctfile* keyword to the queue definition stanza in */etc/qconfig*:

```
laser:
device = dlas1,dlas2
header = group
trailer = never
acctfile = /var/adm/qacct
...
```

This line may be added with a text editor, by using the chque command, or by using SMIT, but in any case, the queue should be stopped first (for example, with enq -D) and then restarted after reconfiguration (see Chapter 13 for more information).

 Merely defining the accounting file field will not in itself cause accounting records to be created. The facility requires support for accounting data from the filter(s) used to process the print jobs. There are many filters available that include this functionality. See Chapter 13 for more information about filters. Printing accounting, including techniques for generating the required data for modern printers, is also discussed in detail in *Network Printing*, by Todd Radermacher and Matthew Gast (O'Reilly & Associates).

By default, pac displays total usage of the current printer (as designated in an environment variable or as the system default printer) for each user on each host over the lifetime of the printer's accounting files. The units are pages for printers and linear feet for plotters and similar raster devices. You can combine all the host-specific entries for each user by including -m, since you seldom care where print jobs were spooled from.

You can specify what price to charge per unit with -p (the default is two cents, cheap even for the mid-1970s), where a unit is one page or one foot of continuous output. In addition, on systems using the *printcap* file, the *pc* entry can be used for the same purpose (its units are .01 cents). Thus, the example printcap entry at the beginning of this section set a page charge of 10 cents.

For example, this command produces a report of printer usage for the *listings* printer (specified as usual with -P), with one entry per user and a charge of 12 cents per page:

```
# pac -m -p0.12 -Plistings
    Login           pages/feet    runs          price
  chavez               132.00     50        USD 15.84
  silk                 114.00      9        USD 13.68
  harvey                16.00      2        USD  1.92
  ...
  total               5361.00    378        USD 643.32
```

A total line for all users appears at the bottom of the report. pac is quite picky about its syntax, requiring options to follow the option letter immediately and not allowing you to concatenate options behind a single minus sign.

You can limit the report to specific users by including one or more usernames at the end of the pac command line. pac's other report-related options are -c, which sorts output by cost rather than username, and -r, which reverses the sort ordering in either mode. It also has a -s option, which produces a summary file from the raw data file; the summary file has the name of the raw data file with *_sum* appended to it.

If you want date-based printer accounting reports, you'll have to generate them yourself. For example, the following script produces a printer-account report for the current week (it is designed to be run via the cron facility):

```
#!/bin/sh
# pracct - run printing accounting report
cd /var/adm
while [ $# -gt 0 ]; do
    file="$1.`date +%m-%d-%y`"
    echo "Printing Usage Report for Printer $1" > $file
    echo "Covering the week ending `date +%m-%d-%y`" >> $file
    /usr/sbin/pac -m -p0.12 -P$1 >> $file
    if [ -s $1_lastweek ]; then
        mv -f $1_lastweek $1_prevweek
    fi
    /usr/sbin/pac -s
    mv $1_sum $1_lastweek
done
```

The script saves pac's output to a file named for the printer and the current date after writing two header lines to it. It then creates a (smaller) summary file from the current printer accounting file (assumed to be named the same as the printer), which it renames, so that its data will not appear in future pac output (if a file is present, summary file data is included). This script arranges to save the summary files for the past two weeks online by renaming last week's file (if it exists) before creating the current week's summary file.

Printer Accounting Under LPRng

LPRng uses the same field for specifying the accounting file as the LPD system: *af*. In addition, it provides some additional flags:

- The flags *la* (enable local accounting) and *ar* (enable remote job transfer accounting). The former is on by default.

- The *as* and *ae* fields specify a script to be run at the start and end of each print job. Typically, these are used to record the beginning and ending page counts and essential information about the print job. The LPRng package provides the *accounting.pl* Perl script as an example.

Typical accounting records from the example program look something like this:

```
start -p100 -Fo -kjob ...        Start of print request (-Fo); counter is 100.
start -p100 -Ff -kjob ...        Start of first component file (-Ff).
end -p10 -q 110 -Ff -kjob ...    End of first file (10 pages).
start -p110 -Ff -kjob ...        Start of second component file.
end -p5 -q115 -Ff -kjob ...      End of second job (5 pages).
end -p115 -Fo -kjob ...          End of print request; counter is 115.
```

Each line displays the current print counter setting (*-p* in start lines and *-q* in end lines), and a flag indicating whether the entry applies to a print request or an actual printed file, and other information about the job (the job ID, submitting user and host, and the like).

See the LPRng documentation for full details on its printer accounting capabilities.

The Profession of System Administration

We'll conclude this book as we began: by considering the system administrator's job, this time considering it as a profession.

I find system administrators to be a very interesting group of people. One of the reason is that system administrators as a group tend to have diverse and varied backgrounds. Many people come to system administration after being educated and/or working in other areas. It's only relatively recently that system administration has been available as an "official" educational track and career path.

Whatever their backgrounds, though, system administrators are valuable technical professionals, and they should be treated as such (and also should act accordingly). Sadly, the contributions of system administrators are not always respected or even noticed. The way to address this oversight lies in greater visibility for the profession as a whole.

SAGE, the System Administrators Guild, is an organization that works very hard at doing just that. It also provides many valuable services to the individual system administrators that are its members.

SAGE: The System Administrators Guild

For almost a decade, SAGE has served the needs of system administrators around the world.* One of SAGE's main goals is the increase of visibility and recognition of system administration as a profession. To this end, SAGE has published as series of short topics handbooks. All of them are excellent. A good one to start with is *Job Descriptions for System Administrators* (Revised and Expanded Edition), edited by Tina Darmohray. This work provides detailed job descriptions for system administration positions at various levels. As such, it is very useful for evaluating both your skills and your present position in light of general practices.

* Thanks to Rob Kolstad, SAGE's Executive Director, for most of the descriptive text in the SAGE section.

Along the same lines, SAGE committees are currently working on the *System Administration Book of Knowledge*, which includes a listing of all the tasks a system administrator might encounter (but not how to do them), and they are also working on a university curriculum for new system administrators. Complementing these is a vendor-neutral certification program developed as a "career certification" instead of the usual "product certification."

Organized as a special technical group of USENIX, SAGE's thousands of members share information, technical tips, and white papers on SAGE's website. Many of SAGE's services are available for no charge at the SAGE portal *http://www.sage.org*. They include:

SAGEwire
> An online discussion forum with daily updates of news for and about system administration.

SAGEweb
> Items of long-term interest, including SAGE's activities, member services, and organizational news.

SAGEnews
> An email periodical with just the right amount of summarization on system administration news.

SAGE co-sponsors many conferences, including the popular LISA conference for system administrators. LISA, the Large Installation System Administration conference, is excellent and very relevant to all system administrators, regardless of the size of their site. Held annually, it is preceded by three days of optional, in-depth tutorials on various system administration topics. The conference itself also runs three days and includes a variety of technical sessions—including both well-known speakers and ordinary system administrators sharing their experience—and social activities. Overall, the conference is both informative and a lot of fun. For more information about LISA, see *http://www.usenix.org/events/*.

All system administrators are welcome at SAGE. Check us out and see what SAGE has to offer you.

Administrative Virtues

I'll close this brief consideration of the profession and professionalism with the full list of administrative virtues. This time, we'll take a somewhat more humorous tack than we have previously:

Flexibility
> Being able to wriggle out of tight spots and escape when irate users seem to have you cornered.

Ingenuity

Realizing that you can use syslog to send messages to your friend on another system.

Patience

Remaining capable of waiting until the final sendmail configuration bug is fixed.

Persistence

The compulsion to try just-one-more-thing to fix a problem before going home.

Adherence to Routine

Insisting on real cream and sugar-in-the-raw in your coffee (which is Kona or nothing).

Attention to Detail

Noticing that the clock on one of your systems is using Aleutian time, and changing all the others to match.

Laziness

Writing a 250-line Perl script to avoid typing 15 characters.

What these alternative definitions are designed to highlight is the fact that system administration is not only challenging and sometimes frustrating, but can also be fun. In fact, this is my last piece of advice for you:

     Don't forget to have fun. Life is too short.

Administrative Shell Programming

The purpose of this appendix is to review major Bourne shell (sh) programming features. *It is not intended as a comprehensive treatment of shell programming or of the features of the various shells*. Rather, it will enable you to understand and modify the system administration scripts on your system, most of which are Bourne shell scripts (although this is slowly changing).

In the course of this appendix, we will look at many examples drawn from actual system scripts, as well as some other simple examples to illustrate basic features. Some of the latter examples use shell commands executed at the command prompt (although the corresponding commands could obviously appear just as easily in scripts).[*]

With the exception of AIX and Linux, the Unix versions we are considering use the Bourne shell for system scripts. AIX uses the Korn shell (ksh), and Linux uses the Bourne-Again shell (bash). Linux system scripts also frequently use bash features that are not part of the standard shell. Since they are extensions to sh, however, the most important of these features are now described in this appendix.[†] When I mention bash features here, I am doing so in a descriptive sense only—not in an historical sense—in comparison to what is offered in the *standard* Bourne shell. The feature in question may also be present in other shells and may very well have originated in a shell other than bash.

The books *UNIX in a Nutshell: System V Edition*, by Arnold Robbins, and *Learning the bash Shell*, by Cameron Newham and Bill Rosenblatt (both published by O'Reilly & Associates) are excellent references for sh and bash, respectively.

Discussing Korn shell features is beyond the scope of this appendix; consult the book *Learning the Korn Shell* by Bill Rosenblatt and Arnold Robbins (O'Reilly & Associates) for a detailed discussion of this shell.

---

[*] Not all examples will necessarily run in every sh implementation.

[†] This discussion covers bash Version 2.04 or later.

As much as possible, the examples in this appendix come from actual system scripts. Thus, while there are many useful techniques illustrated in the examples, they should not generally be viewed as recommendations of shell programming style, and many readers may quibble or disagree with them at some points.

Basic Syntax

This section reviews some basic syntactic features of the Bourne shell, in a somewhat arbitrary order.

Lines in shell scripts beginning with number signs are comments:

```
# Start or stop the lp scheduler
```

In fact, comments can begin anywhere on a line:

```
grep ':00*:' /etc/passwd     # Check for UID=0 accounts
```

The first line of a shell script usually looks like this:

```
#!/bin/sh
```

This identifies the shell that should run the script, in this case, the Bourne shell. The path location can vary.

 The best practice is to begin every shell script with a line identifying the shell to be used to run it. If this line is not present, /bin/sh is assumed.

The Bourne shell offers some syntactic flexibility over other shells. For example, quotes remain in effect across physical lines, as in this example we looked at in Chapter 7:

```
echo "*** Non-root UID=0 or GID=0 accounts:"
grep ':00*:' /etc/passwd | \
   awk -F: 'BEGIN        {n=0}
            $1!="root"   {print $0 ; n=1}
            END          {if (n==0) print "None found."}'
```

Note that the arguments to the awk command extend across three lines, which is much more readable than forcing them onto a single line.

I/O Redirection

Another construct you'll see quite often is this redirection of standard output to a file and of standard error to standard output (and thus to the same file):

```
/usr/lib/lpshut > /dev/null 2>&1
```

In this case the file is */dev/null*, but the concept applies whether output goes to a real disk file, to */dev/console*, or gets thrown out.

Note that standard output and error can also be redirected to separate destinations:

```
/sbin/rc.local  1>> boot.log  2> /dev/console
```

In general, the form *n> file* redirects file descriptor *n* to the specified file; *file* may also be replaced by a second file description, as in the form *n1>&n2*.

Some Bourne shells and bash support more complex I/O-redirection syntax. For example, the following command redirects all future standard input and all output to the system console (which is the target of the *CONSOLE* environment variable):

```
exec 0<> $CONSOLE 1>&0 2>&0
```

bash also offers additional I/O-redirection features. One of the most useful is illustrated in this example:

```
/etc/shutdown.local >| /var/adm/shutdown.log 2>&1
```

This command runs the specified script, placing all of its output into the indicated file even if the file already exists and the *noclobber* shell variable, which inhibits accidental overwriting of existing files, is set.

The dot Command

The so-called *dot command*—consisting of a single period—is used to run commands from a file in the same shell as the script itself. The file specified as a dot command's argument thus functions as an include file. For example, the following command executes the contents of */etc/rc.config* as if they were part of the calling script:

```
. /etc/rc.config
```

Placing some commands in a separate file can have many purposes: isolating their function, allowing them to be used in multiple scripts, and so on.

bash provides source as a synonym for the dot command. The return command may be used to return to the calling script at any point within a script executed with the dot command.

Return Codes and the exit Command

On Unix systems, commands return a value of zero when they terminate normally and a nonzero value when they don't. The exit command may be used in scripts to return an explicit value; it takes the return value as its argument.

Here is a typical use of exit:

```
echo "configure network FAILED"
exit 1
```

This command, from a TCP/IP startup file, terminates the script and returns a non-zero value (indicating an error).

Compound Commands

The forms && and || are used to create conditional compound commands. When the shell encounters one of these operators, it checks the exit value of the command on the left of the operator before deciding whether to execute the command on the right. For &&, the second command is executed only if the first one completed successfully; for ||, the second command executes when the first one fails. Here is an example with &&:

```
grep chavez /etc/passwd && grep chavez /etc/group
```

If the string "chavez" is found in the password file, the same string is searched for in the group file; if it isn't found, the second command doesn't execute.

The two constructs can be used together:

```
/usr/local/cksecret && echo "Everything ok." || mail root < slog
```

If the script cksecret returns 0, a message is sent to standard output; otherwise, the contents of the *slog* file are mailed to *root*. The && has to come before the || for this to work correctly.

Command Substitution

Back quotes may be used to place the output of one command into a separate command. For example, this command defines the variable *otty* as the output of the stty command:

```
otty=`stty -g`
```

bash and some Bourne shells also support the following more readable syntax:

```
otty=$(stty -g)
```

Argument Symbols and Other $ Abbreviations

Bourne shell scripts can be passed arguments like any Unix command. The first nine arguments can be referred to by the abbreviations $1 through $9. The shift command is one way to access later arguments. Here is an example of how it works:

```
$ cat show_shift
#!/bin/sh
echo $1 $2 $3
shift
echo $1 $2 $3
$ show_shift a1 a2 a3 a4
a1 a2 a3
a2 a3 a4
```

After the `shift` command, all parameters are shifted one parameter position to the left (or down, depending on how you want to look at it), and their parameter numbers are reduced by one.

bash provides a simplified syntax for accessing arguments beyond the ninth: ${*n*}. Thus, `echo ${12}` would display the value of the twelfth argument.

$0 refers to the command or script name, as in this example:

```
restart)
  $0 stop && $0 start
  ;;
```

These lines are from a boot script. They are part of a case statement in which the various options correspond to possible arguments that may be passed to the script. In this case, when the script argument is "restart", it calls itself with the argument "stop" and then calls itself again with the argument "start", provided that the first command was successful.

The form $# is a shorthand for the number of arguments. Thus, for the `show_shift` command in the previous example, $# was 4 before the `shift` command was executed and 3 afterwards.

There are two shorthand forms for all the arguments passed to a script: $@ and $*. $@ keeps the individual arguments as separate entities; $* merges them into a single item. Quoting the two of them illustrates this clearly:

```
"$*" = "$1 $2 $3 $4 ... $n"
"$@" = "$1" "$2" "$3" "$4" ... "$n"
```

You'll usually see the $@ form in system scripts.

There are a few other dollar-sign abbreviations that appear from time to time. Although they're not related to script arguments, I'll list them here:

$?

Exit status of previous command

$$

PID of this shell's process

$!

PID of the most recently started background job.

We'll see examples of some of these later in this appendix.

Variable Substitution

Shell scripts can also define variables, using the same syntax as environment variables:

```
name=value     No spaces allowed around the = sign.
```

Variables are dereferenced by putting a dollar sign in front of their name: *$name*. The variable name may be surrounded with braces to protect it from surrounding text. For example:

```
$ cat braces
#!/bin/sh
item=aaaa
item1=bbbb
echo $item1 ${item}1
$ braces
bbbb aaaa1
```

The first command displays the value of the variable *item1*, while the second command displays the value of the variable *item*, followed by a 1.

There are more complex ways of conditionally substituting variable values. They are summarized in Table A-1.

Table A-1. Conditional variable substitution

| Form | Return Value (Action Taken) | |
	If *var* is set[a]	If *var* is unset
${*var-string*}	*$var*	*string*
${*var+string*}	*string*	null
${*var=string*}	*$var*	*string (set var=string)*
${*var?string*}	*$var*	(display var:*string* only)

a "Set" means "defined," regardless of value (i.e., even if null).

Here are some examples:

```
$ name=rachel                          Assign value to variable name.
$ echo ${name-tatiana}                 name is set, so use its value.
rachel
$ echo ${name2-tatiana}                name2 is unset, so use "tatiana".
tatiana
$ echo ${name=tatiana}                 name is set, so use it.
rachel
$ echo ${n2=tatiana}; echo $n2         n2 is unset, so use "tatiana"...
tatiana
tatiana                                ...and give n2 that value too:
$ echo ${name+tatiana}                 name is set, so use "tatiana".
tatiana
$ echo name3=${name3+tatiana}          name3 is unset, so return nothing.
name3=
$ name4=${name3?"no name given"}       name3 is unset, so display message...
name3: no name given
$ echo name4=$name4                    ...note name4 is not set.
name4=
$ dir=${name-`pwd`}; echo $dir         name is set, so use it (pwd not run).
rachel
$ dir=${name3-`pwd`}; echo $dir        name3 is unset, so set dir to `pwd`.
/home/chavez
```

As the final two examples indicate, commands can be included in the *string*, and they will be executed only if that portion of the construct is actually used.

bash variable substitution extensions

The bash shell and some Bourne shell implementations provide additional variable substitution possibilities:

- Placing a colon before the operator character in the various items in Table A-1 tests whether the variable is set to a non-null value. Thus, echo ${var:-apple} displays the value of variable *var* if it is set to something other than an empty string (null value); it displays "apple" otherwise.

- The form ${var:offset:length} may be used to extract substrings from a variable. *offset* indicates which character to start with (numbering begins at 0); if *offset* is negative, character counting begins from the end of the string (e.g., −1 starts extracting at the penultimate character). *length* indicates how many characters to extract, and it is optional; if it is omitted, all remaining characters are extracted. It must be greater than zero.

  Here are some examples:

  ```
  $ names="applepearplum"
  $ echo ${names:5}
  pearplum
  $ echo ${names:5:4}
  pear
  $ echo ${names:(-4):4}        Negative numbers must be parenthesized to
  plum                          avoid confusion with the :- operator.
  ```

- The form ${#var} may be used to determine the length of the specified variable's value. For example, ${#names} is 13.

- The form ${var#pattern} may be used to remove substrings from a variable, returning the remaining string. The following commands illustrate its use:

  ```
  $ names="applepearplum"
  $ echo ${names#apple}
  pearplum
  $ echo ${names#a*p}           The pattern can include wildcards.
     plepearplum
  $ echo ${names#pear}          Patterns only match the beginning of the string.
  applepearplum
  ```

  Note that the pattern must match the beginning of the string.

  There are several variations on this form: ${var##pattern}, ${var%pattern} and ${var%%pattern}. The number sign says to match the beginning of the string, and the percent sign says to match the end of the string. The single character forms remove the shortest matching substring, and the double character forms remove the longest matching substring, as in these examples:

  ```
  $ echo ${names##a*p}          Remove longest match.
     lum
  $ echo ${names%%e*m}
  appl
  ```

Here is a real-world example:

```
rex="[0-9][0-9]"
for i in $prerc/K${rex}*; do
  service=${i#*/K$rex}            # extract service name
  ...
done
```

This loop runs over the K-file boot scripts in whatever directory *prerc* resolves to. For each script, the variable *service* is set to the name of the facility being started by removing the initial path and *Knn* portion from the variable *i*.

• The preceding syntax can be extended to perform general search-and-replace operations within strings, using constructs of the form: ${*var/pattern/repstr*}. This form replaces the longest string matching the pattern with *repstr*. If the initial slash is replaced by two slashes, all matching substrings are replaced. If *repstr* is null, the matching substrings are simply deleted.

By default, matching occurs anywhere within the string. Precede the pattern with a number sign or percent sign to force matches to be at the beginning/end of the string.

Here are some examples:

```
$ names="applepearplum"
$ echo ${names/p/X}
aXplepearplum
$ echo ${names//p/X}
aXXleXearXlum
$ echo ${names/%plum/kumquat}
applepearkumquat
```

You can do such pattern matching and replacement on the script argument list by using @ as the variable name.

Variable Double Dereferencing

It's very common to come across code like this:

```
netdev="NETDEV_"
iconfig="IFCONFIG_"

# Set up environment variables for each network device
. /etc/rc.config

num=0
while [ $num -le $NUM_NETDEVS ]; do
  curr_dev=`eval echo $netdev$num`        # NETDEV_n
  eval device=\$$curr_dev                 # value of NETDEV_n
  if [ "$device" != '' ]; then
    curr_opts=`eval echo $iconfig$num`    # IFCONFIG_n
    eval options=\$$curr_opts             # value of IFCONFIG_n
    /sbin/ifconfig $device $options up
  fi
  num=`expr $num + 1`
done
```

This script fragment initializes all the network interfaces on a system. The device names are stored in a series of environment variables named *NETDEV_0*, *NETDEV_1*, and so on, and the corresponding ifconfig options are stored in *IFCONFIG_n*. The while loop configures each interface in turn. The variable *num* holds the number of the current interface, and the variables *netdev* and *iconfig* hold the beginning part of the environment variable names. The value of the proper environment variable is extracted into the variables *device* and *options* (which are used in the ifconfig command) via a two-step process: for the *NETDEV* case, the name of the environment variable is constructed first and saved in the variable *curr_dev*. Then *curr_dev* is itself dereferenced, and its value—which is the value stored in *NETDEV_n*—is assigned to the variable *device*. If you've ever wondered how to get to the value of the value of variable, this is one way.

Here is a similar example from a Linux system:

```
. /etc/rc.config
locale_vars="\
  LANG        \
  LC_ALL      \
  ...         \
  LC_MONETARY"
```

```
for var in $locale_vars; do        Loop over locale-related environment variables.
  if eval test -z "\$$var"         Is the variable's value undefined or null?
  then
    eval $var="\$RC_$var"          If so, set its value to the same RC_ variable.
    export $var
  fi
done
```

Consider the first trip through the loop. The loop variable *var* is set to *LANG*. If the *LANG* environment variable is not set, then *LANG*'s value is set to that of *RC_LANG* variable (defined in */etc/rc.config*) via the second eval command, and the environment variable is exported.

The if Statement

In this section, we begin looking at Bourne shell control structures: programming features seldom used on the command line. The first construct we will consider is if, used for conditional command execution. Here is the simplest syntax of an if statement and a simple if example:

```
if condition
then
    commands
fi
```

```
if test -x /sbin/sendmail ; then
    /sbin/sendmail $SENDMAIL_OPTIONS
fi
```

The if command runs the commands in *condition*. If they return a true value (zero exit status), the *commands* are executed; on a false, nonzero status, the script jumps to the command after fi.

The preceding example uses the test command to check for the file */sbin/sendmail* and starts the daemon if it's present and executable. We'll look at constructing conditions more closely a little later. For now, notice the placement of the then command. then must appear to the shell as a separate command, or you'll get an error. So it must be on a new line after the if command, or it must be separated from the if command by a semicolon. The same rules hold true for the fi command that ends the if construct.

There are more complex forms of if:

```
strings /vmunix | grep Unix > /tmp/motd
i=`head -1 /etc/motd | grep -c Unix`
if [ $i -eq 0 ]
then
    cat /etc/motd >>/tmp/motd
else
    tail +2 /etc/motd >>/tmp/motd
fi
mv /tmp/motd /etc/motd
```

This example illustrates the if-then-else construct. It updates the Unix version string in the message-of-the-day file. First, it gets the current Unix version string out of the kernel file */vmunix* and puts it in the file */tmp/motd*. Then, it checks whether the string "Unix" appears in the first line of */etc/motd*. If it doesn't, the entire contents of */etc/motd* are appended to */tmp/motd* by the tail command. Otherwise— when "Unix" does appear in the first line of */etc/motd*—all but its first two lines are appended to */tmp/motd*. Finally, the new message file replaces the current one.

Here is an example of the most complex form of if:

```
set `who -r`                              Determine previous run level.
if [ "$9" = "S" ]                         Previous level was single-user mode.
then
    echo "The system is coming up."
elif [ "$7" = "2" ]; then                 Target run level is level 2.
    echo "Changing to state 2."
else
    echo "Changing to state 3."
fi
```

The elif command allows if statements to be chained together. It functions as an else for the current if and as the beginning of a new if. The final else covers the case of all false conditions and ends the entire chain.

The test Command (a.k.a. [ )

The most common way to construct a condition for an if command is with the test command. It has two forms:

```
test condition
[ condition ]
```

test evaluates *condition* and returns 0 or 1, depending on whether the condition is true (0) or false (1). (This polarity matches up with if's sense of true and false.)

The open bracket ([) command is a link to test and works in exactly the same way. It makes for more readable scripts, so you'll seldom see test. If the [form is used, a final closed bracket (]) is included to keep test from complaining. Note that there must be spaces after [and before].

Table A-2 lists the various options and operators that may be used to construct conditions with test and [. The shaded items are extensions available in only some shell implementations.

Table A-2. Constructing conditions

Construct	Meaning
-s *file*	File has greater than 0 length.
-r *file*	File is readable.
-w *file*	File is writable.
-x *file*	File/directory is executable.
-f *file*	File exists and is a regular file.
-d *file*	File is a directory.
-c *file*	File is a character special file.
-b *file*	File is a block special file.
-p *file*	File is a named pipe.
-u *file*	File has SETUID bit set.
-g *file*	File has SETGID bit set.
-k *file*	File has sticky bit set.
-t *n*	File descriptor *n* refers to a terminal.
-e *file*	File exists.
-O *file*	You own the file.
-G *file*	Your group owns the file.
-L *file*	File is a symbolic link.
-S *file*	File is a socket.
-N *file*	File has been modified since it was last read.
file1 -ef *file2*	Files reside on the same device and refer to the same inode number.
file1 -ot *file2*	First file is older than second file.
file1 -nt *file2*	First file is newer than second file.

Table A-2. Constructing conditions (continued)

Construct	Meaning
-z *string*	String's length is 0.
-n *string*	String's length is greater than 0.
string1 = *string2*	The two strings are identical.
string1 != *string2*	The two strings are different.
string	String is not null.
string1 > *string2*	First string is lexically before second string.
string1 < *string2*	First string is lexically after second string.
int1 -eq *int2*	The two integers are equal.
int1 -ne *int2*	The two integers are not equal.
int1 -gt *int2*	*int1* is greater than *int2*.
int1 -ge *int2*	*int1* is greater than or equal to *int2*.
int1 -lt *int2*	*int1* is less than *int2*.
int1 -le *int2*	*int1* is less than or equal to *int2*.
! *condition*	NOT logical operator: negates the condition.
cond1 -a *cond2*	AND logical operator: returns true only if both conditions are true.
cond1 -o *cond2*	OR logical operator: returns true if either condition is true.
( )	Used for grouping conditions.

Many of the items in Table A-2 require quoting to protect them from the shell (as we'll see).

Here are some simple examples:

```
if [ "$9" = "S" ]            If the 9th argument is S
if [ -s /etc/ptmp ]          If /etc/ptmp is not empty
if [ $# -lt 4 ]              If the number of arguments is < 4
if [ ! -f /etc/.fsckask ]    If the plain file /etc/.fsckask does not exist
if [ $? -eq 0 ]              If the last command succeeded
if [ $? -ne 0 ]              If the last command failed
```

Here are some examples placed in context:

```
# get pid of lpsched
pid=`/bin/ps -e | grep ' lpsched$' | sed -e 's/^ *//' -e 's/ .*//'`
if [ $(pid) != "" ]          If we found an lpsched process ...
then
    /bin/kill $(pid)         ... kill it.
fi

if [ $1x = autobootx ]       If script argument was "autoboot",
    run fsck
fi

if [ -d /etc/rc0.d ]         If there is a directory named /etc/rc0.d
then
    run the K files
```

```
        fi

        if [ -x /sbin/inetd ]; then    If the file /sbin/inetd is executable…
            /sbin/inetd                 …start the daemon
            echo inetd started
        fi

        if [ "$(BOOT)" = "yes" -a -d /etc/rc0.d ]
        then                            If this is a boot and there is an rc0.d directory
            Run the files in /etc/rc0.d
        fi
```

Note that constructs such as the following are used to prevent errors from occurring when a script's expected argument turns out to be null:

```
        if [ $1x = autobootx ]
```

There are, of course, other ways of handling this contingency, but this approach is quite common in system scripts, especially older ones.

Here's a tricky one; try to figure out what this does:

```
        interface_names="`echo /etc/dhcp.*[0-9] 2>/dev/null`"
        if [ "$interface_names" != '/etc/dhcp.*[0-9]' ]; then
            Configure the network interfaces with DHCP
        fi
```

A common mistake to make is to think the *interface_name* must always be the same as the filename string. The key here is to notice that the second operand to the not-equal operator in the `if` condition is a literal value: specifically, a string of characters and not a wildcarded filename. If there are any files of the form *dhcp.xxxn* in */etc* (where *xxx* is a string and *n* is a number), the echo command returns the list of file-names. Otherwise, the literal string "/etc/dhcp.*[0-9]" is returned and becomes the value of *interface_names*.

The `if` command figures out which of these has happened. If *interface_names* has any value other than the literal wildcard string, the variable can be assumed to contain a list of filenames to be processed. On the other hand, if the variable holds only the wildcard string, then no files were found, and nothing needs to be done, so the commands in the body of the `if` block are skipped.

Other Control Structures

This section describes other important Bourne shell and bash control structures.

The while and until Commands

The `while` statement is one way to create a loop. It has two forms:

```
        while condition
        do
            commands
        done
```

```
until condition
do
    commands
done
```

In the while form, the *commands* are executed until the *condition* becomes false. In the until form, they are executed until the *condition* becomes true. Here is an example of while:

```
cat /etc/fstab |
while read DEVICE MOUNT_DIR READONLY FS DUMMY1 DUMMY2
do
    fsck (if required) and mount the device
done
```

This loop takes each line of */etc/fstab* in turn (sent to it via cat) and performs an appropriate action for the corresponding device. The while loop will end when read (described later) returns a nonzero status, indicating an end-of-file.

Here is another very similar example, taken from a recent Linux system:

```
while read des fs type rest; do
  case "$fs" in
    /) break;;
    *)      ;;
  esac
done < /etc/fstab
if [ -e "$des" -a "$type" != "resiserfs" ]
then
    run fsck
fi
```

Note that the input to the while loop is provided via I/O redirection following the done statement.

The case Command

The case command is a way to perform a branching operation. Here is its syntax:

```
case str in
  pattern_1)
    commands
    ;;

  pattern_2)
    commands
    ;;
  ...
  pattern_n)
    commands
    ;;

  *)
    commands
    ;;
esac
```

The value in *str* is compared against each of the patterns. The corresponding commands are executed for the first match that is found. The double semicolons are used to end each section. Wildcards are allowed in the patterns, and a pattern consisting of a single asterisk can serve as a default if no other pattern is matched; it must be placed at the end of the case command.

Here is an example of the case command:

```
/etc/fsck -p >/dev/console
case $? in                        Select action based on fsck return value.
    0)
      date >/dev/console
      ;;
    2)
      exit 1
      ;;
    4)
      /sbin/reboot -n
      ;;
    *)
      echo "Unknown error in reboot" > /dev/console
      exit 1
      ;;
esac
```

In this example, different commands are run depending on the return value from fsck.

Another typical use of case is found in the files in */etc/init.d* on systems with System V–style boot scripts. Here is an abbreviated example:

```
#! /bin/sh
# Start or stop the lp scheduler

case "$1" in
  'start')
      /usr/lib/lpsched # and other commands
      ;;

  'stop')
      /usr/lib/lpshut > /dev/null 2>&1
      ;;

  'restart')
      $0 stop && $0 start
      ;;

  *)
      echo "usage: $0 {start|stop}"
      ;;
esac
```

This script takes different actions depending on the keyword specified as its argument. The argument it gets at boot time depends on whether it is invoked as an S-file or a K-file (as we noted in Chapter 4).

The for Command

The for command is another way to create loops. Here is its syntax:

```
for var [ in list ]
do
    commands
done
```

If a *list* is included, the variable *var* is set to each value in turn, and the command in the loop are executed. If no list of values is specified, $@ (all script arguments) is used.

Here is an example:

```
for d in /tmp /usr/tmp /chem/tmp ; do
    find $d ! -name tmp -type d -exec rmdir {} \;
done
```

This loop removes empty subdirectories from under */tmp*, */usr/tmp*, and */chem/tmp* in turn, while not removing those directories themselves (via ! -name tmp—of course, it won't remove */tmp/tmp* either).

The bash arithmetic for loop

bash also offers an arithmetic-style for loop, with the following syntax:

```
for (( start ; test ; incr )) ; do
    commands
done
```

start is an expression evaluated when the loop starts, *test* is an expression evaluated at the end of each loop iteration, and *incr* is an expression evaluated whenever the test condition is false. The loop terminates when the test condition is true.

Here is a simple example:

```
for (( i=1 ; i<10 ; i++ )); do
    echo $i
done
```

This loop displays the numbers 0 through 9.

The Null Command

Occasionally, you'll run across a command consisting of just a colon:

```
:
```

This null command is typically used when all the work is done in the control statement, and the body of the loop is empty.

Sometimes this command is used as a comment character (since its arguments will be ignored), as in this ancient example:

```
: attempt to ship remaining files
uucico -r
```

However, this practice is not recommended, because a line such as the following:

```
: Hourly cleanup script @(#)cleanup.hourly 2/4/90
```

(part of which was produced by a source-code control system) produces an error:

```
./cleanup.hourly: syntax error at line 2: `(' unexpected
```

This is because syntax checking is still done on the arguments to the null command.

Getting Input: The read Command

The read command reads one line from standard input and assigns the next word in the line to each successive variable specified as its arguments; extra words are assigned to its final argument. For example, these commands:

```
cat file.dat | \
while read x y z
do
    echo $x $y $z
done
```

produce output like this:

```
a b c
d e f
...
```

read can be used either for reading sequentially through a file (as in the earlier example with while) or for getting runtime input from the user. Here is an example using read for command input:

```
echo "fsck all disks? [y] \c"
read ans < /dev/console
```

The bash select command

bash provides the select command for prompting the user to select an item from a menu, as in this example:

```
$ cat choose.bash
#!/bin/bash

PS3="Choose an operating system: "
select os in "aix" "hp-ux" "solaris" "tru64" "linux" "freebsd"
do                                Loop until a valid choice is entered.
  if [ $os ]; then
    echo You chose $os which was choice number $REPLY
    break
  else
    echo -e "\nInvalid choice -- try again.\n"
  fi
done
$ choose.bash
1) aix
```

```
   2) hp-ux
   3) solaris
   4) tru64
   5) linux
   6) freebsd
Choose an operating system: 2
You chose hp-ux which was choice number 2
```

This code fragment also illustrates the bash echo command's -e option, which allows
you to include backslash escape sequences such as \n.

Other Useful Commands

This section briefly describes other commands that you may encounter in system
scripts.

set

The set command sets the values of $1 through $n to the words given as its arguments. It is often used with a backquoted command to assign the argument identifiers to the command's output. Here is an example of its use:

```
$ who -r
.  run-level 2  Aug 21 16:58    2    0    S
$ set `who -r`
$ echo $6
16:58
```

The unset command may be used to remove a defined variable.

eval

The eval command executes its argument as a shell command. It is used to execute
commands generated by multiple levels of indirection. Here is a silly example:

```
$ a=c; b=m; c=d; cmd=date
$ echo $a$b$c
cmd
$ eval $`echo $a$b$c`
Sun Jun  3 19:37:30 EDT 2001
```

Here is a real example that we looked at in Chapter 12:

```
$ eval `tset -sQ -m ":?vt100"`
```

This eval command runs the commands generated by tset -s. As we say, they are
used to set the *TERM* and *TERMCAP* environment variables.

The command eval resize provides a similar example for xterm windows.

printf

The printf command is used to produce formatted output strings, and you will occasionally see it used in system scripts. It takes two arguments: a format-specification string and a list of items to be printed using that format. Here is an example command used to create a record in a printer accounting file:

```
# pages=21; host=hamlet; user=chavez
# printf '%7.2f\t%s:%s\n' "$pages" "$host" "$user"
   21.00        hamlet:chavez
```

This command creates a line in which the number of pages is printed as a floating point number containing two decimal places, followed by a tab and then the hostname and username joined by a colon.

Format specification strings are comprised of field definitions and literal characters, and each successive item in the print list is formatted according to the corresponding field in the format string. In our example, %7.2f and %s (twice) were the field definitions, and the tab (\t), colon, and newline character (\n) were literal characters.

Field definitions always begin with a percent sign. Their simplest syntax is:

```
%n[.m]z
```

n indicates the minimum width of the field, m indicates the number of decimal places (if applicable), and z is a code letter indicating the type of field data. The most important codes are d for signed integer, f for floating point, c for the first character of the argument, s for a character string and x or X for a hexadecimal number (depending on whether you want the alphabetic digits to appear in lowercase or uppercase). A percent sign is specified with %%.

At output time, field widths are automatically expanded when more space is needed, and output that is smaller than the specified width is padded on the left.

The printf command also allows some optional flags to be placed between the percent sign and the field width:

- The minus-sign flag tells the command to pad the output on the right rather than the left (in other words, make the field left-aligned rather than right-aligned).

- The plus-sign flag indicates that positive numbers should be preceded by an explicit plus sign. The space flag similarly indicates that positive numbers should be preceded by a space. These flags are useful for creating columns of aligned numbers regardless of sign (the default is not to place any character in front of a positive number). Note that this is an issue only when items are left-aligned.

- The 0 flag indicates that zeros should be used for padding instead of blanks.

Here are some examples illustrating some of these flags:

```
# n=27; n1=-23
# printf '*%7.1f*  *%-7.1f* \n' $n $n
```

```
*   27.0*  *27.0   *
# printf '%-5.1f\n%-5.1f\n%-+5.1f\n%- 5.1f\n' $n $n1 $n $n
27.0
-23.0
+27.0
 27.0
```

expr

The expr command is used to evaluate various expressions. It has a lot of uses, but one common one in shell scripts is integer arithmetic. Here is a very simple example of its use in this mode:

```
$ cat count_to_5
#!/bin/sh
i=1
while [ $i -le 5 ] ; do
  echo $i
  i=`expr $i + 1`            # add one to i
done
$ count_to_5
1
2
3
4
5
```

See the manual page for full details on expr.

bash integer arithmetic

Integer arithmetic is included within the bash shell (so we can hope that constructions like the preceding will eventually go away). Here are some simple examples:

```
$ echo $(( 5+8/2-1 ))
8
$ a='1+2'; echo $a
1+2
$ let a='1+2'; echo $a
3
$ declare -i a; a='1+2'; echo $a
3
```

The first command illustrates the $(( )) operator, which forces the enclosed expression to be interpreted as integer arithmetic. Note that the usual operator precedence rules apply.

The second command illustrates that simply constructing an integer expression is not sufficient for it to be evaluated. You must use the $(( )) operator, precede the variable with let, or declare the variable to be of type integer (indicated by -i). The declare command may also be used to specify other variable types (see the documentation for details).

Table A-3 lists the supported arithmetic operators.

Table A-3. bash integer operators

Math operator	Meaning	Bitwise operator	Meaning	Logical operator	Meaning
+	add	>>	shift right	&&	logical AND
-	subtract	<<	shift left	||	logical OR
*	multiply	&	bitwise AND	==	equals
/	divide	|	bitwise OR	!=	not equals
%	modulus	~	bitwise NOT	<, <=	less than (or =)
**	exponentiation	^	bitwise XOR	>, >=	greater than (or =)
++	increment			!	logical NOT
--	decrement				
c?t:f	conditional assignment				

A few notes on these operators:

- In general, the operators have the same meanings and precedence as they do in C. Parentheses should be used for explicit grouping.

- The increment and decrement operators (++ and --) may either precede or follow the variable to which they are applied: *var*++ or ++*var*. Their placement determines whether the variable is modified before or after it is used.

- The conditional assignment operator tests the condition (*c*), returning the value *t* if it is true or *f* if it is false.

- Finally, the unary and bitwise operators can precede the equal sign in an assignment statement. For example, this statement adds three to the current value of *counter*:

      counter += 3

- Note that only integer values are returned by integer expressions. Thus, 5 / 10 = 0.

bash arrays

The bash shell also supports array variables. They are not very prevalent in system scripts at present, so we will present just a brief overview of their use via some examples:

```
$ a=(aaa bbb [5]=eee ddd)        Define an array and some values.
$ echo ${a[4]} ${a[5]}
ddd eee
$ echo ${a[3]:-undefined}
undefined                         Arrays can have "holes": undefined elements.
$ a=(x y z); echo ${a[4]:-undefined}
undefined                         Redefining an array replaces all elements.
```

```
$ for i in ${a[@]}; do              Loop over array elements.
> echo $i; done
x
y
z
$ echo ${#a[@]}                     Number of non-null elements in array a.
3
```

See the bash documentation for more information about arrays.

Shell Functions

Bourne shell scripts can define functions. Functions have all the same syntactic features as the scripts themselves, including their own arguments. Within a function, the argument and other shorthand forms refer to its own arguments.

The basic function syntax is:

```
name ( )
{
    commands
}
```

Here is a sample function from an AIX system, followed by an example of its use:

```
sserv( )
{
# sserv: function to start a server
# args: $1=daemon pathname; $2!="" means use startsrc
#
if [ $# = 0 ] ; then
  echo "sserv: server name required."; return 1
fi
if [ ! -x $1 ] ; then return 1 ; fi
if [ -n "$2" ] ; then
    startsrc -s `basename $1`
else
$1
fi
}

...

sserv /sbin/syslogd $USE_SRC
```

The sserv function starts a server process on an AIX system, either conventionally from the command line or via the startsrc command (which uses the system resource controller subsystem, a general server management facility). The pathname of the server to start is specified as sserv's first argument, and whether to use startsrc is specified by the second argument (any non-null value uses it).

The function begins by making sure it was passed one argument; the function exits this is not the case. Note that return is used instead of exit in functions. Then the function makes sure the pathname it was passed is executable, and then finally it starts the daemon.

The example invocation of sserv uses an environment variable *USE_SRC* as its second argument. If *USE_SRC* is defined, then startsrc will be used; otherwise, only one argument will be passed to sserv.

bash Local Variables

bash functions may define local variables—variables whose scope is limited to the function and have no meaning in or effect on the script as a whole—via its local command, which takes the desired variable names as its arguments. Note also that any variables declared within a function are automatically local variables.

Index

We'd like to hear your suggestions for improving our indexes. Send email to *index@oreilly.com*.

base permissions (AIX), 354
bash, 244
    initialization files, 241
    invocation options, 244
batch command, 977
batch processes, 55
batch systems, 977–978
    AIX, 857
Bellovin, Steven M., 374, 383
belt-and-suspenders firewall
        configuration, 385
Berkeley Internet Name Domain (see BIND)
biff command, 614
big endian, 741
BIND, 417, 420, 422
    Version 8, 422
    Version 9, 422, 429, 438–439, 445, 446
    versions, 420–421, 430
binlogd daemon (Tru64), 110
biod daemon, 696
biometric devices, 340
BIOS, 128
BITNET, 334
blacklist_recipients sendmail feature, 562
blacklists, electronic mail, 562, 589–590
block special files, 47, 63
Boleyn, Erich, 1040
boot process, 127
    customizing, 165
    disabling parts of, 166
    DNS and, 423
    failures, 175
    from CD-ROM, 134–137
    manual, 133
    messages, 138
    multiuser mode, 130
    network interface configuration, 204
    networking and, 148
    phases of, 128, 130, 137
    scripts, 131
    single-user mode, 131
    starting daemons, 146
boot program, 128
boot scripts, 131, 140
    adding to, 165
    AIX, 164
    BSD-style, 151
    directories for, 155
    disabling, 166
    Linux, 164
    modifying, 168

    rc*, 155, 159
    S and K files, 160
    Solaris, 163
    starting daemons in, 146
    System V–style, 152, 159
    Tru64, 164
boot0cfg command (FreeBSD), 1029
/boot directory (Linux), 70
/boot/grub/grub.conf configuration file
        (Linux), 1041
/boot/loader.conf configuration file
        (FreeBSD), 1029
boot.message configuration file
        (Linux), 1040
Borg designation, 315
bounds checking, 331
Bourne shell, 241
    example scripts, 886–893, 897–898
Bourne-Again shell (see bash)
Braun, Rob, 380
breaches, security, 405
breakout box, 796
bridges, 201
broadcast addresses, 195
btcreate command (Tru64), 765
buffer cache, 987
buffer overflows, 331
bugs, 331, 373
bundles (HP-UX), 119
Burgess, Mark, 921
bzip2 package, 123

C

C programs, 919
C shell, 241
    example scripts, 893–897
C2 security level, 227
cables, maximum length
    network, 184
    SCSI, 640
Cables to Go, 780
cache, DNS, 418
caching-only name servers, DNS, 419
caller ID, faxes and, 803
cancel command, 830, 833
canonical name records, DNS, 429
capabilities (Linux and FreeBSD), 367
capacity planning, backups, 710
cap_mkdb command (FreeBSD), 251
captive user accounts, 239
Carnegie Mellon University, 488, 539

F

facilities (syslog), 102
fake shutdowns, 172
Farmer, Dan, 374, 401, 403
Fast File System (FFS), 618
    soft updates, 619–620
fastpaths in SMIT (AIX), 19
fax2ps command, 803
faxaddmodem command, 799
faxadduser command, 806
faxalter command, 803
faxcron command, 800
faxdeluser command, 806
faxes (see HylaFAX)
faxgetty daemon, 800
faxinfo command, 803
faxqclean command, 800
faxrm command, 802
FAXSERVER environment variable, 801
faxsetup command, 799
faxstat command, 802
fbackup command (HP-UX), 734
fdformat command (Solaris), 690
fdisk command
    DOS, 1043
    FreeBSD, 645
    Linux, 896
FEATURE macros, 549
    access_db, 562
    allmasquerade, 551
    always_add_domain, 557
    blacklist_recipients, 562
    dnsbl, 562
    generics_entire_domain, 557
    genericstable, 556
    ldap_routing, 557
    local_lmtp, 553
    masquerade_envelope, 551
    msp, 568
    nocanonify, 554
    nullclient, 555
    redirect, 558
    relay_entire_domain, 554
    smrsh, 553
    summary table, 576–578
    use_cw_file, 550
    virtusertable, 559
fetchmail package, 596–598
    authentication, 597
    configuration file, 598
    configuring, 597

    security, 597
    syslog and, 597
.fetchmailrc configuration file, 598
fiber optic cable, 182–183
FIFOs, 52
file command, 53
file locking bit, 43
files, 33–53
    access, 37
    accounting, 1050, 1058
    backing up, 113
    boot scripts, 131
    checksums, computing, 397
    commands, relation to, 59
    core, 960
    deleting unusual, 87
    DHCP leases, 208
    font, 879
    group, 223
    group owner, 33
    identifying types, 52
    include, 71
    inodes, 46
    links, 48
    locating, 79
    log, 73, 112, 1011
    modes, 36–37, 42–43
    monitoring log, 114
    named pipes, 52
    open, 625
    ownership, 33
    paging, 998
    password, 223, 234
    PostScript, 817
    protection, 36, 39, 348
    rotating log, 114
    shadow password, 223
    skeleton initialization, 242
    sockets, 51
    special, 47, 65
    static routes, 218–219
    symbolic links, 48
    systemwide login initialization, 246
    types, 52
    user account initialization, 241
    user owner, 33
    (see also configuration files)
filesystem paging, 998
filesystems, 141
    administering, 616
    backing up system, 759–760
    backups of, 731

K

K files, 160
kcmdhcpd package, 463
KDE
    ksysv command, 167
    memory usage utility, 982
    system administration tools, 26
    user manager, 270
keeping, 374
Kerberos, 345–348
    OpenLDAP and, 326
    overview, 345
    PAM and, 307
    tickets, 348
    time synchronization and, 469
kernel
    build directories, 1026
    building, 1024–1047
    configuring, 1024–1047
    functions of, 1024
    listing parameters, 896
    locations, 129
    modularized, 1024
    modules, 1024, 1029, 1036, 1044–1046
    names of, 129
/kernel directory (Solaris), 70
key rings, 365
keyboard shifting, 280
keys, encryption
    DNS, 443
    public/private pairs, 363
kill command, 962
KILL signal, 963
killall command, 962
Kipling, 176
kldstat command (FreeBSD), 1029
Klingon, 278
kludges, 282, 907
Kmoch, David, 511
kmtune command (HP-UX), 991
kmupdate command (HP-UX), 1031
Knaff, Alain, 690
knowing what normal is, 391, 946
Kolstad, Rob, 1069
Kona coffee, 1071
Korn shell, 241, 244
.kshrc file, 241
kstat command (Solaris), 993
ksysguard command, 982
ksysv command (Linux), 167
kuser command, 270

L

Lamm, Holger, 536
LAN (local area network), 180
lanscan command (HP-UX), 184
last command, 409–410
lastcomm command, 409–411
layers, networking, 186
laziness, 886
LDAP, 313–328
    attributes, 315
    daemons, 314
    data interchange format, 315
    distinguished name, 315
    email-related attributes, 558
    entries, 315
    LDIF, 315, 317
    objectClass attribute, 315
    Postfix and, 588
    records, 315
    schemas, 316
    searching, 318
    sendmail and, 557
    terminology, 314–315
    (see also OpenLDAP)
LDAP data interchange format (see LDIF)
ldapadd command, 318
LDAPMAP macro, 557
LDAP_ROUTE_DOMAIN macro, 557
ldap_routing sendmail feature, 557
ldapsearch command, 318
LDIF, 315, 317
leap seconds, 470
leases (DHCP), 207
    files listing current, 208, 459
LeFebvre, William, 956
Leffler, Sam, 799
Leres, Craig, 481
/lib directory, 70
Libes, Don, 911
libpam_unix module (HP-UX), 312
libpam_updbe module (HP-UX), 312
libraries, media, 721
Lightweight Directory Access Protocol (see
    LDAP)
lilo boot loader (Linux), 136, 1036–1040
    password, 133
    Windows 2000 partitions and, 1038
lilo.conf configuration file
    (Linux), 1037–1040
limit command, 959
lines of defense, 336

About the Author

Æleen Frisch has been a system administrator for over 20 years, tending a plethora of VMS, Unix, and Windows systems over the years. Her current system administration responsibilities center on looking after a very heterogeneous network of Unix and Windows NT/2000/XP systems. She is also a writer, lecturer, teacher, marketing consultant, and occasional database programmer. She has written eight books, including *Essential System Administration* (now in its third edition), *Essential Windows NT System Administration*, and the *Windows 2000 Commands Pocket Reference* (all from O'Reilly & Associates), and *Exploring Chemistry with Electronic Structure Methods* (Gaussian, Inc.). Currently, she writes the "Guru Guidance" column for *Linux Magazine*. She also writes poetry and is working on her first novel.

Æleen is a native Californian living in exile in Connecticut with her partner Mike and her cats Daphne, Susan, Lyta, and Talia. She has a B.S. in Literature from Caltech and a Ph.D. in Cultural Studies from Pitt. When she's not writing technical books and articles, marketing literature, or computer programs, she enjoys watercolor painting and creating murder mystery games.

Æleen can be reached by email at *aefrisch@lorentzian.com*. Her home page is *http://www.aeleen.com*. If you'd like to receive the free ESA3 newsletter, you can sign up at *http://www.aeleen.com/esa3_news.htm*.

Colophon

Our look is the result of reader comments, our own experimentation, and feedback from distribution channels. Distinctive covers complement our distinctive approach to technical topics, breathing personality and life into potentially dry subjects.

The animal featured on the cover of *Essential System Administration*, Third Edition, is an armadillo. This insect-eating mammal is native to South America and has spread through the southern United States. Unlike most insectivores, the armadillo has teeth—rootless pegs set far back in its mouth. These teeth allow it to supplement its diet of termites, scorpions, and other insects with snakes, poultry, fruit, and eggs.

The armadillo's name, "little armored thing," was given to it by the Spanish when they invaded the New World. This "armor" is an outer layer consisting of numerous bony plates with a horny covering. This shell is hinged at the middle of the back, allowing the front and hind sections freedom of movement. In some species, this covering extends over the face and tail as well as the torso and limbs.

Armadillos range in size from the great armadillo, at 5 feet in length, to the fairy armadillo, at 5 inches. The most common of the armadillos, the 9-banded armadillo, is about the size of a house cat.

Leanne Soylemez was the production editor and copyeditor for *Essential System Administration*, Third Edition. Sheryl Avruch, Jane Ellin, Colleen Gorman, and Darren Kelly provided quality control. Æleen Frisch wrote the index.

The cover image is a 19th-century engraving from the Dover Pictorial Archive. Emma Colby produced the cover layout with QuarkXPress 4.1 using Adobe's ITC Garamond font.

David Futato designed the interior layout. This book was converted to FrameMaker 5.5.6 with a format conversion tool created by Erik Ray, Jason McIntosh, Neil Walls, and Mike Sierra that uses Perl and XML technologies. The text font is Linotype Birka; the heading font is Adobe Myriad Condensed; and the code font is LucasFont's TheSans Mono Condensed. The illustrations that appear in the book were produced by Robert Romano and Jessamyn Read using Macromedia FreeHand 9 and Adobe Photoshop 6. The note and warning icons were drawn by Christopher Bing.

The book also still benefits from the work that Sheryl Avruch, Nicole Gipson, Seth Maislin, Kismet McDonough, Lenny Muellner, Kiersten Nauman, Dominic Newman, Clairemarie Fisher O'Leary, Chris Reilley, Mike Sierra, Ellen Siever, Mary Anne Weeks Mayo, Norm Walsh, and Frank Willison did on the second edition, and that Kismet McDonough and Ellie Cutler performed on the first edition. Edie Freedman designed the cover of the book, forever linking system administration and armadillos.